FUNDAMENTALS OF
SECURITIES REGULATION

FUNDAMENTALS OF
SECURITIES
REGULATION

LOUIS LOSS

William Nelson Cromwell Professor of Law
Harvard University

LITTLE, BROWN AND COMPANY   Boston and Toronto

Library of Congress Catalog Card No. 82-083733

ISBN No. 0-316-53328-9

HAL

Published simultaneously in Canada
by Little, Brown & Company (Canada) Limited

Printed in the United States of America

SUMMARY OF CONTENTS

APPENDIXES

CONTENTS

CHAPTER 1

DEVELOPMENT OF THE SEC STATUTES

CHAPTER 2

DISTRIBUTION OF SECURITIES

CHAPTER 3

A WHAT! A "SECURITY" (HEREIN OF "ISSUER" AS WELL)

CHAPTER 4

"OFFER," "SALE," "UNDERWRITER,"
AND "DEALER"

CHAPTER 5

SECURITIES ACT EXEMPTIONS

CHAPTER 6

"CONTROL" CONCEPTS UNDER THE SEC STATUTES

CHAPTER 7

REGISTRATION AND POSTREGISTRATION PROVISIONS OF THE 1934 ACT

CHAPTER 8

MARKET REGULATION

CHAPTER 9

"FRAUD" AND MANIPULATION

C H A P T E R   10

CIVIL LIABILITY

CHAPTER 11

THE SEC LAWYER

APPENDIXES

PREFACE

This book is designed both as a teaching tool and as an up-dating of the fundamentals of my Securities Regulation, which was last supplemented with the publication of Volumes IV-VI in 1969.

As a teaching tool the book differs from the traditional case-book (or "cases and materials") in that (1) less than a quarter of the pages consists of cases, SEC releases, and miscellaneous materials such as American Bar Association reports and an excellent article on the "national market system" (all appropriately edited) and (2) the rest, constituting some 900 pages, comes from my own pen.

From the student's point of view, this format is designed to give him or her a more coherent and smooth-flowing treatment of the basics of the entire field and to make it possible for the instructor to save precious classroom hours for the more abstruse aspects of the subject. That is to say, students should be able to get a good deal from their reading; it is worth recalling that our forebears at the Bar "read" law. At any rate, I used a copy of the manuscript in my Fall 1982 course, and its format did make it possible to cover considerably more subject matter than I had ever covered before.

From the practitioner's point of view, this is first cousin to a third edition of my treatise, following substantially the same ar-rangement of chapters. It is self-contained, not a supplement. But obviously it is not as comprehensive, whether for the pre-1969 period or since. So great has been the proliferation of cases and other literature in the almost fifteen years since the December 1, 1968, cut-off date of Volumes IV-VI that a new edition in the style of the treatise would probably extend to eight or ten volumes. As I said in the preface to the 1969 Supplement, "It may be that the one-man treatise, at least in a rapidly changing and expanding field like this, is a dying 'art form.'" This is not altogether bad: winnowing the leading cases and other material out of the mass (or mess) should serve to improve readability.

A note for teachers: Although I have the impression that many instructors (like myself) cover the essentially corporate law aspects of securities regulation (proxies, tender offers, and insider trading) in the basic Corporations course, I have treated them quite fully here for several reasons: some instructors do cover these materials in their courses on Securities Regulation; others may try using the book for the SEC aspects of the basic course as well as the Securities Regulation course that follows; and the book is designed also for the profession. I was able in my Fall 1982 course, extending for thirty-nine hours, to cover the whole book quite comfortably except for Chapters 7D (proxies), 7F (insider trading under §16), 8F (a national market system, which I suggested as optional reading), 9B (Rule 10b-5), and 10I-J (statutes of limitations and miscellaneous aspects of civil liability).

So far as the Federal Securities Code is concerned, a detailed treatment would not be justified until its enactment seems more imminent. At the same time, one must nurture one's faith that, with due allowance for the political process, there will some day be a code that will be recognizably the work produced by The American Law Institute and approved by the American Bar Association as well as (with not too basic changes) both the "Carter Commission" and the "Reagan Commission." Meanwhile the courts are treating parts of the Code as if it were a clarification and restatement of existing law — which in substantial measure is what it amounts to — and the Code has also encouraged administrative reform. Consequently, Chapter 1 contains a detailed account of how the Code was produced, and the more important substantive changes are mentioned at the places where there is a discussion of the law that would be changed.

I owe warm thanks to a number of highly expert lawyers who gave me the benefit of their reading of specialized portions of the manuscript: Milton P. Kroll and Gary O. Cohen for the Investment Company Act discussion in Chapter 1E and, along with Margaret R. Loss, the variable annuity and insurance discussion in Chapter 3E; David S. Henkel for the discussion of distribution techniques in Chapter 2A; Edward F. Greene, at the time General Counsel of the SEC, for all but the accounting portion of the discussion of the 1933 Act's registration scheme in Chapter 2B-D; Milton H. Cohen for the discussion of options and commodity futures in Chapters 3K-L and 10D; and Milton V. Freeman as well as my colleague, Andrew L. Kaufman, for the discussion of "the SEC lawyer" in Chapter 11. In addition, most of the manuscript was read by Professor Joel Seligman. There is no inference, however, that these people agree with what they have read. The responsibility is mine alone.

I am grateful also to two very able and patient editors at Little, Brown and Company (Nancy Campbell and Rosemary Winfield); to a number of student assistants who are far more at home with computerized research than I am (John T. Atkins, Ronald O. Campbell, Molly Liskow, Lewis K. Loss, and Sheldon G. Nussbaum); and most particularly to a remarkable secretary, Julia Stephanian, who not only typed the entire manuscript but also saw to much of the "engineering" that is hidden in the recesses of a work of this sort.

The book speaks generally as of January 1, 1983, although there are occasional references to later cases.

L. L.

Cambridge, Massachusetts
March 1983

A NOTE ON
FOOTNOTE NUMBERING

(1) The writer's footnotes are numbered consecutively in each subchapter (c. 1A, 1B, etc.).

(2) The writer's footnotes are interspersed with whatever footnotes are incorporated from cases or other materials that are set out substantially in full. Those footnotes are numbered as in their sources.

(3) The writer's own footnotes to such materials are identified by letters rather than numbers, together with the symbol, "ED."

CHAPTER 1

DEVELOPMENT OF THE
SEC STATUTES

A. OF BUBBLES AND GIANTS

The Securities Act of 1933 did not spring full grown from the brow of any New Deal Zeus. It followed a generation of state regulation and several centuries of legislation in England. For the problems at which modern securities regulation is directed are as old as the cupidity of sellers and the gullibility of buyers.

A statute of Edward I, in 1285, authorized the Court of Aldermen to license brokers in the City of London, and there are said to be records of a number of prosecutions against unlicensed brokers before the year 1300.[1] Four centuries later, but still eighty years before the American Revolution, Parliament passed "An act to restrain the number and ill practice of brokers and stock jobbers."[2] And it was not long after that statute of 1697 that the "Bubble Mania" swept over France and England.

The story has often been told of the Mississippi Company, organized by the crafty John Law, and the South Sea Company, granted a monopoly by the British Government of the trading with South America and the Pacific Islands — and of how the two companies undertook to pay off the French and British public debts.[3] The bursting of the South Sea Bubble ruined thousands in all ranks of

C. 1A   [1] S. Killik, The Work of the Stock Exchange (2d ed. 1934) 12.
   [2] 8 & 9 Wm. 3 (1697) c. 32; see Lane, The Years before the Stock Exchange, 7 History Today (1957) 760, 761.
   [3] On the fascinating story of Law's Mississippi Company, see J. Francis, History of the Bank of England, Its Time and Traditions (1862) c. 7. See also P. Strong, Jessamy John (1947), a novel based on Law's life. The most scholarly treatment of the South Sea Bubble is in 1 W. Scott, The Constitution and Finance of English, Scottish and Irish Joint-Stock Companies to 1720 (1912) cc. 21-22. For popular accounts, see B. Melville, The South Sea Bubble (1921); G. Erleigh, The South Sea Bubble (1933).

1

society. Reputations in the financial and political world were destroyed wholesale. And the national disaster was aggravated by the numerous hoaxes that were developed by imitators. A thousand persons are said to have paid two guineas each in one morning as a first installment on a share in a company "for carrying on an undertaking of great importance, but nobody to know what it is."[4]

The result of all this was enforcement of the vague and prolix "Bubble Act" of 1720 — a piece of legislation that, ironically, had its origin in the political power of the South Sea Company itself and its desire to suppress less favored rivals without royal charters. In Maitland's words, "A panic-stricken Parliament issued a law, which, even when we now read it, seems to scream at us from the statute book."[5] The statute's recitals referred to "persons who contrive or attempt such dangerous and mischievous undertakings or projects, under false pretences of publick good, do presume * * * to open books for publick subscriptions, and draw in many unwary persons to subscribe therein towards raising great sums of money, whereupon the subscribers or claimants under them do pay small proportions thereof."[6] The act prohibited the use of false or irregular charters and the taking of subscriptions for such enterprises. It declared such matters to be a public nuisance subject to penalties and forfeitures. Brokers trading in such unlawful shares were rendered liable to lose their licenses. And (as if foreshadowing the American antitrust laws) merchants and traders whose business was injured by such unlawful organizations were given the right to sue for treble damages.

The Bubble Act was gradually whittled away and finally was repealed in 1825[7] — though as recently as 1906 counsel attempted, unsuccessfully, to have the statute applied as part of the received law of Idaho.[8] But with the growth of legitimate corporate enterprise Parliament in the Companies Act of 1844 enacted the first modern prospectus requirement. This followed a landmark report (the first of a series of such reports about a generation apart) by a Select Committee on Joint Stock Companies under the chairmanship of Gladstone, who was then the young Tory President of the Board of Trade (now the Department of Trade and Commerce).[9]

---

[4] Melville, op. cit. supra n. 3, at 97.
[5] 3 Maitland, Collected Papers (1911) 390.
[6] 6 Geo. 1, c. 18, §18.
[7] 6 Geo. 4, c. 91. See A. DuBois, The English Business Company after the Bubble Act 1720-1800 (1938).
[8] Spotswood v. Morris, 12 Idaho 360, 85 Pac. 1094 (1906).
[9] 7 B. P. P. 1844.

The 1844 act introduced the principle of compulsory disclosure through the registration of prospectuses inviting subscriptions to corporate shares.

In 1890 Parliament passed the Directors Liability Act (subsequently incorporated into the Companies Act), whose purpose it was to modify the common law of deceit, as it had been applied by the House of Lords the previous year in *Derry* v. *Peek*,[10] in order to subject corporate directors and promoters to civil liability for untrue statements in the prospectus without proof of scienter. And by the early 1900s, when the first American legislation made its appearance, the Companies Act of 1900 — which introduced an elaborate prescription of the contents of the prospectus — had pretty well fixed the British pattern as enforcement of a certain amount of affirmative disclosure going considerably beyond the negative injunction against fraud.

The financial life of the United States developed later, of course, than that of England. But John Law had his spiritual descendants in the Daniel Drews, Jim Fisks, and Jay Goulds.[11] And the growth of corporate enterprise produced much the same problems and abuses as had been met earlier in Great Britain.

The role of government in the protection of investors in the American economy of the closing decades of the twentieth century extends considerably beyond the proscription of fraud, or even the policing of affirmative disclosure of corporate information. This is not to say that those two ends are not the basic foundation of any system of investor protection. Indeed, the disclosure problem is exacerbated by the very factors that have necessarily expanded government's role beyond those ends — the growth of the corporate giants and supergiants in modern society,[12] with the concomitant dispersion of stock ownership and divorcement of ownership from control. Deft pens have written the story of "other people's money" and absentee ownership.[13] And by now a half-century of literature

[10] 14 A. C. 337 (1889).

[11] For some very readable accounts, see F. Davis, What Price Wall Street? (1932); S. Holbrook, The Age of the Moguls (1953); M. Josephson, The Robber Barons (1934); H. Larson, Jay Cook (1936); R. O'Connor, Gould's Millions (1962); B. White, The Book of Daniel Drew (1911).

[12] We live in an economy in which it was possible for Ford and General Motors to *lose* $468 million and $412 million, respectively, in just the second quarter of 1980, without serious danger to their continued corporate existence. N. Y. Times, Sept. 30, 1980, p. 1, col. 1.

[13] See Brandeis, Other People's Money (1914); T. Veblen, Absentee Ownership and Business Enterprise in Recent Times (1923); W. Ripley, Main Street and Wall Street (1927).

has built on the classic study in which Berle and Means traced the evolution of the corporate system as a "major social institution."[14]

Whether or not the economy is becoming increasingly concentrated, there is no doubt that it is now highly concentrated.[15] The "managerial revolution" that was in process when Berle and Means conducted their study in 1929 was said by 1966 to be "close to complete"; the portion of the 200 largest nonfinancial corporations that were under management control had increased from 44 percent in 1924 to 84.5 percent in 1963.[16] Indeed, Professor Berle in the late 1950s traced the progression from "ownership control" through "working control" and "management control" into a fourth stage: control by a relatively small group of institutions through their management of the spectacularly growing (and today far more huge) pension funds. The only right of the pensioner or policyholder is to receive money, a right depending "on a status position of some kind based on his having fulfilled a stated set of conditions." Thus it is, says Berle (with a touch of hyperbole), that "divorce between men and industrial things is becoming complete. A Communist revolution could not accomplish that more completely."[17]

The other side of the dispersion-of-ownership coin is the New York Stock Exchange estimate that 30 million individuals owned

[14] Berle and Means, The Modern Corporation and Private Property (1932), esp. bk. 1.

[15] See Senate Com. on Governmental Affairs, 96th Cong., 2d Sess., Structure of Corporate Concentration: Institutional Shareholders and Interlocking Directorates among Major U. S. Corporations (Com. Print 1980).

[16] See Larner, Ownership and Control in the 200 Largest Nonfinancial Corporations, 1929 and 1963, 56 Am. Econ. Rev. 777, 786-87 (1966).

[17] Berle, Power without Property (1959) 75-76. The following make good reading: J. Livingston, The American Stockholder (1958) esp. c. 2; Manning, Book Review, 67 Yale L. J. 1477 (1958); E. Mason (ed.), The Corporation in Modern Society (1959); Manne, The "Higher Criticism" of the Modern Corporation, 62 Colum. L. Rev. 399 (1962), with a rebuttal in Berle, Modern Functions of the Corporate System, 62 Colum. L. Rev. 433 (1962).

Berle was prescient. Institutional ownership grew from 8.5 percent of the value of all outstanding securities listed on the New York Stock Exchange in 1933 [Securities Industry Study Report, S. Doc. No. 13, 93d Cong., 1st Sess. (1973) 113] to 35 percent by the end of 1979 [39 SEC Statistical Bull. 28 (July 1980)]. And institutional *trading* reached 70 percent of total dollar volume in the first quarter of 1976. N. Y. Stock Exchange, Public Transaction Study (1976) 10.

It has been reported that this tendency toward institutionalization of the stock market — which has created its own problems in securities regulation — "is likely to continue, though probably at a more moderate pace." M. Blume and I. Friend, The Changing Role of the Individual Investor (1978) 186; in general, see SEC, Institutional Investor Study Report, H. R. Doc. No. 92-64, 92d Cong., 1st Sess. (1971).

shares of publicly held corporations in 1980, up from 6.5 million in early 1952, when the first such study was made by The Brookings Institution. This figure represents about one in every four American adults, and it is apart from the approximately 133 million persons with an indirect stake in the market through their pension plans, life insurance, and other intermediaries.[18]

These figures have inspired the discovery in some quarters that the United States now has a new form of economy, "People's Capitalism" — a slogan that would seem to combine the best of both East and West.[19] It also has been suggested that the cloud has a silver lining after all. It may be that the very emancipation of the corporate manager from the concerns of ownership has been making him, as the editors of Fortune have put it, "a professional in the sense that like all professional men he has a responsibility to society as a whole."[20] Indeed, as far back as the middle 1920s Keynes referred to "the tendency of big enterprise to socialise itself" by management's considering the general stability and reputation of the institution more than maximum profit for the dissociated stockholders.[21] Even if the executives of large enterprises are no longer restrained by the owners, they cannot be impervious to "the subtle but all-pervasive influences exercised on them by the standards, values, and myths of the broader community in which they function."[22] It may even be, as Professor Berle himself ultimately discovered, that the modern enterprise is developing something surprisingly like a corporate soul.[23]

---

[18] L. Kimmel, Share Ownership in the United States (Brookings Institution 1952) 85, 89; N. Y. Stock Exchange, Shareownership 1980 (1981) *i*.

[19] "The expression was developed by the Advertising Council, which prepared a 'People's Capitalism' exhibit, shown internationally under the auspices of the United States Information Agency." Perlo, "People's Capitalism" and Stock-Ownership, 48 Am. Econ. Rev. 333 (1958).

[20] Editors of Fortune (in collaboration with Davenport), U. S. A.: The Permanent Revolution (1951) 79.

[21] Keynes, The End of Laissez-Faire (1926) 42, republished in Keynes, Essays in Persuasion (1931) 314-15.

[22] Papandreou, Some Basic Problems in the Theory of the Firm, in 2 Am. Econ. Assn., A Survey of Contemporary Economics (Haley ed. 1952) 183, 198; cf. P. Drucker, The New Society (1949) 34-35, 339-43.

[23] Berle, The 20th Century Capitalist Revolution (1954) esp. cc. 3, 5. In the concluding lecture incorporated in this book, Professor Berle gracefully concedes that his well-known controversy with Professor E. Merrick Dodd in the early 1930s "has been settled (at least for the time being) squarely in favor of Professor Dodd's contention." Id. at 169; see Berle and Means, The Modern Corporation and Private Property (1932) bk. II, c. 7, bk. IV, esp. cc. 1, 4; Dodd, For Whom Are Corporate Managers Trustees?, 45 Harv. L. Rev. 1145 (1932); Berle, For Whom Corporate Managers *Are* Trustees: A Note, 45 Harv. L. Rev. 1365 (1932); Dodd, Is Effective Enforcement of the Fiduciary

As to all this the debate is far from over. Remarking that the "managerial" writers view business "as a kind of game in which profit has approximately the same significance as one's golf score," Professor Mason has contended that the managerial literature has not yet produced an ideology that justifies today's economic system — a system in which managers are supposed to manage for some diffuse, multivalued objective — as satisfactorily as classical economics performed the task for a nineteenth-century enterprise system committed solely to the profit objective.[24]

This much seems clear under any view: The important *law-shaping* factors in recent decades have in fact been the dispersion of ownership among great masses of stockholders — who clearly do *not* control regardless of who does — and the size of modern corporate entities.

At the same time, these are not the only antecedents of the SEC statutes: A collateral aspect of the separation of ownership and control was the development of the institution of "dummy directors" whose function it was to provide "snobbery appeal"[25] — "guinea-pig directors," as they have been called in England because of the once traditional fee of a guinea per meeting, accompanied by a free lunch.[26] And many other problems required legislative attention.

One of the foremost was the failure to furnish essential information to prospective investors when they were invited to buy securities. Others were the common law limitations on civil recovery by injured investors; the inadequacy of current information concerning companies with publicly held securities; the abuse of the proxy device by self-perpetuating managements; the abuse by corporate "insiders" of their favored position in order to trade in their corporations' securities for their own profit; the "private club" atmosphere of the Nation's securities exchanges; the ease with which the securities markets could be manipulated; the lack

---

Duties of Corporate Managers Practicable?, 2 U. Chi. L. Rev. 194 (1935). Dodd was already arguing that corporate powers were held in trust for the entire community, whereas Berle was reluctant to abandon the view that business corporations exist solely to make profit for their stockholders until there was offered "a clear and reasonably enforceable scheme of responsibilities to someone else." 45 Harv. L. Rev. at 1367.

[24] Mason, The Apologetics of "Managerialism," 31 J. Bus. U. Chi. 1, 7, 9 (1958); see also E. Mason (ed.), The Corporation in Modern Society (1959) c. 1.

[25] See Douglas, Directors Who Do Not Direct, 47 Harv. L. Rev. 1305 (1934).

[26] H. Samuel, Shareholders' Money (1933) 111 n. 1.

of financial safeguards for brokers and dealers; the disproportionate amount of the Nation's available credit that at times was
channeled into the securities markets at the expense, it was thought,
of direct financing of commerce and industry; the practices of
protective committees in corporate reorganizations; the abuses of
the holding company and investment company devices; and the
irresponsibility of trustees under corporate bond indentures.

The eight statutes under which the SEC operates — and it must
be remembered that they are not an integrated code passed at a
single legislative sitting — do not attack these problems with any
single philosophy.

One recurrent group of themes centers around an assumption
that various institutions operate according to certain "ideal" concepts: If directors are made civilly liable for misleading prospectuses unless they can affirmatively show that they exercised due
care, they will really direct and not spread themselves too thin —
so the theory goes. Trustees under corporate indentures should
be made to act like real trustees. Other persons in a fiduciary
position should be held to fiduciary standards — whether they are
corporate "insiders" trading in their corporations' securities, or
the managers or advisers of investment companies, or protective
committee members in corporate reorganizations. There is also
something of the idea that corporations ought to be run on the
"town meeting" principle — a concept that, for all its naïveté,
cannot be easily abandoned without an agonizing reappraisal of
the major premise of Anglo-American corporation law to the effect
that management is accountable to the owners of the enterprise.

A second (and somewhat overlapping) group of themes seems to
be aimed at safeguarding the economy generally from the operation of the securities sector: Because of the "trigger" proclivities
of the stock exchanges, they must be cleansed of manipulative influences and transformed into genuinely public institutions. Margin trading must be regulated as an integral part of supervising
the Nation's banking and credit structure. And the crazy-quilt
pattern of electric and gas holding companies built up in the 1920s,
with their extreme separation of voting power from control, must
undergo geographical integration and simplification of their capital structures with a view to protecting consumers as well as
investors.

Then, too, there is the recurrent theme throughout these sta utes
of disclosure, again disclosure, and still more disclosure. Substantive regulation has its limits. But "The truth shall make you free."

B. STATE REGULATION OF SECURITIES: THE BLUE SKY LAWS

1. THE UNIFORM SECURITIES ACT

Securities regulation in this country began around the turn of the century with public utility regulation, and most states still exempt public utility issues from the general securities statutes. The first securities statute with teeth was enacted in Kansas in 1911. Kansas had been a stronghold of the Populist philosophy, and to this day the relative strictness of the Midwestern and Western securities statutes is probably a carryover from the era when an "Agrarian West" was bled by a "Moneyed East." Indeed, it was in Kansas, apparently, that the term "blue sky law" first came into general use to describe legislation aimed at promoters who "would sell building lots in the blue sky in fee simple."[1]

The fashion set by Kansas soon spread, so that today blue sky laws of one kind or another are found in every state, the District of Columbia, Puerto Rico, and all the Canadian provinces. In the *Blue Sky Cases* of 1917 the Supreme Court held that a number of these statutes neither violated the Fourteenth Amendment nor unduly burdened interstate commerce.[2] And, far from preempting the field, Congress in the SEC statutes specifically preserved the state legislation.

In 1956 the National Conference of Commissioners on Uniform State Laws and the American Bar Association — after an unsuccessful experience with a 1929 Uniform Sale of Securities Act — promulgated a new Uniform Securities Act, which was drafted principally by the present writer after a two-year Study of State Securities Regulation conducted at the Harvard Law School under his direction.[3] That Act (which is in the process of revision) has

C. 1B   [1] Mulvey, Blue Sky Law, 36 Can. L. T. 37 (1916).

[2] Hall v. Geiger-Jones Co., 242 U. S. 539 (1917); Caldwell v. Sioux Falls Stock Yards Co., 242 U. S. 559 (1917); Merrick v. N. W. Halsey & Co., 242 U. S. 568 (1917).

[3] 7A U. L. A. 561 (master ed. 1978); see L. Loss and E. Cowett, Blue Sky Law (1958). Roughly the first half of that book treats the blue sky laws as they then were, and the second half is the text of the Uniform Act with the official comments as well as the more extensive comments of the draftsmen. The second part was republished, with an up-to-date bibliography by states, as Loss, Commentary on the Uniform Securities Act (1976). Although only the two bodies that promulgated the Uniform Act can officially change it, in late 1981 the North American Securities Administrators Association, an organization of state and Canadian provincial administrators, voted a number of not

now been adopted, with the greater or lesser modifications that seem to be the curse of all "uniform" legislation, by thirty-six states in addition to the District of Columbia and Puerto Rico.[4] A number of additional states have adopted portions of the Act. This is particularly true of California, where the draftsman of the Corporate Securities Law of 1968 is understood to have borrowed as much of the Uniform Act as he thought would survive that state's relatively inhospitable climate for uniform legislation generally.

The Uniform Act is in four parts. The first three reflect the three traditional blue sky approaches: (I) antifraud provisions, (II) regulation of brokers and dealers (and more recently investment advisers), and (III) registration of securities. Part IV contains the definitions, exemptions, and other provisions of general applicability, and tables indicate how much of Part IV is required depending on whether a state adopts only Part I or Parts I and II or all three parts. An additional table permits several different treatments of investment advisers.

Thus the Uniform Act is really several uniform acts in one. This reflects the great diversity that previously existed, to the point where it was not considered feasible to draft a single statute that would achieve general acceptance. In fact, however, except for the District of Columbia's omission of Part III, all the jurisdictions that have adopted the Uniform Act have taken all four parts (*mutatis mutandis*), and most have adopted the broadest version with respect to investment advisers, treating them like brokers and dealers.[5]

To describe the first three parts of the Act in general terms:

Part I, Fraudulent and Other Prohibited Practices, contains only two sections: §101 outlaws fraudulent practices in connection with the *sale or purchase* of a security, and §102 has to do with fraudulent and other undesirable *investment advisory* activities. There are no exemptions from Part I. The sanctions are found in other parts of the Act. They include (1) criminal prosecution in the event of a willful violation, (2) injunction, and (3) adminis-

---

too major amendments, whose text is set out with comments at CCH Blue Sky L. Rep. ¶¶5512.05 et seq.

[4] The states that have *not* adopted the Act are Arizona, California, Florida, Georgia, Illinois, Louisiana, Maine, New York, North Dakota, Ohio, Rhode Island, South Dakota, Texas, and Vermont.

[5] Nevada and New Jersey register only intrastate offerings, and the Colorado Uniform Act was amended in 1981 to register only those securities and broker-dealers not registered with the SEC.

trative proceedings to deny, suspend, or revoke registration when the violator is a broker-dealer, an agent of a broker-dealer or of an issuer, or an investment adviser. Moreover, although there is no civil liability for violation of Part I as such, provision is made in Part IV (§410(a)(2)) for civil liability in the case of *sales* made through fraud or misstatement.[6]

Part II, Registration of Broker-Dealers, Agents, and Investment Advisers, contains four sections. Section 201 requires the annual registration of broker-dealers, their agents, and investment advisers. Most of the exemptions from *securities* registration in Part IV do not apply. Any registered broker-dealer may act as an investment adviser without registering separately in that capacity if his application so states and the administrator does not condition his registration. An issuer distributing its own securities does not have to register as a broker-dealer,[7] but the employees who represent the issuer in making the offering must register as "agents" as that term is defined in §401(b). The registration procedure is set out in §202, with provisions whereby the administrator by rule may require broker-dealers and investment advisers to maintain a minimum capital and may specify surety bonds for *all* registrants. Applications for registration automatically become effective on the thirtieth day after filing unless the administrator either accelerates the effective date or institutes a proceeding to deny registration. Section 203 contains a number of postregistration provisions having to do with books and accounts, financial reports, and the administrator's inspection or visitatorial power. Section 204 specifies eleven grounds on which the registration of a broker-dealer, agent, or investment adviser may be denied, suspended, or revoked, provided always that the administrator finds it in the public interest to take such action. One of these grounds is lack of qualification, and §204(b) provides, among other things, that in that connection the administrator may require applicants to take examinations.

Part III, Registration of Securities, contains six sections. Section 301 requires the registration of any security before it is offered or sold in the state unless the security or transaction is exempted under §402. Sections 302-04 provide for three types of registration — by "notification," "coordination," and "qualification."[8] The first and third were quite common before the Uniform Act.

---

[6] Civil liability is treated in Chapter 10.

[7] See p. 16 infra.

[8] In California the generic term has traditionally been "qualification" rather than "registration," and what is "registration by qualification" elsewhere is "qualification by permit" in California.

Under §302 the notification procedure is reserved for (1) issuers that have been in continuous operation for five years with no default or any senior security during the past three years and with a three-year average net earnings record of 5 percent on their common stock and (2) certain distributions of outstanding securities, whether or not they meet the first test. The registration statement in a notification case is substantially limited to the information that is essential to permit application of the statutory standards governing effectiveness under §306. In addition, the registration statement automatically becomes effective at a fixed hour on the second full business day after filing unless the administrator accelerates or institutes a stop-order proceeding to deny effectiveness. A number of Uniform Act jurisdictions have deleted the notification procedure in the light of the new coordination procedure.

The coordination procedure under §303 is limited to issues for which a registration statement has been filed with the SEC under the Securities Act of 1933. This reform, perhaps the most important in the entire statute, has been adopted by several non-uniform states (California, Ohio, South Dakota, and Texas). A special procedure for such cases was relatively novel in the blue sky laws before the Uniform Act — although a measure of such coordination had been informally achieved in quite a few states, at least by those law firms with counsel who specialize in blue sky practice. The purpose of §303 was essentially to regularize this informal technique and to arrive at a coordination procedure that is definite and uniform. The section does this by streamlining the *content* of the registration statement and the *procedure* by which it becomes effective, but not the *substantive standards* governing its effectiveness.

The concept is essentially a simple one. If the SEC prospectus (together with such additional information filed with the SEC as the administrator may require) is filed in time, the registration statement becomes effective automatically at the state level the moment it becomes effective in Washington unless the administrator takes the affirmative step of instituting a stop-order proceeding under the substantive standards of the Uniform Act. There is also a special exemption designed to permit offers (but not sales) to be made during the waiting period between the filing and the effectiveness of the registration statement to the extent that such offers are permitted under the federal statute.[9] A coordination procedure was thus achieved without sacrificing the traditional

---

[9] §402(b)(12).

regulatory philosophy of the states to the disclosure philosophy of the federal statute.

The qualification procedure under §304 *must* be used when neither of the other procedures is available and *may* be used in any case. Here the administrator has plenary power to require information and to decide when the registration statement becomes effective, as well as to require the use of a prospectus.

Section 305 contains a number of provisions that are applicable to all or most registrations. For example, the administrator is authorized by rule or order to require escrow of securities, impounding of proceeds, and the use of a specified contract form as conditions upon registration by qualification or coordination.

Section 306 specifies nine grounds on which the administrator may issue a stop order denying, suspending, or revoking effectiveness of a registration statement if he finds it in the public interest to do so. These grounds apply equally to all three types of registration. The draftsmen's commentary has this to say about them:

> The *standards* in §306(a) are a cross-section of the existing standards somewhere between the two extremes: the simple "fraud" test exemplified by the Georgia statute and the "fair, just and equitable" or "sound business principles" language of states like California[10] and formerly Kansas. This is not a mere practical compromise. Administrative flexibility is important in this area, but it must always be balanced against the proper claim of legitimate business to as great a degree of specificity as the public interest will permit. Clause (F) of §306(a) refers to "unreasonable" *selling expenses or promoters' participation or options;* this one clause should take care of many of the classic abuses which led to the development of such a thing as blue sky law. Among other grounds for action under §306(a), Clause (E) contains a *fraud* standard, Clause (A) contains a *full disclosure* standard, and Clause (B) refers to *violations* by the issuer and various other persons.[11]

---

[10] ED.: Today in California the Commissioner of Corporations may refuse to issue a permit unless he finds, among other things, that "the proposed plan of business of the applicant and the proposed issuance of securities are fair, just, and equitable, [and] that the applicant intends to transact its business fairly and honestly," except that (1) when he takes the initiative to suspend or revoke a permit that has already been issued, or in the first instance when the issuer has used the "notification" or "coordination" procedure, as well as in all nonissuer offerings, the *Commissioner* has the burden of showing that the proposed plan of business or issuance "is *not* fair, just, or equitable," and (2) neither standard applies in the case of a cash offering pursuant to a firm commitment underwriting in which the issue and all the underwriters are registered with the SEC. Cal. Corp. Code §25140.

[11] Loss, Commentary on the Uniform Securities Act (1976) 83-84. Other

2. NEW YORK AND OTHER ATYPICAL JURISDICTIONS

Because it would not be feasible to rely on local counsel in each state in which a multistate offering is to be made, a single lawyer or law firm will see to the registration of the offering wherever it is needed. This means that blue sky counsel must be familiar not only with the law of his own state but with all fifty-two statutes.[12] Students of the subject, therefore, will be relieved to know that, taken broadly, all fifty-two statutes are comparable — which is not surprising in view of the fact that the Uniform Act basically followed existing patterns — except for seven jurisdictions that require separate mention:

Although the District of Columbia does not register securities, it does authorize the administrator to call for data by order in specific cases. This authority has been seldom if ever exercised.

Maine and Rhode Island are the last two states that register all securities under a "notice of intention" procedure — what is generally called "registration by notification" — in the sense that the issuer must file a registration statement, which is subject to administrative proceedings designed to stop the offering, but is not required to await affirmative clearance.

New York's Martin Act,[13] passed in 1921, was supplemented in 1932 by very simple filing provisions with respect both to broker-dealers and to the securities they sell. But it is commonly referred to as a fraud act and falls primarily in that category. The basic provision, §352, is a grant of investigatory power to the Attorney General. The section has a majestic, one-sentence sweep: Whenever it appears to the Attorney General that, in connection with any security (or commodity) or investment advice, any person

> shall have employed, or employs, or is about to employ any device, scheme or artifice to defraud or for obtaining money or property by means of any false pretense, representation or promise, * * * shall have made, makes or attempts to make within or from this

---

aspects of the Uniform Act, and of the blue sky laws generally, are considered in later portions of this book by way of comparison with the federal statutes.

[12] The North American Securities Administrators Association has achieved a considerable amount of uniformity of forms in cooperation with the SEC. As of mid-1981 thirty-odd states were participants in a computerized Central Registration Depository for some 200,000 registered salespersons. The depository is operated by the National Association of Securities Dealers, Inc. (NASD), a self-regulatory organization for the over-the-counter market, under an agreement with the NASAA.

[13] Gen. Bus. Law, Art. 23-A.

state fictitious or pretended purchases or sales of securities or commodities or * * * shall have employed, or employs, or is about
to employ, any deception, misrepresentation, concealment, suppression, fraud, false pretense or false promise, or shall have engaged in or engages in or is about to engage in any practice or
transaction or course of business relating to the purchase, exchange, investment advice or sale of securities or commodities
which is fraudulent or in violation of law and which has operated
or which would operate as a fraud upon the purchaser, * * *
any one or all of which devices, schemes, artifices, fictitious or pretended purchases or sales of securities or commodities, deceptions,
misrepresentations, concealments, suppressions, frauds, false pretenses, false promises, practices, transactions and courses of business are hereby declared to be and are hereinafter referred to as a
fraudulent practice or fraudulent practices[,] or he believes it to
be in the public interest that an investigation be made, he may in
his discretion either require or permit such person * * * to file
with him a statement in writing under oath or otherwise as to all
the facts and circumstances concerning the subject matter which
he believes it is to the public interest to investigate * * * .

The Attorney General or his representative may subpoena witnesses, examine them under oath before himself or a magistrate
or court of record, and require the production of books and papers. When the Attorney General believes "from evidence satisfactory to him" that any person "has engaged in, is engaged in
or is about to engage in any * * * fraudulent practices," or (under a 1958 amendment) whenever he shows a conviction anywhere
of a crime involving securities or of any felony, he may bring an
action in the name of the people against any person participating
in any such practices to enjoin their continuation, and he may include an application to enjoin the defendant permanently from
selling any securities in any capacity within the state. The court
may grant as much of the relief sought as it "may deem proper."
Refusal to testify or produce relevant papers in an investigation
is *prima facie* proof of "fraudulent practices" so as to sustain a
permanent injunction. Violation of an injunction, in addition to
being contempt of court and a misdemeanor, may result in a civil
penalty of $3000. And the court may appoint a receiver for
"property derived * * * by means of * * * fraudulent practices," as well as any commingled property that cannot be identified, "for the benefit of all persons intervening * * * and establishing an interest in such property."

The New York courts have painted with a broad brush. As
early as 1926 the Court of Appeals unanimously held that the

term "fraud" includes "all deceitful practices contrary to the plain rules of common honesty." In the light of the legislative purpose, the words "fraud" and "fraudulent practice" are given "a wide meaning, so as to include all acts, although not originating in any actual evil design or contrivance to perpetrate fraud or injury upon others, which do by their tendency to deceive or mislead the purchasing public come within the purpose of the law." Hence a complaint for injunction is good if it alleges merely "a species of conduct commonly, although perhaps inaccurately, called equitable fraud, although the facts alleged do not connote what is commonly known as actual or intentional or legal fraud; i. e., false representations knowingly made and acted on, resulting in damage."[14]

On the broker-dealer front, the New York scheme is unquestionably the simplest. Every "dealer" or "broker" must file several documents, all of them quite simple: (1) A "state notice," containing merely the dealer's or broker's name and address, the state of incorporation, if any, and the names of the partners, if any, must be filed in the Department of State. (2) In addition, every dealer or broker must file a "broker-dealer statement" in the Department of Law, and (3) every salesman must file in the same place a "salesman's statement," containing "such information pertaining to the business history for the last preceding five years, criminal record and educational background of the applicant and [in the case of the broker-dealer statement] his or its partners, officers, directors or other principals thereof deemed pertinent by the attorney-general."[15] (4) The Attorney General may provide by rule or order for the filing of supplemental broker-dealer or salesman's statements to keep this information reasonably current. And (5) registration must be renewed every four years. (6) Finally, there must be filed in the Department of State a "further state notice" identifying each security offered by the dealer and giving the name, address, and state of incorporation of its issuer. A number of categories of securities are exempted from this last requirement, and the manager of an underwriting or selling syndicate who maintains an office in the state normally files the "further state notice" on behalf of all members of the syndicate.

Violation of any of these filing requirements is defined as a "fraudulent practice" by §352. But, except for a 1963 amendment

---

[14]People v. Federated Radio Corp., 244 N. Y. 33, 38-39, 41, 154 N. E. 655, 657, 658 (1926). This is one of the leading cases on the concept of fraud in securities legislation, state or federal.

[15]§359-e(3)(a), (b).

that requires every broker-dealer to maintain net capital of
$5000,[16] there are no provisions concerning financial responsibility
or even the filing of periodic financial statements. There is no
authority anywhere to deny or revoke or suspend registration on
any standards. And the total information available from all the
required filings does not amount to very much. In short, the
registration requirements are merely an adjunct to the fraud
provisions.

At the same time, New York defines "dealer" to include a
"corporation selling or offering for sale * * * to the public
within or from this state securities issued by it."[17] This kind of
provision was quite common before the Uniform Act. One must
not be surprised, however, when this Alice in Wonderland type
of drafting — "When I use a word, it means just what I choose
it to mean"[18] — produces strange results: It is understood to be
the Attorney General's position that every corporation, domestic
or foreign, that issues stock to employees in New York in connection with an employee stock option plan must register as a "dealer"
unless an exemption is granted on application.[19]

The fraud and broker-dealer registration provisions aside, New
York since late 1968 has required *securities* registration of intrastate offerings on a disclosure basis and with a notification procedure. In thus complementing the federal scheme, which exempts
intrastate offerings, New York resembles Colorado, New Jersey,
and Nevada. Both New Jersey and New York, however, go further in requiring the registration of real estate syndication offerings generally.[20] And, apart from the blue sky law, New York has
a similar Theatrical Syndication Financing Act dating from 1964.[21]

3. INSURANCE SECURITIES

Regulation of insurance securities is frequently a world of its
own. About a dozen jurisdictions have provisions in their *insurance* laws that regulate the issuance and sale of insurance securities
quite comprehensively, generally with definitions, conditions for

---

[16] §352-k1.
[17] §359-e1(a).
[18] Carroll, Through the Looking-Glass and What Alice Found There, c. 6.
[19] The exemption provision is §359-f2(e).
[20] N. Y. §352-e. The New Jersey statute, though modeled closely on New
York's, is not a part of the blue sky law. N. J. Stat. Ann. (1970) §49:3-27 *et seq.*
[21] Gen. Bus. Law §§309-b et seq.

the issuance of permits and licenses, provisions for their revocation, filing fees, prohibitions of false advertising, penalties for issuance without a license or permit, limitations on organizational expenses, bond requirements, and provisions for subsequent financing.[22] About the same number of insurance laws have securities provisions of lesser scope.[23] Moreover, these provisions in the insurance statutes are apart from special provisions on insurance company securities that are occasionally found in the blue sky laws themselves.[24]

The net result is that regulation of insurance securities is sometimes within the exclusive jurisdiction of the insurance authorities, sometimes within the exclusive jurisdiction of the blue sky authorities (wherever there are no special provisions on insurance securities), and sometimes under the concurrent jurisdiction of both. Some of the statutes also distinguish between domestic and foreign or between authorized and unauthorized insurers.

Section 51 of the New York Insurance Law deserves special mention because it prohibits the unlicensed public sale of any security of an insurance company not authorized to do business in the state until one year from the first date upon which the security was "offered to the public" in New York. In the early 1960s it was held that that section's "endeavor to protect the public is * * * so emphatic that allowance of rescission in a proper case is in our opinion essential to carry out the Legislature's intent."[25] The court accordingly denied the defendant's motion for summary judgment. But the defendant won at trial on the ground that the exemption was satisfied by quotations in the "sheets"[26] indicating that the security had been traded over the counter for at least a year, from which the defendant might justifiably have inferred, had he checked, that there had been a public offering at least a year previously. In other words, the court thought that it did not have to determine whether there had been a "public offering" during the one-year period in the sense in which newly issued securities are formally presented to the public; nor did it think it had to ascertain whether there had been actual sales in New York within

[22] E. g., Cal. Ins. Code §§820-60; Ill. Rev. Stat. c. 73, esp. §§627-44, 759.1, 759.2; Pa. Stat. Ann. (Purdon) Tit. 40, §§389-400.

[23] E. g., N. J. Rev. Stat. §17B:18-6; N. Y. Ins. Law §§48, 51. All these provisions are collected in CCH Blue Sky L. Rep.

[24] E. g., Ohio Rev. Code §1707.32.

[25] Atkin v. Hill, Darlington & Grimm, 15 A. D. 2d 362, 366, 224 N. Y. S. 2d 553, 557 (1st Dept. 1962), aff'd per curiam, 12 N. Y. 2d 940, 188 N. E. 2d 790 (1963).

[26] This refers to the National Daily Quotation Service, published by the National Quotation Bureau, Inc., which is a subsidiary of Commerce Clearing House, Inc.

that period.[27] This judgment was affirmed, the Appellate Division apparently concluding on the basis of the trial as distinct from what could be ascertained on motion for summary judgment:

> It is not every sale in derogation of the statute that can be rescinded. The purpose of the statute is, we believe, to prevent unlicensed foreign insurance companies from getting financing by offering their stock here by public sale. This court held that any buyer caught in such an operation could rescind the sale. The statute was not designed to allow a speculator to buy stock in such a company from a third person — neither the company nor one engaged in distributing its stock — and rest secure in the knowledge that if the stock turned out to be an advantageous investment he could keep it, and if not he could force the seller to take it back. In our opinion the record reveals just such a situation.[28]

Two members of the court dissented but wrote simply on the question of the exemption, disagreeing that it had been established by proof of only three sales and five over-the-counter quotations in New York during the year 1957.

4.   CONFLICT OF LAWS

The increasingly interstate nature of the securities business has produced a complex congeries of problems in the conflict of laws: A broker-dealer in Boston sends sales literature to persons in California. Does the California statute apply? The Massachusetts statute? Both? A broker-dealer in New York calls a customer who lives in Connecticut or is vacationing in Florida. A contract between issuer and underwriter, or between dealer and customer, is signed in one state after preliminary negotiations in another. A corporation whose stockholders have preemptive rights and live in many states wants to raise additional capital through a public stock offering, and the blue sky administrators in one or more states refuse registration or insist on changes in the terms of the offering that are distasteful to the corporation and are not required in most states. A purchaser of an installment or periodic payment plan certificate issued by an investment company moves, before his payments are completed, to a state where the certificates cannot qualify for registration. A broker-dealer or investment adviser or issuer inserts an advertisement in the Wall Street Journal or For-

---

[27] 44 Misc. 2d 863, 254 N. Y. S. 2d 867 (Sup. Ct. 1964).
[28] 23 A. D. 2d 331, 332, 260 N. Y. S. 2d 482, 484 (1st Dept. 1965), *aff'd per curiam,* 18 N. Y. 2d 980, 224 N. E. 2d 723 (1966).

tune, which circulate all over the country. In all these instances, and others, if a court should ultimately decide that there had been a violation of the law of one of the states that had a more or less peripheral relation to the transaction or the issue of securities, serious questions would arise of both civil and criminal liability and — perhaps most important of all as a practical matter — of enforceability of contract.

Because the thirty-five or forty reported blue sky decisions that predated the Uniform Securities Act defied generalization,[29] the proponents of the Uniform Act chose the codification route:

UNIFORM SECURITIES ACT, RELEVANT PROVISIONS OF PART IV

SECTION 401. [DEFINITIONS.]

When used in this act, unless the context otherwise requires:

*   *   *

["BROKER-DEALER."]

(c) * * * "Broker-dealer" does not include * * * (4) a person who has no place of business in this state if (A) he effects transactions in this state exclusively with or through (i) the issuers of the securities involved in the transactions, (ii) other broker-dealers, or (iii) banks, savings institutions, trust companies, insurance companies, investment companies as defined in the Investment Company Act of 1940, pension or profit-sharing trusts, or other financial institutions or institutional buyers, whether acting for themselves or as trustees, or (B) during any period of twelve consecutive months he does not direct more than fifteen offers to sell or buy into this state in any manner to persons other than those specified in clause (A), whether or not the offeror or any of the offerees is then present in this state.

*   *   *

["INVESTMENT ADVISER."]

(f) * * * "Investment adviser" does not include * * * (6) a person who has no place of business in this state if (A) his only

---

[29] These cases are collected and analyzed in Loss, The Conflict of Laws and the Blue Sky Laws, 71 Harv. L. Rev. 209 (1957).

clients in this state are other investment advisers, broker-dealers, banks, savings institutions, trust companies, insurance companies, investment companies as defined in the Investment Company Act of 1940, pension or profit-sharing trusts, or other financial institutions or institutional buyers, whether acting for themselves or as trustees, or (B) during any period of twelve consecutive months he does not direct business communications into this state in any manner to more than five clients other than those specified in clause (A), whether or not he or any of the persons to whom the communications are directed is then present in this state * * * .

* * *

SECTION 414.   [SCOPE OF THE ACT AND SERVICE OF PROCESS.]

[SELLERS.]

(a) Sections 101, 201(a), 301, 405, and 410 [which prohibit fraud, require the registration of broker-dealers, agents and securities, prohibit any representation of official approval, and create certain civil liabilities] apply to persons who sell or offer to sell when (1) an offer to sell is made in this state, or (2) an offer to buy is made and accepted in this state.

[BUYERS.]

(b) Sections 101, 201(a), and 405 apply to persons who buy or offer to buy when (1) an offer to buy is made in this state, or (2) an offer to sell is made and accepted in this state.

[OFFER IN THIS STATE.]

(c) For the purpose of this section, an offer to sell or to buy is made in this state, whether or not either party is then present in this state, when the offer (1) originates from this state or (2) is directed by the offeror to this state and received at the place to which it is directed (or at any post office in this state in the case of a mailed offer).

[ACCEPTANCE IN THIS STATE.]

(d) For the purpose of this section, an offer to buy or to sell is accepted in this state when acceptance (1) is communicated to the offeror in this state and (2) has not previously been communicated to the offeror, orally or in writing, outside this state; and acceptance is communicated to the offeror in this state, whether or not either party is then present in this state, when the offeree directs it to the offeror in this state reasonably believing the offeror to be in this state and it is received at the place to which it is directed (or at any post office in this state in the case of a mailed acceptance).

[PUBLICATIONS, RADIO, AND TELEVISION.]

(e) An offer to sell or to buy is not made in this state when (1) the publisher circulates or there is circulated on his behalf in this state any bona fide newspaper or other publication of general, regular, and paid circulation which is not published in this state, or which is published in this state but has had more than two-thirds of its circulation outside this state during the past twelve months, or (2) a radio or television program originating outside this state is received in this state.

[INVESTMENT ADVICE.]

(f) Section 102 and 201(c), as well as section 405 so far as investment advisers are concerned, apply when any act instrumental in effecting prohibited conduct is done in this state, whether or not either party is then present in this state.

[CONSENT TO SERVICE OF PROCESS.]

(g) Every application [*sic:* applicant] for registration under this act and every issuer which proposes to offer a security in this state through any person acting on an agency basis in the common-law sense shall file with the [Administrator], in such form as [he] by rule prescribes, an irrevocable consent appointing the [Administrator] or [his] successor in office to be his attorney to receive service of any lawful process in any non-criminal suit, action, or proceeding against him or his successor, executor or administrator which arises under this act or any rule or order hereunder after the consent has been filed, with the same force and validity as if served personally on the person filing the consent. A person who has filed such a consent in connection with a previous registration need not file another. Service may be made by leaving a copy of the process in the office of the [Administrator], but it is not effective unless (1) the plaintiff, who may be the [Administrator] in a suit, action, or proceeding instituted by [him], forthwith sends notice of the service and a copy of the process by registered mail to the defendant or respondent at his last address on file with the [Administrator], and (2) the plaintiff's affidavit of compliance with this subsection is filed in the case on or before the return day of the process, if any, or within such further time as the court allows.

[SUBSTITUTED SERVICE OF PROCESS.]

(h) When any person, including any nonresident of this state, engages in conduct prohibited or made actionable by this act or any rule or order hereunder, and he has not filed a consent to service of process under subsection (g) and personal jurisdiction over him cannot otherwise be obtained in this state, that conduct shall be considered equivalent to his appointment of the [Administrator] or [his] successor in office to be his attorney to receive service of any lawful process in any non-criminal suit, action, or proceeding against him or his successor, executor or administrator which grows out of that conduct and which is brought under this act or any rule or order hereunder, with the same force and validity as if served on him personally. Service may be made by leaving a copy of the process in the office of the [Administrator], and it is not effective unless (1) the plaintiff, who may be the [Administrator] in a suit, action, or proceeding instituted by [him], forthwith sends notice of the service and a copy of the process by registered mail to the defendant or respondent at his last known address or takes other steps which are reasonably calculated to give actual notice, and (2) the plaintiff's affidavit of compliance with this subsection is filed in the case on or before the return day of the process, if any, or within such further time as the court allows.

KREIS v. MATES INVESTMENT FUND, INC.
United States Court of Appeals, Eighth Circuit, 1973
473 F. 2d 1308

Before BRIGHT and STEPHENSON, Circuit Judges, and TALBOT SMITH, District Judge.

PER CURIAM.

The matter before us is an action for rescission. The plaintiff, Fred P. Kreis, Jr. (hereafter "Kreis"), a citizen and resident of Missouri, bought shares of the defendant Mates Investment Fund,

Inc. (hereafter, the "Fund") by mail, relying upon a glowing account thereof published in Barron's National Business and Financial Weekly in the issue dated June 3, 1968.[1] Eventually Kreis became unhappy with his purchase. Hence this action.

The ground of rescission asserted was non-compliance by the Fund with the registration provisions of the Missouri Uniform Securities Act, Chapter 409, RS Mo. 1969 (hereafter the Act, or the "new" Act), V. A. M. S.

* * *

It was the holding of the District Court that, upon the facts * * * stipulated, although there was an offer by Kreis to buy the shares of the Fund under Section 409.415(c), there was no acceptance thereof in Missouri and hence that the Act does not apply to the purchase. In addition, it was held that the stock dividend of 952 shares was outside the coverage of the Act, being exempt under Section 409.401(j)(6) thereof. The Court thus having concluded that the Fund was not liable to Kreis with respect to the sale of the original 2,178 shares or the stock dividend of 952 shares, did not reach the issue of the liability of Frederick S. Mates, asserted by reason of his being the controlling officer and director of the Fund.

The principal issues on appeal turn on the interpretation of the terms offer and acceptance under the Act. The appellant, Kreis, argues that the Court below erred in holding that the offer to buy the securities was not both made and accepted in Missouri. The appellee Fund asserts that neither the offer nor the acceptance can be deemed to have occurred in Missouri.

The "new" Missouri Uniform Securities Act represents a substantial adoption of the Uniform Securities Act. The portion with which we are here principally concerned is a separate section dealing with what was aptly termed (by the draftsmen of the Uniform Act) to be the "bewildering state of affairs"[4] in the case law governing transactions which crossed state lines. "In order to resolve many uncertainties in this area of conflict of laws, the draftsmen undertook in Section 414 of the Uniform Act [Section 415 of the new Missouri Act] to codify basic rules to determine the applicabil-

[1] This Weekly was at the time published and printed entirely without the State of Missouri. Its circulation in the state was less than one-third of its total circulation. See Section 409.415(e) R. S. Mo. 1969.
[4] Loss and Cowett, Blue Sky Law, 1958 ed., 186.

ity of the substantive provisions of the Act to interstate securities transactions and to define the jurisdiction of the courts over non-residents in actions under the Act."[5]

The Act provides in part as follows:

409.415   Scope of the act and service of process

(c) *For the purpose of this section,* an offer to sell or to buy is made in this state, whether or not either party is then present in this state, when the offer (1) originates from the state or (2) is directed by the offeror to this state and received at the place to which it is directed (or at any post office in this state in the case of a mailed offer); provided however, if an offer is directed to an offeree in a state other than this state and that offer would be lawful if made in such other state, then for the purposes of this section such offer is not made in this state.

(d) *For the purpose of this section,* an offer to buy or to sell is accepted in this state when acceptance (1) is communicated to the offeror in this state and (2) has not previously been communicated to the offeror, orally or in writing, outside this state; and acceptance is communicated to the offeror in this state, whether or not either party is then present in this state, when the offeree directs it to the offeror in this state reasonably believing the offeror to be in this state and it is received at the place to which it is directed (or at any post office in this state in the case of a mailed acceptance) [emphasis supplied].

It is clear that what the Act is here seeking is to bring both order and predictability into an area in which decisions in the various states heretofore rendered, "defy generalization."[6] Common law contract concepts, where supplanted by the Act, obviously no longer control in the applicable areas.

With respect to offer and acceptance (with which we are particularly concerned) the Act, as quoted above, defines its own terms but solely, it must be stressed, "[f]or the purpose of this section," that is to say for the scope of the applicability of the new Act and service of process thereunder. For these purposes, "an offer to sell or to buy is made in this state . . . when the offer (1) originates from this state . . . ." Stopping at this point it would seem clear upon our facts that Mr. Kreis made an offer in Missouri. But the statute contains a proviso (not found in the Uniform Act) and it is this proviso that gives rise to the controversy over the term "offer." The proviso, according to Jensen and

---

[5] Bateman, [The Missouri Securities Act, 34 Mo. L. Rev. 463 (1969)].
[6] Loss and Cowett, supra note 4, at 186.

Mills in their article in 24 J. Mo. Bar 60 (1968), had its origin in the problem presented (to use their terms) where a Missouri broker offered to sell to a customer in Illinois a security which was registered under the Securities Law of Illinois but not registered in Missouri. As the Act stood without the proviso the Missouri broker would be violating Missouri law. To eliminate the problem the following proviso was added to the new Act:

> . . . provided, however, if an offer is directed to an offeree in a state other than this state and that offer would be lawful if made in such other state, then for purposes of this section such offer is not made in this state.

The issue as to construction arises over the content of the word "offer" in the clause of the proviso stating "if an offer is directed to an offeree in a state other than this state. . . . " Does the word offer, so used, mean offer to buy, offer to sell or both?

We turn to the defining section of the Act, Section 409.401(j)(2). There we find the word "offer" defined in terms of an offer to sell and equated to an "offer to sell." The District Court concluded, under the plain words of such definition, that the word "offer," so used, applies only to offers to sell and not to offers to buy. Such construction, moreover, makes sense not only in the light of what the draftsmen of the Act were seeking to accomplish, supra, but also in the practical realities of the market since offers to buy, as such, would rarely be illegal under any law. We conclude, with the District Court, that "the plaintiff made an offer to buy the Fund shares in Missouri within the meaning of Section 409.415(c)."

With regard to acceptance, again it is to be stressed that the Act does not speak in terms of general contract law, with all of the complexities and subtleties acquired over years of classroom hypothetical questions (can the offer to pay $100 for touching the top of the flagpole be revoked as the offeree's hand reaches out for the touch?), but solely as to "acceptance in this state" and "[f]or the purpose of this section," that is, for scope of coverage under the new Act and service of process. In the subsection devoted to acceptance, Section 409.415(d), the stress is upon communication. Substantially, an offer is accepted here in Missouri when it is "communicated to the offeror in this state" (and has not theretofore been communicated outside the state). And it is "communicated to the offeror in this state" when the offeree directs it to him here and it is received where directed. At that point, for the purpose of the new Act, the offer has been accepted in Missouri.

In construing the above Subsection (d) the appellee urges that the mailing of the confirmation into Missouri "would constitute acceptance in this state only if that confirmation constituted the Fund's 'acceptance' of appellant's offer to buy." But, it goes on, such confirmation was not an acceptance, since acceptance had already been "accomplished by the Fund's performance."

The difficulty with the argument is that it ignores the plain language of the Act. We are concerned with 1) acceptance "in this state" 2) for the purposes of this Act, and, as we have noted, such acceptance turns upon communication. Consequently, whether there has been a prior acceptance under orthodox contracts principles in New York, or whether acceptance is accomplished by the precise contents of some communication relating thereto, is not material to the resolution of the applicability of the new Act to the transaction. For, in either event, it is communication to the Missouri offeror that is the critical requirement. When that takes place the offer "is accepted in this state," provided, of course, that there has been no previous communication "to the offeror, orally or in writing, outside this state."

We note, in passing, that such is also the interpretation stated in Logan's Blue Sky Ways and Byways in Missouri, 25 J. Mo. Bar 460, 464 (1969), in these terms: "Furthermore, the situs of an acceptance is Missouri if it was originally communicated to the offeror in Missouri." The official comments to the Act also support such interpretation. Comment 8 thereto states:

> If the selling dealer in State S merely sends a confirmation or delivers a security into State B, or the buyer in State B sends a check in payment from within State B, the statute of State B does not apply *except when under 414(d) the confirmation or delivery constitutes the seller's acceptance of the buyer's offer to buy.* (Emphasis supplied.)

Section 414(d), referred to in the quoted Comment is, it will be noted, the acceptance subsection of the Uniform Securities Act, with its stress upon communication "to the offeror in this state."

In view of the stipulated fact that the only communication received by Kreis as to the action taken upon his offer, namely its acceptance in New York, was the written confirmation of the purchase, mailed by the Fund to Kreis, addressed to him, and received by him, at his home in Missouri, we hold that under the terms of Section 409.415(d) there was acceptance in this state. We need not, then, explore appellant's arguments that the terms of his offer were not exactly complied with, involving thus a rejection, a counter-offer, and the completion of the contract only upon Kreis' acceptance of the allegedly modified terms. Such orthodox contractual complexities have, wisely we think, been discarded by the terms of the Act for purposes of the scope and enforcement thereof.

The appellee, in closing, urges that if we find both offer and acceptance to have taken place in Missouri, we go further and hold that "the Missouri Act would unconstitutionally deprive the Fund of due process of law, through the extraterritorial abrogation of contract rights which arose in New York." So far as our study of this record reveals, no such issue was pleaded below, if argued it is not adequately reflected in the record before us, and it is not touched upon in the trial court's opinion. We thus decline the invitation tendered. Ludwig v. Marion Laboratories, Inc., 465 F. 2d 114 (8th Cir. 1972). Nor do we rule upon the disposition of the stock dividend, or the value thereof, received by Kreis, such issues not having been reached by the District Court in the light of its liability ruling.

Reversed and remanded for further proceedings not inconsistent with this opinion.

5. PARTIAL PREEMPTION UNDER THE FEDERAL SECURITIES CODE

The proponents of The American Law Institute's Federal Securities Code considered three possibilities with respect to federal-state relations:[30]

(a) The first is complete preemption, as in §11361(a) (formerly §20a) of the Interstate Commerce Act (49 U. S. C. §11361(a); see 1 Loss 418-19) or, with modifications, the Commodity Futures Trading Act (7 U. S. C. §2). If the period 1890-1914 had seen the enactment of federal securities laws along with the antitrust and ICC legislation, there might never have been any blue sky laws. Nevertheless, it is impossible to ignore the more than sixty years of blue sky history. Moreover, the blue sky authorities can continue to serve an important (if not indispensable) function with respect to essentially local offerings as well as local broker-dealers

---

[30] 2 ALI, Federal Securities Code (1980) 966-67 (hereinafter cited as "Code"), copyright 1980 by The American Law Institute and reprinted with its permission. On the Code, see p. 38 infra. The Code's comments, in referring to today's section numbers as well as SEC releases, use S for the Securities Act, X for the Securities Exchange Act, U for the Public Utility Holding Company Act, T for the Trust Indenture Act, N for the Investment Company Act, R for the Investment Advisers Act, and SIP for the Securities Investor Protection Act.

and investment advisers. And even with respect to nationwide offerings, there is no reason to assume that Congress would have been satisfied with a disclosure statute in 1933 if the blue sky laws had not already gone further in most states: that is to say, their complete replacement now would require that serious consideration be given to the insertion of substantive standards, at least along the lines of the Uniform Securities Act's, in Part V of the Code. For all these reasons, the Code does not follow the route of complete preemption.

(b) The second possibility is a continuation of the status quo: duplicate regulation except in the rare instance of a conflict. [Citations omitted.] But, whatever the claims of history, they must be balanced against a decent regard for the principles of federalism in a country of fifty-odd jurisdictions with a view to both the legitimate needs of capital formation and the maximum effectiveness of the federal-state regulatory apparatus as a whole.

(c) What remains is the limited use of the Supremacy Clause to achieve what is not so much parital preemption (except in a constitutional sense) as federal-state integration or harmonization with reduction of unnecessary duplication of regulation. That is the philosophy of §1904, taken together with §514.

Whereas §1904 is designed to emphasize federal control of multistate distributions, §514 (which is a substantial expansion of the intrastate exemption in the Securities Act of 1933)[31] is an attempt to enhance the states' responsibility with respect to local distributions. The two sections evolved in the course of several years of collaboration with the North American Securities Administrators Association, which in 1977 endorsed the Code's federal-state scheme.[32]

The Code's first endeavor was to strengthen the Uniform Securities Act's scheme of registration by coordination[33] and make it nationwide. The commentary to the Code (brought current here to reflect the subsequent adoption of the Uniform Act by Mississippi and New Hampshire as well as Colorado's subsequent limitation to intrastate offerings) observes that the coordination technique has already been adopted, either verbatim or in substance, in Puerto Rico and thirty-seven states; that four more states accept the SEC prospectus in lieu of the information otherwise required;[34] that the District of Columbia registers only broker-

[31] See p. 319 infra.
[32] 2 Code 967-69.
[33] See p. 11 supra.
[34] Ariz. Rev. Stat. §44-1896; La. Rev. Stat. §51-708(10), 2d ¶; Me. Rev. Stat. Tit. 32, §871.5; N. D. Cent. Code §10-04-08, ¶4; cf. Ill. Rev. Stat. c. 121-1/2, §137.5A-B (registration by "notification" or "description").

dealers, not securities; that Nevada registers only intrastate issues; that the only interstate offerings registrable in New Jersey and New York are those of real estate securities; that Florida and Georgia provide an "exemption" on filing of an effective registration statement under the 1933 Act (or in Georgia the notification and offering circular under one of the "small issue" exemptions) together with a "notice of intention to sell";[35] and that this leaves only two states (Rhode Island and Vermont, plus New Jersey and New York with respect to real estate offerings and perhaps Illinois) that would be substantially affected by a federally imposed coordination procedure. The Code would accordingly legislate complete preemption with respect to distribution of securities in the case of any state whose registration procedure was not substantially coordinated with the procedure under the Code by a date two years after the Code's enactment.[36]

There is also a preemption provision with respect to "blue chip" distributions as defined in the Code, "on the theory (a) that they almost universally get by the states' substantive requirements anyway, (b) that virtually all states already afford exemption to securities of a class listed on the New York Stock Exchange or frequently other specified exchanges * * * , and (c) that the present scheme makes for much unnecessary paper-shuffling that not only complicates the lives of blue sky lawyers but also (and this is more important) diverts the limited manpower of the blue sky administrators from those regulatory tasks for which they are perhaps better equipped than the SEC."[37] Finally, there would be complete preemption with respect to tender offers.[38]

C. THE BATTLE OF THE PHILOSOPHIES

When the Crash of 1929, followed by the Great Depression, finally led to the passage of the Securities Act of 1933 during the hundred "Glorious Days" of President Roosevelt's New Deal, the first problem was determining what the role of the federal government should be in the protection of investors. In addition to a couple of decades of experience with the blue sky laws — which

---

[35] Fla. Stat. §517.061(19); Ga. Code §10-5-9(5).

[36] §§1904(a), 2010(a).

[37] 2 Code 975.

[38] Because the federal provisions on tender offers (see c. 7E infra) were "not completed and in light of pending litigation," the NASAA was not asked to express a view on preemption in that area. 2 Code 968.

varied, as we have seen, from New York's mild antifraud approach to California's "fair, just, and equitable" standard — Congress had available the English history of prospectus disclosure, the experience with capital control during World War I, the regulation of railroad securities by the Interstate Commerce Commission since 1920, and a long history of various federal incorporation and licensing proposals.

During its six-month life in 1918, the Capital Issues Committee (consisting of two members of the Federal Reserve Board, the Comptroller of the Currency, and four bankers) passed on more than 2000 applications to issue new securities, of which about 20 percent were disapproved.[1] But this was not investor protection. It was purely a rationing of capital to give effect to the Government's policy of "war business first."

Another result of the war was the Transportation Act of 1920, which was an incident of the return of the railroads to "private" ownership. That statute adopted a long-standing recommendation of the Interstate Commerce Commission by adding §20a to the Interstate Commerce Act in order to subject the purposes and uses of railroad issues to ICC authorization.[2] The same progression that had earlier marked the state legislation was thus repeated on the national scene. General securities registration was preceded by legislation of the public service variety dealing with the financing of railroads. Indeed, 1920 also saw the passage of the Federal Water Power Act, which authorized the Federal Power Commission (now the Federal Energy Regulatory Commission, for the time being in the Department of Energy) to regulate the amount and character of securities to be issued by public service licensees.[3]

The investor-protection aspects of the ICC securities provision — which was extended to motor carriers by the Motor Carrier Act of 1935 — are indirect. That provision is neither a blue sky law, in the sense that the ICC's primary interest is in giving investors a "fair shake" for their money, nor a disclosure statute. It takes its coloration from the Interstate Commerce Act and from its purpose of preventing a recurrence of the notorious financial scandals with their destruction of confidence in railroad investment. Accordingly, the statutory standards are phrased in terms of the contribution that the particular plan of financing would make to

---

C. 1C [1] Report of Capital Issues Committee, H. R. Doc. No. 1485, 65th Cong., 3d Sess. (1918) 1, 5.

[2] Now 49 U. S. C. §11301.

[3] See 1 Loss 423-26.

a healthy railroad system for the Nation. At the same time, the legislative history demonstrates that there was "universal recognition of the interrelation of sound railroad financing and the protection of investors, the latter being essential to maintaining confidence in railroad investment."[4] Without benefit of rule, moreover, it is the ICC's practice to require a prospectus comparable to that required by the SEC.[5]

Considerably deeper than any of these roots was the discussion, going back to 1885, of federal licensing or incorporation.[6] The Taft-Wickersham Permissive Federal Incorporation Bills were introduced in 1910[7] (Wickersham was Attorney General), and President Taft sent two messages to Congress on the subject that year and the next. It is an interesting footnote to history that in the 1912 campaign, when the Bull Moose platform declared for federal incorporation, Taft changed his attitude on the ground of undue concentration of power. Nevertheless, in his 1911 message he had recommended that corporations taking out federal charters should "be subject to rigid rules as to their organization and procedure, including effective publicity, and to the closest supervision as to the issue of stock and bonds by an executive bureau or commission in the Department of Commerce and Labor, to which in times of doubt they might well submit their proposed plans for future business."[8]

In recent years federal incorporation and licensing proposals of various sorts have received a boost from the current concern with respect to "corporate governance."[9] Today's proponents of federal

[4] Breswick & Co. v. United States, 156 F. Supp. 227, 234 n. 15 (S. D. N. Y. 1957), *rev'd on other grounds* sub nom. Alleghany Corp. v. Breswick & Co., 355 U. S. 415 (1958). The classic treatise is I. Sharfman, The Interstate Commerce Commission (1931). For a summary discussion of the securities provision, see 1 Loss 412-23.

[5] In contrast to the express preservation of state jurisdiction in the later SEC statutes, Congress made the ICC's jurisdiction "exclusive and plenary," to the point, apparently, where even the general corporation law of the state of incorporation may be ignored with respect to "anything relevant and material to the issuance of the securities and the corporate financial structure of the applicant." New York Central R. R., 295 ICC 19, 26 (1955). In Schwabacher v. United States, 334 U. S. 182 (1948), the Court held that an ICC order approving a merger overrode state statutes on dissenters' appraisal rights.

[6] 69-A FTC, Utility Corporations, S. Doc. No. 92, 70th Cong., 1st Sess. (1934) 137 et seq. The whole volume is devoted to this subject.

[7] S. 6186 and H. R. 20,142, 61st Cong., 2d Sess. (1910).

[8] See 16 Messages and Papers of the Presidents 7455, 7457, 7522 (1910), 17 id. 7652, 7654 (1911); 69-A FTC, Utility Corporations, S. Doc. No. 92, 70th Cong., 1st Sess. (1934) 8 et seq.; H. Cherrington, The Investor and the Securities Act (1942) 40.

[9] The American Law Institute is now studying the law relating to the

incorporation of the largest corporations seem more interested in using that device not by way of corporate law reform or securities regulation but largely as a handle for such ends as more effective antitrust enforcement and protection of consumers and the environment.[10] Be that as it may, Congress in the SEC statutes opted for what is essentially a scheme of federal licensing: corporations may keep their state charters, but various SEC provisions (not all of them limited to disclosure, as we shall see) apply *on top of* the state corporation law if corporations want to distribute securities to the public or engage in the brokerage or investment company business or various other activities. This is not federal licensing in the broad sense in which that technique is currently being advanced as an answer to the states' charter-mongering.[11] But it is certainly licensing in the generic sense.

The basic question that Congress faced in 1933 when at long last it got to the point of legislating was what the *standards* of the limited federal licensing should be. The diehards, who opposed *any* licensing or registration requirement, wanted to settle for a fraud act of the New York type — or, preferably, stern enforcement of the penal laws without even the power somewhere to enjoin frauds. Any preventive law, even of the purely injunctive type, would not work, it was said, and would only hinder honest business. Indeed, it has since been charged that if the SEC "had had jurisdiction during the early days of the development of the west we would have had no mining industry in the United States today"[12] — a statement that may well be true in its implication that securities regulation as we know it is a luxury that an earlier stage of "acquisitive" capitalism could not have afforded.

At the other extreme, not unnaturally, the merit philosophy of the blue sky laws had its proponents — and still does.[13] Professor

---

fiduciary obligations of corporate officers, directors, and controlling stockholders. See D. Schwartz (ed.), Commentaries on Corporate Structure and Governance: The ALI-ABA Symposiums 1977-1978 (1979); ALI, Principles of Corporate Governance and Structure: Restatement and Recommendations, Tentative Draft No. 1 (1982); see also p. 524 infra.

[10] See R. Nader, M. Green, and J. Seligman, Taming the Giant Corporation (1976); Schwartz, Federal Chartering of Corporations: An Introduction, 61 Geo. L. J. 71 (1972).

[11] Cary, Federalism and Corporate Law: Reflections upon Delaware, 83 Yale L. J. 663 (1974).

[12] Telegram from Secretary of Arizona Small Mine Operators Association in opposition to American-Canadian extradition treaty covering securities violations, Canada, Minutes of Proceedings and Evidence before H. C. Standing Comm. on External Affairs, No. 6 (Nov. 23, 1945) 147.

[13] See Hueni, Application of Merit Requirements in State Securities Regulation, 15 Wayne L. Rev. 1417, esp. at 1417-21, 1444-45 (1969); Goodkind, Blue

William O. Douglas, as he then was, published a pungent critique of the Securities Act of 1933 a few years before he was to be charged with its administration as Chairman of the SEC.[14] Although he considered it "sheer nonsense to talk of repealing the Securities Act or even of making substantial amendments," he also thought three propositions were "tolerably clear":

> First, that the Securities Act falls far short of accomplishing its purposes. Second, that in any programme for the protection of investors and in any genuine and permanent correction of the evils of high finance an Act like the Securities Act is of a decidedly secondary character. And, third, that a vigorous enforcement of the Act promises to spell its own defeat because it is so wholly antithetical to the programme of control envisaged in the New Deal and to the whole economy under which we are living.

As to the first two points, the "glaring light of publicity" on which the Act is based is not enough, Douglas wrote, because

> those needing investment guidance will receive small comfort from the balance sheets, contracts, or compilation of other data revealed in the registration statement. They either lack the training or intelligence to assimilate them and find them useful, or are so concerned with a speculative profit as to consider them irrelevant.

This means that the results of the act for the investor are primarily twofold: the disclosure requirement will in itself prevent some fraudulent transactions that cannot stand the light of publicity, and the judgment of those who do understand will be reflected in the market price and will seep down to the investor through his advisers. In addition, the stringent civil liability provisions of the act are a great advance over the hypertechnical common law. But this chief virtue of the statute is also one of its greatest weaknesses; for history teaches that "terroristic methods are notoriously feeble instruments for continuous control." Witness the Eighteenth Amendment.

The Act is also "superficial," Douglas went on to say. Registration will be hardest for well-established going concerns — "businesses with far flung units, with complicated details, with kaleidoscopic activities" — and easiest for "the oil well scheme,

---

Sky Law: Is There Merit in the Merit Requirements?, [1976] Wis. L. Rev. 79; Tyler, More about Blue Sky, 39 Wash. & Lee L. Rev. 899 (1982). Contrast Mofsky and Tollison, Demerit in Merit Regulation, 60 Marq. L. Rev. 367 (1977).

[14] Douglas, Protecting the Investor, 23 Yale Rev. (N. S.) 521 (1934).

the gold mine venture, the holding company set-up, or the investment trust, in fact, any enterprise which is just beginning or whose
activities, assets, and relations are simple." And at best the registration statement will be discounted shortly after its effectiveness
"by a host of other bearish or bullish factors." There is no machinery for periodic reports,[15] nothing to control the power of self-
perpetuating management or to protect the rights of minorities,
nothing on the soundness or unsoundness of capital structure or
on "the problem of mobilizing the flow of capital to various pro-
ductive channels."

To be sure, the Act is but a first step. This, said Douglas, is
where the third point comes in. The whole business is essentially
a "nineteenth-century piece of legislation" that unrealistically
envisages a return to "Main Street business." This explains,
among other things, "the great reliance placed on truth about
securities, as if the truth could be told to people who could understand it — a supposition which might be justified if little units
of business were seeking funds and people were buying shares
with the modicum of intelligence with which they are supposed
to buy wearing apparel or horses." We cannot "turn back the
clock" to simpler days. We must perfect a plan for control of
our present forms of organization so as to harness the "instruments of production not only for the ancient purpose of profit but
also for the more slowly evolving purpose of service in the sense
of the public good." At the same time, although the type of control embodied in the state blue sky laws should not be condemned,
it would if transplanted to the federal scene engage a government
agency in "activity a thousand fold more complex than the analogous activity of the Interstate Commerce Commission in the railroad field." "The control needed is one which would combine
regulation by industry with supervision by government." For example, a company that had cleared its security through the Code
Authority and the supervisory governmental agency (these were
the days of the NRA) would gain the benefits of a moderated Securities Act.[16] And ultimately there must be some form of control
over access to the capital market. Thus spake Douglas.

Those who today discount the efficacy of the prospectus similarly stress its complexity, and refer to the proverbial horse who

---

[15] Reporting came with the Securities Exchange Act of 1934.

[16] Something of this idea was later to be incorporated in the 1938 Maloney
Act amendment of the 1934 Act, which provided a measure of self-regulation
of the business practices of the over-the-counter securities industry under the
general aegis of the SEC. See p. 687 infra.

is led to the water's edge. Moreover, there is always the question of disclosure to whom. To Aunt Minnie or Uncle Gus in Oshkosh (whose English cousin, the author recently learned, is Aunt Jane at Land's End)? Or to the financial analyst on the "creep down" theory? The difference is the gulf between arithmetic and atomic physics.

Despite these limitations, Congress opted for the British disclosure philosophy over the native merit philosophy of the blue sky laws. "Show up the roguery," as The Times had put it in connection with the debate on the 1844 Companies Act, "and it is harmless."[17] Congress was conscious also of Louis D. Brandeis' statement seventy years later, in Other People's Money,[18] strongly urging publicity as a remedy for social and industrial diseases generally and for excessive underwriters' charges specifically. "Sunlight is said to be the best of disinfectants; electric light the most efficient policeman." At the same time, the law should not try to keep investors from making bad bargains; it should not even undertake (except incidentally in connection with railroads and public service corporations) to fix bankers' profits. He cited the Pure Food Law as an example: it does not guarantee quality or prices, but it does help the consumer to judge quality by requiring the disclosure of ingredients. The length and complexity of some SEC prospectuses make one wish that Brandeis had recognized that *excessive* sunlight can cause skin cancer. Nevertheless, if any single person was the spiritual father of the Securities Act, it was he.

Two quotations a scant thirty-three years apart demonstrate the revolution in thinking. In hearings held in 1900 by the so-called Industrial Commission that had been created two years earlier, this exchange occurred between a member of the Commission and the president of American Sugar Refining Company:

> Q: You think, then, that when a corporation is chartered by the State, offers stock to the public, and is one in which the public is interested, that the public has no right to know what its earning power is or to subject them to any inspection whatever, that the people may not buy this stock blindly?
> A: Yes; that is my theory. Let the buyer beware; that covers the whole business. You can not wet nurse people from the time they are born until the time they die. They have got to wade in

---

[17] The Times, July 4, 1844, quoted in B. Hunt, The Development of the Business Corporation in England 1800-1867 (1936) 95 n. 12.
[18] C. 5, esp. 1st ¶.

and get stuck, and that is the way men are educated and cultivated.[19]

In the debate on the bill that became the Securities Act of 1933, Representative (later Speaker) Rayburn stated simply:

> The purpose of this bill is to place the owners of securities on a parity, so far as is possible, with the management of the corporations, and to place the buyer on the same plane so far as available information is concerned, with the seller.[20]

As the Supreme Court has since put it, the SEC statutes embrace a "fundamental purpose * * * to substitute a philosophy of full disclosure for the philosophy of *caveat emptor* and thus to achieve a high standard of business ethics in the securities industry."[21] In short, Congress did not take away from the citizen "his inalienable right to make a fool of himself." It simply attempted to prevent others from making a fool of him.[22]

It must not be thought, however, that Disclosure and Merit are two gods that sit on separate but equal thrones. On the one hand, the Uniform Securities Act has a disclosure component, and most states today require the delivery of prospectuses. On the other hand, the indirect regulatory effect of a policed system of full and fair disclosure should not be underestimated: people who are forced to undress in public will presumably pay some attention to their figures.

Nevertheless, there *is* a difference, which is illustrated by the federal and state approaches to stock options. A registration guide published by the SEC in 1968 stated:

> If a material amount of options or warrants has been or is to be issued to promoters, underwriters, finders, principal stockholders, officers or directors, certain disclosure in regard thereto should be made in the prospectus, in addition to that required by Item 18 of Form S-1. Such additional disclosure should ordinarily include the following: that for the life of the options or warrants the holders thereof are given at nominal cost, the opportunity to

---

[19] 1 Industrial Com., Preliminary Report on Trusts and Industrial Combinations, H. R. Doc. No. 476, 56th Cong., 1st Sess. (1900) 123.

[20] 77 Cong. Rec. 2918 (1933).

[21] SEC v. Capital Gains Research Bureau, Inc., 375 U. S. 180, 186 (1963); Affiliated Ute Citizens of Utah v. United States, 406 U. S. 128, 151 (1972).

[22] The language is from the 1935 Report of the [Canadian] Royal Commission on Price Spreads (p. 38), although the recommendations of that commission came closer to the merit than the disclosure philosophy.

profit from a rise in the market for securities of the class subject thereto, with a resulting dilution in the interest of security holders; that the terms on which the issuer could obtain additional capital during that period may be adversely affected; and that the holders of such options or warrants might be expected to exercise them at a time when the issuer would, in all likelihood, be able to obtain any needed capital by a new offering of securities on terms more favorable than those provided for by the options or warrants. Similar disclosure should also be made where securities with conversion privileges are issued to the above persons.[23]

By contrast, the North American Securities Administrators Association has this policy:

> Warrants or stock purchase options to those other than the purchasers of securities will hereafter be looked upon with great disfavor and will be considered as a basis for denial of the application except in unusual instances and the burden shall always rest on the applicant to justify their issuance. The number of warrants sought to be issued, the exercisable price, the term in which they are exercisable and the absence or adequacy of a step-up rate in the exercisable price will all be taken into consideration.[24]

All this is not to say that the only critics of the disclosure philosophy today would go further. There is an economic school that argues powerfully that "the costs to society of government-required disclosure exceed the benefits."[25] Moreover, the "Effi-

---

[23] Sec. Act Rel. 4936 (1968). This is now reflected in Reg. S-K, Item 201(a)(2), and Sec. Act Rel. 6383, 24 SEC Dock. 1262, 1278-79 (1982).

[24] CCH Blue Sky L. Rep. ¶5211.

[25] Benston, An Appraisal of the Costs and Benefits of Government-Required Disclosure: SEC and FTC Requirements, 41 Law & Contemp. Prob. 30, 60 (1977); see also Bentson, Required Disclosure and the Stock Market: An Evaluation of the Securities Exchange Act of 1934, 63 Am. Econ. Rev. (No. 1) 132 (1973); S. Phillips and J. Zecher, The SEC and the Public Interest (1981); Jarrell, The Economic Effects of Federal Regulation of the Market for New Security Issues, 24 J. L. & Econ. 613 (1982); compare Stigler, Public Regulation of the Securities Markets, 19 Bus. Law. 721, 37 J. Bus. U. Chi. 117 (1964), with a reply in Friend and Herman, The S. E. C. through a Glass Darkly, 37 J. Bus. U. Chi. 382 (1964); and for a general critique of the SEC's approach to life, particularly in the accounting field, see H. Kripke, The SEC and Corporate Disclosure: Regulation in Search of a Purpose (1979).

For a critique of the second Benston study's methodology and conclusions, see Friend and Westerfield, Required Disclosure and the Stock Market: Comment, 65 Am. Econ. Rev. (No. 3) 467 (1975); see also Benston, Required Disclosure and the Stock Market: Rejoinder, 65 Am. Econ. Rev. (No. 3) 473 (1975). In M. Blume and I. Friend, The Changing Role of the Individual Investor (1978) 208, the authors conclude that "economic as well as equity considerations seem to support the general value to investors of the greater financial disclosure that has taken place under the stimulus of Federal securities regulations." For a recent reexamination of the earlier studies, together with an cient Capital Market Hypothesis," which has occupied a prominent place in the economics and finance literature of the last decade and more, implies not only that the SEC's mandated disclosure and its insider trading restrictions are ineffective but also that the very goal of egalitarian disclosure may be inappropriate.[26]

Be all this as it may — and the SEC's disclosure policy continues to evolve — there is little likelihood as this is written that any legislative change will be in the direction of *more* basic regulation.[27]

D. THE SEC STATUTES IN A NUTSHELL AND THE FEDERAL SECURITIES CODE

LOSS, CODIFICATION OF THE FEDERAL SECURITIES LAW IN THE UNITED STATES: A CASE STUDY IN LEGISLATIVE REFORM[a]

This is an account of a project to codify the federal securities law of the United States — a story primarily of procedure rather than substance.

The underlying legislation is administered by the Securities

---

analysis of some of the later ones, see Friend, Economic and Equity Aspects of Securities Regulation (Rodney L. White Center for Financial Research, Wharton School, U. Pa., Working Paper No. 7-82, 1982).

[26] For a basic treatment, see T. Dyckman, D. Downes, and R. Magee, Efficient Capital Markets and Accounting: A Critical Analysis (1975). For a more technical treatment, see Fama, Efficient Capital Markets: A Review of Theory and Empirical Work, 25 J. Fin. 383 (1970). For a brief in support of the hypothesis, see Note, The Efficient Capital Market Hypothesis, Economic Theory and the Regulation of the Securities Industry, 29 Stan. L. Rev. 1031 (1977). For a bibliography, see Fischel, Finance Theory in Securities Fraud Cases Involving Actively Traded Securities, 38 Bus. Law. 1, 4 n. 9 (1982).

[27] The Advisory Committee on Corporate Disclosure — a group of thirteen lawyers, accountants, academics, financial executives, analysts, and other users of information, under the chairmanship of former Commissioner Sommer — concluded in 1976 (although not all its members agreed unreservedly) that the disclosure system of the 1933 and 1934 Acts as developed by the SEC "is sound and does not need radical reform or renovation," although the Commission should not be "indifferent to research which some would suggest has already or may in the future suggest a radical modification of this disclosure system," and that "Market forces and self-interest cannot be relied upon to assure a sufficient flow of timely and reliable information." 1 Report of the Advisory Committee on Corporate Disclosure to the Securities and Exchange Commission (1977) 2, I-II.

C. 1D [a] ED.: This article was published in K. Ludwig and A. Soellner (eds.), Europäisches Rechtsdenken in Geschichte und Gegenwart (*Festschrift* in honor of Professor Helmut Coing of the University of Frankfurt, 1982).

and Exchange Commission. The SEC, as an "independent" agency of five members appointed by the President and confirmed by the Senate for staggered five-year terms, exercises not only executive but also quasi-legislative (rulemaking) and quasi-judicial powers. There are seven related but separate statutes.[b] The first six were enacted between 1933 and 1940; the seventh came in 1970; and most of them have been repeatedly amended.

The Securities Act of 1933 adapted the disclosure philosophy of the British prospectus provisions of 1929 by requiring the registration with the SEC of *distributions* of securities.

The Securities Exchange Act of 1934 was addressed to post-distribution *trading*. The static disclosure of the 1933 Act was thus transposed into a philosophy of continuous disclosure through the registration of all securities traded on exchanges, with rulemaking authority in the Commission to require the filing of periodic reports by both issuers and certain insiders (directors, officers and 10 percent holders) as well as to regulate the solicitation of proxies. In 1964 and later these provisions were extended to certain securities traded in the over-the-counter market: any class of equity security held by at least 500 persons and issued by a company with at least $1,000,000 of gross assets [since increased by rule to $3 million]. Then in 1968 Congress added regulation of "tender offers" ("takeover bids" as they are known in England and Canada and increasingly in the United States) to the statutory scheme.

In addition, the 1934 Act from the beginning has had three other themes: regulation of the exchange and over-the-counter markets; prevention of fraud[c] and market manipulation; and control of securities credit by the Board of Governors of the Federal Reserve System as part of its authority over the Nation's credit generally.

Finally, the 1934 Act was virtually doubled in size in 1970 (and

[b] ED.: There is an eighth statute under which the Commission functions, but it is not included in the Code because it is part of the bankruptcy statute. Under Chapter 11 of the new statute effective October 1, 1979 (11 U. S. C.) — as under the predecessor statute's Chapter X, dating from 1938 — the Commission serves as adviser to the court in corporate reorganization proceedings in which there is a substantial public interest. See 2 Loss c. 4B. As Judge Jerome Frank (who was Chairman of the SEC before he went to the Second Circuit) put it, Congress recognized that "reorganization is only in its superficial aspects litigation *inter partes* and that fundamentally it is an administrative problem of business and finance." Frank, Epithetical Jurisprudence and the Work of the Securities and Exchange Commission in the Administration of Chapter X of the Bankruptcy Act, 18 N. Y. U. L. Q. Rev. 317 (1941).

[c] ED.: The broadest of the several antifraud provisions is the famous Rule 10b-5, which covers fraud, misstatement, or half-truth in connection with the purchase *or* sale of *any* security by *any* person.

greatly complicated as a result of the patchwork process) by broadening the market regulation provisions, with a direction to the Commission to develop a national market system, and inserting the Commission for the first time into the clearance and settlement processes as well as regulation of the markets in municipal securities.

A major theme of the 1934 Act is self-regulation under the general aegis of the SEC. There are now four types of "self-regulatory organizations": the national securities exchanges; the National Association of Securities Dealers, Inc., which is registered with the Commission as a "national securities association" to regulate participants in the over-the-counter market; since 1970, registered clearing agencies; and also since 1970, the Municipal Securities Rulemaking Board.

The next of the seven statutes in chronological order, the Public Utility Holding Company Act of 1935, pervasively regulates electric and gas holding companies and their subsidiaries in order to assure their compliance with the statutory standards of geographical integration and corporate simplification.[d]

The Trust Indenture Act of 1939 supplements the 1933 Act when a distribution consists of debt securities. A trust indenture must be filed and qualified with the Commission, with a mass of specified provisions that are designed to impose appropriate obligations on the trustee, particularly in the event of default. And there must be a corporate trustee that satisfies a batch of stringent tests to assure its independence from both the obligor and every underwriter.[e]

---

[d] ED.: In December 1981 the Commission, pointing out that its "task of reorganizing the Nation's gas and electric companies was completed twenty years ago," unanimously recommended repeal of this Act as having "served its basic purpose." Letter of Dec. 21, 1981, from Chairman Shad to Senator D'Amato, 14 Sec. Reg. L. Rep. 56 (1982).

[e] ED.: The Trust Indenture Act is peculiar in its enforcement technique. Once an indenture that purports to meet the statutory standards is qualified, the Commission is *functus officio.* Congress presumably thought that, particularly with an independent trustee as potential plaintiff, it could rely on the ordinary functioning of the law of contracts and trusts to assure that the indenture would be enforced. And for thirty-six years it was generally supposed that the applicable law would be state law, to be applied in state courts unless the usual requirements of federal diversity jurisdiction were satisfied, though the legislative history would be relevant as one of the sources of interpretation of the contract and presumably error in that respect could ultimately be reviewed by the Supreme Court. See Note, Hybrid State Law in the Federal Courts, 83 Harv. L. Rev. 280, 318-19 (1969).

Beginning in 1975, however, a series of District Court cases concluded that "this legislation must be viewed as an indirect method of imposing nationally uniform and clearly defined obligations upon those associated with the issu-

The Investment Company Act of 1940 is a complex piece of legislation for the still expanding and evolving investment company industry.[f] * * *

Concurrently with the enactment of the Investment Company Act of 1940, Congress passed the Investment Advisers Act of 1940. This is the shortest and simplest statute in the series. It requires the registration of investment advisers of all types — ranging from the "investment counselors" at one extreme, whose individualized advisory clients are substantial institutional and individual investors, to the publishers of various sorts of market letters — and regulates a few of their practices.

The last of the seven statutes, the Securities Investor Protection Act of 1970, insures customers against their brokers' insolvency up to $500,000 for each account, except that the maximum is $100,000 to the extent that a claim is for cash rather than securities. This is made possible by a requirement that every broker or dealer registered with the SEC be a member of the Securities Investor Protection Corporation, which, though not a Government agency, was created by Congress and operates under some supervision by the

---

ance of corporate debt"; that the very exclusion of the Commission from an enforcement role made it easier to imply a private right of action as a matter of federal law; and that the courts would apply federal law to "those questions of interpretation and enforcement of the indenture agreement to which the statute is specifically addressed, leaving the purely business aspects to state regulation, or to the pendent jurisdiction of the district courts." Morris v. Cantor, 390 F. Supp. 817, 822 (S. D. N. Y. 1975); see also In re Equity Funding Corp. of America Securities Litigation, 416 F. Supp. 161, 203 (C. D. Cal. 1976); Zeffiro v. First Pa. Banking & Trust Co., 473 F. Supp. 201 (E. D. Pa. 1979); cf. Caplin v. Marine Midland Grace Trust Co., 439 F. 2d 118, 123 n. 5 (2d Cir. *en banc* 1971), *aff'd,* 406 U. S. 416, 426-27 n. 17 (1971).

Whether or not those cases correctly construe the present law, the Federal Securities Code that is about to be examined reaches the same result in a more radical and more logical way: If it were possible to conceive of the drafting of this twenty-part Code without the background of the present SEC statutes, it is hardly likely that Part XIII (Trust Indentures) would be singled out for purely private enforcement. Consequently, Part XIII shifts from contract to statute: that is to say, instead of requiring a qualified indenture to contain such-and-such provisions, Part XIII merely declares that such-and-such (the substance of those provisions) *is* the law governing qualified indentures; and the Code further provides, in effect, that Part XIII (as distinct from the nonstatutory, business portions of the indenture) "shall be interpreted, applied, and enforced exclusively as a matter of Federal law" (§1305(c)) and that "an action that alleges a violation of or a failure to comply with" Part XIII comes within the Code's jurisdictional provision, which (with a few exceptions not here relevant) gives the federal and state courts concurrent jurisdiction (the state courts, of course, to apply federal law). §§1719(a), 1822(a); see 1 Code xxxvii-xl.

[f] ED.: For a summary of the salient provisions of the Investment Company Act, see c. 1E infra.

SEC; an annual assessment of the members; and backing from the United States Treasury (which thus far has not had to be used) to the extent of $1 billion.

The inevitable result of this episodic kind of legislation, enacted often in response to crises, is a great many inconsistencies, a considerable number of both gaps and overlaps, and in general needless complexity in a field of the law that would not make light bedtime reading at best. In many areas, moreover, such as proxy solicitation and market stabilization, the statutory provisions are essentially a skeletal framework for elaborate SEC rules, which have all the force of law. And there have been some thousands of judicial decisions, not to mention cases decided by the Commission itself.

This state of affairs has made it apparent for some time that ultimately there would have to be a reexamination of the field of securities regulation as a whole, resulting ideally in the preparation of a code that would replace all the existing statutes, with incidental substantive changes, and that would also put appropriate portions of both the administrative rulemaking structure and the jurisprudence into legislative form. The writer of this essay confronted the problem in a personal way as early as 1947, when he started to work on the first edition of his treatise on Securities Regulation. In the interest of an orderly presentation he treated the then six statutes as a single piece of legislation, which, as he stated in the preface, "is ideally what they should be."[1] Indeed, as early as 1939, when William O. Douglas left the Chairmanship of the Commission to become an Associate Justice of the Supreme Court of the United States, he stated in a letter to President Roosevelt that "eventually it should be possible to merge or consolidate the various registration or reporting requirements of the [then] three Acts to the end that information filed by a corporation under one statute would serve the purposes of all three statutes."[2]

The question was how, as a practical matter, the major body of law that had developed by the late 1960s was to be refashioned, particularly in a country without a parliamentary system.

*   *   *

[1] Loss, Securities Regulation (1951) vi.

[2] The writer of this essay first learned of this letter, dated April 12, 1939, about two years ago from Professor Joel J. Seligman of Northeastern University Law School, who discovered it in the Douglas files at the SEC in connection with his writing a history of the Commission. J. Seligman, The Transformation of Wall Street (1982).

In 1966 Mr. Milton H. Cohen of the Chicago Bar, who had directed the "Special Study of Securities Markets,"[g] published an article called " 'Truth in Securities' Revisited," which was a brilliant plea for integration of the two basic statutes of 1933 and 1934.[6] "Though the mills of God grind slowly,"[7] this article set in train a series of events that culminated in the drafting of the proposed Federal Securities Code. Shortly after the article's publication, the Committee on Federal Regulation of Securities of the American Bar Association's Section of Corporation, Banking and Business Law, in a conference held in Chicago in late 1966, reached a consensus in favor of a broad codification study.[8] An approach was then made to The American Law Institute.

* * *

In late 1968 the Council of the Institute, with informal promises of cooperation from both the SEC and the Council of the American Bar Association's Section of Corporation, Banking and Business Law, undertook to produce a Federal Securities Code. Following its usual practice, the Institute's Council appointed a "Reporter" (the author of this essay), several "Consultants," and a larger group of "Advisers." Altogether both categories of the advisory group grew eventually to thirty-odd persons, including several Consultants for particular portions of the Code. It was a superb group, counting among its number two United States Court of Appeals judges, the present Chief Justice of the Supreme Judicial Court of the State of Maine, four former Chairmen and three former members of the SEC, a sitting member of the SEC (happily, the only one of 1968 vintage, when he was the General Counsel, to stay on the Commission throughout the work), a state securities commissioner who acted as liaison with the North American Securities Administrators Association (an organization of American state and Canadian provincial officials), several law professors who are well known for their work in the securities field

---

[g] ED.: See Report of Special Study of Securities Markets, H. R. Doc. No. 95, 88th Cong., 1st Sess. (5 vols. 1963). This most comprehensive study since the enactment of the 1933 and 1934 Acts was ordered by §19(d) of the 1934 Act, enacted in 1961. And it led, among other things, to the Securities Acts Amendments of 1964. See 4 Loss 2306-13.

[6] 79 Harv. L. Rev. 1340 (1966).

[7] Friedrich von Logau, Sinngedichte, III.ii.24, translated into English by H. W. Longfellow. * * * The writer had no idea of [the German origin of this quotation until he checked it] in the course of writing this essay.

[8] Proceedings, Conference on Codification of Federal Securities Laws, 22 Bus. Law. 793 (1967).

(including Professor L. C. B. Gower from London, who provided comparative insights into the British thinking, particularly with regard to "insider trading"), and a number of highly knowledgeable practitioners from various parts of the country.[10]

It is a firm tradition of the Institute that advisers serve in their individual capacities, not as representatives of various constituencies. However, members of the staffs of the SEC and of the appropriate subcommittees of both Houses of Congress were invited to meet with the advisory group on occasion. And the Reporter frequently went outside the advisory group either for assistance on specialized subjects — help that was always promptly and graciously given, sometimes under unforgivable time pressure from the Reporter — or in order to ascertain the views of the self-regulatory organizations, various trade associations, and the federal bank regulatory agencies. Indeed, Part XII of the Code, entitled "Broker-Dealer Insolvency," was drafted in close cooperation with the Reporter's colleague, Professor Vern Countryman, who specializes in bankruptcy law, and Mr. Theodore H. Focht, General Counsel of the Securities Investor Protection Corporation.[11]

The Consultants and Advisers were no letterhead group. The Reporter called on the Consultants both individually and collectively, sometimes by telephone and sometimes for meetings of two or three days' duration. The Consultants and Advisers together attended several similar meetings each year. And all of the larger meetings, as well as some of the smaller, were attended also by the Director of the Institute, Professor Herbert Wechsler of Columbia University, whose very lack of expertise with respect to securities regulation (although that lack rapidly disappeared as the work progressed) provided insights that unraveled more than one knot.

*   *   *

The Reporter, when he first set pen to paper during a sabbatical term that he spent at the Institute of Advanced Legal Studies in London during the fall of 1969, started by outlining a Code in sixteen parts, which ultimately grew to twenty.[h] After this outline

---

[10] The entire group is listed in 1 Code v-vi.

[11] Another colleague, Professor Victor Brudney, was appointed Assistant Reporter for Part XIV (Investment Companies).

[h] ED.: An enumeration of the twenty parts will convey some idea of the Code's scope:
    I.   Legislative Findings and Declarations.
    II. Definitions.
    III. Exemptions.

had been approved by the Consultants, he began to draft those parts that were designed to replace the registration and prospectus provisions of the Securities Act of 1933, including the definitions and exemptions, some of them in equal parts archaic and arcane. The Reporter began there not so much because the 1933 Act was the first of the seven statutes but rather because this subject matter has historically been as difficult as any confronting the Commission, so that an attempt to codify in this area would test the feasibility of the entire project.

Four "Preliminary Drafts" of this portion of the Code were reviewed at joint meetings of the Advisers and Consultants, and three more were reviewed at intermediate meetings of the Consultants alone. An eighth draft was reviewed at a two-day meeting attended by fifty or sixty members of the American Bar Association's Committee, which acted as a further advisory group throughout the project, together with a majority of the Advisers and Consultants and several key staff people from the SEC. A ninth draft was then reviewed by the Council of the Institute. And only then was a tenth draft printed as "Tentative Draft No. 1" for presentation to the Institute at its annual meeting in April 1972, where it was approved with some changes. Nonmember lawyers were given the floor (though, of course, without voting privileges) at all annual meetings; and a considerable number took advantage of the invitation, lending important value to the debate.

In this manner additional parts of the Code evolved into "Tentative Drafts Nos. 2-6," all of which were approved at the Institute's annual meetings in 1973-77, although the number of "Preliminary Drafts" that preceded each "Tentative Draft" was

---

IV. Issuer Registration.
V. Distributions.
VI. Postregistration Provisions.
VII. Broker, Dealer, and Investment Adviser Registration and Qualifications.
VIII. Self-Regulatory Organizations.
IX. Market Regulation.
X. National Market and Clearance-Settlement Systems.
XI. Municipal Securities.
XII. Broker-Dealer Insolvency.
XIII. Trust Indentures.
XIV. Investment Companies.
XV. Utility Holding Companies.
XVI. Fraud, Misrepresentation, and Manipulation.
XVII. Civil Liability.
XVIII. Administration and Enforcement.
XIX. Scope of the Code.
XX. General.

reduced somewhat as all concerned got into the swing of the work. On the other hand, individual provisions went through many more than eight or ten drafts before the language was found to be generally acceptable.

*   *   *

[A "Proposed Final Draft"] was reviewed in a four-day meeting of the advisory group followed by a three-day meeting of the American Bar Association's Committee. And that draft, with a few changes, was approved at the Institute's annual meeting of May 1978 with only one or two negative votes.[12] The Official Draft — which is to say, the *Institute's* final product — is the "Proposed Official Draft" as changed to reflect (1) comments received before and at the May 1978 meeting, (2) action taken at the meeting, (3) adjustments required by the subsequently enacted bankruptcy statute, which the Reporter was authorized to make with the Council's concurrence by the vote approving the Code, and (4) postmeeting changes of an editorial or technical nature that the Reporter was likewise authorized by that vote to make in accordance with the Institute's practice.

The Code's mass is reflected in the fact that, in bill form as it has been printed by the subcommittee of the House of Representatives, it comes to 756 pages. Altogether there are upwards of 1000 subsections.   There are considerable efficiencies of space when certain provisions that are reflected in several or all of the seven existing statutes are unified in the Code structure. But that shortening is counterbalanced by the fact that the Code for the first time puts a great deal of the case law and the Commission's regulations into statutory form.

This involved procedure of multiple reviews and repeated redrafting — sometimes *ad nauseam,* as it seemed to the Reporter — is nevertheless indispensable to a job of the Code's magnitude and complexity. Although the many subsections are so interrelated that it was highly desirable for one person to be responsible for all the *drafting,* no single person could possibly have produced such a document without the continual critiques and revisions that occurred.   In the words of a well known and sympathetic commentator from Paris, the Institute's procedure is *"assez lourde, mais très sûre."*[13]

12 The Institute's discussion of the seven Tentative Drafts and the Proposed Final Draft may be found in the Institute's Proceedings for 1972-79.
13 Tunc, La révision du droit fédéral des sociétés aux États-Unis, 25 Rev. int. dr. comp. 693 (1973).

Even so, "final" is not always final.

First of all, there was the matter of who would undertake the considerable task of attempting to get the Code enacted. It is the Institute's practice not to engage in legislative activities. Who, then, were to be the spokesmen for the Code in approaching members of Congress, in soliciting support from interested organizations, and in responding to whatever opposition might develop during the legislative process? *Faute de mieux,* several members of the advisory group together with the Reporter — making it very plain that they were acting only for themselves and without authority to speak for the Institute or the American Bar Association or anybody else — formed themselves into a self-anointed working group dedicated to the adoption of the Code. And that group has been generally accepted as if it had the sort of official standing that it lacks.

There was also the matter of funding the not inconsiderable expenses for travel, printing, telephone and so on. In the eight years of the Code's preparation, the Institute spent almost $500,000, which it raised from several charitable foundations. And this included no compensation for the members of the advisory group. They were merely reimbursed for their expenses. And the members of the American Bar Association's Committee paid even their own expenses for a total of fifteen days of meetings over a period of seven years. In short, the *production* of the Code, up to the time of the Institute's approval, cost several million dollars of free time in addition to what the Institute raised and expended. And, fortunately, the subsequent expenses of the working group have been funded by the American Bar Association's Section of Corporation, Banking and Business Law; the Association is not subject to the Institute's strictures against engaging in legislative activities. If law reform is not for the short of wind — as the late Chief Justice Vanderbilt of the New Jersey Supreme Court is reputed to have said — it is also not for the impoverished.

The working group's first task was to obtain the approval of the American Bar Association's Committee on Federal Regulation of Securities, which had had a great deal to do with the origination of the project. An unconditionally favorable vote could not be assumed, because that body was being asked to accept the Institute's version of the Code not merely in principle but as it had been approved by the Institute and yet without the opportunity that the Institute's membership had had to make changes. Nevertheless, the Committee did endorse the Code by a postal ballot majority of some 93 percent. And in December 1978 the Council of the Section of Corporation, Banking and Business Law voted unanimously to recommend that the Association's House of Delegates approve the Code and "recommend its prompt introduction, consideration and enactment by the Congress." That resolution was adopted by the House of Delegates, again unanimously, in February 1979.

With the Institute and the American Bar Association thus in agreement, the task force faced the more formidable task of seeking the official endorsement of the SEC. The Reporter had maintained close contact with the Commission and its staff during the drafting process. But most of those who had been consulted were gone by the time the Code was approved by the Institute. And those currently in authority at the Commission quite naturally were unwilling to take the Code on faith. Indeed, the staff was almost uniformly suspicious, if not hostile. Perhaps this was only natural. For here was a group of "outsiders" asking the Commission to join in recommending to Congress a complete restructuring of the Commission's very own statutes — and, worse yet, it was a veritable revolution that was not within the Commission's control.

At the same time, for the proponents of the Code to go to Congress without having attempted to secure the official views of the Commissioners then in office would have been unthinkable. In the first place, although historically the Commission has not always been able to get what it wants from Congress, it has been pretty effective in barring what it does not want. The members of the working group tried to impress upon the people at the Commission that they could not assume that they would have an effective veto over a measure so unprecedented as the Code. But of course, neither side could be sure of its ultimate strength in Congress. And the subcommittee chairmen in Congress made it plain that they would want to know the Commission's views.

So, beginning in December 1978, members of the working group met first for several days with the Commission's General Counsel and others from his office; then separately (at the Chairman's suggestion) with each of the five operating divisions; after that with the entire Commission in three meetings that were open to the public; and finally with the Chairman and a few key staff people in a series of discussions that lasted several months.

The staff had hundreds of comments. Indeed, by the spring of 1980 the members of the working group were sufficiently discouraged by what they perceived to be the lack of movement that they consulted the two appropriate subcommittee chairmen in the House of Representatives with a view to their simply introducing the Code and asking the Commission to state its comments. But by that time the members of the working group had agreed that a number of changes, emanating both from within and from without the Commission, would *improve* the Code; and the subcommittee chairmen said that they would prefer to introduce the Official Draft as altered to reflect those changes, with a side enumeration of the Commission proposals that the working group considered unacceptable.

It was at about this time that the Commission's Chairman, Harold M. Williams, together with its General Counsel, took personal charge of the negotiations. And things began to move to a culmination beyond the working group's fondest expectations. Nobody concerned with the preparation of the Code had dared hope that it would be found to be completely acceptable to the Commission; for it contained many changes whose effect was deregulatory. The hope was that the Commission's objections might be limited to ten or fifteen discrete questions that would be presented to the legislative committees for their resolution. But the agreement reached between the Commission and the working group was complete. On September 18, 1980, the Commission publicly announced that it had "determined to support enactment of the Federal Securities Code as revised to incorporate certain changes which reflect agreements reached in discussions between the Commission and the ALI's Reporter and a group of his advisers."[14] The Commission went on to state in its release:

> In considering the ALI's draft, the Commission was sensitive to the importance of preserving the underlying framework, the structure of particular sections, and the reforms embodied in the ALI's document to the greatest extent possible. While not every provision is cast in the manner which the Commission might prefer, the Commission believes that the proposal which has resulted from this effort would be consistent with the spirit and goals of the existing federal securities laws and would contribute to the state of the law.
> * * * The Commission, therefore, believes that enactment of this proposal would, on the whole, promote greater predictability and certainty in the interpretation of the federal securities laws and would, thus, promote investor protection, the integrity of our Nation's securities markets, and the capital formation process.[i]

---

[14] Rel. 33-6242, 20 SEC Dock. 1483 (1980), reprinted in 1 ALI, Federal Securities Code (2d Supp. 1981) 13, with appendixes at 1 and 17.

[i] ED.: In January 1982 the Commission, after a review of the Code with the agreed changes that the Commissioners had undertaken because three of them had been appointed since the release of September 1980, "strongly" reaffirmed

Attached as an appendix to the Commission's release was a list, prepared by the Reporter, of some 60 changes aside from 20 or so of an essentially technical nature. And the Reporter broke down those 60-odd changes into 11 that originated altogether outside the Commission (some of them with members of the working group themselves), some 35 that the Reporter considered minor, another 14 that he considered a bit more substantial, and only 6 that in his view might be considered *relatively* major.

Altogether these changes affected only some 5 percent of the total number of subsections in the Code, and none of them was thought by the working group to have a significant impact on any of the Code's major reforms. This *entente cordiale* was made possible not only by a series of compromises in which both sides yielded ground but also by the Commission's reservation of the right to bring six "separable issues" to the attention of Congress at any time *apart from* the Code. These are issues of high political and emotional content, such as whether the Commission should be given explicit authority (which it has always considered to be implicit in the present statutes) to discipline lawyers and accountants practicing before it. Since the Commission recognized, realistically, that any one of those issues would be likely to derail the entire codification effort, it did not insist on their resolution in connection with Congress' consideration of the Code.

Even at this point the Code was not yet mechanically ready for Congress. First, the Official Draft, which was approved by the Institute subject to the Reporter's editorial and technical changes, reflects a painstaking and valuable review, over a period of some months, by the Office of Legislative Counsel of the House of Representatives. Secondly, the legislative world has not stood still during the almost twelve years of the Code's development. That is to say, the drafting has had to be done against a moving target. Quite apart from administrative and judicial developments, both of which have picked up volume in the past decade, there have been several major amendments of the existing statutes since 1969 in addition to the enactment of the Securities Investor Protection Act of 1970 and *its* later amendment. As recently as December 1980, during the closing days of its last session, Congress amended

---

its support, stating that it "encourages others, including affected industry and professional groups, to join in this effort to improve the securities laws," and calling the Code "an enormous simplification." Sec. Act Rel. 6377, 24 SEC Dock. 670, 671 (1982). This release assumed that the Code would reflect any action Congress might take in response to the Commission's earlier recommendation that the Holding Company Act be repeated. See p. 40 supra.

the Investment Company Act by incorporating in it the Small Business Investment Incentive Act of 1980, and also subjected the SEC to the Right to Financial Privacy Act of 1978 in addition to raising the insurance limits under the Securities Investor Protection Act. All that had to be incorporated into the Code's structure and cleared for technical accuracy with both the SEC staff and the Office of House Legislative Counsel.

The result of all these emendations is that the Code as one hopes it will be introduced in Congress will differ substantially from the Official Draft as approved by the Institute.[15] That draft was published in 1980 in two volumes that — with the Reporter's introduction and commentary, as well as source notes accompanying each section, a cross-reference table from the Code back to existing law, and a table of cases — come to 1162 pages.[16] The two volumes contained pockets that did not stay empty long. Within a matter of months the Institute published a "First Supplement" that contained the SEC's release (with the Reporter's analysis of the changes attached) together with the text of all the amendments of the Official Draft that were required to reflect that release. And in June 1981 the Institute published a "Second Supplement" that contains everything in the First Supplement together with the text changes necessary to reflect the legislative amendments of late 1980 as well as a few miscellaneous amendments of a minor nature. In short, the two volumes as amended by the Second Supplement reflect the text of the Code as it is expected to be introduced in Congress[j] — subject, of course, to further changes that may be necessary to reflect any amendments of the existing statutes that might be adopted before the Code is introduced.

This is not the place for a description of the Code's major reforms. Suffice it merely to list a few: (1) a functional arrangement in twenty parts, written in straightforward English, with section and subsection headings and numerous cross-references that facilitate comprehension; (2) *company* registration, with continuous disclosure, as a substitute for multiple registration of *securities;* (3) a considerable degree of deregulation through the inclusion of provisions that would replace several of the Commission's most abstruse rules; (4) codification of the complex area of extraterri-

---

[15] Since it was not considered practicable to clear the changes in the Official Draft with either the Institute or the American Bar Association, their approval goes only to the version as it appears in the Official Draft.

[16] ALI, Federal Securities Code (1980).

[j] ED.: This is the version of the Code that is described in this book.

toriality;[17] (5) a significant degree of "preemption" of the state securities laws, achieved with the endorsement of the North American Securities Administrators Association;[18] and (6) a logical restructuring of the entire field of civil liability. This last category does not completely codify the law of "insider trading" — some of which must be allowed to continue to evolve *ad hoc* in the common law tradition — but nevertheless gives fairly precise answers to some twenty-five questions[19] raised by the ubiquitous Rule 10b-5,[20] whose development puts to shame the German resort to the "general clauses."[21]

As a matter of general approach, the Reporter and the advisory groups were guided by five basic policies: (1) achieving an appropriate balance between the conflicting *desiderata* of certainty and equity; (2) a decent regard for precedent, but with freedom to overrule those cases, including Supreme Court decisions, that were thought to be inconsistent with the brave new world of the Code; (3) the art of the practical, which requires a realization that the best is the enemy of the good; (4) restricting the scope of the Code's reforms to what might loosely be called "lawyers' law," with respect to which Congress might be expected to defer to the expertise of the Institute and those associated with the drafting process, as distinct from basically political questions, such as the traditional disclosure philosophy *versus* the "efficient capital market theory"[22] or the continuation of retail price maintenance in the sale of investment company shares *versus* open competition; and (5) the danger of *over*codification.[23] Needless to say, all of these policies could serve only as general guidelines.

To continue with the Code's progress, there was the matter of a national election in November 1980, which, among other

[17] See [c. 1F infra].

[18] The text of the Association's resolution appears in 2 ALI, Federal Securities Code (180) 967-69.

[19] See 2 id. 656-67.

[20] See Loss, The Fiduciary Concept As Applied to Trading by Corporate Insiders in the United States, 33 Mod. L. Rev. 34 (1970), also published as Le Concept de Fiducie Appliqué aux Opérations des Dirigeants sur les Titres de leur Société dans le Droit des États-Unis, [1969] Rev. int. dr. comp. 743. Professor Coing was the senior German representative at an Anglo-American-Franco-German conference on insider trading that was held in London in 1975. See Loss (ed.), Multiple Approaches — Corporate Insiders (1976).

[21] See J. Hedemann, Die Flucht an die Generalklauseln (1933) esp. at 1-4, 6-12, 46-52.

[22] [See pp. 37-38 supra.]

[23] For example, relatively precise measures of damages are supplemented by §1723(e), which, with certain exceptions, permits the court to vary the statutory measure on a showing that a different measure "would be plainly more appropriate on consideration of such factors as the plaintiff's loss, the defendant's profit, and the deterrent effect of the particular type of liability."

things, resulted in the selection of a newly elected Senator as chairman of the appropriate Senate subcommittee. Moreover, one of the two subcommittee chairmen who were to preside over the hearings on the House side was defeated for reelection, and the entire subcommittee was merged into another, so that the second of the former subcommittee chairmen is no longer a member of the subcommittee now in charge of securities legislation. Had these events not occurred, there was every indication that the Code would be introduced, at least on the House side, in the new Congress that convened in January, with immediate hearings. As it is, members of the working group have been cordially received by the present subcommittee chairmen in both the Senate and the House. But the new people start with somewhat different priorities, and they realize that they lack the education with respect to the Code that their predecessors gained over some period of time.

There seems little doubt that the Code will be introduced and brought to hearings (if that will not have occurred by the time this essay is published). But it is also quite clear that there will be opposition. In an ideal world everybody affected would compare the Code *as a whole* with existing law *as a whole* rather than with some imaginary and unattainable version that would be ideal from his parochial point of view. But that is too much to expect in the real world, in which various groups, such as banks, insurance companies, investment companies and securities firms, may be expected to embrace quietly what they like but to be voluble in criticizing the provisions they do not like.

There are also two other obstacles to be overcome. One, which faces any measure as extensive as the Code, is the creation of a coalition of dissentients, the sum of whose individual objections might cause Congress to throw up its collective hands; that is to say, although perhaps 90 percent of the Code's bulk is common ground, different groups may be expected to oppose different provisions within the remaining 10 percent. The other obstacle is simple inertia, which is expressed in several themes: One comes down to "Better the devil you know." A variant is "Don't rock the boat." Another — which, interestingly enough has been heard from both SEC staff and the "Wall Street Bar" — goes like this: "The Code might be acceptable if we could be sure it would be enacted as it stands, but God knows what Congress will do to it." Still another is, of course, a time-honored technique for killing any reform: "The Code may be sound in principle, but it needs more study." And — "the most unkindest cut of all" — the argument is heard that the administrative reforms and judicial developments of the past decade, some of them induced by the Code, are such that "the Code has achieved its purpose" without all the unsettling of precedent that would be caused by its enactment.

All these themes, it should go without saying, are as nihilistic as they are familiar. Surely Hammurabi's draftsmen heard them as they chiseled away on their stone tablets. Basically, after all, there are two kinds of people in the world: a minority whose imagination rises to the challenge of new ideas, and the majority, who always see reasons for not disturbing the familiar. The Reporter, after almost twelve years of work on the Code and several more in prospect as it goes through the legislative process, may be pardoned for his tendency to classify the Code's proponents in the former category and its opponents in the latter.

There will be delays and frustrations. And changes will be worked by the political process that all legislation must undergo. But one is entitled to a degree of optimism that within a few more years there will be a Federal Securities Code on the statute book, and that it will be recognizably the Code in its present form. The important thing is the Code's *structure*. That structure could survive many changes in particular sections, as it already has accommodated many suggestions during the Code's development. It must not be forgotten that codification is compromise.

Surely it would be a sad state of affairs if, after almost a half-century of frequently fortuitous development of a complex field of the law, it were not possible to bring to fruition a decade-long reexamination of the field as a whole by highly qualified experts drawn from the Bench, the practicing Bar, the world of Academia and the Government itself. Fortunately, the reception that the Code's proponents have received so far from the responsible persons in Congress — this session as well as the last — indicates that they are aware of their responsibilities.

E. SALIENT FEATURES OF THE INVESTMENT COMPANY ACT OF 1940

The Investment Company Act (often called "the 1940 Act" despite the Investment Advisers Act of the same year) cannot be treated here as extensively as the 1933 and 1934 Acts. But it *is* referred to from time to time in the exposition of those two statutes. Hence this summary, which does not purport to be complete.[1]

C. 1E   [1] For an exhaustive study, see T. Frankel, The Regulation of Money Managers: The Investment Company Act and the Investment Advisers Act (4 vols. 1979-80).

1.   THE "INVESTMENT COMPANY" CONCEPT

The Investment Company Act is definitely a regulatory statute for an industry that was thought to require something more than the disclosure treatment of the 1933 and 1934 Acts. Investment companies — or "investment trusts" as they used to be termed — engage primarily in the business of investing and reinvesting in securities of other companies. They are basically institutions that provide a medium for public investment in pools of corporate securities. Their *raison d'être* is diversification of risk with professional management. In theory they are the "poor man's" investment counselors. In origin largely Scottish via Boston, they have emerged as an important element in the financial world only within the last fifty or sixty years.

The several types of investment companies are classified by the statute into three basic groups. Some of the Act's provisions apply to all investment companies, others only to one or two classes or subclasses:

a.   Face-Amount Certificate Companies

These companies issue face-amount installment certificates, which, in essence, are unsecured obligations to pay either (1) a specified amount to the holder at a fixed future date if all the required payments are made or (2) a cash surrender value on surrender of the certificate prior to maturity.[2]

b.   Unit Investment Trusts

In the "unit" or "fixed" investment trusts there is no obligation to pay any specified amount. Typically the holder of a share in such a trust has merely an undivided interest in a package of specified securities that are held by a trustee or custodian. There is no board of directors, and management discretion in the management of the portfolio is entirely eliminated or reduced to a minimum.[3] Indeed, the trust's sole asset is almost always the shares of a single open-end investment company (a type to be described in a moment), and the unit investment trust issues "periodic pay-

[2] §§2(a)(15), 4(1).
[3] §4(2).

ment plan certificates" that represent the indirect interest of the trust's investors in the shares of the underlying investment company.[4] There is thus a "trust on a trust," the certificates of the unit investment trust forming the underlying security for the periodic payment plan certificates.

c.   Management Companies

The residual and largest group of investment companies — all those that are not face-amount certificate companies or unit investment trusts — consists of the "management companies."[5] They are organized as corporations, or occasionally business trusts, and they normally have a board of directors or trustees with considerable freedom in selecting the types and amounts of investment. They issue certificates or shares that are equity securities representing a fluctuating interest in a fund (as in the case of unit investment trusts) rather than a fixed obligation to pay a specified amount (as in the case of face-amount certificate companies).

Management investment companies are subdivided into "open-end" companies (popularly called "mutual funds") and "closed-end" companies, and each of these is in turn subdivided into "diversified" and "non-diversified" companies.[6] An open-end company is one that is offering or has outstanding any "redeemable security" — defined as a security that entitles the holder on demand to receive approximately his proportionate share of the issuer's net assets or its cash equivalent.[7] Almost all open-end companies continuously offer new shares to the public in order to cover redemptions and to increase their funds available for investment. Closed-end companies do not have redeemable securities; they may occasionally offer new securities to the public as any industrial company does, but the usual way to acquire their shares is on the open market. The definition of a "diversified" management company is based on a mathematical test of the degree of diversification of the portfolio. Most open-end companies are in fact diversified.

As of September 30, 1980, 1461 registered investment companies were active, of which 907 were open-end, 163 were closed-end,

---

[4] §2(a)(26).
[5] §4(3).
[6] §5.
[7] §2(a)(31).

386 were unit trusts, and 5 were face-amount certificate companies, and the approximate market value of the assets of all these companies aggregated $160 billion.[8]

2. HISTORY OF THE ACT

The problems of the industry flow from the very nature of the assets of investment companies. Because those assets are usually liquid and readily negotiable, control of the companies' large funds of cash and securities offered many opportunities for exploitation by unscrupulous management. The industry's problems and abuses were thoroughly explored by the SEC in a four-year study that had been ordered by Congress in §30 of the Public Utility Holding Company Act.[9] The Investment Company Act evolved from a bill that was based on the conclusion and recommendations in the Commission's report. After hearings had been held on a bill drafted by the Commission, the industry and the Commission worked out a compromise bill that passed without a dissenting vote — and that statute stood substantially without amendment for thirty years.

In 1962 the Wharton School of Finance and Commerce in the University of Pennsylvania completed a study that the SEC had commissioned in 1958,[10] and in December 1966 the Commission sent its own report to Congress.[11] All this eventuated in the Investment Company Amendments Act of 1970, which introduced considerable change. And in late 1980 the Small Business Investment Incentive Act amended the 1940 Act in order to relieve from a number of the statutory restrictions in the interest of financing relatively small business ventures.[12]

---

[8] "Variable annuity separate accounts" (see p. 218 infra) accounted for 59 of the open-end companies and 83 of the unit investment trusts. 49 SEC Ann. Rep. 118 (1980).

[9] SEC, Report on the Study of Investment Trusts and Investment Companies, in 5 parts with 6 supplemental reports, all cited in 1 Loss 147 n. 52; see the findings in Inv. Co. Act §1.

[10] A Study of Mutual Funds Prepared for the Securities and Exchange Commission by the Wharton School of Finance and Commerce, H. R. Rep. No. 2274, 87th Cong., 2d Sess. (1962). The study was later updated and expanded. I. Friend, M. Blume, and J. Crockett, Mutual Funds and Other Institutional Investors: A New Perspective (1970).

[11] SEC, Public Policy Implications of Investment Company Growth, H. R. Rep. No. 2337, 89th Cong., 2d Sess. (1966).

[12] See Thomas and Roye, Regulation of Business Development Companies under the Investment Company Act, 55 So. Cal. L. Rev. 895 (1982).

3. THE REGISTRATION AND REGULATORY PROVISIONS

As under the other SEC statutes, the technique of the Investment Company Act is first of all to require registration — in this case, registration of all investment companies that make use of the mails or interstate facilities — so as to have a handle for the regulatory scheme. Most of the required information is similar to that contained in registration statements filed under the 1933 and 1934 Acts, from which investment companies are not exempted. But the 1940 Act registration statement must also recite the registrant's policy with respect to specified subjects — such as diversification, issuance of senior securities, borrowing and lending money, engaging in underwriting, and investing in real estate or commodities — that may not be changed without the vote of a majority of the outstanding voting securities.[13]

The very first task of the draftsmen of the statute was to create a definition of "investment company" precise enough to distinguish those companies subject to the registration requirement from holding companies on the one hand and operating companies on the other. Their solution was a quantitative definition in terms of the portion of a company's assets that are "investment securities." Thus, one of the several definitions is a company that "is engaged or proposes to engage in the business of investing, reinvesting, owning, holding, or trading in securities" and owns "investment securities" exceeding 40 percent of its total assets (exclusive of Government securities and cash); and the term "investment securities" is in turn defined to exclude securities of majority owned subsidiaries that are not themselves investment companies.[14] There is a declaratory order procedure whereby a company that comes within this definition is given an opportunity to establish that it is engaged in some other business, either directly or through majority owned subsidiaries or controlled companies.[15]

---

[13] §§8(b), 13; cf. §21.

[14] This rule of thumb has given rise to the phenomenon of the inadvertent investment company, which falls within the 40 percent test either (1) during its start-up period, when it may temporarily invest the proceeds of its initial distribution in securities until it can begin its non-investment company operations, or (2) as a result of the sale of an operating division for securities (or cash that is temporarily invested in securities) or an unsuccessful tender offer. See Rosenblat and Lybecker, Some Thoughts on the Federal Securities Laws Regulating External Investment Management Arrangements and the ALI Federal Securities Code Project, 124 U. Pa. L. Rev. 587, 601-03 (1976). The problem is solved in the Code by means of a temporary exclusion from the definition. §202(80)(C); cf. Rules 3a-1, 3a-2.

[15] §§3(a), (b).

Several categories are automatically excluded from the definition, notably any issuer whose outstanding securities (other than short-term paper) are beneficially owned by not more than 100 persons and that "is not making and does not presently propose to make a public offering of its securities."[16] The Act also contains a number of exemptions in addition to giving the Commission the broadest authority to exempt any person, security, or transaction or any class of persons, securities, or transactions — by rule or order, conditionally or unconditionally — from any or all the provisions of the Act.[17]

The regulatory provisions that attach to all registered companies (absent some exemption) are designed to accomplish five main objectives: (1) honest and unbiased management, (2) greater participation in management by security holders, (3) adequate and feasible capital structures, (4) sound financial statements and accounting practices, and (5) correction of abuses in selling practices.[18]

The amendments of 1970 gave the Commission a good deal, but not all, of what it wanted:

SEC, 37th ANNUAL REPORT
1971

In proposing mutual fund legislation in 1967, the Commission recognized that most of the specific abuses aimed at in the Investment Company Act had been substantially eliminated. However, the dramatic growth of the industry and accompanying changes created new situations which were not anticipated in 1940. While the industry accepted or even welcomed many of the changes proposed by the Commission, it took exception to the principal recommendations of the Commission, and as a result these were modified in the legislation passed by Congress. The most significant aspects of that legislation, which also included certain amendments of the Investment Advisers Act of 1940, are described below.

INVESTMENT ADVISORY FEES

The 1970 Act amends the Investment Company Act by adding a new Section 36(b) (effective June 14, 1972) which specifies that

---

[16] §3(c)(1).
[17] §6, esp. §6(c).
[18] 10 SEC Ann. Rep. 162-63 (1944).

the investment adviser of a registered investment company has a fiduciary duty with respect to the receipt of compensation for services or payments of a material nature paid by such company or its shareholders to the adviser or an affiliate of the adviser. An action for breach of this duty may be brought in a Federal court by the Commission or by a shareholder on behalf of the company. * * * Section 36(b) further provides that the court is to give such consideration as it deems appropriate to approval of the compensation or payments in question by the board of directors and to approval or ratification by the shareholders.[a]

*   *   *

While the Commission had originally recommended adoption of a standard of "reasonable" management compensation, it considered the fiduciary standard finally agreed upon and adopted as equivalent in substance. Clearly, the new provision represents a significant improvement over the prior standards of "corporate waste" and "gross abuse of trust" applicable under state and federal law, respectively.

SALES CHARGES

In the area of sales charges imposed on investors in mutual fund shares, the 1970 Act amended Section 22(b) of the Investment Company Act to provide that the National Association of Securities Dealers, Inc. (NASD) may by rule prohibit its members from offering such shares at a price which includes an "excessive sales load but shall allow for reasonable compensation for sales personnel, broker-dealers, and underwriters, and for reasonable sales loads to investors." Previously, the NASD was authorized only to prohibit an "unconscionable or grossly excessive sales load." The 1970 Act also provides that at any time after 18 months from the date of its enactment, or after the NASD has adopted rules under amended Section 22(b), the Commission may alter or supplement the rules of the NASD. * * *[b]

---

[a] ED.: This section will be considered in the Civil Liability chapter. See p. 1162 infra.

[b] ED.: See NASD Rules of Fair Practice, Art. III, §26, CCH NASD Manual ¶2176; SEC Rule 22c-1.

The typical open-end investment company is virtually unique on the American scene in that it is externally managed pursuant to a management contract made with a close corporation that is organized by the investment company's

THE FRONT-END LOAD ON CONTRACTUAL PLANS

Other significant amendments of the 1940 Act relate to the so-called "front-end load" on periodic payment plan certificates (i. e., certificates issued in connection with contractual plans for the accumulation of fund shares on an installment basis). Formerly, there was no right to a refund for an investor who did not want or was unable to continue payments to the end of the plan under which as much as 50 percent of the payment made during the first year could be deducted for sales charges. Thus, planholders who did not complete their payments were disadvantaged in terms of the portion of their payments actually invested in shares.

The 1970 Act, through amendment of Section 27 of the 1940 Act, provides a desirable improvement in investor protection in this area. Under the new provisions, sales charges on contractual plans may be imposed under either of two alternative methods. Under the so-called "spread load" alternative (which must be elected by written notice to the Commission), the sales load is restricted to not more than 20 percent of any payment and not more than an average of 16 percent over the first 4 years of the plan. Under the other alternative, periodic payment plan certificates may still be sold with a 50 percent front-end load, but plan sponsors must refund, to any investor surrendering his certificate within the first 18 months of the plan, that portion of the sales charges which exceeds 15 percent of the gross payments made, as well as paying him the value of his account. The 1970 Act further provides that, regardless of the alternative followed, an investor is entitled to a full refund of the value of his account plus all sales charges if he cancels his plan within 45 days from the mailing by the custodian bank of notice of the charges to be deducted and of his cancellation right. Such a notice must be mailed within 60

---

promoters to function as investment adviser and is affiliated with the principal underwriter of the investment company's shares.

Section 15 of the Act requires that any contract with an investment adviser be approved initially by a majority of the outstanding voting securities, and that any contract with either an adviser or a principal underwriter be approved annually by such a vote or by the board of directors if the contract is to continue for more than two years. Moreover, an advisory contract may be terminated at any time on sixty days' notice, without penalty, by either the investment company's board or a vote of stockholders.

So far as the investment company's board itself is concerned, §10 limits "interested persons" (as broadly defined in §2(a)(19)) to 60 percent of all the directors. And, in effect, a *majority* of the board must be independent if certain inside persons are principal underwriters or regular brokers for the investment company. On top of this, §17 prohibits certain transactions in which there is a conflict of interest.

days after issuance of his certificate. The Commission is authorized to make rules requiring contractual plan sponsors to maintain specified reserves to meet refund obligations and specifying the notice to be given to investors regarding their refund rights.

FUND HOLDING COMPANIES

Provisions of the Investment Company Act relating to fund holding companies (i. e., investment companies whose portfolios consist either entirely or largely of the securities of other investment companies) were also amended, so as to limit the creation of new fund holding companies and the further enlargement of existing companies. Concern with such companies has centered on the fact that they result in "layering" of sales charges and administrative and other expenses to investors and may have a disruptive effect on the funds whose securities are held in their portfolios. Section 12(d)(1) of the 1940 Act formerly prohibited a registered investment company, subject to certain exceptions, from purchasing more than 3 percent of the outstanding voting stock of another investment company unless it already owned at least 25 percent. This limitation was inadequate, since it applied only to purchases by *registered* investment companies. Hence, a foreign-based fund holding company not subject to registration under the Act could make unlimited investments in registered investment companies.

Under the 1970 amendments, no investment company may have more than 10 percent of the value of its assets invested in securities of other investment companies. However, that limitation is made inapplicable to a *registered* investment company if certain conditions are met, principally that: (1) not more than 3 percent of the outstanding stock of any one investment company is owned by the holding company, and (2) the sales load of the holding company cannot exceed $1\frac{1}{2}$ percent. In addition, the portfolio fund is not obligated to redeem its securities held by the holding company in an amount exceeding 1 percent of its outstanding securities in any period of less than 30 days.

PERFORMANCE FEE ADVISORY CONTRACTS

The 1970 Act, in accordance with the Commission's recommendation, amended the Investment Advisers Act by deleting the exemption from the coverage of its provisions formerly provided for an investment adviser whose only clients are registered investment companies. The Advisers Act was further amended so as to prohibit an investment adviser from performing or entering into an advisory contract with a registered investment company providing for certain types of "performance fees," i. e., compensation based on the realized or unrealized appreciation of the investment company's portfolio.

The Commission had originally recommended a flat prohibition of performance fee arrangements between investment advisers and registered investment companies. It considered that such arrangements give advisers incentives to take undue risks and noted that many fee arrangements were unfair or so complex that it was virtually impossible to understand them. However, after discussion with industry representatives, the Commission agreed to an exception for certain limited types of performance fees. The amendments as adopted exempt from the prohibition against performance fee compensation an arrangement based on a percentage of a registered investment company's net asset value averaged over a specified period, which provides for proportionate increases and decreases in compensation on the basis of investment performance of the company as measured against an appropriate index of securities prices or such other measure of investment performance as the Commission may specify.

EXPANDED COMMISSION ENFORCEMENT AUTHORITY

The 1970 Act added a new subsection (b) to Section 9 of the Investment Company Act to provide additional grounds for disqualification of persons from affiliation with an investment company. Formerly only persons subject to certain convictions or injunctions were so disqualified. The new provision parallels comparable provisions in the Securities Exchange and Investment Advisers Acts providing for remedial action through administrative proceedings. It empowers the Commission, after notice and opportunity for hearing, to prohibit any person, either permanently or for such time as may be appropriate, from serving a registered investment company in the capacities of employee, officer, director, member of an advisory board, investment adviser, depositor or principal underwriter or as an affiliated person of its investment adviser, depositor, or principal underwriter. The Commission may take such action if it finds (1) that such person has willfully violated, or willfully aided and abetted violations by another, of any provision of the Securities Act, Securities Exchange Act, Investment Company Act, or Investment Advisers Act, or any rule or regulation thereunder, or has willfully made or caused to be made a materially false or misleading statement in any registration statement, application or report filed under the Investment Company Act, and (2) that such action is in the public interest.

F. TRANSNATIONAL TRANSACTIONS

1. GENERAL

The extraterritorial reach of various provisions of the SEC statutes has engaged the courts (and occasionally the Commission) in upwards of fifty reported cases, most of them decided in the last decade or so. And in an electronic age in which "world class" securities are listed on exchanges around the globe, so that they are traded twenty-four hours a day, the volume of transnational securities business is bound to increase in the 1980s and beyond.

There are five leading cases in the Second Circuit, Judge Lumbard writing in the first and Judge Friendly in the others.[1] And all fifty-odd cases have been litigated with little guidance from either the statutes themselves or the Commission's rules. The Commission has never used its rulemaking authority under §30(b) of the 1934 Act, the only extraterritorial provision of anything like general applicability, which makes that statute inapplicable "to any person insofar as he transacts a business in securities without the jurisdiction of the United States, unless he transacts such business in contravention of such rules and regulations as the Commission may prescribe as necessary or appropriate to prevent the evasion of this title."[2]

The unsure and at times contorted growth of judicial doctrine in this area pointed to a provision on extraterritoriality in the Code that would, it was hoped, combine and distill the best of the judicial and rulemaking processes. Except for its rulemaking aspect, §1905 of the Code was drafted as if it were a restatement of existing law:

C. 1F [1]Schoenbaum v. Firstbrook, 405 F. 2d 200 (2d Cir. 1968), *modified on other grounds,* 405 F. 2d 215 (2d Cir. *en banc* 1968), *cert. denied* sub nom. Manley v. Schoenbaum, 395 U. S. 906; Leasco Data Processing Equipment Corp. v. Maxwell, 468 F. 2d 1326 (2d Cir. 1972); Bersch v. Drexel Firestone, Inc., 519 F. 2d 974 (2d Cir. 1975), *cert. denied* sub nom. Bersch v. Arthur Andersen & Co., 423 U. S. 1018; IIT v. Vencap, Ltd., 519 F. 2d 1001 (2d Cir. 1975); IIT v. Cornfeld, 619 F. 2d 909 (2d Cir. 1980).
[2]See also Sec. Ex. Act §§7(f) (infra p. 726), 12(g)(3) (infra p. 76), 30(a); Holding Co. Act §10(c)(2); Inv. Co. Act §7(d); Sec. Inv. Prot. Act §3(a)(2).

FEDERAL SECURITIES CODE §1905 WITH COMMENTS[a]

Sec. 1905. (a) Application Extraterritorially

(1) Within the limits of international law, this Code * * * applies —

(A) with respect to —

(i) a sale or purchase of a security, an offer to sell or buy a security, or an inducement not to buy or sell a security;

(ii) a proxy solicitation or other circularization of security holders;

(iii) a tender offer or a recommendation to security holders in favor of or opposition to a tender offer; or

(iv) any activity as an investment adviser

that occurs within the United States although it is initiated outside the United States;

(B) with respect to a nonresident of the United States that has a status described in section 1902(b),[b] to the extent that the Code attaches consequences to such a status;

(C) for purposes of section 1821,[c] with respect to an attempt, solicitation, or conspiracy outside the United States to commit a violation of this Code within the United States; and

(D) with respect to any other prohibited, required, or actionable conduct (i) whose constituent elements occur to a significant (but not necessarily predominant) extent within the United States, or (ii) some or all of whose constituent elements occur outside the United States but cause a substantial effect within it (of a type that this Code is designed to prevent) as a direct and reasonably foreseeable result of the conduct.

(2) Within the limits of international law, part XVI[d] applies with respect to an act specified in section 1905(a)(1)(A) that is initiated within the United States although it occurs outside the United States.

---

[a] Ed.: Copyright 1980 by The American Law Institute and reprinted with its permission. The comments collect all the relevant cases, but most citations are here omitted without further indication. See also Loss, Extraterritoriality in the Federal Securities Code, 20 Harv. Int'l L. J. 305 (1979), which is based on the commentary to §1905.

[b] Ed.: This section refers to a person registered under the Code in any capacity, a person who has to file ownership or tender offer reports under §605 or 606 (so far as those sections are concerned), a participant in a registered clearing agency, or an associate or person acting on behalf of any such person.

[c] Ed.: This is the penal section.

[d] Ed.: Part XVI is entitled "Fraud, Misrepresentation, and Manipulation."

(B) NONAPPLICATION EXTRATERRITORIALLY

(1) Except as provided in section 1905(a)(2), this Code * * * does not apply with respect to an act specified in section 1905 (a)(1)(A) that occurs outside the United States although it is initiated within the United States.

(2) Section 702[e] does not apply with respect to a broker, dealer, municipal broker, municipal dealer, or investment adviser, not a resident of the United States, to the extent that he does business with (A) a person outside the United States, or (B) a non-national of the United States who is present as a nonresident within the United States and was previously a customer or client.

(3) Section 702 does not apply with respect to a broker or dealer, not a resident of the United States, to the extent that he participates in a distribution or a limited offering if his only connection with the United States as a broker or dealer, so far as the distribution or limited offering is concerned, consists of (A) taking down securities for sale outside the United States, and (B) participating solely through his group membership in group activities of a principal underwriter who is a registered broker or dealer.

(C) RULEMAKING AUTHORITY

Within the limits of international law and section 1905(a)(1)(D), and in the light of the significance of effects within the United States of particular acts or conduct, the Commission, by rule —

(1) may provide (A) that this Code does not apply with respect to the subject matter of section 1905(a), (B) that it does apply with respect to the subject matter of section 1905(b), and (C) that it does or does not apply with respect to any other subject matter; and

(2) shall prescribe the extent to which section 402[f] applies with respect to an issuer that is not a resident of the United States.

*   *   *g

COMMENT

(1) There are several possible solutions to the variegated problems of extraterritoriality that have produced a substantial amount of litigation in recent years:

[e] ED.: This section requires the designated persons to register.
[f] ED.: This section is the successor to §12(g) of the 1934 act (infra p. 465), which requires the registration of any company with $1 million of assets (raised to $3 million by Commission rule) and 500 security holders.
[g] ED.: The remainder of §1905 codifies the Foreign Corrupt Practices Act

(a) The Code could simply perpetuate X30 * * * and for the rest leave the matter to the courts. But, aside from the fact that X30 covers only a relatively narrow band of the SEC spectrum, that section is both equivocal and illogical.

It is equivocal in referring to a person insofar as he transacts a business in securities "without the jurisdiction of the United States"; for it is not stated whether this refers to the territorial jurisdiction of the United States or its extraterritorial jurisdiction in the international law or the American constitutional law sense. Presumably it means the former in view of the authority of the Commission to adopt rules, which could hardly go beyond the several jurisdictional bases of the statute such as use of the mails or registration as a broker-dealer. But in *SEC* v. *United Financial Group, Inc.,* 474 F. 2d 354, 357-58 (9th Cir. 1973), the court without discussion read it the other way.

X30(b) is, in any event, illogical in the sense that it has been interpreted to exclude the transacting of "a business in securities" but not an isolated act outside the territorial limits of the United States. *Schoenbaum* v. *Firstbrook,* 405 F. 2d 200, 207 (2d Cir. 1968), *modified on other grounds,* 405 F. 2d 215 (2d Cir. *en banc* 1968), *cert. denied* sub nom. *Manley* v. *Schoenbaum,* 395 U. S. 906.

*   *   *

(b) An early draft of §1905(a), along the lines of §§17 and 18 of the Restatement of Foreign Relations Law of the United States, consisted simply, in substance, of §§1905(a)(1)(D) and 1905(c), without the introductory reference to the limits of international law (which is borrowed from §3(3) of the Restatement):

(i) The situation in §1905(a)(1)(D)(ii) — and the more extreme of the two — was litigated in the *Schoenbaum* case (supra Comment (1)(a)). That was a stockholder's derivative action under Rule 10b-5 in which the plaintiff alleged that the directors of a Canadian corporation *with its stock listed on the*

(§1905(d), now in part Sec. Ex. Act §30A), and provides for *in personam* jurisdiction with notice abroad (§1905(e)-(f)). See the text and commentary in 2 Code 996-1006. It should be noted in this connection that all of the first six Acts provide a broad choice of venue — in the case of the 1934 Act, the district where "any act or transaction constituting the violation occurred," or the district where the defendant "is found or is an inhabitant or transacts business" — and that process may be served "in any other district of which the defendant is an inhabitant or wherever the defendant may be found." Sec. Ex. Act §27. This literally permits worldwide service so far as American law is concerned. And the courts have given the venue provisions a broad reading. See 3 Loss 2007-12; 6 id. 4143-56.

American Stock Exchange had authorized the sale of treasury shares *in Canada* at a price that was inadequate in the light of certain oil discoveries not yet disclosed to the public. The court stated:

> We believe that Congress intended the Exchange Act to have extraterritorial application in order to protect domestic investors who have purchased foreign securities on American exchanges and to protect the domestic securities market from the effects of improper foreign transactions in American securities. In our view, neither the usual presumption against extraterritorial application of legislation nor the specific language of Section 30(b) show Congressional intent to preclude application of the Exchange Act to transactions regarding stocks traded in the United States which are effected outside the United States, when extraterritorial application of the Act is necessary to protect American investors.

405 F. 2d at 206.

In Sec. Act Rel. 5068 (1970), the Commission justified guidelines with respect to the applicability of the statutes to the sale of mutual fund shares abroad by referring, *inter alia,* to the possibility that "Loss of confidence in the integrity of American registered investment companies could trigger widespread redemptions resulting in losses to foreign and domestic investors and damage to the United States securities market." * * *

The leading case here, of course, is *United States* v. *Aluminum Co. of America,* 148 F. 2d 416, 444 (2d Cir. 1945), which held that certain agreements made by foreign companies outside the United States were illegal under §1 of the Sherman Act. But cf. *Bersch* v. *Drexel Firestone, Inc.,* 519 F. 2d 974, 989 (2d Cir. 1975), *cert. denied* sub nom. *Bersch* v. *Arthur Andersen & Co.,* 423 U. S. 1018, where Judge Friendly said that "there is subject matter jurisdiction of fraudulent acts relating to securities which are committed abroad only when these result in injury to purchasers or sellers of those securities in whom the United States has an interest, not where acts simply have an adverse effect on the American economy or American investors generally."[h]

(ii) The situation in §1905(a)(1)(D)(i) — where *some* of the constituent elements occur in the United States — is illustrated by *Leasco Data Processing Equipment Corp.* v. *Maxwell,* 468

---

[h] Ed.: See also IIT v. Cornfeld, 619 F. 2d 909, 916-17 (2d Cir. 1980), decided after publication of the Code. A number of countries later took defensive measures against the American "effects" doctrine. See, e. g., U. K. Limitation Amendment Act 1980, 27 & 28 Eliz. 2, c. 24.

F. 2d 1326 (2d Cir. 1972), *on remand,* 68 F. R. D. 178 (S. D. N. Y. 1974), also a Rule 10b-5 action, this one for damage allegedly resulting from the purchase of shares of a British company on the London Stock Exchange. If all the alleged misrepresentations had occurred in England, Judge Friendly stated, "we would entertain most serious doubt whether, despite [the *Aluminum* and *Schoenbaum* cases], §10(b) would be applicable simply because of the adverse effect of the fraudulently induced purchases in England of securities of an English corporation, *not traded in an organized American securities market,* upon an American corporation whose stock is listed on the New York Stock Exchange and its shareholders." 468 F. 2d at 1334 (italics supplied). But "it tips the scales in favor of applicability when substantial misrepresentations were made in the United States" (id. at 1337), as they allegedly were not only by agents physically within the United States but also by telephone and mail. The court saw no reason why, "for purposes of jurisdiction to impose a rule, making telephone calls and sending mail to the United States should not be deemed to constitute conduct within it." Id. at 1335.

*   *   *

But cf. *Bersch* v. *Drexel Firestone, Inc.,* supra Comment (1)(b)(i), 519 F. 2d at 987 (United States activities that "are merely preparatory or take the form of culpable nonfeasance and are relatively small in comparison to those abroad" do not suffice);[i] *Ogdeninvest, A. G.* v. *Hessische Landesbank-Giro-zentrale,* CCH Fed. Sec. L. Rep. ¶96,555 at 94,321 (S. D. N. Y. 1978) (when both parties are foreign corporations, fraudulent acts themselves must be performed in United States "in the absence of a more than negligent effect upon the United States or its citizens").

*   *   *

(c) Section 1905(a)-(c), accordingly, proceeds on a four-way basis: (i) §1905(a)(1)(A)-(C) attempts a statutory formulation of the rules of international law with respect to the extraterritorial application of the most significant areas of the Code; (ii) §1905(a)(1)(D) subjects the residue to the undefined limits of international law;

---

[i] ED.: Such activities assume a different aspect when they involve United States securities. Id. at 918.

(iii) §1905(b) specifies certain areas in which the Code does *not* apply extraterritorially; and (iv) §1905(c)(1) gives the Commission rulemaking authority that permits it not only to reverse the rebuttable "in" and "out" presumptions (as it were) of §1905(a)-(b) but also to fill the gap covered by neither (a) nor (b). All this is subject to the introductory limitation to "international law," however ascertained, as well as §1905(a)(1)(D). See Comment (11)(a) and (e).

This pattern not only blends the judicial expertise in international law (public and private) with the administrative expertise in the securities aspects of international commerce, but also recognizes that it is essential to distinguish between *power* in the international law sense and *policy*. See *Bersch,* supra Comment (1)(b)(i), 519 F. 2d at 985. This §1905 does by making the coverage of the Code quite broad (at least *prima facie*) and relying largely on Commission rules to tailor that expression of power to the appropriate policy considerations in the myriad contexts that could result in litigation (as many already have) under the Code. At the same time, the draft neither exhausts the limits of international law nor attempts to anticipate more than the more common and repetitive factual configurations.

(2) §§1905(a)(1)(A), 1905(a)(2), 1905(b): The pattern here is — in terms, for example, of a simple offer into or out of the United States — to cover both cases so far as "fraud" is concerned (§1905 (a)(2)), but, so far as Part V[j] is concerned, to reach only the offer *into* the United States (§1905(a)(1)(A)), not the offer *out* of the United States (§1905(b)). But all this is true only *prima facie,* in the absence of contrary rules (within the limits of international law) under §1905(c).

(3) §1905(a)(1)(A): (a) * * *

(b) Presumably everybody would agree that the making of an offer from another country into the United States by mail or telephone is subject to S5 and 17(a) [the registration and fraud provisions] even though neither the seller nor an agent of the seller sets foot in the United States. * * * This is the classic case of the shot across a boundary — the so-called "subjective territorial principle." See Restatement §18, Comment c, Illus. 2.

(c) Presumably the same would be true of proxy solicitations or tender requests made in the United States from a point outside solely by use of the mails or telephone, whether or not the statutory

---

[j] ED.: Part V, entitled "Distributions," is basically today's 1933 Act registration and prospectus scheme.

provisions were limited to registered securities (as, for example, X14(e) is not).

(4) §§1905(a)(2), 1905(b): The converse situation — the offer *from* the United States — is just as clearly covered by the "*objective* territorial principle*" of international law. That is to say, there is no question of the propriety of a state's applying its laws so as to avoid its territory's being used as a base to injure persons in other states. Restatement §17(a), esp. Comment a, Illus. 2; *IIT* v. *Vencap, Ltd.*, 519 F. 2d 1001, 1017 (2d Cir. 1975); *Continental Grain (Australia), Pty. Ltd.* v. *Pacific Oilseeds, Inc.*, 592 F. 2d 409 (8th Cir. 1979).

See also *SEC* v. *Kasser*, 548 F. 2d 109 (3d Cir. 1977), *cert. denied* sub nom. *Churchill Forest Industries (Manitoba), Ltd.* v. *SEC*, 431 U. S. 938. "We are reluctant to conclude," Judge Adams [there] stated, "that Congress intended to allow the United States to become a 'Barbary Coast,' as it were, harboring international securities 'pirates.' "

This accounts for §1905(a)(2), which so applies the "fraud" provisions. But *policy* does not require that Part V (successor to the registration and prospectus provisions of the 1933 act) extend as far as it might under international law. In the past the Commission has attacked this problem by construing S4(2) as exempting from registration transactions not involving any public offering *within the United States.* 1 Loss 368-70; 4 id. 2407-11. More recently its counsel have disclaimed that position, relying instead, apparently, on the Commission's withholding action in these cases as a matter of prosecutor's discretion. See Answering Brief of SEC, p. 47, n. 47 (1972), in *SEC* v. *United Financial Group, Inc.*, 474 F. 2d 354 (9th Cir. 973).[k]

Section 1905(b) is an elaboration of this policy, subject to rules that might provide otherwise under §1905(c)(1).

(5) §1905(a)(1)(B): (a) This section rests on a person's *status* rather than his acts. See *Fontaine* v. *SEC*, 259 F. Supp. 880 (D. P. R. 1966), *stay denied,* CCH Fed. Sec. L. Rep. ¶91,892 (1st Cir. 1967), described in 5 Loss 3410-11. With respect to the reference to §1902(b)(3) * * * in *Roth* v. *Fund of Funds, Ltd.*, 405 F. 2d 421 (2d Cir. 1968), *cert. denied,* 394 U. S. 975, a Canadian corporation with its offices in Switzerland was held liable under X16(b) [which provides for the recapture of certain insiders' short-term trading profits] when as a more-than-10 percent holder it

---

[k] ED.: Under either approach, the securities sold abroad must not seep back into the United States; the securities must "come to rest" abroad. Ibid.

had bought and sold on an American exchange, using New York brokers and paying for the purchases through a New York bank. But (subject to the introductory limitation to international law and the Commission's rulemaking authority to provide otherwise) §1905(a)(1)(B) would produce the same result even with respect to purchases and sales abroad.

(b) However, the "to the extent" clause contemplates only provisions that attach to status — for example, §1714 (successor to X16(b)) and the broker-dealer hypothecation and recordkeeping rules. International *offers* and other *transactions* that are effected by brokers or dealers, whether they are American or foreign and whether the offers are into or out of the United States, are governed by §1905(a)(1)(A), (a)(2) and (b) rather than (a)(1)(B).

*   *   *

(7) §1905(a)(1)(D): See Comment (1)(b)(i)-(ii). The "conduct" may consist of culpable nonfeasance. And the "constituent elements" phrase is not limited to acts essential to the establishment of the "prohibited, required, or actionable conduct." Thus, Clause (i) is broad enough, in the context of §1602(a)(1), to cover a sale consummated in England pursuant to negotiations in both England and the United States even though the only misrepresentations occurred in the negotiations abroad. But in such a case the emphasis is on "significant * * * extent." Cf. *Bersch,* supra Comment (1)(b)(i), 519 F. 2d at 987; *IIT,* supra Comment (4), 519 F. 2d at 1018. As here used, that phrase contemplates a qualitative rather than a merely quantitative analysis — just as the "constituent elements" phrase refers generally to the various acts that make up the conduct in question instead of being limited to such discreet steps in the conduct as offer, acceptance, and so on.

(8) §1905(b)(2)(A): This reflects *Schoenbaum* (supra Comment (1)(a)). And the negative implication reflects the holding in *SEC v. Myers,* 285 F. Supp. 743, 746 (D. Md. 1968), that a Canadian investment adviser could be enjoined from violating the registration provision of the Advisers Act if he were conducting a "business" *in the United States.* See also 2 Loss 1291, n. 15, 4th ¶.

*   *   *

(9) §1905(b)(2)(B): This contemplates, for example, the Canadian broker who uses the telephone to service a customer who is vacationing in Florida. If only Canadian brokers were involved,

this clause might be limited to customers who were themselves Canadian nationals; but the clause is phrased in terms of any non-national of the United States in deference particularly to European or Japanese brokers, who are perhaps increasingly likely to have a multinational clientele. The further limitation to persons who were *previously* customers or clients is designed to preclude a nonresident broker's building up a business with aliens more or less permanently in the United States unless he registers, and it does so more simply than would be the case with a fixed time limitation on the customer's presence in the United States.

(10) §1905(b)(3): This reflects the administrative construction, but without limitation to buyers who are non-nationals of the United States. Sec. Act Rel. 4708 (1964) 2, following Report to the President of the United States from the Task Force on Promoting Increased Foreign Investment in United States Corporate Securities and Increased Foreign Financing for United States Corporations Operating Abroad (1964) 7; see also 5 Loss 3353-54.

(11) §1905(c)(1): (a) The introductory language of §1905(a)(1)-(2) and (c) reflects Chief Justice Marshall's admonition that "an act of Congress ought never to be construed to violate the law of nations if any other possible construction remains." *The Charming Betsy,* 2 Cranch 64, 118 (1804), quoted in *McCulloch v. Sociedad Nacional de Marineros de Honduras,* 372 U. S. 10, 21 (1963).

That concept, of course, leaves the not insignificant question of determining what the international law is in a given context. See, e. g., in connection with the originally proposed rules for foreign issuers under X12(g), 21 Record of N. Y. C. B. A. 240, 252 (1966). Moreover, there is the risk — which the Commission presumably will consider under the "public interest" and other standards of §1804(b) [the rulemaking provision] — that excessive extraterritoriality might damage the country's trade position. But it is precisely in the grey area that Commission rules under §1905(c)(1) may be expected to be particularly helpful.

(b) Today some situations are clearly covered without benefit of express statutory provisions or rules. * * *

(c) Other cases are in a grey area under present law — for example, the Canadian newspaper that sells a relatively small number of copies in Miami hotels to Canadians vacationing in Florida. Literally a security advertised for sale in the newspaper is the subject of an "offer" in Florida. But does S12(1) apply if only one or two copies are mailed to Canadian subscribers while temporarily in Florida? The solution in §414(e)(1) of the Uniform Securities Act is a provision to the effect that there is no "offer" in the state when "the publisher circulates * * * in this state any bona fide newspaper or other publication of general, regular, and paid circulation which is not published in this state or which is published in this state but has had more than two-thirds of its circulation outside this state during the past twelve months." Without suggesting that this approach would be appropriate in the context of Part V, it is an indication of one sort of rule that the Commission might adopt under §1905(c)(1).

(d) So far there have been a number of negative cases to counterbalance the affirmative cases that have been cited * * * .

*   *   *

(e) In short, §1905(c)(1) does not give the Commission a completely free hand. * * *

(f) Rules could also consider the *nationality* basis of jurisdiction under international law. Restatement §30; X7(f). That is to say, an act not otherwise within the Code might be brought within it if the actor were an American national. But normally nationality alone is not considered sufficient to establish that a particular statute extends that far. And the nationality principle does not necessarily apply, for example, to transactions abroad merely because they are with American servicemen or other nationals. For "A state does not have jurisdiction to prescribe a rule of law attaching legal consequences to conduct of an alien outside its territory merely on the ground that the conduct affects one of its nationals." Restatement §30(2).

*   *   *

(12) §1905(c)(2): This is X12(g)(3). * * * [1]

2. REGISTRATION OF FOREIGN SECURITIES [§12(g)(3) AND RULE 12g3-2]

Foreign securities, whether governmental or corporate, are exempted neither from the 1933 Act nor from §12(a) of the 1934 Act, which requires the registration of securities listed on ex-

---

[1] ED.: The Commission's rules under §12(g)(3) are considered infra pp. 76-78. Section 7(f) of the 1934 Act, with respect to margin trading, is reflected in the margin section of the Code. §918(d).

changes.[3] Quite the contrary, the Commission sometimes uses Rule 408 under the 1933 Act — which requires a registration statement to include, in addition to the specified information, whatever "further material information * * * may be necessary to make the required statements * * * not misleading" — in order to call for disclosure with respect to various economic, political, and legal considerations pertaining to such matters as taxation, risks of expropriation and currency devaluation, and stockholders' rights. The Commission nevertheless has made some practical concessions with respect to disclosure of management remuneration: it accepts aggregate figures when disclosure of individual remuneration is not made under the customs and practices of the particular foreign country.[4] It also has allowed some deviation in financial reporting. In adopting a new Form 20-F in 1979 by way of consolidating the 1934 Act registration and annual report forms for certain foreign private issuers at a level somewhere between the prior forms and the general Forms 10 and 10-K, the Commission stated that its staff stood ready to discuss modifications in particular cases.[5]

So far as §12(g) is concerned, the problem is much more difficult. For the foreign issuer is not seeking access to the American capital market by way of either a distribution or a listing on a stock exchange. It is *prima facie* subject to the registration requirement if it has $3 million of assets and a class of equity security held of record by 500 persons. The Commission, out of considerations of enforcement difficulties, protection of existing markets in foreign securities, and greater flexibility,[6] would have preferred the Senate's formula, which would have exempted all foreign securities unless the Commission, by either rule or order, should find "that a substantial public market for the equity securities of such issuer

---

[3] Foreign *governmental* securities are exempted from §15(d) of the 1934 Act.

[4] Form 20-F, Item 6; see Garrett, Is the SEC a Barrier to New York's Role in International Finance?, Sec. Reg. L. Rep. No. 257, p. D-2 (1974).

[5] Sec. Ex. Act Rel. 16,371, 18 SEC Dock. 1118, 1119 (1979). Form 20-F facilitated the later extension of the integrated disclosure system under the 1933 and 1934 Acts to foreign private issuers eligible for that form. Sec. Act Rel. 6360, 24 SEC Dock. 3, 5 (1981); Sec. Act Rel. 6437, 26 SEC Dock. 964 (1982), infra c. 2D n. 5. The Commission thus "sought to balance the policies of protecting investors by requiring substantially the same disclosure from domestic and foreign issuers and of promoting the public interest by encouraging foreign issuers to register their securities with the Commission." Id. at 965.

[6] 1 Investor Protection, Hearings on H. R. 6789 before Subcom. of House Com. on Int. and For. Commerce, H. R. 6793, S. 1642, 88th Cong., 1st Sess. (1963) 179.

or of a class of issuers which includes such issuer exists in the United States and that continued exemption * * * is not in the public interest or consistent with the protection of investors."[7] The House turned the formula around, however, so that §12(g)(3) as enacted makes no distinction *prima facie* between domestic and foreign securities. Instead it authorized the Commission, either by rule or on its own motion (after notice and opportunity for hearing) by order, to exempt any foreign security, including a certificate of deposit for a foreign security, "if the Commission finds that such exemption is in the public interest and is consistent with the protection of investors."

After inviting comment on a set of proposed rules that produced protests by the British and Canadian Governments, as well as an opinion by the Committee on International Law of The Association of the Bar of the City of New York that the proposed rules would violate international law as they applied to foreign corporations without securities either listed or publicly offered in the United States,[8] the Commission in 1967 adopted a considerably revised set of rules and forms that reflected its view that

> the continuing improvement in the quality of the information now being made public by foreign issuers, together with the improvement which may reasonably be expected to result from recent changes and current proposals for change in relevant requirements, warrants the provision of an exemption from Section 12(g) for those foreign companies which have not sought a public market for their securities in the United States through public offering or stock exchange listing, and which furnish the Commission certain information which they publish abroad pursuant to law or stock exchange requirement or which they send to their security holders.[9]

Under this scheme of things:[10]

(1) American depositary receipts for foreign securities are exempted from §12(g) outright.

(2) Any class of securities of a foreign issuer (which is defined by Rule 3b-4 to mean a foreign government, a foreign national, or a corporation or other organization incorporated or organized under the laws of a foreign country) is likewise exempted if it has fewer than 300 holders resident in the United States.

---

[7] §12(g)(2)(E) as contained in S. 1642, 88th Cong. (1963); see S. Rep. No. 379, 88th Cong., 1st Sess. 29-31 (1963).

[8] 21 Record A. B. C. N. Y. 240, 252 (1966).

[9] Sec. Ex. Act Rel. 8,066 (1967). A temporary exemptive rule had been in effect meanwhile.

[10] See Rule 12g3-2.

(3) All other foreign private issuers except those that are essentially United States companies are automatically exempted if information of specified categories is furnished to the Commission. A foreign issuer is considered to be essentially a United States company

> if at the end of the last fiscal year of the issuer (i) more than 50 percent of the outstanding voting securities of such issuer are held of record either directly or through voting trust certificates or depositary receipts by residents of the United States and (ii) the business of such issuer is administered principally in the United States or 50 percent or more of the members of its Board of Directors are residents of the United States.

In addition, the required information is limited to whatever during the last fiscal year (a) has been made public by the issuer pursuant to the law of the country of its domicile or organization or by a stock exchange in which its securities are traded or (b) has been distributed by the issuer to its security holders. An English translation or substantially equivalent English version must be furnished only if one has been prepared.

(4) Thus far — that is to say, with respect to foreign issuers that have not sought a public market for their securities in the United States, either by registering under the 1933 Act or by listing on an American exchange — there is no discrimination against North American issuers. A distinction is made with respect to foreign companies that *have* sought an American market in one of those ways. In general, those companies, since they must already report under either §13 or §15(d),[11] are exempted from §12(g) unless they are essentially United States companies in the sense here described. But this exemption is not available to a North American issuer that is listed on a United States exchange, though it is to one that is subject to §15(d). Moreover, insofar as a foreign private issuer has registered under §12(b) (in connection with exchange listing) rather than §12(g), Rule 3a12-3 affords an exemption from §§14 and 16 (the proxy and insider trading provisions), again except for essentially United States companies; and that exemption, too, is unavailable to North American issuers with securities registered under §12(b) in connection with an exchange listing.

(5) In order to inform brokers, dealers, and investors of the unavailability of information in the United States with respect to certain foreign issuers, the Commission undertook from time

---

[11] On these reporting requirements, see pp. 487, 490 infra.

to time to issue lists of issuers from which it had received information. It added that, although no sanction would attach to any broker or dealer by reason of transactions in securities listed as neither registered nor exempt, "the Commission expects that brokers and dealers will consider this fact in deciding whether they have a reasonable basis for recommending these securities to customers."[12] The latest published list includes 227 issuers.[13]

The saving grace in this maze — and the description here is not complete — is that it is inevitably more difficult to attempt to present a composite picture than it is for one to pick his way through the various registration, reporting, proxy, tender offer, and insider trading provisions and the relevant exemptions once he has a particular kind of foreign issuer in mind (with regard, for example, to whether or not it is Canadian, whether or not it has a security listed or wants to list on an American exchange, and whether or not it has registered under the 1933 Act so as to be subject to the reporting requirement under §15(d) of the 1934 Act). At best, however, this complex of rules and forms is not calculated to reassure foreign businessmen and lawyers who already have a mental image of a multi-tentacled monster with its head in Washington and the oddly vinous name, SEC.

G. ADMINISTRATIVE LAW ASPECTS

When writing in a field like securities regulation — which is an amalgam of everything from contracts and torts to corporations and international law — it is difficult to draw precise boundary lines around the subject matter. Administrative law — judicial review, rulemaking, investigation, subpoena enforcement, and the governmental injunction — is a case in point. Some of this matter is more or less peculiar to the SEC. Thus we cover (or at least touch) at appropriate places the administrative enforcement procedures of the SEC and the self-regulatory organizations,[1] judicial review of the Commission's final orders in the Courts of Appeals,[2] and the availability of various kinds of ancillary relief in SEC injunctive proceedings.[3] So far as the bulk of administra-

---

[12] Sec. Ex. Act Rel. 8066 (1967).
[13] Sec. Ex. Act Rel. 17,169, 21 SEC Dock. 8 (1980).

C. 1G [1] See pp. 699-703 infra.
[2] See p. 703; see 3 and 6 Loss, c. 12C.
[3] See p. 842 n. 64 infra. On the prerequisites for an injunction itself, see

tive law is concerned, however, the SEC is simply another administrative agency — and so we leave that matter to the writers on administrative law.[4]

SEC v. National Student Marketing Corp., 457 F. Supp. 682 (D. D. C. 1978), set out infra p. 1176-78. The overwhelming proportion of SEC-initiated injunctions are entered by consent with a statement that the defendant "neither admits nor denies" the Commission's allegations. This pressure to settle can only be aggravated by Parklane Hosiery Co., Inc. v. Shore, 439 U. S. 322 (1979), where the Court held that a defendant found to have violated in a *litigated* SEC injunctive action is collaterally estopped from relitigating the same factual issue in a class action brought against him by a private plaintiff with respect to the same transaction. Other questions, like reliance and causation, may still be open but the plaintiff will obtain a partial summary judgment to the effect that the defendant committed the violation alleged by the Commission. On the exceptions to the *Parklane* case, see Chemetron Corp. v. Business Funds, Inc., 682 F. 2d 1149, 1188-92 (5th Cir. 1982), *vacated and remanded on other grounds,* — S. Ct. — (1983).

[4] See 3 and 6 Loss, c. 12; Code, Part XVIII.

CHAPTER 2

DISTRIBUTION OF SECURITIES

A. DISTRIBUTION TECHNIQUES

The registration and prospectus provisions of the Securities Act of 1933 can be understood — and their effectiveness evaluated — only on the background of the techniques by which securities are distributed in the United States.[1] There are three basic types of so-called underwriting that are in common use, sometimes with variations.

1. STRICT OR "OLD-FASHIONED" UNDERWRITING

Under the traditional English system of distribution — which is no longer common in that country — the issuer did not sell to

---

C. 2A   [1] *Caveat:* Chapter 2A describes the traditional distribution techniques as of the spring of 1982, when the Commission adopted Rule 415 on an experimental basis. Since that rule and its potentially vast implications for capital formation and investment banking practices could not possibly be understood without an analysis of the 1933 Act and the administrative practices that led to the rule's adoption, its consideration must be postponed until later in Chapter 2. See p. 140 infra. At any rate, the traditional distribution techniques are not dead; and, however much they may change under the impact of Rule 415, they are at the very least essential background.

For the rest, Chapter 2A is limited to distributions — which is to say, *public* offerings — of corporate securities. Many of the techniques and procedures used in the distribution of municipal and industrial revenue bonds differ substantially from those followed in the corporate area. On private placements, see c. 5E infra. On offerings of outstanding shares by means of "block distributions," see 1 Code 273-77. Other techniques that in recent years have accounted for a substantial volume have been dividend reinvestment plans, "TRASOPs," and employee thrift plans. In fact, dividend reinvestment plans have enabled companies, particularly utilities, to raise such large amounts of equity capital that utility common stock issues in the traditional manner have decreased in number. TRASOPs are a special form of employee stock ownership plan created by the Tax Reduction Act of 1975. §301(d), Int. Rev. Code §409A, 26 U. S. C. §409A. "From the employee's

81

an investment banking house for resale to the public, either directly or through a group of dealers. Instead a designated "issuing house" advertised the issue and received applications and subscriptions from the public on the issuer's behalf after an announced date. When sufficient applications had been received, an announcement was made that "the lists are closed," and the issuer proceeded to allot the securities directly to the applicants or subscribers, using various methods of proration in the event of an oversubscription. Securities firms normally subscribed to new issues not for their own accounts with a view to resale at a profit, but only as brokers for the accounts of their customers. Before the public offering was thus made, the issue was "underwritten" in order to ensure that the company would obtain the amount of funds it required.

This was underwriting in the strict insurance sense. For a fee or premium, the underwriter agreed to take up whatever portion of the issue was not purchased by the public within a specified time. And, just as insurance companies frequently reinsure large underwritings with other companies in order to distribute the risk, so the initial underwriter often protected himself by agreements with sub-underwriters, to which the issuer was not a party. The typical underwriting syndicate was not limited to investment bankers or so-called issuing houses. It included or might consist entirely of insurance companies or investment trusts or other institutions, or even large individual investors, who thus obtained large blocks of securities at less than the issue price. Accordingly, the underwriters planned to hold for investment any securities they might be required to take. Even the issuing houses that found themselves required to take up unsubscribed portions of issues were included to hold them temporarily until they found a buyer on favorable terms, instead of trying to resell them immediately, at a loss if necessary, as underwriters generally do in this country when issues get "sticky."

This method of distribution is called in the United States "strict" or "old-fashioned" or "standby" underwriting. It is seldom if ever used here except in connection with offerings to existing stockholders by means of warrants or rights. But in that field its use, though with important modifications, is common. Usually stockholders are thus given a prior opportunity to pur-

---

standpoint, they are a combined stock bonus and stock purchase plan. That is, employees can receive shares of the employer at no cost to them under such a plan, and they also may be given the opportunity to purchase additional shares of the employer at half the prevailing market price." Sec. Act Rel. 6188, 19 SEC Dock. 465, 484 (1980).

chase at a price below the market. If the discount is sufficiently large, and especially if the issuer is well established, the services of investment bankers may be dispensed with entirely. But it is common practice for the issuer to enter into a "standby agreement" with an investment banker.

Almost invariably the agreement is made with a syndicate of such bankers formed by the firm that is first approached, in which event that firm generally acts as syndicate manager. The trend has been toward larger and larger syndicates; they sometimes number well over a hundred members. The underwriters may receive by way of compensation a fixed percentage of the entire issue for assuming the risk of standing by during the week or so of the rights offering, or a smaller percentage so computed plus an additional concession (sometimes called the "work-out" cost) on any portion of the issue unsubscribed by security holders and hence required to be taken up by themselves. The method of compensation has been subject to a good deal of variation.

In the last few decades this standby technique for the handling of rights offerings has been developed to a fine point. In order to reduce the market risk of standing by during the rights period, the underwriters often purchase rights that are offered in the market by security holders who do not wish to acquire the new securities, exercise the rights themselves, and offer the stock for sale without waiting for the expiration of the rights offering. This also avoids an unfavorable reception of the public offering by reason of the market impact of a large block of unsubscribed stock.

Another — and less common — method of rights offerings is the so-called dealer-manager plan. The issuer merely arranges with one or more investment banking firms to pay a per-share commission to any dealers who promote the exercise of rights during the subscription period and whose names appear on the exercised warrants. This is a form of best-efforts arrangement, but sometimes it is combined with an ordinary standby agreement.

Rights offerings generally have undergone a good deal of experimentation, and the procedures are far from uniform. Their popularity is largely accounted for, presumably, by the substantial saving in costs as compared with other methods of distribution through investment bankers.

2.   FIRM-COMMITMENT UNDERWRITING

With respect to public financing otherwise than by rights offerings, the most prevalent type of American "underwriting" is the "firm-commitment" variety. It is not technically underwriting in the classic insurance sense. But its purpose and effect are much the same in that it assures the issuer of a specified amount of money at a certain time (subject frequently to specified conditions precedent in the underwriting contract) and shifts the risk of the market (at least in part) to the investment bankers. Traditionally the issuer would simply sell the entire issue outright to a group of securities firms, represented by one or several "managers" or "principal underwriters" or "representatives"; they in turn would sell at a price differential to a larger "selling group" of dealers; and they would sell at another differential to the public. In a very limited sense the process is comparable to the merchandising of beans or automobiles or baby rattles. The issuer is the manufacturer of the securities; the members of the underwriting group are the wholesalers; and the members of the selling group are the retailers. But it is not quite so simple. Except in the case of open-end investment companies, securities of particular issuers are distributed not continually but once in a long time, and then in a large batch. And the securities market is quite a different animal from the market for canned beans.

Before the Securities Act of 1933 — particularly during the period of tremendous industrial and business expansion that began roughly in 1900 — the procedure underwent an elaborate development. The risk of handling the increasingly large securities offerings of the Nation's industrial units had to be spread, and methods had to be developed to merchandise the securities among the ever-growing numbers of investors spread across the continent.

Jay Cooke is credited with having introduced the "underwriting syndicate" into this country in the sale of a $2 million bond issue by the Pennsylvania Railroad in 1870.[2] By the turn of the century it was common in the case of large offerings for a single investment banker to do the "origination" — that is, carry on the preliminary negotiations with the issuer, make the investigations deemed necessary, and then purchase the issue from the issuer. The banker was chosen (and still is to a large extent except when the law requires competitive bidding) on the basis of his past relationships with the issuer and his past performance. The "origination" stage was followed by the process of "syndication": In order to spread the commitment, the originating banker would immediately sell the issue to a small "original purchase group."

---

[2] See H. Larson, Jay Cooke (1936) 314 et seq.

And that group would in turn sell to a larger "banking group"; or the members of the latter group might occupy the status of "old-fashioned underwriters." The originating banker would become a member of the purchase group; the members of that group would likewise become members of the banking group; and the originating banker would manage both groups. When the issue was not too large, the intermediate group might be omitted. In either event, the two or three steps followed each other very closely. The function of both groups was to spread the risk — although the process also permitted the originating banker to make participations available on favorable terms to large distributors, to those firms that had reciprocated in the past or might do so in the future, to those he might count on in less favorable times, and to those suggested by the issuer. In any event, these groups were not designed primarily to do the actual distributing; often the members of the groups were not organized for retailing purposes. The public sale would be effected, for the account of whichever group last bought the issue, by the manager (the originating banker) through an organization of employees and agents, which would sometimes include those members of the purchase and banking groups who were geared for retail distribution.

With the increase in the number and size of securities issues during World War I, as well as the development of coast-to-coast telephone and wire systems, both groups tended to grow in membership and, in order to facilitate the actual mechanics of distribution, it became customary to add still another step to the elaborate process: Instead of the originating banker's selling through agents and employees, a much larger and more dispersed "selling group" or "selling syndicate" would take the issue from the banking group; those members of the earlier group or groups with distributive facilities would join this new group; and it, too, would be managed by the originating banker. These developments also tended to speed up the distribution process and shorten the lives of the several groups.

The passage of the Securities Act of 1933, as well as the new federal securities transfer taxes that were imposed in 1932, made for a simplification of this system.[3] Under the statute only negotiations between the issuer and "underwriters" are permitted before the filing of the registration statement. Until then the securities may not be offered to the public or even to dealers who are not "underwriters" within the statutory definition. And until

---

[3] There has been no federal stock transfer tax since year-end 1965. 79 Stat. 136 (1965).

the actual effective date of the registration statement, no sales or contracts may be made except with underwriters. This, in practice, means that today the interval between the signing of the underwriting contract and the effectiveness of the registration statement, during which whoever is committed to purchase at a fixed price cannot legally shift his liability against a decline in a frequently volatile market, has been reduced to an hour or two. Another result of the Securities Act and the former transfer taxes has been a tendency to reduce the number of transfers between groups and to enlarge the number of "underwriters" who bear the initial risk. In effect, the originating banker and the purchase and banking groups have all been combined into a single "underwriting syndicate or group."

It is difficult to generalize about the practice today, because it may vary substantially from issue to issue. Each of the prominent banking houses tends to develop variations of its own. Nevertheless, certain patterns are familiar. Quite early the underwriter, specifically negativing any obligation, gives the issuer sufficient assurance orally (or sometimes by a "letter of intent") to warrant the issuer's going ahead with the extensive work and expenses that are necessary. The single underwriting group is then created by a contract among its members (usually called the "agreement among purchasers" or the "agreement among underwriters") whereby they agree to be represented in their negotiations with the issuer by one or two or three of their number, whom it is currently the style to call merely the "representatives of the underwriters." It is the latter who, as successors to the old originating bankers, take the initiative and run the show. Through them all the underwriters enter into a "purchase contract" directly with the issuer. In order to limit exposure under §11 of the 1933 Act,[4] the liability of each underwriter to the issuer is several rather than joint. The trend has been toward larger underwriting groups, whose members are more and more able to do their own distributing. For that reason, and because of the tremendous expansion of the retail capability of many of the underwriting houses, there has also been a tendency to deemphasize formal "selling groups."

Typically the underwriters authorize their representatives to reserve out of the syndicate account (the "pot") whatever amount of the issue the latter choose for sale to selling-group dealers — sometimes termed simply "selected dealers" — as well as institutional investors.[5] The dealers are usually selected by the

---

[4] See p. 1029 infra.

[5] Also, in many debt issues, underwriters arrange for "delayed delivery

representatives, or in any event approved by them if suggested by other members of the underwriting group. The degree of formality that surrounds the organization of the selling group (if there is one) or the selection of the "selected dealers" depends largely on the predilections of the representatives. Usually the dealers sign some sort of uniform "dealer offering letter" that is sent to them by the representatives.

The method of determining the participants of the several underwriters is by no means fixed. How much a particular house gets is apt to depend on its prestige, its capital, its distributing capacity, its geographical location, whether it has any special outlets (perhaps connections with large pension funds or the like), and frequently the issuer's wishes. The participation of a given house is not necessarily related to the amount it can distribute. Some houses join the group primarily as underwriters, with a view to making a profit out of assuming their shares of the risk, and they may give up most or all of their participations for sale by the representatives, for their account, to institutions and dealers. In other words, the amount reserved for such sale is not always prorated among the accounts of all the underwriters. Sometimes it is, but sometimes each member of the group indicates to the representatives what proportion of its share it would like to have for its own retail distribution. The portion that particular houses thus distribute at retail usually varies between 25 and 75 percent. Those underwriters who want more for their own retail distribution become "selected dealers." Not infrequently, too, the representatives reserve the right, in checking on the progress of the distribution, to take securities away from those underwriters that are slow and allocate them to members of the selling group whose distribution has been more successful. In any event the representatives are obligated under the "agreement among purchasers" to notify each underwriter, on or before the public offering date, of the amount of its securities that has not been reserved for offering to institutions and dealers, so that the several underwriters will know how much they have to distribute.

As often as not the representatives are authorized, as the syndicate managers were before 1933, to "stabilize" the market on behalf of the underwriting group, although in practice the authority

---

contracts" between institutional buyers and the issuer. These contracts, which are subject to the issuer's approval, relieve the underwriters from the obligation to buy the amount of securities that the contracts cover. The issuer assumes the credit risk of the institutions, and the underwriters are paid a commission in lieu of a spread with respect to those securities.

frequently remains unused especially in debt issues; this is a complicated process (strictly regulated under the 1934 Act) whose purpose is to "peg" or put a floor under the market so as to prevent the overhanging supply of securities that are being distributed from depressing the market before and during the distribution. There has also been a continuation of the practice whereby during the life of the underwriting syndicate all the underwriters and participating dealers make a concurrent public offering at a uniform price and at uniform concessions allowed by them to other dealers, although the representatives usually reserve the right to terminate price restrictions even during the life of the syndicate. The public offering price (within the limits negotiated with the issuer) and all dealers' concessions and discounts are determined by the representatives — usually with the concurrence of a specified proportion of the underwriters, and sometimes with discretion in the former (which is not customarily used) to change the price. Although the liability of each underwriter to the issuer is several, the members of the group are responsible for their proportionate shares of the underwriting expenses, including carrying costs, and they participate *pro rata* in the stabilizing account.

In recognition of the representatives' directing the whole process (like the old originating banker), the are usually paid, out of the gross spread on the entire issue, a management fee of perhaps one-quarter of a point on a bond or some fixed percentage of the spread. This fee, which is split if there is more than one representative, is beyond the regular concession on whatever securities they underwrite or retail for their own account. For example, the underwriters may buy a million shares of stock from the issuer at 23 and sell part of them to selected dealers at, say, 23.8 with a view to a public offering price of 25. The nonmanaging underwriters may allow the representatives 5 percent of their spread of .8. And the selected dealers may sell at a discount of one-quarter of a point (in other words, at $24\frac{3}{4}$) to any other dealer who is a member of the National Association of Securities Dealers (NASD) or frequently foreign dealers on certain conditions. To the extent that any underwriter sells at retail, it gets the entire spread of 2 points, less the management fee, the discount, if any, that it allows to dealers generally, and, of course, its share of the expenses of the syndicate. The spreads in this illustration are arbitrary. Depending on all the circumstances, particularly how much selling effort the issue is expected to require, the retailers may get either more or less than half of the entire spread. In general, their portion of the entire spread seems to have increased in recent years.

In 1941 the SEC adopted Rule 50, a competitive bidding rule for underwritings (with some exceptions) under the Public Utility Holding Company Act. The ICC and a dozen states, including New York, have similar requirements for utility issues in at least some cases. And in one form or another competitive bidding has been the accepted method of financing for municipal and public instrumentality bonds since the beginning of the century, Massachusetts having led the way by statute in 1870. This method of underwriting is rarely used, at least for industrial common stock issues, when it is not required. But in total dollar amount it looms large.[6]

Suffice it to say that competitive bidding works in much the same way as firm-commitment underwriting of the negotiated variety, except for the initial stage. The houses interested in a particular issue that is to be offered at competitive bidding organize their respective underwriting syndicates for the purpose of submitting bids. The manager of each bidding syndicate holds a

---

[6] Some years ago this method was followed by many utilities even though they no longer were subjected to Rule 50 or to a state regulatory requirement. With the phenomenon of highly volatile debt markets, however, the technique has proven in many instances to be very costly. As a result it is seldom used unless required by law, and even in those cases regulatory authorities have often granted exemptions.

In recent years a novel form of competitive bidding has made its appearance, the so-called Dutch Auction:

> The Dutch Auction differs in certain material respects from the practice of competitive bidding. Principally, the bids which are submitted need not cover the entire amount of the offering in order to be accepted. Each bidder, including institutions and individuals as well as registered broker-dealers, indicates the amount of the offering which is wanted, and the yield [which is a function of price and interest rate]. Each bid received will, on the final date designated for entry of bids, become an irrevocable offer to purchase the amount of bonds indicated unless the bid is withdrawn.
>
> In addition, the offering price is based upon the yields specified in the bids. After closing the invitation period, the bids are listed in ascending order of yields. The bid with the lowest yield is accepted first, and then other bids at successively higher yields are accepted up to those bids with the highest yield required to reach the total amount of the offering. The highest accepted yield is the yield at which all of the bonds are awarded. Upon determination of the yield, the interest rate and price are fixed by the issuer. The securities will be awarded to the successful bidders at a uniform price based upon the accepted yield.
>
> Finally, there is no managing underwriter creating an underwriting syndicate, and no underwriting discount or commissions. There are no agreements entered into covering resale prices. As a result, prices can vary among resellers.

Exxon Corp., CCH Fed. Sec. L. Rep. ¶81,198 at 88,159 (letter 1977).

meeting of the members to determine the price they will bid. Then the syndicate with the successful bid distributes in the usual manner.[7]

3.   BEST-EFFORTS UNDERWRITING

Companies that are not well established are not apt to find an underwriter that will give a firm commitment and assume the risk of distribution. Of necessity, therefore, they customarily distribute their securities through firms that merely undertake to use their best efforts.[8] Paradoxically, this type of distribution is also preferred on occasion by companies that are so well established that they can do without any underwriting commitment, thus saving on cost of distribution. The securities house, instead of *buying* the issue *from* the company and reselling it as principal, *sells* it *for* the company as agent; and its compensation takes the form of an agent's commission rather than a merchant's or dealer's profit. There may still be a selling group to help in the merchandising. But its members likewise do not buy from the issuer; they are subagents. This, of course, is not really underwriting; it is simply merchandising.[9]

[7] From the point of view of the structuring of the legal profession, it is interesting that issuers that are subject to Rule 50 follow the practice of designating independent counsel to act for the bidders with the understanding that they will be compensated by the successful bidders. After a special study the Commission early concluded that "the existing practice of designation by the issuer of independent counsel to represent the bidders will be permitted to continue, but that adequate disclosure of such matters as the identity of the independent counsel and the proposed fees of such counsel to be paid by the successful bidders will be required and close scrutiny will be given to the reasonableness of such fees and to the relationship of the independent counsel to the issuer." Holding Co. Act Rel. 3118 (1941).

[8] It must not be assumed that every promotional company can find even a best-efforts underwriter. The problems of financing "small business" are profound. See p. 337 infra. In the Small Business Investment Incentive Act of 1980 Congress amended the Investment Company Act to encourage the formation of "business development companies" ("venture capital companies," as they are known in the street) that would invest in new ventures, and also added an exemption in §4(6) of the 1933 Act (infra p. 339).

[9] The term "best efforts" is used also in a broader sense to include all offerings through investment bankers, whether or not on an agency basis, otherwise than by "firm" agreements to purchase for resale. In this sense the term includes (1) offerings on an agency basis (through rights or otherwise) of high-grade securities not requiring underwriting, (2) offerings through purchases and resales by a dealer firm acting as principal but without any commitment to buy more than it can resell, or more than a specified portion of the offering, and (3) investment company shares that are similarly sold on a continuous dealer basis.

4. AMERICAN INVESTMENT BANKING IN GENERAL

There is nothing immutable about these three general methods of distribution. The investment banking industry, being very much alive, is continually studying and developing new techniques. One generalization, however, is safe. The formal underwriters in this country are invariably investment bankers. Commercial banks and trust companies and their affiliated securities companies used to underwrite in large volume. But all companies engaged "in the business of receiving deposits" had to stop (except for Government and municipal securities and a few other special types) with the divorcement of commercial and investment banking in the Banking Act of 1933 (the Glass-Steagall Act). Insurance companies, commercial banks and, to a lesser extent, investment companies and other institutional investors do play a prominent part in the financing of many companies, particularly in the case of high-grade bonds. But they are not syndicate members as they once were in both England and America. They are commonly consulted by the investment bankers and have portions of certain issues reserved for them by the syndicate manager, as we have seen, so that they are in a sense silent partners in the syndicate. Or in many cases the issuer, instead of making a public offering, merely effects a "private placement" of its bonds (sometimes through an investment banker that obtains a commission of perhaps one point) with a number of institutional investors for their own portfolios.

With rare exceptions, the insurance companies, the largest investors of all, do not even bid for bonds that are offered competitively. This was one of the Government's complaints in its antitrust action against seventeen prominent investment banking firms — although Judge Medina ultimately found in 1953 that the Government had not proved its allegation that a number of large insurance companies had entered into a noncompeting agreement with most of the defendant firms at a series of meetings held in the office of the New York Superintendent of Insurance in December 1941, after three large life insurance companies had won a $90 million issue of American Telephone & Telegraph debentures.[10]

---

[10] United States v. Morgan, 118 F. Supp. 621, 823-26, esp. 826 (S. D. N. Y. 1953).

B. REGISTRATION AND PROSPECTUS PROVISIONS OF THE 1933 ACT

1. THE STATUTORY PATTERN

The 1933 Act is concerned primarily with *distributions*. Post-distribution *trading* was to be the subject of further legislation, which turned out to be the 1934 Act.

The registration and prospectus provisions aside, there are only four sections in the 1933 Act that make conduct unlawful or actionable, and three of them may be disposed of summarily at this point: Section 17, which will be considered in a later chapter, is a general antifraud provision — applicable to the sale of all securities, whether registered or exempt from registration — that was a harbinger of what was to come the next year; and that section has a civil liability analogue in §12(2). Section 23 prohibits misrepresentation with respect to the effect of registration. And §24 makes it a crime not only willfully to violate any other provision (§17 or 23 or 5, the registration section) but also willfully to include a misstatement or half-truth in a registration statement.

The entire balance of the statute serves merely to implement the central registration provision, §5. That scheme of involuted drafting does not facilitate comprehensibility. One begins, naturally enough, with §5 itself. But that section covers the universe: read alone, it makes it unlawful for a humble investor named John Doe ("any person") to use the mails or any means of interstate commerce to sell 100 shares of General Motors (or, for that matter, part or all the outstanding stock of Doe Corp., Doe's family business) to his friend, Richard Roe, unless a registration statement is in effect and he delivers a specified prospectus. But that can't be right: Doe was presumably one of the class to be *protected* by the statute, not *regulated*.

The answer lies in §4(1), which exempts "transactions by any person other than an issuer, underwriter, or dealer."[1] Doe seems to be in the clear, because the "issuer" is Doe *Corp.* and certainly Doe, one supposes, is neither a "dealer" nor an "underwriter."

C. 2B [1] The 1954 and 1964 amendments require caution in considering pre-1954 literature. The principal purpose in 1954 was to permit offers, as distinct from sales, during the waiting period between the filing and the effectiveness of a registration statement, and this entailed adding a §5(c); the original Act made no distinction between the prefiling and waiting periods. Also, until 1964 what is now §§4(1), 4(2), and 4(3) was all §4(1) with three unnumbered clauses, and the present §4(4) was §4(2). Section 4(5) was added in 1975 and §4(6) in 1980.

But slow down. These are all defined terms, and §2(11) makes an "underwriter" out of anyone (whether or not he owns a pair of striped trousers) who has purchased a security, "with a view to [its] distribution," either from the "issuer" or from anybody who is in a "control" relationship with the issuer; and, whatever "control" and "distribution" (which are *not* defined terms) may mean, (1) Doe may well be a controlling person of his family corporation, so that (2) Roe, if he contemplates a reoffering of the stock to the highest bidder he can find, may well be engaged in a "distribution" so as to become an "underwriter," with the result that (3) the §4(1) exemption is lost after all.

If this is not bad enough, Doe's lawyer will find that §5(c) prohibits any "offer" of a security unless a registration statement has been *filed,* and that §2(3) defines "offer" to include "every attempt or offer to dispose of * * * a security" — which is a far cry from what he learned as a first-year law student. And among other artificialities, he will discover that, when §5 refers to a "prospectus," that term, as defined in §2(10), includes any communication that either offers or "confirms" the sale of a security.

The artichoke will have to be addressed layer by layer:

Section 5 was designed to place the facts before the investing public in two ways: First, adequate and accurate information in the form of a "registration statement" was to be made a matter of public record for a period of twenty days; this waiting or "cooling" period was to be used only to inform prospective investors about the issue and not to attempt to sell it. Secondly, underwriters and dealers were to furnish prospective investors with a prospectus based on the information in the registration statement. This is still the basic pattern of the statute, except that it was amended in 1954 to permit certain types of *offers* (but not *sales*) during the waiting period.

As amended in 1954, §5 is in three parts, which do not altogether coincide with the three stages in the registration process: the prefiling stage, the waiting period, and the posteffective stage.

Before a registration statement has been filed, §5(c), which was added in 1954, prohibits any use of interstate facilities or the mails to "offer to sell." Since that term is defined in §2(3) to include "every attempt or offer to dispose of, or solicitation of an offer to buy, a security or interest in a security, for value," it goes well beyond the common law concept of an offer. *A fortiori* it would be unlawful to *sell* or *deliver* a security in the prefiling stage even if the statute said nothing more. But §5(a) expressly prohibits sales or deliveries at any time before the *effective* date of the registration statement, which of course includes the prefiling stage. And the term "sale" is defined by §2(3) to include "every contract of sale or disposition of a security or interest in a security, for value."

During the waiting period between filing and effectiveness, §5(b)(1) prohibits the use of interstate facilities or the mails to transmit any "prospectus" unless it meets the requirements of §10, which prescribes the contents of the statutory prospectus. Since the term "prospectus" is defined by §2(10) to mean a *written* offer (with certain exceptions), there is no prohibition against *oral* offers (even by *inter*state telephone) during the waiting period as there is before filing. And, as we shall see, §§10 and 2(10) contemplate rules permitting the use of certain types of documents that are considerably less extensive than the full statutory prospectus. But §5(b)(1) prohibits the use of interstate facilities or the mails to transmit any other *written* offers during the waiting period; §5(a) prohibits the use of interstate facilities or the mails to *sell* or *deliver,* as in the prefiling stage; and §5(c) prohibits the use of interstate facilities or the mails even to make *offers* while any public examination or proceeding looking toward a "stop order" or "refusal order" under §8 is pending during the waiting period or, of couse, while such an order is operative.

After the effective date sales may be freely made. But *offers* are limited by §5(b) as in the waiting period, except that the term "prospectus" is defined in §2(10) with a view to permitting supplementary selling literature (that is, literature accompanied or preceded by a full §10 prospectus) only *after* the effective date. In any event, the full prospectus must accompany any interstate or mailed *delivery* of the security under §5(b)(2) if it has not *preceded* delivery. And the actual *entry* of a stop order or refusal order bars the use of interstate facilities or the mails even to make *offers,* although the mere *pendency* of a proceeding or examination under §8 does not have this effect except during the waiting period.

Section 5 must be read in the light of the definitions contained in §2 and the exemptions contained in §§3 and 4. We have already noticed §4(1) and its interreaction with the definition of "underwriter" in §2(11) to bring *underwritten* secondary distributions in *control* situations within §5.[2] Now suppose Doe is a dealer in securities by profession, but it has been years since General Motors has issued any new securities. He must then look

2 See pp. 92-93 supra. A primary distribution is a distribution of securities (including treasury shares) by the issuer, and a secondary distribution is a distribution of outstanding securities by their owner.

to §4(3), which exempts all "transactions by a dealer" (and the term "dealer" is defined in §2(12) to include a broker) *except* that (1) dealers that are participants in the distribution are subject to §5 for as long as it may take them to get rid of their unsold allotments or subscriptions and (2) *all* dealers (even those that have played no role whatever in the distribution proper) are subject to §5 for a minimum of forty days after the effective date (ninety days if securities of the issuer have not previously been sold pursuant to an earlier effective registration statement) unless the Commission shortens either period by rule or order.

This is the provision that indicates "that the act is, in the main, concerned with the problem of distribution as distinguished from trading."[3] Congress felt that there had to be some minimum posteffective period during which all dealers, whether members of one of the distributing groups or not, should be required to use a statutory prospectus in order to avoid a particular dealer's claiming "that the securities he was offering for sale were not acquired by him in the process of distribution but were acquired after such process had ended"; and in 1933 Congress arbitrarily picked a period of one year "because, generally speaking, the average public offering has been distributed within a year, and the imposition of requirements upon the dealer so far as that year is concerned is not burdensome."[4] The period was reduced to a minimum of forty days in the 1954 amendments, and the 1964 amendments not only extended the period to ninety days for first registrations but also authorized the Commission by rule or order to shorten the forty-day period as well as the ninety-day period.

Then there is §4(2), which exempts "transactions by an issuer not involving any public offering."[5]

In other words, §5 (quite apart from the other definitions and exemptions) must be read as if it applied to *any transaction by an issuer or underwriter in connection with a "primary" distribution* (that is, a *public* offering) *by the issuer, or a "secondary" distribution by a person in a control relationship with the issuer, or any transaction by a dealer within forty* (sometimes ninety) *days after the beginning of such a distribution* (unless the period is shortened by the Commission) *or during such longer period as he personally may be engaged in distributing*. And even this statement must be limited by a clause in §2(3) that excepts from the definitions of the terms "offer" and "sale" any "preliminary negotiations or

[3] H. R. Rep. No. 85, 73d Cong., 1st Sess. (1933) 15.
[4] Id. at 16.
[5] See c. 5E infra.

agreements" with underwriters. This has the effect of permitting the formation of the underwriting group before the effectiveness or even the filing of the registration statement, although there is no exemption for "offers" or "sales" by underwriters to selling-group dealers.

The method and procedure of registration are specified in §§6 and 8, and the contents of the registration statement and prospectus are prescribed, subject to the Commission's rulemaking power, in §§7 and 10 and Schedule A of the Act (Schedule B in the case of securities issued by foreign governments). Under §8 the registration statement automatically becomes effective on the twentieth day after filing unless the Commission fixes an earlier date; the filing of an amendment before the effective date of the registration statement starts the twenty-day period running again unless the amendment is filed with the consent of the Commission (a process popularly called "acceleration"); and if the registration statement is materially deficient, the Commission, after notice and hearing, may at any time enter a stop order suspending its effectiveness, subject to judicial review in the appropriate Court of Appeals under §9.

Section 11 of the act imposes civil liability on the issuer, its officers and directors, the underwriters, accountants, engineers, and other experts in the event the registration statement contains material misstatements or omits to state material facts; §12(1) imposes civil liability upon any person who offers or sells a security in violation of §5; and §12(2) imposes civil liability upon any person who offers or sells any security (whether or not registered) by means of material misstatements or omissions to state material facts. The rest of the statute contains investigation, injunction, criminal penalty, rulemaking, and a few miscellaneous provisions.

2. THE JURISDICTIONAL BASE OF §5

For constitutional reasons §5, as well as the antifraud provisions of §§12(2) and 17 and of the 1934 Act, refer (not always in the same connective language) to use of the mails or interstate commerce.

Although Congress, in the judicial atmosphere of the day, may have "meant to exert its power to the full constitutional extent permitted by the commerce clause and the postal clause,"[6] it now seems fairly clear that the jurisdictional base of the section could be constitutionally expanded so that it would apply to all steps

[6] Schillner v. H. Vaughan Clark & Co., 134 F. 2d 875, 878 (2d Cir. 1943).

in the process of selling — from offer to delivery and payment —
if the mails or interstate facilities were used in any one step. And
that is what the Code would do.[7] As it is, each of the five prohibitions in §5 stands alone so far as the jurisdictional base is concerned — and in this respect no change was effected by the 1954
amendments. That is to say, a dealer may offer or sell in any
manner he likes, whether before filing or without a prospectus
after filing, as long as he does not use the mails or interstate facilities to do so — even though they may later be used in sending a
confirmation of the transaction or delivering the security. This
is apart, of course, from the fact that *oral* offers are now permitted
during the waiting period even by *inter*state telephone, as they
always were after the effective date.

Thus it is possible in many cases to offer and sell without even
a technical violation, either before or after effective registration,
and deliver a statutory prospectus for the first time with the confirmation or the security — if, indeed, the mails or interstate facilities are used at that stage. This is hardly the kind of informed
investing that was contemplated when the Securities Act was
passed. A prospectus that comes with the security does not tell
the investor whether or not he should buy. It tells him whether
he has acquired a security or a lawsuit. As an English investment
banker is said to have remarked, "What you chaps have is not a prospectus but a retrospectus."[8] Indeed, one may question whether
the ordinary investor will examine the prospectus at all after
skillful sales talk has already convinced him to part with his money.
It is therefore irrelevant that the oral contract of sale may not be
legally enforceable against the buyer, either because of the statute
of frauds or because of difficulties of proof. The fact is that an
investor who is psychologically committed is much less apt to study
the prospectus than one who is trying to make up his mind.

For these reasons the Code would rationalize the prospectus
delivery requirement by moving in two directions. When the
issuer is a "one-year registrant" — which is to say, a company (under the Code's scheme of registering companies rather than securities) that has been registered, and hence is subject to the Code's
continual reporting provisions, for at least a year — there would
be no prospectus requirement at all except for sales out of underwriters' or selling group dealers' allotments or subscriptions.[9] On
the other hand, with respect to securities of *non*-one-year registrants

---

[7] §1902(d).

[8] SEC, Disclosure to Investors (The Wheat Report) (1969) 106.

[9] §512(3). A company would register (1) on acquiring $1 million of assets
and 500 security holders, (2) on the first "distribution" of its securities, (3)
on becoming an investment company, or (4) on becoming a utility holding

— which is to say, those new or relatively new to the marketplace
— the buyer would have a privilege of disaffirmance for two business days after he had received a prospectus (or, during the waiting
period, a so-called "preliminary prospectus."[10]

All this is not to imply a grudging construction of §5 as it stands.
It is now fairly well established in the lower courts (1) that the
use of a common carrier or even a private car or one's own two
feet to cross a state line suffices, since a highway or a bridge that
joins two states (if not the vehicle or the pedestrian's feet) is a
means of interstate commerce;[11] (2) that, on the rationale of the
mail fraud cases, use of the mails or interstate commerce in *making payment* is their use "to offer" and "to sell" within the meaning of §§5(c) and 5(a)(1) on the theory that payment is an essential
element of a sale and that the seller should reasonably have foreseen that payment might be made by one of the jurisdictional
means;[12] and (3) that even the *intra*state telephone is a means or
instrument of communication "in interstate commerce" notwithstanding the arguably broader reference in §10(b) of the 1934 Act,
that statute's general fraud provision, to a means or instrumentality "of" interstate commerce.[13]

---

company (see Part IV); all four categories would then be equally subject to
the continuous disclosure requirements of Part VI, except that investment
and utility holding companies would be subject to substantive regulation
under Parts XIV and XV; and today's 1933 Act registration statement would
become a much simpler "offering statement" (see Part V).

[10] §504(b).

[11] E. g., MacClain v. Bules, 275 F. 2d 431, 433 (8th Cir. 1960); Hill York
Corp. v. American Int'l Franchises, Inc., 448 F. 2d 680, 693 (5th Cir. 1971).
The term "interstate commerce" is defined in §2(7) of the 1933 Act.

[12] E. g., Lennerth v. Mendenhall, 234 F. Supp. 59, 63 (N. D. Ohio 1964)
(mailing a check was "indispensable to the whole transaction"); cf. United
States v. Wolfson, 405 F. 2d 779, 783-84 (2d Cir. 1968) (selling broker's mailing of confirmation to *seller*). Under the mail fraud statute, see, e. g., United
States v. Roylance, 690 F. 2d 164 (10th Cir. 1982).

[13] E. g., Lennerth v. Mendenhall, 234 F. Supp. 59, 63 (N. D. Ohio 1964);
Ingraffia v. Belle Meade Hospital, Inc., 319 F. Supp. 537 (E. D. La. 1970);
Clarence E. Thornton, 42 SEC 751, 753 n. 4 (1965); Loveridge v. Dreaugoux,
678 F. 2d 870 (10th Cir. 1982). *Contra:* e. g., Franklin Savings Bank v. Levy,
406 F. Supp. 40, 42 (S. D. N. Y. 1975), *rev'd on other grounds,* 551 F. 2d 521
(2d Cir. 1977). The fraud provisions of the 1933 Act, §§12(2) and 17, likewise say "in."

The affirmative cases are perhaps weakened by the 1975 amendment of the
definition of "interstate commerce" in §3(a)(17) of the 1934 Act, but not
§2(7) of the 1933 Act, to include "intrastate use of (A) any facility of a national securities exchange or of a telephone or other interstate means of
communication, or (B) any other interstate instrumentality." Quite clearly
that amendment merely codified existing law so far as Rule 10b-5 is concerned.
Myzel v. Fields, 386 F. 2d 718, 727 n. 2 (8th Cir. 1967), *cert. denied,* 390 U. S.
951; Lawrence v. SEC, 398 F. 2d 276, 279 n. 2 (1st Cir. 1968); Kerbs v. Fall
River Industries, Inc., 502 F. 2d 731, 737-38 (10th Cir. 1974); Aquionics Ac-

3.   THE PREFILING PERIOD

Before we proceed further, a word of caution: Everything said in the remainder of this Chapter 2B, as well as Chapter 2C on the registration *procedure,* is subject to the recent adoption of Rule 415, which in certain circumstances permits registration "for the shelf" instead of the traditional registration for specified offerings to be made essentially forthwith.[14] "Shelf" registration may turn out to be the rule rather than the exception. At this writing it is too early to say. At any rate, an exegesis of the historical norm is essential to an understanding of the "shelf" phenomenon.

a.   Preliminary Negotiations with Underwriters

Before a registration statement has been filed, §§5(a)(1) and 5(c) prohibit the use of the mails or interstate facilities not only to sell the security but also "to offer to sell or offer to buy through the use or medium of any prospectus or otherwise." But §2(3) excepts from the definitions of the terms "sell" and "offer to sell," as well as the term "offer to buy" as used in §5(c), "preliminary negotiations or agreements between an issuer (or any person directly or indirectly controlling or controlled by an issuer, or under direct or indirect common control with an issuer) and any underwriter or among underwriters who are or are to be in privity of contract with an issuer (or any person indirectly or directly controlling or controlled by an issuer, or under direct or indirect common control with an issuer)." Before the 1954 amendments, when the prohibition against the use of the mails or interstate facilities to offer to sell or buy extended until the effectiveness rather than the filing of the registration statement, this exception was even more essential as a means of getting the distribution under way.

Just as the express exception for preliminary negotiations between issuer and underwriter was a clear indication that Congress intended in the original act to "delay the actual organization of the selling group and the disposition of the security to the dealers until the registration statement shall have become effective,"[15] it should be equally clear now that the organization of the selling group must be delayed until the registration statement has been

---

ceptance Corp. v. Kollar, 503 F. 2d 1225 (6th Cir. 1974); Gower v. Cohn, 643 F. 2d 1146, 1151 (5th Cir. 1981). Section 3(a)(17) was not mentioned in *Dreaugoux,* supra.

[14] See pp. 140-47 infra.

[15] H. R. Rep. No. 85, 73d Cong., 1st Sess. (1933) 12.

filed. In fact, it is clear from the legislative history that the "offer to buy" prohibition was originally inserted solely for the purpose of preventing *dealers* from making offers to buy from underwriters during the waiting period — or, as §5 has now been amended, before the filing of the registration statement. "Otherwise," the House committee observed, "the underwriter, although only entitled to accept such offers to buy, after the effective date of the registration statement, could accept them in the order of their priority and thus bring pressure upon dealers, who wish to avail themselves of a particular security offering, to rush their orders to buy without adequate considerations of the nature of the security being offered."[16] In other words, an ordinary investor is not prohibited from making an offer to buy a security from the issuer or an underwriter or dealer before the filing date, although no person in these three categories may solicit or accept his offer or make any attempt to sell to him.

Quite apart from the legislative history, any such offer to buy is exempted by §4(1) as a transaction "by any person other than an issuer, underwriter, or dealer"; for, even though the offeree is the issuer or an underwriter or dealer, the word "transactions" in the several exemptions under §4 is simply a shorthand term for offers (including offers to buy) and sales, which are all that §5 prohibits and consequently all that §4 needs to exempt from. Again, since §2(3) permits an issuer to make an offer to sell to a prospective underwriter before the filing date, there should certainly be no objection in principle to a prospective underwriter's approaching an issuer in the first instance with an offer to buy. When the issuer itself is making an offer to buy its own securities — at least when the offer goes to a substantial number of security holders — §5(c) would seem literally to apply in the sense that there is no specific exemption or exclusion; for that *is* an offer (and hence a transaction) "by an issuer." On the other hand, however tempting it might have been before the special legislation of 1968 to reinforce Rule 10b-5 under the 1934 Act by using §5(c) to attack the problems of inadequate disclosure by issuers in public tender offers, not merely the legislative history of §5(c) but the whole registration structure of the 1933 Act is utterly inconsistent with any concept of issuers' registering public offerings to buy.

Now that it is clear that the exception in §2(3) does *not* extend to negotiations or agreements *beyond* the underwriting level, there remains the question of what it does encompass. The juxtaposi-

[16] Id. at 11.

tion of the word "preliminary" is somewhat ambiguous. Apparently it does not modify the word "agreements" — or perhaps it means merely that the agreements must be preliminary to the effectiveness of the registration statement — because the House committee report states that "Underwriting agreements can thus be entered into prior to the time of the filing of the registration statement."[17] In practice the SEC has not interfered with the making of firm contracts to sell between issuer and underwriter at any time. Indeed, it has always insisted on having the registration statement disclose the underwriting date before it becomes effective. But it is not common for the securities actually to be transferred to the underwriters until after effectiveness.

Since §2 introduces all the definitions by the phrase "unless the context otherwise requires,"[18] it is arguable that the "preliminary negotiations" clause, though it literally excludes from the definitions of "sell" and "offer to sell," should be treated like a §4 exemption so as not to extend to the fraud provisions.[19] At any rate, the Code cuts through the entire morass by simply exempting from the Code's successor to §5 "an offer or sale to an underwriter."[20]

b.   "Beating the Gun"

The 1954 legitimation of "offers" during the waiting period substantially solved one important aspect of the old problem of "beating the gun." For there is no longer much pressure in the prefiling days personally to solicit and accept "indications of interest" — a euphemism for the making of "offers" in the statutory sense — in view of the few weeks that will be available for the making of "offers" while the registration statement is being processed. The aspect of the problem that survived the 1954 amendments was the practice that some issuers, underwriters, and dealers followed of "conditioning the market" before the filing of a registration statement through such devices as press interviews, speeches, special reports to stockholders, market letters, and so on. This is a problem that arises not only in the prefiling stage but also during the waiting period and even after effectiveness, because the

---

[17] Id. at 12.

[18] See p. 261 infra.

[19] In any event, there is no reference at all to agreements with underwriters in the 1934 Act.

[20] §512(1).

method of offering is restricted at least as long as the distribution continues.

In 1969 the Commission had this to say:

> * * * the increasing obligations and incentives of corporations to make timely disclosures concerning their offerings raise a question as to a possible conflict between the obligation to make timely disclosure and the restriction on publication of information concerning an issuer which may have securities "in registration." The Commission believes that such a conflict may be more apparent than real. Events resulting in a duty to make prompt disclosure under the anti-fraud provisions of the securities laws or timely disclosure policies of self-regulatory organizations at a time when a registered offering of securities is contemplated are relatively infrequent and normally may be effected in a manner which will not unduly influence the proposed offering. Disclosure of a material event would ordinarily not be subject to restrictions under Section 5 of the Securities Act if it is purely factual and does not include predictions or opinions.[21]

And in 1971:

> It has been suggested that the Commission promulgate an all inclusive list of permissible and prohibited activities in this area. This is not feasible for the reason that determinations are based upon the particular facts of each case. However, the Commission as a matter of policy encourages the flow of factual information to shareholders and the investing public. Issuers in this regard should:
>
> 1. Continue to advertise products and services.
>
> 2. Continue to send out customary quarterly, annual and other periodic reports to stockholders.
>
> 3. Continue to publish proxy statements and send out dividend notices.
>
> 4. Continue to make announcements to the press with respect to factual business and financial developments; i. e., receipt of a contract, the settlement of a strike, the opening of a plant, or similar events of interest to the community in which the business operates.
>
> 5. Answer unsolicited telephone inquiries from stockholders, financial analysts, the press and others concerning factual information.
>
> 6. Observe an "open door" policy in responding to unsolicited inquiries concerning factual matters from securities analysts, financial analysts, security holders, and participants in the communications field who have a legitimate interest in the corporation's affairs.

[21] Sec. Act Rel. 5009 (1969).

7. Continue to hold stockholder meetings as scheduled and to answer shareholders' inquiries at stockholder meetings relating to factual matters.

In order to curtail problems in this area, issuers in this regard should avoid:

1. Issuance of forecasts, projections, or predictions relating but not limited to revenues, income, or earnings per share.

2. Publishing opinions concerning values.

In the event a company publicly releases material information concerning new corporate developments during the period that a registration statement is pending, the registration statement should be amended at or prior to the time the information is released. If this is not done and such information is publicly released through inadvertence, the pending registration statement should be promptly amended to reflect such information.[22]

The issuer confronts still other §5 problems in the course of its corporate life:

(1) A corporation in need of additional capital requires a vote of shareholders to authorize additional shares, and those shareholders have preemptive rights.

(2) The same corporation is informed by a prospective underwriter that its interest is conditioned on a *waiver* of preemptive rights.

(3) A corporation would like to inform its shareholders of a contemplated rights offering — which, absent §5, would be the decent thing to do in order to avoid the possibility of some shareholders' selling their shares and missing out on the value of the rights.

(4) A prospective underwriter that wants to get rid of an outstanding issue of callable preferred that is overhanging the market insists that the stock be called, and the issuer, again out of a sense of sound shareholder relations, would like to inform its preferred shareholders when making the call that they will be given an opportunity to subscribe to a new issue for a limited time after the effective date of the registration statement.

The Commission interposed no objection to any of these practices. And today the answer is found in Rule 135, adopted in 1955 with respect to rights offerings and ultimately extended in 1970 to *all* offerings. That rule provides that a person proposing to make a public offering is not considered to make an "offer," so far as §5 is concerned, if the notice states that the offering will be made only by means of a prospectus and contains no more than six categories of information. But six does not mean seven: there

---

[22] Sec. Act Rel. 5180 (1971).

is no reference to price, and a divided Second Circuit held that
the announcement of a target company (Piper Aircraft) in a hostile
takeover attempt by Chris-Craft Industries that a package exchange
offer by a friendly third company (Bangor Punta) would be valued
at "$80 or more" overstepped Rule 135 and violated §5:

> When it is announced that securities will be sold at some date
> in the future and, in addition, an attractive description of these
> securities and of the issuer is furnished, it seems clear that such
> an announcement provides much the same kind of information
> as that contained in a prospectus. See *SEC* v. *Arvida Corp.,* 169
> F. Supp. 211 (S. D. N. Y. 1958). Doubtless the line drawn between
> an announcement containing sufficient information to constitute
> an offer and one which does not must be to some extent arbitrary.
> A checklist of features that may be included in an announce-
> ment which does not also constitute an offer to sell serves to guide
> the financial community and the courts far better than any ju-
> dicially formulated "rule of reason" as to what is or is not an
> offer. Rule 135 provides just such a checklist, and if the Rule
> is not construed as setting forth an exclusive list, then much of
> its value as a guide is lost.
>
> Moreover, it is reasonable to conclude that the assigning of a
> value to offered shares constitutes an offer to sell. One of the evils
> of a premature offer is its tendency to encourage the formation
> by the offeree of an opinion of the value of the securities before
> a registration statement and prospectus are filed. There is then
> no information on file at the SEC by which the Commission can
> check the accuracy of the information which forms the basis of
> the offeror's estimate of value, and any offeree, such as the reader
> of a press release, is encouraged to form a premature opinion
> of value without benefit of the full set of facts contained in a
> prospectus.
>
> Here a statement of the value of the securities Bangor Punta
> offered was made directly in the announcement. It is true that
> the value which the reader of the May 8 press releases could be
> expected to accept is a value based upon the opinion of a repu-
> table financial corporation and not upon general and necessarily
> speculative facts about the nature of the offeror's business, as in
> *Arvida,* supra. However, the true significance of the $80 value
> which Bangor Punta claimed for its securities package was none-
> theless unclear. Chris-Craft charges that the figure constituted an
> outright misrepresentation inasmuch as most readers would con-
> strue the figure as representing the market value of the package.
> In fact, Chris-Craft charges, some of the securities in the package
> had not previously been sold on the market at all, and the market
> value of Piper shares never reached $80 in response to the Bangor
> Punta exchange offer, so that the Bangor Punta securities did not

have an $80 market value and could not honestly have been thought to have such a value.[23]

On the other hand, Rule 135 does not exhaust the Commission's discretion. This is evident from a development under the 1968 addition of §14(d) to the 1934 Act in order to give the Commission jurisdiction over tender offers.[24] Sometimes two companies agree in principle to a merger, after which one of them (the "acquiring company") makes a cash tender offer for less than all the equity securities of the other (the "acquired company"), with the idea that, if the acquiring company does not obtain as many shares as it wants in the tender offer, stockholders of the acquired company may elect, before the vote on the merger, to receive cash in lieu of securities of the acquiring company. This presents something of a dilemma, in that the very disclosure of these merger negotiations that is required with respect to the tender offer pursuant to §14(d)(1) of the 1934 Act might be said to be a form of "gun-jumping" with respect to the securities of the acquiring company emanating from the subsequent statutory merger. But the Commission has released a staff letter reversing its affirmative position on that question.[25]

Dealers face similar line-drawing problems with respect to recommending, or including in their market letters, securities that are in registration. For them the Commission adopted a *series* of rules in 1970:[26]

> *Rule 137.* This new rule is designed to clarify the status of dealers not participating in a distribution. It permits publication and distribution by a dealer in the regular course of business of information, opinions, or recommendations regarding securities of a reporting company [under the 1934 Act] which has filed or proposes to file a registration statement under the [1933] Act.

---

[23] Chris-Craft Industries, Inc. v. Bangor Punta Corp., 426 F. 2d 569, 574-75 (2d Cir. *en banc* 1970). A 1982 amendment permits information with respect to interest rate, conversion ratio and subscription price, in the case of a rights offering of a security listed on an exchange or quoted in NASDAQ (see p. 675 infra), to be disseminated through the facilities of the consolidated transaction reporting system (see p. 675 infra) or NASDAQ or the Dow Jones broad tape if the information is already disclosed in a registration statement on file. Rule 135(c).

[24] See c. 7E infra.

[25] United Technologies Corp., CCH Fed. Sec. L. Rep. ¶81,679 (letter 1978); Sec. Act Rel. 4927, 14 SEC Dock. 894 (1978). The acquiring company may not go beyond the disclosure required by §14(d)(1) by, for example, issuing press releases or granting interviews. Id. at 898; cf. Sheinberg v. Fluor Corp., 514 F. Supp. 134 (S. D. N. Y. 1981).

[26] Sec. Act Rel. 5101 (1970).

Rule 138. New Rule 138 permits a broker-dealer participating in an offering of non-convertible senior securities [that meet specified conditions, primarily a three-year reporting history under the 1934 Act] to publish opinions or recommendations concerning the issuer's common stock, and vice versa. [The rationale of this rule lies in the fact that the market for senior securities is largely institutional.]

Rule 139. New Rule 139 permits a broker-dealer participating in an offering to publish at regular intervals, as part of a comprehensive list of securities, opinions or recommendations concerning the issuer provided it is a reporting company. The opinion or recommendation, however, must not be given special prominence, and must not be more favorable than the last previous opinion distributed before the broker-dealer became a participant.

The Commission has said in proposing Rule 139:

> Some relaxation of restrictions in this area appears necessary, particularly with respect to issuers which are continuously "in registration." Otherwise investors may be deprived of the broker-dealer's opinion when buying or selling securities in the trading markets.[27]

All this, however, is in a particular state of flux because of the "shelf registration" rule. For the time being, at least, the Commission is permitting research reports beyond Rule 139 until three business days before the commencement of sales.[28]

4. THE WAITING PERIOD

a. The Offer-Sale Distinction

Actual contracts of sale are still illegal under §5(a)(1) and not merely unenforceable if entered into before the effective date. But issuers, underwriters and dealers should find no difficulty in so regulating their conduct during the waiting period as to avoid making "sales." Obviously no such person should make an offer in the common law sense that, if accepted by the buyer before the effective date, would create an illegal contract. And the acceptance

---

[27] Sec. Act Rel. 5010 (1969). Oddly enough, Rule 139 refers only to "the securities so registered or proposed to be registered." But the rule, in principle, is only an interpretation of "offer to sell" that should extend *a fortiori* to recommendations with respect to one class of securities of an issuer that has another class in registration.

[28] Sec. Act Rel. 6383, 24 SEC Dock. 1262, 1294 n. 94 (1982).

of funds, or the segregation of funds held previously for a customer, would presumably be evidence of an illegal contract.

Perhaps the safest technique is to solicit offers to buy, which the seller can then accept after the effective date. But this is not the only possible technique. The 1954 legislative reports refer also to the possibility of "conditioning offers."[29] An offer to sell that is conditioned merely on the effectiveness of the registration statement, and that is accepted on the same condition, might well be held to result in a contract to sell — a contract that is conditioned on effective registration, but still a contract and hence a violation of §5(a)(1). Nevertheless, since the offeror is the lord of his offer, he can presumably make a conditional and revocable offer to sell if it is made clear that the offer cannot be accepted until the effective date. Or he can simply "offer" in the statutory sense by soliciting "indications of interest" and state that no offer for a contract (in the common law sense) will be made until the effective date. The advantage of the latter procedure, which is the most common, is that there is no common law offer outstanding that the statutory offeror will have to revoke if he changes his mind before the effective date.

We turn now to a consideration of the several ways in which offers (in the statutory sense) may legally be made during the waiting period.

b. Types of Statutory Offers: Introduction

DISKIN v. LOMASNEY & COMPANY
United States Court of Appeals, Second Circuit, 1971
452 F. 2d 871

Before FRIENDLY, Chief Judge, FEINBERG, Circuit Judge, and DAVIS, Associate Judge.

FRIENDLY, Chief Judge. During the summer of 1968 plaintiff Diskin had conversations with defendant Lomasney, general partner of defendant Lomasney & Co., a broker-dealer, with respect to securities of two companies, Ski Park City West, S. I. and Continental Travel, Ltd. Lomasney & Co. had agreed to sell up to 60,000 common shares of the former on a "best efforts" basis and was the principal underwriter for the sale of 350,000 common shares of the latter. A preliminary registration statement with respect to the shares of Continental Travel had been filed with the

---

[29] S. Rep. No. 1036 at 15 and H. R. Rep. No. 1542 at 23, 83d Cong., 2d Sess. (1954).

Securities and Exchange Commission on August 28, 1968, but did not become effective until February 11, 1969. On September 17, 1968, Lomasney sent Diskin a final prospectus for the Ski Park City West, S. I., stock, along with a letter, the body of which read as follows:

> I am enclosing herewith, a copy of the Prospectus on SKI PARK CITY WEST. This letter will also assure you that if you take 1,000 shares of SKI PARK CITY WEST at the issue price, we will commit to you the sale at the public offering price when, as and if issued, 5,000 shares of CONTINENTAL TRAVEL, LTD.

On the same day Diskin placed an order for the 1,000 shares of Ski Park City West and received a written confirmation. He later paid for these, and the validity of their offer and sale is unquestioned.

On February 12, 1969, Lomasney sent Diskin a confirmation of the sale of 5,000 shares of Continental Travel at $12 per share, apparently without any further communication. Diskin received from Lomasney a final prospectus and registration statement for these shares prior to February 28, 1969, when he paid the bill of $60,000, and received delivery. On November 19, 1969, Diskin demanded rescission. Having received no answer, he brought this action [under §12(1)] in the District Court for the Southern District of New York on January 6, 1970, claiming that the letter of September 17, 1968, insofar as it related to shares of Continental Travel, was a violation of §5(b)(1) of the Securities Act of 1933. * * *

[The District Court dismissed on the ground that the Continental portion of the letter came within the exclusion in the last sentence of §2(3).]

*   *   *

We have considered whether, despite the error in dismissing the complaint on this ground, the judgment could be affirmed on the basis that a registration statement concerning the Continental Travel shares had been filed prior to September 17, 1968, although it had not yet become effective. See §5(c). However, the mere filing of a registration statement does not ensure the legality of *any* written offer made during the post-filing, pre-effective period; to be lawful, such written offers must be made by way of a "prospectus" which meets the requirements of §10. See §5(b)(1). See also H. R. Rep. No. 1542, reprinted in U. S. Code Cong. & Admin.

News, 83d Cong., 2d Sess. 2973, 2983, 2996-2997 (1954). We perceive no basis for disagreeing with Professor Loss' summary of the law in this respect:

In sum, there are five legal ways in which offers may be made during the waiting period even if the mails or interstate facilities are used: by means of (1) oral communication, (2) the "tombstone ad," whether the old-fashioned variety under §2(10)(b) or the expanded type under Rule 134 (successor to the old "identifying statement"), (3) the preliminary prospectus under Rule 433 [issued pursuant to §10(b)]ᵃ (successor to the "red herring prospectus"), (4) the "buff card" type of summary prospectus independently prepared under §10(b) and Rule 434, and (5) the summary prospectus filed as part of the registration statement under §10(b) and Rule 434a (successor to the old "newspaper prospectus" but not limited to newspapers).ᵇ

I Loss, Securities Regulation 243 (2d ed. 1961). See also Jennings & Marsh, Securities Regulation 89-92 (2d ed. 1968). The letter of September 17, 1968, was none of these. Indeed, the confirmation of February 12, 1969, was a further violation unless a prospectus had been furnished, see §§2(10) and 5(b)(1), which the agreed statement does not say.

We pass therefore to the arguments which defendants made in their memorandum, which the district court did not reach. These were (1) that the letter was not an "offer" but was a mere expression of willingness to sell; (2) that the violation was cured by Diskin's receipt of a prospectus prior to the actual purchase; and (3) that the action was brought more than one year after the violation and was thus untimely under §13 of the Securities Act.

Although there is a paucity of authority on these issues, we think none constituted a valid defense. The statutory language defining "offer" in §2(3) "goes well beyond the common law concept of an offer." I Loss, supra, at 181; cf. Carl M. Loeb, Rhoades & Co., Securities Exch. Act Release No. 5870, at 7-8 (1959); *People* v. *Jacques*, 137 Cal. App. 2d 823, 832, 291 P. 2d 124, 129-130 (1955). Consequently, we entertain no doubt that the portion of the letter of September 17 dealing with the Continental Travel shares constituted an "offer" within §2(3). Moreover, whether or not a dealer can lawfully "make a conditional and revocable offer to sell [without employing any of the five established procedures] if it is made clear that the offer cannot be accepted until the

ᵃ ED.: Brackets are the court's. This rule was renumbered 430 in 1982.
ᵇ ED.: The 1982 former Rules 434 and 434a were consolidated into Rule 131. See p. 115 infra.

effective date," see I Loss, supra, at 224, the offer of September 17 did not measure up to that standard since it was not revocable. This case, where Lomasney apparently confirmed the sale without any further word from Diskin, would be a peculiarly unattractive one for endeavoring to carve out an exception to the statutory words. Indeed, as previously indicated, the confirmation, if unaccompanied by a prospectus, was itself a violation of §5(b)(1).

On the second point, we again agree with Professor Loss that "[w]hatever doubt there may once have been as to the applicability of §12(1) to illegal offers [followed by legal sales] was resolved when the original definition of sale was split into separate definitions of 'sale' and 'offer' in 1954, with the incidental amendment of §12(1) to refer to any person 'who offers or sells a security in violation of section 5' so as 'to preserve the effect of the present law' by not excluding the newly permissible pre-effective offers from liabilities under §12." III Loss, supra, at 1695-96. With respect to the one-year period of limitation, although §13 dates this from the "violation" in cases of claims under §12(1), it would be unreasonable to read §13 as starting the short period for an action at a date before the action could have been brought — a construction which might lead in some extreme cases to a running of the statute of limitations before the claim had even arisen. Furthermore, the limitation argument would be wholly drained of force if, as seems likely, the confirmation of February 12, 1968, was itself a violation.

The result here reached may appear to be harsh, since Diskin had an opportunity to read the final prospectus before he paid for the shares. But the 1954 Congress quite obviously meant to allow rescission or damages in the case of illegal offers as well as of illegal sales. Very likely Congress thought that, when it had done so much to broaden the methods for making legal offers during the "waiting period" between the filing and the taking effect of a registration statement, it should make sure that still other methods were not attempted. Here all Lomasney needed to have done was to accompany the September 17, 1968 letter with any one of the three types of prospectus for the Continental shares mentioned in the extract we have quoted from Professor Loss' treatise. Very likely Congress thought a better time for meaningful prospectus reading was at the time of the offer rather than in the context of confirmation and demand for payment. In any event, it made altogether clear that an offeror of a security who had failed to follow one of the allowed paths could not achieve absolution simply by returning to the road of virtue before receiving payment.

The judgment dismissing the complaint is reversed, with instructions to enter judgment for the plaintiff that, upon delivery of 5,000 shares of Continental Travel, Ltd., he shall receive $60,000 with interest from February 28, 1969, and costs.

c.   Oral Offers

The only prohibition in §5(b)(1) runs to the use of a "prospectus" relating to a security with respect to which a registration statement has been filed unless the prospectus meets the requirements of §10. This makes it important to determine precisely what is meant by the term "prospectus" as used in §5(b)(1). The draftsmen of the statute employed two terms that must not be confused. Section 5(b)(1) refers to a "prospectus that meets the requirements of section 10" — the section that specifies (or permits the Commission by rule to specify) the contents of several types of prospectuses required or permitted to be used in connection with the registration process. They include the full, final prospectus (sometimes referred to as a complete or formal or statutory prospectus) as well as (for some purposes) the so-called "preliminary prospectus" and two types of summary prospectuses (all of which will be discussed later). On the other hand, §5(b)(1) also uses the one word "prospectus," and that term is defined in §2(10) to mean, with certain exceptions, "any prospectus, notice, circular, advertisement, letter, or communication, written or by radio or television, which offers any security for sale or confirms the sale of any security." Any writing that in fact offers a security for sale (in the statutory sense) comes within this definition, notwithstanding an attempted disclaimer to the effect that it is not to be construed as an offer to sell or that the securities are being offered only by a prospectus that will be furnished on request.

But there is another side to this coin. Since §5(b)(1) speaks in terms of a "prospectus," and that term is defined in §2(10) as an offer made in writing (or by radio or television), it is perfectly lawful to make *oral* offers at any time after the filing date even though they are not accompanied or preceded by a §10 prospectus. This has nothing to do with the jurisdictional base. A pre*filing* offer made by personal contact is legal only because it involves no use of the mails or of any interstate facilities. But after the filing date an oral offer may be made even by *inter*state telephone because an oral offer is in no case a "prospectus." It is in such a case — when there is an oral offer during the waiting period followed by a contract entered into orally either after the effective date or without use of the interstate telephone during the waiting period —

that §5(b)(2), with its requirement that the *delivery of the security* be accompanied or preceded by a complete prospectus, becomes significant.

d.   The "Tombstone Ad" [§2(10)(b), Rule 134]

In any event, if any person subject to §5 does make use of the mails or interstate facilities to send a "prospectus" after the filing date, §5(b)(1) demands that the "prospectus" meet the requirements of §10. But there is an important exception to the definition. Section 2(10)(b) provides that "a notice, circular, advertisement, letter, or communication in respect of a security shall not be deemed to be a prospectus if it states from whom a written prospectus meeting the requirements of section 10 may be obtained and, in addition, does no more than identify the security, state the price thereof, state by whom orders will be executed, and contain such other information as the Commission, by rules or regulations deemed necessary or appropriate in the public interest and for the protection of investors, and subject to such terms and conditions as may be prescribed therein, may permit." The last clause, giving the Commission authority to expand the contents of the document by rule, was added in the 1954 amendments. Because of the format that advertisements took under the pre-1954 language — and still do for the most part — they are universally if somewhat mournfully known as "tombstone ads."[30]

The reason for the extreme strictness as to the content of the "tombstone ad" in 1933 was that it was not designed as selling literature. That was to be the function of the §10 prospectus. Section 2(10)(b) was designed to afford merely a devise for screening out those prospective customers who might be sufficiently interested in the particular security to ask for a statutory prospectus. The rulemaking power was inserted in 1954 in view of "the wide variations in the types of issuers, securities, and offerings subject to the Securities Act" and was designed "to permit appropriate variation in the contents of such advertisements under such safeguards as may be necessary in the circumstances."[31] But the Commission emphasized, in proposing the adoption of its Rule 134

---

[30] Not infrequently the "tombstone ad" announces that the issue has already been sold. In that event its function is merely to advertise the underwriters rather than the security.

[31] S. Rep. No. 1036 at 13 and H. R. Rep. No. 1542 at 22, 83d Cong., 2d Sess. (1954).

in 1955, "that such communications are intended to be limited to announcements identifying the existence of a public offering and the availability of a prospectus and they are not to be selling literature of any kind."[32]

Rule 134 permits a document, without constituting a "prospectus," to include fourteen categories of information. But it does not permit the sender of the communication to solicit an indication of interest unless (1) the communication is accompanied or preceded by a §10 prospectus and (2) it contains a statement to the effect that until the effective date no offer can be accepted, no part of the purchase price can be received, any offer to buy may be withdrawn or revoked, and any indication of interest will involve no obligation or commitment of any kind.[33] Nevertheless, it can only further the purpose of the statute and rule to include a detachable form, as is sometimes done, on which the recipient may simply request a copy of the prospectus (or before the effective date, the "preliminary prospectus," which will be examined next).

e.   The Preliminary Prospectus [§10(a), Rule 430]

The "tombstone ad" aside, the only offer in writing (or by radio or television) that §5(b)(1) permits in the waiting period is a prospectus meeting the requirements of §10. Section 10(a) governs the contents of the full statutory prospectus, and §10(b), which will be examined next, directs the Commission to adopt rules permitting the use of an abbreviated or summary prospectus for certain purposes. But the Commission has always had ample power elsewhere in §10 to add to or subtract from the contents of the full prospectus.[34] And, of course, §5(b)(1) as amended in 1954 permits the use of a §10 prospectus at any time after the filing date, not merely after the effective date as it had previously read. Consequently, without finding it necessary to advert to its new §10(b) power, the Commission in 1954 adopted Rule 433, renumbered 430 in 1982, to the effect that "A form of prospectus filed as a part of the registration statement shall be deemed to meet the requirements of section 10 of the Act for the purpose of section 5(b)(1) thereof prior to the effective date of the registration statement" if it contains substantially the information required to be

---

[32] Sec. Act Rel. 3535 (1955).
[33] Rule 134(d).
[34] §§10(a)(4), 10(c), 10(d).

included in the full prospectus under §10(a) "except for the omission of information with respect to the offering price, underwriting discounts or commissions, discounts or commissions to dealers, amount of proceeds, conversion rates, call prices, or other matters dependent upon the offering price." The caption "Preliminary Prospectus" and the following legend must appear in red ink on the outside front cover:

> A registration statement relating to these securities has been filed with the Securities and Exchange Commission but has not yet become effective. Information contained herein is subject to completion or amendment. These securities may not be sold nor may offers to buy be accepted prior to the time the registration statement becomes effective. This prospectus shall not constitute an offer to sell or the solicitation of an offer to buy nor shall there be any sale of these securities in any State in which such offer, solicitation or sale would be unlawful prior to registration or qualification under the securities laws of any such State.[35]

f.   Summary Prospectuses [§10(b), Rule 431]

The new §10(b) that was inserted in 1954 provides:

> In addition to the prospectus permitted or required in subsection (a), the Commission shall by rules or regulations * * * permit the use of a prospectus for the purposes of subsection (b)(1) of section 5 which omits in part or summarizes information in the prospectus specified in subsection (a). A prospectus permitted under this subsection shall, except to the extent the Commission by rules or regulations * * * otherwise provides, be filed as part of the registration statement but shall not be deemed a part of such registration statement for the purposes of section 11. * * *

The exception from §11 liability was designed to encourage the use of summary prospectuses. Of course, any deficiency that carries through to the full §10(a) prospectus despite the Commission's processing would create liability under §11. Section 11(a) in any event extends liability only to any part of the registration statement that was deficient "when such part became effective." Consequently, §10(b) was not necessary in order to immunize from §11 liability in the case of summary prospectuses used be-

[35] This requirement now appears in Regulation S-K, infra p. 153, Item 501(c)(8).

fore the effective date. Moreover, apart from the new suspension power in §10(b) itself, 10(b) prospectuses remain subject, not only to the Commission's stop-order and other administrative powers under §8, but also to the general provisions of §§12(2) and 17(a), which impose civil and criminal sanctions upon a person who sells any security by means of fraud or half-truths. It seems odd, nevertheless, to exempt from civil liability under §11 the issuer and underwriters, who are responsible for what goes into a summary prospectus, but to impose civil liability under §12(2) upon the dealer, who will have to use a summary prospectus (if at all) as he finds it.

In 1982 a single Rule 431 replaced two old ones, Rule 434 for summaries prepared by independent statistical organizations and Rule 434a for summaries prepared as part of the registration statement if the particular form so provided. The present Rule 431, which likewise applies only if the particular form so provides, requires that summary prospectuses of both kinds be filed as a part of the registration statement. In any event, the rule is available only if the registrant has reported for the past three years under the 1934 Act and has had a default-free record since the end of the last fiscal year. A summary prospectus *must* contain whatever information is specified in the instructions to the particular form; *may* reflect other information contained in the registration statement or specified in Rule 134(a), the "tombstone ad" rule; may employ "such condensed or summarized form as may be appropriate in the light of the circumstances under which the [summary] prospectus is to be used"; and must be captioned a "Preliminary Summary Prospectus" when used before the effective date. There is a filing requirement as part of the registration statement in terms of five business days before use, subject to acceleration.

It must not be overlooked that summary prospectuses are considered to meet the requirements of §10 only for the purpose of §5(b)(1). That is to say, a summary prospectus meeting the requirements of the rule may be sent through the mails or interstate channels even before either a preliminary or a final statutory prospectus, but the rule does not affect the requirement of §5(b)(2) that the complete §10(a) prospectus precede or accompany any *delivery* of the security that is effected by use of the mails or interstate means.

In any event, summary prospectuses have not been widely used, at least in recent years. Standard & Poor's Corporation, which used to be the prime user of the old Rule 434, in 1968 gave up its practice of summarizing filed prospectuses on folded-over cards and selling them in bulk to dealers for distribution to their customers during the waiting period. And — whether because of the cost of even a column or less in a national newspaper or because institutional investors, at least, want to see the entire preliminary prospectus — other summaries are rarely used except perhaps for some local offerings. Even so, the Commission included instructions with respect to summary prospectuses in the new forms it adopted in 1982.[36]

g. State Blue Sky Laws

Opening up the SEC waiting period in 1954 to offers aggravated a problem that had always existed under the blue sky laws, because most of the state statutes (including the Uniform Securities Act)[37] incorporate the pre-1954 federal formula of prohibiting offers and sales alike before effective registration. The Uniform Securities Act has a special exemption for "any offer (but not a sale) of a security for which registration statements have been filed under both this act and the Securities Act of 1933 if no stop order or refusal order is in effect and no public proceeding or examination looking toward such an order is pending under either act"[38] — leaving it to the federal statute and rules to regulate the types of offers. And there is a variety of "outs" in states that have not adopted that exemption, including (so far as offers to *dealers* are concerned) the quite common exemption (found in the Uniform Act)[39] for offers and sales to dealers.

5. THE POSTEFFECTIVE PERIOD

a. In General

Since §5(b)(1) as amended in 1954 applies to all transactions after the filing date, the waiting-period and posteffective problems substantially overlap. The permissible methods of offering are the

---

[36] See p. 151 infra. There is also a special rule for investment company advertisements in a newspaper or magazine or on radio or television. Rule 482. Use of the summary prospectus by itself is apart from the Commission's encouraging the inclusion of summaries as part of lengthy or complex prospectuses. See p. 132 n. 13 infra.

[37] §301.

[38] §402(b)(2).

[39] §402(b)(8).

same, except that (1) the "preliminary prospectus" under Rule
430 and the preliminary summary prospectus under Rule 431 are
limited by their nature to the waiting period, (2) the full §10(a)
prospectus is, of course, available, and (3) there is (as we shall
see) one device, supplemental selling literature, that is peculiar
to the posteffective period. But the big difference is that the effectiveness of the registration statement terminates the prohibition in §5(a) against using the mails or interstate facilities to *sell*
or *deliver* the security.

b.   Prospectus with Delivery or Confirmation

It is here that §5(b)(2) enters the picture for the first time:
Unless the buyer has already received a complete §10(a) prospectus, it is unlawful to *deliver* the security through the mails
or in interstate commerce without sending such a prospectus along
with it. There is no requirement that the buyer must have
received the full prospectus *from the seller himself*. But the seller
would be wise to obtain a receipt for the earlier prospectus.

Moreover, the buyer's prior receipt of a *summary* §10(b) prospectus will not satisfy §5(b)(2), because the reference there is to
"a prospectus that meets the requirements of subsection (a) of
section 10" and Rule 431 applies expressly "for the purpose of section 5(b)(1)," not §5(b)(2). Nor will it suffice that the buyer received during the waiting period a *preliminary* 10(a) prospectus
without price and related data; for Rule 430 similarly permits
such a prospectus only "for the purpose of section 5(b)(1)." And
a "tombstone ad" under Rule 134, expanded or otherwise, obviously is not "a prospectus that meets the requirements of subsection (a) of section 10"; it is not a "prospectus" at all. Indeed,
even if the buyer has previously received a *complete* 10(a) prospectus, he must presumably be given another one with delivery
of the security if in the interim the earlier prospectus has been
changed so that it is no longer current.

Now suppose the seller mails a *confirmation* of the transaction
before he mails the security. In 1941 the Commission's General
Counsel expressed the opinion that the term "prospectus" as used
in §5(b)(1) was defined in §2(10) broadly enough to include an
ordinary confirmation.[40] Under this view, the net result of §§5
(b)(2) and 5(b)(1) combined is that a full prospectus must precede or accompany delivery or confirmation, whichever *first* occurs

---

[40] Op. Gen. Counsel, Sec. Act Rel. 2623 (1941).

by use of the mails or interstate facilities.[41] Whether or not this was an unduly broad reading of §2(10) as it then stood — and the interpretation was never formally challenged — it has now been codified by the 1954 expansion of the definition of "prospectus" in §2(10) to include any written communciation that "confirms the sale of any security."

c. The Statutory Prospectus

The Second Circuit had held that "implicit in the statutory provision that the prospectus contain certain information is the requirement that such information be true or correct," so that a prospectus "does not meet the requirements of §10(a) * * * if information required to be disclosed is materially false or misleading."[42] At first blush this seems logical enough. Certainly one is not entitled to file an utterly inadequate document and have it considered a §10(a) prospectus. But *query:* There is no apparent need to find a violation of §5(b) when by hypothesis there is a more serious violation of §17(a), the fraud provision. And to consider *every* material defect to destroy the document's status as a §10(a) prospectus ignores an important distinction between the civil liability provisions of §§12(1) and 12(2). A violation of §5 creates strict liability under §12(1), whereas proof of a material misstatement does not entitle the §12(2) plaintiff to a judgment if the defendant sustains his reasonable care defense.[43]

[41] Since §5(b)(1) refers to a prospectus that meets the requirements of §10 — not, as does §5(b)(2), to a prospectus that meets the requirements of §10(a) — it may seem at first blush that a confirmation may properly be sent along with or after a *summary* prospectus. It is perfectly true that since §5(b)(1) does refer broadly to a §10 prospectus and since a summary prospectus under Rule 431 does meet the requirements of subsection (b) of §10, mailing the summary prospectus as such would not violate §5(b)(1). But a confirmation is itself a "prospectus" as defined in §2(10) unless, under §2(10)(a), "a written prospectus meeting the requirements of *subsection (a)* of section 10" accompanies or has preceded it. (Italics supplied.) Hence the mailing of the *confirmation* would violate §5(b)(1) although the mailing of the Rule 431 prospectus would not. (This is perhaps as good an example as any of the need for some statutory simplification in this area.)

[42] SEC v. Manor Nursing Centers, Inc., 458 F. 2d 1082, 1098 (2d Cir. 1972); cf. Great Sweet Grass Oils, Ltd., 37 SEC 683, 684 n. 1 (1957), *aff'd per curiam* sub nom. Great Sweet Grass Oils, Ltd. v. SEC, 256 F. 2d 893 (D. C. Cir. 1958) (reporting requirement under Sec. Ex. Act §13(a) "necessarily embodies the requirement that such reports be true and correct"); GAF Corp. v. Milstein, 453 F. 2d 709, 720 (2d Cir. 1971) (ownership reports under Sec. Ex. Act §13(d)).

[43] Similarly, so far as the 1934 Act is concerned, an action (including a private action if implied) for *failure* to file might avoid the scienter element

d. Supplementary Selling Literature

We have seen that §5(b)(1) prohibits the use of the mails or interstate facilities to send any non-§10 "prospectus" after the *filing* date, and that the term "prospectus" is defined in §2(10) to mean, in substance, any written offer. There are two exceptions to this definition. One is the provision in §2(10)(b) for the "tombstone ad," which may be used at any time after the *filing* of the registration statement. The other appears in §2(10)(a), which provides that "a communication sent or given *after* the effective date of the registration statement (other than a prospectus permitted under subsection (b) of section 10)[44] shall not be deemed a prospectus if it is proved that prior to or at the same time with such communication a written prospectus meeting the requirements of subsection (a) of section 10 at the time of such communciation was sent or given to the person to whom the communication was made." The purpose of this clause is to permit the use of supplementary selling literature *after* the effective date if it goes along with or follows the full §10(a) prospectus but does not precede it. It need not be filed so far as the 1933 Act is concerned.[45] But §24(b) of the Investment Company Act requires the filing of selling literature of investment companies (other than those of the closed-end type) within ten days *after* its use.

---

in an action for a *false* filing under §18(a) or Rule 10b-5. And both §24 of the 1933 Act and §32(a) of the 1934 Act make it a crime willfully (and knowingly in the case of the 1934 Act) to make any materially false statement in a filing under those statutes.

The view expressed in the text was followed in SEC v. Southwest Coal & Energy Co., 624 F. 2d 1312, 1317-19 (5th Cir. 1980); see also SEC v. Blazon Corp., 609 F. 2d 960, 968-69 (9th Cir. 1979).

[44] The parenthetical clause was presumably inserted in the 1954 amendments because of the peculiar language of §12(2), which imposes civil liability for misstatements in "a prospectus or oral communication." But it does not follow that a §10(b) prospectus is a §2(10) "prospectus" for purposes of §5(b)(1), where "the context otherwise requires" as stated in the introductory clause of §2, so as to prohibit the use of a §10(b) prospectus as supplemental selling literature after the effective date.

[45] The Commission spot-checks. In addition, the NASD requires its members to file their sales literature with the Association ten days before use (1) until they have done so for a year or (2) on a determination by a District Business Conduct Committee that there is a reasonable likelihood that the member has departed and is reasonably likely to depart again from the "fair dealing" standards of the NASD's rule. NASD Rules of Fair Practice, §35, CCH NASD Manual ¶2195. The statutory fraud provisions apply, of course, and in 1979 the SEC adopted an interpretative rule for investment company sales literature (Rule 156) that replaced a considerably more detailed "Statement of Policy." The reason for the shift was to emphasize the industry's principal responsibility in the area.

e. Delivery to Buyer's Broker

Is delivery of a prospectus to the buyer's *broker* sufficient compliance with §5(b) by the seller and his broker even though the buyer's broker never delivers the prospectus to his principal? Presumably it is if the buyer's broker is authorized or otherwise empowered under general principles of agency law to receive delivery.

In the case of transactions effected on a stock exchange during the forty-day period a Commission rule excuses the selling member (that is, the seller's broker) from delivering a prospectus in the usual way to the buying member (that is, the buyer's broker) if the issuer or an underwriter has complied with requests made by the exchange from time to time to deliver to the exchange as many copies of the full prospectus as appear reasonably necessary to comply with the requests of its members and if the exchange delivers a copy to any member on his written request.[46]

Whether the buyer's broker (in a transaction on or off an exchange) is himself under a statutory duty to deliver the prospectus to his principal will depend, within the forty-day period, on whether or not he has done any soliciting. A buyer's broker who has not solicited the buy order does not *"sell"* to the buyer even within the broad definition in §2(3); he *buys for* him. Hence he is not covered by §5.

f. The Dealers' Exemption

(i) *In general:* Transactions by the issuer or an underwriter are always subject to §5(b) whenever they occur. But what dealers are subject to the prospectus requirement and for how long? We have already noticed the requirement in the original Act (now Clause (B) of §4(3)) that all dealers, whether or not engaged in the distribution in the usual sense, comply with the prospectus provisions with respect to all transactions for one year after the first public offering of a registered security — a period arbitrarily selected as marking the line between distribution and post-distribution trading — as well as the further requirement (now in Clause (C)) that dealers participating in the distribution comply with the prospectus provision for as long as it might take them to get rid of their unsold allotments or subscriptions. We have noticed also

---

[46] Rule 153. This has been called a "formal genuflection." Cohen, "Truth in Securities" Revisited, 79 Harv. L. Rev. 1340, 1351 (1966).

the reduction of the arbitrary period to forty days in 1954 and its 1964 extension to ninety days for first offerings, with authority in the Commission to shorten either period by rule or order.[47]

Although it was assumed that most offerings would begin during the waiting period, it was contemplated that an occasional offering might be postponed on account of market conditions or otherwise for some time after the effective date. For this reason what is now Clause (B) was reworded in the 1954 amendments so as to subject *all* dealers to the prospectus provision for forty days after the effective date or forty days after the posteffective offering to the public by the issuer or by or through an underwriter, whichever occurs later.

If the draftsmen had stopped here, however, dealers generally might never have been able to begin lawful trading in securities that had been illegally offered to the public without registration; or perhaps, anomalously, the statute would have been read literally to exempt dealers' transactions *immediately* after an illegal public offering. This made it necessary to insert another clause (now (A)) in order to make the dealers' exemption applicable forty days after "the first date upon which the security was bona fide offered to the public by the issuer or by or through an underwriter" without the filing of a registration statement. Clause (A) is not limited in so many words to transactions after illegal public offerings. But the language in question, apart from permitting dealers' transactions immediately after an *exempt* public offering, could serve no other purpose, and the legislative history makes it clear that the purpose was as here described.[48]

The forty-day and ninety-day periods do not apply to a dealer still acting as an underwriter, since §4(3) exempts only transactions by dealers *qua* dealers and not transactions by dealers *qua* underwriters. At the same time, the exemption applies by its terms to a transaction by "an underwriter no longer acting as an underwriter in respect of the security involved in such transaction."

In 1964 the Commission exercised its new rulemaking authority in §4(3) by adopting Rule 174. Subject to the dealer's overriding obligation to deliver a prospectus while acting as an underwriter or disposing of an allotment or subscription, as well as the statutory exclusion of any stop-order interval in computing the prospectus-delivery period, the rule affords a number of dispensations:

---

[47] See p. 95 supra.

[48] S. Rep. No. 1036 at 14 and H. R. Rep. No. 1542 at 22, 83d Cong., 2d Sess. (1954); see Sec. Act Rel. 4726 (1964) 2 n. 3; Atkin v. Hill, Darlington & Grimm, 15 A. D. 2d 362, 370 n., 224 N. Y. S. 2d 553, 561 n. 1 (1st Dept. 1962), aff'd *per curiam*, 12 N. Y. 2d 940, 188 N. E. 2d 790 (1963).

(1) The statutory periods are waived altogether if the issuer is a reporting company under the 1934 Act or the registration statement covers American depositary receipts or voting trust certificates without registration of the underlying securities. (2) When a registration statement relates to offerings to be made from time to time — in the case of so-called shelf registrations — no new period applies for dealers trading after the period of forty or ninety days following the *first* offering for the account of any person under the registration statement. (3) The rule also preserves the Commission's authority under §4(3) to vary the statutory periods on application or on its own motion; and the Commission has delegated this authority to the Director of the Division of Corporation Finance, along with authority to reduce either the ninety-day or the forty-day period.

Finally, in order to inform dealers more readily of their obligation to deliver a prospectus, there must be a statement in bold face or italic type on the inside front or outside back cover page of the prospectus stating the date on which the relevant statutory period will expire.[49]

(ii) *Investment company securities:* As part of the 1954 legislative program, §24(d) of the Investment Company Act was amended to require, in effect, that all dealers in investment company securities of the types that are continually being offered (namely, securities issued by face-amount certificate companies or redeemable securities issued by open-end management companies or unit investment trusts) be subject to the prospectus provisions as long as any security of the same class as the registered security is being offered. Because such companies normally registered once a year under the original Act, the one-year period during which all dealers had to use prospectuses was continually being renewed. If the reduction to forty days had applied in this context, independent dealers engaged in making a market for such shares would have been subject to the prospectus requirements for forty days in each year, whereas dealers engaged in the distribution would always have had to use prospectuses.

This possibility was neither desirable in the public interest nor relished by the investment companies, which had to think of the competitive disadvantage it would entail for their regular distributors. Consequently, §24(d) was amended to provide that the dealers' exemption in the Securities Act does not apply to any transaction in an investment company security of any of the types here referred to "if any other security of the same class is currently

---

[49] Reg. S-K, Item 502(e).

being offered or sold by the issuer or by or through an underwriter
in a distribution which is not exempted from section 5." At the
same time, in order to mitigate any discrimination that might be
suffered by independent dealers who should be unable to obtain
prospectuses from the issuer of an underwriter, §24(d) was drafted
to give the Commission power by rule to extend the dealers' exemption "with respect to any class of persons, securities, or transactions."

There is also a Rule 135a, which is directed to the problem
of generic advertising. An advertisement or communication (normally by a booker or dealer looking for business) that does not
refer specifically by name to a particular investment company or
its securities (or to any nonexempted securities) is not considered
to offer any security for sale if it is limited to specified categories
of information with respect to investment companies generally.

g. Offering of Additional Securities of an Outstanding Class

Not infrequently an issuer registers and distributes additional
securities of a class already outstanding. A corporation, for example, has a million shares of common stock that have been outstanding and traded on a stock exchange or over the counter for
years, and it issues an additional 300,000 shares. Or perhaps one
of its controlling persons dies and his executor has to sell a large
block of stock to meet estate taxes, so that a registration statement
is filed for that purpose. Common sense tells us that a certificate
for 100 shares of the old stock and a certificate for 100 shares of the
new (or of the control block) are as fungible as two bushels of
September wheat or two one-dollar bills. And so the law treats
securities of the same class for most purposes. But not the Securities Act. Any dealer who sells one of the *new* shares within
the statutory periods must use a prospectus. There is no warrant
in the Act for excepting such a transaction merely because like
securities are already outstanding. If the dealer is sure he is selling
one of the *old* shares, on the other hand, there is likewise no warrant in the Act for subjecting him to the prospectus requirement
just because additional shares of the same class have recently been
distributed. But as a practical matter how is he to tell? Even if
the old and new certificates are distinguished by serial numbers,
ready differentiation is incompatible with the realities of securities
trading. Over-the-counter dealers, for example, customarily solicit
and obtain buy orders for securities that they do not carry in

inventory, and then go out and acquire them in the market. How can a dealer tell when he solicits his customer's buy order whether he will be delivering a new or an old security? In the one case his solicitation must comply with §5(b)(1); in the other case it need not.

The short answer is that the only thing the dealer can do is play safe and comply with §5(b) in all his trading for the applicable period. This is not an altogether satisfactory solution. When the new issue is a fraction of the size of the old — perhaps a relatively small secondary distribution — to subject all trading to the prospectus requirement for the statutory period is definitely a case of tail wagging dog. But the problem is not nearly so serious as it was when dealers had to use prospectuses for an entire year, particularly in the light of Rule 174.[50] Under the present statutory framework, moreover, there seems to be no complete solution short of eliminating any arbitrary period altogether, which would be a case of avoiding tail-wag-dog at the price of having baby-thrown-out-with-the-bath.

6. BASIS FOR A SOCRATIC DIALOGUE

1. *X* Corp., which is not a reporting company under the 1934 Act, has 1 million shares of common stock owned by 400 persons and traded inactively in the over-the-counter market. *D,* a New York dealer, has just been told by a friend in *X* Corp. that it is about to file a registration statement under the 1933 Act for an offering of an additional 300,000 shares with *U* as principal underwriter. Would *D* violate any part of §5 (and, if so, which) if he:

(a) telephoned *U* at his home in Connecticut (*U* having invited *D* into four of his last five selling groups) to urge that he be included in the selling group;

(b) mailed a letter to *C,* an old friend and customer, telling him of the forthcoming offering;

(c) telephoned *C* at his home in New Jersey instead;

(d) telephoned *C* at his office in Manhattan to tell him about it;

(e) told *C* about it during their weekly golf game?

2. The registration statement was filed yesterday. Suppose *D:*

(a) acted as in ¶ 1(a)-(c);

(b) made an offer to *C* in their telephone conversation, con-

---

[50] See p. 121 supra.

ditioning the offer on an effective registration statement, and *C* accepted;

(c) solicited *C*'s offer to buy 1000 shares;

(d) followed up his call by mailing *C* a copy of the entire registration statement as filed;

(e) took a telephone call *from C,* during which it was agreed that *D* would see that *C* got 1000 shares when the registration statement became effective?

3.   The registration statement became effective yesterday. Suppose *D:*

(a) mailed *C* a letter soliciting an order;

(b) solicited an order a week later, during the first golf game after the effective date;

(c) did the same by telephoning *C* at his home in New Jersey;

(d) followed up his telephone call with a two-page letter emphasizing the appropriateness of *X* common for *C*'s portfolio;

(e) got *C*'s order at the "nineteenth hole" and delivered the stock certificates during their next game, without any prospectus;

(f) acted as in (e) but mailed *C* a confirmation of the transaction in between the two golf games;

(g) acted as in (e) but delivered certificates whose serial numbers identified them as previously outstanding?

C.   THE REGISTRATION PROCEDURE

1.   A Study in Administrative Technique

a.   The Statutory Pattern

If an experienced English solicitor specializing in company law were asked for the first time to examine the 1933 Act and describe how the registration machinery worked, this is what he would say: "Under §§6 and 7 one files with the SEC something called a 'registration statement,' which contains information specified by Commission rule, is accompanied by a filing fee, and is signed by specified persons. Under §8(a) there is a twenty-day waiting period between filing and effectiveness, and the filing of a preeffective amendment starts the twenty-day period running again, unless in either case the Commission declares otherwise.[1]

C. 2C [1] The Commission's giving its "consent" under §8(a) to the filing of an amendment (it never exercises its "order" power under that section) is popularly called "acceleration."

Apparently the Commission examines the registration statement, because §8(d) provides for something you chaps call a 'stop order' to prevent effectiveness if the Commission concludes after some sort of hearing that the registration statement is materially deficient. And under §9 a stop order may be reviewed, on a substantial evidence basis, in one of your Courts of Appeals, subject to further review on certiorari in the Supreme Court."

This is a perfectly accurate description. But, if the Commission had followed this procedure literally, the Act would have been a disaster, especially during the period from 1933 to 1954 when §5 prohibited "offers" as well as sales during the waiting period. It required four great administrative inventions — monuments to the vaunted flexibility of the administrative process — to make the Act work.

b.   The "Red Herring" Fiction

Section 5 was based on a conceptual dilemma that plagued both Commission and industry for twenty-one years. Although any form of preeffective solicitation by use of the mails or interstate facilities was categorically forbidden, the whole theory of the waiting period was that the information contained in the registration statement would be disseminated so that the investing public would be able to make an intelligent determination whether to buy when the statement became effective. This "cooling" period as it was known — something not found in the English model — reflected Congress's view that the process of distribution must be slowed down:

> The compulsory 30-day inspection period before securities can be sold is deliberately intended to interfere with the reckless traditions of the last few years of the securities business. It contemplates a change from methods of distribution lately in vogue which attempted complete sale of an issue sometimes within 1 day or at most a few days. Such methods practically compelled minor distributors, dealers, and even salesmen, as the price of participation in future issues of the underwriting house involved, to make commitments blindly. This has resulted in the demoralization of ethical standards as between these ultimate sales outlets and the securities-buying public to whom they had to look to take such commitments off their hands. This high-pressure technique has assumed an undue importance in the eyes of the present generation of securities distributors, with its reliance upon deli-

cate calculations of day-to-day fluctuations in market opportunities and its implicit temptations to market manipulation, and
must be discarded because the resulting injury to an underin-
formed public demonstrably hurts the Nation. It is furthermore
the considered judgment of this committee that any issue which
cannot stand the test of a waiting inspection over a month's average of economic conditions, but must be floated within a few
days upon the crest of a possibly manipulated market fluctuation,
is not a security which deserves protection at the cost of the public as compared with other issues which can meet this test.[2]

But how was dissemination to be distinguished from solicitation? An underwriter with a firm commitment — or a dealer
who hoped to have a firm commitment immediately upon effectiveness — was apparently expected to disseminate information
without in any way puffing his wares. Salesmen, however, are not
educators, and the concept of a reluctant salesman soon proved to
be as chimerical as the dream of a nation without a thirst.

Nevertheless, the administrators of the statute had a job to do.
Consequently, before the Act was many months old, the Federal
Trade Commission (which administered the 1933 Act until the
SEC was created by the 1934 Act) took a hint from the report
of the House committee and issued a release to the effect that,
although the making and acceptance of offers conditioned upon
the effectiveness of the registration statement "would obviously
fly in the face of the general purposes of the Act," it would be
permissible during the waiting period, and indeed would carry
out the general purposes of the statute, for an issuer or underwriter to distribute circulars that described the security as in a
§10 prospectus but were "clearly and unmistakably marked to
indicate that they are informative only, negativing without equiv-
ocation either impliedly or expressly an intent to solicit offers to
buy or to make an offer to sell."[3]

This release was the origin of the so-called "red herring prospectus" — a document that got its name from a legend superimposed on each page to the effect that a registration statement had
been filed with the SEC but had not yet become effective, that the
information in the circular was subject to correction and change
without notice, that under no circumstances was the circular to be
considered an offer to sell or a solicitation of an offer to buy, and

---

[2] H. R. Rep. No. 85, 73d Cong., 1st Sess. (1933) 7-8. The thirty-day period
was reduced to twenty before passage.

[3] Sec. Act Rel. 70 (1933); see H. R. Rep. No. 85, 73d Cong., 1st Sess. (1933)
12-13.

that no offer to buy or sell should be made and no order would be accepted until the effective date of the registration statement. This is now history, except that the "red herring prospectus" was the seed of today's "preliminary prospectus" under Rule 430 and, although one no longer has to indulge in the "red herring" fiction since the 1954 legalization of waiting period offers, these documents are still referred to quite commonly as "red herring prospectuses."[4]

c.   The Letter of Comment

In practice the heavy artillery of §8(d) is reserved for flagrant cases.[5] Instead, without benefit of specific statutory authority, the Commission early developed a very workable examination procedure. For many years every registration statement was examined by the security analysts, lawyers, and accountants in one of the branches of what is now called the Division of Corporation Finance. Except for some companies that have repeatedly registered earlier offerings, relatively few registration statements are found to be in entirely acceptable shape when they are filed.

In the overwhelming majority of cases, however, no thought is given to the institution of a formal proceeding. Instead, the examining branch drafts a letter of comment (originally, and more candidly, called a "deficiency letter") specifying the respects in which it appears that the registration statement is deficient. Nonroutine letters are reviewed by an Assistant Director of the Division in order to coordinate the work of the several branches, and novel questions of policy may be considered by the Director or Associate Director or the entire Commission. The staff is available for personal or telephonic conferences after receipt of the letter of comment. Almost invariably an amendment is filed, and it is unnecessary to resort to formal proceedings against the registration statement. Amendments are examined in the same manner as the registration statement, and sometimes a further letter of comment and one or more additional amendments are required.

If the statement could not be appropriately amended within the statutory twenty-day period, the issuer used to be asked to file

---

[4] See p. 99 supra. Of the many treatments of the "red herring prospectus," one deserves mention if only because of its title. Kennedy, Labor Pains in the Birth of a Red Herring, 34 U. K. C. L. Rev. 198 (1966).

[5] A stop order proceeding may be initiated "at any time," either before or after the effective date. The Commission has never used the alternative preeffective procedure under §8(b).

a simple "delaying amendment" by telegram or letter, which served under §8(a) to start the twenty-day period running again. But Rule 473, which prescribed that procedure, was amended in 1961 to make available an optional procedure, usually followed, whereby a single filing serves in effect as a series of constructive delaying amendments until the Division is satisfied with the registration statement.

In 1968, because of the logjam caused by increased volume of filings, the Commission announced an "emergency" procedure whereby, after a cursory review by a staff officer, counsel would be advised in one of three ways (later increased to four): (1) that the registration statement was so poorly drafted or otherwise presented problems so serious that no further review would be made (a hint that the registration statement should be withdrawn); (2) that the staff had made only a cursory review and would provide no written or oral comments; (3) that limited comments would be given; or (4) that the filing would be subject to the regular review process.[6] The time saving was dramatic. In June and July 1969 about 40 percent of the registration statements received expedited or summary treatment, and for them the median time between filing and notification of either minor comment or none was 8 days, in contrast to 49 days between filing and comment letter with respect to those registration statements that got regular treatment.[7] Then in late 1980 the Commission went over to a concept of what it calls "selective review": All first-time registrants, but only about 5 percent of repeat registrants, receive a thorough review. Certain others are not reviewed at all. The registrant is notified within two or three days after the filing whether its registration statement will be reviewed. If not, it will become effective at any time more than forty-eight hours after filing that the registrant requests.

To be sure, there is another angle to all this informality from the point of view of the science of government. Although in theory the Commission's staff merely "suggests" amendments, the practicalities of financing do not allow any real alternative to complying. The privilege of testing the staff's views by defending a stop-order proceeding is an expensive one in terms of the success of the financing. And, although the Commission's final order is subject to judicial review, a court proceeding that may take a year or more is hardly a realistic way to determine whether a

[6] Sec. Act Rels. 4934 (1968), 5231 (1972).
[7] Smith (SEC Commissioner), An Overview of the Registration Statement Process (address before Practising Law Institute, New York, Sept. 18, 1969) 7.

company in need of financing is right in insisting that a particular item of information may properly go in the footnotes rather than the text of the financial statements.[8] Besides, the registrant that receives less than a full review must pay a dual price: (1) The comment letter process is something of an insurance policy against potentially ruinous liability under §11. (2) Counsel for, say, a cement company cannot be sure, when he follows the time-honored technique of using the last effective registrant statement for a cement company as a model, that it passed through the staff's fire!

d. The Price Amendment

In practice, particularly in the case of large issues, the required information concerning the offering price and related matters (the specific terms of the securities, redemption and sinking fund provisions, call and conversion prices), as well as the underwriting arrangements, is normally filed by amendment after the rest of the statement has been reviewed and informally cleared by the staff, or after notification that the registration statement will not be reviewed, and only a short time before the anticipated offering date. In order to avoid the necessity of fixing the price and terms of the security several days or perhaps several months before the anticipated offering, and because underwriters simply would not accept a firm commitment and run the risk of market changes during all that time, or would demand exorbitant compensation for doing so, it is customary for the underwriters to sign their purchase contract with the issuer only after they receive notice of staff clearance (or nonreview notification), to file the so-called price amendment immediately, and to request that it be accelerated so that the statement will become effective within, typically, an hour or two.[9] The contract is conditioned on a specified effective date and hour. And it is the Commission's policy to grant such acceleration requests ordinarily, whether or not the

---

[8] In the entire history of the Commission only one stop order has been judicially reviewed on its merits, and it was affirmed. Oklahoma-Texas Trust v. SEC, 100 F. 2d 888 (10th Cir. 1939).

[9] Another reason for minimizing the interval between the signing of the underwriting contract and the effectiveness of the registration statement, so far as the underwriters are concerned, is that immediately upon the signing, the Commission's capital rule for broker-dealers under the 1934 Act deducts from the underwriter's net capital as a liquidity factor (depending on the type of securities) specified percentages of the value of the securities representing the underwriter's open contractual commitment. Rule 15c3-1.

registration statement has been reviewed.[10] This practice also permits the issuer and underwriters to "hit the market" — that is, select an effective date in the light of what they regard to be favorable market conditions.

e.   Acceleration

Finally, there is the acceleration power itself. But apart from its implementing the price amendment technique, the Commission has used it to develop a fine-honed tool for accomplishing more effective disclosure — and, some have said on occasion, has abused it for other ends.[11] That is to say, there is decidedly another side to the acceleration coin. To the extent that acceleration of the price amendment is a valuable privilege — one indispensable to the issuer's ability to obtain a firm underwriting commitment — the Commission's authority to deny acceleration in specific cases gives it an effective sanction.[12] How has that authority been used in practice?

(i)   One cannot cavil, under the disclosure philosophy, with the Commission's statement of policy in Rules 460 aand 461:

> 460(a) Pursuant to the statutory requirement that the Commission in ruling upon requests for acceleration of the effective date of a registration statement shall have due regard to the adequacy of the information respecting the issuer theretofore

---

[10] See Rule 461(b).

[11] Oddly, the §8(a) standards are found only in the sentence that permits the Commission to reduce the twenty-day period between filing and effectiveness, a grant of authority that until recently has rarely been used. Nevertheless, the Commission has always assumed that those standards must be read into the second sentence, on acceleration of preeffective amendments. Presumably the courts would so read the second sentence in order to avoid a constitutional question of delegation of legislative power.

[12] The Commission has authorized the Director of the Division of Corporation Finance to grant but not deny acceleration.

The best-efforts underwriter, of course, can more readily wait out the twenty days. Indeed, even the firm-commitment underwriter is not vitally dependent on acceleration of the price amendment when there is no preexisting market for the securities to be offered. In that situation the negotiated price can be inserted in the original filing, with an "out" clause in the underwriting agreement to take care of an abrupt change in market conditions generally during the waiting period.

Registration statements on Form S-8, which applies to certain employee offerings, become effective on the twentieth day after filing regardless of any preeffective amendments, and delaying amendments are not permitted. Rules 473(d), 475(a). This is also the practice with respect to dividend reinvestment plans.

available to the public, the Commission may consider whether the persons making the offering have taken reasonable steps to make the information contained in the registration statement conveniently available to underwriters and dealers who it is reasonably anticipated will be invited to participate in the distribution of the security to be offered or sold.

(b) As a minimum, reasonable steps to make the information conveniently available would involve the distribution, to each underwriter and dealer who it is reasonably anticipated will be invited to participate in the distribution of the security, a reasonable time in advance of the anticipated effective date of the registration statement, of as many copies of the proposed form of preliminary prospectus permitted by Rule 430 as appears to be reasonable to secure adequate distribution of the preliminary prospectus.

(c) The granting of acceleration will not be conditioned upon

(1) The distribution of a preliminary prospectus in any state where such distribution would be illegal * * *

461 * * *

(b) * * * the following are included in the situations in which the Commission considers that the statutory standards of section 8(a) may not be met and may refuse to accelerate the effective date:

(1) Where there has not been a bona fide effort to make the prospectus reasonably concise and readable, so as to facilitate an understanding of the information required or permitted to be contained in the prospectus.[13]

(2) Where the form of preliminary prospectus, which has been distributed by the issuer or underwriter, is found to be inaccurate or inadequate in any material respect, until the Commission has received satisfactory assurance that appropriate correcting material has been sent to all underwriters and dealers who received such preliminary prospectus or prospectuses in quantity sufficient

---

[13] Without specific reference to its acceleration power, the Commission requires a summary "where the length or complexity of the prospectus makes such a summary appropriate," as well as the inclusion, when "appropriate," of an introductory "discussion of the specific factors that make the offering speculative or one of high risk," with a cross-reference on the outside front cover. Reg. S-K, Items 501(c)(4), 503(a) and (c). This so-called "poison pen summary" with respect to high risk issues is a bit debatable if it is to lay the ground for a stop order as distinguished from nonacceleration. Arguably, as long as all the required information is set out in a logical order that stresses neither the favorable nor the unfavorable data, the Commission is no more justified in insisting on concentrating all the poison at the beginning than the registrant would be in concentrating the honey there and relegating the poison to the back pages.

for their information and the information of others to whom the inaccurate or inadequate material was sent.[14]

(ii) The Commission has sometimes required a broader distribution. In the case of most speculative new issues, for example, it has conditioned acceleration on the distribution of a properly amended preliminary prospectus not only among selling-group dealers but also to each customer to whom the underwriters and selling-group dealers expect to confirm. And when the issuer is not a reporting company under the 1934 Act, Rule 15c2-8, one of the over-the-counter antifraud rules under §15(c)(2) of that Act, requires the dealer to deliver a preliminary prospectus at least *forty-eight hours before* the anticipated mailing of confirmations.[15]

(iii) Rule 461 warns further that the Commission "may refuse" to accelerate when (A) the issuer, a controlling person, or an underwriter is under investigation; (B) a firm-commitment underwriter fails to meet the financial responsibility requirements of Rule 15c3-1 under the 1934 Act; (C) persons connected with the offering may have manipulated the market; or (D) the NASD has not issued a "no objection" statement when it is required by its rules to review the underwriters' compensation or any other arrangements among the registrant and securities firms participating in the distribution. All this seems logical enough, at least if the NASD clause is not read as a basis for denial of acceleration when the NASD considers the disclosed compensation or other arrangements to be improper.[16]

(iv) Somewhat more controversial has been the Commission's use of its acceleration power to enforce its view that indemnification of an officer or director (or a person in control of the issuer) against statutory liabilities is unenforceable, however valid the

---

[14] As with the former "red herring prospectus," the risk of being required to circulate corrected material can be substantially reduced or eliminated by merely holding up any circulation of preliminary prospectuses until receipt of the staff's first letter of comment.

[15] See also Sec. Act Rel. 4968 (1969). Rule 15c2-8 provides further that "a broker-dealer participating in a distribution must take reasonable steps to see to it that any person desiring a copy of a preliminary or final prospectus receives a copy. Each salesman who is expected to offer the securities must receive a copy of the preliminary prospectus and, if he is expected to offer the securities after the effective date of the registration statement, he must receive a copy of the final prospectus. The managing underwriter must take reasonable steps to see that broker-dealers participating in the distribution receive a sufficient number of copies of the prospectus to comply with the rule and with" §5(b). Sec. Act Rel. 5101 (1970).

[16] Rule 461(b)(3)-(7).

indemnification may be as a matter of state law, because it tends to frustrate the *in terrorem* purpose of individual liability under §11 for negligent deficiencies in the registration statement. When there is provision for such indemnification and it has not been waived, the Commission will not accelerate unless the registration statement includes a statement of the Commission's view and an undertaking to the effect that any claim for indemnification (other than payment of the expenses of a successful defense) will not be honored without a judicial test.[17] This policy will be considered in the chapter on Civil Liability as part of the indemnification-contribution-insurance complex under the SEC statutes generally.[18]

(v)   As early as 1945 the Commission announced that it considered that the statutory standard for acceleration was "not met in cases where the selling stockholder does not bear his equitable proportion of the expense of registration."[19] And occasionally the Commission experimented with other types of cases. For example, the Commission for some years denied acceleration when the registration statement related to a preferred stock with a par or stated value substantially less than its liquidation preference (or any equity security junior thereto) unless an agreement was made to restrict surplus (so as to prevent dividends on any junior security) until the total capital and surplus at least equalled the amount of the liquidation preference.[20] The Commission justified that policy on the grounds that the description of the terms of the several classes of securities in such cases was apt to give a misleading impression of the registrant's capitalization notwithstanding disclosure of the disparity between liquidation preference and par or stated value, and that the "public interest" standard of §8(a) was not satisfied when the capital structure was such that the contributions of one class of stockholders might be distributed to another class in the form of dividends.

Although these two practices were included when the Commission first proposed to formalize its policy,[21] they were abandoned without explanation when it took final action in the form of a note to Rule 460 (replaced in 1982 by Rule 461).[22] Particularly since those policies were the hardest to defend, there was

---

[17] This is sometimes called the Johnson & Johnson formula after an early registration statement in which it was developed.
[18] See p. 1198 infra.
[19] Sec. Act Rel. 3055 (1945).
[20] Sec. Act Rel. 3672 (1956).
[21] Proposed note to Rule 460, ibid.
[22] Sec. Act Rel. 3791 (1957).

an inference that the note was meant to be exclusive. But that was not done expressly.[23] And the suspicion grew that the Commission intended to leave the door open at least a crack when the Chairman publicly stated in 1958 that there was a clear inference, from the Commission's action in abandoning some of the proposals that "really had little to do with disclosure problems," that acceleration would be granted if the papers were otherwise in order and the note were satisfied — "unless legal ingenuity has thought up some new gadget."[24]

In 1949 a Hoover Commission "task force" cited the indemnification policy, as well as the Commission's policy on "bail-outs" by controlling stockholders, in support of its conclusion that the Commission had exceeded its statutory authority by thus attempting through its acceleration power to achieve objectives unrelated to the principle of disclosure.[25] And in 1958 the American Bar Association's criticism went to the point of suggested legislation to except the price amendment altogether from the power to deny acceleration.[26]

This criticism, of course, assumes the major premise that the Commission's authority under §8(a) is strictly limited to considerations of disclosure. Quite apart from acceleration, the registration statement is supposed to be accurate and adequate if a stop order is to be avoided under §8(d). Consequently, it seems reasonable to suppose that §8(a) requires something more than ordinary disclosure when it imposes on the Commission the duty to consider how readily the facts in the registration statement can be understood by the investing public in less time than the full statutory period.

It may be assumed that in statutory context these general standards alone do not suffice to turn what is basically a disclosure statute into a piece of legislation that gives the Commission authority to approve or disapprove securities on their merits.[27] But

[23] Any doubt was dispelled when the Commission stated in 1968, after referring to the note to Rule 460: "Other instances occur from time to time which cause the Commission to deny acceleration requests." Sec. Act Rel. 4910 (1968).

[24] Gadsby, Proposed Legislation Regarding Acceleration Policies, 187 Com. & Fin. Chron. 2171, 2190 (1958).

[25] Task Force Report on Regulatory Commissions [Appendix N] Prepared for the Commission on Organization of the Executive Branch of the Government (1949) 148-49.

[26] See 83 A. B. A. Rep. 839-42 (1958).

[27] Standards like "the public interest and the protection of investors" must be read in statutory context. New York Central Securities Corp. v. United States, 287 U. S. 12, 24-25 (1932) ("public interest" in Interstate Commerce

the Commission has never claimed this power. And it has now abandoned the two policies — in the "bail-out" and restricted surplus cases — that, however sound they were as a matter of corporation law, were the hardest to justify under disclosure-oriented standards. Insofar as the policies on indemnification, investigations, market manipulation and underwriters' financial responsibility go beyond the disclosure philosophy, there is probably enough flexibility in the standards of §8(a) to justify them.

2. POSTEFFECTIVE PROBLEMS

a. Date As of Which Registration Statement Speaks

Query: As of what date does the registration statement speak? On this fundamental question the statute is not too clear on its face. Section 8(d) authorizes a stop order "If it appears to the Commission at any time that the registration statement includes any untrue statement * * * ." It does not use the past tense, "included." This would seem consistent with the statement of the House committee that, "In determining whether a stop order should issue, the Commission will naturally have regard to the facts as they then exist and will stop the further sale of securities even though the registration statement was true when made, [and] it has become untrue or misleading by reason of subsequent developments."[28] On the other hand, §11 imposes civil liability on the issuer and other persons "In case any part of the registration statement, when such part became effective, contained an untrue statement * * * ." The two sections can be reconciled with each other — although §11 cannot be reconciled with the statement of the House committee — by reading the phrase "at any time" in §8(d), in accordance with its position as a matter of syntax, to modify the verb "appears" rather than "includes." At any rate, the second reported opinion of the Federal Trade Commission decided that the registration statement was required to be true and adequate only as of its effective date.[29]

Under this approach the primary purpose, at least, of the posteffective amendment procedure in §8(c) is to permit posteffective

---

Act §5(2)); Pan American World Airways, Inc. v. United States, 371 U. S. 296, 308-09 (1963) (Civil Aeronautics Act).

[28] H. R. Rep. No. 85, 73d Cong., 1st Sess. (1933) 20.

[29] Charles A. Howard, 1 SEC 6, 9-10, 18 FTC 626, 630-31 (1934). If the state of the registrant's knowledge or the facts change between the filing and effective dates, the registration statement must be corrected by amendment.

correction of belatedly discovered deficiencies that existed as of the effective date. As we shall see, however, the practice has come a long way from this static concept.

First it is necessary to look at the mechanics of §8(c) itself.[30] The filing of a posteffective amendment does not suspend the effectiveness of the registration statement. It may indicate that the statement as unamended is deficient. But in the absence of a stop order the statement remains in effect and sales may legally be made so far as §5 is concerned. The question of the effective date of the amendment is important chiefly from the point of view of civil liability under §11. Until the amendment is declared effective by the Commission, it cannot be the basis of liability under the language of that section. By the same token a person who buys between the filing and the effectiveness of the amendment can recover on the basis of the unamended registration statement if it is deficient (unless, knowledge always being a defense under §11, the defendant is able to prove that the filing of the amendment itself brought knowledge of the deficiencies in the registration statement to the buyer); on the other hand, whether a person who buys after the effectiveness of the amendment can similarly recover is at least open to question.

All this is not to say that the issuer, underwriters, and dealers can ignore all posteffective developments that materially alter the picture presented in the registration statement. Posteffective amendment is not the only means of achieving currency. The Federal Trade Commission put it this way:

> Let us suppose that the registration statement contained a statement to the effect that the registrant owned 500 acres of timbered land, and that after the registration statement became effective a forest fire destroyed the timber on 250 of these acres. The statement made by the registrant would still reflect the truth as of the time that the registration statement became effective and thus would give no ground for the issuance of a stop order. Vendors, who knew or should have known of this fact, would, however, thereafter be under a duty to disclose that fact to their customers in order to avoid the liabilities of Section 12(2); and the Commission could proceed by injunction against such non-disclosing vendors under Section 17(a). On the other hand, let us suppose that the statement that the registrant owned 500 acres

---

[30] A posteffective amendment becomes effective "on such date as the Commission may determine." Posteffective amendments to registration statements for employee offerings on Form S-8 become effective on filing. Rule 464. And this is also the practice with respect to dividend reinvestment plans. Cf. n. 12 supra.

was based upon a mistaken survey, and that after the registration statement became effective a second and correct survey disclosed that the registrant only owned 250 acres. In such a case, the statement would be untrue as of the time that the registration statement became effective, and the Commission could proceed by stop order unless appropriate amendments were made to the registration statement.[31]

The Commission might have referred to the possibility of still further sanctions attendant on use of a prospectus that did not disclose the fire: a common law deceit action, various blue sky liabilities, and criminal prosecution under §17(a), the mail fraud statute, and state statutes on obtaining money or property by false pretenses (not to mention Rule 10b-5 if the Commission had been prescient).

The traditional procedure was to disclose the posteffective change (the fire in the FTC's example) by putting a sticker on the prospectus and filing copies as required by SEC rule,[32] not by way of an amendment that might be subject to a stop order or §11 liability. On the other hand, because §10(a) of the Act requires the prospectus to "contain the information contained in the registration statement," the registrant must file the later prospectus as a posteffective amendment to the registration statement if the new information is *substituted* for the old and not merely *added* to it. And, when numerous and significant changes since the original effective date have made the original prospectus obsolete, the Commission has said, " 'supplementation' of the outmoded prospectus necessarily results in an obscure and uncoordinated presentation."[33] Beyond that, it has been true for some time that "the staff generally requires that posteffective amendments be filed to reflect material changes."[34] Indeed, Commission counsel in 1972 characterized the line of cases going back to the FTC as not dictated by statutory interpretation at all but as based on a series of discretionary refusals to exert statutory authority for reasons of policy and convenience. The Commission, its counsel contended, had never followed the old FTC approach when posteffective developments involved "a major and substantial change in the basic nature and terms of the public offering which was

[31] Charles A. Howard, 1 SEC 6, 10, 18 FTC 626, 631 (1934).

[32] Rule 424(c).

[33] Franchard Corp., 42 SEC 163, 184-85 (1964). In that case a supplemented prospectus was in fact filed as an amendment and the Commission found that its form was misleading.

[34] Sec. Act Rel. 6276, 21 SEC Dock. 1052, 1075 (1980).

deliberately, willfully and voluntarily effected by the issuer and selling shareholders."[35]

Whatever the merit of this argument, there is nevertheless one statutory exception to the rule that the registration statement must be amended whenever the prospectus is changed rather than supplemented. Section 10(a)(3) provides that, "when a prospectus is used more than nine months after the effective date of the registration statement, the information contained therein shall be as of a date not more than sixteen months prior to such use, so far as such information is known to the user of such prospectus or can be furnished by such user without unreasonable effort or expense." There is no requirement that this so-called "nine-month prospectus" be filed as an amendment to the registration statement, even though a Commission rule permits (but does not require) the omission from such a prospectus of any information previously required to be contained in the prospectus insofar as the prospectus contains later information on the same subjects (including the latest available certified financial statements) as of a date not more than sixteen months prior to its use; for §10(a)(3) obviously cuts across the clause in the first part of §10(a) to the effect that the prospectus shall "contain the information contained in the registration statement." It is necessary merely to file ten copies of the prospectus with the Commission.[36] In other words, whereas the substitution of information in a prospectus used *less* than nine months after the effective date requires a posteffective amendment, the same substitution *after* nine months does not. This means, of course, that nine-month prospectuses are not subject to stop order or to civil liability under §11.

Gradually, however, a series of exceptions has been eating up the rule that the nine-month prospectus need not be filed as an amendment. Under §24(e)(3) of the Investment Company Act, nine-month prospectuses of investment companies that make continuous offerings do have to be filed as posteffective amendments. That special class of issuer aside, the Commission developed the practice over the years, in the case of various kinds of deferred or continuous offerings, of requiring an undertaking to file any nine-month prospectuses as posteffective amendments.[37] In time the Commission began to introduce a posteffective amendment re-

---

[35] Brief for Appellees, pp. 47-48, SEC v. Manor Nursing Centers, Inc., 458 F. 2d 1082 (2d Cir. 1972).

[36] Rules 427, 424(c).

[37] See pp. 140-41, 143 infra.

quirement with respect to §10(a)(3) prospectuses in a series of specialized forms.[38] And it normally follows the practice whenever there is only a best-efforts underwriter or none at all.

One can readily understand the Commission's exacting the post-effective amendment procedure as a condition of recognizing the exigencies of certain types of deferred or continuous offerings. It is considerably more difficult to understand, in the light of the juxtaposition of §§7, 8(c), and 10(a)(3), a general requirement that would in effect transpose §10(a)(3) to §7. That end *would* be achieved by the Code, which would also require a posteffective amendment *whenever* the prospectus was "supplemented or changed" or whenever an amendment was necessary "to correct (A) a material deficiency in the offering statement [today's registration statement] as of its effective date, or (B) a statement of a material fact in the offering statement that becomes a misrepresentation by reason of a subsequent event."[39]

b.   Registration "for the Shelf"

In any event, §10(a)(3) is not designed to permit issuers to register unlimited amounts of securities with the thought of presently distributing some and having the rest conveniently registered in the event that a need for further capital should arise in the indefinite future. Section 6(a) of the act concludes by stating that "A registration statement shall be deemed effective only as to the securities specified therein as proposed to be offered." In order to avoid the registration of securities "for the shelf," the Commission has traditionally construed this provision, in the context of the statute as a whole, as if the word "presently" (in the sense of "soon") preceded the phrase "proposed to be offered." The Commission, accordingly, has made it clear by rule that the registration of additional securities, even though they are of the same class as other securities which are already effectively registered, must be effected through a separate statement rather than by way of amendment of the earlier statement.[40] The same policy explains

---

[38] Form S-8, Undertaking B; Form S-11, Undertaking C; Form S-14, Item 6(b).

[39] §508.

[40] Rule 413. *Query* when a company registers and distributes all of its authorized common stock in 1978, reacquires some of those shares in 1980, and desires to offer them to the public in 1982; or when an individual acquires enough of those shares in 1980 to become a controlling stockholder

the Commission's practice of requiring a registrant to include in the registration statement an undertaking to file a posteffective amendment reducing the amount of securities registered in certain contingencies. This practice is followed, for example, in conversion situations with respect to securities not taken down at the expiration of the conversion period.

It used to be followed also in the case of open-end investment companies, which continuously stand ready to redeem their outstanding shares and, usually, to sell new shares to the public. So that they would never run out of registered shares, they used to follow the practice of filing approximately once a year a registration statement that covered as many shares as they expected to be able to sell during the following year. Since they naturally tended to err on the side of plenty, the Commission customarily required an undertaking that any shares remaining unsold after eighteen months would be "deregistered" by a posteffective amendment. In the 1954 amendment program, however, a new §24(e) was added to the Investment Company Act so as to permit those investment companies engaged in continuous offerings (most open-end management companies, face-amount certificate companies, and unit investment trusts) to register additional securities under the 1933 Act either by filing a new registration statement as they formerly did or by filing an appropriate amendment, approximately once a year, to the latest effective registration statement for securities of the same class.[41]

The open-end investment company is the classic case of the continuous offering. But the practical exigencies presented by a number of other types of either continuous or deferred offerings — the latter are more properly "shelf registrations" though the two categories blur into each other — have persuaded the Commission to bend the last sentence of §6(a) so as to ameliorate the burden of filing successive registration statements. In 1982 the Commission, after stating that its substantial experience with various types

---

and desires to make a secondary distribution thereafter through an underwriter.

[41] The filing of current information as a part of the registration statement at approximately yearly intervals is assured by providing, as we have seen (supra p. 139), that no nine-month prospectus relating to a security issued by any such company, within the meaning of §10(a)(3) of the Securities Act, is considered to meet the requirements of §10 unless it has been filed as part of a posteffective amendment that has become effective. In 1970 the Investment Company Act was further amended by the addition of §24(f), which, in effect, permits *nunc pro tunc* registration of oversales in addition to authorizing the Commission by rule to permit the registration of an indefinite number of securities in the first instance. See Rules 24e-1, 24e-2, 24f-1, 24f-2.

of shelf registrations had not made it aware of major abuses and that a restrictive policy was not necessary or appropriate, formalized and radically liberalized the administrative practice in a new Rule 415, which has three conditions designed to assure "[1] a bona fide intention to offer and sell, [2] accurate current information and [3] liability protection under the Securities Act."[42]

The first condition limits the amount of registerable securities to what "is reasonably expected to be offered and sold within two years," whether in a primary or in a secondary distribution,[43] with exceptions that codify past practice.[44] The types of continuous and deferred offerings that will be candidates for the new two-year formula will presumably include at least those that have been over the years: for example, the issuance of securities in connection with a continuing acquisition program[45] or, in connection with mergers and the like, to persons defined as underwriters by the rule that governs such events.[46] Moreover, the rule "contemplates an issuer's selling the securities registered on the shelf in a succession of different kinds of offerings."[47] But the rule breaks new

[42] Sec. Act Rel. 6276, 21 SEC Dock. 1052, 1073 (1980); Sec. Act Rel. 6334, 23 SEC Dock. 387 (1981). The rule was adopted in Sec. Act Rel. 6383, 24 SEC Dock. 1262, 1288-94 (1982).

[43] Rule 415(a)(1)(i). "According to SEC staff, the offering may extend beyond the two-year period so long as it was reasonably expected, upon initial registration, to culminate within two years." Ferrara and Sweeney, Shelf Registration under SEC Temporary Rule 415, 5 Corp. L. Rev. 308, 310 (1982).

[44] Rule 415(a)(1)(ii)-(vii). These exceptions are for (ii) secondary offerings in noncontrol situations (which is to say, when the seller is a statutory "underwriter"), (iii) dividend, interest reinvestment or employee benefit plans, (iv) rights offerings, (v) conversions, (vi) securities pledged as collateral, and (vii) American depositary receipts.

Although Rule 415(b) makes the rule inapplicable to foreign governments, the Commission in practice follows substantially the Rule 415 procedure. Sec. Act Rel. 6424, 26 SEC Dock. 20 (1982).

The Commission, in its various attempts over the years to adjust the last sentence of §6(a) to the exigencies of warrants and convertible securities, has had to ignore the two anomalies in that sentence: (1) The clear negative implication is that the issue of a right that *is* immediately exercisable does involve a present offer of the security it calls for; this would seem to be so even though the right, though immediately exercisable as a legal matter, will not be exercised for some time as a practical matter, if ever, because the exercise price is substantially higher than the current market price of the stock called for. (2) The delayed "offer" concept applies only when the right is "originally issued or transferred with a security"; thus, when warrants are issued independently of any other security, there is again by negative implication an immediate "offer" of the security they call for although they may not be immediately exercisable even as a legal matter.

[45] Sec. Act Rel. 6383, 24 SEC Dock. 1262, 1288 (1982).

[46] Rule 145(c), infra p. 316; see Sec. Act Rel. 6276, 21 SEC Dock. 1052, 1072, 1076 n. 86 (1981).

[47] Sec. Act Rel. 6383, 24 SEC Dock. 1262, 1288 (1982). "The use of a single

ground in permitting offerings to be made from time to time during the two-year period "at the market," through the facilities of an exchange or an over-the-counter marketmaker, if, in the case of a primary offering of equity securities, (1) the securities are sold through one or more underwriters named in the statutory prospectus;[48] (2) the registrant meets the applicable requirements of the contemporaneously adopted Form S-3 (which is to say, the securities are widely followed by financial analysts),[49] and (3) the amount of securities registered, when voting stock, does not exceed 10 percent of the nonaffiliate "float."[50]

The second of the three conditions of Rule 415 (accurate current information) requires undertakings to file posteffective amendments reflecting material postregistration events (any "fundamental change" so far as the prospectus is concerned) as well as the nine-month prospectus provision in §10(a)(3).[51] The term "fundamental," the Commission said, "is intended to reflect current staff practice under which posteffective amendments are filed when major and substantial changes are made to information contained in the registration statement." Numerous small changes can become cumulatively "fundamental." But a short sticker will continue to be permitted for material changes that are not "fundamental" and can be stated accurately and succinctly in that form.[52]

---

shelf registration statement for widely diverse plans of financing may be inappropriate in cases where a complete description of each plan of distribution to which the filing relates, together with a discussion of the impact on the issuer of such plan alone and in combination with the other contemplated financings, becomes so complex as to reduce substantially the effectiveness of the disclosures. In such cases, more than one registration statement may be necessary." Id. at 1291.

[48] "The SEC has required underwriter participation because it asserts that the direct involvement of an underwriter provides discipline upon [at-the-market] offerings of equity securities and helps to ensure that accurate and current disclosure is made to investors in the prospectus and that the prospectus delivery requirements of the Securities Act are met." Ferrara and Sweeney, Shelf Registration under SEC Temporary Rule 415, 5 Corp. L. Rev. 308, 313 n. 22 (1982).

For the Commission's views on the status of various market professionals as "underwriters" in this context, see Sec. Act Rel. 6334, 23 SEC Dock. 387, 397 (1981), *reaffirmed* in Sec. Act Rel. 6383, 24 SEC Dock. 1262, 1293 (1982).

[49] See p. 152 infra.

[50] Rule 415(a)(3). The "float" refers to the amount of stock outstanding and available for trading after deduction of large blocks (whether or not held by affiliates) that are not likely to enter the market.

[51] Rule 415(a)(2); Reg. S-K, Item 512(a)(1). It is the administrative practice to require a two-day wait before *any* posteffective amendment becomes effective.

[52] Sec. Act Rel. 6383, 24 SEC Dock. 1262, 1290 (1982). " * * * there is no need to maintain an accurate and current, or 'evergreen,' prospectus when no offers or sales are being made pursuant to the shelf registration." Id. at

The third condition of Rule 415 (liability protection) requires a further undertaking

> That, for the purpose of determining any liability under the Securities Act of 1933, each such post-effective amendment shall be deemed to be a new registration statement relating to the securities offered therein, and the offering of such securities at that time shall be deemed to be the initial bona fide offering thereof.
> To remove from registration by means of a post-effective amendment any of the securities being registered which remain unsold at the termination of the offering.[53]

A number of prominent underwriting houses strenuously objected that the two-year innovation might have serious impacts on the capital raising process. The new Form S-3 is so skeletal, as we shall see in a moment, that any of some 2000 companies eligible for that form may file a single registration statement designating the amount of bonds and stocks it wants to put on its "shelf" for issuance during the next two years and, when it considers interest rates and other factors to be propitious, may quite readily enter the market with relatively small chunks of securities. The result, in the words of a financial journalist, could be not only to "alter the style and role of investment bankers" but also to "tear asunder some of the traditional relationships and pecking orders that have governed the nation's capital markets since the early 20th century." Without time, necessarily, for lead underwriters to form syndicates, and with smaller amounts involved, the "blue chip" issuers would have "much greater flexibility and incentive to shop around for investment banks" — indeed, the syndicate might be eliminated — and investment bankers might be eschewed entirely in favor of selling the entire issue to one or a few institutional buyers (a so-called "bought deal").[54]

The Commission's language in response was more bland. "Recognizing the importance of the views and concerns of the commentators,"[55] it inserted the S-3 and 10 percent float conditions

---

1289. An example is a rights offering when the market price of the stock is substantially below the exercise price. Sec. Act Rel. 6334, 23 SEC Dock. 387, 394 (1981).

[53] Rule 415(a)(2); Reg. S-K, Item 512(a)(2)-(3).

[54] See Friedman, Investment Banks' New Day, N. Y. Times, Mar. 11, 1982, p. D1, col. 3; Ehrbar, Upheaval in Investment Banking, 106 Fortune 90 (Aug. 23, 1982). For a wryly incisive comparison of primary stock distributions twenty-five years ago and today, thanks largely to Rule 415, see Pryor and Smith, Significant Changes in Primary Stock Distributions over the Last 25 Years, Nat. L. J., Aug. 9, 1982, p. 21; Pryor and Smith, Disclosure and Capital Formation Policies, Nat. L. J., Aug. 16, 1982, p. 15.

[55] Sec. Act Rel. 6383, 24 SEC Dock. 1262, 1288 (1982).

with respect to primary offerings of equities;[56] adopted the rule for only a nine-month period, to expire December 10, 1982; and promised public hearings and a further opportunity to comment during that period.[57]

In the light of these hearings and a great many diverse comments, the Commission extended the rule to year-end 1983 with only one modification: removal of the posteffective amendment requirement to reflect the addition or deletion of a "managing underwriter," because of "the lack of clarity in this area and the difficulty of interpretation and operation of the managing underwriter concept."[58]

At this writing one can only speculate about the impact of Rule 415 on capital formation and investment banking practices. The deregulation aspects are clear: gun-jumping questions with respect to securities taken off the shelf are eliminated; and, except for the relatively rare case where a posteffective amendment is required, underwriters and dealers may confirm sales orally immediately after the terms of the particular offering are agreed to without waiting for the filing of a price amendment or SEC processing or declaration of effectiveness. But there are also a number of legal considerations: the issuer that wants to offer debt securities must qualify an indenture that is "open-ended"; regulated companies, such as public utilities, must work out procedures for authorization in advance; and issuers must also make their peace with the state blue sky administrators. Moreover, the potential changes in techniques of capital formation loom large: the more frequent offering of securities in smaller batches may lead to semiprivate placements effected through single underwriters without syndication, as we have already noticed;[59] we may even see the development of some form of competitive bidding; and institutional investors may come to play a more direct role in capital formation.[60]

---

[56] See pp. 142-43 supra.

[57] Sec. Act Rel. 6383, 24 SEC Dock. 1262, 1288-89 (1982). In Sec. Act Rel. 6391, 24 SEC Dock. 1502 (1982), the Commission set forth a substantial number of issues on which it invited comment at hearings to begin on June 28, 1982.

[58] Sec. Act Rel. 6423, 26 SEC Dock. 2, 8 (1982).

[59] See p. 144 supra.

[60] These and other considerations — including the impact on regional broker-dealers, the risk of aggravating the trend toward institutionalization of the markets, and the risk to underwriters' due diligence and the disclosure system generally — led Commissioner Thomas to write an extensive opinion dissenting from the extension of the rule without substantial change. 26 SEC Dock. at 9.

Even apart from Rule 415, the propriety and enforceability of the Commission-exacted extrastatutory undertakings are moot questions, since the Commission's authority seems never to have been challenged. In principle, it is not easy to answer the trenchant criticism of the entire practice made by a former General Counsel of the SEC: "But it would seem that, to the extent that an undertaking (other than one specifically prescribed by statute) does no more than obligate an issuer to do what is required by law, it is unnecessary; and that, to the extent that an undertaking imposes an obligation to do something not required by law, it is unwarranted."[61] The pragmatic answer is that it may be too much to expect complete logic and philosophic consistency in a field as complex as this. Perhaps the important thing is that all this seems to work. Indeed, to the extent that the undertaking technique represents an attempt to accommodate the policy and requirements of the statute to the exigencies of certain types of offerings that raise questions under the last sentence of §6(a) — to say nothing of the attempt to facilitate capital formation by the new Rule 415 — the Commission has managed to soften the impact of that statutory provision and still to achieve substantially the statutory purpose of providing investors with current information, subject to the sanctions of the Act, at a time close to the actual sales activity or investment decision.

Nevertheless, altogether apart from logical symmetry, all this creates practical problems:

(1) Since the undertakings are given by the issuer but many of the acts bringing them into play are acts by the underwriter that may occur in the future, the issuer should protect itself by appropriate agreement with the underwriter. And conversely, the underwriter will want an appropriate registration covenant from the issuer.[62]

(2) A posteffective amendment designed to make only minor changes may nevertheless have the effect of reaffirming other facts that were true when the registration statement originally became effective but have since become untrue. Therefore, care must be taken that the contents of the entire registration statement are accurate and complete as of the effective date of the posteffective amendment.

(3) As long as the Commission uses its §4(3) authority to waive delivery of prospectuses after expiration of the forty-day or ninety-

---

[61] Throop, Recent Developments with Respect to Rule 133, 15 Bus. Law. 119, 127 (1959).
[62] See p. 416 infra.

day period following the *first* of several "shelf" offerings,[63] it is an academic question whether the Commission through this undertaking technique could extend the statutory periods during which all dealers must deliver prospectuses under §4(3). But the problem remains whether the statute of limitations imposed upon §11 actions by §13 can be extended by any such process of self-levitation. When Congress wanted to accomplish a similar result in connection with the 1954 amendment of §24(e) of the Investment Company Act to permit the registration of additional securities of open-end companies to be effected under the Securities Act by amending an earlier registration statement instead of filing a new one, it expressly extended the statute of limitations. And the Code cuts through the present statutory morass with a series of short and simple provisions.[64]

c.   A Bit More Socraticism, This Time Centering about Warrants

Y Corp. wants to make a public offering of its $5 par preferred stock at par with warrants attached to buy common share for share at $2. The common stock has no market. (Assume in all these questions that no "small issue" exemption is available under §3(b).)
   1.   Should *Y* Corp. register anything besides the preferred on the assumption that the warrants are exercisable:
   (a) immediately;
   (b) only after two years;
   (c) immediately, but on the further assumption that some of the common stock has recently been sold privately at $1?

[63] Rule 174(c); see p. 122 supra.
[64] Section 507 provides:

   (a) *Continuous Distributions.* — Except as the Commission provides otherwise by rule, (1) an issuer may include as many continuously offered securities in an offering statement as it specifies, either initially or by amendment, and (2) a registered investment company may include retroactively in an offering statement, by amendment, continuously offered securities already issued.

   (b) *Deferred Distributions.* — The Commission, by rule or order, may permit the filing of an offering statement by any issuer, or its pre-effective or posteffective amendment to increase the amount of securities offered, in connection with a deferred distribution.

   (c) *Ninety-day Rule.* — Except as provided in section 507(a) or (b) or by rule or order, an offering statement may be filed only if it is proposed to begin the offering of the securities by the ninetieth day after its effective date and the offering statement so states.

2. Assume that the common shares were registered. Two years have elapsed. *Y* Corp. has prospered and the book value of its common stock is now $2.50. *P*, a holder of 100 shares of preferred, presents his warrants for exercise. What, if anything, does §5 require *Y* Corp. to do before it mails a certificate for 100 shares of common stock to *P?*

3. Assume all the facts as in Question 2 except that the interval is six months instead of two years and *Y* Corp. has just had a patent-infringement action for $1 million filed against it.

4. Five years have gone by and 80,000 shares of common have been issued on exercise of warrants. *Y* Corp. now wants to offer 200,000 shares of common to the public at $5 per share.

(a) What, if anything, must *Y* Corp. do to comply with §5?

(b) Assume that 80,000 shares are registered. A month later *D*, a dealer in Oshkosh who has never been in a selling group, sells *C* 100 shares of *Y* Corp. stock and mails him a certificate without a prospectus. Has *D* violated §5?

(c) Any difference if *D* acted as *C*'s *broker?*

D. CONTENTS OF THE REGISTRATION STATEMENT AND PROSPECTUS (HEREIN OF THE SEC'S ACCOUNTING ROLE)

1. INTEGRATION OF THE DISCLOSURE PROVISIONS OF THE 1933 AND 1934 ACTS

This is not the place for a detailed treatment of how to prepare a registration statement. That is more art than science in any event, and it is learned in the doing. All we can profitably do here is tune the fiddle before placing it in the learner's hands.[1]

Section 7 provides, in substance, that the registration statement shall contain the information, and be accompanied by the documents, specified in Schedule A (or Schedule B in the case of securities issued by a foreign government or one of its political subdivisions), except that the Commission may by rule add to or

---

C. 2D [1]Limitation of space prevents setting out the excellent description of the entire process of "going public" in Wheat and Blackstone, Guideposts for a First Public Offering, 15 Bus. Law. 539 (1960). On the advantages and disadvantages of going public in the first place, see Schneider, Manko, and Kant, Going Public — Practice, Procedure and Consequences, 27 Vill. L. Rev. (1981).

subtract from the specified information and documents with respect to any class of issuers or securities. Similar flexibility marks §10, which provides that the statutory prospectus shall contain "the information contained in the registration statement" except for certain documents referred to in the schedules and subject to the Commission's power to adopt rules adding, subtracting and classifying. Additional authority is given the Commission by §19(a), the general provision on rulemaking, to define "accounting, technical, and trade terms" used in the Act and to prescribe the form in which required information shall be set forth and the methods to be followed in the preparation of accounts and financial statements. The Commission has used this authority from the beginning not only to adopt a number of general rules but also to adapt the specifications of Schedule A to the circumstances of particular types of issuers by promulgating a substantial number of separate forms.[2]

Much as new law school professors are reputed to prepare very strict examinations and to become less exacting as they mellow, the Commission has found it possible, as it has accumulated experience, to relax the requirements substantially without impairing the interests of investors — though this is not to say, of course, that experience has not also dictated a tightening of requirements here and there. There has always been a substantial variety of forms for different types of issues and, to some extent, issuers of different qualities. But it is possible to discern four stages in the maturation process:

(1) Until the early 1940s all the forms consisted of the registration statement proper, in question-and-answer form, and the prospectus, which had to repeat much the same information in narrative form.

(2) In 1942 the Commission adopted Form S-1, which, after many modifications, is still the residual form. That form and others in the "S" series made the prospectus the basic part of the registration statement and simply required additional information to be included as Part II. Part II, which has remained in question-and-answer form, is a public document that is used by analysts and financial services, but it does not have to be delivered to anyone. A "hooker" in Part II is a requirement for disclosure of

---

[2] So far as Schedule B is concerned, the Commission has never adopted a form for foreign government issues. Each registration is handled *ad hoc*. When foreign governments guarantee the principal and interest of securities issued by state-owned utilities or other entities, Schedule B is applied to the guaranteed securities as well as the guarantees. Sec. Act Rel. 6424, 26 SEC Dock. 20 (1982).

recent sales of unregistered securities and a statement of the exemption relied on. The result is sometimes the inclusion in the financial statements of a substantial contingent liability under §12(1), or even deferral of the offering.

(3) In 1970 the Commission adopted Form S-16, and later extended its scope on an optional basis to cover issuers that (among other conditions) had a three-year reporting history under the 1934 Act and a specified income record. The prime characteristic of Form S-16 was a highly condensed prospectus, with incorporation by reference of all reports and proxy statements filed under the 1934 Act (including such material filed in the future) together with a statement of any material changes of an adverse nature in the registrant's affairs since the date of the latest certified financials.[3] This was an important step in integration of the filing requirements of the 1933 and 1934 Acts.[4] Some registration statements on Form S-16 became effective in as little as forty-eight hours.

(4) Form S-16 disappeared and the integration program was carried a great step further in 1982 — about as far as possible short of the Code's registration of *companies:*

SECURITIES ACT RELEASE NO. 6383: ADOPTION OF INTEGRATED DISCLOSURE SYSTEM
24 SEC Dock. 1262
Securities and Exchange Commission, 1982

*   *   *

* * * It was long clear that the transaction-oriented framework of the Securities Act and the disclosure system which developed thereunder often overlap with, and produce disclosure duplicative of, that prepared independently in response to the status-oriented framework of the Exchange Act and the continuous disclosure system operating thereunder. * * *

*   *   *

---

[3] Sec. Act Rel. 5117 (1970). Form S-16 followed a recommendation of the "Wheat Report," prepared by an SEC staff group under the direction of then Commissioner Wheat. Disclosure to Investors: A Reappraisal of Federal Administrative Policies under the '33 and '34 Acts (1969).

[4] See Cohen, "Truth in Securities" Revisited, 79 Harv. L. Rev. 1340 (1966), supra p. 43; Sec. Act Rel. 6235, 20 SEC Dock. 1175 (1980).

New Forms S-1, S-2 and S-3 provide the basic framework for the registration of securities under the Securities Act. These Forms establish three categories for registration statements. The same information will be required to be part of Securities Act registration statements in all categories, either presented in, or delivered with, the prospectus or incorporated by reference from another document. Differences among the three Forms reflect the Commission's determination as to (1) when this required information must be presented in full in the prospectus delivered to investors, (2) when certain of the delivered information may be presented on a streamlined basis and supplemented by documents incorporated by reference, and (3) when certain information may be incorporated by reference from documents in the Exchange Act continuous reporting system without delivery to investors.

Generally, it is the registrant-oriented portion of the information relating to a public offering, as opposed to the transaction-specific information, which sometimes may be satisfied otherwise than through full prospectus presentation. Much of this registrant-oriented information is the same as that which is required to be presented in annual reports to the Commission on Form 10-K and in annual reports to security holders, as well as in quarterly and current reports on Forms 10-Q (17 CFR 249.308a) and 8-K (17 CFR 249.308), respectively. Information about the offering, however, will not have been reported on in any other disclosure document or otherwise have been publicly disseminated and thus will be required to be presented in the prospectus in all cases.

The registration statement for the first category is Form S-1. It requires complete disclosure to be set forth in the prospectus and permits no incorporation by reference. Form S-1 is to be used by registrants in the Exchange Act reporting system for less than three years and also may be used by any registrants who choose to do so or for whom no other form is available.

The second category of registration statement is Form S-2, which combines reliance on incorporating Exchange Act reports by reference with delivery to investors of streamlined information. Registrants in the Exchange Act reporting system for three years may use this Form, which allows them to choose to either: (1) deliver a copy of their annual report to security holders along with the prospectus describing the offering or (2) present registrant-oriented information comparable to that of the annual report in the prospectus along with the description of the offering. In either case, the more complete information in the Form 10-K is incorporated by reference into the prospectus.

Form S-3, in reliance on the efficient market theory, allows maximum use of incorporation by reference of Exchange Act reports and requires the least disclosure to be presented in the prospectus and delivered to investors. Generally, the Form S-3 prospectus will present the same transaction-specific information as will be presented in a Form S-1 or S-2 prospectus. Information concerning the registrant will be incorporated by reference from Exchange Act reports. The prospectus will not be required to present any information concerning the registrant unless there has been a material change in the registrant's affairs which has not been reported in an Exchange Act filing or the Exchange Act reports incorporated by reference do not reflect certain restated financial statements or other financial information.

*   *   *

Form S-3 is available, in substance, for American companies (and under certain circumstances foreign private issuers) that have reported under the 1934 Act for the past three years and have had a default-free record since the end of the last fiscal year, but only if (1) the nonaffiliate float is at least $150 million or (2) the voting stock held by nonaffiliates has an aggregate value of at least $100 million and an annual trading volume of at least 3 million shares. In addition, because investment grade debt securities are generally bought on the basis of interest rates and security ratings, they (as well as investment grade preferred stocks) are eligible for Form S-3 regardless of the float.[5]

Underwriters were said to be reluctant to have Form S-16 used out of fear of §11 liability for incorporated documents with whose preparation they had not been involved.[6] And, if they insisted on beefing up the prospectus with additional information such as a description of the issuer's business and summary financial information, they increased the risk of liability, arguably, by picking and choosing without benefit of SEC guidelines. Here the Commission took a leaf out of the Code by adopting a rule to the effect that one of the circumstances to be considered in deter-

---

[5] There are also special provisions for (1) secondary offerings, (2) rights offerings, dividend or interest reinvestment plans, and conversions, (3) majority-owned subsidiaries, and (4) rights offerings by foreign private issuers. And in late 1982 the Commission extended the integrated disclosure system to most foreign private issuers through the adoption (*inter alia*) of Forms F-1, F-2, and F-3. Sec. Act Rel. 6437, 26 SEC Dock. 964 (1982).

[6] See Sec. Act Rel. 5879, 13 SEC Dock. 509, 511 (1977).

mining whether a defendant acted reasonably is "Whether, with respect to a fact or document incorporated by reference, the particular person had any responsibility for the fact or document at the time of the filing from which it was incorporated."[7]

With respect to the forms generally:

(1) There are a number of specialized forms: for example S-4, S-5, and S-6 for various investment companies, S-8 for certain employee offerings, and S-18, an experimental form adopted in 1979 for cash offerings up to $5 million.

(2) In the 1982 integration amendments the Commission expanded Regulation S-K, which it had adopted in 1977,[8] to provide a reservoir of all substantive data (other than financial statements, which are the subject of Regulation S-X, the general accounting regulation) from which registration statements under both Acts, together with reports and proxy statements under the 1934 Act, draw.[9] Accordingly, counsel will first select the proper registration (or report) form, which will direct him to the appropriate sections of Regulation S-K for that form's (or report's) specific disclosure requirements, and he will then look to Regulation C (or Regulation 12B under the 1934 Act) for the preparation and filing *procedures.*

(3) Traditionally the Commission's staff discouraged disclosure of security ratings except in limited circumstances. But in the 1982 integration program the Commission *permitted* registration statements and reports (as well as "tombstone ads") to disclose ratings assigned by nationally recognized rating organizations to classes of debt securities (whether or not convertible) and preferred stock.[10]

(4) Rule 408 requires, in addition to the specific items in a registration statement, the inclusion of such further material information, if any, as may be necessary to make the required statements, in the light of the circumstances under which they are made, not misleading.

---

[7] Rule 176(h); Code §1704(g)(6); see also Rule 412; Sec. Act Rel. 6383, 24 SEC Dock. 1262, 1296 (1982). An underwriter that has an ongoing relationship with a particular company may also perform its §11 "due diligence" by having its counsel participate in the preparation of the annual and quarterly reports under the 1934 Act and obtaining an accountant's "comfort letter" when the reports are filed.

[8] Sec. Act Rel. 5893, 13 SEC Dock. 1217 (1977).

[9] A number of industry guides are attached at the end of Regulation S-K. Items 801-02.

[10] Rules 134(a)(14), 436(g); Reg. S-K, Item 10(d) (Commission policy); Sec. Act Rel. 6383, 24 SEC Dock. 1262, 1282-85 (1982). Indeed, the availability of Form S-3 is conditioned on such ratings.

(5) After its first public offering a company must file reports on Form S-R, semiannually until termination of the offering, to cover (a) the status of the offering when there is a best-efforts underwriter and (b) application of the proceeds.[11]

2. DISCLOSURE STANDARDS

It remains to consider briefly a few troublesome matters of philosophical approach to type of disclosure.

A chronic problem, perhaps endemic to any disclosure system, is a tendency toward prolixity in prospectuses. This has been due partly to the conservatism of lawyers who worry about the broad liabilities under §11 and partly to the Commission staff's insistence on "hard information." A former Chairman of the Commission had a little fun with what he called the "lugubrious approach to life and company affairs" that has marked prospectuses from the beginning:

> Or suppose General Eisenhower's D-Day order had to be filed with the SEC. "The officers who planned this assault, including myself, have never before planned anything like this. In fact, I have never commanded any troops in combat. The airborne and other methods being employed have never before been tried by our Army. The weather forecast is only slightly favorable and such forecasts have a high degree of unreliability. Therefore, there is no assurance that any of you will reach Normandy alive, or, if you do, that you can secure the beach."[12]

Things have improved somewhat in this respect since the Commission in the early 1970s lifted its previous ban against established corporate symbols or trademarks, as well as photographs of management, principal properties and important products.[13] A Boston Gas Company prospectus of September 1, 1971 — which was innovative also in its relatively bold use of color in a map and picture — abbreviated 35 pages of text and financial information into an opening summary of 4 pages. Not surprisingly, that was promptly dubbed the "Mother Goose summary." Nevertheless, the problem, as two lawyers highly experienced in this area have observed, is perhaps intractable:

---

[11] Rule 463.

[12] Garrett, Public Relations and Corporate Disclosures (address to Public Relations Society of America, Los Angeles, Sept. 25, 1975).

[13] Sec. Act Rel. 5171 (1971).

The prospectus is a somewhat schizophrenic document, having two purposes which often present conflicting pulls. On the one hand, it is a selling document. It is used by the principal underwriters to form the underwriting syndicate and a dealer group, and by the underwriters and dealers to sell the securities to the public. From this point of view, it is desirable to present the best possible image. On the other hand, the prospectus is a disclosure document, an insurance policy against liability. With the view toward protection against liability, there is a tendency to resolve all doubts against the company and to make things look as bleak as possible. In balancing the purposes, established underwriters and experienced counsel, guided at least in part by their knowledge of the SEC staff attitudes, traditionally lean to a very conservative presentation. They avoid glowing adjectives, subjective evaluations and predictions about the future. The prospectus is limited to provable statements of historic fact. The layman frequently complains that all the glamor and romance has been lost. "Why can't you tell them," he says, "that we have the most aggressive and imaginative management in the industry?" It takes considerable client education before an attorney can answer this question to his client's satisfaction.[14]

Another philosophical problem that defies neat solution in a disclosure system is the extent to which there should be a disclosure of the integrity and ability of management. In *Franchard Corp.*, a leading case decided in 1964, the Commission started with the premise, "Of cardinal importance in any business is the quality of its management."[15] And it thought that the very difficulty of disclosing management's integrity or ability in any meaningful way, which made generalization misleading, made specific disclosures all the more important. Therefore, it found that a registration statement was misleading because of its failure to disclose (1) the issuer's transfers to its controlling stockholder and chief executive officer of large sums that he used in his own ventures and (2) pledges of his stock by that stockholder, a man whose reputation as a real estate syndicator was an important investor attraction, as security for high-interest loans that placed him in a strained financial condition, created a likelihood of a shift in control, and gave rise to potential conflicts of interests with shareholders in fixing the issuer's financial policy. The Commission considered it irrelevant that the omitted facts were unknown to the other officers and directors.

---

[14] Schneider and Manko, Going Public — Practices, Procedures and Consequences, 15 Vill. L. Rev. 283, 293 (1970).
[15] 42 SEC 163, 169 (1964).

Nevertheless, the Commission thought, too, that the required identification of the members of the board was not an implied representation that they would exercise the degree of diligence that might be required by the varying standards of state corporation law. Despite the standard of care specified in §11, the Act does not purport "to define federal standards of directors' responsibility in the orderly operations of business enterprises and nowhere empowers us to formulate administratively such regulatory standards."[16] Particularly because the state courts for various reasons, including the complexity and diversity of business activities, have shown "a marked reluctance to interfere with good faith business judgments," a general requirement of "information in Securities Act prospectuses as to whether directors have performed their duties in accordance with the standards of responsibility required of them under state law would stretch disclosure beyond the limitations contemplated by the statutory scheme and necessitated by considerations of administrative practicality."[17] The Commission observed that it had required disclosure concerning directors' performance in situations involving a virtual abdication of responsibility or when the prospectus had made affirmative representations by which their performance could be tested. "But the disclosures sought here by the staff would require evaluation of the entire conduct of a board of directors in the context of the whole business operations of a company in the light of diverse and uncertain standards. In our view, this is a function which the disclosure requirements of the Securities Act cannot effectively discharge. It would either result in self-serving generalities of little value to investors or grave uncertainties both on the part of those who must enforce and those who must comply with that Act."[18]

Judge Frankel put it more dramatically a few years later:

> * * * it is bemusing, and ultimately pointless, to charge that directors perpetrated a "material omission" when they failed to (a) discover and adjudge faithless motives for their actions and (b) announce such a discovery in reporting the products of their managerial efforts and judgment. The securities laws, while their central insistence is indeed upon disclosure, were never intended to attempt any such measures of psychoanalysis or reported self-analysis. The unclean heart of a director is not actionable, whether or not it is "disclosed," unless the impurities are trans-

[16] Id. at 176.
[17] Id. at 178.
[18] Ibid.

lated into actionable deeds or omissions both objective and external.[19]

But the Commission itself soon distinguished *Franchard* in a disciplinary proceeding against a broker-dealer firm that acted as investment adviser and underwriter for two investment companies. In view of the failure to provide unaffiliated directors of each investment company with relevant information on important investments and other transactions, the Commission found that the implication inherent in each prospectus that those directors were discharging their responsibilities to the other member of the board and to shareholders, and that investors were being accorded the benefits of responsible and objective observation and consideration of the investment company's activities by affiliated directors, was materially misleading. In *Franchard*, by contrast, not only was the board regularly informed as to the company's affairs; it was also obvious that a single individual would exercise the dominant role in managing the operations.[20]

There are no neat answers here. In 1980 the Commission's General Counsel expressed the view that "*Franchard* is best captured as a philosophical rumination of the Commission on the corporate governance process at an early point in time."[21] And the Commission's concern became painfully apparent to many companies in connection with the post-Watergate disclosures of what were euphemistically called "questionable payments" abroad — a development that resulted in the outlawry of such practices by the Foreign Corrupt Practices Act of 1977.[22] In its 1976 "Report to Congress on Questionable and Illegal Payments," the Commission,

[19] Stedman v. Storer, 308 F. Supp. 881, 887 (S. D. N. Y. 1969). Cf. the discussion of motive in the context of Exchange Act Rule 14a-9, the proxy "fraud" rule, infra p. 543.

[20] Imperial Financial Services, Inc., 42 SEC 717 (1965).

[21] Ferrara, Current Issues between Corporations and Shareholders: Federal Intervention into Corporate Governance, 36 Bus. Law. 759, 769 (1980); see also Ferrara, Disclosure of Management Integrity and Competency — Sliding Down the "Slippery Slope" of Materiality, in L. Gower, L. Loss and A. Sommer (co-chairmen), New Trends in Company Law Disclosure (London conference under auspices of Law & Business, Inc., New York, and Institute of Advanced Legal Studies, U. of London, 1980) 148.

[22] 91 Stat. 1494 (1977). That Act amended §13(b) of the 1934 Act with respect to accounting standards (see p. 162 infra), added §30A to the 1934 Act in order to forbid foreign bribes with respect to companies reporting under that Act, and, altogether apart from the SEC, authorized the Attorney General to institute injunctive (as well as criminal) proceedings in the event of foreign bribes by "domestic concerns" that were not reporting companies under the 1934 Act.

stating that "investors should be vitally interested in the quality and integrity of management," emphasized that disclosure of conflicts of interest and special perquisites to management

> reflects the deeply held belief that the managements of corporations are stewards acting on behalf of the shareholders, who are entitled to honest use of, and accounting for, the funds entrusted to the corporation and to procedures necessary to assure accountability and disclosure of the manner in which management performs its stewardship.[23]

As the court stated in holding that a corporation's failure to disclose an insider's kickbacks from one of its suppliers violated both the reporting and proxy rules under the 1934 Act, "One does not elect as a director an individual who is using the corporation he represents for personal gain."[24] On the other hand, the Ninth Circuit in 1981, speaking to the proxy rules under §14 of the 1934 Act, drew

> a sharp distinction * * * between allegations of director misconduct involving breach of trust or self-dealing — the nondisclosure of which is presumptively material — and allegations of simple breach of fiduciary duty/waste of corporate assets — the nondisclosure of which is never material for §14(a) purposes. * * *
>   * * * The distinction between "mere" bribes and bribes coupled with kickbacks to the directors makes a great deal of sense, indeed, is fundamental to a meaningful concept of materiality under §14(a) and the preservation of state corporate law.

*   *   *

> Absent credible allegations of self-dealing by the directors or dishonesty or deceit which inures to the direct, personal benefit of the directors — a fact that demonstrates a betrayal of trust to the corporation and shareholders and the director's essential unfitness for corporate stewardship — we hold that director misconduct of the type traditionally regulated by state corporate law need not be disclosed in proxy solicitations for director elections. This type of mismanagement, unadorned by self-dealing,

---

[23] Senate Comm. on Banking, Housing & Urban Affairs, 94th Cong., 2d Sess. (Comm. Print 1976).

[24] SEC v. Kalvex, Inc., 425 F. Supp. 310, 315 (S. D. N. Y. 1975). Nor does one "elect as a trustee or director an individual *who knows, or should know,* that other directors or trustees are using the corporation for a personal gain and vote in favor of such transactions, or raise no objection to such transactions." Perelman v. Pennsylvania Real Estate Investment Trust, 432 F. Supp. 1298, 1303-04 (E. D. Pa. 1977).

is simply not material or otherwise within the ambit of the federal securities laws. * * *[25]

3. THE SEC AND ACCOUNTING

If this is not the place for a "how to do it" discussion of how to register, *a fortiori* there is room for only a minimal treatment of the SEC's role in the world of accounting. That role goes far beyond the matter of financial data required to be included in the 1933 Act registration statement. For comprehensive financial statements are required also by the 1934 Act and the Holding Company and Investment Company Acts. Moreover, both the 1933 and 1934 Acts authorize the Commission to define accounting terms and to prescribe "the items or details to be shown in the balance sheet and earning statement, and the methods to be followed in the preparation of accounts, in the appraisal or valuation of assets and liabilities, in the determination of depreciation and depletion, in the differentiation of recurring and nonrecurring income, in the differentiation of investment and operating income, and in the preparation, where the Commission deems it necessary or desirable, of consolidated balance sheets or income accounts of any person" in a control relationship with the issuer.[26]

[25] Gaines v. Haughton, 645 F. 2d 761, 776-79 (9th Cir. 1981), *cert. denied,* 454 U. S. 1145; but cf. Decker v. Massey-Ferguson, Ltd., 681 F. 2d 111, 115-19 (2d Cir. 1982). The impact of Santa Fe Industries, Inc. v. Green, 430 U. S. 462 (1977), set out infra p. 928, is apparent.
This and other cases have led two commentators to conclude:

> Despite litigation during the past ten years regarding the independent standing of integrity of management disclosures under the federal securities laws, the primary issues remain unresolved. The case law has failed to develop uniform standards of analysis and in some instances appears to be inconsistent with the general standards of materiality articulated by the Supreme Court. Thus, the case law is instructive only in those isolated instances of corporate misconduct that conform to familiar factual patterns viewed as material in prior decisions by both the courts and the commission; namely, misconduct that (1) involves self-dealing or concurrent financial materiality, or (2) is the subject of pending proceedings or has already resulted in convictions, fines, or administrative sanctions against the corporation or individual members of senior management. In such instances, the weight of authority requires disclosure. The statutes, case law, and commission's regulations, however, provide no definitive guidance relating to disclosure of illegal conduct by members of senior management that falls outside those boundaries.

Branch and Rubright, Integrity of Management Disclosures under the Federal Securities Laws, 37 Bus. Law. 1447, 1478-79 (1982).
[26] Sec. Act §19(a); Sec. Ex. Act §13(b); cf. Inv. Co. Act §38(a); see also

To the extent of its jurisdiction as so prescribed, one would expect the Commission's impact on accounting principles and practices to be substantial. For what is the purpose of accounting if not full and fair disclosure? Indeed, if it is true (as the saying went) that the SEC "made a lady out of Wall Street," it is equally true that it had a great deal to do with raising public accountancy to the status of a genuine profession.

Actually the Commission's impact has been considerably broader than a literal reading of the statutes would indicate. In the first place, accountants that develop certain habits in preparing financial statements for filing with the SEC are apt to carry those habits over to non-SEC work. The Commission's stringent view on auditors' independence has also influenced the profession generally. And, although the SEC cannot directly regulate the reports sent to stockholders as distinct from those filed under the several statutes, we shall see later that the Commission (perhaps dubiously) has used its proxy rules under §14 of the 1934 Act to assert a significant measure of *indirect* control over the financial statements contained in stockholders' reports.[27]

For some years — partly but not entirely because of the pressure of an inflationary economy on historical cost concepts — the accounting world has been in ferment. There has been an explosion of litigation — SEC disciplinary proceedings, civil actions, both SEC-initiated[28] and private,[29] and even criminal prosecutions of partners in leading firms of accountants. Most disciplinary proceedings, brought under Rule 2(e) of the Commission's Rules of Practice,[30] have resulted, like the typical injunctive action, in settlements calling for such steps as review of the firm's auditing procedures by persons satisfactory to the Commission's Chief Accountant, completion of continuing professional education programs, and "peer review."[31] And the Second Circuit has permitted

---

id., §§30(e), 31(c), 32. The "bible" here is L. Rappaport, SEC Accounting Practice and Procedure (3d ed. 1972). The Code in §1805 gathers the accounting and records provisions of all the SEC statutes with some changes.

[27] See p. 488 infra.

[28] In Peat, Marwick, Mitchell & Co., Acctg. Ser. Rel. 173, 7 SEC Dock. 301 (1975), *modified*, Acctg. Ser. Rel. 173A, 12 SEC Dock. 361 (1977), the Commission announced a settlement of four injunctive actions with respect to four separate audits. The settlement contemplated, among other things, a comprehensive investigation of the firm's audit practices by a committee selected by the firm and the Commission's staff.

[29] E. g., Herzfeld v. Laventhol, Krekstein, Horwath & Horwath, 540 F. 2d 27 (2d Cir. 1976).

[30] The validity of this rule as applied to accountants was sustained in Touche, Ross & Co. v. SEC, 609 F. 2d 570 (2d Cir. 1979).

[31] E. g., Benjamin Botwinick & Co., Acctg. Ser. Rel. 168 (1975).

a criminal jury to find that financial statements did not fairly present the facts even though they followed "generally accepted accounting principles" (GAAP).[32] The Commission is fond of quoting Judge Friendly's statement: "In our complex society the accountant's certificate and the lawyer's opinion can be instruments for inflicting pecuniary loss more potent than the chisel or the crow-bar."[33]

Another cause of the ferment has gone to the essence of the Commission's role in the establishment of accounting principles. Apart from its general accounting regulation, Regulation S-X — which specifies the financial statements to be included in the registration and reporting forms and, insofar as it requires a particular method of accounting, is not believed to conflict "with the basic policy of relying on the FASB [the Financial Accounting Standards Board] for leadership in establishing financial accounting and reporting standards"[34] — the Commission has chosen to rely for the most part on the profession to establish generally accepted accounting principles. This approach goes back to the famous Accounting Series Release 4 of 1938 — the "great treaty" as Chairman Garrett called it.[35]

In 1972 a study committee appointed under the chairmanship of former Commissioner Wheat by the American Institute of Certified Public Accountants rejected the idea of a new government rulemaking authority in favor of a Financial Accounting Standards Board of seven full-time members selected by a Financial Accounting Foundation that would also see to the Board's financing and review its operations.[36] With this apparatus in place,

---

[32] United States v. Simon, 425 F. 2d 796 (2d Cir. 1969), *cert. denied,* 397 U. S. 1006; see also United States v. Natelli, 527 F. 2d 311 (2d Cir. 1975), *cert. denied,* 425 U. S. 934.

[33] United States v. Benjamin, 328 F. 2d 854, 863 (2d Cir. 1964), *cert. denied* sub nom. Howard v. United States, 377 U. S. 953.

[34] Sec. Act Rel. 6233, 20 SEC Dock. 1115, 1118 (1980).

[35] SEC Codification of Financial Reporting Policies §101; Garrett, The Accounting Profession and Accounting Principles (address before Second Annual Robert M. Trueblood Memorial Conference, Ill. C. P. A. Foundation, Chicago, Oct. 3, 1975) 5. The Commission, however, has been historically in advance of the profession so far as standards of accountants' independence are concerned. See, e. g., Acctg. Ser. Rel. 296, 23 SEC Dock. 566 (1981), SEC Codification, supra, §§601.01, 604.01.

In Financial Reporting Release 1, 25 SEC Dock. 2 (1982), the Commission announced the publication of a codification of the relevant portions of the 100 Accounting Series Releases. SEC Codification of Financial Reporting Policies (1982). The Accounting Series Releases were then replaced by two new series: Financial Reporting Releases for accounting and auditing matters of general interest, and Accounting and Auditing Enforcement Releases for enforcement matters. See AAER 1, 25 SEC Dock. 4 (1982).

[36] AICPA, Establishing Financial Accounting Standards (1972).

the Commission announced that it would regard only those principles, standards and practices promulgated in the FASB's "statements and interpretation" as having substantial authoritative support for purposes of Release 4.[37]

This self-abnegation has been attacked from various quarters, both legislative[38] and private.[39] But in a series of reports the SEC has stuck to its guns, relying primarily on the establishment in 1977 of a new SEC Practice Section within the AICPA Division of CPA Firms, whose work is overseen by a Public Oversight Board of non-accountants.[40]

Still another bone of contention — this time between the Commission and the profession — grew out of §13(b)(2) of the 1934 Act, which found its way into the law as part of the Foreign Corrupt Practices Act of 1977. That section requires every reporting company to "(A) make and keep books, records, and accounts, which, in reasonable detail, accurately and fairly reflect the transactions and dispositions of the assets of the issuer," and (B) maintain a system of internal accounting controls sufficient to provide those "reasonable assurances" that the section specifies.[41] Proposed SEC rules that would have required all annual reports

---

[37] Acctg. Ser. Rel. 150, 3 SEC Dock. 275 (1973), SEC Codification of Financial Reporting Policies §101; see also Acctg. Ser. Rel. 280, 20 SEC Dock. 1115 (1980), SEC Codification, loc. cit. supra.

[38] See Federal Regulation and Regulatory Reform, Report by Subcom. on Oversight & Investigations, House Com. on Int. & For. Commerce, 94th Cong., 2d Sess. (the "Moss Report") (1976) 18, 32-39, 51-52; Subcom. on Reports, Acctg. & Mgmt. of Senate Com. on Gov't Operations, The Accounting Establishment: A Staff Study, 95th Cong., 1st Sess. (1977), leading to the report of the subcommittee itself, Improving the Accountability of Publicly Owned Corporations and Their Auditors (the "Metcalf Report") (1977); see also Oversight of the Accounting Profession: Hearings before Subcom. on Governmental Efficiency & the District of Columbia of the Senate Com. on Governmental Affairs, 96th Cong., 1st Sess. (1979) (successor to Metcalf subcommittee).

[39] Some have complained that the Commission has not gone far enough. See Arthur Andersen & Co., Establishing Accounting Principles — A Crisis in Decision Making (1965) 3, 9 and passim; Kripke, The SEC, the Accountants, Some Myths and Some Realities, 45 N. Y. U. L. Rev. 1151, 1175-1204 (1970). At the other extreme, it has been asserted that "the SEC's accounting disclosure requirements are of small, if any, relevance to investors * * * ." Benston, The Effectiveness and Effects of the SEC's Accounting Disclosure Requirements, in H. Manne (ed.), Economic Policy and the Regulation of Corporate Securities (1968) 23, 50.

[40] SEC, Report to Congress on the Accounting Profession and the Commission's Oversight Role, 95th Cong., 2d Sess. (Com. Print 1978), reprinted without appendixes and the much longer SEC *staff* report, CCH Fed. Sec. L. Rep. ¶81,634. Two more reports under the same title were submitted in 1979 and 1980.

[41] See [ABA] Committee on Corporate Law and Accounting, A Guide to the New Section 13(b)(2) Accounting Requirements of the Securities Exchange Act of 1934, 34 Bus. Law. 307 (1978); same committee, Practical Implications

filed with the Commission or mailed under the proxy rules to include a management statement on internal accounting control, reported on by an independent accountant, encountered substantial opposition and were withdrawn, the Commission later noting the significant private sector initiatives in the area.[42]

There has also been a radical change in the SEC's views with respect to "soft information," notably profit forecasts. Traditionally the Commission disallowed forecasts in prospectuses and proxy statements as distinct from shareholders' reports or discussions with financial analysts. Then a number of cases gave pause. In one, brought under §11, the court held that a registration statement filed in connection with a takeover bid should have disclosed the target insurance company's "surplus surplus" (that is to say, the surplus in excess of the amount required by the state insurance authorities) despite counsel's advice that the estimates were too unreliable; for the surplus surplus was one of the principal reasons for the takeover attempt.[43] In another case the court rejected a complaint against a chemical company because the shortfall had been due to a recession that had hit synthetic fiber producers with particular impact, and the company over a period of years had carefully developed internal forecast figures that were consistent with the published figures, and the published forecast had fit into a continuing framework of regular dissemination of company news, good or bad.[44]

Partly at least under the impact of these cases, it must be presumed, the Commission announced in 1973, after a public rulemaking proceeding, that it would permit but not require

---

of the Accounting Provisions of the Foreign Corrupt Practices Act of 1977, and Recent Developments (transcript of a program), 35 Bus. Law. 713 (1980).

[42] Sec. Ex. Act Rel. 15,772, 17 SEC Dock. 421 (1979); Sec. Ex. Act Rel. 16,877, 20 SEC Dock. 310 (1980); Sec. Ex. Act Rel. 18,451, 24 SEC Dock. 746 (1982). The Commission, however, did use its new authority to adopt Rules 13b-1 and 13b-2, which prohibit the falsification of corporate records or accounts as well as a director's or officer's making materially false, misleading or incomplete statements to an accountant in connection with an audit or examination or the preparation or filing of required reports. Sec. Ex. Act Rel. 15,570, 16 SEC Dock. 1143, 1147-48 (1979).

[43] Feit v. Leasco Data Processing Equipment Corp., 332 F. Supp. 544 (E. D. N. Y. 1971).

[44] Dolgow v. Anderson, 53 F. R. D. 64 (E. D. N. Y. 1971), aff'd per curiam, 464 F. 2d 437 (2d Cir. 1972); see also Polin v. Conductron Corp., 552 F. 2d 797, 806 n. 28 (8th Cir. 1977), cert. denied, 434 U. S. 857. Contrast this "rule of reason" approach with the "highly probable" realization test of Beecher v. Able, 374 F. Supp. 341 (S. D. N. Y. 1974) — which supported the worst expectations of those who opposed forecasts as too dangerous legally — although the court after trial found that there was no recklessness as required by Rule 10b-5 as long as there was *some* basis for the prediction. Id., CCH Fed. Sec. L. Rep. ¶95,303 (S. D. N. Y. 1975).

reasonably based projections, under rules to be issued for comment, in the case of companies with a history of reported earnings and internal budgeting.[45] But then the Commission began to back and fill a bit. In 1976, because of the questioning comments[46] it had received on a set of proposed "safe harbor" rules[47] and the diversity of views expressed, the Commission withdrew its proposal and said it would neither encourage nor discourage forecasts. The Commission added, nevertheless, that it would not object to good faith projections that had a reasonable basis and an appropriate format and were accompanied by information adequate to enable investors to make their own judgments. The Commission also went out of its way to express its belief that appropriate projections should not create civil liability simply because they turned out to be erroneous.[48]

By late 1978 the Commission had apparently developed enough confidence to publish a comprehensive release together with staff guides[49] and alternative versions of a proposed "safe harbor rule."[50] Among other things, the release discussed the duty to correct projections known to have become misleading. But the Commission imposed no reporting or operating history or other status criteria, and it stated that, although disclosure of assumptions underlying projections was desirable, it was not essential.[51]

Finally, in order to encourage projections both in filings and generally, the Commission in mid-1979 adopted "safe harbor" rules under the 1933 and 1934 Acts, to the effect that a "forward looking statement" is not a "fraudulent statement" unless the plaintiff shows a lack of reasonable basis or good faith.[52] Although the rules as proposed for comment would have put the burden of proof with respect to reasonableness and good faith on the

---

[45] Sec. Act Rel. 5362, 1 SEC Dock. No. 1, p. 4 (1973).
[46] See Financial Executives Research Foundation, Public Disclosure of Business Forecasts (1972), a two-part study by a management consulting firm and a law firm, which reported that more than 97 percent of the responding companies prepared sales, expense, and earnings forecasts but that all companies expressed concern over the consequences of releasing their internal figures.
[47] Sec. Act Rel. 5581, 6 SEC Dock. 746 (1975).
[48] Sec. Act Rel. 5699, 9 SEC Dock. 472 (1976).
[49] Sec. Act Rel. 5992, 16 SEC Dock. 81 (1978).
[50] Sec. Act Rel. 5993, 16 SEC Dock. 90 (1978).
[51] In 1982 the Commission promulgated a detailed statement of its policy with respect to projections in all disclosure documents. Reg. S-K, Item 10(b).
[52] Rules 175 and 3b-6, adopted by Sec. Act Rel. 6084, 17 SEC Dock. 1048 (1979).

defendant, the Commission deferred to the recommendation of its Advisory Committee on Corporate Disclosure.[53]

The Code's solution is a definition of "fact" to include "a promise, prediction, estimate, projection, or forecast," with a provision that such a fact "is not a misrepresentation if it (i) is made in good faith, (ii) has a reasonable basis when it is made, and (iii) complies with any applicable rule so far as underlying assumptions or other conditions are concerned."[54]

[53] See p. 38 n. 27 supra.

[54] §§202(55)(B), 202(96)(B). On burden of proof, see 1 Code 158, Comment (e). On duty to correct, see §1602(b)(2).

CHAPTER 3

A WHAT! A "SECURITY" (HEREIN OF "ISSUER" AS WELL)

A. A PRELIMINARY THOUGHT OR TWO

The definition in §2(1) of the 1933 Act borrowed from the earlier blue sky definitions, which had already developed something of a judicial gloss. And §401(l) of the Uniform Securities Act is identical with §2(1) except for the oil and gas language and the exclusion of orthodox insurance and annuities from §401(l).[1] But there are enough variations, with additional phrases in some of the state statutes, to indicate caution with respect to interchangeability of federal and state precedents. Indeed, the 1933 and 1934 federal definitions themselves are not identical, as we shall see in a moment.

Even so, such is the complexity of the financial world that after seven decades and more of securities regulation there is still a constant stream of cases that seek to draw the line between "securities" and real property or tangible or intangible personal property or various hybrids emanating from the banking and insurance industries. The definition has been before the Supreme Court no fewer than eight times. Interestingly, the Court reversed in all eight cases. Even more interestingly, the reversals in the first five cases resulted in affirmative holdings and the last three in negative.

Two of these cases may be disposed of here. In *Tcherepnin* v. *Knight* depositors in a savings and loan association that was in voluntary liquidation were able to void their purchases for violation of Rule 10b-5 (the general antifraud rule under the 1934 Act), and thus to get themselves in a creditor position, on the ground that withdrawable and transferable (but nonnegotiable)

C. 3A [1] See p. 215 infra.

capital shares issued to evidence savings accounts were securities.[2] In *Marine Bank* v. *Weaver*, which involved a fixed-interest certificate of deposit issued by a bank, the Court distinguished *Tcherepnin* on the grounds (1) that buyers there not only had voting rights but also received dividends based on profits, not a fixed rate of interest, and (2) that a bank certificate of deposit differed from other long-term debt obligations because of federal bank regulation and insurance, so that there was no need for SEC-type protection against fraud.[3]

B. NOTES

SECURITIES AND EXCHANGE COMMISSION v. DIVERSIFIED INDUSTRIES, INC.
United States District Court
for the District of Columbia, 1979
465 F. Supp. 104

CHARLES R. RICHEY, District Judge.

In the Spring of 1975, the Securities and Exchange Commission (hereinafter, "the Commission") began investigating charges arising out of a proxy contest between Penn-Dixie Industries, Inc. (hereinafter, "Penn-Dixie") and Diversified Industries, Inc. (hereinafter, "Diversified"). * * *

* * *

Counts IV through VI relate to a fraudulent real estate transaction. Count IV charges the defendants Castle, Aronoff, Penn-Dixie and the JDL Trust with violations of section 10(b) of the Securities Exchange Act of 1934 (hereinafter, "the Act"), 15 U. S. C.

---

[2] 389 U. S. 332 (1967).

[3] 102 S. Ct. 1220 (1982); but cf. Wolf v. Banco Nacional de México, 549 F. Supp. 841 (N. D. Cal. 1982) (time deposits in a Mexican bank were securities under both 1933 and 1934 Acts). The definition of "security" in §3(a)(10) of the 1934 Act does not include the phrase "evidence of indebtedness" that appears in §2(1) of the 1933 Act. But the Supreme Court did not rely on this omission. See the dissenting opinion of Cummings, J., below, 371 F. 2d 374, 380 n. 3 (1967): "The author of the 1934 Act may have decided that inclusion of 'evidence of indebtedness' would be poor draftsmanship, that term being inconsistent with the exclusion of 'any note, draft, bill of exchange, or banker's acceptance.'" But cf. Zeller v. Bogue Electric Mfg. Corp., 476 F. 2d 795, 800-01 (2d Cir. 1973), *cert. denied*, 414 U. S. 908 (absence of the phrase precluded an open-account loan from being a security).

§78j(b) (1976) and Rule 10b-5, 17 C. F. R. 240.10b-5 (1978). The Commission alleges that Aronoff conspired with Castle, then President and Chairman of the Board of Penn-Dixie, to arrange for the purchase of undrainable Florida swampland by Penn-Dixie for over five million dollars from the JDL Trust, a trust set up by Aronoff for the benefit of his parents and children. According to the complaint, the defendants conspired to defraud the shareholders of Penn-Dixie by fraudulently inducing a public corporation to issue a security, the mortgage for the land, in connection with the acquisition of this investment property.

* * * Count VI charges Castle and Penn-Dixie with violations of section 14(a) of the Act, 15 U. S. C. §78n(a) (1976) and Rule 14a-9, 17 C. F. R. 240.14a-9 (1978) for filing false and misleading proxy statements which also failed to disclose the alleged swampland fraud.

*   *   *

I. THE PURCHASE MONEY MORTGAGE PENN-DIXIE ISSUED TO THE JDL TRUST IS A "SECURITY" WITHIN THE MEANING OF THE FEDERAL SECURITIES LAW

The defendants in their papers in support of their motion to dismiss and in their oral argument before Judge Waddy have tried to characterize this case as an attempt by the Commission to convert the securities laws into a general remedy for real estate fraud. The defendants contend that if the Court finds that the securities laws apply in this case every homeowner who sells his or her home would be subject to the anti-fraud provisions of the 1934 Securities Exchange Act. The Commission distinguishes this situation from the average homeowner's case by pointing to three factors: (1) the note was issued for the acquisition of an investment asset, (2) the note was issued by a public company, and (3) the note was not initially issued to a bank or other party in the business of making loans.

To render the Securities Exchange Acts of 1933 or 1934 applicable to a transaction, a "security" must be exchanged. The Commission relies on the ten-year purchase money mortagage note Penn-Dixie issued to the JDL Trust as part payment for the Florida real estate to satisfy this requirement.

Although there are slight differences in wording between the 1933 and 1934 Acts, the definitions of "security" in the two acts have been treated as functionally equivalent. See *Tcherepnin* v.

Knight, 389 U. S. 332, 335-336 (1967); *National Bank of Commerce* v. *All American Assurance Co.*, 583 F. 2d 1295 (5th Cir. 1978); *United California Bank* v. *THC Financial Corp.*, 557 F. 2d 1351, 1356 (9th Cir. 1977); *Great Western Bank & Trust* v. *Kotz*, 532 F. 2d 1252, 1255 (9th Cir. 1976).

The definitional section of the Securities Exchange Act of 1934, 15 U. S. C. §78c(a)(10) (1976), provides that, "unless the context otherwise requires — * * * (10) The term 'security' means any note * * * but shall not include * * * any note * * * which has a maturity date at the time of issuance of not exceeding nine months * * * ." The definitional section of the 1933 Act has a similar definition of "security" with the exception of the nine-month limitation. 15 U. S. C. §77b(1) (1976). Although the statutes on their faces are readily discernible, judicial interpretation has clouded their clarity. In the words of a recent commentator:

> The courts have recently made it clear that despite the apparently contrary language of (the definitional statutes), (1) not all notes of more than 9 months' duration are "securities" and not all notes of less than such duration are not "securities,"[2] (2) the decisive factor in the determination of whether notes fall within the 1933 or 1934 Act is the type of note, and not its duration, and (3) this decisive factor is itself not readily determinable.[a]

Kaplan, Promissory Notes as Securities Under §2(1) of Securities Act of 1933 (15 U. S. C. §77b(1)), and §3(a)(10) of Securities Exchange Act of 1934, 39 A. L. R. Fed. 357, 365 (1978).

Unfortunately, the U. S. Circuit Courts of Appeals that have confronted this issue have devised somewhat different tests to

---

C. 3B [a] ED.: More specifically, although the definitions of "security" in both §2(1) of the 1933 Act and §3(a)(10) of the 1934 Act include any 'note' without qualification," §3(a)(3) of the 1933 Act merely *exempts from registration* (as distinct from the fraud provisions) "Any note, draft, bill of exchange, or bankers' acceptance which arises out of a current transaction or the proceeds of which have been or are to be used for current transactions, and which has a maturity at the time of issuance of not exceeding nine months, exclusive of days of grace, or any renewal thereof the maturity of which is likewise limited," whereas §3(a)(10) of the 1934 Act (without reference to the "current transaction" test) *excludes* such short-term paper *from the definition*, so that one would expect even the fraud provisions of the 1934 Act to be inapplicable. But on the premise that the two definitions are *in pari materia*, the courts in Rule 10b-5 cases have ignored the maturity factor in favor of the investment-commercial test. See McClure v. First National Bank of Lubbock, Tex., 497 F. 2d 490 (5th Cir. 1974), *cert. denied*, 420 U. S. 930, where the court conceded that "The original scrivener of the definitional section [3(a)(10)] may well wonder what happened to his carefully drawn exemption on the way to the courthouse * * * ." 497 F. 2d at 495.

determine whether a note constitutes a "security," and the judges of this circuit court have yet to address this problem. Accordingly, the Court must examine the varying approaches taken by the different circuits to the problem before the Court.

A.   THE COMMERCIAL/INVESTMENT DICHOTOMY TEST OF THE THIRD, FIFTH, SEVENTH, AND TENTH CIRCUITS

The "investment/commercial dichotomy test," which has been followed in the Third, Fifth, Seventh, and Tenth Circuits, is premised on the view that Congress's concern is enacting the securities laws was with practices associated with investment transactions and that the securities laws were not designed to regulate commercial transactions. See *C. N. S. Enterprises, Inc.* v. *G. & G. Enterprises, Inc.* 508 F. 2d 1354, 1359 (7th Cir.) *cert. denied* 423 U. S. 825 (1975). The decision of the U. S. Court of Appeals for the Seventh Circuit in *C. N. S. Enterprises, Inc.* contains a helpful description of the investment/commercial test:

> The ultimate question is whether the plaintiffs are simply borrowers in a commercial transaction who are not protected by the 1934 Act or investors in a securities transaction who are protected.
>
> In one sense every lender of money is an investor since he places his money at risk in anticipation of a profit in the form of interest. Also in a broad sense every investor lends his money to a borrower who uses it for a price and is expected to return it one day.
>
> On the other hand, the polarized extremes are conceptually identifiable: buying shares of common stock of a publicly-held corporation, where the impetus for the transaction comes from the person with the money, is an investment; borrowing money from a bank to finance the purchase of an automobile, where the impetus for the transaction comes from the person who needs the money, is a loan. In between is a grey area which, in the absence of further congressional indication of intent or Supreme Court construction, has been and must be in the future subjected to case-by-case treatment.

Id. at 1359. (citations omitted).

Although a case-by-case approach has been adopted under the commercial/investment dichotomy approach, courts have focused on certain factors to guide the application of the test. Despite the defendants' contentions to the contrary, one of the factors the courts have focused on in applying the test is the nature of the assets acquired in exchange for the notes. The defendants are correct in pointing out that every time an investment asset is acquired, the notes have not been determined to be securities under this test. See *Lino* v. *City Investing Co.,* 487 F. 2d 689 (3d Cir. 1973) (franchise); *C. N. S. Enterprises, Inc.* v. *G. & G. Enterprises, Inc.,* 508 F. 2d 1354 (7th Cir.) *cert. denied,* 423 U. S. 825 (1975) (dry cleaning business); *Bellah* v. *First National Bank,* 495 F. 2d 1109 (5th Cir. 1974) (cattle business). Nevertheless, the asset acquired has been recognized to be an important, and often determinative, factor in the court's determination. In *McClure* v. *First National Bank,* 497 F. 2d 490 (5th Cir. 1974), *cert. denied,* 420 U. S. 930 (1975), Judge Roney analyzed prior federal decisions and concluded:

> [W]here notes have been deemed securities within the meaning of the securities laws, either of two factors * * * usually indicated the investment overtones of the underlying transaction. * * * [The] notes were [either] offered to some class of investors, [or] were * * * acquired * * * for speculation or investment. * * * Second, * * * the borrower [obtained] investment assets, directly or indirectly, in exchange for its notes.

Id. at 493-94. [Citations omitted.] * * *

The Court finds that the note issued by Penn-Dixie in part payment for the real estate would qualify as a security under the investment/commercial test. First the land was not acquired to provide housing for a family or to build a new corporate headquarters, but was acquired for purely investment purposes. Second, the note was issued by a publicly held corporation, Penn-Dixie, to a trust not normally in the business of making loans, the JDL Trust. See *Lino* v. *City Investing Co.,* 487 F. 2d 689, 696 (3d Cir. 1973). Third, the duration of the note, ten years, signifies a long-term stake in the progress of the investment, since the collateral for the loan, the land itself, would fluctuate in value with the success of the venture. Therefore, the Court finds that in the "complete context of [this] transaction," id. at 696 n. 15, the note was a security under the investment/commercial dichotomy test of the Third, Fifth, Seventh, and Tenth Circuits.

B.   THE RISK CAPITAL TEST OF THE NINTH CIRCUIT

The U. S. Court of Appeals for the Ninth Circuit applies a risk capital test in determining whether a note is a security.[b] See *Amfac Mortgage Corp.* v. *Arizona Mall, Inc.,* 583 F. 2d 426 (9th Cir.

[b] ED.: On the origin of this test, see p. 213 infra.

1978). Under this test, the ultimate inquiry is whether the lender has contributed risk capital subject to the entrepreneurial or managerial efforts of others. *United California Bank* v. *THC Financial Corp.*, 557 F. 2d 1351, 1358 (9th Cir. 1977); *Great Western Bank & Trust* v. *Kotz*, 532 F. 2d 1252, 1257 (9th Cir. 1976). Six factors have been considered in *Amfac Mortgage, Great Western,* and *United California Bank* to determine if the lender has contributed risk capital. The factors focused on are: (1) time, (2) collateralization, (3) form of the obligation, (4) circumstances of issue, (5) relationship between the amount borrowed and the size of the borrower's business, and (6) the contemplated use of the funds. In this case, the mortgage was for an extended period (ten years). The collateralization was intertwined with the success or failure of the venture. The obligation took the form of the seller providing the loan to facilitate the sale. The circumstances of issuance were such that one not normally in the business of making loans made the loan to a publicly held corporation. The amount borrowed was a significant portion of the value of the venture. Finally, the funds were used to obtain an investment asset. The Court finds that in combination these factors demonstrate that the lender, the JDL Trust, has contributed risk capital subject to the entrepreneurial and managerial efforts of Penn-Dixie. Therefore, the purchase money note is a security under the risk capital test of the Ninth Circuit.

C. THE LITERAL APPROACH OF THE SECOND CIRCUIT

The broadest approach to determining whether a note constitutes a security under the federal securities laws has been taken by the U. S. Court of Appeals for the Second Circuit. In *Exchange National Bank* v. *Touche Ross & Co.*, 544 F. 2d 1126 (2d Cir. 1976), Judge Friendly, writing for the court, held that a party asserting that a note with a maturity longer than nine months is not a security within the 1934 Act [or that a note with a shorter maturity is within it], has the burden of proving that the "context" requires that result. In the course of his opinion, Judge Friendly offered some guidance for future cases:

> One can readily think of many cases where [the context otherwise requires][c] — the note delivered in consumer financing, the note secured by a mortgage on a home, the short-term note secured by a lien on a small business or some of its assets, the note evidencing

[c] ED.: These brackets are Judge Richey's.

a "character" loan to a bank customer, short-term notes secured by an assignment of accounts receivable, or a note which simply formalizes an open-account debt incurred in the ordinary course of business (particularly if, as in the case of the customer of a broker, it is collateralized). When a note does not bear a strong family resemblance to these examples and has a maturity date exceeding nine months, §10(b) of the 1934 Act should generally apply.

Id. at 1138 (citation omitted).[d]

Since the mortgage in this case is on land held for investment purposes, instead of a home, as in Judge Friendly's example, the note would plainly constitute a security under the Second Circuit's test.

The Court feels that the Second Circuit's approach is most consistent with the language of the statute and Congressional intent and is by far the easiest test to apply. * * *

*　　*　　*

Accordingly, the Court finds that the purchase money note issued by Penn-Dixie to the JDL Trust as part payment for the Florida real estate is a security within the meaning of the federal securities laws as construed by all of the available standards.

*　　*　　*

Query: Might a *participation* in a loan be a security even though the underlying note is not?[1] This question indicates cau-

---

[d] ED.: Judge Friendly went on at this point to say that a "more desirable solution" would be for Congress to adopt the Code's treatment. Section 202 (150)(B)(iii), as slightly reworded in the final draft since Judge Friendly wrote, excludes from the definition "a note or evidence of indebtedness issued in a primarily mercantile or consumer, rather than investment, transaction not involving a distribution." In addition, §302(11) exempts from registration "Commercial paper with a denomination of at least $100,000," thus substituting a flat dollar test for the unworkable "current transactions" test of the present §3(a)(3). "Commercial paper" is defined in §202(25) to mean "a note or banker's or trade acceptance that is payable on demand or matures or is renewed for not more than nine months, exclusive of days of grace, after the date of issue or renewal, as the case may be."

[1] Compare Commercial Discount Corp. v. Lincoln First Commercial Corp., 445 F. Supp. 1263, 1267 (S. D. N. Y. 1978) (yes), with Provident National Bank v. Frankford Trust Co., 468 F. Supp. 448 (E. D. Pa. 1979) (no). For a tabular analysis of a dozen cases, see Scholl and Weaver, Loan Participations: Are They "Securities"?, 10 Fla. St. U. L. Rev. 215, 224-25 (1982).

tion on the part of lead banks in syndicated loans — a matter that may have international ramifications.[2]

FIRST NATIONAL BANK OF LAS VEGAS, NEW MEXICO v. ESTATE OF RUSSELL
United States Court of Appeals, Fifth Circuit, 1981
657 F. 2d 668

Before COLEMAN, GARZA and JOHNSON, Circuit Judges.
JOHNSON, Circuit Judge.

Plaintiff First National Bank of Las Vegas, New Mexico, appeals from the district court summary judgment in favor of defendants in this securities fraud case. The district court granted summary judgment for defendants, finding that the notes involved in the transaction at issue were not securities and that the transaction was not a purchase and sale of a security. We vacate and remand.

"In considering the propriety of summary judgment, plaintiff's factual version must be taken as true." *Shores* v. *Sklar*, 647 F. 2d 462, 464 (5th Cir. 1981) (en banc). As the *Shores* Court further noted, "Reciting the facts most favorably to the plaintiff, as we do below, does not imply that he can prove his allegations." Id. With that in mind, the facts indicate that the following transactions occurred.

Russell, Kennedy & Hodgden, Inc., was incorporated in 1973 and began doing business as a broker-dealer in United States government and municipal securities. The firm apparently was unprofitable from the start. According to the plaintiff, to generate funds to cover losses suffered by the brokerage firm and by its president, and to provide the firm with working capital, the brokerage firm initiated a plan involving a series of repurchase transactions. A repurchase transaction is a sale of securities coupled with a concurrent agreement by the seller to repurchase securities of the same description on a date subsequent to the initial transaction.[2] Russell, Kennedy & Hodgden offered to sell

---

[2] See Note, International Loan Syndications, the Securities Acts, and the Duties of a Lead Bank, 64 Va. L. Rev. 897 (1978).

[2] For an in-depth explanation of the nature of the repurchase transaction generally, see SEC v. Miller, 495 F. Supp. 465 (S. D. N. Y. 1980). The *Miller* court concluded that "[f]rom a purely economic perspective * * * , a repro [repurchase agreement] is essentially a short-term collateralized loan, and the parties to these transactions tend to perceive them as such." Id. at 467 (footnote omitted). We note, however, that whether that court considered the transaction to be an actual sale or a collateralized loan, §10(b) of the 1934 Act was applicable since the Second Circuit holds that a pledge of securities

United States Treasury Notes to its customers, and to repurchase the securities at par plus a greater rate of interest than that payable on the Treasury Notes. The customers of the repurchase transactions were small banks and other financial institutions that had previously purchased and sold securities through Russell, Kennedy & Hodgden.

The Plan was to operate basically as follows. The customers were instructed to wire their money to Bossier Bank & Trust Company, a Louisiana bank. They were told to expect a safekeeping receipt in the mail. Following their acceptance of the sale and repurchase offers, the customers would receive two confirmations, one confirming the sale of the securities and one confirming the repurchase of the securities.

Between January 20, 1976 and May 26, 1977, Russell, Kennedy & Hodgden entered into at least twenty-seven agreements to sell and repurchase United States Treasury Notes. The brokerage firm, however, did not own and never acquired the securities in question, and did not deliver them to the purchasing institutions. Obligations to repurchase were extended by rolling over[5] the transactions or were settled with funds obtained from the next purchaser. By paying a repurchase transaction with an insufficiently funded check, the brokerage firm gained additional time to find a purchaser to wire funds to Bossier Bank in an amount sufficient to pay the check.

In May 1977, First National Bank of Las Vegas, which had previously purchased securities through Russell, Kennedy & Hodgden, was solicited by representatives of the brokerage firm to enter into a repurchase transaction. In connection with this transaction, the brokerage firm agreed, either for itself or as an agent for Bossier Bank, to sell Treasury Notes to First National Bank in the aggregate principal amount of $600,000. The brokerage firm also agreed to repurchase the Notes, with settlement of the repurchase deferred for thirty days, for the sale price plus interest at $6\frac{1}{2}$ percent, or a sum of $603,141.67. Ivan Hilton, president of First National Bank, understood that he would receive a safekeeping

constitutes a sale for purposes of the 1934 Act. Thus, the jurisdictional question present in this case was not raised in *Miller*. See United States v. Gentile, 530 F. 2d 461, 466-67 (2d Cir.), *cert. denied*, 426 U. S. 936 (1976). In this Circuit, on the other hand, in a transaction that is considered to involve only a collateralized loan, it is unlikely that there would be a "purchase or sale" of a security as required by §10(b). See McClure v. First Nat'l Bank of Lubbock, 497 F. 2d 490, 495 (5th Cir. 1974), *cert. denied*, 420 U. S. 930 (1975).

[5] The term "rolling over" refers to "entering into a superseding repurchase agreement." Cosmopolitan Credit & Inv. Corp. v. Blyth Eastman Dillon & Co., 507 F. Supp. 954, 956 (S. D. Fla. 1981).

receipt evidencing First National Bank's ownership, custody, and control of the Treasury Notes.

The record indicates that the transaction was treated by First National Bank in all relevant respects as a purchase and sale of securities. There was no commercial banking relationship between First National Bank and Russell, Kennedy & Hodgden; rather, First National Bank was a customer of the brokerage firm. Hilton testified in his deposition that he considered the transaction as an investment and not as a loan. First National Bank did not investigate the credit of the brokerage firm, request documentation with respect to the firm's financial condition, or take any other action customary in the banking business before making a loan. No promissory note evidencing a loan existed and the parties did not enter into a pledge agreement. Rather, on May 26, 1977, First National Bank transferred $600,000 by wire to Bossier Bank for the account of Russell, Kennedy & Hodgden in payment of the purchase price of the securities. In turn, the brokerage firm sent to First National Bank two confirmation slips, one confirming the sale of the Treasury Notes to First National Bank and the other confirming the repurchase of the Notes by the brokerage firm with settlement thirty days thereafter. The confirmations did not expressly restrict First National Bank's right to sell or otherwise dispose of the Notes and to fulfill its obligation to the brokerage firm by delivering securities of a like kind at the specified date.

Russell, Kennedy & Hodgden's repurchase arrangement with First National Bank was its last. Pinemont Bank, a previous purchaser of securities from Russell, Kennedy & Hodgden in a repurchase transaction, threatened to hold Bossier Bank accountable for recommending as a safe investment the $600,000 repurchase transaction that Pinemont entered into with the brokerage firm. In response to Pinemont's threats, Bossier Bank closed the brokerage firm's clearing account on May 23, 1977. On May 26, 1977, when First National Bank wired its $600,000 to Bossier Bank to purchase the securities, Bossier Bank immediately wired the money to Pinemont. Russell, Kennedy & Hodgden never delivered the Treasury Notes to First National Bank or paid First National Bank the repurchase price for the Treasury Notes. On September 19, 1977, Russell, Kennedy & Hodgden was adjudicated a bankrupt as a result of involuntary bankruptcy proceedings instituted in July 1977.

First National Bank commenced this securities fraud action on October 5, 1977, alleging violations of section 10(b) of the Securities Exchange Act of 1934, 15 U. S. C. A. §78j(b), and Rule 10b-5,

17 C. F. R. §240.10b-5. Named as defendants were various individuals alleged to have been officers, employees, and controlling persons of Russell, Kennedy & Hodgden, Bossier Bank, three individuals associated with Bossier Bank, and the Pinemont Bank of Houston, Texas. First National Bank sought to recover for the losses it sustained as a result of the repurchase transaction it entered into with Russell, Kennedy & Hodgden.

* * * On November 19, 1979, the district court denied plaintiff's motion for partial summary judgment and granted defendants' motion for summary judgment. * * * In its memorandum opinion, the district court concluded that (1) "the notes were not securities within the meaning of the Federal Securities Act" and (2) "the transaction does not rise to the dignity of a purchase and sale of a security for Section 10(b) purposes." * * *

Section 10(b) of the Securities Exchange Act of 1934 and Rule 10(b)-5 thereunder prohibit fraud in connection with the "purchase or sale" of "any security." The term "security" is broadly defined in section 3(a)(10) of the 1934 Act to encompass a wide variety of instruments including notes, bonds, and debentures. The district court stated that "[n]otes which are reflective of individual commercial transactions are generally outside the purview of the Act." * * * The district court found that the money paid by First National Bank "was repayable at an agreed time in fixed amounts equal to principal plus interest at the agreed rate." Record, vol. 8, at 1784. From this, the district court concluded that "the notes were not securities within the meaning of the Federal Securities Act." Id.

It is not entirely clear exactly what notes the district court was referring to in this statement. The Treasury Notes that Russell, Kennedy & Hodgden was purporting to sell were not short-term, thirty-day obligations reflective of a private loan between Russell, Kennedy & Hodgden and First National Bank. As described by the brokerage firm, they were scheduled to mature on February 15, 1978 — not thirty days after the purchase. Finally, the Notes described by the brokerage firm were offered originally to a large class of investors. Purchasers and sellers of Treasury Bonds issued by the United States Government are entitled to the protection of section 10(b). *Superintendent of Insurance of New York* v. *Bankers Life & Casualty Co.*, 404 U. S. 6, 10 n. 6 (1971). The plaintiff claims that Treasury Notes, which are identical in all relevant respects to Treasury Bonds,[15] should also fall within the

---

[15] The United States Treasury issues a number of different types of obligations to the investing public in order to finance its deficit and refinance its

definition of a security. Indeed, the defendants expressly concede that the Treasury Notes actually were securities. * * *

If the district court's finding that the "notes were not securities" was based upon an assumption that First National Bank received from Russell, Kennedy & Hodgden a thirty-day note representing the firm's repurchase obligation, then both the assumption and the fact finding were incorrect. There was no promissory note involved in this repurchase transaction. The only written instruments received by First National Bank were the two confirmations verifying the agreement to purchase and sell the securities. Whatever notes the district court was referring to in its memorandum opinion, its conclusion that the notes were not securities is incorrect.

The only remaining inquiry — and the inquiry addressed by the parties on appeal — is whether the district court properly granted summary judgment for defendants on the ground that there was no purchase or sale of a security in this transaction. * * *

Section 3(a)(14) of the 1934 Act defines "sale" to "include any contract to sell or otherwise dispose of" securities. 15 U. S. C. A. §78c(a)(14). Section 3(a)(13) defines "purchase" to "include any contract to buy, purchase, or otherwise acquire" securities. Id. §78c(a)(13). This Court has noted that the terms "purchase" and "sale" are to be broadly construed to effectuate the purpose of the Act. *Herpich* v. *Wallace*, 430 F. 2d 792, 806-07 (5th Cir. 1970). Whether a repurchase transaction is a purchase or sale is a question of first impression in this Circuit.

In this case, the record indicates that Russell, Kennedy & Hodgden, a brokerage firm that engaged in the business of selling United States Government securities, deliberately structured the repurchase transaction as a sale and repurchase of Treasury Notes. The firm solicited First National Bank to invest in the securities. The parties executed no side agreements that would suggest that a sale was not contemplated or that First National Bank would not assume ownership of the securities. Title, and all incidents of ownership, were apparently intended to pass to First National Bank. This Court has generally found section 10(b) to be applicable when there is a surrender of ownership or control of the security.

Bossier Bank contends that there was no purchase or sale in the

---

debt. The Treasury issues interest-bearing bills with maturities of up to one year, 31 U. S. C. A. §754, interest-bearing notes with maturities from one to ten years, id. §753, and interest-bearing bonds with maturities as long as thirty years, id. §752.

instant case because the repurchase transactions were, in substance, loans. Defendants argue that the circumstances of the so-called sale must be examined to determine whether, in economic reality, the transaction was a sale. As a basis for this analysis, defendants rely upon the investment-commercial dichotomy that has been applied in this Circuit. This Court has applied the investment-commercial dichotomy in the context of examining whether a note falls within the definition of a security within the meaning of the securities acts. * * * Defendants argue that the investment-commercial dichotomy is equally applicable to an examination of whether a transaction constitutes a sale.

To support its contention that the transaction was, in reality, a collateralized loan rather than a sale, Bossier Bank points to several factors that have generally been considered by this Court in applying the investment-commercial dichotomy. Thus, Bossier Bank notes that: (1) First National Bank was obligated to resell the securities to Russell, Kennedy & Hodgden at a fixed principal amount plus interest. According to Bossier Bank, this indicates that First National Bank was not investing in the Treasury Notes since any gain or loss in the market value of the Notes would accrue to the brokerage firm and not to the bank. (2) The resale obligation fell due on a fixed date after a relatively short term, a factor that tends to characterize commercial lending rather than investment transactions. (3) The transaction was entered into with a lending institution and was not offered to a large class of investors. See *All American Assurance,* 583 F. 2d at 1301; *McClure,* 497 F. 2d at 493-94. (4) The bank was not investing in the brokerage firm's operations. (5) The principal amount of the transaction was the par value of the Notes, which was less than their market value. According to Bossier Bank, if Russell, Kennedy & Hodgden had intended to sell the Treasury Notes, it could have obtained a higher price on the market. (6) First National Bank was to earn interest on the Treasury Notes at a negotiated market rate that was different from the coupon rate of the Treasury Notes.

Defendants contend that these factors indicate that the transaction between First National Bank and Russell, Kennedy & Hodgden was commercial in nature and was therefore not a sale within the meaning of the 1934 Act. It is true that this Court has recognized that the "securities acts have as their fundamental purpose the protection of *investors.*" *McClure,* 497 F. 2d at 495 (emphasis added). See *Shores* v. *Sklar,* 647 F. 2d at 470. In determining whether a transaction is a sale, however, this Court has examined such factors as whether the transaction affects the securities industry, *McClure*, 497 F. 2d at 495, and "whether the purposes of section 10(b) of the Exchange Act and Rule 10(b)-5 thereunder would be advanced by their application" to the transaction. *Herpich*, 430 F. 2d at 812. Thus, it would appear that the factors pointed out by Bossier Bank are not dispositive of the issue before this Court.

Regardless of the extent to which the factors identified by Bossier Bank relate to the question whether this repurchase transaction constituted a sale, the summary judgment rendered by the district court was improper. A fact finder could have found that the repurchase transaction in this case was a purchase or sale. Since genuine issues of material fact as to the proper characterization of this transaction did exist, summary judgment was improper.[24]

The order granting summary judgment for defendants and dismissing plaintiff's pendent state law claims is vacated. The case is remanded for further proceedings.

SECURITIES ACT RELEASE NO. 6351: THE ISSUANCE OF "RETAIL REPURCHASE AGREEMENTS" BY BANKS AND SAVINGS AND LOAN ASSOCIATIONS
Securities and Exchange Commission, 1981
23 SEC Dock. 1000

The use of so-called "retail repurchase agreements" ("retail repos") as a means for banks and savings and loan associations to raise short-term capital is becoming increasingly widespread in the U. S. financial markets. These retail repos typically are, in economic reality, debt obligations of banks and savings and loan associations that are collateralized by an interest either in a security that is a direct obligation of, or is guaranteed as to principal and interest by, the United States or any agency thereof ("government security"), or a pool of such securities. Retail repos are issued to the general public in denominations of less than $100,000 and with maturities of less than 90 days.

* * * In view of the growing interest in this area and the novel issues raised by retail repo transactions, the Commission has authorized its Division of Corporation Finance to issue the no-action letters which are set forth herein.

*   *   *

[24] In reaching the conclusion that summary judgment for the defendants was improper in this case, we express no opinion on whether a court could find that, as a matter of law, a repurchase transaction is a purchase or sale within the meaning of the 1934 Act.

The following statement by the Comptroller of the Currency would appear to have particular relevance to the adoption of sound disclosure practices in connection with retail repo programs:

* * * The customer should be advised (1) that the Retail Repo is an obligation of the issuing bank and that the underlying security serves as collateral; (2) that the bank will pay a fixed amount, including interest on the purchase price, regardless of any fluctuation in the market price of the underlying security; (3) that the interest rate paid is not that of the underlying security; and (4) that general banking assets will most likely be used to satisfy the bank's obligation under the Retail Repo rather than proceeds from the sale of the underlying security. In addition, the customer should be advised at the time of purchase of the actual or approximate market value of the underlying security interest and he should be clearly warned that the Retail Repo is not a deposit, is not FDIC insured, and is not guaranteed in any way by the U. S. Government or any agency thereof. Language generally associated with deposits must be avoided to prevent creating the impression that insured deposits are being offered. The customer must be informed that he may become an unsecured creditor of the bank to the extent the market value of his security interest falls below the amount of the funds invested.

* * * In addition, the no-action positions contained in the letters do not apply to transactions in which the issuer of the retail repos holds itself out as offering an investment, as opposed to a collateral, interest in a government security or pool of such securities. Characterizing an arrangement as involving a bank's or savings and loan association's "money market fund" or otherwise implying that retail repos are investment interests in a government security or pool of such securities may therefore raise disclosure and other questions under the securities laws.

The no-action letters set forth herein deal solely with retail repos, which are a relatively recent phenomenon. The letters do not discuss more traditional repurchase agreements that have been in use for a number of years. These traditional repurchase agreements essentially are short-term contracts to sell and repurchase entire government securities in large denominations. While the primary purpose of this release is to address the application of the federal securities laws to retail repos, the Commission believes it also would be useful to indicate briefly its views on these other types of repos.

Traditional repurchase agreements differ from retail repos in several significant respects. For example, traditional repos usually have a shorter duration (one day is not untypical), involve larger amounts (one million dollars is not uncommon), are privately negotiated rather than mass marketed, and involve entire government securities which often are delivered directly to the purchaser, an event which rarely, if ever, occurs in a retail repo transaction.

The economic realities of traditional repurchase agreements suggest that such agreements are not themselves separate securities. For purposes of the federal securities laws, however, they are deemed to involve the purchase and sale of the U. S. government securities to which they relate. As a result, the antifraud provisions of such laws would apply to the offer, sale and purchase of U. S. government securities occurring in connection with traditional repurchase agreements.[a]

*   *   *

C. OIL AND GAS

Oil and gas financing is a strange world with a vocabulary all its own. Established companies normally issue the usual types of securities. But in the century and more since the beginnings of the commercial petroleum industry certain peculiar forms of financing have evolved. In the typical case the development of an area with an oil potential is dependent on a favorable geologist's report, although the established companies are apt to get large amounts of acreage under option even before doing any geological or geophysical work. If the report is favorable, the process of leasing or "blocking" the tract begins. Representatives of one or more producers or speculators obtain leases to the oil and gas rights on as many of the individual tracts as they can. The tracts are typically "granted, demised, leased and let" to the lessee "for the sole and only purpose of mining and operating oil and gas and laying pipelines" during a stated term of years. The lessor receives, in addition to an immediate "cash bonus" in some cases, a promise on the part of the lessee to pay a stated rental per acre for every year in which a well is not drilled, and a further promise

[a] ED.: See Fidelity Financial Corp., Sec. Ex. Act Rel. 18,927, 25 SEC Dock. 1056 (1982) (report of investigation). For an analysis from the point of view of banking and other bodies of law as well as securities regulation, see Porter, Eighty-Nine-Day Agreements for the Sale and Repurchase of Fractional Interests in Governmental Securities, 98 Banking L. J. 343 (1981); Porter, Retail Repurchase Agreements Revisited, 99 Banking L. J. 676 (1982).

of a stated percentage, usually one-eighth, of the oil and gas actually produced and sold or its value at the prevailing market price. This one-eighth interest is the "landowner's royalty interest," and it commonly finds its way into the securities markets in lots of fractional undivided portions after having been transferred to banks as collateral for loans or having been sold to an oil royalty dealer. Thus the sale of these interests is not a device for financing the drilling of a well. It is merely a method of sharing the risk involved, or receiving the immediate enjoyment of an income that would otherwise be spread over a number of years, or both.

The *lessee*'s interest is termed the "working interest." If the lessee is an established producing company, it may retain all of the working interest. On the other hand, if it does not have independent resources, it may sell fractional undivided shares of the lease to raise working capital, or it may give a part interest in the lease to a drilling contractor, who in turn may sell all or part of his share to finance the drilling. As in the case of the "landowners' royalty interests," which are fractions of the one-eighth portion, these "working interests," which are fractions of the seven-eighths portion, may nominally give rights of participation either in the oil or gas or in the proceeds from its sale. If the fractional undivided interests in the seven-eighths portion are not subject to any of the expense of development, operation, or maintenance, they are commonly known as "overriding royalty interests." If they *are* subject to any part of that expense, they are known simply as "working interests" — or, in certain circumstances that are not typical, "participating interests." Occasionally, too, interests called "oil or gas payments" may be created out of the seven-eighths interest; these resemble "overriding royalty interests" in that they are not subject to any portion of the expense, but they are limited to a maximum amount fixed either in barrels of oil or in cubic feet of gas or in dollars. This precise terminology is not too fixed, but it has been adopted by the Commission.[1]

Both the landowner's royalty interest and the working interest are *sui generis*. Their precise nature, and particularly the problem whether they are realty or personalty, have much occupied the courts in connection with taxation, inheritance, dower and curtesy, and the formal prerequisites of legal instruments. The answers have varied from state to state and within particular states, depending upon the legal ends sought to be subserved.

For purposes of the Securities Act, however, it is irrelevant whether these interests are real or personal property, and it is

---

C. 3C   [1] Reg. B, Rule 300; Form S-10.

equally irrelevant whether they are transferred by deed or by contract. Section 2(1) was amended in 1934 to make clear that it covers any "fractional undivided interest in oil, gas, or other mineral rights." The Federal Trade Commission thereupon took the position that "The word 'rights' is broad enough to make the definition applicable to interests which are regarded as giving ownership of the oil or gas in place as well as to interests which merely afford the owner the right to produce oil or gas."[2] However, there is no "fractional undivided interest" if the *whole* landowner's royalty interest is transferred, even though under the terms of the lease the holder may be entitled to only one-eighth or some other portion of the production.

The 1934 amendments also supplied a special definition of the term "issuer" with respect to these fractional undivided interests to mean "the owner of any such right or of any interest in such right (whether whole or fractional) who creates fractional interests therein for the purpose of public offering."[3] If there is no "public offering" by an issuer, an exemption is available in any event under §4(2). But the exemptions generally do not apply to the antifraud provisions in §§12(2) and 17. So it is necessary to decide whether a "security" is involved when an owner of an entire leasehold creates fractional interests (or an owner of fractional interests creates smaller fractional interests) for the purpose of a *private* offering that he makes *fraudulently.* This question was answered affirmatively in a case in which the court permitted recovery under §12(2) but not under §12(1).[4] In other words, there can be a "security" without an "issuer," the definition of the latter term being important only because the "issuer" must sign the registration statement under §6(a) and is absolutely liable for material defects in it under §11. By contrast, §§12 and 17(a) refer to any "person" who sells.

At the state level, the draftsmen of the Uniform Securities Act substituted the phrase, "any certificate of interest or participation in an oil, gas, or mining title or lease or in payments out of production under such a title or lease," because some such phraseology was common in the state statutes.[5] The "certificate of interest or participation" locution was also substituted for the "fractional undivided interest" phrase in §3(a)(10) of the 1934 Act.[6]

---

[2] Sec. Act Rel. 185 (1934).
[3] Woodward v. Wright, 266 F. 2d 108 (10th Cir. 1959).
[4] Ibid.
[5] §401(l); see Loss, Commentary on the Uniform Securities Act (1979) 106.
[6] It is nevertheless the administrative view that the ordinary oil royalty is a security under the 1934 Act — if not under this portion of the definition, then under the catchall phrases. Indeed, the 1934 Act definition may well go

The "fractional undivided interest" phrase in §2(1) has been applied in a number of cases. But the financing techniques in this area are so variegated that it is not always clear whether a particular transaction involves a "security" by virtue of either that phrase or some other portion of the definition. Can it be assumed on the one hand, for example, that every transfer of a fractional undivided working interest in an oil or gas leasehold results in a "security" if what is involved essentially is a development contract among only a few persons, especially if they are equally sophisticated in oil and gas matters? Can it be assumed, on the other hand, that a public offering of small portions of a leasehold does *not* involve a "security" under some other portion of the definition merely because they are divided by metes and bounds instead of being "fractional undivided interests"? The first question was answered in the negative by a sharply divided Illinois Supreme Court, whose dissenters accused the majority of having "left the world of realism."[7] And the second question produced the first case on the definition of "security" in the Supreme Court of the United States:

SECURITIES AND EXCHANGE COMMISSION v. C. M. JOINER LEASING CORPORATION
Supreme Court of the United States, 1943
320 U. S. 344

MR. JUSTICE JACKSON delivered the opinion of the Court.

The Securities and Exchange Commission brought this action in District Court to restrain respondents from further violations of §§5(a) and 17(a)(2) and (3) of the Securities Act of 1933. The District Court denied relief and the Circuit Court of Appeals affirmed upon a construction of the statute which excludes from its operation all trading in oil and gas leases. 133 F. 2d 241. As this presents a question important to the administration of the Act we granted certiorari.

Respondents and one Johnson, a defendant against whom a decree was taken by consent, engaged in a campaign to sell assignments of oil leases. The underlying leases, acreage from which was being sold, are not in the record. They required, as appears from the assignments, annual rental in case of delayed drilling of $1

---

further than its 1933 Act counterpart in the sense that a "certificate of interest * * * in any * * * lease" is perhaps broad enough to include any portion of an entire leasehold interest, whether or not an undivided portion.

[7] Hammer v. Sanders, 8 Ill. 2d 414, 429, 134 N. E. 2d 509, 517 (1956), *cert. denied,* 352 U. S. 878.

per year. It also seems that these leases were granted by the land-owners on an agreement that a test well would be drilled by the lessees. One Anthony blocked up leases on about 4,700 acres of land in McCulloch County, Texas, in consideration of drilling a test well. Defendant Joiner testified that he acquired 3,002 of these acres for "practically nothing except to drill a well." Anthony was a driller and agreed to do the drilling which the Joiner Company undertook to finance, expecting to raise most of the funds for this purpose from the resale of small parcels of acreage. The sales campaign was by mail addressed to upwards of 1,000 prospects in widely scattered parts of the country and actual purchasers, about fifty in number, were located in at least eighteen states and the District of Columbia. Leasehold subdivisions offered never exceeded twenty acres and usually covered two and a half to five acres. The prices ranged from $5 to $15 per acre. The largest single purchase shown by the record was $100, and the great majority of purchases amounted to $25 or less. All buyers were given the opportunity to pay these sums in installments, and some did so.

The sales literature nowhere mentioned drilling conditions which the purchaser would meet or costs which he would incur if he attempted to develop his own acreage. On the other hand, it assured the prospect that the Joiner Company was engaged in and would complete the drilling of a test well so located as to test the oil-producing possibilities of the offered leaseholds. The leases were offered on these terms: "You may have ten acres around one or both wells at $5 per acre cash payable by August 1st, 1941 and $5 per acre additional payable November 1st, 1941 or thirty days after both wells are completed." Other language in the advertising literature emphasized the character of the purchase as an invest-ment and as a participation in an enterprise.

The trial court made findings of what amounted to fraud, and the Circuit Court of Appeals approved, saying, "the evidence would justify stronger findings of fraud." However, both courts refused injunction because, as the Court of Appeals stated, it could "find simply sales and assignments of legal and legitimate oil and gas leases, i. e., sales of interests in land." It was thought that these assignments could not be proved to be "securities" or "investment contracts" under §2(1) of the Act.

Undisputed facts seem to us, however, to establish the con-clusion that defendants were not, as a practical matter, offering naked leasehold rights. Had the offer mailed by defendants omitted the economic inducements of the proposed and promised exploration well, it would have been a quite different proposition. Purchasers then would have been left to their own devices for realizing upon their rights. They would have anticipated waiting an indefinite time, paying delayed drilling rental meanwhile until some chance exploration proved or disproved the productivity of their acres. Their alternative would have been to test their own leases at a cost of $5,000 or more per well.

But defendants offered no such dismal prospect. Their proposition was to sell documents which offered the purchaser a chance, without undue delay or additional cost, of sharing in discovery values which might follow a current exploration enterprise. The drilling of this well was not an unconnected or uncontrolled phenomenon to which salesmen pointed merely to show the possibilities of the offered leases. The exploration enterprise was woven into these leaseholds, in both an economic and a legal sense; the undertaking to drill a well runs through the whole transaction as the thread on which everybody's beads were strung. * * *

*   *   *

It is clear that an economic interest in this well-drilling undertaking was what brought into being the instruments that defendants were selling and gave to the instruments most of their value and all of their lure. The trading in these documents had all the evils inherent in the securities transactions which it was the aim of the Securities Act to end.

It is urged that the definition of "security" which controls the scope of this Act falls short of including these transactions. Respondents invoke the *"ejusdem generis* rule" to constrict the more general terms substantially to the specific terms which they follow. And they invoke the ancient maxim *"expressio unius est exclusio alterius"* to exclude sales of leasehold subdivisions by the acre because the statute expressly includes sales of leasehold subdivisions by undivided shares.

Some rules of statutory construction come down to us from sources that were hostile toward the legislative process itself and thought it generally wise to restrict the operation of an act to its narrowest permissible compass. However well these rules may serve at times to aid in deciphering legislative intent, they long have been subordinated to the doctrine that courts will construe the details of an act in conformity with its dominating general purpose, will read text in the light of context and will interpret the text so far as the meaning of the words fairly permits so as to carry out in particular cases the generally expressed legislative policy.[8]

In the Securities Act the term "security" was defined to include by name or description many documents in which there is common trading for speculation or investment. Some, such as notes, bonds, and stocks, are pretty much standardized and the name alone carries well-settled meaning. Others are of more variable character and were necessarily designated by more descriptive terms, such as "transferable share," "investment contract," and "in general any interest or instrument commonly known as a security." We cannot read out of the statute these general descriptive designations merely because more specific ones have been used to reach some kinds of documents. Instruments may be included within any of these definitions, as matter of law, if on their face they answer to the name or description. However, the reach of the Act does not stop with the obvious and commonplace. Novel, uncommon, or irregular devices, whatever they appear to be, are also reached if it be proved as matter of fact that they were widely offered or dealt in under terms or courses of dealing which established their character in commerce as "investment contracts," or as "any interest or instrument commonly known as a 'security.' " The proof here seems clear that these defendants' offers brought their instruments within these terms.

It is urged that because the definition mentions "fractional undivided interest in oil, gas or other mineral rights," it excludes sales of leasehold subdivisions by parcels. Oil and gas rights posed a difficult problem to the legislative draftsman. Such rights were notorious subjects of speculation and fraud, but leases and assignments were also indispensable instruments of legitimate oil exploration and production. To include leases and assignments by name might easily burden the oil industry by controls that were designed only for the traffic in securities. This was avoided by including specifically only that form of splitting up of mineral interests which had been most utilized for speculative purposes. We do not think the draftsmen thereby immunized other forms of contracts and offerings which are proved as matter of fact to answer to such descriptive terms as "investment contracts" and "securities."

Nor can we agree with the court below that defendants' offerings were beyond the scope of the Act because they offered leases and assignments which under Texas law conveyed interests in real

---

[8] This Court has refused to follow the *"ejusdem generis"* rule, even in

estate. In applying acts of this general purpose, the courts have not been guided by the nature of the assets back of a particular document or offering. The test rather is what character the instrument is given in commerce by the terms of the offer, the plan of distribution, and the economic inducements held out to the prospect. In the enforcement of an act such as this it is not inappropriate that promoters' offerings be judged as being what they were represented to be.

Finally it is urged that we must interpret with strictness the scope of this Act because violations of it are crimes. Some authority is cited and a great array could be assembled to support the general proposition that penal statutes must be strictly construed. An almost equally impressive collection can be made of decisions holding that remedial statutes should be liberally construed. What, then, shall we say of the construction of a section like this which may be the basis of either civil proceedings of a preventive or remedial nature or of punitive proceedings, or perhaps both?

Different courts have given different answers to the general question. * * * The weight of authority is committed to a liberal construction, although some courts tend toward strict construction, and some have seemed to differentiate according to the use being made of the statute, inclining to a strict construction when a criminal penalty is being imposed and a more liberal one when civil remedies are being applied.

* * *

In the present case we do nothing to the words of the Act; we merely accept them. It would be necessary in any case for any kind of relief to prove that documents being sold were securities under the Act. In some cases it might be done by proving the document itself, which on its face would be a note, a bond, or a share of stock. In others proof must go outside the instrument itself as we do here. Where this proof is offered in a civil action, as here, a preponderance of the evidence will establish the case; if it were offered in a criminal case, it would have to meet the stricter requirement of satisfying the jury beyond reasonable doubt.

We hold that the court below erred in denying an injunction

---

criminal cases, where its application seemed to conflict with the general purpose of an act. [Citations omitted.]

It has also treated the maxim *"expressio unius est exclusio alterius"* as but an aid to construction. [Citations omitted.]

under the undisputed facts of this case and its findings. The judgment is *reversed*.

MR. JUSTICE ROBERTS is of the opinion that the judgment should be affirmed.

MR. JUSTICE DOUGLAS took no part in the consideration or decision of this case.

The Fifth Circuit later said:

In [*SEC v. W. J. Howey Co.*, 328 U. S. 293 (1946), set out infra p. 192] the element of expectation of "profits solely from the efforts of the promoter or a third party," which are "to come solely from the efforts of others" [citations omitted], as well as that case's restatement of the Joiner holding in the broadest of terms, certainly overcomes any imputation that language in Joiner that the "drilling of this well was not an unconnected or un-controlled phenomenon" etc. meant to require that the col-lateral activity be that of the seller or one under his control. Loss, Securities Regulation, 1955 supp. p. 149, as much as says so: "Mr. Justice Jackson's statement that 'The exploration enter-prise was woven into these leaseholds, in both an economic and a legal sense,' would seem to apply equally in principle whether the exploration is being done under the seller's control or by a third person." * * * [8]

The last few decades have seen the development of a new method of financing, the "oil program," in which the security is not an undivided interest in *one* well but an interest, under a variety of contractual arrangements, in a joint venture or limited partnership whose function is to develop a *number* of profitable drilling prospects. These programs are sold for the purpose of raising funds to acquire leases on prospect acreage and to drill wells, although producing properties are sometimes acquired as well. Ultimately fractional undivided interests in the completed wells may be distributed to the participants. And additional pay-ments may be required for completion and exploration costs, at the risk of forfeiture for nonpayment. Customarily the programs are created at annual or more frequent intervals, with emphasis on the tax advantages flowing from "pass-through" treatment of drilling costs and certain other deductions.

As these programs increased in number and dollar amount, they began to take on the characteristic of investment companies whose portfolio "securities" were various kinds of oil and gas

---

[8] Roe v. United States, 287 F. 2d 435, 439 n. 5 (5th Cir. 1961).

interests rather than stocks. But §3(c)(9) of the Investment Company Act excludes "Any person substantially all of whose business consists of owning or holding oil, gas, or other mineral royalties or leases, or fractional interests therein, or certificates of interest or participation in or investment contracts relative to such royalties, leases, or fractional interests." And there are so many differences from the typical mutual fund that application of many of the provisions of the Investment Company Act would raise serious problems. For one thing, the conflict between that Act's philosophy of an investor-controlled management and the philosophy of the passive investor implicit in the limited partnership arrangement presents difficulties.

The upshot was that the Commission in 1972 transmitted to Congress a proposed Oil and Gas Investment Act, which was intended to deal only with "blind pool" oil programs that provide pass-through tax treatment and generally offer their securities or participations to the public.[9] But legislation of that kind does not seem likely in the foreseeable future. For that reason the Code preserves the exclusion.[10]

D. THE "INVESTMENT CONTRACT" CONCEPT

1. GENERAL

For some reason Justice Jackson seemed reluctant in *Joiner* to adopt in so many words the interpretation of "investment contract" that had been widely followed by the state courts. That was left for the next Supreme Court case three years later:

SEC v. W. J. HOWEY COMPANY
Supreme Court of the United States, 1946
328 U. S. 293

MR. JUSTICE MURPHY delivered the opinion of the Court.

This case involves the application of §2(1) of the Securities Act of 1933 to an offering of units of a citrus grove development coupled with a contract for cultivating, marketing and remitting the net proceeds to the investor.

---

[9] S. 3884, 92d Cong., U. S. Cong. Rec. 26,967 (1972).
[10] §202(8o)(B)(x); 1 Code 125.

The Securities and Exchange Commission instituted this action to restrain the respondents from using the mails and instrumentalities of interstate commerce in the offer and sale of unregistered and non-exempt securities in violation of §5(a) of the Act. The District Court denied the injunction, 60 F. Supp. 440, and the Fifth Circuit Court of Appeals affirmed the judgment, 151 F. 2d 714. We granted certiorari on a petition alleging that the ruling of the Circuit Court of Appeals conflicted with other federal and state decisions and that it introduced a novel and unwarranted test under the statute which the Commission regarded as administratively impractical.

Most of the facts are stipulated. The respondents, W. J. Howey Company and Howey-in-the-Hills Service, Inc., are Florida corporations under direct common control and management. The Howey Company owns large tracts of citrus acreage in Lake County, Florida. During the past several years it has planted about 500 acres annually, keeping half of the groves itself and offering the other half to the public "to help us finance additional development." Howey-in-the-Hills Service, Inc., is a service company engaged in cultivating and developing many of these groves, including the harvesting and marketing of the crops.

Each prospective customer is offered both a land sales contract and a service contract, after having been told that it is not feasible to invest in a grove unless service arrangements are made. While the purchaser is free to make arrangements with other service companies, the superiority of Howey-in-the-Hills Service, Inc., is stressed. Indeed 85% of the acreage sold during the 3-year period ending May 31, 1943, was covered by service contracts with Howey-in-the-Hills Service, Inc.

The land sales contract with the Howey Company provides for a uniform purchase price per acre or fraction thereof, varying in amount only in accordance with the number of years the particular plot has been planted with citrus trees. Upon full payment of the purchase price the land is conveyed to the purchaser by warranty deed. Purchases are usually made in narrow strips of land arranged so that an acre consists of a row of 48 trees. During the period between February 1, 1941, and May 31, 1943, 31 of the 42 persons making purchases bought less than 5 acres each. The average holding of these 31 persons was 1.33 acres and sales of as little as 0.65, 0.7 and 0.73 of an acre were made. These tracts are not separately fenced and the sole indication of several ownership is found in small land marks intelligible only through a plat book record.

The service contract, generally of a 10-year duration without option of cancellation, gives Howey-in-the-Hills Service, Inc., a leasehold interest and "full and complete" possession of the acreage. For a specified fee plus the cost of labor and materials, the company is given full discretion and authority over the cultivation of the groves and the harvest and marketing of the crops. The company is well established in the citrus business and maintains a large force of skilled personnel and a great deal of equipment, including 75 tractors, sprayer wagons, fertilizer trucks and the like. Without the consent of the company, the land owner or purchaser has no right of entry to market the crop;[2] thus there is ordinarily no right to specific fruit. The company is accountable only for an allocation of the net profits based upon a check made at the time of picking. All the produce is pooled by the respondent companies, which do business under their own names.

The purchasers for the most part are non-residents of Florida. They are predominantly business and professional people who lack the knowledge, skill and equipment necessary for the care and cultivation of citrus trees. They are attracted by the expectation of substantial profits. It was represented, for example, that profits during the 1943-1944 season amounted to 20% and that even greater profits might be expected during the 1944-1945 season, although only a 10% annual return was to be expected over a 10-year period. Many of these purchasers are patrons of a resort hotel owned and operated by the Howey Company in a scenic section adjacent to the groves. The hotel's advertising mentions the fine groves in the vicinity and the attention of the patrons is drawn to the groves as they are being escorted about the surrounding countryside. They are told that the groves are for sale; if they indicate an interest in the matter they are then given a sales talk.

* * *

Section 2(1) of the Act defines the term "security" to include the commonly known documents traded for speculation or investment. This definition also includes "securities" of a more variable character, designated by such descriptive terms as "certificate of interest or participation in any profit-sharing agreement," "investment contract" and "in general, any interest or instrument commonly known as a 'security.'" The legal issue in this case turns upon a determination of whether, under the circumstances, the land sales

---

C. 3D [2]Some investors visited their particular plots annually, making suggestions as to care and cultivation, but without any legal rights in the matters.

contract, the warranty deed and the service contract together constitute an "investment contract" within the meaning of §2(1). An affirmative answer brings into operation the registration requirements of §5(a), unless the security is granted an exemption under §3(b). The lower courts, in reaching a negative answer to this problem, treated the contracts and deeds as separate transactions involving no more than an ordinary real estate sale and an agreement by the seller to manage the property for the buyer.

The term "investment contract" is undefined by the Securities Act or by relevant legislative reports. But the term was common in many state "blue sky" laws in existence prior to the adoption of the federal statute and, although the term was also undefined by the state laws, it had been broadly construed by state courts so as to afford the investing public a full measure of protection. Form was disregarded for substance and emphasis was placed upon economic reality. An investment contract thus came to mean a contract or scheme for "the placing of capital or laying out of money in a way intended to secure income or profit from its employment." *State* v. *Gopher Tire & Rubber Co.,* 146 Minn. 52, 56, 177 N. W. 937, 938. This definition was uniformly applied by state courts to a variety of situations where individuals were led to invest money in a common enterprise with the expectation that they would earn a profit solely through the efforts of the promoter or of some one other than themselves.

By including an investment contract within the scope of §2(1) of the Securities Act, Congress was using a term the meaning of which had been crystallized by this prior judicial interpretation. It is therefore reasonable to attach that meaning to the term as used by Congress, especially since such a definition is consistent with the statutory aims. In other words, an investment contract for purposes of the Securities Act means a contract, transaction or scheme whereby a person invests his money in a common enterprise and is led to expect profits solely from the efforts of the promoter or a third party, it being immaterial whether the shares in the enterprise are evidenced by formal certificates or by nominal interests in the physical assets employed in the enterprise. Such a definition necessarily underlies this Court's decision in *S. E. C.* v. *Joiner Corp.,* 320 U. S. 344, and has been enunciated and applied many times by lower federal courts. It permits the fulfillment of the statutory purpose of compelling full and fair disclosure relative to the issuance of "the many types of instruments that in our commercial world fall within the ordinary concept of a security." H. Rep. No. 85, 73rd Cong., 1st Sess., p. 11. It embodies a flexible rather than a static principle, one that is capable of adaptation to meet the countless and variable schemes devised by those who seek the use of the money of others on the promise of profits.

The transactions in this case clearly involve investment contracts as so defined. The respondent companies are offering something more than fee simple interests in land, something different from a farm or orchard coupled with management services. They are offering an opportunity to contribute money and to share in the profits of a large citrus fruit enterprise managed and partly owned by respondents. They are offering this opportunity to persons who reside in distant localities and who lack the equipment and experience requisite to the cultivation, harvesting and marketing of the citrus products. Such persons have no desire to occupy the land or to develop it themselves; they are attracted solely by the prospects of a return on their investment. Indeed, individual development of the plots of land that are offered and sold would seldom be economically feasible due to their small size. Such tracts gain utility as citrus groves only when cultivated and developed as component parts of a larger area. A common enterprise managed by respondents or third parties with adequate personnel and equipment is therefore essential if the investors are to achieve their paramount aim of a return on their investments. Their respective shares in this enterprise are evidenced by land sales contracts and warranty deeds, which serve as a convenient method of determining the investors' allocable shares of the profits. The resulting transfer of rights in land is purely incidental.

Thus all the elements of a profit-seeking business venture are present here. The investors provide the capital and share in the earnings and profits; the promoters manage, control and operate the enterprise. It follows that the arrangements whereby the investors' interests are made manifest involve investment contracts, regardless of the legal terminology in which such contracts are clothed. The investment contracts in this instance take the form of land sales contracts, warranty deeds and service contracts which respondents offer to prospective investors. And respondents' failure to abide by the statutory and administrative rules in making such offerings, even though the failure result from a bona fide mistake as to the law, cannot be sanctioned under the Act.

This conclusion is unaffected by the fact that some purchasers choose not to accept the full offer of an investment contract by declining to enter into a service contract with the respondents. The Securities Act prohibits the offer as well as the sale of unregistered, non-exempt securities. Hence it is enough that the respondents merely offer the essential ingredients of an investment contract.

We reject the suggestion of the Circuit Court of Appeals, 151 F. 2d at 717, that an investment contract is necessarily missing where the enterprise is not speculative or promotional in character and where the tangible interest which is sold has intrinsic value independent of the success of the enterprise as a whole. The test is whether the scheme involves an investment of money in a common enterprise with profits to come solely from the efforts of others. If that test be satisfied, it is immaterial whether the enterprise is speculative or non-speculative or whether there is a sale of property with or without intrinsic value. See *S. E. C.* v. *Joiner Corp.,* supra, 352. The statutory policy of affording broad protection to investors is not to be thwarted by unrealistic and irrelevant formulae.[a]

The *Howey* formula has not been limited by any means to the production of vitamin C. Many schemes have been held with almost monotonous consistency to involve "investment contracts" on the basis of a purported sale or lease of some form of tangible property subject to an arrangement whereby the seller retains possession and control of the property with a view to earning a profit for the nominal owners or lessees. Proof of some sort of pooling arrangement among investors (as in the *Howey* case) helps, but it is not essential.[1] And the catalogue is as variegated as the imaginations of promoters.

Many of them involve animals, preferably of either a fecund or a fur-bearing variety. A person "sells" pairs of silver foxes, for

[a] ED.: Justice Frankfurter dissented on the ground that the Supreme Court should not disturb the findings in which both lower courts had concurred.

See also Marine Bank v. Weaver, 102 S. Ct. 1220, 1225 (1982), supra p. 168, where the Court held that an agreement under which two investors pledged a bank certificate of deposit to enable a company to obtain working capital in return for a 50 percent interest in the company's anticipated profits was not a "security," because it was a "unique agreement, negotiated one-on-one by the parties," that was neither designed for public trading nor meant for a number of potential investors.

[1] E. g., El Khadem v. Equity Security Corp., 494 F. 2d 1224, 1229 (9th Cir. 1974); Pacific Coast Coin Exchange of Canada, Ltd. v. Ontario Securities Commission, [1978] 2 S. C. R. 112, 80 D. L. R. 3d 529 (Sup. Ct. Can.); Union Home Loans, Sec. Ex. Act Rel. 19,346, 26 SEC Dock. 1346, 1348 (1982). On the question whether an interest in a discretionary commodities account with a broker is a security only if there is "horizontal commonality" (some sort of "common enterprise" among customers similarly situated) as distinct from "vertical commonality" (a "common enterprise" between broker and customer), see p. 255 infra.

example, with the idea that he will supply the expert care (for a charge, of course) and in due time nature will supply lots of pups — one is tempted to say "a true stock dividend."[2] But the technique has been applied even to the considerably less glamorous, but more reliable, barnyard cow, which offers not only earnings from her milk but also capital gains on her calves and — when her milking days are but a nostalgic memory and she makes the supreme sacrifice — on her own poor carcass as well.[3] Indeed, the latest zoological medium seems to be earthworms, which rate high on the fecundity scale because their bisexuality makes it possible for any two worms to reproduce.[4]

The courts attempt to draw the line, however, where neither the element of a common enterprise nor the element of reliance on the efforts of another is present. For example, no "investment contract" is involved when a person invests in real estate, with the hope perhaps of earning a profit as the result of a general increase in values concurrent with the development of the neighborhood, as long as he does not do so as part of an enterprise whereby it is expressly or impliedly understood that the property will be developed or operated by others.[5]

We cannot consider here all the permutations of the "investment contract" phenomenon. But we shall examine developments in the most significant areas.

2. PARTNERSHIPS

It seems clear, from the reference to partnerships in §2(2) as well as the specification in Schedule A of the partners' names and addresses "if the issuer be a partnership," that interests in partnerships *may* be securities. Here, too, some sort of line must be drawn. The easy case is the public offering of freely transferable limited partnership interests, which is functionally equivalent to

---

[2] SEC v. Payne, 35 F. Supp. 873 (S. D. N. Y. 1940).

[3] E. g., McLish v. Harris Farms, Inc., 507 F. Supp. 1075 (E. D. Cal. 1980); see also Comment, Equine Syndications: Are They Securities?, 6 N. Ky. L. Rev. 361 (1979) (thoroughbred stallions).

[4] Smith v. Gross, 604 F. 2d 639 (9th Cir. 1979); Sec. Ex. Act Rel. 15,345, 16 SEC Dock. 221 (1978).

[5] Gordon v. Terry, 684 F. 2d 736, 740 n. 4 (11th Cir. 1982). The holding in that case was that an investor might show sufficient dependence on the promoter's expertise to establish an investment contract despite the written agreement's giving the investor substantial control, but that the investor had the burden of proving such dependency, with respect to each defendant separately, as to render him incapable of exercising the power that the agreement vested in him.

a public offering of preferred stock.[6] But such interests have been treated like securities for purposes of the fraud provisions even without the public element.[7] Indeed, even interests in something called a *general* partnership may be securities when the venture, though a general partnership *de jure,* functions *de facto* like a limited partnership.[8]

In short, it is substance, not form, that controls here, too. Conversely, therefore, it by no means follows that a security is involved in even a public advertisement for one or more persons who will be *bona fide* general partners. The problem, as Judge Frank put it when he was Chairman of the SEC, is to distinguish between the public offering of securities parading as "limited partnership interests" and "an offering of a half interest in a hamburger stand."[9]

3.   REAL ESTATE (HEREIN OF SALE OF A BUSINESS)

UNITED HOUSING FOUNDATION, INC. v. FORMAN
Supreme Court of the United States, 1975
421 U. S. 837

MR. JUSTICE POWELL delivered the opinion of the Court.

The issue in these cases is whether shares of stock entitling a purchaser to lease an apartment in Co-op City, a state subsidized and supervised nonprofit housing cooperative, are "securities" within the purview of the Securities Act of 1933 and the Securities Exchange Act of 1934.

I

Co-op City is a massive housing cooperative in New York City. Built between 1965 and 1971, it presently houses approximately

---

[6] E. g., SEC v. Murphy, 626 F. 2d 633, 640-41 (9th Cir. 1980).

[7] McGreghar Land Co. v. Meguiar, 521 F. 2d 822 (9th Cir. 1975); Goodman v. Epstein, 582 F. 2d 388, 408-09 (7th Cir. 1978). When a corporation is organized to be the general partner of a series of limited partnerships — a common phenomenon in recent years in the perpetual search for "tax shelters" — the corporation might be the "issuer" (or at least a co-issuer) of the limited partnership interests as the entity responsible for the success or failure of the enterprise. Cf. SEC v. Murphy, 626 F. 2d 633, 642-44 (9th Cir. 1980); SEC v. Holschuh, 694 F. 2d 130, 139 (7th Cir. 1982).

[8] Williamson v. Tucker, 645 F. 2d 404, 422-24 (5th Cir. 1981), *cert. denied,* 454 U. S. 897; Morrison v. Pelican Landing Development, CCH Fed. Sec. L. Rep. ¶98,863 (N. D. Ill. 1982).

[9] 212 Saturday Evening Post 28 (Apr. 27, 1940), 26 (June 1, 1940), 26 (June 15, 1940).

50,000 people on a 200-acre site containing 35 high-rise buildings and 236 town houses. The project was organized, financed, and constructed under the New York State Private Housing Finance Law, commonly known as the Mitchell-Lama Act, enacted to ameliorate a perceived crisis in the availability of decent low-income urban housing. In order to encourage private developers to build low-cost cooperative housing, New York provides them with large long-term, low-interest mortgage loans and substantial tax exemptions. Receipt of such benefits is conditioned on a willingness to have the State review virtually every step in the development of the cooperative. See N. Y. Priv. Hous. Fin. Law §§11-37, as amended (1962 and Supp. 1974-1975). The developer also must agree to operate the facility "on a nonprofit basis," §11-a(2a), and he may lease apartments only to people whose incomes fall below a certain level and who have been approved by the State.

The United Housing Foundation (UHF), a nonprofit membership corporation established for the purpose of "aiding and encouraging" the creation of "adequate, safe and sanitary housing accommodations for wage earners and other persons of low or moderate income," * * * was responsible for initiating and sponsoring the development of Co-op City. Acting under the Mitchell-Lama, Act, UHF organized the Riverbay Corporation (Riverbay) to own and operate the land and buildings constituting Co-op City. Riverbay, a nonprofit cooperative housing corporation, issued the stock that is the subject of this litigation. UHF also contracted with Community Services, Inc. (CSI), its wholly owned subsidiary, to serve as the general contractor and sales agent for the project. As required by the Mitchell-Lama Act, these decisions were approved by the State Housing Commissioner.

To acquire an apartment in Co-op City an eligible prospective purchaser must buy 18 shares of stock in Riverbay for each room desired. The cost per share is $25, making the total cost $450 per room, or $1,800 for a four-room apartment. The sole purpose of acquiring these shares is to enable the purchaser to occupy an apartment in Co-op City; in effect, their purchase is a recoverable deposit on an apartment. The shares are explicitly tied to the apartment: they cannot be transferred to a nontenant; nor can they be pledged or encumbered; and they descend, along with the apartment, only to a surviving spouse. No voting rights attach to the shares as such: participation in the affairs of the cooperative appertains to the apartment, with the residents of each apartment being entitled to one vote irrespective of the number of shares owned.

Any tenant who wants to terminate his occupancy, or who is forced to move out, must offer his stock to Riverbay at its initial selling price of $25 per share. In the extremely unlikely event that Riverbay declines to repurchase the stock, the tenant cannot sell it for more than the initial purchase price plus a fraction of the portion of the mortgage that he has paid off, and then only to a prospective tenant satisfying the statutory income eligibility requirements. See N. Y. Priv. Hous. Fin. Law §31-a (Supp. 1974-1975).

In May 1965, subsequent to the completion of the initial planning, Riverbay circulated an Information Bulletin seeking to attract tenants for what would someday be apartments in Co-op City. After describing the nature and advantages of cooperative housing generally and of Co-op City in particular, the Bulletin informed prospective tenants that the total estimated cost of the project, based largely on an anticipated construction contract with CSI, was $283,695,550. Only a fraction of this sum, $32,795,550, was to be raised by the sale of shares to tenants. The remaining $250,900,000 was to be financed by a 40-year low-interest mortgage loan from the New York Private Housing Finance Agency. After construction of the project the mortgage payments and current operating expenses would be met by monthly rental charges paid by the tenants. While these rental charges were to vary, depending on the size, nature, and location of an apartment, the 1965 Bulletin estimated that the "average" monthly cost would be $23.02 per room, or $92.08 for a four-room apartment.

Several times during the construction of Co-op City, Riverbay, with the approval of the State Housing Commissioner, revised its contract with CSI to allow for increased construction costs. In addition, Riverbay incurred other expenses that had not been reflected in the 1965 Bulletin. To meet these increased expenditures, Riverbay, with the Commissioner's approval, repeatedly secured increased mortgage loans from the State Housing Agency. Ultimately the construction loan was $125 million more than the figure estimated in the 1965 Bulletin. As a result, while the initial purchasing price remained at $450 per room, the average monthly rental charges increased periodically, reaching a figure of $39.68 per room as of July 1974.

These increases in the rental charges precipitated the present lawsuit. Respondents, 57 residents of Co-op City, sued in federal court on behalf of all 15,372 apartment owners, and derivatively on behalf of Riverbay, seeking upwards of $30 million in damages, forced rental reductions, and other "appropriate" relief. Named as defendants (petitioners herein) were UHF, CSI, Riverbay, several individual directors of these organizations, the State of New York, and the State Private Housing Finance Agency. The heart of respondents' claim was that the 1965 Co-op City Information Bulletin falsely represented that CSI would bear all subsequent cost increases due to factors such as inflation. Respondents further alleged that they were misled in their purchases of shares since the Information Bulletin failed to disclose several critical facts. On these bases, respondents asserted two claims under [§17 (a) of the 1933 Act and Rule 10b-5]. * * *

Petitioners, while denying the substance of these allegations, moved to dismiss the complaint on the ground that federal jurisdiction was lacking. They maintained that shares of stock in Riverbay were not "securities" within the definitional sections of the federal Securities Acts. * * *

The Distrtict Court granted the motion to dismiss. * * * It held that the denomination of the shares in Riverbay as "stock" did not, by itself, make them securities under the federal Acts. The court further ruled, relying primarily on this Court's decisions in *SEC* v. *C. M. Joiner Leasing Corp.,* 320 U. S. 344 (1943), and *SEC* v. *W. J. Howey Co.,* 328 U. S. 293 (1946), that the purchase in issue was not a security transaction since it was not induced by an offer of tangible material profits, nor could such profits realistically be expected. * * *

The Court of Appeals for the Second Circuit reversed. * * *

In view of the importance of the issues presented we granted certiorari. 419 U. S. 1120 (1975). As we conclude that the disputed transactions are not purchases of securities within the contemplation of the federal statutes, we reverse.

II

* * * In providing [the definition of "security" in §2(1) of the 1933 Act] Congress did not attempt to articulate the relevant economic criteria for distinguishing "securities" from "nonsecurities." Rather, it sought to define "the term 'security' in sufficiently broad and general terms so as to include within that definition the many types of instruments that in our commercial world fall within the ordinary concept of a security." H. R. Rep. No. 85, 73d Cong., 1st Sess., 11 (1933). The task has fallen to the Securities and Exchange Commission (SEC), the body charged with administering the Securities Acts, and ultimately to the federal courts to decide which of the myriad financial transactions in our society come within the coverage of these statutes.

In making this determination in the present case we do not write on a clean slate. Well-settled principles enunciated by this Court establish that the shares purchased by respondents do not represent any of the "countless and variable schemes devised by those who seek the use of the money of others on the promise of profits," *Howey*, 328 U. S., at 299, and therefore do not fall within "the ordinary concept of a security."

A

We reject at the outset any suggestion that the present transaction, evidenced by the sale of shares called "stock," must be considered a security transaction simply because the statutory definition of a security includes the words "any * * * stock." Rather we adhere to the basic principle that has guided all of the Court's decisions in this area:

> [I]n searching for the meaning and scope of the word "security" in the Act[s], form should be disregarded for substance and the emphasis should be on economic reality. *Tcherepnin* v. *Knight*, 389 U. S. 332, 336 (1967).

See also *Howey*, supra, at 298 [p. 195 supra].

The primary purpose of the Acts of 1933 and 1934 was to eliminate serious abuses in a largely unregulated securities market. The focus of the Acts is on the capital market of the enterprise system: the sale of securities to raise capital for profit-making purposes, the exchanges on which securities are traded, and the need for regulation to prevent fraud and to protect the interest of investors. Because securities transactions are economic in character Congress intended the application of these statutes to turn on the economic realities underlying a transaction, and not on the name appended thereto. Thus, in construing these Acts against the background of their purpose, we are guided by a traditional canon of statutory construction:

> [A] thing may be within the letter of the statute and yet not within the statute, because not within its spirit, nor within the intention of its makers. *Church of the Holy Trinity* v. *United States*, 143 U. S. 457, 459 (1892).

See also *United States* v. *American Trucking Assns.*, 310 U. S. 534, 543 (1940).[14]

---

[14] * * * See * * * 1 L. Loss, Securities Regulation 493 (2d ed. 1961) ("substance governs rather than form: * * * just as some things which look like real estate are securities, some things which look like securities are real estate").

Respondents' reliance on *Joiner* as support for a "literal approach" to defining a security is misplaced. The issue in *Joiner* was whether assignments of interests in oil leases, coupled with the promoters' offer to drill an exploratory well, were securities. Looking to the economic inducement provided by the proposed exploratory well, the Court concluded that these leases were securities even though "leases" as such were not included in the list of instruments mentioned in the statutory definition. In dictum the Court noted that "[i]nstruments *may* be included within [the definition of a security], as [a] matter of law, if on their face they answer to the name or description." 320 U. S., at 351 (emphasis supplied). And later, again in dictum, the Court stated that a security *"might"* be shown "by proving the document itself, which on its face would be a note, a bond, or a share of stock." Id. at 355 (emphasis supplied). By using the conditional words "may" and "might" in these dicta the Court made clear that it was not establishing an inflexible rule barring inquiry into the economic realities underlying a transaction. On the contrary, the Court intended only to make the rather obvious point that, in contrast to the instrument before it which was not included within the explicit statutory terms, most instruments bearing these traditional titles are likely to be covered by the statutes.

In holding that the name given to an instrument is not dispositive, we do not suggest that the name is wholly irrelevant to the decision whether it is a security. There may be occasions when the use of a traditional name such as "stocks" or "bonds" will lead a purchaser justifiably to assume that the federal securities laws apply. This would clearly be the case when the underlying transaction embodies some of the significant characteristics typically associated with the named instrument.

In the present case respondents do not contend, nor could they, that they were misled by use of the word "stock" into believing that the federal securities laws governed their purchase. Common sense suggests that people who intend to acquire only a residential apartment in a state-subsidized cooperative, for their personal use, are not likely to believe that in reality they are purchasing investment securities simply because the transaction is evidenced by something called a share of stock. These shares have none of the characteristics "that in our commercial world fall within the ordinary concept of a security." H. R. Rep. No. 85, supra, at 11. Despite their name, they lack what the Court in *Tcherepnin* deemed the most common feature of stock: the right to receive "dividends contingent upon an apportionment of profits." 389 U. S., at 339. Nor do they possess the other characteristics traditionally associated with stock: they are not negotiable; they cannot be pledged or hypothecated; they confer no voting rights in proportion to the number of shares owned; and they cannot appreciate in value. In short, the inducement to purchase was solely to acquire subsidized low-cost living space; it was not to invest for profit.

B

The Court of Appeals, as an alternative ground for its decision, concluded that a share in Riverbay was also an "investment contract" as defined by the Securities Acts. Respondents further argue that in any event what they agreed to purchase is "commonly known as a 'security' " within the meaning of these laws. In considering these claims we again must examine the substance — the economic realities of the transaction — rather than the names that may have been employed by the parties. We perceive no distinction, for present purposes, between an "investment contract" and an "instrument commonly known as a 'security.' " In either case, the basic test for distinguishing the transaction from other commercial dealings is

> whether the scheme involves an investment of money in a common enterprise with profits to come solely from the efforts of others. *Howey,* 328 U. S., at 301.[16]

This test, in shorthand form, embodies the essential attributes that run through all of the Court's decisions defining a security. The touchstone is the presence of an investment in a common venture premised on a reasonable expectation of profits to be derived from the entrepreneurial or managerial efforts of others. By profits, the Court has meant either capital appreciation resulting from the development of the initial investment, as in *Joiner,* supra (sale of oil leases conditioned on promoters' agreement to drill exploratory well), or a participation in earnings resulting from the use of investors' funds, as in *Tcherepnin* v. *Knight,* supra

---

[16] This test speaks in terms of "profits to come *solely* from the efforts of others." (Emphasis supplied.) Although the issue is not presented in this case, we note that the Court of Appeals for the Ninth Circuit has held that the "word 'solely' should not be read as a strict or literal limitation on the definition of an investment contract, but rather must be construed realistically, so as to include within the definition those schemes which involve in substance, if not form, securities." SEC v. Glenn W. Turner Enterprises, 474 F. 2d 476, 482, *cert. denied,* 414 U. S. 821 (1973). We express no view, however, as to the holding of this case.

(dividends on the investment based on savings and loan association's profits). In such cases the investor is "attracted solely by the prospects of a return" on his investment. *Howey,* supra at 300. By contrast, when a purchaser is motivated by a desire to use or consume the item purchased — "to occupy the land or to develop it themselves," as the *Howey* Court put it, ibid. — the securities laws do not apply. See also *Joiner,* supra.

In the present case there can be no doubt that investors were attracted solely by the prospect of acquiring a place to live, and not by financial returns on their investments. The Information Bulletin distributed to prospective residents emphasized the fundamental nature and purpose of the undertaking * * * . * * * Nowhere does the Bulletin seek to attract investors by the prospect of profits resulting from the efforts of the promoters or third parties. On the contrary, the Bulletin repeatedly emphasizes the "nonprofit" nature of the endeavor. It explains that if rental charges exceed expenses the difference will be returned as a rebate, not invested for profit. It also informs purchasers that they will be unable to resell their apartments at a profit since the apartment must first be offered back to Riverbay "at the price * * * paid for it."[19] Id., at 163a. In short, neither of the kinds of profits traditionally associated with securities was offered to respondents.

The Court of Appeals recognized that there must be an expectation of profits for these shares to be securities, and conceded that there is "no possible profit on a resale of [this] stock." 500 F. 2d, at 1254. The court correctly noted, however, that profit may be derived from the income yielded by an investment as well as from capital appreciation, and then proceeded to find "an expectation of 'income' in at least three ways." Ibid. Two of these supposed sources of income or profits may be disposed of summarily. We turn first to the Court of Appeals' reliance on the deductibility for tax purposes of the portion of the monthly rental charge applied to interest on the mortgage. We know of no basis in law for the view that the payment of interest, with its consequent deductibility for tax purposes, constitutes income or profits.[20]

---

[19] This requirement effectively insures that no apartment will be sold for more than its original cost. Consonant with the purposes of the Mitchell-Lama Act, whenever there are prospective buyers willing to pay as much as the initial purchase price for an apartment in Co-op City, Riverbay will repurchase the apartment and resell it at its original cost. See App. 138a. If, for some reason, Riverbay does not purchase the apartment the tenant still cannot make a profit on his sale. See supra, at 842-843.

[20] Even if these tax deductions were considered profits, they would not be the type associated with a security investment since they do not result from

These tax benefits are nothing more than that which is available to any homeowner who pays interest on his mortgage. See §216 of Internal Revenue Code, 26 U. S. C. §216; *Eckstein* v. *United States,* 196 Ct. Cl. 644, 452 F. 2d 1036 (1971).

The Court of Appeals also found support for its concept of profits in the fact that Co-op City offered space at a cost substantially below the going rental charges for comparable housing. Again, this is an inappropriate theory of "profits" that we cannot accept. The low rent derives from the substantial financial subsidies provided by the State of New York. This benefit cannot be liquidated into cash; nor does it result from the managerial efforts of others. In a real sense, it no more embodies the attributes of income or profits than do welfare benefits, food stamps, or other government subsidies.

The final source of profit relied on by the Court of Appeals was the possibility of net income derived from the leasing by Co-op City of commercial facilities, professional offices and parking spaces, and its operation of community washing machines. The income, if any, from these conveniences, all located within the common areas of the housing project, is to be used to reduce tenant rental costs. Conceptually, one might readily agree that net income from the leasing of commercial and professional facilities is the kind of profit traditionally associated with a security investment. See *Tcherepnin* v. *Knight,* supra. But in the present case this income — if indeed there is any — is far too speculative and insubstantial to bring the entire transaction within the Securities Acts.

Initially we note that the prospect of such income as a means of offsetting rental costs is never mentioned in the Information Bulletin. Thus it is clear that investors were not attracted to Co-op City by the offer of these potential rental reductions. See *Joiner,* 320 U. S., at 353. Moreover, nothing in the record suggests that the facilities in fact return a profit in the sense that the leasing fees are greater than the actual cost to Co-op City of the space rented. The short of the matter is that the stores and services in question were established not as a means of returning profits to tenants, but for the purpose of making essential services available for the residents of this enormous complex. By statute these facilities can only be "incidental and appurtenant" to the housing

---

the managerial efforts of others. See Rosenbaum, The Resort Condominium and the Federal Securities Laws — A Case Study in Governmental Inflexibility, 60 Va. L. Rev. 785, 795-796 (1974); Note, 62 Geo. L. J. 1515, 1524-1526 (1974).

project. N. Y. Priv. Hous. Fin. Law §12(5) (Supp. 1974-1975).
Undoubtedly they make Co-op City a more attractive housing
opportunity, but the possibility of some rental reduction is not
an "expectation of profit" in the sense found necessary in *Howey*.[24]

There is no doubt that purchasers in this housing cooperative
sought to obtain a decent home at an attractive price. But that
type of economic interest characterizes every form of commercial
dealing. What distinguishes a security transaction — and what is
absent here — is an investment where one parts with his money
in the hope of receiving profits from the efforts of others, and
not where he purchases a commodity for personal consumption
or living quarters for personal use.[25]

[24] Respondents urge us to abandon the element of profits in the definition
of securities and to adopt the "risk capital" approach articulated by the
California Supreme Court in Silver Hills Country Club v. Sobieski, 55 Cal.
2d 811, 361 P. 2d 906 (1961). Cf. El Khadem v. Equity Securities Corp., 494
F. 2d 1224 (C. A. 9), *cert. denied*, 419 U. S. 900 (1974). See generally Coffey,
The Economic Realities of a "Security": Is There a More Meaningful Formula?, 18 W. Res. L. Rev. 367 (1967); Long, An Attempt to Return "Investment Contracts" to the Mainstream of Securities Regulation, 24 Okla. L. Rev.
135 (1971); Hannan & Thomas, The Importance of Economic Reality and
Risk in Defining Federal Securities, 25 Hastings L. J. 219 (1974). Even if we
were inclined to adopt such a "risk capital" approach we would not apply it
in the present case. Purchasers of apartments in Co-op City take no risk in
any significant sense. If dissatisfied with their apartments, they may recover
their initial investment in full. See n. 5, supra.

*   *   *

[25] The SEC has filed an *amicus curiae* brief urging us to hold the federal
securities laws applicable to this case. Traditionally the views of an agency
charged with administering the governing statute would be entitled to considerable weight. * * * But in this case the SEC's position flatly contradicts
what appears to be a rather careful statement of the Commission's views in
a recent release. In Release No. 33-5347, 38 Fed. Reg. 1735 (Jan. 18, 1973),
applicable to the "sale of condominium units, or other units in a real estate
development," the SEC stated its view that only those real estate investments
that are offered and sold with emphasis on the economic benefits to the purchaser to be derived from the managerial efforts of the promoter, or a third
party designated or arranged for by the promoter," are to be considered securities. Id., at 1736. In particular, the Commission explained that the Securities
Acts do not apply when "commercial facilities are a part of the common
elements of a residential project" if "(a) the income from such facilities is
used only to offset common area expenses and (b) the operation of such facilities is incidental to the project as a whole and are not established as a primary income source for the individual owners of a condominium or
cooperative unit." Ibid. * * *

Several commentators have noted the inconsistency between the SEC's
position in the above release and the decision by the Court of Appeals in
this case, which the SEC now supports. * * * In view of this unexplained
contradiction in the Commission's position we accord no special weight to
its views. * * * [The ellipses indicate omitted citations.]

III

* * * We decide only that the type of transaction before us, in which the purchasers were interested in acquiring housing rather than making an investment for profit, is not within the scope of the federal securities laws.

Since respondents' claims are not cognizable in federal court, the District Court properly dismissed their complaint. The judgment below is therefore reversed.

MR. JUSTICE BRENNAN, with whom MR. JUSTICE DOUGLAS and MR. JUSTICE WHITE join, dissenting.

*   *   *

More recently claims have been made that the condominium is superior to the stock cooperative.[10] A condominium is a multi-unit building in which each occupant owns his apartment in fee simple together with a proportionate undivided interest in the common areas.[11] In any event, at the other extreme from either device is the syndication of an office building or of a residential development in which the investor's interest is not equated with residence; the Empire State Building, in effect, "went public" in 1961 by means of the registration of $39 million of participations in the partnership interests of several general partners in Empire State Building Associates, which was to acquire a net 114-year lease on the building and land.[12]

In between is the Florida vacation home that *is* lived in during

[10] See Comment, Community Apartments: Condominium or Stock Cooperative?, 50 Calif. L. Rev. 299 (1962).

[11] On condominiums generally, see Berger, Condominium: Shelter on a Statutory Foundation, 63 Colum. L. Rev. 987 (1963).

[12] SEC File No. 2-18741 (1961). See generally Kroll, The Why and the How of Real Estate Syndications, 14 Record A. B. C. N. Y. 71 (1959), 5 Prac. Law. 70 (Mar. 1959); Berger, Real Estate Syndication: Property, Promotion, and the Need for Protection, 69 Yale L. J. 725 (1960).

Whether or not the SEC statutes apply in the real estate context, the Interstate Land Sales Full Disclosure Act, enacted as Title XIV of the Housing and Urban Development Act of 1968, as amended, 15 U. S. C. §§ 1701 et seq., provides, on the model of §5 of the 1933 Act, that developers selling or leasing ninety-nine or more unimproved lots pursuant to a common promotional plan must file a "statement of record" with the Department of Housing and Urban Development and give each buyer a "property report" forty-eight hours in advance of his commitment. And there is a fraud provision, modeled on §17(a) of the 1933 Act, that applies when the number of unimproved lots is 25 or more. There is also at the state level a Uniform Land Sales Practice Act. 7A U. L. A. 371 (1966).

the winter months but rented out during most of the year. In the release cited by the Supreme Court[13] the Commission published guidelines:[14]

> * * * Resort condominiums are one of the more common interests in real estate the offer of which may involve an offering of securities. However, other types of units that are part of a development or project present analogous questions under the federal securities laws. Although this release speaks in terms of condominiums, it applies to offerings of all types of units in real estate developments which have characteristics similar to those described herein.

*   *   *

> * * * The "profits" that the purchaser is led to expect may consist of revenues received from rental of the unit; these revenues and any tax benefits resulting from rental of the unit are the economic inducements held out to the purchaser.

*   *   *

> In summary, the offering of condominium units in conjunction with any one of the following will cause the offering to be viewed as an offering of securities in the form of investment contracts:
>
> 1. The condominiums, with any rental arrangement or other similar service, are offered and sold with emphasis on the economic benefits to the purchaser to be derived from the managerial efforts of the promoter, or a third party designated or arranged for by the promoter, from rental of the units.
> 2. The offering of participation in a rental pool arrangement; and
> 3. The offering of a rental or similar arrangement whereby the purchaser must hold his unit available for rental for any part of the year, must use an exclusive rental agent or is otherwise materially restricted in his occupancy or rental of his unit.

> In all of the above situations, investor protection requires the application of the federal securities laws.
>
> If the condominiums are not offered and sold with emphasis on the economic benefits to the purchaser to be derived from the managerial efforts of others, and assuming that no plan to avoid

---

[13] 421 U. S. at 858 n. 25.
[14] Sec. Act Rel. 5347 (1973); see Mosher v. Southbridge Associates, Inc., 552 F. Supp. 1231 (W. D. Pa. 1982).

the registration requirements of the Securities Act is involved, an owner of a condominium unit may, after purchasing his unit, enter into a non-pooled rental arrangement with an agent not designated or required to be used as a condition to the purchase, whether or not such agent is affiliated with the offeror, without causing a sale of a security to be involved in the sale of the unit. Further a continuing affiliation between the developers or promoters of a project and the project by reason of maintenance arrangements does not make the unit a security.

In situations where commercial facilities are a part of the common elements of a residential project, no registration would be required under the investment contract theory where (a) the income from such facilities is used only to offset common area expenses and (b) the operation of such facilities is incidental to the project as a whole and are [*sic*] not established as a primary income source for the individual owners of a condominium or cooperative unit.

*   *   *

Another in-between case is stock in a *private* cooperative that *is* the holder's residence — the classic cooperative apartment that has been described as a "child of a marriage of a long-term lease with a stock certificate,"[15] and that, unlike Co-op City, presents the same possibility of capital appreciation as any real estate investment. There the Second Circuit has said there is no security.[16]

Housing cooperatives and condominiums aside, the Supreme Court's perfectly sound conclusion has considerably broader implications: If not all stock is "stock," what about the sale of a *business* (or part of a business) that simply takes the form of a stock transfer. The cases are split, but several courts have read *United Housing Foundation* as applying the *Howey* approach not merely to the "investment contract" phrase but generally — even to the word, "stock."[17]

---

[15] Isaacs, "To Buy or Not to Buy: That Is the Question" * * * What Is a Cooperative Apartment?, 13 Record A. B. C. N. Y. 203, 210 (1958).

[16] Grenader v. Spitz, 537 F. 2d 612 (2d Cir. 1976).

[17] At the appellate level alone: Chandler v. Kew, Inc., 691 F. 2d 443 (10th Cir. 1977); King v. Winkler, 673 F. 2d 342 (11th Cir. 1982); Sutter v. Groen, 687 F. 2d 197 (7th Cir. 1982) (expressly disagreeing with *Golden,* infra). *Contra:* Coffin v. Polishing Machines, Inc., 596 F. 2d 1202 (4th Cir. 1979), *cert. denied,* 444 U. S. 868; Glick v. Campagna, 613 F. 2d 31, 35 n. 3 (3d Cir. 1979); Golden v. Garafolo, 678 F. 2d 1139 (2d Cir. 1982); Cole v. PPG Industries, Inc., 680 F. 2d 549, 555-56 (8th Cir. 1982) (Arkansas statute). There are also negative holdings under the state statutes. Fox v. Ehrmentraut, 28 Cal. 3d 127, 615 P. 2d 1383 (1980); Tech Resources, Inc. v. Estate of Hubbard, 246 Ga. 583, 272 S. E. 2d 314 (1980); Condux v. Neldon, 83 Ill. App. 3d 575, 404 N. E. 2d 523 (1980). Compare Karjala, Realigning Federal and State

This somehow goes against the grain. It is one thing to say that the typical cooperative apartment dweller has bought a home, not a security; or that not every installment purchase "note" is a security; or that a person who charges a restaurant meal by signing his credit card slip is not selling a security even though his signature is an "evidence of indebtedness." But *stock* (except for the residential wrinkle) is so quintessentially a security as to foreclose further analysis. One difficulty with the negative view in the sale-of-business case is that it comes dangerously close to the heresy of saying that the fraud provisions do not apply to private transactions;[18] for nobody, apparently, has had the temerity to argue that the sale of a *publicly* owned business for stock of the acquiring corporation that is distributed to the shareholders of the selling corporation as a liquidating dividend does not involve a security.

4. FRANCHISES

Many of *Howey's* progeny have involved various franchise arrangements. Indeed, one case grew out of a franchise operation on how to run franchise operations.[19] Although *Howey* without more would have sufficed in those cases in which the franchisee virtually sat on his hands and relied "solely" on the franchisor to earn him a return on his investment, the courts have developed two theories for covering even those cases in which the franchisee "makes the hamburgers."

One, which arose under the Hawaii Uniform Securities Act, read the "solely" of *Howey* as referring to the *managerial* efforts of the franchisor. That is to say, since in fact *Howey* involved *no* investment participation, the "solely" was dictum.[20] That holding was soon adopted by the SEC,[21] and at least *obiter* by the Supreme

---

Roles in Securities Regulation through the Definition of a Security, 1982 U. Ill. L. F. 413 (affirmative), with Thompson, The Shrinking Definition of a Security: Why Purchasing All of a Company's Stock Is Not a Federal Security Transaction, 52 N. Y. U. L. Rev. 225 (1982) (negative). See also Rapp, Federal Securities Laws Should Protect Some Purchases of All or Substantially All of a Corporation's Stock, 32 Case W. Res. L. Rev. 59 (1982).

[18] On the other hand, there are holdings under the blue sky laws (as well as contrary holdings, depending on the circumstances) to the effect that one of several promoters of a close corporation has no action against the others based on the "sale" of a "security." See pp. 242-43 infra.

[19] Lino v. City Investing Co., 487 F. 2d 689 (3d Cir. 1973).

[20] State v. Hawaii Market Center, Inc., 52 Hawaii 642, 485 P. 2d 108 (1971).

[21] Sec. Act Rel. 5211 (1971).

Court when it referred in the cooperative housing case to the "entrepreneurial or managerial efforts of others."[22]

The other technique for extending *Howey* — which the Hawaii court used in tandem with the first[23] — is the so-called "risk capital" theory. That theory, which originated in a 1961 opinion of Justice Traynor of the California Supreme Court, has it that a security is involved regardless of the franchisee's activities when the franchisees provide the "risk capital" for the business."[24]

California and a number of other states now have special franchise investment statutes that interrelate in various ways with their blue sky laws.[25]

E. INSURANCE AND BANK HYBRIDS

1. INSURANCE HYBRIDS[1]

The current trend toward "one-stop financial marketing," together with the increasing competition of the securities, insurance, and banking industries for the business of managing the billions of private pension funds, has resulted in the development of interesting — and to no little extent perplexing — hybrids.

[22] United Housing Foundation, Inc. v. Forman, 421 U. S. 837, 852 (1975); see also id. at 852 n. 16. For a square holding under the federal legislation, see SEC v. Glenn W. Turner Enterprises, Inc., 474 F. 2d 476 (9th Cir. 1973), *cert. denied,* 414 U. S. 821; SEC v. Koscot Interplanetary, Inc., 497 F. 2d 473 (5th Cir. 1974).

[23] See also Pacific Coast Coin Exchange of Canada v. Ontario Securities Commission, [1978] 2 S. Ct. Can. 112, 80 D. L. R. 2d 529, a case involving the sale of bags of silver coins.

[24] Silver Hills Country Club v. Sobieski, 55 Cal. 2d 811, 814-16, 361 P. 2d 906, 908-09 (1961), followed in 49 Ops. Cal. Att. Gen. 124, CCH Blue Sky L. Rep. ¶70,747 (1967). At the time of these opinions the California definition included any "beneficial interest or title to property, profits, or earnings." In its original form §2(1) included the comparable phrase, "certificate of interest in property, tangible or intangible," which was removed in the 1934 amendments as perhaps involving "too broad and uncertain application." H. R. Rep. No. 1838, 73d Cong., 2d Sess. (1934) 39. Moreover, Justice Traynor's opinion involved memberships in a new country club. But the Attorney General's opinion was directed to franchise operations. See also, e. g., Mitzner v. Cardet Int'l, Inc., 358 F. Supp. 1262 (N. D. Ill. 1973); but cf. Bitter v. Hobey Int'l, Inc., 498 F. 2d 183 (9th Cir. 1974). See generally Stevenson and O'Leary, Definition of a Security: Risk Capital and Investment Contracts in Washington, 3 U. Puget Sound L. Rev. 83 (1980).

[25] See Cal. Franchise Investment Law, Cal. Corp. Code §§31,000-19.

C. 3E   [1] In order to discount for a possible bias, the reader should know that for some years the writer has been special counsel on securities matters to the American Council of Life Insurance and one of its predecessors, the American Life Convention.

Our story starts with §3(a)(8) of the 1933 Act, which exempts "Any insurance or endowment policy or annuity contract or optional annuity contract, issued by a corporation subject to the supervision of the insurance commissioner, bank commissioner, or any agency or officer performing like functions, of any State or Territory of the United States or the District of Columbia."

This is a perfect example of how it sometimes does not pay to be too cautious. True, all forms of insurance except term have some investment element, and insurance companies are among the largest institutional investors. But without this exemption, and without any specific reference to insurance policies in the definition of "security," and at a time when *Paul* v. *Virginia* was still the law of the land,[2] it is hardly conceivable that Congress would have subjected insurance policies to federal control *sub silentio,* even control of the disclosure variety. As it is, §3(a)(8) seems on its face to create a negative implication that insurance policies *are* securities, which are exempt from the registration requirements but are subject to the antifraud provisions. Nevertheless, the Commission early took the position that insurance or endowment, policies or annuity contracts issued by regularly constituted insurance companies were not intended to be securities, and that in effect §3(a)(8) is supererogation.[3] This undoubtedly carries out the legislative intention; for the House report states that the purpose of the exemption "makes clear what is already implied in the act, namely, that insurance policies are not to be regarded as securities subject to the provisions of the act."[4] And it has been held under a number of the blue sky laws that orthodox annuity contracts issued by life insurance companies are not securities.[5]

The question of categorization as between the two major fields

---

[2] 8 Wall. 168 (U. S. 1869), overruled by United States v. South-Eastern Underwriters Assn., 322 U. S. 533 (1944).

[3] See the writer's testimony on behalf of the Commission in Securities Exchange Acts Amendments, Hearings before Subcom. of Senate Com. on Banking & Currency on S. 2408, 81st Cong., 2d Sess. (1950) 33. The Supreme Court has referred *obiter* to the exemption as "clearly supererogation." Tcherepnin v. Knight, 389 U. S. 332, 342 n. 30 (1967); see also Grainger v. State Security Life Ins. Co., 547 F. 2d 303, 305 (5th Cir. 1977), *rehearing denied,* 563 F. 2d 215 (5th Cir. 1977), *cert. denied,* 436 U. S. 932.

[4] H. R. Rep. No. 85, 73d Cong., 1st Sess. (1933) 15, cited in SEC v. Variable Annuity Life Ins. Co. of America, 359 U. S. 65, 74 n. 4 (1959) (Brennan, J., concurring).

[5] E. g., Haberman v. Equitable Life Assurance Society, 224 F. 2d 401, *corrected on rehearing,* 225 F. 2d 837 (5th Cir. 1955), *cert. denied,* 350 U. S. 948 (phrase "or other evidence of indebtedness" must be construed *ejusdem generis* in Texas act; nor is annuity "any other instrument commonly known as a security").

of insurance (in the generic sense of the term as including annuities) and securities arose most acutely with the development of the so-called "variable annuity" in the mid-1950s. The variable annuity was the answer of an important segment of the insurance industry to the problem of tailoring the traditional annuity to an inflationary economy. The distinguishing feature of the variable annuity is that the annuitant's payments purchase units in a fund of securities, much as in the case of an open-end investment company. The accumulation in the annuitant's account is valued at maturity, and the insurance company promises to pay him thereafter not a fixed number of dollars monthly but the dollar value, fluctuating with each monthly payment as the value of the portfolio fluctuates, of the annuity units to which it is determined at maturity that the annuitant is entitled on the basis of capital contribution, age, and sex. That is to say, the first payment after maturity is determined by reference to standard annuity tables, on the basis of an assumed net investment rate of a certain percentage per annum, but the figure thus obtained is converted to annuity units by dividing it by the then value of an annuity unit. Thereafter the number of annuity units held by the annuitant remains constant, but the dollar value of a unit and hence the amount of subsequent monthly payments fluctuate as the value of the portfolio goes up or down.[6]

Of course, this marriage of the insurance and mutual fund concepts would not work unless the buyers' funds were invested in common stocks. But today all the the states, as well as Congress for the District of Columbia, have adjusted their insurance statutes or regulations in one way or another to permit the issuance of variable contracts.

At the state level the Uniform Securities Act made explicit what seemed to be the view of the great majority of blue sky administrators in the mid-1950s to the effect that variable annuities were securities, which should not be exempted from registration. But the appropriate clauses were inserted in brackets in 1958, so that they could be deleted by any state that might conclude that variable annuities were sufficiently regulated by the insurance authorities to warrant excluding them from the blue sky law along with

[6] See generally G. Johnson and D. Grubbs, The Variable Annuity (2d ed. 1970); Frankel, Variable Annuities, Variable Insurance and Separate Accounts, 51 B. U. L. Rev. 173 (1971); T. Frankel, The Regulation of Money Managers: The Investment Company Act and the Investment Advisers Act (1978) *passim;* Proceedings of Conference on Variable Annuities and Variable Life Insurance, 32 Bus. Law. 675 (1977).

orthodox annuities.[7] And the original version is now law in only a handful of jurisdictions.

The problem at the federal level was more difficult, not only because §3(a)(8) of the Securities Act exempts any "annuity contract" issued by a corporation subject to the supervision of some insurance authority, without further qualification, but also because Congress, promptly after the Supreme Court had overruled *Paul v. Virginia* in 1944, had declared in the McCarran-Ferguson Insurance Regulation Act that "No Act of Congress shall be construed to invalidate, impair or supersede any law enacted by any State for the purpose of regulating the business of insurance."[8] Nevertheless, the SEC in 1956 sued in the District of Columbia to enjoin a local life insurance company, Variable Annuity Life Insurance Company (known as VALIC), from selling variable annuities without registration under both the Securities Act and the Investment Company Act. The District Court, finding that the contracts had characteristics of both securities and insurance, concluded that both statutes would apply "if it were not for the clear and explicit language of the McCarran Act and the fact that the defendants [a second similar company had intervened] are licensed and regulated by the insurance departments of this District and the States where they operate." The Court of Appeals affirmed on the ground that "The definitions in the Securities Act and the Investment Company Act indicate that if the insurance commissioner of a state subjects the business to his supervision, it is the business of insurance." The Supreme Court reversed by a vote of five to four. The majority, though bowing to the long tradition of regulating "insurance" at the state level, emphasized that the words "insurance" and "annuity" had to be construed as federal terms in a federal statute. And they concluded that, although those concepts should not be frozen into the mold they fitted when the federal statutes were passed, "the concept of 'insurance' involves some investment risk-taking on the part of the company" — "a guarantee that at least some fraction of the benefits will be payable in fixed amounts." The dissenters, emphasizing that these were not cases where the label "annuity" had simply been attached to a securities scheme in an effort to avoid federal regulation, were unable to join in what was termed the majority's "preoccupation with a constricted 'color matching' approach to the construction of the relevant federal statutes which fails to take adequate account

[7] §§401(l), 402(a)(5).
[8] §2, 15 U. S. C. §1012.

of the historic congressional policy of leaving regulation of the business of insurance entirely to the States."[9]

The *VALIC* case inevitably left a number of both conceptual and practical problems in its wake, particularly with respect to the application of the Investment Company Act, which our "story line" cannot ignore despite our primary concern with the Securities Act. At times during and after the litigation, as it later appeared, the Commission was perhaps overinclined to analyze the variable annuity in terms of whether its investment or insurance characteristics predominated. But it soon recognized that a variable annuity was neither solely an investment contract nor solely an insurance contract, and that the insurance and investment elements could be segregated with sufficient precision so that the former might be regulated by the state insurance authorities and the latter by the Commission.

VALIC was organized to be purely a variable annuity company. The typical structure that the Commission contemplated in the case of an established insurance company that sought to sell variable annuities (backed by the assets in a legally separate account for the benefit of variable annuity contract holders) was the incorporation by the insurance company of an investment fund as an open-end management investment company that would be registered under the 1940 Act, with the insurance company holding the shares of the "investment company," and as a practical matter controlling it, but with a "pass-through" of voting power from the insurance company to the contract holders; and the insurance company might enter into an advisory contract with the "investment company." Under the practice that has evolved, however,

[9] SEC v. Variable Annuity Life Ins. Co. of America, 155 F. Supp. 521, 526 (D. D. C. 1957), *aff'd,* 257 F. 2d 201, 205 (D. C. Cir. 1958), *rev'd,* 359 U. S. 65, 71, 96 (1959). The concurring opinion of Justice Brennan contains a more reasoned exposition of the insurance-security dichotomy than Justice Douglas's opinion for the Court. Dean Landis, one of the principal draftsmen of the 1933 Act, wrote after this case that no member of the conference committee, where the exemption originated, "could possibly have envisaged that some two decades later the traditional annuity contract would be turned into this type of a pro rata interest in a group of securities," and that Justice Harlan's dissenting opinion misread the history of the Act in several respects. Landis, The Legislative History of the Securities Act of 1933, 28 Geo. Wash. L. Rev. 29, 47 n. 24 (1959).

Of course, the Supreme Court's ruling that variable annuities were "securities" within the 1933 Act is necessarily a holding that the McCarran-Ferguson Act does not bar the application of that statute to the issuance of securities by insurance companies. For a later interpretation of the McCarran-Ferguson Act, in the context of the SEC's proxy rules, see SEC v. National Securities, Inc., 393 U. S. 453 (1969).

there have been certain modifications of this pattern, as we shall
see.

Prudential, the champion of the variable annuity among the
traditional insurance companies, ultimately conceded that it was
governed by the Supreme Court decision as far as registration
under the Securities Act was concerned notwithstanding the fact
that its long-established business in standard insurance would
dwarf its proposed business in variable annuities. But it insisted
that, even though a company that sold variable annuities exclusively might not come within the categorical exclusion of any
"insurance company" from the definition of an "investment company" by §3(c)(3) of the 1940 Act, Prudential certainly was an
"insurance company." It accordingly sought a declaratory order
from the Commission to that effect, or in the alternative a number
of exemptions. The Commission denied the application, and its
order was affirmed on judicial review.

Prudential, the Commission said, "is not itself an investment
company, but it is the creator of one — and proposes to be its
'investment adviser' and 'principal underwriter.' "[10] Insurance
companies, in its view, were excluded from the definition of "investment company" only because they would otherwise fall within
the statute by reason of the investment activities that were a necessary ingredient of their insurance business. In short, the fact that
a pure variable annuity life insurance company might itself register as an "investment company" did not mean that the same means
of compliance with the statute should apply to a company like
Prudential. In its case the "investment company" that would register would be not a subsidiary corporation but the separate fund
created by Prudential to make possible the sale of variable annuities; for §3(a) of the Investment Company Act defines "investment
company" to mean any "issuer" that does certain things and
§2(a)(21) defines "issuer" in terms of a "person" and §2(a)(27)
defines "person" to include a "company" and §2(a)(8) defines
"company" to include a "fund."

Thus was born what has become irreverently known as the
Commission's "ectoplasmic theory." The fund may or may not
have a legal identity for ordinary purposes. For example, the
enabling provision in the New York Insurance Law, on the one
hand, insulates the separate account from the other business of
the company[11] and, on the other hand, specifies that the assets in

---

[10] Prudential Ins. Co. of America, 41 SEC 335, 340-41 (1963), *aff'd sub nom.*
Prudential Ins. Co. of America v. SEC, 326 F. 2d 383 (3d Cir. 1964), *cert.
denied,* 377 U. S. 953.

[11] §227.1(d).

all separate accounts "shall be the property of the insurer."[12] But, be that as it may, for purposes of the Investment Company Act the separate account is an "investment company" distinct from the insurance company. And it seems to be the Commission's view that the "security" is not the variable contract but the "accumulation unit," which "must be located, despite any difficulty in the wording of a particular form of contract."[13] If all this startles at first blush, it must be remembered that a corporation, too, is a *persona ficta;* one gets used to the idea.

By now a considerable number of these "ectoplasms" have been registered, although sometimes, for a variety of reasons, the insurance company creates a wholly owned subsidiary that in turn creates a separate account to be the registrant under both Acts,[14] with the subsidiary acting as its investment adviser and underwriter. Some sort of committee is created to act as the fund's "board of directors," and it is the members of that pseudo-board rather than the directors of the insurance company itself that (1) are elected by the contract holders so as to meet the requirement in §16(a) of the Act and (2) have to comply with §10, on affiliations of directors.

It is not easy to reconcile the "ectoplasmic" concept of an autonomous management for the separate account with (1) the common requirement of the insurance laws (like the corporation laws generally) that the corporation's board of directors is responsible for the conduct of its affairs and (2) the difficulties with respect to any blanket delegation of that responsibility. But the variable annuity laws and regulations of many states now provide for control of the separate account's assets by its board of managers. And, for the rest, the difficulty of fitting an "ectoplasm" on the 1940 Act's Procrustean bed — an image that is a pretty good test of a legal mind — has been ameliorated by the Commission's use of its plenary power under §6(c) of that Act to exempt by either rule or order.[15]

Meanwhile the question remains, even under the 1933 Act, of determining *how much* risk an insurance company must assume in order to avoid SEC jurisdiction. A so-called Flexible Fund Annuity that was obviously designed, by an old-line insurance

---

[12] §227.1(j).

[13] Prudential Ins. Co. of America, supra n. 10, 41 SEC at 347.

[14] The administrative view is that the insurance company (or the subsidiary) is a co-issuer. See p. 681 n. 16 infra; 4 Loss 2522.

[15] In 1969 the Commission adopted a series of rules to codify some of its *ad hoc* exemptions. See Inv. Co. Act Rel. 5738.

company (as distinct from a company like VALIC), to impose just enough investment risk-taking on the company to satisfy the VALIC formula resulted in a second Supreme Court decision ten years later, this time by a bench that followed *VALIC* unanimously.[16] So far as the Investment Company Act is concerned, the Court adopted the Commission's suggestion that it remand the case for further consideration of the question — which the courts below had not reached because of their view that the contract itself was exempt — whether the "Flexible Fund" was an "investment company." In observing that this question was a "difficult one"[17] and that United Benefit, unlike VALIC, was in the main an insurance company exempted from the Investment Company Act, without citing the Third Circuit's opinion in the *Prudential* case, the Court seems to have invited the Court of Appeals to consider as a fresh issue the status under the Investment Company Act of a conventional insurance company that issues a security in the nature of a variable annuity. At that point, however, United Benefit Life apparently lost its stomach for litigation, so that this particular symphony will remain unfinished.

Still another congeries of "security" and related problems is presented by the diversity of *group* annuity contracts with a variable element that have been developed in recent years, to some extent in response to the Self-Employed Individuals Tax Retirement Act of 1962, popularly known as the Keogh Act or "H. R. 10," which permits self-employed persons to enjoy in some measure the tax deferral privileges available to corporate employees in connection with qualified pension plans.[18]

The *Prudential* case provides no direct teaching with respect to group contracts. For, although Prudential intended to offer group as well as individual variable contracts, the Third Circuit followed the Commission in excluding group plans from the scope of its opinion in the light of the fact that the Commission was dealing with the problems of group plans in its administrative capacity.[19] In this state of affairs all that can be said is that these

[16] SEC v. United Benefit Life Ins. Co., 387 U. S. 202 (1967), *rev'g* 359 F. 2d 619 (D. C. Cir. 1966); see also Peoria Union Stock Yards Co. Retirement Plan v. Penn Mutual Life Ins. Co., 698 F. 2d 320 (7th Cir. 1983); cf. Grainger v. State Security Life Ins. Co., 547 F. 2d 303 (5th Cir. 1977), *rehearing denied,* 563 F. 2d 215 (5th Cir. 1977); but cf. Olpin v. Ideal National Ins. Co., 419 F. 2d 1250 (10th Cir. 1969), *cert. denied,* 397 U. S. 1074.

[17] 387 U. S. at 212.

[18] 76 Stat. 809 (1962), amending Int. Rev. Code §401, 26 U. S. C. §401, etc.; for a succinct description of that act, see Mundheim and Henderson, Applicability of the Federal Securities Laws to Pension and Profit-Sharing Plans, 29 Law & Contemp. Prob. 795, 797-800 (1964).

[19] 326 F. 2d at 384 n. 1.

contracts seem sufficiently different from *variable* annuities sold *individually* — in their historical development from the group annuity contracts that have been written for over forty years (with participation by the employer one way or another in the insurer's experience with respect to investment earnings, mortality and expenses), in the material risks assumed by the insurer, in the motivation and character of the persons (usually substantial employers) to whom the contracts are sold, and in the general manner of their negotiation and sale — so that it certainly cannot be assumed that the Supreme Court would follow *VALIC* and its sequel. After all, the SEC won *VALIC* by one vote, and there have been changes in the Court.

At any rate, after the Commission had experimented with exemptive rules, Congress in 1970 amended §3(a)(2) of the 1933 Act and §3(a)(12) of the 1934 Act so that (as further amended in essentially technical respects in 1980) they exempt "any security arising out of a contract issued by an insurance company" in connection with employee plans that come within specified sections of the Internal Revenue Code. Congress likewise amended §3(c)(11) of the Investment Company Act (as it is now numbered) to exclude substantially the same plans from the definition of "investment company." But the 1933 Act exemption does not apply (1) if any part of the corpus or income in excess of the employer's contribution is allocated to the purchase of securities of the employer or an affiliate or (2) with respect to "Keogh plans."[20] The former exception precludes use of exempt employee plans as an indirect method of financing the employer, and the second reflects the thought that self-employed persons unsophisticated in the securities field should have at least the disclosure protections of the 1933 Act in view of the fairly complex nature of "Keogh plans" as an equity investment.

Section 3(a)(2) does provide that the Commission in its discretion "shall" exempt interests in "Keogh plans" by rule or order. And the Commission, after repeatedly exercising its order authority in the case typically of law or brokerage or accounting partnerships that did not fall within the statutory exemption for corporate plans,[21] adopted Rule 180 in late 1981 in order essentially to codify these *ad hoc* exemptions.[22] It also took the occasion to endorse

---

[20] See p. 220 supra.

[21] E. g., Salomon Brothers Profit Sharing Plan, Sec. Act Rel. 5852, 12 SEC Dock. 1462 (1977). Quite a few "Keogh plans" also function under either the intrastate exemption in §3(a)(11) (infra c. 5C) or the private offering exemption (infra c. 5E).

[22] Sec. Act Rel. 6363, 24 SEC Dock. 68 (1981).

its staff's view that there are two securities in these cases, both of which fall within the exemption: the interest of the plan in the trust or insurance company separate account in which plan assets are invested, and, when employees voluntarily contribute, their interests in the plan.[23]

So far we have been speaking of variable annuities. Now what about variable life insurance?[24] Equity-linked insurance policies have been available in different forms in the Netherlands since about 1960, in Great Britain since about 1970, and more recently in Canada.

The Commission and the industry disagree on the applicability of the *VALIC* case. The industry contends that, "as long as insurance protection and mortality considerations are dominant, principal and central, and investment aspects are subordinate, secondary, and auxiliary," there is no security.[25] At the same time, the industry is trying to live with the Commission's view: that apart from limited exemptions from the Investment Company Act,[26] variable life insurance is subject to regulation under all the SEC statutes (including the 1934 Act's broker-dealer registration provisions and the Investment Advisers Act) in conjunction with state insurance laws and regulations.[27]

[23] Sec. Act Rel. 6188, 19 SEC Dock. 465, 467 (1980); see also Sec. Act Rel. 6281, 21 SEC Dock. 1372, 1378-79 (1981).

[24] In addition to the citations in n. 6 supra, see D. Olson and H. Winkleboss (eds.), Variable Life Insurance: Current Issues and Developments (1971).

[25] The quotation is from Kroll and Cohen, The Insurance-Security Identity Crisis, 46 Geo. Wash. L. Rev. 790 (1978), a perceptive essay on the drawing of the line.

[26] See Rules 6c-3, 6e-2, adopted by Inv. Co. Act Rel. 9482, 10 SEC Dock. 751 (1976). Rule 6e-2 defines "variable life insurance contract." These exemptions are based in part on the exemptions granted by order in Equitable Variable Life Ins. Co., Inv. Co. Act Rel. 8888, 7 SEC Dock. 588 (1975). That was the first company to offer variable life insurance. Today there are four, with several more in registration. Unlike the situation with respect to variable annuities, where the "security" is considered to be the "accumulation unit" rather than the variable contract (see p. 219 supra), the "security" here is necessarily the life insurance policy itself. For here the policy holder has no ownership interest in the separate account. Rather, the separate account is used as an index in the sense that the policy holder's benefits may go up (or down) in accordance with the results of the separate account.

[27] Inv. Co. Act Rel. 7644, 1 SEC Dock. No. 1, p. 1 (1973). The Code excludes from the definition of "security" — so that even the fraud provisions do not apply — any "insurance policy" issued by an "insurance company" as defined, as well as any "annuity contract" under which an "insurance company" "promises to pay one or more sums of money that are fixed or vary in accordance with a cost-of-living index or on any other basis specified by rule." §202(150)(B)(vi)-(vii). And the comments state:

(b) Section 202(150)(B)(vii) does nothing more than recognize the holdings in SEC v. Variable Annuity Life Ins. Co. of America, 359 U. S.

More recently the life insurance industry has been developing other novel products. In 1977 the Commission invited comment with respect to the offer and sale of certain contractual arrangements issued by life insurance companies and generally known as "guaranteed investment, interest or income contracts, tax deferred annuity contracts and similar products":

> The contracts which are the subject of study by the staff take a variety of forms but, in general, they provide for the payment of money to a life insurance company (in a single sum or in installments); include promises by the insurer to pay interest at a guaranteed rate with or without the possibility of excess interest; and permit the purchase of an annuity at a future date at an annuity purchase rate which may or may not be guaranteed in the contracts. They appear to be of two basic types: contracts which guarantee a low rate of interest and provide for the possibility that excess interest will be credited by the insurance company ("excess interest contracts") and contracts which guarantee a relatively high rate of interest and generally are written for a short period of time (5 to 12 years) ("high interest contracts").

> *   *   *

> * * * the emphasis in the advertising and marketing of these contracts is clearly on their use as investment vehicles for the accumulation of capital. * * * In addition, an insurance company may have its own agents distributing all its other products but choose to have these new contracts distributed through broker-dealers.[28]

Two years later, however, the Commission opted for guidelines rather than rulemaking.[29] Stating that §3(a)(8) requires a "significant assumption of *both* kinds of risks," mortality and investment, and that it will often be necessary to review the promotional materials and sales methods, the Commission expounded specifically on so-called deposit funds:

---

65 (1959), and SEC v. United Benefit Life Ins. Co., 387 U. S. 202 (1967). and is intended to be illustrative, not exclusive. That is to say, the question whether other non-traditional insurance company products are "securities" is not foreclosed. At the same time, the language has been phrased to exclude from the definition annuities that vary with some cost-of-living index — a type of variable that clearly does not create a security — or on any other basis specified by rule.

(c) With respect to variable *insurance,* which is still in the process of gestation, it seems best to leave the language unelucidated.

28 Sec. Act Rel. 5838, 12 SEC Dock. 915, 916-17 (1977).
29 Sec. Act Rel. 6050, 17 SEC Dock. 182 (1979).

Certain deposit fund riders, which may be marketed in conjunction with either a life insurance policy or an annuity contract, appear to be designed to function as an alternative to a bank savings account. Such arrangements ordinarily provide that: (1) a basic premium must be paid for the annuity or life insurance; (2) additional sums contributed by the investor are held on deposit by the insurance company; and (3) interest is credited on such deposits at a rate which might change from time to time. The contract may provide that sums accumulated during the accumulation period may be used, at a later date, to purchase an annuity at guaranteed purchase rates or to purchase other forms of insurance protection. Often, the investor is permitted to withdraw money from the deposit fund at will.

* * * the fact that a deposit fund rider is attached to, or made a non-integral, merely incidental feature of, a life insurance or annuity contract entitled to rely on Section 3(a)(8), cannot by itself bring within Section 3(a)(8) those deposit fund riders which are offered primarily as investments where the purchaser assumes substantial investment risks.[30]

The §3(a)(2) exemption is broad enough since the 1980 amendments to include guaranteed investment contracts and other arrangements sold to tax-qualified plans that are funded by an insurance company's *general* account (as distinct from a separate account).[31]

The difficulty with all these insurance hybrids — and there will be more — is that, in the last analysis, there is no escaping the fact that there is a continuous spectrum from a one-year term life insurance policy, which is pure insurance, through the various forms of straight life and endowment policies, to annuities and life insurance, both fixed and (in varying degrees) variable, to mutual fund shares and ultimately common stock, which represent pure investment.

2. Bank Hybrids

The variable annuity experience, together with the 1962 statute that transferred authority over the trust powers of national banks from the Board of Governors of the Federal Reserve System to

---

[30] Sec. Act Rel. 6051, 17 SEC Dock. 190, 194 (1979). But cf. Olpin v. Ideal National Ins. Co., 419 F. 2d 1250 (10th Cir. 1969), *cert. denied*, 397 U. S. 1074.

[31] The staff had previously taken a "no action" position with respect to guaranteed investment contracts if specified conditions were met. Sec. Act Rel. 6188, 19 SEC Dock. 465, 468 (1980).

the Comptroller of the Currency,[32] forced the SEC to take a position with respect to the activities of banks when they commingle customers' investments in one form or another.

The Board's Regulation F did not prohibit national banks from operating *individual* "managing agency accounts" (that is to say, accounts in which banks act not as trustees but simply as investment advisers on an agency basis) for a fee. It simply limited *commingling* of those accounts to "common trust funds" (that is to say, as the term was defined in Regulation F[33] and still is in §584(a) of the Internal Revenue Code, funds maintained by a bank "exclusively for the collective investment and reinvestment of monies contributed thereto by the bank in its capacity as a trustee, executor, administrator, or guardian") or, when authorized by the trust instrument or court order, employee plans.[34] But banks could not accept small managing agency accounts as a practical matter because they were too expensive to administer. And the operation of common trust funds "as investment trusts for other than strictly fiduciary purposes" was prohibited, as was any publicizing of the earnings of the funds or the value of their assets.

Even then the Commission had an uneasy feeling about interests in these commingled funds. For, quite apart from the fraud provisions, the §3(a)(2) exemption for "any security issued or guaranteed by any bank," as well as the exclusion of any "bank" from the definition of "investment company" in §3(c)(3) of the 1940 Act, has always been understood as applying to the bank itself and securities with a claim against the bank's assets (a construction substantially confirmed in the 1970 amendment of §3(a) (2) to the effect that "a security issued or guaranteed by a bank shall not include any interest or participation in any collective trust fund maintained by a bank"). Rightly or wrongly, the Commission's rationale for staying its hand in those days was the exemption in §4(2) of the Securities Act for transactions "not involving any public offering." This rationale also served to reenforce the position of nonaction under the Investment Company Act insofar as §3(c)(1) of that statute excludes from the definition of "investment company" any issuer whose outstanding securities are beneficially owned by not more than one hundred persons and "which is not making and does not presently propose to make a public offering of its securities."

The Commission's hand was forced when the Comptroller of

---

[32] 76 Stat. 668, 12 U. S. C. §92a.
[33] §10(c), 2 Fed. Reg. 2976 (1937), as amended, 20 Fed. Reg. 3305 (1955).
[34] Id., §17(a).

the Currency in 1963 revised his Regulation 9 (as the Board's Regulation F had been redesignated) by not only abandoning the Board's "bona fide fiduciary purpose" concept but also permitting collective investment (when not in contravention of local law) in (1) a fund consisting of assets of tax-exempt trusts or (2) a so-called "common trust fund, maintained by the bank exclusively for the collective investment and reinvestment of monies contributed thereto by the bank in its capacity as managing agent under a managing agency agreement expressly providing that such monies are received by the bank in trust."[35]

It is still provided that no bank administering a collective investment fund may "issue any certificate or other document evidencing a direct or indirect interest in such fund in any form."[36] But the passage of the Keogh Act very substantially expanded the tax-exempt category, and the other was specifically intended to permit the commingling of managing agency accounts.[37]

All this led to a clash between the Comptroller and the Commission in both the courts and Congress. The *banks'* objections to SEC encroachment were probably based not only on a natural enough disinclination to become subject to the jurisdiction of yet another federal regulatory agency, but also on the fear that their submission might be construed as an admission that they were violating the Glass-Steagall Banking Act of 1933, which divorced commercial from investment banking. That fear proved to be well founded, as we shall see in a moment.

The logjam began to break in late 1963. Prudential filed a registration statement under the Securities Act for interests in a "Keogh fund." A few weeks later, the National Bank of Detroit ruptured the banking industry's solid front by filing a similar registration statement. Soon a number of registrations became

[35] Reg. 9, §9.18(a), 12 C. F. R. §9.18(a).

[36] Id., §9.18(b)(13).

[37] The Comptroller redefined "managing agent" in a 1964 amendment of Regulation 9 as a relationship that imposes upon the bank "the fiduciary responsibilities imposed upon trustees under will or deed"; and that is when the description of the managing agency common trust fund was changed to require that the managing agency agreement provide expressly that the bank shall hold the monies received "in trust." §§9.1(g), 9.18(a)(3). These amendments were intended to facilitate the ruling that the Internal Revenue Service had issued in early 1964 to the effect that a collective managing agency fund maintained pursuant to Regulation 9 would qualify as a "common trust fund" under §584 of the Code. Rev. Rul. 64-59, [1964]-1 Cum. Bul. 193. Since a common trust fund would be financially improbable without this tax exemption and §584 extends only to funds that comply with the regulations governing common trust funds of national banks, Regulation 9 actually affects all banks, state as well as national, that establish common trust funds.

effective for commingled bank funds used as the investment media for "Keogh plans" sponsored by associations like the American Bar Association and the American Medical Association. And finally, in August 1965, the First National City Bank of New York (now Citibank), having obtained the Comptroller's approval of a collective investment fund for managing agency accounts with a minimum value of $10,000, applied for a number of exemptions from the Investment Company Act, with a view to registering under the Securities Act if its application should be granted, as it was.[38]

The Commission's order followed by a day the opening of hearings on the most recent of a series of exemptive bills, and the Comptroller inexplicably canceled his appearance. This combination of the First National City Bank exemptive order and the Comptroller's *volte face* seemed to put the quietus on the pending bill.

A few weeks later, however, the NASD sought judicial review of the Commission's order in the Court of Appeals for the District of Columbia Circuit, and the Investment Company Institute (together with a few of its members) sued the Comptroller of the Currency in the District Court for the District of Columbia for a declaratory judgment to the effect that his permitting national banks to sponsor their own mutual funds violated the provisions of the Banking Act on divorcement of investment and commercial banking. The ICI won below. The Court of Appeals, deciding both cases together, sustained both the SEC and the Comptroller. On the banking laws, the court held that the words "security" and "underwriter" in the Securities Act were "terms of art with a high gloss" whose "expansive definitions under the Securities Act cannot be imported wholesale into the Glass-Steagall Act when the two statutes serve different purposes." The Supreme Court took the opposite view and reversed the *ICI* case, thus vacating the *NASD* case as moot.[39]

It seems quite clear from Justice Stewart's opinion that, if the banking laws were to be amended to allow pooled managing agency accounts, the SEC statutes would apply. Meanwhile, just as United Benefit Life tested the boundaries of *VALIC*,[40] First

---

[38] First National City Bank, 42 SEC 924 (1966), *rehearing denied,* Inv. Co. Act Rel. 4563 (1966).

[39] Investment Company Institute v. Camp, 274 F. Supp. 624 (D. D. C. 1967), *rev'd* sub nom. NASD v. SEC, 420 F. 2d 83, 89 (D. C. Cir. 1969), *rev'd* sub nom. Investment Company Institute v. Camp, 401 U. S. 617 (1971).

[40] See pp. 219-20 supra.

National City Bank tested the *ICI* case by introducing a Special Investment Advisory Service whereby the Bank gave Merrill Lynch investment direction over a group of accounts, each at least $25,000 in size, to be managed on a uniform basis. Merrill Lynch charged nothing for custody and bookkeeping, since its compensation came from commissions. The SEC alleged in a complaint for injunction that the Service was an unregistered "investment company" with a present value of some $35 million and more than 1000 security holders. And the case was settled on terms that left the bank free to offer a service, on a nondiscretionary basis only, pursuant to which it would make investment recommendations for a fee and any person deciding to act on the recommendations would transfer an order to a broker-dealer selected from a list of at least three provided by the bank.[41]

The Comptroller has also permitted various kinds of automatic investment services, which permit customers to buy any of a preselected list of common stocks by means of a predetermined monthly charge to their checking accounts, as well as dividend reinvestment plans by arrangement with issuers.[42] The SEC status of these mutations is not yet clear. There have been some "no action" letters, although the question seems a bit closer with respect to dividend reinvestment plans because of the issuer's involvement.[43]

So far as tax-exempt plans are concerned, Congress treated banks as it did insurance companies in 1970.[44] And the Code proposes a novel treatment of the "mini-account" problem — how to provide a needed service to the investor who cannot quite afford custom-tailored investment advice — by defining "mini-account client" and relying on regulation of the investment advisory rather than the Securities Act and Investment Company Act types.[45]

[41] SEC v. First National City Bank, Litig. Rel. 4534 (S. D. N. Y. 1970).

[42] Comptroller of Currency letter, June 10, 1974, CCH Fed. Sec. L. Rep. ¶79,817.

[43] See Sec. Act Rel. 5515, 4 SEC Dock. 623 (1974).

[44] See p. 221 supra. Congress concurrently amended §3(a)(2) of the 1933 Act and §3(a)(12) of the 1934 Act to exempt "any interest or participation in any common trust fund or similar fund maintained by a bank exclusively for the collective investment and reinvestment of assets contributed thereto by such bank in its capacity as trustee, executor, administrator, or guardian." See the definition of "common trust fund" in Securities Act Rule 132 and Exchange Act Rule 3a12-6.

[45] §§202(80)(B)(xiv), 202(95), 202(150)(B)(ix), 914(c); see 1 Code 396-407. See generally Wade, Bank-Sponsored Collective Investment Funds: An Analysis of Applicable Federal Banking and Securities Laws, 35 Bus. Law. 361 (1980).

F. EMPLOYEE BENEFIT PLANS

With respect to those benefit plans of various kinds that are *not* administered or funded through an insurance company or a bank or an investment company, there may be two separate securities, as we have seen,[1] and the §3(a)(2) exemption may apply to both: the participation interests of the *plans* in the collective investment vehicles in which they invest their assets, and the *employees'* interests in their respective plans. The former are always securities; they have been considered in the last section of this chapter, in the discussion of the insurance and banking hybrids. The latter (whether in combination with the former or whether the particular employer administers its own plan) may or may not be securities; it is this question that we now explore.[2]

INTERNATIONAL BROTHERHOOD OF TEAMSTERS, CHAUFFEURS, WAREHOUSEMEN & HELPERS OF AMERICA v. DANIEL

Supreme Court of the United States, 1979
439 U. S. 551

MR. JUSTICE POWELL delivered the opinion of the Court.

This case presents the question whether a noncontributory, compulsory pension plan constitutes a "security" within the meaning of the Securities Act of 1933 and the Securities Exchange Act of 1934 (Securities Acts).

I

In 1954 multiemployer collective bargaining between Local 705 of the International Brotherhood of Teamsters, Chauffeurs, Warehousemen, and Helpers of America and Chicago trucking firms produced a pension plan for employees represented by the Local. The plan was compulsory and noncontributory. Employees had no choice as to participation in the plan, and did not have the option of demanding that the employer's contribution be paid directly to them as a substitute for pension eligibility. The employees paid nothing to the plan themselves.

C. 3F   [1] See pp. 221-22 supra.

[2] The Commission has published two exhaustive releases of its staff's views on all aspects of employee benefit plans. Sec. Act Rel. 6188, 19 SEC Dock. 465 (1980); Sec. Act Rel. 6281, 21 SEC Dock. 1372 (1981).

The collective-bargaining agreement initially set employer contributions to the Pension Trust Fund at $2 a week for each man-week of covered employment. The Board of Trustees of the Fund, a body composed of an equal number of employer and union representatives, was given sole authority to set the level of benefits but had no control over the amount of required employer contributions. * * * At the time respondent brought suit, employers contributed $21.50 per employee man-week and pension payments ranged from $425 to $525 a month depending on age at retirement.[3] In order to receive a pension an employee was required to have 20 years of continuous service, including time worked before the start of the plan.

The meaning of "continuous service" is at the center of this dispute. Respondent began working as a truckdriver in the Chicago area in 1950, and joined Local 705 the following year. When the plan first went into effect, respondent automatically received 5 years' credit toward the 20-year service requirement because of his earlier work experience. He retired in 1973 and applied to the plan's administrator for a pension. The administrator determined that respondent was ineligible because of a break in service between December 1960 and July 1961.[4] Respondent appealed the decision to the trustees, who affirmed. Respondent then asked the trustees to waive the continuous-service rule as it applied to him. After the trustees refused to waive the rule, respondent brought suit in federal court against the International Union (Teamsters), Local 705 (Local), and Louis Peick, a trustee of the Fund.

Respondent's complaint alleged that the Teamsters, the Local, and Peick misrepresented and omitted to state material facts with respect to the value of a covered employee's interest in the pension plan. Count I of the complaint charged that these misstatements and omissions constituted a fraud in connection with the sale of a security in violation of §10(b) of the Securities Exchange Act of 1934, 48 Stat. 891, 15 U. S. C. §78j(b), and the Securities and Exchange Commission's Rule 10b-5, 17 C. F. R. §240.10b-5 (1978).

---

[3] Because the Fund made the same payments to each employee who qualified for a pension and retired at the same age, rather than establishing an individual account for each employee tied to the amount of employer contributions attributable to his period of service, the plan provided a "defined benefit." See 29 U. S. C. §1002(35); Alabama Power Co. v. Davis, [431 U. S. 581, 593 n. 18 (1977)].

[4] Respondent was laid off from December 1960 until April 1961. In addition, no contributions were paid on his behalf between April and July 1961, because of embezzlement by his employer's bookkeeper. During this 7-month period respondent could have preserved his eligibility by making the contributions himself, but he failed to do so.

Count II charged that the same conduct amounted to a violation of §17(a) of the Securities Act of 1933, 48 Stat. 84, as amended, 15 U. S. C. §77q. Other counts alleged violations of various labor-law and common-law duties. Respondent sought to proceed on behalf of all prospective beneficiaries of Teamsters pension plans and against all Teamsters pension funds.

The petitioners moved to dismiss the first two counts of the complaint on the ground that respondent had no cause of action under the Securities Acts. The District Court denied the motion. 410 F. Supp. 541 (N. D. Ill. 1976). It held that respondent's interest in the Pension Fund constituted a security within the meaning of §2(1) of the Securities Act, 15 U. S. C. §77b(1), and §3(a)(10) of the Securities Exchange Act, 15 U. S. C. §78c(a)(10), because the plan created an "investment contract" as that term had been interpreted in *SEC* v. *W. J. Howey Co.*, 328 U. S. 293 (1946). It also determined that there had been a "sale" of this interest to respondent within the meaning of §2(3) of the Securities Act, as amended, 15 U. S. C. §77b(3), and §3(a)(14) of the Securities Exchange Act, 15 U. S. C. §78c(a)(14). It believed respondent voluntarily gave value for his interest in the plan, because he had voted on collective-bargaining agreements that chose employer contributions to the Fund instead of other wages or benefits.

The order denying the motion to dismiss was certified for appeal pursuant to 28 U. S. C. §1292(b), and the Court of Appeals for the Seventh Circuit affirmed. 561 F. 2d 1223 (1977). Relying on its perception of the economic realities of pension plans and various actions of Congress and the SEC with respect to such plans, the court ruled that respondent's interest in the Pension Fund was a "security." According to the court, a "sale" took place either when respondent ratified a collective-bargaining agreement embodying the Fund or when he accepted or retained covered employment instead of seeking other work. The court did not believe the subsequent enactment of the Employee Retirement Income Security Act of 1974 (ERISA), 88 Stat. 829, 29 U. S. C. §1001 et seq., affected the application of the Securities Acts to pension plans, as the requirements and purposes of ERISA were perceived to be different from those of the Securities Acts. We granted certiorari, 434 U. S. 1061 (1978), and now reverse.

II

"The starting point in every case involving construction of a statute is the language itself." *Blue Chip Stamps* v. *Manor Drug*

Stores, 421 U. S. 723, 756 (1975) (Powell, J., concurring); see *Ernst & Ernst* v. *Hochfelder,* 425 U. S. 185, 197, 199, and n. 19 (1976). In spite of the substantial use of employee pension plans at the time they were enacted, neither §2(1) of the Securities Act nor §3(a)(10) of the Securities Exchange Act, which define the term "security" in considerable detail and with numerous examples, refers to pension plans of any type. Acknowledging this omission in the statutes, respondent contends that an employee's interest in a pension plan is an "investment contract," an instrument which is included in the statutory definitions of a security.[11]

To determine whether a particular financial relationship constitutes an investment contract, "[t]he test is whether the scheme involves an investment of money in a common enterprise with profits to come solely from the efforts of others." *Howey,* 328 U. S., at 301. This test is to be applied in light of "the substance — the economic realities of the transaction — rather than the names that may have been employed by the parties." *United Housing Foundation, Inc.* v. *Forman,* 421 U. S. 837, 851-852 (1975). Accord, *Tcherepnin* v. *Knight,* 389 U. S. 332, 336 (1967); *Howey,* supra, at 298. Cf. *SEC* v. *Variable Annuity Life Ins. Co.,* 359 U. S. 65, 80 (1959) (Brennan, J., concurring) ("[O]ne must apply a test in terms of the purposes of the Federal Acts . . ."). Looking separately at each element of the *Howey* test, it is apparent that an employee's participation in a noncontributory, compulsory pension plan such as the Teamsters' does not comport with the commonly held understanding of an investment contract.

A. INVESTMENT OF MONEY

An employee who participates in a noncontributory, compulsory pension plan by definition makes no payment into the pension fund. He only accepts employment, one of the conditions of which is eligibility for a possible benefit on retirement. Respondent contends, however, that he has "invested" in the Pension Fund by permitting part of his compensation from his employer to take the form of a deferred pension benefit. By allowing his employer to pay money into the Fund, and by contributing his labor to his employer in return for these payments, respondent asserts he has

---

[11] * * * respondent here does not seriously contend that a "certificate of interest * * * in any profit-sharing agreement" has any broader meaning under the Securities Acts than an "investment contract." In *Forman,* supra, we observed that the *Howey* test, which has been used to determine the presence of an investment contract, "embodies the essential attributes that run through all of the Court's decisions defining a security." 421 U. S., at 852.

made the kind of investment which the Securities Acts were intended to regulate.

In order to determine whether respondent invested in the Fund by accepting and remaining in covered employment, it is necessary to look at the entire transaction through which he obtained a chance to receive pension benefits. In every decision of this Court recognizing the presence of a "security" under the Securities Acts, the person found to have been an investor chose to give up a specific consideration in return for a separable financial interest with the characteristics of a security. See *Tcherepnin,* supra (money paid for bank capital stock); *SEC* v. *United Benefit Life Ins. Co.,* 387 U. S. 202 (1967) (portion of premium paid for variable component of mixed variable- and fixed-annuity contract); *Variable Annuity Life Ins. Co.,* supra (premium paid for variable-annuity contract); *Howey,* supra (money paid for purchase, maintenance, and harvesting of orange grove); *SEC* v. *C. M. Joiner Leasing Corp.,* 320 U. S. 344 (1943) (money paid for land and oil exploration). Even in those cases where the interest acquired had intermingled security and nonsecurity aspects, the interest obtained had "to a very substantial degree elements of investment contracts * * * ." *Variable Annuity Life Ins. Co.,* supra, at 91 (Brennan, J., concurring). In every case the purchaser gave up some tangible and definable consideration in return for an interest that had substantially the characteristics of a security.

In a pension plan such as this one, by contrast, the purported investment is a relatively insignificant part of an employee's total and indivisible compensation package. No portion of an employee's compensation other than the potential pension benefits has any of the characteristics of a security, yet these noninvestment interests cannot be segregated from the possible pension benefits. Only in the most abstract sense may it be said that an employee "exchanges" some portion of his labor in return for these possible benefits.[12] He surrenders his labor as a whole, and in return receives a compensation package that is substantially devoid of aspects resembling a security. His decision to accept and retain covered employment may have only an attenuated relationship, if any, to perceived investment possibilities of a future pension. Looking at the economic realities, it seems clear that an employee is selling his labor primarily to obtain a livelihood, not making an investment.

---

[12] This is not to say that a person's "investment," in order to meet the definition of an investment contract, must take the form of cash only, rather than of goods and services. See *Forman,* supra, at 852 n. 16.

Respondent also argues that employer contributions on his behalf constituted his investment into the Fund. But it is inaccurate to describe these payments as having been "on behalf" of any employee. The trust agreement used employee man-weeks as a convenient way to measure an employer's overall obligation to the Fund, not as a means of measuring the employer's obligation to any particular employee. Indeed, there was no fixed relationship between contributions to the Fund and an employee's potential benefits. A pension plan with "defined benefits," such as the Local's, does not tie a qualifying employee's benefits to the time he has worked. See n. 3, supra. One who has engaged in covered employment for 20 years will receive the same benefits as a person who has worked for 40, even though the latter has worked twice as long and induced a substantially larger employer contribution. Again, it ignores the economic realities to equate employer contributions with an investment by the employee.

B.   EXPECTATION OF PROFITS FROM A COMMON ENTERPRISE

As we observed in *Forman,* the "touchstone" of the *Howey* test "is the presence of an investment in a common venture premised on a reasonable expectation of profits to be derived from the entrepreneurial or managerial efforts of others." 421 U. S., at 852. The Court of Appeals believed that Daniel's expectation of profit derived from the Fund's successful management and investment of its assets. To the extent pension benefits exceeded employer contributions and depended on earnings from the assets, it was thought they contained a profit element. The Fund's trustees provided the managerial efforts which produced this profit element.

As in other parts of its analysis, the court below found an expectation of profit in the pension plan only by focusing on one of its less important aspects to the exclusion of its more significant elements. It is true that the Fund, like other holders of large assets, depends to some extent on earnings from its assets. In the case of a pension fund, however, a far larger portion of its income comes from employer contributions, a source in no way dependent on the efforts of the Fund's managers. The Local 705 Fund, for example, earned a total of $31 million through investment of its assets between February 1955 and January 1977. During this same period employer contributions totaled $153 million. Not only does the greater share of a pension plan's income ordinarily come from new contributions, but unlike most entrepreneurs who manage other people's money, a plan usually can count on increased employer contributions, over which the plan itself has no control, to cover shortfalls in earnings.

The importance of asset earnings in relation to the other benefits received from employment is diminished further by the fact that where a plan has substantial preconditions to vesting, the principal barrier to an individual employee's realization of pension benefits is not the financial health of the fund. Rather, it is his own ability to meet the fund's eligibility requirements. Thus, even if it were proper to describe the benefits as a "profit" returned on some hypothetical investment by the employee, this profit would depend primarily on the employee's efforts to meet the vesting requirements, rather than the fund's investment success. When viewed in light of the total compensation package an employee must receive in order to be eligible for pension benefits, it becomes clear that the possibility of participating in a plan's asset earnings "is far too speculative and insubstantial to bring the entire transaction within the Securities Acts," *Forman*, 421 U. S., at 856.

III

The court below believed that its construction of the term "security" was compelled not only by the perceived resemblance of a pension plan to an investment contract but also by various actions of Congress and the SEC with regard to the Securities Acts. In reaching this conclusion, the court gave great weight to the SEC's explanation of these events, an explanation which for the most part the SEC repeats here. Our own review of the record leads us to believe that this reliance on the SEC's interpretation of these legislative and administrative actions was not justified.

A.   ACTIONS OF CONGRESS

The SEC in its *amicus curiae* brief refers to several actions of Congress said to evidence an understanding that pension plans are securities. A close look at each instance, however, reveals only that Congress might have believed certain kinds of pension plans, radically different from the one at issue here, came within the coverage of the Securities Acts. There is no evidence that Congress at any time thought noncontributory plans similar to the one before us were subject to federal regulation as securities.

The first action cited was the rejection by Congress in 1934 of an amendment to the Securities Act that would have exempted employee stock investment and stock option plans from the Act's registration requirements. The amendment passed the Senate but was eliminated in conference. The legislative history of the defeated proposal indicates it was intended to cover plans under which employees contributed their own funds to a segregated investment account on which a return was realized. [Citations omitted.] In rejecting the amendment, Congress revealed a concern that certain interests having the characteristics of a security not be excluded from Securities Act protection simply because investors realized their return in the form of retirement benefits. At no time, however, did Congress indicate that pension benefits in and of themselves gave a transaction the characteristics of a security.

The SEC also relies on a 1970 amendment of the Securities Act which extended §3's exemption from registration to include "any interest or participation in a single or collective trust fund maintained by a bank * * * which interest or participation is issued in connection with * * * a stock bonus, pension, or profit-sharing plan which meets the requirements for qualification under section 401 of title 26, * * * " §3(a)(2) of the Securities Act, as amended, 84 Stat. 1434, 1498, 15 U. S. C. §77c(a)(2). It argues that in creating a registration exemption, the amendment manifested Congress' understanding that the interests covered by the amendment otherwise were subject to the Securities Acts. It interprets "interest or participation in a single * * * trust fund * * * issued in connection with * * * a stock bonus, pension, or profit-sharing plan" as referring to a prospective beneficiary's interest in a pension fund. But this construction of the 1970 amendment ignores that measure's central purpose, which was to relieve banks and insurance companies of certain registration obligations. The amendment recognized only that a pension plan had "an interest or participation" in the fund in which its assets were held, not that prospective beneficiaries of a plan had any interest in either the plan's bank-maintained assets or the plan itself.

B.   SEC INTERPRETATION

The court below believed, and it now is argued to us, that almost from its inception the SEC has regarded pension plans as falling within the scope of the Securities Acts. We are asked to defer to what is seen as a longstanding interpretation of these statutes by the agency responsible for their administration. But there are limits, grounded in the language, purpose, and history of the particular statute, on how far an agency properly may go in its interpretative role. Although these limits are not always easy to discern, it is clear here that the SEC's position is neither longstanding nor even arguably within the outer limits of its authority to interpret these Acts.[20]

As we have demonstrated above, the type of pension plan at issue in this case bears no resemblance to the kind of financial interests the Securities Acts were designed to regulate. Further, the SEC's present position is flatly contradicted by its past actions. Until the instant litigation arose, the public record reveals no evidence that the SEC had ever considered the Securities Acts to be applicable to noncontributory pension plans. In 1941, the SEC first articulated the position that voluntary, contributory plans had investment characteristics that rendered them "securities" under the Acts. At the same time, however, the SEC recognized that noncontributory plans were not covered by the Securities Acts because such plans did not involve a "sale" within the meaning of the statutes. Opinions of Assistant General Counsel, [1941-1944 Transfer Binder] CCH Fed. Sec. L. Serv. ¶75,195 (1941); Hearings before the House Committee on Interstate and Foreign Commerce on Proposed Amendments to the Securities Act of 1933 and to the Securities Exchange Act of 1934, 77th Cong., 1st Sess., 895, 896-897 (1941) (testimony of Commissioner Purcell).[21]

In an attempt to reconcile these interpretations of the Securities Acts with its present stand, the SEC now augments its past position with two additional propositions. First, it is argued, noncontributory plans are "securities" even where a "sale" is not involved. Second, the previous concession that noncontributory plans do not involve a "sale" was meant to apply only to the registration and

---

[20] * * * On a number of occasions in recent years this Court has found it necessary to reject the SEC's interpretation of various provisions of the Securities Acts. [Citations omitted.]

[21] Subsequent to 1941, the SEC made no further efforts to regulate even contributory, voluntary pension plans except where the employees' contributions were invested in the employer's securities. Cf. n. 19, supra. It also continued to disavow any authority to regulate noncontributory, compulsory plans. See letter from Assistant Director, Division of Corporate Finance, May 12, 1953, [1978] CCH Fed. Sec. L. Rep. ¶2105.51; letter from Chief Counsel, Division of Corporate Finance, Aug. 1, 1962, [1978] CCH Fed. Sec. L. Rep. ¶2105.52; Hearings before the Senate Committee on Banking and Currency, supra n. 19, at 1326; 1 L. Loss, Securities Regulation 510-511 (2d ed. 1961); 4 id., at 2553-2554 (2d ed. 1969). * * *

reporting requirements of the Securities Acts; for purposes of the antifraud provisions, a "sale" is involved. As for the first proposition, we observe that none of the SEC opinions, reports, or testimony cited to us address the question. As for the second, the record is unambiguously to the contrary.[22] Both in its 1941 statements and repeatedly since then, the SEC has declared that its "no sale" position applied to the Securities Act as a whole. [Citations omitted.] Congress acted on this understanding when it proceeded to develop the legislation that became ERISA. * * * As far as we are aware, at no time before this case arose did the SEC intimate that the antifraud provisions of the Securities Acts nevertheless applied to noncontributory pension plans.

IV

If any further evidence were needed to demonstrate that pension plans of the type involved are not subject to the Securities Acts, the enactment of ERISA in 1974, 88 Stat., 829, would put the matter to rest. Unlike the Securities Acts, ERISA deals expressly and in detail with pension plans. ERISA requires pension plans to disclose specified information to employees in a specified manner, see 29 U. S. C. §§1021-1030, in contrast to the indefinite and uncertain disclosure obligations imposed by the antifraud provisions of the Securities Acts, see *Santa Fe Industries, Inc.* v. *Green,* 430 U. S. 462, 474-477 (1977); *TSC Industries, Inc.* v. *Northway, Inc.,* 426 U. S. 438 (1976). Further, ERISA regulates the substantive terms of pension plans, setting standards for plan funding and

---

[22] On occasion the SEC has contended that because §2 of the Securities Act and §3 of the Securities Exchange Act apply the qualifying phrase "unless the context otherwise requires" to the Acts' general definitions, it is permissible to regard a particular transaction as involving a sale or not depending on the form of regulation involved. See 1 L. Loss, Securities Regulation 524-528 (2d ed. 1961); 4 id., at 2562-2565 (2d ed. 1969). The Court noted the contention in SEC v. National Securities, Inc., 393 U. S. 453, 465-466 (1969). On previous occasions the SEC appears to have taken a different position: In 1943 it submitted an *amicus* brief in the Ninth Circuit arguing that a transaction must be a sale for all purposes of the Securities Act or for none, and it did not begin to rely on its "regulatory context" theory until 1951. See Brief for the SEC in National Supply Co. v. Leland Stanford Junior University, No. 10270 (C. A. 9 Apr. 1, 1943); 1 L. Loss, supra, at 524 n. 211; Cohen, Rule 133 of the Securities and Exchange Commission, 14 Record of N. Y. C. B. A. 162, 164-165 (1959). We also note that, with respect to statutory mergers, the area in which the SEC originally developed its theory as to the bifurcated definition of a sale, the SEC since has abandoned its position and finds the presence of a "sale" for all purposes in the case of such mergers. See 17 C. F. R. §230.145 (1978). In view of our disposition of this case, we express no opinion as to the correct resolution of the divergent views on this issue.

limits on the eligibility requirements an employee must meet. For example, with respect to the underlying issue in this case — whether respondent served long enough to receive a pension — §203(a) of ERISA, 29 U. S. C. §1053(a), now sets the minimum level of benefits an employee must receive after accruing specified years of service, and §203(b), 29 U. S. C. §1053(b), governs continuous-service requirements. Thus, if respondent had retired after §1053 took effect, the Fund would have been required to pay him at least a partial pension. The Securities Acts, on the other hand, do not purport to set the substantive terms of financial transactions.

The existence of this comprehensive legislation governing the use and terms of employee pension plans severely undercuts all arguments for extending the Securities Acts to noncontributory, compulsory pension plans. Congress believed that it was filling a regulatory void when it enacted ERISA, a belief which the SEC actively encouraged. Not only is the extension of the Securities Acts by the court below unsupported by the language and history of those Acts, but in light of ERISA, it serves no general purpose. See *Califano v. Sanders*, 430 U. S. 99, 104-107 (1977). Cf. *Boys Markets, Inc.* v. *Retail Clerks*, 398 U. S. 235, 250 (1970). Whatever benefits employees might derive from the effect of the Securities Acts are now provided in more definite form through ERISA.

V

We hold that the Securities Acts do not apply to a noncontributory, compulsory pension plan. Because the first two counts of respondent's complaint do not provide grounds for relief in federal court, the District Court should have granted the motion to dismiss them. The judgment below is therefore reversed.

MR. JUSTICE STEVENS took no part in the consideration or decision of these cases.

MR. CHIEF JUSTICE BURGER, concurring.

*   *   *

Query how much of the Commission's traditional view survives Mr. Daniel's misfortune:

(1) Although the Court expressed no opinion on the Commission's "bifurcated sale" arguments,[3] the Commission has aban-

[3] 439 U. S. at 567-68, n. 22, supra p. 238.

doned that concept. It now construes the term "sale" no more broadly for the fraud provisions than for registration purposes.[4]

(2) Otherwise the face of *Daniel,* where the plan was both compulsory and noncontributory, requires no change in the Commission's traditional position — which it tried to enlarge in its *amicus curiae* capacity — to the effect that there is no "sale" unless a plan is both voluntary and contributory. Lower courts have applied *Daniel* in the compulsory-contributory case[5] and even in the voluntary-contributory case that the Commission would cover.[6] But much may still depend on the circumstances.[7] Notwithstanding the Commission's view that it is irrelevant to the "security" question whether the plan is a "defined benefit plan" (one that pays fixed or determinable benefits without regard to the plan's earnings) rather than a "defined contribution plan" (one in which benefits vary with the investment success of the plan and perhaps other factors),[8] even a voluntary-contributory plan does not look like a "security" when one's pension is not based on the plan's income; consequently, cases of that type[9] may be distinguished from even voluntary-contributory cases that are not defined benefit plans.

(3) So far as indirect distribution of the employer's own securities is concerned,[10] very few *pension* plans are funded by investment in company stock with employee money. All of such plans that have been registered (and quite a few have been) are so-called thrift plans, which are almost always optional rather than compulsory, although they are structured as "profit-sharing plans" to qualify them under §401 of the Internal Revenue Code. They often provide from two to four investment media, including a portfolio of common stocks, Government bonds, and securities of the employer, whichever the employee chooses. Many plans are expressly designed to limit the amount that can be used to pur-

---

[4] Sec. Act Rel. 6188, 19 SEC Dock. 465, 483 (1980).

[5] Black v. Payne, 591 F. 2d 83, 87-88 (9th Cir. 1979), *cert. denied,* 444 U. S. 867.

[6] Tanuggi v. Grolier, Inc., 471 F. Supp. 1209 (S. D. N. Y. 1979); Newkirk v. General Electric Co., CCH Fed. Sec. L. Rep. ¶97,216 (N. D. Cal. 1979); O'Neil v. Marriott Corp., 538 F. Supp. 1026 (D. Md. 1982); Coward v. Colgate-Palmolive Co., 686 F. 2d 1230 (7th Cir. 1982); Cunha v. Ward Foods, Inc., 545 F. Supp. 94 (D. Hawaii 1982).

[7] See Faulk v. Bagley, 88 F. R. D. 153, 164 (M. D. N. C. 1980).

[8] Sec. Act Rel. 6188, 19 SEC Dock. 465, 471-72 (1980).

[9] See the *Black, Tanuggi, Coward,* and *Cunha* cases, supra nn. 5, 6.

[10] See p. 221 supra; and see generally H. Weyher and H. Knott, the Employee Stock Ownership Plan (1982).

chase the employer's securities to the amount of the employer's contribution for the express purpose of avoiding registration.

(4) What is the significance to all this of the exclusion in §3(c) (11) of the 1940 Act of any "employee's stock bonus, pension, or profit-sharing trust" that meets certain requirements, as well as the direction to the Commission in §6(b) of the 1940 Act to exempt any "employees' security company" on application to whatever extent it considers appropriate under specified standards? If these things are not *prima facie* "investment companies," why exclude or exempt them? And can it be that interests in an investment company are not "securities"?

The Code's Reporter breathed a sigh of relief when *Daniel* was decided and promptly recommended that the Code say nothing on the question, thus leaving it to the courts to prick out *Daniel's* boundaries. But the Code's comments evidence a clear preference for amending ERISA to the extent that the protection it affords is not as adequate as the SEC's — on the theory that "the SEC should no more be in the business of regulating *bona fide* pension (or pension-related) plans (even on a 'fraud' basis) than orthodox insurance policies or annuities."[11]

G. PREORGANIZATION CERTIFICATES OR SUBSCRIPTIONS (HEREIN OF "JOINT ADVENTURES")

"There is more reason for the application of this [blue sky] law to unorganized business concerns," the Oregon Supreme Court has said, "than to those having a recognized legal entity."[1] This was said without benefit of any statutory reference to preorganization subscriptions. The promoters were simply held to be selling stock in a corporation as yet unborn. The specific reference to any "preorganization certificate or subscription" in §2(1) represents a concession on the part of Congress as much as it does assurance of complete coverage. Without it there would be no way legally to solicit the public in advance of incorporation, since there would be no "issuer" to sign the registration statement. As the statute

---

[11] See 1 Code 225-27.

C. 3G [1] State v. Whiteaker, 118 Ore. 656, 661, 247 Pac. 1077, 1079 (1926).

stands, the preorganization certificates or subscriptions are securities distinct from the ultimate stock, and their issuers are the promoters, who may thus effect registration before the corporation is organized. However, since this does not preclude the necessity of filing a separate registration statement for the stock after the corporation is formed, promoters normally incorporate first in order to avoid double registration. It has been many years since any preorganization subscriptions have been registered, and few have ever been.

It seems clear that, although a "preorganization certificate" requires a writing, a "preorganization subscription" does not. It is specifically recognized in the legislative history that there may be a "security" under some parts of the definition even though all the negotiations are oral.[2]

There is a nice question of determining the extent to which the preorganization subscription rationale should be applied to the formation of a close corporation. And the question is complicated by the theory developed by some of the state courts — and implicit, as we have seen, in the delineation of the "investment contract" phrase in §2(1) of the 1933 Act — that no "security" is involved in a "joint adventure," at least if nothing has yet been incorporated when the joint venture is put together.[3] The federal exemption for private offerings would normally preclude the necessity of registration in this kind of case. But the identical question could arise in an action under §12(2) or Rule 10b-5 — or conceivably in

---

[2]This was said with reference to the 1934 amendment that added the words "interest or" in the present clause, "any interest or instrument commonly known as a 'security.'" "It is also intended to apply the Act to interests commonly known as 'securities,'" the conference report said, "whether or not such interests are represented by any document or not [sic]. Thus the statute will apply to inscribed shares, and its provisions cannot be evaded by simply refraining from issuing to the subscriber any documentary evidence of his interest." H. R. Rep. No. 1838, 73d Cong., 2d Sess. (1934) 39. In SEC v. W. J. Howey Co., 328 U. S. 293, 299 (1946), the Court said it was "immaterial whether the shares in the enterprise are evidenced by formal certificates or by nominal interests in the physical assets employed by the enterprise." But "The absence of a physical document presents difficulties for the plaintiff because it must nonetheless prove the existence of subject matter jurisdiction based on the existence of a written or oral security not available for examination by the court." Canadian Imperial Bank of Commerce Trust Co. v. Fingland, 615 F. 2d 465, 467 (9th Cir. 1980).

[3]E. g., Nicholl v. Ipsen, 130 Cal. App. 2d 452, 458-59, 278 P. 2d 927, 930 (1955), and cases cited; but cf., e. g., Brown v. Cole, 155 Tex. 624, 291 S. W. 2d 704 (1956). Under the express statutory exemptions for joint adventures that exist in a few states, see, e. g., Grabendike v. Adix, 335 Mich. 128, 55 N. W. 2d 761 (1952).

an enforcement proceeding under §17(a) — for misstatements in the alleged sale of subscriptions.

A 1952 decision of the California Supreme Court (*Holmberg* v. *Marsden*) is typical of one point of view as applied to one type of case. The plaintiff and the two defendants had agreed to organize a corporation, each taking a one-third interest. When this company went the way of many other new businesses, the plaintiff tried to get his money back on the ground that no permit had been secured for the issuance of the stock at the time of his payment. He prevailed in the appellate court, but the California Supreme Court reversed, holding that there was evidence to support the factual findings of the trial court to the effect that the defendants had not offered or sold preorganization subscriptions to the plaintiff but had merely participated with him in organizing the enterprise. The fact that the proposal had originated with the defendants was not considered conclusive when weighed against the circumstances that the plaintiff had participated actively in the business. "Whether the three men, as among themselves, be termed partners, joint venturers, or copromotors [*sic*] of a corporation * * * it is obvious that the trial court was justified in concluding that they stood on an equal footing as entrepreneurs."[4] Consequently there appeared to the court to be no more reason for the defendants to reimburse the plaintiff than the other way around.

In most of the state cases thus far cited the statutory definition did not explicitly include preorganization subscriptions. But the blue sky laws have sometimes been applied to preorganization solicitations nevertheless. Might it not follow, conversely, that the explicit inclusion of preorganization subscriptions is no assurance that the statute *will* apply to every promotion of a close corporation? Certainly a respectable argument could be made for reaching the same result arrived at by the California court in the *Holmberg* case if in similar circumstances one of the organizers of the corporation were to sue the others under §12(2) of the federal statute. We have noticed and shall notice other instances when a cautious use of the introductory phrase in §2 — to the effect that the several definitions apply "unless the context otherwise requires" — had led to a result different from that produced by a literal reading of the statutory words but more consistent with the statutory purpose.[5]

[4] Holmberg v. Marsden, 39 Cal. 2d 592, 597, 248 P. 2d 417, 419-20 (1952); cf. Goodman v. DeAzoulay, 539 F. Supp. 10 (E. D. Pa. 1981); but cf., e. g., Trump v. Badet, 84 Ariz. 319, 327 P. 2d 1001 (1958). For additional blue sky cases both ways, see 4 Loss, Securities Regulation (Supp. 1969) 2490-91.

[5] See c. 3B supra; pp. 243-44 infra.

H. VOTING TRUST CERTIFICATES, CERTIFICATES OF DEPOSIT, AND RECEIPTS

The ordinary voting trust certificate or certificate of deposit — the latter is usually but not always issued by a protective committee in the course of a corporate reorganization — is recognizable enough.[1] But certain types of solicitation may well result in the offer of such certificates — or at least securities in the nature of such certificates — even though the particular words are not used. Thus, although the ordinary solicitation of a corporate proxy or of a power of attorney by a protective committee raises no question under the 1933 Act, there may be circumstances in which it amounts to an offer of a "security." For example, proxies might be solicited under an arrangement amounting to a voting trust. Or a committee might seek authority not merely to represent bondholders or stockholders in a pending reorganization proceeding, but also to bind them to a particular plan of reorganization or to accept new securities without any further assent on their part. If there is difficulty in saying this amounts to an offering of "certificates of deposit" when there are no certificates, there are other toeholds: The committee would seem to be offering "preorganization subscriptions" to the securities of the reorganized corporation. Or, if the outstanding securities are stamped to indicate that they are subject to a lien for their *pro rata* share of the committee's expenses, the stamp would seem to be a "receipt" for a security. Or, as a last resort, there is the clause, "any interest * * * commonly known as a 'security,'" which was presumably intended as a catchall for this sort of contingency.

Conversely, not all instruments that are in form "receipts" for securities are themselves "securities." Congress could not have intended to require registration when the issuer of the receipt acts in a purely ministerial capacity and has only the obligations of an ordinary bailee. For example, a bank or trust company, retained to act as depositary by a corporation or a committee of security holders, may issue receipts as part of the mechanics of a voluntary reorganization, the receipts merely evidencing the depositors' right either to receive certain new securities or to have their old securities returned depending on specified contingencies (such as the number of securities deposited by a given date). The new securities called for by the plan will be registered (unless an exemption

---

C. 3H [1] A bank "certificate of deposit" that is a debt of the bank itself is a very different animal.

is available), but the receipts themselves are hardly "securities."
In other words, the phrase "receipt for" a security is more or less
ejusdem generis with "certificate of deposit," and is essentially another statutory handle to cover instruments that are certificates
of deposit in substance without being so termed. In close cases
this may draw a fine line. But the touchstone should always be
substance rather than form — whether it operates to include or
to exclude.

So far as identifying the "issuer" of these types of securities is
concerned — a matter that is important not only in determining
who must sign the registration statement but also in assessing the
issuer's virtually absolute liability under §11 — there is a specific
provision in §2(4):

> * * * with respect to certificates of deposit, voting-trust certifi-
> cates, or collateral-trust certificates, or with respect to certificates
> of interest or shares in an unincorporated investment trust not
> having a board of directors (or persons performing similar func-
> tions) or of the fixed, restricted management, or unit type,[2] the
> term "issuer" means the person or persons performing the acts
> and assuming the duties of depositor or manager pursuant to the
> provisions of the trust or other agreement or instrument under
> which such securities are issued * * *

This makes it clear that the physical issuer of these types of securities — the depositary — is not the "issuer." It is not clear
whether that is all that this clause means — in which event the
"issuer" is the voting trust or the committee as an entity — or
whether the voting trustees or the committee members were intended to be the "issuer" in either their official or their personal
capacities. It is probably the former, but this question is not too
important, since §2(4) goes on to say that

> in the case of an unincorporated association which provides by its
> articles for limited liability of any or all of its members, or in
> the case of a trust, committee, or other legal entity, the trustees
> or members thereof shall not be individually liable as issuers of
> any security issued by the association, trust, committee, or other
> legal entity.

In any event, in determining who is "performing the acts and
assuming the duties of depositor or manager," it is necessary once
again to look to the substance of the arrangements in each case,
however desirable it would be to have a more definite criterion.

---

[2] See p. 55 supra.

Take the so-called American depositary receipt, which goes back to the "substitute certificates" developed by the financial community in the 1920s as a device to facilitate American trading in foreign securities.[3] The Commission early adopted Form C-3, still in effect, for the registration of "American Certificates (for example, so-called American Depositary Receipts for foreign shares or American Participation Certificates in foreign bonds or notes) issued against securities of foreign issuers deposited or to be deposited with an American depositary (whether physically held by such depositary in America or abroad) and of the foreign securities so deposited."[4] Part I of the form must be signed by the issuer of the American certificates, and Part II, which must be filed only if the sale of the underlying securities would require registration when made directly rather than through the means of American certificates, requires information concerning the issuer of the underlying securities and must be signed by that issuer.[5]

In the 1920s, the depositor was generally an American investment house that was anxious to facilitate the sale of a block of shares it held in a foreign company. It would enter into an agreement with a domestic bank as depositary. The foreign company would not be a party to the agreement, but the American investors would automatically become parties by purchasing the

---

[3] See Williams, Trading in the United States in Foreign Securities and Securities Distributed outside the United States without Registration under the Securities Act of 1933, in 6 Practising Law Institute, Sixth Annual Institute on Securities Regulation (1975) 327, 333.

"ADRs" are convenient not only when the shares are in bearer form but also when the normal unit of trading in the foreign market is not suited to the American market, or when there are inconvenient requirements of foreign law such as the British prohibition of a foreign registry or the Japanese requirement of maintaining an agent and having a mailing address in Japan. Stephenson and Williams, A Lawyer's Guide to International Business Transactions (2d ed. 1980) 70.

Actually foreign equity securities are traded in three forms in the United States: (1) as issued in the country of incorporation ("ordinary shares"); (2) as issued specifically for use in the United States and frequently with different procedural rights ("American shares"); and (3) most commonly in the form of ADRs.

There have also been quite a few converse instances where banks have issued bearer depositary receipts in foreign countries ("Continental Depositary Receipts") against securities of American corporations in order to accommodate them to the European custom of trading in bearer instruments.

[4] Instr. Book for Form C-3, Rules as to the Use of Form C-3.

[5] Ibid. The "which" clause in the text refers to the situation in which the American depositary receipts are a means of effecting a distribution of the underlying security by its issuer or an underwriter, in which event the dealers' exemption in §4(3) would not be applicable to secondary trading in the underlying securities themselves within the United States until some time after the public offering.

receipts. The depositor normally reserved the right to exercise managerial control over the deposit, and the depositary bank undertook merely to hold the foreign shares and to issue receipts against them. Under such an arrangement the "issuer" was clearly the depositor rather than the depositary.

In practice Form C-3 has never been widely used. Today it is common for the depositary bank to assume the initiative by announcing that it stands ready to issue receipts against the deposit of designated foreign securities. The depositors, who are generally domestic dealers or private shareholders, then undertake to have their foreign securities lodged with the depositary's foreign agent in return for American depositary receipts to be issued by the depositary bank. There is no longer a formal deposit agreement, except as it may be evidenced in the receipts themselves. And the foreign company is still not involved, except that the depositary bank normally receives its permission in advance to issue the receipts. Under this state of affairs the "issuer" is just as clearly the depositary bank rather than the depositors. But if there is a depositor who retains managerial authority, both the depositary and the depositor might be regarded as co-issuers.

Thus, depending on all the circumstances, the "issuer" may be the depositor or the depositary or both. And since 1955 there has been a fourth possibility. In response to the pressure to facilitate the banks' offering of American depositary receipts, the Commission at that time adopted a new Form S-12, which applies when (1) the holder of a receipt may withdraw the deposited securities at any time and (2) the deposited securities would not be subject to registration if sold directly in the United States.[6] If either of these conditions is not satisfied, Form C-3 must still be used. But, when Form S-12 is available, the entire prospectus, which consists of only four items of information specified in the form, may be embodied in the receipts themselves.[7] Under this form, when no

---

[6] The second condition means that the American depositary receipts are not a means of effecting a distribution of the underlying stock by the issuer or an underwriter, and that the dealers' exemption in §4(3) would be applicable to secondary trading in the underlying securities themselves within the United States. This is the converse of the situation referred to in note 5 supra. Rule 174(a) (supra pp. 121-22) excuses ordinary dealers (those that are not underwriters and are not disposing of unsold allotments or subscriptions) from delivering a prospectus altogether in S-12 cases as long as registration of the deposited securities is not required; but, of course, Form S-12 is not supposed to be used at all when such registration *is* required.

[7] The form requires undertakings to file and transmit certain information from time to time.

person performs the acts or assumes the duties of depositor or manager pursuant to the instrument under which the receipts are issued, the "issuer" of the receipts is specified to be the altogether fictitious "entity created by the agreement"; and the form provides specifically that the depositary is not to be deemed an issuer or a person controlling the issuer notwithstanding its signing the registration statement in the name of the "entity." This awe-inspiring (and altogether laudable) demonstration of administrative flexibility means that nobody has the liability of an "issuer" under §11 so far as Form S-12 is concerned.[8]

I. EQUIPMENT TRUST CERTIFICATES

There is still another special provision in §2(4) for "equipment-trust certificates or like securities," with respect to which "the term 'issuer' means the person by whom the equipment or property is or is to be used." This is to make it clear that the issuer is the carrier that thus finances its rolling stock, whoever may be the physical issuer of the certificates. The manufacturer of the equipment transfers title to a trustee, who is the nominal issuer of equipment trust certificates. The certificates are secured by a lease or conditional sale agreement under which the railroad obtains possession of the equipment. The purpose of this financing device is, by placing title in the trustee, to avoid subjecting the equipment to the lien of the after-acquired property clauses that are typical in railroad mortgages.[1] Although equipment trust certificates are not included *eo nomine* in §2(1), any doubt that they are "securities" is set at rest by the special provision defining their "issuer" in §2(4) as well as their exemption by §3(a)(6).

A financial writer claimed in 1955 that equipment trust certificates as a vehicle of financing have been applied to only one type of commercial property aside from railroad and trolley cars, buses, and airplanes — namely, "jukeboxes."[2] The exaggeration in that

---

[8] On the S-12 analogy, the Code defines "issuer" in these non-board investment company cases as "the trust, if any, and otherwise the agreement or instrument under which the security is issued," rather than the "depositor or manager" under the trust. §202(85)(C).

C. 31 [1] In general, see Hawks and Wood, Marketing Railroad Equipment Trust Certificates, 45 ICC Prac. J. 466 (1978).
[2] M. Mayer, Wall Street: Men and Money (1955) 38.

statement is only slight.[3] At any rate, an example of the "like securities" referred to in the equipment trust clause of §2(4) would presumably be a lease-back arrangement where for tax purposes a corporation conveys certain land and buildings in fee to a trustee and takes back a perpetual or long-term lease. If the trustee issues certificates of beneficial interest in the property, the "issuer" would seem to be the lessee.

Since all the purposes of equipment trust certificates can be equally served without the formality of a trust by conditional sales contracts[4] — which was not true in all states before the Uniform Commercial Code — equipment trust certificates may well be on their way to extinction. Whether or not conditional sales contracts are "like securities" today — as they probably are — the Code's definitions of both "security" and "issuer" refer specifically to an "equipment trust certificate (including a conditional sale contract or similar interest or instrument serving the same purpose)."[5]

J. GUARANTEES

The reference to a "guarantee" of a security in the 1934 amendment of §2(1) makes it clear that the guarantor is the issuer only of the guarantee and not of the security guaranteed.[1] The House committee report on the amendment also emphasizes that "the omission of specific mention of guarantors [in the definition of the term 'issuer'] * * * will make it clear that guarantors are to be treated as issuers of securities only if the guarantees are incorporated in securities distributed to investors."[2] Presumably the guarantee may be of either principal or interest or both.

The statute does not refer specifically to the "assumption" by *B* of securities issued by *A*. But obviously, if the holders of *A*'s securities have anything to say about the assumption, *B* is in substance offering its securities in exchange for *A*'s, and registration of *B*'s securities is required unless some exemption is available.

---

[3] For scattered instances outside the transportation industries, see 1 Dewing, The Financial Policy of Corporations (5th ed. 1953) 207-08. This means that most equipment trust certificates are exempted anyway under §3(a)(6).

[4] See Sec. Act §3(a)(6) as amended in 1976.

[5] §§202(85)(D), 202(150)(A). The definition of "issuer" refers to a "similar security" rather than a "similar interest or instrument."

C. 3J [1] H. R. Rep. No. 1838, 73d Cong., 2d Sess. (1934) 39. See Hugo Stinnes Corp., 7 SEC 622, 635 (1940).

[2] H. R. Rep. No. 1838, 73d Cong., 2d Sess. (1934) 39.

K. WARRANTS, OPTIONS, AND COMMODITY FUTURES

Until October 1982 the relevant part of the definition in both the 1933 and 1934 Acts referred only to any "warrant or right to subscribe to or purchase" any of the previously mentioned securities. The 1982 amendment inserted before this language

> any put, call, straddle, option, or privilege on any security, certificate of deposit, or group or index of securities (including any interest therein or based on the value thereof), or any put, call, straddle, option, or privilege entered into on a national securities exchange relating to foreign currency.[1]

The story of how this came about, as well as how the question of option securities came to be affected by the world of commodity futures. is best told historically.

The original definition clearly covered the ordinary warrants or rights to purchase shares of the same corporation — or occasionally a related corporation — that are customarily traded both on the exchanges and in the over-the-counter market.[2] Moreover, although "warrant" may be a term of art that assumes some sort of certificate, undoubtedly rights to purchase securities are themselves "securities" even when they are not evidenced by any writing but are announced in a letter to security holders. However announced or evidenced, warrants and rights have a dual personality. They are themselves "securities" at the same time that they represent offers to sell other securities.

In a 1961 decision, the first case in which the Commission allowed restricted stock options under the Holding Company Act, it held that the options were nonetheless "securities" under that

---

C. 3K [1] In contrast to this language, which covers an *option* on a certificate of deposit, the definitions in the two 1940 Acts were concurrently amended to include a certificate of deposit itself. This variation is designed to make an "investment company," under the 40 percent test of §3(a)(3) of the Investment Company Act (see 58 n. 14 supra), out of any "money fund" that invests heavily in certificates of deposit.

[2] See Entel v. Guilden, 223 F. Supp. 129, 130 n. 4 (S. D. N. Y. 1963): "The Atlas Corporation has for many years used perpetual warrants as a major means of acquiring equity capital." In permitting a warrant holder to bring a derivative action under §17(e) of the Investment Company Act, the court there pointed out that the definition of "security" in §2(a)(35) included any "warrant or right to subscribe to or purchase" any stock. "An Atlas warrant, thus, can be fairly described as a 'distilled' share of Atlas common — the sweet liquor of speculation concentrated with some of the dregs of investment 'responsibility' left behind." Id. at 130.

Act by virtue of their being nontransferable.[3] Nevertheless, it is still arguable, as in the case of the ordinary promissory note given to a bank or another private lender, that a literal reading is not always indicated and that a nontransferable option that is incident to a contract for personal services is not a "security" even for purposes of the fraud provisions of the 1933 Act. This leaves another unavoidable shadow area.

In financial jargon "puts" and "calls" are in a different category from "warrants" and "rights," although all are forms of options. A put is an option to sell at a certain price within a certain period, and a call is a similar option to buy. The economic *raison d'être* of these options is to serve as a hedge (a form of insurance) against future market movements. For example, a person who is long may buy a put as insurance that he will be able to sell if the market falls to a certain level, and a person who is short may buy a call to ensure that he will be able to cover (buy) if the market rises to a certain figure. At the same time, these instruments provide a cheap form of speculation.[4] Since they had served as manipulative devices, the Commission was given authority in the 1934 Act to regulate puts and calls by rule.[5]

Until 1973 these instruments were generally written in bearer form by more or less professional investors, endorsed by stock exchange houses, and then bought and sold in the over-the-counter market. This procedure continues to some extent. But the main ballgame has undergone a radical change since the creation of the Chicago Board Options Exchange in 1973, followed by options trading on the American, Philadelphia and Pacific Stock Exchanges. The CBOE pioneered two concepts: (1) contract standardization so that options were made fungible by fixing the exercise months and exercise ("striking") prices, and (2) establishment (and now joint ownership by all the options exchanges) of The Options Clearing Corporation, which is the issuer, as well as the guarantor, of the traded options.[6]

[3] Middle South Utilities, Inc., 40 SEC 509, 511-12 (1961).
[4] A 1961 SEC staff report stated: "From the data collected and from interviews, it appears that only a small number of options are bought for insurance. * * * The brokers interviewed were unanimous in the opinion that the reason most persons bought options was the opportunity it afforded them for speculation on a small amount of capital." SEC, Div. of Trading & Exchanges, Report on Put and Call Options (1961) 76-77.
[5] §9(b)-(d), infra p. 990.
[6] See Report of the Special Study of the Options Markets to the Securities and Exchange Commission, House Com. Print 96-IFC3, 96th Cong., 1st Sess. (1978), discussed in Lipton, The Special Study of the Options Market: Its

How, then, do these instruments stand under §5 of the 1933 Act? A call is a "right to * * * purchase" a security within the literal language of the original definition; but a put is a right to *sell*. The Sixth Circuit has held without elucidation that this language "clearly includes options to purchase or sell stock."[7] Alternatively, both types of option are such an integral part of securities trading that it seemed entirely reasonable to subsume them under the phrases, "investment contract" and "interest or instrument commonly known as a 'security.' "

At any rate, the definition was evidently thought sufficient to include options for purposes of broker-dealer registration, and might have been thought sufficient all along for registration purposes under the 1933 Act. Presumably one reason for the Commission's not requiring 1933 Act registration, or perhaps never squarely facing the question, was that pre-1973 options were not issued as classes of fungible securities and were not subjects of public offerings in any significant sense.

When the mechanisms for offering and trading of fungible options were inaugurated in 1973, after close Commission scrutiny under both Acts, it was thought essential to have a disclosure document covering rights to sell as well as rights to buy (and, interestingly, containing disclosures for the benefit of writers of options, which is to say, sellers, not merely purchasers). At this point the SEC staff insisted, and apparently no one questioned, that options had to be registered under the 1933 Act, as they have been by The Options Clearing Corporation in the capacity of issuer.[8]

Then in 1982 the Commission adopted an optional Form S-20 for the registration of standardized options, together with Rule 9b-1 under the 1934 Act by way of providing an *Exchange* Act "dis-

---

Findings and Recommendations, 7 Sec. Reg. L. J. 299 (1980); Poser and Brodsky, Amex Options Regulation, 8 Rev. Sec. Reg. 959 (1975). For the basics, see Johnson, Is It Better to Go Naked on the Street? A Primer on the Options Market, 55 Notre Dame Law. 7 (1979). On the role of organized options markets in capital formation, see Mendelson, Exchange Traded Options and the Supply of Capital, 2 J. Comp. L. & Sec. Reg. 65 (1979); Rubinstein, An Economic Evaluation of Organized Options Markets, 2 J. Comp. L. & Sec. Reg. 49 (1979).

[7] Mansbach v. Prescott, Ball & Turbin, 598 F. 2d 1017, 1026 n. 40 (6th Cir. 1979). The Code expressly covers a right to "buy or sell." §202(150)(A).

[8] The Corporation's current prospectus contains a full description of the trading mechanism.

closure document" for use along with the new form.[9] That document, which contains general information concerning standardized options and option trading, is prepared by *the options markets,* is filed with the Commission in preliminary form sixty days before its use,[10] and is "intended to enhance investor understanding of standardized options by presenting all essential information about such options in a more readable Exchange Act disclosure document."[11] At the same time, a prospectus is available for investors who are interested in more detailed information about the *issuer* of the options; but another new rule, 153b under the 1933 Act, provides that the prospectus delivery requirement is satisfied by depositing copies of the prospectus with each options market on which the options are traded.[12]

Enter the Commodity Futures Trading Commission Act of 1974,[13] which amended the Commodity Exchange Act by expanding its coverage beyond edible commodities and transferring its administration from the Department of Agriculture to the newly created Commodity Futures Trading Commission. In the process Congress defined "commodity" to mean a couple of dozen edible items, "and all other goods and articles" (except onions for some reason)[14]

> and all services, rights, and interests in which contracts for future delivery are presently or in the future dealt in: *Provided,* That the [Commodity Futures Trading] Commission shall have exclusive jurisdiction with respect to accounts, agreements (including any transaction which is of the character of, or is commonly known to the trade as, an "option", "privilege", "indemnity", "bid", "offer", "put", "call", "advance guaranty", or "decline

---

[9] Sec. Act Rel. 6426, 26 SEC Dock. 136 (1982).

[10] The document must be kept current by the filing of amendments thirty days before use; and both the original document and any amended document must be filed in definitive form not later than their use. The Commission may accelerate either period.

[11] Sec. Act Rel. 6426, 26 SEC Dock. 136 (1982).

[12] Cf. Rule 153, supra p. 120. The Commission concurrently adopted Rule 135b in order to exclude the disclosure document from §12(1) liability by providing that it "shall not be deemed to constitute an offer to sell or offer to buy any security" for purposes of §5, and adopted Rule 134a in order similarly to exclude from a "prospectus" status, under certain conditions, any materials "limited to explanatory information, describing the general nature of the standardized options markets or one or more strategies."

[13] 88 Stat. 1389 (1974), scattered in 7 U. S. C.

[14] In Board of Trade of the City of Chicago v. SEC, 677 F. 2d 1137, 1142 n. 9 (7th Cir. 1982), *vacated as moot,* 103 S. Ct. 434 (1982), the court could not resist suggesting "a physiological basis for the onion producers' crying."

guaranty"), and transactions involving contracts of sale of a commodity for future delivery, traded or executed on a contract market designated pursuant to section 7 of this title or any other board of trade, exchange, or market * * * : *And provided further,* That, except as hereinabove provided, nothing contained in this section shall (i) supersede or limit the jurisdiction at any time conferred on the Securities and Exchange Commission or other regulatory authorities under the laws of the United States or of any State, or (ii) restrict the Securities and Exchange Commission and such other authorities from carrying out their duties and responsibilities in accordance with such laws. Nothing in this section shall supersede or limit the jurisdiction conferred on courts of the United States or any State. Nothing in this chapter shall be deemed to govern or in any way be applicable to transactions in foreign currency, security warrants, security rights, resales of installment loan contracts, repurchase options, government securities, or mortgages and mortgage purchase commitments, unless such transactions involve the sale thereof for future delivery conducted on a board of trade. * * * [15]

We shall first explore the security-commodity line apart from the ambit of the CFTC's exclusive jurisdiction and then consider the impact of the commodity legislation on that question:

(1) Clearly the term "security" does not comprehend a commodity futures contract *per se*[16] any more than it does an orthodox life insurance policy.[17] The security and commodity worlds, like the world of insurance, were so distinct in 1933 that Congress would expressly have included commodity futures in the definition, as a few states have,[18] if it had so intended.

(2) *Discretionary* commodity accounts, however, may involve the kind of reliance on the broker's efforts that will result in "investment contracts."[19] For that matter, so may discretionary *securities* accounts.[20] And the discretionary authority need not be

[15] 7 U. S. C. §2.
[16] Sinva, Inc. v. Merrill Lynch, Pierce, Fenner & Smith, Inc., 253 F. Supp. 359, 366-67 (S. D. N. Y. 1966); Berman v. Dean Witter & Co., Inc., 353 F. Supp. 669 (C. D. Cal. 1973) (Japanese yen futures); Rasmussen v. Thomson & McKinnon Auchincloss Kohlmeyer, Inc., 608 F. 2d 175, 177 (5th Cir. 1979) (commodities adviser does not have to register under Investment Advisers Act).
[17] See p. 214 supra.
[18] E. g., N. Y. Gen. Bus. Law, Art. 23-A, §352; Wis. Stat., c. 189, §551.02-(13)(a). *Contra:* Cal. Ad. Code, Tit. 10, c. 3, Rule 260.019, CCH Blue Sky L. Rep. ¶ 11,750 ("security" does not include "any discretionary account maintained by a customer with a commodity broker").
[19] Commercial Iron & Metal Co. v. Bache & Co., Inc., 478 F. 2d 39 (10th Cir. 1973); Moody v. Bache & Co., Inc., 570 F. 2d 523, 526 (5th Cir. 1978).
[20] Alvord v. Shearson Hayden Stone, Inc., 485 F. Supp. 848, 851-53 (D.

embodied in a formal contract as long as the broker in fact controls the account.[21]

(3) The cases are in disarray with respect to the kind of "common enterprise" required to make an "investment contract" out of a discretionary account. The broadest view is satisfied with "vertical commonality"; that approach recognizes a "common enterprise" between broker and customer, without insisting on any sort of pooling among customers' accounts.[22] A stricter view does insist on such pooling: "horizontal commonality."[23] The strictest view is not satisfied, at least with merely vertical commonality, unless the broker himself shares in the enterprise apart from his commissions.[24]

(4) There is authority for the proposition that a commodity futures contract for a Government security involves a "contract to buy" the underlying security and hence constitutes, within §3(a)(13) of the 1934 Act, a "purchase" of a security for purposes of Rule 10b-5.[25]

Conn. 1980); Savino v. E. F. Hutton & Co., 507 F. Supp. 1225, 1235-39 (S. D. N. Y. 1981).

[21] Scheer v. Merrill Lynch, Pierce, Fenner & Smith, Inc., CCH Fed. Sec. L. Rep. ¶95,086 (S. D. N. Y. 1975).

[22] SEC v. Continental Commodities Corp., 497 F. 2d 516, 520-23 (5th Cir. 1974) (options on commodity futures); Troyer v. Karcagi, 476 F. Supp. 1142, 1147-48 (S. D. N. Y. 1979), and cases cited at 1147 n. 7; Alvord v. Shearson Hayden Stone, Inc., 485 F. Supp. 848, 853 (D. Conn. 1980). This view is supported by the holdings that pooling of accounts is not a prerequisite to other kinds of investment contracts. See p. 197 supra.

[23] Milnarik v. M-S Commodities, Inc., 457 F. 2d 274 (7th Cir. 1972), *cert. denied*, 409 U. S. 887; Curran v. Merrill Lynch, Pierce, Fenner & Smith, Inc., 622 F. 2d 216, esp. at 224-25 (6th Cir. 1980), *aff'd on other grounds* sub nom. Merrill Lynch, Pierce, Fenner & Smith, Inc. v. Curran, 456 U. S. 353 (1982) (even though the account was misrepresented as including the essential elements of horizontal commonality); Salcer v. Merrill Lynch, Pierce, Fenner & Smith, Inc., 682 F. 2d 459 (3d Cir. 1982); cf. Marine Bank v. Weaver, 102 S. Ct. 1220, 1225 (1982), supra p. 197 n. a.

[24] Meyer v. Thomson & McKinnon Auchincloss Kohlmeyer, Inc., 686 F. 2d 818 (9th Cir. 1982), *cert. denied,* — S. Ct. — , and earlier 9th Cir. cases cited; Savino v. E. F. Hutton & Co., 507 F. Supp. 1225, 1237-38 (S. D. N. Y. 1981); Kaufman v. Magid, 539 F. Supp. 1088, 1097 (D. Mass. 1982). The cases cited supra n. 22 do not consider this question.

[25] Paine, Webber, Jackson & Curtis, Inc. v. Conaway, 515 F. Supp. 202, 210 (N. D. Ala. 1981); Fisher v. Dean Witter Reynolds, Inc., 526 F. Supp. 558 (E. D. Pa., Giles, J., 1981). *Contra:* P & C Investment Club v. Becker, 520 F. Supp. 120 (E. D. Pa., Ditter, J., 1981). The SEC staff has taken a "no action" position under the several statutes to the extent that investments in futures contracts on financial instruments, as well as any advice with respect to such contracts, are limited to futures contracts on Treasury instruments, GNMA certificates [which are described in Board of Trade of City of Chicago v. SEC, 677 F. 2d 1137, 1138-39 (7th Cir. 1982), *vacated as moot*, 103 S. Ct. 434 (1982)], and commercial paper, all of which are exempted from registration

(5) Commodity *options* are no more securities *per se* than are commodity futures contracts.[26] But "naked" options — calls not backed by ownership of the commodity futures called for — have been held to be investment contracts, apparently because of the introduction of a substantial, investor "enterprise risk," as well as the seller's undertaking to advise customers with respect to the most opportune moment to sell or exercise their options or to sell specific futures contracts.[27]

The impact on all this of the "exclusive jurisdiction" language in the CFTC Act's definition of "commodity" was unclear.[28] Several District Courts read that phrase to preclude even private actions with respect to discretionary commodity accounts under the SEC's *rules* (notably Rule 10b-5) as distinct from the statutory provisions.[29] But the two Commissions jointly announced in December 1981 that, pending the enactment of clarifying amendments to the securities and commodities laws, they had "resolved a range of issues regarding their respective jurisdictions * * * over a host of instruments generally described as 'financial futures' or 'financial options' ":[30]

(1) The agreement left untouched the CFTC's exclusive juris-

---

under the 1933 Act. Boston Futures Fund 1, CCH Com. Fut. L. Rep. ¶20,915 (1979) (letter).

[26] Glazer v. National Commodity Research & Statistical Service, 547 F. 2d 392 (7th Cir. 1977); but cf. SEC v. American Commodity Exchange, Inc., 546 F. 2d 1361, 1366 (10th Cir. 1976) (purported commodity options sold as part of a scheme to generate fees).

[27] SEC v. Continental Commodities Corp., 497 F. 2d 516 (5th Cir. 1974); SEC v. Commodities Options Int'l, Inc., 553 F. 2d 628 (9th Cir. 1977); Searsy v. Commercial Trading Corp., 560 S. W. 2d 637 (Tex. 1977) (state act). See generally Long, The Naked Commodity Option Contract As a Security, 15 Wm. & Mary L. Rev. 211 (1973); Long, Commodity Options — Revisited, 25 Drake L. Rev. 75 (1976).

[28] See p. 253 supra. In general, see Bromberg, Commodities Law and Securities Law — Overlaps and Preemptions, 1 J. Corp. L. 217 (1976); Guttman, The Futures Trading Act of 1978: The Reaffirmation of CFTC-SEC Coordinated Jurisdiction over Security/Commodities, 28 Am. U. L. Rev. 1 (1978).

[29] Hofmayer v. Dean Witter & Co., Inc., 459 F. Supp. 733 (N. D. Cal. 1978) (court held simply that there could be no resort to Rule 10b-5); Mullis v. Merrill Lynch, Pierce, Fenner & Smith, Inc., 492 F. Supp. 1345, 1349-51 (D. Nev. 1980); Westlake v. Abrams, 504 F. Supp. 337, 345-46 (N. D. Ga. 1980); American Grain Assn. v. Canfield, Burch & Mancuso, 530 F. Supp. 1339, 1346 (W. D. La. 1982).

[30] SEC and CFTC press release (CFTC Rel. 853-81), Dec. 7, 1981, CCH Fed. Sec. L. Rep. ¶83,062; see Longstreth (SEC Commissioner), The SEC-CFTC Accord: Accommodation in the Public Interest (remarks to Securities and Commodities Law Committees of Chicago Bar Assn., Chicago, Apr. 16, 1982).

diction over the trading on boards of trade of *futures contracts* (or options on futures contracts) on securities issued or guaranteed by the United States Government or other SEC-exempted securities (except municipals).

(2) On the other hand, the agreement recognized the SEC as the sole federal regulator of the securities *options* markets. And, in recognition of the SEC's unique responsibilities over the markets for corporate and municipal securities, the two agencies specified certain criteria to govern approval by the CFTC of futures trading in a *group* or *index* of such securities, in addition to affording the SEC an opportunity for an oral hearing before the CFTC (together with judicial review) in order to present the bases for any objection.

This estimable example of administrative harmony hit a snag, however, in the Seventh Circuit. In early 1981 the SEC had approved proposed rule changes by the Chicago Board Options Exchange, a securities exchange,[31] designed to accommodate trading in options on GNMA securities.[32] On petition of the Chicago Board of Trade, which had traded GNMA *futures* since 1975, the Seventh Circuit in a split decision reversed. The majority not only held that the SEC was without jurisdiction because of the CFTC statute — the two Commissions could not by agreement "reapportion their jurisdiction in the face of a clear, contrary statutory mandate"[33] — but also went on, gratuitously, to say that GNMA options were not even "securities" despite the "right to * * * purchase" language of the definition.[34]

This case was promptly overruled by the enactment of the October 1982 amendments.[35] The Commission thereupon approved a number of changes in the rules of the Chicago Board Options Exchange and the American and Philadelphia Stock Exchanges to allow them to begin trading in various financial instruments,[36] and the Supreme Court vacated the Seventh Circuit

---

[31] See p. 251 supra.

[32] Chicago Board Options Exchange, Inc., Sec. Ex. Act Rel. 17,577, 22 SEC Dock. 186 (1981). See n. 25 supra.

[33] Board of Trade of the City of Chicago v. SEC, 677 F. 2d 1137, 1142 n. 8 (7th Cir. 1982), *vacated as moot,* 103 S. Ct. 434 (1982).

[34] 677 F. 2d at 1155-61.

[35] See p. 250 supra.

[36] Sec. Ex. Act Rels. 19,125-34, 26 SEC Dock. 464-92 (1982); see also American Stock Exchange, Inc., Sec. Ex. Act Rel. 19,263, 26 SEC Dock. 1027 (1982) (options on certificates of deposit); American Stock Exchange, Inc., Sec. Ex. Act Rel. 19,264, 26 SEC Dock. 1033 (1982) (options on various stock indexes on Amex, CBOE, and NYSE, marking the NYSE's first entry into the listed

decision as moot.[37] Then, as part of the Future Trading Act of 1982, Congress enacted the SEC-CFTC "treaty" into law.[38]

L. JUDGE OR JURY?

In principle, the line between the functions of judge and jury on the "security" question would seem to be drawn as follows:

(1) If the underlying facts are in dispute in a criminal case, they must go to the jury, and it is reversible error for the judge to instruct flatly that there is an "investment contract" instead of instructing that the jury should find an "investment contract" if it credits certain facts essential to constitute such a "security." "The plea of not guilty puts all in issue, even the most patent truths. In our federal system, the Trial Court may never instruct a verdict either in whole or in part."[1]

(2) This is equally true with respect to a civil action at law, except that the burden of proof is in terms of a preponderance of the evidence rather than the reasonable doubt rule.

(3) When the underlying facts on the "security" question are sufficiently one-sided in a civil action at law so that a verdict for the other side would have to be set aside, the judge (if the other elements of the action are established) may direct a verdict for the first side.[2]

---

options market); Options Clearing Corp., Sec. Ex. Act Rel. 19,274, 26 SEC Dock. 1051 (1982) (foreign currency options). Releases 19,263-64 discuss the economic functions of these various interests, the Commission expressing its belief that, unless serious regulatory concerns were identified, "the market-place generally should be permitted to determine whether a particular contract meets the needs of market participants." Sec. Ex. Act Rel. 19,263, 26 SEC Dock. at 1029.

[37] Board of Trade of the City of Chicago v. SEC, 103 S. Ct. 434 (1982).

[38] See H. R. Rep. No. 97-964 (1982); Rosen, The Impact of the Futures Trading Act of 1982 on Commodity Regulation, 15 Sec. Reg. L. Rep. 142 (1983). The statute departs from the "treaty" in giving the SEC an effective veto over any application submitted to the CFTC on or after December 9, 1982, for designation of a stock index future or an option on such a future. The statute also prohibits the designation of future contracts and options on such contracts based on individual corporate or municipal securities.

C. 3L   [1] Roe v. United States, 287 F. 2d 435, 440-41 (5th Cir. 1961), cert. denied, 368 U. S. 824; see also Farrell v. United States, 321 F. 2d 409, 414-16 (9th Cir. 1963), cert. denied, 375 U. S. 992 (court approved jury instruction on question whether certain trust deed notes were "notes" or "evidences of indebtedness" or "investment contracts"); Gibbs v. United States, 559 F. 2d 28 (10th Cir. 1976), cert. denied, 434 U. S. 1015.

[2] Ahrens v. American-Canadian Beaver Co., Inc., 428 F. 2d 926, 928 (10th

(4) So far as the esoteric types of "security" are concerned, the question is far less likely to be determinable as a practical matter from the face of a written instrument alone.[3] But when that is so under the conceded facts, it is not error, even in a criminal case, to refuse an instruction giving an abstract definition of "security" in the language of the statute.[4]

(5) In any case, the "security" question under the federal statute is to be determined as a matter of federal law, regardless of the impact of state law.[5]

M. A FEW FINAL WORDS ABOUT STATUTORY CONSTRUCTION

Justice Jackson's language in the *Joiner* case rejecting the liberal-strict construction approach[1] in favor of reading "text in the light of context" was a breath of fresh air that one hoped might counter the pressure, as Justice Schaefer of the Illinois Supreme Court put it, toward "a jurisprudence of words or phrases divorced from facts and capable of generating new words and phrases with

---

Cir. 1976); Great Western Bank & Trust Co. v. Kotz, 532 F. 2d 1252, 1255 (9th Cir. 1976). Cf. also SEC v. W. J. Howey Co., 328 U. S. 293 (1946), supra p. 192, an action for injunction that the Commission lost on the "investment contract" point in both lower courts but won in the Supreme Court. Justice Frankfurter dissented on the ground that the majority had ignored the federal two-court rule with respect to findings of fact. But the majority obviously thought that it was free to decide the question as one of law, since it said that "Most of the facts are stipulated." Id. at 294.

[3] Aldrich v. McCulloch Properties, Inc., 627 F. 2d 1036, 1039 (10th Cir. 1980).

[4] Tarvestad v. United States, 418 F. 2d 1043, 1048 (8th Cir. 1969) (no more specific instruction was requested); United States v. Austin, 462 F. 2d 724, 735-36 (10th Cir. 1972), *cert. denied*, 409 U. S. 1048 (court conceded that *Roe,* supra n. 1, was substantially indistinguishable, but "in this six-week trial * * * establishing guilt beyond all reasonable doubt, we do not believe that reversal would be justifiable"); United States v. Carman, 577 F. 2d 556, 562-63 (9th Cir. 1978). See also, under the California statute, People v. Skelton, 109 Cal. App. 3d 691, 716, 167 Cal. Rptr. 636, 649 (1980), and cases cited.

[5] SEC v. C. M. Joiner Leasing Co., 320 U. S. 344, 352 (reversing holding below that "defendants' offerings were beyond the scope of the Act because they offered [oil] leases and assignments that under Texas law conveyed interests in real estate"); SEC v. Variable Annuity Life Ins. Co. of America, 359 U. S. 65, 69 (1959); Farrell v. United States, 321 F. 2d 409, 416 (9th Cir. 1963), *cert. denied*, 375 U. S. 992 (California law limiting personal liability of makers of trust deed notes *held* not determinative).

C. 3M   [1] 320 U. S. at 350-51, supra p. 190.

independent lives."[2] And one does occasionally find echoes of this suspicion of maxims.[3] But not all judges seem eager to be liberated from the ratrace that caused a Texas court to say that the blue sky law "should be considered as a penal statute when it is sought to enforce the penalty, and as a remedial statute when it is sought to enforce the [civil] remedy."[4] In short, the old maxims have a good deal of staying power, and advocates may be pardoned for following the judges' rhetoric when it suits their purpose.[5] Indeed, three short years after *Joiner* an appellate court quoted from Justice Jackson's opinion to support the proposition that the Securities Act "should be liberally construed"![6]

The further Jackson adjuration to read "text in the light of context"[7] is reflected in the statutes themselves insofar as their definitional sections apply "unless the context requires otherwise."[8] The Supreme Court has referred to this phrase in stating that "Congress itself has cautioned that the same words may take on a different coloration in different sections of the securities laws."[9] In that case the Court did not have to decide whether the

[2] Schaefer, Book Review, 84 Harv. L. Rev. 1558, 1559-60 (1971); cf. Pound, Common Law and Legislation, 21 Harv. L. Rev. 383, 386-87, 401-02 (1908).
[3] See Herman & MacLean v. Huddleston, 103 S. Ct. 683, 690 n. 23 (1983), set out infra p. 1141, at p. 1146 n. 23; United States v. Charnay, 537 F. 2d 341, 348 (9th Cir. 1976), *cert. denied*, 429 U. S. 1000; United States v. Chiarella, 588 F. 2d 1358, 1368 n. 16 (2d Cir. 1978), *rev'd on other grounds* sub nom. Chiarella v. United States, 445 U. S. 222 (1980). As Justice White has said (in a non-SEC case) of the maxim that penal statutes should be strictly construed:

> But that canon "is not an inexorable command to override common sense and evident statutory purpose," United States v. Brown, 333 U. S. 18, 25 [1948], and does not "require that the act be given the 'narrowest meaning.' It is sufficient if the words are given their fair meaning in accord with the evident intent of Congress." United States v. Raynor, 302 U. S. 540, 552 [1938] * * *

United States v. Cook, 384 U. S. 257, 262-63 (1966).
[4] Dempsey-Tegeler, Inc. v. Flowers, 465 S. W. 2d 208, 211 (Tex. Civ. App. 1971).
[5] See p. 1105 infra. Contrast Murphy, J., in M. Kraus & Bros., Inc. v. United States, 327 U. S. 614, 626 (1946) ("certainly a criminal conviction [under the Emergency Price Control Act of 1942] ought not to rest upon an interpretation reached by the use of policy judgments rather than by the inexorable command of relevant language"), with Warren, C. J., in Tcherepnin v. Knight, 389 U. S. 332, 336 (1967) ("we are guided by the familiar canon of statutory construction that remedial legislation should be construed broadly to effectuate its purposes").
[6] Creswell-Keith, Inc. v. Willingham, 264 F. 2d 76, 80 (8th Cir. 1959).
[7] 320 U. S. at 351, supra p. 188.
[8] Sec. Act §2; Sec. Ex. Act §3(a); Holding Co. Act §2(a); Trust Ind. Act §303; Inv. Co. Act §2(a); Inv. Adv. Act §202(a); see also Code §201(a).
[9] SEC v. National Securities, Inc., 393 U. S. 453, 465-66 (1969).

Commission's former Rule 133, its so-called "no sale rule" with respect to mergers and the like,[10] precluded a sale for purposes of Rule 10b-5, because the rule itself was limited to §5. And it later left open the question whether the "context" language permitted different interpretations of "sale" for purposes of applying the registration and fraud provisions to interests in employee pension plans.[11] Nevertheless, a number of lower courts have applied the word "context" as referring not only to the context of the statute itself but also to "the surrounding factual circumstances.[12] And there is support for that view in the legislative history.[13]

[10] See p. 316 infra.

[11] International Brotherhood of Teamsters v. Daniel, 439 U. S. 551, 567 n. 22 (1979), set out supra p. 229, at p. 238.

[12] E. g., Emisco Industries, Inc. v. Pro's, Inc., 543 F. 2d 38, 39 (7th Cir. 1976); Exchange National Bank v. Touche Ross & Co., 544 F. 2d 1126, 1137-38 (2d Cir. 1976), supra p. 173, *semble*.

[13] Early versions of the 1933 bills said: "unless the *text* requires otherwise." S. 875 and H. R. 4314, §2, 73d Cong. (1933). The "context" language was substituted in H. R. 5480.

CHAPTER 4

"OFFER," "SALE," "UNDERWRITER," AND "DEALER"

A. "SALE" AND "OFFER" [§2(3)]

1. EXCHANGES OF SECURITIES AND ALTERATIONS OF THEIR TERMS

The Commission has not attempted any metaphysical distinction between "value" and "consideration." By now, however, it is pretty well understood that certain types of disposition are regarded as made for "value" and others not. Thus, it is clear on the face of the statute that an exchange of one security for another is a sale: witness the exemptions provided by §§3(a)(9) and 3(a)(10) for certain types of exchange offerings,[1] as well as the reference in the definition of "security" to certificates of deposit, voting trust certificates, and receipts, which are normally issued only in exchange for outstanding securities. The Commission has likewise held that securities issued in settlement of open-book or contract obligations are issued for value.[2] The stamping of outstanding bonds to evidence their holders' consent to an extension of maturity has been treated by the courts as if it were an exchange of new bonds for old and hence a sale; the absence of a new certificate is regarded as irrelevant.[3] On the same rationale it is equally

C. 4A [1] See pp. 301, 308 infra.
[2] Resources Corp. Int'l, 7 SEC 689, 730 (1940).
[3] SEC v. Associated Gas & Electric Co., 99 F. 2d 795 (2d Cir. 1938). This case was decided under the Holding Company Act, which defines the term "sale" even more broadly to include "any sale, disposition by lease, exchange or pledge, or other disposition," with no mention of "value." §2(a)(23). Moreover, that Act requires an effective declaration not only in order to "sell" any security but also in order to "issue" any security or "to exercise any privilege or right to alter the * * * rights of the holders of an outstanding security." §6(a). But the court spoke only in terms of a "sale" within the

263

unimportant that the extension may not even be evidenced by any stamping; dissenters' bonds, for example, may be bought in and the maturity of the others extended by means of an amendment of the underlying indenture.

There is always the question, however, whether the rights of security holders have been so substantially affected by the particular change in the terms of the outstanding security that it becomes a new security. For example, a change in interest or dividend rate or liquidation preference or underlying security, or a change in the identity of the issuer, would seem quite clearly to result in a new security. On the other hand, there is likely to be agreement that a mere change in the name of the security (perhaps from common to Class B stock), or a change in the name of the issuer without a change of identity, or certain types of charter amendment affecting the powers of the directors, do not make a new security. In between come a great variety of other changes — for example, from par to no par or vice versa, changes in par or stated value, changes in redemption or cumulative or conversion features, various changes in voting rights. There the answer must depend on the context, and in fact it varies in different contexts under the SEC statutes themselves.

2.   GIFTS

It would be hard to make a "sale" out of a *bona fide* gift.[4] Thus, just as the Commission regarded noncontributory employee plans as not involving a "sale" of an investment contract,[5] so, too, with respect to *stock* issued to employees as a bonus (that is to say, without any contractual commitment). But the situation is otherwise when stock is offered as a reward for meeting certain sales quotas or other measures of performance. And it must be remembered that even a *gift* of a *warrant* involves an "offer" of the security it calls for, so that the registration and prospectus provisions must be satisfied for the latter security before the gift is made of the warrant. Since it is no extra trouble, it is customary (though not necessary) to register the gift warrants along with the ultimate securities.

---

meaning of the Holding Company Act, and it is impossible to read the opinion without concluding that its rationale applies equally to the Securities Act.

[4] Cf. Shaw v. Dreyfus, 172 F. 2d 140 (2d Cir. 1949), *cert. denied,* 337 U. S. 907 (Sec. Ex. Act §16(b)).

[5] See p. 240 supra.

3. Pledges

RUBIN v. UNITED STATES

Supreme Court of the United States, 1981
449 U. S. 424

Chief Justice Burger delivered the opinion of the Court.

We granted certiorari in this case to decide whether a pledge of stock to a bank as collateral for a loan is an "offer or sale" of a security under §17(a) of the Securities Act of 1933, 15 U. S. C. §77q(a).

I

Late in 1972, petitioner became vice president of Tri-State Energy, Inc., a corporation holding itself out as involved in energy exploration and production. At the time, Tri-State was experiencing serious financial problems. Petitioner approached Bankers Trust Company, a bank with which he had frequently dealt while he had been affiliated with an accounting firm. Bankers Trust initially refused a $5 million loan to Tri-State for operating a mine. Nevertheless, it lent Tri-State $50,000 on October 20, 1972, for 30 days with the understanding that if Tri-State could produce adequate financial information and sufficient collateral, additional financing might be available.

Petitioner assisted other officers of Tri-State in preparing a financial statement for submission to the bank. The balance sheet, which listed a net worth of $7.1 million, was false and misleading in several respects. Tri-State also submitted inflated projections of future earnings based in large measure on sham contracts and forged documentation. Subsequently, petitioner personally paid the loan officer $4,000 and another official $1,000 as inducements for further loans. Tri-State borrowed an additional $425,000 over a brief period. Ultimately, the loans were consolidated into a single demand note for $475,000, dated February 26, 1973.

Bankers Trust required collateral for each new loan; between October 20, 1972, and January 19, 1973, Tri-State pledged stock in six companies. The stocks were represented as being good, marketable, and unrestricted and valued at a total of approximately $1.7 million; in fact, they were practically worthless. Many shares were issued by "shell" companies. Most were simply "rented" — i. e., borrowed from the owner for a fee — to show to the bank or were otherwise restricted. In one instance, petitioner arranged for fictitious quotations to appear in a service reporting over-the-counter transactions and used by the bank in evaluating pledged securities; in another, Tri-State planted, through others, a fictitious advertisement in an overseas newspaper and showed it to the bank, representing it to be a quotation. Trading of one issue was suspended shortly after the pledge when the issuing company could not account for 900,000 shares of its stock; Tri-State replaced this collateral before Bankers Trust learned of the difficulty. Petitioner acted as Tri-State's agent for most of these transactions.

A Justice Department request for information about Tri-State received February 28, two days after the consolidated note was signed, prompted Bankers Trust on March 5 to demand payment in full within three days. No payment of this demand was made, and in May another officer of Tri-State met with bank officials and tried to forestall foreclosure. After rejecting Tri-State's request for a further loan, the bank sued on the note.

Bankers Trust also proceeded against petitioner personally as a guarantor of the loans. Petitioner signed a confession of judgment against himself in the amount of the unpaid loans, plus accrued interest, but thereafter filed a petition for bankruptcy. The bank recovered only about $2,500, plus interest and expenses, on its $475,000 loan.

Petitioner was indicted on three counts of violating and conspiring to violate various federal antifraud statutes, including §17(a) of the Securities Act of 1933, 15 U. S. C. §77q(a). Following a jury trial in the United States District Court for the Southern District of New York, petitioner was convicted on the conspiracy count. On appeal to the Court of Appeals for the Second Circuit, petitioner raised several grounds, including whether a pledge of stock as collateral for a bank loan is an "offer or sale" under §17(a). The Court of Appeals affirmed. 609 F. 2d 51 (C. A. 2 1979). We granted certiorari limited to the question whether such a pledge is an "offer or sale." 445 U. S. 960 (1980).

II

Section 17(a) of the Securities Act of 1933 [prohibits fraud or misrepresentation *"in the offer or sale of any securities."*]

Petitioner does not deny that he engaged in a conspiracy to commit fraud through false representations to Bankers Trust concerning the stocks pledged; he does not deny that the shares were "securities" under the Act. Rather, he contends narrowly that these pledges did not constitute "offers" or "sales" under §17(a) of the Act. Tr. of Oral Arg. 6. To sustain this contention, petitioner argues that Tri-State deposited the stocks with the bank only as collateral security for a loan, not as a transfer or sale. From this he argues that the implied power to dispose of the stocks could ripen into title and thereby constitute a "sale" only by effecting foreclosure of the various pledges, an event that could not occur without a default on the loans.

We begin by looking to the language of the Act. E. g., *Ernst & Ernst v. Hochfelder,* 425 U. S. 185, 197 (1976). The terms "offer" and "sale" in §17(a) are defined in §2(3) of the Act * * * .

Obtaining a loan secured by a pledge of shares of stock unmistakably involves a "disposition of * * * [an] interest in a security, for value." Although pledges transfer less than absolute title, the interest thus transferred nonetheless is an "interest in a security." The pledges contemplated a self-executing procedure under a power that could, at the option of the pledgee (the bank) in the event of a default, vest absolute title and ownership. Bankers Trust parted with substantial consideration — specifically, a total of $475,000 — and obtained the inchoate but valuable interest under the pledges and concomitant powers. It is not essential under the terms of the Act that full title pass to a transferee for the transaction to be an "offer" or a "sale." See, e. g., *United States v. Gentile,* 530 F.2d 461, 466 (C. A. 2), *cert. denied,* 426 U. S. 936 (1976).

III

When we find the terms of a statute unambiguous, judicial inquiry is complete, except "in 'rare and exceptional circumstance.' " [Citations omitted.] No such circumstances are present here, for our reading of the statute is wholly consistent with the history and the purposes of the Securities Act of 1933. The Uniform Sale of Securities Act, a model "blue sky" statute adopted in many states,[a] defined "sale" in language almost identical to that now appearing in §2(3). In *Cecil B. De Mille Productions, Inc. v. Woolery,* 61 F. 2d 45 (C. A. 9 1932), the Court of Appeals for the Ninth Circuit construed this provision of the model statute as adopted by California and held that the definition of "sale" embraced a pledge. Congress subsequently enacted the definition from the uniform Act almost verbatim. [Citations omitted.] Petitioner has cited nothing to suggest that Congress did not intend the broad scope

[a] ED.: This was an earlier uniform act that was withdrawn when the present Uniform Securities Act was promulgated in 1956.

that cases arising under the Uniform Act, such as *Woolery,* supra, had given the definition of "sale." [Citations omitted.]

Treating pledges as included among "offers" and "sales" comports with the purpose of the Act and, specifically, with that of §17(a). We frequently have observed that these provisions were enacted to protect against fraud and promote the free flow of information in the public dissemination of securities. E. g., *United States* v. *Naftalin,* 441 U. S. 768, 774 (1979); *Ernst & Ernst* v. *Hochfelder,* supra, at 195. The economic considerations and realities present when a lender parts with value and accepts securities as collateral security for a loan are similar in important respect to the risk an investor undertakes when purchasing shares. Both are relying on the value of the securities themselves, and both must be able to depend on the representations made by the transferor of the securities, regardless of whether the transferor passes full title or only a conditional and defeasible interest to secure repayment of a loan.

Petitioner would have us interpret "offer" and "sale" in a way that not only is cramped but conflicts with the plain meaning of the statute and its purpose as well. We therefore hold that the pledges here were "offers" or "sales" under §17(a); accordingly, the judgment of the Court of Appeals is affirmed.

Justice BLACKMUN, concurring in the judgment.

While I agree that a pledge of stock to a bank as collateral for a loan is an "offer or sale" of a security within the meaning of §17(a) of the Securities Act of 1933, 15 U. S. C. §77q(a), I reach that conclusion by a slightly different route than does the Court. The Court holds that a pledge confers an "interest in a security," and that therefore a pledge of shares of stock as collateral for a loan constitutes a "disposition of * * * [an] interest in a security, for value" within the meaning of §2(3) of the Act, 15 U. S. C. §77b(3). Ante, at 701. I would hold simply that a pledge of stock as collateral is a type of "disposition" within the meaning of §2(3). See *United States* v. *Gentile,* 530 F. 2d 461, 466 (C. A. 2) *cert. denied,* 426 U. S. 936 (1976) (interpreting §2(3) of the 1933 Act). Cf. §3(a)(14) of the Securities Exchange Act of 1934, 15 U. S. C. §78c(a)(14) ("[t]he terms 'sale' and 'sell' each include any contract to sell or otherwise dispose of"); *Mansbach* v. *Prescott, Ball & Turben,* 598 F. 2d 1017, 1029 (C. A. 6 1979) (interpreting §3(a)(14) of the 1934 Act).[b]

---

[b] ED.: See also SEC v. Guild Films Co., Inc., 279 F. 2d 485 (2d Cir. 1960), *cert. denied* sub nom. Santa Monica Bank v. SEC, 364 U. S. 819, set out infra p. 283.

4. STOCK AND LIQUIDATING DIVIDENDS

A stock dividend "does not distribute property but simply dilutes the shares as they existed before."[6] That is to say, it just cuts the same pie into smaller slices. At the same time — perhaps because enough people think that enough other people will be deluded by stock dividends — "the market may in some instances place value on them."[7]

Presumably the 1933 conference committee was aware of this Janus-faced phenomenon when it omitted a House provision exempting stock dividends because "they do not constitute a sale, not being given for value."[8] And the General Counsel of the Commission early expressed the opinion that, although "the waiver or surrender of a right or claim" ordinarily constitutes "value," there is no sale when a dividend is declared in cash or stock in the alternative and a stockholder's election of the stock waives his right to the cash.[9] He distinguished the case, however, where the board gives stockholders an opportunity to waive a cash dividend that has already been declared and to receive it in the form of securities, since stockholders ordinarily acquire the vested rights of creditors on the public declaration of a cash dividend out of surplus. The same rationale would seem to apply to securities offered in exchange for accrued dividends on preferred stock.

A like analysis should apply in principle to dividends payable in *portfolio* securities, which are really partial liquidations, as long as it is not a case where certain classes of existing security holders are "bought out" by the distribution of portfolio securities in exchange, each holder being permitted to decide for himself whether or not to accept the offer.[10] But in the late 1960s the

---

[6] Hafner v. Forest Laboratories, Inc., CCH Fed. Sec. L. Rep. ¶91,443 at 94,741 (S. D. N. Y. 1964), *aff'd*, 345 F. 2d 167 (2d Cir. 1965). So, too, with respect to a stock split (or, presumably, a reverse stock split). Gurvitz v. Breyman & Co., 379 F. Supp. 1283 (S. D. N. Y. 1974). The title of one article adhering to this view is exceptionally expressive: Sosnick, Stock Dividends Are Lemons, Not Melons, 3 Calif. Mgmt. Rev. 61 (Winter 1961).

[7] Hafner v. Forest Laboratories, Inc., supra n. 6, 345 F. 2d at 168.

[8] H. R. Rep. No. 152, 73d Cong., 1st Sess. (1933) 25; Sec. Act Rel. 3728 (1956) 3.

[9] Sec. Act Rel. 929 (1936). The Uniform Securities Act has an express provision to this effect. §401(j)(6)(B). And it is on this theory that open-end investment companies do not deliver prospectuses in distributions pursuant to dividend investment programs when each stockholder has the option of taking the dividends in cash or shares. SEC, Public Policy Implications of Investment Company Growth, H. R. Rep. No. 2337, 89th Cong., 2d Sess. (1966) 216.

[10] Cf. pp. 924-25 ¶(8) infra. The Uniform Act provision (supra n. 9) applies "whether the corporation distributing the dividend is the issuer of the stock or not."

Commission became aware that some people had developed corporate shell games out of this spin-off technique in order to obtain the advantages of a public market by the back door rather than through registration. The Commission addressed perhaps the simplest model in:

SECURITIES ACT RELEASE NO. 4982: APPLICATION OF THE SECURITIES ACT OF 1933 AND THE SECURITIES EXCHANGE ACT OF 1934 TO SPIN OFFS OF SECURITIES AND TRADING IN THE SECURITIES OF INACTIVE OR SHELL CORPORATIONS
Securities and Exchange Commission, 1969

The Securities and Exchange Commission today made publicly known its concern with the methods being employed by a growing number of companies and persons to effect distributions to the public of unregistered securities in possible violation of the registration requirements of the Securities Act of 1933 and of the anti-fraud and anti-manipulative provisions of the Securities Act of 1933 and the Securities Exchange Act of 1934. The methods employed can take and in fact have taken a variety of patterns.

I

Frequently, the pattern involves the issuance by a company, with little, if any, business activity, of its shares to a publicly-owned company in exchange for what may or may not be nominal consideration. The publicly-owned company subsequently spins off the shares to its shareholders with the result that active trading in the shares begins with no information on the issuer being available to the investing public. Despite this lack of information, moreover, the shares frequently trade in an active market at increasingly higher prices. Under such a pattern, when the shares are issued to the publicly-owned or acquiring company, a sale takes place within the meaning of the Securities Act and if the shares are then distributed to the shareholders of the acquiring company, that company may be an underwriter within the meaning of Section 2(11) of the Act as a person "who purchased from an issuer with a view to . . . the distribution of any security" or as a person who "has a direct or indirect participation in any such undertaking."

While the distribution of the shares to the acquiring company's shareholders may not, in itself, constitute a distribution for the purposes of the Act, the entire process, including the redistribution in the trading market which can be anticipated and which may indeed be a principal purpose of the spin off, can have that consequence. It is accordingly the Commission's position that the shares which are distributed in certain spin offs involve the participation of a statutory underwriter and are thus, in those transactions, subject to the registration requirements of the Act and subsequent transactions in the shares by dealers, unless otherwise exempt, would be subject to the provisions of Section 5 requiring the delivery of a prospectus during the forty or ninety day period set forth in Section 4(3).

The theory has been advanced that since a sale is not involved in the distribution of the shares in a spin off that registration is not required and that even if it is required, no purpose would be served by filing a registration statement and requiring the delivery of a prospectus since the persons receiving the shares are not called upon to make an investment judgment.

This reasoning fails, however, to take into account that there is a sale by the issuer and the distribution thereafter does not cease at the point of receipt by the initial distributees of the shares but continues into the trading market involving sales to the investing public at large. Moreover, it ignores what appears to be primarily the purpose of the spin off in numerous circumstances which is to create quickly, and without the disclosure required by registration, a trading market in the shares of the issuer. Devices of this kind contravene the purpose, as well as the specific provisions, of the Act which, in the words of the statutory preamble, are "to provide full and fair disclosure of the character of the securities sold in interstate and foreign commerce and through the mails, and to prevent frauds in the sale thereof." In the circumstances of a spin off, when the shares are thereafter traded in the absence of information about the issuer, the potential for fraud and deceit is manifest.

This release does not attempt to deal with any problems attributable to more conventional spin offs, which do not involve a process of purchase of securities by a publicly-owned company followed by their spin off and redistribution in the trading markets.[11]

*   *   *

Variations on the theme tend toward the Byzantine.[12] For example:

[11] See also Sec. Ex. Act Rel. 19,284, 26 SEC Dock. 1145 (1982).
[12] See Schneider, Shell Corporations and Spin-Offs, in Practising Law Institute, First Annual Institute on Securities Regulation (1979) c. 15.

SECURITIES AND EXCHANGE COMMISSION v. DATRONICS ENGINEERS, INC.

United States Court of Appeals, Fourth Circuit, 1973
490 F. 2d 250, *cert. denied,* 416 U. S. 937

Before BRYAN, Senior Circuit Judge, and FIELD and WIDENER, Circuit Judges.

BRYAN, Senior Circuit Judge.

The Securities and Exchange Commission in enforcement of the Securities Act of 1933, §20(b), 15 U. S. C. §77t(b), and the Securities Exchange Act of 1934, §21(e), 15 U. S. C. §78u(e), sought a preliminary injunction to restrain Datronics Engineers, Inc., its officers and agents, as well as related corporations, from continuing in alleged violation of the registration and antifraud provisions of the Acts. The breaches are said to have been committed in the sale of unregistered securities, §5 of the 1933 Act, 15 U. S. C. §77e, and by the employment of false representations in their sale, §10(b) of the 1934 Act, 15 U. S. C. §78j, and Rule 10b-5 of the Commission, 17 C. F. R. 240.10b-5.

Summary judgment went for the defendants, and the Commission appeals. We reverse.

Specifically, the complaint charged transgressions of the statutes by Datronics, assisted by the individual defendants, in declaring, and effectuating through the use of the mails, "spin-offs" to and among its stockholders of the unregistered shares of stock owned by Datronics in other corporations. With exceptions to be noted, and since the decision on appeal rests on a motion for summary judgment, there is no substantial dispute on the facts. Datronics was engaged in the construction of communications towers. Its capital stock was held by 1000 shareholders and was actively traded on the market. All of the spin-offs occurred within a period of 13 months — from November 1, 1968 to December 31, 1969 — and the spin-off stock was that of nine corporations, three of which were wholly owned subsidiaries of Datronics and six were independent corporations.

The pattern of the spin-offs in each instance was this: Without any business purpose of its own, Datronics would enter into an agreement with the principals of a private company. The agreement provided for the organization by Datronics of a new corporation, or the utilization of one of Datronics' subsidiaries, and the merger of the private company into the new or subsidiary corporation. It stipulated that the principals of the private company would receive the majority interest in the merger-corporation. The remainder of the stock of the corporation would be delivered to, or retained by, Datronics for a nominal sum per share. Part of it would be applied to the payment of the services of Datronics in the organization and administration of the proposed spin-off, and to Datronics' counsel for legal services in the transaction. Datronics was bound by each of the nine agreements to distribute among its shareholders the rest of the stock.

Before such distribution, however, Datronics reserved for itself approximately one-third of the shares. Admittedly, none of the newly acquired stock was ever registered; its distribution and the dissemination of the false representations were accomplished by use of the mails.

I

Primarily, in our judgment each of these spin-offs violated §5 of the Securities Act * * * in that Datronics caused to be carried through the mails an unregistered security "for the purpose of sale or for delivery after sale." Datronics was actually an issuer, or at least a co-issuer, and not exempted from §5 by §4(1) of the Act, 15 U. S. C. §77d as "any person other than an issuer."

Datronics and the other appellees contend, and the District Court concluded, that this type of transaction was not a sale. The argument is that it was no more than a dividend parceled out to stockholders from its portfolio of investments. A noteworthy difference here, however, is that each distribution was an obligation. Their contention also loses sight of the definition of "sale" contained in §2 of the 1933 Act, 15 U. S. C. §77b. As pertinent here that definition is as follows:

> When used in this subchapter, unless the context otherwise requires —
>
> *   *   *
>
> (3) The term "sale" or "sell" shall include every contract of sale or *disposition* of a security or interest in a security, *for value.* The term "'offer to sell," "offer for sale," or "offer" shall include every attempt or offer to dispose of, or solicitation of an offer to buy, a security or interest in a security, *for value.* . . . (Accent added.)[a]

As the term "sale" includes a "disposition of a security," the dissemination of the new stock among Datronics' stockholders was

---

[a] ED.: The parenthetical phrase is the court's.

a sale. However, the appellees urged, and the District Court held, that this disposition was not a statutory sale because it was not "for value," as demanded by the definition. Here, again, we find error. Cf. *Securities and Exchange Commission* v. *Harwyn Industries Corp.*, 326 F. Supp. 943, 954 (S. D. N. Y. 1971). Value accrued to Datronics in several ways. First, a market for the stock was created by its transfer to so many new assignees — at least 1000, some of whom were stockbroker-dealers, residing in various States. Sales by them followed at once — the District Judge noting that "[i]n each instance dealing promptly began in the spun-off shares." This result redounded to the benefit not only of Datronics but, as well, to its officers and agents who had received some of the spun-off stock as compensation for legal or other services to the spin-off corporations. Likewise, the stock retained by Datronics was thereby given an added increment of value. The record discloses that in fact the stock, both that disseminated and that kept by Datronics, did appreciate substantially after the distributions.

This spurious creation of a market whether intentional or incidental constituted a breach of the securities statutes. Each of the issuers by this wide spread of its stock became a publicly held corporation. In this process and in subsequent sales the investing public was not afforded the protection intended by the statutes. Further, the market and the public character of the spun-off stock were fired and fanned by the issuance of shareholder letters announcing future spin-offs, and by information statements sent out to the shareholders.

Moreover, we think that Datronics was an underwriter within the meaning of the 1933 Act. Hence its transactions were covered by the prohibitions, and were not within the exemptions, of the Act. §§3(a)(1) and 4(1) of the 1933 Act, 15 U. S. C. §§77c, 77d. By definition, the term underwriter "means any person who has purchased from an issuer with a view to, or offers or sells for an issuer in connection with, the distribution of any security, or participates or has a direct or indirect participation in any such undertaking . . . ." §2(11) of the 1933 Act, 15 U. S. C. §77b(11). Clearly, in these transactions the merger-corporation was an issuer; Datronics was a purchaser as well as a co-issuer; and the purchase was made with a view to the distribution of the stock, as commanded by Datronics' preacquisition agreements. By this underwriter distribution Datronics violated §5 of the 1933 Act — sale of unregistered securities.

II

*   *   *

* * * a summary of the activities of Datronics is conclusively convincing that they violated the statutes in question, and should now be restrained to prevent recurrences. To begin with, it is noteworthy that they were not isolated or minimal transgressions. There were, to repeat, nine sales and distributions of unregistered stocks in little more than a year. They were huge in volume, ranging from 75,000 to 900,000 shares. The distribution was not confined to a small number of recipients; nor was it incidental to Datronics' corporate functions. Concededly, none of the several distributions had a business purpose. In short, the spin-offs seemingly constituted the major operation of Datronics at the time.

*   *   *

We cannot read the releases or letters of the Commission or its abstention from earlier suits as evincing express or implied approval of the repeated and large-scale violations as are here. The releases do not approve or condone a campaign, such as Datronics engaged in, to develop means and opportunities to promote spin-offs. Indeed, one of Datronics' agents was a "finder" of opportunities for spin-offs.

*   *   *

Vacated with directions.

WIDENER, Circuit Judge (concurring).
I concur in the issuance of the temporary injunction because I believe the existence of the agreements between Datronics and the various companies whose stock found its way to the market through Datronics, on account of the agreements, with no apparent business purpose which has been expressed to us, other than the creation of a public market for the stock, points to the fact that Datronics may have been a willing catspaw in a device or scheme to avoid the statute. * * *

*   *   *

I note that the opinion of the court may not be broadly enough read to cast doubt upon the legitimate business acquisition of one company by another, or the legitimate business merger of two companies, although a market for securities spun off as a consequence of the transfer may be thereby created; for, as the opinion of the court recites, the market created by Datronics' spin-offs was spurious, doubtless meaning illegitimate, however actual it might have been, and Datronics caused the consummation of the transactions complained of without any business purpose of its own.

In my opinion, the root of this case is the pre-existing agreement between Datronics and the various companies whose stocks it spun off with no apparent purpose other than the incidental benefits of creation of a public market for the stock. If the transactions were with a view to creating a public market for the stock which the various companies could not otherwise do absent compliance with the statute, then I think Datronics may be held to be an underwriter. The value requirement of a sale, 15 U. S. C. §77b(3), for the issuer (15 U. S. C. §77b(4)) did receive value, I think, may be satisfied by the exchange of stock of the various companies with Datronics or by the exchange of stock of the various companies for services of Datronics. See also 58 Va. L. Rev. 1451.[b]

Query: Was Datronics "an issuer, or at least a co-issuer," as the court twice stated, in order to preclude the §4(1) exemption?[13] "Issuer" is defined in §2(4), as we have seen, to mean "every person who issues or proposes to issue any security." Were not the issuers, rather, the companies whose shares were the subject of the dividends? And was not Datronics merely (1) a "controlling" person within the second sentence of §2(11),[14] so that any person who "purchased" the dividend shares from Datronics "with a view to * * * distribution" (or who *sold* them *for* Datronics "in connection with [a] distribution") would be an "underwriter," or (2) an "underwriter" itself as having purchased the shares with a view to their distribution as a dividend? The presence of an

---

[b] ED.: On a petition for reconsideration the court remanded for a determination in the District Court's discretion whether a preliminary injunction should issue, instead of itself requiring an injunction. In SEC v. Harwyn Industries Corp., 326 F. Supp. 943 (S. D. N. Y. 1971), the court had held that §§2(3) and 5 did not require that the "value" flow from the immediate parties who got the stock, but had denied a preliminary injunction because, among other reasons, the defendants had relied on advice of counsel in the light of prevailing business practices and of the Commission's past acquiescence in unregistered spin-offs. See United States v. Rubinson, 543 F. 2d 951, 958 n. 18 (2d Cir. 1976), *cert. denied* sub nom. Chester v. United States, 429 U. S. 850.

[13] Ibid.

[14] See p. 278 infra.

"underwriter" is just as effective to destroy the §4(1) exemption as the presence of an "issuer."

At any rate, the Commission in 1971, using its antifraud rule-making authority under §15(c)(2) of the 1934 Act[15] to reinforce the disclosure scheme of the 1933 Act, adopted Rule 15c2-11, which prohibits broker-dealers from publishing over-the-counter quotations unless specified information is available with respect to the security and its issuer. The Commission referred to shell distributions through the spin-off device as one of the occasions for the rule.[16]

More recently Commission counsel are understood to be taking the position that *any* spin-off requires registration unless the issuer of the dividend security is a reporting company under the 1934 Act. This position is perhaps more straightforward than defensible under the present statutory structure and the saving references in both the 1969 release and Judge Widener's concurring opinion in *Datronics.* A simple, bright line test requires legislation, and the Code supplies it in defining "offer" and "sale" to *include* "a dividend consisting of a security of another company that is not a one-year registrant" and to *exclude* any other "security dividend."[17]

B. "UNDERWRITER" [§2(11)]

1. GENERAL

The determination whether a particular person is an "underwriter" is important for a number of reasons. Underwriters are subject to civil liability under §11 for deficiencies in the registration statement. Various items of the registration forms call for information concerning each underwriter. And, as we have already seen, whether a person is an "underwriter" sometimes determines the availability of both the "preliminary negotiations" clause in §2(3) and the §4(1) exemption for "transactions by any person other than an issuer, underwriter, or dealer."[1]

The term "underwriter" is defined not with reference to the

---

[15] See p. 805 infra.

[16] Sec. Ex. Act Rel. 9310 (1971).

[17] §202(143)(F)(iv) and (G)(iv). The definition excludes also "a split or reverse split." §202(143)(G)(v). A two-for-one split is, of course, the equivalent of a 100 percent stock dividend.

C. 4B [1] See pp. 92-93, 99 supra.

particular person's general business but on the basis of his relationship to the particular offering. No distinction is made between professional investment bankers and rank amateurs. Any person who performs one of the specified functions in relation to the offering is a statutory underwriter even though he is not a broker or dealer. Conversely, even a professional investment banker is *not* a statutory underwriter in effecting a distribution on behalf of a person not in a control relationship with the issuer, or in arranging a private placement on behalf of the issuer or a person in a control relationship with the issuer.

The language of the definition is broad enough to cover at least the three basic types of underwriting that have been described in the preceding chapter: firm-commitment, best-efforts and "old-fashioned." Section 2(11) reads as follows (the letters are added to indicate the six elements of the definition):

> The term "underwriter" means any person who [a] has purchased from an issuer with a view to, or [b] offers or sells for an issuer in connection with, [c] the distribution of any security, or [d] participates or has a direct or indirect participation in any such undertaking, or participates or has a participation in the direct or indirect underwriting of any such undertaking; but [e] such term shall not include a person whose interest is limited to a commission from an underwriter or dealer not in excess of the usual and customary distributors' or sellers' commission. [f] As used in this paragraph the term "issuer" shall include, in addition to an issuer, any person directly or indirectly controlling or controlled by the issuer, or any person under direct or indirect common control with the issuer.

2.   THE CONTROL CLAUSE

The second sentence of §2(11) tends to confuse because the introductory clause, "As used in this paragraph," is overlooked. A person in a control relationship with the issuer is *not* an "issuer" *except* for purposes of reading the control language into the *first* sentence. The draftsmen were simply trying to avoid a single, long sentence. In other words, it is as if §2(11) defined the term "underwriter" to mean any person who bought from or sold for either the issuer or a person in a control relationship with the issuer, and so on.

The second sentence nevertheless has two functions:

> The first function is to require the disclosure of any underwriting commission which, instead of being paid directly to the under-

writer by the issuer, may be paid in an indirect fashion by a subsidiary or affiliate of the issuer to the underwriter. Its second
function is to bring within the provisions of the bill redistribution
whether of outstanding issues or issues sold subsequently to the
enactment of the bill. All the outstanding stock of a particular
corporation may be owned by one individual or a select group of
individuals. At some future date they may wish to dispose of
their holdings and to make an offer of this stock to the public.
Such a public offering may possess all the dangers attendant upon
a new offering of securities. Wherever such a redistribution
reaches significant proportions, the distributor would be in the
position of controlling the issuer and thus able to furnish the
information demanded by the bill. This being so, the distributor
is treated as equivalent to the original issuer and, if he seeks to
dispose of the issue through a public offering, he becomes subject to the act.[2]

It is the second of these two functions that is the more significant, and that has created the problems under the "control" clause.
Since the same or similar questions of control pervade all the SEC
statutes, the discussion of what constitutes control within the meaning of §2(11) will be reserved for a later chapter.[3] In general, the
Commission has applied the pragmatic test: Is the particular person in a position to obtain the required signatures of the issuer
and its officers and directors on a registration statement? No other
criterion would do, since the controlling person himself is not an
"issuer" except for purposes of §2(11).

3. PURCHASING FROM AN ISSUER

The term "purchased," which is not separately defined in the
Act, presumably is complementary to the word "sold" or "sell."[4]
Clearly it includes an exchange.[5] The substance of the transaction
controls. The Commission held that a firm was an underwriter
under this language because it had loaned money to an individual
to enable him to exercise an option to buy a controlling block of
stock and the firm was to share in the profits and risks of the undertaking.[6] In another case the issuer's president was held to be an

---

[2] H. R. Rep. No. 85, 73d Cong., 1st Sess. (1933) 13-14.
[3] See c. 6 infra.
[4] See SEC v. Guild Films Co., Inc., 279 F. 2d 485, 489 (2d Cir. 1960),
cert. denied sub nom. Santa Monica Bank v. SEC, 364 U. S. 819.
[5] Hayes Mfg. Corp., 23 SEC 574, 576-77 (1946).
[6] Sweet's Steel Co., 4 SEC 589 (1939).

underwriter because his activities in connection with two previous registrations justified the inference that he would exercise purchase warrants and resell the registered stock in substantial volume, as he did, even though he received no price differential and was treated no differently from other stockholders.[7]

The status of a large warrant holder who wishes to exercise his warrants and distribute the underlying securities, but who is not connected with the issuer in any way, is unclear. He does fall literally within the definition of "underwriter," even though he may be the last person in the world the issuer would choose to act in that capacity in the usual sense. Indeed, the humble investor who buys 100 shares of a registered issue with the hope of a quick turnaround profit by reselling on the stock exchange likewise falls literally within the definition, because she has purchased "with a view to * * * distribution"; the term "distribution" is more or less synonymous with "public offering,"[8] and a sell order given to a stock exchange broker results in an offer to the highest bidder anywhere in the world, which is certainly a "public offering." But surely that result would be even more inane than to say that a tremendous shareholder who exercises stock purchase rights can *never* be an underwriter."

How, then, to separate the big from the small potatoes? Commission counsel have tried a number of pragmatic solutions. For a while they applied a rule of thumb in terms of 10 percent of the issue. Gradually they began to consider that percentage as simply one factor together with other circumstances such as the total amount of the issuer's securities outstanding, the size of the "float," and whether the issuer was a reporting company under the 1934 Act. And in recent years "no action" letters have tended simply to apply the volume figures in Rule 144, which is considered in a later chapter: the greater of (1) 1 percent of the amount outstanding or (2) the average weekly reported volume of trading during the last four weeks.[9] But, as we shall see there, this area is something of a morass.

4.   SELLING FOR AN ISSUER

This part of the definition, too, is broad enough to cover a person who solicits exchanges of securities on behalf of the issuer.[10]

---

[7] Kinner Airplane & Motor Corp., Ltd., 2 SEC 943, 946-48 (1937).

[8] See H. R. Rep. No. 1838, 73d Cong., 2d Sess. (1934) 41; Gilligan, Will & Co. v. SEC, 267 F. 2d 461, 466-68 (2d Cir. 1959), *cert. denied*, 361 U. S. 896. On "public offering," see c. 5E infra.

[9] Rule 144(e), infra p. 426.

[10] Chair Stores Depot Corp., 7 SEC 1015, 1024 (1940).

However, the ordinary protective committee in reorganization is not considered to be an "underwriter"; when it delivers the new securities to its depositors, it is acting for them and not for the issuer.[11] Whether directors or officers or employees of the issuer who sell on its behalf are underwriters or are merely performing their official corporate functions is a question of fact in each case. If their selling activity is only an incidental function of their regular duties and they receive no additional compensation, they are not regarded as underwriters, since a corporation can act only through individuals.[12] But a different conclusion is required when they spend a major part of their time and effort in selling activities and receive special compensation.[13] It should be highly relevant also whether they are specially hired in connection with the company's selling activities, particularly if they have a background in the securities business either as professional promoters or otherwise.[14]

The Second Circuit has made it clear that a person may be an underwriter under this part of the definition even though it has no contractual relationship or understanding with the issuer. The first holding to this effect was made in the course of reversing a District Court judgment that had dismissed the Commission's complaint for an injunction to restrain future violations of §5 by a Chinese benevolent association. The association had received some $600,000 from members of various Chinese communities in the Eastern states for the purpose of acquiring Chinese "Liberty Bonds." The association would deliver the money to the New York agency of the Bank of China, together with written applications for bonds by the respective purchasers, and the New York agency would transmit the funds to its branch in Hong Kong, which would return the bonds to the New York branch. Neither the association nor any of its members had ever received any compensation from any source. The motive was purely patriotic. A majority of the court nevertheless concluded:

> Whether the Chinese government as issuer authorized the solicitation, or merely availed itself of gratuitous and even unknown acts

[11] Commonwealth Bond Corp., 1 SEC 13, 17, 18 FTC 635, 641 (1934).
[12] Free Traders, Inc., 7 SEC 913, 921-22 (1940).
[13] Beta Frozen Food Storage, Inc., 37 SEC 387, 392 (1956). It would also be evidentiary of an "underwriter" status, presumably, if they rather than the issuer were to hire or pay salesmen, or pay any part of the selling expenses, or maintain separate offices for handling sales.
[14] Cf. American Gyro Co., 1 SEC 83, 93 (1935) (several stock salesmen engaged at 25 percent commission). A related question is whether an officer, director, or employee of the issuer selling its securities must be registered as a broker under the 1934 Act. See p. 681 infra.

on the part of the defendant whereby written offers to buy, and the funds collected for payment, were transmitted to the Chinese banks does not affect the meaning of the statutory provisions which are quite explicit. In either case the solicitation was equally for the benefit of the Chinese government and broadly speaking was for the issuer in connection with the distribution of the bonds.[15]

5.   DONEES AND PLEDGEES

The question whether a donee or pledgee may be an "underwriter" implicates both the "purchasing from" and the "selling for" parts of the definition. There have been registrations for secondary distributions effected by charitable donees of controlling persons. The theory, presumably, was that registration would have been required if the controlling person had himself distributed the shares through an underwriter for cash and contributed the cash to a charitable institution — a procedure that would not be nearly so favorable for him from the tax point of view. Even so, secondary distributions by controlling persons are exempted under §4(1) unless there is an "underwriter" in the picture. And one may question whether a court would agree that a charitable donee was a person that had "purchased from" or was "selling for" the controlling person within the meaning of §2(11).[16]

The case for finding an "underwriter" is stronger, for example, when securities are given to a university on condition that a building be named after the donor, or when the donee is a charitable foundation identified in name and purpose with the donor. The case for making a "sale" out of a charitable gift may also be a bit stronger where there was a prior pledge to make the gift, though there is undeniably a bootstrap quality about this approach. But apparently the Commission does not stop with either of these situations. It has referred publicly to a letter of Commission counsel estating that the answer "may be given only after consideration of all the relevant facts including the intents and purposes of the donor, any understandings or agreements between the donor and donee, and the needs and policies of the donee," and that, "As a general rule, registration may be required when a gift of securities is made by a control person under circumstances in

---

[15] SEC v. Chinese Consolidated Benevolent Assn., Inc., 120 F. 2d 738, 740 (2d Cir. 1941), cert. denied, 314 U. S. 618.

[16] See pp. 279-82 supra.

which a redistribution to the public by the donee may reasonably be anticipated."[17]

The fact is that the charitable gift cases that have been registered so far have involved gifts requiring the immediate use of cash, for example, to build a library. But this test exalts account-juggling, in that the donee can simply use unrestricted funds or sell other securities out of its portfolio in order to finance the donor's project and hold the donor's securities for investment.

The donor, of course, may always condition his gift on the donee's holding for investment — though that may reduce its value for income tax purposes. Or the donee may avoid an "underwriter" status by reselling privately for investment — though, here again, unless the donor were to restrict his gift accordingly, he might be involved in a distribution by the donee as "underwriter" in accordance with the Commission's view, and any such restriction would presumably diminish the value of the gift for tax purposes.

The case of a noncharitable donee — for example, a daughter of the controlling person who, in order to diversify her portfolio, sells a substantial block of securities that she has received from her father as a wedding gift — is different still. On the one hand, the lack of any tax advantage to the donor weakens the Commission's case. But on the other hand, the family relationship makes it easier to say that the daughter is an "underwriter" in the sense that she is "selling for" her father.[18]

SECURITIES AND EXCHANGE COMMISSION v. GUILD FILMS COMPANY, INC.
United States Court of Appeals, Second Circuit, 1960
279 F.2d 485, *cert. denied* sub nom. Santa Monica Bank v. SEC,
364 U. S. 819

Before MOORE, Circuit Judge, and SMITH and HERLANDS, District Judges.

MOORE, Circuit Judge.

This is an appeal under 28 U. S. C. A. §1292(a) from an order by the district court, 178 F. Supp. 418, granting a preliminary injunction to restrain the sale of 50,000 shares of Guild Films Company, Inc. common stock by two of the appellants, the Santa

---

[17] Letter of Chief Counsel, Div. of Corp. Fin., Aug. 8, 1962, CCH Fed. Sec. L. Rep. ¶1551.60, cited in Sec. Act Rel. 4669 (1964) 3 n. 5.

[18] Compare the charitable and noncharitable gift cases under §16(b) of the 1934 Act. See 2 Loss 1082-84.

Monica Bank and The Southwest Bank of Inglewood. Pending a final determination of this action, the preliminary injunction was issued "unless and until" a registration statement should be filed under the Securities Act of 1933, 15 U. S. C. A. §77a et seq.

Section 5 of the Act makes it unlawful for anyone, by any interstate communication or use of the mails, to sell or deliver any security unless a registration statement is in effect. Section 4 provides, however, that "the provisions of section 5 * * * shall not apply to * * * (1) Transactions by any person other than an issuer, underwriter, or dealer." The banks claim that they come within this exemption to the registration requirements. The district court rejected this claim, holding that the banks were "underwriters" within the meaning of the Act. While the issue involved can be simply stated, a rather complete discussion of the facts is necessary.

[In September 1958 Hal Roach, Jr., obtained a short-term loan from two banks, pledging shares of F. L. Jacobs Co., Inc., of which he was a controlling stockholder. The Jacobs stock having dropped in value after the New York Stock Exchange had suspended trading, the banks on December 9, 1958, demanded payment by December 15, the due date. Roach was in financial difficulties, and after considerable negotiations the banks again demanded payment on January 28, 1959, this time by February 3. Meanwhile Roach had arranged a deal on January 23 whereby Guild Films Co., Inc., was to issue 400,000 shares of stock and some notes to a Roach subsidiary in exchange for certain film rights. On the deadline date of February 3 Roach wired the banks that he would furnish 50,000 shares of Guild Films stock as additional collateral, and a certificate in that amount, executed in blank, was delivered to the banks on February 12. Pending registration of the shares issued to the Roach subsidiary, the subsidiary warranted that the 400,000 shares were being acquired for investment, so that the private offering exemption in §4(2) would be available. And on the instruction of Guild Films the transfer agent put on the face of the 50,000-share certificate a restrictive legend to the effect that the shares had not been registered, had been acquired for investment, and could not be "sold, transferred, pledged or hypothecated" without an effective registration statement or an opinion of the issuer's counsel that registration was not required. On February 11, the day before delivery of the Guild Films certificate to the banks, the SEC had suspended all trading in the stock. And on February 12 the banks wired Roach that they were calling the loan and would sell the stock if payment were not received within four days. Payment was not made. The banks tried to sell the stock on the American Stock Exchange. The transfer agent refused to transfer because of the restrictive legend. The banks (without the SEC's knowledge) obtained an order in the New York Supreme Court directing a transfer. They then began a public sale notwithstanding notice by the Commission's staff that a sale without registration would be unlawful. And the Commission brought this action for an injunction.

[The District Court (referring to the bank that had arranged the loan on behalf of itself and the other bank) stated that, if it were "a bona fide pledgee now seeking to sell collateral it acquired in good faith to secure the debt, it would not appear to come within the statutory prohibition." 178 F. Supp. 418 (S. D. N. Y. 1959). And the court continued:

> The fact that a pledge as such is not exempt by the Act is not significant, since the activities proscribed by their terms exclude a pledge transaction. The touchstone to the transaction is the good faith of the parties — a good faith consisting not of an absence of intent to evade the statute, but an absence of intent on the part of the one delivering the property that it be sold and an absence of intent on the part of the one receiving it, at the time he receives the property[,] to sell it.

But the court found the conclusion inescapable that Roach had purchased the stock in order to have the bank sell it for his benefit, since he himself could not do so; that this made him an "underwriter"; that the bank in turn was no more interested than Roach in acquiring stock that it could not liquidate promptly; that clearly it was no longer hoping for payment from him; that the bank's action, "while for its direct benefit, was ultimately for the benefit of Roach who in exchange for an extension on a past due debt of $120,000 planned to be able to sell 'tainted' stock through the Bank"; and that consequently the bank, too, became an "underwriter."]

The Securities Act of 1933 was primarily intended to "protect investors by requiring registration with the Commission of certain information concerning securities offered for sale." *Gilligan, Will & Co. v. S. E. C.*, 2 Cir., 1959, 267 F. 2d 461, 463. An exemption from the provisions of §5 of the Act was provided by §4(1) for "transactions by any person other than an issuer, underwriter or dealer" because it was felt that no protection was necessary in these situations. See H. R. Rep. No. 85, 73rd Cong., 1st Sess. (1933) at p. 15. The primary question involved in this case is: were appellants issuers, underwriters or dealers within this exemption?

An "underwriter" is defined in §2(11), 15 U. S. C. A. §77b(11), as "any person who has purchased from an issuer with a view to, or sells for an issuer in connection with, the distribution of any security, * * * or participates or has a participation in the direct or indirect underwriting of any such undertaking * * * ." The burden of proof is on the one seeking an exemption. *Gilligan, Will & Co. v. S. E. C.,* supra.

The banks cannot be exempted on the ground that they did not "purchase" within the meaning of §2(11). The term, although not defined in the Act, should be interpreted in a manner complementary to "sale" which is defined in §2(3) as including "every * * * disposition of * * * a security or interest in a security, for value * * * ." In fact, a proposed provision of the Act which expressly exempted sales "by or for the account of a pledge holder or mortgagee selling or offering for sale or delivery in the ordinary course of business and not for the purpose of avoiding the provisions of the Act, to liquidate a bona fide debt, a security pledged in good faith as collateral for such debt," was not accepted by Congress. S. 875, 73rd Cong., 1st Sess. (1933) §126. Cf. Throop & Lane, Some Problems of Exemption Under the Securities Act of 1933, 4 Law & Contemp. Prob. 89, 124 n. 103 (1937).

Nor is it a defense that the banks did not deal directly with Guild Films. This court has recently stated that "the underlying policy of the Act, that of protecting the investing public through the disclosure of adequate information, would be seriously impaired if we held that a dealer must have conventional or contractual privity with the issuer in order to be an 'underwriter.' " *S. E. C. v. Culpepper,* 2 Cir., 1959, 270 F. 2d 241, 246, following *S. E. C. v. Chinese Consol. Benev. Ass'n,* 2 Cir., 1941, 120 F. 2d 738, *certiorari denied,* 1942, 314 U. S. 618. It was held in these two cases that §4(1) "does not in terms or by fair implication protect those who are engaged in steps necessary to the distribution of a security issue. To give Section 4(1) the construction urged by the defendant would afford a ready method of thwarting the policy of the law and evading its provisions." *S. E. C. v. Chinese Consol. Benev. Ass'n,* supra, 120 F. 2d at page 741.

The banks have contended that they were "bona fide pledgees" and therefore "entitled upon default to sell the stock free of restrictions." They assume that "good faith" in accepting the stock is a sufficient defense. See Loss, Securities Regulation, 346 (1951). But the statute does not impose such a "good faith" criterion. The exemption in §4(1) was intended to permit private sales of unregistered securities to investors who are likely to have, or who are likely to obtain, such information as is ordinarily disclosed in registration statements. See *S. E. C.* v. *Ralston Purina Co.,* 1953, 346 U. S. 119. The "good faith" of the banks is irrelevant to this purpose. It would be of little solace to purchasers of worthless stock to learn that the sellers had acted "in good faith." Regardless of good faith, the banks engaged in steps necessary to this public sale, and cannot be exempted.

Without imputing to the banks any participation in a preconceived scheme to use the pledge of these securities as a device for unlawful distribution, it may be noted that when the 50,000 shares of Guild Films stock were received on February 12, 1959, the banks knew that they had been given unregistered stock and that the issuer had specifically forbidden that the stock "be sold, transferred, pledged or hypothecated in the absence of an effective registration statement for the shares under the Securities Act of 1933 or an opinion of counsel to the company that registration is not required under said Act." Furthermore, from Roach's prior unfulfilled promises, the banks should have known that immediate sale was almost inevitable if they were to recoup their loans from the security received. On February 11, 1959, the day before the stock was received, the S. E. C. suspended trading in the Jacobs stock. And on the very day that the stock was received, appellants wired Roach that they would call the loan unless payment were made. For months the banks had threatened action but declined to act; circumstances finally required action. The banks cannot now claim that this possibility was unforeseeable. The district court properly enjoined the threatened violation.

Affirmed.

Query:

(1) Does *Rubin*[19] foreclose any critique of *Guild Films?* That is to say, does *Rubin* decide either the question whether a pledge is a "sale" or the question whether a pledgee is an "underwriter" for purposes of §5 of the 1933 Act? The §5 question may arise in a number of ways even though banks do not ordinarily make loans to companies that are collateralized by their own shares. For quite commonly the borrower does pledge the stock of a subsidiary in order to obtain funds for the operations of that subsidiary, or of the parent borrower itself or of some other subsidiary. Indeed, the borrower may borrow in order to *acquire* control of a company whose shares he pledges to secure the loan. Or the pledged shares may be controlled by a *guarantor* of the

---

[19] Set out supra p. 265.

loan, as in the case where a bank makes a loan to a closely held corporation but asks for the personal guarantees of the owners and takes a pledge of the stock of the borrowing company in order to protect itself against a change in ownership.

(2) On the assumption that *Rubin* does not *govern* in these §5 contexts, it is still easier probably, under the language of §2(3), to say that a pledge involves a "sale" to the pledgee than that it does not.[20] Even so, is it not a *non sequitur* to say that the pledgee is an "underwriter" as having purchased "with a view to * * * distribution"? For does it not require a forced reading of that phrase to say that a *bona fide* lender is calculating more on foreclosure than on repayment? So, if the pledgee is a purchaser but is *not* an underwriter, is not the §4(2) exemption available? And, if the pledgee *is* an "underwriter" *arguendo,* is not the pledge itself excluded from the definition of "sale" by the "preliminary negotiations" clause of §2(3)?

(3) On the other hand, even if the pledge itself is not a "sale" and the pledgee is not *ab initio* an "underwriter" for purposes of §5, is it not persuasive to argue that the pledgee does purchase *on foreclosure* and, if it forecloses "with a view to * * * distribution," becomes an "underwriter" at that time? Alternatively, can the foreclosing pledgee be brought under the "sells for" phrase in §2(11) because of its obligation to account to the pledgor for any amount by which the proceeds of the foreclosure sale exceed the debt; or does the "sells for" phrase contemplate more than that?

(4) What if the pledgor loses control of the issuer between date of pledge and date of foreclosure?

(5) Until *Guild Films* it had been generally considered that a *bona fide* pledge did not involve an "offer" or "sale" and that, in any event, a foreclosure sale by a *bona fide* pledgee of securities deposited as collateral by the issuer or a control affiliate was exempt under §4(1) unless the pledgee was himself in a control relationship with the issuer and also used an underwriter.[21] The Commission argued as appellee in that case that every pledgee did engage

---

[20] There is a series of 10b-5 cases so holding. See Kerbs v. Fall River Industries, Inc., 502 F. 2d 731, 739 (10th Cir. 1974); Mallis v. Federal Deposit Ins. Corp., 568 F. 2d 824, 828-30 (2d Cir. 1977), *cert. dismissed* sub nom. Bankers Trust Co. v. Mallis, 435 U. S. 381; Mansbach v. Prescott, Ball & Turben, 598 F. 2d 1017, 1029 (6th Cir. 1979); but cf. McClure v. First National Bank of Lubbock, Tex., 497 F. 2d 490 (5th Cir. 1974), *cert. denied,* 420 U. S. 930. The Code makes a pledge a "sale" for fraud purposes, §202(143)(F)(v). And the Code's successor to 1933 Act registration no longer turns on the presence of an "underwriter." See 1 Code xxxii-xxxiii.

[21] See Throop and Lane, Some Problems of Exemption under the Securities Act of 1933, 4 Law & Contemp. Prob. 89, 124 (1937).

in a "purchase" within the meaning of §2(11), but that whether registration would be required for a *bona fide* foreclosure sale "is not the issue here, because clearly these are not the facts in the instant case."[22] If, therefore, the appellate court had affirmed on the lower court's reasoning to that effect, the case would have been of little consequence. Since the last paragraph of the appellate opinion did, in effect, agree that this was not a case of a *bona fide* pledge, can the rest of the opinion be regarded as dictum?[23]

(6) Why was the Second Circuit so eager to address itself to a question of great importance that was not at all necessary to the decision — a question that could not have been fully argued, with all its implications for the world of commercial banking, and that one cannot assume would have been decided the same way after a proper argument directed to the facts of an altogether different case? With great respect to those who joined in the opinion, would it not have been better if they had heeded the Supreme Court's admonition:

> Courts should avoid passing on questions of public law even short of constitutionality that are not immediately pressing. Many of the same reasons are present which impel them to abstain from adjudicating constitutional claims against a statute before it effectively and presently impinges on such claims.[24]

(7) The SEC for its part, although it had not requested the appellate court to go so far, eagerly clasped the entire opinion to its corporate bosom. "Although we believe, as the court below held, that registration would be required even if this had been an ordinary collateral situation," the Commission stated in its brief in opposition to the banks' unsuccessful petition for certiorari, "there can be no doubt that registration is required where the securities to be sold were actually transferred and taken with the specific intention that they be distributed in order to obtain repayment of the loan."[25] Was this statement fair to the Supreme Court, or was it an example of overzealous advocacy that came

---

[22] Brief for SEC, pp. 16, 23. That is to say, a *bona fide* pledgee is a bank that "takes unregistered securities as collateral for a loan which the debtor plans to pay at maturity, and which the bank can reasonably expect will be so retired, but because of unforeseen and untoward circumstances the debtor is unable to pay, compelling the bank to resort to the collateral." Id. at 23.

[23] See Lincoln National Bank v. Herber, 604 F. 2d 1038 (7th Cir. 1979).

[24] Eccles v. Peoples Bank of Lakewood Village, Cal., 333 U. S. 426, 432 (1948).

[25] Brief for SEC in Opposition, pp. 7-8, Santa Monica Bank v. SEC, 364 U. S. 819 (1960).

dangerously close to a half-truth in not indicating how recently the Commission had decided so to "believe"?

(8) What should a bank (or other lender) do to protect itself in view of both *Rubin* and *Guild Films?* The first answer that generally comes to mind, when the borrower is an issuer or control affiliate, is to obtain an immediate "shelf" registration, or the borrower's promise to use his best efforts to obtain registration if required, or both.[26] Even the former, however, requires an undertaking with the Commission to file a posteffective amendment to reflect any "fundamental change"; and a registration covenant is cold comfort at best when by hypothesis the lender will be dealing with a registrant that in the event of foreclosure will be probably hostile and possibly insolvent. Therein, indeed, lies the greatest danger of the *Guild Films* case — that borrowers may find it more difficult to finance by pledging the shares of controlled companies, registration covenants notwithstanding. But the person who does decide to lend should consider these protective measures for what they are worth. Moreover, although it might be argued that the pledgor's good faith is not so essential to the exemption as the pledgee's, it is understood to have been the administrative view for some period even before *Guild Films* that both parties must contemplate in good faith, when the loan is made, that it will be repaid. Consequently, the careful lender will also see to it (as he normally will quite apart from the Securities Act) that there is objective evidence of the borrower's probable ability to make repayment.

There are other devices that may be used either as alternatives or in addition to a registration covenant:

(a) The Uniform Commercial Code authorizes the disposition of collateral after default "by public or private proceedings" as long as "every aspect of the disposition including the method, manner, time, place and terms" are "commercially reasonable" and (unless the collateral is perishable "or threatens to decline speedily in value or is of a type customarily sold on a recognized market")

---

[26] See p. 142 supra. Rule 415(a)(1)(vi) permits "shelf" registration for securities "pledged as collateral." Under either alternative, in order for the bank to protect itself against the possibility that the borrower may lose control otherwise than through a disposition of the pledged securities, an act that, of course, is under the bank's control, the borrower might be asked to get the appropriate promises from the issuer itself. Or, at the very least, the pledgor should agree, by way of minimizing the possibility of his loss of control, that he will not sell or pledge any of his unpledged holdings before discharging the loan; and any such agreement, in order to bind innocent buyers or pledgees of those holdings, should be accompanied by a legend on the shares restricting transferability.

the debtor is given "reasonable notification of the time * * * after which any private sale * * * is to be made."[27] Moreover, "The fact that a better price could have been obtained by a sale at a different time or in a different method from that selected by the secured party is not of itself sufficient to establish that the sale was not made in a commercially reasonable manner."[28] Indeed, the lender may ask the borrower to secure a "take out" or "pick up" letter from a satisfactory third party who will agree with the lender that upon the lender's demand or the pledgor's default he will either buy, or seek or secure somebody who will buy, the pledged securities for investment.[29]

(b) Since a private sale for investment is apt to entail a substantial discount below the market price, banks normally buttress the right of private sale by a specific provision in the loan agreement. Although §9-501(3) of the Uniform Commercial Code generally precludes waiver or variation of the Code's safeguards of the debtor's rights, it does permit the parties by agreement to "determine the standards by which the fulfillment of these rights and [the secured party's] duties is to be measured if such standards are not manifestly unreasonable."

(c) When the loan is collateralized by securities in addition to the "control" stock, the lender can simply liquidate the other collateral first and realize on the "control" stock only as a last resort. Here again, in order to avoid any question of the lender's right to determine which collateral to dispose of first, a suitable provision might be written into the loan agreement.

(d) The Commission permits a pledgee to sell "control" stock through a broker under the brokerage exemption in §4(4) as elucidated by Rule 144.[30] Once more, an agreement permitting the use of that procedure may prevent a later complaint by the debtor that a less restricted method of sale might have brought a higher price. Moreover, it may be well to obtain agreements by the controlling stockholders to file the reports necessary to activate Rule 144.

(e) Subject to a similar agreement, the pledgee might try to

---

[27] §9-504(3).

[28] §9-507(2).

[29] See, e. g., Meadow Brook National Bank v. Levine, CCH Fed. Sec. L. Rep. ¶91,496 (N. Y. Sup. Ct. 1965). It has been said that "This is not a practical solution." Lehr, Some Securities Law Issues in Lending on Pledged Stock, 38 Bus. Law. 91, 119 n. 139 (1982).

[30] See pp. 401, 426-27 infra; Hueter, The Plight of the Pledgee under Rule 144, 3 Sec. Reg. L. J. 111 (1975).

use the intrastate exemption[31] rather than the private offering exemption in selling the security on foreclosure. But, insofar as the application of that exemption to secondary distributions by controlling persons is treated differently from its application to primary distributions,[32] a sale on foreclosure of a loan made to the *issuer* would probably be considered in the primary category on the theory that the lender (i) is an "underwriter" rather than a controlling person and (ii) is, under the law of pledge, selling for the issuer.

6. PARTICIPATION IN AN UNDERWRITING

The House report, after referring to the other portions of the "underwriter" definition, went on to say:

> The definition of underwriter is also broad enough to include two other groups of persons who perform functions, similar in character, in the distribution of a large issue. The first of these groups may be designated as the underwriters of the underwriter, a group who, for a commission, agree to take over pro rata the underwriting risk assumed by the first underwriter. The second group may be termed participants in the underwriting or outright purchase, who may or may not be formal parties to the underwriting contract, but who are given a certain share or interest therein.[33]

It seems quite clear, therefore, that the language of §2(11) is intended to cover the "old-fashioned underwriter."[34] Whether he is an underwriter only with respect to the amount sold, or also with respect to the unsold portion he takes down, is not clear; the former is understood to be the administrative construction if the portion taken down by the underwriter is held for investment. In any event, the Commission's Rule 142 has the effect of excluding an "old-fashioned underwriter" from the definition if his sole function in the distribution is confined to an undertaking entered into with one of the principal underwriters (*not with the issuer itself*) to purchase all or some specified proportion of the securities remaining unsold after the lapse of some specified period of time, and if he purchases those securities for investment. It is required also that he have no affiliation of any kind with any of the principal underwriters. The Commission's General Counsel has observed that this rule was "adopted in recognition of the

---

[31] See c. 5C infra.
[32] See p. 323 infra.
[33] H. R. Rep. No. 85, 73d Cong., 1st Sess. (1933) 13.
[34] For a description of this type of underwriting, see p. 81 supra.

value of secondary capital in facilitating the flow of investment funds into industry, and of the fact that the owners of such secondary capital cannot practicably perform the duty of thorough investigation and analysis imposed by the Act on the underwriter proper." In emphasizing that the rule "in no way limits the responsibility of the underwriter who actually serves as a conduit for the distribution of securities to the public," this opinion points out that "Disproportionate commissions or service fees would raise a serious doubt whether the functions of the persons concerned were in fact confined as prescribed in the rule."[35]

Section 2(11), particularly the clause here marked [d], also extends beyond the "old-fashioned underwriter." The section was amended in conference "to make clear that a person merely furnishing an underwriter money to enable him to enter into an underwriting agreement is not an underwriter."[36] The report went on to say: "The test is one of participation in the underwriting undertaking rather than that of a mere interest in it." The Commission has accordingly applied the definition to a person appointed by the principal underwriter as "exclusive selling agent," as well as a person who by arrangement with the principal underwriters undertook to see that a daily print would be made on the stock exchange tape.[37] Presumably the definition applies likewise to a "sub-underwriter" whom the principal underwriters put in charge of the distribution in a particular area of the country. Certainly there is no requirement of privity of contract with the issuer (or a person in a control relationship with the issuer).[38]

The ordinary "finder" who receives a cash fee from either the issuer or the underwriter or both for bringing them together is not himself an underwriter if he does not otherwise participate in the distribution.[39] On the other hand, "Whenever the finder is deemed to be an underwriter by reason of the receipt of securities for services, or otherwise, he should be identified as such in the prospectus."[40] But it does not follow that the receipt of securities for a finder's services will automatically make the finder an underwriter. He will not be an underwriter if he takes the securities

[35] Sec. Act Rel. 1862 (1938).

[36] H. R. Rep. No. 152, 73d Cong., 1st Sess. (1933) 24. But cf. Sweet's Steel Co., 4 SEC 589 (1939), supra n. 6.

[37] Reiter-Foster Oil Corp., 6 SEC 1028, 1036-41 (1940).

[38] The Commission has found it convenient to refer in its registration forms to the "principal underwriter." That term is defined in Rule 405 to mean "an underwriter in privity of contract with the issuer * * * ."

[39] South Umpqua Mining Co., 3 SEC 233, 241 (1938); Sec. Act Rel. 4936 (1968) ¶ 11.

[40] Sec. Act Rel. 4936 (1968) ¶ 11.

for investment, although (1) the securities he receives should be included in the registration statement and (2) it will be more difficult for a finder *who is engaged in the securities business* to persuade the Commission on the eventual resale of his securities that he is not an underwriter despite his investment undertaking.[41]

7. THE USUAL AND CUSTOMARY COMMISSION

The "usual and customary * * * commission" clause of §2(11) seeks to draw the line between "sub-underwriters" and ordinary selling group dealers. And Rule 141 settles most of the questions by providing that the term "commission" includes the remuneration, commonly known as a "spread," that is received by a dealer who buys and sells as *principal;* that the term "commission from an underwriter or dealer" includes any commission paid by an underwriter or dealer who is in a control relationship with the issuer;[42] that the "usual and customary" commission may not exceed the amount allowed to other persons for comparable services; and that a person *is* an underwriter, regardless of the amount of his commission, if his function "is the management of the distribution of all or a substantial part of the particular issue" or if he "performs the functions normally performed by an underwriter or underwriting syndicate." Section 2(11) itself is specific that the commission may not be received from the issuer.

C. "DEALER" [§2(12)]

Two propositions are apparent on the face of the definition of "dealer" as "any person who engages either for all or part of his time, directly or indirectly, as agent, broker, or principal, in the business of offering, buying, selling, or otherwise dealing or trading in securities issued by another person":

[41] It has been under the California statute that, when a finder goes beyond bringing a buyer and seller together so that they may make their own contract without aid from him, any participation by him in the negotiations, however slight, will make him a "broker," who cannot recover a fee without registration as such. Evans v. Riverside Int'l Raceway, 237 Cal. App. 2d 666, 675-76, 47 Cal. Rptr. 187, 192 (1965).

[42] This makes it clear that the fact that the underwriter is an "issuer" within the meaning of the second sentence of §2(11) does not *per se* place any dealer receiving a commission from him in the "underwriter" category.

(1) In contrast to the definition of "underwriter," this definition does depend on the person's general activities rather than his conduct in the particular offering. And it is settled in a variety of contexts, as has been said of §2(12), that the concept of "doing business" requires a degree of continuity — certainly more than an isolated transaction.[1]

(2) Although in common parlance a dealer is a principal and a broker is an agent, and although §4(4) exempts certain "brokers' transactions" without defining "broker," §2(12) defines "dealer" to include a "broker." This overeconomy of language was corrected in the 1934 Act, which separately defines the two terms in accordance with the English language.[2] "The sole object of this definition," the 1933 House report states, "is thus to subject brokers to the same advertising restrictions [and, it might have added, to the same prospectus delivery requirement pursuant to the dealers' exemption in the present §4(3)] that are imposed upon dealers, so as to prevent the broker from being used as a cloak for the sale of securities."[3]

The brokerage portion of the definition is broad enough to include an auctioneer who is regularly (although not necessarily exclusively) engaged in the business of auctioning securities. Moreover, although banks are specifically excluded from the 1934 Act definitions of "broker" and "dealer," they are not excluded from the definition in §2(12) of the 1933 Act. Presumably, therefore, the ordinary commercial bank, which under the federal banking laws can legally act as broker though not (except, basically, in governments and municipals) as dealer, is a "dealer" under the §2(12) definition, and hence must deliver a prospectus in executing a customer's buy order that it has solicited (so that the exemption for unsolicited brokerage transactions in §4(4) is not available).[4] In a case in which the Commission censured a bank for aiding and abetting an illegal distribution by selling 20,000 shares of common stock for a customer through an account that it maintained with a New York Stock Exchange member firm, the Commission stated:

C. 4C [1] deBrun v. Andromeda Broadcasting Systems, Inc., 465 F. Supp. 1276, 1279 (D. Nev. 1979).

[2] §§3(a)(4), 3(a)(5), discussed infra p. 678.

[3] H. R. Rep. No. 85, 73d Cong., 1st Sess. (1933) 14.

[4] Cf. Hyman v. Gregory & Sons, 44 Misc. 2d 102, 252 N. Y. S. 2d 919 (Sup. Ct. 1964), where the court applied the brokerage exemption to a bank executing an unsolicited buy order for a customer without considering whether the bank was a "dealer" in the first place.

In our opinion, if banks wish to maintain brokerage accounts for the convenience of their customers or others, it is incumbent upon them to take precautions to avoid the use of such accounts in connection with unlawful distributions or unregistered securities. * * * Generally speaking, it would seem that the bank would be expected to follow procedures substantially equivalent to those which we have required brokers-dealers to establish and maintain * * * . We would consider that, alternatively, a bank could meet its responsibilities by requesting the broker-dealer with which it maintains its account to conduct the necessary investigation of the circumstances surrounding a proposed securities transaction, of course with the full cooperation of the bank.[5]

---

[5] Southern Cal. First National Bank of San Diego, 44 SEC 652, 653-54 (1971).

CHAPTER 5

SECURITIES ACT EXEMPTIONS

A.   GENERAL

The exemption in §3(a)(1) for offerings pending in 1933 has long since spent its force. The exemptions in §§3(a)(2), (3), (6), and (8), as well as §§4(1) and 4(3), have already been referred to.[1] And the exemptions in §§3(a)(4) and (5) for securities issued by certain eleemosynary institutions, savings and loan associations, and farmers' cooperatives, as well as the §4(5) exemption for certain first-lien notes, require no discussion here. That leaves for consideration (the letters indicating subchapters) (B) the exchange and reorganization exemptions in §§3(a)(7), (9), and (10) and the bankruptcy statute, (C) the intrastate exemption in §3(a)(11), (D) the exemptions for "small" issues in §4(6) and the rules under §§3(b)-(c), (E) the nonpublic offering exemption in §4(2), and (F) the brokers' exemption in §4(4). But first a number of general observations:

1.   EXEMPTED SECURITIES VERSUS EXEMPTED TRANSACTIONS

A moment's glance at §§3 and 4 will reveal that the dichotomy between the "exempted securities" and the "exempted transactions" was not carefully considered. The exemptions in §§3(a)(2) to 3(a)(8) are genuine security exemptions. But there is nothing peculiar about the securities, or the issuers of the securities, that are exempted under §§3(a)(1), 3(a)(9)-(11), 3(b), and to some extent 3(c). All those exemptions were created because (or in the case of §3(c) partly because) of the circumstances surrounding the particular offering.

C. 5A   [1] See pp. 120, 170 n. a, 174 n. d, 214, 221, 224, 228 n. 44, 248 supra; p. 400 infra.

The fact is that the present 3(a)(9) and 3(a)(10) exemptions were originally §4(3) and that the present 3(a)(11) exemption was originally §5(c). It was essentially a legislative accident that placed these two exemptions among the "exempted securities" in the 1934 amendments. The express purpose of the shift was merely to codify the Federal Trade Commission's previous interpretation[2] that, when the issuer was excused from registration under §4(3) or §5(c), dealers could trade immediately notwithstanding the non-applicability of the dealers' exemption in the then §4(1) (now §4(3) as renumbered in 1964, which is not to be confused with the original §4(3) of 1933-34 vintage) to transactions within "one year [now forty days] after the first date upon which the security was bona fide offered to the public."[3] As sometimes happens when statutes are amended, the attempt to solve one problem created another that was even more serious — namely, the anomaly of having several transaction exemptions included among the security exemptions. What should have been done, of course, was to amend the dealers' exemption to make it clear that the nonexempt period applies only when the particular issue is subject to the registration requirement.[4]

It is not simply a matter of statutory neatness. If these few sections are to be read literally as exempting the securities themselves, presumably a control affiliate's distribution of securities previously issued under one of these exemptions (or a redistribution after a reacquisition by the issuer) would itself be exempt. On the basis of the legislative history the Commission's General Counsel early took the position that a secondary distribution would not be exempt, because §§3(a)(9), 3(a)10), and 3(a)(11) were in substance transaction exemptions.[5] Later this view was formally adopted by the Commission itself.[6]

2.   FRAUD PROVISIONS

None of the exemptions in either §3 or §4 extends to the fraud provisions of §17 or the provision in §12(2) creating civil liability

---

[2] Sec. Act Rel. 97, part 7 (1933).
[3] H. R. Rep. No. 1838, 73d Cong., 2d Sess. (1934) 40.
[4] See Code §512(2).
[5] Op. Gen. Counsel, Sec. Act Rel. 646 (1936).
[6] Thompson Ross Securities Co., 6 SEC 1111, 1117-18 (1940); Sec. Act Rel. 4434 (1961) (§3(a)(11)); Gearhart & Otis, Inc., 42 SEC 1, 27 (1964), aff'd sub nom. Gearhart & Otis, Inc. v. SEC, 348 F. 2d 798 (D. C. Cir. 1965) (§§3(a)(1), 3(b)).

for the sale of securities by misleading statements or omissions.[7] There is one exception to this statement: §12(2) is by its terms inapplicable to the governmental, bank, and other securities exempted under §3(a)(2), not to mention the fraud provisions of the 1934 Act.[8] But even those securities are subject to §17. In other words, it is unlawful for any person to employ any fraudulent scheme in the sale of even a United States Government bond by use of the mails or any facilities of interstate commerce. This conclusion, of course, is subject to whatever may be the general law with respect to (1) presumption of substantive inapplicability of statutes to the Government itself and (2) sovereign immunity of the Government and its agents.[9]

3. BURDEN OF PROOF

In 1938 the Ninth Circuit said of the private offering exemption that "the terms of such an exception to the 'general policy' of the act must be 'strictly construed' against the claimant of its benefit."[10] This was before the *Joiner* Case.[11] Whether or not the injunction of the Supreme Court to look to statutory context rather than maxims of construction applies to this statement of the Ninth Circuit, the more important holding of the Court of Appeals — since repeated by the Supreme Court itself in the context of the same exemption — was that the burden of proving an exemption is on the person who claims it.[12] That is the generally accepted view under the blue sky laws as well.[13] By the same token, the

---

[7] §17(c) and introductory clauses of §§3(a) and 4; see, e. g., United States v. Tallant, 547 F. 2d 1291, 1297 (5th Cir. 1977), *cert. denied*, 434 U. S. 889.

[8] Harmsen v. Smith, 693 F. 2d 932, 939-40 (9th Cir. 1982).

[9] All the statutes *except* the 1933 Act and its first cousin, the 1939 Act, codify the first proposition. Sec. Ex. Act §3(c); Holding Co. Act §2(c); Inv. Co. Act §2(b); Inv. Adv. Act §202(b). On both propositions, see Code §304 and cases cited in the comment.

[10] SEC v. Sunbeam Gold Mines Co., 95 F. 2d 699, 701 (9th Cir. 1938); see also, e. g., Hill York Corp. v. American Int'l Franchises, Inc., 448 F. 2d 680, 691-92 (5th Cir. 1971); Quinn & Co. v. SEC, 452 F. 2d 943, 945-46 (10th Cir. 1971), *cert. denied*, 406 U. S. 957.

[11] SEC v. C. M. Joiner Leasing Corp., 320 U. S. 344, 350-51 (1943), set out supra p. 186.

[12] SEC v. Ralston Purina Co., 346 U. S. 119, 126 (1953); see also FTC v. Morton Salt Co., 334 U. S. 37, 44-45 (1948) (a "general rule of statutory construction"). In Whitehall Corp., 38 SEC 259, 268-70 (1958), the Commission carried this rule to the point of finding a violation *without any evidence of offers to nonresidents* simply because the respondent had not sustained the burden of proving that the offers represented by certain interim certificates had been restricted to residents.

[13] E. g., Commonwealth v. David, 365 Mass. 47, 53-54, 309 N. E. 2d 484,

burden of pleading the exemption is also upon the defendant; it is not necessary to negative all the statutory exemptions in an indictment or any other initial pleading.[14]

All this seems reasonable and fair enough as applied to genuine exemptions like those for bank securities, short-term commercial paper, and so on. The defendant has the burden simply of going forward with evidence of his pleaded exemption. The plaintiff retains the ultimate burden of proof by a preponderance of the evidence or, in a criminal case, beyond a reasonable doubt.[15] But suppose, for example, that the question is whether the defendant was a controlling person of the issuer within the meaning of §2(11). Even in a civil action under §12(1), and *a fortiori* in a criminal prosecution, it might still be argued that, when a statute is drafted with a universal prohibition like §5 and a §4(1) type of "exemption" that looks in turn to the last sentence of §2(11), to permit the plaintiff to prove merely a sale of an unregistered security to him by use of the mails and to shift to the defendant the burden of proving lack of control are so far at odds with the usual burden of proof that Congress would have been more specific if it had intended such a departure. So, too, with respect to the nonpublic offering exemption in §4(2). The exemptions altogether, including §§4(1)-(4), probably cover more than 99 percent of all transactions in securities. In short, they are not really exemptions at all but simply "a drafting technique used to extract, from the overall universe of sales, that small segment which is in fact subject to registration."[16]

Admittedly the line between genuine and formal exemptions for purposes of assigning the burden of going forward (and presumably of pleading) would not be easy to draw. In the criminal law generally the Supreme Court held in 1975 that the Maine rule that required a homicide defendant to prove that he acted in the heat of passion or with sudden provocation in order to avoid a mandatory life sentence for murder violated the due process requirement that the prosecution prove beyond a reasonable doubt every fact necessary to constitute the crime charged.[17] Then two

---

488 (1974); Brown v. Cole, 155 Tex. 624, 634, 291 S. W. 2d 704, 711 (1956). The Uniform Securities Act codifies the rule. §402(d); see People v. Dempster, 396 Mich. 700, 242 N. W. 2d 381 (1976) (not an unconstitutional burden); cf. State v. Fairchild, 298 S. E. 2d 110 (W. Va. 1982).

[14] Edwards v. United States, 312 U. S. 473 (1941).

[15] People v. Dempster, 396 Mich. 700, 242 N. W. 2d 381 (1976).

[16] Section 4(2) and Statutory Law: A Position Paper of the Federal Regulation of Securities Committee, Section of Corporation, Banking and Business Law of the American Bar Association, 31 Bus. Law. 485, 503 (1975). This entire paper is set out infra p. 376; see esp. p. 395 infra.

[17] Mullaney v. Wilbur, 421 U. S. 684 (1975).

years later the Court distinguished the 1975 case, stating: "To recognize at all a mitigating circumstance does not require the State to prove its nonexistence in each case in which the fact is put in issue, if in its judgment this would be too cumbersome, too expensive, and too inaccurate."[18] The securities cases, state and federal, reflect this perplexity.[19]

B.   EXCHANGES AND REORGANIZATIONS

1.   VOLUNTARY EXCHANGES [§3(a)(9)]

Section 3(a)(9) exempts "Any security exchanged by the issuer with its existing security holders exclusively where no commission or other remuneration is paid or given directly or indirectly for soliciting such exchange." The philosophy of this exemption is not altogether easy to understand in view of the skepticism that the legislative history reflects concerning voluntary reorganizations. The following rather weak explanation in the conference report indicates that the exemption may represent little more than a horse-trade compromise between the two houses:

> The House provision * * * exempting * * * the sale of stock to stockholders is omitted from the substitute * * * . Sales of stock to stockholders become subject to the act unless the stockholders are so small in number that the sale to them does not constitute a public offering. The Senate agreed that the mere exchange with its security holders of one form of security for another by an

---

[18] Patterson v. New York, 432 U. S. 197, 209 (1977).

[19] In United States *ex rel.* Shott v. Tehan, 365 F. 2d 191, 194 (6th Cir. 1966), *cert. denied,* 385 U. S. 1012, a *habeas corpus* proceeding by a lawyer who had been convicted in Ohio of failing to register a single promissory note as well as failing to register as a dealer in that connection, the court held that shifting the burden of proving an exemption for notes "not offered * * * for sale to the public" was "not unreasonable, nor does it offend any principle of justice, nor does it constitute a denial of due process of law." See also State v. Frost, 57 Ohio St. 2d 121, 387 N. E. 2d 235 (1979); United States v. Abrams, 29 F. R. D. 178, 181 (S. D. N. Y. 1961), *convictions aff'd,* 357 F. 2d 539 (2d Cir. 1966), *cert. denied,* 384 U. S. 1001; Pennaluna & Co., Inc. v. SEC, 410 F. 2d 861, 865 (9th Cir. 1968), *cert. denied,* 396 U. S. 1007. Contrast United States v. Re, 336 F. 2d 306, 317 (2d Cir. 1964), *cert. denied,* 379 U. S. 904 (conviction on §5 count *rev'd* for failure to prove that controlling person was source of shares sold); United States v. Prince, 496 F. 2d 1289, 1291 (5th Cir. 1974), *cert. denied,* 419 U. S. 1107 (court without comment stated that lower court had granted one defendant's post-conviction motion for a judgment of acquittal because prosecution had failed to prove that the stock was not exempt); Gaskin v. State, 248 Ark. 168, 179, 450 S. W. 2d 557, 563 (1970).

issuer where no commission or other remuneration is paid, shall be exempt. This exemption is considered necessary to permit certain voluntary readjustment of obligations. Inasmuch as any exchange that involves the payment of a commission of any sort is not exempt, there is no danger of the provision being used for purposes of evasion.[1]

In any event, the exemption is quite narrow: (a) The issuer of both securities must be the same. (b) Under the administrative construction no part of the offering may be made to persons other than existing security holders or even to existing security holders other than by way of exchange. (c) There may be no paid solicitation.

a. Identity of the Issuer

The reference to exchanges "by the issuer with its existing security holders" precludes application of the exemption in such instances as when a parent offers its securities in exchange for those of a subsidiary or vice versa, or when a successor corporation offers its securities in exchange for those of a predecessor, or when certificates of deposits are issued by a committee in exchange for the securities deposited, or when the securities of a successor corporation are issued in exchange for certificates of deposit representing securities of a predecessor corporation, or when voting-trust certificates are issued in exchange for the securities that are placed in trust. In all these cases the issuer of the security being "sold" is different from the issuer of the security being received in exchange.

Changes in the composition of a committee that has issued certificates of deposit or in the trustees under a voting trust would not seem to result in a change of identity of the "issuer" if effected in accordance with the provisions of the deposit agreement or the trust instrument. This would seem to be equally true with respect to the renewal of a voting trust pursuant to a provision in the original trust instrument.[2] On the other hand, when the original trust instrument contains no renewal provision or when none is permitted by the local law, solicitation of the holders of the expiring voting-trust certificates to deposit their underlying securities

---

C. 5B [1] H. R. Rep. No. 152, 73d Cong., 1st Sess. (1933) 25.
[2] Some corporation statutes expressly provide for a renewal of the term. E. g., Del. Gen. Corp. Law, Del. Code, Tit. 8, §218(b); N. Y. Bus. Corp. L. §621(d).

in a new trust requires registration because the new trust is a different "issuer" from the old.[3]

b.   Exclusively in Exchange

It is not clear from the position of the word "exclusively" whether it modifies "exchanged" or the phrase "with its existing security holders." The Commission has made the word do double duty. Under its construction — which seems as logical as any, and as much as an exemption of such parenthood deserves — the exemption is lost if existing security holders of the issuer are asked to give up anything in addition to their old securites *or* if any part of the new offering is made (whatever the consideration) to persons other than the issuer's security holders.

So far as the first of these conditions is concerned, the Commission has two interpretative rules. One defines the term "exchanged" so that the issuer may require the surrender of the outstanding securities "to be accompanied by such payment in cash by the security holder as may be necessary to effect an equitable adjustment, in respect of dividends or interest paid or payable on the securities involved in the exchange, as between such security holder and other security holders of the same class accepting the offer of exchange."[4] The other, in substance, permits the *issuer* to make payments to its security holders in connection with an exchange; in other words, although anything of value (other than the old securities) coming from the *security holders* will destroy the exemption, except as permitted by the first of these two rules, the payment of cash by the *issuer* will not.[5]

Query: Are the securities issued in "exchange" when the consideration is the waiver of unpaid interest coupons? Should a distinction be drawn between unpaid interest coupons — which, if severed from the bonds and assigned by the bondholders, would presumably be considered "evidences of indebtedness" and hence securities in their own right for purposes of applying the fraud provisions — and unpaid interest not evidenced by coupons? Are accrued but unpaid dividends on preferred stock, or cash dividends declared on preferred or common, different? Undeclared dividends, even though accrued and cumulative, are not a debt.

---

[3] Reserve Life Ins. Co. v. Provident Life Ins. Co., 499 F. 2d 715, 722 (8th Cir. 1974), *cert. denied,* 419 U. S. 1107.

[4] Rule 149.

[5] Rule 150.

So far as the second condition is concerned — that the offering be made exclusively to existing security holders — there is no requirement that it be made to all members of a given class of holders. On the other hand, when part of an issue is offered in exchange with existing security holders and the rest, say, is offered for cash to a sufficiently small number of nonholders that that part considered alone would not involve a public offering, the 3(a)(9) exemption is considered to be destroyed. Inherent in this proposition are two questions:

First, what is an "issue" of securities? The term "issue," which is read into §3(a)(9) by interpretation of the word "exclusively," is explicit in two other exemptions that will be examined shortly.[6] It is a word that is widely used in the financial world without much attention to its precise meaning. It used to be the Commission's general approach that a difference *either* between classes[7] *or* between plans of financing in time and circumstances[8] resulted in a separate "issue" so long as in either event the difference was substantial.[9] For example, if new Series B bonds were offered in exchange for outstanding Series A bonds, and new Series C bonds differing substantially from the Series B were sold to a few insurance companies in order to raise the funds necessary to redeem those Series A bonds whose holders did not accept the exchange offer, the Series B would be exempted under §3(a)(9) and the Series C as a private offering under §4(2). Again, so far as different segments of the *same* class are concerned, the Commission put it this way in discussing one of the other exemptions that expressly involves the "issue" concept:

> The determination whether securities are being offered as part of a single "issue" will depend upon a consideration of various factors concerning the methods of sale and distribution employed to effect the offerings and the disposition of the proceeds. If the offerings may be segregated into separate blocks, as evidenced by material differences in the use of the proceeds, in the manner and terms of distribution, and in similar related details, each offering

---

[6] §§3(a)(11), 3(b), infra c. 5C and p. 341.
[7] Op. General Counsel, Sec. Act Rel. 2029 (1939). Cf. the definition of "class" in Sec. Ex. Act §§12(g)(5) and 15(d) as including "all securities of an issuer which are of substantially similar character and the holders of which enjoy substantially similar rights and privileges."
[8] Unity Gold Corp. 3 SEC 618 (1938); see also Sec. Act Rel. 4434 (1961) (§3(a)(11)).
[9] Hillsborough Investment Corp. v. SEC, 276 F. 2d 665 (1st Cir. 1960); SEC v. Murphy, 626 F. 2d 633, 645 (9th Cir. 1980).

will be a separate "issue." In the main, of course, each case must be determined upon the basis of its own facts.[10]

More recently the Commission has taken the position that a genuine difference in *class* is not conclusive but merely one factor to be considered.[11] In any event, two batches of securities without substantial differences are considered a single "issue": to use SEC jargon, they are "integrated."

Secondly, on the assumption that there *is* a single issue (that is, a single *class* of securities being offered in a single *plan of financing*), under what circumstances may different exemptions be combined? The answer to this question depends on which exemptions are being considered. Naturally both of the exemptions that are sought to be combined must be capable of combination if registration is to be avoided. So far as §3(a)(9) is concerned, it is not capable of combination with any other exemption, as we have seen.

Another problem under this branch of the 3(a)(9) exemption is created by the provision in §2(3) to the effect that the issuance of a security pursuant to a delayed conversion privilege is not a "sale" until the privilege is exercised. In such a case, clearly, the 3(a)(9) exemption is available for the future conversions. On the other hand, when a company issues preferred stock *immediately* convertible into common (regardless of the practicability of immediate conversion from the point of view of market prices), there is a present "offer" of the common. What, then, is the status of the common under §3(a)(9)? In a sense, the consideration given for the common is simply the preferred stock. On the other hand, when a purchaser pays $100 for a share of convertible preferred that he immediately converts into common, it does not seem altogether realistic to consider that he did not have his eye in part on the common when he parted with his money. The administrative construction has gone from one extreme to the other and has now come pretty solidly to rest in the middle. The Federal Trade Commission required immediate registration of both securities, even to insisting on a double registration fee. Then for a while SEC counsel followed the view that the exemption was available notwithstanding immediate convertibility. But for many years the Commission has

[10] Unity Gold Corp., 3 SEC 618, 625 (1938). In the context of the increased use of limited partnerships as financing vehicles, see Integration of Partnership Offerings: A Proposal for Identifying a Discrete Offering, 37 Bus. Law. 1591 (1982) (position paper of an ABA committee).

[11] The Commission has so read Sec. Act Rel. 4552 (1962). See Sec. Act Rel. 6274, 21 SEC Dock. 1013, 1020 (1980); Prelim. Note 3 to Rule 146. The Code's definition of "offering" would restore the old position. §202(110)(A).

required registration of the common along with the preferred on the ground that the *initial offer* (in the common law sense) is not an exchange transaction, while regarding the actual *sale* (in that sense) as exempt. In other words, although §3(a)(9) is not considered to exempt the initial offer of the common stock from the *registration* provisions of §§5(a) and 5(c), it is considered to exempt its actual issuance from the *prospectus* provisions of §5(b). More than that, the exemption extends also to the *continuing* offer of the common inherent in the convertible securities once they have all been issued, so that it is not necessary for the issuer to use a series of nine-month prospectuses under §10(a)(3) as long as the convertible security is outstanding.

Query: Suppose the issuer offers common stock to the public for cash at the same time that it is offering preferred immediately convertible into common. Or suppose an offering of common by way of conversion is outstanding when additional common is offered for cash. Does the cash offering of the common automatically destroy the §3(a)(9) exemption for the issuance of the common upon conversion?

c.   Nonpayment of Remuneration for Soliciting Exchanges

The problems that arise with respect to this final condition of the §3(a)(9) exemption are somewhat simpler. The predecessor exemption in the original Act had prohibited the payment of remuneration "in connection with such exchange" rather than "for soliciting such exchange." The latter language was substituted in the 1934 amendments in order to codify the Federal Trade Commission's interpretation that fees paid, for example, to lawyers or accountants or printers did not destroy the exemption.

The exemption will still be destroyed, however, when any remuneration is paid "directly or indirectly" for soliciting exchanges. This presumably covers remuneration received by the solicitors from sources other than the issuer, whether directors, officers, employees, or outsiders. The question whether the issuer's employees or officers or directors may solicit is much the same as whether they are "underwriters."[12]

Query:

(1) Does the condition with respect to the absence of remuneration preclude the issuer's using paid solicitors to obtain the se-

---

[12] See p. 281 supra.

curity holders' *authorization* of the new issue that is then offered to them by way of exchange?[13]

(2) Not infrequently an issuer forces conversions by calling the convertible security for redemption and seeks to protect its cash position, in the event of an unfavorable market break that could cause many shareholders to let their shares be redeemed, by retaining one or more investment bankers to buy the convertible security at a fraction over the call price, convert, and distribute the underlying security. Is this activity precluded by §3(a)(9)?

d. The Exemption in General

(i)   *When-issued trading:*   So far as when-issued trading in the contemplated securities is concerned, the Commission has interposed no objection, presumably on the theory that the dealers' exemption under §4(3) is available when the ultimate issuance will be exempt under §3(a)(9).[14] On the other hand, it is clear that the dealers' exemption is not available for when-issued trading in advance of an offering that is subject to the registration requirement, since it would be a form of "beating the gun." Consequently, the dealer who offers or sells a security on a when-issued basis in contemplation of an offering under §3(a)(9) is at the mercy of the issuer's failing to comply with all the conditions of the exemption, as well as the issuer's changing its plans and registering the securities after all. Either of these eventualities would put the dealer in the position of having retroactively violated §5, with a consequent contingent liability to his buyers under §12(1) even if the Commission should take no action against him.[15]

---

[13] Cf. p. 103 supra.

[14] See Loss and Vernon, When-Issued Securities Trading in Law and Practice, 54 Yale L. J. 741, 782-86 (1945).

[15] Certain dealers actually found themselves in this predicament in connection with a Brazilian debt refunding in 1944. The Brazilian Government had five series of bond issues outstanding and various political subdivisions had twenty-five series. According to a plan of readjustment that was originally proposed, the federal government was to issue five series of new bonds in exchange for the five old series of its own bonds, and the bonds of the political subdivisions were to be refunded by new bonds that were to be issued by those subdivisions and guaranteed by the federal government. The refunding of the federal bonds was entitled to an exemption under §3(a)(9), but a registration statement was filed to cover the federal guarantee of the subdivisions' twenty-five series. After a substantial amount of when-issued trading had occurred in the new federal bonds that it was thought would be exempted under §3(a)(9), the registration statement was amended to reflect a radical change in the plan of readjustment: the federal government offered

(ii) *The requirement of good faith:* It goes without saying that "Section 3(a)(9) is applicable only to exchanges which are bona fide, in the sense that they are not effected merely as a step in a plan to evade the registration requirements of the Act." This view was early expressed by the Commission's General Counsel in an opinion in which he stated that the determination of the *bona fides* of the exchange would depend on

> factors such as the length of time during which the securities received by the issuer were outstanding prior to their surrender in exchange, the number of holders of the securities originally outstanding, the marketability of such securities, and also the question whether the exchange is one which was dictated by financial considerations of the issuer and not primarily in order to enable one or a few security holders to distribute their holdings to the public.[16]

(iii) *Code treatment:* The Code rationalizes the 3(a)(9) exemption in both directions by (A) limiting it to securities of "one-year registrants" and (B) in that area deleting the exclusivity requirement with respect to nonconversion exchanges and opening the exemption to securities issued on the exercise of warrants as well as conversions so long as there is no paid solicitation.[17] As a substitute for the delivery of a prospectus on exercise, holders of warrants and convertible securities will receive whatever reports the Commission requires to be sent.[18]

2. Judicially or Administratively Approved Exchanges
[§§3(a)(7), 3(a)(10), and 11 U. S. C. §§364(f), 1125(e), 1145]

Until October 1, 1979, §3(a)(10) and the exemptions in §§264, 393, and 518 of Chapters X-XII of the old Bankruptcy Act sub-

---

thirty new series of its own bonds in exchange for all the outstanding series. Since there was to be a single new federal issue part of which was to be exchanged with persons other than existing security holders of the federal government, there could be no 3(a)(9) exemption for any part of the new bonds, and a serious question arose as to the status of outstanding when-issued contracts. In view of the fact that the trading had occurred in good faith in reliance on the original plan, the Commission did not interfere with the consummation of the contracts. N. Y. Herald Tribune, May 27, 1944, p. 17, col. 6; N. Y. Times, July 3, 1944, p. 18, col. 6. No opinion was expressed, however, on the legality of these contracts; the buyers were left to whatever civil remedies they might have.

[16] Op. Gen. Counsel, Sec. Act Rel. 646 (1936).
[17] §512(7)-(8).
[18] §§602(a)(2), 602(e).

stantially overlapped, as §77(f) of that Act, the exemption for "reorganization rails," substantially overlapped §3(a)(6) of the 1933 Act. But the Bankruptcy Reform Act as it is popularly called — it is officially Title 11 of the United States Code — repealed §77 and Chapters X-XII in favor of a single new chapter on reorganization, Chapter 11. And in the process Congress amended §3(a)(10) (and also §3(a)(9)) to exclude from the exemption "a security exchanged in a case under Title 11." This codified the Commission's lately developed view (of dubious merit) under the pre-1979 version of §§3(a)(9) and 3(a)(10).

Otherwise §3(a)(10) embodies none of the restrictions that surround the 3(a)(9) exemption. There is no requirement of identity of the issuers. The new securities may be issued in exchange for claims or property interests as well as outstanding securities; indeed, the consideration may *in part* be cash.[19] Although the exemption does not apply to the issuance of securities *entirely* for cash, there is nothing in its language to prevent combining it with another exemption (if one can be found that does not itself suffer from a marital disability). Finally, the 3(a)(10) exemption is not destroyed by the payment of remuneration for soliciting exchanges.

Section 3(a)(10), on the other hand, does have peculiar conditions and raise peculiar problems of its own:

(a) The syntax requires the construction that a *state* governmental authority must be *expressly* authorized by law to approve not only the terms and conditions of the exchange but also their *fairness*.[20] This is not so with respect to a court or a *federal* official or agency. But the court or the federal official or agency must still hold the requisite hearing on the fairness of the terms and conditions and presumably have jurisdiction to do so.[21] And there is implicit in the language of §3(a)(10) a requirement of adequate notice to all persons to whom it is proposed to issue securities.[22]

(b) The exemption does not apply to the issuance of certificates of deposit unless the court or agency expressly approves the terms and conditions of their issuance after the same type of hearing

---

[19] *Query:* Does a judicial or quasi-judicial determination of the issuer's insolvency render its stock valueless so as to destroy the exemption for new securities issued in consideration of the shares and cash?

[20] Op. Gen. Counsel, Sec. Act Rel. 312 (1935). Although it is a corollary of this position that the approving authority must be expressly authorized to hold the hearing, it is unnecessary that the hearing be mandatory under the applicable state law. Ibid. All this applies equally to state bank and insurance authorities. Institutional Corp. of America, CCH Fed. Sec. L. Rep. ¶78,133 (letter 1971).

[21] Op. Gen. Counsel, Sec. Act Rel. 312 (1935).

[22] Ibid.

that is specified for any other securities that are to be exempted. The courts on occasion have held such hearings so that deposits might be solicited by committees under the exemption.[23]

(c) Just as it is unlawful to offer securities on condition of their future registration, it is the Commission's position that there may be no solicitation of exchanges in advance of the approval that is expected under §3(a)(10). This statement must be qualified, however, to the extent that the particular statute or procedure governing the hearing requires tentative indications of approval of a plan by security holders before the court or authority will give its approval. Otherwise the operation of §3(a)(10) would be stymied. In such cases even formal receipts or certificates of deposit are unobjectionable if their legal effect is equivalent solely to the requisite indication of approval.[24]

The new bankruptcy statute contains three relevant sections. Since they are fairly complex and are yet to be construed, they will be set out in full text with explanatory comments in the footnotes:

RELEVANT PROVISIONS OF TITLE 11, UNITED STATES CODE

§364. Obtaining Credit

(a) If the trustee is authorized to operate the business of the debtor under section 721, 1108, or 1304 of this title, unless the court orders otherwise, the trustee may obtain unsecured credit

---

[23] In re Saenger Theatres, Inc., CCH Bktcy. L. Rep. ¶308 (E. D. La. 1934). Any "court" will do; it may be foreign. And the matter *sub judice* need not be a reorganization. It may be a judicially approved settlement of a class or derivation action. See Ash, Reorganizations and Other Exchanges under Section 3(a)(10) of the Securities Act of 1933, 75 Nw. U. L. Rev. 1, 37-40 (1980). For the first use of §3(a)(10) in settling an action brought by the SEC itself, see SEC v. Blinder, Robinson & Co., Inc., 511 F. Supp. 799 (D. Colo. 1981); for a discussion of the "fairness" criteria there applied, see Glanzer, Schiffman and Packman, Settlement of Securities Litigation through the Issuance of Securities without Registration: The Use of Section 3(a)(10) in SEC Enforcement Proceedings, 50 Ford. L. Rev. 533 (1982).

SEC administrative action under the Holding Company Act may also do the trick. Utah Power & Light Co., Holding Co. Act Rel. 13,748 (1958) 10, n. 7; Holding Co. Act Rel. 16,081 (1968).

A few states have specifically adjusted their blue sky laws to conform to the language of §3(a)(10). Cal. Corp. Code §24142; N. C. Gen. Stat. §78A-30; Ohio Rev. Code §1707.04; Ore. Rev. Stat. 59.220. And since the late 1960s a substantial number of states have enacted insurance legislation directed to the acquisition of control of an insurance company through an exchange offer by a holding company created by it for that purpose. See Ash, supra, at 51-59.

[24] Op. Gen. Counsel, Sec. Act Rel. 296 (1935).

and incur unsecured debt in the ordinary course of business allowable under section 503(b)(1) of this title as an administrative expense.[a]

* * *

(f) Except with respect to an entity that is an underwriter as defined in section 1145(b) of this title, section 5 of the Securities Act of 1933 (15 U. S. C. 77e), the Trust Indenture Act of 1939 (15 U. S. C. 77aaa et seq.), and any State or local law requiring registration for offer or sale of a security or registration or licensing of an issuer of, underwriter of, or broker or dealer in, a security does not apply to the offer or sale under this section of a security that is not an equity security.

* * *

§1125.   POSTPETITION DISCLOSURE AND SOLICITATION

(a) In this section —

(1) "adequate information" means information of a kind, and in sufficient detail, as far as is reasonably practicable in light of the nature and history of the debtor and the condition of the debtor's books and records, that would enable a hypothetical reasonable investor typical of holders of claims or interests of the relevant class to make an informed judgment about the plan; and

(2) "investor typical of holders of claims or interests of the relevant class" means investor having —

(A) a claim or interest of the relevant class;

(B) such a relationship with debtor as the holders of other claims of interests of such class generally have; and

---

[a] ED.: The purpose of this exemption is to finance the reorganization. Section 3(a)(7) of the 1933 Act remains, presumably because it covers certificates issued by a receiver as well as by a trustee in bankruptcy. And that section is not limited, as §364(f) is, to non-equity securities and non-underwriter transactions. But the first limitation is superfluous in view of the practice of financing reorganizations only with debt securities. And, even if the non-underwriter limitation is not read into §3(a)(7), the receiver or trustee relying on that section would not have the advantage of the preemption clause in §364(f), which is new. On the Code's integration of the two sections, see §302(13).

(C) such ability to obtain such information from sources other than the disclosure required by this section as holders [of] claims or interest in such class generally have.

(b) An acceptance or rejection of a plan may not be solicited after the commencement of the case under this title from a holder of a claim or interest with respect to such claim or interest, unless, at the time of or before such solicitation, there is transmitted to such holder the plan or a summary of the plan, and a written disclosure statement approved, after notice and a hearing, by the court as containing adequate information. The court may approve a disclosure statement without a valuation of the debtor or an appraisal of the debtor's assets.

(c) The same disclosure statement shall be transmitted to each holder of a claim or interest of a particular class, but there may be transmitted different disclosure statements, differing in amount, detail, or kind of information, as between classes.

(d) Whether a disclosure statement contains adequate information is not governed by any otherwise applicable nonbankruptcy law, rule, or regulation, but an agency or official whose duty is to administer or enforce such a law, rule, or regulation may be heard on the issue of whether a disclosure statement contains adequate information. Such an agency or official may not appeal from an order approving a disclosure statement.

(e) A person that solicits, in good faith and in compliance with the applicable provisions of this title, or that participates, in good faith and in compliance with the applicable provisions of this title, in the offer, issuance, sale, or purchase of a security, offered or sold under the plan, of the debtor, of an affiliate participating in a joint plan with the debtor, or of a newly organized successor to the debtor under the plan, is not liable, on account of such solicitation or participation, for violation of any applicable law, rule, or regulation governing the offer, issuance, sale, or purchase of securities.[b]

*   *   *

---

[b] ED.: Section 1125(e) is not an exemption for the securities coming out of a reorganization — that is the function of §1145 — but a limitation on civil liability. This section is not only directed to the proxy rules but also designed to preclude civil liability for good faith solicitations of sales and purchases of securities in connection with a plan, on the theory that the policing of the solicitations would be by the court.

§1145.　EXEMPTION FROM SECURITIES LAWS

(a) Except with respect to an entity that is an underwriter as defined in subsection (b) of this section, section 5 of the Securities Act of 1933 (15 U. S. C. 77e) and any State or local law[c] requiring registration for offer or sale of a security or registration or licensing of an issuer of, underwriter of, or broker or dealer in, a security[d] does not apply to —

(1) the offer or sale under a plan of a security of the debtor, of an affiliate participating in a joint plan with the debtor, or of a successor to the debtor under the plan —

(A) in exchange for a claim against, an interest in, or a claim for an administrative expense in the case concerning, the debtor or such affiliate; or

(B) principally[e] in such exchange and partly for cash or property;

(2) the offer of a security through any warrant, option, right to subscribe, or conversion privilege that was sold in the manner specified in paragraph (1) of this subsection, or the sale of a security upon the exercise of such a warrant, option, right, or privilege;

(3) the offer or sale, other than under a plan, of a security of an issuer other than the debtor or an affiliate,[f] if —

(A) such security was owned by the debtor on the date of the filing of the petition;

(B) the issuer of such security is —

(i) required to file reports under section 13 of the Securities Exchange Act of 1934 (15 U. S. C. 78m); and

(ii) in compliance with all applicable requirements for the continuance of trading in such security on the date of such offer or sale; and

---

[c] ED.: This preemption clause, like that in §364(f), is new.

[d] ED.: Title 11 has its own definition of "security" in §101(35), which includes an "investment contract or certificate of interest or participation in a profit-sharing agreement or in an oil, gas, or mineral royalty or lease" only if the contract or interest is registered under the 1933 Act or exempted pursuant to §3(b).

[e] ED.: Note that §3(a)(10) says "partly" in exchange.

[f] ED.: This limited exemption for the sale of a *portfolio* security of the debtor is new.

(C) such offer or sale is of securities that do not exceed —

(i) during the two-year period immediately following the date of the filing of the petition, four percent of the securities of such class outstanding on such date; and

(ii) during any 180-day period following such two-year period, one percent of the securities outstanding at the beginning of such 180-day period; or

(4) a transaction by a stockholder [stockbroker]^g in a security that is executed after a transaction of a kind specified in paragraph (1) or (2) of this subsection in such security and before the expiration of 40 days after the first date on which such security was bona fide offered to the public by the issuer or by or through an underwriter, if such stockbroker provides, at the time of or before such transaction by such stockholder [stockbroker], a disclosure statement approved under section 1125 of this title, and, if the court orders, information supplementing such disclosure statement.

(b)(1) Except as provided in paragraph (2) of this subsection, an entity is an underwriter under section 2(11) of the Securities Act of 1933 (15 U. S. C. 77b(11)), if such entity —

(A) purchases a claim against, interest in, or claim for an administrative expense in the case concerning, the debtor, if such purchase is with a view to distribution of any security received or to be received in exchange for such a claim or interest;

(B) offers to sell securities offered or sold under the plan for the holders of such securities;

(C) offers to buy securities offered or sold under the plan for the holders of such securities, if such offer to buy is —

(i) with a view to distribution of such securities; and

---

^{g} ED.: The word "stockholder" here and in the seventh line is obviously a typographical error for "stockbroker"; and, perhaps to keep lawyers on the *qui vive*, §101(39) of Title 11, in contrast to the definition of "dealer" in §2(12) of the 1933 Act to include a broker, defines "stockbroker" to include a dealer. At any rate, this new exemption supplements the dealers' exemption in §4(3) of the 1933 Act, which does not apply, under its Clause (A), to transactions during the forty-day period covered by §1145(a)(4) (although §1145 (a)(4) seems to overlook the fact that §4(3) is inapplicable for *ninety* days in the case of a first registrant).

(ii) under an agreement made in connection with the plan, with the consummation of the plan, or with the offer or sale of securities under the plan; or

(D) is an issuer, as used in such section 2(11), with respect to such securities.

(2) An entity is not an underwriter under section 2(11) of the Securities Act of 1933 or under paragraph (1) of this subsection with respect to an agreement that provides only for —

(A)(i) the matching combination of fractional interests in securities offered or sold under the plan into whole interests; or

(ii) the purchase or sale of such fractional interests among entities receiving such fractional interests under the plan; or

(B) the purchase or sale for such entities of such fractional or whole interests as are necessary to adjust for any remaining fractional interests after such matching.

(3) An entity other than an entity of the kind specified in paragraph (1) of this subsection is not an underwriter under section 2(11) of the Securities Act of 1933 with respect to any securities offered or sold to such entity in the manner specified in subsection (a)(1) of this section.[h]

(c) An offer or sale of securities of the kind and in the manner specified under subsection (a)(1) of this section is deemed to be a public offering.[i]

---

[h] ED.: Section 1145(a) exempts only the issuance of the securities in the reorganization; it is a transaction exemption, not a securities exemption. In our discussion of the 1933 Act's definition of "underwriter" we have noticed the problem whether a person who takes a large part of a registered issue with a view to distribution is an "underwriter" so as to preclude the §4(1) exemption. See p. 280 supra. And we shall later notice the same problem with respect to a person who takes a large block in an exempted exchange under §§3(a)(9) or 3(a)(10) or in a private offering exempted under §4(2). See pp. 406, 439-40 infra. Section 1145(b)(3) solves the problem, to the extent of a non-"underwriter" within §1145(b)(1), in the context of securities coming out of a Chapter 11 reorganization.

[i] ED.: The purpose of this provision is understood to be to prevent a construction of Rule 144, along the lines of former Rule 155 as interpreted in Sec. Act Rel. 4248 (1960) (see p. 417 n. a infra), so as to impose restrictions on the resale of convertible securities received in a reorganization.

(d) The Trust Indenture Act of 1939 (15 U. S. C. 77aaa et seq.) does not apply to a commercial note issued under the plan that matures not later than one year after the effective date of the plan.[j]

---

3. MERGERS AND SIMILAR EVENTS [RULE 145]

Despite the perceived presence of a "sale" in exchanges of securities and significant alterations of their terms,[25] and despite the definitional implication from the registration exemptions in §§3 (a)(9) and 3(a)(10) for various exchange offerings by way of reorganization or otherwise, the SEC, almost from its first day, took the view that the ordinary merger or consolidation or sale of assets for securities (as well as the ordinary reclassification of a single company's capital structure) did not involve an "offer" or "sale" if under the applicable law or charter provision a vote of a specified majority bound the entire class (subject only to any dissenters' statutory appraisal rights). This so-called "no sale theory" was premised on the concept that stockholders participating in a class vote were simply acting as one of the corporate organs, without the element of *individual* volition that is essential to a "sale."

Both on that account and because the theory did not apply to reorganizations that took the form of share-for-share exchanges, the theory was unforgivably formalistic. And the hole it created was a wide one. Consequently, although the Ninth Circuit early sustained the theory with only a reference to the Commission's brief as *amicus curiae*,[26] the short (really the long) of it is that, after gradually whittling away at the rule that embodied the theory (former Rule 133), the Commission in 1972 finally screwed up the courage to repeal that rule in favor of a new Rule 145 that says there *is* a "sale."[27]

The Committee on Administrative Law of the Association of the Bar of the City of New York — happily — could not resist a reminder, when the Commission had earlier proposed to repeal

---

[j] ED.:The draftsman of Title 11 necessarily worked on the basis of today's Securities Act. On the substantially different — and, one hopes, simpler — treatment of secondary (that is to say, nonissuer) transactions in the Code, see p. 429 infra.

[25] See p. 263 supra.

[26] National Supply Co. v. Leland Stanford Jr. University, 134 F. 2d 689, 694 (9th Cir. 1943), *cert. denied,* 320 U. S. 773.

[27] Sec. Act Rel. 5316 (1972). For the history, see 1 Loss 518-39.

Rule 133, that what it called "a serious legal problem" had been similarly solved in Sir William S. Gilbert's Iolanthe:

> QUEEN: * * * And yet (*unfolding a scroll*) the law is clear — every fairy must die who marries a mortal!
> LORD CHANCELLOR: Allow me, as an old Equity draftsman, to make a suggestion. The subleties of the legal mind are equal to the emergency. The thing is really quite simple — the insertion of a single word will do it. Let it stand that every fairy shall die who doesn't marry a mortal, and there you are, out of your difficulty at once![28]

In 1959, when the Commission had amended Rule 133 to limit its application, it had adopted Form S-14 as an optional form for use when registration was required in a merger-type transaction. That form requires the same information as a "proxy statement" or "information statement" under §14 of the 1934 Act.[29] And, when such a statement is sent to the security holders who are to vote, as it must be if their security is registered under the 1934 Act, there may be a "wrap-around" prospectus consisting of the proxy or information statement inside an S-14 cover.[30]

Rule 145 does not apply to a reclassification consisting simply of a "stock split, reverse stock split, or change in par value" or to a merger or consolidation whose sole purpose is to change an issuer's domicile.[31] But the release adopting the rule[32] states that a "short-form merger"[33] involves a "sale" despite the absence of *any* vote of the subsidiary's stockholders and despite the silence of the rule itself. This view is reflected in the Code because it is sound in policy:

[28] Act II, quoted in Purcell, A Consideration of the No-Sale Theory under the Securities Act of 1933, 24 Brooklyn L. Rev. 254, 279 n. 78 (1958).

[29] See p. 522 infra.

[30] Rule 153a defines "preceded by a prospectus" in §5(b)(2) to take into account changes in the body of stockholders between the date of voting and the date of delivery of a prospectus. And there is a "tombstone ad" provision in Rule 145(b)(1). In 1980, as part of its program of integrating filings under the 1933 and 1934 Acts, the Commission adopted Form S-15, which in certain cases permits the delivery of an abbreviated prospectus together with the latest annual report to stockholders, certain portions of which are incorporated by reference into the registration statement. Sec. Act Rel. 6232, 20 SEC Dock. 1092 (1980).

[31] On the scope of the rule's application to transfers of assets for securities, see Rule 145(a)(3).

[32] Sec. Act Rel. 5316 (1972).

[33] See, e. g., Del. Gen. Corp. L., Tit. 8, §253, which permits the merger of a 90 percent subsidiary into its parent without a stockholder vote, subject to dissenters' appraisal rights.

Even a short-form merger comes within the definition. This is consistent with the disclosure philosophy; for the minority holders should be able to make up their minds intelligently whether to demand their statutory appraisal rights or seek injunctive relief. That is to say, the mere fact that they have no vote on the merger is no more significant than it is in an ordinary merger in which the surviving company already owns more than the percentage of shares required for approval.[34]

Whether a short-form merger involves a "sale" today is another question. The Second Circuit in a case under Rule 10b-5 has held that it does.[35]

As that case demonstrates, bringing mergers and the like within the definition of "sale" has an important impact on state corporation law with respect to mergers. Even before the adoption of Rule 145, the "no sale theory," as the Commission took pains to point out when it codified the theory as Rule 133, was limited to §5 as distinct from the fraud provisions of the 1933 and 1934 Acts.[36] This makes Rule 10b-5 and the other fraud provisions available as a basis for attacking mergers and the like, and since state law cannot foreclose federal remedies, to do so even when the merger statute declares that the appraisal remedy is exclusive.[37]

If an exemption is available under §3(a)(9)-(11) or 4(2), nothing in Rule 145 affects that result.[38]

An early draft of the Uniform Securities Act attempted to codify the SEC's then "no sale theory" by *exempting* mergers and the like only from the *registration* requirement.[39] But the final draft excludes mergers and the like from the *definitions* of "offer" and "sale," even for fraud purposes — this on the dual theory that merger provisions at the state level should be relegated to the corporation statutes, and that fraud may be attacked at the state level by means of all the usual remedies at common law and in equity.[40]

The Code is explicit that "offer" and "sale" include the issuance

34 1 Code 188.
35 Vine v. Beneficial Finance Co., Inc., 374 F. 2d 627 (2d Cir. 1967), *cert. denied,* 389 U. S. 970.
36 Sec. Act Rel. 3420 (1951).
37 Swanson v. American Consumer Industries, Inc., 415 F. 2d 1326, 1332-33 (7th Cir. 1969).
38 Sec. Act Rel. 5463, 3 SEC Dock. 600, 601-02 (1974).
39 Harvard Law School Study of State Securities Regulation — A Proposed Uniform Securities Act — Second Draft (Loss and Cowett 1955) §§401(j)(7), 402(b)(8).
40 §401(j)(6)(C); see Loss, Commentary on the Uniform Securities Act (1976) 102-04.

of a security "pursuant to a merger, consolidation, recapitalization, or acquisition of assets."[41]

C. INTRASTATE ISSUES [§3(a)(11)]

SECURITIES ACT RELEASE NO. 4434: SECTION 3(a)(11) EXEMPTION FOR LOCAL OFFERINGS
Securities and Exchange Commission, 1961

The meaning and application of the exemption from registration provided by Section 3(a)(11) of the Securities Act of 1933, as amended, have been the subject of court opinions, releases of the Securities and Exchange Commission [Release Nos. 33-1459 (1937) and 33-4386 (1961)], and opinions and interpretations expressed by the staff of the Commission in response to specific inquiries. This release is published to provide in convenient and up-to-date form a restatement of the principles underlying Section 3(a)(11) as so expressed over the years and to facilitate an understanding of the meaning and application of the exemption.[1]

*   *   *

"Issue" Concept[a]

A basic condition of the exemption is that the *entire issue* of securities be offered[b] and sold exclusively to residents of the state in question. Consequently, an offer to a non-resident which is considered part of the intrastate issue will render the exemption unavailable to the entire offering.

Whether an offering is "a part of an issue," that is, whether it

---

[41] §202(143)(F)(iii)(I).

C. 5C [1] Since publication of the 1937 release, the Investment Company Act of 1940 was enacted, and under Section 24(d) thereof, the Section 3(a)(11) exemption for an intrastate offering is not available for an investment company registered or required to be registered under the Investment Company Act. [But the Commission may exempt specific issues from §24(d) as it may from any other provision of the 1940 Act.]

[a] Ed.: See p. 304 supra.

[b] Ed.: An offer to a nonresident destroys the exemption for the entire issue even if no sales are made to nonresidents. SEC v. Hillsborough Investment Corp., 173 F. Supp. 86, 87-88 (D. N. H. 1958), *permanent injunction,* 176 F. Supp. 789 (D. N. H. 1959), *aff'd on other grounds* sub nom. Hillsborough Investment Corp. v. SEC, 276 F. 2d 665 (1st Cir. 1960). On the other hand, mere delivery to a nonresident who had been a resident at the time of the sale, or acceptance of payment from such a person, should not be fatal.

is an integrated part of an offering previously made or proposed to be made, is a question of fact and depends essentially upon whether the offerings are a related part of a plan or program. *Unity Gold Corporation*, 3 S. E. C. 618, 625 (1938); *Peoples Securities Company*, SEA Release No. 6176, Feb. 10, 1960. Thus, the exemption should not be relied upon in combination with another exemption for the different parts of a single issue where a part is offered or sold to non-residents.

*   *   *

Moreover, since the exemption is designed to cover only those security distributions, which, as a whole, are essentially local in character, it is clear that the phrase "sold only to persons resident" as used in Section 3(a)(11) cannot refer merely to the initial sales by the issuing corporation to its underwriters, or even the subsequent resales by the underwriters to distributing dealers. To give effect to the fundamental purpose of the exemption, it is necessary that the entire issue of securities shall be offered and sold to, and come to rest only in the hands of residents within the state. If any part of the issue is offered or sold to a non-resident, the exemption is unavailable not only for the securities so sold, but for all securities forming a part of the issue, including those sold to residents. Securities Act Release No. 201 (1934); *Brooklyn Manhattan Transit Corporation*, 1 S. E. C. 147 (1935); *S. E. C. v. Hillsborough Investment Corp.*, 173 F. Supp. 86 (D. N. H. 1958); *Hillsborough Investment Corp. v. S. E. C.*, 276 F. 2d 665 (C. A. 1, 1960); *S. E. C. v. Los Angeles Trust Deed & Mortgage Exchange, et al.*, 186 F. Supp. 830, 871 (S. D. Cal., 1960), aff'd 285 F. 2d 162 (C. A. 9, 1960).[e] It is incumbent upon the issuer, underwriter, dealers and

---

[e] ED.: *Cert. denied*, 366 U. S. 919. The Commission has repeatedly held that a single sale (or presumably, under its view, a single offer) to a non-resident destroys the exemption for the entire issue. E. g., Armstrong, Jones & Co., 43 SEC 888, 890-94 (1968), *rehearing denied*, 43 SEC 993 (1968), aff'd sub nom. Armstrong, Jones & Co. v. SEC, 421 F. 2d 359 (6th Cir. 1970), *cert. denied*, 398 U. S. 958 (underwriter had reason to believe that two residents who signed subscription agreement were nominees for nonresidents). Part of a single issue may not be sold under the 3(a)(11) exemption even if the balance is registered. Sec. Act Rel. 97, part 10 (1933); see Texas Glass Mfg. Corp., 38 SEC 630, 634 (1938); cf. Unity Gold Corp., 3 SEC 618, 625-26 (1938). In such a case, however, the Commission would be unlikely to take any action except to require the registration statement to disclose a contingent liability under §12(1) for selling in violation of §5 — though there would seem to be no defense to such liability.

Presumably a *gift* could be made to a nonresident. SEC v. Hillsborough Investment Corp., supra, 173 F. Supp. at 90 n. 2. And nonresidents could be other persons connected with the offering to make sure that it does not become an interstate distribution through resales. It is understood to be customary for such persons to obtain assurances that purchases are not made with a view to resale to non-residents.

DOING BUSINESS WITHIN THE STATE

In view of the local character of the Section 3(a)(11) exemption, the requirement that the issuer be doing business in the state can only be satisfied by the performance of substantial operational activities in the state of incorporation. The doing business requirement is not met by functions in the particular state such as bookkeeping, stock record and similar activities or by offering securities in the state.[d] Thus, the exemption would be unavailable to an offering by a company made in the state of its incorporation of undivided fractional oil and gas interests located in other states even though the company conducted other business in the state of its incorporation. While the person creating the fractional interests is technically the "issuer" as defined in Section 2(4) of the Act, the purchaser of such security obtains no interest in the issuer's separate business within the state. Similarly, an intrastate exemption would not be available to a "local" mortgage company offering interests in out-of-state mortgages which are sold under circumstances to constitute them investment contracts. Also, the same position has been taken of a sale of an interest, by a real estate syndicate organized in one state to the residents of that state, in property acquired under a sale and leaseback arrangement with another corporation organized and engaged in business in another state.

If the proceeds of the offering are to be used primarily for the purpose of a new business conducted outside of the state of incorporation and unrelated to some incidental business locally conducted, the exemption should not be relied upon. *S. E. C.* v.

---

bought out for cash. West Side National Bank of San Angelo, 563 Sec. Reg. L. Rep. C-3 (letter 1980). When a nonresident stockholder has preemptive rights, there would seem to be no alternative to arranging a waiver or abandoning the exemption or risking an action by the stockholder for damages or perhaps injunction. A *bona fide* attempt to obtain a waiver should not be regarded as an "offer" to the nonresident. See p. 103 supra. It might be feasible to reserve the nonresident's shares until he found himself in the state and purchase, payment, and delivery could all be effected without use of the mails or interstate facilities; but it would be illegal to use the mails or interstate facilities even indirectly in arranging the sale or delivery.

[d] ED.: Mark E. O'Leary, 43 SEC 842, 847 (1968), *aff'd* sub nom. O'Leary v. SEC, 424 F. 2d 908 (D. C. Cir. 1970).

Truckee Showboat, Inc., 157 F. Supp. 824 (S. D. Cal. 1957). So also, a Section 3(a)(11) exemption should not be relied upon for each of a series of corporations organized in different states where there is in fact and purpose a single business enterprise or financial venture whether or not it is planned to merge or consolidate the various corporations at a later date. *S. E. C.* v. *Los Angeles Trust Deed & Mortgage Exchange, et al.,* 186 F. Supp. 830, 871 (S. D. Cal. 1960), *aff'd* 285 F. 2d 162 (C. A. 9, 1960).[e]

RESIDENCE WITHIN THE STATE

Section 3(a)(11) requires that the entire issue be confined to a single state in which the issuer, the offerees and the purchasers are residents. Mere presence in the state is not sufficient to constitute residence as in the case of military personnel at a military post. *S. E. C.* v. *Capital Funds, Inc.,* No. A46-60 [Litig. Rel. 1805], D. Alaska, 1960.[f] The mere obtaining of formal representations of residence and agreements not to resell to non-residents or agree-

---

[e] ED.: See also SEC v. Freeman, CCH Fed. Sec. L. Rep. ¶96,361 at 93,243 (N. D. Ill. 1978).

[f] ED.: This reflects a construction of "resident" to mean "domiciled" in the conflict-of-laws sense. The legislative committees, in connection with the 1954 amendments that added the words "offered and," stated that "the exemption * * * has not been considered available unless the entire issue of securities was offered and sold exclusively to persons domiciled in the one State." For this statement the reports cited a 1937 opinion of the General Counsel (Sec. Act Rel. 1459), which did go into the "offer" point but was silent on the meaning of "resident." S. Rep. No. 1036 at 13 and H. R. Rep. No. 1542 at 22, 83d Cong., 2d Sess. (1954). What obviously happened is that the SEC lawyers who drafted the legislative reports employed one of the recognized bootstrap techniques of making "legislative history" by having the committees "approve" an administrative construction. To be sure, the interpretation of "resident" as a statutory term depends on the statutory context. 1 Beale, The Conflict of Laws (1935) §10.3. But one is intrigued by the picture of a securities salesman's examining a prospective buyer on his *animus manendi* before making him an "offer." And today the Commission construes "residence" in terms of "principal residence." Rule 147(d)(2), infra p. 331. The Code defines "resident" in terms of "(A) a natural person * * * resident but not necessarily domiciled in a specified place, (B) a corporation, business trust, or limited partnership organized in a specified place, or (C) any other company with its principal place of business in a specified place." §202(141). There is no residence requirement with respect to the underwriter. Whitehall Corp., 38 SEC 259, 268-71 (1958), *semble* (Commission did not question the use of a Texas underwriter for a purportedly Arkansas issue). So, too, with respect to the transfer agent. Letter from Acting Chief Counsel, Div. of Corp. Fin., SEC, Sept. 28, 1956, CCH Fed. Sec. L. Rep. ¶76,411. Presumably, however, there would be some question in the case of a nonresident underwriter not selling as agent but buying for resale, at least if the underwriter retained any part of the issue after completing the distribution. In the case of buyers who take the security in two or more names, whether the tenure is joint, common or by the entirety, presumably both or all must

ments that sales are void if the purchaser is a non-resident should not be relied upon without more as establishing the availability of the exemption.

An offering may be so large that its success as a local offering appears doubtful from the outset. Also, reliance should not be placed on the exemption for an issue which includes warrants for the purchase of another security unless there can be assurance that the warrants will be exercised only by residents. With respect to convertible securities, a Section 3(a)(9) exemption may be available for the conversion.

A secondary offering by a controlling person in the issuer's state of incorporation may be made in reliance on a Section 3(a)(11) exemption provided the exemption would be available to the issuer for a primary offering in that state. It is not essential that the controlling person be a resident of the issuer's state of incorporation.

RESALES

From these general principles it follows that if during the course of distribution any underwriter, any distributing dealer (whether or not a member of the formal selling or distributing group),[g] or any dealer or other person purchasing securities from a distributing dealer for resale were to offer or sell such securities to a non-resident, the exemption would be defeated. In other words, Section 3(a)(11) contemplates that the exemption is applicable only if the entire issue is distributed pursuant to the statutory conditions. Consequently, any offers or sales to a non-resident in connection with the distribution of the issue would destroy the exemption as to all securities which are a part of that issue, including those sold to residents regardless of whether such sales are made directly to non-residents or indirectly through residents who

---

be residents. But, if the one who is a resident supplies the entire purchase price, he might be considered to be making a gift of a part interest to the other without destruction of the exemption. Needless to say, the exemption does not permit offers or sales to resident agents of nonresident principals. Sec. Act Rel. 97, part 9 (1933). In the case of buyers on an installment basis who become nonresidents before all the installments are paid, the legality of accepting further installment payments and making delivery to the former residents should depend on whether there was a mutually enforceable sale in the first instance with a mere postponement of delivery until completion of payment, in which event payment and delivery could be completed, or whether there was in substance a series of separate sales, in which event obviously none could be effected after termination of residence. SEC v. American Founders Life Ins. Co. of Denver, Colo., CCH Fed. Sec. L. Rep. ¶90,861 (D. Colo. 1958).

[g] ED.: J. A. Hogle & Co., 36 SEC 460, 463-64 (1955).

as part of the distribution thereafter sell to non-residents. It would furthermore be immaterial that sales to non-residents are made without use of the mails or instruments of interstate commerce. Any such sales of part of the issue to non-residents, however few, would not be in compliance with the conditions of Section 3(a) (11), and would render the exemption unavailable for the entire offering including the sales to residents. *Petersen Engine Co., Inc.,* 2 S. E. C. 893, 903 (1937); *Professional Investors,* 37 S. E. C. 173, 175 (1956); *Universal Service,* 37 S. E. C. 559, 563-564 (1957); *S. E. C.* v. *Hillsborough Investment Corp.,* 173 F. Supp. 86 (D. N. H. 1958); *Hillsborough Investment Corp.* v. *S. E. C.,* 276 F. 2d 665 (C. A. 1, 1960).[h]

This is not to suggest, however, that securities which have actually come to rest in the hands of resident investors, such as persons purchasing without a view to further distribution or resale to non-residents, may not in due course be resold by such persons, whether directly or through dealers or brokers, to non-residents without in any way affecting the exemption. The relevance of any such resales consists only of the evidentiary light which they might cast upon the factual question whether the securities had in fact come to rest in the hands of resident investors. If the securities are resold but a short time after their acquisition to a non-resident this fact, although not conclusive, might support an inference that the original offering had not come to rest in the state, and that the resale therefore constituted a part of the process of primary distribution; a stronger inference would arise if the purchaser involved were a security dealer. It may be noted that the non-residence of the underwriter or dealer is not pertinent so long as the ultimate distribution is solely to residents of the state.

USE OF THE MAILS AND FACILITIES OF INTERSTATE COMMERCE

The intrastate exemption is not dependent upon non-use of the mails or instrument of interstate commerce in the distribution. Securities issued in a transaction properly exempt under this provision may be offered and sold without registration through the mails or by use of any instruments of transportation or communication in interstate commerce, may be made the subject of

---

[h] ED.: Clearly, however, only those buyers (resident or nonresident) to whom sales *are* made by use of the mails can recover under §12(1). That is to say, a sale (whether to a resident or to a nonresident) cannot itself violate §5 if no use is made of the jurisdictional means in any step of the transaction; but even a fact-to-face sale to a nonresident makes illegal those sales (whether to residents or to nonresidents) that do involve some use of the mails or interstate facilities.

general newspaper advertisement (provided the advertisement is appropriately limited to indicate that offers to purchase are solicited only from, and sales will be made only to, residents of the particular state involved), and may even be delivered by means of transportation and communication used in interstate commerce, to the purchasers.[i] * * *

CONCLUSION

In conclusion, the fact should be stressed that Section 3(a)(11) is designed to apply only to distributions genuinely local in character. From a practical point of view, the provisions of that section can exempt only issues which in reality represent local financing by local industries, carried out through local investments. Any distribution not of this type raises a serious question as to the availability of Section 3(a)(11). Consequently, any dealer proposing to participate in the distribution of an issue claimed to be exempt under Section 3(a)(11) should examine the character of the transaction and the proposed or actual manner of its execution by all persons concerned with it with the greatest care to satisfy himself that the distribution will not, or did not, exceed the limitations of the exemption. Otherwise the dealer, even though his own sales may be carefully confined to resident purchasers, may subject himself to serious risk of civil liability under Section 12(1) of the Act for selling without prior registration a security not in fact entitled to exemption from registration. In Release No. 4386, we noted that the quick commencement of trading and prompt resale of portions of the issue to non-residents raises a serious question whether the entire issue has, in fact, come to rest in the hands of investors resident in the state of the initial offering.

* * *

SECURITIES ACT RELEASE NO. 5450: NOTICE OF ADOPTION OF RULE 147 UNDER THE SECURITIES ACT OF 1933[a]
Securities and Exchange Commission, 1974
3 SEC Dock. 349

The Securities and Exchange Commission today adopted Rule 147 which defines certain terms in, and clarified [*sic*] certain

---

[i] ED.: Coastal Finance Corp. v. Coastal Finance Corp. of North Providence, 387 A. 2d 1373, 1376 (R. I. 1978).
[a] ED.: 3 SEC Dock. 249 (1974).

conditions of, Section 3(a)(11) of the Securities Act of 1933 ("the Act"). * * *

In developing the definitions in, and conditions of, Rule 147 the Commission has considered the legislative history and judicial interpretations of Section 3(a)(11) as well as its own administrative interpretations. The Commission believes that adoption of the rule, which codifies certain of these interpretations, is in the public interest, since it will be consistent with the protection of investors and provide, to the extent feasible, more certainly in determining when the exemption provided by that Section of the Act is available. Moreover, the Commission believes that local businesses seeking financing solely from local sources should have objective standards to facilitate compliance with Section 3(a)(11) and the registration provisions of the Act, and that the rule will enable such businesses to determine with more certainty whether they may use the exemption in offering their securities. The rule also will give more assurance that the intrastate offering exemption is used only for the purpose that Congress intended, i. e., local financing of companies primarily intrastate in character. * * *

*   *   *

BACKGROUND AND PURPOSE

Congress, in enacting the federal securities laws, created a continuous disclosure system designed to protect investors and to assure the maintenance of fair and honest securities markets. The Commission, in administering and implementing these laws, has sought to coordinate and integrate the disclosure system with the exemptive provisions provided by the laws. Rule 147 is a further effort in this direction.

Section 3(a)(11) was intended to allow issuers with localized operations to sell securities as part of a plan of local financing. Congress apparently believed that a company whose operations are restricted to one area should be able to raise money from investors in the immediate vicinity without having to register the securities with a federal agency. In theory, the investors would be protected both by their proximity to the issuer and by state regulation. Rule 147 reflects this Congressional intent and is limited in its application to transactions where state regulation will be most effective. The Commission has consistently taken the position that the exemption applies only to local financing provided by local investors for local companies. To satisfy the exemption, the entire issue must be offered and sold exclusively to residents of the state in which the issuer is resident and doing business. An offer or sale of part of the issue to a single non-resident will destroy the exemption for the entire issue.

Certain basic questions have arisen in connection with interpreting Section 3(a)(11). They are:

1. what transactions does the Section cover;

2. what is "part of an issue" for purposes of the Section;

3. when is a person "resident within" a state or territory for purposes of the Section; and

4. what does "doing business within" mean in the context of the Section?

The courts and the Commission have addressed themselves to these questions in the context of different fact situation and some general guidelines have been developed. Certain guidelines were set forth by the Commission in Securities Act Release No. 4434 and, in part, are reflected in Rule 147. However, in certain respects, as pointed out below, the rule differs from past interpretations.

*   *   *

Synopsis of Rule 147

1. PRELIMINARY NOTES

The first preliminary note to the rule indicates that the rule does not raise any presumption that the Section 3(a)(11) exemption would not be available for transactions which do not satisfy all of the provisions of the rule. The second note reminds issuers that the rule does not affect compliance with state law. The third preliminary note to the rule briefly explains that rule's purpose and provisions.

As initially proposed, the rule was intended not to be available for secondary transactions. In order to make this clear the fourth preliminary note indicates that the rule is available only for transactions by an issuer and that the rule is not available for secondary transactions. However, in accordance with long standing administrative interpretations of Section 3(a)(11), the intrastate offering exemption may be available for secondary offers and sales by controlling persons of the issuer, if the exemption would have been available to the issuer.

2. TRANSACTIONS COVERED — RULE 147(a)

Paragraph (a) of the rule provides that offers, offers to sell, offers for sale and sales of securities that meet all the conditions of the rule will be deemed to come within the exemption provided by Section 3(a)(11). Those conditions are: (1) the issuer must be resident and doing business within the state or territory in which the securities are offered and sold (Rule 147(c)); (2) the *offerees* and purchasers must be resident within such state or territory (Rule 147(d)); (3) resales for a period of 9 months after the last sale which is part of an issue must be limited as provided (Rule 147(e) and (f)). In addition, the revised rule provides that certain offers and sales of securities by or for the issuers will be deemed not "part of an issue" for purposes of the rule only (Rule 147(b)).

3. "PART OF AN ISSUE" — RULE 147(b)

Subparagraph (b)(1) of the rule provides that all securities of the issuer which are part of an issue must be offered, offered for sale or sold only in accordance with all of the terms of the rule. For the purposes of the rule only, subparagraph (b)(2) provides that all securities of the issuer offered, offered for sale or sold pursuant to the exemptions provided under Section 3 or 4(2) of the Act or registered pursuant to the Act, prior to or subsequent to the six month period immediately preceding or subsequent to any offer, offer to sell, offer for sale or sale pursuant to Rule 147 will be deemed not part of an issue provided that there are no offers, offers to sell or sales of securities of the same or similar class by or for the issuer during either of these six month periods. If there have been offers or sales during the six months, then in order to determine what constitutes part of an issue, reference should be made to the five traditional integration factors discussed above.[b]

As initially proposed the rule would have deemed all securities of the issuer, its predecessors and affiliates offered or sold by the issuer, its predecessors and affiliates within any consecutive six month period to be part of the same issue. On reconsideration, the Commission believes this would be too restrictive and has revised the rule as discussed above. Since subparagraph (b)(2) does not define "part of an issue," a note has been added to paragraph (b) which refers to the discussion of the five factors to be considered in determining whether a transaction is part of an issue. These factors are discussed in the third preliminary note to the

[b] ED.: These go to whether there is "a single plan of financing," to whether there is a single class of security, and to time, type of consideration, and general purpose of the offerings. See Sec. Act Rel. 4434 (1961).

rule, and should be considered in determining whether any offers and sales falling outside the scope of subparagraph (b)(2) and offers and sales made in reliance on the rule must be integrated. Neither Section 3(a)(11) nor Rule 147 can be relied upon in combination with another exemption for different parts of a single issue where a part is offered or sold to non-residents.

4. NATURE OF THE ISSUER — RULE 147(c) — "PERSON RESIDENT WITHIN" — RULE 147(c)(1)

Subparagraph (c)(1) of the rule defines the situations in which issuers would be deemed to be "resident within" a state or territory. A corporation, limited partnership or business trust must be incorporated or organized pursuant to the laws of such state or territory. Section 3(a)(11) provides specifically that a corporate issuer must be incorporated in the state. A general partnership or other form of business entity that is not formed under a specific state or territorial law must have its principal office within the state or territory.[e] The rule also provides that an individual who is deemed an issuer, e. g., a promoter issuing preincorporation certificates, will be deemed a resident if his principal residence is in the state or territory. As initially proposed, the rule provided that in a partnership, *all* the general partners must be resident within such state or territory. The Commission has reconsidered this provision in light of the provisions applicable to corporations and determined to treat all business entities in a similar manner.

5. NATURE OF THE ISSUER — RULE 147(c) — DOING BUSINESS WITHIN — RULE 147(c)(2)

Subparagraph (c)(2) of the rule provides that the issuer will be deemed to be "doing business within" a state or territory in which the offers and sales are to be made if: (1) at least 80 percent of its gross revenues and those of its subsidiaries on a consolidated basis (a) for its most recent fiscal year (if the first offer of any part of the issue is made during the first six months of the issuer's current fiscal year) or (b) for the subsequent six month period, or for the twelve months ended with that period (if the first offer of any part of the issue is made during the last six months of the issuer's current fiscal year) were derived from the operation of a business or

---

[e] ED.: See Grenader v. Spitz, 390 F. Supp. 1112, 1117 (S. D. N. Y. 1975), *reaff'd*, CCH Fed. Sec. L. Rep. ¶95,300 (S. D. N. Y. 1975), *rev'd on other grounds*, 537 F. 2d 612 (2d Cir. 1976), *cert. denied*, 429 U. S. 1009.

property located in or rendering of services within the state or territory; (2) at least 80 percent of the issuer's assets and those of its subsidiaries on a consolidated basis at the end of the most recent fiscal semi-annual period prior to the first offer of any part of the issue are located within such state or territory; (3) at least 80 percent of the net proceeds to the issuer from the sales made pursuant to the rule are intended to be and are used in connection with the operation of a business or property or the rendering of services within such state or territory; and (4) the issuer's principal office is located in the state or territory.

*   *   *

The provisions of paragraph (c) are intended to assure that the issuer is primarily a local business. Many comments were received requesting more elaboration with respect to the above standards. The following examples demonstrate the manner in which these standards would be interpreted:

Example 1. X corporation is incorporated in State *A* and has its only warehouse, only manufacturing plant and only office in that state. *X*'s only business is selling products throughout the United States and Canada through mail order catalogs. *X* annually mails catalogs and order forms from its office to residents of most states and several provinces of Canada. All orders are filled at and products shipped from *X*'s warehouse to customers throughout the United States and Canada. All the products shipped are manufactured by *X* at its plant in State *A*. These activities are *X*'s sole source of revenues.

Question. Is *X* deriving more than 80 percent of its gross revenues from the "operation of a business or * * * rendering of services" within State *A*?

Interpretive Response. Yes, this aspect of the "doing business within" standard is satisfied.

Example 2. Assume the same facts as Example 1, except that *X* has no manufacturing plant and purchases the products it sells from corporations located in other states.

Question. Is *X* deriving more than 80 percent of its gross revenues from the "operation of a business or * * * rendering of services" within State *A*?

Interpretive Response. Yes, this aspect of the "doing business within" standard is satisfied.

Example 3. Y Corporation is incorporated in State *B* and has its only office in that state. *Y*'s only business is selling undeveloped land located in State *C* and State *D* by means of brochures mailed from its office throughout the United States.

Question. Is *Y* deriving more than 80 percent of its gross revenues from the "operation of a business or of property or rendering of services" within State *B*?

Interpretive Response. There are not sufficient facts to respond. If *Y* owns an interest in the developed land, it might not satisfy the "80 percent of assets" standard as well as the "80 percent of gross revenues" standard. Moreover, *Y* could not use more than 20 percent of the proceeds of any offerings made pursuant to the rule in connection with the acquisition of the undeveloped land.

Example 4. Z company is a firm of engineering consultants organized under the laws of State *E* with its only office in that state. During any year, *Z* will provide consulting services for projects in other states. 75 percent of *Z*'s work in terms of man hours will be performed at *Z*'s offices where it employs some 50 professional and clerical personnel. *Z* has no employees located outside of State *E*. However, professional personnel visit project sites and clients' offices in other states. Approximately 50 percent of *Z*'s revenue is derived from clients located in states other than State *E*.

Question. Is *Z* deriving more than 80 percent of its gross revenues from "rendering services" within State *E*?

Interpretive Response. Yes, this aspect of the "doing business within" standard is satisfied.

Example 5. The facts are the same as in Example 4. In addition, at the end of *Z*'s most recent fiscal quarter 25 percent of its assets are represented by accounts receivable from clients in other states.

Question. Does *Z* satisfy the "assets" standard?

Interpretive Response. Yes, *Z* satisfies the "assets" standard. For purposes of the rule, accounts receivable arising from a business conducted in the state would generally be considered to be located at the principal office of the issuer.

6. OFFEREES AND PURCHASERS: PERSONS RESIDENT — RULE 147(d)

Paragraph (d) of the rule provides that offers and sales may be made only to persons resident within the state or territory. An individual offeree or purchaser of any part of an issue would be deemed to be a person resident within the state or territory if such person has his principal residence in the state or territory. Temporary residence, such as that of many persons in the military service, would not satisfy the provisions of paragraph (d). In addition, if a person purchases securities on behalf of other persons, the residence of those persons must satisfy paragraph (d). If the offeree or purchaser is a business organization its residence will be deemed the state or territory in which it has its principal office, unless it is an entity organized for the specific purpose of acquiring securities in the offering, in which case it will be deemed to be a resident of a state only if all of the beneficial owners of interests in such entity are residents of the state.

As initially proposed, subparagraph (d)(2) provided that an individual, in order to be deemed a resident, must have his principal residence in the state and must not have any present intention of moving his principal residence to another state. The Commission believes that it would be difficult to determine a person's intentions, and accordingly, has deleted the latter requirement. In addition, as initially proposed, the rule would have deemed the residence of a business organization to be the state in which it was incorporated or otherwise organized. The Commission believes that the location of a company's principal office is more of an indication of its local character for purposes of the offeree residence provision of the rule than is its state of incorporation. Section 3(a)(11) requires that an issuer corporation be incorporated within the state, but there is no similar requirement in the statute for a corporation that is an offeree or purchaser.

7.   LIMITATIONS ON RESALES — RULE 147(e)

Paragraph (e) of the rule provides that during the period in which securities that are part of an issue are being offered and sold and for a period of nine months from the date of the last sale by the issuer of any part of the issue, resales of any part of the issue by any person shall be made only to persons resident within the same state or territory. This provides objective standards for determining when an issue "comes to rest." The rule as initially proposed limited both *reoffers* and resales during a twelve month period after the last sale by the issuer of any part of the issue. However, the Commission believes that it would be difficult for an issuer to prohibit or even learn of reoffers. Thus, the limitation on reoffers would be impractical because, if any purchaser made a reoffer outside of such state or territory, the issuer would lose the exemption provided by the rule. In addition, the Commission determined that a shorter period would satisfy the coming to rest test for purposes of the rule. Thus, the twelve month period has been reduced to nine months.

Persons who acquire securities from issuers in transactions complying with the rule would acquire unregistered securities that could only be reoffered and resold pursuant to an exemption from the registration provisions of the Act.

* * * As an additional precaution, a note to paragraph (e) reminds dealers that they must satisfy the requirements of Rule 15c2-11 under the Securities Exchange Act of 1934 prior to publishing any quotation for a security, or submitting any quotation for publication in any quotation medium.[d]

A note to the rule indicates that where convertible securities are sold pursuant to the rule, resales of either the convertible security, or if it is converted, of the underlying security, could be made during the period specified in paragraph (e) only to residents of the state. However, the conversion itself, if pursuant to Section 3(a)(9) of the Act, would not begin a new period. In the case of warrants and options, sales upon exercise, if done in reliance on the rule, would begin a new period.

8.   PRECAUTIONS AGAINST INTERSTATE OFFERS AND SALES — RULE
      147(f)

Paragraph (f) of the rule requires issuers to take steps to preserve the exemption provided by the rule, since any resale of any part of the issue before it comes to rest within the state to persons resident in another state or territory will, under the Act, be in violation of Section 5. The required steps are: (i) placing a legend on the certificate or other document evidencing the security stating that the securities have not been registered under the Act and setting forth the limitations on resale contained in paragraph (e); (ii) issuing stop transfer instructions to the issuer's transfer agent, if any, with respect to the securities, or, if the issuer transfers its own securities, making a notation in the appropriate records of the issuer; and (iii) obtaining a written representation from each purchaser as to his residence. Where persons other than the issuer are reselling securities of the issuer during the time period specified in paragraph (e) of the rule, the issuer would, if the securities are presented for transfer, be required to take steps (i) and (ii). In addition, the rule requires that the issuer disclose in writing the

---

[d] ED.: This is an antifraud rule, adopted under §15(c)(2) of the 1934 Act (infra p. 805), which prohibits brokers or dealers from publishing quotations unless specific information is available.

limitations on resale imposed by paragraph (e) and the provisions of subsections (f)(1)(i) and (ii) and subparagraph (f)(2).

OPERATION OF RULE 147

Rule 147 will operate prospectively only. The staff will issue interpretative letters to assist persons in complying with the rule, but will consider requests for "no action" letters on transactions in reliance on Section 3(a)(11) outside the rule only on an infrequent basis and in the most compelling circumstances.

The rule is a nonexclusive rule. However, persons who choose to rely on Section 3(a)(11) without complying with all the conditions of the rule would have the burden of establishing that they have complied with the judicial and administrative interpretations of Section 3(a)(11) in effect at the time of the offering. The Commission also emphasizes * * * that Rule 147 is available only for transactions by issuers and is not available for secondary offerings.

In view of the objectives and policies underlying the Act, the rule would not be available to any person with respect to any offering which, although in technical compliance with the provisions of the rule, is part of a plan or scheme by such person to make interstate offers or sales of securities. In such cases, registration would be required. In addition, any plan or scheme that involves a series of offerings by affiliated organizations in various states, even if in technical compliance with the rule, may be outside the parameters of the rule and of Section 3(a)(11) if what is being financed is in effect a single business enterprise.

*   *   *

Rule 147 makes for considerable certainty. But the exemption is still no bargain: witness, for example, the transformation of "doing business" — which to the man in the street would mean *some* business, possibly a *substantial* portion of the total business, and *conceivably* the *primary* portion[1] — into a triple 80 percent test. As it is, the several conditions and their strict reading by the Commission quite justify the Chairman's statement in 1958 that "as a practical matter the intrastate exemption is loaded with

---

[1] In Chapman v. Dunn, 414 F. 2d 153 (6th Cir. 1969), the court concluded that the issuer "must conduct a predominant amount of his business" within the state. But, since all the land covered by the oil and gas leases managed by a Michigan office were in Ohio, the Michigan activities in fact were apparently insubstantial.

dynamite and must be handled with very great care."[2] Its limited usefulness is all the more apparent in the light of other exemptions. If the offering is not over $5 million, an exemption may well be available in many cases pursuant to §4(6) or 3(b), with none of the risk inherent in §3(a)(11). And, if the offering is larger, it is difficult to see how the very restrictive conditions of §3(a)(11) can be satisfied unless the entire issue is placed with a relatively few persons for investment, in which event the exemption for private offerings under §4(2) will be available without regard to the residence of the issuer or the buyers.

Nevertheless, the exemption is there. It was presumably intended to be used. And it is in fact used. This inevitably raises the question: If a single sale or offer (or, indeed a single resale or reoffer by a resident buyer before the expiration of thte nine-month period of the rule) to a nonresident destroys the exemption forevermore for the entire issue, what are the practical consequences of a mistake made in good faith, or of a properly supervised salesman's disregard of his instructions to confine his activities to residents? There can be no criminal liability without proof of willfulness, and there have been relatively few criminal prosecutions of any kind under §5 alone. But in a proceeding to revoke a broker-dealer's registration under the 1934 Act, which requires a finding both of willfulness and of public interest, the Commission held that evidence of the broker-dealer's reliance on advice of counsel and of his effort in good faith to restrict the offering to residents was relevant only to the question whether the public interest required the imposition of a sanction and did not negative a finding of a willful violation.[3] By the same token, it is the Commission's policy, once the exemption has been lost under its view, however innocently, to threaten injunctive proceedings if the offering is continued without registration, to require that the registration statement disclose a contingent liability under §12(1) with respect to the shares already sold in violation of §5, and to insist that the issuer offer rescission to those persons on the basis of a statutory prospectus.

One can understand the enforcement agency's attitude that it should construe all exemptions strictly until the courts hold otherwise. And it is true, almost by hypothesis, that the Commission, when it examines the prospectuses that are used in purportedly exempt offerings (if, indeed, any prospectuses are used at all), will

---

[2] Gadsby, The SEC and the Financing of Small Business, 14 Bus. Law. 144, 148 (1958).
[3] Whitehall Corp., 38 SEC 259, 273-74 (1958).

find misstatements or omissions to state material facts as compared with the prospectuses that buyers would have received in the event of registration. Yet it is difficult to believe that Congress intended to make the issuer an absolute insurer of every offeree's residence and of every salesman's integrity. Unless the standard is one of due care — which includes reasonable supervision of all selling agents and may well require something more than an automatic acceptance of the buyer's representation — the exemption is virtually read out of the statute. Perhaps it should be. But that presumably is why Congress sits. Meanwhile, although it is usually impracticable to litigate with the Commission when an issuer is primarily interested in completing its financing — and although prudent counsel, with the potentialities of strict liability under §12(1) and of class actions in mind, will think twice before counseling reliance on §3(a)(11) (with or without Rule 147), particularly in the case of a substantial public offering — a seller against whom a claim is made for rescission or damages under §12(1) would be well advised to defend if he thinks he used reasonable care.

In the preparation of the Code it was early decided to develop a successor exemption "that would serve the need without undue risk to either the user or the investor"[4] or, if that turned out to be impracticable, to delete the exemption altogether as little more than a trap for the unwary. As matters turned out after several false starts, a considerable expansion of the exemption was the other side of the partial preemption coin.[5] This effort to enhance the states' responsibility with respect to local distributions produced an endorsement of the Code's federal-state balance by the North American Securities Administrators Association.[6]

The Code's §514 exempts a "local distribution":

(1) As long as *sales* are *substantially* restricted to residents or persons with their *primary employment* in the state, the section is not concerned with mere *offers* that do not ripen into sales. And "substantially" is so defined that the exemption is available if 95 percent of all buyers holding of record at least 95 percent of the securities[7] are persons who are resident or have their primary employment in the state; this formula "is designed not only as a safety valve to preclude a 'one sale to a nonresident and you're out'

---

[4] 2 Code 970.

[5] See §§514, 1904.

[6] See 2 Code 966-81.

[7] This second 95 percent figure was 80 percent in the Code as approved by the ALI and the ABA, but the group that negotiated the SEC's endorsement of the Code (see pp. 48-50 supra) accepted this one change.

rule but also as a way to permit, for example, an offering to a class of persons (perhaps employees) of whom a small number are *known* to be nonresidents."[8]

(2) As long as the issuer has or proposes to have its "principal place of business" in the state (or whatever multistate area may be permitted by rule), the exemption applies "regardless of where it is organized."[9]

(3) The resale problem is relegated to rulemaking, with a maximum period of one year.

(4) "An original seller or a reseller who in good faith accepts from his buyer a written undertaking that is reasonably designed to avoid an illegal distribution and complies with any rule adopted under this section is not considered to be a participant in any such distribution."[10]

D.   "SMALL" ISSUES [§§3(b), 4(6)]

1.   THE "SMALL BUSINESS" DILEMMA

"Small business" is the darling of Congress and the essence of the American dream. But "small business" is also the source of many of the frauds and other problems at which securities regulation is directed. In a 1941 report to Congress the Commission stated that its "experience demonstrates that the evils of high-pressure salesmanship and of selling on the basis of inadequate information are particularly prevalent in small issues."[1] It is not that "captains of industry" are inherently more saintly than struggling entrepreneurs or promoters. It is simply that successful business people, like successful politicians, sometimes become statesmen, whereas new business enterprises inevitably have a high mortality rate. Partly on that account, new businesses — and to a lesser extent old businesses that are relatively small — find it hard to obtain financing, and more expensive when they do.

Still, a healthy capitalist system dare not allow small enterprise to dry up. And so over the years both Congress and the SEC have

---

[8] 2 Code 971.
[9] §514(a)(2).
[10] §514(d)(2).

C. 5D   [1] SEC, Report on Proposals for Amendments to the Securities Act of 1933 and the Securities Exchange Act of 1934, H. R. Com. Print, Com. on Int. & For. Commerce, 77th Cong., 1st Sess. (1941) 17.

addressed the problem of financing small business in various (not always consistent) ways. For example:

Under the Small Business Investment Act of 1958, "small business investment companies," themselves financed in part by the Small Business Administration, were designed to provide a source of both equity capital and loan funds to eligible small business;[2] and Congress concurrently added §3(c) to the 1933 Act, under which the SEC adopted Regulation E in order conditionally to exempt offerings by SBA-licensed small business investment companies up to $500,000 each year (except that no single nonissuer offering may exceed $100,000). Again, the Regulatory Flexibility Act of 1980 requires each agency, among other things, to publish a plan for periodic review of all rules with a significant impact on a substantial number of small entities.[3] And the Small Business Investment Incentive Act of 1980 amended the Investment Company Act by establishing a new regulatory system for certain investment companies called "business development companies."[4]

As part of the same piece of legislation Congress enacted also the Omnibus Small Business Capital Formation Act of 1980[5] and the Small Business Issuers' Simplification Act of 1980.[6]

The former Act added §19(c) to the 1933 Act in order to encourage cooperation between the SEC and state securities authorities by way of achieving "maximum uniformity in Federal and State standards" (including uniform forms and a uniform registration exemption for "small issuers") and "minimum interference with the business of capital formation." Toward these ends the Commission is directed to conduct, at least annually, a conference with representatives of associations of state securities officials, self-regulatory organizations, and private organizations involved in capital formation. And other provisions (which are not mechanically incorporated into any of the existing SEC statutes) direct the Commission to "gather, analyze, and make available to the public, information with respect to the capital formation needs, and the problems and costs involved with new, small, medium-

---

[2] 15 U. S. C. §§661-96.

[3] 5 U. S. C. §§601-12; see Sec. Act Rel. 6323, 22 SEC Dock. 1319 (1981).

[4] 94 Stat. 2275 (1980). Section 2(a)(48) of the 1940 Act defines a "business development company," in effect, as a domestic, closed-end company that (1) is operated for the purpose of making investments in small and developing as well as financially troubled businesses, (2) makes available significant managerial assistance to its portfolio companies, and (3) has notified the Commission of its election to be subject to the system of regulation established by §§55-65 of the 1940 Act.

[5] 95 Stat. 2291 (1980), scattered in U. S. C.

[6] 15 U. S. C. §§77b, 77d(6).

sized, and independent businesses,"[7] and to make the results available to the Small Business Administration; to "conduct an annual Government-business forum to review the current status of problems and programs relating to small business capital formation"; and to "use its best efforts to identify and reduce the costs of raising capital in connection with the issuance of securities by firms whose aggregate outstanding securities and other indebtedness have a market value of $25,000,000 or less."

The Small Business Issuers' Simplification Act of 1980 added §4(6) to the 1933 Act in order to exempt

> transactions involving offers or sales by an issuer solely to one or more accredited investors, if the aggregate offering price of an issue of securities offered in reliance on this paragraph does not exceed the amount allowed under section 3(b) of this title, if there is no advertising or public solicitation in connection with the transaction by the issuer or anyone acting on the issuer's behalf, and if the issuer files such notice with the Commission as the Commission shall prescribe.[8]

The term "accredited investor" is defined in a new §2(15) of the 1933 Act to mean, in substance, a bank, registered investment company, or licensed small business investment company, or any other person specified by Commission rule "on the basis of such factors as financial sophistication, net worth, knowledge, and experience in financial matters, or amount of assets under management qualifies."[9] This is substantially the Code's definition of "institutional investor" for purposes of its "limited offering" concept.

Even before this legislation, the SEC, for its part, held a series of hearings throughout the country in 1978-79 with respect to the effects of its rules and the disclosure requirements of the statutes on the ability of small businesses to raise capital.[10] And in 1979 it adopted a simplified Form S-18 for cash offerings up to $5 million by certain domestic or Canadian corporate issuers that are not already reporting companies under the Exchange Act. The narrative disclosure called for is somewhat less extensive than it is in Form S-1. And audited financial statements, which are required

---

[7] Code §1903(g)(1) substitutes "independent businesses that are (A) new, or (B) small or medium-sized" — wording that better expresses what is understood to have been intended.

[8] The §3(b) amount (see p. 340 infra) is now $5 million, and the notice requirement is reflected in Form D.

[9] The Commission has further defined the term in Rule 215. See n. 60 infra.

[10] Sec. Act Rel. 5914, 14 SEC Dock. 314 (1978).

for only two rather than the three fiscal years of Form S-1, must comply only with generally accepted accounting principles, not with Regulation S-X.[11]

Much earlier than all this the joint effort of Congress *and* Commission produced a series of "small issue" exemptions from §5 of the 1933 Act. Section 3(b) gives the Commission rulemaking authority to exempt any "issue" up to a maximum amount that has grown in stages from $100,000 in 1933-45 to $5 million since late 1980. And the Commission has adopted a series of exemptions under that section that provide a panoply from which to choose in accordance with the facts of the particular case.

2.　REGULATION A

a.　Maximum Offering Price

The principal exemption under §3(b) (at least until recent years) has always been Regulation A, which now consists of Rules 251-64.[12] It is often referred to as "short-form registration." But, of course, it is not registration at all. It is a conditional exemption. Among other differences, §11 liability for false registration statements does not attach to selling literature used in Regulation A offerings; there only §12(2) and Rule 10b-5[13] apply by way of civil liability.

Although the §3(b) authority now goes to $5 million — which is also the maximum in Form S-18 — the Regulation A limit is $1.5 million in aggregate offering price (inclusive of any securities offered or sold pursuant to any other exemption under §3(b) or in violation of §5(a) within a year before the commencement of the proposed offering). But that figure applies only when the offering is for the account of (1) the issuer, (2) the estate of a decedent who owned the securities at his death if they are offered within two years after that date, or (3) a control affiliate of the issuer (except that the maximum is $100,000 for the account of any single affiliate other than an estate). Otherwise the maximum is $300,000 rather than $1.5 million (with the same limitation per

---

[11] Sec. Act Rel. 6049, 17 SEC Dock. 153 (1979).

[12] See p. 807 infra.

[13] For what is substantially a treatise on Regulation A as it then stood, written by a lawyer who was in charge of Regulation A interpretations in the SEC's New York Regional Office, see Weiss, Regulation A under the Securities Act of 1933 — Highways and Byways, 8 N. Y. L. F. 3 (1962); Weiss, Highways and Byways Revisited, 15 N. Y. L. F. 218 (1969).

affiliate).[14] In any event, when portions of a "hot issue" are withheld or taken by insiders and then sold at a higher price in the market shortly after the initial offering, one must guard against the limitation's being exceeded; for the distribution is not completed until the stock "ultimately comes to rest in the hands of the investing public."[15]

b.   The "Issue" Concept

The §3(b) limitation is imposed on any "issue" — the same term used in §3(a)(11). The Commission early refused to construe that term "to permit the exemption of small portions of large financing operations" — either by claiming exemption for a small portion and registering the remainder or by the formality of successive yearly filings under the regulation if the shares otherwise constituted a single "issue." This view, expounded in the leading *Unity Gold* case,[16] has not been changed so far as the "issue" concept in the intrastate exemption or the similar concept read into the 3(a)(9) exemption is concerned.[17] But it was expressly abandoned — presumably under the Commision's statutory power to define "technical" terms[18] — in the 1941 revision of Regulation A.[19] The 1941-53 regulation specifically permitted the full amount to be offered in any twelve-month period, year after year, or that amount might be offered under the exemption and the balance immediately registered, without regard to whether the successive offerings constituted an integrated plan of financing.[20] And this is still the Commission's view, although the specific provision was omitted, presumably as surplusage, in the revised regulation.

Nevertheless, in 1948, when the limit was $100,000, the Commission repeated its *Unity Gold* language almost word for word in order to hold that there had been a single "issue," all of which had been sold in violation of §5, when 74,000 shares of stock had been offered under Regulation A at $1 and five months later 50,000

---

[14] Rule 254.

[15] R. A. Holman & Co. v. SEC, 366 F. 2d 446, 449, 450 (2d Cir. 1966), *amended on rehearing,* 377 F. 2d 665 (2d Cir. 1967), *aff'g* R. A. Holman & Co., 42 SEC 866, 869 (1965), *cert. denied,* 389 U. S. 991. Par value is irrelevant. Mines & Metals Corp. v. SEC, 200 F. 2d 317, 319-20 (9th Cir. 1952), *cert. denied,* 345 U. S. 941.

[16] Unity Gold Corp., 3 SEC 618, 625 (1938).

[17] See pp. 304, 319 supra.

[18] §19(a).

[19] Sec. Act Rel. 2410 (1940).

[20] Former Rule 220(e), Sec. Act Rel. 2410 (1940).

additional shares had been offered without benefit of registration or any other exemption.[21] Of course, the 50,000 shares were sold illegally under any view. But the Commission's going out of its way to hold that the first 74,000 shares had also been sold in violation can mean only that the relaxation of the "issue" concept incorporated in the 1941 revision of Regulation A is not to be extended by interpretation.[22] Moreover, under a special rule that the Commission adopted in the 1956 revision for promotional companies and those without a specified earnings record, the "issue" includes, unless a specified escrow or similar arrangement is made,

> (1) all securities issued prior to the filing of the offering statement,[23] or proposed to be issued, for a consideration consisting in whole or part of assets or services and held by the person to whom issued; and
>
> (2) all securities issued to and held by or proposed to be issued, pursuant to options or otherwise, to any director, officer or promoter of the issuer, or to any underwriter, dealer or security salesman.[24]

There are, however, limited exclusions in computing the aggregate offering price.[25]

c.   Filing Requirements

Unless the Commission accelerates the period on a written request, no securities may be offered under Regulation A until ten business days after the filing with the appropriate Regional Office of an offering statement on Form 1-A in three parts: (I) Notification; (II) Offering Circular; and (III) Exhibits.[26] As with a registration statement, the filing of an amendment starts the period running anew unless the Commission accelerates.

There are also provisions modeled on the "tombstone ad," preliminary prospectus, and post-offering report rules, as well as the nine-month prospectus provision.[27] But Regulation A goes even further in requiring (1) that the offering circular be furnished, in the case of a company that does not report under the 1934 Act,

---

[21] Herbert R. May, 27 SEC 814, 817-20 (1948).
[22] Cf. Batkin & Co., 38 SEC 436, 448 (1958).
[23] See p. 342 infra.
[24] Rule 253(c).
[25] Rule 254(d).
[26] Rule 255.
[27] See pp. 112, 113, 139, 154 supra.

forty-eight hours before the confirmation is mailed,[28] and (2) that copies of all sales literature be filed five days before use.[29]

On the other hand, no offering circular is required at all with respect to an offering of not more than $100,000 by a nonpromotional company, except for the filing (not the use) of the nonfinancial information normally required in an offering circular.[30]

d.   Exclusions and Suspensions

In substance, Regulation A is available only to issuers that are incorporated and also have their principal business operations in the United States or Canada.[31] Investment company securities and fractional undivided interests in oil, gas, or mineral rights are excluded.[32] Certain criminal, injunctive, or disciplinary records bar access to the exemption.[33] So does noncompliance with the reporting requirements of the 1934 Act when they apply.[34] And the Commission has reserved the authority temporarily or permanently to suspend the exemption on certain findings.[35]

e.   The Crystal Ball

As the Commission has been relaxing the registration route via Form S-18 and lightening the exemption route via Regulation A, the two extremes are beginning to meet. Both Form S-18 and §3(b) have the same $5 million limit. And the Commission has prescribed substantially the same financial information in both contexts.[36] Regulation A does not require an audit. But state authorities and underwriters frequently do, and the SEC *encourages* audits. In any event, the issuer, if not already a registrant under §12(g) of the 1934 Act,[37] is apt to become one, and thus to have to have an audit, after completion of the offering. And the cost of an audit to a start-up company is not great.

[28] Rule 256(a).
[29] Rule 258.
[30] Rule 257.
[31] Rule 252(a).
[32] Rule 252(b).
[33] Rule 252(c)-(e).
[34] Rule 252(f).
[35] Rule 261.
[36] See pp. 339-40 supra.
[37] See p. 465 infra.

It will be interesting to see which of the two alternatives — an evolving Form S-18 and an evolving Regulation A — will predominate. In August 1981 the Commission announced that it was considering the advisability of merging Regulation A into a revised Form S-18, with a substantial reduction in audited financial statements for offerings under $3 million.[38]

It will be interesting to see also whether Form S-18 offerings will escape the mild odor that surrounds Regulation A offerings in some investment bankers' and lawyers' minds.[39] Frauds there have been here. But, quite apart from the fact that Regulation A is used by some relatively small but established companies, its reputation reflects to a large extent the inevitable risk of investing in new and unproved enterprises.

3. SPECIALIZED §3(b) EXEMPTIVE RULES

There are three more exemptions under §3(b) that are specialized in one way or another:

(1) Regulation B (Rules 300-46) conditionally exempts offerings of various species of fractional undivided interests in oil or gas rights up to $250,000 per year. Among other conditions, there may be no sales or payment until forty-eight hours after delivery of a specified "offering sheet," which must also be filed, and the Commission requires satisfactory assurance that notification of the offering has been furnished to the authorities in each state in which it is to be made.[40]

(2) In 1959, concurrently with the adoption of an interpretative rule to the effect that the levying of an assessment on assessable stock involves an "offer" and "sale," the Commission adopted Regulation F (Rules 651-56) in order to exempt (1) "Assessments on assessable stock of any corporation incorporated and having its "principal business operations" in the United States and (2) "Assessable stock of any such corporation offered or sold at public auction or otherwise for the purpose of realizing the amount of an assessment levied thereon." In computing the $300,000 maximum per-

---

[38] Sec. Act Rel. 6339, 23 SEC Dock. 446, 452 (1981).

[39] 1 SEC, Report of Special Study of Securities Markets, H. R. Doc. No. 95, 88th Cong., 1st Sess. (1963) 496-97. These offerings have also suffered from the "hot issue" aroma. See CCH NASD Manual ¶2151.06; Grienenberger, The "Hot Issue" Amendments and New Disclosure Guides, in Practising Law Institute, Fifth Annual Institute on Securities Regulation (1974) c. 4.

[40] Rule 310(e). This requirement applies even though a particular state itself requires no filing. Sec. Act Rel. 5662, 8 SEC Dock. 807 (1975).

mitted in any twelve-month period by the regulation, there must be included "all assessments levied on assessable stock of the issuer" and all securities offered under any §3(b) exemptive rule or sold in violation of §5(a). There are filing and suspension procedures.[41]

(3) Rule 236 conditionally exempts a reporting company's share offerings up to $300,000 to provide funds to be distributed to the issuer's shareholders in lieu of issuing fractional shares or scrip certificates in connection with a stock dividend or merger or the like.

4. OTHER §3(b) EXEMPTIVE RULES OF GENERAL APPLICABILITY

Finally, there are several more exemptions of general applicability:

In 1972 the Commission adopted Rule 237, stating:[42]

> Rule 237 exempts from registration outstanding securities held by persons, other than the issuer, control persons or brokers or dealers, if the following conditions are met:
>
> > The issuer is a domestic issuer and has been actively engaged in business as a going concern for at least five years;
> > The securities have been beneficially owned and paid for by the seller for at least five years and are bona fide sold in negotiated transactions otherwise than through a broker or dealer.[43]
>
> The amount of securities of the issuer, its predecessors, and all of its affiliates which can be sold during any period of one year cannot exceed the lesser of the gross proceeds from the sale of one percent of the securities of the class outstanding or $50,000 [now $100,000] in aggregate gross proceeds. If during such year the person selling the securities has sold securities under any other exemption under Section 3(b) of the Act or under Rule 144, the amount sold must be deducted from the amount sold under Rule 237. In computing such amounts sales by certain family members and related interests must be taken into consideration.

[41] In April 1982 the Commission solicited comment concerning the continued usefulness of Regulation F. Sec. Act Rel. 6393, 24 SEC Dock. 1646 (1982).

[42] Sec. Act Rel. 5224 (1972). This rule was adopted in connection with Rule 144, infra p. 417.

[43] The basis for the negotiated transactions requirement has never been stated. One can speculate that it was included because of the belief that direct negotiations would give the buyer a better opportunity to protect his interests. See Romeo, Resale of Restricted Securities, 12 Rev. Sec. Reg. 847 (1979).

Any person intending to sell securities under Rule 237 is required to file a notice, on a form prescribed therefor, with the appropriate Regional Office of the Commission 10 business days before the sale. A copy of the notice would have to be sent or given to the issuer at the same time.

The purpose of the rule is to provide a means whereby persons who have held securities for five years or more may dispose of them otherwise than in the trading market without requiring the purchasers to take them under the limitations of a private placement. * * *

In 1975 the Commission adopted a Rule 240 in order conditionally to exempt certain offerings up to $100,000 annually by closely held issuers.[44] And effective in February 1980 it adopted a much broader Rule 242, which on certain conditions exempted issues up to $2 million in a six month period if the number of buyers (not offerees) was limited to thirty-five apart from "accredited persons" as defined.[45] In 1982, the Commission adopted Regulation D as an amalgam of those two rules (with changes) and the former Rule 146 with respect to the statutory exemption for nonpublic offerings.[46] Regulation D consists of six rules. Rules 504-06 replace Rules 240, 242, and 146. And Rules 501-03 contain definitions and conditions that apply to the regulation generally (that is to say, to all three exemptions). Consequently, Rules 504 and 505 will be discussed here, and Rule 506 will be discussed in the next subchapter in connection with the private offering exemption in §4(2).

Rule 504, since it is "an effort by the Commission to set aside a clear and workable exemption for small offerings by small issuers to be regulated by state 'Blue Sky' requirements" and to be subject only to antifraud provisions at the federal level,[47] is limited to primary offerings of securities whose issuers are neither reporting companies under the 1934 Act nor investment companies.[48] The limit is $500,000 in twelve months, inclusive of all offerings made under any §3(b) exemptive rule or in violation of §5.[49] There is the same type of "integration" provision, in terms of six months on either side of the offering, that appears in Rule 147, the intrastate exemption "safe harbor" rule.[50] Although there is no preoffer

[44] Sec. Act Rel. 5560, 6 SEC Dock. 132 (1975).
[45] Sec. Act Rel. 6180, 19 SEC Dock. 295 (1980).
[46] Sec. Act Rel. 6389, 24 SEC Dock. 1166 (1982).
[47] Id. at 1168.
[48] Rule 504(a).
[49] Rule 504(b)(2).
[50] Rule 502(a); see p. 328 supra. The Commission went out of its way to

filing requirement, notices of sales must be filed on Form D at specified times.[51] There may be no "general solicitation or general advertising."[52] And, so far as resales are concerned, the securities have the status of those acquired in a private offering.[53] But these last two conditions do not apply to offers and sales made exclusively in one or more states in accordance with their requirements of registration and pre-sale delivery of a disclosure document[54] — a conditional bow to state regulation that is a bit inconsistent philosophically with the express negation in Rule 504 of any requirement that specific information be furnished to buyers.[55]

The Rule 505 exemption applies to primary offerings by any issuer other than an investment company or an issuer disqualified under Rule 252(c)-(f) of Regulation A,[56] and it extends to the full $5 million permitted by §3(b) (with the same "integration" treatment as in Rule 504).[57] Moreover, the treatment with respect to general solicitation or advertising, resales, and filings is the same in both rules (without the bow to state law that is in Rule 504). But the greater liberality of Rule 505 is balanced by additional conditions: The issuer must "reasonably believe" that there are not more than thirty-five buyers,[58] with an elaborate prescription of how to calculate the number,[59] a prescription that excludes an "accredited investor" from the count.[60] And, except for sales only to "accredited investors," the issuer must furnish each buyer, before the sale, with prescribed information centered basically around (1) the last annual report to stockholders and various

---

note that (unlike apparently the situation with respect to Regulation A, supra pp. 341-42) the failure of one transaction under Rule 504 to meet the $500,000 limitation does not affect the exemption for the prior transactions considered in computing the limitation. Rule 504(b)(2), Note 2.

[51] Rule 503.
[52] Rule 502(c).
[53] Rule 502(d).
[54] Rule 504(b)(1).
[55] Rule 502(b)(1)(i).
[56] Rules 505(a), 505(b)(2)(iii).
[57] Rule 505(b)(2)(i).
[58] Rule 505(b)(2)(ii). This formula was borrowed from the Code's concept of a "limited offering." See pp. 396-98 infra.
[59] Rule 501(e).
[60] The statutory definition of this term in §2(15) (see p. 339 supra) is enlarged in Rule 215 to include (among others) any director, executive officer, or general partner of the issuer, any buyer of at least $150,000 of securities if that amount does not exceed 20 percent of his net worth, and any natural person whose net worth exceeds $1 million or who had more than $200,000 of income in each of the two past years and reasonably expects to do as well in the current year; and the entire definition from §2(15) and Rule 215 is repeated in Rule 501(a) for ease of reference. The rich, apparently are honorary financial sophisticates.

filings under the 1934 Act when the issuer is a reporting company under that Act and (2) Part I of Form S-18[61] in other cases.[62]

Regulation D was expressly designed, in part, to achieve uniformity between state and federal exemptions in order to facilitate capital formation consistent with the protection of investors. And in 1982 the North American Securities Administrators Association adopted a uniform limited offering exemption modeled on Rule 505 that each state, depending on its regulatory scheme, might either substitute for or add to any other available exemption.[63]

5. Limited Sales to "Accredited Investors" [§4(6)]

Cutting across all this, as we have already noticed,[64] is Congress' 1980 gift of §4(6). That exemption, which is, of course, self-operative except for the Commission's authority (reflected in Form D) to require the filing of notice, extends to offerings up to the §3(b) limit (now $5 million) to "accredited investors." Section 4(6) is thus a hybrid that combines elements of §3(b) (small size) and §4(2) (private offerings). But, as the following colloquy demonstrates, the gift was not too generous:

> Mr. Fleischer [of the New York Bar]: If Section 4(2) is presently available for sales to institutions, why would one bother using the 4(6) exemption?
>
> Ms. Wertheimer [of the Dallas Bar]: One would not, and the exemption has limited utility.
>
> Remember that much of the impetus for Section 4(6) came from the White House Small-Business Conference. Partnerships had been complaining about not being able to use Rule 242, which was already in existence, and this exemption may have been a bone that was thrown them, although in its present form it is limited to institutional sales. Mickey, do you know any more about the background than that?
>
> Ms. Beach [Associate Director, Division of Corporation Finance, SEC]: Not really. I think you are right, that it may very well be that this is not a significant extension of the existing Rule 242 exemption. In many ways it is more restrictive than Rule 242, since no securities may be sold to individuals and no big-ticket purchasers are included as accredited investors. As

---

[61] See p. 339 supra.
[62] Rule 502(b).
[63] CCH Blue Sky L. Rep. ¶¶5294, 5294A.
[64] See p. 339 supra.

Art said, if you sell only to institutions, Section 4(2) probably presents no problem.[65]

E. PRIVATE OFFERINGS [§4(2)]

1. THE EXEMPTION BEFORE ANY "SAFE HARBOR" RULE

Section 4(2) exempts "transactions by an issuer not involving any public offering." These nine words support a substantial gloss. The legislative history is of little help except insofar as the general tone may be set by the House committee's reference to this exemption as permitting "an issuer to make a specific or an isolated sale of its securities to a particular person," and to the exemption generally as directed to transactions "where there is no practical need for [the bill's] application or where the public benefits are too remote."[1]

The administrative construction was early set in an opinion of the SEC's General Counsel to the effect that the determination whether a particular transaction involves a public offering depends on all the surrounding circumstances. Apart from the number of offerees, he said, important factors are their relationship to each other and to the issuer, the number of units offered, and the manner of offering.[2]

In that opinion, which was written in the context of a proposed offering of $1,766,000 of preferred stock to twenty-five persons, the General Counsel had thought it "a much wiser policy for me not to express an opinion * * * as to whether a public offering is involved." Nevertheless, while emphasizing the necessity of considering all surrounding circumstances, he did not withdraw the opinion referred to by him as having been expressed by his office that "under ordinary circumstances an offering to not more than approximately 25 persons is not an offering to a substantial number and presumably does not involve a public offering." And in the case of an offering to institutional investors the Commission was known not to object to a hundred or more offerees.

That was the rubric until:

[65] Wertheimer, Small Offerings: Recent SEC and Legislative Initiatives, in Practising Law Institute, Twelfth Annual Institute on Securities Regulation (1981) c. 17 at 293. In addition, §4(6) (like Rules 505 and 506 but unlike Regulation A) is limited to primary offerings by issuers.

C. 5E [1] H. R. Rep. No. 85, 73d Cong., 1st Sess. (1933) 5, 7, 15-16.
[2] Sec. Act Rel. 285 (1935).

SECURITIES AND EXCHANGE COMMISSION v.
RALSTON PURINA CO.
Supreme Court of the United States, 1953
346 U. S. 119

Mr. Justice Clark delivered the opinion of the Court.

Section 4(1) [now §4(2)] of the Securities Act of 1933 exempts "transactions by an issuer not involving any public offering" from the registration requirements of §5. We must decide whether Ralston Purina's offerings of treasury stock to its "key employees" are within this exemption. On a complaint brought by the Commission under §20(b) of the Act seeking to enjoin respondent's unregistered offerings, the District Court held the exemption applicable and dismissed the suit. The Court of Appeals affirmed. The question has arisen many times since the Act was passed; an apparent need to define the scope of the private offering exemption prompted certiorari. 345 U. S. 903.

Ralston Purina manufactures and distributes various feed and cereal products. Its processing and distribution facilities are scattered throughout the United States and Canada, staffed by some 7,000 employees. At least since 1911 the company has had a policy of encouraging stock ownership among its employees; more particularly, since 1942 it has made authorized but unissued common shares available to some of them. Between 1947 and 1951, the period covered by the record in this case, Ralston Purina sold nearly $2,000,000 of stock to employees without registration and in so doing made use of the mails.

In each of these years, a corporate resolution authorized the sale of common stock "to employees * * * who shall, without any solicitation by the Company or its officers or employees, inquire of any of them as to how to purchase common stock of Ralston Purina Company." A memorandum sent to branch and store managers after the resolution was adopted advised that "The only employees to whom this stock will be available will be those who take the initiative and are interested in buying stock at present market prices." Among those responding to these offers were employees with the duties of artist, bakeshop foreman, chow loading foreman, clerical assistant, copywriter, electrician, stock clerk, mill office clerk, order credit trainee, production trainee, stenographer, and veterinarian. The buyers lived in over fifty widely separated communities scattered from Garland, Texas, to Nashua, New Hampshire, and Visalia, California. The lowest salary bracket of those purchasing was $2,700 in 1949, $2,435 in 1950 and $3,107 in 1951. The record shows that in 1947, 243 employees bought stock, 20 in 1948, 414 in 1949, 411 in 1950, and the 1951 offer, interrupted by this litigation, produced 165 applications to purchase. No records were kept of those to whom the offers were made; the estimated number in 1951 was 500.

The company bottoms its exemption claim on the classification of all offerees as "key employees" in its organization. Its position on trial was that "A key employee * * * is not confined to an organization chart. It would include an individual who is eligible for promotion, an individual who especially influences others or who advises others, a person whom the employees look to in some special way, an individual, of course, who carries some special responsibility, who is sympathetic to management and who is ambitious and who the management feels is likely to be promoted to a greater responsibility." That an offering to all of its employees would be public is conceded.

The Securities Act nowhere defines the scope of §4(1)'s private offering exemption. Nor is the legislative history of much help in staking out its boundaries. The problem was first dealt with in §4(1) of the House Bill, H. R. 5480, 73d Cong., 1st Sess., which exempted "transactions by an issuer not with or through an underwriter; * * * ." The bill, as reported by the House Committee, added "and not involving any public offering." H. R. Rep. No. 85, 73d Cong., 1st Sess. 1. This was thought to be one of those transactions "where there is no practical need for [the bill's] application or where the public benefits are too remote." Id., at 5. The exemption as thus delimited became law. It assumed its present shape with the deletion of "not with or through an underwriter" by §203(a) of the Securities Exchange Act of 1934, 48 Stat. 906, a change regarded as the elimination of superfluous language. H. R. Rep. No. 1838, 73d Cong., 2d Sess. 41.

Decisions under comparable exemptions in the English Companies Acts and state "blue sky" laws, the statutory antecedents of federal securities legislation, have made one thing clear — to be public an offer need not be open to the whole world.[7] In *Securities and Exchange Comm'n v. Sunbeam Gold Mines Co.*, 95 F. 2d 699 (C. A. 9th Cir. 1938), this point was made in dealing

---

[7] Nash v. Lynde, [1929] A. C. 158; In re South of England Natural Gas and Petroleum Co., Ltd., [1911] 1 Ch. 573; cf. Sherwell v. Combined Incandescent Mantles Syndicate, Ltd., 23 T. L. R. 482 (1907). See 80 Sol. J. 785 (1936).

People v. Montague, 280 Mich. 610, 274 N. W. 347 (1937); In re Leach, 215 Cal. 536, 12 P. 2d 3 (1932); Mary Pickford Co. v. Bayly Bros., 68 P. 2d 239 (1937), *modified*, 12 Cal. 2d 501, 86 P. 2d 102 (1939).

with an offering to the stockholders of two corporations about to
be merged. Judge Denman observed that:

> In its broadest meaning the term "public" distinguishes the
> populace at large from groups of individual members of the
> public segregated because of some common interest or character-
> istic. Yet such a distinction is inadequate for practical purposes;
> manifestly, an offering of securities to all red-headed men, to all
> residents of Chicago or San Francisco, to all existing stockholders
> of the General Motors Corporation or the American Telephone &
> Telegraph Company, is no less "public," in every realistic sense
> of the word, than an unrestricted offering to the world at large.
> Such an offering, though not open to everyone who may choose
> to apply, is none the less "public" in character, for the means
> used to select the particular individuals to whom the offering is
> to be made bear no sensible relation to the purposes for which
> the selection is made. * * * To determine the distinction be-
> tween "public" and "private" in any particular context, it is
> essential to examine the circumstances under which the distinc-
> tion is sought to be established and to consider the purposes
> sought to be achieved by such distinction. 95 F. 2d, at 701.

The courts below purported to apply this test. The District
Court held, in the language of the *Sunbeam* decision, that "The
purpose of the selection bears a 'sensible relation' to the class
chosen," finding that "The sole purpose of the 'selection' is to
keep part stock ownership of the business within the operating
personnel of the business and to spread ownership throughout
all departments and activities of the business." The Court of Appeals treated the case as involving "an offering, without solicitation, of common stock to a selected group of key employees of the
issuer, most of whom are already stockholders when the offering
is made, with the sole purpose of enabling them to secure a
proprietary interest in the company or to increase the interest already held by them."

Exemption from the registration requirements of the Securities
Act is the question. The design of the statute is to protect investors
by promoting full disclosure of information thought necessary to
informed investment decisions. The natural way to interpret the
private offering exemption is in light of the statutory purpose.
Since exempt transactions are those as to which "there is no practical need for [the bill's] application," the applicability of §4(1)
should turn on whether the particular class of persons affected
needs the protection of the Act. An offering to those who are
shown to be able to fend for themselves is a transaction "not involving any public offering."

The Commission would have us go one step further and hold that "an offering to a substantial number of the public" is not exempt under §4(1). We are advised that "whatever the special circumstances, the Commission has consistently interpreted the exemption as being inapplicable when a large number of offerees is involved." But the statute would seem to apply to a "public offering" whether to few or many.[11] It may well be that offerings to a substantial number of persons would rarely be exempt. Indeed nothing prevents the commission, in enforcing the statute, from using some kind of numerical test in deciding when to investigate particular exemption claims. But there is no warrant for superimposing a quantity limit on private offerings as a matter of statutory interpretation.

The exemption, as we construe it, does not deprive corporate employees, as a class, of the safeguards of the Act. We agree that some employee offerings may come within §4(1), e. g., one made to executive personnel who because of their position have access to the same kind of information that the Act would make available in the form of a registration statement.[12] Absent such a showing of special circumstances, employees are just as much members of the investing "public" as any of their neighbors in the community. Although we do not rely on it, the rejection in 1934 of an amendment which would have specifically exempted employee stock offerings supports this conclusion. The House Managers, commenting on the Conference Report, said that "the participants in employees' stock-investment plans may be in as great need of the protection afforded by availability of information concerning the issuer for which they work as are most other members of the public." H. R. Rep. No. 1838, 73d Cong., 2d Sess. 41.

Keeping in mind the broadly remedial purposes of federal securities legislation, imposition of the burden of proof on an issuer who would plead the exemption seems to us fair and reasonable.

---

[11] See Viscount Sumner's frequently quoted dictum in Nash v. Lynde: " 'The public' * * * is of course a general word. No particular numbers are prescribed. Anything from two to infinity may serve: perhaps even one, if he is intended to be the first of a series of subscribers, but makes further proceedings needless by himself subscribing the whole." [1929] A. C. 158, 169.

[12] This was one of the factors stressed in an advisory opinion rendered by the Commission's General Counsel in 1935. "I also regard as significant the relationship between the issuer and the offerees. Thus, an offering to the members of a class who should have special knowledge of the issuer is less likely to be a public offering than is an offering to the members of a class of the same size who do not have this advantage. This factor would be particularly important in offerings to employees, where a class of high executive officers would have a special relationship to the issuer which subordinate employees would not enjoy." 11 Fed. Reg. 10952.

Schlemmer v. *Buffalo, R. & P. R. Co.*, 205 U. S. 1, 10 (1907). Agreeing, the court below thought the burden met primarily because of the respondent's purpose in singling out its key employees for stock offerings. But once it is seen that the exemption question turns on the knowledge of the offerees, the issuer's motives, laudable though they may be, fade into irrelevance. The focus of inquiry should be on the need of the offerees for the protections afforded by registration. The employees here were not shown to have access to the kind of information which registration would disclose. The obvious opportunities for pressure and imposition make it advisable that they be entitled to compliance with §5.

Reversed.

THE CHIEF JUSTICE and MR. JUSTICE BURTON dissent.

MR. JUSTICE JACKSON took no part in the consideration or decision of this case.

DORAN v. PETROLEUM MANAGEMENT CORP.
United States Court of Appeals, Fifth Circuit, 1977
545 F. 2d 893

Before GOLDBERG, DYER and SIMPSON, Circuit Judges.

GOLDBERG, Circuit Judge.

In this case a sophisticated investor who purchased a limited partnership interest in an oil drilling venture seeks to rescind. The question raised is whether the sale was part of a private offering exempted by §4(2) of the Securities Act of 1938, 15 U. S. C. §77d(2) (1970), from the registration requirements of that Act. See Securities Act of 1933, §§5, 12(1), 15 U. S. C. §§77e, 77l(1).[1] We hold that in the absence of findings of fact that each offeree had been furnished information about the issuer that a registration statement would have disclosed or that each offeree had effective access to such information, the district court erred in concluding that the offering was a private placement. Accordingly, we reverse and remand.

I. FACTS

Prior to July 1970, Petroleum Management Corporation (PMC) organized a California limited partnership for the purpose of

---

[1] * * * The SEC's adoption of Rule 146, 17 C. F. R. §230.146 (1976), which establishes a sufficient set of conditions for coming within the exemption, does not bear directly on the case at bar. The transaction at issue began in 1970, and the plaintiff filed suit in 1972. Rule 146 was not adopted until 1974. It applies to offers commencing on or after June 10, 1974.

drilling and operating four wells in Wyoming. The limited partnership agreement provided for both "participants," whose capital contributions were to be used first to pay all intangible expenses incurred by the partnership, and "special participants," whose capital contributions were to be applied first to pay tangible drilling expenses.

PMC and Inter-Tech Resources, Inc., were initially the only "special participants" in the limited partnership. They were joined by four "participants." As found by the district court, PMC contracted only four other persons with respect to possible participation in the partnership. All but the plaintiff declined.

During the late summer of 1970, plaintiff William H. Doran, Jr., received a telephone call from a California securities broker previously known to him. The broker, Phillip Kendricks, advised Doran of the opportunity to become a "special participant" in the partnership. PMC then sent Doran the drilling logs and technical maps of the proposed drilling area. PMC informed Doran that two of the proposed four wells had already been completed. Doran agreed to become a "special participant" in the Wyoming drilling program. In consideration for his partnership share, Doran agreed to contribute $125,000 toward the partnership. Doran was to discharge this obligation by paying PMC $25,000 down and in addition assuming responsibility for the payment of a $113,643 note owed by PMC to Mid-Continent Supply Co. Doran's share in the production payments from the wells was to be used to make the installment payments on the Mid-Continent note.

Pursuant to this arrangement, on September 16, 1970, Doran executed a promissory note, already signed by the President and Vice President of PMC in their individual capacities, for $113,643 payable to Mid-Continent. On October 5, 1970, Doran mailed PMC a check for $25,000. He thereby became a "special participant" in the Wyoming drilling program.

On July 16, 1971, the balance on the note to Mid-Continent became due. The parties renegotiated the loan. A new note for $66,292.24 was executed by PMC, the two PMC officers, and Doran. Pursuant to a written agreement of February 9, 1971, however, Doran had agreed to hold PMC and its officers harmless for any liability arising from the Mid-Continent note. The July renegotiation did not alter Doran's obligation.

During 1970 and 1971, PMC periodically sent Doran production information on the completed wells of the limited partnership. Throughout this period, however, the wells were deliberately overproduced in violation of the production allowances established by the Wyoming Oil and Gas Conservation Commission. As a consequence, on November 16, 1971, the Commission ordered the partnership's wells sealed for a period of 338 days. On May 1, 1972, the Commission notified PMC that production from the wells could resume on August 9, 1972. After August 9, the wells yielded a production income level below that obtained prior to the Commission's order.

Following the cessation of production payments between November 1971 and August 1972 and the decreased yields thereafter, the Mid-Continent note upon which Doran was primarily liable went into default. Mid-Continent subsequently obtained a state court judgment against Doran, PMC, and the two signatory officers of PMC for $50,815.50 plus interest and attorney's fees.

On October 16, 1972, Doran filed this suit in federal district court seeking damages for breach of contract, rescission of the contract based on violations of the Securities Acts of 1933 and 1934, and a judgment declaring the defendants liable for payment of the state judgment obtained by Mid-Continent.

The court below found that the offer and sale of the "special participant" interest was a private offering because Doran was a sophisticated investor who did not need the protection of the Securities Acts. The court also found that there was no evidence that PMC, its officers, or Kendrick made any misrepresentation or omissions of material facts to Doran. Finally, the court found that the overproduction of the wells was not a breach of the partnership agreement, but in any event there was no evidence that Doran suffered any losses as a result of the overproduction. The court concluded that all relief requested by Doran should be denied. Doran filed this appeal.

II. THE PRIVATE OFFERING EXEMPTION

No registration statement was filed with any federal or state regulatory body in connection with the defendants' offering of securities. Along with two other factors that we may take as established — that the defendants sold or offered to sell these securities, and that the defendants used interstate transportation or communication in connection with the sale or offer of sale — the plaintiff thus states a prima facie case for a violation of the federal securities laws. See *Hill York Corp.* v. *American International Franchises, Inc.*, 448 F. 2d 680, 686 (5th Cir. 1971).

The defendants do not contest the existence of the elements of plaintiff's prima facie case but raise an affirmative defense that the relevant transactions came within the exemption from registration found in §4(2), 15 U. S. C. §77d(2). Specifically, they contend that the offering of securities was not a public offering. The defendants, who of course bear the burden of proving this affirmative defense, must therefore show that the offering was private. See *SEC* v. *Ralson Purina Co.*, 346 U. S. 119, 126 (1953); *Hill York Corp.* v. *American International Franchises, Inc.*, supra, 448 F. 2d at 690; *Lively* v. *Hirschfeld*, 440 F. 2d 631, 632 (10th Cir. 1971); *United States* v. *Custer Channel Wing Corp.*, 376 F. 2d 675, 678 (4th Cir.), *cert. denied*, 389 U. S. 850 (1967).

This court has in the past identified four factors relevant to whether an offering qualifies for the exemption. The consideration of these factors, along with the policies embodied in the 1933 Act, structure the inquiry. *Hill York Corp.* v. *American International Franchises, Inc.*, supra, 448 F. 2d at 687-88; *Henderson* v. *Hayden, Stone Inc.*, 461 F. 2d 1069, 1071 (5th Cir. 1972); *SEC* v. *Continental Tobacco Co. of South Carolina*, 463 F. 2d 137, 158 (5th Cir. 1972); see also *Woolf* v. *S. D. Cohn & Co.*, 515 F. 2d 591, 609 (5th Cir. 1975), *vacated on other grounds*, 426 U. S. 944 (1976). The relevant factors include the number of offerees and their relationship to each other and the issuer, the number of units offered, the size of the offering, and the manner of the offering. Consideration of these factors need not exhaust the inquiry, nor is one factor's weighing heavily in favor of the private status of the offering sufficient to ensure the availability of the exemption. Rather, these factors serve as guideposts to the court in attempting to determine whether subjecting the offering to registration requirements would further the purposes of the 1933 Act.

The term, "private offering," is not defined in the Securities Act of 1933. The scope of the §4(2) private offering exemption must therefore be determined by reference to the legislative purposes of the Act. In *SEC* v. *Ralston Purina Co.*, supra, the SEC had sought to enjoin a corporation's offer of unregistered stock to its employees, and the Court grappled with the corporation's defense that the offering came within the private placement exemption. The Court began by looking to the statutory purpose:

> Since exempt transactions are those as to which "there is no practical need for * * * [the bill's] application," the applicability of [§4(2)] should turn on whether the particular class of persons affected need the protection of the Act. An offering to those who are shown to be able to fend for themselves is a transaction "not involving any public offering."

346 U. S. at 124. According to the Court, the purpose of the Act was "to protect investors by promoting full disclosure of information thought necessary to informed investment decisions." Id. at 124. It therefore followed that "the exemption question turns on

the knowledge of the offerees." Id. at 126-27. That formulation remains the touchstone of the inquiry into the scope of the private offering exemption. It is most nearly reflected in the first of the four factors: the number of offerees and their relationship to each other and to the issuer.

In the case at bar, the defendants may have demonstrated the presence of the latter three factors. A small number of units offered, relatively modest financial stakes, and an offering characterized by personal contact between the issuer and offerees free of public advertising or intermediaries such as investment bankers or securities exchanges — these aspects of the instant transaction aid the defendants' search for a §4(2) exemption.

Nevertheless, with respect to the first, most critical, and conceptually most problematic factor, the record does not permit us to agree that the defendants have proved that they are entitled to the limited sanctuary afforded by §4(2). We must examine more closely the importance of demonstrating both the number of offerees and their relationship to the issuer in order to see why the defendants have not yet gained the §4(2) exemption.

A. THE NUMBER OF OFFEREES

Establishing the number of persons involved in an offering is important both in order to ascertain the magnitude of the offering and in order to determine the characteristics and knowledge of the persons thus identified.

The number of offerees, not the number of purchasers, is the relevant figure in considering the number of persons involved in an offering. *Hill York Corp.* v. *American International Franchises, Inc.*, supra, 448 F. 2d at 691. A private placement claimant's failure to adduce any evidence regarding the number of offerees will be fatal to the claim. *SEC* v. *Continental Tobacco Co.*, supra, 463 F. 2d at 161; *Henderson* v. *Hayden, Stone Inc.*, supra, 461 F. 2d at 1071-72; *Repass* v. *Rees*, 174 F. Supp. 898, 904 (D. Colo. 1959). The number of offerees is not itself a decisive factor in determining the availability of the private offering exemption. Just as an offering to few may be public, so an offering to many may be private. *SEC* v. *Ralston Purina Co.*, supra, 346 U. S. at 125. Nevertheless, "the more offerees, the more likelihood that the offering is public." *Hill York Corp.* v. *American International Franchises, Inc.*, supra, 448 F. 2d at 688. In the case at bar, the record indicates that eight investors were offered limited partnership shares in the drilling program — a total that would be entirely consistent with a finding that the offering was private.

The defendants attempt to limit the number of offerees even further, however. They argue that Doran was the sole offeree because all others contacted by PMC were offered "participant" rather than "special participant" interests. The district court, which did not issue a finding of fact or conclusion of law with respect to this argument, appears to have assumed that there were eight offerees.

The argument is, in any event, unsupported by the record. The only evidence that the defendants adduced to show the number of offerees established merely that offers of "participant" interests were made to four investors who accepted, and that offers of "limited partnership" interests were made to three other prospective investors who declined. Because both "participant" and "special participant" interests were limited partnership interests, we are unable to discern from the record whether the three declining investors were offered "special participant" interests. Moreover, we have no evidence that the four "participants" were not also offered "special participant" interests. The defendants have the burden of proof regarding the number of offerees. We must therefore reject the argument that Doran was the sole offeree.[9]

In considering the number of offerees solely as indicative of the magnitude or scope of an offering, the difference between one and eight offerees is relatively unimportant. Rejecting the argument that Doran was the sole offeree is significant, however, because it means that in considering the need of the offerees for the protection that registration would have afforded we must look beyond Doran's interests to those of all his fellow offerees. Even the offeree-plaintiff's 20-20 vision with respect to the facts underlying the security would not save the exemption if any one of his fellow offerees was in a blind.

---

[9] Even had the defendants shown that Doran was the only investor to have been offered a "special participant" interest, however, it is doubtful that the defendants would thereby have established that Doran was the sole offeree with respect to the security in question. The two kinds of limited partnership interests were (1) offered as part of a single scheme of financing contemplated by the limited partnership agreement; (2) they appear to have been offered within a time span of a few months (3) for the same kind of consideration (4) and for the same general purpose. The only difference between the two kinds of limited partnership interests that appears on the record was that the "participants" were able to take a greater portion of intangible drilling deductions. Otherwise, according to the limited partnership agreement, the two kinds of limited partnership interests were identical. Accordingly, on the present state of the record we shall treat the eight offers of limited partnership shares in the Wyoming drilling venture as an integrated offering for purposes of determining the availability of the §4(2) exemption. See generally Schwartz, The Private Offering Exemption — Recent Developments, 37 Ohio St. L. J. 1, 8-11 (1976).

B.   THE OFFEREES' RELATIONSHIP TO THE ISSUER

Since *SEC* v. *Ralston*, supra, courts have sought to determine the need of offerees for the protections afforded by registration by focusing on the relationship between offerees and issuer and more particularly on the information available to the offerees by virtue of that relationship. Id., 346 U. S. at 126-27. Once the offerees have been identified, it is possible to investigate their relationship to the issuer.

The district court concluded that the offer of a "special participant" interest to Doran was a private offering because Doran was a sophisticated investor who did not need the protections afforded by registration. It is important, in light of our rejection of the argument that Doran was the sole offeree, that the district court also found that all four "participants" and all three declining offerees were sophisticated investors with regard to oil ventures.

The need of the offerees for the protection afforded by registration is, to be sure, a question of fact dependent upon the circumstances of each case. *Hill York Corp.* v. *American International Franchises, Inc.*, supra, 448 F. 2d at 687. Nevertheless, the trial court's conclusion with respect to the availability of the private offering exemption may be set aside if induced by an erroneous view of the law. See *SEC* v. *Continental Tobacco Co.*, supra, 463 F. 2d at 156-57; *Henderson* v. *Hayden, Stone Inc.*, supra, 461 F. 2d at 1071.

1.   The Role of Investment Sophistication

The lower court's finding that Doran was a sophisticated investor is amply supported by the record, as is the sophistication of the other offerees. Doran holds a petroleum engineering degree from Texas A&M University. His net worth is in excess of $1,000,-000. His holdings of approximately twenty-six oil and gas properties are valued at $850,000.

Nevertheless, evidence of a high degree of business or legal sophistication on the part of all offerees does not suffice to bring the offering within the private placement exemption. We clearly established that proposition in *Hill York Corp.* v. *American International Franchises, Inc.*, supra, 448 F. 2d at 690. We reasoned that "if the plaintiffs did not possess the information requisite for a registration statement, they could not bring their sophisticated knowledge of business affairs to bear in deciding whether or not to invest * * * ." Sophistication is not a substitute for access to the information that registration would disclose. *United States* v. *Custer Channel Wing Corp.*, supra, 376 F. 2d at 678. As we said in *Hill York,* although the evidence of the offerees' expertise "is certainly favorable to the defendants, the level of sophistication will not carry the point. In this context, the relationship between the promoters and the purchasers and the 'access to the kind of information which registration would disclose' become highly relevant factors." 448 F. 2d at 690.[10]

In short, there must be sufficient basis of accurate information upon which the sophisticated investor may exercise his skills. Just as a scientist cannot be without his specimens, so the shrewdest investor's acuity will be blunted without specifications about the issuer. For an investor to be invested with exemptive status he must have the required data for judgment.

2. *The Requirement of Available Information*

The interplay between two factors, the relationship between offerees and issuer and the offerees' access to information that registration would disclose, has been a matter of some conceptual and terminological difficulty. For purposes of this discussion, we shall adopt the following conventions: We shall refer to offerees who have not been furnished registration information directly, but who are in a position relative to the issuer to obtain the information registration would provide, as having "access" to such information. By a position of access we mean a relationship based on factors such as employment, family, or economic bargaining power that enables the offeree effectively to obtain such information. See SEC Rule 146(e), 17 C. F. R. §280.146(e) (1976).[a] When offerees, regardless of whether they occupy a position of access, have been furnished with the information a registration statement would provide, we shall say merely that such information has been disclosed. When the offerees have access to or there has been disclosure of the information registration would provide, we shall say that such information was available.

---

[10] We do not intimate that evidence of the offerees' sophistication is required in all cases to establish a private offering exemption under §4(2). Indeed, we have said that SEC Rule 146, 17 C. F. R. §230.146 (1976), is "more restrictive than the cases in this Circuit in that it requires that the offeree either be sophisticated or advised by an offeree representative who is, in addition to the requirement that offerees receive or have access to information that registration would disclose." Woolf v. S. D. Cohn & Co., supra, 515 F. 2d at 611-12 n. 14. In other words, in *Hill York* we said that the "sophistication" of the offerees was not a sufficient condition for the availability of the private offering exemption; Rule 146 says that "sophistication" is a necessary but not a sufficient condition.

[a] ED.: This rule has since given way to Rule 506. See p. 373 supra.

The requirement that all offerees have available the information registration would provide has been firmly established by this court as a necessary condition of gaining the private offering exemption. Our decisions have been predicated upon *Ralston Purina,* supra, where the Supreme Court held that in the absence of a showing that the "key employees" to whom a corporation offered its common stock had knowledge obviating the need for registration, the offering did not qualify for the private offering exemption. The Court said that an employee offering would come within the exemption if it were shown that the employees were "executive personnel who because of their position have access to the same kind of information that the act would make available in the form of a registration statement." Id. 346 U. S. at 125-26.

In *Hill York Corp.* v. *American International Franchises, Inc.,* supra, 448 F. 2d at 689, this court approved jury instructions that "correctly stated the ultimate test. . . . that every offeree had to have information equivalent to that which a registration statement would disclose." In subsequent cases we have adhered to that test. See *Woolf* v. *S. D. Cohn & Co.,* supra, 515 F. 2d at 613; *SEC* v. *Continental Tobacco Co.,* supra, 463 F. 2d at 158-61; *Henderson* v. *Hayden, Stone Inc.,* supra, 461 F. 2d at 1071. Because the district court failed to apply this test to the case at bar, but rather inferred from evidence of Doran's sophistication that his purchase of a partnership share was incident to a private offering, we must remand so that the lower court may determine the extent of the information available to each offeree.

More specifically, we shall require on remand that the defendants demonstrate that all offerees, whatever their expertise, had available the information a registration statement would have afforded a prospective investor in a public offering. Such a showing is not independently sufficient to establish that the offering qualified for the private placement exemption, but it is necessary to gain the exemption and is to be weighed along with the sophistication and number of the offerees, the number of units offered, and the size and manner of the offering. See *SEC* v. *Continental Tobacco Co.,* supra, 463 F. 2d at 160; see also *Woolf* v. *S. D. Cohn & Co.,* supra, 515 F. 2d at 610-613. Because in this case these latter factors weigh heavily in favor of the private offering exemption, satisfaction of the necessary condition regarding the availability of relevant information to the offerees would compel the conclusion that this offering fell within the exemption.

The cornerstone of the regulatory structure envisaged by the authors of the Securities Act is disclosure. The Act is practical and pragmatic, not dogmatic and doctrinaire. It is designed to give a panoply of protection to the investor, but also to allow play in the marts of trade for offers of securities that do not require the oversight of the Securities and Exchange Commission. In suggesting the scope of that exemption, we cannot divine all the variables of a formula that might enable a trial court precisely to determine whether a given offering falls within or without its perimeter. There are few certitudes, and in interpreting the statute we must permit ourselves room for the ifs, the perhapes, and the maybes in commercial relationships and variegated investor postures. The question of exemption remains one of fact reserved in the first instance for the trial court. Nevertheless, it cannot be doubted that within or without the perimeter of the private offering exemption, the policies of the Securities Act mandate that the courts focus on the information available to the offerees of a security.

C.   ON REMAND: THE ISSUER-OFFEREE RELATIONSHIP

In determining on remand the extent of the information available to the offerees, the district court must keep in mind that the "availability" of information means either disclosure of or effective access to the relevant information. The relationship between issuer and offeree is most critical when the issuer relies on the latter route.

To begin with, if the defendants could prove that all offerees were actually furnished the information a registration statement would have provided, whether the offerees occupied a position of access pre-existing such disclosure would not be dispositive of the status of the offering. If disclosure were proved and if, as here, the remaining factors such as the manner of the offering and the investment sophistication of the offerees weigh heavily in favor of the private status of the offering, the absence of a privileged relationship between offeree and issuer would not preclude a finding that the offering was private. Any other conclusion would tear out of context this court's earlier discussions of the §4(2) exemption and would conflict with the policies of the exemption.

Alternatively it might be shown that the offeree had access to the files and record of the company that contained the relevant information. Such access might be afforded merely by the position of the offeree or by the issuer's promise to open appropriate files and records to the offeree as well as to answer inquiries regarding material information. In either case, the relationship between offeree and issuer now becomes critical for it must be shown that the offeree could realistically have been expected to take advantage of his access to ascertain the relevant information.[12] Similarly the investment sophistication of the offeree assumes added importance, for it is important that he could have been expected to ask the right questions and seek out the relevant information.

In sum, both the relationship between issuer and offeree and the latter's investment sophistication are critical when the issuer or another relies on the offeree's "access" rather than the issuer's "disclosure" to come within the exemption. We shall first show that this formulation is consistent with the current state of private offering law in this and other circuits. Second, we shall examine the misconception that our cases require a privileged or "insider" relationship between issuer and offeree as a necessary condition of coming within the §4(2) exemption. Once the distinction between "access" and "disclosure" is fully recognized, our caselaw should not be construed to embody such a requirement.

1. Disclosures or Access: A Disjunctive Requirement

That our cases sometimes fail clearly to differentiate between "access" and "disclosure" as alternative means of coming within the private offering exemption is, perhaps, not surprising. Although the *Ralston Purina* decision focused on whether the offerees had "access" to the required information, 346 U. S. at 127, the holding that "the exemption question turns on the knowledge of the offerees," id. at 126, could be construed to include possession as well as access. Such an interpretation would require disclosure as a necessary condition of obtaining a private offering notwithstanding the offerees' access to the information that registration would have provided.

Both the Second and the Fourth Circuits, however, have interpreted *Ralston Purina* as embodying a disjunctive requirement. Thus, for example, in *Gilligan, Will & Co. v. SEC,* 267 F. 2d 461, 466 (2nd Cir. 1959), *cert. denied,* 361 U. S. 896 (1960), the court observed that *Ralston Purina* "held that the governing fact is whether the persons to whom the offering is made are in such a position with respect to the issuer that they either actually have such information as a registration would have disclosed, or have access to such information." See also *SEC* v. *Tax Service, Inc.,* 357 F. 2d 143, 144 (4th Cir. 1966).

The cases in this circuit are not inconsistent with this view.

---

[12] For example, the offeree's ability to compel the issuer to make good his promise may depend on the offeree's bargaining power or on his family or employment relationship to the issuer.

In *Woolf* v. *S. D. Cohn & Co.*, supra, 515 F. 2d at 612-13, we admittedly read *Continental* as "requiring that there be disclosure of the information registration would have revealed to each offeree . . . ." Because the court in *Continental* found neither disclosure to all offerees of the information registration would provide nor their access to such information, however, the case does not hold that when sophisticated offerees have access to the requisite information by virtue of their privileged relationship to the issuer, actual disclosure is nonetheless necessary. Only if the defendants in *Continental* had demonstrated that all offerees were sophisticated and that all had access to the relevant information, but the court had nevertheless required actual disclosure, could *Continental* foreclose the view we express in the case at bar.

Similarly, in *Woolf* we found that because it was not clear "what information was disclosed to whom at what time," we were obliged to remand the case. Because the defendants in *Woolf* did not argue that the offerees' access to information qualified the offering for private status even without actual disclosure, we did not and could not hold that disclosure was the only means of coming within the exemption.

Woolf refers to Rule 146 as a "useful frame of reference to an appellate court in assessing the validity of §4(2) exemptions claimed . . . prior to its effective date." 515 F. 2d at 612. Since *Woolf* elsewhere notes specifically that Rule 146 would permit the issuer to show either access or disclosure, it is inconceivable that the court in *Woolf* would establish more stringent requirements for this circuit or would interpret *Continental* to establish such requirements. Rather, *Woolf* observes correctly that Rule 146 does not purport to be an exclusive definition of the circumstances under which the exemption is available, implying that there will be a class of placements that do not satisfy the more stringent criteria of the Rule 146 safe harbor but are nevertheless to be accorded private status. Id at 612.

Although Rule 146 cannot directly control the case at bar, we think its disjunctive requirement that the private offering claimant may show either "access" or "disclosure" expresses a sound view that this court has in fact implicitly accepted. For example, in *Hill York Corp.* v. *American International Franchises, Inc.*, supra, 448 F. 2d at 690-91, this court thought it necessary to show that the offerees neither possessed the information registration would afford nor had access to such information. See also 1 Loss, Securities Regulation 657 n. 53 (2d ed. 1961), quoted in *Hill York*, supra, 448 F. 2d at 698. And in *Henderson* v. *Hayden, Stone Inc.*, supra, 461 F. 2d at 1072, the court clearly separates the questions: "Did [the offerees] possess the same information as would be found in a registration statement? Did they have access to such information?"[17]

2. The Role of Insider Status

Once the alternative means of coming within the private placement exemption are clearly separated, we can appreciate the proper role to be accorded the requirement that the offerees occupy a privileged or "insider" status relative to the issuer. That is to say, when the issuer relies on "access" absent actual disclosure, he must show that the offerees occupied a privileged position relative to the issuer that afforded them an opportunity for effective access to the information registration would otherwise provide.[18] When the issuer relies on actual disclosure to come within the exemption, he need not demonstrate that the offerees held such a privileged position. Although mere disclosure is not a sufficient condition for establishing the availability of the private offering exemption, and a court will weigh other factors such as the manner of the offering and the investment sophistication of the offerees, the "insider" status of the offerees is not a necessary condition of obtaining the exemption.

Because the line between access and disclosure has sometimes been obscured, some have interpreted this court's decision in *Con-*

---

[17] One argument for requiring actual disclosure as opposed to access is that the existence of a written disclosure statement makes it easier subsequently to evaluate the accuracy of the information imparted. Because any misleading information will be recorded, the issuer may have a greater incentive to be careful. Despite the force of this argument when ordinary investors are concerned, with respect to sophisticated investors the additional protection may be unnecessary. Sophisticated investors will be more able to discern a fraud or misrepresentation and will presumably have the acumen successfully to invoke the securities laws even if evidence of the misrepresentation is not as easily preserved.

[18] That all offerees are in certain respects "insiders" does not ensure that the issuer will gain the private placement exemption. An insider may be an insider with respect to fiscal matters of the company, but an outsider with respect to a particular issue of securities. He may know much about the financial structure of the company but his position may nonetheless not allow him access to a few vital facts pertaining to the transaction at issue. If Doran had effective access to all information that registration would provide, he would be a transactional insider. That is all we require regarding the availability of information. If, on the other hand, his insider knowledge was incomplete or his access ineffective, he would be a transactional outsider despite the fact that we might consider him an "insider" for other purposes.

tinental as limiting the §4(2) exemption to insider transactions. As we pointed out in our recent decision in *Woolf,* however, such fears are unfounded. 515 F. 2d at 610.

The language from *Continental* that gave rise to those fears consists in the court's findings that "Continental did not affirmatively prove that all offerees of its securities had received both written and oral information concerning Continental, that all offerees of its securities had access to any additional information which they might have required or requested, and that all offerees of its securities had personal contacts with the officers of Continental." 463 F. 2d at 160. It is possible to read this as a list of the necessary conditions for coming within the §4(2) exemption, and therefore to infer that a private placement claimant must show the "insider" status of the offerees. Properly viewed in context, however, these statements were not clearly intended to establish necessary conditions, but only to point to the manifold weaknesses of the defendant's claim which, taken together, precluded private offering status.

In *Continental,* the court admittedly agreed with the SEC's position that even if the prospectus that Continental had sent to purchasers contained all the information registration would disclose, that fact alone would not justify the exemption. 463 F. 2d at 160. That is doubtless true, since even if all the purchasers of Continental's securities had received full disclosure, the defendant would not have established that all offerees had received full disclosure. Because Continental had failed to sustain its burden of demonstrating the number of offerees, moreover, even the fact that all known offerees might have received disclosure would still have been insufficient to ensure the availability of the exemption. But the court's language in *Continental* should not be read as requiring in addition to full disclosure to all offerees a demonstration of the offerees' insider status.

Rather, the court's language regarding Continental's failure to show that all offerees had access to the requisite information and that all offerees had personal contacts with Continental's officers may be read as foreclosing the possible alternative route to the §4(2) exemption. Because the prospectus did not contain all the information registration would provide and because it was not established that all offerees received the prospectus, it was clear that Continental could not rely upon actual disclosure. The additional language in *Continental,* though admittedly subject to other interpretations, may be read as making clear that there was in that case no privileged relationship between the offerees and the issuer that might have compensated for the defendant's palpable failure to disclose.

Although the disjunctive nature of the requirement is, to be sure, not made explicit in *Continental,* it is important that the pertinent conclusion of fact held clearly erroneous in that case was that "the offerees . . . were furnished and/or provided access to the same type of information that would have been provided in a registration statement . . . ." 463 F. 2d at 159. In order to hold this conclusion clearly erroneous, it was thus necessary to show that the defendant had failed to prove either disclosure or access.

In any event, absent a clear and unambiguous indication to the contrary, we do not read *Continental* as requiring insider status. We think that any such requirement would inhibit the ability of business to raise capital without the expense and delay of registration under circumstances in which the offerees did not need the protection of registration. The enactment of Rule 146 represents the SEC's recognition of this legitimate business need. We think that it would be unwise to adopt in this circuit a requirement of insider status notwithstanding disclosure or that of actual disclosure notwithstanding effective access. Such requirements would constrict the scope of the private offering exemption more narrowly than does Rule 146 and would retard necessary capital investment without a corresponding benefit to those investors who need the protection of registration.

Rule 146 offers some rays of sunlight into the limbos and uncertain depths of §4(2). The cases cast at best a faint beacon toward the horizon of decision. While we appreciate full well that the test we have fashioned remains too fluid to enable the would-be private offering issuer to feel entirely secure, we are confident that, at long last, the safe harbor of Rule 146 will provide that security and that few private placement claimants will stray far from that harbor. Rule 146 is a serotine development. More than two decades passed after *Ralston* before the SEC sufficiently elaborated on the definitional concepts behind §4(2). With respect to those transactions that antedate the effective date of Rule 146, this case and those preceding it in this circuit establish as the critical factor in determining whether the exemption applies to a particular offering the availability of information of all offerees. The privileged status of the offerees must be demonstrated only when it is necessary to the claimant's efforts to establish that the requisite information was in fact available.

III. BREACH OF CONTRACT

We affirm that portion of the district court's judgment rejecting Doran's claim that he was damaged by the defendants' overproduction of the wells in breach of the partnership agreement.

*   *   *

IV. CONCLUSION

An examination of the record and the district court's opinion in this case leaves unanswered the central question in all cases that turn on the availability of the §4(2) exemption. Did the offerees know or have a realistic opportunity to learn facts essential to an investment judgment? We remand so that the trial court can answer that question.

This opinion focuses on facts because the Securities Act focuses on facts — facts disclosed, facts known, or access to facts. "Insider" or "outsider" labels are not determinative. Traditional forms are not determinative. In adjusting the generalities of §4(2) to the realities of the contemporary market, we have seized on the availability to all offerees of pertinent facts. We have conditioned the private offering exemption on either actual disclosure of the information registration would provide or the offerees' effective access to such information. If the issuer has not disclosed but instead relies on the offerees' access, the privileged status of the offerees relative to the issuer must be shown.

We are conscious of the difficulty of formulating black letter law in this area in light of the multiplicity of security transactions and their multifarious natures. Securities regulation is often a matter of the hound chasing the hare as issuers devise new ways to issue their securities and the definition of a security itself expands. We do not want the private offering exemption to swallow the Securities Act, and we must resolve doubtful cases against the private placement claimant and in favor of the Act's paramount value of disclosure. By the same token, we must heed the existence and purposes of the exemption, and be cautious lest we discourage private avenues for raising capital. Our present emphasis on the availability of information as the *sine qua non* of the private offering is an attempt to steer a middle course.

We must reverse in part the judgment of the district court and remand for proceedings not inconsistent with this opinion.[b]

---

[b] Ed.: See also Lawler v. Gilliam, 569 F. 2d 1283, 1289-91 (4th Cir. 1978).

Query:

(1) True, the language of §4(2) came out of the British Companies Act 1929.[3] But, both §4(2) and the legislative history being as sparse as they are, was there any policy reason to follow the House of Lords in worrying about number and type of offerees rather than buyers? How is an offeree hurt if he does not buy?

(2) Suppose an offering is made to ten "self-fending" types, all of whom buy, and one "*non*-self-fender" who does *not* buy. Should the first ten be able to recover under §12(1)?

(3) When the *Ralston* approach is carried to the point where an offer to a single person becomes a "public" offering,[4] have we not left the world of reason — or, at least, abandoned the English language?

(4) In considering whether an offering to not more than a relatively small number of persons (perhaps twenty-five) may safely be assumed to be private notwithstanding any other factors, arguably the Court's rejection of a quantity limit was not directed to a number *below* which an offering might be deemed *private* but was by way of reply to the Commission's argument that the substantial number of offerees in the *Ralston* case conclusively established without more that the offering was *public*. In other words, the Court, still arguably, rejected a rule of thumb on the top side, not the bottom side.

At least as late as 1961, the present writer thought it "apparent from an examination of the subsequent cases and other expressions of the Commission's views" that "On the pragmatic rather than the semantic level, * * * the Supreme Court's opinion seems to have had little effect on the traditional position taken by the Commission except perhaps to strengthen it."[5] By 1969, however, he had to say: "Since 1958 or so, * * * the number of Commission disavowals of any safe numerical test, though mostly dicta, has grown to the point that one can no longer assume as a practical

---

[3] Now 11 & 12 Geo. 6, c. 38, §38(3)(b) (1948).

[4] G. Eugene England Foundation v. First Federal Corp., 663 F. 2d 988, 990 (10th Cir. 1973); see also Klapmeier v. Telecheck Int'l, Inc., 482 F. 2d 247, 254 (8th Cir. 1973) (stock-for-stock exchange with seven persons, all represented by one of them in negotiating a merger); Meadow Brook National Bank v. Levine, CCH Fed. Sec. L. Rep. ¶91,496 at 94,870 (N. Y. Sup. Ct. 1965) (dictum that, taken out of context, indicates the possibility that an offering to a single person in need of protection might not be exempted); but see Milnarik v. M-S Commodities, Inc., 320 F. Supp. 1149, 1153 (N. D. Ill. 1970), aff'd on *other grounds*, 457 F. 2d 274 (7th Cir. 1972), *cert. denied*, 409 U. S. 887 (despite *Ralston*, "an offering has never been held to be a public offering when it has been extended to only one person").

[5] 1 Loss 661-62 (1961).

matter that an offering to not more than some twenty-five persons (or any lesser number) will be considered exempt even so far as Commission intervention as distinct from civil liability under §12(1) is concerned."[6]

What happened in the interim was the series of cases cited in *Doran* — most of them, as chance had it, in the Fifth Circuit — which gradually narrowed the exemption to the point where the court in *Doran* went out of its way to emphasize that its earlier decisions had not meant to lay down any categorical requirement that every offeree be an "insider"[7] (presumably in the sense of the law that has developed under Rule 10b-5).[8] The "insider" approach is precisely what SEC counsel had argued in one of the earlier Fifth Circuit cases cited in *Doran*,[9] although a member of the Commission was quick to make a public disavowal.[10]

(5) It has been the accredited doctrine for some time that statutes should not be read literally, or even construed in accordance with a "legislative intention" that is often (as in this case) mythical or at best unclear, but that the correct approach is that enjoined on us by Justice Jackson in *Joiner:* to fathom the "dominating general purpose" and to go ahead with the business of interpretation "so far as the meaning of the words fairly permits so as to carry out in particular cases the generally expressed legislative policy."[11] Even so, do the two simple English words,

---

[6] 4 Loss 2644 (1969). The Commission's General Counsel did say in December 1970: "As a rule, the Commission does not take after small transactions in the situation where the Supreme Court said we might. Unless we feel that there is more to it than a registration problem, we do not normally object, at least in court, to situations where the securities are offered to some fifteen or twenty people." Loomis, The Federal Securities Laws, 7 Ga. S. B. J. 353, 361 (1971). But see Thomas D. Conrad, Jr., 44 SEC 725 (1971), where the Commission held that, when the offerees were unsophisticated and "clearly did not have access to the same kind of information that registration would have supplied," the fact that there were only nine offerees and that the bonds were by their terms nontransferable did not suffice to make the offering private.

[7] 545 F. 2d at 906-08, supra pp. 366-68.

[8] See c. 9B infra.

[9] "Before the statutory protections may be safely eliminated, in any case, the issuer must affirmatively demonstrate by 'explicit, exact' evidence that each person to whom unregistered securities were offered was able to 'fend' for himself — in other words, that each offeree had a relationship to the company tantamount to that of an 'insider' in terms of his ability to know, to understand and to verify for himself all of the relevant facts * * *." Brief of SEC at 28, SEC v. Continental Tobacco Co. of S. C., 463 F. 2d 137 (5th Cir. 1972).

[10] Owens, A Look at the Private Offering Exemption As It Approaches Its Fortieth Birthday, Sec. Reg. L. Rep., No. 152, p. G-1 at G-2 (1972).

[11] SEC v. C. M. Joiner Leasing Corp., 320 U. S. 344, 350-51 (1943), set out supra p. 186, at pp. 188-89.

"public offering," fairly permit the supersophisticated gloss that has surrounded them? At least from hindsight, would it not have been better if the Justice in *Ralston* had acted a bit less "professorial," simply agreeing with the Commission's position that at some point the number of offerees is so large (or presumably so small) as not to permit of debate, and had left the in-between cases to be decided on the basis of all the relevant circumstances as the Commission's General Counsel had viewed the matter in 1935?[12]

(6) If a person keeps lions in his backyard and one of them chews up a neighbor, it is altogether reasonable to hold him liable without proof of negligence; for the man-eating propensities of wild beasts are well known. But, when a §12(1) imposes liability on one who violates §15 — a question that raises all sorts of difficult subsidiary questions under §§2-4 — isn't the combination of strict liability and a fuzzy substructure an abominable kind of jurisprudence?

The fact is — a point made with his usual felicity by the late Ray Garrett, Jr., a few years before he was to become Chairman of the SEC — that the Fifth Circuit series involved promotional offerings, which are but one of four discernible *loci classici* under the §4(2) rubric. The other three are offerings to employees, the issuance of securities in payment of acquisitions of other companies, and (foremost of all) institutional placements. *Ralston* furnishes adequate guide for the employee category. But acquisition offerings are vastly different, in that the offerees are usually identified and finite in number and negotiations are usually extensive. And institutional investors are well able to care for themselves without all the "sophistication" and "access" paraphernalia erected on the foundation of Ralston's annual offerings to "chow loading foremen" and other management-anointed "key employees."[13]

2. The "Safe Harbor" of Rule 506

The situation cried out for rulemaking. The Bar uttered appropriate cries. And in 1974 the Commission responded, perhaps not altogether in a way that the Bar wished, with Rule 146, which

---

[12] See p. 349 supra.

[13] Garrett, Private Offerings under the Securities Act of 1933 (unpublished address before 11th Annual Corporate Counsel Institute, Chicago, Oct. 5, 1972), condensed in Garrett, The Private Offering Exemption Today, in Practising Law Institute, Fourth Annual Institute on Securities Regulation (1973) c. 2.

was replaced by a somewhat simpler Rule 506 as part of the Regulation D that was adopted in 1982.

Rule 506, with its condition of reasonable belief that there are not more than thirty-five buyers apart from an unlimited number of "accredited investors,"[14] is not too different from Rule 505[15] — which presumably accounts for their integration into the same Regulation D, to the point where most of the conditions of Rule 506 are found in Rules 501-03. This includes the treatment with respect to "integration," general solicitation or advertising, resales, filings, and disclosure to buyers.[16] The basic differences are two:

(1) Since Rule 506 is based on §4(2), not §3(b), there is no limitation with respect to aggregate offering price.

(2) The issuer must "reasonably believe immediately prior to making any sale that each purchaser who is not an accredited investor * * * has such knowledge and experience in financial and business matters that he is capable of evaluating the merits and risks of his prospective investment."[17] The rule, however, perpetuates the former Rule 146's invention of a "purchaser representative" whose knowledge and experience (and there may be more than one) may supplement or be substituted for the purchaser's. That term is elaborately defined to insure independence from the issuer (except when the purchaser is a relative of his representative or a trust, estate, or corporation related in a specific manner to its representative) as well as knowledge and experience.[18]

The language of the rule itself must be carefully studied, of course, since each of the highly structured conditions must be satisfied by one who wants to enter its "safe harbor." A number of those conditions deserve special mention:

(1) Significantly, the Commission in Rule 146 shifted for the first time to maximum number of *buyers* rather than offerees. An early version of the Code referred to thirty-five buyers plus an unlimited number of "institutional investors."[19] This was designed basically as a return to the very early administrative view except

---

[14] See p. 339 supra.
[15] See p. 347 supra.
[16] See pp. 346-47 supra. If the offering exceeds $5 million, so that Form S-18 cannot be used as a point of reference (see p. 153 supra), and the issuer is not a reporting company under the 1934 Act, the reference is to Part I of whatever form the issuer would be entitled to use. Rule 502(b)(2)(i)(B).
[17] Rule 506(b)(2)(ii).
[18] Rule 501(h).
[19] Code §§202(41)(B), 202(74).

for the increase from twenty-five to thirty-five. Rule 506(b)(2)(i) follows this approach.

(2) The "official representative" concept that found its way into securities regulation with Rule 146 led the staff to say that a lawyer who is included in a list of such representatives and receives compensation for his advisory services is not excluded from the definition of "investment adviser" as a "lawyer * * * whose performance of such [legal] services is solely incidental to the practice of his profession,"[20] and hence he must register under the Investment Advisers Act.[21]

(3) Although §4(2) does not contain the word "issue" that is found in §§3(a)(11) and 3(b),[22] the "issue" or "integration" concept is read into the word "involving" just as it is read into the word "exclusively" in §3(a)(9). The Commission has stated that "it is clear that the private offering exemption [§4(2)] cannot be available for a *portion* of a 'single' offering."[23] But Regulation D contains a six-month "safe harbor," like that in Rule 147(b) with respect to intrastate offerings, on either side of the D offering.[24]

(4) In 1978 the Commission, stating that its experience with Rule 146 had demonstrated "the need to be able to perceive misuses of the rule and, thus, to become aware of, and prevent, frauds in their incipient stages," added a requirement, now reflected in Rule 503, that certain reports of sales be filed.[25] The filing burden

[20] Inv. Adv. Act §202(a)(11)(B).

[21] Winstead, McGuire, Sechrest & Trimble, CCH Fed. Sec. L. Rep. ¶80,131 (letter 1975).

[22] See pp. 319-20, 341 supra.

[23] Herbert R. May, 27 SEC 814, 819-20 (1948); Crowell-Collier Publishing Co., Sec. Act Rel. 3825 (1957) 5. The Commission has made two exceptions to the integration doctrine by rule so far as the private offering exemption is concerned. One of them is Rule 254(d)(2) of Regulation A, to the effect that securities offered to a single majority-control parent of the issuer in connection with a *pro rata* offering to stockholders may be segregated from the other securities involved in the offering. The other is a special rule that affords a *locus poenitentiae* to an issuer that starts with a private offering and *subsequently* decides to make a public offering or file a registration statement; in such a case the exemption is considered to apply to the transactions not involving any public offering at the time that they were effected. Rule 152. There is no similar dispensation for an issuer that thinks it can get by under §3(a)(9) or §3(a)(11) but finds it necessary to register in order to complete the financing. In such a case, at least in principle and presumably so far as civil liability under §12(1) is concerned, there is a single issue no part of which qualifies for exemption.

[24] See pp. 328-29 supra.

[25] Sec. Act Rel. 5912, 14 SEC Dock. 306, 307 (1978). This requirement followed a strong recommendation in a General Accounting Office report that had described a rash of private placement frauds. General Accounting Office, Action Needed to Better Protect Investors from Fraud in Purchasing Privately Placed Securities (1980).

is not great. But there is no indication that the Commission took into account the *dis*advantages of a reporting requirement in an exemptive rule: Congress intended all the statutory exemptions to work automatically. And, once more, there is the specter of strict liability under §12(1) if a report is filed a day late. Indeed, in the ordinary case, as Professor Kripke pungently put it, of "one pizza twirler who sells to another pizza twirler for $75,000 the capital stock of a corporation which owns a pizza parlor," counsel, at least if not expert in the law and lore of securities regulation, normally will not even think of a federal registration requirement, let alone the conditions his client must meet if he wants to be sure to gain an exemption.[26]

(5) To get back to Genesis, where does the Commission get the authority to adopt a rule like 506 (as implemented by Rules 501-03)? In theory the rule is interpretative, not substantive. But is a detailed rule that runs for several columns in the SEC Docket, complete with filing requirements, a definition of a "technical" or "trade" term, or does it otherwise fall within the scope of §19 (a) of the Act — a provision that authorizes "such rules and regulations as may be necessary to carry out the provisions of this title, including rules and regulations governing registration statements and prospectuses * * * , and defining accounting, technical, and trade terms used in this title"?

(6) The Commission has emphasized that the rule is a "safe harbor."[27] Compliance with every condition assures the §4(2) exemption. But the Commission did not (and, aside from what a court might consider to be a proper use of its rulemaking authority, could not) take away anything that Congress gave in §4 (2).[28] One who relies on §4(2) *apart* from the rule is simply on his own, as if there had never been a rule. Since it is unnecessary to choose between §4(2) *per se* and Rule 506, prudent counsel who uses the rule will so structure the offering as to be able to establish a §4(2) defense if it turns out that one or more conditions of the rule have not been satisfied.[29]

---

[26] Kripke, SEC Rule 146: A "Major Blunder," N. Y. L. J., July 5, 1974, p. 1, col. 3.

[27] Sec. Act Rel. 6389, 24 SEC Dock. 1166, 1178 n. 33 (1982).

[28] Mary S. Krech Trust v. Lake Apartments, 642 F. 2d 98, 102 (5th Cir. 1981).

[29] In 1976 the Commission invited comment on the operation of then Rule 146 and whether it should be rescinded or revised. Sec. Act Rel. 5779, 11 SEC Dock. 1116 (1976). Fifteen months later the Commission stated that the majority of comments favored retention of the rule and "did not indicate that the rule impedes the flow of venture capital or facilitate the fraudulent offering of securities." Sec. Act Rel. 5913, 14 SEC Dock. 310, 311 (1978).

3.   THE STATUTORY EXEMPTION TODAY

As evidence that §4(2) lives, consider:

SECTION 4(2) AND STATUTORY LAW: A POSITION PAPER OF THE FEDERAL REGULATION OF SECURITIES COMMITTEE, SECTION OF CORPORATION, BANKING AND BUSINESS LAW OF THE AMERICAN BAR ASSOCIATION*
31 Business Lawyer 485 (1975)[a]

*   *   *

INTRODUCTION

*   *   *

In the Release announcing adoption of the Rule, the Commission emphasizes that Rule 146 is not the exclusive basis for determining whether the Section 4(2) exemption is available. Additionally, issuers may continue to rely on the exemption "by complying with the relevant administrative and judicial interpretations in effect at the time of the transaction." For a number of reasons discussed below, the body of law relevant to the availability of the Section 4(2) exemption otherwise than in reliance upon Rule 146, referred to in this position paper as "Statutory Law," is and will continue to be important notwithstanding the adoption of Rule 146. For example, institutional private placements of straight debt issues routinely continue to rely on statutory law. We anticipate that issuers and their attorneys in noninstitutional private placements as well will continue to rely on Statutory Law in many situations, sometimes by choice, sometimes by necessity and finally sometimes through accident or inadvertence.

Unfortunately, there have been differing views expressed, even among experienced securities lawyers, as to the state of the Statutory Law on certain points. There is considerable uncertainty as to the effect and force of the existing judicial interpretations, many of which have been influenced by extreme positions taken by the

---

*Note: Attached to this paper are two appendices. Appendix A contains a survey of the literature with respect to Section 4(2). Appendix B lists a number of cases dealing with the section.

[a] ED.: Copyright 1975, American Bar Association. Reprinted with the permission of the Association and its Section of Corporation, Banking, and Business Law. Some citations are omitted and citation style is here adjusted.

Commission in litigation. In large part as a result of these litigation positions, there is also considerable uncertainty as to the administrative interpretations. The legislative history of Section 4(2) is scanty, as is apparent from the present confused state of the law, and is susceptible of widely differing interpretations. There have been relatively few published administrative interpretations of Section 4(2) by the Commission. In any event, the authority of the Commission in this area is somewhat circumscribed by relevant judicial decisions. Furthermore, the judicial precedents are not particularly helpful because many involve fact situations where the result — usually the denial of the exemption and therefore a victory for the purchaser of the unregistered securities — could well be justified on other grounds, such as fraud or a material misrepresentation or omission in connection with the sale, in addition to a relatively broad distribution of securities. Additionally, many of the cases have been decided more on procedural than on substantive grounds, and, some of the most troublesome judicial pronouncements in the decisions constitute dicta rather than clear holdings.

We recognize, therefore, that it is difficult, if not impossible, to state accurately what the Statutory Law is. Nevertheless, we have set forth in this position paper practical guidelines which represent what we believe is an interpretation of Statutory Law which is consistent with the language of the Securities Act of 1933, the legislative history of Section 4(2), the purposes and policies of the Act and the principal judicial decisions on the subject. We believe that the interpretations discussed herein should be followed by the courts.

SOURCES OF STATUTORY LAW

LEGISLATIVE HISTORY

In our search for Statutory Law, there are several sources upon which we can draw. First, there is the legislative history, which referred to:

[A] Specific or isolated sale . . . to a particular person.
[W]here there is no practical need for the bill's application.
[W]here the public benefits are too remote.
[U]nless the stockholders are so small in number that the sale to them does not constitute a public offering.[6]

---

[6] H. R. Rep. No. 85, 73d Cong., 1st Sess. (1933) 5-7, 15-16; see also H. R. Rep. No. 152, 73d Cong., 1st Sess. (1933) 1-29.

ADMINISTRATIVE

An early opinion of the SEC General Counsel[7] set the interpretative stage for many years. This opinion focused on the number of offerees as a prime consideration, indicating that under ordinary circumstances an offering to approximately 25 or fewer persons would presumably not involve a public offering. It went on to enumerate the following factors as being relevant:

> The number of offerees;
> The relationship of the offerees to each other;
> The relationship of the offerees to the issuer;
> The number of units offered;
> The size of the offering; and
> The manner of the offering.

An administrative interpretation in 1962[8] stressed another aspect found in earlier interpretations, namely, that the offerees must have access to information about the issuer. We believe that the requirement of access to information might be satisfied independent of the transaction by virtue of a preexisting relationship — for example, where the purchaser is an executive officer of the issuer. Or, access to information can arise through the economic bargaining power of an offeree who did not have prior first hand knowledge of the issuer. Thus, in the traditional institutional private placement, purchasers who had no prior information about the issuer could obtain the information they desired as a result of their economic bargaining power.

Access through economic bargaining power seemed to be a generally accepted approach until doubt was cast upon the doctrine, at least as far as the Commission's position was concerned, by the Commission's appellate brief in *SEC v. Continental Tobacco Co., Inc.* That brief reiterated every restriction that any of the authorities had mentioned over the years, including the suggestion that a qualified offeree was required to have "a relationship to the company tantamount to that of an 'insider.' "[10] The Commission's reply brief raised further doubts regarding certain generally accepted notions (discussed below) with respect to offeree qualification. The reply brief suggested that a desire to consult counsel tends to disqualify an offeree by asserting: "Indeed, the very fact

---

[7] Sec. Act Rel. 285 (1935).

[8] Sec. Act Rel. 4552 (1972).

[10] Brief for Appellant at 28. This interpretation was expressly rejected in Woolf v. S. D. Cohn & Co., 515 F. 2d 591 (5th Cir. 1975), *vacated on other grounds* sub nom. S. D. Cohn & Co. v. Woolf, 426 U. S. 944 (1976).

that investors consider it is necessary to rely upon an attorney in their purchase of stock demonstrates that the investors are unfamiliar with the company, cannot 'fend for themselves' and therefore need the 'protections afforded by registration.' "[11] Contrary to the Commission's contention, it is the highly sophisticated investors, those least needing the benefits of a registration statement, who are most likely to rely on counsel.

JUDICIAL PRECEDENTS

Turning to the judicial precedents, *SEC* v. *Ralston Purina Co.,* focused on the offerees' lack of need for the Act's protection. It articulated the test in terms of the offerees' ability to "fend for themselves," and "access" to the "kind of information which registration would disclose." The court did not elaborate upon the meaning of the term "access." The case, however, involved an offering to hundreds of employees. It was clear that many of them had neither economic bargaining power nor a relationship to the company which would give them an independent means of obtaining necessary information.

The subsequent judicial precedents have not been particularly helpful. In most of the reported cases decided since *Ralston Purina,* the issuers and their control persons lost. Many of these cases involved egregious fact situations, typically tainted with a clearly public distribution and misrepresentation, in which the issuers should have lost. The courts, however, have used extremely broad dicta which, if taken literally, would leave little viability in the exemption under the statute. The narrow holdings of many of these cases turn on a simple procedural aspect of the cases — the failure of the issuer to offer evidence necessary to carry the burden of proving that the exemption was available. In many of the cases, the issuer offered no evidence regarding crucial factors necessary to establish the exemption, such as the method by which the offering was made, the number of offerees or their qualifications.

In those cases where the issuer prevailed on the merits, it is clear that the courts did not require full compliance with the dicta enunciated in those cases where the issuers lost.

We add a caveat. Certain of the early cases which were decided favorably to the issuers might not be decided the same way today, in the light of later circuit court precedents. Also, it is noteworthy that some of these cases involve interests in oil and gas ventures

---

[11] Reply Brief for Appellant at 2.

where a purchaser, asserting a Section 5 violation, was refusing to honor his purchase commitment when the holes were dry. The courts might have found the equities in that factual setting to be somewhat different from the equities in the normal rescission suit. Nonetheless, we believe it is fair to conclude that a distinctly different attitude toward the exemption emerges from a reading of the cases in which the issuers prevailed, as contrasted with the more numerous cases where the exemption was held to be unavailable. When the facts were more favorable to the issuer, the courts seemed to interpret the requirements for exemption in a less demanding manner.

SEC Chairman Garrett, at the PLI Fourth Annual Securities Institute (when he was still a private practitioner) characterized the result of the various authorities, legislative, judicial, and administrative, as:

> [A] kind of mishmash. The issuer is now told that all of these factors have something to do with whether he has an exemption under Section 4(2), but he is never given a hint as to the proper proportions in the brew. The saving recipe is kept secret, a moving target which he can never be sure he has hit.[15]

GUIDELINES

Where does this leave us? We believe that there are only four attributes of any real significance in determining whether the exemption is available under Statutory Law. This combination of factors provides a reasonable test to identify those transactions where the registration provisions of the Act are not needed to implement its statutory purpose. The other factors frequently mentioned in the precedents are of very minor significance, or none at all. We believe the four essential attributes relate to the following — (1) offeree qualification; (2) availability of information; (3) manner of offering; and (4) absence of redistribution. Each of these will be discussed separately. We further believe, as more fully noted below, that all of the four foregoing attributes must be approached flexibly and in recognition of the fact that they do not constitute abstract concepts whose parameters are fixed. Furthermore, these four attributes are intimately related; indeed, the question of qualification of offerees and the manner in which information is imparted to such offerees may justifiably be regarded

---

[15] Garrett, The Private Offering Exemption Today, in Practising Law Institute, Fourth Annual Institute on Securities Regulation (1973) c. 2 at 10-11.

as correlatives from the standpoint of determining the applicability of the exemption to a specific private placement under Statutory Law.

While we suggest some practical guidelines below, we are not attempting to lay down precise tests on any of the four relevant factors. This position paper is not intended to be an exact definition of Statutory Law, in the sense that compliance with all of the suggestions herein would necessarily assure the availability of the exemption or, conversely, that failure to comply in some detail would necessarily result in the unavailability of the exemption. As it has evolved, the exemption has become far too complex and the transactions in which it may be relied upon far too varied to permit any precise and all-encompassing definition of its exact limits in anything but the most abstract terms. This no doubt explains why Rule 146 was cast in terms of a non-exclusive safe harbor.

The analysis below is designed to be consistent with the basic public policy objective, which is to provide registration for investors who need the Act's protections through the rather burdensome registration process. The conclusions reached below attempt to balance the practical needs of various classes of investors for the benefits of registration (over and above the protections arising under the federal securities anti-fraud provisions), and the burdens on issuers of compliance with the registration process. Hopefully, the guidelines set forth should provide a basis of exemption for various broad categories of transactions for which the registration process seems inappropriate or unnecessary — among them, the institutional private placement, and the financing of a small business among individuals closely associated with the venture.

To a large extent, our discussion focuses on the type of equity private placements which are typically sold to individuals or others who are not professional investors or venture capitalists, and which often involve a relatively high degree of risk. So-called institutional private placements have been undertaken for many years in a fairly standardized pattern. Such transactions involve sophisticated institutional investors making relatively large purchases of debt or, less often, equity securities. No significant interpretive problems have been experienced in applying the provisions of Section 4(2) to such institutional transactions, and nothing in this position paper is intended to cast doubt on the propriety of prevailing practices in the institutional private placement field.

We note in passing that newly-adopted Rule 240[b] should furnish some relief from the burdens of registration for small financings of closely held companies. We feel strongly, however, that the existence of this exemptive Rule, promulgated under another statutory provision (Section 3(b)), should not preempt or otherwise narrow the interpretation of the Section 4(2) exemption.

We also note in passing that issuers effecting private placements may have additional requirements to satisfy under state blue sky laws, which are beyond the scope of the present discussion. Parenthetically, we note that several state blue sky authorities recently have published rules or statements of policy, in proposed or final form, which appear to condition their exemptions for private placements upon compliance by issuers with all of the provisions of Rule 146. We believe that these actions by state blue sky administrators are inappropriate, and overlook the sound policy reasons which prompted the SEC to make Rule 146 non-exclusive. We believe that there are many transactions which, as a policy matter, should be exempt from both federal and state registration requirements, even though they do not meet the many technical requirements of Rule 146.

OFFEREE QUALIFICATION

From the standpoint of framing precise or objective standards, qualification of offerees is probably the most troublesome of all the attributes of the exemption. We believe that offerees in a private placement should be deemed qualified on any one of several bases. They may be qualified on the basis of their ability to understand the risk. This attribute is sometimes called "sophistication." They may be qualified on the basis of their ability to assume the investment risk, so called "wealth." Or, they may be qualified on the basis of a personal relationship to the issuer or a promoter. The qualifying relationships include, but are not necessarily limited to, family ties, friendship, an employment relationship or a pre-existing business relationship. In our view, *Ralston Purina* does not exclude these alternative approaches. Because of the personal relationship factor, Promoter *X* might be justified in allowing a close family member, his best friend and his right-hand man in the business to participate in a private placement, while Promoter *Y*, who is a stranger to these people, would not be justified in including them in an otherwise identical offering which relied

[b] ED.: Now Rule 504. See p. 346 supra.

upon the Section 4(2) exemption. We believe that the public benefits are too remote and there is no practical need for the burdens of applying the registration provisions (as contrasted with anti-fraud provisions) when the offerees have such close relationships to the offeror. We note that when such close personal ties exist, a decision to make an investment may be motivated, wholly or in part, by non-economic factors unrelated to financial risks and benefits of the investment.

We suggested above that an offeree might qualify solely on the basis of his ability to assume the risk. We add a caveat. We might have serious reservations about including a very wealthy person as an offeree in a highly risky private placement, based solely upon his ability to assume the risk, if he had no understanding of financial matters, and no competent advisor. On the other hand, if an equally wealthy offeree was an experienced business man with some general understanding of financial matters, we would consider him qualified as an offeree based upon his ability to assume the risk, even though he lacked a high degree of sophistication.

Several other observations concerning offeree qualification are relevant.

(1) *Risk-Bearing Ability:* First, with respect to the offeree's ability to assume the risk, we believe it is relevant to consider, in very broad and general terms, the extent of the risk of loss in judging whether the offeree can assume it. There have been expressions from the Commission that the appropriate inquiry is whether the offeree can afford to lose all of the money to be invested. Nothwithstanding such suggestions, under Statutory Law as well as Rule 146, we believe that both the total amount of money invested, and also the likelihood that all or part of it will be lost, must be considered.[c]

Specifically, other things being equal, it may well be that Offeree X is qualified to participate in a private placement of a high-grade mortgage bond, where the likelihood of substantial loss is minimal, but not in a highly speculative common stock offering involving a significant probability of total loss. In short, risk-bearing ability may require a judgment regarding the general level of the risks inherent in the particular investment, not merely a reference to the total amount invested.

(2) *The Offeree Representative Principle:* We believe that Statutory Law gives some recognition to the offeree representative principle which is formalized in Rule 146 — that is, a person other

[c] ED.: Rule 506 eliminated the risk test in former Rule 146(d) as an alternative to knowledge and experience.

than an offeree may be able to advise an offeree or otherwise protect the offeree's interests so as to qualify the offeree. Two cases
seem to recognize this principle in the acquisition setting.[18] The
point is also recognized tangentially in at least one non-acquisition
case.[19] In *Klinkel* v. *Krekow*,[20] an unreported U. S. District Court
memorandum decision, the court accepted the parties' agreement
in a rescission suit that information disclosed to the son of the
plaintiff-purchaser was deemed known by plaintiff and "to the extent sophistication and investment philosophy of an offeree are
relevant, those of [the son] should control."

(3) *Manner of Disclosure:* We suggest that a determination of
the offeree's ability to understand the risk may well vary with the
manner and scope of the disclosure made to him. The more careful, painstaking and detailed the disclosure is, the more readily
one may find that a particular offeree is able to understand the risk.
Consider any business which is not particularly well known to the
investing public generally. Without the availability of appropriate information to the offeree, by way of access or as a result of
being furnished by the issuer, most persons would not be able to
qualify as offerees on the basis of ability to understand the risk.
On the other hand, if a carefully prepared disclosure document is
submitted to them, the same group of investors might well qualify
as persons who can understand the risk.

This point may have an important bearing in preparing disclosure materials. If the offerees are all thoroughly familiar with
the particular business, it may be sufficient to disclose only distinctive aspects of the particular issuer. On the other hand, if the
offerees are not familiar with the issuer's business, the disclosure
should also give them more general information about the industry and type of business.

(4) *Degrees of Sophistication:* We consider it important to recognize that there are degrees of sophistication. The inquiry as to
whether an offeree is adequately sophisticated should not be approached in a categorical or absolute fashion, since the concept
entails weighing of relative factors. All those who are not sufficiently sophisticated to qualify as offerees of every type of security
for every type of offering should not be lumped together. The
unsophisticated range from the total incompetent in financial

---

[18] Klapmeier v. Telecheck Int'l, Inc., 482 F. 2d 247 (8th Cir. 1973); Bowers
v. Columbia General Corp., 336 F. Supp. 609 (D. Del. 1971).
[19] See Woodward v. Wright, 226 F. 2d 108, 115 (10th Cir. 1959). [ED.: For
a later square holding, see Barry v. Ceres Land Co., CCH Fed. Sec. L. Rep.
¶99,008 (D. Minn. 1978).]
[20] W. D. Wash., No. 317-71C2, Aug. 16, 1974.

matters, and possibly other matters as well, to the worldly man of business who knows a good deal about money matters but who has had limited experience in corporate finance and private placements. A good many presidents of companies going public are not "sophisticated" in matters of corporate finance, in the normal sense of the term "sophisticated."

Indeed, we suggest that the term "sophistication" is somewhat misused in this context. It is a shorthand way of expressing a rather complex thought, and quite possibly the use of the term is not entirely accurate. The relevant inquiry should be whether the investor can understand and evaluate the nature of the risk based upon the information supplied to him. The relevant inquiry should not be whether the investor is *au courant* in all of the latest nuances and techniques of corporate finance. To the extent that the term "sophistication" raises inquiries of the latter type, the use of the term may tend to becloud the inquiry.

(5) *Non-Qualified Offerees:* Is the exemption lost for the entire transaction where one or more of the offerees (or purchasers) fails to meet the appropriate tests? The question may arise in a variety of factual settings, as illustrated by the following extreme hypotheticals. Assume that the issue concerning the availability of the exemption is raised in each case in a Section 12(1) rescission suit brought by a qualified purchaser, who is seeking a return of his purchase price after the investment turns out to be unprofitable. The plaintiff charges that the offering as a whole did not qualify for the exemption.

> *Case No. 1:* The offeror makes the offers with total disregard as to the qualifications of the offerees. In fact, most of the offerees and purchasers are not qualified.
>
> *Case No. 2:* The offeror uses a high degree of care in pre-clearing offerees. In hindsight, it appears that only one offeree was not appropriately qualified. When the offer was made to him, the offeror had reasonable grounds to believe that the offeree was qualified, relying in part on information supplied by the offeree which was subsequently discovered to be untrue. Prior to the sale, when the true facts were discovered, the non-qualified offeree was eliminated from the private placement and the securities were sold only to qualified offerees, but no effort was made to terminate the pending offering as to the qualified offerees.

The language in the case discussing the point indicates that the exemption is unavailable unless every offeree (even those who did not become purchasers) meets the qualification test.[21] However, virtually all such cases more closely resemble Case No. 1 above, rather than Case No. 2. If the issue were to arise in a circumstance similar to Case No. 2, we believe that a court should, and probably would, either find the exemption available vis-à-vis the plaintiff, or find some other basis for denying the plaintiff the right to rescind his transaction.[22]

There is not enough precedent to make specific predictions concerning the broad range of circumstances which might be presented. We think, however, it would be appropriate for courts to consider, in passing on the availability of the exemption, such factors as the status of the plaintiff (e. g., whether he is qualified as an offeree), whether the defendant acted reasonably in making offers to offerees who were not in fact qualified, the extent of the offers which were made to non-qualified offerees, what remedial action, if any, was taken by the defendant upon learning of the non-qualification, and the procedural setting in which the issue arises.

Note that the exemption remains available under Rule 146 even if a sale was made to a non-qualified person, as long as the issuer had reasonable grounds to believe and, after making reasonable inquiry, did believe that each offeree-purchaser was qualified. The general philosophy of protecting an issuer, and ultimately its existing investors, when the issuer acts reasonably was further emphasized by the SEC in its recent amendment of Rule 146(g).[23] Prior to the amendment, the 35 purchaser ceiling was absolute, and the benefits of the Rule were lost if there were more, despite the issuer's reasonable and good faith belief to the contrary. As amended, the Rule remains available where there are more than 35 purchasers, so long as the issuer has reasonable grounds to believe, after making reasonable inquiry, that there are no more than 35 purchasers.

(6) *Economic Bargaining Power:* The concept of economic bargaining power has become a widely accepted concept under Statutory Law, and is used in a somewhat imprecise way to describe an attribute of offerees who have "access" to information.[24]

---

[21] E. g., Lively v. Hirschfeld, 440 F. 2d 631, 633 (10th Cir. 1971); Repass v. Rees, 174 F. Supp. 898 (D. Colo. 1959).

[22] See A. C. Frost & Co. v. Coeur D'Alene Mines Corp., 312 U. S. 38 (1941); Value Line Fund, Inc. v. Marcus, CCH Fed. Sec. L. Rep. ¶91,523 (S. D. N. Y. 1965); Schneider and Zall, Section 12(1) and the Imperfect Exempt Transaction: The Proposed I & I Defense, 28 Bus. Law. 1011 (1973).

[23] Sec. Act Rel. 5585, 6 SEC Dock. 829 (1975).

[24] See, e. g., Note to Rule 146(e), which states: "Access can only exist by

If the plain meaning of the expression "economic bargaining power" is considered, the term would seem to have no necessary connection with the sophistication of the offeree or his background in financial matters, as illustrated by the following two examples:

(a) A small privately held company desperately needs funds, and the only potential investor identified by the sole stockholder is his neighbor. The neighbor has $20,000 to invest but little experience in finance. The stockholder offers a 20 percent interest in the company for $20,000, and the neighbor wants 30 percent. Given the relative position of the company and the neighbor, arguably the neighbor has great leverage, or economic bargaining power, to impose his terms and conditions and satisfy his other requirements, before he parts with his money.

(b) A small insurance company is invited by a lead institution to purchase a $1,000,000 unit in a $50,000,000 placement of high grade debt securities. As a practical matter, the insurance company may have very little ability to negotiate any terms in the transaction with the issuer or make any independent investigation. Its alternatives are to accept or reject the deal as packaged by the lead institutional investor based upon the offering memorandum supplied, and it knows that any efforts to act too independently might well decrease the likelihood of its being invited into future transactions. Arguably, the insurance company has very little economic bargaining power in this transaction.

Notwithstanding the foregoing analysis, however, we think the term economic bargaining power, as used in the private placement context, should be understood as a term of art. It is, to a large extent, an attribute which an offeree may be presumed to have based upon several factors including, but not necessarily limited to, available resources, financial experience and history as an investor. It is not to be determined primarily from a factual analysis of the relative bargaining strengths of a particular issuer vis-à-vis a particular offeree in a given factual setting.

---

reason of the offeree's position with respect to the issuer. Position means an employment or family relationship or economic bargaining power that enables the offeree to obtain information from the issuer in order to evaluate the merits and risks of the prospective investment." [Rule 146(e) referred to each officer's access to "the same kind of information that is specified in Schedule A of the Act" as an alternative to his being furnished with that kind of information prior to sale. Rule 506 does not refer to "access," although it does not require any information to be furnished to an "accredited investor" (Rule 502(b)(1)(i)), which includes any director, executive officer, or general partner of the issuer (Rule 501(a)(4)).]

INFORMATION

A second general attribute relates to the scope and manner of disclosure of information. It is generally considered necessary that each offeree have some information about the issuer, or at least access to that information, prior to the sale. It is not necessary in all cases for the offeree to have had the information prior to, and independent of, the transaction. In some situations, the information may be supplied to the offeree in connection with the transaction at the time the offering is made.

It is difficult to set forth a precise standard to determine when the information requirement can be satisfied by having the information supplied, in connection with the transaction, to offerees who did not previously have such information. Clearly supplying the information is a generally accepted practice where institutional type offerees are involved. Institutions normally are presumed to have "access" to the information by virtue of their economic bargaining power. In addition, the practice of supplying information is acceptable in certain instances where qualified individual offerees are involved; otherwise, individuals could never participate in a private placement of an issuer which has not made extensive prior public disclosures, unless the individuals had pre-existing relationships which made them privy to information about the issuer. In practice, the law has not been interpreted so restrictively. To the contrary, the participation of individuals in the private placement of a private company has been widely accepted for a long time, even if the offerees had no knowledge about the issuer prior to their receipt of information in connection with the transaction.

The information required to be supplied need not be nearly as extensive as the information called for by Schedule A of the 1933 Act, or by Form S-1, although the Form S-1 requirements provide a useful guideline. The statutory exemption does reflect a legislative policy decision that occasions exist where there is no need for the expense and delay of providing a registration statement, or its non-filed equivalent. It is probably adequate to give basis information concerning the issuer's financial condition, results of operations, business, property and management.

Indeed, it is doubtful whether all of the foregoing categories of information are required in every case. Many private placements by a small closely-held company are completed with little or no formal disclosure documentation. If the buyer shows no interest in information regarding executive compensation, for example, the exemption should not be lost by the failure of the issuer to supply such information, especially if the remuneration is reasonable and just about what the buyer would have expected had he considered the matter.

In some private placements, especially those involving closely held companies, even more basic information in reliable form may be unavailable. *Livens* v. *William D. Witter, Inc.,*[25] held that a private placement was proper despite the absence of reliable financial statements, since the buyer was advised that reliable financial statements were unavailable and he was willing, in effect, to take the risk. Significantly, in *Livens* the exemption applied although the court found that at the time of the purchase no one, neither the sellers nor the purchaser, appreciated the full extent of the deficiency in the issuer's financial records, and in a sense the purchaser was misled, albeit unintentionally, by the seller.

Statutory Law does not require that disclosures be made, or that information be conveyed, in writing, if the result can be accomplished in another manner such as an oral presentation, a tour of physical facilities, inspection of products, or allowing the offeree to communicate directly with others such as customers, suppliers and bankers. In fact, most private companies which accept an occasional new investor do not prepare a narrative prospectus-type disclosure document. Many supply no written material at all to the investor, subject to the possible exception of financial statements which have been prepared for other purposes.

Of course, written disclosures are very helpful as a matter of proof, to establish what information was conveyed. In some cases, it may well be helpful to concentrate the written disclosures on what is, essentially, a list of risk factors such as one might find in a so-called "introductory statement" to a statutory prospectus. The purchaser may be asked for written acknowledgment that he is aware of these risk factors. He might also be requested to acknowledge that he is familiar with the business, has had an opportunity to ask questions and has received the information requested. (We do not suggest, however, that inviting the offeree to ask for any information he wishes adequately substitutes in all cases for supplying him with information in written or other readily usable form.) In some cases, as a mechanical matter, these suggested acknowledgments can be incorporated into a simple subscription agreement which the investor signs at the time of the purchase.

[25] 374 F. Supp. 1104 (D. Mass. 1974).

MANNER OF THE OFFERING

The third general attribute of a proper private placement under Statutory Law relates to the manner of offering. In general,
the offering should be made through direct communication with
qualified offerees or their representatives, whether by the issuer
itself or through an agent of the issuer. All forms of general advertising and mass media circulation should be avoided. The number of offers made may have evidentiary significance, as discussed
below, in determining whether the manner of an offering was
proper.

A related question is the determination of when an offer is
made. At one extreme, we find nothing objectionable if a full
service brokerage firm advertises generally for customers, even
though some of them may eventually become offerees in a specific
private placement. A detailed discussion of this subject is beyond
the scope of this paper except for the following generalizations.
On the one hand, "offer" for purposes of Statutory Law is defined
broadly and might include attempts to sell specific investments
which fall far short of an offer capable of acceptance under traditional contract law principles. On the other hand, inquiries to
screen preliminary indications of general interest in a broad category of investments do not amount to offers. In *SEC* v. *Universal
Major Industries Corp.*,[26] the Court indicated that it was not the
manner of the offering, but rather the class of offerees which determines whether the exemption is available. Read in context,
we do not interpret this case as holding that the manner of offering
is irrelevant, but merely that an offering made in a proper manner
will nonetheless fail to qualify if the class of offerees is inappropriate.

ABSENCE OF REDISTRIBUTION[d]

*   *   *

SIGNIFICANCE OF THE FACTORS

If all the foregoing attributes are met — qualification of the
offerees, availability of information, manner of the offering and
absence of a redistribution — the exemption should apply to the

---

[26]CCH Fed. Sec. L. Rep. ¶95,229 at 98,210 (S. D. N. Y. 1975), *aff'd on
other grounds*, 546 F. 2d 1044 (2d Cir. 1976).
 [d]ED.: See pp. 406-17, 427-28 infra.

transaction notwithstanding the failure of that transaction to meet some of the other tests sometimes articulated in the traditional sources.

The Release promulgating Rule 146 noted that none of the foregoing factors, standing alone, would assure the availability of the exemption. We agree with the Release in this respect. However, the Release does not comment on the proposition which we have just made — that the presence of all of the factors together would normally satisfy the terms of the exemption.

For purposes of discussion and analysis, we have separated four attributes of a private placement, but we do not consider them to be totally self-contained and unrelated criteria. Rather, we view them as interrelated factors, the composite effect of which should result in an exempt transaction complying with the underlying statutory objective. To illustrate this interrelationship, we have noted the correlation between the scope and care of the information disclosures, on the one hand, and the qualification of an offeree based upon his ability to understand the risk, on the other hand.

To a large extent, this position paper reviews minimum requirements necessary to establish the Section 4(2) exemption. Assuming that the events have already occurred, we believe that the principles set forth should be of assistance in predicting how a court may decide if a transaction is challenged. We do not necessarily imply, however, that sound counseling or good business judgment dicates the planning of transactions to meet only the minimal standards. To the contrary, we have suggested that good practice might, in certain circumstances, suggest additional steps in order to assure the availability of the exemption — for example, see the discussion above regarding the desirability of legends. Additionally, we note that the cases which have been presented to the courts have typically involved complex fact situations and numerous interrelated issues. It may be difficult as a practical matter to defend the availability of the exemption if a transaction is planned to meet only the barest minimum standards. As an illustration, while Statutory Law does not require that written evidence be maintained concerning the identity and qualification of each offeree, the absence of such documentation may be very damaging to an issuer whose reliance upon the exemption is later challenged.

We emphasize that this position paper deals only with the applicability of the exemption under Section 4(2) of the Securities Act from the registration provisions of Section 5. In planning any private placement, other bodies of law should be considered. These include the anti-fraud provisions, state blue sky laws (which, as noted above, often define their private placements exemptions in terms more restrictive than Statutory Law under Section 4(2)), laws relating to professionals in the securities business such as broker dealers or investment advisers, and the special professional responsibilities applicable to counsel.

NUMBER OF OFFEREES

*   *   *

A much discussed subject regarding private placements is the significance of the number of offerees. It is the official dogma that the number of offerees (or purchasers) is not conclusive as to the availability or unavailability of the exemption. For many years, however, experienced counsel attached great significance to the number of offerees. Assuming an otherwise proper transaction, traditionally 25 qualified offerees was a widely accepted rule of thumb as an appropriate ceiling, at least when the non-institutional type of offeree was involved. However, in *Ralston Purina*, the Supreme Court pointedly rejected the SEC contention that there could be a *maximum* number which could never be *exceeded* for the exemption to remain available. Indeed, if the 1933 Act itself imposes a maximum limit on the number of offerees, Rule 146 would be invalid under the Act, since it has no such limitation, although the Act appears to impose (and the Rule clearly does impose) a limit on the manner of the offering.

We believe that the adoption of Rule 146 will inevitably affect interpretations under Statutory Law. In the future, we expect that there will be much less concern among experienced counsel regarding the number of offerees as such. Rather, the focus of attention will be directed more to the manner of the offering. The total number of offerees may be considered relevant, if at all, primarily as evidence of the matter in which the offering was made.

As a practical matter, we believe there has always been some relationship between the number of offerees considered acceptable and the level of the offerees' sophistication. Other things being equal, most counsel would feel comfortable with a larger number of offerees and purchasers, where the offerees are all sophisticated institutions rather than individuals. It is widely known that institutional private placements have occurred involving well over

100 purchasers.[e] We doubt that many experienced counsel would have felt comfortable with a private placement involving the same number of individual purchasers under similar circumstances.

The discussion throughout this position paper relates to a single offering. Consideration should also be given to the integration doctrine, which deals generally with the question of whether two or more transactions should be viewed as parts of the same offering.

SUBSTANTIAL COMPLIANCE WITH RULE 146

This analysis leads us to the question of whether substantial, but not total, compliance with Rule 146 will qualify a transaction for exemption under Statutory Law. We believe, as a policy matter, that this question should be answered in the affirmative in most cases, since the Rule is essentially, in its broad concepts (subject to exceptions — especially, but not exclusively, those dealing with documentation), an articulation of our understanding of Statutory Law. Of course, it becomes essential in any given case to consider the particular defect in the transaction under the Rule, in order to determine whether the statutory exemption applies.

If the Rule has made any significant departure from the Statutory Law, as it had been understood previously, it probably related to the number of offerees permitted. However, as previously indicated, this factor is likely to be one of declining significance under Statutory Law, as long as the matter of offering is appropriate and the number of offerees does not become excessive.

Rule 146 gave express recognition to the offeree representative concept, in order to qualify an offeree who was not independently sophisticated. As previously indicated, however, we believe that this principle had some support in Statutory Law.

Under Rule 146, there are many mechanical requirements. Various items of documentation and record keeping are essential under the Rule. While these procedures are, by and large, desirable practices to follow, we do not consider them to be essential in order to establish the exemption under Statutory Law.

Turning to another point, the Rule has several requirements that the issuer have certain beliefs and/or reasonable grounds for certain beliefs — for example, that the offerees are qualified. We

[e] ED.: See Institutional Private Placements under the Securities Act of 1933, A Paper of the Committee on Developments in Business Financing, Section of Corporation, Banking and Business Law of the American Bar Association, 31 Bus. Law. 515 (1975).

do not believe that Statutory Law has similar requirements. Specifically, we suggest that if the offerees are in fact qualified, the exemption would not be lost under Statutory Law because the issuer lacked a reasonable ground for so believing in advance.

Let us hasten to add that we would not advise clients to go into private placements without considerable care. Every effort should be made to make sure that the issuer has the beliefs required by the Rule, and that such beliefs are reasonably based. We are suggesting, however, that if counsel is consulted after the fact and is asked to render an opinion, the absence of a reasonable belief in advance by the issuer should not be a fatal defect if the circumstances were, in fact, as they should have been for the exemption to apply. We stress again, however, that it would be foolhardy to plan a transaction without forming appropriate beliefs in advance.

RELATIONSHIP BETWEEN SECTION 4(2) AND THE ANTI-FRAUD RULES

The issue of whether the disclosure is fraudulent is a different issue from whether a transaction violates the registration requirements. We do not believe that any fraud in connection with a private placement should automatically render Section 4(2) inapplicable — thereby converting every Section 12(2) case in a private placement into a Section 12(1) case as well — despite certain judicial intimations to the contrary.[31] But, as a practical matter, there is likely to be a close connection between the factors which determine whether Section 5 was violated and whether disclosure was adequate. That is, the more adequate, careful and painstaking the disclosure, the more likely it is that a court will find that the Section 4(2) exemption applied, including the fact that there were proper and qualified offerees who could understand the risks based upon the disclosures made to them. On the other hand, the more defective the disclosure, the more likely it is, we believe, that a court will find the transaction to be non-exempt under Section 4(2).

*   *   *

BURDEN OF PROOF[f]

We would like to add a brief comment on the burden of proof. Following *Ralston Purina,* many cases have held that the burden

---

[31] See Hill York Corp. v. American Int'l Franchises, Inc., 448 F. 2d 680 (5th Cir. 1971). [See also p. 1023 n. 6 supra.]

[f] ED.: See also p. 299 supra.

of proof to establish the availability of the exemption is on the party relying upon it. It is reasoned that the Act is "remedial" and that "exemptions" are to be viewed narrowly. This analysis tends to ignore the fact that every sale of a security, public or private, is prima facie subject to registration if the jurisdictional means are used. This includes all of the millions of shares traded every day on the stock exchanges. The exemptions cover 99 + % of all of the transactions. Viewed in this light, they are not really "exemptions" in the normal sense of exceptions to the general principle. Rather, they are a drafting technique used to extract, from the overall universe of sales, that small segment which is in fact subject to registration.

In any event, traditional statements about burden of proof make sense where the defendant makes no effort to demonstrate general compliance with the exemption. These statements are questionable, once the defendant has shown that the offering was conducted generally in a proper manner and that the plaintiff himself was a proper purchaser. If the law were otherwise, the defendant could never win a Section 12(1) case in a private placement context until he had presented affirmative evidence regarding such matters as the qualifications of each and every person to whom an offer was made. Once the defendant demonstrates that the overall procedures of the offering were properly conducted, is it likely that a court would impose such a burdensome requirement, or permit such a waste of judicial time? At some point, the burden should shift back to the plaintiff for him to show some defects in the transaction. In *Grenader* v. *Spitz*,[35] the court held that the defendant was entitled to rely on the intra-state offering exemption. The court apparently placed the burden on the plaintiff to show that the offerees were *not* residents of the State in question. Query whether a minor defect in a transaction, which does not involve the plaintiff, should ever permit the plaintiff to rescind, if the transaction was generally conducted in a proper manner.

The way to test our hypothesis with respect to the burden of proof would be to consider the following hypothetical case: Assume that the defendant issuer is attempting to establish the availability of the exemption. The issuer proves affirmatively that the offering was conducted in a proper manner, with one minor exception with respect to one offeree. It also offers into evidence written questionnaires signed by each purchaser and offeree which, in every case but one, establish that the person was fully qualified. However, one purchaser, who was not the one seeking rescission

[35] 390 F. Supp. 1112 (S. D. N. Y. 1975).

of the transaction, simply completed the questions regarding current annual income and net worth by stating "more than $10,000." Let us further assume that such purchaser would not have qualified if his current annual income and net worth actually had been barely $10,000, although there is no reason from the record to suspect that the relevant amounts for him were in fact that low. After the record is closed, is it likely that any court would grant the plaintiff a directed verdict on the grounds that the defendant failed to carry the burden of proof regarding the qualifications of the particular offeree — not the plaintiff — who was reluctant to give specific information? We very much doubt it.

We believe that at some point practical realities and equitable considerations will prevail. Regardless of the language employed by the courts, once the party relying on the exemption has shown that the transaction was generally conducted in a proper manner, the burden of going forward should and probably will shift to the adverse party to demonstrate some material defect in the transaction.

CONCLUSION

The Section 4(2) exemption covers a wide variety of circumstances, ranging from the equity financing of small privately held companies among employees, relatives and friends, through the multi-million dollar institutional private placement of high grade debt securities. It is difficult to articulate, in specific terms, the precise requirements of the exemption as it applies to each type of transaction within the broad range. Our attempt in this position paper has been to examine those attributes which should be significant in identifying transactions where the registration process is not necessary in order to implement the statutory purpose. We trust that the foregoing discussion will be of assistance to counsel and to courts in applying the statutory exemption and implementing the statutory purpose.[g]

4. THE CODE

This is one of the areas in which those who worked on the Code saw the greatest need for simplification and objectization. The

---

[g] ED.: For an updated version of the substance of this ABA position paper written by the paper's principal draftsman, see Schneider, The Statutory Law of Private Placements, 14 Rev. Sec. Reg. 869 (1981).

Code's approach — aside from the treatment of the second (resale) stage, which we shall consider later[30] — has five elements:

(1) The Code's successors to §5 apply only "in connection with a distribution."[31] That term is defined to mean "an offering other than (i) a limited offering or (ii) an offering by means of one or more trading transactions."[32] Clause (ii) need not detain use here.[33] The term "limited offering" is in turn defined as one in which "the initial buyers of the securities are institutional investors or not more than thirty-five other persons or both, or the seller reasonably so believes."[34]

(2) We have already noticed the Code's definition of "institutional investor," which is in part statutory and in part left to Commission rule.[35]

(3) We have noticed also the Code's scheme of *company* registration and the "one-year registrant."[36] When the issuer is *not* a one-year registrant, the Commission, by rule, may modify the definition of "limited offering" and "impose additional conditions, considering (I) the type of issuer and security, (II) the kind of market if any, and (III) similar criteria."[37]

(4) When the issuer *is* a one-year registrant, the Code's working group agreed with the Commission to amend the ALI-ABA-approved draft as the Code would go to Congress by giving the Commission the limited authority to require by rule that the most recent annual report (and all subsequent reports) be given to each non-institutional buyer unless (i) the security is traded in specified markets or (ii) the issuer has been a registrant for *three* years.[38] This reflects the view that there should be added to the one-year registrant's continuous disclosure rationale "some assurance that the market adequately reflects that disclosure."[39]

(5) The Code preserves the strict liability of §12(1)[40] as tempered by reducing the absolutism of today's substantive provisions. On this approach the presence of a "limited offering" is not con-

---

[30] See p. 429 infra.
[31] §§502(a), 503(a), 504(a).
[32] §202(41)(A).
[33] See p. 430 ¶(5) infra.
[34] §202(41)(B)(i)(I). There are two more conditions, which will be considered below because they are directed to the "second stage." See pp. 429-30 ¶(4) infra.
[35] §202(74); see p. 339 supra.
[36] See p. 98 n. 9 supra.
[37] §202(41)(B)(iii).
[38] §202(41)(B)(iv).
[39] 1 Code (2d Supp.) 23.
[40] Code §1702.

ditioned on the absence of "general advertising," a fairly slippery
term. Instead it is simply made "unlawful," subject to the usual
sanctions, "for any person in connection with a limited offering
* * * to engage in general advertising in contravention of the
rules of the Commission."[41]

5. State Blue Sky Laws

Whether today or under the Code, counsel will not be able to
rest when he finds an exemption under §4(2), with or without
Rule 506. If he is to avoid registration altogether, he must find
some exemption also in every state (a term that as here used includes the District of Columbia and Puerto Rico) in which the
offering is to be made. Each of the 52 states has one or more
comparable exemptions except the District of Columbia, which
does not register securities. And they follow several themes (sometimes more than one in the same state), though with considerable
variations even among the 38 states[42] that have adopted basically
the Uniform Securities Act:

(1) The Uniform Act — partly because of the difficulties inherent in the undefined federal criterion of a "public offering"
and partly because those states that previously had any sort of
general exemption in this area usually phrased it in terms of a
maximum number of buyers or offers or security holders — exempts offers to ten persons (other than institutional investors and
broker-dealers) in the state during any twelve-month period, but
only if the seller "reasonably believes that all the buyers in this
state are purchasing for investment" and no remuneration is paid
for soliciting, with authority in the administrator by rule or order
to withdraw or further condition the exemption, or change the
number of offerees permitted, or waive any of the conditions.[43]
This is the basic theme in 44 states, 32 of those with the Uniform
Act[44] and 12 others.[45] The number of offerees remains at 10 in

---

[41] §503(b).

[42] See p. 9 n. 4 supra.

[43] §402(b)(9); see Loss, Commentary on the Uniform Securities Act (1976)
124-30.

[44] All except the District of Columbia, Nevada, New Mexico, Utah, Virginia, and Washington. The Kansas exemption applies only to Kansas corporations.

[45] California, Florida, Georgia (limited number of *buyers* rather than offerees), Illinois, Louisiana (if there is no "public offering"), Nevada, New
York (with respect to real estate issues), North Dakota, Ohio, South Dakota,
Texas, and Vermont (if there are no more than twenty-five security holders
on the completion of the offering).

only 13 of those 44 states (except that in Connecticut "the total number of purchasers of all securities of the issuer" may not exceed 10). Elsewhere the number is 5 in 1 state, 15 in 7, 20 in 1, 25 in 12, 35 in 10, and 40 in 1 (New York with respect to real estate securities).

(2) Seven states have exemptions that limit the total number of security holders at the end of the offering rather than the number of offerees.[46]

(3) Only 9 states make general use of the undefined federal criterion of a "public offering."[47] Some of these incorporate most of the federal exemptions by reference. In the latter group presumably the federal precedents are binding, not merely persuasive, as a matter of state (not federal) law. And a substantial number of states have incorporated part or all of former Rule 146, or its successor, Rule 506, either by statute or administratively.[48]

(4) A few states with the almost universal exemption for an "isolated transaction" do not limit that exemption to nonissuer transactions. This is particularly important in Kansas, whose exemption of the Uniform Act type is limited to domestic corporations.

(5) The only comparable exemption in Rhode Island, aside from sales to institutional investors,[49] is for "isolated sales which in the judgment of the [administrator] do not come under the provisions of this chapter."[50]

(6) It is also relevant here that most of the statutes contain some sort of exemption for offerings to existing security holders — usually offers of additional *stock* to existing *stockholders* and only on condition that no commissions be paid. The comparable exemption in the Uniform Act is broader in that (a) it covers any offer to existing security holders, (b) it permits payment of "a standby commission," and (c) it waives the condition with repect to the payment of other remuneration if the issuer first files a notice specifying the terms of the offer and the administrator

[46]California, Maine, Missouri, New Mexico, Oklahoma, Texas, and Virginia.

[47]Arizona, Connecticut, Maine, New York, North Carolina, Ohio, Oklahoma, Utah, and Washington.

[48]See Regulation of Real Estate Securities, Including the Applicability of Federal Rule 146 and Its Use in State Blue Sky Laws, Report of Subcommittee on Syndications and Joint Ventures of the Committee on Real Estate Financing, American Bar Association, 13 Real Est., Probate & Trust J. 841, 846-52 (1978).

[49]An exemption of that kind is contained also in §402(b)(8) of the Uniform Act and in the great majority of the states.

[50]R. I. Gen. Laws (1956) §7-11-9(a).

does not by order disallow the exemption within the next five full business days.[51]

F. TRADING TRANSACTIONS AND SECONDARY DISTRIBUTIONS

In this subchapter we examine various kinds of transactions whose common denominator is that the issuer is not a party. This includes "secondary distributions" of outstanding securities by their owner. It includes also the matter of resales after either a primary or a secondary offering, whether the offering is public or private — what we referred to in the §4(2) discussion as the "second stage" in the consideration of the private offering exemption,[1] although the resale problem extends well beyond the §4(2) context.

1. PRIVATE NONISSUER TRANSACTIONS [§4(1)]

Section 4(1) exempts "Transactions by any person other than an issuer, underwriter, or dealer." We have already noticed the definitions of these three terms and the interrelation between this exemption and the definition of "underwriter" so as to bring within §5 any secondary distribution of outstanding securities when the security holder is in a control relationship with the issuer and the distribution involves an underwriter.[2] Since §5 covers the universe — all persons and all transactions — this exemption is essential to permit Jones to sell his 100 shares of General Motors stock to Smith. Even if Jones's sale is of 1 million shares to thousands of Smiths, there is still an exemption under §4(1) unless (1) Jones is an affiliate of General Motors (that is to say, there is a control relationship between them within the meaning of the second sentence of §2(11)), in which event anyone acting for him in making the distribution becomes an "underwriter," or (2) Jones is himself an "underwriter" because he purchased the security from General Motors with a view to distribution or because the circumstances warrant the conclusion that he is making the distribution for the benefit of General Motors. If Jones is neither an affiliate nor an underwriter, there is no limit on the size of a distribution he may

[51] §402(b)(11).

C. 5F   [1] See p. 397 supra.
[2] See pp. 92-96 supra.

make under the §4(1) exemption, even through an investment banking syndicate, because the investment bankers will not be "underwriters."

If Jones *is* an affiliate, arguably he may make a direct distribution — which is to say, a *public* offering — so long as he does not use an underwriter. But suppose that we metamorphose Jones into Jones *Corp.*, which wants to offer the stock of its subsidiary to its own thousands of shareholders. Would not a person who took even a few of the subsidiary's shares for resale on a market rise become literally an "underwriter"? And, since §4(1) exempts *transactions*, not *persons*,[3] would not such an "underwriter's" participation in the transaction destroy the exemption so as to involve Jones Corp. in an illegal transaction?[4] This raises the same question of drawing the line between big and little buyers from the issuer itself that we have met in discussing the definition of "underwriter."[5] Significantly, the public utility holding companies that made secondary offerings of their subsidiaries' securities to their own security holders pursuant to §11(e) plans under the Holding Company Act took the prudent course of causing the securities to be registered.

2.   BROKERS' TRANSACTIONS [§4(4)]

What, then, is the impact on all this of §4(4), which exempts "Brokers' transactions" effected without the solicitation of customers' orders? As we have seen, the term "broker" is not separately defined.[6] All brokers are included within the definition of "dealer" in §2(12). It follows that the §4(4) exemption depends not upon a firm's generally acting as a broker but upon the capacity in which it executes the particular transaction. It follows also that the exemption is of no consequence at such times as the dealers' exemption in §4(3) is available. Its significance is that it permits an investor to cut his losses at any time, even while a stop order is in effect, by calling his broker.[7]

---

[3] SEC v. Chinese Consolidated Benevolent Assn., Inc., 120 F. 2d 738, 741 (2d Cir. 1941), *cert. denied*, 314 U. S. 618 (1941), supra pp. 281-82; see also SEC v. Culpepper, 270 F. 2d 241, 247 (2d Cir. 1959); SEC v. Holschuh, 694 F. 2d 130, 137 (7th Cir. 1982).

[4] The word "transaction" has always been read in the global sense of the entire offering rather than the sale from issuer to *A* and from *A* to *B*.

[5] See p. 280 supra.

[6] See p. 295 supra.

[7] H. R. Rep. No. 85, 73d Cong., 1st Sess. (1933) 16.

The brokers' exemption does not extend to the selling customer. It was established by the Federal Trade Commission that the exemption is limited to the broker's part of the transaction.[8] Thus, an *issuer* cannot avoid registration simply by having its securities sold through a broker, even though the issuer merely wishes to sell 100 shares of treasury stock on a stock exchange. Nor is the exemption available when the broker's principal is an *underwriter* or *dealer*. Whether or not the broker is liable in such cases as a participant in, or aider and abettor of, his *principal's* nonexempt transaction — as he is if he knows or has reasonable ground to believe that his principal is an issuer, underwriter, or dealer — the *principal* clearly violates §5. Conversely, when the principal is *not* an issuer, underwriter, or dealer, a §4(1) exemption for the principal's part of the transaction goes hand in hand with a §4(4) exemption for the broker's part.

Does this mean that an affiliate (who is not himself an underwriter or dealer) may sell his securities without limit as long as he does so through unsolicited brokers' transactions? Until 1946 the Commission followed this line: The fact that a broker effects an isolated transaction for an affiliate of the issuer does not make the broker an underwriter, even though he is selling for an "issuer" within the meaning of §2(11).[9] This assumes, however, that the broker does not exceed ordinary brokerage functions. If he does, he becomes an underwriter, with the result that his part of the transaction loses the 4(4) exemption and the affiliate's part loses the 4(1) exemption. What constitutes ordinary brokerage functions is a question of fact. Presumably the delegation of unusual discretion as to the time and manner of executing the affiliate's order, or the payment of more than the customary brokerage commission, would be fatal. And, although solicitation would normally seem to be part of the ordinary brokerage function, any solicitation that destroys the 4(4) exemption for the broker's part of the transaction destroys also the 4(1) exemption for the affiliate's part.[10]

---

[8] Sec. Act Rel. 131 (1934).

[9] True, an affiliate's broker who sells even 100 shares on a stock exchange is engaged in a "distribution" if that term is synonymous with "public offering." An implied exception is simply read into §2(11) for brokers when they execute transactions exempted under §4(4).

[10] It is a nice question whether the affiliate would be held to have engaged in an illegal transaction if he had had no knowledge or reasonable ground to believe that the broker had done any soliciting or in any way exceeded normal brokerage functions. This is in a sense the correlative of the question whether a particular broker participates in an illegal transaction when he does solicit or exceed normal brokerage functions but he has no knowledge or reasonable ground to believe that his selling customer is the issuer or in

The caveat was always added, however, that a broker engaged in distributing any substantial block of securities would probably be compelled to perform functions beyond those normally exercised by brokers.

This caveat seemed adequate to draw the line between sporadic trading and secondary distributions until the "bull" market of 1945 and 1946. It became apparent, however, that large blocks of securities could be sold in that market without solicitation or any particular sales effort. For example, in a series of three orders entered between late December 1945 and May 1946, the Commission granted exemptions under the Holding Company Act for the sale by The United Corporation on the New York Stock Exchange of a total of almost 600,000 shares of the common stock of its subsidiary, Columbia Gas & Electric Corporation. Since there was clear control and no registration statement had been filed under the Securities Act, it was obvious from the Commission's silence that exemption was assumed under §§4(1) and 4(4).[11]

A few months later, in the *Haupt* case, the Commission repudiated the implications of these orders and restated its position under §4(4). From December 15, 1943, to June 1, 1944, Ira Haupt & Company, a New York Stock Exchange member firm, had sold approximately 93,000 shares of the common stock of Park & Tilford, Inc., on behalf of the Schulte interests, who together owned some 91 percent of the outstanding stock. On December 15, 1943, Schulte had publicly announced that Park & Tilford was contemplating a distribution of whiskey to its shareholders at cost. (One must remember the date; whiskey was so scarce during the war that some thought Prohibition would come back *de facto*.) The stock advanced from $57\frac{5}{8}$ on that day to a high of $98\frac{1}{4}$ on May 26. On that day Park & Tilford offered to sell to its stockholders at a reduced price six cases of whiskey for each share of stock. On May 31 the Office of Price Administration limited the negotiability of the purchase rights and the maximum profits on the resale of the liquor. The price of the stock dropped $10\frac{1}{8}$ points that day and reached a low of $30\frac{5}{8}$ in June. All the Schulte sales during this period were effected on the New York Stock Exchange through the Haupt firm. At first the firm received a series of orders

---

any way related to the issuer. Obviously there would be no criminal liability or basis for administrative disciplinary proceedings or injunctive action in either case. Whether there would be civil liability under §12(1) is an open question.

[11] United Corp., Holding Co. Act Rels. 6337 (1945), 6409 (1946), 6649 (1946). The first 200,000 shares were sold in only twenty-six days. Holding Co. Act Rel. 6409, supra.

to sell 200 or 300 shares at a time at a limited price. On March 7, however, the firm was authorized to sell up to 50,000 shares at 80 or better, and this number was later increased to 73,000 shares. It was stipulated that, during the period of $5\frac{1}{2}$ months when the 93,000 shares were sold, 10 customers' men or representatives of the Haupt firm had solicited 21 customers, who had purchased approximately 4000 shares, and that the firm's chief statistician had prepared a written analysis of the stock for a customer, who had thereupon purchased 100 shares. This was the only evidence in the record with respect to solicitation.

In an administrative proceeding against the Haupt firm under the 1934 Act, the Commission stated:

> We conclude that Section [4(4)] cannot exempt transactions by an underwriter executed over the Exchange in connection with a distribution for a controlling stockholder. Respondent has suggested that this conclusion is contrary to administrative interpretations issued by our staff and to the implications in recent orders issued in connection with applications of *The United Corporation* under the Public Utility Holding Company Act with respect to United's sale of common stock of a subsidiary through brokers on the New York Stock Exchange. The administrative interpretations referred to were to the general effect that an underwriter selling for a controlling stockholder over the exchange might conceivably be entitled to the exemption under Section [4(4)] if his activities were confined strictly to the usual brokerage functions, but that, as a practical matter, his activities could not be so confined in connection with a distribution of any substantial block of securities. These interpretations arrived at the same ultimate result as that which we have reached here. But the theory and the qualification of the interpretations — which we agree are inconsistent with our conclusion herein — were developed against the background of a very different market than is now prevalent. It has been only comparatively recently that the problem has been presented in the context of a market in which large blocks can frequently be sold without solicitations or other sales activity. In that context, the invalidity of the theory on which the interpretations were based has become apparent. We have reached our present conclusion on this phase of the case after careful consideration of the entire problem and, to the extent that the administrative interpretations referred to and the principle involved in the *United* case may be inconsistent with that conclusion, they must be overruled.[12]

The Commission had little trouble tying the Haupt firm into the violation. It found "no validity in the argument that a predeter-

[12] Ira Haupt & Co., 23 SEC 589, 604-06 (1946).

mination of the precise number of shares which are to be publicly dispersed is an essential element of a distribution." "Nor do we think," the Commission said, "that a 'distribution' loses its character as such merely because the extent of the offering may depend on certain conditions such as the market price." The Commission also rejected the firm's claim that it was not aware of the distribution intended by the Schulte interests. The Commission pointed out that only 7000 shares of the stock had been traded on the Exchange in the entire month of November; that 24,500 shares had been traded in the first two days following the announcement of the impending whiskey dividend; and that an additional 115,000 shares had been traded during the rest of that month. Under all the circumstances, the Commission found that "The only reasonable conclusion that could have been reached by respondent was that it was intended that a large block would be sold."[13]

Although it could not be convincingly argued for a moment that Congress did not intend this kind of distribution to be subject to the registration requirement, the absence of any precise line between a nonexempt secondary distribution and the kind of brokerage transaction on behalf of an affiliate of an issuer that might still come within the brokerage exemption caused a good deal of concern among the brokerage fraternity. The argument was occasionally heard that, since "distribution" was supposed to be synonymous with "public offering," no broker could feel safe any longer in executing an order to sell 100 shares of stock on behalf of some officer or director of a corporation who might conceivably be deemed to be a member of a controlling group.

The upshot was the Commission's adoption eight years later, in 1954, of a Rule 154 (since replaced, as we shall see), which defined the term "broker's transactions" in §4(4) to include transactions by a broker acting as agent for a person in a control relationship with the issuer if, in addition to otherwise meeting the conditions of that section, he was "not aware of circumstances indicating that his principal is an underwriter in respect of the securities or that the transactions are part of a distribution of securities on behalf of his princpal." And by way of "a ready guide for routine cases involving trading as distinguished from distributing transactions," the rule provided that there was not deemed to be a "distribution" if the transaction in question and all other sales of the same class of securities by or on behalf of the same person within the preceding six months did not exceed approximately 1 percent of the shares or units of an over-the-counter security and, in the case of a security traded on an exchange,

[13] Id. at 598.

the lesser of that amount or the aggregate reported volume of exchange trading during any week within the preceding four weeks. Whether transactions exceeding this formula constituted a "distribution" would depend on whether they involved an amount that was "substantial in relation to the number of shares or units of the security outstanding and the aggregate volume of trading in such security."[14]

3. RESALES AFTER PRIVATE OFFERINGS

Roughly the same period saw the playing out of another drama: what has here been referred to as the "second stage" of the private offering exemption in §4(2). That is to say, on the assumption that the number of initial offerees and all the other relevant factors are such as to justify the conclusion that the first stage of the transaction does not involve a public offering, it is still necessary to consider whether the purchasers' intent is to take for resale. If so, obviously, it is the number and type of *ultimate* offerees that are significant; otherwise a distribution by means of a sale to two or three firm-commitment underwriters for distribution would be a private offering.

The purchaser's intent is a question of fact, of which his own statement is evidentiary (not, of course, conclusive). The fact that a buyer does resell is not conclusive that he so intended when he bought. The private offering exemption does not impose an indefinite restraint on alienation — though naturally, the shorter the period before resale, the stronger would be the inference that there had been an intention to resell from the beginning unless the original purchaser could show some plausible reason why he had changed his mind. This came to be known as the "change of circumstances doctrine." Time, in other words, is relevant on the question of intent, but not conclusive.[15] Other factors, too, are very relevant: Whereas "insurance and investment companies * * * could quite readily sustain the burden of proof that they

---

[14] Although the rule was expressly directed at §4(4), it was obviously contemplated that the seller's part of the transaction would be considered to be exempt under §4(1) whenever the broker's part came within the rule.

[15] In Vohs v. Dickson, 495 F. 2d 607, 620-21 (5th Cir. 1974), where the court (*obiter*) found support for the finding below that the defendant had taken with investment intent, the court talked about the relevance of length of time, an investment letter, an unforeseen change of circumstances, the nature of the defendant's past investment and trading processes, and the character and scope of his business.

had purchased for investment," the nature of the business ordinarily carried on by a dealer or an investment banking house "would create an extremely strong presumption of purchase for resale."[16] If the buyer is neither an institutional investor on the one hand nor a securities firm on the other, the question must be asked whether his purchase of a block of securities of the particular size for investment is consistent with his general operations. Indeed, most of the factors enumerated in the 1935 opinion of the General Counsel[17] other than the number of offerees are hardly relevant except "where there are indications that the securities have been purchased for redistribution and hence a public offering may be involved even though the initial offering is to an insubstantial number of offerees."[18]

In a 1938 opinion the General Counsel had expressed the view that retention of the securities for as long as a year "would create a strong inference that they had been purchased for investment." But he had added that even such an inference would fall, for example, "in the face of evidence of a pre-arranged scheme to effect a distribution at the end of the year."[19] The Commission later elaborated on this caveat:

> Holding for the six months' capital gains period of the tax statutes, holding in an "investment account" rather than a "trading account," holding for a deferred sale, holding for a market rise, holding for sale if the market does not rise, or holding for a year, does not afford a statutory basis for an exemption and therefore does not provide an adequate basis on which counsel may give opinions or businessmen rely in selling securities without registration.
>
> Purchasing for the purpose of future sale is nonetheless purchasing for sale and, if the transactions involve any public offering even at some future date, the registration provisions apply unless at the time of the public offering an exemption is available.[20]

It would seem to follow that the length of the holding that is required to negative an inference of an intent to distribute is affected by the relatively speculative or stable nature of the issuer.

---

[16] Op. Gen. Counsel, Sec. Act Rel. 1862 (1938).

[17] Op. Gen. Counsel, Sec. Act Rel. 285 (1935).

[18] Brief of SEC, p. 38 n. 28, SEC v. Ralston Purina Co., 346 U. S. 119 (1953).

[19] Op. Gen. Counsel, Sec. Act Rel. 1862 (1938).

[20] Crowell-Collier Publishing Co., Sec. Act Rel. 3825 (1957) 6-7. See also Gilligan, Will & Co. v. SEC, 267 F. 2d 461, 468 (2d Cir. 1959), *cert. denied*, 361 U. S. 896, where the court affirmed disciplinary action taken by the Commission against one of the broker-dealers in the *Crowell-Collier* case.

But, in the case of an established issuer with relatively stable earnings, it seems considerably less clear that (as asserted by a member of the Commission) "the happening or non-occurrence of an event in the affairs of the company or within the industry of which the company is a part, or that affects the general economy, is generally, in the absence of other persuasive factors, not the type of emergency or hardship situation that justifies reliance upon the change of circumstance doctrine."[21] One can understand the Commission's not being persuaded "that a person who had acquired a large block of securities in an airplane manufacturer but desired to sell his holdings upon learning of the launching of the first sputnik, because he suddenly believed that the age of missiles would supplant the use of aircraft, had originally taken the securities for investment."[22] But the mere fact that an unanticipated technological advance affects an entire industry hardly precludes an inference that there has been a change of circumstances. Indeed, if it is to be taken as literally true that the exemption is destroyed by a vague intention to sell upon a substantial market movement in either direction, it is difficult to see how a resale could ever be made with safety except in the event of death, bankruptcy, or other personal disaster.

In their search for a crutch to lean on, some lawyers talked for a time of a "Cohen two-year rule," in reliance on remarks made by then Commissioner Manuel F. Cohen (later Chairman)[23] as well as a case in which a District Court concluded that a two-year holding was "an insuperable obstacle" to a finding that the defendant had taken the shares with a view to distribution "in the absence of any relevant evidence from which I could conclude he did not take the shares for investment."[24] But Commissioner Cohen indicated that certain factual situations would negative any two-year presumption, and the court might have been influenced by the necessity in a criminal contempt proceeding of proving "beyond a reasonable doubt" that the defendant's transactions had violated the court's injunction. Some lawyers then followed their own house rules in terms of three years or even five. But the Commission insisted that no specific period was conclusive or even presumptive of a "change of circumstances."

All this left a conscientious lawyer in a difficult position if he

21 Orrick, Non-public Offerings of Corporate Securities — Limitations on the Exemption under the Federal Securities Act, 21 U. Pitt. L. Rev. 1, 16 (1959).
22 Id. at 17.
23 See C. Israels (ed.), S. E. C. Problems of Controlling Stockholders and in Underwritings (1962) 30-31.
24 United States v. Sherwood, 175 F. Supp. 480, 483 (S. D. N. Y. 1959).

examined the issuer or the prospective buyers too closely on the question of investment intent; for few investors could honestly survive the examination, and a prospective buyer's very act of inquiring of counsel how long he must hold before reselling might require the answer that he has already entertained the fatal thought. For that matter, the prudent buyer's exaction of a registration covenant from the issuer in the event of a resale might itself damn the transaction. And it is difficult to see how a buyer acting in a *fiduciary* capacity could ever make the necessary representation consistently with his duty regularly to examine his investments with a view to making whatever changes are indicated. The late Ray Garrett put it very well some years before he became Chairman of the SEC:

> For reasons which will appear, one of the financial lawyer's most intriguing tasks is that of explaining, for example, to a man who has just sold his business for stock, the precise state of mind which is appropriate for a good investment letter. The lawyer begins by saying that he must take for investment purposes, not for resale. And the dialogue runs: "Does that mean I can't ever sell it?" "No." "When, then?" "Only later when your reselling is consistent with your present investment intent." "In 6 months?" "No." "How long?" "Theoretically tomorrow if there is some change in circumstances — but don't you dare try it!" "What is a change of circumstances?" "Something basic and unforeseen." "Like needing the cash for a trip around the world?" "Do you expect to take a trip around the world?" And so on, ad infinitum.[25]

In this difficult state of affairs the Bar developed a number of safeguards:

(1) Every first-tier buyer is asked to sign an investment letter, which should be carefully drafted to explain what the buyer is being asked to sign. Some lawyers advise that a written explanation be given and that each buyer acknowledge in writing that it has been read. More properly, these letters should state negatively, more or less in the language of §2(11), that the buyers are *not* taking with a view to *distribution;* for a promise to hold for investment, or not to *resell,* would be inconsistent with a *private* resale for *investment,* which would not necessarily destroy the exemption (although even such resales are apt to increase the number of offerees dangerously by reason of the factor of geometric progression). And one should by all means avoid phrasing the letter in terms of holding for a fixed period. In principle even a long

---

[25] Garrett, Federal Securities Act — An Introduction to Jurisdiction, [1961] U. Ill. L. F. 267, 293 n. 85.

period would be worse than none; for it might be taken to indicate a present intention to resell at the end of the period.

(2) Transfer of the securities is restricted, with a notation on each certificate in order to meet the requirement of the Uniform Commercial Code for binding third persons.[26] A legend along these lines should be adequate when the seller has sufficient bargaining power to get it:

> These shares have been purchased for investment within the meaning of the Securities Act of 1933 and they may not be sold, transferred, pledged or hypothecated without an effective registration statement under that Act or an opinion of counsel satisfactory to the company to the effect that the proposed transaction will be exempt from registration.

Depending on the relative bargaining power of the parties, the buyer, on the one hand, may have to agree to be bound by the opinion of the seller's counsel, and the seller, on the other hand, may have to agree to accept an opinion of the buyer's counsel or, conceivably, any counsel without further designation. Indeed, the buyer may be unwilling to accept legended certificates at all.[27]

(3) Sometimes a restriction on transfer is impracticable, or at least awkward, as, for example, when the seller is a controlling per-

---

[26] §8-204.

[27] Alternatively, since it is not so much a pledge itself as a possible resale by the pledgee that must be guarded against (see p. 288 supra), it should be sufficient, if the buyer objects to the broader language, to substitute: " * * * they may not be sold or transferred by any person, including a pledgee, without * * * ." In that event it may also be advisable, depending on the circumstances, to insert "or a donee" after "a pledgee," since the Commission has sometimes made "underwriters" out of donees as we have seen (supra pp. 282-83) and the specific inclusion of a pledgee in the legend may create an undesirable negative implication.

Regulation D recites that the reasonable care that the issuer must exercise to assure that its buyers are not underwriters includes reasonable inquiry as to investment purpose, written disclosure of resale limitations, and an appropriate legend on the certificate. §502(d).

An issuer may not delay registration of a transfer by unreasonably refusing to honor an opinion of counsel (or a "no action" letter from the SEC staff if that was bargained for). Kanton v. U. S. Plastics, Inc., 248 F. Supp. 353 (D. N. J. 1965). And an opinion of counsel may not be unreasonably withheld, at least when his refusal is "part of a deliberate and unwarranted attempt to forestall plaintiff's transfer of his stock while permitting favored shareholders to transfer their shares." Singer v. Whitman & Ransom, 83 A. D. 2d 862, 863, 442 N. Y. S. 2d 26, 27 (2d Dept. 1981). But, if the parties bargained for an opinion of counsel, a "no action" letter does not afford the same protection. Kenler v. Canal National Bank, 489 F. 2d 482 (1st Cir. 1973). In any exent, a Securities Act barrier to a transfer does not necessarily defeat a claim for damages under UCC §8-204. Edina State Bank v. Mr. Steak, Inc., 487 F. 2d 640 (10th Cir. 1973), *cert. denied*, 419 U. S. 883.

son who wants to rely on §4(1) for the sale of outstanding securities. In that event, an alternative to a restriction on transfer — or in any event a device to supplement the stamped certificate technique — is to deliver a "stop transfer notice" to the company or its transfer agent, with instructions to hold up transfer when a certificate affected by the notice is presented for registration of transfer until counsel for the company can pass on the matter.[28]

(4) It may be advisable, depending on the reliability of the buyers and the relative bargaining power of the parties, to require a statement of each buyer's financial condition by way of showing, for example, whether the amount of securities purchased is unduly large in relation to his financial means, or whether he borrowed to finance the purchase so that he might intend or be forced to resell in the near future in order to repay his loan. Prudence would seem also to dictate some inquiry, before making a sale, into the prospective buyer's record with respect to holding securities for long-term investment in the past.

In the last analysis, of course, the value of all such safeguards rests on the ability to persuade a court or the SEC that they are not empty rituals. But they may be particularly important with respect to civil or other liabilities:

(a) If first-tier buyers resell pursuant to a registration statement, there is no retroactive violation in the issuer's (or affiliate's) sale to them, because they turn out to have been "underwriters" within the expansive reading of the "preliminary negotiations" clause of §2(3).[29] Indeed, if the initial offering would be exempted under §4(2) (or §4(1) in the case of an affiliate) except for the fact that at least some of the buyers contemplate the possibility of a delayed distribution, it is questionable whether registration would be *proper* before the distribution (Rule 415 aside); for the last sentence of §6(a) indicates that the registration process was intended to have its impact at the point of *public offering.* By the same token, an investment representation hardly seems appropriate in such a case; instead the opinion of counsel for the issuer (or the affiliate) should more properly be couched in terms of the preliminary negotiations clause of §2(3) rather than §4(2) (or §4(1)). When the buyers are such that a §4(2) (or §4(1)) exemption would clearly be available if they were in fact taking for investment, but they want to be free to resell at any time subject to registration,

---

[28] For a discussion of the complexities raised by the Uniform Commercial Code, see Israels, in Current Problems of Securities Underwriters and Dealers, 18 Bus. Law. 27, 85-89 (1962).

[29] See pp. 99-101 supra.

there is no reason why the opinion of counsel cannot be phrased under both sections in the alternative; for the mere fact that only time will tell whether these candid persons did in fact buy "for investment" or were "underwriters" is no reason why the initial transaction should fall between two stools. Of course, if even one of the initial buyers takes for immediate distribution, there is no choice but to register; in that event, the technique of an undertaking to file a posteffective amendment before any delayed distribution by the others affords a practical solution to the dilemma.

(b) On the other hand, an *illegal* resale by first-tier buyers who purported to take for investment raises different questions as far as the issuer's (or affiliate's) involvement in the violation is concerned, depending presumably on whether the issuer (or affiliate) had reasonable ground to question the initial investment representation. If so, the issuer (or affiliate) violates §5 along with the person reselling, either directly by virtue of participating in a nonexempt sale or as an aider and abettor. For these reasons, an issuer (or its transfer agent) should be particularly careful before registering a transfer of shares out of the names of persons who purported to buy from the issuer (or from an affiliate, though the *issuer's* involvement is somewhat less in that event) for investment. It may, of course, hold up a request to transfer for a reasonable time in order to investigate its legality. But it is not a proposition unique to §5 of the Securities Act that the issuer (or its transfer agent) may in either event guess wrong at the issuer's peril (if not the agent's as well) — whether it improperly registers a transfer or improperly declines to do so.

(c) The Commission's staff has spoken forcefully about the *broker-dealer's* duty of investigation before he participates in an unregistered distribution:

SECURITIES ACT RELEASE NO. 5168: SALES OF UNREGISTERED SECURITIES BY BROKER-DEALERS
Securities and Exchange Commission, 1971

The Director of the Division of Trading and Markets takes this occasion to reaffirm certain basic standards of conduct required of registered broker-dealers in meeting their responsibilities in connection with sales of significant amounts of unregistered securities.

A number of instances have recently come to the attention of the Division of Trading and Markets in which brokerage firms, including members of national securities exchanges, have failed to meet applicable standards of conduct in investigating whether sales of securities would result in registration or anti-fraud violations of the federal securities laws. A firm's participation in an unregistered public distribution has frequently been a major factor in the success of this unlawful activity since the firm affords sellers access to the market place and may create an appearance of propriety and substance otherwise lacking. The potential harm to the public is particularly acute when securities of a little-known issuer, or one concerning which reliable information is not readily available, are sold to the public on the over-the-counter market.

The Division is aware of recent instances in which brokerage firms have purported to rely upon opinion letters which fail to describe the facts underlying counsel's conclusion that the shares sold are freely tradeable. Similar reliance has been claimed even when the firm itself had reason to question whether a valid exemption from registration existed. On another occasion, a registered broker-dealer considered the fact that shares were put through transfer to be the definitive test of free transferability. Customers have also occasionally succeeded in selling substantial amounts of securities in unregistered public distributions because the firm's compliance procedures either did not include scrutiny of sales transactions or were inadequate to detect substantial sales of a particular issue by one or more accounts. Frequently, these sales were made by new customers who opened a brokerage account specifically to effect such unlawful transactions.

As the Commission has stated,[2]

> * * * [a] dealer who offers to sell, or is asked to sell a substantial amount of securities must take whatever steps are necessary to be sure that this is a transaction not involving an issuer, person in a control relationship with an issuer or an underwriter. For this purpose, it is not sufficient for him merely to accept "self-serving statements of his sellers and their counsel without reasonably exploring the possibility of contrary facts."
>
> The amount of inquiry called for necessarily varies with the circumstances of particular cases. A dealer who is offered a modest amount of a widely traded security by a responsible customer, whose lack of relationship to the issuer is well known to him, may ordinarily proceed with considerable confidence. On the other hand, when a dealer is offered a substantial block of a little-known

---

[2] Distributions by Broker-Dealers of Unregistered Securities, Securities Exchange Act Release No. 6721, Securities Act Release No. 4445 (February 2, 1962), pages 2 and 3, footnote omitted. See also S. E. C. v. Culpepper, 270 F. 2d 241 (C. A. 2, 1959) and S. E. C. v. Mono-Kearsarge Consolidated Mining Company, 167 F. Supp. 248 (D. Utah, 1958).

security, either by persons who appear reluctant to disclose exactly where the securities came from, or where the surrounding circumstances raise a question as to whether or not the ostensible sellers may be merely intermediaries for controlling persons or statutory underwriters, then searching inquiry is called for.

While "the amount of inquiry called for necessarily varies with the circumstances of particular cases," all registered broker-dealers should establish minimum standard procedures to prevent and detect violations of the federal securities laws and to ensure that the firm meet its continuing responsibility *to know* both its customers and the securities being sold. There should be written supervisory procedures that cover *sales as well as purchases*. These must be made known to salesmen and be sufficient to reveal promptly to supervisory officials transactions which may, when examined individually or in the aggregate, indicate that sales in a security should be halted immediately pending further inquiry.

Registered broker-dealers should also establish standard procedures as an initial step in their general investigation into the background of prospective customers and the source of the securities to be traded. In the case of a new customer, a new account form identifying the customer and describing his financial condition and investment objectives should be completed before sales are made. A firm should not permit accounts to be opened by third persons or orders accepted from third persons on behalf of a customer without the customer's express authorization. In addition, registered broker-dealers should make certain routine inquiries of customers, including for example: whether the customer has direct or indirect connections with any publicly owned company or with the issuer; what his financial condition is (so that the broker-dealer may determine whether it is consistent with the value of the securities to be sold); whether the customer's securities were acquired on the open market; whether he is the true beneficial owner of them; whether he has non-public information about the issuer and whether he is currently selling or attempting to sell the same securities through other brokerage houses.

Basic information concerning the issuer such as its address, business activities, principals, products, assets, financial condition and number of shares of stock outstanding, should be obtained independently as a matter of course. Where public information concerning the company is not available from the Commission or standard research sources, the extent of inquiry required to reasonably assure the broker or dealer that the proposed transaction complies with applicable legal requirements will be correspondingly greater. Moreover, the Commission has "repeatedly held that it is a violation of the anti-fraud provisions for a broker-dealer to recommend a security unless there is an adequate and reasonable basis for the recommendations and, further, that such recommendation should not be made without disclosure of facts known or reasonably ascertainable, bearing upon the justification for the recommendation."

The customer's responses or other particular circumstances may reasonably indicate that there is a duty to make further inquiries and verify the information received. The most obvious situations are where a previously unknown customer may be seeking to sell a significant amount of securities and the issuer may be relatively unknown to the public. In this regard, it should be noted that information received from little-known companies or their officials, transfer agent or counsel must be treated with great caution as these are the very parties that may be seeking to deceive the firm. When circumstances suggest that further inquiry and verification by the broker or dealer is necessary, the firm may consider it prudent to document its investigative efforts. The customer could be required, for example, to supply in writing the information suggested above and state that it is accurate and complete. Such a signed statement might not necessarily mean that the information received was inherently more reliable but could supplement the investigatory efforts otherwise required.

Where it appears that securities to be sold were not acquired by open-market purchases, it must be determined whether their sale is exempted from registration under the Securities Act of 1933. Any determination that such an exemption exists should only be made after the broker-dealer has reviewed the facts surrounding the acquisition of the shares and competent outside counsel having no proprietary interest in the offering has furnished a supporting opinion describing the relevant facts in sufficient detail to provide an explicit basis for the legal conclusions stated. Of course, any firm receiving a sell order where the circumstances raise questions as to the propriety of the transactions should, in the exercise of its responsibilities, immediately alert the nearest Commission office.[a]

* * *

---

[a] ED.: See also Rule 144(g)(3), infra pp. 426-27, which deems the term "brokers' transactions" in §4(4) to include a transaction in which (among other conditions) the broker "after reasonable inquiry is not aware of circumstances indicating that the person for whose account the securities are sold is an

Violations are one thing and sanctions are another. A violation is not a crime, nor may it be the basis for administrative disciplinary proceedings against a broker-dealer, unless it was committed "willfully."[30] And an injunction requires "equity" — "some cognizable danger of recurrent violation."[31] *Civil* liability under §12(1) runs only to the seller's immediate buyer. When a lying first-tier buyer sues an innocent issuer (or affiliate), the doctrine of *in pari delicto* should apply, though this is less certain when *both* parties are playing games.[32] But an issuer (or affiliate) that in good faith had accepted investment representations from both X and Y might well be held liable to an innocent Y if only X had misrepresented his intention and distributed the security. Whether a *dealer* who acted reasonably but got caught up in an illegal distribution would be liable to *his* buyers is a nice question — literally yes, with a right over presumably against the violators in common law tort.

Thus far we have been examining the resale problem from the issuer's (or affiliate's) point of view. The first-tier buyer, from his point of view, will want a registration covenant from the issuer (not just from the affiliate that is making a private offering under §4(1), since that very offering may weaken or destroy his control) in case the buyer will want to resell at a time or under circumstances when everybody agrees that registration is required (or, at any rate, when the issuer's counsel is of that opinion). A well-drafted registration covenant will consider many variables and, again, will reflect the relative bargaining powers of the parties.[33] Sometimes, for example, the initial buyers from the issuer will have to be satisfied with a "piggyback" arrangement, whereby the issuer, instead of agreeing to register on a specified demand, agrees merely to give the initial buyers an opportunity to participate in any registration statement that the issuer may file in the future, with appropriate provisions with respect to payment of the expenses of registration and so on. These covenants are subject to specific performance whenever that relief is appropriate under

---

underwriter with respect to the securities or that the transaction is a part of a distribution of securities of the issuer." And the Commission has spoken on the meaning of "reasonable inquiry" in this context. Sec. Act Rel. 5223 (1972) 11. The Commission's further animadversions with respect to the role of counsel are considered infra c. 11A.

[30] Sec. Act §24; Sec. Ex. Act §15(b)(4)(D).

[31] United States v. W. T. Grant Co., 345 U. S. 629, 633 (1953).

[32] See 2 Code 805-06 and authorities cited.

[33] See Schneider and Manko, Rule 145, 5 Rev. Sec. Reg. 811, 821 n. 59 (1972).

the law of contracts.[34] But it is not always easy to get these agreements, because they may interfere with the issuer's future financing.

4. RULE 144

In 1972 the two tracks we have traveled in the last two sections of this subchapter — transactions by affiliates' brokers and resales after issuers' private offerings — converged in Rule 144. In the former aspect the rule replaced Rule 154. In the latter aspect Rule 144 is new. Both aspects are reflected in the rule's definition of "restricted securities" to mean securities "acquired directly or indirectly from the issuer, or from an affiliate of the issuer, in a transaction or chain of transactions not involving any public offering, or securities acquired from the issuer that are subject to the resale limitations of Regulation D under the Act, or securities that are subject to the resale limitations of Regulation D and are acquired in a transaction or chain of transactions not involving any public offering."[35]

SECURITIES ACT RELEASE NO. 5223: NOTICE OF ADOPTION OF RULE 144 RELATING TO THE DEFINITION OF THE TERMS "UNDERWRITER" IN SECTIONS 4(1) AND 2(11) AND "BROKERS' TRANS-ACTIONS" IN SECTION 4(4) OF THE SECURITIES ACT OF 1933, ADOPTION OF FORM 144, AND RESCISSION OF RULES 154 AND 155ª UNDER THAT ACT
Securities and Exchange Commission, 1972

*   *   *

In brief, the rule provides that any affiliate or other person who sells restricted securities of an issuer for his own account, or any

[34] See, e. g., Kupferman v. Consolidated Research & Mfg. Corp., CCH Fed. Sec. L. Rep. ¶91,197 (S. D. N. Y. 1962); Siegler v. Living Aluminum, Inc., CCH ¶91,266 (N. Y. Sup. Ct. 1963); Waste Management, Inc. v. Deffenbaugh, 534 F. 2d 126 (8th Cir. 1976); Madison Fund, Inc. v. Charter Co., 427 F. Supp. 597 (S. D. N. Y. 1977) (breach of "piggyback" agreement); Canfield v. Reynolds, 631 F. 2d 169, 178 (2d Cir. 1980).
[35] Rule 144(a)(3). Rule 506 of Regulation D is, of course, a private offering rule; and Rules 504 and 505, though adopted under §3(b), have something of the private offering flavor.
ª ED.: Rule 155, adopted in 1962, was designed to make clear, in the form

person who sells restricted or any other securities for the account of an affiliate of the issuer, is not deemed to be engaged in a distribution of the securities, and therefore is not an underwriter as defined in Section 2(11) of the Act, if the securities are sold in accordance with all the terms and conditions of the rule. * * *

A number of persons have commented that it is not clear whether the rule, as proposed, was intended to be the exclusive means for selling restricted securities without registration under the Securities Act. In this connection, certain commentators asserted that the Commission does not have the statutory authority to adopt such an exclusive rule while others stated that the Commission had such power and urged it to adopt an exclusive rule. The Commission does not believe it is necessary to reach these questions relating to its statutory authority at this time, since the rule as adopted is not exclusive. However, persons who offer or sell restricted securities without complying with Rule 144 are hereby put on notice by the Commission that in view of the broad remedial purposes of the Act and of public policy which strongly supports registration, they will have a substantial burden of proof in establishing that an exemption from registration is available for such offers or sales and that such persons and the brokers and other persons who participate in the transactions do so at their risk.

Moreover, with respect to restricted securities acquired after the effective date of the rule, the staff will not issue "no-action" letters relating to resales of such securities. Further, in connection with such resales, the Commission hereby puts all persons including brokers and attorneys on notice that the "change in circumstances" concept should no longer be considered as one of the factors in determining whether a person is an underwriter. The Commission recognizes that this concept has been in existence in one form or another for a long period of time. However, administrative agencies as well as courts from time to time change their interpretation of statutory provisions in the light of new considerations and changing conditions which indicate that earlier interpretations of such provisions are no longer in keeping with the statutory objectives. Thus, the "change in circumstances" concept in the

---

of a definition of the phrase "transactions by an issuer not involving any public offering," that the exemption did not apply either (1) to a public offering of the convertible security itself, if it was at that time immediately convertible into another security of the same issuer, by or on behalf of any person that had purchased the convertible security directly or indirectly from the issuer as part of a nonpublic offering, or (2) to any public offering, by or on behalf of any such person, of the security acquired on conversion unless it had been acquired under such circumstances that the person was not an "underwriter." 4 Loss 2659; see the background discussion in 1 Loss 673-86.

Commission's opinion fails to meet the objectives of the Act, since the circumstances of the seller are unrelated to the need of investors for the protections afforded by the registration and other provisions of the Act.

Further, with respect to restricted securities acquired after the effective date of the rule but not sold pursuant to the provisions of the rule, the Commission hereby gives notice that in deciding whether a person is an underwriter, the length of time the securities have been held will be considered but the fact that securities have been held for a particular period of time does not by itself establish the availability of an exemption from registration.

* * *

Background and Purpose

* * *

Rule 144 is designed to implement the fundamental purposes of the Act as expressed in its preamble:

> To provide full and fair disclosure of the character of the securities sold in interstate commerce and through the mails, and to prevent fraud in the sale thereof * * *

The rule would also operate to inhibit the creation of public markets in securities of issuers concerning which adequate current information is not available to the public. At the same time, where adequate current information concerning an issuer is available to the public, the rule would permit the public sale in ordinary trading transactions of limited quantities of securities owned by persons controlling, controlled by or under common control with the issuer (hereinafter "affiliate") and by persons who have acquired restricted securities of the issuer.

This approach is consistent with the philosophy underlying the Act, that a disclosure law would provide the best protection for investors. In other words, if the investor had available to him all the material facts concerning a security, he would then be in a position to make an informed judgment whether or not to buy. In order to provide such information to investors, Congress determined that a distribution of securities requires the filing of a registration statement with the Commission and the delivery to investors of a prospectus containing accurate and current information concerning the issuer and its securities.

* * *

Resales of securities acquired in private placements are frequently made under claims of an exemption pursuant to Section 4(1) of the Act, that is, a transaction by a person other than an issuer, underwriter, or dealer. This Section was intended to exempt only trading transactions between individual investors with respect to securities already issued and not to exempt distributions by issuers or acts of other individuals who engage in steps necessary to such distributions.

Generally the majority of questions arising under this Section have dealt with whether the seller is an "underwriter." The term underwriter is broadly defined in Section 2(11) of the Act to mean any person who has purchased from an issuer with a view to, or offers or sells for an issuer in connection with, the distribution of any security, or participates or has a direct or indirect participation in any such undertaking, or participates or has a participation in the direct or indirect underwriting of any such undertaking. The interpretation of this definition has traditionally focused on the words "with a view to" in the phrase "purchased from an issuer with a view to * * * distribution." Thus, an investment banking firm which arranges with an issuer for the public sale of its securities is clearly an "underwriter" under that Section. Not so well understood is the fact that individual investors who are not professionals in the securities business may be "underwriters" within the meaning of that term as used in the Act if they act as links in a chain of transactions through which securities move from an issuer to the public. It is difficult to ascertain the mental state of the purchaser at the time of his acquisition, and the staff has looked to subsequent acts and circumstances to determine whether such person took with a view to distribution at the time of his acquisition. Emphasis has been placed on factors such as the length of time the person has held the securities ("holding period") and whether there has been an unforeseeable change in circumstances of the holder. Experience has shown, however, that reliance upon such factors as the above has not assured adequate protection of investors through the maintenance of informed trading markets and has led to uncertainty in the application of the registration provisions of the Act.

Moreover, the Commission hereby emphasizes and draws attention to the fact that the statutory language of Section 2(11) is in the disjunctive. Thus, it is insufficient to conclude that a person is not an underwriter solely because he did not purchase securities from an issuer with a view to their distribution. It must also be established that the person is not offering or selling for an issuer in connection with the distribution of the securities and that the person does not participate or have a participation in any such undertaking, and does not participate or have a participation in any such underwriting of such an undertaking.

Rule 144, together with the other related rules and amendments, is designed to provide full and fair disclosure of the character of securities sold in trading transactions and to create greater certainty and predictability in the application of the registration provisions of the Act by replacing subjective standards with more objective ones.

EXPLANATION AND ANALYSIS OF THE RULE

* * *

* * * In determining when a person is deemed not to be engaged in a distribution several factors must be considered.

First, the purpose and underlying policy of the Act to protect investors requires, in the Commission's opinion, that there be adequate current information concerning the issuer, whether the resales of securities by persons result in a distribution or are effected in trading transactions. Accordingly, the availability of the rule is conditioned on the existence of adequate current public information.

Secondly, a holding period prior to resale is essential, among other reasons, to assure that those persons who buy under a claim of a Section 4(2) exemption have assumed the economic risks of investment, and therefore, are not acting as conduits for sale to the public of unregistered securities, directly or indirectly, on behalf of an issuer. It should be noted that there is nothing in Section 2(11) which places a time limit on a person's status as an underwriter. The public has the same need for protection afforded by registration whether the securities are distributed shortly after their purchase or after a considerable length of time.[5]

---

[5] The Commission is aware that certain commentators have asserted that the absence of a cut-off period would constitute an unreasonable restraint on the alienation of personal property. Generally speaking, the Commission does not concur in this view. As mentioned below, the rule would operate prospectively and permits limited resales of securities in trading transactions consistent with the purposes of the Act. Such limitation is reasonable since the holder of unregistered securities may resell his securities to persons who have access to adequate and current information concerning the issuer, and who do not need the protection of registration or he may contract for registration or for filing under Regulation A for subsequent resales, if he desires

A third factor, which must be considered in determining what is deemed not to constitute a "distribution," is the impact of the particular transaction or transactions on the trading markets. It is consistent with the rationale of the Act that Section 4(1) be interpreted to permit only routine trading transactions as distinguished from distributions. Therefore, a person reselling securities under Section 4(1) of the Act must sell the securities in such limited quantities and in such a manner so as not to disrupt the trading markets. The larger the amount of securities involved, the more likely it is that such resales may involve methods of offering and amounts of compensation usually associated with a distribution rather than routine trading transactions. Thus, solicitation of buy orders or the payment of extra compensation are not permitted by the rule.

In summary, if the sale in question is made in accordance with all the provisions of the rule, as outlined below, any person who sells restricted securities shall be deemed not to be engaged in a distribution of such securities and therefore not an underwriter thereof. The rule also provides that any person who sells restricted or other securities on behalf of a person in a control relationship with the issuer shall be deemed not to be engaged in a distribution of such securities and therefore not to be an underwriter thereof, if the sale is made in accordance with all the conditions of the rule.

* * *

RELATED RULES AND OTHER AMENDMENTS

RULE 237[b]

The Commission recognized that noncontrolling persons owning restricted securities of issuers which do not satisfy all of the conditions of Rule 144 might have difficulty in selling those securities due to circumstances beyond their control. Accordingly, in

---

to distribute his restricted securities. In addition, as discussed below, the Commission has adopted Rule 237 under Section 3(b) of the Act which permits noncontrolling persons who have owned for five years or more securities of an issuer, which is actively engaged in business as a going concern, to make offerings of such securities in amounts not exceeding the lesser of the gross proceeds from the sale of one percent of the securities of the class outstanding or \$50,000 in aggregate gross proceeds during any twelve-month period by filing a simple notification with the appropriate regional office of the Commission, provided the securities are sold in negotiated rather than trading transactions.

[b] ED.: This exemption is described supra p. 345 in connection with the other "small issue" exemptions.

order to avoid unduly restricting the liquidity of such investments, the Commission has adopted Rule 237 under Section 3(b) of the Act. * * *

*   *   *

USE OF LEGENDS AND STOP-TRANSFER INSTRUCTIONS

Precautions by issuers are essential to assure that a public offering does not result from resale of securities initially purchased in transactions claimed to be exempt under Section 4(2) of the Act. (Attention is directed to Securities Act Release No. 5121 [1970] which discusses the use of legends and stop-transfer instructions as evidence of a non-public offering.) Although such assurance cannot be obtained merely by the use of an appropriate legend on stock certificates or other evidences of ownership, or by appropriate instructions to transfer agents, these devices serve a useful policing function, and the use of such devices is strongly suggested by the Commission and will be considered a factor in determining whether in fact there has been a private placement.

CONTRACTUAL REGISTRATION OR OTHER RIGHTS FOR RESALE OF RESTRICTED SECURITIES

Issuers, brokers, dealers, private placees and other holders of restricted securities are hereby put on notice that the Commission deems it appropriate that such persons when acquiring such securities, should consider contracting for registration or other rights, so that, if they desire to distribute their securities rather than resell in trading transactions pursuant to the rule, they can do so in a manner consistent with the provisions of the Act, i. e., by filing a registration statement or a notification under Regulation A. If the issuer does not file reports pursuant to Sections 13 or 15(d) of the Exchange Act, such persons should consider obtaining an agreement by the issuer to register voluntarily under that Act so that Rule 144 may be available.

*   *   *

Rule 144 is detailed and complex, to the point where it is the subject of an entire book — whose second edition was published in 1977 in 452 pages plus appendixes, only to see the rule amended since![36] As Chairman Casey, under whose chairmanship the rule was adopted, later stated: " * * * the price of clarity and predictability has been great."[37] A Lexis search in late 1978 revealed more than 4000 interpretations.[38] And two highly qualified commentators, concluding in 1977 that the rule "has proven a success," stated:

> In the last five years, the securities bar has been inundated with a veritable flood of interpretive letters which have penetrated virtually every crevice and cavity in the rule in which a latent ambiguity might be lurking. As of this late date, one might say that the unresolved interpretive questions which remain under the rule are generally of mind-boggling insignificance.[39]

So the partial summary here of the rule's six conditions must be taken with more than a grain of salt:[40]

(1) *Current public information:* There must be "adequate public information." This condition is satisfied if the issuer has been a reporting company under the 1934 Act for at least ninety days and has filed all required reports for twelve months (or for whatever shorter period it was required to file reports). If the issuer is not a reporting company, specified portions of the information required by Rule 15c2-11[41] must be publicly available. The rule provides that "the person proposing to sell securities or the broker through whom they are to be sold shall be entitled to rely upon the issuer's statement in the latest * * * report that all required reports have been filed or upon a written statement from the issuer that all such reports have been filed, unless he knows or has reason to believe that the issuer has not complied with such requirements."

(2) *Holding period:* As stated in the Commission's release:

---

[36] D. Goldwasser, A Guide to Rule 144 (2d ed. 1977); see also Lipton, Fogelson, and Warnken, Rule 144 — A Summary Review after Two Years, 29 Bus. Law. 1183 (1974); Sec. Act Rel. 6099, 17 SEC Dock. 1422 (1979) (summary of principal interpretations); Dept. of Commerce and SEC, Rule 144 Sales in the OTC Market: A Preliminary Analysis of the Impact of Rule 144 Sales in the OTC Market (1980); Fogelson, Rule 144 — A Summary Review, 37 Bus. Law. 1519 (1982).

[37] Casey, SEC Rules 144 and 146 Revisited, 43 Brooklyn L. Rev. 571, 587 (1977).

[38] H. Kripke, The SEC and Corporate Disclosure: Regulation in Search of a Purpose (1979) 42-43.

[39] Borden and Fleischman, The Continuing Development of Rule 144: Significant SEC Staff Interpretations, in Practising Law Institute, Eighth Annual Institute on Securities Regulation (1977) c. 4 at 91.

[40] All quotations are from Sec. Act Rel. 5223 (1972).

[41] See p. 333 n. d supra.

Securities sold in reliance upon the rule must have been beneficially owned and fully paid for by the seller for a holding period
of at least two years prior to his sale as specified below. This
condition is designed to assure that the registration provisions of
the Act are not circumvented by persons acting, directly or indirectly, as conduits for an issuer in connection with resales of
restricted securities. In order to accompish this, the rule provides that such persons be subject to the full economic risks of
investment during the holding period. Accordingly, the rule
provides that giving the person from whom the securities were
purchased promissory notes or other obligations to pay the purchase price, or entering into an installment purchase contract
with such person, will not constitute payment of the purchase
price unless certain conditions are met. These conditions are that
the promissory note, obligation or contract must provide for full
recourse against the purchaser of the securities, must be adequately secured by collateral other than the securities purchased
and must have been discharged by payment in full prior to the
sale of the securities.

*   *   *

There have been various holding periods provided for in proposed rules and applied over the years by administrative interpretations. After reexamination and reconsideration, the Commission
believes, in keeping with the purposes of the Act in preventing
the distribution of unregistered securities to the public, that the
holding period should be two years in the context of the other
provisions of the rule. The definitive holding period provided
in the rule may be relied on only in connection with sales made
pursuant to the rule.

For the purpose of the rule, the doctrine of "fungibility" will
not apply. That is, the acquisition during the two-year period of
other securities of the same issuer, whether restricted or non-
restricted, will not start the holding period running anew.[a] How-

---

[a] ED.: Before Rule 144, and perhaps still when one is not relying on the
theoretically nonexclusive rule, one who bought a block of securities from
the issuer could not avoid the status of an "underwriter" by retaining that
block for investment and simultaneously distributing another block of securities acquired from the issuer some time previously. See, e. g., Thomas C.
Bennett, Jr., 43 SEC 75, 81-82 (1966). For this purpose — and the same result
might follow in principle if the one block was sold shortly *before* the other
block was purchased — the two blocks were considered fungible despite the
statutory nonfungibility that we have noticed is unavoidable for other purposes (see p. 123 supra). But there was considerable grey in this area. See
4 Loss 2578. There is an old rule, for example, to the effect that a person
whose business consists chiefly of buying the securities of any one issuer
with the proceeds of the sales of its own securities is to be regarded as

ever, a new provision has been added to the rule dealing with short sales, puts or other options to sell securities. The provision requires that if the securities sold are equity securities there shall be excluded in determining the holding period any period during which the seller had a short position in, or any put or other option to dispose of, any securities of the same class or any securities convertible into securities of such class. If the securities sold are nonconvertible debt securities, there must be excluded any period during which the seller had a short position in, or any put or other option to dispose of, any nonconvertible debt securities of the same issuer.

Certain securities acquired in connection with, or as a result of, ownership or acquisition of other securities, are deemed to have been acquired when such other securities were acquired. These include stock dividends (including stock dividends on securities initially acquired as stock dividends), stock splits, stock acquired in recapitalizations, conversions or contingent issuances of securities. The rule, as adopted, includes provision for contingent issuance of securities in a stock for stock transaction as well as in the stock for assets transaction provided for in the rule as proposed.

The holding periods of pledgor-pledgee-purchaser on default, donor-donee, settlor-trustee-beneficiary, and decedent-estate-legatee may be tacked.[42] But, as stated in the release, "A purchaser in a private placement or series of private placements would not be permitted to tack the holding period of the prior owner."

(3) *Amount of securities sold:* The amount of securities that normally may be sold in reliance on the rule during any three-month period is the greater of 1 percent of the outstanding class or average weekly reported volume during the past four calendar weeks. Here the pledge, gift, trust, and estate situations that enjoy tacking for purposes of computing the holding period are *accumulated* for purposes of applying the amount limitations. As stated in the release, "The rule permits sales within successive 6-month [now 3-month] periods, but no accumulation [is] permitted."

(4) *Manner of sale:* Sales must be made in "brokers' transactions" within §4(4) (as elaborated in the rule) or in transactions directly with a "market maker" as defined in §3(a)(38) of the 1934

---

engaged in the distribution of the securities of that issuer so as to become an underwriter of those securities. Rule 140. On the Code's treatment of the fungibility problem, see 1 Code 89-90.

[42] There is no holding period at all if the estate or selling legatee is not an affiliate of the issuer.

Act (in substance, a dealer who holds himself out as being willing to buy and sell a particular security for his own account on a regular basis).[43] As stated in the release:

> * * * The broker may not solicit buy orders, but he may inquire of other brokers or dealers who have indicated an interest in the securities within the preceding 60 days.
>
> In addition, the rule provides that the broker shall make a reasonable inquiry to ascertain whether the seller is engaged in a distribution. Reasonable inquiry should include, among other matters, inquiry as to the length of time the seller has held the securities; the amount of securities the seller and "chargeable" persons have sold in the past six months; whether he intends to sell securities of the same class through any other means; the number of shares of the class outstanding or the relevant trading volume; and whether the seller has solicited or made any arrangement for the solicitation of buy orders, or has made any payment to any other person in connection with the proposed transaction.

(5) *Notice of offering:* The seller must file a prescribed notice with the Commission and the principal exchange (if any) on which the securities are traded. But there is a *de minimis* exception in terms of 500 shares or $10,000 of aggregate sale price.

(6) Bona fide *intention to sell:* Along the lines of the last sentence of §6(a), the "anti-shelf" provision, the person filing the notice must "have a bona fide intention to sell * * * within a reasonable time * * * ."

In the case of sales by a nonaffiliate who has been a beneficial owner for *three* years, the conditions with respect to the amount, manner of sale, and notice are waived, so that the only conditions aside from holding period are those relating to publicly available information and *bona fide* intention to sell.

As with respect to the impact of Rule 506 on the statutory exemption in §4(2), the question arises here of how much of the pre-144 gloss on §4(1) together with §2(11) survives Rule 144. The Commission in 1979 added Rule 144(j) to codify its repeated statements that the rule is not exclusive.[44] But, as we have seen, the release adopting Rule 144 (1) emphasized the "substantial burden of proof" in establishing exemption apart from the rule, (2) withheld the comfort of "no action" letters, (3) rejected *any* time period as itself establishing an exemption, and (4) announced that "the 'change in circumstances' concept should no longer be

---

[43] This condition does not apply to securities sold for an estate or its beneficiary that is not an affiliate.

[44] Sec. Act Rel. 6032, 16 SEC Dock. 1261, 1264 (1979).

considered as one of the factors in determining whether a person is an underwriter."[45] One's heart grows cold!

The rule *has* elevated a good deal of prior lore into written form and thus has made things more predictable. But aside from the price in complexity, as well as the question we noticed with respect to Rule 506 whether the definitional and implemental rule-making authority in §19(a) justifies so substantive a rule, it is not easy to comprehend how the Commission can abandon the "change of circumstances" concept that is so clearly implicit in 2(11)'s "with a view to * * * distribution." It is never possible to decide questions that lurk in a person's mind, like intention or motive, except by circumstantial evidence. It is not a matter of the Commission's not being absolutely bound by *stare decisis* or of the abandoned concept's being inconsistent with the need for investor protection — the two rationales mentioned in the adopting release. It is a matter simply of how far statutory language may be stretched.

It follows that, if the person who bought from an issuer (or affiliate) has held the securities long enough to make credible his assertion that he did not take them with a view to distribution — so that, as it used to be said, the securities have "come to rest" in his hands — he should not be brought within the "has purchased from" portion of the "underwriter" definition in §2(11), and his later distribution should be exempted under §4(1).

The securities Bar, understandably, seems loathe to do battle on this front. But *private* sales of restricted securities outside Rule 144 are fairly common, and neither the Commission nor the Bar seems to be much troubled by them. Because the SEC staff often has required such resales to meet some of the *Ralston*-type criteria for §4(2) offerings by an issuer, this variety of sale has been dubbed a "Section 4(1-½)" transaction. But the answer, of course, is simply §4(1). Section 4(2) with its reference to "transactions by an issuer" can have no application to a resale unless the securities have not yet "come to rest" in the reseller's hands. In that event, it is appropriate for the sophistication and access criteria to be applied, but only for the purpose of assuring that the issuer's original §4(2) exemption has not been lost.[46]

---

[45] See p. 418 supra.

[46] See The Section "4(1-1/2)" Phenomenon: Private Resales of "Restricted" Securities, A Report to the [ABA] Committee on Federal Regulation of Securities from the Study Group on Section "4(1-1/2)" of the Subcommittee on 1933 Act — General, 34 Bus. Law. 1961 (1979). This report does not consider the "change of circumstances" doctrine. But with respect to private resales it is consistent with the views here expressed. It also thought that

There is a more fundamental objection to the entire "140 series" of rules: They represent an administrative philosophy that will not suffer the smallest mouse to escape the trap. In terms of cost-benefit analysis they ignore the inordinate price in complexity of catching the few smallest mice. Certainly this whole area, with or without the "140 series" of rules (now including Rule 506), is one of the best arguments for a code that will cut through the half-century accumulation of underbrush and emancipate both Government and the citizen from an archaic and tyrannic statutory structure.

5. Nonissuer Transactions under the Code

, The Code's treatment of resales and secondary distributions — which marks a substantial departure from existing law — follows this scheme:

(1) The "control" test is abandoned altogether except for purposes of civil liability and disclosure (as well as block trades to a limited extent).

(2) All distributions (primary as well as secondary) up to $200,-000 are categorically *exempted* from the offering statement requirement as *de minimis* (subject to SEC rulemaking authority only in the $100,000-$200,000 range).[47] And the Commission's general authority to exempt any person, security, or transaction by rule or order from any or all provisions of the Code[48] will enable it to exempt even larger distributions with or without conditions.

(3) We have already noticed the "one-year registrant" concept;[49] the definition of "distribution" as "an offering other than (i) a limited offering or (ii) an offering by means of one or more trading transactions"; and the definition of "limited offering" in terms of 35 buyers and an unlimited number of "institutional investors."[50] This applies equally to *secondary* offerings.

(4) The difficult problem with respect to holding period is simplified by a provision to the effect that there may be free and unlimited transfers within or outside the initial group of buyers as long as there are no more than thirty-five buyer-owners (apart

---

a three-year holding period should be "well-nigh conclusive." Id. at 1975 n. 69.

[47] §512(5).
[48] §303.
[49] See p. 97 supra.
[50] §202(41), supra p. 397.

from institutional investors) at any time for a year in the case of a one-year registrant or three years in other cases.[51] This is a much easier restriction on transferability both to interpret and to police, and after the one-year or three-year period there is no restriction at all. Moreover, the restriction itself, like the initial test of thirty-five, is expressed not in absolute terms but in terms of reasonable belief.[52]

(5) Whereas §4(4) today exempts only unsolicited *brokers'* transactions, and Rule 144 as amended a few years ago extends to transactions directly with marketmakers, the new "trading transaction" includes all routine dealer transactions as a matter of statute.[53]

(6) All secondary *distributions* not exempted by reason of small amount are treated alike. But in the case of a one-year registrant all that is required is the filing by the secondary distributor (not the issuer) of a very short "distribution statement" that contains simply the facts with respect to the secondary distributor and the terms of the distribution, together with a certification that the secondary distributor does not know any additional information that he would have to disclose under the antifraud provisions; and the distribution statement becomes effective on the third day after filing.[54]

(7) With respect to *non*-one-year registrants, the issuer must file a regular offering statement (today's registration statement), together with a company registration statement if it is not already a registrant, on demand. But this requirement is subjected to a number of qualifications designed, on the one hand, to avoid locking in market buyers and, on the other hand, to protect the issuer's legitimate interests:[55]

(a) The issuer has sixteen months to comply with the demand.

(b) The secondary distributor must pay the costs.

(c) The issuer has a right of indemnification against any underwriters with respect to material supplied by them.[56]

(d) The demand provision carries no "piggy-back" rights.

(e) The demand provision does not apply if the secondary distributor executes an express waiver of his rights, is contractually

---

[51] §202(41)(B)(i)-(ii). Moreover, the Commission is given rulemaking authority, which is considerably narrower with respect to one-year registrants. §202(4)(B)(iv)-(v). See p. 397, ¶¶(3)-(4) supra.

[52] §202(41)(B)(i)(I) and (viii).

[53] §202(41)(C).

[54] §510.

[55] §502(b).

[56] §1724(e)(1).

or legally bound by a restriction on transfer that would be violated by the proposed distribution, or acquired the securities with knowledge that his seller executed such a waiver.

(f) The secondary distributor must present a reasonably supported opinion of counsel to the effect that the distribution could not otherwise be legally made.

(g) The issuer has the alternative of offering (or arranging for someone else to offer) to buy out the secondary distributor at a price to be determined by arbitration.

(8) There is a special exemption for block trades in securities of one-year registrants if, among other conditions, (a) the secondary distributor owns or reasonably believes that he owns not more than 15 percent of the voting securities and (b) in the event of 5-15 percent ownership he is not in a control relationship with the issuer and forwards a brief report of beneficial ownership to the SEC by the next business day after the contract to sell.[57]

6.   NONISSUER TRANSACTIONS UNDER THE STATE BLUE SKY LAWS

Once more the lawyer's task is not finished until he examines the law with respect to nonissuer transactions in every state in which an offer is to be made.

Section 305 of the Uniform Securities Act provides:

[*Effective Period, Withdrawal, and Non-Issuer Distributions.*]

(i) Every registration statement is effective for one year from its effective date, or any longer period during which the security is being offered or distributed in a non-exempted transaction by or for the account of the issuer or other person on whose behalf the offering is being made or by any underwriter or broker-dealer who is still offering part of an unsold allotment or subscription taken by him as a participant in the distribution, except during the time a stop order is in effect under section 306. All outstanding securities of the same class as a registered security are considered to be registered for the purpose of any non-issuer transaction (1) so long as the registration statement is effective and (2) between the thirtieth day after the entry of any stop order suspending or revoking the effectiveness of the registration statement under section 306 (if the registration statement did not relate in whole or in part to a non-issuer distribution) and one year from the effective date of the registration statement. A registration statement may not be withdrawn for one year from its

[57] §512(4).

effective date if any securities of the same class are outstanding. A registration statement may be withdrawn otherwise only in the discretion of the [Administrator].

[*Reports.*]

(j) So long as a registration statement is effective, the [Administrator] may by rule or order require the person who filed the registration statement to file reports, not more often than quarterly, to keep reasonably current the information contained in the registration statement and to disclose the progress of the offering.

LOSS, COMMENTARY ON THE UNIFORM SECURITIES ACT (1976) 72-79

Draftsmen's Commentary to §305(i), §305(j) and Related Sections Referring to Non-issuer Distributions

Perhaps the most difficult aspect of the area of securities registration, and often the most ambiguous under the present statutes, is the application of the registration provisions to secondary distributions or other transactions not involving the issuer of the security. In many statutes it is difficult or impossible to say with any certainty when registration is required in such a case; who must or may register; how many units of the security should be registered; who may sell once a registration becomes effective; and, as a result, who is civilly liable. A related question is how long a registration statement remains in effect. These questions are dealt with in §305(i), §305(j) and a number of other provisions throughout the statute.

This is one of the few areas in which this Act breaks new ground, although part of the statutory scheme can be traced to existing patterns. Thus, most of the present statutes provide that a registration remains effective for one year. But the statutes are silent for the most part as to the effect of registration upon trading in outstanding securities of the class. A registration statement usually relates to a fixed number of shares sold at a specified price, or an indeterminate number of shares aggregating no more than a specified dollar amount. The status of resales of the registered securities by their initial purchasers is ambiguous. Quite a few statutes contain exemptions for resales when the security is listed in a recognized manual * * * , when an exemption is specially applied for * * * , or when the outstanding security meets some other test * * * . When registration is clearly required before outstanding securities may be resold, the statutes not infrequently specify a special method of registration * * * . * * *

One solution for many of these problems would be to restrict the registration provisions to primary offerings * * * . * * * The Securities Act of 1933 is similarly restricted to primary offerings, except that registration is required when a person in a control relationship with the issuer makes a secondary distribution through an underwriter. And the Illinois statute is to the same effect. But, aside from the great difficulty in determining when "control" exists * * * , the tradition of registering outstanding securities is too strong in most states to be easily disturbed. The statutory scheme of this Act is essentially in that tradition, but it incorporates a number of devices which are designed to make for less unnecessary red tape and more certainty:

1. Section 301(a) applies broadly to any offer or sale by any person. Thus, it is literally unlawful for Jones to sell five shares of *X* Corp. to Smith unless there is registration or an exemption.

2. The term "non-issuer" is defined in §401(h) to mean simply "not directly or indirectly for the benefit of the issuer." * * *

3. Section 402(b)(1) exempts from registration "any isolated non-issuer transaction, whether effected through a broker-dealer or not." Some sort of "isolated transaction" exemption is universal or virtually so today, and a considerable body of case law has been developed. This exemption takes care of Jones's sale of *X* Corp. to Smith, but obviously does not cover something like the offering of Ford stock by the Ford Foundation. Whether it covers something in between — say, Jones's sale of 500 or 1000 shares of *X* Corp. to several people more or less concurrently — depends on the construction of the word "isolated." In Massachusetts, where the exemption in §3(a) for "Any isolated sale" is qualified, as this type of exemption usually is, by a provision that "this exemption shall not include a sale made in the course of repeated and successive transactions of a like character," the Supreme Judicial Court has stated that "two sales of securities, made one after the other within a period of such reasonable time as to indicate that one general purpose actuates the vendor and that the sales promote the same aim and are not so detached and separated as to form no part of a single plan, would be 'repeated and successive transactions.'" *Kneeland* v. *Emerton*, 280 Mass. 371, 389, 183 N. E. 155, 163 (1932); followed in *Gales* v. *Weldon*, 282 S. W. 2d 522, 526 (Mo. 1955) (five sales in two months) * * * . * * *

4. On the other hand, there are in this statute, as there often are in the existing acts, other exemptions which frequently make

resort to this exemption unnecessary. When the non-issuer distribution is something more than an "isolated transaction," however that phrase is construed, it may still be exempted under §402(a)(8) if the security is listed on a stock exchange, under §402(b)(3) if the distribution is effected through a registered broker-dealer who does not solicit orders or offers to buy, under §402(b)(6) if the transaction is by an executor or one of the other persons there enumerated, under §402(b)(7) if it is a transaction by a *bona fide* pledgee, under §402(b)(8) if the offer is made solely to institutional buyers and broker-dealers, or under §402(b)(9) if it is made to a limited number of persons. * * *

5. These exemptions of general applicability aside, §402(b)(2) affords an exemption which is specifically designed for certain non-issuer distributions. That exemption applies to

> any non-issuer distribution of an outstanding security if (A) a recognized securities manual contains the names of the issuer's officers and directors, a balance sheet of the issuer as of a date within eighteen months, and a profit and loss statement for either the fiscal year preceding that date or the most recent year of operations, or (B) the security has a fixed maturity or a fixed interest or dividend provision and there has been no default during the current fiscal year or within the three preceding fiscal years, or during the existence of the issuer and any predecessors if less than three years, in the payment of principal, interest, or dividends on the security.

*   *   *

Apart from these existing types of exemption, the "manual" exemption for secondary distributions which is incorporated in Clause (A) of §402(b)(2) is of ancient vintage in some states, and it has been spreading in recent years. * * * The exemption in §402(b)(2)(A) is not so restricted as most of the existing manual exemptions. Not infrequently they apply only to sales by registered dealers, or require that the sale be at a price "reasonably related to the current market price," or contain other restrictions. On the other hand, not all of them provide, as this Act does, that the exemption may be denied or revoked by the Administrator. Under §402(c) the Administrator may deny or revoke the exemption for a particular non-issuer distribution if he finds, in the language of §412(b), that denial or revocation "is necessary or appropriate in the public interest or for the protection of investors and consistent with the purposes fairly intended by the policy and provisions of this act." This same authority applies to all of the other exemptions enumerated in paragraph 4 of this commentary except the exemption for listed securities. * * * Moreover, there are other safeguards: The Administrator may define the term "recognized securities manual" by rule under §412(a). The fraud provisions of §§101 and 410(a)(2) apply. Broker-dealers and their agents who effect transactions exempted under §402(b)(2) are subject to the registration provisions of Part II and the Administrator's policing thereunder. And an Administrator who chooses to do so may keep track of the securities sold under this exemption by requiring under §203(a) that registered broker-dealers prepare and keep lists of those securities.

6. If no exemption is available for the non-issuer distribution, the security must be registered. This is when §305(i) becomes significant. Under the first sentence of that section every registration statement is effective for at least one year and for any longer period during which the security is being distributed, except while a stop order is in effect. To this extent, §305(i) is in the existing pattern, except that it is more specific. What is new is the second sentence. Under Clause (1) of that sentence all outstanding securities "of the same class" as the registered security are considered to be registered for the purpose of any non-issuer transaction so long as the registration statement remains effective. When the Administrator has permitted a registration statement to become effective, it seems perfectly safe to permit secondary trading in the same class of security without further ado for a period of at least one year. Compare the present exemptions described in paragraph 5 of this commentary. * * *

Moreover, since §305(j) gives the Administrator power by rule or order to require the registrant to file reports as long as the registration remains effective, current information will always be obtainable in respect of offerings which take more than one year to complete, and hence it seems proper to permit secondary trading for however long a registration remains in effect. Section 305(j) is actually somewhat broader than the average reporting provision in the statutes today, but it is basically consistent with the prevailing pattern. There are also other statutory protections: injunction under §408 against continued or threatened sales which would violate the antifraud provisions of §101; entry of a stop order under §306(a); criminal prosecution under §409 for fraudulent sales; and revocation of the registration of any broker-dealer who engages in such transactions under §304(a)(2)(B).

The net effect of this class registration technique is that whenever a registration statement has become effective, no matter who has filed it or how many units of the class have been registered, all securities *of the same class* can be legally traded by anybody *as if they were registered.* Whether the security being traded is "of the same class" as the registered security notwithstanding changes in its terms during the year presents a question of construction. * * *

7. It remains to explain Clause (2) of the second sentence of §305(i). This is designed to take care of the situation where the Administrator finds it necessary to enter a stop order during the year after the effective date. Obviously, when the registration which thus becomes the subject of a stop order was itself filed in connection with a non-issuer distribution, it would substantially nullify the effect of the stop order to continue to permit a secondary market on the class registration theory of the first sentence of §305(i). But, when the registration statement related entirely to a primary distribution by the issuer, and a substantial part of the offering was made in the state before the stop order was entered, there should be some way to avoid indefinitely locking in those people who were unfortunate enough to be buyers. On the one hand, it would not be in the public interest freely to permit this one set of unfortunates to dump their securities into the hands of another set of unfortunates. But, on the other hand, forever to stop all secondary trading after the entry of a stop order except for "isolated transactions" under §402(b)(1) would come very close to establishing a restraint on alienation, perhaps even with constitutional overtones under the due process clauses. Cf. *People* v. *Pace,* 73 Cal. App. 548, 238 Pac. 1089 (1925) * * * . The proposed solution is Clause (2).

8. The next problem under the class registration theory of the first sentence of §305(i) is raised by the possibility of withdrawal. For the reason stated in paragraph 8 of the official comment, §305(i) provides that a registration statement may not be withdrawn for one year from its effective date if any securities of the same class are outstanding. Under any other circumstances withdrawal is discretionary with the Administrator.

9. If no exemption is available for a non-issuer distribution and *a registration statement for securities of the same class is not effective,* there arises for the first time the necessity of filing a *special* registration statement to permit a non-issuer distribution. As in the case of a distribution for the account of the issuer, registration may be effected here by coordination, or by notification under *either* §302(a)(2) or §302(a)(1),[a] or as a last resort by quali-

---

[a] ED.: Section 302(a)(2) makes the notification procedure available for a

fication. In any event, a registration for a non-issuer distribution, like any other registration, is deemed to register all outstanding securities of the same class, and thus to permit *anybody* to trade for a minimum of one year or however much longer it may take to complete the registered non-issuer distribution. It is thus immaterial, as stated in paragraph 9 of the official comment, whether the registration statement specifically covers 100 shares or 100,000 shares, because the Administrator may not permit the registration statement to become effective unless the statutory standards are satisfied.

*   *   *

10.   There is one final problem with respect to non-issuer distributions, which is dealt with in §305(f). That section provides:

> In the case of a non-issuer distribution, information may not be required under section 304 or 305(j) unless it is known to the person filing the registration statement or to the persons on whose behalf the distribution is to be made, or can be furnished by them without unreasonable effort or expense.

This provision is designed only to take care of the case where the seller simply cannot obtain certified financial statements and other data normally required. It is a problem which is apparently worked out today at a pragmatic level. But it is a problem which cannot be ignored. Cf. *People* v. *Pace,* 73 Cal. App. 548, 238 Pac. 1089 (1925). If a person owns 5 percent of the stock of a company and decides to sell out precisely because he cannot get along with the management, there must be some way out of the impasse which results when the Administrator insists on information that the stockholder simply cannot obtain. The phrase "without unreasonable effort or expense" is borrowed from §10(a)(3) of the Securities Act of 1933, 15 U. S. C. §77j(a)(3), which is derived from a provision that was inserted by amendment in 1934 in order to prevent the blocking in of dealers who might still be subject to the statutory requirement that an up-to-date prospectus be used without being able to supply the required up-to-date information. The SEC has taken the position that, when the issuer itself or an underwriter or dealer who does have access to current information is

---

nonissuer distribution, apart from the quality standards of §302(a)(1), "if (A) any security of the same class has ever been registered under this act or a predecessor act, or (B) the security being registered was originally issued pursuant to an exemption under this act or a predecessor act."

still selling after the time when the prospectus must be brought up to date, the "unreasonable effort or expense" clause was not intended to apply to that expense which is merely incident to the correlation of the new information and the reprinting of the prospectus. * * * Similarly here, in the case of a non-issuer distribution by a person who is in a control relationship with the issuer or otherwise has access to required information, the "unreasonable effort or expense" clause is not meant to apply to that expense which is merely incident to supplying the information required to register. * * *

7.   THE RESALE PROBLEM IN OTHER CONTEXTS UNDER THE 1933 ACT

a.   Registered Securities and "Small Issues"

We have yet to consider the matter of resales by buyers of *registered* securities or of securities received in an intrastate offering, a merger or the like, or an exchange or reorganization.

Why worry about the buyer of a *registered* security who wants to resell? The answer, conceptually, is that, though in form an issuer registers its *securities,* in substance it registers *offerings* — or, more precisely perhaps, securities *with respect to* specified offerings. Surely an issuer that registered its stock and went public ten years ago and then five years ago "went private" by rebuying the public's stock, which thus became treasury shares, could not now go public once more without a fresh registration statement by arguing "once registered always registered." The same result would follow if one bought enough of the registered shares to become a controlling shareholder and now wanted to make a secondary distribution through an underwriter. These would be altogether different offerings from the original distribution, and a fresh registration would be required. By the same token, an institution, let us say, that bought a large (though noncontrolling) block of a registered issue and later wanted to reoffer it publicly, even while the registration statement was fresh so far as its description of the *issuer* was concerned, would be an "underwriter" making a very different *offering* from the *issuer's.*

This is so *conceptually.* And, as we noticed in considering whether a large warrant holder who exercises his warrants and acquires registered shares with a view to their public resale is an "underwriter," the Commission has experimented with various pragmatic solutions.[58] No definitive answer is possible at the moment beyond saying that staying within the recently expanded Rule 144 formula should afford a safe harbor by analogy.

Presumably all this is equally true of resales after public offerings pursuant to Regulation A or one of the other "small issue" exemptions except Rules 504 and 505. Since those two rules are based in part on the private offering rationale, the securities acquired are "deemed to have the same status as if they had been acquired in a transaction pursuant to Section 4(2)," and Rule 144 is expressly made applicable to their resale.[59]

b.   Mergers and Similar Events [Rule 145]

Rule 145 defines "underwriter" for purposes of that rule to include any company (other than the issuer) whose assets or capital structure is affected by a merger or the like, as well as any control affiliate of any such company.[60] But there is an exception if (1) the securities are resold pursuant to all the conditions of Rule 144 except the two-year holding period and the notice requirement or (2) the reseller is not an affiliate of the *issuer* and the issuer has been a reporting company for at least twelve months and has filed all required reports during that period.[61] With this much explicitness, it is not likely that any *non*affiliate of a constituent company would be considered an "underwriter" regardless of how large a block of the issuer's securities he acquired.

c.   Voluntary Exchanges [§3(a)(9)]

If the §3(a)(9) offering, though an exempted exchange, was not a public offering — that is to say, if the §4(2) exemption also fit — the securities are "restricted securities" within Rule 144(a)(3). But the holding period dates back to the date of acquisition of the security surrendered for conversion.[62]

If the §3(a)(9) offering was a *public* offering, presumably the answer — or lack of answer — should be the same in principle as it is with respect to the resale of large blocks of *registered* securities.

[58] See p. 280 supra.
[59] Rules 144(a)(3), 502(d), 504(b)(1); see p. 417 supra.
[60] Rule 145(c).
[61] Rule 145(d).
[62] Rule 144(d)(4)(B).

d. Judicially or Administratively Approved Exchanges [§3(a)(10); 11 U. S. C. §1145]

Here again, the Commission applies the volume formula of Rule 144 by analogy with respect to resales of securities acquired pursuant to the §3(a)(10) exemption, as it used to with respect to the exemptions in Chapters X and XI of the old Bankruptcy Act. The fact is that most *trade* creditors, at least, do take, in all probability, for distribution.

So far as Chapter 11 of the new bankruptcy statute is concerned, the text of an elaborate exemptive provision, with a special definition of "underwriter," has already been set out.[63] Under §1145 (b)(3), in substance, one who does not fall within the *special* definition of "underwriter" in §1145(b)(1) is not a §2(11) underwriter, so that the §4(1) exemption is available with respect to resales of securities of the debtor (or an affiliate participating with it in a joint plan, or a successor to the debtor) received in the reorganization at least principally in exchange for claims against the debtor (or affiliate). In addition, §1145(a)(3) exempts, on conditions that are self-explanatory, an offer or sale of the debtor's (or an affiliate's) portfolio securities apart from a plan.

e. Intrastate Issues [§3(a)(11]

The answer with respect to the resale of securities received in an intrastate offering is mercifully simple. Rule 147(e), as we have seen, provides a nine-month gestation period before the securities can be said to "come to rest" so that they may be sold to non-residents.[64]

f. The Code

With the Code's treatment of resales without regard to the presence of either an "underwriter" or "control," all these pieces fall readily into place. Each proposed resale is judged separately to see whether a "distribution" is involved.[65]

---

[63] See p. 313 supra.
[64] Sec. Act Rel. 5450, 3 SEC Dock. 349, 353 (1974), supra p. 328.
[65] See p. 429 supra.

CHAPTER 6

"CONTROL" CONCEPTS UNDER THE SEC STATUTES

A. THE STATUTORY CONTEXTS

The concept of "control" of a corporation or other entity pervades the statutes administered by the SEC. The context — perhaps also the meaning of the concept — varies from statute to statute and sometimes within a particular statute.

In the Securities Act the concept figures most prominently in determining which secondary distributions must be registered. For purposes of the definition of "underwriter" only, as we have seen, the term "issuer" includes "any person directly or indirectly controlling or controlled by the issuer, or any person under direct or indirect common control with the issuer."[1] There is also a provision — to be examined in the chapter on civil liabilities — to the effect that, when any person is civilly liable under the statute, the same liability extends in general to "Every person who, by or through stock ownership, agency, or otherwise, or who, pursuant to or in connection with an agreement or understanding with one or more other persons by or through stock ownership, agency, or otherwise, controls" the first person.[2] Finally, the registration forms require information with respect to the issuer's "parents," "subsidiaries," "affiliates," and "associates";[3] for this purpose the Commission's rules define an "affiliate" as "a person that directly, or indirectly through one or more intermediaries, controls or is controlled by, or is under common control with, the

---

C. 6A [1] See p. 278 supra.

[2] §15, infra page 1179. There is a similar provision in the Exchange Act except that the reference is merely to "Every person who, directly or indirectly, controls any person liable * * *." §20(a).

[3] See Sec. Act Sch. A(25); §19(a) (consolidated financial statements for issuer and any person in a control relationship).

person specified," and define "parent" and "subsidiary" as controlling and controlled affiliates respectively.[4]

The Trust Indenture Act, in disqualifying a proposed trustee who has any control relationship with an obligor or underwriter, borrows the language used to define "underwriter" in the Securities Act.[5]

The same language appears also in the sections of the Exchange Act that require registration statements for securities to contain specified categories of information with respect to the registrant and any person in a control relationship.[6] The provision in the Advisers Act on disclosure of education refers to "any controlling person."[7] The provisions of the Exchange and Advisers Acts on discipline and qualifications refer repeatedly to any "person associated" with a broker-dealer, exchange member or adviser,[8] a term defined in both Acts to include "any person directly or indirectly controlling or controlled by" the broker-dealer, member, or adviser.[9] And the Exchange Act provisions on registered securities associations and municipal securities are replete with the "person associated" phrase.[10] In addition, the tender offer provision of the Exchange Act directs the Commission to exempt offers that do not have the purpose or effect of "changing or influencing the control of the issuer";[11] the provision on issuers' purchases of their own shares apply equally to purchases by a person with the kind of control relationship described in the Securities Act (or "a person subject to the control of the issuer or any such person");[12] and the Commission has a rule under one of the fraud provisions of the Exchange Act that, in substance, requires any broker or dealer in a control relationship with the issuer of any security purchased or sold to disclose to the customer "the existence of such control."[13]

In neither the Securities Act (as supplemented by the Trust Indenture Act) nor the Exchange Act is "control" defined. In the two essentially regulatory statutes, the Holding Company and Investment Company Acts, the scheme is different. Both statutes refer repeatedly to the control concept, and they contain elaborate

[4] Rule 405; see also Sec. Ex. Act Rule 12b-2.
[5] §310(b)(3); see also §310(b)(7).
[6] §§12(b), 12(g)(1).
[7] §203(c)(1).
[8] Sec. Ex. Act §§15(b)(1), 15(b)(2)(A), 15(b)(4), 15(b)(6), 15(b)(7)(A), 19(d)(1), 19(e)(1), 19(f)(h); Inv. Adv. Act §§203(e), 203(f). See n. 16 infra.
[9] Sec. Ex. Act §§2(a)(18), 2(a)(21); Inv. Adv. Act §202(a)(17).
[10] §§15A, 15B.
[11] §14(d)(8)(C).
[12] §13(e)(2); see also Sec. Ex. Act Rule 10b-18(a)(1), infra p. 1003.
[13] Rule 15cl-5.

definitions, with provision for declaratory orders by the Commission. In both cases the purpose is to establish relationships in which the absence of arm's-length dealing may exist, with opportunity for unfair treatment of investors.

The Holding Company Act does not define "control" as such, but it contains definitions of "holding company," "subsidiary company," and "affiliate" that determine the status of persons under the Act generally.[14] For purposes of the first two definitions, which are correlatives, Congress adopted as a point of departure a rule of thumb based upon 10 percent ownership. In substance, a 10 percent stockholder is presumed to be a holding company unless it proves that it is not, whereas any other company is presumed not to be a holding company unless the Commission establishes that it is. More particularly, any "company which directly or indirectly owns, controls, or holds with power to vote," 10 percent of the outstanding voting securities of a public utility company (that is, an electric or gas company) or of another holding company is itself a holding company unless the Commission, upon application, finds that it

(i) does not, either alone or pursuant to an arrangement or understanding with one or more other persons, directly or indirectly control a public-utility or holding company either through one or more intermediary persons or by any means or device whatsoever, (ii) is not an intermediary company through which such control is exercised, and (iii) does not, directly or indirectly, exercise (either alone or pursuant to an arrangement or understanding with one or more other persons) such a controlling influence over the management or policies of any public-utility or holding company as to make it necessary or appropriate in the public interest or for the protection of investors or consumers that the applicant be subject to the obligations, duties, and liabilities imposed in this title upon holding companies.

On the other hand, regardless of the 10 percent figure, the Commission may declare "any person" to be a holding company upon a determination, after notice and opportunity for hearing, that it exercises such a controlling influence, either alone or with other persons.

The term "affiliate" is defined to include any person that "directly or indirectly owns, controls, or holds with power to vote, 5 per centum or more of the outstanding voting securities" of a specified company; or any company of whose outstanding voting

---

[14] §§2(a)(7), 2(a)(8), 2(a)(11); see also §2(b).

securities that percentage is so owned, controlled, or held by a specified company; or any person or class of persons that the Commission determines, after notice and opportunity for hearing, to stand in such relation to a specified company "that there is liable to be such an absence of arm's-length bargaining in transactions between them as to make it necessary or appropriate in the public interest or for the protection of investors or consumers that such person be subject to the obligations, duties, and liabilities imposed in this title upon affiliates of a company."[15]

The Investment Company Act does define "control" as such. The scheme is roughly similar to that of the Holding Company Act except that Congress chose the figure 25 percent rather than 10 percent:

> "Control" means the power to exercise a controlling influence over the management or policies of a company, unless such power is solely the result of an official position with such company.
>
> Any person who owns beneficially, either directly or through one or more controlled companies, more than 25 per centum of the voting securities of a company shall be presumed to control such company. Any person who does not so own more than 25 per centum of the voting securities of any company shall be presumed not to control such company. A natural person shall be presumed not to be a controlled person within the meaning of this title. Any such presumption may be rebutted by evidence, but except as hereinafter provided, shall continue until a determination to the contrary made by the Commission by order either on its own motion or on application by an interested person. If an application filed hereunder is not granted or denied by the Commission within sixty days after filing thereof, the determination sought by the application shall be deemed to have been temporarily granted pending final determination of the Commission thereon. The Commission, upon its own motion or upon application, may by order revoke or modify any order issued under this paragraph whenever it shall find that the determination embraced in such original order is no longer consistent with the facts.[16]

[15] §2(a)(11). A number of other sections of the Holding Company Act refer to "control" without elaboration or definition, as in the 1933, 1934, and 1939 Acts. For example, §11(b)(1), on geographical integration, requires the Commission to permit a registered holding company to "continue to control" more than one integrated utility system if it makes certain findings. See also §§1(a)(4), 1(b)(3); cf. §§4(a)(6), 10(a)(1)(C), (F).

[16] §2(a)(9). The Commission borrowed the 25 percent test in Rule 19g2-1(b)(2), which has to do with enforcement by exchanges and the NASD of compliance with the statute by members and "persons associated," and borrowed the 10 percent test in Rule 19h-1(f)(2), which has to do with notice

One impact of these determinations of a person's status comes under the provision of the Act that (with certain exceptions) prohibits "any registered investment company and any company or companies controlled by such registered investment company" from acquiring more than specified percentages of the voting stock of any other investment company or any insurance company unless the first company and any companies it controls already own in the aggregate at least 25 percent of the total outstanding voting stock of the company in question.[17] Other impacts come under the sections of the statute concerned with affiliations of directors and transactions of affiliated persons of registered investment companies.[18]

Oddly enough, the Investment Company Act sometimes puts the shoe on the other foot so far as control is concerned. Thus, a person is defined not to be an "investment company" if the Commission upon application declares that it is primarily engaged in a business other than that of investing, owning, or trading in securities "either directly or (A) through majority-owned subsidiaries or (B) through controlled companies conducting similar types of businesses." There it is to the applicant's advantage to prove control in order to escape registration under the statute.[19]

The Investment Advisers Act — which, in addition to the provisions already mentioned,[20] prohibits any transfer of "a controlling block" of a corporate investment adviser's voting securities without the consent of each client[21] — repeats the first sentence of the Investment Company Act's definition of "control," omitting the balance of that definition with its rebuttable presumption.[22]

B. DETERMINANTS OF "CONTROL"

It has been generally recognized, back far further than 1933, that practical control of a corporation does not require ownership of 51 percent of its voting securities — or anything like that

---

by a self-regulatory organization of membership or participation or association notwithstanding a statutory disqualification, finding "important distinctions between the policies underlying the two rules." Sec. Ex. Act Rel. 18,278, 24 SEC Dock. 76, 85 (1981).

[17] §12(d).
[18] §§10, 17(a), 17(d), 17(e).
[19] §3(b)(2).
[20] See notes 7-9 supra.
[21] §§202(a)(1), 205(2).
[22] §202(a)(12).

amount. We have already noticed in the opening chapter the rarity of control by majority ownership so far as the country's largest corporations are concerned, and the frequency of control by management with little or no voting power.[1] In 1912 the Supreme Court said in the Government's suit against the Union Pacific Railroad under the Sherman Act: "It may be true that in small corporations the holding of less than a majority of the stock would not amount to control, but the testimony in this case is ample to show that, distributed as the stock is among many stockholders, a compact, united ownership of 46% is ample to control the operations of the [Southern Pacific Railroad Company]."[2] As Judge Cardozo (as he then was) put it for the New York Court of Appeals in 1918, "A dominating influence may be exerted in other ways than by a vote."[3]

The legislative history demonstrates, consistently with this approach, that Congress took a broad view of control, even in the basic statutes in which it did not define the term. The House

---

C. 6B [1] See pp. 3-5 supra.

[2] United States v. Union Pacific R. R. Co., 226 U. S. 61, 95-96 (1912). In Natural Gas Pipeline Co. v. Slattery, 302 U. S. 300, 307-08 (1937), the Court said, apropos of the control relationship between a gas company and its source of supply as bearing on the fixing of its rates: "We have not said, nor do we perceive any ground for saying, that the Constitution requires such an inquiry to be limited to those cases where common control of the two corporations is secured through ownership of a majority of their voting stock. We are not unaware that, as the statute recognizes, there are other methods of control of a corporation than through such ownership. Common management of corporations through officers or directors, or common ownership of a substantial amount, though less than a majority of their stock, gives such indication of unified control as to call for close scrutiny of a contract between them whenever the reasonableness of its terms is the subject of inquiry." In Denver & Rio Grande Western R. R. Co. v. United States, 387 U. S. 485, 499 (1967), the Court held that acquisition of 20 percent of the stock of Railway Express Agency by The Greyhound Corporation might constitute control.

[3] Globe Woolen Co. v. Utica Gas & Electric Co., 224 N. Y. 483, 489, 121 N. E. 378, 379-80 (1918). In Essex Universal Corp. v. Yates, 305 F. 2d 572, 580 (2d Cir. 1962), which was not an SEC case, Judge Clark (concurring) stated: "Surely in the normal course of events a management which has behind it 28.3 per cent of the stock has working control, absent perhaps a pitched proxy battle which might unseat it." And Judge Lumbard added, speaking only for himself, that in such a case, with a listed company, the person attempting to overcome the presumption of control would have to do more than "raise merely hypothetical possibilities of opposition by the other Republic shareholders to Essex' assumption of management control." Id. at 579. There would have to be a showing that there was "some other organized block of stock of sufficient size to out-vote the block Essex was buying, or else some circumstance making it likely that enough of the holders of the remaining Republic stock would band together to keep Essex from control." Ibid.

committee report stated with reference to the definition of "under-writer" in the Securities Act:

> The concept of control herein involved is not a narrow one, depending upon a mathematical formula of 51 percent of voting power, but is broadly defined to permit the provisions of the act to become effective wherever the fact of control actually exists.[4]

The same committee stated, in speaking of the concept of control as used in the registration and civil liability provisions of the Exchange Act:

> * * * when reference is made to "control," the term is intended to include actual control as well as what has been called legally enforceable control. * * *[5] It was thought undesirable to attempt to define the term. It would be difficult if not impossible to enumerate or to anticipate the many ways in which actual control may be exerted. A few examples of the methods used are stock ownership, lease, contract, and agency. It is well known that actual control sometimes may be exerted through ownership of much less than a majority of the stock of a corporation either by the ownership of such stock alone or through such ownership in combination with other factors.[6]

In the absence of a statutory definition of control in these two Acts, as well as the Trust Indenture Act,[7] the Commission has supplied its own definition by rule. There are rules under the three Acts, as well as the accounting regulation, that define "control" to mean "the possession, direct or indirect, of the power to direct or cause the direction of the management and policies of a person, whether through the ownership of voting securities, by contract, or otherwise."[8] There are also rules under these three Acts, as well as the Investment Company Act, that permit the registrant to disclaim the existence and any admission of control if its existence "is open to reasonable doubt," but in any event

---

[4] H. R. Rep. No. 85, 73d Cong., 1st Sess. (1933) 14.
[5] Citing Handy & Harmon v. Burnet, 284 U. S. 136 (1931).
[6] H. R. Rep. No. 1383, 73d Cong., 2d Sess. (1934) 26.
[7] This does not make the concept of "control" stock unconstitutionally vague for criminal purposes. "The meaning of 'control' under the [1933] act is no different than it is in normal everyday usage." United States v. Re, 336 F. 2d 306, 316 (2d Cir. 1964), *cert. denied,* 379 U. S. 904.
[8] Sec. Act Rule 405; Sec. Ex. Act Rule 12b-2; Trust Ind. Act Rule 0-2; Reg. S-X, Rule 1-02. Although these definitions were adopted for purposes of registration or qualification, they presumably apply by analogy in so far as the term "control" is used in other contexts.

the registrant must state "the material facts pertinent to the possible existence of control."[9]

The Communications Act of 1934 uses the identical control language that is found in the Securities Act definition of the term "underwriter." The Federal Communications Commission is denied jurisdiction over any carrier "engaged in interstate or foreign communication solely through physical connection with the facilities of another carrier not directly or indirectly controlling or controlled by, or under direct or indirect common control with such carrier."[10] There is likewise no statutory definition of "control." In sustaining an order that found that one company controlled another, the Supreme Court set the tone for subsequent discussion of "control" in administrative contexts when it said in the *Rochester Telephone* case:

> The record amply justified the Communications Commission in making such findings. Investing the Commission with the duty of ascertaining "control" of one company by another, Congress did not imply artificial tests of control. This is an issue of fact to be determined by the special circumstances of each case. So long as there is warrant in the record for the judgment of the expert body it must stand. The suggestion that the refusal to regard the New York ownership of only one third of the common stock of the Rochester as conclusive of the former's lack of control of the latter should invalidate the Commission's finding, disregards actualities in such intercorporate relations. Having found that the record permitted the Commission to draw the conclusion that it did, a court travels beyond its province to express concurrence therewith as an original question. "The judicial function is exhausted when there is found to be a rational basis for the conclusions approved by the administrative body." [Citations omitted.][11]

The precedent is a particularly close one so far as the SEC acts are concerned, even to the point that the FCC spoke of "power to control the functions of Rochester,"[12] just as the SEC rule speaks of "power to direct * * * management and policies."

There has been relatively little litigation with respect to control, however, under the 1933, 1934, and 1939 Acts themselves. Most of the SEC control cases that have gone to court have arisen under the Holding Company Act. The Commission has won all

---

[9] Sec. Act Rule 410; Sec. Ex. Act Rule 12b-22; Trust Ind. Act Rule 7a-26; Inv. Co. Act Rule 8b-22.

[10] §2(b), 47 U. S. C. §152(b).

[11] Rochester Telephone Corp. v. United States, 307 U. S. 125, 145-46 (1939).

[12] See 307 U. S. at 145.

of them, although the margin in one case was too close for comfort: The Ninth Circuit first affirmed, by a vote of two to one, the Commission's order denying an application by Pacific Gas & Electric Company to be declared not to be a subsidiary of The North American Company; it then reheard the case *en banc* and affirmed by an evenly divided court; and the Supreme Court divided evenly in turn.[13] In these cases, however, the accent is on "controlling influence," which the Commission and the courts have said means "something less in the form of influence over the management or policies of a company than 'control' of a company." Whereas the existence of "control" constitutes an absolute bar under §2(a)(7) to the entry of an order declaring a company not to be a holding company, the existence of a "controlling influence" precludes such an order only under specified "public interest" standards.

The courts have held under the Holding Company Act that "latent power" is sufficient to constitute a "controlling influence";[14] that a "controlling influence may be effective without accomplishing its purpose fully";[15] and that the concept means essentially "susceptibility to domination."[16] As Justice Murphy stated for the Supreme Court in sustaining the constitutionality of the geo-

---

[13] Pacific Gas & Electric Co., 10 SEC 39 (1941), *aff'd sub nom.* Pacific Gas & Electric Co. v. SEC, 127 F. 2d 378 (9th Cir. 1942), *aff'd per curiam on rehearing, with a dissenting opinion,* 139 F. 2d 298 (9th Cir. 1943), *aff'd per curiam,* 324 U. S. 826 (1945).

[14] Koppers United Co. v. SEC, 138 F. 2d 577, 580-81 (D. C. Cir. 1943), and cases cited.

[15] Detroit Edison Co. v. SEC, 119 F. 2d 730, 738-39 (6th Cir. 1941), *cert. denied,* 314 U. S. 618. "This phrase should be construed in the light of the purpose of the Act of which it is a part, and when understood in this setting and in the light of its ordinary signification, it means the act or process, or power of producing an effect which may be without apparent force or direct authority and is effective in checking or preventing action, or exercising restraint or preventing free action. The phrase as here used, does not necessarily mean that those exercising controlling influence must be able to carry their point." Ibid.

[16] See cases cited in American Gas & Electric Co. v. SEC, 134 F. 2d 633, 643 n. 22 (D. C. Cir. 1943), *cert. denied,* 319 U. S. 763. "Under some circumstances 'controlling influence may spring as readily from advice constantly sought as from command arbitrarily imposed.'" Id. at 642, citing Manchester Gas Co., 7 SEC 57, 62 (1940). Judge Stephens insisted in his dissenting opinion, on the other hand, that "control" and "controlling influence" are "two different types of presently effective control" — the first referring to control through "structural means" such as stock ownership, voting trusts, or interlocking officers or directors or the like, and the second referring to "such control as might result from the command of one mind over another, or from station or prestige, or from habituation to the policies of another." 134 F. 2d at 648-49.

graphical integration requirement in §11(b)(1): "Historical ties and associations, combined with strategic holdings of stock, can on occasion serve as a potent substitute for the more obvious modes of control. [Citations omitted.] Domination may spring as readily from subtle or unexercised power as from arbitrary imposition of command."[17] It has also been held by the Commission that the presumption of control cannot be rebutted merely by asserting the existence of control in others, since the "potentiality of exercising a controlling influence in the determination of the course of action of a company may exist in more than one person at the same time or from time to time.[18]

Yet, once it is admitted that control does not require ownership of a majority of the voting stock — and that, like "controlling influence," it may take many different forms[19] — many of the factors that determine the existence of a "controlling influence" apply equally to the determination whether there is "control." Just as the cases under the Holding Company Act emphasize "latent power," the Commission's rules under the 1933, 1934, and 1939 Acts speak of the "power to direct * * * management." Control, the Commission has held under the Securities Act, "is not synonymous with direct operation of an enterprise"; it "may be inferred from the conduct of the parties."[20] As the Commission

---

[17] North American Co. v. SEC, 327 U. S. 686, 693 (1946).

[18] M. A. Hanna Co., 10 SEC 581, 589 (1941) (Inv. Co. Act); see also Investors Mutual, Inc., 42 SEC 1071, 1086 (1966), *aff'd sub nom.* Phillips v. SEC, 388 F. 2d 964 (2d Cir. 1968) (control by each of two hostile groups); DeMarco v. Edens, CCH Fed. Sec. L. Rep. ¶91,856 at 95,935 (S. D. N. Y. 1966), *aff'd,* 390 F. 2d 836 (2d Cir. 1968) (vice-president of broker-dealer corporation, who *inter alia* had loaned large sums to president, was himself a controlling person despite president's being sole stockholder); United States v. Corr, 543 F. 2d 1042, 1050 (2d Cir. 1976).

[19] American Gas & Electric Co. v. SEC, 134 F. 2d 633, 641 n. 14 (D. C. Cir. 1943), *cert. denied,* 319 U. S. 763, and cases cited. A brokerage firm has been held civilly liable for a wire correspondent's violations of various provisions of the Exchange Act on the theory that it controlled the correspondent, even though the court expressly found no agency relationship. Hawkins v. Merrill Lynch, Pierce, Fenner & Beane, 85 F. Supp. 104, 123 (W. D. Ark. 1949). See also DeMarco v. Edens, CCH Fed. Sec. L. Rep. ¶91,856 at 95,934 (S. D. N. Y. 1966), *aff'd,* 390 F. 2d 836 (2d Cir. 1968) (court held that issuer controlled best-efforts underwriter because it had selected the underwriter, fixed the offering price and drafted the offering circular).

[20] Reiter-Foster Oil Corp., 6 SEC 1028, 1044 (1940). It does not follow, regardless of the literal definition of "parent" and its cross-reference to controlling persons, that the officers and directors as a group must always be listed as a "parent" in the registration statements and annual reports. For otherwise *every* corporation would have a "parent" in the form of its board and management. When a group of individuals or a family or several families control, the question becomes closer. An individual can also be a *controlled*

put it in its Report on Investment Trusts, "the word 'control' does
not mean day-to-day management of the portfolio company, but
means rather that major decisions are probably seldom taken without consulting the investment company or its sponsors, or that the
control is at least potential and equivalent at all times to unusual
influence."[21] Again, "past history" has been emphasized not only
as evidence of "controlling influence,"[22] but also as evidence of
"control" itself. One of the leading Commission decisions on
"control" is the *Morgan* case under the Trust Indenture Act,
where the then J. P. Morgan & Co. Incorporated and Morgan
Stanley & Co. Incorporated were held to be under common control
so as to prevent the former, under §310(b)(3), from acting as indenture trustee when the latter acted as underwriter.[23] The Commission emphasized such factors as the origin and sponsorship of
Morgan Stanley by J. P. Morgan & Co., the common Morgan name,

person. See SEC v. North American Research & Development Corp., 424 F. 2d
63, 67, 72 (2d Cir. 1970), where an individual was held to be an "issuer" under
§2(11) because of his control of a woman who in turn controlled the company.

[21] SEC, Report on the Study of Investment Trusts and Investment Companies, Part 4, Control and Influence over Industry and Economic Significance
of Investment Companies. H. R. Doc. No. 246, 77th Cong., 1st Sess. (1941) 2,
quoted in Chicago Corp., 28 SEC 463, 468 (1948). In a very different context,
cf. Communist Party of the U. S. A. v. Subversive Activities Control Board,
367 U. S. 1, 36-38 (1961):

* * * Under §3(3) of the Act an organization cannot be found to
be a Communist organization unless it is "substantially directed, dominated, or controlled by the foreign government or foreign organization
controlling the world Communist movement . . . ." * * *
We agree that substantial direction, domination, or control of
one entity by another may exist without the latter's having power, in
the event of noncompliance, effectively to enforce obedience to its
will. * * *
* * * A foreign government "dominates" or "controls" the "direction" of the world Communist movement through very different means
and in very different ways than one organization "dominates" or "controls" another, or than an individual "dominates" or "controls" an
organization. These differences do not deprive the concepts "domination" and "control" of ample meaning. Throughout various manifestations these concepts denote a relationship in which one entity so much
holds ascendancy over another that it is predictably certain that the
latter will comply with the directions expressed by the former solely by
virtue of that relationship, and without reference to the nature and
content of the directions. * * *

[22] American Gas & Electric Co. v. SEC, 134 F. 2d 633, 636 n. 8 (D. C. Cir.
1943), *cert. denied,* 319 U. S. 763, and cases cited; Chicago Corp., 28 SEC 463
(1948).

[23] J. P. Morgan & Co., 10 SEC 119 (1941). This case followed the Commission's order under the Holding Company Act, Dayton Power & Light
Co., 8 SEC 950 (1941), which was affirmed in Morgan Stanley & Co. v. SEC,

the business relationships between the two firms,[24] their retaining of the same counsel,[25] and the family relations such as husband-wife and father-son among the several family groups that in the aggregate controlled both firms.

Certainly the additional factors that the Commission considered in its 1948 decision in the *Chicago Corporation case* under the Investment Company Act[26] are equally relevant in determining the existence of *A*'s "control" over *B* under those acts that do not define the term. There the Commission emphasized the amount of stock held;[27] the number of *A*'s representatives on *B*'s board of di-

---

126 F. 2d 325 (2d Cir. 1942). The *Dayton* case involved the Commission's former Rule U-12F-2, which, in general, prohibited the payment of any underwriters' fees to any affiliate of the issuer, or to any person found to stand in such relation to the issuer "that there is liable to be or to have been an absence of arm's-length bargaining with respect to the transaction," unless the underwriter had been awarded the securities as the most favorable bidder in open competition. The Commission had applied this rule in denying an underwriting fee to Morgan Stanley in connection with an offering of securities by Dayton Power & Light Company. The Commission's order, affirmed by the court, was based on the following four steps: (1) Dayton was wholly owned by Columbia Gas & Electric Corporation. (2) Columbia was controlled by United Corporation, which owned 19.6 percent of its stock. (3) United had been organized in 1929 by J. P. Morgan & Co. and another house, which had chosen the man who was still president; the court said that this was the most tenuous step but held that there was substantial evidence to support the Commission's conclusion. (4) Morgan Stanley had been created by J. P. Morgan & Co., whose partners still held 45 percent of its preferred stock. This stock was disposed of to members of their families between the date of the Commission's opinion in the *Dayton* case and the date of its opinion in the proceeding under the Trust Indenture Act.

24 See also United States v. E. I. du Pont de Nemours & Co., 366 U. S. 316, 332 (1961).

25 This factor did not impress Judge Stephens, who said in his dissenting opinion in American Gas & Electric Co. v. SEC, 134 F. 2d 633, 654 (D. C. Cir. 1943), *cert. denied,* 319 U. S. 763: "The existence of a common law firm * * * of itself proves nothing."

26 28 SEC 463 (1948).

27 The Commission has elsewhere expressed doubt that "a voting trust (except possibly a voting trust established solely for the purpose of liquidation) can ever operate effectively to insulate the control which ownership of a block of stock carries." H. M. Byllesby & Co., 6 SEC 639, 654 (1940) (Holding Co. Act). Certainly control is not affected when the voting trustees are not completely independent of the depositors. Ibid. When they *are* independent of or perhaps even hostile to the beneficial owners and the termination of the trust is not imminent, the beneficial owners may indeed be insulated from control. And stock in a voting trust, or securities held otherwise in a representative capacity, might be considered along with other factors in determining whether the voting trustees or other representatives are themselves in control. The question is inevitably one of fact in each case. For example, the SEC has recognized that a stockholder that has given a proxy that is irrevocable until a specified event not within the stockholder's control (for example, the exhaustion of coal mines) is no longer in control. Clearfield

rectors; *A*'s strategic position through the number of representatives on the executive committee;[28] *A*'s demonstrated influence;[29] *A*'s position as banker of the controlled company when that is the case; the relative size and prestige of *A* and *B*; *A*'s veto power over mergers or consolidations through ownership of preferred stock; and *A*'s power to "break quorum" by abstaining from attending the stockholder's meeting or giving a proxy. Still another factor that may evidence control is a strong position as creditor.[30]

A person's clear ability to control the proxy machinery of a corporation when the stockholders are widely scattered is strong evidence of control.[31] At the same time, a determination of control by no means requires a showing that the person in question could win a proxy fight against the management. Both court and Commission have rejected any such "blood and thunder" concept of control. As long as the putatively controlling person and the management of the putatively controlled company are friendly and cooperative, there is no point in speculating on the results of a proxy fight.[32]

Bituminous Coal Corp., 1 SEC 374 (1936); cf. Boise Gas Light & Coke Co., 2 SEC 269 (1937) (when preferred stock has elected a majority of the board for ten years because of failure of earnings, and imminent reorganization will leave 100 percent common stockholder with only 5 percent of the common, that stockholder no longer controls).

[28] Appointment or domination of the officers or members of the executive committee of the board is strong evidence of control, especially when the board seldom meets. Resources Corp. Int'l, 7 SEC 689, 716-18 (1940).

[29] Cf. SEC v. Franklin Atlas Corp., 154 F. Supp. 395 (S. D. N. Y. 1957) (manager of real estate venture who was not director, officer, or stockholder was found to be in "actual control" for purposes of Sec. Act §2(11)). Absence of a stock interest does not preclude a control finding. M. J. Merritt & Co., 42 SEC 1021, 1030-31 (1966), *aff'd per curiam* sub nom. Vickers v. SEC, 383 F. 2d 343 (2d Cir. 1967), and sub nom. Walker v. SEC, 383 F. 2d 344 (2d Cir. 1967) (partner of firm whose broker-dealer registration had been revoked had in effect continued its business through a corporate successor with a brother in the management).

[30] See In re Falstaff Brewing Corp. Antitrust Litigation, 441 F. Supp. 62, 68 (E. D. Mo. 1977) (Sec. Act §20(a)); Touche, Niven, Bailey & Smart, 37 SEC 629, 662-67 (1957) (Reg. S-X, control flowing from *former* creditor position). See generally Enstam and Kamen, Control and the Institutional Investor, 23 Bus. Law. 289, 319-25 (1968); Bartlett and Lapatin, The Status of a Creditor As a "Controlling Person," 28 Merc. L. Rev. 639 (1977).

[31] Chicago Corp., 28 SEC 463, 476 (1948); Thompson Ross Securities Co., 6 SEC 1111, 1120-21 (1940) (Sec. Act); Moulton v. Field, 179 Fed. 673, 675 (7th Cir. 1910), *cert. denied* sub nom. Gray v. Field, 219 U. S. 586; Berle, "Control" in Corporate Law, 58 Colum. L. Rev. 1212, 1213 (1958). Everything else being equal, the amount of stock required to give a particular person control decreases as the number of other holders increases and as the amount of stock usually represented at the annual meetings decreases.

[32] American Gas & Electric Co. v. SEC, 134 F. 2d 633, 639 (D. C. Cir. 1943), *cert. denied*, 319 U. S. 763; Chicago Corp., 28 SEC 463, 474-75 (1948).

It follows that control may rest with a *group* of persons, such as the members of the corporation's management (both directors and officers) and their families, or the members of one or more families not directly in the management, or a number of business associates. As we have noticed with reference to the Securities Act, the House report itself, by way of explaining the "control" clause in the definition of "underwriter," observed that "All the outstanding stock of a particular corporation may be owned by one individual or a select group of individuals."[33] This approach has been taken in a number of cases.[34] And it was the Commission's theme, of course, in the *Morgan* case under the Trust Indenture Act — the theme of common control by a number of family groups united by social and business connections.[35] It does not follow, however, that one member of such a group controls in all contexts. For example, whether a secondary distribution by one member requires registration under the Securities Act raises essentially a question of fact in each case whether that person has enough influence with the group to be able to obtain the issuer's signature on a registration statement. Hence it is for the jury when a jury sits.

The question has been much mooted whether a person's status as an officer or director in itself makes him a controlling person for purposes, for example, of registration under the Securities Act or disclosure by a broker-dealer of a control relationship with the issuer under the Commission's Exchange Act fraud rules. The Investment Company Act, as we have seen, specifically negatives control when the "power to exercise a controlling influence * * * is solely the result of an official position."[36] But even there the Commission held that an individual was a controlling person when his being president was the *result* rather than the *source* of his power; in that case the president owned less than 3 percent of

[33] H. R. Rep. No. 85, 73d Cong., 1st Sess. (1933) 13-14, supra p. 279; see also Temporary National Economic Committee, Investigation of Concentration of Economic Power, Monog. No. 29, Distribution of Ownership in the 200 Largest Nonfinancial Corporations (1940) 101.

[34] Landay v. United States, 108 F. 2d 698, 704 (6th Cir. 1939), *cert. denied*, 309 U. S. 681 ("appellants by voting their shares of stock in a block completely dominated the corporation" and hence were properly convicted under Sec. Act §5); SEC v. Micro-Moisture Controls, Inc., 148 F. Supp. 558 (S. D. N. Y. 1957) (preliminary injunction), *reargument denied*, CCH Fed. Sec. L. Rep. ¶90,805 (S. D. N. Y. 1957), *final injunction*, 167 F. Supp. 716 (S. D. N. Y. 1958), *aff'd sub nom.* SEC v. Culpepper, 270 F. 2d 241 (2d Cir. 1959) (a broker-dealer who had bought shares with a view to distribution from two persons owning only 1½ percent of the stock was an "underwriter" because those two were part of a larger controlling group).

[35] J. P. Morgan & Co., 10 SEC 119 (1941).

[36] §2(a)(9), supra p. 444.

the company's voting stock, but he had the confidence of four family groups that together accounted for over 31 percent.[37] Accordingly, although a person's being an officer or director does not create any *presumption* of control, it is a sort of red light. It may take only one or two questions to bring out that a particular officer has no substantial influence, or that a particular director represents a minority interest (perhaps as the result of cumulative voting) that is out of sympathy with the controlling block. On the other hand, the answer to the first few questions may demonstrate the need for a fairly extensive inquiry into the entire relationship of the particular officer or director to the rest of the managing group.[38]

There is also food for thought here so far as estate planners are concerned: Does control cease with death? If control resulted solely from stock ownership, presumably it passes to the estate. Otherwise, presumably it does not. On the other hand, when an executor or administrator is an officer or director or otherwise a controlling person, the estate may well be under *common* control. Or a bank might be an executor of several estates or a trustee under a number of testamentary (or, for that matter, *inter vivos*) trusts that in the aggregate carry enough voting power to constitute control. As a writer with a literary bent put it in another connection, "some holders, it seems, are born to control, some achieve control, and some have control thrust upon them."[39]

In sum, the available authority seems to impel the conclusion that the difference between "control" and "controlling influence" is one of degree. This is so much so that it is the Commission's policy not to permit its lawyers to express any views as to the existence or nonexistence of control except in the clearest cases. Once the meaning of "control" in a particular statutory context is understood, the parties themselves and their attorneys are in a much

[37] Transit Investment Corp., 23 SEC 415 (1946).

[38] Obviously the *resignation* of a substantial stockholder as an officer or director cannot be conclusive that he no longer controls, since it may have had nothing to do with a disagreement on managerial policy.

[39] Note, Rule 144: SEC Regulation of Dispositions of Securities by Controlling Persons and Private Places, 25 Vand. L. Rev. 845, 857 (1972). On these estate complications, see Rifkind, Securities Problems of the "Locked-in" Estate, 25 Bus. Law. 169 (1969). Cf. Barclays Bank, Ltd. v. Inland Revenue Commissioners, [1960] 3 W. L. R. 280 (H. L.), noted in Pennington, Control of a Company, 104 Sol. J. 1088 (1960) (testator who died owning beneficially 1100 shares out of a total of 8350, and holding 3650 other shares with three other persons as trustees under a trust created by him nineteen years earlier for his wife and children, *held* to have "the control of the company" for estate tax purposes, so that the 1100 shares should be valued by apportioning the value of the company's assets rather than on the basis of market).

better position to determine whether or not control exists than any outside counsel.[40]

C. THE CODE

The Code sweeps this Augean stable reasonably clean:

(1) It abandons "control" as a criterion for determining which distributions must be the subject of an offering statement (the Code's successor to today's 1933 Act registration statement).

(2) It contains a single Code-wide definition of "control" for disclosure and civil liability purposes, in terms of "controlling influence."

(3) That definition adapts the 25 percent formula of the Investment Company Act as a rebuttable presumption one way or the other.

(4) In addition to retaining the declaratory order procedure now in the Investment Company Act, which is obligatory on the Commission, the Code gives the Commission discretion to entertain applications for declaratory orders generally.

FEDERAL SECURITIES CODE §202(29)

(29) CONTROL —

(A) *General.* — "Control" means the power, directly or indirectly, to exercise a controlling influence over the management or policies of a company or the activities of a natural person (either alone or pursuant to an arrangement or understanding with one or more other persons), whether through the ownership of voting securities, through one or more intermediary persons, by contract, or otherwise.

(B) *Presumptions.* — (i) A person who (either alone or pursuant to an arrangement or understanding with one or more other persons) owns or has the power to vote more than 25 percent of the outstanding voting securities of a company (or more than 25 percent of total equity if the company has no voting securities) is presumed to control.

---

[40] For a thorough analysis and collection of authorities, see 1 T. Frankel, The Regulation of Money Managers: The Investment Company Act and the Investment Advisers Act (1978) 489-529.

(ii) Any other person is presumed not to control by virtue solely of his ownership or power to vote.

(iii) For purposes of part XIV, a natural person is presumed not to be controlled.

(iv) Any such presumption may be rebutted by evidence.

(C) *Declaratory orders.* — On application by an investment company or a person with an interest in an investment company the Commission shall, and on its own motion for any purpose under this Code the Commission may, declare by order whether or not control exists. A court of competent jurisdiction need not await an application or order under this subsection.

CHAPTER 7

REGISTRATION AND POSTREGISTRATION PROVISIONS OF THE 1934 ACT

This chapter considers those provisions of the 1934 Act — relating essentially to continuing disclosure by the issuer — that supplement the 1933 Act. Under §12 the issuer must register every nonexempt security that (1) is listed on an exchange or (2), since a 1964 amendment, is an equity security held of record by at least 500 persons if the issuer has total assets exceeding $3 million[1] (and if it is engaged in interstate commerce or in a business affecting interstate commerce, or any of its securities are traded by use of the mails or any means of interstate commerce).

Unlike the 1933 Act, whose disclosure scheme is transaction-oriented and hence episodic, registration under the 1934 Act is designed to afford more or less continuous disclosure. This it does in four ways (which in some respects go beyond disclosure into substantive regulation): (1) Periodic reports must be filed under §13 (and in some cases under §15(d)). (2) Under §14(a) the solicitation of proxies with respect to registered securities must comply with the Commission's rules. (3) The Williams Act provisions, §§13(d)-(e) and 14(d)-(f), which were added in 1968 and amended in 1970, regulate tender offers and require certain beneficial ownership reports. (4) Section 16 imposes certain controls over insider-trading practices. These will be considered in the order indicated.

A. REGISTRATION

1. Exchange-Listed Securities

Section 12(a) makes it unlawful for an exchange member or a broker or dealer to effect a transaction in any nonexempt security on a national securities exchange "unless a registration is effective as to such security for such exchange." The Exchange Act is not tied in with the Securities Act as is the Trust Indenture Act. Although the Commission has taken heroic steps in recent years to integrate the disclosure requirement of the 1933 and 1934 Acts,[1] registration under the one statute does not excuse registration under the other when it is otherwise required. If a particular security is offered to the public and forthwith listed on an exchange, it must be registered under both Acts. Indeed, a debt security offered to the public by a public utility holding company or a subsidiary and listed on an exchange must comply with four separate SEC statutes — the Securities Act, the Exchange Act, the Trust Indenture Act, and the Holding Company Act — except insofar as an exemption may be available under one or more of the statutes. By the same token, Exchange Act registration is required when the issuer desires to list on an exchange, even though the security has never been registered under the Securities Act because the security was publicly held before 1933 or was issued under a Securities Act exemption. Registration is effected by the issuer's filing an application *with the exchange,* duplicate originals being filed with the Commission.[2] The Exchange Act, unlike the Securities Act, contains no signature requirement, but in 1980 the Commission required the basic *annual report* form, Form 10-K, to include the signatures not only of the issuer's principal executive, financial, and accounting officers but also of a majority of the directors. This requirement, taken over from §6(a) of the Securities Act, was incidental to the Commission's integration movement: "The Commission believes that just as its rules and the administrative focus of the Division of Corporation Finance are being realigned to reflect the shift in emphasis toward relying on periodic disclosure under the Exchange Act, so too the attention of the private sector, including management, directors, accountants, and attorneys, must also be refocused towards Exchange Act filings if a sufficient degree of discipline is to be instilled in the system to make it work."[3]

Amendments may be filed either before or after registration becomes effective,[4] which is thirty days after the Commission's receipt of certification by the exchange authorities that the security

---

C. 7   [1] The statutory figure in §12(g)(1) is $1 million, but it has been increased by rule to $3 million. See p. 465 infra.

C. 7A   [1] See pp. 145-53 supra.
    [2] §12(b).
    [3] Sec. Act Rel. 6231, 20 SEC Dock. 1059, 1067 (1980).
    [4] Rule 12b-15.

has been approved for listing and registration "or within such shorter period of time as the Commission may determine."[5] There is no statutory standard governing acceleration, and in practice most applications are accelerated under the following statement of policy:

> The Commission will consider requests for acceleration of the effective date of registration of securities in cases where, in its opinion, adequate and reasonably current information concerning the issuer has previously been filed and made available to the general public under any Act administered by the Commission. However, in passing upon requests for acceleration the Commission will also consider the following additional factors:
>
> (a) The adequacy of disclosure in the application for registration and its general compliance with the requirements of the Act and the rules and regulations thereunder;
>
> (b) The distribution of the securities being registered or the distribution of other securities related thereto;
>
> (c) The operation of the exchange's trading mechanism in relation to the date on which effective registration is requested;
>
> (d) Compliance with the registration requirements of the Securities Act of 1933;
>
> (e) Any other factors pertinent to the particular case, such as required stockholder approval; qualification under applicable State "Blue-sky" laws; authorization by appropriate State and Federal Agencies having jurisdiction; Court proceedings; and similar matters connected with the securities being registered or with other securities related thereto.
>
> Requests for acceleration of the effective date of registration of securities may be made either by the registrant or its authorized representatives or by the exchange on which registration is sought. Every request should be in writing and should state the grounds upon which it is based and the approximate date on which effective registration is desired.
>
> While the Commission will cooperate with registrants and with exchanges by acting upon requests for acceleration as promptly as possible, consistent with the public interest and the protection of investors, applications for registration should be filed early enough to allow at least ten days for examination of the application and consideration of the request for acceleration by the Commission.[6]

Until 1954 the procedure was to register, as under the 1933 Act, only as many units of a class of securities as had been issued (including treasury shares) rather than the entire class. In that year the Commission adopted a system of registration of entire *classes*

---

[5] §12(d), 1st sentence, as implemented by Reg. 12D1.
[6] Sec. Ex. Act Rel. 3985 (1941). The penultimate paragraph of this quotation is codified in Rule 12d1-2.

of securities.[7] All applications for registration, past and future, are now "deemed to apply for registration of the entire class," and registration once effective automatically extends, without further application or exchange certification or Commission order, to additional securities *of the same class* "upon issuance." This is so even when the additional securities have not been authorized until after the effective registration of the class pursuant to the original application.[8] In view of the annual and current reporting requirements of §13, the Commission concluded that the filing of a new application was not necessary in the interest of investors except in the case of a new class (or a new series with different terms). But, since the Commission's new procedure affects only the *statutory* requirement of *registration,* the exchanges as part of their own *listing* procedures still require issuers to notify them how many securities of the class or series have actually been issued.

As in the case of the Securities Act, the Commission has adopted a number of specialized forms and a residual form, Form 10, which corresponds to the Securities Act's Form S-1. And we have already noticed the adoption of Regulation S-K in 1977, together with its expansion in 1982, as a repository for the types of information required in filings under both statutes.[9]

2.   OVER-THE-COUNTER SECURITIES

a.   The Statutory Scheme

For thirty years after enactment of the Exchange Act there was a double standard of investor protection — a standard that resulted, more by accident than by design, from the piecemeal adoption of the SEC statutes but that nevertheless glowed with an incandescent illogic: If an investor happened to be a stockholder of a listed company, or a public utility holding company or a subsidiary of such a company, or an investment company, he had the protections afforded by the reporting requirements as well as (with some exceptions) the proxy rules and the insider-trading provisions. If, on the other hand, he happened to hold a security that did not fall within any of these categories but that had been offered to the public and registered under the 1933 Act since 1936, he was likely to have current information by virtue of §15(d) of

---

[7] Sec. Ex. Act Rel. 4990 (1954).
[8] Rule 12d1-1.
[9] See p. 153 supra.

the Exchange Act, but that was all; §15(d), enacted that year, subjected certain *Securities* Act registrants to the reporting requirement of the Exchange Act but not to the proxy or insider-trading provisions.[10] The third investor, who held an unlisted security in an industrial corporation that had not done any public financing since 1936, was still further from the fire; so far as he was concerned, the whole series of SEC statutes might just as well not have existed except for a few fraud provisions, no matter how large the corporation or how widely distributed its securities.

The limitation of §§12, 13, 14, and 16 of the original Exchange Act to listed securities was not due to any conviction on the part of Congress that similar safeguards were not equally essential with respect to securities traded in the over-the-counter market. The several exchanges were concrete, organized institutions that one could see and touch, and it was a relatively simple matter to condition the use of those markets upon compliance with the registration and other provisions. By contrast, the over-the-counter market was an amorphous thing that did not present a ready platform on which to base similar provisions. As the Commission had occasion to observe in 1936: "Prior to the enactment of the statute, the over-the-counter market was one of the enigmas of our financial system. Authentic data were lacking with respect to its nature, its function, its size, and the technique of its operation."[11] It was not surprising, therefore, that, after setting up a fairly detailed system of regulation of the organized exchanges, Congress threw the entire problem of the over-the-counter market into the lap of the newly created Commission. Section 15 of the original Exchange Act simply made it unlawful, in contravention of whatever rules the Commission might prescribe as necessary or appropriate in the public interest and "to insure to investors protection comparable to that provided by and under authority of this title in the case of national securities exchanges," for any broker or dealer to use the mails or interstate facilities for the purpose of making a market otherwise than on an exchange. The Commission was authorized under the original §15 to provide, among other things, for registration of brokers or dealers making such a market, as well as registration of the *securities* there traded.[12]

[10] See p. 490 infra.

[11] SEC, Report on the Feasibility and Advisability of the Complete Segregation of the Functions of Dealer and Broker (1936) 78.

[12] 48 Stat. 895-96 (1934). "This power is vitally necessary to forestall widespread evasion of stock exchange regulation by the withdrawal of securities from listing on exchanges, and by transferring trading therein to 'over-the-counter' markets where manipulative evils could continue to flourish, un-

Under this section the Commission adopted rules requiring the registration of over-the-counter brokers and dealers, as well as a few rudimentary antifraud rules. But in 1936 the Commission in a report to Congress referred to the impracticability of enforcing a registration requirement against the *issuers* of securities by prohibiting *brokers and dealers* from trading in securities not registered.[13] One of the solutions it suggested was requiring future registrants of substantial size under the Securities Act to undertake to make periodic reports thereafter. Accordingly, Congress added §15(d) (since amended), on reports by certain Securities Act registrants, and further amended §15 by codifying the Commission's rules on *broker-dealer* registration. But — solely for want of a practicable sanction — Congress omitted any reference to the registration of *securities* traded in the over-the-counter market.

It was a strange sort of regulatory scheme that gave individual members of the class to be regulated the power to decide whether the regulation should apply to them. This is apart from the dislocation of the traditional relationship between the exchanges and the over-the-counter market that was an inevitable result of regulating the one market and not the other. For, just as surely as water flows downhill, business will move from a regulated to an unregulated market.[14] The Wall Street Journal, resorting to another metaphor, saw "no reason why the laws for the protection of investors * * * should make fish of one group of corporations and fowl of another."[15]

Legislative hearings were held on a number of occasions between 1941 and 1957, and a series of SEC reports documented the inadequate reporting and proxy-soliciting practices of many large,

---

checked by any regulatory authority. Since the necessity for regulation of 'over-the-counter' markets will depend largely on the extent to which activities prohibited on exchanges are transferred to such markets, provision for their regulation has been made as flexible as possible." S. Rep. No. 792, 73d Cong., 2d Sess. (1934) 6. See also the legislative findings in §2, which do not discriminate between the two markets.

[13] SEC, Report on Trading in Unlisted Securities upon Exchanges (1936) 17-21, infra p. 669 n. d.

[14] An early comparative study referred to the experience under the German Stock Exchange Law of 1896, which, on the theory that the original incorporators would normally list on the Exchange in order to redistribute, safeguarded that channel very strongly, thus increasing the temptation of many incorporators to use other channels for distribution. See Kessler, The American Securities Act and Its Foreign Counterparts: A Comparative Study, 44 Yale L. J. 1133, 1140-41 (1935).

[15] Wall St. J., Feb. 8, 1950, p. 8, col. 1.

publicly held over-the-counter companies.[16] Finally — as if to prove once more that reform legislation, at least of the SEC variety, is hostage to some crisis — a delinquent child of the American Stock Exchange set the stage for a legislative solution. The Commission's expulsion of two partners of a member firm for fraud and market manipulation[17] resulted in an SEC investigation of the exchange, which was merged into a broader study that Congress ordered in late 1961. That was the famous "Special Study of Securities Markets" that we have already noticed.[18] And its recommendations ultimately produced the Securities Acts Amendments of 1964, which added §12(g)-(i) to the 1934 Act.

The technique seems simple on the background of the Commission's 1936 confession that no statutory mechanism could be found. It reflects, of course, a later constitutional milieu. Section 12(g)(1) provides simply that "every issuer which is engaged in interstate commerce, or in a business affecting interstate commerce, or whose securities are traded by use of the mails or any means or instrumentality of interstate commerce[19] shall," within 120 days after the last day of its fiscal year on which it has "total assets exceeding $1,000,000 and a class of equity security (other than an exempted security) held of record by" 500 or more persons, register that security; and in 1982 the Commission used its §12(h) exemptive authority to recognize eighteen years of inflation by raising the $1 million figure to $3 million.[20] The registration statement becomes effective sixty days after filing, with authority in the Commission to accelerate.

The interrelation of §§12(b) and 12(g) is such that a particular company may be subject to both registration requirements. Section 12(g)(2)(A) exempts any security listed and registered on an exchange under §12(b). But a company of the requisite size with its common stock listed and an unlisted class of preferred held by at least 500 persons must register the preferred under §12(g). Moreover, §12(g)(1) specifically *permits* an issuer to register any class of equity security even though it is not required to be registered. The ordinary human does not willingly put his head in

---

[16] See 2 Loss 1152-64.

[17] Re, Re & Sagarese, 41 SEC 230 (1962).

[18] See p. 43 supra.

[19] See Bastian v. Lakefront Realty Corp., 581 F. 2d 685, 688 (7th Cir. 1978).

[20] Sec. Ex. Act Rel. 18,647, 25 SEC Dock. 49 (1982). The 500 figure was 750 for the first two years in order to ease the Commission's burden. The Code incorporates the §12(g)(1) formula as one basis for requiring company registration, except that the 500 figure applies (consistently with the concept of *company* registration) to all nonexempted securities in the aggregate. §402.

the lion's mouth. But even before the 1964 amendments, companies were occasionally known to list on an exchange in anticipation of a proxy contest so as to subject the opposition's material to the proxy rules, and today the tender offer provisions give some protection to a company that is an unwilling target. Again, it is conceivable that an underwriter will require registration before undertaking a distribution. And the privilege of voluntary registration will also take care of the company with almost 500 stockholders that prefers the lion's mouth to the cliff's edge.

It is from the point of view of the regulatory philosophy that §12(g) is particularly significant. For it is the first instance of compulsory registration in the 1933 and 1934 Acts. Companies could previously avoid registration — at a price, of course — by not going to the public or listing on an exchange. But a company that meets the size and ownership standards of §12(g) has no choice.

Apart from the reflection of a later constitutional atmosphere, one implication of the compulsory factor is that, whereas there are ready devices for the issuer's delaying the effectiveness of a registration statement under the 1933 Act or §12(b) of the 1934 Act until it is reasonably sure from the staff's comments (if any) that the registration statement is not materially deficient, an issuer cannot postpone the operative effect of §12(g) by merely deferring its public offering or its listing until the deficiencies are cured. The fact that a §12(g) registration statement may become effective after sixty days in deficient form presents no particular problem for the *Commission*. It has ample sanctions for obtaining amendments from a recalcitrant issuer with an effective registration statement. It is the issuer itself that may be in an uncomfortable position. Although the possibility of criminal prosecution under §32 for filing false or misleading statements may be discounted unless the issuer is utterly indifferent to its responsibilities, the issuer risks civil liability under §18 — not to mention Rule 10b-5.

b.   Due Date of Registration Statement

The critical date under §12(g)(1) for application of the size and ownership criteria is the last day of the fiscal year.[21] Two propositions follow from this arbitrary choice: (1) Exceeding either or both figures *during* a fiscal year is irrelevant unless *both* criteria

---

[21] McAlinden v. Wiggins, 543 F. Supp. 1004, 1005 (S. D. N. Y. 1982).

are satisfied on the last day. (2) If both criteria are met on the last day of the fiscal year, a registration statement must be filed within 120 days even though by then the company has less than $3 million of assets and fewer than 500 record holders of any class of equity security; the company (unless it obtains an exemptive order under §12(h) must then look to the quite different standards governing *termination* of registration.

At first blush it would seem to be equally clear that there is nothing illegal or otherwise improper about having either the issuer or one or more stockholders buy out enough record holders to keep the total safely below 500 on the last day of the fiscal year. But this device presents a number of problems. First, any re-purchases by the issuer itself would have to comply, of course, with the appropriate provisions of the state of incorporation governing repurchases with respect to capital and various kinds of surplus. Secondly, a question might be raised, normally in a stockholder's derivative action, whether a repurchase by the company, particularly when the company had never repurchased before, had been for a proper corporate purpose as a matter of state law. Thirdly, §20(c) of the 1934 Act, which was appropriately amended in 1964 in the light of the adoption of §12(g), makes it "unlawful for any director or officer of, or any owner of any securities issued by, any issuer required to file any document, report, or information under this title or any rule or regulation thereunder without just cause to hinder, delay, or obstruct the making or filing of any such document, report, or information." And, in any event, careful attention would have to be paid to Rule 12g5-1(b)(3):

> If the issuer knows or has reason to know that the form of holding securities of record is used primarily to circumvent the provisions of section 12(g) or 15(d) of the Act, the beneficial owners of such securities shall be deemed to be the record owners thereof.[22]

This is obviously a catch-all provision that is aimed at deterring the organization of holding companies, subsidiaries, or trusts for the primary purpose of avoiding registration. Finally, since an issuer or stockholder buying on the market would have no way of knowing whether the seller was selling out completely, any purchases for the purpose of reducing the number of shareholders would have to be negotiated transactions, and this would increase the likelihood of a court's finding a violation of Rule 10b-5,

---

[22] See Tankersley v. Albright, 374 F. Supp. 551, 557 (N. D. Ill. 1974).

perhaps on the basis of a failure to disclose that the purpose of the purchases was to avoid the rights of investors flowing from registration.

Even so, it is by no means clear that reducing the number of stockholders below the statutory figure would not be considered a proper avoidance of an arbitrary statutory test, comparable to avoiding §16(b) by holding a security for six months before selling it. It is not unknown for public companies to "go private" quite apart from §12(g).[23] Nevertheless, any management that ventured on this virgin territory should tread warily. And certainly an issuer that had to do so repeatedly would be well advised to give up and register.

There are similar questions of avoidance and evasion with reference to the assets test. For example, a company with a seasonable business might legitimately avoid registration by adopting a natural fiscal year, ending on a date when reduced inventories have not been replenished and both receivables and bank loans are usually at their low points for the year. On the other hand, paying off a substantial bank debt just before the close of the fiscal year and then reborrowing the money early in the next fiscal year would be an obvious evasion. In between there is inevitably another gray area.

Do §§13, 14, and 16 apply when a class of security should be registered under §12(g) but has not been? The Code adopts the administrative construction[24] as sound in policy by making it generally "unlawful for a person who is required to be registered under any provision of this Code but is not so registered to do any act that it would be unlawful for him to do if he were registered."[25] And that view has some judicial support under existing law.[26] On the other hand, a negative answer today is suggested not only by a literal reading of §§13, 14, and 16, which apply only to "registered" securities, but also by the language of prior bills,[27] which would have applied the three sections to securities "registered or required to be registered." And there is presumably some limit to the administrative or judicial rewriting of statutes

---

[23] On the "going private" phenomenon, see pp. 585-87 infra.

[24] See Townsend Corp. of America, 42 SEC 282, 316-17 (1964) (Inv. Co. Act).

[25] §2006(b); see 2 Code 1022.

[26] Reserve Life Ins. Co. v. Provident Life Ins. Co., 499 F. 2d 715, 724 (8th Cir. 1974), cert. denied, 419 U. S. 1107; but cf. Upson v. Otis, 155 F. 2d 606, 610 (2d Cir. 1946); Bastian v. Lakefront Realty Corp., 581 F. 2d 685, 689-91 (7th Cir. 1978).

[27] See 2 Loss 1153-62; 4 Loss 2310.

in order to repair drafting oversights. In any event, injunctive and criminal proceedings would still lie, of course, for violation of §12(g)(1) itself.

The question assumes practical importance, therefore, only in the context of civil liability. So far as §16(b) is concerned, the statute of limitations would be tolled pending the required registration.[28] And the plaintiff that would otherwise seek private relief for violation of the proxy rules might be well advised to argue, at least in the alternative, not (1) that §14 could be or had been violated by an unregistered company but (2) that a company that was about to solicit or had solicited proxies when it was in violation of the registration requirement of §12(g)(1) should no more be permitted to enjoy the fruits of its violation than a company whose proxy solicitation had violated §14. Moreover, this latter argument should be equally available to the Commission itself in an injunctive action directed to the proxy solicitation of a company that was in violation of the registration requirement.

c. Banks

Banks and insurance companies[29] were the areas that created the greatest difficulty in connection with the 1964 legislation.

On the one hand, bank securities had always been exempted from registration under the 1933 Act. This in turn had precluded operation of the reporting requirement in §15(d) of the 1934 Act.[30] And, although bank stocks had never been exempted from the registration requirement in §12(a) of the 1934 Act, the Commission had early created a "temporary" exemption from §12(a) for bank securities listed on June 30, 1935 (or securities of the same issuer exchanged for them), until the adoption of a special form[31] and had never adopted a form. In any event, a tendency to withdraw bank stocks from listing had set in well before 1934. And, although several bank *holding companies* have stocks listed on the New York Stock Exchange, by 1963 there were only five listed bank stocks (all on the then Philadelphia-Baltimore-Washington Stock Exchange) in addition to fifteen that were traded on the Honolulu, Richmond, and Wheeling Stock Exchanges, all ex-

---

[28] See p. 606 infra; Whittaker v. Whittaker Corp., 639 F. 2d 516, 527-30 (9th Cir. 1981), *cert. denied*, 454 U. S. 1031.

[29] With respect to insurance companies, see p. 477 infra.

[30] See pp. 477-82 supra.

[31] Former Rule 12a-1, adopted by Sec. Ex. Act Rel. 291 (1935), and repealed as obsolete by Sec. Ex. Act Rel. 18,853, 25 SEC Dock. 794 (1982).

empted exchanges.[32] Furthermore, all banks are regulated by federal or state banking authorities or both.[33] And the country's banks could not be expected to relish another layer of regulation, which might interfere with customary accounting methods and other operating practices.

On the other hand, existing regulation was oriented toward the protection of depositors rather than investors and the integrity of the market.[34] And the Special Study had marshalled impressive evidence that the financial reporting and proxy solicitation practices of banks fell far short of the standards imposed by §§13 and 14 of the Exchange Act.[35]

At some point the Commission apparently concluded that the most statesmanlike policy consistent with principle would be to recommend that the registration and other provisions of the bill should extend to bank securities but should be administered by the respective federal bank agencies. The result was §12(i), which — as amended in 1968 to add references to the new tender offer provisions in the Williams Act, and as extended to insured savings and loan institutions by the Depository Institutions Act of 1974[36] — vests the SEC's "powers, functions, and duties * * * to administer and enforce" §§12, 13, 14(a), (c), (d), and (f), and 16 in (1) the Comptroller of the Currency with respect to national and District of Columbia banks, (2) the Board of Governors of the Federal Reserve System with respect to all other member banks of the Federal Reserve System, (3) the Federal Deposit Insurance Corporation with respect to all other insured banks, and (4) the Federal Home Loan Bank Board with respect to institutions insured by the Federal Savings and Loan Insurance Corporation. The 1974 statute also amended §12(i) to require these agencies to adopt rules "substantially similar" to the SEC's unless they publish detailed reasons for their findings to the contrary.

The "powers, functions, and duties" referred to in §12(i) include authority to adopt definitional and other rules under §§3(b) and 23(a) and to act just as the Commission would with respect

---

[32] 3 SEC, Report of Special Study of Securities Markets, H. R. Doc. No. 95, 88th Cong., 1st Sess. (1963) 36.

[33] SEC Legislation, Hearings before Subcom. of Com. on Banking & Currency on S. 1642, 88th Cong., 1st Sess. (1963) 172-75 (description by Comptroller of the Currency of disclosure requirements applicable to national banks in 1963).

[34] See Murane, SEC, FTC, and the Federal Bank Regulators: Emerging Problems of Administrative Jurisdictional Overlap, 61 Geo. L. J. 37 (1972).

[35] 3 Special Study, op. cit. supra n. 32, at 35-39.

[36] §105, 88 Stat. 1500, 1503-04 (1974).

to the investigatory, injunctive, and criminal provisions as well as the several administrative sanctions.[37] Moreover, the Senate made it clear that the bill in no way limited other provisions of law giving authority to the federal and state banking agencies.[38] The SEC, however, retains a considerable amount of jurisdiction in this area.

First of all, most of the larger banks are now subsidiaries of bank holding companies, which (together with their affiliates) come within the SEC's jurisdiction if they fall within the standards of §12(g), since they are not "banks" as defined in §3(a)(6). This inevitably gives the Commission an indirect say on the financial and other disclosures acquired with respect to the subsidiary banks.[39]

Secondly, the enumeration of only a few sections in §12(i) leaves jurisdiction in the SEC to apply the various investigatory provisions and sanctions as far as any other sections, including the fraud and manipulation provisions, are concerned.[40] Moreover, since the bank agencies are given no authority to register over-the-counter broker-dealers under §15(b), it is clear that only the SEC may discipline registered broker-dealers for violation of *any* provision of the Exchange Act — including even those specified in §12(i) — in connection with bank securities. And it is the Commission's view that, although the bank agencies have the authority normally vested in the Commission under §§12(j) and 12(k) to delist or summarily suspend trading in securities within their jurisdiction for violation of the provisions specified in §12(i), they have no authority under those provisions that affect exchange trading in securities generally as well as the organization and administration of the exchanges.[41]

The Code abandons the concept of §12(i) for two reasons: "In principle the disclosure-oriented provisions of the Code as they

---

[37] S. Rep. No. 379, 88th Cong., 1st Sess. (1963) 63-64.

[38] Id. at 35-36.

[39] See Third National Corp., Sec. Ex. Act Rel. 11,396, 6 SEC Dock. 852 (1975).

[40] See Local 734 Bakery Drivers Pension Fund Trust v. Continental Ill. National Bank of Chicago, CCH Fed. Sec. L. Rep. ¶94,565 at 95,960 (N. D. Ill. 1973) (Rule 10b-5). On the symbiosis of the SEC and banking provisions with respect to insiders, see Buchalter and Allen, Bank Insider Abuses: When Does the Ax Fall?, 96 Banking L. J. 804 (1979). In SEC and Comptroller of the Currency v. National Bank of Ga. and Lance, Litig. Rel. 8395, 14 SEC Dock. 1029 (N. D. Ga. 1978), both agencies sued jointly, alleging violations of the fraud, reporting, and proxy provisions of the SEC statutes.

[41] 2 Investor Protection, Hearings before Subcom. of House Com. on Int. & For. Commerce on H. R. 6789, H. R. 6793, S. 1642, 88th Cong., 1st Sess. (1963) 1365-66.

apply to bank securities * * * should be centrally administered and enforced by the Commission, as the Federal Reserve Board suggested in 1964" in order to avoid a fragmentation of responsibility and a loss of efficiency.[42] And "most of the larger banks have to conjure today with dual regulation as subsidiaries of bank *holding* companies."[43]

d.   Definitions[44]

(i) *"Class"*: Section 12(g)(5) borrowed a special definition from §15(d):

> For the purposes of this subsection the term "class" shall include all securities of an issuer which are of substantially similar character and the holders of which enjoy substantially similar rights and privileges.

This general problem keeps cropping up in a number of contexts. We have met it in connection with the "new security" question[45] and the voluntary exchange exemption;[46] and we shall meet it again in connection with §15(d)[47] and especially §16, on insider trading, which refers to beneficial holders of more than 10 percent of "any class of any equity security."[48] In terms of maximizing the statutory coverage, there is a built-in stress and strain. For purposes of §§12(g) and 15(d) — as well as the intrastate and private offering exemptions in §§3(a)(11) and 4(2) of the 1933 Act to the extent that different classes constitute separate "issues" or "offerings"[49] — it is in the Commission's interest to play down relatively minor differences between "Class A Common" and "Class B Common," or between two formally separate "classes" of convertible debentures, so as to produce one big, widely held "class." So, too, when it is a matter of matching a purchase of Class A against a sale of Class B for purposes of §16(b). But that approach cuts in the opposite direction as far as the 10 percent test in §16 is concerned. Presumably there is some limit to the freedom to give the same term different constructions in different sections of the same statute, particularly since the existence of a single

---

[42] See 2 id. at 1362.
[43] 2 Code 825-26.
[44] The definition of "equity security" is considered infra p. 651.
[45] See p. 264 supra.
[46] See pp. 301-04 supra.
[47] See p. 490 infra.
[48] See p. 652 infra.
[49] See pp. 319-20, 328-29, 374 supra.

"class" for purposes of §12(g) may be the sole basis for applying §16. And maximization of coverage itself may not be a strong enough solvent. Yet §3(a) of the 1934 Act, like §2(a) of the 1933 Act, introduces all the general definitions with the words, "unless the context otherwise requires." And — more to the point here — the definition of "class" in §§12(g)(5) and 15(d) is specifically limited to "the purposes of this subsection."

There is not much that has so far emerged in the way of guidelines. As always, of course, "form" must yield to "substance." This means that securities denominated "preferred" and "common" *may* constitute a single class. The mere fact that one security is convertible into another, does not make them one class. On the other hand, the result is apt to be different when both securities are of the same basic type, which is to say, common stock, preferred stock, unsecured debt, or secured debt. Convertibility aside, when, for example, two preferred issues differ with respect to one or more of their basic characteristics — voting rights, dividend preference, and preference on liquidation — an approach in terms of the purpose of the differences in the particular case, which would be roughly analogous to the "business purpose" test in tax law, would seem to be superior to the sort of "color matching" approach that Justice Harlan disparaged in his dissenting opinion in the variable annuity case,[50] even though the latter approach seems to be invited by the "substantially similar character" language of §12(g)(5).

(ii) *"Held of record"* [Rule 12g5-1]: Consistently with the reference in §12(g)(1) to holders "of record," this definitional rule simply supplies a series of explanations and qualifications, only a few of which require comment:

Securities held by two or more persons as co-owners, or as co-fiduciaries with respect to a single trust, estate, or account are considered to have a single record holder. It follows, for example, that, when John Doe holds some securities in his own name and others as trustee, there are two record holders; that, when John and Mary Doe hold securities as co-owners (whether the type of tenancy is joint or common or by the entirety or unknown) and each of them holds other securities in his or her own name, there is a total of three record holders; and that, when securities are held by John Doe, by Mary Doe, by John and Mary Doe as co-owners, by John Doe as custodian for a minor child, and by John

---

[50] SEC v. Variable Annuity Life Ins. Co. of America, 359 U. S. 65, 96 (1959).

and Mary Doe as trustees, there is a total of five record holders.

"Each outstanding unregistered or bearer certificate shall be included as held of record by a separate person, except to the extent that the issuer can establish that, if such securities were registered, they would be held of record, under the provisions of this rule, by a lesser number of persons." Since a convertible bond is defined as an "equity security" by §3(a)(11), this clause applies equally to convertible bonds in bearer form. That is to say, it is simply a matter of counting the number of bonds outstanding, regardless of denomination.

"Securities held, to the knowledge of the issuer, subject to a voting trust, deposit agreement or similar arrangement shall be included as held of record by the record holders of the voting trust certificates, certificates of deposit, receipts or similar evidences of interest in such securities: *Provided however,* That the issuer may rely in good faith on such information as is received in response to its request from a nonaffiliated issuer of the certificates or evidences of interest." Note the limiting words, "to the knowledge of the issuer." When that limitation is satisfied, the record holders of the voting-trust certificates or similar securities are counted twice, once to determine the number of holders of the underlying shares and again to determine the number of holders of the voting-trust certificates, which are themselves included within the definition of "equity security" under §3(a)(11). On the other hand, the rule as adopted does not, as the Commission originally proposed, look through brokers, dealers, banks, or their nominees to include the number of separate customers' accounts. That is to say, the brokerage firm that holds stock in "street name" for fifty customers is counted as a single holder. The Commission, apparently assuming that its authority in §12(g)(5) to define "held of record" *could* be stretched to include beneficial holders of this sense, stated that it had abandoned its original proposal in the interest of simplification but would "determine in the light of experience whether inclusion of these accounts at a future date is necessary or appropriate to prevent circumvention of the Act and to achieve the intended coverage on a uniform and acceptable basis."[51] Similar considerations underlay the Commission's decision not to include employees with a direct beneficial interest in securities held by an employee plan.[52]

(iii)   *"Total assets"* [Rule 12g5-2]: The assets test in §12(g)(1), too, presents a bit of a dilemma for both the Commission and cor-

[51] Sec. Ex. Act Rel. 7492 (1965).
[52] Ibid.

porate management. The Commission for its part must balance the conflicting policies of furthering the statutory coverage, which in an inflationary economy would tend to support asset revaluations, and encouraging conservative accounting, which would tend in the opposite direction. Conversely, management now has an incentive to make accounting adjustments downward in order to reduce total assets below the $3 million figure and thus avoid registration.

As long as the accounting principles followed by the company are supported by substantial authority, are adequately disclosed, do not unfairly portray the company's financial condition and do not contravene a position expressed in a Commission rule or release, it is difficult to see how the Commission could object to this kind of avoidance. For, consistently with its general approach to accounting principles, the Commission has not prescribed detailed rules under §12(g) for valuing assets or computing reserves. Although this may result in some lack of uniformity in the application of the section, that consideration alone has not persuaded the Commission to undertake the formidable task of choosing between alternative methods of valuation when there is a substantial difference of opinion within the profession. Its definitional rule makes only two points:

(1) The term "total assets" refers to either the corporate or the consolidated balance sheet, whichever shows the larger figure, as required to be filed on the proper registration form and as prepared in accordance with Regulation S-X. This formula, of course, makes more acute the question whether consolidated statements should be prepared in the first place. Clearly the fact that a company may not have prepared consolidated financial statements in the past cannot be determinative for purposes of the $3 million test when generally accepted accounting principles would have dictated consolidated statements.

(2) "Where the security is a certificate of deposit, voting trust certificate, or certificate or other evidence of interest in a similar trust or agreement, the 'total assets' of the issuer of the security held under the trust or agreement shall be deemed to be the 'total assets' of the issuer of such certificate or evidence of interest." This means that the assets test is met by a voting trust that has half the stock of a company with $4 million of assets.

One thing that is perfectly clear is that the existence of a capital deficit is irrelevant as long as "total assets" exceed $3 million. On this basis registration might be required even on the part of a company that was insolvent in the bankruptcy sense.

3. EXEMPTIONS

a. General

The treatment of exemptions in the 1934 Act is quite different from that in the 1933 and 1939 Acts, essentially because the 1934 Act contains so many different kinds of substantive provisions:

(1) Section 3(a)(12) *defines* the term "exempted security" to include, in effect, only "direct obligations of or obligations guaranteed as to principal or interest" by an American governmental authority,[53] certain industrial development bonds by reference to the Internal Revenue Code,[54] and whatever other securities the Commission may exempt, conditionally or unconditionally, by rule. The Commission has broadly construed the term "direct obligations" as standing in contradistinction to the phrase "obligations guaranteed as to principal or interest," and hence has regarded state and municipal revenue bonds and special assessment bonds as exempt. Rules adopted under a section that excludes "exempted securities" obviously cannot be made applicable to the securities that are so defined by §3(a)(12). But the converse does not necessarily follow. The Commission apparently considers that its power to classify securities in the general rulemaking provisions is sufficiently broad to permit it to exclude "exempted securities" from rules adopted under provisions that do *not* exclude them.[55]

(2) Apart from those few securities that come within the definition of "exempted securities" in §3(a)(12), there is a considerable panoply of exemptions peculiar to §12(g). These include securities of investment companies, savings and loan associations, nonprofit issuers, cooperatives, insurance companies, and foreign issuers. In some respects these exemptions differ from their analogues in the 1933 Act.

(3) All these exemptions flow automatically from statute or rule. In addition, although §3(a)(12) limits the Commission to acting

---

[53] Only the Secretary of the Treasury may designate for exemption securities issued or guaranteed by "corporations in which the United States has a direct or indirect interest," and that authority has been used sparingly.

[54] The Internal Revenue Code references comprehend industrial revenue bonds issued (1) for certain specific purposes or (2) in the face amount of not more than $1 million (or in certain cases $5 million). See Sec. Act Rel. 5103 (1970). On the various kinds of industrial development bonds, see Note, The Liability of Municipalities for State and Federal Securities Fraud in the Issuance of Industrial Development Bonds, 30 Okla. L. Rev. 704, 705-11 (1977).

[55] See Rules 10b-6(d), 10b-7(n), which exclude "exempted securities" from the regulations on trading during distributions and on market stabilization although they are not excluded by §10(b).

by rule rather than by order, the Commission has given itself an *ad hoc* exemptive authority in certain rules, for example, those on trading during distributions, market stabilization, and distributions through rights.[56] And §12(h), added in the 1964 amendments, authorizes exemption, by rule *or order*, from not only §12(g) but also §§13, 14, 15(d), and 16.

As a result of this statutory scheme, one who wishes to determine whether a particular kind of security or transaction is or may be exempted from a particular substantive provision of the statute must see first whether that provision by its terms excludes "exempted securities" or contains any special exemptions or exemptive authority. Then, in either event, he must determine whether the Commission has adopted an exemptive rule under that section. And, finally, either the particular section or a rule thereunder or §12(h) may afford him an opportunity to seek an exemptive *order*.

b.   Insurance Companies [§12(g)(2)(G)]

Most of the §12(g) exemptions do not require discussion here. But one that does, because of both its intrinsic importance and its implications for federalism, is the exemption in §12(g)(2)(G) for securities of insurance companies.

We have already noted that, along with banks,[57] insurance companies were the area of greatest difficulty for Congress in connection with the 1964 legislation. The ultimate solutions, though philosophically similar in that jurisdiction over both categories was shifted for the most part from the SEC to the bank and insurance regulatory authorities, took quite different forms. Because there was no federal insurance agency on the scene to which jurisdiction could be transferred as it was to the federal bank agencies by §12(i), the device used was an exemption from §12(g)(1) that was made conditional on the existence of substantially similar regulation in the domiciliary state.

The SEC has never had jurisdiction over *mutual* insurance companies except on their occasional issuance of debt securities, because they do not issue stock and §3(a)(8) of the 1933 Act exempts insurance policies and annuities, which (as we have seen) are normally not "securities" in any event.[58] However, before

---

[56] Rules 10b-6(h), 10b-7(o), 10b-8(f).
[57] See pp. 469-70 supra.
[58] See p. 214 supra.

1964 there was no exemption from either the 1933 Act or the 1934 Act for insurance company *securities*. That was the entire point of the variable annuity controversy. Consequently a considerable number of insurance companies had registered issues under the 1933 Act. And, as a result, 169 insurance companies were reporting to the Commission under §15(d) of the 1934 Act as of June 30, 1963, though only two additional companies were listed on an exchange (and thus reporting under §13) on that date.[59] (In 1965 The Insurance Company of North America became the first new insurance company to be listed on the New York Stock Exchange since 1916; today there are some 26.)

So far as the merits are concerned, the Commission's "Special Study" of 1963, finding that "Insurance companies as a group * * * exhibit all of the inadequacies in reporting and proxy solicitations characteristic of the total group studied," concluded that they did not present a case for special treatment with respect to §§13, 14, and 16.[60] And in 1960 a group within the National Federation of Financial Analysts Societies concluded that annual stockholders' reports of the life insurance industry "are the poorest of any major industry in the United States."[61]

Nevertheless, the National Association of Insurance Commissioners (NAIC), representing the insurance regulatory authorities of all the states, the District of Columbia, and Puerto Rico, took a firm position that insurance companies should be exempted in accordance with the tradition of state regulation. The commissioners recognized that there was some validity to the contention that their procedures were directed primarily to the protection of policy holders rather than investors. But they sought an opportunity to demonstrate their ability effectively to protect investors as well.[62] And the Commission, as it did with the banks, went along presumably to avoid the danger of a serious floor fight on the entire bill. But, again as with banks, jurisdiction over insurance *holding* companies remains with the SEC.

Unhappily, perhaps because it was a relatively late insertion in the bill, §12(g)(2)(G) is not as precisely drafted as one might wish when it exempts

> any security issued by an insurance company if all of the following conditions are met:

---

[59] 1 Investor Protection, supra n. 41, at 176 n. 5.

[60] 3 SEC, Report of Special Study of Securities Markets, H. R. Doc. No. 95, 88th Cong., 1st Sess. (1963) 42.

[61] SEC Legislation, 1963, Hearings before Subcom. of Senate Com. on Banking & Currency on S. 1642, 88th Cong., 1st Sess. (1963) 25.

[62] H. R. Rep. No. 1418, 88th Cong., 2d Sess. (1964) 10.

(i) Such insurance company is required to and does file an annual statement with the Commissioner of Insurance (or other officer or agency performing a similar function) of its domiciliary State, and such annual statement conforms to that prescribed by the National Association of Insurance Commissioners or in the determination of such State commissioner, officer or agency substantially conforms to that so prescribed.

(ii) Such insurance company is subject to regulation by its domiciliary State of proxies, consents, or authorizations in respect of securities issued by such company and such regulation conforms to that prescribed by the National Association of Insurance Commissioners.

(iii) After July 1, 1966, the purchase and sales of securities issued by such insurance company by beneficial owners, directors, or officers of such company are subject to regulation (including reporting) by its domiciliary State substantially in the manner provided in section 16 of this title.[63]

Citations to the relevant laws of all three categories in the fifty-two jurisdictions are readily available.[64] Suffice it here to note the pitfalls in all three clauses:

Two points are worth noting with respect to the first clause:

(1) Unlike the second and third clauses, the first clause requires not merely that the insurance company be "subject to" specified regulation but also that it comply by actually filing. This raises the question whether a late filing would destroy the exemption. Presumably every commissioner's control over the required filings is great enough to authorize him to grant reasonable extensions, which would prevent non-compliance as a matter of state law and hence avoid any question under Clause (i). In any event, it is difficult to conceive of a company's failing to file its report for a given year until the last day of its next fiscal year, which is presumably the date for determining the availability of the exemption.[65] But the short answer would seem to be that any failure to file that was not excused as a matter of state law *would* hazard the exemption, at least if the failure extended beyond the end of the next fiscal year.

(2) Timing aside, the insurance commissioner's determination (at least in the absence of a genuine abuse of discretion on his part) is made conclusive on the question of substantive compliance.

---

[63] In addition, Congress in §3(a)(19) incorporated the definition of "insurance company" from §2(a)(17) of the Investment Company Act.

[64] See the chart in CCH Fed. Sec. L. Rep. ¶23,310; for the text of the provisions, see CCH Blue Sky L. Rep., where they are collected along with the "insurance securities laws."

[65] Cf. §12(g)(1)(B) (due date of registration statement).

That is to say, Congress has not only delegated a legislative function, as it were, to an organization of state administrative officials;
it has also precluded the SEC and the federal courts from examining (except perhaps in extreme cases) the question of compliance
in an individual case.

In contrast with Clause (i), which quite clearly did not require
additional state legislation, Clause (iii) just as clearly did. Accordingly, the NAIC adopted a model insider trading act. That model
or similar legislation based on §16 of the Exchange Act has now
been adopted in all fifty-two jurisdictions. And the NAIC also
adopted and recommended a set of rules and forms closely modeled
on the SEC's. But problems remain aside from the variations that
seem to plague all "uniform" state legislation. For example, since
Clause (iii) refers to local regulation "substantially in the manner
provided in" §16, there is a question how much weight the word
"substantially" will bear. The SEC, for example, has adopted a
pretty rigid rule defining beneficial ownership in various trust
situations.[66] Although Clause (iii) does not require compliance
with any regulations prescribed by the NAIC as Clause (i) does,
any insurance commissioner who did not adopt the NAIC's model
forms and rules — which for this reason were copied as closely as
possible from the SEC's forms and rules — would be hazarding the
exemption for companies incorporated in his jurisdiction. Even
so, the NAIC and all the commissioners must watch carefully for
future SEC rule or form amendments that tighten §16 and, therefore, automatically affect Clause (iii) of the exemption. And, forms
and rules aside, what about judicial construction? The federal
courts have developed an extremely strict test for computing the
recoverable profits under §16(b) in cases of multiple transactions,
refusing to permit either the tracing of certificates or a first-in-
first-out presumption as under the tax laws.[67] The state courts are
not bound to follow these federal precedents in interpreting state
statutes as such, but they may well risk destruction of the entire
exemption if they do not.

It is Clause (ii) that presents perhaps the toughest problems.
To be sure, it is the only one of the three clauses that does not
require that the state regulation conform "substantially" to either
the NAIC or the SEC pattern. In the event, virtually all fifty-two
jurisdictions have enacted enabling legislation to authorize their
insurance commissioners to adopt the proxy rules, basically but

---

[66] Rule 16a-8.
[67] See p. 630 infra.

not altogether like the SEC's, that the NAIC "strongly recommended" (it did not use the statutory word "prescribed") and that all fifty-two jurisdictions have adopted. But, unfortunately, the NAIC did not recommend a model proxy act as it did a model insider trading act; and the inevitable result is a hodgepodge.

It must not be overlooked, moreover, that the exemptive scheme in §12(g)(2)(G) is on an all-or-none basis. That is to say, failure to comply with Clause (ii), for example, destroys the exemption not only with respect to §14 but also with respect to the reporting and insider trading provisions of §§13 and 16. Therefore, the absence or insufficiency of the proxy regulation required by Clause (ii) in a particular state may mean, for example, that a director that has diligently filed the required insider trading reports with the insurance commissioner will find himself sued several years later under §16(b) on the theory that no exemption was available and that the two-year statute of limitations in §16(b) was tolled during the period that he did not file reports with the SEC. Conversely, suppose that a state court — perhaps relishing its independence of the Supreme Court of the United States and the lower federal courts — reads the state statute's insider trading provisions less stringently than the federal precedents go. Having in mind the Supreme Court's holding that in a proper case a trial court, as a matter of federal law, may set aside any action taken by means of illegally solicited proxies,[68] a company that is soliciting proxies for some extraordinary event like a merger might well give serious consideration to the advisability of registering under §12(g) and complying with the SEC proxy rules. Whatever the reason, a number of insurance companies have done so.

All in all, counsel for one of the large insurance companies concluded after a detailed survey of the action taken by the NAIC and the insurance commissioners in the light of §12(g)(2)(G):

> It seems doubtful that any of the industry or NAIC representatives who worked so diligently and effectively to secure the provisional insurance company exemption foresaw the multiplicity of problems posed by incorporation of the federal regulatory pattern in all the states. * * * If Congress should amend Section 16, presumably all the states will have to do likewise. If the SEC revises its rules under that section, at least if such revision should have the effect of narrowing exemptions, insurance commissioners will almost certainly have to follow suit. Eternal, unflagging vigilance will be the price of continued liberty, and to the extent that state regulation is as effective as it must be to

---

[68] J. I. Case Co. v. Borak, 377 U. S. 426 (1964), set out infra p. 1059.

maintain the exemption the liberty purchased may be largely illusory.[69]

The only observation one can add is that this proliferation of jurisdiction among fifty-two insurance commissioners and judicial systems, not to mention four federal bank and savings and loan agencies, does little to improve the disposition of a writer on the subject.

c.   Exemptive Orders [§12(h)]

The authority under §12(h) to exempt by order is not limited to §12(g). It may be applied separately to §13, 14, or 15(d), whether the security is registered under §12(g) or under §12(b). And the Commission has used the authority in a great variety of cases, often granting exemption partially and conditionally.

In one case, for example, the Commission rejected contentions that an exemption was warranted by (1) the fact that only 456 of the 599 shareholders of record were residents of the United States, (2) the fact that 466 shareholders owned five shares or less, and (3) the very limited trading interest. But the Commission recognized that, in view of the absence of a continuing or professional market interest, the financial community that seeks out and disseminates information on file would not be served by compliance with the reporting requirements of §13(a) in the particular case. It accordingly exempted from that section, and waived certain of the financial requirements in connection with the filing of a registration statement, but also imposed a number of conditions: (a) that the financial statements included in the annual reports to shareholders and certified in accordance with generally accepted accounting principles be deemed incorporated by reference in the company's proxy or information statements so that §18 would be made applicable; (b) that the company, when acting as middleman between seller and buyer, furnish every offeree a copy of the most recent proxy or information statement and annual report; and (c) that the company inform the Commission annually of all sales and advise it promptly of any material change in the factual situation.[70]

---

[69] Kenney, Securities Regulation in the Insurance Business or S-X and the Single Standard, 19 Assn. Life Ins. Counsel Proc. 1, 52 (1965). For a discussion of the additional complexities in the event that an insurance commissioner should seek to enforce his state's proxy or insider trading legislation in the courts of another state, see 5 Loss 2758-59.

[70] National Dollar Stores, Ltd., 43 SEC 881 (1968).

4. NONSTATUTORY LISTING REQUIREMENTS OF THE EXCHANGES

Long before the Exchange Act the several exchanges had their own varying requirements for listing. These are unaffected by the Exchange Act, except for a residual power in the Commission (which was enlarged in the 1975 amendments) to disapprove new rules or rule changes generally before they become effective and to make changes in exchange rules.[71]

The development of the exchanges' listing rules was gradual. For many years all that the New York Stock Exchange demanded to know was that a company really existed and that its securities were authentic. The old viewpoint was that the function of an exchange was not to reform corporate practices but to maintain a "free and open" market for securities. The trend toward the modern disclosure requirements — like so many developments in this field — followed the increasing divorcement of management and ownership. Although the New York Stock Exchange was trying as early as the 1860s to get financial reports from companies whose securities were dealt in, and by 1909 was obtaining agreements to distribute annual financial statements to stockholders as a condition of listing, the development did not proceed in earnest until the boom that ended with the 1929 crash had got well under way, and it was then accentuated by the depression. Thus the New York Stock Exchange has required since 1933 that the financial statements accompanying listing applications and those subsequently published or sent to stockholders be audited under specified standards by public accountants. And its requirements with respect to the publication of quarterly earnings and the sending of annual reports to stockholders antedate the SEC.

The disclosure requirements of the New York Stock Exchange largely, but not entirely, parallel those under the Exchange Act.[72] But the conditions of listing go beyond disclosure. The Exchange itself has described its requirements this way:

> The company must be a going concern or be the successor to a going concern. While the amount of assets and earnings and the aggregate market value are considerations, greater emphasis is placed on such questions as the degree of national interest in the company, the character of the market for its products, its relative stability and position in its industry, and whether or not it is

---

[71] §§19(b)(1)-(3), 19(c); see Code §805(a)-(c), (e), (f).
[72] The listing application obligates the issuer to "furnish to the Exchange on demand such information concerning the Corporation as the Exchange may reasonably require." N. Y. Stock Ex. Company Manual A-34.2, ¶13.

engaged in an expanding industry with prospects for maintaining its position.[73]

The Exchange has repeatedly raised its *minimum* numerical standards so that it now looks in general for 1 million publicly held shares; 2000 holders (including beneficial holders of stock held in "street name") of 100 shares or more; demonstrated earning power under competitive conditions of $2.5 million before taxes during the latest year and $2 million during the preceding two years; and an aggregate market value of $8 million for the publicly held shares.[74]

There are also a number of other conditions:[75]

SECURITIES EXCHANGE ACT RELEASE NO. 13,346: ORDER APPROVING PROPOSED RULE CHANGE
11 SEC Docket 1945
Securities and Exchange Commission, 1977

On February 1, 1977, the New York Stock Exchange, Inc. (the "NYSE"), filed with the Commission, pursuant to Section 19(b) of the Securities Exchange Act of 1934 (the "Act"), and Rule 19b-4 thereunder, copies of a proposed rule change concerning the requirements applicable to issuers with stock listed on the exchange. The proposed rule change would require each domestic company with common stock listed on the NYSE, as a condition of initial and continued listing of its securities on the NYSE, to establish not later than June 30, 1978, and maintain thereafter, an audit committee comprised solely of directors independent of management and free from any relationship that, in the opinion of the board of directors, would interfere with the exercise of independent judgment as a committee member.

*   *   *

The NYSE listing agreement, which has traditionally been a principal means by which the NYSE enforces its listing standards, was first adopted by the NYSE in 1899. That agreement, and the

[73] Id. at B-3.
[74] CCH N. Y. Stock Ex. Guide ¶2495B.
[75] For the current form of listing agreement, see N. Y. Stock Ex. Company Manual A-34 to A-34.5. See generally Comment, Stock Exchange Listing Agreements As a Vehicle for Corporate Governance, 129 U. Pa. L. Rev. 1427 (1981).

policies set forth in the NYSE Company Manual, have developed gradually over the years and impose a wide variety of requirements for initial and continued listing. Those policies frequently require a listed company to take action which it would not otherwise be required to take and prevent a listed company from taking action which would otherwise be permitted.[6] Furthermore, the NYSE has a general policy calling for timely and adequate disclosure of corporate affairs and has in past urged listed companies to consider the desirability of having at least two outside directors whose functions on the board would include giving particular attention to full disclosure of corporate affairs.

Consistent with its overall approach to listing policies, the NYSE, and the accounting profession, major corporations and others, including the Commission, have for many years recognized the advantages of corporate audit committees.[9] Stronger support

[6] For example, since 1926, the NYSE has refused to list non-voting common stock, and currently it will delist the voting common stock of a company which creates a class of non-voting common stock or fails to solicit proxies for meetings of its stockholders. [N. Y. Stock Ex. Co. Manual] at xxi, A-280, A-134. As a matter of policy, the NYSE refuses to list a class of stock whose voting rights are subject to unusual restrictions. Id., at A-280 et seq. Certain redemption schemes are prohibited. Id., at A-30. In authorizing additional shares distributed by a stock dividend, a company can be required to transfer from earned surplus to permanent capitalization an amount equal to the fair value of such shares. Id., at A-235. A company whose board of directors is divided into more than three classes may not list its shares; if the board is divided into classes, they should be of approximately equal size and tenure, and the directors' terms of office should not exceed three years. Id., at A-280. Since 1940, listed preferred stock must have certain minimum provisions enabling holders to obtain board representation in the event of dividend default, and must be protected against compulsory change in rights and preferences. Id., at 281, 282. Shareholder approval is a prerequisite to listing securities to be used in connection with options or other remuneration plans for directors, officers, or employees; actions resulting in a change in the control of a company; and certain acquisitions. Id., at A-283, 284. Where stockholder approval is needed for listing any additional securities, over 50 percent of all securities entitled to vote must be represented in the vote, and approval must be by a majority of votes cast. Id., at A-284, 285. Before a class of securities eligible for continued listing may be delisted, the proposed withdrawal must have been approved by a substantial percentage of the outstanding shares (generally 66-2/3 percent) and not opposed by a substantial number of individual holders (generally 10 percent of the individual holders). Id., at A-294.1, 294.2. * * *

[In late 1968 the Exchange solicited comment with respect to supermajority voting requirements designed to ward off tender offers. But it ultimately decided to keep the matter under study instead of adopting a formal policy. See Mullaney, Guarding against Takeovers — Defensive Charter Provisions, 25 Bus. Law. 1441 (1970).]

[9] The NYSE first suggested the concept of an audit committee in 1940, and in recent years has strongly recommended that each listed company form an audit committee preferably composed exclusively of outside directors.* * *

for audit committees independent of management developed in the wake of recent revelations of questionable and illegal corporate payments. In particular, the Commission has urged strengthening the independence and vitality of corporate boards of directors and has suggested that, at least initially, those principles could be implemented by amending the listing requirements of the NYSE and other self-regulatory organizations, rather than by direct Commission action. * * *

The NYSE's revision of its listing policies appears to be an appropriate way to implement, at this time, an independent audit committee requirement. Exchange rules are, among other things, required to be designed to remove impediments to and perfect the mechanism of a free and open market, to prevent fraudulent and manipulative acts and practices and, in general, to protect investors and the public interest. * * * While independent audit committees will not eliminate all instances of abuse, their establishment can be an important step in a broader effort to remedy the problems of corporate accountability and disclosure that have been uncovered.

* * * While the current proposal applies only to domestic companies, their compliance should not be deemed to place them at any inappropriate competitive disadvantage.[17]

* * *

IT IS THEREFORE ORDERED, pursuant to Section 19(b)(2) of the Act, that the above-mentioned proposed rule change be, and it hereby is, approved.

In 1956 the Exchange announced a formal statement of policy covering so-called backdoor listings to codify its objection to indirect listings of companies that cannot meet the original listing standards: When an unlisted company proposes to combine with and into a listed company under circumstances that in the opinion of the Exchange constitute an acquisition of a listed company by an unlisted company, the resulting company must meet the standards for original listing or the Exchange will refuse to list additional shares of the listed company for the purpose.[76]

---

[17] It would, however, be helpful to have the NYSE's reasons for confining its proposal to domestic companies in order to assist the Commission in considering the appropriateness of extending the concept to foreign issuers. * * *

[76] N. Y. Stock Ex. Company Manual B-11.

The American Stock Exchange (formerly the New York Curb Exchange) has a similar policy.[77] But its requirements generally are somewhat less strict, in line with its tradition as a "seasoner" for the "Big Board." Each case is considered on its merits. Some issues of corporations still in the development stage, and without demonstrated earning power, have been listed. Important factors in such cases are the company's management, the adequacy of its financing, and its prospects. The other exchanges run the gamut.

Whatever may be the rights of *stockholders* as third-party beneficiaries of a corporation's listing agreement, it has been held that a *prospective purchaser* has no such right that is enforceable in an action against the corporation for damages resulting from breach of its agreement with the Exchange to publish promptly its decision to pass a dividend. The market price had dropped after the delayed publication of the passed dividend, and the plaintiff claimed that she would have canceled an order to buy additional shares "good till canceled" if the decision to pass the dividend had been promptly published.[78]

B. REPORTS

1. IN CONNECTION WITH EXCHANGE ACT REGISTRATION

Section 13(a) of the Exchange Act requires every issuer of a security registered on an exchange to file with the Commission and the exchange (1) such information as the Commission may by rule require "to keep reasonably current" the information filed in registering and (2) such annual and quarterly reports as the Commission may by rule prescribe. The Commission has held that §13(a) "necessarily embodies the requirement that such reports be true and correct."[1]

---

[77] CCH Am. Stock Ex. Guide ¶ 10,032.

[78] Mackubin v. Curtiss-Wright Corp., 190 Md. 52, 57 A. 2d 318 (1948). Corbin says: "It would have been helpful if the court had analyzed the purposes for which the exchange exacted the promise as a condition of listing." 4 Corbin, Contracts (1951) 49.

On the exemption for foreign securities, see pp. 76-77 supra.

C. 7B   [1] Great Sweet Grass Oils, Ltd., 37 SEC 683, 684 n. 1 (1957), *aff'd per curiam* sub nom. Great Sweet Grass Oils, Ltd. v. SEC, 256 F. 2d 893 (D. C. Cir. 1958); see p. 118 supra, where this approach is *queried.*

a. Annual Reports

A Commission rule requires the filing of an annual report, normally within ninety days after the close of the fiscal year, for each year after the last full fiscal year for which financial statements were filed in the application for registration.[2] The basic annual report form, corresponding to Form 10 for registration, is Form 10-K, and there are other forms in the "K" series corresponding to each of the specialized registration forms.

Information may be incorporated by reference from a proxy statement or from a report to security holders or from a prospectus into a 1934 Act registration statement or report.[3] And issuers are encouraged to integrate their annual reports to shareholders and those filed with the Commission. We have already noticed in the subchapter on accounting[4] that the Commission, without any direct authority over reports to security holders, has managed to assert a significant measure of indirect control by resort to its rulemaking authority with respect to proxy solicitations — this on the theory that the annual report to security holders, more than the occasional prospectus or even the proxy statement, should be recognized as "the most effective means of communication between management and security holders."[5]

The proxy rules have gradually been tightened so that today a proxy solicitation on behalf of the issuer with respect to an annual meeting for the election of directors must be accompanied or preceded by an annual report to security holders that includes (*inter alia*) (1) balance sheets for two years and income statements for three, all audited and prepared on a consolidated basis in substantial compliance with Regulation S-X, (2) selected financial data, and (3) management's analysis of financial condition and results of operations.[6] Unless the report itself satisfies Form 10-K, either the report or the proxy statement must contain an undertaking to supply a copy of the 10-K report on request without charge.[7] Copies of the report to security holders must also be mailed to the Commission "solely for its information," which is to say, the report is not considered to be filed for purposes of civil liability

---

[2] Rule 13a-1; Form 10-K, Gen. Inst. A.

[3] Rule 12b-23. Financial statements incorporated by reference must satisfy the requirements of the form or report in which they are incorporated. Rule 12b-23(a)(1).

[4] See p. 160 supra.

[5] Sec. Ex. Act Rel. 11,079, 5 SEC Dock. 356, 357 (1974).

[6] Rule 14a-3(b)(1)-(9).

[7] Rule 14a-3(b)(10).

under §18.[8] And a company that has no securities registered under the 1934 Act but that is subject to §15(d), so that the proxy rules do not apply, must likewise furnish to the Commission (but not "file") any annual report or proxy material that *is* distributed, or must state that that is not the case.[9]

The Code recognizes the security holders' report as "the central device for continuous disclosure" by giving the Commission direct authority over its contents.[10]

b.　Quarterly and Current Reports

Every issuer that is required to file an annual report on Form 10-K (with a few exceptions) must file a quarterly report on Form 10-Q within forty-five days after the end of its first three fiscal quarters,[11] and a "current report" on Form 8-K within fifteen days after the occurrence of specified events of an extraordinary character that have not been reported previously.[12]

The *quarterly* report must include condensed financial data, which need not be audited but must follow generally accepted accounting principles,[13] together with a management analysis of financial condition and results of operations.[14] That much of the report is not considered to be "filed" for purposes of civil liability under §18.[15] But, in addition, the report must include specified information with respect to legal proceedings, material changes in registered securities, defaults on senior securities, and matters submitted to a vote of security holders.

The extraordinary events that call for the filing of a *current* report are a change in control, the acquisition or disposition of a

---

[8] Rule 14a-3(c). This is without prejudice to the question whether Rule 10b-5 might apply.

[9] This requirement appears at the end of Form 10-K itself.

[10] §602(a)(2); see 1 Code 293-95.

[11] Rule 13a-13; Form 10-Q, Gen. Instr. A2. Separate publication of the results of operations for the fourth quarter is not required but is encouraged. Sec. Ex. Act Rel. 9559 (1972).

[12] Rule 13a-11; Form 8-K, Gen. Instr. B. Registrants are "encouraged" to make voluntary reports of further events "promptly." Id., Gen. Instr. B2. And the Commission's staff encourages the practice, voluntarily adopted by some companies, of announcing the availability of their current reports on request and in some cases distributing copies to their stockholders and other interested persons. Sec. Ex. Act Rel. 10,547, 3 SEC Dock. 210 (1973).

[13] Reg. S-X, §10-01.

[14] Reg. S-K, Item 11(b).

[15] Rule 13a-13(d).

significant amount of assets, bankruptcy or receivership proceedings, a change of auditors, and a director's resignation because of
a policy dispute.

When §13, together with the annual and current reporting rules
and forms, was attacked in a criminal case as casting the defendants
"into a hopelessly tangled rat maze," Judge Edelstein concluded:
"The statutory and regulatory scheme is certainly more involved
than the injunction, 'Thou shalt not steal.' But the conditions of
society giving rise to the necessity for regulation are more involved
than in the days of the patriarchs."[16]

2. In Connection with Securities Act Registration

Section 13 applied only to listed companies until the 1964 adoption of §12(g), although there are comparable reporting provisions
with respect to registered holding companies and mutual service
companies in the Holding Company Act[17] and the Investment
Company Act specifically incorporates §13(a) of the Exchange Act
among other reporting requirements.[18] We have already noticed
the 1936 adoption of §15(d) of the Exchange Act.[19] That section
survived in amended form the 1964 adoption of §12(g), because
§15(d) is not limited, as §12(g) is, to classes of securities with 500
holders or to equity securities. Since the original version continues
to apply to pre-1964 registrants under the 1933 Act, our description
of the section must start there.

In salient portion §15(d) as adopted in 1936 provided:

> Each registration statement hereafter filed pursuant to the Se-
> curities Act of 1933, as amended, shall contain an undertaking by
> the issuer[20] of the issue of securities to which the registration state-
> ment relates to file with the Commission, in accordance with such

[16] United States v. Guterma, 189 F. Supp. 265, 274 (S. D. N. Y. 1960). In
the same case Judge Edelstein held (id. at 273) that a series of counts charging violations in connection with the filing of annual reports and current
reports was not duplicitous under the "course of conduct" theory that the
Supreme Court had expounded in United States v. Universal C. I. T. Credit
Corp., 344 U. S. 218 (1952).

[17] §14; Rule 1(c); Form U5S.

[18] §30(a)-(e).

[19] See pp. 462-63 supra.

[20] This is the only "undertaking" provision that has ever appeared in any
of the SEC statutes, as distinct from the extrastatutory undertakings that are
sometimes required under the 1933 Act. See pp. 143-47 supra. The sanction for
enforcement of §15(d) undertakings is equally unique. Congress concurrently
amended the penal section of the statute to provide that, in lieu of any criminal penalty for failure to comply with an undertaking under §15(d), the issuer

rules and regulations as the Commission may prescribe as necessary or appropriate in the public interest or for the protection of investors, such supplementary and periodic information, documents, and reports as may be required pursuant to section 13 of this title in respect of a security listed and registered on a national securities exchange; but such undertaking shall become operative only if the aggregate offering price of such issue of securities, plus the aggregate value of all other securities of such issuer of the same class (as hereinafter defined) outstanding, computed upon the basis of such offering price, amounts to $2,000,000 or more. The issuer shall file such supplementary and periodic information, documents, and reports pursuant to such undertaking, except that the duty to file shall be automatically suspended if and so long as * * * the aggregate value of all outstanding securities of the class to which such issue belongs is reduced to less than $1,000,000 computed upon the basis of the offering price of the last issue of securities of said class offered to the public. * * *

Section 15(d) was considerably simplified in the 1964 amendments so far as its prospective operation is concerned. Although the original version remains in force for purposes of determining the operative effect, under the old $2 million and $1 million tests, of undertakings contained in registration statements filed before August 20, 1964 (the "date of enactment" of the 1964 amendments), the reporting duty with respect to registration statements filed since that date flows directly from the section. Except for the old cases, the "awkward" undertakings under §15(d) are thus a thing of the past.[21]

Regulation 15D generally parallels Regulation 13A. The §12(h) exemptive authority[22] has occasionally been used to exempt from §15(d) *ad hoc.* And the Commission's authority to enforce the statute by "mandamus"[23] (mandatory injunction under the Federal Rules of Civil Procedure) extends to §15(d).[24]

"shall forfeit to the United States the sum of $100" for every day the failure to comply continues. The forfeiture is "recoverable in a civil suit in the name of the United States." §32(b). The section has been a dead letter.

[21] S. Rep. No. 379, 88th Cong., 1st Sess. (1963) 69. A company with two or more registration statements effective under the 1933 Act, one or more filed on or before August 20, 1964, and one or more since that date, must report under §15(d) if (and as long as) required *either* by any of the undertakings in the older registration statements *or* by the amended §15(d). Id. at 67-69.

[22] See p. 482 supra.

[23] §21(e); see SEC v. Union Corp. of America, 205 F. Supp. 518 (E. D. Mo. 1962), *aff'd per curiam* sub nom. Union Corp. of America v. SEC, 309 F. 2d 93 (8th Cir. 1962).

[24] For a discussion of some nice questions of interpretation of the scope of §15(d), see 5 Loss 2784-87.

C. GETTING OUT ONCE YOU'RE IN

1. VOLUNTARY DELISTING

Although listing and registration are entirely discretionary with the issuer in the first instance, the issuer has no unqualified right to delist. Section 12(d) provides that "A security registered with a national securities exchange may be withdrawn or stricken from listing and registration in accordance with the rules of the exchange and, upon such terms as the Commission may deem necessary to impose for the protection of investors, upon application by the issuer or the exchange to the Commission."

All that the Commission's rules require is the filing of an application or notice in the event of something like a redemption or retirement.[1] And in other cases deregistration on application of an exchange (as distinct from the issuer) is granted automatically after a short time interval unless the Commission orders a hearing with respect to the possible imposition of terms.[2] Although the exchanges' status as self-regulatory organizations requires that an issuer that opposes delisting be given a hearing that satisfies the Fifth Amendment,[3] they also have "broad latitude * * * in making the critical judgment of when a company has failed to fulfill its responsibilities to such an extent that dealing on the Exchange in the security is unwarranted."[4] Listing "is not a vested right which may not be terminated by changes in the importance of the company and its stock in the investment community."[5]

The New York Stock Exchange's delisting guidelines (which do not operate automatically) contain both numerical criteria and others: for example, a common stock might be delisted if the company issues a debt security with inadequate interest coverage and common stock equity of less than 25 percent.[6]

Application by exchanges normally raise no particular problem, because they have a selfish interest in retaining appropriate listings. Nor do issuers' applications when the securities have little value, or when they are to remain listed on another exchange. And

---

C. 7C   [1] Rule 12d2-2(a)-(b).
  [2] Rule 12d2-2(c).
  [3] Intercontinental Industries, Inc. v. American Stock Exchange, 452 F. 2d 935, 940-41 (5th Cir. 1971).
  [4] Id., 452 F. 2d at 940.
  [5] Atlas Tack Corp. and Exchange Buffet Corp., 37 SEC 362, 365 (1956), aff'd sub nom. Exchange Buffet Corp. v. New York Stock Exchange, 244 F. 2d 507 (2d Cir. 1957), and Atlas Tack Corp. v. SEC, 246 F. 2d 311 (1st Cir. 1957).
  [6] N. Y. Stock Ex. Company Manual §A-16, esp. at A-294, ¶17.

initially, except for a few cases where the Commission dismissed
factually misleading applications (without prejudice to their renewal) on the ground that security holders might have been misled
into not appearing and objecting,[7] the only term the Commission
imposed in granting the application was a brief delay. But, in
order to counter what seemed to be a wave of delisting applications
from regional exchanges that were motivated by a desire to avoid
the disclosure impact of the statute, the Commission in 1944 imposed for the first time, as a "term" in granting the application
under §12(d), the requirement of a shareholder vote; and, in view
of the "grave questions" whether deregistration "would deprive
the shareholders of substantial advantages without giving them or
the [issuer] itself compensatory benefits,"[8] the Commission required a vote not only by a majority of shares but also by a majority of shareholders *per capita*. The fact that the issuer was a
Massachusetts trust, whose shareholders had no vote at all under
state law, emphasizes the supremacy of federal law here.[9]

---

[7] E. g., Automobile Finance Co., 9 SEC 571 (1941).

[8] Shawmut Assn., 15 SEC 1028, 1035, 1038 (1944), *aff'd* sub nom. Shawmut
Assn. v. SEC, 146 F. 2d 791 (1st Cir. 1945), *motion to modify terms of vote
denied*, 19 SEC 719 (1945). Most of the exchanges have their own voting
requirements, which must be complied with under §12(d) before the issuer
can apply for deregistration. But Boston, where Shawmut was listed, did not.

[9] Id., 146 F. 2d at 795; cf. Phillips v. SEC, 153 F. 2d 27 (2d Cir. 1946),
cert. denied, 328 U. S. 860 (plan under Holding Co. Act §11(e) need *not*
provide for a stockholders' vote although it normally would be *required* by
state law).

Cf. also United Funds, Inc. v. Carter Products, Inc., CCH Fed. Sec. L. Rep.
¶91,288 (Md. Cir. Ct. 1963), a non-SEC case of considerable significance as far
as delisting is concerned. Carter had only one class of stock, with 3 million
shares authorized and 2.6 million outstanding, of which Hoyt owned slightly
more than 50 percent. In 1957 Hoyt and members of his family had made a
public distribution of 500,000 shares, the prospectus stating that the company
intended to apply for listing on the New York Stock Exchange. The plaintiffs,
three investment companies, bought their shares in the public offering or
afterwards. In 1962 the board recommended, and the shareholders after a
solicitation under the SEC proxy rules approved, an amendment of the articles
to create a new class of nonvoting common, of which 4 million shares were
authorized, with an announcement that the board would declare a stock
dividend share for share. Before that board meeting, the Exchange had advised that it would delist the common stock if the amendment became effective.

The court enjoined consummation of the proposed plan, holding (1) that
the statement about listing, which had been made for the company's benefit
as well as that of the sellers, had been meant to make the stock more attractive
to investors and, under the usage and custom of the market, had been accepted
as a promise that the listing would be continued in the absence of a proper
corporate reason for discontinuance, and that the plaintiffs had relied upon
that statement in buying, so that the promissory estoppel doctrine of §90 of
the Restatement of Contracts applied without regard to absence of privity
(an underwriter having intervened between the defendants and the plaintiffs);

This and two similar cases that followed — in all three of which management ultimately decided not to go to shareholders — effectively checkmated the delisting trend.[10] And since the 1964 adoption of §12(g), of course, few companies would escape regulation by delisting.

2. INVOLUNTARY DELISTING AND COMPLIANCE ORDERS

The same statute that denies management the unqualified right to withdraw voluntarily from exchange listing and registration authorizes the Commission to impose involuntary delisting as one of the sanctions. Section 12(j) (successor to the pre-1975 §19(a)(2)) authorizes the Commission to suspend for not more than twelve months, or to revoke, registration on a finding (after notice and

---

(2) that this contractual obligation of Carter applied equally to Hoyt in view of his implied representation and promise that through his control he would see that Carter complied with his stated intention; (3) that Hoyt had an additional obligation, apart from the law of contracts, based on the fiduciary duty of a majority holder toward the minority not to use his voting power for some ulterior purpose adverse to the interests of the company and its stockholders; (4) that the only real purpose was to enable the Hoyt family to diversify or reduce its large investment in Carter without reduction of its majority control; (5) that perpetuation of majority voting control in a single stockholder was not a proper corporate purpose; (6) that Exchange listing was a valuable corporate asset, so that delisting would cause special damage to minority stockholders, as contrasted with Hoyt and his family, by depriving them of the benefit of §§14 and 16, and hence injustice could be avoided only by the enforcement of the promise pursuant to §90; (7) that these conclusions with respect to the company's and Hoyt's contractual obligations applied also to the determination whether Hoyt had committed a breach of his fiduciary obligation; and (8) that, in conclusion, the proposed issuance of nonvoting common would violate the company's and Hoyt's contractual obligations, as well as Hoyt's duty as a fiduciary, and would substantially damage the plaintiffs, who had no adequate legal remedy.

[10] Torrington Co., 19 SEC 39 (1945); Suburban Electric Securities Co., 23 SEC 5, 11 (1946) (*two-thirds* majorities by shares and *per capita*). A few companies that did submit delisting proposals to their shareholders — either because of exchange rules or because they realized the Commission would insist on a vote — managed to obtain substantial majorities, in terms of shareholders as well as shares, notwithstanding their inclusion of a statement of the disadvantages of delisting in the proxy statements required to be sent to shareholders under the Commission's proxy rules. Apparently shareholders follow management here as in most matters. But one can only speculate on how a full and fair disclosure would have worked in the three cases in which the Commission wrote opinions — whether, to take one of them as an example, any substantial number of shareholders would have been sufficiently ill-advised, or sufficiently magnanimous, to vote for delisting in the face of disclosure that the management thought the price of the shares on the exchange was too high and expected that the price would go down in the event of delisting! Id. at 5.

opportunity for hearing) that the issuer "has failed to comply with any provision of this" Act.

The remedy is Draconian. When management fails to comply with some provision of the statute or the Commission's rules, it makes little sense to visit the sin on the innocent security holders by depriving them of an exchange market, not to mention the statutory advantages of registration. More than that, the remedy is unnecessary in view of the availability of a judicial action for mandatory injunction to require the filing of adequate reports.[11]

Indeed, the 1975 amendments added a new *administrative* remedy in §15(c)(4), which authorized the Commission, if it finds (after notice and opportunity for hearing) that any person subject to the registration or reporting provisions "has failed to comply with" any such provision "in any material respect," to publish its findings and order compliance on whatever terms it specifies.

At first blush it seems odd to provide for an order that is not self-enforcing in the sense that failure to comply would subject any person either to contempt proceedings of any kind or to criminal prosecution. But §21(e) gives the District Courts jurisdiction to command compliance not only with the statute and rules but also with "orders thereunder." And §15(c)(4) serves the important function of permitting the Commission to resolve complex factual, accounting, and other technical questions in its own forum, just as it may use §12(j) with respect to listed securities.[12] That is to say, §15(c)(4) makes it possible for the Commission to appear in court as a lower tribunal whose quasijudicial orders are being reviewed instead of as an ordinary plaintiff in an injunctive action. This, of course, is not unimportant.

Most of the §15(c)(4) orders have been entered by consent,[13] just as §12(j) orders have normally resulted in compliance rather than delisting, presumably because most managements are not anxious to lose their exchange market or, in any event, dislike the aroma of being *thrown* off.[14] In other words, the deregistration procedure, as applied to companies with securities actively traded,

---

[11] SEC v. Atlas Tack Corp., 93 F. Supp. 111 (D. Mass. 1950).

[12] See S. Rep. No. 379, 88th Cong., 1st Sess. (1963) 66. Actually, although §15(c)(4) came into the law in 1964 in connection with §12(g), it is not limited to §12(g) registration and in fact it has been used against exchange-registered securities. Crescent Corp., 43 SEC 551 (1967).

[13] E. g., Hycel, Inc., Sec. Ex. Act Rel. 14,981, 15 SEC Dock. 315 (1978).

[14] See, e. g., Adolf Gobel, Inc., 35 SEC 535, 539 (1954). In the early years most orders under the former §19(a)(2), now §12(j), involved small companies with negligible assets and little or no investor interest, which had no business being on an exchange. 10 SEC Ann. Rep. 47 (1944).

seemed to be developing into an administrative "means of correcting faulty statements."[15]

This makes it harder to understand a number of proceedings beginning in the late 1950s — proceedings not explicable in terms of getting rid of the "deadwood" in some exchanges' lists — that the Commission pursued to the bitter end of deregistration, emphasizing that use of the facilities of a national securities exchange was a "privilege involving important responsibilities," whose abuse violated "the integrity of the exchange market," and observing that regard must be had to the interests of potential investors as well as existing stockholders.[16] Whatever their explanation, presumably those cases may be consigned to history in view of the Commission's statement in the hearings that led to the enactment of §15(c)(4):

> The sanction of delisting for failure to comply with the provisions of the act has been imposed only infrequently by the Commission because delisting would have the effect of relieving the issuer of the duty of complying with the disclosure provisions of the act and would deprive investors of an exchange market for the trading of their securities.[17]

3.   TERMINATION OF §12(g) REGISTRATION

Under §12(g)(4), registration of any class of security is terminated ninety days after the issuer files a certification that the number of holders of record of that class of security is reduced below 300. But in 1982 the Commission by rule (concurrently with its increase of the statutory assets figure to $3 million) added an *alternative* deregistration standard in terms of falling below 500 holders if the issuer's total assets have not exceeded $3 million on the last day of each of the three most recent fiscal years.[18] The

---

[15] Associated Gas & Electric Co., 11 SEC 975, 1062 (1942).

[16] Great Sweet Grass Oils, Ltd., 37 SEC 683, 697-98 (1957), *aff'd per curiam* sub nom. Great Sweet Grass Oils, Ltd. v. SEC, 256 F. 2d 893 (D. C. Cir. 1958); see also Kroy Oils, Ltd., 37 SEC 683, 697-98 (1957).

[17] SEC Legislation, 1963, Hearings before Subcom. of Senate Com. on Banking & Currency on S. 1642, 88th Cong., 1st Sess. (1963) 402-03; 1 Investor Protection, Hearings before Subcom. of House Com. on Int. & For. Commerce on H. R. 6789, H. R. 6793, S. 1642, 88th Cong., 1st Sess. (1963) 183. *Query* SEC v. American Realty Trust, 429 F. Supp. 1148, 1178 (E. D. Va. 1977), *rev'd on other grounds*, 586 F. 2d 1001 (4th Cir. 1978), where the court (without discussion) cited §15(c)(4) as one reason for declining to order the filing of corrected annual reports.

[18] Rule 12g-4(a); Sec. Ex. Act Rel. 18,647, 25 SEC Dock. 49 (1982).

Commission may accelerate the ninety-day period. And, if it finds that the statutory certification is untrue, it is required (after notice and opportunity for hearing) to deny termination of registration, in which event termination is deferred pending final decision on the question of denial. Once a company becomes registered under §12(g), the mere fact that its assets fall below $3 million is irrelevant.

The first characteristic of this section that strikes the eye, in comparison with both §12(g)(1), under which the 500 test for initial registration is determined as of the last day of each fiscal year, and §15(d), under which the reporting requirement is suspended if there are fewer than 300 record holders of the particular class of securities at the *beginning* of a particular fiscal year, is that the statutory certification under §12(g)(4) may be filed at any time during the fiscal year. Furthermore, unless termination is denied on a finding that the certification with respect to the number of holders is untrue, the registration is *terminated*, not merely suspended like the reporting duty under §15(d).

Literally this would seem to be so even if the number of holders rises above 300 (or 500 under the rule's alternative) once more during the period between the filing of the certification and the effectiveness of the termination. But, of course, the security will have to be registered anew if there are as many as 500 holders (as well as $3 million of assets) by the end of the fiscal year during which registration was terminated or the end of any succeeding fiscal year. Moreover, the legislative history emphasizes that after termination of registration the Commission may still require the filing of reports with respect to periods while the security was registered.[19] Finally, because of the differences in the critical date for applying the statutory test of 300 stockholders under §15(d), it is quite possible that a reporting duty under §15(d) may for a short time survive the termination of §12(g) registration under the statutory test.

4. SUSPENSION OF §15(d) REPORTING

Suspension of the reporting duty under §15(d) is now governed by a test in terms of 300 record holders of any class of securities to which the registration statement relates rather than the old

---

[19] S. Rep. No. 379, 88th Cong., 1st Sess. (1963) 62; 1 Investor Protection, Hearings before Subcom. of House Com. on Int. & For. Commerce on H. R. 6789, H. R. 6793, S. 1642, 88th Cong., 1st Sess. (1963) 215.

$1 million test.[20] This is so with respect to all registration statements filed before or after August 20, 1964, except that (1) the old $1 million test continues to apply to those registration statements filed before that date as an *additional* "out" in accordance with the provisions of the undertaking,[21] and (2) in 1982 the Commission by rule added an *alternative* suspension standard comparable to the new alternative deregistration standard with respect to §12(g).[22]

5. SUSPENSION OF TRADING

Apart from the fact that the Commission's authority under §12(j) extends to the temporary suspension as well as the withdrawal of the *registration* of a security, there are certain circumstances under which either the exchange or the Commission may suspend *trading*. The difference between the two types of suspension is that a security that is suspended from trading still retains its registered status.

a.   Suspension of Trading by Exchange

The Act is silent on the point. But a rule of the Commission permits the exchanges to suspend trading in accordance with their own rules. It is required merely that the exchange promptly notify the Commission of the effective date of the suspension and of the restoration to trading, as well as the reasons for ordering or continuing the suspension. It goes without saying that any such suspension may not be continued to the point where it appears to the Commission that it is designed to evade the delisting provisions of §12(d).[23]

Brief exchange suspensions are frequent — almost three per trading day on the average — and typically they occur either when there is a substantial influx or imbalance of buy or sell orders or in the event of a news announcement considered to have

---

[20] The duty to file is automatically suspended for any fiscal year (after the year in which the registration statement becomes effective) at whose beginning there are fewer than 300 record holders of each registered class.

[21] S. Rep. No. 479, 88th Cong., 1st Sess. (1963) 67.

[22] Rule 15d-6(a)(2); see p. 496 supra.

[23] Rule 12d2-1.

significant implications for price.[24] Sometimes a suspension is initiated by a request from the issuer itself.[25]

b. Suspension of Trading by SEC

In addition, an emergency suspension power is given the Commission directly by §12(k) (successor to the pre-1975 §19(a)(4)). That section authorizes the Commission, if in its opinion the public interest and the protection of investors so require,

> to suspend trading in any security (other than an exempted security) for a period not exceeding ten days, or with the approval of the President, summarily to suspend all trading on any national securities exchange or otherwise, in securities other than exempted securities, for a period not exceeding ninety days.

Although the New York Stock Exchange had to close for some four months in 1914 and again on fourteen scattered days in 1928 and November 1929 because of volume activity, as well as eleven days during the bank moratorium of March 1933,[26] it has not yet been necessary to invoke the emergency power to suspend all trading.

The story with respect to individual suspensions is very different. The Commission never used its summary power until 1944. The first order was entered on the day the company's president committed suicide, and it was followed by an investigation and public hearing with respect to the adequacy of the company's recent filings under both the 1933 and 1934 Acts.[27]

For a while the Commission regarded summary suspension as a

---

[24] See Hopewell and Schwartz, Temporary Trading Suspensions in Individual NYSE Securities, 33 J. Fin. 1355, 1372 (1978). See also, e. g., Wall St. J., May 3, 1966, p. 7, col. 2: Apparently because of an error by one or more specialists in establishing a post-merger opening price at about one-third what it should have been, the Exchange not only halted trading at 11:23 A. M. but also ordered all previous transactions cancelled, and trading did not reopen until the next day, after appointment of "a new temporary specialist."

[25] Cf. State Teachers Retirement Board v. Fluor Corp., 654 F. 2d 843 (2d Cir. 1981).

[26] N. Y. Stock Ex., Fact Book (1966) 37, 44-45. The Exchange closed without any action by the Commission twenty-eight minutes after President Kennedy's assassination on Friday, November 22, 1963, and most of the other exchanges followed. The weekend and a national day of mourning intervened before the resumption of trading the following Tuesday.

[27] Elastic Stop Nut Corp. of America, Sec. Ex. Act Rel. 3635 (1944).

highly extraordinary remedy, designed essentially for crisis situations. But over the years this authority developed into another disclosure device. After a warning by the Commission that it would consider temporary suspension of trading in securities of issuers that were delinquent in filing reports,[28] nearly 200 of the 279 suspension orders in fiscal 1974 fell in that category.[29] Between 1964 and November 1976 alone, the Commission suspended trading in 941 securities.[30] More than that:

(1) By 1959 the Chairman found it possible to say, by way of explaining a legislative proposal to insert a *pendente lite* suspension power in the then §19(a)(2), predecessor of today's §12(j), that "Lately, this grant of power [then §19(a)(4), now §12(k)] has been used to keep in effect a suspension of trading pending final disposition of delisting proceedings," although "No express authority for such action is contained in Section 19(a)(4).[31]

(2) The original §19(a)(4) covered only exchange trading. But from the beginning the Commission managed to extend its authority to the over-the-counter market by adopting an appropriate fraud-prevention rule under §15(c)(2)[32] and simply finding, whenever it suspended exchange trading, that the purpose of the suspension was "to prevent fraudulent, deceptive or manipulative acts or practices." That practice was regularized by the 1964 amendments' adoption of an over-the-counter suspension authority in a §15(c)(5), which in the 1975 amendments was combined with the original §19(a)(4) into the present §12(k). The Senate committee said of the new §15(c)(5) in 1964:

> As under section 19(a)(4), the Commission could invoke this suspension power in those cases in which fraudulent or manipulative practices of the issuer or other persons have deprived the security of a fair and orderly market, or where some corporate event makes informed trading impossible and provides opportunities for the deception of investors. Trading would be resumed as soon as adequate disclosure and dissemination of the facts material to informed investment decision were achieved.[33]

[28] Sec. Ex. Act Rel. 10,214 (1973).
[29] 40 SEC Ann. Rep. 77-78 (1974).
[30] Petition for cert., SEC v. Sloan, 436 U. S. 103 (1978).
[31] Gadsby, Current S. E. C. Legislative and Related Problems, 189 Com. & Fin. Chron. 1863, 1903 (1959). Sometimes the Commission also acted to prevent trading until it might obtain appropriate injunctive relief, usually against fraud or manipulation or an unregistered distribution in violation of §5 of the 1933 Act.
[32] Former Rule 15c2-2 as adopted in Sec. Ex. Act Rel. 3587 (1944). On §15(c)(2), see p. 805 infra.
[33] S. Rep. No. 379, 88th Cong., 1st Sess. (1963) 66.

In recent years the Commission has exercised its suspension authority primarily in the over-the-counter market, relying on the exchanges to act in their own markets.

(3) Another construction of the Con.mission ultimately led to a sharp defeat in the Supreme Court. Although the suspension power has always been limited to ten days, the Commission from the beginning followed the policy of entering a series of orders until it considered that adequate information was available. Then, except when the suspension culminated in a delisting order or a final suspension order under former §19(a)(2) (now §12(j)), it timed the lifting of its suspension so that the public would have some opportunity to be informed of the facts before the resumption of exchange trading. It was perhaps not unreasonable for the Commission to conclude that a single ten-day suspension order did not exhaust its summary power with respect to the particular security if it made a new determination every ten days of the necessity of continuing the suspension under the statutory standards.[34] But the practice got out of hand. Consecutive orders were entered in 235 of the 941 suspensions between 1964 and November 1976.[35] And many lasted the better part of a year. The result was predictable:

SECURITIES AND EXCHANGE COMMISSION v. SLOAN
Supreme Court of the United States, 1978
436 U. S. 103

MR. JUSTICE REHNQUIST delivered the opinion of the Court.

* * * the Commission issued a series of consecutive orders suspending trading in the common stock of Canadian Javelin, Ltd. (CJL), for over a year. The Court of Appeals for the Second Circuit held that such a series of suspensions was beyond the scope of the Commission's statutory authority. 547 F. 2d 152, 157-158 (1976). We granted certiorari to consider this important question, 434 U. S. 901 (1977), and, finding ourselves in basic agreement with the Court of Appeals, we affirm. We hold that even though there be a periodic redetermination of whether such action is required by "the public interest" and for "the protection of in-

---

[34] The Senate committee accepted this construction in connection with the 1964 amendments, while counseling "restraint" and action "with all diligence to develop the necessary facts in order that any suspension can be terminated as soon as possible." S. Rep. No. 379, 88th Cong., 1st Sess. (1963) 66-67.

[35] Petition for cert., SEC v. Sloan, 436 U. S. 103 (1978).

vestors," the Commission is not empowered to issue, based upon a single set of circumstances, a series of summary orders which would suspend trading beyond the initial 10-day period.

I

On November 29, 1973, apparently because CJL had disseminated allegedly false and misleading press releases concerning certain of its business activities, the Commission issued the first of what was to become a series of summary 10-day suspension orders continuously suspending trading in CJL common stock from that date until January 26, 1975. App. 109. During this series of suspensions respondent Sloan, who owned 13 shares of CJL stock and had engaged in substantial purchases and short sales of shares of that stock, filed a petition in the United States Court of Appeals for the Second Circuit challenging the orders on a variety of grounds. On October 15, 1975, the court dismissed as frivolous all respondent's claims, except his allegation that the "tacking" of 10-day summary suspension orders for an indefinite period was an abuse of the agency's authority and a deprivation of due process. It further concluded, however, that in light of two events which had occurred prior to argument, it could not address this question at that time. The first event of significance was the resumption of trading on January 26, 1975. The second was the commencement of a second series of summary 10-day suspension orders, which was still in effect on October 15. This series had begun on April 29, 1975, when the Commission issued a 10-day order based on the fact that the Royal Canadian Mounted Police had launched an extensive investigation into alleged manipulation of CJL common stock on the American Stock Exchange and several Canadian stock exchanges. App. 11-12. This time 37 separate orders were issued, suspending trading continuously from April 29, 1975, to May 2, 1976. The court thought the record before it on October 15 inadequate in light of these events and dismissed respondent's appeal "without prejudice to his repleading after an administrative hearing before the SEC * * * ," which hearing, though apparently not required by statute or regulation, had been offered by the Commission at oral argument. 527 F. 2d 11, 12 (1975), *cert. denied,* 426 U. S. 935 (1976).

Thereafter respondent immediately petitioned the Commission for the promised hearing. The hearing was not forthcoming, however, so on April 23, 1976, during the period when the second series of orders was still in effect, respondent brought the present action pursuant to §25(a)(1) of the Act, 15 U. S. C. §78y(a)(1) (1976 ed), challenging the second series of suspension orders. He argued, among other things, that there was no rational basis for the suspension orders, that they were not supported by substantial evidence in any event, and that the "tacking" of 10-day summary suspension orders was beyond the Commission's authority because the statute specifically authorized suspension "for a period not exceeding ten days." The court held in respondent's favor on this latter point. It first concluded that despite the fact that there had been no 10-day suspension order in effect since May 2, 1976, and the Commission had asserted that it had no plans to consider or issue an order against CJL in the foreseeable future, the case was not moot because it was " 'capable of repetition, yet evading review.' " 547 F. 2d, at 158, quoting from *Southern Pacific Terminal Co. v. ICC*, 219 U. S. 498, 515 (1911).

The court then decided that the statutes which authorized summary suspensions — §12(k) and its predecessors — did not empower the Commission to issue successive orders to curtail trading in a security for a period beyond the initial 10-day period. 547 F. 2d, at 157-158.[a] We granted certiorari, specifically directing the attention of the parties to the question of mootness, 434 U. S. 901 (1977), to which we now turn.

II

[This part of the opinion concludes that the case is not moot.]

III

A

Turning to the merits, we note that this is not a case where the Commission, discovering the existence of a manipulative scheme affecting CJL stock, suspended trading for 10 days and then, upon the discovery of a second manipulative scheme or other improper activity unrelated to the first scheme, ordered a second 10-day suspension. Instead it is a case in which the Commission issued a series of summary suspension orders lasting over

---

[a] ED.: Presumably because there was no effective order to set aside, the Second Circuit's opinion concluded with a direction to the Commission — something extraordinary if not unique in its experience — "to discontinue forthwith its adoption and use of successive ten-day suspension orders * * * ." *Sloan v. SEC*, 547 F. 2d 152, 158 (2d Cir. 1976), *cert. denied*, 434 U. S. 821.

a year on the basis of evidence revealing a single, though likely sizable, manipulative scheme. Thus, the only question confronting us is whether, even upon a periodic redetermination of "necessity," the Commission is statutorily authorized to issue a series of summary suspension orders based upon a single set of events or circumstances which threaten an orderly market. This question must, in our opinion, be answered in the negative.

The first and most salient point leading us to this conclusion is the language of the statute. Section 12(k) authorizes the Commission "summarily to suspend trading in any security . . . *for a period not exceeding ten days* . . . ." 15 U. S. C. §78*l*(k) (1976 ed.) (emphasis added). The Commission would have us read the underscored phrase as a limitation only upon the duration of a single suspension order. So read, the Commission could indefinitely suspend trading in a security without any hearing or other procedural safeguards as long as it redetermined every 10 days that suspension was required by the public interest and for the protection of investors. While perhaps not an impossible reading of the statute, we are persuaded it is not the most natural or logical one. The duration limitation rather appears on its face to be just that — a maximum time period for which trading can be suspended for any single set of circumstances.

Apart from the language of the statute, which we find persuasive in and of itself, there are other reasons to adopt this construction of the statute. In the first place, the power to summarily suspend trading in a security even for 10 days, without any notice, opportunity to be heard, or findings based upon a record, is an awesome power with a potentially devastating impact on the issuer, its shareholders, and other investors. A clear mandate from Congress, such as that found in §12(k), is necessary to confer this power. No less clear a mandate can be expected from Congress to authorize the Commission to extend, virtually without limit, these periods of suspension. But we find no such unmistakable mandate in §12(k). Indeed, if anything, that section points in the opposite direction.

* * * In light of the explicit congressional recognition in other sections of the Act, both past and present, that any long-term sanctions or any continuation of summary restrictions must be accompanied by notice and an opportunity for a hearing, it is difficult to read the silence in §12(k) as an authorization for an extension of summary restrictions without such a hearing, as the Commission contends. The more plausible interpretation is that Congress did not intend the Commission to have the power to extend

the length of suspensions under §12(k) at all, much less to repeatedly extend such suspensions without any hearing.

B

*   *   *

This very case belies the Commission's argument that injunctions cannot be sought in appropriate cases. At exactly the same time the Commission commenced the first series of suspension orders it also sought a civil injunction against CJL and certain of its principals, alleging violations of the registration and antifraud provisions of the Securities Act of 1933, violations of the antifraud and reporting provisions of the Securities Exchange Act of 1934, and various other improper practices, including the filing of false reports with the Commission and the dissemination of a series of press releases containing false and misleading information. App. 109. And during the second series of suspension orders, the Commission approved the filing of an action seeking an injunction against those in the management of CJL to prohibit them from engaging in further violations of the Acts. Id., at 101.

* * * Even assuming that it is proper to suspend trading simply in order to enhance the information in the marketplace, there is nothing to indicate that the Commission cannot simply reveal to the investing public at the end of 10 days the reasons which it thought justified the initial summary suspension and then let the investors make their own judgments.

Even assuming, however, that a totally satisfactory remedy — at least from the Commission's viewpoint — is not available in every instance in which the Commission would like such a remedy, we would not be inclined to read §12(k) more broadly than its language and the statutory scheme reasonably permit. Indeed, the Commission's argument amounts to little more than the notion that §12(k) *ought* to be a panacea for every type of problem which may beset the marketplace. This does not appear to be the first time the Commission has adopted this construction of the statute. As early as 1961 a recognized authority in this area of the law called attention to the fact that the Commission was gradually carrying over the summary suspension power granted in the predecessors of §12(k) into other areas of its statutory authority and using it as a *pendente lite* power to keep in effect a suspension of trading pending final disposition of delisting proceedings. 2 L. Loss, Securities Regulation 854-855 (2d ed. 1961).

The author then questioned the propriety of extending the summary suspension power in that manner, id., at 854, and we think those same questions arise when the Commission argues that the summary suspension power should be available not only for the purposes clearly contemplated by §12(k), but also as a solution to virtually any other problem which might occur in the marketplace. We do not think §12(k) was meant to be such a cure-all. It provides the Commission with a powerful weapon for dealing with certain problems. But its time limit is clearly and precisely defined. * * *

*   *   *

* * * The absence of any truly persuasive legislative history to support the Commission's view, and the entire statutory scheme suggesting that in fact the Commission is not so empowered, reinforce our conclusion that the Court of Appeals was correct in concluding no such power exists. Accordingly, its judgment is affirmed.

MR. JUSTICE BRENNAN, with whom MR. JUSTICE MARSHALL joins, concurring in the judgment.

*   *   *

I

The Court's opinion does not reveal how flagrantly abusive the Security and Exchange Commission's use of its §12(k) authority has been. * * * the Commission has used §12(k), or its predecessor statutes, * * * to suspend trading in a security for up to 13 years. * * * And, although the 13-year suspension is an extreme example, the record is replete with suspensions lasting the better part of a year. I agree that §12(k) is clear on its face and that it prohibits this administrative practice. But even if §12(k) were unclear, a 13-year suspension, or even a 1-year suspension as here, without notice or hearing so obviously violates fundamentals of due process and fair play that no reasonable individual could suppose that Congress intended to authorize such a thing. * * *

Moreover, the SEC's procedural implementation of its §12(k) power mocks any conclusion other than that the SEC simply could not care whether its §12(k) orders are justified. So far as this record shows, the SEC never reveals the reasons for its suspension orders. * * * Nonetheless, when the SEC finally agreed to give respondent a hearing on the suspension of Canadian Javelin stock, it required respondent to state, in a verified petition (that is, *under oath*) why he thought the unrevealed conclusions of the SEC to be wrong. This is obscurantism run riot.

Accordingly, while we today leave open the question whether the SEC could tack successive 10-day suspensions if this were necessary to meet first one and then a different emergent situation, I for one would look with great disfavor on any effort to tack suspension periods unless the SEC concurrently adopted a policy of stating its reasons for each suspension. Without such a statement of reasons, I fear our holding today will have no force since the SEC's administration of its suspension power will be reviewable, if at all, only by the circuitous and time-consuming path followed by respondent here.

*   *   *

MR. JUSTICE BLACKMUN, concurring in the judgment.

I join the Court in its judgment, but I am less sure than the Court is that the Congress has not granted the Securities and Exchange Commission at least some power to suspend trading in a nonexempt security for successive 10-day periods despite the absence of a new set of circumstances. The Congress' awareness, recognition, and acceptance of the Commission's practice * * * , at the time of the 1964 amendments, blunts, it seems to me, the original literal language of the statute. * * *

Here, the Commission indulged in 37 suspension orders, all but the last issued "quite bare of any emergency findings," to borrow Professor Loss' phrase. Beyond the opaque suggestion in an April 1975 Release, No. 11,383 [6 SEC Dock. 780], that the Commission was awaiting the "dissemination of information concerning regulatory action by Canadian authorities," shareholders of CJL were given no hint why their securities were to be made non-negotiable for over a year. Until April 22, 1976, see Release No. 12,361 [9 SEC Dock. 482], the SEC provided no opportunity to shareholders to dispute the factual premises of a suspension, and, in the absence of any explanation by the Commission of the basis for its suspension orders, such a right to comment would be useless. As such, I conclude that the use of suspension orders in this case exceeded the limits of the Commission's discretion.

Given the 1975 amendments, a year-long blockade of trading without reasoned explanation of the supposed emergency or opportunity for an interim hearing clearly exceeds Congress' intention.

The Commission is now very careful to find a different ground for a second order.[36] And it has continued the practice of cautioning broker-dealers who trade after termination of the suspension to consider all available information, including any subsequently issued by the company, and not to enter quotations in violation of the minimum information requirements of Rule 15c2-11.[37]

The Code developed, before the *Sloan* decision, a novel solution designed to recognize the time constraints on the Commission while being fair to the issuer. Section 903(d) provides:

> (2) The Commission, by order, may summarily suspend trading in any security other than a Government or municipal security.

> (3) The issuer or any other person with an interest may request the Commission at any time to terminate a suspension under section 903(d)(2). The Commission's failure to grant such a request within ten days is a final order denying the request for purposes of judicial review under section 1818(a). See especially section 1818(a)(9).

The comments explain:

> (2) * * * So far as the second sentence of §903(d)(3) is concerned, the review, under the special provision of §1818(a)(9), will be on a limited record * * * unless the court uses its authority to procure evidence by remanding the matter under §1818(a)(6). And the scope of review will be limited to abuse of discretion. Consequently, it should not be easy to persuade the court to interfere with the administrative determination. But that is as it should be. It is simply essential to have some limited right of review, if only for the outrageous case, in order to prevent the whole procedure from being meaningless. Moreover, §1818(a)(8) expressly withholds review of the summary suspension order itself.

> (3) In view of the §903(d)(3) procedure, there is no ten-day limitation in §903(d)(2).

[36] See McDowell Enterprises, Inc., Sec. Ex. Act Rel. 16,682, 19 SEC Dock. 938 (1980) (no interval between the two suspension periods); Olympic Gas & Oil, Inc., Sec. Ex. Act Rel. 16,738, 19 SEC Dock. 1213 (1980) (three-week interval).

[37] Ibid.; on Rule 15c2-11, see p. 333 n. d supra.

(4) Section 1817(d)(1)(B) requires every suspension order to include the reasons for its entry. * * *

(5) There will be nothing — except common sense — to prevent either (a) a series of suspension-lifting requests, no matter how many previous requests there have been, or (b) a further suspension after a judicial reversal. But in either case, the shorter the interval, the less will be the need for the Commission or the court (as the case may be) to do more than refer to its last order (or judgment).

(6) A related problem that has occasionally arisen is the Commission's *refusal* to order or continue a suspension, typically pending a reorganization of the issuer, when those in control of the issuer *want* a suspension. Whether such a refusal is subject to judicial review is left to whether it constitutes "other final action" within §1818(b).

D.   PROXIES

1.   THE PROBLEM (HEREIN OF COSTS OF SOLICITATION)

Corporate practice has come a long way from the common law's nonrecognition of the proxy device. The widespread distribution of corporate securities, with the concomitant separation of ownership and management, puts the entire concept of the stockholders' meeting at the mercy of the proxy instrument. This makes the corporate proxy a tremendous force for good or evil in our economic scheme. Unregulated, it is an open invitation to self-perpetuation and irresponsibility of management. Properly circumscribed, it may well turn out to be the salvation of the modern corporate system.

In the old days the stockholder typically received once a year a finely printed proxy card that he was urged to sign and return. Ordinarily the proxy authorized one or more persons to vote the stockholder's shares to elect directors and take any other action that was considered desirable. This was the sum and substance of the corporate owner's solemn right of suffrage. It was an accepted practice before the SEC proxy rules, as an eminent member of the corporate bar has pointed out,

> to give the proxies power to approve, adopt, ratify and confirm all of the minutes of the board of directors since the date of the last annual meeting and all acts and transactions of the directors or officers taken pursuant thereto, although a detailed description

of such minutes or action was customarily not included in the notice. Corporate practice varied as to whether at the meeting the presiding officer would merely state that the minute books were at hand and available for inspection by the stockholders prior to action upon the customary motion for approval and ratification, or whether a clerk would read the minutes aloud for several hours while the proxies designated by the stockholders sat around in bored silence. Some lawyers and managements regarded this so-called ratification by the stockholders of the acts of the management even though not set forth in detail in the notice of the meeting as being of great efficacy.[1]

Management had every advantage, moreover, if insurgent groups should have the temerity to wage a "proxy fight." It had the stockholders' lists. It stood to gain from stockholder inertia. And it had the overwhelming strategic advantage of access to the corporate treasury for the sometimes substantial costs of solicitation. As a British writer has put it, "it is easier to upset a Ministry than a Board of Directors, so long as a company remains a going concern."[2]

So far as the matter of costs is concerned, the relatively few cases in both the United States and England follow the general approach — an approach that had its inception before the day of campaign expenses running sometimes into seven figures — that reasonable expenditures in the interest of an intelligent exercise of the stockholders' judgment on the corporate policies to be followed may properly be charged to the corporation, whereas expenditures that are solely in the interest of the directors' maintaining themselves in office may not. But, the courts say, even though the formal issue may be an election of directors, it does not necessarily follow that no question of corporate policy is involved.[3]

A 1955 New York case that might have clarified the general problem of solicitation costs produced an anticlimactic three-way split in the Court of Appeals without a majority opinion. The difficulty was that the plaintiff, in a derivative action to require reimbursement of the corporation, challenged various expenses — including professional proxy solicitation,[4] public relations counsel,

C. 7D   [1] Dean, Non-compliance with Proxy Regulations — Effect on Ability of Corporation to Hold Valid Meeting, 24 Corn. L. Q. 483, 490 (1939).

[2] H. Parkinson, Scientific Investment (1932) 134.

[3] E. g., Hall v. Trans-Lux Daylight Picture Screen Corp., 20 Del. Ch. 78, 171 Atl. 226 (Ch. 1934); Campbell v. Australian Mutual Provident Society, 99 L. T. 3 (P. C. 1908).

[4] For a brief description of one of the leading firms of proxy solicitors, Georgeson & Co., see The Old Touch, 30 New Yorker 24 (Mar. 27, 1954).

entertainment, and chartered airplanes and limousines — as improper *per se,* conceding that they were "fair and reasonable" in amount.[5] Judge Froessel for himself, Chief Judge Conway, and Judge Burke followed the policy test and saw no need for the trial court to examine each of the challenged items in view of the concession as to their reasonableness. Judge Desmond concurred in the result only because the plaintiff, in failing to introduce any "evidentiary bases for a determination as to either lawfulness or reasonableness," had not made out a *prima facie* case; the record, as he saw it, did not present the "highly important" question whether it is lawful for a corporation to pay the expenses of a proxy contest, although he did go on to say that a heavy vote of stockholder ratification would not immunize "intrinsically unlawful" expenditures from attack.[6] Judges Van Voorhis, Dye, and Fuld dissented. They thought it quite possible that the existence of a contest warranted the management "in circularizing the stockholders with more than ordinarily detailed information."[7] But they rejected the policy test as impracticable. In their view the plaintiff's concession of reasonableness did not relieve the defendants of the burden of going forward with evidence justifying their expenditures "once plaintiff had proved facts from which an inference of impropriety might be drawn."[8]

At any rate, even if the sauce goes to the ganders and *successful* insurgents may reimburse themselves from the treasury once the "outs" have become "ins" — a point on which the law is far from clear — there is still a great difference between the management's dipping into the corporate till at the outset and the insurgents'

---

[5] Rosenfeld v. Fairchild Engine & Airplane Corp., 309 N. Y. 168, 172, 128 N. E. 2d 291, 292 (1955). Professor Eisenberg takes the view that, if the statutory principal of a limited term of office is to be respected, the directors must be regarded "as acting not as officeholders but as officeseekers"; that, in terms of fiduciary duties as distinct from authority, the rationale of the traditional test "loses sight of the crucial fact that toward the expiration of his term an incumbent director assumes the capacity of officeseeker as well as officeholder, thereby creating an irreconcilable conflict of interest"; that consequently the presence of a policy issue should not in itself justify board access to the corporate proxy machinery; and that a preferable approach would be a matching test under which management would not be allowed to use the corporate proxy machinery to wage a campaign that substantially exceeds that of the insurgents (so that, for example, management should be allowed to employ public relations counsel or proxy solicitors only if the insurgents do so or it is reasonably foreseeable that they will). Eisenberg, Access to the Corporate Proxy Machinery, 83 Harv. L. Rev. 1489, 1494-1502 (1970).

[6] 309 N. Y. at 174, 175, 176, 128 N. E. 2d at 293, 294, 295.

[7] 309 N. Y. at 179, 128 N. E. 2d at 296.

[8] 309 N. Y. at 178, 128 N. E. 2d at 296.

raising the funds themselves with a view to reimbursement *if* they win.

Altogether, a writer in the London Economist put it well when he said on Christmas Day in 1937:

> Company meeting procedure is a fitting topic for the festival of Christmas. Outwardly, it is a conglomeration of paradoxes whose superb unreason best suits the moment when paper hats are put on and logic leaves by the chimney. Approximately five thousand British public companies invite their shareholders, once every year, to a folk *moot*. If half the proprietors of even a moderate-sized company attended, the chairman would have a larger audience than Signor Mussolini ever addressed from the Palazzo Venezia. No hall in England could possibly contain the 150,000 ordinary shareholders of Imperial Chemical Industries. But no secretary ever lost sleep on that account; for shareholders simply do not come trooping by battalions. Contrary to all theatrical canons, the best shows draw the thinnest houses. Only a passed dividend, a heavy loss or a reconstruction scheme can really pack the hall; a crowded meeting is usually an angry meeting. Shareholders who cannot attend, however, are given special facilities for voting in favour of the chairman's policy before they have heard his speech.[9]

2. THE REGULATORY SCHEME

In §14(a) of the Exchange Act, Congress, abandoning the more specific standards of the original bills,[10] left the solicitation of proxies to SEC rulemaking under broad "public interest" standards. Neither the statute nor the rules are limited to ensuring full disclosure. The statutory language is considerably more general than it is under the specific disclosure philosophy of the 1933 Act. But the Commission's basic philosophy here has been one of disclosure. At any rate, it has analogized its rules to the disclosure requirements of the Securities Act — the rules *are* in a sense a little Securities Act — and has emphasized that its power under §14(a), unlike its authority under the Holding Company

---

[9] "The Chairman Said * * * ," 129 Economist 646 (1937).

[10] §13(a), S. 2693, H. R. 7852, 7855, 73d Cong., 2d Sess. (1934). See also Holding Co. Act §§12(e), 12(g)(3); Inv. Co. Act §§14(a), 20(a). With respect to §15(d) companies, see p. 463 supra. The Code codifies the more basic concepts that have long characterized the proxy rules, especially the exemptions. §§202(128), 202(158), 603. And in July 1982 the Commission began a review of the entire system of proxy regulation. Sec. Ex. Act Rel. 18,878, 25 SEC Dock. 924 (1982).

Act, does not extend to passing on the fairness or merits of any plan presented to security holders.[11] Within its authority, however, the Commission has recognized that the stockholder today "can only address the assembled proxies which are lying at the head of the table."[12] Notwithstanding Professor Berle's characterization of the shareholders' meeting as "a kind of ancient, meaningless ritual like some of the ceremonies that go on with the mace in the House of Lords,"[13] the Commission has designed its rules so as to make the proxy device the closest practicable substitute for attendance at the meeting.

The Commission's approach to its quasi-legislative function under §14(a) has been an empirical one, but its philosophy has been consistent. The first rudimentary rules of 1935 set the basic three-way approach that has survived several general revisions and many amendments: (1) There must be a "brief description" of the matters to be considered, together with the action proposed to be taken by the holder of the proxy. (2) Nonmanagement solicitation must be facilitated. (3) A general fraud rule prohibits the making of any materially false or misleading statements.

As Regulation 14A stands, it consists of twelve fairly detailed rules, together with a Schedule 14A that specifies in twenty-two items the information required in the proxy statement and a Schedule 14B that specifies the information to be included in the statement required to be filed for each "participant" in a *contested* election.

In 1956 the Second Circuit upheld both the constitutionality of §14(a) and the validity of the rules "as applied either to management or to insurgent stockholder groups." The court rejected a defense that the section and rules were "unconstitutional as unauthorized delegations of legislative power and otherwise," the "otherwise" evidently referring to the argument of prior restraint under the First Amendment.[14]

---

[11] Sec. Ex. Act Rel. 1350 (1937).

[12] Testimony of SEC Chairman Purcell in Securities and Exchange Commission Proxy Rules, Hearings before House Com. on Int. & For. Commerce on H. R. 1493, H. R. 1821, and H. R. 2019, 78th Cong., 1st Sess. (1943) 174.

[13] A. Berle, Economic Power and the Free Society (Fund for the Republic 1957) 7.

[14] SEC v. May, 229 F. 2d 123, 124 (2d Cir. 1956). In Curtis Publishing Co. v. Butts, 388 U. S. 130, 150 (1967), the Court stated: "Federal securities regulation, mail fraud statutes, and common-law actions for deceit and misrepresentation are only some examples of our understanding that the right to communicate information of public interest is not unconditional." Cf. also Donaldson v. Read Magazine, 333 U. S. 178, 191 (1948) (Court, in sustaining the postal fraud order statute, stated that the First Amendment did not inhibit

3. COVERAGE, DEFINITIONS, AND EXEMPTIONS

Although most proxy solicitations are directed to holders of *stock,* §14(a) applies to any kind of security as long as it is registered. Holders of debt securities are not uncommonly solicited to give consents or authorizations in connection with reorganizations or modifications of one kind or another.[15] The rules use the term "proxy" as a generic reference to the statutory trilogy, "proxy or consent or authorization," and it is made clear that the consent or authorization whose solicitation is subject to the rules "may take the form of failure to object or to dissent.[16]

The term "solicitation" is defined[17] to include "(1) any request for a proxy whether or not accompanied by or included in a form of proxy; (2) any request to execute or not to execute, or to revoke, a proxy;[18] or (3) the furnishing of a form of proxy or other com-

---

legislation like the 1934 Act that is designed to prevent fraud or deception of the public with respect to such areas as securities).

[15] Under the Code's scheme of company rather than security registration, §603(a) applies the proxy rules with respect to any class of securities with at least 300 holders. And, to avoid interfering with activities of debt security holders that might be construed as "solicitation" in an attempt to avoid bankruptcy proceedings, §603(i)(2) provides an exemption with respect to a debt security "not traded in an organized market (except when the holders have a right under state law to vote with respect to the particular matter).

[16] Rule 14a-1. In Sargent v. Genesco, Inc., 492 F. 2d 750, 767-68 (5th Cir. 1974), the court held that at the pleading stage this rule did not preclude an adjudication that an "informational" letter sent to shareholders (whose vote was not required) to describe a proposed refinancing plan was a proxy solicitation on the theory that it encouraged shareholder inaction with respect to the plan.

[17] Rule 14a-1.

[18] See, e. g., Gaudiosi v. Mellon, 269 F. 2d 873 (3d Cir. 1959), *cert. denied,* 361 U. S. 902 (insurgent's wires to Swiss banks that were nominees for large blocks warning them not to vote for management without informing owners of contest and giving them an opportunity to determine how their stock should be voted were solicitations).

In Greater Iowa Corp. v. McLendon, 378 F. 2d 783, 796-98 (8th Cir. 1967), the court, characterizing "consent" and "authorization" as "extremely broad words" that were "not limited by the word proxy" (id. at 796), held that a solicitation to enter into a voting trust was so analogous to a proxy solicitation as to be covered by the rules. Cf. also Reserve Life Ins. Co. v. Provident Life Ins. Co., 499 F. 2d 715, 725 (8th Cir. 1974). But voting trust certificates are "securities," and Rule 14a-2(a)(3) exempts any solicitation involved in the offer and sale of securities registered under the 1933 Act (except in connection with a merger-type transaction within Rule 145).

It does not follow that a plaintiff's demand on stockholders in a derivative action, whether made pursuant to Rule 23.1 of the Federal Rules of Civil Procedure or pursuant to a similar requirement of state law, is subject to §14(a). On the other hand, certain types of notices to stockholders in class actions may present a closer question, particularly if the stockholders are asked to contribute toward expenses. Code §603(i)(7) exempts any solicitamunication to security holders under circumstances reasonably calculated to result in the procurement, withholding, or revocation of a proxy."[19] And it is clear that the Commission's authority extends to any writings, whether or not they strictly solicit a proxy, which (in the words of Judge Learned Hand) "are part of a continuous plan ending in solicitation and which prepare the way for its success."[20] Analogy to the problem of "beating the gun" by issuing press releases and making speeches before the filing of a registration statement under the 1933 Act is not inapt.

At the same time, there are a number of activities that quite clearly do *not* amount to solicitation. One is the routine distribution of semiannual and quarterly reports, as well as "other communications containing information and comment concerning the business of the character normally sent to security holders by corporate management during the course of a fiscal year."[21] Again, the term "solicitation" as defined in the rules does not apply to the furnishing of a form of proxy to a security holder upon his unsolicited request, or to the performance of ministerial acts on behalf of a solicitor (such as the physical distribution of the proxy literature or management's required mailing of a security holder's communications).[22] And as a matter of administrative policy the Commission has never questioned the propriety of answering inquiries from the press as long as they have not been "planted" by the persons interested in obtaining proxies.

---

tion in a class or stockholder's derivative action that is "under judicial supervision pursuant to a Federal or State statute or rule."

Query whether the definition extends to a request for tenders when the tender offer is conditioned on the certificate's being deposited along with the proxy and there is no solicitation otherwise. See Rule 14a-2(a)(2). Suppose *X* makes a tender offer for the stock of *Y*, which resorts to the not uncommon stratagem of proposing a merger with *Z*. If *X* continues to press its bid after *Y* or *Z* begins to solicit proxies for the merger, will *X*'s literature amount to a request not to execute, or to revoke, proxies for the merger? Conversely, will *Y*'s literature directed nominally *against* *X*'s offer be considered a solicitation of proxies *for* the merger?

Query further the position of one who permits the use of his name in another's solicitation — as where a person is the proposed buyer of the company soliciting proxies for approval of the sale. Compare Yamamoto v. Omiya, 564 F. 2d 1319, 1323 (9th Cir. 1977), with SEC v. Falstaff Brewing Corp., 629 F. 2d 62, 68-69 (D. C. Cir. 1980).

[19] See Suburban Electric Securities Co., 23 SEC 5, 11 (n. 11) (1946) (attachment of blank proxy form to notice of meeting with statement that proxies were not being solicited).

[20] SEC v. Okin, 132 F. 2d 784, 786 (2d Cir. 1943); see also Studebaker Corp. v. Gittlin, 360 F. 2d 692, 696 (2d Cir. 1966); but cf. Smallwood v. Pearl Brewing Co., 489 F. 2d 579, 600-01 (5th Cir. 1974), *cert. denied*, 419 U. S. 873.

[21] Sec. Ex. Act Rel. 5276 (1956).

[22] Rule 14a-1.

Indeed, presumably because the cry of "free press" had been raised in connection with the Commission's consideration of the 1956 rule amendments, the Director of the Division of Corporation Finance took pains to emphasize in a letter to the General Manager of the American Newspaper Publishers Association that "The proxy rules do not control or regulate what a newspaper publishes."[23] Out of context this says too much. It seems quite clear, as the letter recognizes, that a publisher would be criminally liable (and probably subject to injunction as well) as an aider and abettor if he were willfully to publish, by way of advertisement, any soliciting material that was misleading or that had not been filed when it should have been. The same conclusion would follow in principle if it could be shown that a publisher, through a financial interest in the company being fought over or a business or personal relationship with persons in one camp or the other, had willfully lent himself to unlawful solicitation in the guise of news stories or editorial comment. And it almost goes without saying that the distribution of reprints or reproductions of news stories or editorial comment may subject their distributor to the proxy rules under certain circumstances.[24] But the specific message of the Director's letter is perfectly plain: The proxy rules do not apply to a newspaper's publication of news stories quoting the contending parties, or of editorial comments, or to a publisher's merely permitting reprints of either news or editorial matter from his newspaper.

The means by which the solicitation is made is of no consequence. Section 14(a) applies to any solicitation "by use of the mails or by any means or instrumentality of interstate commerce or of any facility of any national securities exchange or otherwise." This technique was obviously used in order to preserve the rest of the section if the words "or otherwise" should be stricken on constitutional grounds. The question, of course, is whether the dependence of the rules upon registration, which is based on use of the mails or interstate facilities, furnishes a sufficient constitutional foundation for regulating the ordinary word-of-mouth solicitation. Until the 1942 revision of the proxy rules the Commission played it safe and exempted solicitations not effected by use of the mails or interstate or exchange facilities. Since then, however, there has been no such exemption.[25] The constitutional question has not been raised, and it seems fair to conclude that there is no longer any substantial question (if there ever was).

---

[23] See text at n. 14 supra.
[24] Sec. Ex. Act Rel. 5276 (1956).
[25] Sec. Ex. Act Rel. 3347 (1942).

There are nine exemptions apart from the exemptive authority in §12(h).[26] We have already noticed the treatment of certain foreign securities.[27] Three of the exemptions are designed to avoid duplication of regulation; they cover solicitations incident to a bankruptcy reorganization (the rule still refers to Chapter X of the old Bankruptcy Act), or an application or declaration under the Holding Company Act, or the registration of a security under the 1933 Act. There is also an exemption modeled on the "tombstone ad" provision of the Securities Act: this exemption permits any solicitation through the medium of a newspaper advertisement that informs security holders where they may obtain copies of a proxy statement, form of proxy and any other soliciting material, and that does no more than name the issuer, state the reason for the advertisement and identify the proposals to be acted upon by security holders.

Another exemption applies unconditionally to "Any solicitation by a person in respect of securities of which he is the beneficial owner." This permits the buyer to solicit and obtain the seller's proxy when the sale has occurred after the record date for determining the security holders who may vote at the meeting. It also reflects the practice whereby brokers or dealers carry securities in their own names as record owners for the accounts of their customers, usually for the reason that the securities are held in a margin account or that the "street name" facilitates transferability. In these cases the corporation, of course, recognizes only the record owner, and the exemption permits the beneficial owner to solicit a proxy from the broker if he wants to atttend the meeting and vote himself or appoint his own substitute proxy.

Still another exemption contemplates the converse situation, where the broker or other record owner transmits the proxy literature to the customer (the beneficial owner) with a request for instructions. This exemption, which is subject to a number of conditions, complements the rules of the several exchanges with respect to their members' transmittal of proxy literature to their customers, the beneficial owners of the securities.[28]

The final two exemptions do not extend to Rule 14a-9, the general antifraud rule. One permits one person, under certain conditions, to furnish proxy voting advice to another with whom he has a business relationship. The other of these two exemptions

---

[26] See p. 482 supra.

[27] Rule 3a12-3, supra p. 77. The other eight exemptions appear in Rule 14a-2.

[28] See also Rule 14b-1, infra p. 560.

covers *nonmanagement* solicitations of not more than ten persons. As in the case of the private offering exemption under the 1933 Act, the significant factor is the number of persons solicited rather than the number who actually give their proxies. And the maximum of ten solicitations is applicable not to each member of a given nonmanagement group but to the group as a whole. Nor may one piece of soliciting material be sent to one group of ten persons and another piece to ten different persons. By the same token, the exemption does not permit the sending of follow-up material even to fewer than ten persons if more than ten were initially approached as part of the same solicitation campaign. On the other hand, the exemption applies to each of several opposition groups, not just the first. By way of rough analogy, the exception in the 1933 Act for preliminary negotiations with underwriters comes to mind. A beginning must be made somehow.

4.   The Proxy Statement and Form of Proxy

a.   The Filing Requirements

Like the Securities Act, the proxy rules contain, in effect, their "prospectus" requirement and their "registration" requirement, complete with waiting period. No solicitation subject to the rules may be made "unless each person solicited is concurrently furnished or has previously been furnished with a written proxy statement containing the information specified in Schedule 14A."[29] Preliminary copies of the proxy statement and form of proxy, as well as any other soliciting material to be distributed at the same time, must be filed with the Commission at least ten days before the final material is used.[30] In addition, copies of all the literature in definitive form must be mailed, concurrently with its distribution, to the Commission and each exchange on which *any* security of the issuer is listed.[31] When the staff asks for revised preliminary material, it is a matter of prudence whether to wait for "clearance" of the revised material if that takes more than ten days from the first filing; for there is always the "fraud" rule to consider. The practice in such cases is to wait. But in late 1980 the staff stopped examining all preliminary material, so that there is no point in

29 Rule 14a-3(a).
30 Rule 14a-6(a).
31 Rule 14a-6(c).

waiting beyond the ten days unless the staff indicates during that period that there will be comments.

If the proxy statement is analogized to the Securities Act prospectus, the filing requirements so far mentioned already go further than they do under that Act in that supplemental soliciting material that is to accompany the proxy statement must be filed along with it, instead of being left merely to the fraud rule as supplementary selling literature is left to §17(a) of the Securities Act, the model for the proxy fraud rule. But the rules require also that preliminary copies of any "follow-up" material be filed at least two days (exclusive of weekends or holidays) before its use and, if there is to be any personal solicitation, that copies of all written instructions or other materials furnished to the solicitors themselves be filed at least five days before they are so furnished.[32] But *advance* filing of "soliciting material in the form of speeches, press releases and radio or television scripts" is optional.[33] It thus becomes once more a question of prudence whether to take advantage of the privilege not to file in advance and thus to assume the risk that the Commission will insist on the distribution of what it considers to be corrective material.

In the exceptional cases where a contest develops, the Commission's role is in part that of a mediator attempting to obtain the clarification or deletion of questionable statements. Partly to avoid wrangling by the opposing camps when there is a contest, partly because the preliminary material was often filed in incomplete form with a view to amendment during the ten-day waiting period, and partly because disclosure before examination would tend to defeat the very purpose of the rules and also make it harder to secure correction of misleading material, the preliminary material was not made public, whether in contested or uncontested cases, until some time after the passage of the Freedom of Information Act.[34] But in 1976 the Commission amended the pertinent rule to make the preliminary material public (except as confidential treatment might be granted pursuant to that Act and the Commission's rule on confidential treatment)[35] when the definitive material is filed.[36]

---

[32] Rule 14a-6(b), (d).
[33] Rule 14a-6(g).
[34] 5 U. S. C. §552 (1966).
[35] Rule 24b-2.
[36] Rule 14a-6(e), as amended in Sec. Ex. Act Rel. 13,030, 11 SEC Dock. 1075 (1976).

b. The Form of Proxy

The form of proxy itself must indicate in bold-face type whether or not the proxy is solicited on behalf of the board.[37] The rules exclude proxies that confer authority to vote at more than one annual meeting.[38] And, because of the common law rule of agency whereby the latest proxy is the one that counts, the form of proxy must provide a specifically designated blank space for dating the proxy,[39] and there may be no solicitation of "(a) Any undated or post-dated proxy; or (b) Any proxy which provides that it shall be deemed to be dated as of any date subsequent to the date on which it is signed by the security holder."[40]

In addition, the form of proxy must "identify clearly and impartially each matter or group of related matters intended to be acted upon, whether proposed by the issuer or by security holders."[41] And it is required, in substance, that there be a box-type ballot: the form of proxy must permit the security holder to choose "between approval or disapproval of, or abstention with respect to, each matter or group of related matters referred to therein as intended to be acted upon, other than elections to office."[42] So far as elections are concerned, there is usually no point in merely voting *against* a slate; if a security holder does not like the nominees, he can either give his proxy to the opposition, if any, or simply not vote.

As amended in 1979, the rules require the proxy form to provide one of several designated methods for security holders to withhold authority to vote for each nominee.[43] In any event, authority may not be conferred to vote for any person to any office for which a *bona fide* nominee is not named in the proxy statement.

---

[37] Rule 14a-4(a)(1).
[38] Rule 14a-4(d)(2).
[39] Rule 14a-4(a)(2).
[40] Rule 14a-10.
[41] Rule 14a-4(a)(3).
[42] Rule 14a-4(b)(1). Professor Gower, the preeminent British authority on company law, makes the intriguing suggestion that certain types of resolutions ought to be susceptible of being passed only on a postal ballot, with a prohibition against the dispatch of any voting papers until after a meeting had been held and the proposals discussed. "If this were done, meetings would produce a genuine debate instead of the present farce in which a handful of opposing orators harangue a complacent management secure in the knowledge that nothing that is said or left unsaid can affect the result." Gower, Investor Protection in the U. S. A., 15 Mod. L. Rev. 446, 452 (1952).

[43] Rule 14a-4(b)(2), as amended in Sec. Ex. Act Rel. 16,356, 18 SEC Dock. 997 (1979). A few states do count votes cast *against* a nominee in determining whether he has received the requisite number of votes. See Strong v. Fromm

A proxy may confer discretionary authority only within specified limitations:[44] with respect to matters incident to the conduct of the meeting or unanticipated matters that may come before the meeting (including the election of a person to an office for which a *bona fide* nominee named in the proxy statement is unable to serve or "for good cause will not serve"); approval of the minutes of a prior meeting when approval does not amount to ratification of action taken at the meeting; any proposal properly omitted from the proxy statement under the "stockholder proposal" rule that will be examined later or the fraud rule;[45] or any matter as to which the security holder does not specify a choice, if the form of proxy states in bold type how it is intended to vote the shares in each such case.

This last privilege has been attacked on the ground that management is thus enabled to gain an unfair advantage from stockholder inertia, with the result that it is almost impossible for minority proposals to carry if all unmarked ballots are to be counted for the management. The rule has been defended, on the other hand, on the ground (1) that otherwise it would be impossible to obtain the favorable vote of a specified percentage of the outstanding shares as is required by state law for certain types of action, and (2) that it is necessary in order to avoid disfranchising stockholders who inadvertently fail to mark their ballots but who evidence a pro-management position by the very fact that they return proxies to the management.[46]

Along somewhat similar lines, the Commission thus far has also resisted a proposal that rings the bell of "corporate democracy" but would create difficult practical problems in the context of existing corporate laws and procedures — the proposal of a secret ballot. And in the 1948 amendments the Commission failed to adopt still another proposal — this time one that it had itself circulated for comment — to the effect that the form of proxy should contain no recommendation with respect to any matter to be acted upon.[47] At the same time, the Commission warned against "the use of the proxy form to electioneer for or against propositions

---

Laboratories, Inc., 273 Wis. 159, 77 N. W. 2d 389 (1956). In such cases issuers are instructed to provide a means for voting against a nominee in lieu of or in addition to providing a means for withholding authority to vote. Instr. 2 to Rule 14a-4(b).

[44] Rule 14a-4(c).

[45] See pp. 526, 541 infra.

[46] See Dyer v. SEC, 266 F. 2d 33, 39 (8th Cir. 1959), *cert. denied,* 361 U. S. 835.

[47] Sec. Ex. Act Rel. 4114 (1948).

to be voted upon." It stated that it would permit the form of proxy to include nothing beyond a simple statement of the management's favoring or opposing any of the propositions. Among the forbidden devices are arguments or recommendations, as well as "the use of arrows or any other visual device designed to direct the stockholder's attention to the place on the proxy for voting one way and away from the place for voting the contrary, and the switching of boxes in order to procure the result desired by the management."[48] There is no objection to the use of a distinctive color for either the form of proxy or the proxy statement. Indeed, this serves to reinforce the rule that requires the form of proxy to indicate in bold type whether or not it is solicited on behalf of the board.[49] But it does seem to be carrying a good thing a bit far for one side to print all of its materials on white paper with diagonal stripes of red and blue on the side, as a stockholders' committee did in a 1951 contest, and then to urge stockholders to vote "the red, white and blue proxy"![50]

Finally, either the proxy form or the proxy statement must provide "subject to reasonable specified conditions" that the shares will be voted and, when a choice is specified by means of a box-type ballot, that the specification will be honored.[51]

c. Content of the Proxy Statement

The first five items of Schedule 14A apply to proxy statements generally, regardless of the type of action proposed to be taken. They call for information with respect to (1) the revocability of the proxy, (2) dissenters' appraisal rights, (3) the identity of the persons on whose behalf the solicitation is being made and who are bearing its cost, (4) any "substantial interest" of the solicitors and other specified persons in the matters to be acted upon, and (5) the issuer's voting securities and their principal holders. Item 6 specifies in considerable detail the information required in connection with an election of directors; this is at least one of the matters involved in about 90 percent of all the proxy statements filed. And Items 8 through 21 relate to proposals of various other types: the selection of auditors; bonus, profitsharing, and other remunera-

---

[48] Sec. Ex. Act Rel. 4185 (1948).

[49] Rule 14a-4(a)(1).

[50] E. Aranow and H. Einhorn, Proxy Contests for Corporate Control (2d ed. 1980) 175-76.

[51] Rule 14a-4(e); cf. Textron, Inc. v. American Woolen Co., 122 F. Supp. 305 (D. Mass. 1954).

tion plans; pension and retirement plans; options, warrants, or rights; the authorization or issuance of securities otherwise than for exchange; the modification or exchange of securities; mergers, consolidations, acquisitions of another issuer's securities, and similar matters; the acquisition or disposition of property; the restatement of accounts; reports of the management or of committees, as well as minutes of stockholders' meetings; matters submitted to a vote of security holders without any requirement that they be so submitted; and charter and by-law amendments.

Financial statements are required by Item 15 only if action is to be taken with respect to the authorization, issuance, modification, or exchange of securities, or a merger, consolidation, acquisition, or similar matter. And we have already noticed the tie-in that the Commission has developed between proxy statements and reports to security holders.[52]

One item of Schedule 14A remains, and it clutches at the heartstrings. Item 7 (by reference to Regulation S-K) requires the proxy statement to include substantially the same information with respect to management remuneration as in Form 10-K, the basic annual report form: the aggregate remuneration of (1) every director and each of the five highest paid officers or directors whose cash and "cash-equivalent" total remuneration exceeds $50,000 and (2) all directors and officers as a group.[53]

It is the Commission's view that, on the one hand, information specifically required by Schedule 14A must be disclosed regardless of materiality, and that, on the other hand, when omitted information *is* material, the mere fact that it is not specifically called for by the schedule does not foreclose the possibility of a violation of Rule 14a-9, the "fraud" rule.[54]

In view of all this, it is not surprising to find a commentator concluding more than thirty years ago:

> In addition to requiring an adequate disclosure of pertinent information, the proxy rules are inevitably effecting, albeit in a negative way, the establishment of minimal standards of conduct for management; for there is little doubt that many transactions

---

[52] See p. 488 supra.

[53] For a history of the remuneration disclosure requirement and a proposed revision, see Sec. Ex. Act Rel. 19,431, 27 SEC Dock. 2 (1983).

[54] The lower courts are divided on the first proposition. The Commission's view is supported by Lewis v. Dansker, 357 F. Supp. 636 (S. D. N. Y. 1973), *modified on other grounds*, 68 F. R. D. 184 (S. D. N. Y. 1975); cf. Smillie v. Park Chemical Co., 466 F. Supp. 572, 577 (E. D. Mich. 1979) (such omissions "are material as a matter of law"). *Contra*: Kass v. Arden-Mayfair, Inc., 431 F. Supp. 1037, 1046 (C. D. Cal. 1977). On the second proposition, see Zell v. InterCapital Income Securities, Inc., 675 F. 2d 1041, 1044 (9th Cir. 1982).

entered into by a company during the year preceding its annual meeting are undertaken by its management with one eye on the company's forthcoming proxy statement.[55]

Much more recently the Commission, under Chairman Williams, relied primarily on its proxy authority to explore the area of what has come to be called "corporate governance."[56] After soliciting written comments and then posing a series of questions,[57] the Commission in 1978 proposed a number of rules designed, among other things, to increase the information available to investors with respect to the structure, composition, and functioning of boards of directors.[58] And, after extensive public hearings, the Commission in stages adopted a number of these proposals,[59] including the present rule, which we have already noticed, that permits the withholding of authority to vote for individual candidates for the board.[60]

In publishing its 1978 proposals the Commission seemed to go beyond disclosure in expressing its belief that "it is desirable that [the audit, nominating, and compensation committees of the board], which have responsibilities in areas where disinterested oversight is most needed, normally be composed entirely of persons independent of management.[61] But in adopting certain of the 1978 proposals the Commission eschewed any purpose to prescribe the composition of the board or the mechanisms of corporate governance, adding: "While the federal securities laws generally embody a disclosure approach, it has long been recognized that disclosure may have beneficial effects on corporate behavior."[62] And the Commission backed off from the most controversial of its proposals, which would have required an identification of directors as "management director," "affiliated nonmanagement director," and "independent director." Instead it amended Regulation 14A

[55] Caplin, Proxies, Annual Meetings and Corporate Democracy: The Lawyer's Role, 37 Va. L. Rev. 653, 667 (1951).
[56] See SEC, Div. of Corporate Finance, Staff Report on Corporate Accountability, S. Com. on Banking, Housing & Urban Affairs, 96th Cong., 2d Sess. (Com. Print 1980); Sec. Ex. Act Rel. 17,518, 21 SEC Dock. 1551 (1981) (statistical profile of boards of registered issuers).
[57] Sec. Ex. Act Rel. 13,482, 12 SEC Dock. 239 (1977); Sec. Ex. Act Rel. 13,901 (1977), 12 SEC Dock. 1630, with a staff-prepared summary of the comments in CCH Fed. Sec. L. Rep. ¶81,653 (1978).
[58] Sec. Ex. Act Rel. 14,970, 15 SEC Dock. 291 (1978).
[59] Sec. Ex. Act Rel. 15,384, 16 SEC Dock. 348 (1978); Sec. Ex. Act Rel. 16,356, 18 SEC Dock. 997 (1979).
[60] Rule 14a-4(b)(2), supra p. 520.
[61] Sec. Ex. Act Rel. 14,970, 15 SEC Dock. 291, 296-97 (1978).
[62] Sec. Ex. Act Rel. 15,384, 16 SEC Dock. 348, 350 (1978).

to require a brief description of certain economic and personal relationships between each director and the issuer. Indeed, it urged issuers *not* to "label" their directors until an adequate system of categorization might be developed.[63]

5. CONTESTED SOLICITATIONS AND SECURITY HOLDER PROPOSALS

A major problem in any system of proxy regulation is the equalization, so far as practicable, of the rights of management and of opposition security holders. The SEC rules attack this problem in three ways: (a) by assuring access to fellow security holders, (b) by imposing special requirements on all participants in *contested* elections, and (c) by opening the management's own proxy statement to legitimate proposals of security holders.

a.　Lists of Security Holders [Rule 14a-7]

The Commission's rules do not require the disclosure of security holders' lists. Rule 14a-7 neatly side-steps all the state law problems of proper motive by giving management a choice. If it intends to make any solicitation subject to the proxy rules, it must either (1) furnish a list of the names and addresses of the holders of the particular security promptly on the written request of any security holder entitled to vote on the matter or (2) mail his proxy material for him, in either event at his expense.

At the same time, this rule is not preemptive: nothing in it derogates from whatever right the shareholder may have under state law to obtain a list.[64] In most cases, not surprisingly, the management prefers the mailing alternative. And, by the same

---

[63] Id. at 355.

[64] Alabama Gas Corp. v. Morrow, 265 Ala. 604, 93 So. 2d 515 (1957); Western Air Lines, Inc. v. Kerkorian, 254 A. 2d 240, 242 (Del. 1969); Smith v. Republic Pictures Corp., 144 N. Y. S. 2d 142 (Sup. Ct. 1955), *aff'd per curiam,* 286 App. Div. 1000, 145 N. Y. S. 2d 311 (1st Dept. 1955), *leave to appeal to* C. A. *denied,* 286 App. Div. 1089, 147 N. Y. S. 2d 674 (1st Dept. 1955). Conceivably, however, the availability of the right to have management send out the dissident's literature will affect his right to a list as a matter of *state* law. See Sawers v. American Phenolic Corp., 404 Ill. 440, 452, 89 N. E. 2d 374, 381 (1949). *Contra:* Wood, Walker & Co. v. Evans, 300 F. Supp. 171 (D. Colo. 1969), *aff'd on other grounds,* 461 F. 2d 852 (10th Cir. 1972); Kerkorian v. Western Air Lines, Inc., 253 A. 2d 221, 225 (Del. Ch. 1969), *aff'd on other grounds* sub nom. Western Air Lines, Inc. v. Kerkorian, supra.

token, the security holder would prefer a list, not only because he would just as soon not have the management see his material in advance so that it can get a reply into the hands of the security holders simultaneously, but also because he may want to do some personal solicitation, particularly of the larger holders.

b.   Contested Elections [Rule 14a-11 and Sch. 14B]

Aside from the exemption for non-board solicitations of not more than ten persons and the fact that some of the items of information in Schedule 14A (such as management compensation) are by their nature inapplicable to opposition solicitations, the requirement of delivery of a proxy statement applies to all proxy solicitors equally, whether they are for or against the board. Indeed, although hotly contested proxy fights probably give the Commission as much cause as any of its variegated functions do to conclude that "A policeman's lot is not a happy one," it is perhaps a tribute to the Commission's impartial role of umpire that a few companies are said actually to have listed their securities on an exchange in anticipation of a proxy contest with the primary purpose of ensuring that the opposition's proxy material would be filed with the Commission and reviewed by its staff. Nevertheless, nonmanagement proxy statements are a rarity — though the period before the popularity of the tender offer as a form of corporate warfare saw a number of proxy battles that achieved epic proportions.

The result was the adoption in the mid-1950s of Rule 14a-11 and Schedule 14B. Rule 14a-11 applies only to contests for the election or removal of directors, not to contested solicitations on other matters. It requires every "participant" in such a solicitation (a term that is broadly defined except that it does not include the issuer itself) to file with the Commission, as well as each exchange on which *any* security of the issuer is listed, a statement containing the information specified by the schedule. And a summary of the greater part of the schedule must be incorporated in the proxy statement. Rule 14a-11 permits either side to solicit before furnishing a proxy statement, but only under specified conditions.

c.   Security Holder Proposals [Rule 14a-8]

Security holders who are not willing or able to bear the expense of solicitation have another procedure available to them on voting matters not involving elections. Rule 14a-8 formalized the Commission's previous practice of occasionally suggesting that a management on notice of certain stockholder proposals set forth the proposals in its own proxy material, with provision for a yes-no vote, and state that the management intended to vote its stock and the proxies it received against the proposals unless otherwise directed. In salient part the rule provides:

> (a) If any security holder of an issuer notifies the issuer of his intention to present a proposal for action at a forthcoming meeting of the issuer's security holders, the issuer shall set forth the proposal in its proxy statement and identify it in its form of proxy and provide means by which security holders can make the specification required by Rule 14a-4(b).[a] Notwithstanding the foregoing, the issuer shall not be required to include the proposal in its proxy statement or form of proxy unless the security holder (hereinafter, the "proponent") has complied with the requirements of this paragraph and paragraphs (b) and (c) hereof:

*   *   *

> (4) *Number and Length of Proposals.* The proponent may submit a maximum of two proposals of not more than 300 words each for inclusion in the issuer's proxy materials for a meeting of security holders. * * *

> (b) If the issuer opposes any proposal received from a proponent, it shall also, at the request of the proponent, include in its proxy statement a statement of the proponent of not more than 200 words in support of the proposal * * * .

> (c) The issuer may omit a proposal and any statement in support thereof from its proxy statement and form of proxy under any of the following circumstances:

> (1) If the proposal is, under the laws of the issuer's domicile, not a proper subject for action by security holders;

> NOTE. A proposal that may be improper under the applicable state law when framed as a mandate or directive may be proper when framed as a recommendation or request.

> (2) If the proposal would, if implemented, require the issuer to violate any state law or federal law of the United States, or any law of any foreign jurisdiction, to which the issuer is subject, except that this provision shall not apply with respect to any foreign law compliance with which would be violative of any state law or federal law of the United States;

> (3) If the proposal or the supporting statement is contrary to

[a] ED.: See p. 522 supra.

any of the Commission's proxy rules and regulations, including Rule 14a-9, which prohibits false or misleading statements in proxy soliciting materials;

(4) If the proposal relates to the enforcement of a personal claim or the redress of a personal grievance against the issuer or any other person.

(5) If the proposal deals with a matter that is not significantly related to the issuer's business;

(6) If the proposal deals with a matter that is beyond the issuer's power to effectuate;

(7) If the proposal deals with a matter relating to the conduct of the ordinary business operations of the issuer;

(8) If the proposal relates to an election to office;[b]

(9) If the proposal is counter to a proposal to be submitted by the issuer at the meeting;

(10) If the proposal has been rendered moot;

(11) If the proposal is substantially duplicative of a proposal previously submitted to the issuer by another proponent, which proposal will be included in the issuer's proxy materials for the meeting;

(12) If substantially the same proposal has previously been submitted to security holders in the issuer's proxy statement and form of proxy relating to any annual or special meeting of security holders held within the preceding 5 calendar years, it may be omitted from the issuer's proxy materials relating to any meeting of security holders held within 3 calendar years after the latest such previous submission:

Provided, That —

(i) If the proposal was submitted at only one meeting during such preceding period, it received less than 3 percent of the total number of votes cast in regard thereto; or
(ii) If the proposal was submitted at only two meetings during such preceding period, it received at the time of its

---

[b] ED.: This rules out a resolution to censure the incumbent directors and declare them disqualified for reelection. Dyer v. SEC, 289 F. 2d 242, 247 (8th Cir. 1961) (the resolution "was not one of attempt by by-law provision or otherwise to lay down general qualification standards for the office of director * * * "). For a history of the recurrent proposals over the years to permit stockholders to nominate directors in the issuer's proxy statement, see Hinsey, Nomination and Election of Corporate Directors, in Ray Garrett, Jr. Corporate and Securities Law Institute, Northwestern University School of Law, Standards for Regulating Corporate Internal Affairs (1981) 54.

second submission less than 6 percent of the total number of votes cast in regard thereto; or

(iii) If the proposal was submitted at three or more meetings during such preceding period, it received at the time of its latest submission less than 10 percent of the total number of votes cast in regard thereto; and

(13) If the proposal relates to specific amounts of cash or stock dividends.

(d) Whenever the issuer asserts, for any reason, that a proposal and any statement in support thereof received from a proponent may properly be omitted from its proxy statement and form of proxy, it shall file with the Commission, not later than 50 days prior to the date the preliminary copies of the proxy statement and form of proxy are filed pursuant to Rule 14a-6(a), or such shorter period prior to such date as the Commission or its staff may permit, five copies of the following items: (1) the proposal; (2) any statement in support thereof as received from the proponent; (3) a statement of the reasons why the issuer deems such omission to be proper in the particular case; and (4) where such reasons are based on matters of law, a supporting opinion of counsel. The issuer shall at the same time, if it has not already done so, notify the proponent of its intention to omit the proposal from its proxy statement and form of proxy and shall forward to him a copy of the statement of reasons why the issuer deems the omission of the proposal to be proper and a copy of such supporting opinion of counsel.

(e) If the issuer intends to include in the proxy statement a statement in opposition to a proposal received from a proponent, it shall, not later than ten calendar days prior to the date the preliminary copies of the proxy statement and form of proxy are filed pursuant to Rule 14a-6(a), or, in the event that the proposal must be revised to be includable, not later than five calendar days after receipt by the issuer of the revised proposal, promptly forward to the proponent a copy of the statement in opposition to the proposal.

In the event the proponent believes that the statement in opposition contains materially false or misleading statements within the meaning of [Rule 14a-9] and the proponent wishes to bring this matter to the attention of the Commission, the proponent should promptly provide the staff with a letter setting forth the reasons for this view and at the same time promptly provide the issuer with a copy of such letter.

The rule does not permit the security holder himself to do any soliciting on the basis of his hundred-word statement; if he wants to solicit, he must comply with the rules and furnish his own proxy statement. And the management is not limited to any maximum number of words in reply.

A recurrent question is what constitutes "a proper subject for action by security holders" within Rule 14a-8(c)(1). That rule was amended in 1954 to refer expressly to "the laws of the issuer's domicile." As to this the Commission probably has little choice under the statute. When the state law is clear that a particular matter is for the directors alone, that would seem to be decisive. If Congress had intended to give the Commission power to reallocate functions between the two corporate organs, so revolutionary a federal intervention would presumably have been more clearly expressed.[65]

At the same time, the Commission made it clear when it codified the state law test that it considered that standard to be consistent with:

SECURITIES AND EXCHANGE COMMISSION v. TRANSAMERICA CORPORATION
United States Court of Appeals, Third Circuit, 1947
163 F. 2d 511, *cert. denied,* 332 U. S. 847

Before BIGGS and KALODNER, Circuit Judges, and MCGRANERY, District Judge.

BIGGS, Circuit Judge.

There are two appeals at bar. One is that of Transamerica Corporation (No. 9240), the other is the appeal of the Securities and Exchange Commission (No. 9259). Both are from an order of the United States District Court for the District of Delaware entered September 9, 1946. What this order was and what it effected is discussed hereinafter. It seems appropriate to deal with both appeals in one opinion.

Transamerica, a Delaware corporation subject to the provisions of Section 14(a) of the Securities Exchange Act of 1934, 15 U. S. C. A. §78n(a), has outstanding approximately 9,935,000 shares of $2 par value capital stock registered with the Commission and listed on national security exchanges, *viz.,* the New York Stock Exchange, the Los Angeles Stock Exchange and the San Francisco Stock Exchange. Transamerica's shares are held by approximately 151,000 persons.

On January 2, 1946, Gilbert,[a] the owner of record of seventeen

---

[65] This would approach federal incorporation in all but name.

[a] ED.: The Gilbert brothers, Lewis and John, have long played a unique

shares of Transamerica's stock, wrote the management, submitting four[1] proposals which he desired to present for action by shareholders at the next annual stockholders' meeting to be held on April 25, 1946. The first, second and fourth of these proposals were as follows:

(1) To have independent public auditors of the books of Transamerica elected by the stockholders, beginning with the annual meeting of 1947, a representative of the auditing firm last chosen to attend the annual meeting each year.

(2) To amend By-Law 47 in order to eliminate therefrom the requirement that notice of any proposed alteration or amendment of the by-laws be contained in the notice of meeting.

(4) To require an account or a report of the proceedings at the annual meeting to be sent to all stockholders.

It appears that proposal (1) was in the form of a by-law amendment; Gilbert, the Commission and the corporation all so regarding it. Gilbert identified the second proposal also as a by-law amendment. The fourth proposal was designated by Gilbert as "a straight resolution." The Commission demanded of Transamerica that it accede to Gilbert's proposals. The corporation refused the Commission's demands.

The Commission therefore filed a complaint in the court below to enjoin Transamerica and its officers, *inter alia,* from making use of any proxy solicited by it for use at the annual meeting, from making use of the mails or any instrumentality of interstate commerce to solicit proxies or from making use of any soliciting material without complying with the Commission's demands, and for other relief which need not be detailed here.

The court below, finding its jurisdiction based on Sections 14(a), 23(a), as amended by §8, Act of May 27, 1936, and Section 21(e), as amended, and Section 27, as amended, of the Securities Exchange Act of 1934, 15 U. S. C. A. §§78n(a), 78w(a), 78u(e), and 78aa, to enforce compliance with the proxy rules of the Commission, concluded that the primary question in respect to Gilbert's

---

role on the American corporate scene as full-time attenders at stockholder meetings. Lewis Gilbert has been called "the country's most celebrated minority stockholder." For a description of his corporate activities, see Bainbridge, The Talking Stockholder, 24 New Yorker 40 (Dec. 11, 1948), 33 (Dec. 18, 1948).

[1] The third proposal was one to change the place of the annual meeting of the corporation from Wilmington, Delaware, to San Francisco, California. This request became moot on or about April 25, 1946, the directors amending the by-laws to change the place of annual meetings from Wilmington to San Francisco.

proposals was whether they constituted proper subjects for action by stockholders at the annual meeting and stated that the question must be answered "not by federal but by Delaware law." See D. C., 67 F. Supp. 326, 329. No substantial question of fact being in dispute, the learned trial judge disposed of the case on the Commission's motion for summary judgment under Rule 56, 28 U. S. C. A. following section 723c. He concluded as to proposal (1) that nothing in the General Corporation Law of Delaware or in the charter or by-laws of Transamerica required the corporation to give stockholders notice in the notice of meeting of any by-law amendment which a shareholder desired to submit to an annual meeting of stockholders, but that there was "no special reason why the vote on independent auditors should be required to assume the form of a new by-law." He held that such a vote is simply a mandate from the stockholders to the directors which may be carried into execution by following its terms. He ordered management to notice and set forth Gilbert's proposal for independent auditors for a vote of stockholders at the adjourned meeting of the company. As to proposal (2), the court concluded that Transamerica's management was not compelled to give notice in the notice of meeting of a stockholder's proposal to change By-Law 47 and hence the management was entitled to rule, notice not being given, the proposal out of order. As to proposal (4) the court concluded that the Commission was not entitled to make good the demand that an account or a report of the proceedings at annual meetings be sent to all stockholders. He enjoined the corporation from proceeding to hold the annual meeting unless complying with Proxy Rules X-14A-7 and X-14A-2[b] of the Commission by giving notice in the proxy of Gilbert's proposal. Following the hearing and its opinions the court ordered the adjourned meeting to be convened for consideration of the auditor proposal, Gilbert's proposal (1). Both the Commission and Transamerica have appealed; the Commission, from the failure of the court below to enforce its demands respecting Gilbert's proposals (2) and (4); Transamerica, from the court's decision to enforce the Commission's demand as to Gilbert's proposal (1).

* * * Much of the briefs of the parties and most of the argument have been devoted to a discussion of what is "a proper subject" for action by the stockholders of Transamerica. Speaking broadly, it is the position of the Commission that "a proper subject" for stockholder action is one in which the stockholders may

_____

[b] ED.: These are now Rules 14a-8 and 14a-4(b)(1).

properly be interested under the law of Delaware. Transamerica takes the position that a stockholder may interest himself with propriety only in a subject in respect to which he is entitled to vote at a stockholders' meeting when every requirement of Delaware law and of the provisions of the charter and by-laws, including notice, has been fulfilled. Putting Transamerica's position in its full technical abundance, as we understand it, it says that since Section 5(8) of the Delaware Corporation Law provides that a certificate of incorporation may set forth provisions which limit, regulate and define the powers and functions of the directors and stockholders, and since Article XIII of Transamerica's charter states that all the powers of the corporation shall be vested in the board of directors, the power to control corporate acts rests in the board of directors and not in the stockholders; in other words that the incorporators by the notice requirement of By-Law 47[9] curbed the power of the stockholders to vote on any by-law amendment of which notice was not included in the notice of meeting and in effect vested in Transamerica's board of directors the power to decide whether any proposed by-law amendment should be voted on at an annual meeting of stockholders. In short, management insists that it is entitled to use the notice requirement of By-Law 47 as a block or strainer to prevent any proposal to amend the by-laws, which it may deem unsuitable, from reaching a vote at an annual meeting of stockholders.

We will now treat specifically with Gilbert's three proposals, with some of the contentions of the parties in regard to them and with the rulings of the court below. Transamerica contends, as we have indicated, that since Article XIII of Transamerica's charter vests in the Board of Directors all powers of corporate management, not prohibited to them by the law of Delaware, this comprehensive grant renders the question of auditors not a proper subject

---

[9] By-Law 47. — "These by-laws may be altered or amended by the affirmative vote of a majority of the stock issued and outstanding and entitled to vote thereat, at any regular or special meeting of the stockholders if notice of the proposed alteration or amendment be contained in the notice of the meeting, or by a resolution adopted by the affirmative vote of a majority of the whole Board at a regular or special meeting, provided that the amendments so adopted shall first have been proposed by a resolution passed by the vote of a majority of the whole Board at its last preceding meeting * * * ."

It should be observed that on March 26, 1946, the directors amended by-law 47 to provide that a valid by-law amendment would be noticed at the annual meeting if proposed in writing by stockholders holding at least 1% of stock.

*   *   *

for action by Transamerica's stockholders. The court below took the view, in our opinion, fully supportable, that the stockholders as the beneficial owners of the enterprise may prefer to consider the selection of independent auditors to review "what is no more than the trust relationship which exists between the directors and stockholders." See D. C., 67 F. Supp. at page 334. Assuredly, it is no less than this. It is necessary to go no further in order to sustain the Commission's contention that the auditing of the books of a corporation is a proper subject for stockholder consideration and action. Surely the audit of a corporation's books may not be considered to be peculiarly within the discretion of the directors. A corporation is run for the benefit of its stockholders and not for that of its managers.

Stockholders are entitled to employ watchmen to eye the guardians of their enterprise, the directors. Section 9[10] of the Delaware Corporation Law does not militate against this view nor is it important whether Gilbert's proposal be considered as a proposal to amend the by-laws or, as the court below considered it, "a mandate from the stockholders to the directors" to be carried into execution by following its terms. Setting to one side the notice provision of By-Law 47, to be dealt with hereinafter, the employment of independent auditors to be selected by the stockholders beyond any question is a proper subject for action by the stockholders.

As to (2), the proposal to amend By-Law 47 in order to eliminate the requirement that notice be given in the notice of any meeting of any proposed alteration or amendment of the by-laws, the court below decided in favor of Transamerica and against the Commission. As the learned District Judge pointed out, as Transamerica has contended and as has been stated herein, By-Law 47 provides that the by-laws may be altered or amended by an affirmative vote of a majority of the stock issued and outstanding and entitled to vote at any regular or special meeting of stockholders if notice of the proposed alteration or amendment is contained in the notice of the meeting. See note 9, supra. The court below took the view that because notice was not given by management, management was entitled to rule out of order any proposal to amend this By-law. But Gilbert had made his intention plain. He did not intend to deny notice to the stockholders for notice would have been given if Transamerica obeyed the Commission's

---

[10] Rev. Code, Delaware 1935, §2041. "The business of every corporation organized under the provisions of this Chapter shall be managed by a Board of Directors, except as hereinafter or in its Certificate of Incorporation otherwise provided. * * * "

direction and its proxy rules. Gilbert stated to Transamerica that the proposed by-law amendment was "to be introduced only if the management again resorts to what I consider the extremely undemocratic method of trying to avoid a vote, for approval or rejection, of the other resolutions, by ruling them out of order."

That the law of Delaware will permit stockholders of a Delaware corporation to act validly on a stockholder's proposal to amend by-laws is clear beyond any doubt. Section 12 of the General Corporation Law of Delaware provides that "The original by-laws of a corporation may be adopted by the incorporators. Thereafter, the power to make, alter or repeal by-laws shall be in the stockholders, but any corporation may, in the certificate of incorporation, confer that power upon the directors." Transamerica's charter imposes no impediment for Article X of the charter provides:

> In furtherance and not in limitation of the powers conferred by statute, the board of directors is expressly authorized: (a) To make and alter the by-laws of this corporation, without any action on the part of the stockholders; but the by-laws made by the directors and the power so conferred may be altered or repealed by the stockholders.

In short if it were not for the block interposed by the notice provisions of By-Law 47, it would be clear that Gilbert's second proposal would be a proper subject for stockholder action.

As to (4), the proposal to require a report of the proceeding of the annual meeting to be sent to all stockholders, we can perceive no logical basis for concluding that it is not a proper subject for action by the security holders. The security holders numbered approximately 151,000 persons holding approximately 9,935,000 shares of stock. Certainly it is proper for the stockholders to desire and to receive a report as to what transpired at the annual meeting of their company. True it may cost Transamerica $20,000 annually, but accurate information as to what transpired respecting the corporation is an absolute necessity if stockholders are to act for their joint interest. If stockholders cannot act together, they cannot act effectively.

The propriety of proposal (4) seems to us to be scarcely arguable and we conclude that no further discussion is necessary, any question of notice under By-Law 47 aside.

The conclusions reached by the court below in respect to Gilbert's proposals (2) and (4) may be supported only by applying the notice provision of By-Law 47 in all its strictness. Admittedly, so long as the notice provision of By-Law 47 remains in effect unless management see fit to include notice of a by-law amendment proposed by a stockholder in the notice of meeting the proposed amendment can never come before the stockholders' meeting with complete correctness. The same would be true even if one per centum of the stockholders backed the proposed amendment. But Transamerica's position is overnice and is untenable. In our opinion Gilbert's proposals are proper subjects for stockholder action within the purview of Proxy Rule X-14A-7 since all are subjects in respect to which stockholders have the right to act under the General Corporation Law of Delaware.

But assuming arguendo that this was not so, we think that we have demonstrated that Gilbert's proposals are within the reach of security-holder action were it not for the insulation afforded management by the notice provision of By-Law 47. If this minor provision may be employed as Transamerica seeks to employ it, it will serve to circumvent the intent of Congress in enacting the Securities Exchange Act of 1934. It was the intent of Congress to require fair opportunity for the operation of corporate suffrage. The control of great corporations by a very few persons was the abuse at which Congress struck in enacting Section 14(a). We entertain no doubt that Proxy Rule X-14A-7 represents a proper exercise of the authority conferred by Congress on the Commission under Section 14(a). This seems to us to end the matter. The power conferred upon the Commission by Congress cannot be frustrated by a corporate by-law.

Other arguments made by Transamerica need not be discussed in this opinion.

We entertain no doubt that the court below possesses the authority to make any order necessary to enforce liabilities or duties created by the Act or rules promulgated pursuant thereto. Cf. *Deckert* v. *Independence Shares Corporation,* 311 U. S. 282, and *Aldred Inv. Trust* v. *Securities and Exchange Comm.,* 1 Cir., 151 F. 2d 254, 261, *certiorari denied* 326 U. S. 795.

The judgment of the court below will be modified to compel re-solicitation on Gilbert's proposals (2) and (4). The court below has already ordered re-solicitation on Gilbert's proposal (1). If further re-solicitation of proposal (1) be necessary by reason of lapse of time the court below will be authorized to order such re-solicitation. It will be directed to enjoin violation of the Act and the rules by Transamerica in respect to proposals (2) and (4). In all other respects the judgment will be affirmed.

Query:

(1) Suppose the authority to amend the by-laws had been reserved to the board of directors under the statute or the articles or both, as permitted by Delaware law.

(2) The *holding* seems to be that application of By-Law 47 "in all its strictness" would be "overnice" and "untenable" *as a matter of Delaware law.* But then, perhaps because the court realized that it did not have the last word in interpreting the state law, it added — whether by way of an alternative holding or *obiter* — the "But assuming *arguendo*" paragraph, whose implications are not altogether clear. It does seem plain that, at the very least, the Commission's requirement cannot be evaded by means of procedural obstacles that are claimed to be lawful in the state of incorporation. On the other hand, given the *arguendo* assumption that By-Law 47 *would* be enforced "in all its strictness" by the Delaware courts, does not the court's "But" paragraph put the federal camel's nose in the Delaware tent? Or will the camel be allowed to proceed only to the extent that state law might otherwise be regarded as frustrating full implementation of the federal policy — which is to say, only as far as the Supremacy Clause requires? Presumably yes, especially in view of the Commission's subsequent amendment of Rule 14a-8 to refer expressly to "the laws of the issuer's domicile."

(3) This leaves the major question of determining the precise division of authority between stockholders and directors under the applicable state law. But the difficulty is that there is simply not very much state law to use as a guide in these matters. The typical corporation law provides, more or less as in the words of the Delaware statute, that "The business and affairs of every corporation organized under this chapter shall be managed by or under the direction of a board of directors, except as may be otherwise provided in this chapter or in its certificate of incorporation."[66] There may be an occasional provision that specifically requires board action on a given matter — for example, a provision giving the directors authority to amend or repeal by-laws when the certificate of incorporation so provides, as in Delaware, or giving them that authority unless the articles of incorporation provide otherwise, as in Illinois.[67] But, apart from these special provisions, a judicial decision barring shareholder action on a

---

[66] Del. Gen. Corp. Law §141(a).
[67] Id., §109(a); Ill. Bus. Corp. Act §25, 32 Smith-Hurd Ill. Ann. Stat. §157.25.

particular item of business as being contrary to the state's statutory scheme for the conduct of corporate affairs would be highly unusual. Consequently, with the Commission in the position in which the federal courts frequently find themselves under the *Erie* doctrine of guessing what the state courts would say, there is inevitably much room for the exercise of administrative discretion — and for resorting to the "burden of proof" (which the Commission puts on the company) and "benefit of the doubt" techniques in deciding individual cases.

Inevitably the Commission (normally its staff), while purporting to find and apply a generally nonexistent state law, has been building a "common law" of its own as to what constitutes a "proper subject" for shareholder action. It is a "common law" that undoubtedly would yield to a contrary decision of the particular state court. But it is perhaps equally likely that this body of "common law" will influence the state courts themselves when the rare cases come to them.[68] As for the handful of judicial opinions construing the rule, they must be read with care because of the rule's repeated amendment.

It is not easy to generalize in describing the rule's operation.[69] But a number of propositions seem reasonably clear apart from the relatively specific provisions like the exclusion by Rule 14a-8(c)(13)

[68] See Medical Committee for Human Rights v. SEC, 432 F. 2d 659, 680 n. 29 (D. C. Cir. 1970), *vacated as moot,* 404 U. S. 403 (1972).

[69] For recent reviews of positions taken by the Commission's staff, see Warwick, Shareholder Proposals, in Practicing Law Institute, Twelfth Annual Institute on Securities Regulation (1981) c. 5; Eisenberg, Current Applications of the Shareholder Proposal Rule, 15 Rev. Sec. Reg. 903 (1982). Stating that "There is no way for us to write our rules with the surgical precision that preserves solely the values we desire, while foreclosing all possible abuse or inefficiency," and that "the Rule has effectively invested our staff with the power to decide complex issues of law, fact and policy without any real possibility of outside, objective appellate review," Commissioner Longstreth would permit the inclusion of *any* shareholder proposal except "those which state law would exclude (even after they have been expressed in the most acceptable language) and those which relate to the nomination of directors." Longstreth, The S. E. C. and Shareholder Proposals: Simplification in Regulation, CCH Fed. Sec. L. Rep. ¶83,067 at 84,707 (1981).

This later turned up as the last of three proposals on which the Commission sought comment in October 1982 (on the assumption, on which it also invited the public's views, that shareholder access to the issuer's proxy statement should continue to be provided under the 1934 Act rather than being left to regulation under state law):

Proposal I would retain the framework of the current rule with certain revisions proposed to its specific terms, various interpretations thereof proposals with respect to "specific amounts of cash or stock dividends":

(1) There is little question about proposals of the general *Transamerica* or Gilbert type, such as independent auditors and stockholders' ratification of their selection, change of the place of stockholders' meeting, post-meeting reports, and cumulative voting.

(2) As the Commission went out of its way to observe in the note to Rule 14a-8(c)(1): "A proposal that may be improper under the applicable state law when framed as a mandate or directive may be proper when framed as a recommendation or request."

(3) Form is important in the sense that an otherwise ineligible proposal may pass muster if cast in the form of an amendment of the articles or by-laws.

(4) In the 1970s — partly under the impact of the "ethical investor" movement centering around a number of churches and universities[70] — the Gilbert-type proposals gave way largely to the "social" or "ethical" type, such as disinvestment in tobacco stocks, withdrawal from South Africa, female and minority directors, consumer issues, and industrial safety.[71] In 1952 the rule was amended to exclude a proposal submitted "primarily for the purpose of promoting general economic, political, racial, religious, social or similar causes";[72] in 1972, in order to make the exclusion as objective as possible, that clause was amended to refer to any such matter "that is not significantly related to the business of the issuer or is not within the control of the issuer";[73] and in

---

under and some of the staff procedures followed in administering the rule. * * *

Proposal II would permit the issuer, with the approval of its security holders, to vary the procedures specified in the Commission's security holder proposal rule. Under Proposal II, issuers would be permitted to formulate eligibility criteria and bases for exclusion of proposals more or less restrictive than those set forth in the Commission's rule.

Proposal III reflects a view that security holders should have relatively unfettered access to the issuer's proxy statement. Proposal III would require inclusion of a proposal so long as it is proper under state law and does not involve an election of directions, subject to a numerical limit on the aggregate number of proposals required to be included in any proxy statement. * * *

Sec. Ex. Act Rel. 19,135, 26 SEC Dock. 494, 495 (1982).

[70] See J. Simon, C. Powers and J. Gunnemann, The Ethical Investor: Universities and Corporate Responsibility (1972); Blumberg, The Public's "Right to Know": Disclosure in the Major American Corporation, 28 Bus. Law. 1025, 1026-32 (1973).

[71] See Schwartz, The Public-Interest Proxy Contest: Reflections on Campaign GM, 69 Mich. L. Rev. 421 (1971).

[72] Sec. Ex. Act Rel. 4775 (1952).

[73] Sec. Ex. Act Rel. 9784 (1972).

1976 the Commission substituted the present Rule 14a-8(c)(5), which speaks simply of "a matter that is not significantly related to the issuer's business."[74]

In 1970, during the war in Vietnam and while this exclusion was still in its original form, the District of Columbia Circuit remanded to the Commission for more thorough consideration its exclusion of a proposal advanced by a committee of physicians that Dow Chemical Company stop making napalm. "We think," the court said, "that there is a clear and compelling distinction between management's legitimate need for freedom to apply its expertise in matters of day-to-day buisness judgment, and management's patently illegitimate claim of power to treat modern corporations with their vast resources as personal satrapies implementing personal political or moral predilections. It could scarcely be argued that management is more qualified or more entitled to make these kinds of decisions than the shareholders who are the true beneficial owners of the corporation; and it seems equally implausible that an application of the proxy rules which permitted such a result could be harmonized with the philosophy of corporate democracy which Congress embodied in section 14(a) of the Securities Exchange Act of 1934."[75]

(5) Because the National Environmental Policy Act of 1969 requires all federal agencies to consider that Act and administer their own statutes in accordance with that Act "to the fullest extent possible,"[76] environmental proposals must be considered as a distinct species of the "ethical" genus. But it is difficult to say how high a boost this legislation will give to environmental and ecological proposals that might otherwise be dubious under Rule 14a-8. It has been suggested that the Commission has not been as vigorous with respect to *disclosure* in the environmental area as it has been with respect to "questionable payments" abroad.[77]

Stockholder proposals generally are an area in which policy should negate a higgling approach. It is not too important that

[74] Sec. Ex. Act Rel. 12,999, 10 SEC Dock. 1006 (1976).

[75] Medical Committee for Human Rights v. SEC, 432 F. 2d 659, 681 (D. C. Cir. 1970), *vacated as moot*, 404 U. S. 403. But cf. State *ex rel.* Pillsbury v. Honeywell, Inc., 291 Minn. 322, 191 N. W. 2d 406 (1971).

[76] 42 U. S. C. §4332; see Natural Resources Defense Council, Inc. v. SEC, 606 F. 2d 1031 (D. C. Cir. 1979).

[77] See Stevenson, The SEC and the New Disclosure, 62 Corn. L. Rev. 50 (1976); Sec. Act Rel. 5569, 6 SEC Dock. 257 (1975); Sec. Act Rel. 5627, 8 SEC Dock. 41 (1975); Sec. Act Rel. 5704, 9 SEC Dock. 540 (1976).

these proposals are not carried, or that disproportionate use is made of the rule by a few perennial proponents. The very opportunity to submit proposals, even of an advisory nature, affords a safety valve for stockholder expression at a price to management that would seem to be relatively slight. There is said to be "little doubt that the public interest shareholder proposal movement has affected corporate management, raised its consciousness about a number of ethical issues, and caused it to do some things it would not otherwise have done."[78] Moreover, if the rule is anachronistic in a day in which meetings are attended by "a few corporate officials and a heap of proxies,"[79] one should not underestimate its symbolic significance in an area in which no alternative philosophy has yet been developed for the classic theory of managerial responsibility to the owners of the business.

6.　FALSE OR MISLEADING STATEMENTS [RULE 14a-9]

Much as the registration and prospectus requirement of the Securities Act is complemented by a general fraud provision, the regulatory pattern built on the proxy statement is filled out by a rule now numbered 14a-9. This proxy "fraud" rule is the most elaborate formulation of any of the fraud provisions in that it not only combines the 1934 Act's prohibition of "false or misleading" statements (instead of the 1933 Act's narrower "untrue" statements) with the 1933 Act's express concern about omissions, but also introduces the concept of an omission to state any material fact "necessary to correct any statement in any earlier communication * * * which has become false or misleading."[80] And Rule

---

[78] Purcell, Management and the "Ethical" Investor, 57 Harv. Bus. Rev. 24, 30 (Sept.-Oct. 1979); see also Stevenson, The Corporation As a Political Institution, 8 Hofstra L. Rev. 39, 46-47 (1979). It is noteworthy also in this connection that Transamerica Corporation, after strenuously contesting the Commission's ruling, adopted Gilbert's proposals with respect to independent auditors and reports of meetings without submitting them to a stockholder vote. Gilbert abandoned the proposal on amending the by-laws as unnecessary in view of the appellate decision. A fourth Gilbert proposal — that the place of annual meeting be changed from Wilmington to San Francisco — had been adopted by the board's amending the by-laws before the litigation. 14 SEC Ann. Rep. 54 (1948).

[79] Freeman, An Estimate of the Practical Consequences of the Stockholder's Proposal Rule, 34 U. Detroit L. J. 549, 554 (1957).

On the question, common to Rules 14a-7 and 14a-8, of liability for defamatory matter contained in security holders' material distributed by the company, see 2 Loss 913-15; 5 id. 2862-63.

[80] See also Rule 14a-11(c)(5); and see n. 53 supra. This may require the

14a-9 is the portion of the proxy regulation that has most often been to court.

First of all, a note to Rule 14a-9 gives "some examples of what, depending upon particular facts and circumstances, may be misleading within the meaning of this rule":

(a) Predictions as to specific future market values.[81]

(b) Material which directly or indirectly impugns character, integrity or personal reputation, or directly or indirectly makes charges concerning improper, illegal or immoral conduct or associations, without factual foundation.

(c) Failure to so identify a proxy statement, form of proxy and other soliciting material as to clearly distinguish it from the soliciting material of any other person or persons soliciting for the same meeting or subject matter.

(d) Claims made prior to a meeting regarding the results of a solicitation.

One side's omissions are not cured by the other side's disclosures.[82] Similarly, one's omissions are not automatically excused by his own disclosure in an earlier communication. "Perception of future events may take on a different cast as the future approaches, and, what is more important, later correspondence may act to bury facts previously disclosed."[83] This is not to say that previously disclosed facts may not be considered in the balance; "the adequacy of disclosure can be measured only by considering the total mix."[84]

---

postponement of a merger or the like if updating the proxy literature is impractical. See Gerstle v. Gamble-Skogmo, Inc., 478 F. 2d 1281, 1297 n. 15 (2d Cir. 1973). But in General Time Corp. v. Talley Industries, Inc., 403 F. 2d 159, 163 (2d Cir. 1968), cert. denied, 393 U. S. 1026, the court, assuming that Rule 14a-9 might be read as authorizing that type of relief, called it "strong medicine, especially when administered the very day of the stockholders' meeting," so that a correspondingly strong showing of materiality was required. Code §1602(b) substitutes a duty to correct generally, which is to say, with respect to purchases, sales, tender offers, and investment advice as well as proxy solicitations. And cf. p. 829 infra.

[81] Until the 1979 adoption of Rule 3b-6, the "safe harbor" rule for forward projections (see p. 164 supra), Note (a) referred to "market value, earnings, or dividends."

[82] Kohn v. American Metal Climax, Inc., 458 F. 2d 255, 265 (3d Cir. 1972), cert. denied, 409 U. S. 874; Gladwin v. Medfield Corp., 540 F. 2d 1266, 1270 (5th Cir. 1976).

[83] Smallwood v. Pearl Brewing Co., 489 F. 2d 579, 605 (5th Cir. 1974), cert. denied, 419 U. S. 873.

[84] Id., 489 F. 2d at 606. But apparently no case has considered news accounts to be an adequate substitute for disclosure by the proxy solicitor. Bertoglio v. Texas Int'l Co., 488 F. Supp. 630, 643-44 (D. Del. 1980), reargument or modification denied, CCH Fed. Sec. L. Rep. ¶97,373 (D. Del. 1980).

We have earlier considered the extent to which the 1933 Act requires disclosure of the integrity and ability of management.[85] That conundrum is further reflected here in the holdings that motive (for example, entrenchment of control) need not be disclosed[86] so long as the facts are adequately stated and the motive is not "manipulative or deceptive."[87]

In considering what is false or misleading there is some indication that a degree of freedom is permitted in proxy fights along the lines of the traditional concept of "puffing." In the analogous context of a contested tender offer Judge Friendly has cautioned that "Courts should tread lightly in imposing a duty of self-flagellation on officers with respect to matters that are known as well, or almost as well, to the target company; some issues concerning a contested tender offer can safely be left for the latter's riposte."[88] And he has also suggested that "the hurly-burly" of election contests might justify a less strict approach than something like a merger.[89] But the Second Circuit said earlier that it was not "the policy of Congress" to view stockholder's disputes "in the eyes of the law just as are political contests, with each side free to hurl charges with comparative unrestraint, the assumption being that the opposing side is then at liberty to refute and thus effectively deflate the 'campaign oratory' of its adversary."[90] To sum up in Judge Friendly's trenchant prose once more:

> While "corporations are not required to address their stockholders as if they were children in kindergarten," Richland v. Crandall, 262 F. Supp. 538, 554 (S. D. N. Y. 1967), it is not sufficient that overtones might have been picked up by the sensitive antennae of investment analysts.[91]

Counsel will know what rhetoric to employ on either side.

For the rest, the great questions are (1) what is a "material" fact

---

[85] See pp. 155-59 supra.

[86] Golub v. PPD Corp., 576 F. 2d 759, 765 (8th Cir. 1978); Biesenbach v. Guenther, 588 F. 2d 400, 402 (3d Cir. 1978); Rodman v. Grant Foundation, 608 F. 2d 64, 71 (2d Cir. 1979).

[87] Vaughn v. Teledyne, Inc., 628 F. 2d 1214, 1221 (9th Cir. 1980).

[88] Missouri Portland Cement Co. v. Cargill, Inc., 498 F. 2d 851, 873 (2d Cir. 1974), *cert. denied*, 419 U. S. 883. On "puffing" in the sale of securities, see p. 814 infra.

[89] Gerstle v. Gamble-Skogmo, Inc., 478 F. 2d 1281, 1300 n. 19 (2d Cir. 1973), infra p. 553 n. 19; see also Kennecott Copper Corp. v. Curtiss-Wright Corp., 584 F. 2d 1195, 1200 (2d Cir. 1978).

[90] SEC v. May, 229 F. 2d 123, 124 (2d Cir. 1956).

[91] Gerstle v. Gamble-Skogmo, Inc., 478 F. 2d 1281, 1297 (2d Cir. 1973); see also Gould v. American-Hawaiian Steamship Co., 535 F. 2d 761, 770-71 (3d Cir. 1976).

and (2) whether the rule requires proof of negligence or "scienter" or neither:

TSC INDUSTRIES, INC. v. NORTHWAY, INC.
Supreme Court of the United States, 1976
426 U. S. 438

Mr. Justice Marshall delivered the opinion of the Court.

The proxy rules promulgated by the Securities and Exchange Commission under the Securities Exchange Act of 1934 bar the use of proxy statements that are false or misleading with respect to the presentation or omission of material facts. We are called upon to consider the definition of a material fact under those rules, and the appropriateness of resolving the question of materiality by summary judgment in this case.

I

The dispute in this case centers on the acquisition of petitioner TSC Industries, Inc., by petitioner National Industries, Inc. In February 1969 National acquired 34% of TSC's voting securities by purchase from Charles E. Schmidt and his family. Schmidt, who had been TSC's founder and principal shareholder, promptly resigned along with his son from TSC's board of directors. Thereafter, five National nominees were placed on TSC's board; and Stanley R. Yarmuth, National's president and chief executive officer, became chairman of the TSC board, and, Charles F. Simonelli, National's executive vice president, became chairman of the TSC executive committee. On October 16, 1969, the TSC board, with the attending National nominees abstaining, approved a proposal to liquidate and sell all of TSC's assets to National. The proposal in substance provided for the exchange of TSC common and Series 1 preferred stock for National Series B preferred stock and warrants. On November 12, 1969, TSC and National issued a joint proxy statement to their shareholders, recommending approval of the proposal. The proxy solicitation was successful, TSC was placed in liquidation and dissolution, and the exchange of shares was effected.

This is an action brought by respondent Northway, a TSC shareholder, against TSC and National, claiming that their joint proxy statement was incomplete and materially misleading in violation of §14(a) of the Securities Exchange Act of 1934, 48 Stat.

895, 15 U. S. C. §78n(a), and Rules 14a-3 and 14a-9, 17 C. F. R. §§240.14a-3, 240.14a-9 (1975), promulgated thereunder. The basis of Northway's claim under Rule 14a-3 is that TSC and National failed to state in the proxy statement that the transfer of the Schmidt interests in TSC to National had given National control of TSC. The Rule 14a-9 claim, insofar as it concerns us, is that TSC and National omitted from the proxy statement material facts relating to the degree of National's control over TSC and the favorability of the terms of the proposal to TSC shareholders.

Northway filed its complaint in the United States District Court for the Northern District of Illinois on December 4, 1969, the day before the shareholder meeting on the proposed transaction, but while it requested injunctive relief it never so moved. In 1972 Northway amended its complaint to seek money damages, restitution, and other equitable relief. Shortly thereafter, Northway moved for summary judgment on the issue of TSC's and National's liability. The District Court denied the motion, but granted leave to appeal pursuant to 28 U. S. C. §1292(b). The Court of Appeals for the Seventh Circuit agreed with the District Court that there existed a genuine issue of fact as to whether National's acquisition of the Schmidt interests in TSC had resulted in a change of control, and that summary judgment was therefore inappropriate on the Rule 14a-3 claim. But the Court of Appeals reversed the District Court's denial of summary judgment to Northway on its Rule 14a-9 claims, holding that certain omissions of fact were material as a matter of law. 512 F. 2d 324 (1975).

We granted certiorari because the standard applied by the Court of Appeals in resolving the question of materiality appeared to conflict with the standard applied by other Courts of Appeals. 423 U. S. 820 (1975). We now hold that the Court of Appeals erred in ordering that partial summary judgment be granted to Northway.

II

A

As we have noted on more than one occasion, §14(a) of the Securities Exchange Act "was intended to promote 'the free exercise of the voting rights of stockholders' by ensuring that proxies would be solicited with 'explanation to the stockholder of the real nature of the questions for which authority to cast his vote is sought.'" *Mills* v. *Electric Auto-Lite Co.,* 396 U. S. 375, 381 (1970), quoting

H. R. Rep. No. 1383, 73d Cong., 2d Sess., 14 (1934); S. Rep. No. 792, 73d Cong., 2d Sess., 12 (1934). See also *J. I. Case Co.* v. *Borak,* 377 U. S. 426, 431 (1964). In *Borak,* the Court held that §14(a)'s broad remedial purposes required recognition under §27 of the Securities Exchange Act, 15 U. S. C. §78aa, of an implied private right of action for violations of the provision. And in *Mills,* we attempted to clarify to some extent the elements of a private cause of action for violation of §14(a). In a suit challenging the sufficiency under §14(a) and Rule 14a-9 of a proxy statement soliciting votes in favor of a merger, we held that there was no need to demonstrate that the alleged defect in the proxy statement actually had a decisive effect on the voting. So long as the misstatement or omission was material, the causal relation between violation and injury is sufficiently established, we concluded, if "the proxy solicitation itself * * * was an essential link in the accomplishment of the transaction." 396 U. S., at 385. After *Mills,* then, the content given to the notion of materiality assumes heightened significance.

B

The question of materiality, it is universally agreed, is an objective one, involving the significance of an omitted or misrepresented fact to a reasonable investor. Variations in the formulation of a general test of materiality occur in the articulation of just how significant a fact must be or, put another way, how certain it must be that the fact would affect a reasonable investor's judgment.

The Court of Appeals in this case concluded that material facts include "all facts which a reasonable shareholder *might* consider important." 512 F. 2d, at 330 (emphasis added). This formulation of the test of materiality has been explicitly rejected by at least two courts as setting too low a threshold for the imposition of liability under Rule 14a-9. *Gerstle* v. *Gamble-Skogmo, Inc.,* 478 F. 2d 1281, 1301-1302 (C. A. 2 1973); *Smallwood* v. *Pearl Brewing Co.,* 489 F. 2d 579, 603-604 (C. A. 5 1974). In these cases, panels of the Second and Fifth Circuits opted for the conventional tort test of materiality — whether a reasonable man *would* attach importance to the fact misrepresented or omitted in determining his course of action. See Restatement (Second) of Torts §538(2)(a) (Tent. Draft No. 10, Apr. 20, 1964). See also American Law Institute, Federal Securities Code §256(a) (Tent. Draft No. 2, 1973).[8] *Gerstle*

[8] This standard, or a close approximation, has been widely recited in cases involving various sections of the securities laws. [Citations omitted.] In several

v. *Gamble-Skogmo,* supra, at 1302, also approved the following standard, which had been formulated with reference to statements issued in a contested election: "whether, taking a properly realistic view, there is a substantial likelihood that the misstatement or omission may have led a stockbroker to grant a proxy to the solic- itor or to withhold one from the other side, whereas in the absence of this he would have taken a contrary course." *General Time Corp.* v. *Talley Industries, Inc.,* 403 F. 2d 159, 162 (C. A. 2 1968), *cert. denied,* 393 U. S. 1026 (1969).

In arriving at its broad definition of a material fact as one that a reasonable shareholder *might* consider important, the Court of Appeals in this case relied heavily upon language of this Court in *Mills* v. *Electric Auto-Lite Co.,* supra. That reliance was mis- placed. The *Mills* Court did characterize a determination of ma- teriality as at least "embod[ying] a conclusion that the defect was of such a character that it might have been considered important by a reasonable shareholder who was in the process of deciding how to vote." 396 U. S., at 384. But if any language in *Mills* is to be read as suggesting a general notion of materiality, it can only be the opinion's subsequent reference to materiality as a "require- ment that the defect have a significant *propensity* to affect the voting process." Ibid. (Emphasis in original.) For it was that requirement that the Court said "adequately serves the purpose of ensuring that a cause of action cannot be established by proof of a defect so trivial, or so unrelated to the transaction for which approval is sought, that correction of the defect or imposition of liability would not further the interests protected by §14(a)." Ibid. Even this language must be read, however, with apprecia- tion that the Court specifically declined to consider the material- ity of the omissions in *Mills.* Id., at 381 n. 4. The references to materiality were simply preliminary to our consideration of the sole question in the case — whether proof of the materiality of an omission from a proxy statement must be supplemented by a showing that the defect actually caused the outcome of the vote. It is clear, then, that *Mills* did not intend to foreclose further inquiry into the meaning of materiality under Rule 14a-9.[9]

---

of these cases, the courts have also defined materiality to encompass those facts "which in reasonable and objective contemplation might affect the value" of the securities involved. [Citations omitted.] * * *

[9] Nor is Affiliated Ute Citizens v. United States, 406 U. S. 128 (1972), also relied upon by the Court of Appeals, dispositive. There we held that when a Rule 10b-5 violation involves a failure to disclose, "positive proof of reliance is not a prerequisite to recovery. All that is necessary is that the facts with- held be material in the sense that a reasonable investor might have considered

C

In formulating a standard of materiality under Rule 14a-9, we are guided, of course, by the recognition in *Borak* and *Mills* of the Rule's broad remedial purpose. That purpose is not merely to ensure by judicial means that the transaction, when judged by its real terms, is fair and otherwise adequate, but to ensure disclosures by corporate management in order to enable the shareholders to make an informed choice. See *Mills,* 396 U. S., at 381. As an abstract proposition, the most desirable role for a court in a suit of this sort, coming after the consummation of the proposed transaction, would perhaps be to determine whether in fact the proposal would have been favored by the shareholders and consummated in the absence of any misstatement or omission. But as we recognized in *Mills, supra,* at 382 n. 5, such matters are not subject to determination with certainty. Doubts as to the critical nature of information misstated or omitted will be commonplace. And particularly in view of the prophylactic purpose of the Rule and the fact that the content of the proxy statement is within management's control, it is appropriate that these doubts be resolved in favor of those the statute is designed to protect. *Mills, supra,* at 385.

We are aware, however, that the disclosure policy embodied in the proxy regulations is not without limit. See *id.,* at 384. Some information is of such dubious significance that insistence on its disclosure may accomplish more harm than good. The potential liability for a Rule 14a-9 violation can be great indeed, and if the standard of materiality is unnecessarily low, not only may the corporation and its management be subjected to liability for insignificant omissions or misstatements, but also management's fear of exposing itself to substantial liability may cause it simply to bury the shareholders in an avalanche of trivial information — a result that is hardly conducive to informed decisionmaking. Precisely these dangers are presented, we think, by the definition of a material fact adopted by the Court of Appeals in this case — a fact which a reasonable shareholder *might* consider important. We agree with Judge Friendly, speaking for the Court of Appeals in *Gerstle,* that the "might" formulation is "too suggestive of mere possibility, however unlikely." 478 F. 2d, at 1302.

them important in the making of this decision." *Id.,* at 153-154. The conclusion embodied in the quoted language was simply that positive proof of reliance is unnecessary when materiality is established, and in order to reach that conclusion it was not necessary to articulate a precise definition of materiality, but only to give a "sense" of the notion. The quoted language did not purport to do more.

The general standard of materiality that we think best comports with the policies of Rule 14a-9 is as follows: An omitted fact is material if there is a substantial likelihood that a reasonable shareholder would consider it important in deciding how to vote. This standard is fully consistent with *Mills'* general description of materiality as a requirement that "the defect have a significant *propensity* to affect the voting process." It does not require proof of a substantial likelihood that disclosure of the omitted fact would have caused the reasonable investor to change his vote. What the standard does contemplate is a showing of a substantial likelihood that, under all the circumstances, the omitted fact would have assumed actual significance in the deliberations of the reasonable shareholder. Put another way, there must be a substantial likelihood that the disclosure of the omitted fact would have been viewed by the reasonable investor as having significantly altered the "total mix" of information made available.

D

The issue of materiality may be characterized as a mixed question of law and fact, involving as it does the application of a legal standard to a particular set of facts. In considering whether summary judgment on the issue is appropriate, we must bear in mind that the underlying objective facts, which will often be free from dispute, are merely the starting point for the ultimate determination of materiality. The determination requires delicate assessments of the inferences a "reasonable shareholder" would draw from a given set of facts and the significance of those inferences to him, and these assessments are peculiarly ones for the trier of fact. Only if the established omissions are "so obviously important to an investor, that reasonable minds cannot differ on the question of materiality" is the ultimate issue of materiality appropriately resolved "as a matter of law" by summary judgment. *Johns Hopkins University* v. *Hutton,* 422 F. 2d 1124, 1129 (C. A. 4 1970). See *Smallwood* v. *Pearl Brewing Co.,* 489 F. 2d, at 604; *Rogen* v. *Ilikon Corp.,* 361 F. 2d 260, 265-267 (C. A. 1 1966).

III

The omissions found by the Court of Appeals to have been materially misleading as a matter of law involved two general issues — the degree of National's control over TSC at the time of the proxy solicitation, and the favorability of the terms of the proposed transaction to TSC shareholders.

* * *

IV

In summary, none of the omissions claimed to have been in violation of Rule 14a-9 were, so far as the record reveals, materially misleading as a matter of law, and Northway was not entitled to partial summary judgment. The judgment of the Court of Appeals is reversed, and the case is remanded for further proceedings consistent with this opinion.

It is so ordered.

MR. JUSTICE STEVENS took no part in the consideration or decision of this case.

This definition of "material" has been followed (*mutatis mutandis*) in other SEC contexts.[92]

GERSTLE v. GAMBLE-SKOGMO, INC.
United States Court of Appeals, Second Circuit, 1973
478 F. 2d 1281

Before FRIENDLY, Chief Judge, OAKES, Circuit Judge, and DAVIS, Judge.

[Both sides appealed from a judgment in a class action by minority stockholders of an outdoor advertising corporation that was merged into the defendant corporation, the plaintiffs claiming that the merger had been procured by a false and misleading proxy statement and by abuse of the defendant's position as a controlling stockholder.]

FRIENDLY, Chief Judge:

* * *

B. WHAT IS THE STANDARD OF CULPABILITY IN SUITS FOR DAMAGES FOR VIOLATION OF RULE 14a-9?

In contrast to the large quantity of ink that has been spilled on the issue whether a plaintiff seeking damages under Rule 10b-5

---

[92] Alton Box Board Co. v. Goldman, Sachs & Co., 560 F. 2d 916 (8th Cir. 1977) (Sec Act §12(2)); Healey v. Catalyst Recovery of Pa., Inc., 616 F. 2d 641, 647 (3d Cir. 1980) (Rule 10b-5); SEC v. MacDonald, 699 F. 2d 47 (1st Cir. 1982) (same).

must make some showing of "scienter" and, if so, what, there has been little discussion of what a plaintiff alleging damage because of a violation of Rule 14a-9(a) must show in the way of culpability on the part of a defendant.[16] Neither of the Supreme Court decisions concerning private actions under section 14(a), *J. I. Case Co. v. Borak,* supra, 377 U. S. 426, or *Mills* v. *Electric Auto-Lite Co.,* 396 U. S. 375 (1970), casts light on the problem.

Judge Bartels held, 298 F. Supp. at 97, that "the basis for incorporating scienter into a Rule 10b-5 action does not exist in a Rule 14a-9 suit," and that "Negligence alone either in making a misrepresentation or in failing to disclose a material fact in connection with proxy solicitation is sufficient to warrant recovery." The judge agreed in substance with Judge Mansfield's analysis in *Richland* v. *Crandall,* supra, 262 F. Supp. at 553 n. 12, to the effect that one strong ground for holding that Rule 10b-5 requires a showing of something more than negligence in an action for damages is that the statutory authority for the Rule, section 10(b) of the Securities Exchange Act, 15 U. S. C. §78j, is addressed to "any manipulative or deceptive device or contrivance," a point later stressed in the writer's concurring opinion in *SEC* v. *Texas Gulf Sulphur Co.,* 401 F. 2d 833, 868 (2 Cir. 1968), *cert. denied,* 394 U. S. 976 (1969), whereas section 14(a) contains no such evil-sounding language.

We think there is much force in this. See *Gould* v. *American Hawaiian S. S. Co.,* 351 F. Supp. 853, 861-863 (D. Del. 1972); 5 Loss, Securities Regulation 2864-65 (2d ed. supp. 1969). Although the language of Rule 14a-9(a) closely parallels that of Rule 10b-5, and neither says in so many words that scienter should be a requirement, one of the primary reasons that this court has held that this is required in a private action under Rule 10b-5, *Shemtob* v. *Shearson, Hammill & Co.,* 448 F. 2d 442, 445 (2 Cir. 1971); *Lanza* v. *Drexel & Co.,* 479 F. 2d 1277, 1304, 1305 (2 Cir. 1973), is a concern that without some such requirement the Rule might be invalid as exceeding the Commission's authority under section 10(b) to regulate "manipulative or deceptive devices." See *SEC* v.

---

[16] Our discussion of this point is limited to the rights of persons who were invited by a proxy statement to participate in the taking of corporate action involving a change in the character of their securities, as in a sale of assets or a consolidation or merger. It does not include persons who have traded because of information in such a proxy statement, for whom the statement would seem to stand no differently from, say, an annual report to stockholders. We likewise do not pass on the principles that should govern liability of directors and other individuals having some responsibility for such a statement, as distinguished from a controlling corporation which has been the beneficiary of the action that was induced. See Jennings & Marsh, Securities Regulation: Cases and Materials 1358-59 (3d ed. 1972).

Texas Gulf Sulphur Co., supra, 401 F. 2d at 868 (Friendly, J., concurring); *Lanza* v. *Drexel & Co.,* supra, 479 F. 2d at 1305; 3 Loss, supra, at 1766 (2d ed. 1962); 6 id. at 3883-85 (Supp. 1969). In contrast, the scope of the rulemaking authority granted under section 14(a) is broad, extending to all proxy regulation "necessary or appropriate in the public interest or for the protection of investors" and not limited by any words connoting fraud or deception. This language suggests that rather than emphasizing the prohibition of fraudulent conduct on the part of insiders to a securities transaction, as we think section 10(b) does, in section 14(a) Congress was somewhat more concerned with protection of the outsider whose proxy is being solicited. Indeed, it was this aspect of the statute that the Supreme Court emphasized in recognizing a private right of action for violation of section 14(a) in *Borak,* 377 U. S. at 431-432.[17] We note also that while an open-ended reading of Rule 10b-5 would render the express civil liability provisions of the securities acts largely superfluous, and be inconsistent with the limitations Congress built into these sections, see *SEC* v. *Texas Gulf Sulphur Co.,* supra, 401 F. 2d at 867-868; 3 Loss, supra, at 1785, a reading of Rule 14a-9 as imposing liability without scienter in a case like the present is completely compatible with the statutory scheme.[18]

[17] For similar reasons, we do not think that this court's recent holding in Chris-Craft Industries, Inc. v. Piper Aircraft Corp., supra, 480 F. 2d at 362, that scienter must be proved in a private action under section 14(e) of the Securities Exchange Act, in which Congress in 1968 adopted the language of Rule 10b-5 and applied it to tender offers, is inconsistent with the result we reach here. In that connection Judge Mansfield noted, 480 F. 2d at 397:

> Congress' use of the words "fraudulent" "deceptive" and "manipulative" in §14(e), when coupled with the partially similar language and the legislative history of the earlier-enacted §10(b), indicates that its purpose was not to punish mere negligence * * * .

[18] It has been argued that imposing liability for negligent misrepresentations or omissions under Rule 14a-9 would be inconsistent with the congressional intent in enacting section 18 of the 1934 Act, 15 U. S. C. §78r, which expressly creates liability in a private civil action for making materially false or misleading statements in any document filed with the Commission but provides that no liability shall be imposed if the defendant "acted in good faith and had no knowledge that such statement was false and misleading." See Gould v. American Hawaiian S. S. Co., supra, 351 F. Supp. at 863. But section 18 applies broadly to any document filed with the Commission, whereas section 14 was specifically directed at proxy regulation. Moreover, most of the documents within the scope of section 18 are not distributed to stockholders for the purpose of inducing action; we see nothing anomalous about applying a different standard of culpability in actions concerning misrepresentations in proxy statements which are so distributed than in those involving reports which were merely filed with the Commission. In short, we see no incom-

Although this does not mean that scienter should never be required in an action under Rule 14a-9, a number of considerations persuade us that it would be inappropriate to require plaintiffs to prove it in the circumstances of this case. First, many 10b-5 cases relate to statements issued by corporations, without legal obligation to do so, as a result of what the SEC has properly called "a commendable and growing recognition on the part of industry and the investment community of the importance of informing security holders and the public generally with respect to important business and financial developments." Securities Act Release No. 3844 (Oct. 8, 1957). Imposition of too liberal a standard with respect to culpability would deter this, particularly in light of the almost unlimited liability that may result. See *SEC* v. *Texas Gulf Sulphur Co.,* supra, 401 F. 2d at 867. Such considerations do not apply to a proxy statement required by the Proxy Rules, especially to one, like that in the present case, which serves many of the same functions as a registration statement, compare *Gould* v. *American Hawaiian S. S. Co.,* supra, 351 F. Supp. at 863 n. 12. Rather, a broad standard of culpability here will serve to reinforce the high duty of care owned by a controlling corporation to minority shareholders in the preparation of a proxy statement seeking their acquiescence in this sort of transaction, a consideration which is particularly relevant since liability in this case is limited to the stockholders whose proxies were solicited.[19] While "privity" is not required for most actions under the securities laws, its existence may bear heavily on the appropriate standard of culpability. See Ruder, *Texas Gulf Sulphur* — The Second Round: Privity and State of Mind in Rule 10b-5 Purchase and Sale Cases, 63 Nw. U. L. Rev. 423, 437 (1968).

Furthermore, the common law itself finds negligence sufficient

---

patibility between our holding here and the limitations Congress imposed in section 18.

In any event, we note that a corporation in Skogmo's position would be unable to take advantage of the defenses in section 18. The statute requires that both good faith and lack of knowledge be shown to escape liability under that section. But, as Jennings and Marsh point out, note 20 infra, a corporation would be charged with the knowledge of all its agents and it is most unlikely that it could issue a false or misleading proxy statement without "knowledge" of the facts which made it false or misleading.

[19] We are not dealing here with statements issued "in the hurly-burly of election contests," see General Time Corp. v. Talley Industries, supra, 403 F. 2d at 162, but with a statement which defendant had ample time to prepare and revise. A less strict view could well be taken with respect to statements of the former sort, whether this be phrased as requiring more than negligence or as recognizing the need for haste as a factor to be considered in determining negligence.

for tort liability where a person supplies false information to another with the intent to influence a transaction in which he has a pecuniary interest. Restatement (Second) of Torts §552 (Tent. Draft No. 12, 1966); Prosser, Torts §107, at 706-09 (4th ed. 1971); *Gediman* v. *Anheuser Busch, Inc.*, 299 F. 2d 537, 543-546 (2 Cir. 1962). This is particularly so when the transaction redounded directly to the benefit of the defendant, in which case the common law would provide the remedies of rescission and restitution without proof of scienter. See Prosser, supra, §105, at 687-89; 3 Loss, supra, at 1626-27. It is unlikely that section 14(a) and Rule 14a-9 contemplated less.

We thus hold that in a case like this, where the plaintiffs represent the very class who were asked to approve a merger on the basis of a misleading proxy statement and are seeking compensation from the beneficiary who is responsible for the preparation of the statement, they are not required to establish any evil motive or even reckless disregard of the facts. Whether in situations other than that here presented "the liability of the corporation issuing a materially false or misleading proxy statement is virtually absolute, as under Section 11 of the 1933 Act with respect to a registration statement," Jennings & Marsh, Securities Regulation: Cases and Materials 1358 (3d ed. 1972), we leave to another day.

* * *

ADAMS v. STANDARD KNITTING MILLS, INC.
United States Court of Appeals, Sixth Circuit, 1980
623 F. 2d 422, *cert. denied*, 449 U. S. 1067

Before WEICK, ENGEL and MERRITT, Circuit Judges.

MERRITT, Circuit Judge.

In this securities fraud case, Peat, Marwick, Mitchell & Co., herein referred to as "Peat," a firm of certified public accountants, appeals from a judgment of the District Court in the amount of $3.4 million, plus pre-judgment interest, plus attorneys' fees of $1.2 million. The suit is a class action based upon causes of action implied under §§10(b) and 14(a) of the Securities Exchange Act of 1934 and SEC Rules 10b-5 and 14a-9. It is based on an allegedly false proxy solicitation issued in order to gain shareholder approval of a merger between two corporations, Chadbourn, Inc. and Standard Knitting Mills, Inc., herein referred to as "Chadbourn" and "Standard." The primary issue is whether Peat is liable for a negligent error — the failure to point out in the proxy statement sent to stockholders of the acquired corporation that certain restrictions on the payment of dividends by the acquiring corporation applied to preferred as well as common stock. We hold that in the context of this case Peat is not liable for such conduct and reverse the District Court on the issue of liability.

*　　*　　*

II. LIABILITY FOR NEGLIGENT MISREPRESENTATION UNDER SEC RULES 10B-5 AND 14A-9

In view of our conclusion that the District Court's findings of scienter are clearly erroneous, we reverse the imposition of liability under Rule 10b-5. In *Ernst & Ernst* v. *Hochfelder,* 425 U. S. 185 (1976), the Supreme Court settled the issue. It unequivocably held that liability under Rule 10b-5 requires "intentional misconduct." Id. at 201. The Court said that 10b-5 requires "intentional or willful conduct designed to deceive or defraud investors." Id. at 199.

We turn to the question of the standard of liability under Rule 14a-9 pertaining to statements made in proxy solicitations. There has been relatively little case law on the standard of liability following the Supreme Court decision in *J. I. Case Co.* v. *Borak,* 377 U. S. 426 (1964), which established a private right of action under 14(a) and Rule 14a-9. Two circuits have examined the issue. Both have prescribed a negligence standard for the corporation issuing the proxy statement. One held that the negligence standard also applies to outside, non-management directors, *Gould* v. *American-Hawaiian Steamship Co.,* 535 F. 2d 761, 777-78 (3d Cir. 1976); and the other intimated in dicta, without deciding the issue, that a *scienter* standard probably should apply to outside directors and accountants, *Gerstle* v. *Gamble-Skogmo, Inc.,* 478 F. 2d 1281, 1300-1301 (2d Cir. 1973).

In view of the overall structure and collective legislative histories of the securities laws, as well as important policy considerations, we conclude that scienter should be an element of liability in private suits under the proxy provisions as they apply to outside accountants.

It is not simply a question of statutory interpretation. Federal courts created the private right of action under section 14, and they have a special responsibility to consider the consequences of their rulings and to mold liability fairly to reflect the circumstances of the parties. Although we are not called on in this case to decide the standard of liability of the corporate issuer of proxy material, we are influenced by the fact that the accountant here, unlike the corporate issuer, does not directly benefit from the proxy vote and is not in privity with the stockholder. Unlike the corporate issuer, the preparation of financial statements to be appended to proxies and other reports is the daily fare of accountants, and the accountant's potential liability for relatively minor mistakes would be enormous under a negligence standard. In contrast to section 12(2) of the 1933 Act which imposes liability for negligent misrepresentation in a prospectus, Rule 14a-9 does not require privity. In contrast to section 11 of the 1933 Act which imposes liability for negligent misrepresentation in registration statements, Rule 14a-9 does not require proof of actual investor reliance on the misrepresentation. Rule 14a-9, like 10b-5, substitutes the less exacting standard of materiality for reliance, *TSC Ind., Inc.* v. *Northway, Inc.*, 426 U. S. 438 (1976), and in the instant case there was no proof of investor reliance on the notes to the financial statements which erroneously described the restriction on payment of dividends. We can see no reason for a different standard of liability for accountants under the proxy provisions than under 10(b).[6]

* * *

Another important consideration is Congressional intent regarding subsequent amendments that are indirectly linked to 14(a). In passing the Williams Act of 1968 governing tender offers, Congress expressed the desire that proxy statements and tender offers be governed by the *same* rules and regulations. This would logically extend to standards of liability. Because 14(e) pertaining to tender offers requires scienter, we believe there is a strong policy reason for imposing a similar standard on 14(a).

* * *

We conclude that 14(a) and 14(e) should be governed by the same standard of liability insofar as accountants' liability is con-

---

[6] Indeed section 18 of the 1934 Act, dealing with misstatements in reports filed with the SEC, requires *both* scienter *and* reliance for civil liability. Section 14 is much more similar to section 18 than it is to section 11 of the 1933 Act. Under the current regulatory scheme, proxy materials must be filed in advance of the solicitation with the SEC, *see* 17 C. F. R. §240.14a-6, and are therefore subject to the provisions of section 18. In contrast, proxy solicitation *per se* do not put the solicitor within the ambit of section 11.

* * *

cerned, and that an action under 14(a) requires proof of scienter. Finding no evidence of scienter, we reverse the imposition of liability under 14(a) and Rule 14a-9.

*   *   *

The judgment of the District Court should be affirmed.
WEICK, Circuit Judge, dissenting.

*   *   *

Between the dates of the *Gerstle* and *Adams* opinions, the Third Circuit, in a case that involved only injunctive relief, said that, whatever might be the rule with respect to damages or rescission, "we have no hesitancy in recognizing that for prospective relief looking to the protection of the franchise the test for the purposes of Rule 14a-9 is the objective sufficiency of the disclosure."[93]

Apart from these holdings with specific reference to Rule 14a-9, much of what is said in the later chapter on SEC fraud concepts generally is equally applicable here.[94] For example, the classic fact-opinion question that is commonly met in the field of fraud has arisen under the proxy rules — to result in a holding by the Second Circuit that the expression of a statement as an opinion does not preclude a violation when the opinion is groundless.[95]

7.   SECURITIES HELD IN "STREET" NAME [§14(b)]

A 1975 New York Stock Exchange survey reported that some 5 or 6 percent of all equity securities were held in "street" name (a phrase that refers to the form of nominee name that brokers use to register securities they hold for customers or for their own account) and something over 22 percent were held in "nominee" name (a phrase that refers to a partnership formed to act as record holder of securities held by institutional investors and financial intermediaries, mostly banks, for *their* customers or for their own account).[96] Whatever the reasons for this phenomenon — nor-

---

[93] Ash v. LFE Corp., 525 F. 2d 215, 220 (3d Cir. 1975). But cf., under Rule 10b-5, Aaron v. SEC, 446 U. S. 680 (1980), set out infra p. 887.

[94] See c. 9A infra.

[95] SEC v. Okin, 137 F. 2d 862, 864 (2d Cir. 1943).

[96] SEC, Div. of Corporate Finance, Staff Report on Corporate Accountability, S. Com. on Banking, Housing & Urban Affairs, 96th Cong., 2d Sess. (Com. Print 1980) 327-28.

mally, so far as brokers are concerned, because the stock is held in margin accounts or because it is just more convenient for the customers — any split of the legal and beneficial ownership of shares creates a substantial problem when proxies are solicited, because management knows only the stockholders of record. And the problem has been exacerbated by the steps taken by the securities industry in the last decade and more to immobilize stock certificates in depositories in an attempt to cope with the burgeoning paperwork problem — a development that has greatly increased the proportion of shares held in the names of nominees in order to facilitate transfers among participants in a depository.[97]

Congress specifically legislated for this problem in §14(b) to the extent of making it unlawful (as that section was amended in 1964) for an exchange member or a registered broker-dealer to give or withhold a proxy with respect to a registered security in contravention of the Commission's rules. But we have just noticed that banks' record ownership for the account of others exceeds that of brokers several times over.[98] And, even within the scope of §14(b), the Commission, as of the time of the legislative studies leading to the 1975 amendments of the 1934 Act, had left the problem to the exchanges to handle.

The rules of the New York Stock Exchange[99] (and the rules of the other exchanges are more or less similar) require its member firms, upon the proxy solicitor's reimbursing them for out-of-pocket expenses, to transmit copies of all proxy material they receive to beneficial owners within the United States. Along with the proxy material, the member firm must transmit either (1) a request for voting instructions, together with a statement that it may give a proxy in its own discretion if no instructions are received within time periods specified by the rules, or (2) a signed proxy together with a letter informing the beneficial owner of the necessity for completing the proxy form and forwarding it to the proxy solicitor in order that the shares may be represented at the meeting. Except in compliance with these rules or at the direction of the beneficial owner, a member firm may not give a proxy. And in no event may it give a proxy without instructions if the signer of the proxy has knowledge of any contest or if the question

[97] H. R. Rep. No. 92-1537 (1972) 5.

[98] This problem would be readily remedied by the Code's extension of §14(b) to *all* record holders for the account of others and its making express the Commission's rulemaking authority to require registrants to send the necessary materials to such holders. §604.

[99] N. Y. Stock Ex. Rules 450-60, CCH N. Y. Stock Ex. Guide ¶2450-60; see also CCH NASD Manual ¶2151.05.

is the authorization of a merger or consolidation "or any other matter which may affect substantially the rights or privileges" of the stock. When a countersolicitation develops after a member firm has given a discretionary proxy in good faith, the question whether the proxy should be canceled is a matter that the Exchange leaves to each firm to decide for itself.

In general, these rules apply without regard to whether the particular security is subject to the SEC's proxy rules. But, if it is not, there are a number of other requirements: (1) If member firms or their employees solicit proxies (otherwise than by merely forwarding the solicitor's proxy material) or engage in specified other activities, a copy of Schedule B, which is equivalent to the SEC's Schedule 14B, must be filed with the Exchange. (2) Before a member or member firm or one of its employees solicits more than ten security holders to sign a proxy or to vote or abstain from voting on any proposal in connection with a proxy contest, he must also file the information specified in Schedule A, which is equivalent to the SEC's Schedule 14A. (3) He may not even join with any other person in requesting more than ten security holders to sign a proxy, or to vote or abstain from voting on any proposal in connection with a proxy contest, unless the *other* person agrees to file Schedules A and B with the Exchange and to furnish a copy of the information contained in Schedule A (in substance, an SEC-type proxy statement) to each person solicited.

As part of the 1975 amendments Congress in §12(m) directed the Commission to study the problem and to determine (1) whether the practice of nonbeneficial record ownership was consistent with the purposes of the 1934 Act and (2) "whether steps can be taken to facilitate communications between issuers and the beneficial owners of their securities while at the same time retaining the benefits of such practice." The Commission sent two reports to Congress.[100] And in 1977 it finally exercised its §14(b) authority to the extent of adopting Rule 14b-1 concurrently with its revision of Rule 14a-3(d).[101]

Under the latter rule, an issuer that intends to solicit proxies

---

[100] SEC, Preliminary Report on the Practice of Recording the Ownership of Securities in the Records of the Issuer in Other Than the Name of the Beneficial Owner of Such Securities (1975); SEC, Final Report on the Practice of Recording the Ownership of Securities in the Records of the Issuer in Other Than the Name of the Beneficial Owner of Such Securities (1976).

[101] Sec. Ex. Act Rel. 13,719, 12 SEC Dock. 1111 (1977). For further proposals designed to improve the communication process, see Advisory Committee on Shareholder Communications between Issuers and Beneficial Owners of Nominee Held Securities (1982); Sec. Ex. Act Rel. 19,291, 26 SEC Dock. 1150 (1982).

must (1) find out from any broker, dealer, bank, voting trustee, or nominee known to be a record holder how many copies of the soliciting material are needed for the beneficial owners and (2) supply the necessary copies for mailing to beneficial owners at the issuer's expense. Rule 14b-1 simply complements this obligation on the issuer by requiring registered brokers (as the exchange rules require their members) to act accordingly.

The 1975 amendments also added §17A, which for the first time injected the Commission into the clearance and settlement process. Among other things, that section directs the Commission to "facilitate the establishment" of a national clearance and settlement system; requires the registration of clearing agencies and transfer agents[102] as self-regulatory organizations under specified standards and with certain obligations, including the disciplining of participants;[103] gives the Commission broad rulemaking authority with respect to the activities of registered clearing agencies and transfer agents; and goes so far as to direct the Commission to use its authority "to end the physical movement of securities certificates in connection with the settlement among brokers and dealers of transactions in securities."[104] In 1979 the Commission used this rulemaking authority to adopt Rule 17Ad-8, which requires a registered clearing agency on request to provide to each issuer whose securities are held in the name of the clearing agency or its nominee a "securities position listing" of those participants in the clearing agency on whose behalf the agency holds the issuer's securities and the participants' respective positions in those securities as of a specified date.[105]

8.   "INFORMATION STATEMENTS" WHEN PROXIES ARE NOT SOLICITED [§14(c)]

One of the defects of §14(a) was the ready means of avoidance by the simple device of not soliciting proxies — a particularly un-

---

102 The terms are defined in §§3(a)(23) and 3(a)(25).

103 The term is defined in §3(a)(24).

104 All this is reflected in §§202(21), 202(22), 202(169), 803-10, 1002, 1006-08, and 1810 of the Code. Transfer agents that are banks register with the appropriate bank regulator rather than the Commission; and the bank regulators are also given certain rulemaking authority.

105 Sec. Ex. Act Rel. 16,443, 19 SEC Dock. 3 (1979). For a general description of the nominee practice, with recommendations, see Advisory Committee on Shareholder Communications, Improving Communications between Issuers and Beneficial Owners of Nominee Held Securities (1982). Apart from all this, certain 5 percent and 10 percent beneficial owners are required to file reports with the Commission under §§13(d), 13(g), and 16(a). See pp. 579, 605 infra.

fortunate practice because it may prevent the presence of a quorum and thus result in self-perpetuation of management. A number of exchanges began to require all listed companies to solicit proxies, to the point where the New York Stock Exchange in 1962 suspended trading in the one company that had defied all its efforts. But in the 1964 amendments, presumably because the new §12(g) would require the registration of a great many over-the-counter securities, Congress inserted §14(c). That section does not require solicitation but it does require substantially the same filings (in accordance with Commission rules) as if there *were* a solicitation.

A new Regulation 14C, which generally parallels Regulation 14A, requires the filing and transmittal of an "information statement." And the problem of *partial* solicitation is met by simply requiring that those holders that do not receive a proxy statement be given an information statement under Regulation 14C.[106]

When the information statement relates to an annual meeting at which directors are to be elected, there is a stockholders' report rule (14c-3(a)) that corresponds to Rule 14a-3(b). And there is a fraud rule (14c-6) that precisely parallels Rule 14a-9. On the other hand, there is no rule comparable to Rule 14a-7 with respect to security holder lists or the mailing of non-board literature by the issuer. And, aside from the requirement in Item 5 of Schedule 14C that an appropriate statement be made whenever any security holder entitled to vote has submitted a proposal with notice of his intention to present it for action at the meeting, there is nothing in Schedule 14C comparable to the stockholder proposal rule (14a-8).

During fiscal 1977 (the last year for which there are published figures) the Commission received only 149 information statements as compared with 5832 proxy statements (of which 14 were non-board).[107] The relatively small number of information statements is accounted for by the number of small companies that do not hold annual meetings (notably some of the mining companies on the Salt Lake Stock Exchange) and those that have only debt securities registered (particularly public utility subsidiaries whose equity securities are owned by their parents). Moreover, the Commission has used its exemptive authority in §12(h) to issue a number of orders exempting from §14(c).

---

[106] Rule 14c-2.
[107] 43 SEC Ann. Rep. 107 (1977).

9. ENFORCEMENT OF THE PROXY RULES AND STATUS OF ACTION TAKEN BY MEANS OF PROXIES ILLEGALLY SOLICITED[108]

In the overwhelming majority of cases the proxy literature is cleared, without question of formal enforcement, through the same process of examination and letter of comment that is used under the 1933 Act.[109] However, when management or a security holder is adamant in refusing to comply with the rules as the Commission construes them, there is no administrative procedure comparable to the stop order proceeding under the 1933 Act. The Commission may investigate. It may use its statutory power to "publish information concerning * * * violations."[110] It may institute appropriate administrative proceedings of a disciplinary nature when the offender happens to be a registered broker-dealer or investment adviser or an exchange or NASD member or an associate of such a person, as it may when some other statutory provision or Commission rule has been violated.[111] It may even use a violation of §14(a) as a basis for delisting the security. And it may ask the Attorney General to prosecute willful violations. But the principal sanction — and the only practicable way of the Commission's forcing compliance — is the statutory action for injunction.[112]

In the real world all these statutory sanctions have been dwarfed by the courts' implication of *private* actions for violation of the rules. We leave that development until the chapter on civil liability, in which we shall consider the implication of private actions generally. But the quantum of relief is relevant also to SEC injunctive actions. And there is no reason to believe that the relief that a court of equity may grant is any different in the two situations (except for the possibility of awarding damages to private plaintiffs). Consequently the scope of relief in litigation under the proxy rules generally will be explored at this point.

A literal reading of the court's injunctive power would justify restraining only continued or threatened *solicitation* in violation

---

108 For convenience this section will not refer separately to §14(c).

109 In 1978 the Commission announced that its staff normally would not review investment company proxy material that was limited to an uncontested election of directors, ratification of an auditor's selection, and continuation of an investment advisory contract. Inv. Co. Act Rel. 10,447, 15 SEC Dock. 1310 (1978).

110 §21(a).

111 Sec. Ex. Act §§15(b)(4)(D), 19(h)(2)(A)-(B), 19(h)(3); Inv. Adv. Act §§203(e)(4), 203(f).

112 §21(e).

of the proxy rules, since it is the solicitation and not the use of the proxies that is unlawful. But the court's power does not stop there. Once the court's jurisdiction is properly invoked, it has all the inherent powers of a court of equity. Indeed, under §12(2) of the 1933 Act, which makes fraudulent sellers of securities liable to their buyers for rescission or damages, the Supreme Court early sustained a complaint for an accounting, appointment of a receiver, and an injunction *pendente lite.* Pointing out that §22(a) of the 1933 Act gave specified courts jurisdiction "of all suits in equity and actions at law brought to enforce any liability or duty created by" the Act (and as to this §27 of the 1934 Act is identical), the Court stated:

> The power *to enforce* implies the power to make effective the right of recovery afforded by the Act. And the power to make the right of recovery effective implies the power to utilize any of the procedures or actions normally available to the litigant according to the exigencies of the particular case. If petitioners' bill states a clause of action when tested by the customary rules governing suits of such character, the Securities Act authorizes maintenance of the suit, providing the bill contains the allegations the Act requires. That it does not authorize the bill in so many words is no more significant than the fact that it does not in terms authorize execution to issue on a judgment recovered under Section 12(2).[113]

In Chafee prose, "As it is the function of a factory to produce goods, so it is the function of courts to produce justice, and they should feel free to use for that object all or any of the means which long custom and legislation have placed at their disposal."[114]

Accordingly, since equity will not suffer an offender to enjoy the fruits of his illegal action, the courts have enjoined the *use* of proxies obtained through illegal solicitation.[115] This is no more than equity has done quite apart from statute when proxies have been obtained by misrepresentation.[116] And this is where the Rubicon is crossed, in the sense that the statutory text with its reference to enjoining *violations* is left behind. For §14(a), as already noted, does not (in the criminal sense) prohibit the *use* of

---

[113] Deckert v. Independence Shares Corp., 311 U. S. 282, 288 (1940).
[114] Chafee, Some Problems of Equity (1950) 148.
[115] E. g., Henwood v. SEC, 298 F. 2d 641 (9th Cir. 1962), *cert. denied,* 371 U. S. 814; Studebaker Corp. v. Gittlin, 360 F. 2d 692 (2d Cir. 1966).
[116] E. g., Campbell v. Loew's, Inc., 36 Del. Ch. 563, 134 A. 2d 852 (Ch. 1957); Berendt v. Bethlehem Steel Corp., 108 N. J. Eq. 148, 151, 154 Atl. 321, 322 (Ch. 1931); Jackson v. Munster Bank, Ltd., 13 L. R. Ir. 118, 134, 137 (Ch. 1884).

proxies illegally solicited. Thus, the difference between enjoining the use of the proxies in voting on something like a merger and enjoining consummation of the merger itself once the proxies have been voted is a difference of degree. Indeed, the Supreme Court, though cautioning that nothing in the statutory policy "requires the court to unscramble a corporate transaction merely because a violation occurred," recognized that "Possible forms of relief will include setting aside the merger * * * ."[117] And that recognition logically applies to any *lesser* relief.[118]

Clearly the plaintiff will find it harder to arouse the chancellor's conscience as he proceeds from point *A* (injunction against further solicitation in literal violation of the rules) to *B* (injunction against use of the proxies for, say, the approval of a merger) to *C* (injunction against consummation of the merger) to *D* (putting Humpty together again after consummation of the merger, which is to say in "legal English," restoration of the *status quo ante*). And no American case has yet gone the whole way.[119] For one thing, the further along the chain one gets, the more the court is likely to have to consider the right of innocent third persons. But it is all a matter of judicial discretion, not jurisdiction. And, of course, state law can be only persuasive, not binding.[120] There is precedent in the antitrust divestiture cases.[121] And the Supreme Court has said: "In devising retrospective relief for violation of the proxy rules, the federal courts should consider the same factors that would govern the relief granted for any similar illegality or fraud. One important factor may be the fairness of the terms

---

[117] Mills v. Electric Auto-Lite Co., 396 U. S. 375, 386 (1970), set out infra p. 1109, at p. 1115.

[118] Yamamoto v. Omiya, 564 F. 2d 1319, 1323-24 (9th Cir. 1977). In Allyn Corp. v. Hartford National Corp., CCH Fed. Sec. L. Rep. ¶98,646 at 93,007 (D. Conn. 1982), the court enjoined the consummation of a merger until corrected proxy materials were made available.

[119] But see Fogler v. Norcan Oils, Ltd., 47 W. W. R. 257, 261, 43 D. L. R. 2d 508, 512 (Alta. 1964), *rev'd on other grounds* sub nom. Norcan Oils, Ltd. v. Fogler, 49 W. W. R. 321, 46 D. L. R. 2d 630 (Sup. Ct. Can. 1964), where approval of an amalgamation of two companies was set aside because the proxy statement had not disclosed sufficient information to enable shareholders "to judge of the fairness and propriety of the scheme." Cf. Wright v. Heiser Corp., 560 F. 2d 236, 252-54 (7th Cir. 1977), *cert. denied*, 434 U. S. 1066, *on remand*, 802 F. Supp. 503 (N. D. Ill. 1980), a 10b-5 case in which the court did unravel past transactions, including a charter amendment that increased the authorized number of common shares and a pledge.

[120] J. I. Case Co. v. Borak, 377 U. S. 426 (1964), set out infra p. 1059.

[121] E. g., United States v. E. I. duPont de Nemours & Co., 366 U. S. 316, esp. at 328-31 (1961).

of the merger."[122] This includes the possibility of monetary relief.[123]

All this is not to say that every illegally solicited proxy is *ipso facto* invalid so as automatically to void the election or any other action taken by its use. Violation of the proxy rules should stand on the same footing as any other illegality or fraud that might induce a court under appropriate circumstances to invalidate a corporate election or to grant other equitable relief. Thus, a violation consisting of the distribution of the proxy statement on the ninth rather than the tenth day after filing, or the failure to file a piece of follow-up literature in advance, should presumably be insufficient to set aside the vote, whether or not it should suffice for equitable relief *before* the use of the proxies. On the other hand, a proxy obtained by means of a material misstatement or an omission to state a material fact is quite a different animal.

On this approach the courts have framed a great variety of judgments. For example:

In the *Transamerica* case, where the company was found to have illegally excluded stockholder proposals from its proxy statement, the court enjoined the meeting (except for the purpose of electing directors) and ordered resolicitation.[124]

Another court thought that merely requiring the defendant committee to distribute a correction was not the relief best calculated to protect investors, because it would place the onus on the stockholders to revoke their proxies, which they could always do anyway. Accordingly, the court declared the proxies void, adjourned the meeting to permit ample time for resolicitation, and spelled out precisely the corrective statement to be included in the next piece of proxy material.[125]

---

[122] Mills v. Electric Auto-Lite Co., 396 U. S. 375, 386 (1970), set out infra p. 1109, at p. 1115. But fairness does not *preclude* relief, because that would bypass the stockholders. Id. at 381, infra pp. 1112-13.

[123] Id. at 388-89, infra p. 1116. In Gerstle v. Gamble-Skogmo, Inc., 478 F. 2d 1281 (2d Cir. 1973), the court affirmed a judgment for restitutional damages and an accounting with respect to a consummated merger. See also Ohio Drill & Tool Co. v. Johnson, 498 F. 2d 186, 192-93 (6th Cir. 1974); cf. Swanson v. American Consumer Industries, Inc., 475 F. 2d 516, 519-21 (7th Cir. 1973) (Rule 10b-5 in a merger context). The causation element in cases of this type is discussed in the civil liability chapter. See pp. 1109-20 infra.

[124] SEC v. Transamerica Corp., 67 F. Supp. 326 (D. Del. 1946), *modified and aff'd*, 163 F. 2d 511 (3d Cir. 1947), *cert. denied*, 332 U. S. 847, set out supra p. 530.

[125] Central Foundry Co. v. Gondelman, 166 F. Supp. 429, 446 (S. D. N. Y. 1958), *modified* sub nom. SEC v. Central Foundry Co., 167 F. Supp. 821 (S. D. N. Y. 1958). The court ordered that the opposition committee clearly

In a case in which a voting trust had been extended in violation of the proxy rules, the court rescinded the extension.[126]

Even in England, where circulars, though not required, normally do accompany the notice of meeting if anything other than ordinary business is to be transacted, Professor Gower says that "there have been many cases in which resolutions have been set aside on the ground that they were passed as a result of a 'tricky' circular."[127] And these cases are echoed in the United States altogether apart from the SEC laws.[128]

So far as election cases are concerned, the remedy in most states is an action in the nature of *quo warranto*, and the United States District Courts may not issue any of the extraordinary legal writs that are not ancillary to jurisdiction otherwise acquired.[129] But the fact that the federal courts have not reviewed elections as a matter of historic equity is simply a reflection of the fact that there was no need for them to do so until the proxy rules came along. There is no inherent reason why federal equity should not act when there is no adequate *federal* remedy at law.[130]

state in the next piece of proxy material, *inter alia*, that the resolicitation had become necessary because of the court's determination in an action brought by the company and the SEC that the committee's earlier solicitations, written and oral, had been materially misleading and unlawful. See also Gladwin v. Medfield Corp., CCH Fed. Sec. L. Rep. ¶95,013, *modified on other grounds and aff'd*, 540 F. 2d 1266 (5th Cir. 1976), where management's violation of Rule 14a-9 resulted in the court's ordering a new election.

[126] Reserve Life Ins. Co. v. Provident Life Ins. Co., 499 F. 2d 715, 726 (8th Cir. 1974).

[127] L. Gower, The Principles of Modern Company Law (4th ed. 1979) 536; see, e. g., Baillie v. Oriental Telephone & Electric Co., Ltd., [1915] 1 Ch. 503 (C. A.) (suit to set aside ratification of directors' remuneration from subsidiary and to enjoin company and directors from acting thereon for failure to disclose very large amount of remuneration that had been received); Prudential Assurance Co., Ltd., v. Newman Industries, Ltd. (No. 2), [1980] 3 W. L. R. 543, [1980] 2 All E. R. 841 (Ch.).

[128] See, e. g., Lonergan v. Crucible Steel Co. of America, 37 Ill. 2d 599, 229 N. E. 2d 536 (1967).

[129] United States *ex rel.* Wisconsin v. First Federal Savings & Loan Assn., 248 F. 2d 804 (7th Cir. 1957); cf. Marshall v. Crotty, 185 F. 2d 622, 626-27 (1st Cir. 1950) (mandamus). The only exception is the District Court for the District of Columbia, which inherited an independent jurisdiction with respect to the prerogative writs from the Maryland common law. Kendall v. United States *ex rel.* Stokes, 12 Pet. 524, 619-20 (U. S. 1838).

[130] Equity reviewed an election for violation of the proxy rules in Dillon v. Berg, 326 F. Supp. 1214 (D. Del. 1971), *aff'd per curiam*, 453 F. 2d 876 (3d Cir. 1971); see also Dillon v. Scotten, Dillon Co., 335 F. Supp. 566 (D. Del. 1972) (declaratory judgment); cf. Stern v. South Chester Tube Co., 390 U. S. 606 (1968), where the Court held that the federal courts had diversity jurisdiction to enforce a stockholder's right under state law to inspect the corporation's books and records even though the state statute labeled the right of action "mandamus."

The courts must simply be careful, when enjoining the use of proxies unlawfully solicited, to avoid disfranchisement of the innocent security holders who gave the violator their proxies. The solution is to order a postponement of the meeting, unless it is postponed voluntarily, in order to permit resolicitation.[131] In its actions against insurgents, the Commission has sometimes made the company a nominal defendant solely for this purpose.[132] And, in private actions in which the company or members of the management are plaintiffs rather than defendants, the court can either condition the granting of relief on a postponement of the meeting or, for that matter, simply enjoin the plaintiff or plaintiffs, as parties to the litigation, from holding the meeting or taking a vote until there has been time for resolicitation.[133]

So far as preliminary relief is concerned — and here proxy and tender offer cases should be to some extent interchangeable — the courts are torn by conflicting considerations. On the one hand, as Chief Justice Burger said *obiter* in a tender offer case, quoting Judge Friendly's observation, "in corporate control contests the stage of preliminary injunctive relief, rather than post-contest lawsuits, 'is the time when relief can best be given.' "[134] On the other hand, "Experience seems to demonstrate that * * * the grant of a temporary injunction on antitrust grounds at the behest of a target company spells the almost certain doom of a tender offer."[135] The chancellor inevitably has a great deal of discretion.[136]

[131] E. g., Kennecott Copper Corp. v. Curtiss-Wright Corp., 584 F. 2d 1195, 1202 (2d Cir. 1978).

[132] E. g., SEC v. May, 134 F. Supp. 247 (S. D. N. Y. 1955), *aff'd*, 229 F. 2d 123 (2d Cir. 1956).

[133] E. g., Central Foundry Co. v. Gondelman, 166 F. Supp. 429, 435, 447 (S. D. N. Y. 1958), *modified* sub nom. SEC v. Central Foundry Co., 167 F. Supp. 821 (S. D. N. Y. 1958).

[134] Piper v. Chris-Craft Industries, Inc., 430 U. S. 1, 42 (1977), set out infra p. 1070, at p. 1074.

[135] Missouri Portland Cement Co. v. Cargill, Inc., 498 F. 2d 851, 870 (2d Cir. 1974), *cert. denied*, 419 U. S. 833; Jewelcor, Inc. v. Pearlman, 397 F. Supp. 221, 252 (S. D. N. Y. 1975) (in a proxy contest shareholders will misinterpret a preliminary injunction as a determination of improper conduct).

[136] Compare, e. g., Sonesta Int'l Hotels Corp. v. Wellington Associates, 483 F. 2d 247, 250 (2d Cir. 1973) (§14(e) injunction *granted*), with Sherman v. Posner, 266 F. Supp. 871, 873-74 (S. D. N. Y. 1966) (§14(a)).

Section 1713(a) of the Code authorizes the court, in an action by the issuer or a person solicited, to "(1) enjoin a violation or further violation, (2) require compliance, (3) enjoin the use of proxies solicited or given in violation or the consummation of action authorized by their use, (4) set aside action so consummated, (5) award damages against the violator for any loss caused by his

E. TENDER OFFERS

1. THE PHENOMENON

As the age of conglomerates got to the 1960s and the supply of willing merger partners seemed to be dwindling, expansionist minded managements on this side of the ocean discovered that the British were onto a good thing in their preference for the "takeover bid" (or "tender offer," to use the more common American term) rather than the proxy fight as a means of capturing control of a corporation: (1) It was relatively cheaper, because the expenditures, which could be very heavy in a proxy fight, resulted in an investment as well as purchase of control. (2) If the tender offer was not successful, the defeated offeror might well be able to dispose of its block of stock without any loss — if not at a profit — to the target company or to some larger aggregate into which an initially worried and latterly relieved management of the target company had arranged a merger. (3) The offer could be limited to a fixed period of time, so that the resultant speed with which the entire transaction could take place was an influential factor both in preventing the build-up of management defenses and in curbing the expenses of acquiring control. (4) If the offeror was confident of management opposition and did not wish to seek its cooperation, secrecy enabled it to catch the management by surprise. (5) Until 1968, except for certain provisions of the Holding Company and Investment Company Acts that regulate purchases of securities,[1] there was no federal regulation remotely comparable to the proxy rules.

An *exchange* tender offer, of course, has always had to be registered under the 1933 Act, and the prospectus must contain detailed information about the business and financial condition of both companies involved — although the Commission has no choice, when the management of the target company is uncooperative, but to permit the offeror to use the most recent data filed with the Commission by the target. But in the case of a *cash* offer the only potential pitfalls before the 1968 legislation were the fraud and insider trading provisions of Rule 10b-5 and §16.

Gradually, therefore, the Americans have taken over the British

---

violation, or (6) grant other appropriate relief (preliminary or final), including a combination of the types of relief set forth in section 1713(a)."

C. 7E   [1] Holding Co. Act §§9, 10; Inv. Co. Act §23(c); see 6 Loss 3647-49.

takeover. Even the British term "takeover" is gradually replacing the American "tender offer," although technically the American term is broader because not all tender offers seek control.

Tender offers may be made for cash or for paper (typically convertible debentures). But more than 90 percent of all tender offers in 1978-79 were for cash.[2] There are a number of reasons for this aside from avoidance of 1933 Act registration, with an important saving in time as well as money: limitation of the interest deduction on "corporate acquisition indebtedness" by the Tax Reform Act of 1969;[3] accounting reforms that favored the "purchase" over the "pooling" method;[4] and the question of valuation of the offered paper, with its invitation to litigation. But perhaps the most significant development with respect to cash offers was their new "respectability." That is to say, the surprise takeover was labeled "unethical" as long as it was linked with the classic raid aimed at liquidation, but its image changed so that corporate managers and financial executives came to view it as a legitimate procedure for corporate expansion.[5]

This development has produced a great body of both law and practice,[6] which is nothing if not rich in financial slang:[7] "beautiful maiden" or "sleeping beauty" (a ripe target); "casual pass" or "Teddy bear pat" (a notification to the target that a business combination is desired); "bear hug" (an ultimatum out of the blue, with or without a public announcement, in which a formal acquisition or merger proposal is made to target management with

[2] Austin, Tender Offer Update: 1978-1979, 15 Mergers & Acquisitions (No. 2) 13, 14 (1980). Recently there has been an increase in *partial* paper offers. See Robinson, Tender Offers and Takeovers, in SEC '79 (L. J. Seminars-Press, vol. 7, 1979) 66, 72.

[3] Int. Rev. Code §279. This made it harder for "mice" to acquire "elephants" by offering large amounts of their convertible debentures, on which the interest would be fully deductible, in exchange for common stock, on which the mouse would pay income tax only to the extent of 15 percent of dividends received from its elephant subsidiary.

[4] See Acctg. Ser. Rel. 130 (1972).

[5] Nothing is forever. Recently, with high interest rates making it difficult to finance acquisitions and depressed stock prices inviting attacks on management's performance, there has been a resurgence of the proxy contest. See Lewin, Waging Corporate War by Proxy, N. Y. Times, July 4, 1982, p. F1.

[6] The leading works are E. Aranow and H. Einhorn, Tender Offers for Corporate Control (1972); A. Fleischer, Tender Offers: Defenses, Responses, and Planning (1978).

[7] On the origins of some of this jargon, see Gilson, The Case against Shark Repellent Amendments: Structural Limitations on the Enabling Concept, 34 Stan. L. Rev. 775, 775-76 (1982).

the hope of avoiding the necessity for a tender offer); "clamp" (an aggressive form of "bear hug" in which a firm offer is made without significant preconditions); "reverse bear hug" (a target's willingness to negotiate a friendly acquisition but at a far higher price); "sandbag" (a target's agreeing to negotiate after a "bear hug" but with the intention of delaying a tender offer as long as possible); "blitzkrieg" or "Saturday night special" (an unnegotiated, surprise tender offer of short duration); "low ball" (a tender offer at a bargain price); "godfather offer" (one the directors can't afford to refuse); "front-end loaded" or "two-tier" deal (a partial cash offer followed by an offer of securities, valued at less than the cash consideration and sometimes issued by the company to survive a merger, for the rest); "trading stamp" (a security offered in an exchange offer); "toehold" or "creeping" acquisition (a gradual accumulation not involving a statutory "tender offer"); "white knight" or "Prince Charming" or "sweetheart" (a third company that the target persuades to merge with it or to make a competing offer that it hopes will lead to a combination more to its liking); "grey knight" (a competing tender offeror no more acceptable to target management than the original offeror); "black knight" (a third company that comes in to spoil an offer that the target *favors*); "black book" or "Pearl Harbor file" (a combination of defensive materials and procedures); "shark repellent" or "porcupine" provisions (defensive steps such as amendment of the target's articles in an attempt to ward off potential offers by going over to staggered boards or adopting super-majority voting requirements for mergers and the like); "iron maiden" (a resolute target management); "scorched earth" (no-holds-barred defense tactics); "stopper" or "show stopper" (an impediment, such as an antitrust defense, that effectively halts a tender offer); "golden parachute" (a special employment agreement with a target officer affording certain financial assurance in the event of a change in control).

Moreover, a whole galaxy of defenses has been developed from the "shark repellent" provisions just mentioned to selecting a "white knight" whose business will give the target an antitrust argument against the tender offer, and including redeployment of assets by restructuring the target's capitalization or selling a division of the business or effecting a partial liquidation or making a tender offer for the target's own shares.[8] As Judge Friendly put

---

[8] See Schmults and Kelly, Cash Take-over Bids — Defense Tactics, 23 Bus. Law. 115 (1967); Reuben and Elden, How to Be a Target Company, 23 N. Y. L. S. L. Rev. 423 (1978). For an enumeration of defensive measures, with an indication of the disclosure they require in proxy materials looking toward their adoption, see Sec. Ex. Act Rel. 15,230, 15 SEC Dock. 1311 (1978).

it with his usual felicity: "Drawing Excalibur from a scabbard where it would doubtless have remained sheathed in the face of a friendly offer, the target company typically hopes to obtain a temporary injunction which may frustrate the acquisition since the offering company may well decline the expensive gambit of a trial or, if it persists, the long lapse of time could so change conditions that the offer will fail even if, after a full trial and appeal, it should be determined that no antitrust violation has been shown."[9]

It has been claimed that these anti-takeover amendments "are a waste of time and are probably counter-productive";[10] indeed, 85 percent of all tender offers during the twelve months beginning July 1, 1978, were completely or partially successful,[11] although this includes a great many offers that were friendly either *ab initio* or by virtue of a beefed-up price or the intervention of a "white knight."[12] Indeed, there has been much controversy with respect to the propriety, as a matter of corporation law, of a target's taking *any* defensive measures to prevent its stockholders' receiving the benefit of a higher price for their shares resulting from the prospect of higher earnings when the offeror and target companies are combined (the favorite word here is "synergy").[13]

---

[9] Missouri Portland Cement Co. v. Cargill, Inc., 498 F. 2d 851, 854 (2d Cir. 1974), *cert. denied,* 419 U. S. 883.

[10] Flom, in Leiman, Recent Developments in Tender Offers: Defensive Tactics, in Practising Law Institute, Tenth Annual Institute on Securities Regulation (1979) c. 15 at 293-94; see also Cary, Corporate Devices Used to Insulate Management from Attack, 25 Bus. Law. 839 (1970).

[11] Austin, loc. cit. supra n. 2.

[12] See Freund and Greene, Substance over Form S-14: A Proposal to Reform SEC Regulation of Negotiated Acquisitions, 36 Bus. Law. 1483, 1486-87 (1981), which discusses the fortuitous regulatory disparities between negotiated cash tender offers and negotiated cash mergers.

[13] In favor of target management's adopting a *laissez faire* position, see Easterbrook and Fischel, The Proper Role of a Target's Management in Responding to a Tender Offer, 94 Harv. L. Rev. 1161 (1981) (analysis in terms of "efficient market theory"); cf. Gilson, A Structural Approach to Corporations: The Case against Defensive Tactics in Tender Offers, 33 Stan. L. Rev. 819, 879 (1981); Gilson, The Case against Shark Repellent Amendments: Structural Limitations on the Enabling Concept, 34 Stan. L. Rev. 775 (1982). *Contra:* Lipton, Takeover Bids in the Target's Boardroom, 35 Bus. Law. 101 (1979); Lipton, Takeover Bids in the Target's Boardroom: A Response to Professors Easterbrook and Fischel, 55 N. Y. U. L. Rev. 1231 (1980); see also Steinbrink, Management's Response to the Takeover Attempt, 28 Case W. Res. L. Rev. 882 (1978) (the "knee jerk" opposition to a takeover attempt, whatever the price, has gone out of style, id. at 887); cf. Bebchuk, The Case for Facilitating Competing Tender Offers, 95 Harv. L. Rev. 1028 (1982) (disagreeing with Easterbrook and Fischel, supra, to the extent of maintaining that the facilitation of *competing bids* is desirable for both target stockholders and society).

There is controversy, too, with respect to the position of a bank that in one way or another serves both sides. The few holdings thus far reflect a judicial reluctance to interfere, at least in the absence of a bank's actually relaying confidential information it received from a client that is a putative target to another client that is a putative tender offeror.[14] But the SEC has recommended legislation with respect to investment bankers, financial advisers, and securities analysts as well as banks that are engaged to advise a tender offeror after having obtained material nonpublic information from the target company.[15]

2. The Regulatory Scheme

Oddly, apart from Congress's borrowing in 1933 from the British prospectus provision, tender offers are the one area of securities regulation where the British acted before the Americans. As we have seen, they experienced the phenomenon earlier. And there seems to have been an explosion of regulation of one kind or another throughout the capitalist world.[16] But the British, with

---

So far as attacks against management under §14(e) of the 1934 Act are concerned, contrast Panter v. Marshall Field & Co., 646 F. 2d 271 (7th Cir. 1981), where the court applied the business judgment rule to a series of defensive acquisitions designed to create antitrust problems for a tender offeror, with Mobil Corp. v. Marathon Oil Co., 669 F. 2d 366 (6th Cir. 1981), where the court held that two separate options granted by Marathon to United States Steel Corporation (a "white knight") in order to induce it to make an offer to the Marathon shareholders that was better than the initial offer made by Mobil were invalid as "manipulative acts" within the meaning of §14(e) even though the Marathon directors might have acted in good faith and exercised reasonable business judgment in granting the options.

[14] Washington Steel Corp. v. TW Corp., 602 F. 2d 594 (3d Cir. 1979); Humana, Inc. v. American Medicorp, Inc., 445 F. Supp. 613 (S. D. N. Y. 1978); see Note, Regulating the Use of Confidential Information in Tender Offer Financing: A Common Law Solution, 55 N. Y. U. L. Rev. 838 (1980); Note, Bank Financing of Hostile Acquisitions of Corporate Law Customers, 31 Case W. Res. L. Rev. 132 (1981). Both notes recommend a "Chinese wall." See also Sec. Ex. Act Rel. 17,120, 20 SEC Dock. 1241, 1252 (1980). That concept is discussed in another connection at pp. 843-51 infra.

[15] See SEC Report on Tender Offer Laws, S. Com. on Banking, Housing & Urban Affairs, 96th Cong., 2d Sess. (Com. Print 1980) 15-45.

[16] See A. Vice, The Strategy of Takeovers: A Casebook of International Practice (1971); P. Anisman, Takeover Bid Legislation in Canada: A Comparative Analysis (1974); Tan, The Singapore Code on Takeovers and Mergers: An Introduction, 44 Malaya L. J. lxviii (1975); M. Weinberg and M. Blank, Takeovers and Mergers (4th ed. 1977) (United Kingdom); Macgregor, Takeovers Revisited, 95 S. Af. L. J. 329 (1978); Santow, Defensive Measures against Company Takeovers, 53 Aust. L. J. 374 (1979); Lépine, The French General Philosophy Concerning the Transfer of Controlling Interests and

their traditional skepticism about anything approaching an SEC,[17] rely on self-regulation. As early as 1959 a committee of various City groups that had been set up at the suggestion of the Governor of the Bank of England produced a concise code of recommended rules of conduct for "take-over bids."[18] And a Panel on Take-overs and Mergers, created in 1968 with an independent Chairman and Deputy Chairman appointed by the Governor of the Bank of England, administers a Code of "principles" and "rules," functioning since 1978 as one of the twelve arms of the Council for the Securities Industry that was created that year.[19]

Congress finally acted in 1968 by adding §§13(d)-(e) and 14(d)-(f) to the 1934 Act, and these sections (collectively known as the Williams Act) were amended into their present form in 1970. Section 14(d)(1) makes it unlawful for any person "to make a tender offer for, or a request or invitation for tenders of," any class of equity security registered under §12 (or within the insurance company exemption in §12(g)(2)(G) or issued by a closed-end investment company registered under the Investment Company Act), if consummation of the offer would make that person the beneficial owner of more than 5 percent of the class,[20] unless he files with the Commission, concurrently with the first publication of the offer or its first transmission to security holders, whatever information the Commission may prescribe by rule. The five-day

---

the New Takeover Bid Rule, in L. Gower, L. Loss, and A. Sommer (co-chairmen), New Trends in Company Law Disclosure (Law & Business, Inc. 1980) 269; Carvalhosa, The Brazilian Experience with Respect to Tender Offers, 3 J. Comp. L. & Sec. Reg. 103 (1981).

[17] See Report of Committee to Review the Functioning of Financial Institutions ("Wilson Report"), Cmd. 7937 (Law & Business, Inc., 1980) §§1199, 1411. This view is by no means unanimous. See L. Gower, Principles of Modern Company Law (4th ed. 1979) 365 (recommending "a smaller (poor man's) S. E. C.").

[18] See Queensbury Rules for Bids, 193 Economist 440 (1959). In late 1982 the Deputy Chairman of the Council for the Securities Industry was quoted as saying, in the wake of a number of scandals, that "There are bound to be some parts of the self-regulatory system which eventually become law." Wall St. J., Dec. 10, 1982, p. 34, col. 2.

[19] For a history of the Code and Panel written by its Deputy Chairman, see A. Johnson, The City Take-Over Code (1980). Legal control over takeover bid circulars does exist to the extent of rules made by the Department of Trade under the Prevention of Fraud Investments Act 1958. 6 & 7 Eliz. 2, c. 45; Licensed Dealers (Conduct of Business) Rules, S. I. No. 1216 (1960). But these rules rarely apply, because they cover only licensed dealers whereas most bids are made by members of the Stock Exchange or other *exempted* dealers. See L. Gower, Principles of Modern Company Law (4th ed. 1979) 693-99.

[20] The figure was dropped to 5 percent from the original 10 percent in 1970.

advance filing that would have been required in the bill as introduced was abandoned on the ground that "prior review was not necessary and in some cases might delay the offer when time was of the essence."[21] Supplementary soliciting material must be filed and sent to the issuer concurrently with its transmission to security holders, and the contents of any such material are again subject to the Commission's rules.

Section 14(d)(4) authorizes the Commission to regulate any solicitation or recommendation to holders to accept or reject a tender offer. This authorizes the Commission not only to specify the information to be included in any recommendation, whether by the management or others and whether in favor of or in opposition to a tender offer, but also to regulate solicitations by broker-dealers, who are often compensated for shares tendered as a result of their activities and the activities of persons who make competing tender offers or seek to influence investors' decisions on a single tender offer.[22]

A new antifraud provision, §14(e), makes it unlawful for *any* person to make any untrue statement of a material fact (a half-truth being included as in the fraud provisions generally), "or to engage in any fraudulent, deceptive, or manipulative acts or practices," in connection with any tender offer or any solicitation in opposition to or in favor of a tender offer. This section, in the tradition of the general fraud provisions of the 1933 and 1934 Acts, applies to all securities without regard to registration.[23]

---

[21] S. Rep. No. 550, 90th Cong., 1st Sess. (1967) 4. However, the 1933 Act's strictures on offers must, of course, be observed in the case of a paper tender offer; the 1968 exemption for offers pursuant to a 1933 Act registration was deleted in the 1970 amendments. Moreover, §7A of the Clayton Act, added by the Hart-Scott-Rodino Antitrust Improvements Act of 1976, applies if (1) either the tender offeror or the target has $100 million and the other has $10 million in sales or assets, *and* (2) the offering company would end up with 15 percent of the voting securities or $15 million of assets; and, when those two circumstances are present, the offering company must file a premerger notification with the Federal Trade Commission and the Assistant Attorney General in charge of the Antitrust Division fifteen or thirty days before any purchase of target stock, depending on whether or not the offer is for cash. The Government may waive the waiting period, and it may also extend the period within limits in order to accommodate its request for additional material. 15 U. S. C. §18a; see S. Axinn, B. Fogg, and N. Stoll, Acquisitions under the Hart-Scott-Rodino Antitrust Improvements Act (1979).

[22] S. Rep. No. 550, 90th Cong., 1st Sess. (1967) 9; H. R. Rep. No. 1711, 90th Cong., 2d Sess. (1968) 10.

[23] "In effect [§14(e)] applies Rule 10b-5 both to the offeror and to the opposition — very likely, except perhaps for any bearing it may have on the issue of standing, only a codification of existing case law." Electronic Specialty Co. v. International Controls Corp., 409 F. 2d 937, 940-41 (2d Cir.

As with the scheme of proxy regulation, neither the statutory provisions nor the rules are limited to disclosure. So far as substantive provisions are concerned:

Section 14(d)(5) permits persons who have tendered to withdraw within the first seven days after the tender offer or more than sixty days afterwards unless the Commission prescribes otherwise by rule or order. The Commission has in fact extended the period by rule[24] to (1) fifteen *business* days from the date of commencement[25] of the tender offer and (2) ten business days after the date of commencement of a competing offer (other than certain offers for cash or exempt securities within §3 of the 1933 Act or both). And the legislative reports contemplated the Commission's acting by order when, for example, shareholders might need more than seven days to assess correcting material that had been circulated or when the required approval of some regulatory authority might not be obtainable within the sixty days.[26]

Another of the Commission's suggestions — a *pro rata* acceptance requirement in the event of an overacceptance — is reflected in §14(d)(6). The Senate committee was persuaded by the testimony of the New York Stock Exchange, based on its own experience, to limit the *pro rata* requirement to shares offered during the first ten days of the offer, with an additional ten-day period in the event of an increase in price.[27] Nevertheless, and despite the absence of rulemaking authority in §14(d)(6), the Commission has used its fraud-prevention authority under §14(e) not only to extend the proration requirement to the life of the tender offer[28] but

---

1969). But there is a "bug" here. Section 14(e), alone of all the SEC fraud provisions that are not grounded on a registration requirement that is itself conditioned on some use of the mails or interstate commerce, is silent with respect to these assumed prerequisites to federal jurisdiction. It may be that the world of securities is so impregnated with interstate commerce that it is no longer constitutionally necessary to tie every prohibition, directly or indirectly, to use of the mails or interstate facilities, at least when some such use is pleaded and proved in the particular case. Cf. Perez v. United States, 402 U. S. 146 (1971) ("loan sharking" activities). But the omission in §14(e) was apparently inadvertent. Even if the Commission itself is careful in its own cases to allege and prove either (1) some use of the mails or interstate facilities or (2) the target company's registration, there is always the possibility that plaintiffs in private actions will not do so. And, in any event, it is not a foregone conclusion that the severability clause in §33 will save the section's constitutionality, though it should.

[24] Rule 14d-7.

[25] This is a defined term. Rule 14d-2.

[26] S. Rep. at 10 and H. R. Rep. at 10, supra n. 22.

[27] S. Rep. at 4-5, supra n. 22.

[28] Rule 14d-8 as revised in Sec. Ex. Act Rel. 19,336, 26 SEC Dock. 1445 (1982).

also to require all tender offers to be open for at least twenty business days plus ten business days after any increase in the price or the dealer's soliciting fee (unless, in either event, the tender offer is made by the *issuer* otherwise than in anticipation or response to another offer).[29]

It startles a bit to see the §14(e) authority used in this way when Congress was careful to supply specific time periods for both withdrawal and proration purposes. On that account (and also on the merits for Chairman Shad) two of the five Commissioners dissented from the adoption of the proration rule.[30]

The sixty-day withdrawal provision is construed administratively as not applying to the extent that the offeror has purchased the deposited securities, notwithstanding the practice of leaving the offer open for a considerable time in order to pick up odds and ends.

The Senate committee also referred to the abuse of "short tendering." In order to permit acceptance by brokers on behalf of shareholders who are away or otherwise not in a position to deposit their certificates, tender offers commonly provide that the certificates need not be deposited if a bank or a member firm of an exchange guarantees that they will be delivered on demand or at a specified time in the event of acceptance. As a result of this practice, a broker who estimated that only half of the shares tendered would be accepted on a *pro rata* basis could tender twice as many shares as he owned without depositing them. But the committee thought that the Commission had adequate power under the existing antifraud provisions to deal with the problem. And in May 1968, before passage of the bill, the Commission adopted a new Rule 10b-4, which declares it a "manipulative or deceptive device or contrivance" for any person (1) to tender for his own account any security that he does not own or (2) to tender or guarantee the tender of any security on behalf of another person unless (A) the security is in the possession of the person making the tender or giving the guarantee or (B) the latter person has reason to believe that the former owns the security and, as soon as possible without undue inconvenience or expense, will deliver it to the latter. Ownership is defined as in Rule 10a-1, the rule on

---

[29] Rule 14e-1.
[30] Sec. Ex. Act Rel. 19,336, 26 SEC Dock. 1445, 1447-49 (1982). In San Francisco Real Estate Investors v. Real Estate Investment Trust of America, 692 F. 2d 814, 817 (1st Cir. 1982), the court held that, although the "ten-day deadline of §14(d)(6) * * * was not necessarily immutable," it had been enlarged by the District Court without specific reason.

short sales.[31] And special provision is made for convertible securities and rights.[32]

Section 14(d)(7) incorporates into the statute the Commission's further proposal that persons who have already tendered before an increase in the offering price must receive the same price as those who tender after the increase.[33]

Finally, §14(f) is aimed at the practice, to the extent it is permitted by state law, of using the authority of directors to fill vacancies so as to have the entire board resign *seriatim* upon a shift of control. On the theory that the disclosures required by the proxy rules should be made before a new board is installed pursuant to a private agreement for a transfer of control even though the ownership of a majority of the shares makes it unnecessary to solicit proxies, and consistently with the new §14(c) that was added in the 1964 amendments,[34] the new §14(f) requires the issuer in such a case to file with the Commission before any new director takes office, and transmit to all holders of record who would be entitled to vote at a meeting for election of directors, information substantially equivalent to the information that would be required by §14(a) or §14(c) if the directors were to be elected at a meeting of shareholders.[35]

Section 14(d)-(f) is complemented by §13(d)-(e), which is directed to the period *before* a potential tender offer.

Under §13(d)(1) any person who *after acquiring* the beneficial ownership of an equity security registered under §12 (or issued by an insurance company or a closed-end investment company as

---

[31] See p. 716 infra.

[32] See Sec. Ex. Act Rel. 8321 (1968).

[33] In Missouri Portland Cement Co. v. Cargill, Inc., 498 F. 2d 851, 874 (2d Cir. 1974), *cert. denied*, 419 U. S. 883, the court said that §14(d)(7) made it misleading for the target company to say that the offeror might raise its price if it did not get all the stock it wanted at its initial price.

Query: Since this provision applies only when the price is increased "before the expiration of" the offer, what if an offeror announces a new offer at a higher price immediately after the expiration of the original offer. Are there one or two offers? Cf. McDermott, Inc. v. Wheelabrator-Frye, Inc., 649 F. 2d 489 (7th Cir. 1980) (tender offeror's announcement of an increase in the number of shares covered by the offer was not a new tender offer). Code §202(166)(B) treats the offers as separate if they are for different classes of securities or are "substantially distinct on the basis of such factors as manner, time, purpose, price, and kind of consideration." Compare the "integration" problem with respect to certain exemptions under the 1933 Act, supra p. 374.

[34] See p. 560 supra.

[35] See Rule 14f-1; Ratner, Section 14(f): A New Approach to Transfers of Corporate Control, 54 Corn. L. Rev. 65 (1968). Presumably the courts will develop a federal "*de facto* director" doctrine with respect to directors who assume office without compliance with the section.

in §14(d)(1)) becomes the beneficial owner of more than 5 percent of the class must send to the issuer and to each exchange on which the security is traded and also file with the SEC — all within ten days after the acquisition — whatever information the Commission may by rule prescribe with respect to such matters as (A) the background and identity of the buyers, (B) the source and amount of the consideration used, together with a description of any borrowing (except that the name of any bank lending in the ordinary course of business is to be kept confidential on request), (C) any plans to liquidate the issuer, sell its assets, merge it, or make any other major change in its structure if the purpose of the purchases or prospective purchases is to acquire control, (D) the number of shares that the buyer and each associate own beneficially or have a right to acquire, and (E) any contracts or arrangements with any person concerning any securities of the issuer, including transfers, joint ventures, loan or option arrangements, puts or calls, guaranties, division of losses or profits, or giving or withholding of proxies. These disclosures are altogether apart from the ownership reports required by §16(a). Moreover, a new §13(d)(2) authorizes the Commission to adopt rules with respect to amendments to the statement filed in the event of material changes — an authority that goes not only to the form and content of the amendments but also to the time of transmission.[36]

Section 13(e)(1) makes it unlawful for an issuer to buy any of its own equity securities in contravention of the Commission's rules adopted to define, and "to prescribe means reasonably designed to prevent," practices that are "fraudulent, deceptive, or manipulative." The rules under §13(e) may require the issuer to furnish whatever information the Commission deems necessary or material with respect to such matters as the reasons for the purchase, the source of the funds, the number of shares to be purchased, the price, and the method of purchase. Moreover, a purchase by or for any person in a control relationship with the issuer, or a purchase "subject to control of the issuer or any such person," is considered (subject to rulemaking authority to define and exempt) a purchase by the issuer. In contrast to §14(e), however, §13(e) applies only to an issuer that has a class of registered equity securities or that is a closed-end investment company registered under the 1940 Act. The bill as passed by the Senate was

---

[36] There is nothing to prevent making significant additional acquisitions during the ten-day period, and to that extent preserving the element of surprise. The Commission has expressed its concern with respect to the practice. Sec. Ex. Act Rel. 16,420, 18 SEC Dock. 1293, 1304 (1979).

amended before enactment to make it clear that the Commission may not regulate issuers' repurchases apart from the prevention of fraud — a concept borrowed from §15(c)(2), part of the over-the-counter broker-dealer complex.[37]

Apart from the Williams Act provisions but closely related to §13(d) is §13(g), which resulted from the Commission's 1976 report on beneficial ownership[38] and was adopted by the Domestic and Foreign Investment Disclosure Act of 1977.[39] Section 13(g) was designed to close some gaps in §13(d): it applies to every person who "is" a 5 percent beneficial owner, regardless of when he achieved that status or of the exemptions in §13(d)(6) for acquisitions made pursuant to a 1933 Act registration statement or totaling not more than 2 percent of the class in twelve months. It would have been simpler, of course, to amend §13(d). And the Commission has done the next best thing by adopting a single reporting regulation denominated D-G.[40]

To return to the Williams Act, its legislative history makes it clear that "the Act was designed for the benefit of investors and not to tip the balance of regulation either in favor of management or in favor of the person seeking corporate control."[41] In a free economy it is hard to imagine any federal governmental policy *other than* studied neutrality. At the same time, one need not favor deregulation in this area in order to express a mild disquiet.

It is not a matter of steering between the Scylla of understatement when a company is making a tender offer and the Charybdis of overstatement when that same company may shortly thereafter be filing a registration statement under the 1933 Act in order to replenish the capital used up in consummating the tender offer.

---

[37] See p. 805 infra; Code §1613. But the Commission does not view its §13(e) authority as limited to requiring disclosure. Sec. Ex. Act Rel. 17,222, 21 SEC Dock. 212, 217 (1980).

[38] See p. 559 n. 100 supra.

[39] 91 Stat. 1498 (1977). This statute is flavored by the concurrent adoption of the Foreign Corrupt Practices Act, which added §30A to the 1934 Act. See p. 157 n. 22 supra.

[40] Sec. Ex. Act Rel. 15,348, 16 SEC Dock. 228 (1978). Concurrently with the adoption of §13(g), Congress in §13(h) directed the Commission to report with respect to the effectiveness of the ownership reporting requirements contained in the 1934 Act and the desirability of modifying the 5 percent threshhold used in §§13(d)(1) and 13(g). The Commission submitted a report in June 1980 that concluded that the existing reporting requirements in §§13, 14, and 16 were "effective in accomplishing [their] purposes" and that no further legislation was necessary. Report of the Securities and Exchange Commission on Beneficial Ownership Reporting Requirements Pursuant to Section 13(h) of the Securities Exchange Act of 1934 (1980) 8, 39, 66-68.

[41] GAF Corp. v. Milstein, 453 F. 2d 709, 717 n. 16 (2d Cir. 1971), *cert. denied*, 406 U. S. 910.

The requirements of disclosure imposed by Rule 10b-5, actually and potentially, have long tended to make management adept at that kind of seamanship — although some lawyers who have received letters of comment on 1933 Act registration statements from the staff in the past may be bemused when they anticipate letters of comment on tender offer filings suggesting that the offeror has been too modest in describing his own experience and qualifications. The crux of the philosophical difficulty goes deeper. We do after all pretend to a corporate system and an economy in which it is of the essence of shares that they be freely transferable. In principle, "The incumbent management has no protected interest in remaining in power."[42] And, just as not all managements are "stodgy old fools," not all tender offerors are "raiders" or "pirates."[43] But, when a shareholder gets an SEC-processed statement from an offeror who does sound like a raider, presumably he will be more inclined to sell out than he will be when the offeror is a company of impeccable management and an excellent record of taking over and rehabilitating other companies. This is simply to say — since this relatively greater or lesser reluctance to sell will be reflected in the price that will have to be paid in order to obtain control — that one result of full disclosure may well be: the better the reputation and attainment of the offeror, the higher the price he will have to pay.

3. DEFINITIONS AND EXEMPTIONS

a. "Beneficial Owner," "Class," and "Group"

"Beneficial owner" is elaborately defined in Rule 13d-3 in terms basically of "voting power" and "investment power." The definition is quite different from the comparable definition under

---

[42] General Time Corp. v. American Investors Fund, Inc., 283 F. Supp. 400, 403 (S. D. N. Y. 1968), *aff'd* sub nom. General Time Corp. v. Talley Industries, Inc., 403 F. 2d 159 (2d Cir. 1968), *cert. denied*, 393 U. S. 1026.

[43] See Jarrell and Bradley, The Economic Effects of Federal and State Regulations of Cash Tender Offers, 23 J. L. & Econ. 371 (1980). We are told that the reaction of one official of a company that was subject to a takeover bid was: "This type of maneuver, which has been rampant in England, is, in my opinion, a wholly unfair and even an un-American approach." Mundheim, Why the Bill on Tender Offers Should Not Be Passed, 1 Institutional Investor 24 (May 1967). See generally Brudney, A Note on Chilling Tender Solicitations, 21 Rutgers L. Rev. 609 (1967).

§16(a),[44] where the emphasis is on the economic incidence of ownership rather than the ability to shift control.[45]

The three reporting provisions themselves, in identical language, define "class" to exclude securities held by or for the issuer or a subsidiary[46] and provide that two or more persons acting as a partnership "or other group" for the purpose of acquiring, holding, or disposing of securities are considered a "person."[47] It has been variously held that the post-1968 formation of a group is an acquisition by the group "person" from the members of the group, so that the group must file under §13(d)(1) (and presumably §13(g)(1)) within ten days after its members agree to act together even though no member has acquired any security between 1968 and that time;[48] at the other extreme, that there is no acquisition by the group in such a case;[49] and, in the middle, that the duty to report is touched off only when the group *later* agrees to act in concert "to acquire additional shares," but that, once it is shown that a group has agreed to pursue a common objective and that a member has *thereafter* acquired additional shares, that acquisition creates a rebuttable presumption that the acquisition was pursuant to an agreement as of the acquisition date to acquire securities in furtherance of the group's objective.[50] The Commission has codified the first of these views by rule,[51] as the Code would by statute.[52]

In any event, a mere relationship (family, personal, or business) among individuals or entities does not create a group "person." There must be an agreement to act in concert,[53] though that agreement, obviously, need not be in writing.[54]

---

[44] See p. 646 infra.

[45] Beneficial ownership may be disclaimed. Rule 13d-4.

[46] §§13(d)(4), 13(g)(4), 14(d)(3).

[47] §§13(d)(3), 13 (g)(3), 14(d)(2).

[48] GAF Corp. v. Milstein, 453 F. 2d 709 (2d Cir. 1971), *cert. denied,* 406 U. S. 910. The same court later distinguished the case of a *management* group created to stave off a tender offer: "Since the Exchange Act contains a specific provision governing the disclosures required of a target company's management, it would be pointless to superimpose requirements found in another section, which does not deal specifically with management disclosures." Corenco Corp. v. Schiavone & Sons, Inc., 488 F. 2d 207, 218 (2d Cir. 1973).

[49] Ozark Air Lines, Inc. v. Cox, 326 F. Supp. 1113 (E. D. Mo. 1971).

[50] Bath Industries, Inc. v. Blot, 427 F. 2d 97, 108-10 (7th Cir. 1970).

[51] Rule 13d-5(b).

[52] §605(b)(2).

[53] Texasgulf, Inc. v. Canada Development Corp., 366 F. Supp. 374, 403 (S. D. Tex. 1973).

[54] SEC v. Savoy Industries, Inc., 587 F. 2d 1149, 1163 (D. C. Cir. 1978), *cert.*

Query: Once there is a group "person," how does a member dissociate himself? Would it suffice simply to report that fact in a new filing? If the group refuses to make such a filing, could the ex-member do so, though he alone had never filed before? Wouldn't his filing be a self-serving statement? Would he have to go so far as to get rid of his stock?

b. "Tender Offer"

It is odd that, with everything in §14(d)-(f) turning on the existence of a "tender offer," that term is defined by neither statute nor rule. A *release* accompanying amendments to the very first preliminary rules referred to an exclusion (which must have been excised before the adoption of the amendments) of "offers to no more than ten security holders during any period of twelve months."[55] But no such exclusion has ever been adopted. And in 1976, after its tender offer hearings,[56] the Commission said that a definition was neither appropriate nor necessary in view of "the dynamic nature of these transactions and the need * * * to remain flexible."[57] In this state of affairs case law has pretty well settled a number of propositions:

It is clear that the concept is not limited to the classic page in the Wall Street Journal that confronts a surprised chief executive officer over his breakfast coffee. The Commission is on record[58] that "the term is to be interpreted flexibly and applies to special bids;[59] purchase resulting from widespread solicitations by means of mailings, telephone calls and personal visits; and any transaction where the conduct of the person seeking control causes pressures to be put on shareholders similar to those attendant to a conventional tender offer." And that is about as good a generalization

---

denied, 440 U. S. 913; Wellman v. Dickinson, 682 F. 2d 355, 362-63 (2d Cir. 1982).

[55] Sec. Ex. Act Rel. 8392 (1968).

[56] See Sec. Ex. Act Rel. 11,003, 5 SEC Dock. 115 (1974); Sec. Ex. Act Rel. 11,088, 5 SEC Dock. 406 (1974).

[57] Sec. Ex. Act Rel. 12,676, 10 SEC Dock. 143, 145 (1976); see also Sec. Ex. Act Rel. 15,548, 16 SEC Dock. 973, 980 (1979).

[58] Sec. Ex. Act Rel. 12,676, 10 SEC Dock. 143, 145 (1976); see generally Note, The Developing Meaning of "Tender Offer" under the Securities Exchange Act of 1934, 86 Harv. L. Rev. 1250 (1973).

[59] See also Sec. Ex. Act Rel. 16,112, 18 SEC Dock. 67, 71 (1979). This refers to a special stock exchange procedure for filling bids for blocks too large to be filled in the regular auction market. See 2 Loss c. 7F, esp. at 1238-39.

concerning the case law as any.[60] We are reminded that there is no "constitutional requirement that the legislative standards be translated by the Commission into formal and detailed rules of thumb prior to their application in a particular case."[61] Moreover, although *hostile* offers formed the immediate catalyst for the Williams Act, a tender offer is no less a tender offer because it is unopposed by the target; for "there is no reason to assume that the danger [of the stockholders' being misled by the offeror or the target's management] will be lessened when both are on the same side of the fence."[62]

On the other hand, a tender offer does not result *merely* from unsolicited market purchases[63] or privately negotiated transactions at premium prices[64] or both.[65] This legitimates the "creeping tender offer" practice whereby the proposed tender offeror accumulates just under 5 percent and *then* makes its tender offer. But this may not be true with respect to *issuer* tender offers[66] or someone's purchases either to *block* a tender offer or to cement an existing control position.[67]

Statutory mergers and consolidations are not tender offers.[68]

[60] See Cattlemen's Investment Co. v. Fears, 343 F. Supp. 1248, 1251-52 (W. D. Okla. 1972) (alleged "active and widespread solicitation of public shareholders in person, over the telephone and through the mails" seems designed even more than a general newspaper advertisement to force a shareholder into making a hurried investment decision); S-G Securities, Inc. v. Fuqua Investment Co., 466 F. Supp. 1114, 1126-27 (D. Mass. 1978) ("(1) a publicly announced intention by the purchaser to acquire a substantial block of the stock of the target company for purposes of acquiring control thereof; and (2) a subsequent rapid acquistion by the purchaser of large blocks of stock through open market and privately negotiated purchases").

[61] Wellman v. Dickinson, 475 F. Supp. 783, 826 (S. D. N. Y. 1979), *aff'd on other grounds*, 682 F. 2d 355 (2d Cir. 1982), quoting from American Power & Light Co. v. SEC, 329 U. S. 90, 106 (1946).

[62] Smallwood v. Pearl Brewing Co., 489 F. 2d 579, 598 (5th Cir. 1974), *cert. denied*, 419 U. S. 873.

[63] See City Investing Co. v. Simcox, 633 F. 2d 56, 61 n. 11 (7th Cir. 1980) (dictum that no court has so held); Sec. Ex. Act Rel. 16,385, 18 SEC Dock. 1092, 1095 (1979). Support is lent to this conclusion by the impossibility of applying the withdrawal, proration, and equal price provisions of §14(d)(5)-(7) to market purchases.

[64] Kennecott Copper Corp. v. Curtiss-Wright Corp., 584 F. 2d 1195, 1206-07 (2d Cir. 1978).

[65] Brascan, Ltd. v. Edper Equities, Ltd., 477 F. Supp. 773, 789 (S. D. N. Y. 1979).

[66] See Kerr, Corporate Stock Repurchases — Substantive Trading Restrictions, in Practising Law Institute, Sixth Annual Institute on Securities Regulation (1975), 3, 29.

[67] See Lipton in Law, Lipton and Flom, Take-Over Bids: Recent Developments, in Practising Law Institute, Seventh Annual Institute on Securities Regulation (1976), 181, 208.

[68] Sec. Ex. Act Rel. 16,385, 18 SEC Dock. 1092, 1097 (1979).

Nor is an issuer's purchase under a statutory appraisal procedure when preemptive rights are eliminated.[69] And the absence of "a statutory checklist of features" led the Second Circuit to apply a "rule of reason" that led it to conclude that an announcement in the Wall Street Journal that professed not to be a tender offer, and that stated that tenders could be made only after stockholders had received a printed offer, fell short of being a tender offer.[70]

The Code defines the term as the converse, roughly, of the "limited offering" that is excluded from its definition of "distribution":[71]

> "Tender offer" means an offer to buy a security, or a solicitation of an offer to sell a security, that is directed to more than thirty-five persons, unless —
>
> > (i) it (I) is incidental to the execution of a buy order by a broker, or to a purchase by a dealer, who performs no more than the usual function of a broker or dealer, or (II) does no more than state an intention to make such an offer or solicitation; and
> >
> > (ii) it satisfies any additional conditions that the Commission imposes by rule.[72]

There is also outstanding a two-tier definition — partly objective, partly subjective — that the Commission proposed for comment in 1979: *either* (1) one or more offers to buy (or solicitations of offers to sell) more than 5 percent of a single class, directed to more than ten persons during any forty-five-day period (other than market offers at market prices without solicitation or unusual brokers' commissions or dealers' markups), *or* (2) dissemination of an offer in a widespread manner, and with a premium in excess of the greater of 5 percent or $2 above market, without "a meaningful opportunity to negotiate the price and terms."[73]

c. Exemptions

There are no exemptions from §13(e) or 14(e), although the former gives the Commission authority to exempt by rule.

[69] Leighton v. American Telephone & Telegraph Co., 397 F. Supp. 133 (S. D. N. Y. 1975).

[70] Corenco Corp. v. Schiavone & Sons, Inc., 488 F. 2d 207, 216 (2d Cir. 1973). The court referred by analogy to Rules 134 and 135 under the 1933 Act. See pp. 110, 113 supra.

[71] See p. 397 supra.

[72] §202(166)(A).

[73] Sec. Ex. Act Rel. 16,385, 18 SEC Dock. 1092, 1108 (1979).

Section 13(d)(6) exempts offers to buy in consideration of securities registered under the 1933 Act. In addition, both that section and §14(d)(8), apart from giving the Commission rulemaking authority to exempt, afford automatic exemptions for (1) acquisitions up to 2 percent of the class in a twelve-month period and (2) issuer acquisitions of their own equity securities. But the Commission reads the 2 percent exemption as extending only to the initial filing requirement of §13(d)(1), not to the obligation under §13(d)(2) to report any material change; and it *presumes* that an acquisition or disposition of more than 1 percent is material (though less may also be depending on the facts).[74]

4. THE RULES

The late 1970s and early 1980s saw a veritable orgy of rulemaking under the Williams Act provisions as the Commission replaced its temporary rules with an elaborate regulatory structure. Portions of the scheme — for example, the definition of "beneficial owner" in Rule 13d-3 — have already been touched on. Our endeavor here is to present the "big picture" in inevitably summarized and incomplete form.

Regulation D-G, adopted under §§13(d) and 13(g), consists of Rules 13d-1 to 13d-7. And Rule 13d-1 requires the filing of Schedule 13D or 13G as the case may be.[75]

Rule 13e-1 prohibits a target company from buying any of its equity securities during another's tender offer unless it files a statement (and within the past six months has sent or given its equity security holders the substance of the information) with respect to such data as the manner and purpose of the purchases and the source of funds to be used.

There is no Rule 13e-2. A proposed rule under that number that would have imposed both disclosure requirements and substantive purchasing limitations on issuers' stock repurchases was ultimately adopted in different form as Rule 10b-18.[76]

Rule 13e-3 is directed at the "going private" phenomenon. There are ways of "going private" other than by the issuer's or an affiliate's buying up the publicly held stock — notably the "re-

---

[74] Sec. Ex. Act Rel. 17,353, 21 SEC Dock. 775 (1980).

[75] For a collection of staff views, see Sec. Ex. Act Rel. 16,623, 19 SEC Dock. 807 (1980).

[76] See p. 1004 infra.

verse split" and the "freezeout."[77] The Supreme Court aborted an attempt to make a Rule 10b-5 violation out of "a breach of fiduciary duty by majority stockholders, without any deception, misrepresentation, or nondisclosure."[78] But the Commission has tried its hand by way of Rule 13e-3.

In early 1975 the Commission, in giving notice of a public investigation and rulemaking proceeding, suggested alternative versions of a rule: both versions would have turned on "fair value," but, in addition, one would have required two independent valuations and the other a valid business purpose.[79] In adopting Rule 13e-3 more than four years later, the Commission expressed the belief that the fairness question should be deferred until there was an opportunity to determine the efficacy of the new rule.[80] And the Commission also abandoned the idea of valid business purpose. But Schedule 13E-3 requires a statement whether the issuer or affiliate filing the schedule "reasonably believes that the Rule 13e-3 transaction is fair or unfair to unaffiliated security holders," with a discussion in reasonable detail of the enumerated factors on which the belief with respect to fairness is based.[81]

A "Rule 13e-3 transaction" is defined as (1) a purchase of an equity security by the issuer or an affiliate, (2) a tender offer for an equity security made by the issuer or an affiliate, or (3) a solicitation subject to Regulation 14A or 14C in connection with a merger or similar transaction, sale of assets to an affiliate, or reverse stock split involving the purchase of fractional interests, if

---

[77] This refers to the procedure, available under the laws of many states, whereby those in control initiate a merger into a corporate shell that they own and require public holders to take cash or a newly created debt security. But see, e. g., Bryan v. Brock & Blevins Co., Inc., 490 F. 2d 563 (5th Cir. 1974), *cert. denied*, 419 U. S. 844 (Georgia law); Singer v. Magnavox Co., 380 A. 2d 969 (Del. 1977).

In general, see Am. B. Assn., Com. on Corp. Laws, Guidelines on Going Private, 37 Bus. Law. 313 (1981); A. Borden, Going Private (1982). On the incidental problems that arise as a matter of corporation law, see Brudney, A Note on "Going Private," 61 Va. L. Rev. 1019 (1975); Note, Going Private, 84 Yale L. J. 903 (1975).

[78] Santa Fe Industries, Inc. v. Green, 430 U. S. 462 (1977), set out infra p. 928. But cf., e. g., Goldberg v. Meridor, 567 F. 2d 209, *cert. denied*, 434 U. S. 1069 (2d Cir. 1977) (alleged nondisclosure to stockholders when all the directors were part of the alleged deceit); Healey v. Catalyst Recovery of Pa., Inc., 616 F. 2d 641 (3d Cir. 1980).

[79] Sec. Ex. Act Rel. 11,231, 6 SEC Dock. 250 (1975).

[80] Sec. Ex. Act Rel. 16,075, 17 SEC Dock. 1449, 1451 (1979).

[81] Sch. 13E-3, Item 8.

in any such case the transaction has a reasonable likelihood or purpose of causing either (a) termination of reporting obligations by bringing the number of record holders below 300 or (b) a class of equity securities to be neither listed nor authorized to be quoted on an interdealer quotation system.[82]

The next rule, 13e-4 applies to issuer tender offers generally.[83] If Rule 13e-3 applies by its terms, Rule 13e-4 continues to apply as well. Schedule 13E-4 resembles Schedule 14D-1.

Aside from the rules under §13(d)-(e), the Commission adopted a whole new set of rules under §14(d)-(e) effective in January 1980.[84] They are, unhappily, both long — 16 two-column pages in the SEC Docket — and complex. We shall have to settle for a few highlights:

(1) One way that a cash tender offer "commences" is by *any* public announcement that identifies the offeror and the target and states the amount, class, and price range, *unless* within five business days the offeror either (a) publicly reneges or (b) files a Schedule 14D-1, *hands* it to the target and any other offeror that has filed a Schedule 14D-1, and telephones specified information and mails a copy of the schedule to every exchange on which the security is traded (as well as NASDAQ[85] if the security is quoted there); and in the latter event (that is to say, if the offeror acts as in (b)) the date of commencement is the date that specified information is first published or sent to security holders.[86] The effect of this peculiar on-again-off-again formula — as well as, one suspects, its purpose — is to buttress the Commission's preemption argument with respect to those state tender offer statutes that impose a post-filing waiting period and sometimes a hearing procedure before a tender offer may be made.[87]

---

[82] Rule 13e-3(a)(3). For a collection of staff views on the rule, see Sec. Ex. Act Rel. 17,719, 22 SEC Dock. 783 (1981). Although §13(e) is restricted to "an issuer which has a class of equity securities registered pursuant to section 12 of this title, or which is a closed-end investment company registered under the Investment Company Act of 1940," Rule 13e-3(c)(1) extends to an issuer (or its affiliate) within §15(d). *Query* whether the Commission's reliance on §10(b) for this extension (Sec. Ex. Act Rel. 14,185, 13 SEC Dock. 839, 847 (1982) is justified in the face of a §13(e) that is as restricted as it is.

[83] The rule was adopted by Sec. Ex. Act Rel. 16,112, 18 SEC Dock. 67 (1979).

[84] Sec. Ex. Act Rel. 16,384, 18 SEC Dock. 1053 (1979).

[85] See p. 675 infra.

[86] Rule 14d-2.

[87] See pp. 601-03 infra. The conflict "is so direct and substantial as to make it impossible to comply with both sets of requirements as they presently exist." Sec. Ex. Act Rel. 16,384, 18 SEC Dock. 1053, 1060 (1979).

(2) Rule 14d-5 is a stockholder list rule modeled on Rule 14a-7.[88]

(3) Neither the target company nor specified persons connected with it may do any soliciting or recommending without filing a "recommendation statement" on Schedule 14D-9 and circulating copies as specified. There is an exception, however, for a "stop, look, and listen" communication in which the target may request holders to wait up to ten business days for the target's views.[89]

(4) In any event, the target, within ten business days, *must* publish or give security holders a reasoned statement to the effect that it recommends acceptance or rejection, is remaining neutral, or is unable to take a position.[90]

The same day that these new §14(d)-(e) rules were adopted, the Commission invited comment on still further proposals and questions, including the need for rules with respect to the impact of defensive charter amendments on tender offer practice and interested investors.[91]

Finally, the Commission has used its §10(b) authority to adopt two rules that relate to tender offers: Rule 10b-4, which we have already noticed, to prohibit "short tenders,"[92] and Rule 10b-13, which prohibits a person making a cash tender offer or exchange offer for *any* equity security (whether or not registered) from buying or arranging to buy any such security (or any other security that is immediately convertible into any such security) outside the tender or exchange offer — a practice sometimes called buying "alongside" the tender offer.[93] The latter rule is made inapplicable to purchases pursuant to stock option plans within specified sections of the Internal Revenue Code. And the Commission reserves an *ad hoc* exemptive authority.

5.   CONTENT OF THE SCHEDULES

As with respect to other filings,[94] it has been held that the Williams Act filing requirements impose a duty to file truthfully and completely.[95]

---

[88] See p. 525 supra.

[89] Rule 14d-9.

[90] Rule 14e-2. Rule 14e-3, an insider trading rule, is discussed later. See p. 868 infra.

[91] Sec. Ex. Act Rel. 16,385, 18 SEC Dock. 1092 (1979).

[92] See p. 576 supra.

[93] See Burack, When Buying Rights Is Wrong: Purchases of Target Company Stock during Exchange Offers and Mergers, 33 Bus. Law. 605 (1978).

[94] See p. 487 supra.

[95] GAF Corp. v. Milstein, 453 F. 2d 709, 720 (2d Cir. 1971), *cert. denied,*

As with respect to the proxy statement,[96] it is the Commission's position, too, that "Disclosure of material facts is not limited to the specific requirements of" the schedules.[97] For there is always §14(e) as there is Rule 14a-9. It follows that a tender offeror's financial statements of one kind or another might be "material" even if not specifically required by the appropriate schedule.[98] Schedule 14D-1 — as well as Schedules 13E-3 and 13E-4 with respect to issuer tender offers — now refers specifically to financial data of one kind or another.[99] This moots the question to a large extent — but not entirely, because Schedule 14D-1 requires "adequate" financial information only when the offeror is not a natural person and its financial condition is "material" to target stockholders,[100] and Schedule 13E-4 likewise contains the "material" modifier. There is thus some rubber left. Financial information *may* be material under the circumstances even in the case of a cash offer, particularly if it is a partial offer.[101]

6.   FALSE OR MISLEADING STATEMENTS [§14(e)]

Section 14(e) is beginning to rival Rule 10b-5 as the subject of litigation. It would not be an exaggeration to say that there has hardly been a contested tender offer in which both sides have not hurled §14(e) thunderbolts at each other.

The section does not track Rule 14a-9, the proxy fraud rule, as closely as it might. For example, it is an open question whether the "solicitation" of §14(e) is as broad as the "solicit" of §14(a).[102] But much of what has been said in the discussion of Rule 14a-9 applies equally here. For example:

Judge Friendly cautioned in the first appellate opinion on the Williams Act that tender offers, like proxy contests, generally are

---

406 U. S. 910; SEC v. Savoy Industries, Inc., 587 F. 2d 1149, 1165 (D. C. Cir. 1978), *cert. denied*, 440 U. S. 913.

[96] See p. 523 supra.

[97] Sec. Ex. Act Rel. 13,787, 12 SEC Dock. 1256, 1264 n. 22 (1977).

[98] For a review of the cases, see Prudent Real Estate Trust v. Johncamp Realty, Inc., 599 F. 2d 1140 (2d Cir. 1979).

[99] Sch. 13E-3, Item 14; Sch. 13E-4, Item 7; Sch. 14D-1, Item 9.

[100] "The facts and circumstances concerning the tender offer, particularly the terms of the tender offer, may influence a determination as to whether disclosure of financial information is material. However, once the materiality requirement is applicable, the adequacy of the financial information will depend primarily on the nature of the bidder." Sch. 14D-1, Item 9, Instr. 1.

[101] Life Investors, Inc. v. AGO Holding, N. V., — F. 2d —, — (8th Cir. 1981).

[102] See Sargent v. Genesco, Inc., 492 F. 2d 750, 769 (5th Cir. 1974). See p. 514 supra.

contests. "Congress intended to assure basic honesty and fair dealing, not to impose an unrealistic requirement of laboratory conditions that might make the new statute a potent tool for incumbent management to protect its own interests against the desires and welfare of the stockholders."[103] At the same time, the tender offeror may not look to the target to remedy its own disclosure deficiencies.[104]

So far as antitrust implications are concerned, all that is required is "the disclosure of basic facts so that outsiders may draw upon their own evaluated experience in reaching their own investment decisions with knowledge equal to that of the insiders."[105]

There is no reason to believe that materiality does not have the same meaning in the two contexts.[106] But, so far as scienter is concerned, §14(e), though not quite as broad as Rule 14a-9,[107] is, like §17(a) of the 1933 Act and unlike Rule 10b-5, a statute and not a rule. Therefore, the Supreme Court's construction of §17(a) should govern so as to conclude that scienter (whatever its meaning) is required by the "fraudulent" and "deceptive" clause of §14(e), which more or less tracks §17(a)(1) of the 1933 Act and §10(b) of the 1933 Act, but not by the untrue statement clause, which *precisely* tracks §17(a)(2).[108]

7. ENFORCEMENT

What has been said with respect to enforcement of the proxy rules — the absence of an administrative sanction, the quantitative primacy of private litigation, and the breadth of the courts' ancillary jurisdiction with respect to the scope of relief — applies here *mutatis mutandis*.[109] And we shall similarly explore the scope of relief here, because that is relevant to SEC as well as private ac-

---

[103] Electronic Specialty Co., v. International Controls Corp., 409 F. 2d 937, 948 (2d Cir. 1969).
[104] Sonesta Int'l Hotels Corp. v. Wellington Associates, 483 F. 2d 247, 255 (2d Cir. 1973).
[105] Gulf & Western Industries, Inc. v. Great Atlantic & Pacific Tea Co., 476 F. 2d 687, 697 (2d Cir. 1973).
[106] Electronic Specialty Co. v. International Controls Corp., 409 F. 2d 937, 948 (2d Cir. 1969); see TSC Industries, Inc. v. Northway, Inc., 426 U. S. 438 (1976), set out supra p. 544.
[107] See p. 541 supra.
[108] Aaron v. SEC, 446 U. S. 680 (1980), set out infra p. 887. Scienter is *not* required with respect to §13(d)(1), or presumably §14(d)(1). SEC v. Savoy Industries, Inc., 587 F. 2d 1149, 1167 (D. C. Cir. 1978).
[109] See pp. 562-67 supra.

tions, leaving the question of implying private actions to the chapter on civil liability.

RONDEAU v. MOSINEE PAPER CORP.
Supreme Court of the United States, 1975
422 U. S. 49

Mr. Chief Justice Burger delivered the opinion of the Court.

We granted certiorari in this case to determine whether a showing of irreparable harm is necessary for a private litigant to obtain injunctive relief in a suit under §13(d) of the Securities Exchange Act of 1934, 48 Stat. 894, as added by §2 of the Williams Act, 82 Stat. 454, as amended, 84 Stat. 1497, 15 U. S. C. §78m(d). 419 U. S. 1067 (1974). The Court of Appeals held that it was not. 500 F. 2d 1011 (C. A. 1974). We reverse.

I

Respondent Mosinee Paper Corp. is a Wisconsin company engaged in the manufacture and sale of paper, paper products, and plastics. Its principal place of business is located in Mosinee, Wis., and its only class of equity security is common stock which is registered under §12 of the Securities Exchange Act of 1934, 15 U. S. C. §78*l*. At all times relevant to this litigation there were slightly more than 800,000 shares of such stock outstanding.

In April 1971 petitioner Francis A. Rondeau, a Mosinee businessman, began making large purchases of respondent's common stock in the over-the-counter market. Some of the purchases were in his own name; others were in the name of businesses and a foundation known to be controlled by him. By May 17, 1971, petitioner had acquired 40,413 shares of respondent's stock, which constituted more than 5% of those outstanding. He was therefore required to comply with the disclosure provisions of the Williams Act, by filing a Schedule 13D with respondent and the Securities and Exchange Commission within 10 days. That form would have disclosed, among other things, the number of shares beneficially owned by petitioner, the source of the funds used to purchase them, and petitioner's purpose in making the purchases.

Petitioner did not file a Schedule 13D but continued to purchase substantial blocks of respondent's stock. By July 30, 1971, he had acquired more than 60,000 shares. On that date the chairman of respondent's board of directors informed him by letter that his activity had "given rise to numerous rumors" and "seems to have created some problems under the Federal Securities Laws . * * *" Upon receiving the letter petitioner immediately stopped placing orders for respondent's stock and consulted his attorney. On August 25, 1971, he filed a Schedule 13D which, in addition to the other required disclosures, described the "Purpose of Transaction" as follows:

> Francis A. Rondeau determined during early part of 1971 that the common stock of the Issuer [respondent] was undervalued in the over-the-counter market and represented a good investment vehicle for future income and appreciation. Francis A. Rondeau and his associates presently propose to seek to acquire additional common stock of the Issuer in order to obtain effective control of the Issuer, but such investments as originally determined were and are not necessarily made with this objective in mind. Consideration is currently being given to making a public cash tender offer to the shareholders of the Issuer at a price which will reflect current quoted prices for such stock with some premium added.

Petitioner also stated that, in the event that he did obtain control of respondent, he would consider making changes in management "in an effort to provide a Board of Directors which is more representative of all of the shareholders, particularly those outside of present management . * * *" One month later petitioner amended the form to reflect more accurately the allocation of shares between himself and his companies.

On August 27 respondent sent a letter to its shareholders informing them of the disclosures in petitioner's Schedule 13D.[3] The letter stated that by his "tardy filing" petitioner had "withheld the information to which you [the shareholders] were entitled for more than two months, in violation of federal law." In addition, while agreeing that "recent market prices have not reflected the real value of your Mosinee stock," respondent's management could "see little in Mr. Rondeau's background that would qualify him to offer any meaningful guidance to a Company in the highly technical and competitive paper industry."

Six days later respondent initiated this suit in the United States District Court for the Western District of Wisconsin. Its complaint named petitioner, his companies, and two banks which had financed some of petitioner's purchases as defendants and alleged

---

[3] Respondent simultaneously issued a press release containing the same information. Almost immediately the price of its stock jumped to $19-$21 per share. A few days later it dropped back to the prevailing price of $12.50-$14 per share, where it remained.

that they were engaged in a scheme to defraud respondent and its shareholders in violation of the securities laws. It alleged further that shareholders who had "sold shares without the information which defendants were required to disclose lacked information material to their decision whether to sell or hold," and that respondent "was unable to communicate such information to its stockholders, and to take such actions as their interest required." Respondent prayed for an injunction prohibiting petitioner and his codefendants from voting or pledging their stock and from acquiring additional shares, requiring them to divest themselves of stock which they already owned, and for damages. A motion for a preliminary injunction was filed with the complaint but later withdrawn.

After three months of pretrial proceedings petitioner moved for summary judgment. He readily conceded that he had violated the Williams Act, but contended that the violation was due to a lack of familiarity with the securities laws and that neither respondent nor its shareholders had been harmed. The District Court agreed. It found no material issues of fact to exist regarding petitioner's lack of willfulness in failing to timely file a Schedule 13D, concluding that he discovered his obligation to do so on July 30, 1971,[4] and that there was no basis in the record for disputing his claim that he first considered the possibility of obtaining control of respondent some time after that date. The District Court therefore held that petitioner and his codefendants "did not engage in intentional covert, and conspiratorial conduct in failing to timely file the 13D Schedule."[5]

Similarly, although accepting respondent's contention that its management and shareholders suffered anxiety as a result of petitioner's activities and that this anxiety was exacerbated by his failure to disclose his intentions until August 1971, the District Court concluded that similar anxiety "could be expected to accompany any change in management," and was "a predictable

[4] The District Court pointed out that prior to December 10, 1970, a Schedule 13D was not required until a person's holdings exceeded 10% of a corporation's outstanding equity securities, see Pub. L. 91-567, 84 Stat. 1497, and credited petitioner's testimony that he believed the 10% requirement was still in effect at the time he made his purchases. Indeed, the chairman of respondent's board of directors was not familiar with the Williams Act's filing requirement until shortly before he sent the July 30, 1971, letter.

[5] The District Court also concluded that respondent's management was not unaware of petitioner's activities with respect to its stock. It found that by July 1971, there was considerable "street talk" among brokers, bankers, and businessmen regarding his purchases and that the chairman of respondent's board had been monitoring them.

consequence of shareholder democracy." It fell far short of the irreparable harm necessary to support an injunction and no other harm was revealed by the record; as amended, petitioner's Schedule 13D disclosed all of the information to which respondent was entitled, and he had not proceeded with a tender offer. Moreover, in the view of the District Court even if a showing of irreparable harm were not required in all cases under the securities laws, petitioner's lack of bad faith and the absence of damage to respondent made this "a particularly inappropriate occasion to fashion equitable relief . * * *" Thus, although petitioner had committed a technical violation of the Williams Act, the District Court held that respondent was entitled to no relief and entered summary judgment against it.

The Court of Appeals reversed, with one judge dissenting. The majority stated that it was "giving effect" to the District Court's findings regarding the circumstances of petitioner's violation of the Williams Act, but concluded that those findings showed harm to respondent because it "was delayed in its efforts to make any necessary response to" petitioner's potential to take control of the company. In any event, the majority was of the view that respondent "need not show irreparable harm as a prerequisite to obtaining permanent injunctive relief in view of the fact that as issuer of the securities it is in the best position to assure that the filing requirements of the Williams Act are being timely and fully complied with and to obtain speedy and forceful remedial action when necessary." 500 F. 2d, at 1016-1017. The Court of Appeals remanded the case to the District Court with instructions that it enjoin petitioner and his codefendants from further violations of the Williams Act and from voting the shares purchased between the due date of the Schedule 13D and the date of its filing for a period of five years. It considered "such an injunctive decree appropriate to neutralize [petitioner's] violation of the Act and to deny him the benefit of his wrongdoing." Id. at 1017.

We granted certiorari to resolve an apparent conflict among the Courts of Appeals and because of the importance of the question presented to private actions under the federal securities laws. We disagree with the Court of Appeals' conclusion that the traditional standards for extraordinary equitable relief do not apply in these circumstances, and reverse.

II

As in the District Court and the Court of Appeals, it is conceded here that petitioner's delay in filing the Schedule 13D constituted a violation of the Williams Act. The narrow issue before us is whether this record supports the grant of injunctive relief, a remedy whose basis "in the federal courts has always been irreparable harm and inadequacy of legal remedies." *Beacon Theatres, Inc.* v. *Westover*, 359 U. S. 500, 506-507 (1959).

The Court of Appeals' conclusion that respondent suffered "harm" sufficient to require sterilization of petitioner's stock need not long detain us. The purpose of the Williams Act is to insure that public shareholders who are confronted by a cash tender offer for their stock will not be required to respond without adequate information regarding the qualifications and intentions of the offering party. By requiring disclosure of information to the target corporation as well as the Securities and Exchange Commission, Congress intended to do no more than give incumbent management an opportunity to express and explain its position. The Congress expressly disclaimed an intention to provide a weapon for management to discourage takeover bids or prevent large accumulations of stock which would create the potential for such attempts. Indeed, the Act's draftsmen commented upon the "extreme care" which was taken "to avoid tipping the balance of regulation either in favor of management or in favor of the person making the takeover bid." S. Rep. No. 550, 90th Cong., 1st Sess., 3 (1967); H. R. Rep. No. 1711, 90th Cong., 2d Sess., 4 (1968). See also *Electronic Specialty Co.* v. *International Controls Corp.*, 409 F. 2d 937, 947 (C. A. 2 1969).

The short of the matter is that none of the evils to which the Williams Act was directed has occurred or is threatened in this case. Petitioner has not attempted to obtain control of respondent, either by a cash tender offer or any other device. Moreover, he has now filed a proper Schedule 13D, and there has been no suggestion that he will fail to comply with the Act's requirement of reporting any material changes in the information contained therein.[9] 15 U. S. C. §78m(d)(2); 17 C. F. R. §240.13d-2 (1974). On this record there is no likelihood that respondent's shareholders will be disadvantaged should petitioner make a tender offer, or that respondent will be unable to adequately place its case before them should a contest for control develop. Thus, the usual basis for injunctive relief, "that there exists some cognizable danger of

[9] Because this case involves only the availability of injunctive relief to remedy a §13(d) violation following compliance with the reporting requirements, it does not require us to decide whether or under what circumstances a corporation could obtain a decree enjoining a shareholder who is currently in violation of §13(d) from acquiring further shares, exercising voting rights, or launching a takeover bid, pending compliance with the reporting requirements.

recurrent violation," is not present here. *United States* v. *W. T. Grant Co.,* 345 U. S. 629, 633 (1953). See also *Vicksburg Waterworks Co.* v. *Vicksburg,* 185 U. S. 65, 82 (1902).

Nor are we impressed by respondent's argument that an injunction is necessary to protect the interests of its shareholders who either sold their stock to petitioner at predisclosure prices or would not have invested had they known that a takeover bid was imminent. Brief for Respondent 13, 20-21. As observed, the principal object of the Williams Act is to solve the dilemma of shareholders desiring to respond to a cash tender offer, and it is not at all clear that the type of "harm" identified by respondent is redressable under its provisions. In any event, those persons who allegedly sold at an unfairly depressed price have an adequate remedy by way of an action for damages, thus negating the basis for equitable relief.[10] See *Youngstown Sheet & Tube Co.* v. *Sawyer,* 343 U. S. 579, 595 (1952) (Frankfurter, J., concurring). Similarly, the fact that the second group of shareholders for whom respondent expresses concern have retained the benefits of their stock and the lack of an imminent contest for control make the possibility of damage to them remote at best. See *Truly* v. *Wanzer,* 5 How. 141, 142-143 (1847).

We turn, therefore, to the Court of Appeals' conclusion that respondent's claim was not to be judged according to traditional equitable principles, and that the bare fact that petitioner violated the Williams Act justified entry of an injunction against him. This position would seem to be foreclosed by *Hecht Co.* v. *Bowles,* 321 U. S. 321 (1944). There, the administrator of the Emergency Price Control Act of 1942 brought suit to redress violations of that statute. The fact of the violations was admitted, but the District Court declined to enter an injunction because they were inadvertent and the defendant had taken immediate steps to rectify them. This Court held that such an exercise of equitable discretion was proper despite §205(a) of the Act, 56 Stat. 23, 50 U. S. C. App. §925(a) (1940 ed., Supp. II), which provided that an injunction or other order "shall be granted" upon a showing of violation, observing:

> We are dealing here with the requirements of equity practice with a background of several hundred years of history. * * * *The historic injunctive process was designed to deter, not to*

---

[10] The Court was advised by respondent that such a suit is now pending in the District Court and class action certification has been sought. Although we intimate no views regarding the merits of that case, it provides a potential sanction for petitioner's violation of the Williams Act.

punish. The essence of equity jurisdiction has been the power of the Chancellor to do equity and to mould each decree to the necessities of the particular case. Flexibility rather than rigidity has distinguished it. The qualities of mercy and practicality have made equity the instrument for nice adjustment and reconciliation between the public interest and private needs as well as between competing private claims. We do not believe that such a major departure from that long tradition as is here proposed should be lightly implied. 321 U. S., at 329-330. (Emphasis added.)

This reasoning applies *a fortiori* to actions involving only "competing private claims," and suggests that the District Court here was entirely correct in insisting that respondent satisfy the traditional prerequisites of extraordinary equitable relief by establishing irreparable harm. Moreover, the District Judge's conclusions that petitioner acted in good faith and that he promptly filed a Schedule 13D when his attention was called to this obligation support the exercise of the court's sound judicial discretion to deny an application for an injunction, relief which is historically "designed to deter, not to punish" and to permit the court "to mould each decree to the necessities of the particular case." Id. at 329. As Mr. Justice Douglas aptly pointed out in *Hecht Co.*, the "grant of *jurisdiction* to issue compliance orders hardly suggests an absolute duty to do so under any and all circumstances." Ibid. (emphasis in original).

Respondent urges, however, that the "public interest" must be taken into account in considering its claim for relief and relies upon the Court of Appeals' conclusion that it is entitled to an injunction because it "is in the best position" to insure that the Williams Act is complied with by purchasers of its stock. This argument misconceives, we think, the nature of the litigation. Although neither the availability of a private suit under the Williams Act nor respondent's standing to bring it has been questioned here, this cause of action is not expressly authorized by the statute or its legislative history. Rather, respondent is asserting a so-called implied private right of action established by cases such as *J. I. Case Co.* v. *Borak,* 377 U. S. 426 (1964). Of course, we have not hesitated to recognize the power of federal courts to fashion private remedies for securities laws violations when to do so is consistent with the legislative scheme and necessary for the protection of investors as a supplement to enforcement by the Securities and Exchange Commission. Compare *J. I. Case Co.* v. *Borak,* supra, with *Securities Investor Protection Corp.* v. *Barbour,* 421

U. S. 412 (1975). However, it by no means follows that the plaintiff in such an action is relieved of the burden of establishing the traditional prerequisites of relief. Indeed, our cases hold that quite the contrary is true.

In *Deckert* v. *Independence Shares Corp.*, 311 U. S. 282 (1940), this Court was called upon to decide whether the Securities Act of 1933 authorized purchases of securities to bring an action to rescind an allegedly fraudulent sale. The question was answered affirmatively on the basis of the statute's grant of federal jurisdiction to "enforce any liability or duty" created by it. The Court's reasoning is instructive:

> The power *to enforce* implies the power to make effective the right of recovery afforded by the Act. And the power to make the right of recovery effective implies the power to utilize any of the procedures or actions normally available to the litigant according to the exigencies of the particular case. If petitioners' bill states a cause of action when tested by the customary rules governing suits of such character, the Securities Act authorizes maintenance of the suit . * * * 311 U. S. at 288.

In other words, the conclusion that a private litigant could maintain an action for violation of the 1933 Act meant no more than that traditional remedies were available to redress any harm which he may have suffered; it provided no basis for dispensing with the showing required to obtain relief. Significantly, this passage was relied upon in *Borak* with respect to actions under the Securities Exchange Act of 1934. See 377 U. S. at 433-434.

Any remaining uncertainty regarding the nature of relief available to a person asserting an implied private right of action under the securities laws was resolved in *Mills* v. *Electric Auto-Lite Co.*, 396 U. S. 375 (1970). There we held that complaining shareholders proved their case under §14(a) of the 1934 Act by showing that misleading statements in a proxy solicitation were material and that the solicitation itself "was an essential link in the accomplishment of" a merger. We concluded that any stricter standard would frustrate private enforcement of the proxy rules, but Mr. Justice Harlan took pains to point out:

> Our conclusion that petitioners have established their case by showing that proxies necessary to approval of the merger were obtained by means of a materially misleading solicitation implies nothing about the form of relief to which they may be entitled. * * * In devising retrospective relief for violation of the proxy rules, the federal courts should consider the same factors that would govern the relief granted for any similar illegality or

fraud. * * * In selecting a remedy the lower courts should exercise "the sound discretion which guides the determinations of courts of equity," keeping in mind the role of equity as "the instrument for nice adjustment and reconciliation, between the public interest and private needs as well as between competing private claims." 396 U. S., at 386, quoting *Hecht Co.* v. *Bowles,* 321 U. S., at 329.

Considering further the remedies which might be ordered, we observed that "the merger should be set aside only if a court of equity concludes, from all the circumstances, that it would be equitable to do so," and that "damages should be recoverable only to the extent that they can be shown." 396 U. S. at 388, 389.

Mills could not be plainer in holding that the questions of liability and relief are separate in private actions under the securities laws, and that the latter is to be determined according to traditional principles. Thus, the fact that respondent is pursuing a cause of action which has been generally recognized to serve the public interest provides no basis for concluding that it is relieved of showing irreparable harm and other usual prerequisites for injunctive relief. Accordingly, the judgment of the Court of Appeals is reversed and the case is remanded to it with directions to reinstate the judgment of the District Court.

So ordered.

Mr. Justice Marshall dissents.

Mr. Justice Brennan, with whom Mr. Justice Douglas joins, dissenting.

I dissent. Judge Pell, dissenting below, correctly in my view, read the decision of the Court of Appeals to construe the Williams Act, as I also construe it, to authorize injunctive relief upon the application of the management interests "irrespective of motivation, irrespective of irreparable harm to the corporation, and irrespective of whether the purchases were detrimental to investors in the company's stock. The violation timewise is * * * all that is needed to trigger this result." 500 F. 2d 1011, 1018 (C. A. 7 1974). In other words, the Williams Act is a prophylactic measure conceived by Congress as necessary to effect the congressional objective "that investors and management be notified at the earliest possible moment of the potential for a shift in corporate control." Id. at 1016. The violation itself establishes the actionable harm and no showing of other harm is necessary to secure injunctive relief. Today's holding completely undermines the congressional purpose to preclude inquiry into the result of the violation.

It does not follow that the Commission in its own injunctive actions must show "irreparable harm" as distinct from "equity," which gets down to whether the defendant's past conduct indicates — under all the circumstances and not merely in view of the time that has elapsed since the last violation — that there is a reasonable likelihood of further violation in the future.[110] For SEC injunctions are creatures of statute. As the Supreme Court said in *Hecht Co. v. Bowles,* which was relied upon in the *Rondeau* case, "the standards of the public interest, not the requirements of private litigation, measure the propriety and need for injunctive relief in these cases."[111]

At any rate, when the plaintiff establishes that some relief is appropriate, there is a great variety of precedent to choose from.[112] To proceed once more by way of example:

Under §13(d) one formula restrains further purchases until a corrected schedule has been filed,[113] and perhaps for a period of thirty days or so thereafter.[114] The courts, while conceiving of the possibility of divestiture or disfranchisement, seem to regard those remedies as rather harsh.[115]

---

[110] 3 Loss 1976. The court's discretion is particularly broad with respect to preliminary relief.

[111] 321 U. S. 321, 331; cf. SEC v. Capital Gains Research Bureau, Inc., 375 U. S. 180, 192 (1963). See generally 3 Loss 1975-80; 6 id. 4109-17.

[112] See Porter and Hyland, Rondeau v. Mosinee Paper Co. and the Williams Act Injunction, 59 Marq. L. Rev. 743 (1976). The authors enumerate five basic forms of preliminary relief and four of permanent. Id. at 745-46, 762. See, e. g., SEC v. General Refractories Co., 400 F. Supp. 1248, 1260 (D. D. C. 1975), where the court froze certain assets by way of preliminary relief against the likelihood of an ultimate disgorgement of illicit benefits. On the difficulties of framing appropriate relief once the tender offer has been consummated, see Hamilton, Some Reflections on Cash Tender Offer Legislation, 15 N. Y. L. F. 269, 292 (1969).

[113] General Aircraft Corp. v. Lampert, 556 F. 2d 90 (1st Cir. 1977).

[114] Kirsh Co. v. Bliss & Laughlin Industries, Inc., 495 F. Supp. 488, 502 (W. D. Mich. 1980); cf. Rule 13d-1(b)(3)(ii), applied in Jacobs v. Pabst Brewing Co., 549 F. Supp. 1068, 1079-80 (D. Del. 1982). But cf. Corenco Corp. v. Schiavone & Sons, Inc., 488 F. 2d 207 (2d Cir. 1973) (court concluded that a "cooling off" period would not be justified on the facts); Chromalloy American Corp. v. Sun Chemical Corp., 611 F. 2d 240, 248-49 (8th Cir. 1979) (no ninety-day injunction against purchases while information was disseminated to public).

[115] Bath Industries, Inc. v. Blot, 427 F. 2d 97 (7th Cir. 1970); Raybestos-Manhattan, Inc. v. Hi-Shear Industries, Inc., 503 F. Supp. 1122, 1126, 1133 (E. D. N. Y. 1980); cf. Kirsch Co. v. Bliss & Laughlin Industries, Inc., 495 F. Supp. 488, 502-06 (W. D. Mich. 1980) (no rescission offer).

Relief under §14(d)-(e) has included extension of the depositing security holders' statutory right to withdraw,[116] preliminary restraint against transferring or hypothecating deposited shares in order to permit their return if it should ultimately be ordered,[117] and requiring both sides to start over when both have violated.[118]

8. STATE LEGISLATION

Beginning with a Virginia statute that became effective in March 1968,[119] about five months before the federal provisions, some thirty-five states have adopted their own tender offer statutes.[120] Those acts varied a great deal: in the presence or absence of an advance filing requirement or a hearing provision, in their standards as between disclosure and substantive tests, and in their selection of one or more of a number of criteria by way of establishing contact with the particular state (incorporation or doing business or having a "principal" business or substantial assets in the state).[121] But it seems fair to say that, in contrast to the federal provisions, all the state statutes, to a greater or lesser degree, were motivated toward protecting "local" industry against tender offers.[122] The great majority of them, for example, exclude "friendly" tender offers from their restrictions.

After a considerable number of constitutional attacks under the Supremacy and Commerce Clauses had been mounted in both federal and state courts, most of them successfully, the Supreme

[116] Butler Aviation Int'l, Inc. v. Comprehensive Designers, Inc., 425 F. 2d 842 (2d Cir. 1970).
[117] North American Car Corp. v. Flying Tiger Corp., CCH Fed. Sec. L. Rep. ¶92,757 (N. D. Ill. 1970).
[118] Cauble v. White, 360 F. Supp. 1021 (E. D. La. 1973).
[119] L. 1968, c. 119.
[120] All the statutes are collected in CCH Blue Sky L. Rep. For a detailed chart of the then thirty-three statutes, see Bartell, State Takeover Laws: A Survey, in Practising Law Institute, Ninth Annual Institute on Securities Regulation (1978) App. B. The North American Securities Administrators Association (*not* the National Conference of Commissioners on Uniform State Laws) approved a "Uniform Take-Over Act" in October 1981. Id. ¶5295.
[121] See Langevoort, State Tender-Offer Legislation: Interests, Effects, and Political Competency, 62 Corn. L. Rev. 213 (1977).
[122] The writer has elsewhere paid his compliments to the Ohio legislation by calling it "stockingly one-sided, with all the onus on the take-over bidder and none on the management of the target company." Loss, Foreword to Symposium, Controlling Corporate Takeover Bids: State Regulation and the Ohio Approach, 21 Case W. Res. L. Rev. 605, 609, 611 (1970).

Court in 1982 threw out the Illinois statute.[123] But so many flowers bloomed among the seven opinions — partly because four Justices thought the case was moot — as to make this case less than altogether definitive.

In the first place, the only decision that was able to muster a majority of five (and that only because Justice Powell, though in the moot camp, concurred on this one point in view of the decision of a majority to reach the merits) was that the Illinois statute violated the Commerce Clause because the burden it imposed on interstate commerce through its *incidental* regulation was "excessive in light of the local interests the Act purports to further."[124] There was no majority for the anterior proposition that the statute "*directly* regulates transactions which take place across state lines, even if wholly outside the State of Illinois,"[125] and even if the tender offer would not affect a single Illinois stockholder.

The preemption decision was joined in only by the Chief Justice and Justices Blackmun and White, who identified three provisions that "upset the careful balance struck by Congress":[126] (1) the twenty-day waiting period that applied to the offeror but not to the target; (2) the hearing provisions, which introduced extended delay; and (3) the state's passing on the substantive fairness of the offer.[127]

It does not follow, of course, that the six Justices who did not join in the preemption holding disagreed with it. Only Justice Stevens went out of his way to limit his concurring opinion by

[123] Edgar v. MITE Corp., 102 S. Ct. 2629 (1982); see also Telvest, Inc. v. Bradshaw, 697 F. 2d 576 (4th Cir. 1983) (Virginia statute).

[124] 102 S. Ct. at 2640. Those who favored this view noted the complete statutory exemption of the tender offer that the target had made for its own shares — a distinction that "is at variance with Illinois' asserted legislative purpose, and tends to undermine appellant's justification for the burdens the statute imposes on interstate commerce." Id. at 2642. And they brushed aside the argument of state interest in regulating the internal affairs of domestic corporations (the target was incorporated in Illinois) by observing that "Tender offers contemplate transfers of stock by stockholders to a third party and do not themselves implicate the internal affairs of the target company." Id. at 2643. Besides, the statute applied also to foreign corporations with their principal place of business in other states if Illinois stockholders owned 10 percent of the class of equity securities subject to the offer.

[125] Id. at 2641 (italics supplied).

[126] Id. at 2637.

[127] The events in the litigation preceded the promulgation of Rule 14d-2(b), supra p. 587. Id. at 2638 n. 11. And there was "no contention that it would be impossible to comply with both the provisions of the Williams Act and the more burdensome requirements of the Illinois law. The issue thus is * * * whether the Illinois Act frustrates the objectives of the Williams Act in some substantial way."

stating that he was not persuaded "that Congress' decision to follow a policy of neutrality in its own legislation is tantamount to a federal prohibition against state legislation designed to provide special protection for incumbent management."[128] The other five Justices simply did not address the question — four (Justices Brennan, Marshall, Powell, and Rehnquist) because they thought the case was moot and the fifth (Justice O'Connor) because the holding of invalidity under the Commerce Clause made it unnecessary, she thought, to reach the preemption issue. Consequently the preemption question is still altogether open, and even the Commerce Clause holding might be distinguished with respect to statutes of narrower scope.[129]

All of that remains to be seen — as does the possibility of cutting the broad statutes like Illinois' down to size.

9.   LEGISLATIVE PROPOSALS

This aspect of SEC law must be regarded as "soft." That is to say, it is still evolving.

Those who produced the Code concluded that, despite the state laws' anti-takeover coloration, the existing federal provisions required reexamination both (1) by way of incorporating those aspects of the state legislation that would improve the regulatory scheme without sacrificing the neutral approach that is essential in a free economy and (2) in the interest of smoothing the road toward the explicit statutory preemption contemplated by §1904 (c).[130] Among other changes, a new ten-day advance filing requirement is designed to reduce the element of surprise.[131]

---

[128] Id. at 2648.

[129] The First Circuit subsequently reversed a preemption holding with respect to the Massachusetts statute — which it characterized as involving far less conflict with the federal law than the statutes involved in the appellate preemption decisions — and remanded for consideration of the Commerce Clause question in the light of the *MITE* case, which had been decided while the appeal was pending. Agency Rent-A-Car, Inc. v. Connolly, 686 F. 2d 1029 (1st Cir. 1982). But every other Circuit Court case to consider a preemption attack has come out the other way. Great Western United Corp. v. Kidwell, 577 F. 2d 1256 (5th Cir. 1978), *rev'd on other grounds* sub nom. Leroy v. Great Western United Corp., 443 U. S. 173 (1979); MITE Corp. v. Dixon, 633 F. 2d 486 (7th Cir. 1980), *aff'd on other grounds* sub nom. Edgar v. MITE Corp., 102 S. Ct. 2629 (1982); Kennecott Corp. v. Smith, 637 F. 2d 181 (3d Cir. 1980), *on remand*, 507 F. Supp. 1206 (D. N. J. 1981); National City Lines, Inc. v. LLC Corp., 687 F. 2d 1122 (8th Cir. 1982); see also Esmark, Inc. v. Strode, 639 S. W. 2d 768 (Ky. 1982).

[130] 1 Code 316.

[131] §606(d).

Preemption would be complete except for (1) a "regulated industry"[132] and (2) "the law of any State in which (A) the registrant to whose security holders the tender offer is directed has its principal place of business and (B) more than 50 percent of the record or beneficial holders of its outstanding voting securities holding more than 50 percent of those securities are residents." These exceptions should be well within the limits of the Constitution, both as recently expounded by the Supreme Court and otherwise.

This is one of the few "separable issues" that the Commission reserved the right to bring to the attention of Congress apart from the Code.[133] And the Commission has advanced legislation that, among other things, would define "tender offer" to include *all* purchases of a publicly held company's securities looking toward the ownership of 10 percent of any class of equity security, with an exemption (*inter alia*) for privately negotiated acquisitions from not more than ten persons in any twelve-month period; would require offers to remain open for twenty days, with all sellers receiving the highest price paid during that period; would speed up the filing of ownership reports; would repeal §13(g); would preempt and also create a private right of action, as in the Code; and would deal with the participation of banks and other intermediaries in tender offers.[134]

F. INSIDER TRADING

1. INTRODUCTION

The last of the provisions activated by registration under the 1933 Act is §16, which has to do with insider trading.

"Prior to the enactment of the Securities Exchange Act," the Commission has said, "profits from 'sure thing' speculation in the stocks of their corporations were more or less generally accepted

---

[132] This exception "is designed to make the section inapplicable to provisions on acquisitions that are found in the insurance or banking or other specialized statutes." 2 Code 978. On the Insurance Holding Company System Regulatory Act Model Bill, approved by the National Association of Insurance Commissioners in 1969, [1969] 2 NAIC Proc. 737, and since adopted in almost every state, see Kennedy, State Insurance Commissioner Involvement in Takeovers of Insurers: An Overview of Procedures and Some Constitutional Considerations, 17 Forum 374 (1981).

[133] See p. 50 supra.

[134] S. 3188, 97th Cong. (Oct. 1, 1980).

by the financial community as part of the emolument for serving as a corporate officer or director notwithstanding the flagrantly inequitable character of such trading."[1] The 1934 report of the Senate Banking and Currency Committee stated:

> Among the most vicious practices unearthed at the hearings be-fore the subcommittee was the flagrant betrayal of their fiduciary duties by directors and officers of corporations who used their positions of trust and the confidential information which came to them in such positions, to aid them in their market activities. Closely allied to this type of abuse was the unscrupulous employ-ment of inside information by large stockholders who, while not directors and officers, exercised sufficient control over the destinies of their companies to enable them to acquire and profit by infor-mation not available to others.[2]

In one case described in the committee's report on the bill, "the president of a corporation testified that he and his brothers con-trolled the company with a little over 10 percent of the shares; that shortly before the company passed a dividend, they disposed of their holdings for upward of $16,000,000 and later repurchased them for about $7,000,000, showing a profit of approximately $9,000,000 on the transaction."[3]

It was in order to "bring these practices into disrepute and en-courage the voluntary maintenance of proper fiduciary standards" that §16 was enacted.[4] And it reflects a variety of approaches:

(1) Section 16(a) provides that every officer or director of a company with an equity security registered under §12, as well as every person "who is directly or indirectly the beneficial owner of more than 10 per centum of any class of any equity security" so registered, shall file with the Commission, and also any exchange on which the security is listed, an initial report of his holdings of *all* the issuer's equity securities and a further report within ten days after the close of each calendar month in which there has been any change in his holdings. The factor that touches off the reporting requirement is the registration of an *equity* security. If a particular company has only its common stock registered, §16 applies also to its preferred. But the section does not apply to any of the securities — even equity securities — of a company that has only a nonconvertible bond issue registered. Similarly, a 10 per-

C. 7F   [1] 10 SEC Ann. Rep. 50 (1944).
  [2] Stock Exchange Practices, Report of Com. on Banking & Currency, S. Rep. No. 1455, 73d Cong., 2d Sess. (1934) 55.
  [3] S. Rep. No. 792, 73d Cong., 2d Sess. (1934) 9.
  [4] H. R. Rep. No. 1383, 73d Cong., 2d Sess. (1934) 13. All of §16 is incorpo-rated in §30(f) of the Investment Company Act, and §16(a)-(b) is reflected in §17(a)-(b) of the Holding Company Act.

cent owner of an *unregistered* equity security who is neither a director nor an officer is not subject to §16 even with respect to equity securities that are registered.[5]

This is pure disclosure, except that §16(a) serves the further function of facilitating the enforcement of §16(b).

(2) Section 16(b) — a nice example of "native American radicalism" — has a sting:

> For the purpose of preventing the unfair use of information which may have been obtained by such beneficial owner, director, or officer by reason of his relationship to the issuer, any profit realized by him from any purchase and sale, or any sale and purchase, or any equity security of such issuer (other than an exempted security) within any period of less than six months, unless such security was acquired in good faith in connection with a debt previously contracted, shall inure to and be recoverable by the issuer, irrespective of any intention on the part of such beneficial owner, director, or officer in entering into such transaction of holding the security purchased or of not repurchasing the security sold for a period exceeding six months. Suit to recover such profit may be instituted at law or in equity in any court of competent jurisdiction by the issuer, or by the owner of any security of the issuer in the name and in behalf of the issuer if the issuer shall fail or refuse to bring such suit within sixty days after request or shall fail diligently to prosecute the same thereafter; but no such suit shall be brought more than two years after the date such profit was realized. This subsection shall not be construed to cover any transaction where such beneficial owner was not such both at the time of the purchase and sale, or the sale and purchase, of the security involved, or any transaction or transactions which the Commission by rules and regulations may exempt as not comprehended within the purpose of this subsection.[6]

---

[5] Abrams v. Occidental Petroleum Corp., 450 F. 2d 157, 160 n. 6 (2d Cir. 1971), *aff'd on other grounds* sub nom. Kern County Land Co. v. Occidental Petroleum Corp., 411 U. S. 582 (1973).

[6] Cf. Societas Europaea §5, as submitted to EEC Council, [1970] 2 Bul. Eur. Comms. (Supp. to Bul. No. 8). Otherwise, there is apparently nothing quite like §16(b) in the Canadian and European statutes. Japan, which inherited all of §16 as part of the postwar reception of American law, kept §16(b) but repealed §16(a)! Whether on that account or because of cultural differences, there is said to have been only one §16(b) action in Japan, an unreported case that arose from an internal management conflict. See Tatsuta, Enforcement of Japanese Securities Legislation, 1 J. Comp. Corp. L. & Sec. Reg. 95, 112 (1978); see also Tatsuta, Proxy Regulation, Tender Offers, and Insider Trading, in L. Loss, M. Yazawa, and B. Banoff (eds.), Japanese Securities Regulation (1983) c. 8.

On tolling the statute of limitations pending the filing of the required reports, see p. 469 n. 28 supra.

(3) Whereas conduct within §16(b), though it may be expensive, is not *unlawful* in the criminal sense — or even in the sense of permitting injunctive relief at the instance of the SEC — §16(c) does prohibit short sales by §16 insiders. This contrasts also with §10(a), under which short sales generally are simply subject to SEC rulemaking.

It is interesting that the only explicit answer of Congress to the insider trading problem was §16, not some sort of provision (along the lines of the vast jurisprudence that ultimately developed under Rule 10b-5) for civil liability to the other party to an insider's transaction. It is interesting, too, that §16(b) and Rule 10b-5 are at opposite jurisprudential poles on the objective-subjective or predictability-fairness continuum. That must be borne in mind as we examine both provisions — §16(b) here because of its being an integral part of the §16 scheme and Rule 10b-5 in the chapters on fraud and civil liability.

The basic premise of the entire SEC attack on insider trading, under both provisions, has been sharply challenged by able economists. Professor Manne argues (1) that the exploitation and sale of valuable information are necessary as a method of compensating entrepreneurs, so as to guarantee the uninterrupted flow of entrepreneurial abilities into American business enterprise; (2) that no one is really hurt when insiders market valuable information; and (3) that, far from there having been any economic demonstration of the evils of insider trading, it is a good thing.[7] It has been contended, in short, that "speculative trading by insiders may be beneficial in an 'economic' sense."[8] Needless to say, however, the economists are not of one persuasion.[9] And the grievous

---

[7] H. Manne, Insider Trading and the Stock Market (1966); see also Hetherington, Insider Trading and the Logic of the Law, [1967] Wis. L. Rev. 720; Demsetz, Perfect Competition, Regulation, and the Stock Market, in H. Manne (ed.), Economic Policy and the Regulation of Corporate Securities (1968) 11-16; Note, The Efficient Capital Market Hypothesis, Economic Theory and the Regulation of the Securities Industry, 29 Stan. L. Rev. 1031 (1977), supra c. 1C, n. 26. For a more moderate, though dubious, view about it all, see Herman, Equity Funding, Inside Information, and the Regulators, 21 U. C. L. A. L. Rev. 1 (1973).

[8] Wu, An Economist Looks at Section 16 of the Securities Exchange Act of 1934, 68 Colum. L. Rev. 260, 269 (1968).

[9] See Mendelson, The Economics of Insider Trading Reconsidered, 117 U. Pa. L. Rev. 470 (1969); for a debate between Professor Manne, who is a lawyer-economist, and some of his lawyer colleagues, see Painter, Book Rev., 35 Geo. Wash. U. L. Rev. 146 (1966); Schotland, Unsafe at Any Price: A Reply to Manne, *Insider Trading and the Stock Market*, 53 Va. L. Rev. 1425 (1967); Manne, Insider Trading and the Law Professors, 23 Vand. L. Rev. 547 (1970); Ferber, The Case against Insider Trading: A Response to Professor

defect of the strictly economic arguments against insider trading regulation is their apparent scorn for the moral or public opinion factor, which is relegated to the "it's just not right" propositions.[10] This overlooks the fact that it is important for the markets, as it is for the courts, not merely to do equity but to *appear* to do equity. Why should the public enter the market if the rules of the game make it perfectly legitimate for insiders (and their friends and business associates) to play with marked cards?[11]

At any rate, whatever the merit of the economic arguments, the insider trading regulatory structure that is in place requires analysis. And, far from that structure's withering away, its underlying philosophy (to be sure, more along the 10b-5 than along the 16(b) model) is spreading. In the United Kingdom, after a Labor Government had concluded in 1973 that it was essential to insure by legislation, "as far as practically possible, that the market operates freely on the basis of equality between buyer and seller,"[12] a Conservative Government, while eschewing civil liability, criminalized insider trading in the Companies Act of 1980.[13]

Manne, 23 Vand. L. Rev. 621 (1970); Manne, A Rejoinder to Mr. Ferber, 23 Vand. L. Rev. 627 (1970). See also Insider Trading, A Report by Justice (British Section of Int'l Commission of Jurists, 1972) ¶(3), which, referring to the Manne thesis, concluded: "Nevertheless, we think 'insider trading' is wrong and ought to be illegal."

[10] H. Manne, Insider Trading and the Stock Market (1966) 15 and c. 1, n. 42.

[11] The justifications that have been advanced for the attack on insider trading under Rule 10b-5 (see c. 9B infra) apply equally here: A variation of the "fair play" rationale there suggested is that, if the public is loathe to play an unfair game, the markets will suffer and the efficient allocation of capital will be impeded. Under the "informed market" rationale the prohibition of insider trading removes an incentive to *delay* the release of corporate information. There is also the "business property" theory. As to all these, see Scott, Insider Trading: Rule 10b-5, Disclosure and Corporate Privacy, 9 J. Legal Stud. 801 (1980). Most recently still another perspective has been suggested: that the prohibition of insider trading may enhance business decision-making in large corporations. See Haft, The Effect of Insider Trading Rules on the Internal Efficiency of the Large Corporation, 80 Mich. L. Rev. 1051 (1982).

[12] Company Law Reform, Cmd. 5391 (1973) §15.

[13] 28 & 29 Eliz. 2, c. 22, §§68-73 (1980). See also (U. K.) Council for the Securities Industry, Statement on Insider Dealing, in Council Report on the Year to 31st March, 1979, App. A, ¶5: " * * * insiders are expected not to deal in securities likely to be affected, if they are in possession of confidential price-sensitive information, and not to pass on this information to others who might deal." To the same effect, see Commission Recommendation of 25 July 1977 Concerning a European Code of Conduct Relating to Transactions in Transferable Securities, 20 Off. J. Eur. Communities, No. L 212/37, 77/534 EEC (1977) ¶9.

See generally K. Hopt and M. Will, Europäisches Insiderrecht (1973) (the German language seems not to have a word with the precise connotation of

So far as the Code is concerned, the Reporter and his advisers considered the several grounds that some had advanced for abandoning §16(b): "(a) that it is needlessly arbitrary to the point of being quixotic; (b) that it has acted as a trap for the unwary; (c) that the Commission has made insufficient use of its exemptive authority; and (d) that, most of all, the jurisprudence that has developed under Rule 10b-5 (and that is being codified in large part) has rendered obsolete the concept of *automatic* recapture of *certain* short-term profits of *certain* insiders."[14] Instead, on the theory that §16(b) "has a symbolic significance that must be, and deserves to be, recognized," the Code codifies the most important areas of the §16(b) jurisprudence, polishing the rough diamond a bit in the process without derogating from the basic genius of the section, and with the expectation that the Commission will "use its expanded rulemaking authority in order to play a greater quasi-legislative role in this area than it has in the past."[15]

2. FROM THE "OBJECTIVE" TO THE "SUBJECTIVE"

Section 16(b) was described by the Administration's spokesman in the 1934 hearings as a "crude rule of thumb."[16] Consequently,

---

"insider"); Loss (ed.), Multiple Approaches — Corporate Insiders (1976) (edited transcript of an Anglo-American-Franco-German conference); B. Rider and L. Ffrench, The Regulation of Insider Trading (1979) (worldwide treatment). On individual countries, see, e. g., A. Yoran, Insider Trading in Israel and England (1972); Pillai, Insider Trading in Singapore and Malaysia, 16 Malaya L. Rev. 333 (1974); Parsons, The Insider Trading Provisions of the Federal Corporations and Securities Industry Bill, 1975, 12 U. W. Aust. L. Rev. 254 (1976); Hawes, Lee, and Robert, Insider Trading Law Developments: In International Analysis, 14 L. & Pol. in Int'l Bus. 335 (1982) (France, United Kingdom and United States). Even the last bastion seems about to fall: it was reported in January 1982 that the Swiss Finance Ministry was supporting a demand by the Swiss banking authorities that insider trading be made a criminal offense, apparently so that Swiss banks would be freed of Swiss banking secrecy rules under the terms of a treaty with the United States to provide information about clients being investigated by American regulatory authorities. N. Y. Times, Jan. 15, 1982, p. D2, col. 6; 14 Sec. Reg. L. Rep. 104 (1982); see also N. Y. Times, Jan. 3, 1983, p. D1, col. 4 (action by Swiss banks).

[14] 2 Code 751.

[15] 2 id. 751-52.

[16] 15 Stock Exchange Practices, Hearings before Senate Com. on Banking & Currency, 73d Cong., 2d Sess. (1934) 6557 (testimony of Mr. Thomas G. Corcoran). This characterization was approved in Booth v. Varian Associates, 334 F. 2d 1, 5 (1st Cir. 1964), *cert. denied*, 379 U. S. 961. Later characterizations afford counsel a choice of rhetoric: "an extremely crude rule of a most deformed and misshapen thumb" [Provident Securities Co. v. Foremost-McKesson, Inc., 331 F. Supp. 787, 792 (N. D. Cal. 1971), *aff'd*, 506 F. 2d 601

a showing of an actual unfair use of inside information is not required for recovery; the preamble of the section was intended merely as an aid to constitutionality, as well as a guide to the Commission in the exercise of its rulemaking authority.[17] By the same token, no estoppel flows from the fact that the defendant acquired the stock pursuant to an incentive stock option plan initiated by the company,[18] or sold the stock at the issuer's suggestion.[19] The statute uses the corporation as an instrument — perhaps an unwilling one — to effectuate its policy.[20] This being so, the Second Circuit has held that the rights of the company and its innocent stockholders cannot be defeated by attempting to prove that the real party in interest was the plaintiff's attorney, whose sole motive was to obtain a fee, although it did add the caveat that "A showing of misconduct is naturally pertinent to the determination of an appropriate fee."[21] As the District Court later pointed out with evident distaste in awarding a fee in the same case, Congress apparently "regards public policy against proved and repeated violations of fiduciary responsibility by corporate officers at the expense of the public more detrimental to public good than the violation of generally accepted ethics by attorneys."[22]

(9th Cir. 1974), aff'd, 423 U. S. 232 (1976)] or (if one is in a more benign mood) "a placid inlet in the chaotic sea of securities law — a statute designed for easy application" [Cummings v. Commissioner, 506 F. 2d 449, 452 (2d Cir. 1974), cert. denied, 421 U. S. 913].

[17] Smolowe v. Delendo Corp., 136 F. 2d 231, 235 (2d Cir. 1943), cert. denied, 320 U. S. 751; Emerson Electric Co. v. Reliance Electric Co., 434 F. 2d 918, 923-24 (8th Cir. 1970), aff'd on other grounds sub nom. Reliance Electric Co. v. Emerson Electric Co., 404 U. S. 418 (1972).

[18] Jefferson Lake Sulphur Co. v. Walet, 104 F. Supp. 20, 23-24 (E. D. La. 1952), aff'd sub nom. Walet v. Jefferson Lake Sulphur Co., 202 F. 2d 433 (5th Cir. 1953), cert. denied, 346 U. S. 820; cf. Lockheed Aircraft Corp. v. Campbell, 110 F. Supp. 282 (S. D. Cal. 1953) (stock acquired as part of company policy to compensate executives for a drastic salary cut); Sonics Int'l, Inc. v. Johnson, 387 F. Supp. 741, 744 (N. D. Tex. 1975). Contra: Consolidated Engineering Corp. v. Nesbit, 102 F. Supp. 112 (S. D. Cal. 1951), order denying intervention rev'd sub nom. Pellegrino v. Nesbit, 203 F. 2d 463 (9th Cir. 1953).

[19] Magida v. Continental Can Co., Inc., 231 F. 2d 843 (2d Cir. 1956), cert. denied, 351 U. S. 972; Roth v. Fund of Funds, Ltd., 405 F. 2d 421, 422-23 (2d Cir. 1968), cert. denied, 394 U. S. 975 (sale to issuer at its suggestion).

[20] Blau v. Lamb, 314 F. 2d 618, 619-20 (2d Cir. 1963), cert. denied, 375 U. S. 813. The "inure to" phrase in §16(b) suggests also the concept of a constructive trust. See 5 Scott, Trusts (3d ed. 1967) §505; cf. Diamond v. Oreamuno, 24 N. Y. 2d 494, 248 N. E. 2d 910 (1969), set out infra p. 657.

[21] Magida v. Continental Can Co., Inc., 231 F. 2d 843, 848 (2d Cir. 1956), cert. denied, 351 U. S. 972. "If there has been a violation of N. Y. Penal Law §274 as alleged, offenders are liable to its criminal sanction. But the public policy of New York cannot nullify this federally created right * * *." 231 F. 2d at 848.

[22] Magida v. Continental Can Co., Inc., 176 F. Supp. 781, 783 (S. D. N. Y.

On the other hand, the "crude rule of thumb" works two ways. An insider who holds for six months or more before selling does not become liable under §16(b), no matter how much proof is adduced of unfair resort to nonpublic information:

> Congress recognized * * * that §16(b) would not correct all the practices thought to be evil; obviously the six month limitation alone "let many fish out of the net" since the tax laws tend to encourage a holding period longer than six months. * * * One can speculate on whether the moral or ethical values are altered by the passage of 24 hours but the statute makes an honest if not honorable man out of the insider in that period.[23]

As we have been reminded by the Supreme Court, "Liability cannot be imposed simply because the investor structured his transaction with the intent of avoiding liability under §16(b)."[24] There is also no guarantee against evasion by mutual "back-scratching" of insiders in different corporations, or by trading through relatives or friends. Provisions in the early drafts making unlawful the improper disclosure of confidential information by insiders, and providing that any profit made by any person to whom such unlawful disclosure was made should inure to the issuer, were deleted, "presumably because the burden of proof made enforcement unfeasible."[25]

1956). The Second Circuit held in its first §16(b) opinion that the plaintiff was entitled to reimbursement for reasonable counsel fees from the sum recovered, on the analogy of the rule in stockholders' or creditors' representative actions, and that, "Since in many cases such as this the possibility of recovering attorney's fees will provide the sole stimulus for the enforcement of §16(b), the allowance must not be too niggardly." Smolowe v. Delendo Corp., 136 F. 2d 231, 241 (2d Cir. 1943), *cert. denied,* 320 U. S. 751. This risk of champerty led this writer to suggest that Congress consider substituting the SEC as plaintiff. 2 Loss 1053-54. But he sadly yields to Professor Cary's rejoinder to the effect that §16(b) "is an appropriate vehicle for the corporate gadfly." Cary, Book Rev., 75 Harv. L. Rev. 857, 861 (1962). When the chips were down, the writer did not consider it practical to push his suggestion as Reporter for the Code.

[23] Adler v. Klawans, 267 F. 2d 840, 845 (2d Cir. 1959); see also B. T. Babbitt, Inc. v. Lachner, 332 F. 2d 255, 258 (2d Cir. 1964) (interval of six months and one day). The six-month test has been explained on the ground that "Improper use of inside information by corporate insiders is most likely to occur in short-term, in-and-out trading" and that "Congress sought to minimize misuse of confidential information without unduly discouraging bona fide long-term investment." Blau v. Max Factor & Co., 3 2 F. 2d 304, 308 (9th Cir. 1965), *cert. denied,* 382 U. S. 892.

[24] Reliance Electric Co. v. Emerson Electric Co., 404 U. S. 418, 422 (1972), infra p. 637 n. 51.

[25] Smolowe v. Delendo Corp., 136 F. 2d 231, 236 (2d Cir. 1943), *cert. denied,* 320 U. S. 751. In Blau v. Lehman, 368 U. S. 403, 411-12 (1962), infra p. 641, the Court pointed to this history in answer to a policy argument directed to evasion.

At the same time, the provision's very simplicity has undoubtedly had a substantial deterrent effect.[26] Since the elements of the action are so simple, the defendant is apt to find that he has no practicable alternative but to pay up; "the liability is, as a practical matter, inexorable."[27] Consequently the number of reported decisions is probably no criterion of the total amount of short-term profits recaptured or, once the section became well known, simply foregone. Conversely, although there have been quite a few reported cases, they all involved some legal question that counsel obviously thought was worth the expense of a defense. For "There is no rule so 'objective' ('automatic' would be a better word) that it does not require some mental effort in applying it on the part of the person or persons entrusted by law with its application."[28] Witness the "subjective-objective" clash in:

KERN COUNTY LAND CO. v. OCCIDENTAL PETROLEUM CORP.

Supreme Court of the United States, 1973
411 U. S. 582

MR. JUSTICE WHITE delivered the opinion of the Court.

Section 16(b) of the Securities Exchange Act of 1934, 48 Stat. 896, 15 U. S. C. §78p(b), provides that officers, directors, and holders of more than 10% of the listed stock of any company shall be

---

[26] See Whiting v. Dow Chemical Co., 523 F. 2d 680, 689 (2d Cir. 1975).

[27] Anderson v. Commissioner, 480 F. 2d 1304, 1308 (7th Cir. 1973).

[28] Blau v. Lamb, 363 F. 2d 507, 520 (2d Cir. 1966), *cert. denied*, 385 U. S. 1002. For the SEC staff's views on 151 enumerated questions of interpretation that have arisen under §16(a) and (b), see Sec. Ex. Act Rel. 18,114, 23 SEC Dock. 856 (1981).

Since §16(a) requires the filing of a report whenever there is a change of beneficial ownership, it is self-evident that not every transaction reported under §16(a) can be the basis of liability under §16(b). Chemical Fund, Inc. v. Xerox Corp., 377 F. 2d 107, 112 (2d Cir. 1967). But the converse does not follow. In order that "Section 16(b) liability should not be predicated upon any transactions which are not subject to the reporting requirements of Section 16(a)" (Sec. Ex. Act Rel. 4801 (1953)), the Commission adopted Rule 16a-10: "Any transaction which has been or shall be exempted by the Commission from the requirements of section 16(a) shall, in so far as it is otherwise subject to the provisions of section 16(b), be likewise exempted from section 16(b)." See Adler v. Klawans, 267 F. 2d 840, 847 (2d Cir. 1959).

With respect to questions of jurisdiction, venue, procedure, and statute of limitations under §16(b), see 2 Loss 1044-58; 5 id. 3006-21. Section 16(b) merely *resembles* a derivative action in some respects, but it is a statutory action with its own procedural attributes. Dottenheim v. Murchison, 227 F. 2d 737 (5th Cir. 1955), *cert. denied*, 351 U. S. 919. Therefore, the contemporaneous ownership requirement of Rule 23.1 of the Federal Rules of Civil Procedure does not apply. Ibid.

liable to the company for any profits realized from any purchase and sale or sale and purchase of such stock occurring within a period of six months. Unquestionably, one or more statutory purchases occur when one company, seeking to gain control of another, acquires more than 10% of the stock of the latter through a tender offer made to its shareholders. But is it a §16(b) "sale" when the target of the tender offer defends itself by merging into a third company and the tender offeror then exchanges his stock for the stock of the surviving company and also grants an option to purchase the latter stock that is not exercisable within the statutory six-month period? This is the question before us in this case.

I

On May 8, 1967, after unsuccessfully seeking to merge with Kern County Land Co. (Old Kern), Occidental Petroleum Corp. (Occidental) announced an offer, to expire on June 8, 1967, to purchase on a first-come, first-served basis 500,000 shares of Old Kern common stock[4] at a price of $83.50 per share plus a brokerage commission of $1.50 per share. By May 10, 1967, 500,000 shares, more than 10% of the outstanding shares of Old Kern,[10] had been tendered. On May 11, Occidental extended its offer to encompass an additional 500,000 shares. At the close of the tender offer, on June 8, 1967, Occidental owned 887,549 shares of Old Kern.

Immediately upon the announcement of Occidental's tender offer, the Old Kern management undertook to frustrate Occidental's takeover attempt. A management letter to all stockholders cautioned against tender and indicated that Occidental's offer might not be the best available, since the management was engaged in merger discussions with several companies. When Occidental extended its tender offer, the president of Old Kern sent a telegram to all stockholders again advising against tender. In addition, Old Kern undertook merger discussions with Tenneco, Inc. (Tenneco), and, on May 19, 1967, the Board of Directors of Old Kern announced that it had approved a merger proposal advanced by Tenneco. Under the terms of the merger, Tenneco would acquire

---

[4] The Old Kern stock was registered pursuant to §12 of the Securities Exchange Act of 1934, as amended, 15 U. S. C. §78*l*. The stock was a nonexempt, equity security for purposes of §16(b).

[10] New Kern, a Delaware corporation with its principal place of business in California, is the petitioner in this Court and is a wholly owned subsidiary of Tenneco Corp. Tenneco Corp. is, in turn, a wholly owned subsidiary of Tenneco * * * . * * *

the assets, property, and goodwill of Old Kern, subject to its liabilities, through "Kern County Land Co." (New Kern),[10] a new corporation to be formed by Tenneco to receive the assets and carry on the business of Old Kern. The shareholders of Old Kern would receive a share of Tenneco cumulative convertible preference stock in exchange for each share of Old Kern common stock which they owned. On the same day, May 19, Occidental, in a quarterly report to stockholders, appraised the value of the new Tenneco stock at $105 per share.

Occidental, seeing its tender offer and takeover attempt being blocked by the Old Kern-Tenneco "defensive" merger, countered on May 25 and 31 with two mandamus actions in the California courts seeking to obtain extensive inspection of Old Kern books and records. Realizing that, if the Old Kern-Tenneco merger were approved and successfully closed, Occidental would have to exchange its Old Kern shares for Tenneco stock and would be locked into a minority position in Tenneco, Occidental took other steps to protect itself. Between May 30 and June 2, it negotiated an arrangement with Tenneco whereby Occidental granted Tenneco Corp., a subsidiary of Tenneco, an option to purchase at $105 per share all of the Tenneco preference stock to which Occidental would be entitled in exchange for its Old Kern stock when and if the Old Kern-Tenneco merger was closed. The premium to secure the option, at $10 per share, totaled $8,866,230 and was to be paid immediately upon the signing of the option agreement. If the option were exercised, the premium was to be applied to the purchase price. By the terms of the option agreement, the option could not be exercised prior to December 9, 1967, a date six months and one day after expiration of Occidental's tender offer. On June 2, 1967, within six months of the acquisition by Occidental of more than 10% ownership of Old Kern, Occidental and Tenneco Corp. executed the option. Soon thereafter, Occidental announced that it would not oppose the Old Kern-Tenneco merger and dismissed its state court suits against Old Kern.[16]

The Old Kern-Tenneco merger plan was presented to and approved by Old Kern shareholders at their meeting on July 17, 1967. Occidental refrained from voting its Old Kern shares, but in a letter read at the meeting Occidental stated that it had determined prior to June 2 not to oppose the merger and that it did

---

[16] Seeking to prevent its acquisition of Tenneco shares pursuant to the merger from being matched with the sale of those shares upon exercise of the option for purposes of establishing §16(b) liability, Occidental asked that the new Tenneco stock not be immediately registered pursuant to §12 of the Securities Exchange Act of 1934, 15 U. S. C. §78l. See 450 F. 2d 157, 160 n. 6.

not consider the plan unfair or inequitable. Indeed, Occidental indicated that, had it been voting, it would have voted in favor of the merger.

Meanwhile, the Securities and Exchange Commission had refused Occidental's request to exempt from possible §16(b) liability Occidental's exchange of its Old Kern stock for the Tenneco preference shares that would take place when and if the merger transaction were closed. Various Old Kern stockholders, with Occidental's interests in mind, thereupon sought to delay consummation of the merger by instituting various lawsuits in the state and federal courts. These attempts were unsuccessful, however, and preparations for the merger neared completion with an Internal Revenue Service ruling that consummation of the plan would result in a tax-free exchange with no taxable gain or loss to Old Kern shareholders, and with the issuance of the necessary approval of the merger closing by the California Commissioner of Corporations.

The Old Kern-Tenneco merger transaction was closed on August 30. Old Kern shareholders thereupon became irrevocably entitled to receive Tenneco preference stock, share for share in exchange for their Old Kern stock. Old Kern was dissolved and all of its assets, including "all claims, demands, rights and choses in action accrued or to accrue under and by virtue of the Securities Exchange Act of 1934 * * * ," were transferred to New Kern.

The option granted by Occidental on June 2, 1967, was exercised on December 11, 1967. Occidental, not having previously availed itself of its right, exchanged certificates representing 887,549 shares of Old Kern stock for a certificate representing a like number of shares of Tenneco preference stock. The certificate was then endorsed over to the optionee-purchaser, and in return $84,229,185 was credited to Occidental's accounts at various banks. Adding to this amount the $8,886,230 premium paid in June, Occidental received $93,905,415 for its Old Kern stock (including the 1,900 shares acquired prior to issuance of its tender offer). In addition, Occidental received dividends totaling $1,793,439.22. Occidental's total profit was $19,506,419.22 on the shares obtained through its tender offer.

On October 17, 1967, New Kern instituted a suit under §16(b) against Occidental to recover the profits which Occidental had realized as a result of its dealings in Old Kern stock. The complaint alleged that the execution of the Occidental-Tenneco option on June 2, 1967, and the exchange of Old Kern shares for shares of Tenneco to which Occidental became entitled pursuant to the merger closed on August 30, 1967, were both "sales" within the coverage of §16(b). Since both acts took place within six months of the date on which Occidental became the owner of more than 10% of the stock of Old Kern, New Kern asserted that §16(b) required surrender of the profits realized by Occidental. New Kern eventually moved for summary judgment, and, on December 27, 1970, the District Court granted summary judgment in favor of New Kern. *Abrams* v. *Occidental Petroleum Corp.*, 323 F. Supp. 570 (S. D. N. Y. 1970). The District Court held that the execution of the option on June 2, 1967, and the exchange of Old Kern shares for shares of Tenneco on August 30, 1967, were "sales" under §16(b). The Court ordered Occidental to disgorge its profits plus interest. In a supplemental opinion, Occidental was also ordered to refund the dividends which it had received plus interest.

On appeal, the Court of Appeals reversed and ordered summary judgment entered in favor of Occidental. *Abrams* v. *Occidental Petroleum Corp.*, 450 F. 2d 157 (C. A. 2 1971). The Court held that neither the option nor the exchange constituted a "sale" within the purview of §16(b). We granted certiorari. 405 U. S. 1064 (1972). We affirm.

II

*   *   *

Although traditional cash-for-stock transactions that result in a purchase and sale or a sale and purchase within the six-month, statutory period are clearly within the purview of §16(b), the courts have wrestled with the question of inclusion or exclusion of certain "unorthodox" transactions.[24] The statutory definitions of "purchase" and "sale" are broad and, at least arguably, reach many transactions not ordinarily deemed a sale or purchase. In deciding whether borderline transactions are within the reach of the statute, the courts have come to inquire whether the transaction may serve as a vehicle for the evil which Congress sought to prevent — the realization of short-swing profits based upon access to inside information[26] — thereby endeavoring to implement congressional objectives without extending the reach of the statute

---

[24] The term, see 2 L. Loss, Securities Regulation 1069 (2d ed. 1961), has been applied to stock conversions, exchanges pursuant to mergers and other corporate reorganizations, stock reclassifications, and dealings in options, rights, and warrants.

[26] Several decisions have been read as to apply a so-called "objective" test in interpreting and applying §16(b). See, e. g., Smolowe v. Delendo Corp.,

beyond its intended limits. The statute requires the inside, short-swing trader to disgorge all profits realized on all "purchases" and "sales" within the specified time period, without proof of actual abuse of insider information, and without proof of intent to profit on the basis of such information. Under these strict terms, the prevailing view is to apply the statute only when its application would serve its goals. "[W]here alternative constructions of the terms of §16(b) are possible, those terms are to be given the construction that best serves the congressional purpose of curbing short-swing speculation by corporate insiders." *Reliance Electric Co.* v. *Emerson Electric Co.,* 404 U. S., at 424. See *Blau* v. *Lamb,* 363 F. 2d 507 (C. A. 2 1966), *cert. denied,* 385 U. S. 1002 (1967). Thus, "[i]n interpreting the terms 'purchase' and 'sale,' courts have properly asked whether the particular type of transaction involved is one that gives rise to speculative abuse." *Reliance Electric Co.* v. *Emerson Electric Co.,* supra, at 424 n. 4.

In the present case, it is undisputed that Occidental became a "beneficial owner" within the terms of §16(b) when, pursuant to its tender offer, it "purchased" more than 10% of the outstanding shares of Old Kern. We must decide, however, whether a "sale" within the ambit of the statute took place either when Occidental became irrevocably bound to exchange its shares of Old Kern for shares of Tenneco pursuant to the terms of the merger agreement between Old Kern and Tenneco or when Occidental gave an option to Tenneco to purchase from Occidental the Tenneco shares so acquired.[28]

[136 F. 2d 231 (2d Cir. 1943), *cert. denied,* 320 U. S. 751]; Park & Tilford v. Schulte, 160 F. 2d 984 (C. A. 2), *cert. denied,* 332 U. S. 761 (1947); Heli-Coil Corp. v. Webster, 352 F. 2d 156 (C. A. 3 1965). Under some broad language in those decisions, §16(b) is said to be applicable whether or not the transaction in question could possibly lend itself to the types of speculative abuse that the statute was designed to prevent. By far the greater weight of authority is to the effect that a "pragmatic" approach to §16(b) will best serve the statutory goals. See, e. g., Roberts v. Eaton, 212 F. 2d 82 (C. A. 2), *cert. denied,* 348 U. S. 827 (1954); Ferraiolo v. Newman, 259 F. 2d 342 (C. A. 6 1958), *cert. denied,* 359 U. S. 927 (1959); Blau v. Max Factor & Co., 342 F. 2d 304 (C. A. 9), *cert. denied,* 382 U. S. 892 (1965); Blau v. Lamb [363 F. 2d 507 (2d Cir. 1966), *cert. denied,* 385 U. S. 1002]; Petteys v. Butler, 367 F. 2d 528 (C. A. 8 1966), *cert. denied,* 385 U. S. 1006 (1967). * * *

[28] Both events occurred within six months of Occidental's first acquisition of Old Kern shares pursuant to its tender offer. Although Occidental did not exchange its Old Kern shares until December 11, 1967, it is not contended that that date, rather than the date on which Occidental became irrevocably bound to do so, should control. Similarly, although the option was not exercised until December 11, 1967, no liability is asserted with respect to that event, because it occurred more than six months after Occidental's last acquisition of Old Kern stock.

III

On August 30, 1967, the Old Kern-Tenneco merger agreement was signed, and Occidental became irrevocably entitled to exchange its shares of Old Kern stock for shares of Tenneco preference stock. Concededly, the transaction must be viewed as though Occidental had made the exchange on that day. But, even so, did the exchange involve a "sale" of Old Kern shares within the meaning of §16(b)? We agree with the Court of Appeals that it did not, for we think it totally unrealistic to assume or infer from the facts before us that Occidental either had or was likely to have access to inside information, by reason of its ownership of more than 10% of the outstanding shares of Old Kern, so as to afford it an opportunity to reap speculative, short-swing profits from its disposition within six months of its tender-offer purchases.

It cannot be contended that Occidental was an insider when, on May 8, 1967, it made an irrevocable offer to purchase 500,000 shares of Old Kern stock at a price substantially above market. At that time, it owned only 1,900 shares of Old Kern stock, far fewer than the 432,000 shares needed to constitute the 10% ownership required by the statute. There is no basis for finding that, at the time the tender offer was commenced, Occidental enjoyed an insider's opportunity to acquire information about Old Kern's affairs.

It is also wide of the mark to assert that Occidental, as a sophisticated corporation knowledgeable in matters of corporate affairs and finance, knew that its tender offer would either succeed or would be met with a "defensive merger." If its takeover efforts failed, it is argued, Occidental knew it could sell its stock to the target company's merger partner at a substantial profit. Calculations of this sort, however, whether speculative or not and whether fair or unfair to other stockholders or to Old Kern, do not represent the kind of speculative abuse at which the statute is aimed, for they could not have been based on inside information obtained from substantial stockholdings that did not yet exist. Accepting both that Occidental made this very prediction and that it would recurringly be an accurate forecast in tender-offer situations,[29] we

[29] Although a "defensive merger" is one tactic available to incumbent management in its arsenal of antitender-offer weapons, it is by no means a foregone conclusion that it is the response that will be most often, much less invariably, employed. Incumbent management might, for instance, choose to exhort shareholders not to tender, employ various techniques to elevate the market price of the company's stock in order to make the tender offer less attractive, institute legal proceedings, or increase the company's outstanding

nevertheless fail to perceive how the fruition of such anticipated events would require, or in any way depend upon, the receipt and use of inside information. If there are evils to be redressed by way of deterring those who would make tender offers, §16(b) does not appear to us to have been designed for this task.

By May 10, 1967, Occidental had acquired more than 10% of the outstanding shares of Old Kern. It was thus a statutory insider when, on May 11, it extended its tender offer to include another 500,000 shares. We are quite unconvinced, however, that the situation had changed materially with respect to the possibilities of speculative abuse of inside information by Occidental. Perhaps Occidental anticipated that extending its offer would increase the likelihood of the ultimate success of its takeover attempt or the occurrence of a defensive merger. But, again, the expectation of such benefits was unrelated to the use of information unavailable to other stockholders or members of the public with sufficient funds and the intention to make the purchases Occidental had offered to make before June 8, 1967.

The possibility that Occidental had, or had the opportunity to have, any confidential information about Old Kern before or after May 11, 1967, seems extremely remote. Occidental was, after all, a tender offeror, threatening to seize control of Old Kern, displace its management, and use the company for its own ends. The Old Kern management vigorously and immediately opposed Occidental's efforts. Twice it communicated with its stockholders, advising against acceptance of Occidental's offer and indicating prior to May 11 and prior to Occidental's extension of its offer, that there was a possibility of an imminent merger and a more profitable exchange. Old Kern's management refused to discuss with Occidental officials the subject of an Old Kern-Occidental merger. Instead, it undertook negotiations with Tenneco and forthwith concluded an agreement, announcing the merger terms on May 19. Requests by Occidental for inspection of Old Kern records were sufficiently frustrated by Old Kern's management to force Occidental to litigate to secure the information it desired.

There is, therefore, nothing in connection with Occidental's acquisition of Old Kern stock pursuant to its tender offer to indicate either the possibility of inside information being available to Occidental by virtue of its stock ownership or the potential for

---

stock. Any one of these devices might prove more attractive to incumbent management than a defensive merger which could prove to be highly detrimental to the enterprise. See Note, Defensive Tactics Employed by Incumbent Managements in Contesting Tender Offers, 21 Stan. L. Rev. 1104 (1969).

speculative abuse of such inside information by Occidental. Much the same can be said of the events leading to the exchange of Occidental's Old Kern stock for Tenneco preferred, which is one of the transactions that is sought to be classified a "sale" under §16(b). The critical fact is that the exchange took place and was required pursuant to a merger between Old Kern and Tenneco. That merger was not engineered by Occidental but was sought by Old Kern to frustrate the attempts of Occidental to gain control of Old Kern. Occidental obviously did not participate in or control the negotiations or the agreement between Old Kern and Tenneco. Cf. *Newmark* v. *RKO General,* 425 F. 2d 348 (C. A. 2), *cert. denied,* 400 U. S. 854 (1970); *Park & Tilford* v. *Schulte,* 160 F. 2d 984 (C. A. 2), *cert. denied,* 332 U. S. 761 (1947). Once agreement between those two companies crystallized, the course of subsequent events was out of Occidental's hands. Old Kern needed the consent of its stockholders, but as it turned out, Old Kern's management had the necessary votes without the affirmative vote of Occidental. The merger agreement was approved by a majority of the stockholders of Old Kern, excluding the votes to which Occidental was entitled by virtue of its ownership of Old Kern shares. See generally *Ferraiolo* v. *Newman,* 259 F. 2d 342 (C. A. 6 1958), *cert. denied,* 359 U. S. 927 (1959); *Roberts* v. *Eaton,* 212 F. 2d 82 (C. A. 2 1954). Occidental, although registering its opinion that the merger would be beneficial to Old Kern shareholders, did not in fact vote at the stockholders' meeting at which merger approval was obtained. Under California law, its abstention was tantamount to a vote against approval of the merger. Moreover, at the time of stockholder ratification of the merger, Occidental's previous dealing in Old Kern stock was, as it had always been, fully disclosed.

Once the merger and exchange were approved, Occidental was left with no real choice with respect to the future of its shares of Old Kern. Occidental was in no position to prevent the issuance of a ruling by the Internal Revenue Service that the exchange of Old Kern stock for Tenneco preferred would be tax free; and, although various lawsuits were begun in state and federal courts seeking to postpone the merger closing beyond the statutory six-month period, those efforts were futile. The California Corporation Commissioner issued the necessary permits for the closing that took place on August 30, 1967. The merger left no right in dissenters to secure appraisal of their stock. Occidental could, of course, have disposed of its shares of Old Kern for cash before the merger was closed. Such an act would have been a §16(b) sale and would have left Occidental with a prima facie §16(b) liability. It was not, therefore, a realistic alternative for Occidental as long as it felt that it could successfully defend a suit like the present one. See generally *Petteys* v. *Butler,* 367 F. 2d 528 (C. A. 8 1966), *cert. denied,* 385 U. S. 1006 (1967); *Ferraiolo* v. *Newman,* supra; *Lynam* v. *Livingston,* 276 F. Supp. 104 (Del. 1967); *Blau* v. *Hodgkinson,* 100 F. Supp. 361 (S. D. N. Y. 1951). We do not suggest that an exchange of stock pursuant to a merger may never result in §16(b) liability. But the involuntary nature of Occidental's exchange, when coupled with the absence of the possibility of speculative abuse of inside information, convinces use that §16(b) should not apply to transactions such as this one.

IV

Petitioner also claims that the Occidental-Tenneco option agreement should itself be considered a sale, either because it was the kind of transaction the statute was designed to prevent or because the agreement was an option in form but a sale in fact. But the mere execution of an option to sell is not generally regarded as a "sale." See *Booth* v. *Varian Associates,* 334 F. 2d 1 (C. A. 1 1964), *cert. denied,* 379 U. S. 961 (1965); *Allis-Chalmers Mfg. Co.* v. *Gulf & Western Industries,* 309 F. Supp. 75 (E. D. Wis. 1970); *Marquette Cement Mfg. Co.* v. *Andreas,* 239 F. Supp. 962 (S. D. N. Y. 1965). And we do not find in the execution of the Occidental-Tenneco option agreement a sufficient possibility for the speculative abuse of inside information with respect to Old Kern's affairs to warrant holding that the option agreement was itself a "sale" within the meaning of §16(b). The mutual advantages of the arrangement appear quite clear. As the District Court found, Occidental wanted to avoid the position of a minority stockholder with a huge investment in a company over which it had no control and in which it had not chosen to invest. On the other hand, Tenneco did not want a potentially troublesome minority stockholder that had just been vanquished in a fight for the control of Old Kern. Motivations like these do not smack of insider trading; and it is not clear to us, as it was not to the Court of Appeals, how the negotiation and execution of the option agreement gave Occidental any possible opportunity to trade on inside information it might have obtained from its position as a major stockholder of Old Kern. Occidental wanted to get out, but only at a date more than six months thence. It was willing to get out at a price of $105 per share, a price at which it had publicly valued Tenneco preferred on May 19 when the Tenneco-Old Kern agreement was announced. In any event, Occidental was dealing with the putative new owners of Old Kern, who undoubtedly knew more about Old Kern and Tenneco's affairs than did Occidental. If Occidental had leverage in dealing with Tenneco, it is incredible that its source was inside information rather than the fact of its large stock ownership itself.

Neither does it appear that the option agreement, as drafted and executed by the parties, offered measurable possibilities for speculative abuse. What Occidental granted was a "call" option. Tenneco had the right to buy after six months, but Occidental could not force Tenneco to buy. The price was fixed at $105 for each share of Tenneco preferred. Occidental could not share in a rising market for the Tenneco stock. See *Silverman* v. *Landa*, 306 F. 2d 422 (C. A. 2 1962). If the stock fell more than $10 per share, the option might not be exercised, and Occidental might suffer a loss if the market further deteriorated to a point where Occidental was forced to sell. Thus, the option, by its very form, left Occidental with no choice but to sell if Tenneco exercised the option, which it was almost sure to do if the value of Tenneco stock remained relatively steady. On the other hand, it is difficult to perceive any speculative value to Occidental if the stock declined and Tenneco chose not to exercise its option. See generally Note, Put and Call Options Under Section 16 of the Securities Exchange Act, 69 Yale L. J. 868 (1960); H. Filer, Understanding Put and Call Options 96-111 (1959); G. Leffler, The Stock Market 363-378 (2d ed. 1957).

The option, therefore, does not appear to have been an instrument with potential for speculative abuse, whether or not Occidental possessed inside information about the affairs of Old Kern. In addition, the option covered Tenneco preference stock, a stock as yet unissued, unregistered, and untraded. It was the value of this stock that underlay the option and that determined whether the option would be exercised, whether Occidental would be able to profit from the exercise, and whether there was any real likelihood of the exploitation of inside information. If Occidental had inside information when it negotiated and signed the option agreement, it was inside information with respect to Old Kern. Whatever it may have known or expected as to the future value of Old Kern stock, Occidental had no ownership position in Tenneco giving it any actual or presumed insights into the future value of Tenneco stock. That was the critical item of intelligence if Occidental was to use the option for purposes of speculation. Also, the date for exercise of the option was over six months in the future, a period that, under the statute itself, is assumed to dissipate whatever trading advantage might be imputed to a major stockholder with inside information. See Comment, Stock Exchanges Pursuant to Corporate Consolidation: A Section 16(b) "Purchase or Sale?," 117 U. Pa. L. Rev. 1034, 1054 (1969); *Silverman* v. *Landa,* supra. By enshrining the statutory period into the option, Occidental also, at least if the statutory period is taken to accomplish its intended purpose, limited its speculative possibilities. Nor should it be forgotten that there was no absolute assurance that the merger, which was not controlled by Occidental, would be consummated. In the event the merger did not close, the option itself would become null and void.

Nor can we agree that we must reverse the Court of Appeals on the ground that the option agreement was in fact a sale because the premium paid was so large as to make the exercise of the option almost inevitable, particularly when coupled with Tenneco's desire to rid itself of a potentially troublesome stockholder. The argument has force, but resolution of the question is very much a matter of judgment, economic and otherwise, and the Court of Appeals rejected the argument. That court emphasized that the premium paid was what experts had said the option was worth, the possibility that the market might drop sufficiently in the six months following execution of the option to make exercise unlikely, and the fact that here, unlike the situation in *Bershad* v. *McDonough,* 428 F. 2d 693 (C. A. 7 1970), the optioner did not surrender practically all emoluments of ownership by executing the option. Nor did any other special circumstances indicate that the parties understood and intended that the option was in fact a sale.[30] We see no satisfactory basis or reason for disagreeing with

---

[30] In Bershad v. McDonough, 428 F. 2d 693 (C. A. 7 1970), the defendants were directors and greater-than-ten-percent stockholders of Cudahy Co. The defendants, within six months of their acquisition of beneficial ownership of Cudahy, granted an option to Smelting Refining & Mining Co. to purchase their Cudahy stock. The Seventh Circuit held that the grant of the option was a §16(b) "sale" of the Cudahy stock. The Court of Appeals in the present case distinguished *Bershad* as follows:

> That case came before the court of appeals on a finding by the district court that, under the circumstances there presented, the stock had in fact been sold within the six months period, although the option was not formally exercised until later. The district court had relied on a number of circumstances, the most significant being that the optionor gave the optionee an irrevocable proxy to vote the shares and that the optionor and one of his associate directors resigned as directors within a few days after the grant of the option and were replaced by officers

the judgment of the Court of Appeals in this respect.[31]

The judgment of the Court of Appeals is affirmed.

So ordered.

MR. JUSTICE DOUGLAS, with whom MR. JUSTICE BRENNAN and MR. JUSTICE STEWART concur, dissenting.

The Court, in resorting to an *ad hoc* analysis of the "possibility for the speculative abuse of inside information," charts a course for the interpretation of §16(b) of the Securities Exchange Act of 1934, 15 U. S. C. §78p(b), that in my mind undermines the congressional purpose. I respectfully dissent.

I

"The statute is written broadly, and the liability it imposes is strict." *Reliance Electric Co.* v. *Emerson Electric Co.*, 404 U. S. 418, 431 (Douglas, J., dissenting). Except for narrowly drawn exceptions, it is all-inclusive. * * * By its own terms, the section subsumes *all* transactions that are technically purchases and sales and applies irrespective of any actual or potential use of inside information to gain a trading advantage. See *Feder* v. *Martin Marietta Corp.*, 406 F. 2d 260, 262 (C. A. 2 1969). The conclusion seems inescapable that Occidental Petroleum Corp. (Occidental) purchased and sold shares of Kern County Land Co. (Old Kern) within a six-month period and that this "round trip" in Old Kern stock is covered by the literal terms of §16(b).

*   *   *

* * * The term "sale," as used in the Securities Exchange Act, includes "any contract to sell or otherwise dispose of." 15 U. S. C. §78c(a)(14). Clearly, Occidental "disposed" of its Old Kern shares through the Old Kern-Tenneco consolidation. Its status as a shareholder of Old Kern terminated, and it became instead a shareholder of Tenneco, privy to all the rights conferred by the Tenneco shares. See *Newmark* v. *RKO General*, 425 F. 2d 348 (C. A. 2

---

of the optionee. In other words, the district court found in effect that the "option" was accompanied by a wink of the eye, and the court of appeals sustained this. Here there is no such finding, and no basis for one. 450 F. 2d at 165.

[31] With respect to entering judgment for Occidental, the dissent simply has a different, but insufficiently persuasive, view of the facts from that of Judge Friendly and his colleagues.

1970); *Park & Tilford* v. *Schulte,* 160 F. 2d 984 (C. A. 2 1947). In my view, we need look no further. As my Brother Blackmun, then Circuit Judge, stated in dissent in *Petteys* v. *Butler,* 367 F. 2d 528, 538 (C. A. 8 1966):

> My own reaction is that either the statute means what it literally says or that it does not; that if the Congress intended to provide additional exceptions, it would have done so in clear language; and that the recognized purpose and aim of the statute are more consistently and protectively to be served if the statute is construed literally and objectively rather than non-literally and subjectively on a case-by-case application. The latter inevitably is a weakening process.

The majority finesses the literal impact of §16(b) by examining Occidental's willfulness and its access to inside information. It concludes: "But the involuntary nature of Occidental's exchange, when coupled with the absence of the possibility of speculative abuse of inside information, convinces us that §16(b) should not apply to transactions such as this one." Ante, at 600. This approach is plainly contrary to the legislative purpose.

* * * Unlike other remedial provisions of the Act, the most noteworthy being §10(b), 15 U. S. C. §78j(b), Congress drafted §16(b) as an objective rule, designed to have a clearly "prophylactic" effect. * * *

In *Reliance Electric,* supra, the Court noted that "the only method Congress deemed effective to curb the evils of insider trading was a flat rule taking the profits out of a *class of transactions* in which the possibility of abuse was believed to be intolerably great." 404 U. S., at 422 (emphasis added). Certainly, mergers are such a class of transactions. In *Newmark* v. *RKO General,* supra, for example, RKO signed an option contract to purchase shares of the company which was to be merged into a subsidiary of RKO. When the merger was approved by the necessary parties, RKO exercised its option and the merger was consummated. The court found that RKO "not only acquired knowledge of what would transpire but also could exercise substantial influence over the course of events." 425 F. 2d, at 353. "In sum," the court concluded, "the purchase and subsequent exchange of Central shares were fraught with opportunities for the kind of speculative abuse section 16(b) was intended to abort." Id., at 354.

The Securities and Exchange Commission has resisted a rule that would exempt mergers as a class from the operation of §16(b). * * * It is true that in some cases an insider may be required to disgorge profits even though his transactions do not lend themselves to the abuses that underlay the enactment of §16(b). The draftsmen carefully weighed this eventuality and opted for a bright-line rule. As Thomas Corcoran stated: "You have to have a general rule. In particular transactions it might work a hardship, but those transactions that are a hardship represent the sacrifice to the necessity of having a general rule."[9]

The very construction of §16(b) reinforces the conclusion that the section is based in the first instance[10] on a totally objective appraisal of the relevant transactions. * * *

The majority takes heart from those decisions of lower federal courts which endorse a "pragmatic" approach to §16(b). Many involved the question whether a conversion of one security of an issuer into another security of the same issuer constituted a purchase or a sale. It would serve no purpose to parse their holdings because, as Louis Loss describes, they have a "generalization-defying nature."[14] In 1966 the Securities and Exchange Commission exercised its exemptive power under §16(b) to adopt Rule 16b-9,[15] which under specified conditions excludes a conversion from the operation of §16(b). This rule will relieve the courts of much of the burden that has developed from *ad hoc* analyses in this narrow area. But, by sanctioning the approach of these cases, the majority brings to fruition Louis Loss' prophecy that they will "continue to rule us from their graves."[16] for henceforth they certainly will be applied by analogy to the area of mergers and other consolidations.

Thus, the courts will be caught up in an *ad hoc* analysis of each transaction, determining both from the economics of the transaction and the *modus operandi* of the insider whether there exists the possibility of speculative abuse of inside information. Instead of a section that is easy to administer and by its clearcut terms discourages litigation, we have instead a section that fosters litigation because the Court's decision holds out the hope for the insider that he may avoid §16(b) liability. In short, the majority destroys much of the section's prophylactic effect. I would be the

[9] Hearings [before Senate Com. on Banking & Currency, 73d Cong., 2d Sess. (1934)] 6558.
[10] The objective approach may have to yield to a more flexible interpretation of the terms "purchase" and "sale" to include transactions which present the evil Congress sought to eliminate or transactions which are designed to evade §16(b). See discussion, infra, at 612-613.
[14] 5 L. Loss, Securities Regulation 3029 (Supp. to 2d ed. 1969).
[16] 5 L. Loss, Securities Regulation 3029 (Supp. to 2d ed. 1969).

first to agree that "[e]very transaction which can reasonably be defined as a purchase [should] be so defined, if the transaction is of a kind which can possibly lend itself to the speculation encompassed by Section 16(b)." *Ferraiolo* v. *Newman,* 259 F. 2d 342, 345 (C. A. 6 1958) (Stewart, J., then Circuit Judge). See also *Reliance Electric Co. v. Emerson Electric Co.,* 404 U. S., at 424. Certainly we cannot allow transactions which present the possibility of abuse but do not fall within the classic conception of a purchase or sale to escape the confines of §16(b). It is one thing to interpret the terms "purchase" and "sale" liberally in order to include those transactions which evidence the evil Congress sought to eliminate; it is quite another to abandon the bright-line test of §16(b) for those transactions which clearly fall within its literal bounds. Section 16(b), because of the six-month limitation, allows some to escape who have abused their inside information. It should not be surprising, given the objective nature of the rule, if some are caught unwillingly.

*   *   *

* * * It is this "objective standard" that the Court hung to so tenaciously in *Reliance Electric,* but now apparently would abandon to a large extent. In my view, the Court improperly takes upon itself the task of refashioning the contours of §16(b) and changing its essential thrust.

II

[The remainder of the opinion dissents on the option point.]

---

(1) The Second Circuit promptly held "that whether the tender offeror quits fighting when the defensive merger is announced [as in *Kern*] or continues to fight in the hope of winning, his exchange of stock on the merger after he has been defeated is not *ipso facto* a 'sale' for §16(b) purposes."[29] But the Seventh Circuit quite properly distinguished *Kern* where an unsuccessful tender offeror sold to a third person.[30] And a divided Fourth Circuit,

---

[29] American Standard, Inc. v. Crane Co., 510 F. 2d 1043, 1055 (2d Cir. 1974), *cert. denied,* 421 U. S. 1000.

[30] Allis-Chalmers Mfg. Co. v. Gulf & Western Industries, Inc., 527 F. 2d 335 (7th Cir. 1975), *cert. denied,* 423 U. S. 1078, 424 U. S. 928.

in considering whether there was a merger-*purchase* rather than a merger-sale, took into account, in applying the possibility of abuse test, only premerger events (as distinct from the defendant's access to corporate information after the merger); in its view the Supreme Court considered events all the way to the second of the two transactions sought to be matched only because the merger there *was* the second transaction.[31]

(2) Although the adjective "unorthodox" that this writer coined to describe merger and other cases lending themselves to a "possibility of abuse" analysis is itself orthodox enough, it has become something of a term of art.[32] It cannot be overemphasized that it is of no more relevance than in routine cash transactions to consider whether inside information was in fact used. But it does seem to be of considerable consequence to consider whether the circumstances were such that the defendant could possibly have obtained an advantage over the public generally that did not already exist. *Cessante ratione legis, cessat et ipsa lex.*

(3) Justice Douglas was quite correct in reminding the majority that the Court had taken an *objective* approach in the *Reliance Electric* case, where (as he did not point out) the Court had held for the *defendant* in deciding that a 10+ percent holder who sold down to 9.96 percent and then sold the rest of his holdings in a separate transaction, both transactions occurring within less than six months after the defendant's purchase, was not liable with respect to the second sale. A completely reliable lodestar in these cases is hard to find. But can one justify simply taking whichever approach, "objective" or "subjective," gives the case to the plaintiff?

(4) When the market price of a common stock rises above the redemption price of a callable and convertible preferred, the market considers them to be equivalents. And, when the preferred is called and a director converts along with everybody else and shortly thereafter sells the common on the market, the transactions that *should* be paired are not the conversion-purchase and market sale of common,[33] but the purchase of *preferred* and sale of common. For the first pairing would have all the significance of a

---

[31] Gold v. Sloan, 486 F. 2d 340 (4th Cir. 1973), *cert. denied,* 419 U. S. 873.

[32] See 2 Loss 1029. On the §16(b) treatment of (1) conversions, mergers, reclassifications, and other exchanges, (2) rights and other options, and (3) gifts, see 2 id. 1066-84; 5 id. 3027-47. That material reads as of 1969, but the analysis should still be helpful.

[33] See Ferraiolo v. Newman, 259 F. 2d 342, 346 (6th Cir. 1958), *cert. denied,* 359 U. S. 927.

change of a $10 bill into two fives, whereas the purchase and sale in the second pairing could just as readily be based on inside information as (a) a cash purchase and cash sale of common or (b) a cash purchase and cash sale of preferred. Yet covering the first pairing might make it harder, logically, to cover the second. *Query:* Would the *Kern* dissenters cover *both* configurations.

(5) The scant authority on the question of matching a purchase of one security against a sale of another is not conclusive.[34] But, when the Commission in 1966 adopted Rule 16b-9 by way of *exempting* any acquisition or disposition involved in a conversion, it made the exemption inapplicable to the extent that the insider buys (or sells) one of the securities and sells (or buys) the other (otherwise than in the conversion itself or in a transaction exempted by any other rule) within a period of less than six months that includes the date of conversion.[35] The Commission has thus hedged against the possibility that a court might *decline* to match transactions in convertible and conversion securities.

(6) The Code's successor to §16(b) exempts a conversion or merger-like transaction, as well as a share-for-share exchange involving two companies, if the defendant proves that he "*did* not use" (not *could* not have used) inside information.[36] But, on the ground of greater potentiality for abuse, the Code also *covers* the two-security situation in the context not only of conversions but also of warrants, merger-like transactions, voting trust certificates, and certificates of deposit for securities "unless the defendant proves that under the circumstances he *could* not have been advantaged by the use of" insider information.[37]

---

[34] In American Standard, Inc. v. Crane Co., 510 F. 2d 1043, 1057-63 (2d Cir. 1974), *cert. denied*, 421 U. S. 1000, the court refused to match a cash purchase of the merged company's shares against a sale of shares of the surviving company. But in Bershad v. McDonough, 428 F. 2d 693, 697 n. 5 (7th Cir. 1970), *cert. denied*, 400 U. S. 992, the court matched a sale of an option against a prior purchase of the underlying security, stating: "Certainly the interest of simple application of the prohibitions of Section 16(b) does not carry so far as to facilitate evasion of that provision's function by formalistic devices." See also Blau v. Lamb, 363 F. 2d 507, 525 (2d Cir. 1966), *cert. denied*, 385 U. S. 1002 (dictum that under the circumstances the purchase of convertible preferred might be treated as a purchase of common under the statutory definition of "purchase" as including "any contract to buy * * * "); Chemical Fund, Inc. v. Xerox Corp., CCH Fed. Sec. L. Rep. ¶91,653 at 95,419 (W. D. N. Y. 1966), *rev'd on other grounds*, 377 F. 2d 107 (2d Cir. 1967) (court without discussion matched purchases of convertible debentures against sales of common).

[35] Sec. Ex. Act Rel. 7826 (1966).

[36] §1714(h)(1); 2 Code 755-56.

[37] §1714(g); 2 Code 754-55.

3. "PROFIT REALIZED"

SMOLOWE v. DELENDO CORPORATION

United States Court of Appeals, Second Circuit, 1943
136 F. 2d 231, *cert. denied*, 320 U. S. 751

Before SWAN, CHASE, and CLARK, Circuit Judges.
CLARK, Circuit Judge.

*   *   *

The legislative history of the statute is perhaps more significant upon a determination of the method of computing profits — defendants' second line of attack upon the district court's construction of the statute. They urge that even if the statute be not construed to impose liability only for unfair use of inside information, in any event profits should be computed according to the established income tax rule which first looks to the identification of the stock certificate, and if that is not established, then applies the presumption which is hardly more than a rule of administrative convenience of "first in, first out." Defendants rely on the deletion from early drafts of the statute, H. R. 7852, H. R. 8720, and S. 2693, of a provision that profit should be calculated irrespective of certificates received or delivered.[11] H. R. 9323, which was finally passed by the House, failed even to penalize short-swing speculations, other than to prohibit short sales. But H. R. 8720 was never discussed by a House Committee of the Whole, and the omission of the penalty provision in H. R. 9323 suggests at most only an opinion of the Committee on Interstate and Foreign Commerce which drafted it, and one which concerns merely the advisability of any penalty, not the method for its computation.

Actually the Act as passed is a combination of H. R. 9323 and S. 3420. In the process §16(b) was taken bodily from S. 3420 and written into H. R. 9323. S. 3420 was introduced into the Senate after elaborate hearings on S. 2693 were closed. And its failure

----

[11] H. R. 7852 and S. 2693 contained the provision that "profit shall be calculated on the sale or sales by such person of such security made at the highest price or prices and on the purchase or purchases made by such person of such security at the lowest price or prices during the six months' period, irrespective of the certificates for such security received or delivered by such person during such period." H. R. 8720 provided that "the profit shall be the difference between the aggregate amount for which such security was purchased and sold during the six months' period irrespective of the certificates for such security received or delivered pursuant to such purchases and sales." * * *

to specify a method of computation may well be thought more of a sanction of the formula devised in S. 2693 than an expression of hostility towards it.

Such a conclusion may be reached upon the face of the Act. "Purchase" is defined in §3(a)(13), 15 U. S. C. A. §78c(a)(13), to include "any contract to buy," and "sale," in §3(a)(14), to include "any contract to sell." "Equity security" is defined in §3(a)(11) as "any stock or similar security." Section 16(b) then appears simply as a statement that any profit from any contract to purchase and any contract to sell — or vice versa — any stock or similar security shall be recoverable by the corporate issuer. There is no express limitation in this language; its generality permits and points to the matching of purchases and sales followed below. The fact that purchases and sales may be thus coupled, regardless of the intent of the insider with respect to a particular purchase or a particular sale and without limitation to a specific stock certificate, points to an arbitrary matching to achieve the showing of a maximum profit. Thus, where an insider purchases one certificate and sells another, the purchase and sale may be connected, even though the insider contends that he is holding the purchased security for sale after six months.

Defendants seek support for their position from the Senate hearings, where, in answer to Senator Barkley's comment, "All these transactions are a matter of record. It seems to me the simple way would be to charge him with the actual profit," Mr. Corcoran responded: "It is the same provision you have in the income tax law. Unless you can prove the actual relationship between certificates, you take the highest price sold and the lowest price bought." This was an incorrect statement of the income tax law. The rule there is first in, first out, regardless of price, wherever the stock actually purchased and sold is not identifiable. But this does show the rule the proponents had in mind, even though its source is erroneously stated. Analysis will show that the income tax rules cannot apply without defeating the law almost completely. Under the basic rule of identifying the stock certificate, the large stockholder, who in most cases is also an officer or director, could speculate in long sales with impunity merely by reason of having a reserve of stock and upon carefully choosing his stock certificates for delivery upon his sales from this reserve. Moreover, his profits from any sale followed by a purchase would be practically untouchable, for the principle of identity admits of no gain without laboring proof of a subjective intent — always a nebulous issue — to effectuate the connected phases of this type of transaction. In consequence the statute would be substantially emasculated. We cannot ascribe to it a meaning so inconsistent with its declared purpose.

Once the principle of identity is rejected, its corollary, the first-in, first-out rule, is left at loose ends. At best it is a rule of convenience designed originally to hit marginal trading without shares in hand and supplementing the principle of identity. Its rationalization is the same as that for the identification rule, for which it operates as a presumptive principle; and it has no other support. If we reject one, we reject the other and for like reasons. Its application would render the large stockholder with a backlog of stock not immediately devoted to trading immune from the Act.[19] Further, we should note that it does not fit the broad statutory language; a purchase followed immediately by a sale, albeit a transaction within the exact statutory language, would often be held immune from the statutory penalty because the purchase would be deemed by arbitrary rule to have been made at an earlier date; while a sale followed by purchase would never even be within the terms of the rule.[20] We must look elsewhere for an answer to our problem of finding a reasonable and workable interpretation of the statute in the light of its admitted purpose.

Another possibility might be the striking of an average purchase price and an average sale price during the period, and using these as bases of computation. What this rule would do in concrete effect is to allow as offsets all losses made by such trading. This in effect the district court first planned to do, 46 F. Supp. at page 766, although it did not carry it out fully, since its table as to Kaplan's sales shows only an initial loss on the first transaction showing any loss of \$16.98 and does not take into consideration some 1,634 more shares, the losses upon which were not computed. But it corrected this in its supplemental opinion, properly pointing out

---

[20] Defendants suggest, albeit rather obliquely, an intermediate rule limiting the application of the principle only to stock purchased and sold during the chosen six months' period. On the surface this would appear to prevent complete emasculation of the statute, since it assumes to prevent use of an investment backlog. Actually it makes a rule of most uncertain incidence; thus here it would leave the recovery against Seskis untouched, but reduce that against Kaplan by roughly two-thirds. These uncertain results would be increased, of course, if the period during which the officer actually continued his trading was greater than six months; consider its chance application to, say, a fourteen months' period, which might be divided up into three, or even four, six-month periods starting at different times. And once the general income tax rule is rejected (as we have seen it must be), there is surely no basis for developing this original and uncertain gloss upon it, since it does not aid the statutory intent or fit the statutory language.

that the statute provided for the recovery of "any" profit realized and obviously precluded a setting off of losses. Even had the statutory language been more uncertain, this rule seems one not to be favored in the light of the statutory purpose. Compared to other possible rules, it tends to stimulate more active trading by reducing the chance of penalty; thus Kaplan, with his more involved trading, benefits by the rule, whereas Seskis, who bought substantially at one time and sold as a whole, does not. Its application to a case where trading continued more than six months might be most uncertain, depending upon how the beginning of each six months' period was ascertained. It is not a clear-cut taking of "any profit" for the corporation, and we agree with the district court in rejecting it.

The statute is broadly remedial. Cf. *Wright* v. *Securities and Exchange Commission,* 2 Cir., 112 F. 2d 89. Recovery runs not to the stockholder, but to the corporation. We must suppose that the statute was intended to be thorough-going, to squeeze all possible profits out of stock transactions, and thus to establish a standard so high as to prevent any conflict between the selfish interest of a fiduciary officer, director, or stockholder and the faithful performance of his duty. Cf. *Woods* v. *City Nat. Bank & Trust Co. of Chicago,* 312 U. S. 262; *In re Mountain States Power Co.,* 3 Cir., 118 F. 2d 405; *Otis & Co.* v. *Insurance Bldg. Corp.,* 1 Cir., 110 F. 2d 333; *In re Republic Gas Corp.,* D. C. S. D. N. Y., 35 F. Supp. 300. The only rule whereby all possible profits can be surely recovered is that of lowest price in, highest price out — within six months — as applied by the district court. We affirm it here, defendants having failed to suggest another more reasonable rule. Cf. *Snyder* v. *Commissioner of Internal Revenue,* 295 U. S. 134.

*   *   *

Affirmed.

Eight years later the Second Circuit reasserted the lowest-in-highest-out formula after independent analysis in awarding a judgment of some $300,000 although the defendant's trading during various six-month periods had resulted in a *loss* of more than $400,000.[38] Observing that this "crushing" liability "should cer-

---

[38] Gratz v. Claughton, 187 F. 2d 46 (2d Cir. 1951), *cert. denied,* 341 U. S. 920. The loss of $400,000 is mentioned in App. to Defendant-Appellant's Brief, p. 29, and in Adler v. Klawans, 267 F. 2d 840, 847-48 (2d Cir. 1959).

tainly serve as a warning, and may prove a deterrent,"[39] Judge Learned Hand referred[40] to "the doctrine which has been law since the days of the 'Chimney Sweeper's Jewel Case,'[41] that when damages are at some unascertainable amount below an upper limit and when the uncertainty arises from the defendant's wrong, the upper limit will be taken as the proper amount." It might have been more apt to recall the condemned prisoner who, when asked if he had any last words before the noose was pulled, replied: "Yes, sir, this sure is gonna teach me a lesson." At any rate, the formula has been followed virtually without dissent.[42]

More specifically, the calculation proceeds as follows:

> Listed in one column are all the purchases made during the period for which recovery of profits is sought. In another column is listed all of the sales during that period. Then the shares purchased at the lowest price are matched against an equal number of the shares sold at the higest price within six months of such purchase, and the profit computed. After that the next lowest price is matched against the next highest price and that profit is computed. Then, the same process is repeated until all the shares in the purchase column which may be matched against shares sold for higher prices in the sales column have been matched off. Where necessary to accurate computation it would seem proper to split a larger denomination or lot of shares in order to match off part of the lot against an equal amount on the other side. The gross recovery is the sum of the profits thus determined.[43]

But "obviously no transaction can figure in more than one equation."[44] That is to say, if there is a purchase of 100 shares on February 1 followed by a sale of 100 shares on March 1 and another purchase of 100 shares on April 1, the sale on March 1 can be matched against either purchase but not both. On the other hand, if the case were the same except that 200 shares were sold on March 1, presumably 100 of that figure could be matched against the February 1 purchase and the other 100 against the April 1 purchase.

---

[39] Gratz v. Claughton, 187 F. 2d at 52.

[40] Id., 187 F. 2d at 51-52.

[41] Armory v. Delamirie, 1 Strange 505, 93 Eng. Reprint 664 (K. B. 1722).

[42] A single District Court judge who ventured to disagree was reversed, though he found one vote on appeal. Western Auto Supply Co. v. Gamble-Skogmo, Inc., 231 F. Supp. 456, 460-61 (D. Minn. 1964), rev'd, 348 F. 2d 736, 742-43 (8th Cir. 1965), cert. denied, 382 U. S. 987.

[43] Rubin and Feldman, Statutory Inhibitions upon Unfair Use of Corporate Information by Insiders, 95 U. Pa. L. Rev. 468, 482-83 (1947).

[44] Gratz v. Claughton, 187 F. 2d 46, 52 (2d Cir. 1951), cert. denied, 341 U. S. 920.

It is equally obvious that several different six-month periods may be included in the same lawsuit, with the above calculation applied to each period separately, as long as the two-year statute of limitations has not expired. And it is at least arguable that the periods may overlap as long as no transaction is used more than once. For example, if a director were to buy 100 shares at 4 on February 1, sell 100 at 6 on April 1, sell another 100 at 5 on June 1, and buy 100 at 3 on September 1, a court might well match the lowest purchase (September 1) against the highest sale (April 1) and the next lowest purchase (February 1) against the next highest sale (June 1) although the entire period in which the formula were thus applied would have exceeded six months.

The amount of damages awarded is computed net after brokerage commissions and transfer taxes on all transactions that figured in the computation.[45] The same logic permits the deduction of expenses incurred in effecting transactions otherwise than in the usual way.[46] Whether the defendant should be charged with dividends (or interest on convertible debt securities) that he received, or *credited* with dividends or interest that he *failed* to receive because his transactions were sale-purchase rather than purchase-sale, is a question that does not yet permit of a general answer.[47] This is true, too, with respect to the question whether interest will be allowed from the time of realization of profit. More often than not, probably, it is awarded, often without discussion. But some courts have been led to deny interest by the Supreme Court's

---

[45] Falco v. Donner Foundation, Inc., CCH Fed. Sec. L. Rep. ¶90,612 (S. D. N. Y. 1953), *rev'd on other grounds*, 208 F. 2d 600 (2d Cir. 1953).

[46] Blau v. Mission Corp., 212 F. 2d 77, 82 (2d Cir. 1954), *cert. denied*, 347 U. S. 1016; Arkansas La. Gas Co. v. W. R. Stephens Investment Co., Inc., 141 F. Supp. 841 (W. D. Ark. 1956).

[47] See Adler v. Klawans, 267 F. 2d 840, 848 (2d Cir. 1959); Western Auto Supply Co. v. Gamble-Skogmo, Inc., 348 F. 2d 736, 744 (8th Cir. 1965), *cert. denied*, 382 U. S. 987; Blau v. Lamb, 363 F. 2d 507, 528 (2d Cir. 1966), *cert. denied*, 385 U. S. 1002; Allis-Chalmers Mfg. Co. v. Gulf & Western Industries, Inc., 372 F. Supp. 570, 588-89 (N. D. Ill. 1974), *rev'd in part on other grounds*, 527 F. 2d 335 (7th Cir. 1975), *cert. denied*, 423 U. S. 1078; Champion Home Builders Co. v. Jeffress, 385 F. Supp. 245, 250 (E. D. Mich. 1974); Cutler-Hammer, Inc. v. Leeds & Northrop Co., Inc., 469 F. Supp. 1021, 1024 (E. D. Wis. 1979).

Cf. Morales v. Consolidated Oil & Gas, Inc., CCH Fed. Sec. L. Rep. ¶98,796 (S. D. N. Y. 1982), where the court held that profits must be computed without regard to the "incentive income" provisions of §83 of the Internal Revenue Code, whose application to the defendant's purchase by way of a stock option would have resulted in a loss. "In determining the profits to be disgorged it should not be necessary for a court to inquire into an insider's tax bracket, annual income, deductions, etc., matters which are extraneous to the administration of §16(b)." Id. at 94,080.

statement, in a case in which interest had been denied by both lower courts, "that it did not think the denial was either so unfair or so inequitable as to require us to upset it." In a situation of this sort, the Court reminded, "interest is not recovered according to a rigid theory of compensation for money withheld, but is given in response to considerations of fairness."[48]

4.   MEASUREMENT OF THE SIX-MONTH PERIOD

Since the statute refers to "any period of less than six months," the profit realized from a purchase on January 1 and a sale on June 30 would not be recoverable. As Judge Dimock put it — citing Blackstone, who might have been surprised to be told that he would be making law under the Securities Exchange Act of 1934 — the statutory period of "less than six months" means "six months minus one full period from midnight to midnight since the law does not take into account fractions of a day." The phrase "for a period exceeding six months" later on in §16(b) was regarded "as a mere referential inaccuracy which cannot prevail over the language used by Congress in creating the cause of action."[49]

5.   CHANGE OF STATUS

Whatever its rationale — perhaps on the theory that substantial stockholders as such are less likely than directors or officers to have access to inside information unless they are long-term investors — the last sentence of §16(b) excludes "any transaction where such beneficial owner was not such both at the time of the purchase and sale, or the sale and purchase, of the security involved." This, the Supreme Court has held, excludes the purchase that *makes* a person a 10+ percent stockholder.[50] At the other end, the Court has held also that a short-term 10+ percent holder who is careful to get out in two separate sales, the first of which reduces

[48] Blau v. Lehman, 368 U. S. 403, 414 (1962).

[49] Stella v. Graham-Paige Motors Corp., 132 F. Supp. 100, 104 (S. D. N. Y. 1955), *remanded on other grounds*, 232 F. 2d 299 (2d Cir. 1956), *cert. denied*, 352 U. S. 831; see also Colonial Realty Corp. v. MacWilliams, 381 F. Supp. 26 (S. D. N. Y. 1974), *aff'd per curiam*, 512 F. 2d 1187 (2d Cir. 1975), *cert. denied*, 423 U. S. 867.

[50] Foremost-McKesson, Inc. v. Provident Securities Co., 423 U. S. 232 (1976). The lower court, whose judgment the Supreme Court affirmed, added that its

his holding to 10 percent or a bit less, is not liable with respect to any profit resulting from the second sale.[51]

Now suppose the defendant was an *officer* or *director* at the time of his purchase *or* at the time of his sale, but not at both times. The express requirement that a 10+ percent holder have that status at both ends indicates that an officer or director need not. It has been so held both with respect to the person who *becomes* a director[52] and with respect to the person who *ceases* to be a director[53] between the dates of the two transactions. The courts have also imposed liability in the cognate situation in which an equity security of the issuer first becomes registered between the dates of the two transactions.[54]

The Code, on a potentiality of abuse approach, codifies these holdings with respect to officers and directors and registration, but overrules both Supreme Court decisions with respect to 10+ percent stockholders, so as to cover all three categories of insiders equally as long as the defendant had an insider's status at one end

---

reasoning "should not be applied to a transaction that is not an initial purchase but in reality is a repurchase or closing transaction" — for example, a sale to a point below 10 percent followed by a repurchase within less than six months. Provident Securities Co. v. Foremost-McKesson, Inc., 506 F. 2d 601, 614 (9th Cir. 1974).

[51] Reliance Electric Co. v. Emerson Electric Co., 404 U. S. 418 (1972). In that case the two sales were made two weeks apart and to different persons. *Query* two sales to the *same* person *a few minutes* apart. Here again, the lower court, whose judgment the Supreme Court affirmed, cautioned that the factual question whether "a particular sale is a separate and independent sale" would depend on the peculiar facts. Emerson Electric Co. v. Reliance Electric Co., 434 F. 2d 918, 925 (8th Cir. 1970).

The whole question in *Reliance Electric* was rendered moot by the *Foremost-McKesson* case, supra n. 50, four years later. For, if one must be a 10+ percent holder to begin with, he will always have to sell more in the first getting-out transaction than his total exposure under §16(b). For example, the long-term 11 percent owner who buys 5 percent more is liable in any event only to the extent of 5 percent if he sells within less than six months, but as a 16 percent holder he must sell at least 6 percent to take advantage of the *Reliance Electric* holding. The Supreme Court could not consider the *Foremost-McKesson* question in deciding *Reliance Electric*, because the lower court had *included* the transaction that brought the defendant's holdings over 10 percent and there was no cross-petition for *certiorari*.

[52] Adler v. Klawans, 267 F. 2d 840 (2d Cir. 1959); Bershad v. McDonough, 300 F. Supp. 1051, 1055 (N. D. Ill. 1969), *aff'd*, 428 F. 2d 693 (7th Cir. 1970), *cert. denied*, 400 U. S. 992.

[53] Feder v. Martin Marietta Corp., 406 F. 2d 260, 269 (2d Cir. 1969), *cert. denied*, 396 U. S. 1036. *Query* the case of the person who buys, becomes an officer or director, resigns, and sells, all within less than six months.

[54] The latest case is Gold v. Scurlock, 324 F. Supp. 1211, 1216 (E. D. Va. 1971), *aff'd in part and rev'd in part on other grounds* sub nom. Gold v. Sloan, 486 F. 2d 340 (4th Cir. 1973), *cert. denied*, 419 U. S. 873.

or the other.[55] Meanwhile Rule 16a-1 has been amended so that (1) any officer or director who is required to report any change in beneficial ownership occurring within six months after he became an officer or director, or after registration, must reflect in his report of that change all changes that occurred within six months *before* the change that touched off the reporting requirement, and (2) any person who ceases to be an officer or director, or who has that status upon deregistration, must report any *subsequent* change that occurs within six months after any prior change.[56] It has been held that the rule as so amended is valid, but that it provides no basis for applying §16(b) when *both* transactions occur after the defendant ceased to be an officer or director (or, presumably, after deregistration) even though those transactions are reportable.[57]

6. DEFINITIONS

Thus far we have been using the terms "officer," "director," "beneficial owner," "purchase," and "sale," as if their meaning were plain. But life is not so simple.

a. "Officer" [Rule 3b-2]

The Commission has defined the term "officer" to mean "a president, vice-president, treasurer, secretary, comptroller, and any other person who performs for an issuer, whether incorporated or unincorporated, functions corresponding to those performed by the foregoing officers." The General Counsel of the Commission early expressed the opinion

> that an assistant would be an "officer" if his chief is so inactive that the assistant is really performing his chief's functions. However, an assistant, although performing some functions which might be those of his chief, would not be an "officer" so long as these duties were under the supervision of his chief. Temporary absence or brief vacation of an officer during which an assistant performs the officer's duties would not constitute the assistant an "officer."[58]

[55] §1714(c)-(e); 2 Code 752-53.
[56] Rule 16a-1(d) and (e) as amended by Sec. Ex. Act Rel. 8697 (1969).
[57] Lewis v. Varnes, 505 F. 2d 785 (2d Cir. 1974); see also Lewis v. Mellon Bank, N. A., 513 F. 2d 921 (3d Cir. 1975) (no mention of the rule).
[58] Sec. Ex. Act Rel. 2687 (1940).

A Second Circuit dictum cast doubt on the validity of the Commission's definition; the court preferred a more subjective, statute-oriented test in terms of accessibility to inside information.[59] But a proposed revision of the rule in those terms met an unfavorable response.[60] And there is now some authority in support of the rule's validity.[61]

The most recently announced administrative view is as follows:

> Generally, it is not difficult to identify a company's principal officers by their traditional titles and functions. However, an employee who does not possess a title may nevertheless be an officer because of the significant functions he performs; similarly, an employee who holds a title may nonetheless not be an officer because his functions and duties are insignificant, despite his formal position. The staff generally takes the view that anyone holding an appropriate title is an officer for purposes of Section 16(a).[62]

b. "Director" [§3(a)(7)]

The statute itself defines the term "director" to mean "any director of a corporation or any person performing similar functions with respect to any organization, whether incorporated or unincorporated." This is broad enough to cover a trustee of a Massachusetts trust or of a voting trust, or a member of a committee that issues certificates of deposit. But it does extend to an "honorary" director who plays no role with respect to policy issues and has no access to insider information.[63] Presumably, since the

---

[59] Colby v. Klune, 178 F. 2d 872 (2d Cir. 1949).

[60] Sec. Ex. Act Rels. 4718, 4754 (1952).

[61] Lockheed Aircraft Corp. v. Rathman, 106 F. Supp. 810 (S. D. Cal. 1952); Lockheed Aircraft Corp. v. Campbell, 110 F. Supp. 282 (S. D. Cal. 1953).

[62] Sec. Ex. Act Rel. 18,114, 23 SEC Dock. 856, 860-61 (1981). In Merrill Lynch, Pierce, Fenner & Smith, Inc. v. Livingston, 566 F. 2d 1119, 1122 (9th Cir. 1978), involving an "Account Executive" who was one of some 350 "Executive Vice Presidents," the court held: "The title 'Vice President' does no more than raise an inference that the person who holds the title has the executive duties and the opportunities for confidential information that the title implies. The inference can be overcome by proof that the title was merely honorary and did not carry with it any of the executive responsibilities that might otherwise be assumed." The same court later emphasized that "officer" status was determined "by the title [held], with a very limited exception applicable only where the title is essentially honorary or ceremonial." National Medical Enterprises, Inc. v. Small, 680 F. 2d 83, 84 (9th Cir. 1982). For a discussion of the then eight decided cases — there has been none since — see Comment, Section 16(b) of the Securities and [*sic*] Exchange Act of 1934: Is a Vice President an Officer?, 58 Neb. L. Rev. 733 (1979).

[63] Fort Worth National Corp., CCH Fed. Sec. L. Rep. ¶78,309 (letter 1971).

Commission's definition of "officer" is modeled on this statutory definition of "director," much the same considerations govern.

The big question here is whether one who "deputizes" another to be a director is himself a director and, if so, what it takes to "deputize":

FEDER v. MARTIN MARIETTA CORPORATION
United States Court of Appeals, Second Circuit, 1969
406 F. 2d 260, *cert. denied,* 396 U. S. 1036

WATERMAN, Circuit Judge.

Plaintiff-appellant, a stockholder of the Sperry Rand Corporation ("Sperry") after having made the requisite demand upon Sperry which was not complied with, commenced this action pursuant to §16(b) of the Securities Exchange Act of 1934, 15 U. S. C. §78p(b) (1964), to recover for Sperry "short-swing" profits realized upon Sperry stock purchases and sales by the Martin Marietta Corporation ("Martin"). Plaintiff alleged that George M. Bunker, the President and Chief Executive of Martin Marietta, was deputized by, or represented, Martin Marietta when he served as a member of the Sperry Rand Board of Directors and therefore during his membership Martin Marietta was a "director" of Sperry Rand within the meaning of Section 16(b). The United States District Court for the Southern District of New York, Cooper, J., sitting without a jury, finding no deputization, dismissed plaintiff's action. 286 F. Supp. 937 (S. D. N. Y. 1968). We hold to the contrary and reverse the judgment below.

*   *   *

The judicial tendency, especially in this circuit, has been to interpret Section 16(b) in ways that are most consistent with the legislative purpose, even departing where necessary from the literal statutory language. See, e. g., cases cited in *Blau* v. *Oppenheim*, 250 F. Supp. 881, 884-885 (S. D. N. Y. 1966) (Weinfeld, J.). But the policy underlying the enactment of §16(b) does not permit an expansion of the statute's scope to persons other than directors, officers, and 10% shareholders. *Blau* v. *Lehman*, 368 U. S. 403, 410-411 (1962). Cf. *Ellerin* v. *Massachusetts Mut. Life Ins. Co.*, 270 F. 2d 259, 263 (2 Cir. 1959). Through the creation of a legal fiction, however, our courts have managed to remain within the limits of §16(b)'s literal language and yet have expanded the Act's reach.

In *Rattner* v. *Lehman,* 193 F. 2d 564 (2 Cir. 1952), Judge Learned Hand in his concurring opinion planted the seed for a utilization of the theory of deputization upon which plaintiff here proceeds. In discussing the question whether a partnership is subject to Section 16(b) liability whenever a partner is a director of a corporation whose stock the partnership traded, Judge Hand stated:

> I agree that §16(b) does not go so far; but I wish to say nothing as to whether, if a firm deputed a partner to represent its interests as a director on the board, the other partners would not be liable. True, they would not even then be formally "directors"; but I am not prepared to say that they could not be so considered; for some purposes the common law does treat a firm as a jural person. 193 F. 2d at 567.

The Supreme Court in *Blau* v. *Lehman,* 368 U. S. 403, 408-410, (1962), affirming 286 F. 2d 786 (2 Cir. 1960), affirming 173 F. Supp. 590 (S. D. N. Y. 1959) more firmly established the possibility of an entity, such as a partnership or a corporation, incurring Section 16(b) liability as a "director" through the deputization theory. Though the Court refused to reverse the lower court decisions that had held no deputization, it stated:

> Although admittedly not "literally designated" as one, it is contended that Lehman is a director. No doubt Lehman Brothers, though a partnership, could for purposes of §16 be a "director" of Tide Water and function through a deputy * * * . 368 U. S. at 409.

In *Marquette Cement Mfg. Co.* v. *Andreas,* 239 F. Supp. 962, 967 (S. D. N. Y. 1965), relying upon *Blau* v. *Lehman,* the availability of the deputization theory to impose §16(b) liability was again recognized. See also *Molybdenum Corp. of America* v. *International Mining Corp.,* 32 F. R. D. 415, 418 (S. D. N. Y. 1963).

In light of the above authorities, the validity of the deputization theory, presumed to be valid here by the parties and by the district court, is unquestionable. Nevertheless, the situations encompassed by its application are not as clear. The Supreme Court in *Blau* v. *Lehman* intimated that the issue of deputization is a question of fact to be settled case by case and not a conclusion of law. See 368 U. S. at 408-409. Therefore, it is not enough for appellant to show us that inferences to support appellant's contentions should have been drawn from the evidence. Id. at 409. Rather our review of the facts and inferences found by the court below is imprisoned by the "unless clearly erroneous" standard. Fed. R. Civ. P. 52(a).

In the instant case, applying that standard, though there is some evidence in the record to support the trial court's finding of no deputization, we, upon considering the entire evidence, are left with the definite and firm conviction that a mistake was committed. *Guzman* v. *Pichirilo,* 369 U. S. 698, 702 (1962); *United States* v. *United States Gypsum Co.,* 333 U. S. 364, 394-395 (1948). Consequently, we reverse the result reached below.

Bunker served as a director of Sperry from April 29, 1963 to August 1, 1963, when he resigned. During the period December 14, 1962 through July 24, 1963, Martin Marietta accumulated 801,300 shares of Sperry stock of which 101,300 shares were purchased during Bunker's directorship. Between August 29, 1963 and September 6, 1963, Martin Marietta sold all of its Sperry stock. Plaintiff seeks to reach, on behalf of the Sperry Rand Corporation, the profits made by Martin Marietta from the 101,300 shares of stock acquired between April 29 and August 1, all of which, of course, were sold within six months after purchase.

The district court, in determining that Bunker was not a Martin deputy, made the following findings of fact to support its decision: (1) Sperry intially invited Bunker to join its Board two and a half months before Martin began its accumulation of Sperry stock; (2) Bunker turned down a second offer by Sperry at a time when Martin already held 400,000 shares of Sperry stock; (3) Sperry, not Martin, took the initiative to encourage Bunker to accept the directorship; (4) no other Martin man was ever mentioned for the position in the event Bunker absolutely declined; and (5) Bunker's fine reputation and engineering expertise was the prime motivation for Sperry's interest in him. In addition, the testimony of the only two witnesses who testified at trial, Mr. Bunker and a Mr. Norman Frost, a Sperry director and its chief counsel, were fully believed and accepted as truthful by the court. We assume all of the foregoing findings have a basis of fact in the evidence, but we find there was additional, more germane, uncontradicted evidence, overlooked or ignored by the district court, which we are firmly convinced require us to conclude that Martin Marietta was a "director" of Sperry Rand.

First and foremost is Bunkers' testimony that as chief executive of Martin Marietta he was "ultimately responsible for the total operation of the corporation" including personal approval of all the firm's financial investments, and, in particular, all of Martin's purchases of Sperry stock. As the district court aptly recognized, Bunker's control over Martin Marietta's investments, coupled with his position on the Board of Directors of Sperry Rand, placed him in a position where he could acquire inside information concerning Sperry and could utilize such data for Martin Marietta's benefit wthout disclosing this information to any other Martin Marietta personnel. Thus, the district court's findings that Bunker "never disclosed inside information relevant to investment decisions" and that the "information that he obtained while a director 'simply wasn't germane to that question at all' " are not significant. 286 F. Supp. at 946. Nor are these findings totally supported by the evidence. Bunker's testimony revealed that while he was a Sperry director three Sperry officials had furnished him with information relating to the "short-range outlook" at Sperry, and, in addition, Bunker admitted discussing Sperry's affairs with two officials at Martin Marietta and participating in sessions when Martin's investment in Sperry was reviewed. Moreover, an unsigned document concededly originating from the Martin Marietta files, entitled "Notes on Exploratory Investment in Sperry Rand Corporation," describing the Sperry management, evaluating their abilities, and analyzing the merit of Sperry's forecasts for the future, further indicates that Martin Marietta may have benefited, or intended to benefit, from Bunker's association with Sperry Rand.

In contrast, in *Blau* v. *Lehman,* supra, where Lehman Brothers was the alleged "director," the Lehman partner exercised no power of approval concerning the partnership's investment; was not consulted for advice; had no advance knowledge of Lehman Brothers' intention to purchase the stock of the corporation of which he was a member of the board of directors; and never discussed the operating details of that corporation's affairs with any member of Lehman Brothers. 368 U. S. at 406. Similarly, in *Rattner* v. *Lehman,* supra, the court's decision was premised on the assumption that the defendant's purchases and sales were made without any advice or concurrence from the defendant's partner sitting on the Board of the company in whose stock the defendant traded.

It appears to us that a person in Bunker's unique position could act as a deputy for Martin Marietta even in the absence of factors indicating an intention or belief on the part of both companies that he was so acting. We do not hold that, without more, Bunker's control over Martin Marietta, see *Marquette Cement Mfg. Co.* v. *Andreas,* supra at 967, or the possibility that inside information was obtained or disclosed, mandates that Bunker was Martin's deputy. However, additional evidence detailed hereafter which indicates that the managements of Sperry Rand and of Martin Marietta intended that Bunker should act as Martin's deputy on the Sperry Board, and believed he was so acting, lends valuable support to our factual conclusion.

First, in Bunker's letter of resignation to General MacArthur, the Chairman of the Board of Directors of Sperry Rand, he stated:

> When I became a member of the Board in April, it appeared to your associates that the Martin Marietta ownership of a substantial number of shares of Sperry Rand should have representation on your Board. This representation does not seem to me really necessary and I prefer not to be involved in the affairs of Sperry Rand when there are so many other demands on my time * * *

Martin Marietta urges that we should not read this letter to mean what it so clearly says. They would have us believe that this letter was so phrased because Bunker intended "to write a gentle letter of resignation to a great (but elderly) man whom he admired, in terms that he would understand." No matter how advanced in years the Chairman of the Sperry Board may have been, we are puzzled by defendant's contention that he, and only he, of all those on the Sperry Board, considered Bunker to be representing Martin's interests. Furthermore, if, throughout Bunker's service, the Chairman of the Board misunderstood the purpose of Bunker's directorship, why Bunker upon resignation would want this misunderstanding perpetuated is even more perplexing. Certainly the more logical inference from the wording of Bunker's letter of resignation is the inference that Bunker served on the Sperry Board as a representative of Martin Marietta so as to protect Martin's investment in Sperry.

Second, the Board of Directors of Martin Marietta formally consented to and approved Bunker's directorship of Sperry prior to Bunker's acceptance of the position. While Martin's organizational policy required that Bunker secure that Board's approval of any corporate directorship he were offered, the approval was not obtained until, significantly, the Board had been informed by Bunker that Martin had a 10 million dollar investment in Sperry stock at the time. Bunker testified that he "thought the Board would draw the inference that his presence on Sperry's Board would be to Martin's interest." Indeed, as noted by the district court, "the logic behind such an inference is obvious when we stop to consider that a directorship, by its very nature, carries with it potential access to information unavailable to the ordinary investor." 286 F. Supp. at 945. Surely such conduct by the Martin Board supports an inference that it deputized Bunker to represent its interests on Sperry's Board. The trial court's finding to the contrary leaves us with the definite and firm conviction that a mistake was indeed committed.

Finally, Bunker's testimony clearly established that the Martin Marietta Corporation had representatives or deputies who served on the boards of other corporations. The only distinctions drawn by the court below to differentiate Bunker's Sperry relationship from the relationship to Martin Marietta of other Martin Marietta deputies on other corporate boards were that Bunker had no duty to report back to Martin what was going on at Sperry and there was a lesser degree of supervision over Bunker's actions than over the actions of the others. Otherwise Bunker was a typical Martin deputy. In view of Bunker's position of almost absolute authority over Martin's affairs, such differences hardly suffice to refute the evidentiary value of the similarities between the functions of Bunker and those of Martin's representatives on other corporate boards.

In summary, it is our firm conviction that the district court erred in apportioning the weight to be accorded the evidence before it. The control possessed by Bunker, his letter of resignation, the approval by the Martin Board of Bunker's directorship with Sperry, and the functional similarity between Bunker's acts as a Sperry director and the acts of Martin's representatives on other boards, as opposed to the factors relied upon by the trial court, are all definite and concrete indicatives that Bunker, in fact, was a Martin deputy, and we find that indeed he was.

*   *   *

Reversed and remanded.[a]

Query:

(1) Was Bunker's mistake that he asked permission?

(2) If a *corporation* can be a "director" of another corporation, there is no reason to assume that a partnership or individual who "deputizes" cannot be. One may guess, however, that no "director by deputization" has ever filed a §16(a) report or signed a 1933 Act registration statement as a "director."

(3) Is it conceivable — let alone likely — that Congress contemplated a director by "deputization" when it defined the term to

---

[a] ED.: See also Lewis v. Dekcraft Corp., CCH Fed. Sec. L. Rep. ¶94,620 at 96,202 (S. D. N. Y. 1974).

include "any person performing similar functions" to those of a "director of a *corporation*" and defined "person" in §3(a)(9) to include a "partnership"?[64] Is this not the sort of wooden reading of statutes that the courts have so often disapproved? Is it not much more likely that the quoted language was directed simply to trustees of business trusts and active general partners?

The Code's definition of "director" specifically excludes "a person who deputizes another person to be a director" on the ground that the theory is "out of harmony with the spirit" of §16(b).[65] That is to say, this area, unlike the area of mergers and so on, seems more appropriate for an "objective" approach. It seems significant in this respect that early drafts of what became §16(b) not only would have made it unlawful for any of the specified insiders to disclose any confidential information regarding registered securities, but also would have extended to all profits received by *anyone,* insider or not, "to whom such unlawful disclosure" had been made.[66]

c.   Beneficial Ownership

Throughout §16 there is the question of determining who is a 10+ percent "beneficial owner," a phrase that Mr. Corcoran told the Senate committee in 1934 was "the broadest term you can have."[67] In addition, whereas the criterion under §16(b) is whether there have been a "purchase and sale," the criterion under §16(a) for all three types of insiders is beneficial ownership, direct or indirect. Changes in beneficial ownership must be reported whether they result from a purchase or a sale or a gift or any other event. Record ownership alone is of no consequence.

Although the Act does not define "beneficial ownership," there are a number of rules and releases with respect to various relationships:

(i)   *Family relationships:* Intrafamily bookkeeping arrangements are not conclusive. In 1966 the Commission restated the applicable principles as enunciated in a 1935 interpretation of its General Counsel:[68]

Generally a person is regarded as the beneficial owner of secu-

---

[64] The 1975 amendments substituted the word "company."

[65] §202(40); 2 Code 752.

[66] Blau v. Lehman, 368 U. S. 403, 412 (1962).

[67] 15 Stock Exchange Practices, Hearings before Senate Com. on Banking & Currency, 73d Cong., 2d Sess (1934) 6556.

[68] Sec. Ex. Act Rel. 175 (1935); Sec. Ex. Act Rel. 7793 (1966), as corrected by Sec. Ex. Act Rel. 7824 (1966).

rities held in the name of his or her spouse and their minor children. Absent special circumstances such relationship ordinarily results in such person obtaining benefits substantially equivalent to ownership, e. g., application of the income derived from such securities to maintain a common home, to meet expenses which such person otherwise would meet from other sources, or the ability to exercise a controlling influence over the purchase, sale, or voting of such securities. Accordingly, a person ordinarily should include in his reports filed pursuant to section 16(a) securities held in the name of a spouse or minor children as being beneficially owned by him.

A person also may be regarded as the beneficial owner of securities held in the name of another person, if by reason of any contract, understanding, relationship, agreement, or other arrangement, he obtains therefrom benefits substantially equivalent to those of ownership. Accordingly, where such benefits are present such securities should be reported as being beneficially owned by the reporting person. Moreover, the fact that the person is a relative or relative of a spouse and sharing the same home as the reporting person may in itself indicate that the reporting person would obtain benefits substantially equivalent to those of ownership from securities held in the name of such relative. Thus, absent countervailing facts, it is expected that securities held by relatives who share the same home as the reporting person will be reported as being beneficially owned by such person.

A person also is regarded as the beneficial owner of securities held in the name of a spouse, minor children or other person, even though he does not obtain therefrom the aforementioned benefits of ownership, if he can vest or revest title in himself at once, or at some future time [the 1935 opinion had added at this point, "without payment of other than a nominal consideration"].

This 1966 release marked no sharp departure from the published interpretation of 1935 — with its dual approach in terms of a "benefits" test and a "right to recapture" test — except for the statement that, "absent countervailing facts," a person might be considered to derive "benefits substantially equivalent to those of ownership" from the mere fact that his (or his spouse's) relative (presumably of any degree) shared his home. This was apparently designed to correct the impression on the part of many practitioners at that time that one spouse did not have benefits substantially equivalent to those of ownership as far as the other's securities were concerned unless the first spouse had not merely some economic benefit from them but also control over their purchase or sale.

Surely the proverbial case of the wealthy (and perhaps hostile) mother-in-law who moves in with her daughter is a "countervailing fact." The norm with which the release deals, though the rebuttable presumption it creates is not so limited, is the insider's wife (for simplicity we shall make the husband rather than the wife the insider) or minor child. And, even before the 1966 release, the obvious course — as simple as it was prudent — was to include the wife's and minor children's securities with the husband's (except in the event of a divorce or separation or, *perhaps* since the 1966 release, a clear case in which the wife had always been the "moneyed" member of the family in her own right) together with a disclaimer.[69]

There are only a few reported opinions in point. In what is perhaps the closest case, a director of Dow Chemical Company whose wife was a Dow heiress was held to be the beneficial owner of his wife's Dow stock under the harmonious family circumstances, so as to match her sales against his later exercise of an option financed by using the proceeds of her sale, which he borrowed from her at 7 percent interest.[70]

(ii) *Partnerships:* A partnership that is a 10+ percent beneficial owner for its own account must report regardless of whether reports are filed by the partners. Moreover, an individual partner must report as well if he is an officer or director of the issuer, or if his indirect interest in the security through the partnership (together with the amount of the security of which he is otherwise directly or indirectly the beneficial owner) exceeds 10 percent, or if he is the beneficial owner of 10+ percent of some other class

---

[69] This is permitted by Rule 16a-3.

[70] Husband and wife filed joint tax returns and had the same financial advisers. She used his gift tax exclusion. He contributed virtually his entire salary to living expenses. But she was primarily responsible for the style in which they lived, which included the cost of their children's education and maintaining a vacation home. Whiting v. Dow Chemical Co., 523 F. 2d 680 (2d Cir. 1975).

See also Blau v. Potter, CCH Fed. Sec. L. Rep. ¶94,115 (S. D. N. Y. 1973) (judgment for defendant); Altamil Corp. v. Pryor, 405 F. Supp. 1222 (S. D. Ind. 1975); Whittaker v. Whittaker Corp., 639 F. 2d 516 (9th Cir. 1981), cert. denied, 454 U. S. 1030 (director felt free to manage his aged mother's assets as his own); but cf. CBI Industries, Inc. v. Horton, 682 F. 2d 643 (7th Cir. 1982) (distinguishing *Whiting* and *Whittaker* as involving the required "direct pecuniary benefit to the insider").

Not surprisingly, the federal policy in §16(b) has been held to prevail over the local community property law, so that the husband (or presumably the wife if she is an insider) is liable for the entire amount of the profit and not merely half. Jefferson Lake Sulphur Co. v. Walet, 104 F. Supp. 20, 25 (E. D. La. 1952), aff'd on the lower court's "fuller discussion" of this point sub nom. Walet v. Jefferson Lake Sulphur Co., 202 F. 2d 433, 434 (5th Cir. 1953), cert. denied, 346 U. S. 820.

of registered equity security of the same issuer.[71] When a partner reports, he must state the entire amount owned by the partnership, though he may elect to disclose the extent of his interest in the partnership and its transactions.[72]

Absent "deputization," and on the assumption that a partnership buys and sells without the advice or concurrence of the partner who is a director, the partner-director is liable only for his *pro rata* share of the firm's profit.[73] But, however innocent himself, he cannot avoid all liability by disclaiming his interest in the firm's profit.[74]

(iii)   *Holding companies:* Concerning the question of indirect beneficial ownership through a holding company that is itself a 10+ percent beneficial owner, the Commission's General Counsel expressed the view in 1938 that "no consideration need be given by the owner of stock in a holding company to the holdings of that company, except in a case where the holding merely provides a medium through which one person, or several persons in a small group, invest or trade in securities, and where such company has no other substantial business."[75] But a 1981 release seems to tighten up a bit when it considers any "control person of a closely-held company" to be "the beneficial owner of all securities held by that company."[76]

The Commission does have a rule that no report is required of any person with respect to his indirect interest in portfolio securities held by a holding or investment company registered under the 1935 or 1940 Act, a "pension or retirement plan holding securities of an issuer whose employees generally are the beneficiaries of the plan," or a business trust with more than twenty-five beneficiaries.[77]

(iv)   *Trusts [Rule 16a-8]:* About the only simple statement one can safely make about the many different kinds of trust situations is that "beneficial ownership" within the meaning of §16 "must

---

[71]Op. Gen. Counsel, Sec. Ex. Act Rel. 1965 (1938); Sec. Ex. Act Rel. 18,114, 23 SEC Dock. 856, 863 (1981).

[72]Form 3, Instr. 10; Form 4, Instr. 10.

[73]Blau v. Lehman, 368 U. S. 403 (1962).

[74]Blau v. Lehman, 286 F. 2d 786 (2d Cir. 1960), *aff'd on other grounds,* 368 U. S. 403 (1962).

[75]Op. Gen. Counsel, Sec. Ex. Act Rel. 1965 (1938).

[76]Sec. Ex. Act Rel. 18,114, 23 SEC Dock. 856, 863 (1981). See generally Boston & Me. R. R. Co. v. Hillman, CCH Fed. Sec. L. Rep. ¶90,813 (S. D. N. Y. 1957); Blau v. Lamb, 242 F. Supp. 151, 161 (S. D. N. Y. 1965), *aff'd in part and rev'd in part,* 363 F. 2d 507 (2d Cir. 1966), *cert. denied,* 385 U. S. 1002; Morales v. Colt Industries, Inc., CCH Fed. Sec. L. Rep. ¶93,569 (S. D. N. Y. 1972); Popkin v. Dingman, 366 F. Supp. 534, 541 (S. D. N. Y. 1973).

[77]Rule 16a-8(g). See Tomlinson, The Application of Section 16(b) to Tax-Qualified Employee Benefit Plans, 33 Stan. L. Rev. 231 (1981).

be construed in context and is not necessarily identical with similar concepts in other contexts such as tax law, nor does it depend solely upon the form in which the trust is established."[78] But Rule 16a-8 is reasonably straightforward:

Beneficial ownership for purposes of §16(a) is considered to flow from any one of three relationships to a trust:[79] (1) the ownership of securities as a trustee when either the trustee or members of his immediate family have a vested interest in the income or corpus of the trust; (2) the ownership of a vested beneficial interest in a trust; and (3) the ownership of securities as a settlor of a trust in which the settlor has the power to revoke the trust without obtaining the consent of all the beneficiaries.

In addition, the trust and the trustees as such are required to file reports when the trust is a 10+ percent beneficial owner; this, in effect, treats the trust "entity" as the beneficial owner, for which in practice reports are normally filed by the trustee. However, except in so far as the *trust* as a beneficial owner is concerned, the rule provides an exemption with respect to any obligation that would otherwise be imposed solely by reason of ownership as a *settlor* or *beneficiary* when (1) less than 20 percent in market value of the trust's securities having a readily ascertainable market value (determined as of the end of the trust's preceding fiscal year) consists of equity securities with respect to which reports would otherwise be required, or (2) the ownership, acquisition, or disposition of the securities by the trust is made without the settlor's or beneficiary's prior approval.[80]

[78] Sec. Ex. Act Rel. 4720 (1952).

[79] So far as §16(b) is concerned, presumably Rule 16a-10 forestalls its application when Rule 16a-8 makes it clear that the person is *not* a beneficial owner. But it does not follow that a person declared to be a beneficial owner by the rule will be so treated for purposes of 16(b). See Sec. Ex. Act Rels. 4801 (1953), 7824 (1966); CBI Industries, Inc. v. Horton, 682 F. 2d 643 (7th Cir. 1982). In Marquette Cement Mfg. Co. v. Andreas, 239 F. Supp. 962, 967 (S. D. N. Y. 1965), where the defendant was himself beneficiary of one of the trusts of which he was trustee and was also sole trustee of eighteen other trusts of which for the most part members of his family were beneficiaries, the court held him liable only *pro rata* under Blau v. Lehman (supra p. 641), saying that Rule 16a-8 had "only slight significance in assessing insider liability under Section 16(b)." Whether the defendant held a beneficial interest in the stock of the other trusts was considered a question of fact to be determined from all the evidence. His normal interest in seeing that members of his family were well and comfortable did not bring him within §16(b). All the trusts were *bona fide* and irrevocable except the one for his benefit, and all but that one were for the benefit of individuals with recognizably different interests from his.

[80] See also Rule 16a-8(g), supra p. 490, text at n. 17. And there is more. See Sec. Ex. Act Rel. 18,114, 23 SEC Dock. 856, 864, 878-82 (1981).

d. "Equity Security" [§3(a)(11)]

Section 3(a)(11) defines "equity security," in substance, to mean any stock or any security that carries a right to acquire stock, whether by conversion or otherwise, with rulemaking authority to add any security "of similar nature." Until the 1964 amendments, this term was significant *only* with respect to §16. With the use of the term in §12(g)(1) discriminating in favor of issuers of unlisted *nonequity* securities, the Commission in 1965 adopted Rule 3a11-1 to flesh out the statutory definition:[81]

> The term "equity security" is hereby defined to include any stock or similar security, certificate of interest or participation in any profit sharing agreement, preorganization certificate or subscription, transferable share, voting trust certificate or certificate of deposit for an equity security, limited partnership interest, interest in a joint venture, or certificate of interest in a business trust; or any security convertible, with or without consideration, into such a security, or carrying any warrant or right to subscribe to or purchase such a security; or any such warrant or right.

Even before this rule, voting-trust certificates and certificates of deposit were considered to be equity securities whenever the underlying securities were.[82] Hence 10+ percent owners of registered instruments of these types, as well as committee members, voting trustees, and any other persons whose position with the issuer of the instruments corresponds to an officer or director of a corporation, are subject to §16. Moreover, since beneficial ownership of these certificates involves beneficial ownership of the underlying security, persons who beneficially own more than 10 percent of the underlying security (both directly and through beneficial ownership of one of these instruments), as well as officers and directors of the issuer of the underlying security, are subject to §16 with respect to changes in their beneficial ownership of the certificates as well as of the underlying security. This assumes that the underlying security is registered. If so, it is immaterial whether or not the certificates issued against them are registered as well.

Treasury stock is an "equity security" even though it is expressly included in the definition of "security" and not specifically mentioned in the definition of "equity security."[83] And presumably

---

[81] Sec. Ex. Act Rel. 7581 (1965).
[82] See Rule 16a-2(a), infra p. 655, text at n. 94.
[83] Walet v. Jefferson Lake Sulphur Co., 202 F. 2d 433, 435 (5th Cir. 1953), *cert. denied,* 346 U. S. 820.

a warrant to subscribe to a convertible bond would be an equity security, though twice removed. *Query* the status of income bonds and the hybrid instruments.

e. "Class"

We have already considered the definition of "class" in connection with §12(g) registration. But it has a fillip in the §16 context so far as convertible debt securities are concerned.

In the first case to construe "class" in the §16 context, the corporation had two series of cumulative preferred stock and the defendant owned more than 10 percent of the smaller series but not more than 10 percent of both combined. The two series differed in that they had been listed fourteen months apart, they had different dividend rates, redemption prices, and sinking-fund provisions, they were redeemable separately, and a two-thirds vote of the particular series was required for any charter amendment adversely affecting its holders. But neither series was preferred over the other with respect to dividends or liquidation; the par value was the same; on a default in four quarterly dividends, the preferred as a class had the right to elect one-third of the directors; the articles themselves referred to the preferred as a class with provision for its issuance in "series"; and they referred also to a second preferred as a separate class with series, thus unequivocally distinguishing between different classes and different series. Applying the normal distinction between "class" and "series" in corporation law, and pointing out that most of the states specifically provide for the division of "classes" into "series," the Second Circuit concluded that there was but a single "class."[84]

In 1967, however, the same court, disagreeing with the SEC's position as *amicus curiae*, held that convertible debentures were not themselves a "class of any equity security," but were equity securities only in the sense that the class consists of the common stock augmented as to any beneficial holding in question by the

---

[84] Ellerin v. Massachusetts Mutual Life Ins. Co., 270 F. 2d 259, 261 (2d Cir. 1959). Cf. Rule 12d1-1(d): "If a class of security is issuable in two or more series with different terms, each such series shall be deemed a separate class for the purposes of this regulation." Cf. also Sec. Ex. Act §15(d), 4th sentence: "For the purposes of this subsection, the term 'class' shall be construed to include all securities of an issuer which are of substantially similar character and the holders of which enjoy substantially similar rights and privileges." These two provisions, as the court observed, are expressly made applicable only for their own peculiar purposes.

number of shares into which the debentures owned by the particular person are convertible.[85] The *holding* of the case was that a 10+ percent owner of the debentures was not liable for any profit resulting from the matching of purchases of debentures against sales of common stock within less than six months when the defendant had never owned as much as 10 percent of the class under the court's construction. Judge Lumbard found nothing in the legislative history to indicate that the owners of debentures as such ought to be considered "insiders," and saw "no reason whatever to believe that any holder of any Convertible Debentures would, by reason of such holding, normally have any standing or position with the officers, directors or large stockholders of a company so that such holder of Debentures would be the recipient of any inside information."[86] Moreover, the court pointed to the anomaly whereby the defendant, able to command less than 3 percent of the common stock on a hypothetical conversion of all its debentures, would be liable for short-swing profits under the Commission's view although a holder of 9 percent of the common would not be.

The opinion is persuasive. But the anomaly that concerned the court is built into the statute: if (altogether apart from convertibility) a company has twenty times as much Class A stock as Class B stock, the 11 percent holder of B stock (if it is registered) is covered by §16 even though the 1 percent holder of A stock has a far greater equity in the company. And the opinion does leave a number of perplexing questions. There are convertible debentures and convertible debentures. One that is fully protected against dilution[87] and that is traded in the market will be considered by the market to be the substantial equivalent of the common stock, and will rise in price with the common if the market price of the common, on adjustment for the conversion ratio, exceeds the call price of the debentures. We have earlier noticed the desirability of being able to match a purchase (or sale) of the one security against a sale (or purchase) of the other in such a situation.[88] And that would not

---

[85] Chemical Fund, Inc. v. Xerox Corp., 377 F. 2d 107 (2d Cir. 1967). See also Foremost-McKesson, Inc. v. Provident Securities Co., 423 U. S. 232, 236 n. 5 (1976), involving a purchase and sale of a convertible debenture, where the Court stated merely: "The owner of debentures convertible into more than 10% of a corporation's registered common stock is a beneficial owner within the meaning of the Act."

[86] Chemical Fund, Inc. v. Xerox Corp., 377 F. 2d 107, 111 (2d Cir. 1967).

[87] On what constitutes full protection, see Posner, Developments in Federal Securities Regulation, 22 Bus. Law. 645, 664 n. 68 (1967).

[88] See pp. 628-29 supra.

be easy if the two were considered separate "classes" — though §16(b) is not explicit to the effect that the purchase and sale must be of the same "class," and the section *might* be applied to the purchase and sale of different "classes" that were nevertheless substantially similar. At any rate, when conversion of debentures is *not* economical, it is their senior position and fixed interest claim that give them value. At least in that situation, the debentures, until converted, would seem *a fortiori* to be a different "class" of security from the common if a convertible *preferred* (which is indubitably an "equity security" even apart from the convertibility feature) is ever a different "class" from the common;[89] and surely the court is not saying that a convertibility feature automatically makes the preferred and common the same "class."

Presumably, too (apart from the arbitrage exemption in §16(e) in the event of simultaneous transactions), the matching would have been sustained if the defendant *had* owned enough of the debentures (either alone or together with holdings of common stock) to make it a 10+ percent owner of the single class, or if the defendant had been an officer or director. Indeed, the court's single-class approach should greatly facilitate matching in such a case. And it is even clearer that any such person would be liable for profits from short-term trading in the debentures themselves. Again, since the "class," in the court's view, is augmented by the number of shares into which the beneficial holding in question is convertible, not the number of shares into which all outstanding debentures are convertible, one does not come to the case of the person who owns more than 10 percent of the *common stock* alone but less than 10 percent of the common as augmented by the shares into which outstanding debentures are convertible.[90] But what of the short-term trader in convertible debentures (or preferred) who is neither officer nor director and who owns more than 10 percent of the convertible debentures (or preferred) alone but not more

---

[89] But see American Standard, Inc. v. Crane Co., 346 F. Supp. 1153, 1161 (S. D. N. Y. 1972), *rev'd on other grounds*, 510 F. 2d 1043 (2d Cir. 1974), *cert. denied*, 421 U. S. 1000, a case in which a hypothetical conversion on the *Chemical Fund* rationale resulted in a holding of *more* than 10 percent of the common. The court refused to distinguish a convertible preferred from a convertible debenture on the contention that every preferred is *per se* an "equity security."

[90] Jennings and Marsh put this intriguing *query*: "Suppose a corporation has outstanding 1,000,000 shares of listed common stock and an outstanding debenture issue which is convertible into 500,000 shares of common stock, although none of it has been converted. A owns 110,000 shares of common stock, and he purchases and sells common stock within a period of six months. Under the Chemical Fund rationale, is he subject to liability under Section 16(b) as a *10%* holder of a registered security?" R. Jennings and H. Marsh, Securities Regulation Cases and Materials (5th ed. 1982) 1332.

than 10 percent of the "class" in the court's sense? And what of the occasional convertible debentures that have voting rights?

In 1968, in the wake of the *Chemical Fund* case, the Commission recognized the result of that case by adopting a rule to the effect that, for the purpose of determining whether a person is a 10+ percent beneficial owner, he is considered to be the beneficial owner of securities of the class that he has the right to acquire "through the exercise of presently exercisable options, warrants of rights or through the conversion of presently convertible securities."[91] But the Commission has not read *Chemical Fund* as requiring any change in its traditional position that a person who apart from the formula of that case is a beneficial owner of more than 10 percent of a registered security convertible into an equity security (or of a class of stock purchase warrants) is required to file reports under §16(a).[92]

Conversion complexities aside, other questions are determined by an older rule:[93] A class of a given security is considered to consist of the total amount outstanding, exclusive of any securities of the class held by the issuer itself or a subsidiary. However, in the case of voting-trust certificates or certificates of deposit for equity securities, the class of certificates is considered to consist of the entire amount issuable for the class of equity securities that may be deposited, regardless of how many have in fact been deposited.[94]

f. "Purchase" and "Sale" [§§3(a)(13), 3(a)(14)]

In contrast to the 1933 Act, with its elaborate definitions of "sale" and "offer" and no definition at all of "purchase," §§3(a)(13) and 3(a)(14) of the 1934 Act contain parallel language on "purchase" and "sale." But they are not really definitions. All we are told is that ("unless the context otherwise requires") the two terms "include" contracts to buy "or otherwise acquire," or to sell "or otherwise dispose of." Nevertheless, the First Circuit,

---

[91] Rule 16a-2(b); Sec. Ex. Act Rel. 8325 (1968). Securities subject to such rights or conversion privileges are considered for the purpose of computing the percentage of the class owned by the particular person, but not for the purpose of computing the percentage owned by any other person. Ibid.

[92] Sec. Ex. Act Rel. 8202 (1967); Sec. Ex. Act Rel. 18,114, 23 SEC Dock. 856, 868, 873 and n. 57 (1981).

[93] Rule 16a-2(a).

[94] See Chemical Fund, Inc. v. Xerox Corp., 377 F. 2d 107, 110 (2d Cir. 1967), supra p. 652; United States v. Guterma, 281 F. 2d 742, 748-49 (2d Cir. 1960), *cert. denied,* 364 U. S. 871 ("class" does not include unissued shares reserved for exercise of options or conversion rights).

in reading the bonus clause of the 1933 Act into §3(a)(14), saw "no reason to believe that Congress intended, one year after the passage of the Securities Act, to dilute the concept of 'sale' in the Securities Exchange Act."[95]

Nice questions have been litigated with respect to fixing the time of the "purchase" and "sale" for purposes of determining the six-month period as well as computing the profit. And there is the related question of when beneficial ownership starts and stops for purposes of determining when a person who is not an officer or director must file reports under §16(a), as well as determining when any of the persons covered by §16(a) has had a change in his beneficial ownership. The criteria in the two cases, however, are not necessarily the same. The broker's or dealer's confirmation would ordinarily seem determinative in fixing the dates of *purchase and sale*. On the other hand, the opinion was early expressed by the Commission's General Counsel that *beneficial ownership* is acquired or divested when the insider "takes a firm commitment" for the purchase or sale of the security.[96]

This is no longer true so far as options (and convertible securities) are concerned. There, as we have seen, there is a rule for reporting purposes to the effect that a person is considered the beneficial owner of securities that he has a right to acquire through the exercise of currently exercisable options.[97] For §16(b) purposes, however, it is the "established rule * * * that the mere granting of an option to purchase is not a sale [or a purchase]."[98]

---

[95] Lawrence v. SEC, 398 F. 2d 276, 280 (1st Cir. 1968); see also Dasho v. Susquehanna Corp., 380 F. 2d 262, 266 (7th Cir. 1967), *cert. denied* sub nom. Bard v. Dasho, 389 U. S. 977. But cf. SEC v. Sterling Precision Corp., 393 F. 2d 214, 217-18 (2d Cir. 1968), where Judge Friendly said in holding that a redemption was not a "purchase" under §17(a)(2) of the Investment Company Act, which does not define the term:

> "Purchase" is not a peculiarly technical term and "[a]fter all, legislation when not expressed in technical terms is addressed to the common run of men and is therefore to be understood according to the sense of the thing, as the ordinary man has a right to rely on ordinary words addressed to him." Addison v. Holly Hill Fruit Products, Inc., 322 U. S. 607, 618 (1944). A party asserting that a word in a statute should be given a meaning different from what it has in the speech of common men or, in this instance, the common speech of lawyers, has the burden of showing that context or evident purpose requires this.

[96] Op. Gen. Counsel, Sec. Ex. Act Rel. 116 (1935), cited in Stella v. Graham-Paige Motors Corp., 232 F. 2d 299, 301 n. 2 (2d Cir. 1956), *cert. denied*, 352 U. S. 831.

[97] Rule 16a-2(b), supra p. 655, text at n. 91.

[98] Abrams v. Occidental Petroleum Corp., 450 F. 2d 157, 164 (2d Cir. 1971), *aff'd on other grounds* sub nom. Kern County Land Co. v. Occidental Petroleum Corp., 411 U. S. 582 (1973), set out supra p. 612. But cf. Bershad v. McDonough, 428 F. 2d 693 (7th Cir. 1970), *cert. denied*, 400 U. S. 992, which

Can the date of purchase or sale ever be fixed at a time *later* than the date of an option's exercise? In an unusual option case in which it was agreed between the company and an officer that he should be obligated to pay the price specified in the option upon his mailing of notice of exercise, but that payment and delivery might be postponed until the termination of employment, title to remain in the company and the officer to have no rights as a stockholder pending payment, the court held that the purchase had occurred upon the officer's sending of notice. Consequently there was no purchase, at the time of payment and delivery some three years later, that could be matched against a sale less than six months before that time. The court conceded that "The inclusion of executory transactions does not import the exclusion of executed ones." But that, the court said, cannot "justify finding two 'purchases' where in fact but one exists." Judge Clark stated that speculation was the only vice within the purview of §16(b), and the court held as it did on the ground that the important factor was the insider's "firm assurance that a fixed quantity [of stock] can be acquired or disposed of at a fixed price" rather than "who has title or possession or who can vote the stock or receive dividends."[99]

7. THE COMMON LAW

It is wise once in a while — especially when dealing with a body of occasionally esoteric federal law — to return to our Mother, the Common Law. For it turns out that the lady has a remarkable resilience.

DIAMOND v. OREAMUNO
New York Court of Appeals, 1969
24 N. Y. 2d 494, 248 N. E. 2d 910

Chief Judge FULD. Upon this appeal from an order denying a motion to dismiss the complaint as insufficient on its face, the

---

the *Abrams* court characterized as a case where "the 'option' [which was held to be essentially a firm sale with a delayed payment provision] was accompanied by a wink of the eye."

[99] Blau v. Ogsbury, 210 F. 2d 426, 427 (2d Cir. 1954); see also Freeman v. Decio, 584 F. 2d 186, 200 (7th Cir. 1978) (defendant "bought" optioned stock when he exercised his option and made payment, not five years later, when certain restrictions lapsed and the certificates were delivered); but cf. Booth v. Varian Associates, 334 F. 2d 1 (1st Cir. 1964), *cert. denied,* 379 U. S. 961; Newmark v. RKO General, Inc., 425 F. 2d 348 (2d Cir. 1970), *cert. denied,* 400 U. S. 854.

question presented — one of first impression in this court — is whether officers and directors may be held accountable to their corporation for gains realized by them from transactions in the company's stock as a result of their use of material inside information.

The complaint was filed by a shareholder of Management Assistance, Inc. (MAI) asserting a derivative action against a number of its officers and directors to compel an accounting for profits allegedly acquired as a result of a breach of fiduciary duty. It charges that two of the defendants — Oreamuno, chairman of the board of directors, and Gonzalez, its president — had used inside information, acquired by them solely by virtue of their positions, in order to reap large personal profits from the sale of MAI shares and that these profits rightfully belong to the corporation. Other officers and directors were joined as defendants on the ground that they acquiesced in or ratified the assertedly wrongful transactions.

MAI is in the business of financing computer installations through sale and lease back arrangements with various commercial and industrial users. Under its lease provisions, MAI was required to maintain and repair the computers but, at the time of this suit, it lacked the capacity to perform this function itself and was forced to engage the manufacturer of the computers, International Business Machines (IBM), to service the machines. As a result of a sharp increase by IBM of its charges for such service, MAI's expenses for August of 1966 rose considerably and its net earnings declined from $262,253 in July to $66,233 in August, a decrease of about 75%. This information, although earlier known to the defendants, was not made public until October of 1966. Prior to the release of the information, however, Oreamuno and Gonzalez sold off a total of 56,500 shares of their MAI stock at the then current market price of $28 a share.

After the information concerning the drop in earnings was made available to the public, the value of a share of MAI stock immediately fell from the $28 realized by the defendants to $11. Thus, the plaintiff alleges, by taking advantage of their privileged position and their access to confidential information, Oreamuno and Gonzalez were able to realize $800,000 more for their securities than they would have had this inside information not been available to them. Stating that the defendants were "forbidden to use [such] information * * * for their own personal profit or gain," the plaintiff brought this derivative action seeking to have the defendants account to the corporation for this difference. * * *

In reaching a decision in this case, we are, of course, passing only upon the sufficiency of the complaint and we necessarily accept the charges contained in that pleading as true.

It is well established, as a general proposition, that a person who acquires special knowledge or information by virtue of a confidential or fiduciary relationship with another is not free to exploit that knowledge or information for his own personal benefit but must account to his principal for any profits derived therefrom. (See, e. g., *Byrne* v. *Barrett,* 268 N. Y. 199.) This, in turn, is merely a corollary of the broader principle, inherent in the nature of the fiduciary relationship, that prohibits a trustee or agent from extracting secret profits from his position of trust.

In support of their claim that the complaint fails to state a cause of action, the defendants take the position that, although it is admittedly wrong for an officer or director to use his position to obtain trading profits for himself in the stock of his corporation, the action ascribed to them did not injure or damage MAI in any way. Accordingly, the defendants continue, the corporation should not be permitted to recover the proceeds. They acknowledge that, by virtue of the exclusive access which officers and directors have to inside information, they possess an unfair advantage over other shareholders and, particularly, the persons who had purchased the stock from them but, they contend, the corporation itself was unaffected and, for that reason, a derivative action is an inappropriate remedy.

It is true that the complaint before us does not contain any allegation of damages to the corporation but this has never been considered to be an essential requirement for a cause of action founded on a breach of fiduciary duty. (See, e. g., *Matter of People [Bond & Mtge. Guar. Co.],* 303 N. Y. 423, 431; *Wendt* v. *Fischer,* 243 N. Y. 439, 443; *Dutton* v. *Willner,* 52 N. Y. 312, 319.) This is because the function of such an action, unlike an ordinary tort or contract case, is not merely to *compensate* the plaintiff for wrongs committed by the defendant but, as this court declared many years ago (*Dutton* v. *Willner,* 52 N. Y. 312, 319, supra), "to *prevent* them, by removing from agents and trustees all inducement to attempt dealing for their own benefit in matters which they have undertaken for others, or to which their agency or trust relates." (Emphasis supplied.)

Just as a trustee has no right to retain for himself the profits yielded by property placed in his possession but must account to his beneficiaries, a corporate fiduciary, who is entrusted with potentially valuable information, may not appropriate that asset for his own use even though, in so doing, he causes no injury to the corporation. The primary concern, in a case such as this, is not to determine whether the corporation has been damaged but to decide, as between the corporation and the defendants, who has a higher claim to the proceeds derived from the exploitation of the information. In our opinion, there can be no justification for permitting officers and directors, such as the defendants, to retain for themselves profits which, it is alleged, they derived solely from exploiting information gained by virtue of their inside position as corporate officials.

In addition, it is pertinent to observe that, despite the lack of any specific allegation of damage, it may well be inferred that the defendants' actions might have caused some harm to the enterprise. Although the corporation may have little concern with the day-to-day transactions in its shares, it has a great interest in maintaining a reputation of integrity, an image of probity, for its management and in insuring the continued public acceptance and marketability of its stock. When officers and directors abuse their position in order to gain personal profits, the effect may be to cast a cloud on the corporation's name, injure stockholder relations and undermine public regard for the corporation's securities. As Presiding Justice Botein aptly put it, in the course of his opinion for the Appellate Division, "[t]he prestige and good will of a corporation, so vital to its prosperity, may be undermined by the revelation that its chief officers had been making personal profits out of corporate events which they had not disclosed to the community of stockholders." (29 A. D. 2d, at p. 287.)

The defendants maintain that extending the prohibition against personal exploitation of a fiduciary relationship to officers and directors of a corporation will discourage such officials from maintaining a stake in the success of the corporate venture through share ownership, which, they urge, is an important incentive to proper performance of their duties. There is, however, a considerable difference between corporate officers who assume the same risks and obtain the same benefits as other shareholders and those who use their privileged position to gain special advantages not available to others. The sale of shares by the defendants for the reasons charged was not merely a wise investment decision which any prudent investor might have made. Rather, they were assertedly able in this case to profit solely because they had information which was not available to any one else — including the other shareholders whose interests they, as corporate fiduciaries, were bound to protect.

Although no appellate court in this State has had occasion to pass upon the precise question before us, the concept underlying the present cause of action is hardly a new one. (See, e. g., Securities Exchange Act of 1934 [48 U. S. Stat. 881], §16[b]; U. S. Code, tit. 15, §78p, subd. [b]; *Brophy* v. *Cities Serv. Co.,* 31 Del. Ch. 241; Restatement, 2d, Agency, §388, comment *c;* Israels, A New Look at Corporate Directorship, 24 Business Lawyer 727, 732 et seq.; Note, 54 Cornell L. Rev. 306, 309-312.) Under Federal law (Securities Exchange Act of 1934, §16[b]), for example, it is conclusively presumed that, when a director, officer or 10% shareholder buys and sells securities of his corporation within a six-month period, he is trading on inside information. The remedy which the Federal statute provides in that situation is precisely the same as that sought in the present case under State law, namely, an action brought by the corporation or on its behalf to recover all profits derived from the transactions.

* * *

Although the provisions of section 16(b) may not apply to all cases of trading on inside information, it demonstrates that a derivative action can be an effective method for dealing with such abuses which may be used to accomplish a similar purpose in cases not specifically covered by the statute. In *Brophy* v. *Cities Serv. Co.* (31 Del. Ch. 241, supra), for example, the Chancery Court of Delaware allowed a similar remedy in a situation not covered by the Federal legislation. One of the defendants in that case was an employee who had acquired inside information that the corporate plaintiff was about to enter the market and purchase its own shares. On the basis of this confidential information, the employee, who was not an officer and, hence, not liable under Federal law, bought a large block of shares and, after the corporation's purchases had caused the price to rise, resold them at a profit. The court sustained the complaint in a derivative action brought for an accounting, stating that "[p]ublic policy will not permit an employee occupying a position of trust and confidence toward his employer to abuse that relation to his own profit, regardless of whether his employer suffers a loss" (31 Del. Ch. at p. 246). And a similar view has been expressed in the Restatement, 2d, Agency (§388, comment *c*):

    c. *Use of confidential information.* An agent who acquires confidential information in the course of his employment or in violation of his duties has a duty * * * to account for any

profits made by the use of such information, although this does
not harm the principal. * * * So, if [a corporate officer] has
"inside" information that the corporation is about to purchase
or sell securities, or to declare or to pass a dividend, profits made
by him in stock transactions undertaken because of his knowledge
are held in constructive trust for the principal.

In the present case, the defendants may be able to avoid liability
to the corporation under section 16(b) of the Federal law since
they had held the MAI shares for more than six months prior to
the sales. Nevertheless, the alleged use of the inside information
to dispose of their stock at a price considerably higher than its
known value constituted the same sort of "abuse of a fiduciary
relationship" as is condemned by the Federal law. Sitting as we
are in this case as a court of equity, we should not hesitate to permit an action to prevent any unjust enrichment realized by the
defendants from their allegedly wrongful act.

*   *   *

An examination of the Federal regulatory scheme refutes the
contention that it was designed to establish any particular remedy
as exclusive. * * *

Accepting the truth of the complaint's allegations, there is no
question but that the defendants were guilty of withholding material information from the purchasers of the shares and, indeed, the
defendants acknowledge that the facts asserted constitute a violation of rule 10b-5. The remedies which the Federal law provides
for such violation, however, are rather limited. An action could
be brought, in an exceptional case, by the SEC for injunctive relief.
This, in fact, is what happened in the *Texas Gulf Sulphur* case
(401 F. 2d 833, supra). The purpose of such an action, however,
would appear to be more to establish a principle than to provide
a regular method of enforcement. A class action under the Federal
rule might be a more effective remedy but the mechanics of such
an action have, as far as we have been able to ascertain, not yet
been worked out by the Federal courts and several questions relating thereto have never been resolved. These include the definition
of the class entitled to bring such an action, the measure of damages, the administration of the fund which would be recovered
and its distribution to the members of the class. (See Note, 54
Cornell L. Rev. 306, 309, supra.) Of course, any individual purchaser, who could prove his own injury as a result of a rule 10b-5

violation can bring an action for rescission but we have not been referred to a single case in which such an action has been successfully prosecuted where the public sale of securities is involved. The reason for this is that sales of securities, whether through a stock exchange or over-the-counter, are characteristically anonymous transactions, usually handled through brokers, and the matching of the ultimate buyer with the ultimate seller presents virtually insurmountable obstacles. Thus, unless a section 16(b) violation is also present, the Federal law does not yet provide a really effective remedy.

In view of the practical difficulties inherent in an action under the Federal law, the desirability of creating an effective common-law remedy is manifest. "Dishonest directors should not find absolution from retributive justice," Ballantine observed in his work on Corporations ([rev. ed., 1946], p. 216), "by concealing their identity from their victims under the mask of the stock exchange." There is ample room in a situation such as is here presented for a "private Attorney General" to come forward and enforce proper behavior on the part of corporate officials through the medium of the derivative action brought in the name of the corporation. (See, e. g., *Associated Ind.* v. *Ickes,* 134 F. 2d 694, 704; *Cherner* v. *Transitron Electronic Corp.,* 201 F. Supp. 934, 936.) Only by sanctioning such a cause of action will there be any effective method to prevent the type of abuse of corporate office complained of in this case.

There is nothing in the Federal law which indicates that it was intended to limit the power of the States to fashion additional remedies to effectuate similar purposes. Although the impact of Federal securities regulation has on occasion been said to have created a "Federal corporation law," in fact, its effect on the duties and obligations of directors and officers and their relation to the corporation and its shareholders is only occasional and peripheral. The primary source of the law in this area ever remains that of the State which created the corporation. Indeed, Congress expressly provided against any implication that it intended to preempt the field by declaring, in section 28(a) of the Securities Exchange Act of 1934 (48 U. S. Code 903), that "[t]he rights and remedies provided by this title shall be in addition to any and all other rights and remedies that may exist at law or in equity."

Nor should we be deterred, in formulating a State remedy, by the defendants' claim of possible double liability. Certainly, as already indicated, if the sales in question were publicly made, the likelihood that a suit will be brought by purchasers of the shares is quite remote. But, even if it were not, the mere possibility of such a suit is not a defense nor does it render the complaint insufficient. It is not unusual for an action to be brought to recover a fund which may be subject to a superior claim by a third party. If that be the situation, a defendant should not be permitted to retain the fund for his own use on the chance that such a party may eventually appear. A defendant's course, if he wishes to protect himself against double liability, is to interplead any and all possible claimants and bind them to the judgment (CPLR 1006, subd. [b]).

In any event, though, no suggestion has been made either in brief or on oral argument that any purchaser has come forward with a claim against the defendants or even that anyone is in a position to advance such a claim.[1] As we have stated, the defendants' assertion that such a party may come forward at some future date is not a basis for permitting them to retain for their own benefit the fruits of their allegedly wrongful acts. For all that appears, the present derivative action is the only effective remedy now available against the abuse by these defendants of their privileged position.

*   *   *

Order affirmed, etc.

This case confounded those lawyers who had relegated *Brophy,* the 1949 Delaware Chancery case cited by the court,[100] to the indignity of a "sport." It does seem surprising that it took twenty years for another square holding like *Brophy* to find its way into the law reports. Nevertheless, *Diamond* indicates — as a commentator put it who confused the Common Law Mother's sex but was blessed with a deft pen — that, "Like the fertile octogenarian, state law has made a belated comeback."[101] The New York court, un-

---

[1] In the absence of any such appearance by adverse claimants, we need not now decide whether the corporation's recovery would be affected by any amounts which might have to be refunded by the defendant to the injured purchasers.

[100] In Davidge v. White, 377 F. Supp. 1084, 1089-90 (S. D. N. Y. 1974), the court denied a motion to dismiss under Delaware law on the ground that the *Brophy* principle applied even when the defendant had resigned as a director before he finished selling. See also Thomas v. Roblin Industries, Inc. 520 F. 2d 1393, 1399 (3d Cir. 1975) (dictum).

[101] 55 Va. L. Rev. 1520, 1533 (1969).

derstandably, found satisfaction in observing that *its* writ was not limited to specified types of insiders, or to publicly held companies, or to in-and-out (or out-and-in) transactions within a specified interval.

Indeed, it may be contended with considerable cogency that a director who knows that *another* director is buying or selling securities on the basis of confidential information may incur liability for failure to prevent his colleague's action, since a trustee has an obligation to prevent a co-trustee from violating their joint trust.[102] Or the same result might be reached on another line of reasoning: since it is the corporation that has a cause of action against a fiduciary who uses confidential information for his own profit, it is the obligation of each director to protect that corporate asset or he will be liable for failure to do so.

Soon the Second Circuit, applying a nonexistent Florida law, carried *Diamond* a step further by holding the president's "tippees" (one of whom was a "tippee" thrice removed) on a "common enterprise" theory, reenforced by the rule that one who knowingly participates in a breach of fiduciary obligation is liable jointly and severally with the fiduciary.[103] But this thrust forward also planted the seed of something like a counterrevolution. For the Supreme Court remanded with instructions to certify the question of Florida law to the Florida Supreme Court under Florida's reception statute.[104] And the Florida court disavowed not only *Diamond's* extension but also *Diamond* itself.[105] Then the Seventh Circuit, applying Indiana law, came out the same way.[106]

Even so, one may hazard the guess that the future lies with

[102] It was on this line of reasoning that the Court in Mosser v. Darrow, 341 U. S. 267 (1951), surcharged a Chapter X trustee under general equitable principles for profits derived by two employees from trading in securities of the debtor's subsidiaries although he had considered their services indispensable and had expressly agreed that they could continue to trade and there was no hint of personal profit on his part.

[103] Schein v. Chasen, 478 F. 2d 817 (2d Cir. 1973), *vacated* sub nom. Lehman Bros. v. Schein, 416 U. S. 386 (1974); but cf. Frigitemp Corp. v. Financial Dynamics Fund, Inc., 524 F. 2d 275, 278-79 (2d Cir. 1975) (*Diamond* and *Schein* were distinguished under New York law where plaintiff alleged only that defendants had entered into a "special relationship" with the company by receiving confidential information in connection with their purchase of its debentures); Walton v. Morgan Stanley & Co., Inc., 623 F. 2d 796 (2d Cir. 1980) (same result under Delaware law where investment banker for acquiring company used information obtained in confidence from friendly target to buy target stock for its own account).

[104] Lehman Brothers v. Schein, 416 U. S. 386 (1974).

[105] Schein v. Chasen, 313 So. 2d 739 (Fla. 1975).

[106] Freeman v. Decio, 584 F. 2d 186 (7th Cir. 1978).

Diamond rather than its rivals. There is authority for the proposition that directors of an investment company are in breach of
their fiduciary duty when they trade in *portfolio* securities.[107] And
there are signs of movement in the less volatile British courts.[108]

[107] McMenomy v. Ryden, 276 Minn. 55, 148 N. W. 2d 804 (1967); Cambridge Fund, Inc. v. Abella, 501 F. Supp. 598, 631 (S. D. N. Y. 1980) (Del.
law); cf. SEC v. Midwest Technical Development Corp., CCH Fed. Sec. L.
Rep. ¶91,252 (D. Minn. 1963). The 1970 amendments added §17(j) to the
Investment Company Act in order to subject these practices to SEC rulemaking on a fraud-prevention basis. And in 1980 the Commission adopted
Rule 17j-1 in order *(inter alia)* to require registered investment companies,
their advisers, and principal underwriters to adopt written codes of ethics,
which are specifically mentioned in §17(j), and to require "access persons" (as
defined) to report their transactions to their investment companies, advisers
or principal underwriters. Inv. Co. Act Rel. 11,421, 21 SEC Dock. 488 (1980).
Section 12(j) is reflected in Code §1411(e). See 2 Code 568-69.

[108] See cases cited in L. Gower, Principles of Modern Company Law (4th
ed. 1979) 595 n. 65. Thirty years ago Professor Gower cited the *Brophy*
case in support of the view he had long held that principles of agency law
are sufficiently elastic to enable a company to recover from its director any
profit that he has made on share dealings as a result of the misuse of confidential information, although he added that no English company had yet
had the temerity to make such a claim. Gower, Investor Protection in the
U. S. A., 15 Mod. L. Rev. 446, 453 (1952). See also Beck, The Saga of Peso
Silver Mines: Corporate Opportunity Reconsidered, 49 Can. B. Rev. 80 (1971);
Beck, The Quickening of Fiduciary Obligation: Canadian Aero Services v.
O'Malley, 53 Can. B. Rev. 771 (1975).

CHAPTER 8

MARKET REGULATION

A. STRUCTURE OF THE MARKETS

POSER, RESTRUCTURING THE STOCK MARKETS: A
CRITICAL LOOK AT THE SEC'S NATIONAL
MARKET SYSTEM, PART I
56 New York University Law Review 881 (1981)[a]

*   *   *

I. THE STRUCTURE OF THE SECURITIES MARKETS

It is generally believed that the securities markets serve an important economic purpose; they provide a mechanism by which business enterprises obtain equity capital and long-term debt from the public. These markets may be divided into two distinct parts: the new-issue markets, in which companies typically issue securities to the public through syndicates of dealers and underwriters; and the trading markets, in which these securities may be bought and sold after they have been issued.

The economic function of the trading markets is to create liquidity — a market characteristic that enables investors to dispose of or purchase securities at a price reasonably related to the preceding price. For the sale of a new issue of securities to succeed, prospective purchasers must have a reasonable assurance of liquidity in the market for the security. Thus, the success of new-issue markets is dependent on the effectiveness of trading markets. In

C. 8A   [a]ED.: Copyright 1981 by New York University Law Review and reprinted with its permission. This excellent article by Professor Norman S. Poser of Brooklyn Law School, sometimes Assistant Director of the SEC's Division of Trading and Markets and Executive Vice President of the American Stock Exchange, is reprinted from the December 1981 issue of the New York University Law Review with permission of the editors and of Professor Poser. The greater portion of the article appears infra p. 749.

addition, since trading markets are a price setting mechanism, they facilitate the use of securities as collateral for loans, determine the price at which a company is able to issue additional securities, and establish a basis for the valuation of securities for taxation and other purposes. * * *

Crucial to an understanding of the NMS [National Market System] proposal is an appreciation of the differences and relationship between these two types of markets and among the different trading markets. The trading markets consist of ten stock exchanges[b] and the over-the-counter market, a structure that came into existence by an evolutionary process, substantially free of government regulation. During the nineteenth century, stock exchanges were organized in various parts of the country and served as loci for the trading of securities; the stock exchanges were supplemented by a loosely organized "over-the-counter" market, in which brokers and dealers executed transactions in their offices, in coffee houses, and in other public places. The evolution of these markets was affected only minimally by the advent of federal securities regulation in the 1930's. This legislation was designed to protect investors from market abuses rather than to alter the structure of the markets. The growth, combination, and attrition of particular stock exchanges and the over-the-counter market that had occurred prior to the enactment of the Exchange Act continued in the years that followed.

A.   THE STOCK EXCHANGES

A stock exchange provides a place and organized rules and procedures for buying and selling securities that have been admitted to trading. Only members may trade on a stock exchange floor, either for their own accounts or for customers. Since each stock exchange has a limited number of members, a stock exchange membership, or "seat," has a value, and there is a market for exchange seats.

There is no bar to a company's listing its securities on more than one stock exchange.[c] * * *

The securities of a company may also be traded on a stock exchange even though the company has not applied to the stock exchange for a listing and actually opposes being listed. This

[b] ED.: Section 5 of the 1934 Act requires all exchanges to be registered with the SEC as "national securities exchanges" — one of the several categories of "self-regulatory organizations" (see p. 689 infra) — unless they are exempted.

[c] ED.: On the listing requirements, see p. 483 supra.

occurs when a stock exchange on its own initiative admits the company's securities to "unlisted" trading. Since 1934, the granting of such "unlisted trading privileges" has been subject to the approval of the SEC, which has broad discretion as to whether or not to grant applications. For many years, the Commission's policy has been to grant applications by stock exchanges for unlisted trading privileges freely if the class of securities is already listed on another exchange. This SEC policy has made it possible for many securities to be traded on more than one stock exchange (i. e., to be "dually traded").[d]

[d] ED.: All trading, on or off exchanges, started as "unlisted" trading, in the sense that brokers and dealers needed no "by your leave" from an issuer in order to make a market in its outstanding securities. It took time for exchanges to become established and to develop to the point where they were able to exact the filing of listing applications, with certain conditions, from issuers that sought the prestige and advantages of an exchange market. At the same time, the exchanges were reluctant to surrender their unlisted trading. Indeed, except for the New York Stock Exchange (the "Big Board"), most of the exchanges would have had difficulty surviving in 1934 with only listed trading. It was not until 1910 that the New York Stock Exchange abolished its unlisted department, in accordance with the recommendation made the year before in the report of the committee that had been appointed by Governor Hughes of New York to investigate speculation in securities and commodities. J. Meeker, The Work of the Stock Exchange (rev. ed. 1930) 72; Report of the Governor's Committee on Speculation in Securities and Commodities (N. Y. 1909), reprinted in W. Van Antwerp, The Stock Exchange from Within (1913) 415. And in 1934 even the New York Curb Exchange (now the American Stock Exchange), the second largest exchange, was trading 1689 securities unlisted as compared with only 374 that were listed. Stock Exchange Regulation, Hearings before House Com. on Int. & For. Commerce on H. R. 7852 and H. R. 8720, 73d Cong., 2d Sess. (1934) 374.

It was quite natural, therefore, that the Curb should lead the attack, in which most of the smaller exchanges joined, against the proposal of the original 1934 bills to solve the problem of unlisted trading by abolishing it outright. Id. at 367 et seq., 511. As a result, §12(f) of the statute as enacted in 1934 directed the Commission to study the problem and report to Congress with its recommendations by January 3, 1936. See SEC, Report on Trading in Unlisted Securities upon Exchanges (1936). And §12(f), as amended in 1936, again in 1964 and mostly recently in 1975, today specifies three types of unlisted trading, the first two of which have remained fairly constant from the beginning:

(A) Securities that were traded unlisted before July 1, 1964 (originally March 1, 1934), are automatically "grandfathered" in. The theory in 1934 was that the Curb and the regional exchanges should be able to survive the gradual attrition of their unlisted issues as a result of liquidations and mergers and so on while they were building up their listed departments. That theory proved sound, to the extent that §902 of the Code deletes the "grandfather" treatment (subject to the Commission's general exemptive authority) in view of the small number of "unlisted only" issues left: only 38 issues of 37 companies as of September 1, 1978, of which 12 were §12(g) companies and 7 had their common stock listed with unlisted trading privileges for their preferred. 1 Code 365-66.

(B) The second category consists of dually traded securities — those listed

The markets maintained by the stock exchanges are known as "auction" markets because buy and sell orders are executed at a central location at the best available price. Typically, an investor who wishes to buy or sell an exchange-listed security will give the order to an exchange member who, acting as a broker (i. e., agent), executes the order on the floor of the exchange and receives a commission as compensation. Most of these orders are either "market" orders, which require the broker to execute the order promptly at the best available price, or "limit" orders, which require the broker to buy at or below or sell at or above the stated (limit) price. It is possible, then, for the orders of a buying customer and a selling customer, each represented by a broker, to meet on the floor of an exchange without the intervention of a professional dealer (i. e., one who trades for his own account). In 1971, however, forty-five percent of all share volume on the New York Stock Exchange involved a member firm's buying or selling for its own account on one side of the trade; the remaining fifty-five percent represented customers' orders executed without the participation of a member acting as principal.

Specialist units (or specialists), which compose a category of exchange member firms separately registered with the exchange, play a unique and important role in the trading process. When a stock has been admitted to trading, the exchange "allocates" it to a particular specialist. During trading hours, the specialist remains at a particular location, or "post," on the trading floor of the exchange, and any member who wishes to trade in a stock,

---

on one exchange and admitted to unlisted trading on another with the Commission's approval under a "fair and orderly markets" test. See Ludlow Corp. v. SEC, 604 F. 2d 704 (D. C. Cir. 1979). Since listing on the first exchange means full registration, the Commission has acted almost routinely in this area. See Midwest Stock Exchange, Sec. Ex. Act Rel. 16,422, 18 SEC Dock. 1323 (1979) (910 securities).

(C) With the enactment of §12(g) in 1964, the logic of the second category should apply as well to over-the-counter as to listed securities as long as they are registered. But, far from creating a third category of unlisted trading based on §12(g) registration, Congress in 1964 deleted the third category based on §15(d) reporting (see p. 490 supra) that had existed as virtually a dead letter since 1936. It took eleven years and the force of the 1975 amendments for the §12(g) logic to prevail, so that the Commission may today extend unlisted trading privileges to any security registered under §12 if it makes a series of specified findings related (*inter alia*) to competitive factors, "fair and orderly markets," and development of a national market system. Pacific Resources, Inc., Sec. Ex. Act Rel. 17,584, 22 SEC Dock. 283 (1981). (The issuer's consent is not required, although it may petition the Commission under §12(f)(4) for *termination* of unlisted trading privileges.) But the Commission characterized the *Pacific Resources* case, where the stock was concurrently *delisted* on the issuer's application, as a "limited exception to its general policy" of deferring action in Clause (C) cases pending further developments in a national market system. Id. at 284. See p. 791 infra.

either for his own account or for the account of a customer, will go to the post of the specialist in that stock. All trading in the stock takes place at that location.

Exchange transactions in a given stock may be executed between two brokers standing in the trading "crowd" at the post or between a broker and a specialist. The specialist may trade for his own account or for a customer's account. If an order cannot be executed readily at a price reasonably close to the price of the preceding sale (i. e., if a customer cannot be found for the other side of a transaction at such price), the exchange rules require the specialist to buy or sell the securities for his own account. The specialist, using his own capital, thus offsets temporary imbalances between supply and demand by making bids to buy stock and offers to sell stock. His role is essentially passive, in that he buys or sells when approached by an exchange member. For example, a specialist may bid for a stock at a price of fifty and offer stock at a price of fifty and one-half. In that case he will buy when requested to do so at fifty and he will sell at fifty and one-half. His profit is the fifty-cents-per-share difference between the bid and the offer.

The specialist also acts as a broker, handling for other brokers limit order that cannot be executed at the current market price.[e] Typically, a broker holding a customer's limit order to buy at a price below the current market price (or to sell above the current market price) will leave the order with the specialist. If the market moves down (or up) to the customer's limit, the specialist will execute the order for the customer and will receive a portion of the commission paid by the customer. The aggregate of limit orders held by a specialist in a particular stock is known as his "book." Exchange rules "protect" customers' orders left on the book against an inferior execution. Thus, if a customer's buy order at a price of twenty-five is on the book, no transaction may take place on that exchange at a price lower than twenty-five before that customer's order is executed. As we will see, one goal of the NMS is to extend this "public limit order protection" so that customers are protected against inferior executions in any market, not just on the exchange where the order is held.

All exchange transactions, whether or not a specialist participates, are immediately reported to an exchange employee for transmission to the ticker tape and to data reporting services,

---

[e] ED.: Legend has it that the first specialist was a member of the New York Stock Exchange who broke his leg in the 1870s, whereupon he took up a position at the spot where Western Union stock was traded and handled orders there for other members.

which electronically disseminate reports of completed transactions to subscribers. Prices and volume of completed stock exchange transactions are summarized daily in the financial press.

In 1979, over 99.6% of the dollar amount of trading on U. S. stock exchanges occurred on six stock exchanges: the New York [NYSE], American [Amex], Midwest, Pacific, Philadelphia, and Boston stock exchanges.[23] Although these stock exchanges have identical legal statuses since all are registered with the SEC as national securities exchanges, they have very different characteristics and economic functions.

1. The New York Stock Exchange

The NYSE is the dominant stock exchange, and its dominance is perhaps the key determinant of the structure of the securities markets. In 1979, its 374 member firms that do business directly with the public comprised only fifteen percent of all broker-dealer firms doing business with the public and yet accounted for ninety percent of the total assets and eighty-five percent of the gross revenues of such broker-dealer firms. Since most NYSE member firms doing business with the public are also members of the Amex and one or more of the regional stock exchanges, the various exchanges cannot be thought of as separate entities in the sense of distinct groups of firms competing with each other. On the other hand, many of the broker-dealers that act as specialists on the Amex and most of the specialists on the regional exchanges are not members of the NYSE.

The NYSE also is dominant in terms of companies whose shares are traded on it. The 1,915 companies whose securities were listed on the NYSE as of September 30, 1980 include most of the largest industrial and commercial enterprises in the United States. As of December 31, 1979, the value of all common stocks listed on the NYSE was $960.6 billion, compared to $57.8 billion for stocks listed on the Amex and $3.9 billion for stocks exclusively listed on other exchanges. Similarly, the NYSE dwarfs the other stock exchanges in terms of trading activity. In 1979, the NYSE accounted for 83.65% of total dollar volume of trading on U.S. stock exchanges, the Amex 6.93%, and the regional exchanges 9.42%.

2. The American Stock Exchange

The Amex, having lower listing standards than those of the NYSE, generally serves as a market for the securities of smaller,

---

[23] See [1979-1980] SEC Ann. Rep. 126. The other four registered securities exchanges are the Chicago Board Options Exchange and the Cincinnati, Intermountain (in Salt Lake City), and Spokane Stock Exchanges.

newer companies than those listed on the NYSE. As of September 30, 1980, there were 1,034 companies with stocks traded on the Amex. Many Amex-listed companies, when they meet the more stringent NYSE listing requirements, transfer their listings to the latter exchange. Until 1976, rules of the NYSE and Amex prohibited their respective members from dealing on the exchange in any securities listed on the other exchange; in addition, Amex rules provided for automatic delisting of any security whose listing was transferred to the NYSE.

Despite repeal of these rules, there is virtually no trading on the Amex in securities listed on NYSE. Few companies whose securities are listed on the Amex choose to remain listed on that exchange after obtaining a NYSE listing, presumably because they believe that concentration of all trading in a single market will produce more liquidity for their shares. Moreover, the Amex, not wishing to enter into direct competition with its powerful neighbor, has an informal policy of not actively seeking listings or unlisted trading privileges in NYSE-listed securities. Finally, NYSE member firms, many of which are also Amex members, have been unwilling to direct to the Amex any portion of their customers' orders in securities listed on both exchanges. Unlike the four regional exchanges, then, the Amex is not a derivative market, but is, rather, a "primary" market (i. e., the principal market for the securities that are admitted to trading) established on a much smaller scale than the NYSE.

3. *The Regional Exchanges*

The Midwest (MSE), Pacific (PSE), Philadelphia (Phlx), and Boston (BSE) stock exchanges are known as regional exchanges. Although the regional exchanges began their existence as primary markets for the securities of companies of local geographic interest, most trading on the regional exchanges since the 1930's has been in securities whose primary market is the NYSE or, to a lesser extent, the Amex. Despite their concentration in NYSE and Amex issues, the regional exchanges account for only a small percentage of the total trading in shares listed on these two primary markets. In 1980, approximately ten percent of the total share volume in stocks listed on the NYSE represented regional exchange transactions, while the corresponding figure for Amex-listed issues was only about two percent. Dual trading is thus of great importance to the regional exchanges, but the regional exchanges are relatively minor factors in the trading of securities of national importance. The markets for listed stocks thus comprise a high concentrated industry that is dominated by the NYSE and its member firms.

The regional exchanges, like the NYSE and Amex, use the specialist system. The method of trading stocks whose primary market is the NYSE or Amex, however, differs substantially from the trading system in the primary markets. These differences reflect the fact that the regional exchange markets in these stocks are derivative markets. According to a study conducted by the SEC in the 1960's, the prices at which transactions were executed on the regional exchanges normally were based on the prices in the primary markets. Although regional exchange specialists participated as dealers in the overwhelming majority of all transactions, typically they did not publish quotations competing with those on the primary markets; instead, "[a] variety of special arrangements have been developed * * * by which a customer may be enabled to receive a price substantially equivalent to that in the primary market * * * ." Because of these characteristics, the secondary markets that were made on the regional exchanges did not tend to affect the primary market prices of dually traded securities. It is essential to keep in mind this role of the regional exchanges as derivative markets when considering the proposal to establish an NMS.

B.   THE OVER-THE-COUNTER MARKET

The over-the-counter (OTC) market is the residual securities market. All transactions that do not take place on a stock exchange are said to be executed in the OTC market. Like their counterparts in the securities exchanges, brokers and dealers trading in the OTC market are required to register with the SEC, but they need not become stock exchange members. In practice, most broker-dealers serving the public are members of the National Association of Securities Dealers (NASD), a national securities association registered with the SEC.

A broad spectrum of securities is traded OTC, including government and corporate bonds and shares of various industrial and commercial enterprises. Common stocks traded solely OTC tend to represent smaller and newer companies than those listed on stock exchanges. Additionally, there is some OTC trading in securities that are traded on one or more stock exchanges; such trading is referred to as the "third market." In 1980, third market transactions represented just over two percent of all trading in NYSE-listed stocks and one percent of all trading in Amex-listed stocks. The proposal for an NMS contemplates that the OTC market, including the third market, will be an integral part of the system.

OTC transactions are usually executed over the telephone by broker-dealers in their offices.[f] If an investor wishes to buy an OTC security, the broker-dealer handling his account may sell him the security as principal out of the broker-dealer's inventory. If the broker-dealer does not own the security [which is the usual case], he will buy the security from a "market maker" in that security and sell the security to his customer, acting either as an agent and charging a commission, or as a principal and charging a markup to the customer.[45] A market maker is a broker-dealer who holds himself out "as being willing to buy and sell [a] security for his own account on a regular or continuous basis."[46] Market makers' quotations in the 2,700 most active OTC securities are made through the National Association of Securities Dealers Automated Quotations (NASDAQ), a computerized quotations system operated by the NASD.[47]

There are several important differences between the stock exchanges and the OTC market. First and most obvious, each stock exchange provides a central place for trading where all customers' buy and sell orders meet and the highest buy order is matched against the lowest sell order in an auction-type process; the OTC market, on the other hand, is a decentralized market in which

---

[f] ED.: Dealers' counters have gone the way of the grocers.' "Over-the-telephone" would be a more accurate description. Indeed, the German term is precisely that: *Telefonhandel.*

[45] * * * This works the same way when a customer sells a security, except that the broker charges a markdown rather than a markup.

[46] [Sec. Ex. Act §3(a)(38).]

[47] NASDAQ, inaugurated in 1971, displays continuously updated price quotations (i. e., bids and offers) on a real-time basis on cathode ray terminals located in subscribers' offices. There are three kinds of terminals, designated as Levels I, II, and III. Market makers use Level III terminals, consisting of a cathode ray tube ("CRT") screen and a keyboard. Using the keyboard, a market maker can enter, change, or cancel any bid or offer for any stock in which he makes a market. All current bids and offers entered by market makers in that stock are shown on the CRT screen. Level II terminals, used by brokers and dealers who do not act as market makers, provide the same information as Level III terminals but do not permit inputting of bids and offers. Thus, any firm subscribing to the NASDAQ system can see at a glance which market maker in any NASDAQ-quoted stock is disseminating the highest bid and the lowest offer. Level I terminals, which are used by salespeople of brokerage firms, show only a "representative" bid and offer in each NASDAQ-quoted stock and provide both salesperson and customer with an approximate idea of the price at which a security can be bought or sold. When a brokerage firm receives an order from a customer to buy (or sell) a stock that is quoted in the NASDAQ system, it checks the Level II or III screen to ascertain the market maker quoting the best current offer (or bid). The firm then telephones the market maker and executes the transaction with him. In doing so, the brokerage firm will either act as an agent for its customer and charge the customer a commission, or as a principal and purchase the security for its own account and immediately resell at a price markup to the customer who placed the order. * * *

transactions are negotiated among broker-dealers and between broker-dealers and their customers. Second, unlike the stock exchanges, the OTC market provides no way for the orders of a buying customer and a selling customer to meet directly; in virtually every OTC transaction, there is a professional dealer who participates by buying or selling for his own account. The OTC market is therefore known as a "dealer" market.

A third significant difference between the two types of markets is that although there is typically only one specialist allocated to a particular stock on any given stock exchange, it is common for there to be several market makers (sometimes as many as thirty) in a particular OTC stock. A fourth difference is that the specialist at his central location on the exchange floor is in a position to see and participate in all trading, whereas the OTC market maker in his office can become a participant in trading only by issuing competitive quotations that will induce other broker-dealers to trade with him. Finally, the OTC market, unlike the stock exchanges, does not have a ticker tape showing the price and volume of completed transactions as they occur.[49] OTC stock tables appearing in the newspapers provide the daily volume of activity and the bids and offers of market makers, but not the prices of completed transactions.

*   *   *

B.   BROKER-DEALER REGISTRATION

1.   THE REGISTRATION REQUIREMENT

We have already noted the original §15 and the 1936 amendment that, among other things, codified the Commission's rules on broker-dealer registration.[1] As it now reads, §15(a)(1) requires the registration of any broker or dealer that wants to "effect any transactions in, or to induce or attempt to induce the purchase or sale of, any security (other than an exempted security or commercial paper, bankers' acceptances, or commercial bills)."[2] Be-

---

[49] Under SEC rule 11Aa2-1, * * * approximately 40 OTC stocks will be included in the national market system by February 1, 1982. * * * Last-sale information will be shown for these securities. * * *

C. 8B   [1] See p. 463 supra.

[2] See generally N. Wolfson, R. Phillips, and T. Russo, Regulation of Brokers, Dealers and Securities Markets (1977); E. Weiss, Registration and Regulation of Brokers and Dealers (1965).

fore the 1975 amendments this section applied only to transactions "otherwise than on a national securities exchange" — which is to say, over the counter — on the theory that the Commission already had some control over members of registered exchanges. But most member firms registered anyway, if only because they also effect some transactions over the counter. And the over-the-counter limitation was eliminated in 1975.[3]

The Commission has developed a registration application form, Form BD, that is used also by the NASD and virtually all the states.[4] Within 45 days after the filing of an "application" (not, be it noted, a "registration statement"), the Commission must either grant registration or institute denial proceedings, and any proceedings must be concluded within 120 days of filing.[5] Before 1975 there were no qualifications to be met except, since the 1964 amendments, for broker-dealers (and their associates) who were not members of the NASD.[6] In effect, any person who had managed to stay clear of a securities violation had a right to become registered or to be associated with a registered firm.[7] Today §15(b)(7) imposes "operational capability" standards on all registered broker-dealers; requires that they and their natural person associates meet Commission-imposed standards of "training, experience, competence, and * * * other qualifications"; and specifically authorizes the Commission to administer tests to any or all classes of broker-dealers and their associates. But the Commission has yet to take final action on a set of minimum qualifications for all registered broker-dealers and their associates that it proposed in 1977 and again in 1982.[8] Meanwhile it continues to rely on the NASD and the exchanges to examine *their* members together with their associates, and on its own rule for nonmembers of the NASD.[9]

---

[3] The Commission, however, has exempted a specialist's block purchases and sales off the floor when the transactions are approved by the exchange and effected under its rules to help the specialist to maintain a fair and orderly market. This makes it unnecessary for a specialist who effects no other over-the-counter transactions in nonexempted securities to register. Rule 15a-3.

[4] Sec. Ex. Act Rel. 11,424, 7 SEC Dock. 2 (1975).

[5] The Commission may extend the 120 days for a period up to 90 more days. §15(b)(1).

[6] Rule 15b8-1. On the NASD, see p. 689 infra.

[7] The grounds for denial were the same as those for revocation or other discipline of broker-dealers already registered — grounds that were themselves extended somewhat in 1975. See pp. 699-701 infra.

[8] Sec. Ex. Act Rel. 13,629, 12 SEC Dock. 1017 (1977); Sec. Ex. Act Rel. 18,710, 25 SEC Dock. 220 (1982).

[9] That rule, Rule 15b8-1, accepts any examination "deemed by the Com-

For administrative purposes the Commission applies the entity theory to all registrants and applicants for registration, whether they are organized as corporations or partnerships or in some other form. Consistently with that theory, the Commission does not separately register partners, officers, directors, and the like. And, unlike virtually all the state statutes, the 1934 Act does not call for a new registration annually or (except for nonmembers of the NASD, as we shall see) require the separate registration of salesmen, or contain any bonding provision.

2.   DEFINITIONS OF "BROKER" AND "DEALER" [§§3(a)(4), 3(a)(5)]

Unlike the artificial definition of "dealer" in §2(12) of the 1933 Act to include a broker, the 1934 Act defines the two terms separately and in accordance with the normal distinction between agent and principal. Section 3(a)(4) defines a "broker" as "any person engaged in the business of effecting transactions in securities for the account of others." Section 3(a)(5) defines a "dealer" as "any person engaged in the business of buying and selling securities for his own account, through a broker or otherwise"; and, to be on the safe side, it specifically excludes "any person insofar as he buys or sells securities for his own account, either individually or in some fiduciary capacity, but not as a part of a regular business."

a.   What Constitutes a "Business"

The phrase "engaged in the business" is common to both definitions, with the adjective "regular" modifying the word "business" in the second part of the "dealer" definition. With or

---

mission * * * to be a satisfactory alternative." And a great deal of uniformity has developed among the Commission's Rule 15b8-1 examination and those administered by the NASD, the exchanges and most of the states. Sec. Ex. Act Rel. 13,629, 12 SEC Dock. 1017, 1021 n. 22 (1977). Section 15(b)(7), as enacted in 1975, authorizes the Commission to cooperate with the exchanges and the NASD in devising and administering tests, and to require that *their* tests be passed even though they might be more stringent than the Commission's requirements, which were regarded as a floor. For a history of the several examination requirements, see id. at 1018-21. The Commission anticipated in proposing its general rule that it would continue to delegate the responsibility for developing and administering all required examinations to the NASD, subject to the Commission's review. Id. at 1021.

without the adjective, the phrase connotes a certain regularity of participation in purchasing and selling activities rather than a few isolated transactions. But there is no requirement that the purchase and sale of securities be a person's *principal* business or the principal source of his income. It may be a small percentage of his business. A large firm that handles securities, commodities, and perhaps real estate and insurance may do more securities business than a small firm that is exclusively a broker-dealer in securities.

A similar question has been before the Supreme Court under §32 of the Banking Act of 1933,[10] under which the Board of Governors of the Federal Reserve System removed certain persons as directors of a national bank on the ground that they were employees of a firm "primarily engaged" in the underwriting of securities. The firm, Eastman Dillon & Co., had ranked ninth among the ninety-four leading investment bankers in its participation in bond underwritings in 1943 and for a time during that year had ranked first. Nevertheless, for an indefinite period only about 15 percent of its total transactions, in both number and market value of the securities, had consisted of underwriting; and during its preceding two and one-half fiscal years the portion of its total gross income attributable to underwriting had been only 26, 32, and 39 percent, compared with 42, 47, and 40 percent from brokerage. Pointing out that §32 would apply to no one if "primarily" were construed to mean more than half, the Court read it to mean "essentially" or "fundamentally." "One might as well say," Justice Douglas remarked, "that a professional man is not 'primarily engaged' in his profession though he holds himself out to serve all comers and devotes substantial time to the practice but makes the greater share of his income on the stock market."[11] The case is, of course, stronger under the 1934 Act because of the absence of the word "primarily."

There is likewise nothing in the concept of a "business" to preclude a person from being a broker or dealer because he handles, with regularity, only a single issue of securities.[12] In principle, therefore, an issuer selling and buying its own securities with sufficient regularity might itself be a "dealer." Although

---

[10] 48 Stat. 194 (1933), 49 Stat. 709 (1935), 12 U. S. C. §78.

[11] Board of Governors of Federal Reserve System v. Agnew, 329 U. S. 441, 446-47 (1947).

[12] Fogel v. Chestnutt, 533 F. 2d 731, 750-52 (2d Cir. 1975) (investment adviser placing buy and sell orders for investment company's portfolio).

there might be peculiar circumstances that would justify this position, the Commission has apparently considered that no purpose would be served by requiring the ordinary open-end investment company, which is continually issuing and redeeming its securities, to register under §15 of the 1934 Act as well as under the 1933 and 1940 Acts. Moreover, the Commission has not required the registration of trust companies whose business is substantially confined to the investment of trust funds even though transactions of purchase and sale are effected as an incident of that activity.[13]

b.   The Dealer-Trader Distinction

One aspect of the "business" concept is the matter of drawing the line between a "dealer" and a trader — an ordinary investor who buys and sells for his own account with some frequency. This question does not arise so far as a "broker" is concerned, since the ordinary investor does not effect transactions for the account of others. But when do a person's trading activities make him a "dealer"?

There is no ready distinction. However, a dealer has characteristic attributes: He ordinarily tries to obtain a regular clientele. He is apt to transact a substantial portion of his business directly with investors rather than with other dealers or through exchange members, although there are "marketmakers" who trade principally with other professionals. A dealer ordinarily holds himself out as one engaged in buying and selling securities at a regular place of business. And his business (except when he participates in underwriting) is ordinarily characterized by a regular turnover, whereas a trader's transactions are generally more irregular in both volume and time. A trader, on the other hand, does not handle other people's money or securities; he does not "make a market"; and he does not furnish the services that are usually provided by dealers, such as quoting the market, rendering incidental investment advice, extending or arranging for the extension of credit, and lending securities to customers. Needless to say, a person does not have to exhibit all or any given number of these dealer characteristics in order to be considered a dealer.[14]

---

[13] Cf. Sec. Ex. Act Rel. 11,742, 8 SEC Dock. 82 (1975).

[14] Eastside Church of Christ v. National Plan, Inc., 391 F. 2d 357, 361-62 (5th Cir. 1968), *cert. denied* sub nom. Church of Christ v. National Plan, Inc., 393 U. S. 913, *judgment for plaintiff on remand aff'd* sub nom. McGregor Blvd. Church of Christ v. Walling, 428 F. 2d 401 (5th Cir. 1970).

c.   Officials or Salesmen of an Issuer Making a Direct Distribution

Under the state statutes other than the Uniform Securities Act an issuer distributing its securities directly to the public without the intervention of a broker or dealer is sometimes defined as a "dealer" itself, as we have seen.[15] This is not true under the 1934 Act, because such an issuer, even if it is considered to be engaged in the "business" of *selling* securities, does not do any *buying* as required by the definition. However, since buying is not an element of the definition of "broker," the question remains whether the individual officials or employees who do the actual selling for the issuer are themselves required to register. In the states they frequently have to register as salesmen but not, ordinarily, as brokers. Whether they have to register with the SEC as brokers is a question of fact in each case, depending on much the same considerations that determine whether they are "servants" or "independent contractors" at common law. The test for determining whether they are "underwriters" within the meaning of the 1933 Act may be different; for an employee might be considered a person who "sells for" the issuer within the contemplation of §2(11) of the 1933 Act without being "engaged in the business" of selling securities for purposes of §3(a)(5) of the 1934 Act.[16]

d.   Banks

Both definitions exclude banks. The term "bank" as defined in the Act, however, does not include a nonbanking holding com-

---

[15] See p. 16 supra.

[16] The Commission has ruled that an insurance company must register as a broker-dealer if it distributes variable annuities representing interests in a separate account. "Since the insurance company engages in the purchase and sale of its own portfolio securities, will make purchases and sales of securities for the portfolio of the Separate Account, and will distribute the variable annuity interests of which it and the Separate Account are co-issuers [see p. 219 supra], the insurance company would be a 'broker' as defined in Section 3(a)(4) of the Act as well as a 'dealer' as defined in Section 3(a)(5) of the Act." Sec. Ex. Act Rel. 8389 (1968). A substantial number of insurance companies (usually their brokerage affiliates) are registered. But, whatever the validity of the "broker" interpretation, the "dealer" interpretation seems to say too much in the light of the administrative line that the Commission has always drawn between dealers and active traders. See p. 680 supra. Although mutual funds, universities, and other institutional investors likewise engage in the purchase and sale of securities for their portfolios, the Commission has never suggested that they are "dealers" on that account alone.

pany or a subsidiary or other affiliate of a bank.[17] Nor, arguably, does it include a foreign bank.[18]

e. Finders and Investment Advisers

Although a pure finder may "induce the purchase or sale of" a security within the meaning of §15(a), he is not normally a "broker" because he effects no transactions. He merely brings buyer and seller together.[19] Nor is an investment adviser ordinarily a "broker," whether or not he is registered under the Investment Advisers Act. He may even place orders with brokers or dealers for his clients' accounts as long as he receives no special compensation for that service. The question becomes close when his total compensation is based on individual transactions.

3. EXEMPTIONS

Section 15(a) does not apply to a broker or dealer "whose business is exclusively intrastate" or to any transaction in "an exempted security[20] or commercial paper, bankers' acceptances, or commercial bills."

a. Exclusively Intrastate Business

If all the broker's or dealer's securities activities and customers are confined to a single state, he need not register. This precludes him, for example, from selling even once as underwriter for an out-of-state issuer[21] or as broker for an out-of-state customer.[22] And this is equally true with respect to his selling to or buying

---

[17] §3(a)(6).

[18] United States v. Weisscredit Banca Commerciale e d'Investimenti, 325 F. Supp. 1384, 1390-92 (S. D. N. Y. 1971). But cf., under the exemption in §3(a)(2) of the 1933 Act for securities of a "bank" (a term not defined in that Act), Taiyo Kobe Bank, Ltd., CCH Fed. Sec. L. Rep. ¶80,264 (letter 1975); Barclay's Bank Int'l, Ltd., Sec. Reg. L. Rep. No. 488, p. C-2 (letter 1979); Bank of Nova Scotia, 14 Sec. Reg. L. Rep. 116 (letter 1982).

[19] But the emphasis is on "pure." See SEC, Final Report on Bank Securities Activities (1977) 53-54, 101-02; Augustine and Fass, Finder's Fees in Security and Real Estate Transactions, 35 Bus. Law. 485 (1980).

[20] See p. 476 supra.

[21] Professional Investors, Inc., 37 SEC 173, 175-76 (1956).

[22] Whitehall Corp., 38 SEC 259, 271 (1958).

for an out-of-state customer.[23] He may not even offer his customers securities acquired on a stock exchange or mutual fund
shares, since those securities are continually moving in the stream
of interstate commerce.[24] However, as long as the buying and
selling customers are all in the same state, the issuers of the securities need not be local companies.[25] And the exemption is not
destroyed by sending the securities to out-of-state transfer agents.
Nor is it necessary that the *market* in the securities dealt in be
exclusively or predominantly intrastate. That was the test under
the rules adopted by the Commission pursuant to the original
§15, but it was dropped in the 1936 amendment of the statute.[26]

The intrastate exemption is eliminated in the Code, as it would
have been in the bill that passed the Senate in connection with
the 1964 amendments.[27] The Code's comments repeat the reasons
given at that time:

(a) The scope of the exemption is very narrow and only a
small number can avail themselves of it. (b) Intrastate broker-
dealers are subject to $X_{15}(c)(1)$-(3), so that the Commission has
responsibility for their conduct in important respects without
adequate means to discharge that responsibility; it is anomalous
that they are subject to the capital requirements without being
required to keep records in order to show how much capital they
have; as a result, the Commission must devote a disproportionate
amount of time and effort to fraud investigations involving
intrastate firms. (c) They often involve themselves in inadvertent

---

[23] Capital Funds, Inc., 42 SEC 245, 249 (1964), *aff'd* sub nom. Capital Funds,
Inc. v. SEC, 348 F. 2d 582 (8th Cir. 1965).

[24] See SEC Legislation, 1963, Hearings before Subcom. of Senate Com. on
Banking & Currency on S. 1642, 88th Cong., 1st Sess. (1963) 388.

[25] The SEC advised the Senate committee in 1963: "In order to qualify
for the exclusively intrastate exemption, a broker-dealer must not only deal
with customers who are exclusively within the State, but he must deal exclusively in securities originating in the State." Ibid. The Commission, it is
understood, did not mean to imply that the issuer always had to be a local
company. The reference may have been to something like the "coming to
rest" concept in the hands of local *buying* customers. See E. Weiss, Registration and Regulation of Brokers and Dealers (1955) 14-15. That is to say, a
resident who buys out-of-state securities with a view to distribution and
resells them to a dealer in the state destroys the dealer's intrastate exemption,
presumably on the theory that the dealer has been made a step in the distribution of an out-of-state issue.

[26] Sec. Ex. Act Rel. 721 (1936).

[27] The House committee deleted the repeal provision on the ground of
lack of demonstrated need, fortified by the false ground of preemption.
H. R. Rep. No. 1418, 88th Cong., 2d Sess. (1964) 12. But there would have
been no more preemption than there is today with *inter*state broker-dealers
— which is to say, none at all.

violations of X15(a)(1) by overstepping the bounds of the exemption. (d) When they do observe those restrictions, they are limited in the securities they can recommend and sell to customers. (e) If the Commission is to have the authority to suspend for a limited period, a broker or dealer should not be able to ameliorate a suspension by conducting an intrastate business.[28]

To these reasons the Code's comments add two more: the "critically important * * * limitation of SIPC protection[29] to customers of *registered* broker-dealers," and the fact that "many states have no broker-dealer inspection programs."[30]

b. Combination of Exemptions

The intrastate exemption is destroyed by effecting an *inter*state transaction even in an *exempted* security. For the *entire* business of the broker-dealer must be exclusively intrastate. It follows also from the Commission's construction of the intrastate exemption that a broker-dealer relying on it may not effect a transaction on an exchange in another state even though he places the order through a member of that exchange with an office in his own state. Nor may he effect a transaction on an exchange even in the *same* state if the security is in fact sold to or purchased from a person *outside* the state. Since one cannot ordinarily tell who the other party will be in an exchange transaction, a broker-dealer relying on the intrastate exemption is precluded, in effect, from engaging in exchange transactions altogether.[31]

C. GOVERNMENTAL *VERSUS* SELF-REGULATION

1. THE PHILOSOPHY

At best, direct regulation of a complex business through the machinery of government — even with the advantages that the administrative process offers over traditional enforcement by grand jury investigation and criminal prosecution — divides black from white with a buzz saw when the many variations of gray call for a surgeon's scalpel. Although appropriate provisions on regis-

---

[28] 1 Code 324.
[29] See p. 41 supra.
[30] 1 Code 325.
[31] Professional Investors, Inc., 37 SEC 173, 175-76 (1956).

tration and fraud-prevention furnish an indispensable foundation for an adequate system of control, they must be supplemented by regulation on an ethical plane in order "to protect the investor and the honest dealer alike from dishonest and unfair practices by the submarginal element in the industry" and "to cope with those methods of doing business which, while technically outside the area of definite illegality, are nevertheless unfair both to customer and to decent competitor, and are seriously damaging to the mechanism of the free and open market."[1] And regulation of the *ethics* of an industry means a substantial degree of *self*-regulation, properly supervised by government.

Witness the early symbiosis between the Commission under the chairmanship of William O. Douglas and the New York Stock Exchange. In late 1937, after negotiations with the exchanges on their voluntary reorganization had broken down, Mr. Douglas gave a statement to the press in which he stressed the importance of reaching an early decision on where to draw the line between the two kinds of regulation:

> Ideally, of course, it would be desirable to have all national securities exchanges so organized and so imbued with the public interest that it would be possible and even desirable to entrust to them a great deal of the actual regulation and enforcement within their own field, leaving the government free to perform a supervisory or residual role. * * *
>
> At the present time, however, I have doubts as to the desirability, from the standpoint of the public interest, of assigning to exchanges such a vital role in the nation's economic affairs, before they adopt programs of action designed to justify their existence solely upon their value as public market places. I have always regarded the exchanges as the scales upon which that great national resource, invested capital, is weighed and evalued. Scales of such importance must be tamper-proof, with no concealed springs — and there must be no laying on of hands. * * * Such an important instrument in our economic welfare * * * must be surrounded by adequate safeguards. Yet it is also obvious that such restrictions must be consistent with the profit motive, which in final analysis is and must remain the driving force in our economy.

* * *

Operating as private-membership associations, exchanges have always administered their affairs in much the same manner as

C. 8C   [1] S. Rep. No. 1455 at 3 and H. R. Rep. No. 2307 at 4, 75th Cong., 3d Sess. (1938).

private clubs. For a business so vested with the public interest, this traditional method has become archaic.[2]

Elsewhere Mr. Douglas expressed his philosophy as

letting the exchanges take the leadership with Government playing a residual role. Government would keep the shotgun, so to speak, behind the door, loaded, well oiled, cleaned, ready for use but with the hope it would never have to be used.[3]

The New York Stock Exchange responded by appointing a committee to study the need of reorganization. The committee's report of January 1938 recognized the public nature of the exchanges and provided a plan for a modern administrative organization. But Wall Street seems to be synonymous with drama. Six weeks later, before any action could be taken, one of the most spectacular incidents in the financial history of the United States focused the country's attention on the state of the Exchange housekeeping. The firm of Richard Whitney & Co. was suspended by the Exchange for insolvency and Whitney himself was soon on his way to Sing Sing for grand larceny. Whitney was a former president and a pillar of the Exchange. An investigation disclosed that his firm had been insolvent for at least three and a half years, largely as a result of his personal speculations in ventures "involving such widely diverse products as applejack, peat humus, and mineral colloids."[4] To raise funds for these ventures, Whitney had begun misappropriating a customer's securities as far back as 1926, and his misappropriations had become a steady practice by 1936, extending even to securities of the Exchange's gratuity fund, of which he was a trustee. Many persons high in the administration of the Exchange were aware of Whitney's financial difficulty for a considerable time before his suspension, but the "unwritten code of silence" protected him until, as in a detective "thriller," the accident of a groundless rumor led to the discovery of his embezzlement.[5] The Commission immediately began an investigation, during which public hearings were held from time to time during the months of April through June.[6]

In March 1938 the Exchange voted a radically revised constitution, which became effective in May. It provided for a paid non-

---

[2] Douglas, Democracy and Finance (J. Allen, ed. 1940) 64-65.
[3] Id. at 82.
[4] 10 SEC Ann. Rep. 37 (1944).
[5] 1 SEC, In the Matter of Richard Whitney (1938) 181-82.
[6] The Commission published its three-volume report on November 1, 1938. SEC, In the Matter of Richard Whitney (1938).

member president, executive staffs to carry out functions formerly conducted by the governors sitting as committee members, direct representation of the public on the board of governors, increased representation of Exchange firms doing business with the public, and a greatly simplified administrative structure. Similar reorganizations had been effected earlier the same year by the then Detroit and Chicago Stock Exchanges, and the New York Curb Exchange (now the American Stock Exchange) followed early in 1939.[7]

The year 1938 also saw the implementation of the mixed regulatory philosophy when Congress in the Maloney Act added §15A to the 1934 Act in order to provide for the registration of one or more "national securities associations" that would perform for the over-the-counter market the same self-regulatory function performed by the "national securities exchanges." As each of the legislative committees then put it:

> The committee believes that there are two alternative programs by which this problem [of adequate regulation of the over-the-counter market] could be met. The first would involve a pronounced expansion of the organization of the Securities and Exchange Commission; the multiplication of branch offices; a large increase in the expenditure of public funds; an increase in the problem of avoiding the evils of bureaucracy; and a minute, detailed, and rigid regulation of business conduct by law. It might very well mean expanding the present process of registration of brokers and dealers with the Commission to include the proscription not only of the dishonest, but also of those unwilling or unable to conform to rigid standards of financial responsibility, professional conduct, and technical proficiency.[8] The second of these alternative programs, which the committee believes distinctly preferable to the first, is embodied in S. 3255. This program is based upon cooperative regulation, in which the task will be largely performed by representative organizations of investment bankers, dealers, and brokers, with the Government exercising appropriate supervision in the public interest, and exercising supplementary powers of direct regulation. In the concept of a really well organized and well-conducted stock exchange, under the supervision provided by the Securities Exchange Act of 1934, one may perceive something of the possibilities of such a program.[9]

---

[7] See 4 SEC Ann. Rep. 20 (1938); 5 id. 37 (1939).

[8] Congress was to do substantially this in 1975, as we have seen. See p. 677 supra.

[9] S. Rep. No. 1455 at 3-4 and H. R. Rep. No. 2307 at 4-5, 75th Cong., 3d Sess. (1938).

In short, as Senator Maloney of Connecticut emphasized, the scheme is not so much self-regulation as "cooperative regulation."[10]

The idea is encapsulated in the provision in §§6(b)(5) and 15A (b)(6) that has always conditioned registration as a "national securities exchange" or a "national securities association" on its having rules designed "to promote just and equitable principles of trade."[11] The 1975 amendments, which greatly enlarged the statute, altered the mix somewhat away from self-regulation.[12] But the statutory scheme continues to give the Commission considerable discretion in drawing the line between self-regulation and direct governmental supervision.

---

[10] 83 Cong. Rec. 4451 (1938). For a discussion of the two regulatory philosophies in the very similar — yet very different — British milieu, see L. Gower, Review of Investor Protection: A Discussion Document (1982) (commissioned by the Secretary of State for Trade).

[11] See N. Y. Stock Ex. Const., Art. I, §2(a), CCH N. Y. Stock Exchange Guide ¶1002; NASD Rules of Fair Practice, Art. III, §1, CCH NASD Manual ¶2151. In Todd v. SEC, 557 F. 2d 1008, 1013 (3d Cir. 1977), the court sustained the NASD rule against a charge of vagueness. Some of these rules of the NASD are patterned after the Commission's fraud and disclosure rules. Indeed, the NASD has uniformly considered — and properly so in the SEC's view — that violations of the statutes and the Commission's rules on fair dealing and fraud constitute conduct inconsistent with "just and equitable principles of trade" and hence violations of Article III, §1. Valley Forge Securities Co., Inc., 41 SEC 486, 488 (1963); see CCH NASD Manual ¶2152 at 2053.

Other NASD strictures are more specific. One of the most significant is its "suitability" requirement, which will be considered later in connection with the emergent role of the SEC itself in that area. NASD Rules of Fair Practice, Art. III, §2, id., ¶2152. Another, for example, prohibits the payment of any reward to an employee of another firm without that firm's consent. Art. III, §10, id., ¶2160; see H. C. Keister & Co., 43 SEC 164, 166-71 (1966).

The NASD has also issued a number of significant "interpretations" of Article III, §1, dealing with such matters as the review of corporate financing (CCH NASD Manual ¶2151.02) and the "free riding" problem with respect to "hot issues" (id., ¶2151.06), where the aim is to assure a good faith offer to the public for a reasonable time at the prospectus price. On the latter subject, see 5 Loss 3455-61. On the NASD's mark-up policy, see p. 956 infra.

[12] See generally 2 SEC, Study of Unsafe and Unsound Practices of Brokers and Dealers (1971) c. 9, pp. 27-36. "Self-regulation," the Commission there said, "has worked, but not well enough." Id. at 27. For an assessment of the performance of the New York Stock Exchange and the NASD, see Securities Industry Study, H. R. Rep. No. 92-1519 (1972) ("Moss Report") 91-100. That report found the Commission frequently negotiating with the exchanges "as if they were coordinate sovereign bodies." Id. at 113. A concurrent report on the Senate side concluded: "The concept of industry self-regulation, subject to SEC oversight, is well-adapted to dealing with problems of conduct and ethics, but is not well-adapted to dealing with general economic questions involving competitive interrelationships among firms within the industry." Securities Industry Study, Report of Subcom. on Securities, S. Com. on Banking, Housing & Urban Affairs, 93d Cong., 1st Sess. (1973) 2-3.

2. THE SELF-REGULATORY ORGANIZATIONS

a. National Securities Exchanges

There are now four kinds of self-regulatory organizations. The original 1934 Act contemplated only one, the national securities exchanges.

b. National Association of Securities Dealers (Herein of "SECO" Broker-Dealers)

The second came in 1938 with the addition of §15A, which, as we have just seen, invented the "national securities association."

The resemblance of §15A to the 1933 National Industrial Recovery Act — as well as the genesis of the NASD in that short-lived statute — is not accidental. The NRA code of fair competition for investment bankers, which was approved by the President in November 1933, embraced all over-the-counter brokers and dealers. In March 1934 the President approved an amendment to the code that incorporated certain rules of fair practice. After the demise of the NRA in the spring of 1935, representatives of the industry discussed with the Commission the feasibility of a new organization that would undertake to perpetuate the objectives of the code by regulating brokers and dealers in a manner comparable to the exchanges' regulation of their members. The result was the formation in 1936 of the Investment Bankers Conference, Inc., as a Delaware nonprofit corporation. And the Conference and the Commission jointly sponsored the bill that became the Maloney Act. That act was approved June 25, 1938. In the summer of 1939 the Investment Bankers Conference, Inc., became the National Association of Securities Dealers, Inc., also a Delaware nonprofit corporation. On August 7, 1939, after a public hearing, the Commission found that the NASD satisfied the statutory standards and granted its application for registration.[13] No other association has ever applied for registration.

---

[13] National Assn. of Securities Dealers, Inc., 5 SEC 627 (1939). It is interesting, on this background, that no constitutional attack was made on §15A until the early 1950s, when the challenge received short shrift. In the light of the statutory provisions concerning the Commission's power to disapprove the NASD's rules according to reasonably fixed standards, as well as the Commission's review of any disciplinary action, the Second Circuit saw no merit in a contention that §15A involved an unconstitutional delegation of power to the NASD. R. H. Johnson & Co. v. SEC, 198 F. 2d 690, 695 (2d Cir. 1952),

An interesting technique was used to get the great bulk of the over-the-counter broker-dealer community to put their heads in the lion's mouth by subjecting themselves to the risks and expense of an additional regulatory and disciplinary system. First of all, the leaders of the industry — the major underwriting firms that had been active in the Conference — favored the scheme. Secondly, the proponents, in effect, got an antitrust exemption inserted into the statute. Section 15A(i) as enacted in 1938 (now §15A(e)(1) as amended technically in 1975) provides:

> The rules of a registered securities association may provide that no member thereof shall deal with any nonmember professional * * * except at the same prices, for the same commissions or fees, and on the same terms and conditions as are by such member accorded to the general public.

And §15A(n) provided:

> If any provision of this section is in conflict with any provision of any law of the United States in force on the date this section takes effect, the provision of this section shall prevail.

It is these two subsections that afforded the NASD an exemption from the antitrust laws[14] and that, according to the Commission, made it "virtually impossible for a dealer who is not a member of the NASD to participate in a distribution of important size."[15] For the rules of the Association not only require members to treat nonmember brokers and dealers the way they do members of the public, but also forbid members to "join with any non-member broker or dealer in any syndicate or group contemplating the distribution to the public of any issue of securities or any part thereof."[16] It is doubtful whether more than a few hundred of the Association's members engage in underwriting. But, entirely apart from underwriting, members may give each other the bene-

---

cert. denied, 344 U. S. 855; see also First Jersey Securities, Inc. v. Bergen, 605 F. 2d 690, 697 (3d Cir. 1979), *cert. denied* sub nom. First Jersey Securities, Inc. v. Biunno, 444 U. S. 1074; Sorrell v. SEC, 679 F. 2d 1323 (9th Cir. 1982).

[14] See United States v. Socony-Vacuum Oil Co., Inc., 310 U. S. 150, 227 n. 60 (1940); National Assn. of Securities Dealers, Inc., 19 SEC 424, 478 n. 9 (1945); but cf. Harwell v. Growth Programs, Inc., 451 F. 2d 240, 245-47 (5th Cir. 1971), *modified per curiam*, 459 F. 2d 461 (5th Cir. 1972), *cert. denied* sub nom. NASD v. Harwell, 409 U. S. 876.

[15] National Assn. of Securities Dealers, Inc., 19 SEC 424, 441 (1945).

[16] NASD Rules of Fair Practice, Art. III, §25, CCH NASD Manual ¶2175. In its opinion granting the NASD's application for registration, the Commission did not comment on the extension of this rule beyond the literal language of §15A(i) (now §15A(e)(1)). National Assn. of Securities Dealers, Inc., 5 SEC 627, 632 (1939).

fit of special discounts in ordinary trading that they do not give to the general public and hence may not give to nonmember brokers and dealers. And there is the distribution of investment company shares to be considered.[17]

Congress deleted §15A(n) in the 1975 amendments, apparently on the theory that it should be left to the courts to prick out the extent to which an antitrust exemption is to be implied from §15A(e)(1). But everybody seems to be proceeding on the assumption that an exemption survives. Although the Supreme Court said in 1963 that "Repeal [of the antitrust laws] is to be regarded as implied only if necessary to make the Securities Exchange Act work, and even then only to the minimum extent necessary,"[18] it carefully left open the antitrust question as applied to §15A, with its provision for Commission "jurisdiction and ensuing judicial review for scrutiny of a particular exchange ruling."[19] And the Commission later embraced that distinction.[20]

In 1945 the NASD emulated the major exchanges by requiring the registration with itself of members' representatives.[21] And in 1956 it instituted an elementary written examination requirement for all members and representatives, which has been developed since.[22]

"Over the years," the then Chairman of the SEC said in 1975, speaking of both the NASD and the exchanges, "the Commission has had a sort of love-hate relationship with these self-regulators."[23] For they are, after all, only half self-regulatory organizations. And, apart from the inevitable lack of universal harmony even in that capacity, they are half trade associations. "Finlandized" to an extent they may be; but they are not SEC satellites.

At any rate, the Commission, in connection with the events leading to the 1964 amendments, was concerned that a significant number of registered broker-dealers was avoiding the self-regulation component of the statutory scheme by simply not joining the

---

[17] No member may purchase any security of an open-end investment company from a nonmember underwriter at a discount, and no member underwriter may sell any such security to a nonmember broker-dealer at a discount. NASD Rules of Fair Practice, Art. III, §26(c), CCH NASD Manual ¶2176.

[18] Silver v. New York Stock Exchange, 373 U. S. 341, 357 (1963).

[19] Id. at 358 n. 12.

[20] C. A. Benson & Co., Inc., 42 SEC 107, 112 (1964); cf. Gordon v. New York Stock Exchange, Inc., 422 U. S. 659 (1975) (fixed stock exchange commissions).

[21] See National Assn. of Securities Dealers, Inc., 20 SEC 508 (1945), *petition for review denied per curiam,* 4 SEC Jud. Dec. 669 (2d Cir. 1946).

[22] See c. 8B n. 9 supra.

[23] Garrett, The Markets: Nationalization or Centralization? (address before N. Y. Chamber of Commerce & Industry, New York, Mar. 20, 1975) 11.

NASD. As of February 28, 1962, 1035 of the 5785 registered broker-dealers were not members. Of the 1035, about 40 percent were either new firms that had not become active or existing firms that had gone out of business but had not yet withdrawn their registrations; about 9 percent were exchange members that presumably did a very limited over-the-counter business, and that in any event were subject to discipline by their exchanges; and about 20 percent were primarily in businesses like real estate, oil royalties, savings and loan shares, and insurance. But this left some 200 or 300 firms that were actively engaged in the securities business without membership in either the NASD or an exchange. And not all of these were small. Some of the mutual fund selling organizations, for example, were of considerable dimension.[24] So the closing of this gap became one of the objectives of the Securities Acts Amendments of 1964. Just as §12(g) attacked the discrepancy between the exchange and over-the-counter markets as far as the *disclosure*-oriented provisions (§§12, 13, 14, and 16) are concerned, a series of amendments of §§15 and 15A was designed to put the two markets more nearly on the same level as far as the *regulatory* features of the statute are concerned.

One aspect of this regulatory line-straightening took the form of a provision, in the bill as it was passed by the Senate, that would have amended §15(a) simply to require all registered broker-dealers to be members of a registered securities association.[25] Consistently with the position it had taken in 1938, the SEC favored this approach because of its concern about "having the Federal Government get too deeply involved in this question of qualifications of persons."[26] But a number of investment companies objected strenuously to the principle of compulsory membership in any trade association.[27] In the event, they outsmarted themselves. As the then Chairman of the SEC later indicated, some of the investment company lobbyists had not anticipated the suggestion of the Chairman of the House Commerce Committee that the alternative was direct SEC regulation on an *ethical* plane.[28]

That is what eventuated in the form (as renumbered and

[24] SEC Legislation, 1963, Hearings before Subcom. of Senate Com. on Banking & Currency on S. 1642, 88th Cong., 1st Sess. (1963) 43-45.

[25] S. 1642, 88th Cong. (1963) §6(a). This had been recommended by the Special Study. 1 SEC, Report of Special Study of Securities Markets, H. R. Doc. No. 95, 88th Cong., 1st Sess. (1963) 159.

[26] 1 Investor Protection, Hearings before Subcom. of House Com. on Int. & For. Commerce on H. R. 6789, H. R. 6793, S. 1642, 88th Cong., 1st Sess. (1963) 251; see also 2 id. at 1216-19 (1963-64).

[27] H. R. Rep. No. 1418, 88th Cong., 2d Sess. (1964) 3.

[28] W. Cary, Politics and the Regulatory Agencies (1967) 108-10.

amended in 1975) of new §15(b)(8) and (9) — which the industry promptly dubbed the "SECO provisions" (pronounced "see-co") by way of referring to those broker-dealers that are subject to the "SEC only." Roughly paralleling §15A as concurrently amended in 1964 and again in 1975, they gave the Commission a considerable amount of unwanted authority:

(1) SECO broker-dealers were subjected to SEC qualification standards in 1964, eleven years before broker-dealers generally were so treated in the 1975 amendments.[29]

(2) The Commission itself is authorized to adopt rules designed "to promote just and equitable principles of trade" and "to remove impediments to and perfect the mechanism of a free and open market."[30] One of those rules (which parallels the NASD's registration of members' representatives) requires every "SECO" broker-dealer to file a form with the Commission on behalf of every associate.[31]

(3) The Commission is directed to prescribe whatever reasonable fees and charges may be necessary to defray costs of the additional regulatory duties required to be performed by the Commission.[32]

All this, of course, represents a step backward from the 1938 decision to leave the regulation of ethics to the industry itself in the first instance. And, quite apart from regulatory philosophy, it creates anomalies. To be sure, the Commission was inevitably placed in the "ethics business" when the original §15A gave it jurisdiction to review NASD disciplinary proceedings for violation of its ethical strictures. But now a willful violation of the SECO rules is quite literally a *felony* under the penalty provision, §32(a), which covers "any rule or regulation" under the Act. And we shall see in the chapter on civil liability that violation of a self-regulatory organization rule may be less likely to create a private right of action than violation of an SEC rule, even of the SECO variety.[33]

[29] See p. 677 supra.

[30] §15(b)(9); Rules 15b10-1 to 15b10-12. These include a rule requiring "high standards of commercial honor and just and equitable principles of trade" (Rule 15b10-2); a suitability rule (Rule 15b10-3, infra p. 972); and a fidelity bond requirement (Rule 15b10-11). These rules are still numbered "15b10" although the §15(b)(10) of 1964 became §15(b)(9) in 1975.

[31] Rule 15b8-1. A uniform form (U-4) has been developed that is used also by all the exchanges, the NASD and 46 states. Sec. Ex. Act Rel. 11,424, 7 SEC Dock. 2 (1975); Sec. Ex. Act Rel. 17,383, 21 SEC Dock. 977 (1980); see Association of Investment Brokers v. SEC, 676 F. 2d 857 (D. C. Cir. 1982).

[32] §15(b)(8); Rules 15b9-1, 15b9-2.

[33] See p. 1157 infra.

For these reasons those who worked on the Code would have preferred to abandon the SECO concept.[34] But under all the circumstances, including some constitutional doubts that had been expressed, the Code makes no significant change.[35]

c.   Registered Clearing Agencies

One response to the "back office" or "paper crunch" crisis of the late 1960s and early 1970s — when more than a hundred broker-dealers were forced to close their doors or merge not because of too little but because of too much business — was the Commission's being put for the first time into the business of regulating the securities transfer and clearance processes, a subject previously left to state law. In a new §17A Congress, in recognition *(inter alia)* of new data processing and communications techniques, directed the Commission to use its authority "to facilitate the establishment of a national system for the prompt and accurate clearance and settlement of transactions in securities (other than exempted securities)."[36] This more or less parallels the direction in the new §11A (which we examine later) to "facilitate the establishment of a national market system."[37]

Section 17A requires the registration not only of transfer agents[38] but also of clearing agencies.[39] The latter give us our

---

[34] The number of SECO broker-dealers fell from 495 in 1968 to 251 in 1978. For a table breaking the totals down by categories, see 1 Code 376-77.

[35] §905(c).

[36] §17A(a)(2).

[37] §11A(a)(2); see p. 748 infra. The two subjects are treated together, with a minimum of change, in Part X of the Code.

[38] §17A(c); Rule 17Ac2-1.

[39] §17A(b). "Clearing agency" as elaborately defined in §3(a)(23) (Code §202(21)), goes well beyond the old-fashioned clearing agency that exchanges envelopes to "any person, such as a securities depository, who (i) acts as a custodian of securities in connection with a system for the central handling of securities whereby all securities of a particular class or series of any issuer deposited within the system are treated as fungible and may be transferred, loaned, or pledged by bookkeeping entry without physical delivery of securities certificates, or (ii) otherwise permits or facilitates the settlement of securities transactions or the hypothecation or lending of securities without physical delivery of securities certificates." Indeed, Congress made a bow toward the "certificateless society" by directing the Commission to use its authority (without further statutory specification) "to end the physical movement of securities certificates" in connection with settlements among brokers and dealers. §17A(e). And until Nirvana is achieved, §12(l) authorizes the Commission to regulate both the form (that is to say, whether bearer or, in the non-SEC sense, registered) and the format (that is to say, the style) of registered securities.

third category of self-regulatory organizations.[40] The relationship with the Commission here is modeled basically on that of the exchanges and the NASD. But, because so many transfer agents and clearing agencies are banks, a political compromise (reminiscent of the 1964 adoption of §12(i) with respect to the registration of bank securities) split jurisdiction between the SEC and the federal bank regulators (the Comptroller of the Currency for national and District of Columbia banks, the Board of Governors of the Federal Reserve System for state member banks, and the Federal Deposit Insurance Corporation for nonmember banks that it insures) with respect to transfer agents and clearing agencies that are banks.[41]

(1) Bank transfer agents (but not bank clearing agencies) register with their bank regulators rather than the SEC.

(2) With respect to both categories, however, the Commission has a broader rulemaking authority (anything "in furtherance of the purposes" of the statute) than the bank regulators (just "the safeguarding of securities and funds").[42] This, of course, recognizes the essentiality of all transfer agents' playing in accordance with the same rules if there is to be a national clearance and settlement system.

(3) Again with respect to both bank clearing agencies and bank transfer agents, the Commission and the bank regulators are enjoined to cooperate with each other as well as with state banking authorities;[43] and the bank regulators are given "primary responsibility" with respect to inspections and discipline.[44] They also play a role with respect to registration applications by bank clearing agencies,[45] their rule changes,[46] and (as we shall see) disciplinary proceedings.[47]

---

[40] The National Securities Clearing Corporation, the result of a merger of three clearing agencies that were wholly owned subsidiaries of the New York Stock Exchange, the American Stock Exchange, and the NASD, was granted registration in January 1977. National Securities Clearing Corp., Sec. Ex. Act Rel. 13,163, 11 SEC Dock. 1448 (1977), *aff'd and remanded* sub nom. Bradford National Clearing Corp. v. SEC, 590 F. 2d 1085 (D. C. Cir. 1978), *on remand* sub nom. National Securities Clearing Corp., Sec. Ex. Act Rel. 17,562, 22 SEC Dock. 129 (1981). This agency controls by far the preponderance of the market.

[41] It does this by an incredibly complex definition of "appropriate regulatory agency" in §3(a)(34), which the Code manages to condense from six long paragraphs to twenty lines. §202(5); see also §202(12) (definition of "bank regulator").

[42] §17A(d)(1); Rules 17Ad-1 to 17Ad-8.

[43] §17A(d)(3)(A).

[44] §17A(d)(3)(A)(ii).

[45] §19(a)(2).

[46] §19(b)(4).

[47] See p. 703 infra.

d. Municipal Securities Rulemaking Board

Until 1975 the Commission had nothing to do with state or municipal securities (generically "municipals") except for some of the fraud provisions. For they have always been exempted from registration of their securities by §3(a)(2) of the 1933 Act and §§3(a)(12) and 12(a) of the 1934 Act; and municipal broker-dealers were exempted from broker-dealer registration by §15(a)(1) of the 1934 Act. Indeed, §3(a)(2) is the only exemption in the 1933 Act that carries over to §12(2), on civil liability, though not to §17(a);[48] and municipal securities are likewise exempted from the over-the-counter broker-dealer fraud-prevention rules under §15(c)(2), though not from the narrower authority in §15(c)(1) to "define" fraudulent practices.

The 1975 amendments did not disturb this scheme so far as securities registration[49] and the fraud provisions are concerned. But they extended the SEC's jurisdiction to municipal dealers in a new §15B. Here again, the banks — which have never been kept out of the municipal securities business by the banking laws and, insofar as those laws permit them to act as brokers (not dealers) in securities generally, have always been excluded from the definition of "broker" (and, for that matter, "dealer")[50] — did not relish the prospect of SEC regulation of their municipal securities activities.

So, once more, there was a jurisdictional compromise. All municipal dealers, including banks, must register with the SEC.[51]

---

[48] See §§4 (introduction), 17(c).

[49] The so-called Tower Amendment added §15B(d) apparently to make this clear. But the language raises more questions than it answers. See Code §1105; 1 Code 442-43.

[50] In addition, municipal securities are exempted from §15A by §15A(f).

[51] (1) The interrelation of the definitions of "broker," "dealer," "municipal broker," and "municipal dealer" is confusing. See 1 Code 159-60:

> X3(a)(4) and 3(a)(5), which were not amended in 1975, define "broker" and "dealer" in terms of any "person" other than a bank. X3(a)(30) defines "municipal securities dealer" in terms of "any person" *including* a bank (that is not trading as a fiduciary). And X3(a)(31) defines "municipal securities broker" to mean a "broker" in municipals. As a result, one who uses the statute must remember (a) that any provision applicable to a "broker" includes a municipal broker; (b) that, on the other hand, a bank, not being a "broker," is not a "municipal securities broker"; (c) that a *non*bank "municipal securities dealer" comes within the term "dealer" wherever it is used, though a *bank* municipal dealer does not; and (d) that a "municipal securities dealer," as distinct from a "dealer," *may* be a bank.
>
> The Code attempts to achieve greater comprehensibility without substantive change by making the four definitions mutually exclusive

But, instead of giving the Commission rulemaking authority with respect to practices in the municipal securities business (outside the fraud areas of §§10(b) and 15(c)(1)), Congress created the Municipal Securities Rulemaking Board. This fourth of the self-regulatory organizations differs from the other three in that it has

---

(that is to say, limiting the definitions of "broker" and "dealer" in §§202(16) and 202(34) to nonmunicipals) and defining "municipal broker," without reference to the definition of "broker," in terms of any "person" other than a bank. So far as the definition of "municipal dealer" (§202(99)) is concerned, that term is used only when it is meant to cover both bank and nonbank municipal dealers; otherwise this draft refers to a "bank municipal dealer" or a "nonbank municipal dealer" (terms that do not have to be defined since their definitions are implicit in §202(99)).

As a result, it is necessary under the Code to remember only that a bank is not a "broker," "dealer" or "municipal broker" but *can* be a "municipal dealer."

(2) One may also wonder why it is that registration is required only of bank municipal *dealers,* not bank municipal *brokers.* This follows from the fact that banks, under the 1975 amendments, are not "municipal securities brokers" because they are excluded from the definition of "broker," which is used in the §3(a)(31) definition of "municipal securities broker." To refer once more to the Code's comments (1 Code 323):

The arguments against requiring the registration of bank municipal brokers are these:

(i) The problems that led to the regulation of municipals in the 1975 amendments did not concern bank activities as brokers.

(ii) Since banks do not have to register as "brokers" insofar as they effect brokerage transactions in *industrial* securities, it would seem odd to require them to register as *municipal* brokers. Indeed, the banks might well oppose registration as municipal brokers for fear that that requirement would be the entering wedge to their registration as brokers and their subjection in that capacity to the SEC unrelieved by the Municipal Board.

(iii) The Glass-Steagall Act prohibits banks from acting only as dealers, not as brokers, with an exception from the dealer prohibition so far as municipals are concerned. So in a sense it is logical here to require banks to register only insofar as they come within that exception.

The Code preserves existing law in this respect by excluding banks from the definition of "municipal broker."

(3) The term "municipal securities dealer" is defined, in §3(a)(30)(B), (a) to include only those banks that buy and sell municipals for their own account *otherwise than in a fiduciary capacity* and (b) to mean a bank's "separately identifiable department or division" (as defined by the Municipal Board under §15B(b)(2)(H) if that is the way the bank conducts its buying and selling business). The Code extends this concept to insurance companies as well — in defining not only "municipal dealer" but also "broker," "dealer," and "municipal broker" — with the Commission substituted as definer of "separately identifiable department or division." §§202(16)(B), 202(34)(C), 202(98)(B), 202(99)(C).

no members (or, as in the case of the clearing agencies, "participants"). It is purely a rulemaking agency. But to that extent its relationship to the Commission follows roughly the established pattern.

The Board consists of fifteen members appointed initially by the Commission for two-year terms and thereafter by the incumbents for terms specified in the Board's rules.[52] The Board is neatly (and neutrally) divided into thirds — with five members representing bank municipal brokers and dealers, five representing non-bank municipal brokers and dealers, and five persons not associated with a broker, dealer, or municipal dealer, at least two of the last group functioning as "public representatives" (one for municipal issuers and one for municipal security investors).

The rules that the Board is required to adopt apply equally to bank and non-bank municipal dealers *and brokers*. And they have to do with such matters as qualifications (including tests), the promotion of "just and equitable principles of trade," periodic inspections, the form and content of quotations, recordkeeping, and the Board's fees and charges. The Board's rules are enforced by the NASD.[53] But violation of the Board's rules, unlike the rules of the other self-regulatory organizations, is *unlawful;* for §15B(c)(1) provides that "no broker, dealer, or municipal securities dealer shall * * * effect any transaction in * * * any municipal security in contravention of any rule of the Board."[54]

----

[52] The rules specify a three-year term, with the terms of one-third of the Board expiring each year and a prohibition against reelection. MSRB Rule A-3(c), CCH MSRB Manual ¶3011.

[53] §§15A(b)(7), 19(g)(1).

[54] The comment to Code §1103(b), which makes such conduct "unlawful" in so many words, and for good measure extends to a municipal *broker,* states (1 Code 441):

> Any constitutional question presented by making it unlawful (which is to say, criminal subject to the "intentionally" and "recklessly" qualifications of §1821(a)(3)) to violate a rule of a self-regulatory organization is avoided by the Commission's §805 authority over self-regulatory organization rules, especially the provision in §805(b)(1) that conditions the effectiveness of all rules and rule changes on the Commission's approval.

In general, Part VII of the Code integrates today's separate registration provisions for broker-dealers and municipal dealers in §§15 and 15B of the 1934 Act, as well as investment advisers under the Advisers Act, so that a single registration form will do for all three categories. Similarly, whereas today §19 integrates only the registration and oversight provisions with respect to the self-regulatory organizations and for the rest deals separately with the four types of self-regulatory organizations (sometimes with unnecessary inconsistencies) in §§6, 15A, 15B, and 17A, the Code scheme is to gather into Part VIII all those matters that pertain to most or all of the self-regulatory organi-

3. QUALIFICATIONS AND DISCIPLINE

We have already noticed the qualifications for *becoming* one of the self-regulatory organizations. Here we shall examine the qualifications for membership in an exchange or the NASD or participation in a clearing agency, as well as the machinery for disciplining the self-regulatory organizations themselves, their officials, members, members' associates, and participants. All this, again, is manifested at two levels: the governmental (action by the SEC or one of the bank regulators) and the self-regulatory (action by an exchange, the NASD, or a clearing agency). So far as those three self-regulatory organizations are concerned, they may be both *discipliners* and *disciplined.*

(1) Under §15(b)(4) the Commission is required to discipline any registered broker-dealer if it finds in a quasi-judicial administrative proceeding that the respondent or an associate (A) has "willfully"[55] made or caused a material misstatement in any application for registration, required report, or proceeding with respect

---

zations and then in Parts IX-XI, respectively, to deal with the role of the exchanges and the NASD in market regulation, the role of clearing agencies in a national clearance system, and the role of the Municipal Board in the regulation of the municipal securities market.

Because the subject matter of Parts VII-XI had been given a great deal of attention by Congress as recently as 1975, and the amendments of that year embodied many policy determinations and compromises, those parts reflect only a modicum of substantive change.

[55] This word is a much abused legal workhorse, which appears not only in most of the disciplinary provisions but also in all the SEC statutes' penal provisions and in a few miscellaneous sections. See 2 Code 874-76. Its meaning depends on statutory context. United States v. Murdock, 290 U. S. 389, 394-95 (1933). In the §15(b)(4) context it has been held to mean "no more than that the person charged with the duty knows what he is doing." Hughes v. SEC, 174 F. 2d 969, 977 (D. C. Cir. 1949); Stead v. SEC, 444 F. 2d 713, 714-15 (10th Cir. 1971), *cert. denied,* 404 U. S. 1059; Arthur Lipper Corp. v. SEC, 547 F. 2d 171, 180 (2d Cir. 1976), *rehearing en banc denied,* 551 F. 2d 915 (2d Cir. 1977), *cert. denied,* 430 U. S. 1009; Steadman v. SEC, 603 F. 2d 1126, 1135 (5th Cir. 1979), *aff'd on other grounds,* 450 U. S. 91 (1981). But the term may well mean something more in the criminal context. See Tager v. SEC, 344 F. 2d 5, 8 (2d Cir. 1965). See generally Hawes and Sherrard, Reliance on Advice of Counsel As a Defense in Corporate and Securities Cases, 62 Va. L. Rev. 1, 82-93 (1976).

The Code abandons the term in favor of a new phrase, "without reasonable justification or excuse," for the disciplinary provisions (on the theory that that language directs attention to *conduct* rather than state of mind) and the pending Criminal Code's "intentionally or recklessly" for the penal provisions. Inevitably, however — and it is just as well — both phrases "leave room for some play as applied to varying substantive provisions, depending on their relative technicality and perhaps other factors." 2 Code 878, citing United States v. Crosby, 294 F. 2d 928 (2d Cir. 1961), *cert. denied* sub nom. Mittelman v. United States, 368 U. S. 984; see generally 5 Loss 3368-73.

to registration under the statute (or has omitted a material fact required to be stated in such an application or report), (B) has been convicted of a specified securities or similar offense within ten years before applying for registration or while registered, (C) "is" (*not* "has ever been") subject to an injunction (permanent or temporary) entered by "any court of competent jurisdiction" (presumably including a state or even a foreign court) with respect to specified securities or similar conduct, (D) "has willfully violated" any provision of the 1933 or 1934 or either 1940 Act, the rules under one of those Acts, or the rules of the Municipal Board, or "is unable to comply with any such provision," (E) has "willfully" aided or procured any such violation by another person, or "has failed reasonably to supervise" a person subject to his suspension who commits such a violation, or (F) is subject to a Commission order barring or suspending the respondent from being associated with a broker or dealer.

Clause (D) is the most significant in the sense that it empowers the Commission to litigate in its own forum. Consequently, if it appears in court at all, it is there not as an ordinary plaintiff that has to sustain the burden of proof in a District Court but as a quasi-judicial tribunal responding to a petition to review its order in a Court of Appeals, where it not only enjoys the benefit of the substantial evidence rule on questions of fact but also is given considerable deference with respect to choice of sanction.[56]

Although the Commission is *required*, not merely authorized, to act in these cases, the six bases for action are softened by being conditioned on a further finding that the particular sanction is "in the public interest." This gives the Commission a good deal of discretion, which is increased by the wide *choice* of sanctions, from censure to revocation of registration. In between those extremes the Commission may also choose to "place limitations on the [respondent's] activities, functions, or operations" or enter a suspension up to twelve months; and in consent cases (which rep-

---

[56] American Power & Light Co. v. SEC, 329 U. S. 90, 112 (1946); Seaton v. SEC, 670 F. 2d 309 (D. C. Cir. 1982). This is not to say that the sanction is immune from review for harshness. Beck v. SEC, 413 F. 2d 832 (6th Cir. 1969), *bar order reaff'd on remand* sub nom. Commonwealth Securities Corp., Sec. Ex. Act Rel. 8720 (1969), *rev'd* sub nom. Beck v. SEC, 430 F. 2d 673 (6th Cir. 1970) (the bar order was held to be punitive, not remedial); Arthur Lipper Corp. v. SEC, 547 F. 2d 171, 183-84 (2d Cir. 1976), *rehearing en banc denied*, 551 F. 2d 915 (2d Cir. 1977), *cert. denied*, 430 U. S. 1009.

Even in fraud cases it is now settled that the ordinary preponderance of the evidence standard of proof applies, and that violations need not be proved by "clear and convincing evidence" as in some types of proceedings. Steadman v. SEC, 450 U. S. 91 (1981) (administrative proceeding); Herman & Mac Lean v. Huddleston, 103 S. Ct. 683, 690-92 (1983), set out infra p. 1141 (private action).

resent the great bulk of proceedings in recent years) the Commission has been imaginative in fashioning conditions to govern the respondent's future operations.[57]

The Commission's duty under §15(b)(4) to act against the broker or dealer himself (or itself), whether for his (or its) own derelictions or those of an associate, is complemented by a duty under §15(b)(6) to proceed directly against an associate or one seeking to become an associate. If the Commission makes any of the (A)-(E) findings specified in §15(b)(4) with respect to the associate, together with a "public interest" finding, it may enter a censure or limitation-of-activities order or suspend (up to twelve months) or bar the respondent from being associated with a broker or dealer. This is the kind of suspension or bar order that, under §15(b)(4)(F), may result without more in sanctions against a *broker or dealer* who seeks to employ the suspended or barred person.

(2) The Commission is given similar directions with respect to municipal dealers and their associates, with concurrent jurisdiction in the appropriate bank regulator when the municipal dealer is a bank.[58]

(3) There are similar disciplinary and consultation provisions also with respect to transfer agents, except that only the appropriate bank regulator may proceed against a transfer agent that is a bank.[59]

(4) Next there is a group of provisions with respect to action by the Commission or the appropriate bank regulator, as the case may be, against a self-regulatory organization itself (other than the Municipal Board), or an officer, director, or member (or member's associate) of a stock exchange or the NASD, or a participant

---

[57]See, e. g., Hibbard & O'Connor Securities, Inc., Sec. Ex. Act Rel. 12,344, 9 SEC Dock. 411 (1976) (certain stock to be placed in a voting trust satisfactory to SEC with a view to insuring election of three outside directors satisfactory to SEC). For a collection of cases on the factors that the Commission considers under the "public interest" phrase, see O'Leary v. SEC, 424 F. 2d 908, 910 (D. C. Cir. 1970). For a discussion of the Commission's readmission procedure, see Sec. Ex. Act Rel. 11,267, 6 SEC Dock. 346 (1975).

[58]§§15B(c)(2)-(5). Before one agency begins an investigation or proceeding with respect to a bank (or an associate), it must notify and consult with the other agency. §15B(c)(6). This extends not only to violation of §15B or the Board's rules but also, so far as Commission action is concerned, beyond to the Commission's fraud rules under §15(c)(1) or (2) and, so far as Board action is concerned, to any Commission rule with respect to municipal securities or dealers.

With respect to both broker-dealers and municipal dealers, there are also withdrawal, cancellation, and *pendente lite* suspension provisions. §§15(b)(5), 15B(c)(3).

[59]§§17A(c)(3), 17A(d)(2) and (3). Cf. also §11A(b)(6) with respect to "securities information processors" (infra p. 767).

in a clearing agency, or a member or employee of the Municipal Board.[60] In some of these cases it is sufficient to prove only a violation of a self-regulatory organization rule as distinct from a rule of the Commission. It should be understood, of course, that revoking the registration of the New York Stock Exchange would be the financial equivalent of dropping the H-bomb.

(5) Finally, at the level of the self-regulatory organizations themselves (other than the Municipal Board) as *doers* in the business of discipline rather than *done to:*

First, their rules must provide for sanctions similar to those that may be imposed by the Commission[61] if (1) in the case of an exchange or the NASD, a member or associate violates the 1934 Act, the Commission's rules under that Act, or the rules of the exchange or association as the case may be, (2) in the case only of the NASD, a member or associate violates the rules of the Municipal Board, or (3) in the case of a clearing agency, a participant violates the agency's rules.[62]

Secondly, an exchange or the NASD *may* deny membership in the first instance to any person who is subject to a "statutory disqualification" and bar any such person from becoming an associate of a member; a clearing agency *may* deny participation to such a person; and these several self-regulatory organizations *must* do so when the Commission directs.[63] A person is subject to a "statutory disqualification" if, in general, one of the grounds exists for subjecting him to direct disciplinary action by the Commission or he has been found to be a cause of such disciplinary action against a broker, dealer, or municipal dealer.[64]

A final disciplinary or denial or bar order entered by a self-regulatory organization is reviewable by the Commission or the appropriate bank regulator.[65] Although the hearing may consist solely of the record before the self-regulatory organization and argument, the Commission normally reviews the self-regulatory organization's findings of violation *de novo* rather than on a "substantial evidence" basis. The Commission may not *increase* a sanction imposed by a self-regulatory organization. And the Com-

---

[60] §§15B(c)(8), 19(h).
[61] See pp. 699-701 supra.
[62] §§6(b)(6), 15A(b)(7), 17A(b)(3). On the extent to which NASD investigatory and disciplinary action is "governmental action," see Note, Governmental Action and the National Association of Securities Dealers, 47 Ford. L. Rev. 585 (1979).
[63] §§6(c)(2), 15A(g)(2), 17A(b)(4)(A).
[64] §3(a)(39).
[65] §19(d)-(f).

mission's (or bank regulator's) final order, if adverse, is reviewable in an appropriate Court of Appeals like any other final order, which is to say, on a "substantial evidence" basis.[66]

D. SUBSTANTIVE REGULATION

1. PROTECTION OF CUSTOMERS' FUNDS AND SECURITIES

The 1934 Act contains a number of provisions, in the nature of substantive regulation, that are designed to protect customers' funds and securities in the hands of broker-dealers:

a. Recordkeeping and Reports

A registered broker, dealer, municipal dealer, or transfer agent, as well as a self-regulatory organization, must make and keep whatever records, and disseminate whatever reports, the Commission's rules prescribe.[1] Registered clearing agencies and transfer agents are subject to further recordkeeping and reporting requirements laid down by either the Commission or the appropriate bank regulator, as the case may be.[2] And those registered clearing agencies, transfer agents, and municipal dealers that are banks must file copies of their SEC reports with their bank regulators and vice versa.[3]

b. Financial Reports

A registered broker or dealer must file balance sheets and income statements (normally audited) with the Commission annually, together with whatever additional financial information the Commission prescribes by rule, and send copies of its balance sheets and any supplemental financial information to its customers.[4]

---

[66] §25.

C. 8D [1] §17(a)(1). This section extends also to "securities information processors." See p. 767 *infra*. And the Municipal Board has a parallel rulemaking duty with respect to the records of municipal brokers and municipal dealers. §15B(b)(2)(G).
[2] §17(a)(2) and (3).
[3] §17(c)(1) and (2).
[4] 17(e); Rule 17a-5. With respect to municipal brokers and dealers, see 1 Code 841, Comment (1).

In late 1975, after a study by a Commission-appointed Report Coordinating Group, the Commission adopted the FOCUS report (an acronym for a financial and operational combined uniform single report).[5] That report replaced a number of SEC and self-regulatory organization forms and reports. Denominated Form X-17A-5 after the Commission's previous annual report form for broker-dealers, the FOCUS report and a highly articulated Rule 17a-5 together specify who files, and sends to customers, what, and when.[6]

c. Capital Requirements

SECURITIES EXCHANGE ACT RELEASE NO. 18,417:
NET CAPITAL REQUIREMENTS FOR
BROKERS AND DEALERS
24 SEC Dock. 594
Securities and Exchange Commission, 1982

*   *   *

Capital standards based upon liquidity for brokers and dealers have been in effect since at least 1934 when the Securities Exchange Act was adopted. Section 8(b) of the original act made it unlawful for a member of a national securities exchange to allow "in the ordinary course of business as a broker" its aggregate indebtedness to all other persons to exceed such percentage of the net capital employed in the business (but not exceeding in any case 2000%) as the Commission may by rules prescribe as necessary or appropriate. The primary purpose of this section was to prevent a broker from operating on a "shoe-string." Because of inherent limitations in the wording of Section 8(b), it never was more than a general standard of conduct for the securities business.

In 1938, Congress enacted Section 15(c)(3) of the Securities Exchange Act which authorized the Commission to adopt financial responsibility standards for brokers and dealers. In 1942, the Commission adopted Rule X-15C3-1 which incorporated the aggregate indebtedness standards of Section 8(b). The rule exempted from coverage members of national securities exchanges whose rules and practices imposed minimum capital requirements more

[5] Sec. Ex. Act Rel. 11,935, 8 SEC Dock. 808 (1975); see also Sec. Ex. Act Rel. 10,612, 3 SEC Dock. 423 (1974).
[6] See also Rules 17a-10, 17a-11.

comprehensive than those of the Commission. In succeeding years, the Commission was generally satisfied with the financial responsibility program.[a] During the years 1967-1970, however, the securities industry underwent an unprecedented financial and operational crisis. That crisis is extensively detailed in the Commission's Study of Unsafe and Unsound Practices of Brokers and Dealers[4] which the Commission was called upon to prepare for the Congress under Section 11(h) of the Securities Investor Protection Act of 1970. Referring to the operational crisis of the late 1960's, the Study exposed the structural weaknesses of an industry which could not withstand "the stresses and strains placed upon it by events of virtual hurricane force."[5] Out of this period emerged a number of legislative and administrative proposals designed to prevent recurrence of the resulting problems.

The first major development was the passage of the Securities Investor Protection Act of 1970, which was designed to give investors who dealt with brokers and dealers additional protections for their funds and securities, in the event of the insolvency of a broker or dealer. Therein Congress provided additional authority to the Commission to adopt rules relating to the acceptance of custody and use of customer securities and the carrying and use of customers' deposits and credit balances. Pursuant to this authority, the Commission adopted Rule 15c3-3 which requires a broker or dealer to have and maintain possession or control of all fully-paid and excess margin securities carried by it for the account of customers and to use customers' funds or customer-related funds only in "safe" areas of its business related to financing customer transactions and to deposit in a separate bank account any such funds not so used.[b]

In the meantime the Commission also adopted Rule 17a-13, which requires quarterly counts of securities by brokers and dealers in their possession or control, in order to establish a minimum standard as to the location of securities for brokers and dealers.

---

[a] ED.: In 1961 the Fifth Circuit called Rule 15c3-1 "one of the most important weapons in the Commission's arsenal to protect investors." Blaise d'Antoni & Associates, Inc. v. SEC, 289 F. 2d 276, 277 (5th Cir. 1961), *rehearing denied,* 290 F. 2d 688 (5th Cir. 1961), *cert. denied,* 368 U. S. 899. See also Rules 15c3-1a to 15c3-1d.

[4] See Securities and Exchange Commission, Study of Unsafe and Unsound Practices of Brokers and Dealers, H. Doc. No. 92-231, 92nd Cong., 1st Sess. (1971) * * * .

[5] Id. at 11.

[b] ED.: See generally Sec. Ex. Act Rel. 11,094, 5 SEC Dock. 448 (1974); Sec. Ex. Act Rel. 11,497, 7 SEC Dock. 241 (1975); Sec. Ex. Act Rel. 17,208, 21 SEC Dock. 139 (1980).

The Commission also improved its early-warning system to require a broker or dealer to report immediately any net capital violation or the lack of current books and records. The Commission, in addition, revised its reporting provisions to provide for more detailed surveillance of brokers and dealers and to coordinate effectitvely the examination programs of the Commission and the self-regulatory organizations.

Finally, the Commission, responding to Congressional concern, substantially reformed its net capital rule. The Commission eliminated the exemption in its prior net capital rule for all members of national securities exchanges and made virtually all registered brokers and dealers subject to the Commission's capital requirements.[6] The reformed rule continued the basic liquidity concept under which the securities industry had operated for many years. That concept requires a firm to have and maintain designated minimum amounts of liquid assets in relation to its aggregate indebtedness. In addition, the Commission introduced an alternative method to measure the capital adequacy of brokers and dealers. The alternative method linked the capital requirement of a broker or dealer to its customer related business as measured by the requirement of Rule 15c3-3. These reforms were significant steps in the Commission's continuing efforts to structure its rules to provide adequate protection for customers' assets while recognizing the industry's need for flexibility in efficiently allocating capital resources.

The Commission's present net capital rule requires that a broker's or dealer's "aggregate indebtedness" never be more than 1500% of its "net capital," as those terms are defined in the rule. Net capital essentially means the net worth of a broker or dealer reduced by prescribed percentages of the market value of securities owned by the broker or dealer ("haircuts") and reduced by other assets not readily convertible into cash, but including certain subordinated debt, i. e., net liquid assets. Aggregate indebtedness includes all the money liabilities of a broker or dealer, except certain specifically described items. In essence, the rule requires a broker or dealer to cover each dollar of its liabilities with not less than one dollar and six and two-thirds cents of liquid assets.

The alternative method of computing net capital requires a broker or dealer to maintain minimum net capital equal to the greater of $100,000 or 4% of aggregate debit items computed in

[6] Section 15(c)(3) of the Act was amended by the Securities Acts Amendments of 1975 to require the Commission, by September 1, 1975, to establish minimum financial responsibility requirements for all brokers and dealers.

accordance with the Formula for Determination of Reserve Requirements for Brokers and Dealers under Rule 15c3-3 ("Reserve Formula"), 17 C.F.R. 240.15c3-3a. The debit items in the Reserve Formula represent monies owed the broker or dealer in relation to customer transactions. The alternative method is founded on the concept that if the debit items in the Reserve Formula can be liquidated at or near their contract values, these assets, along with any cash required to be on deposit under the net capital rule, will be sufficient to satisfy all customer-related liabilities (which are represented as credit items in the Reserve Formula). As an additional safeguard, election of the alternative method requires a firm to reduce by 3% its aggregate debit items to provide, in essence, a bad debt reserve of firm capital to assure adequate resources to pay customer claims. Election of the alternative also requires that operational charges (stock record differences and suspense account items) be reflected in the Reserve Formula after seven business days, rather than after 30 business days, as permitted for those firms which have not elected the alternative method. These limitations, whether under the basic or the alternative method, allow a firm to increase its customer commitments only insofar as its net capital can support the increases.

*   *   *

d. Hypothecation of Customers' Securities

Section 8(b) of the 1934 Act (which was §8(c) before the 1975 amendments)[7] authorizes the Commission by rule to prohibit the hypothecation or arranging for the hypothecation of

> any securities carried for the account of any customer under circumstances (1) that will permit the commingling of his securities without his written consent with the securities of any other customer, (2) that [regardless of consent] will permit such securities to be commingled with the securities of any person other than a bona fide customer, or (3) that [again regardless of consent] will permit such securities to be hypothecated, or subjected to any lien or claim of the pledgee, for a sum in excess of the aggregate indebtedness of such customers in respect of such securities.

Although §8 applies only to "any member of a national securities exchange, or any broker or dealer who transacts a business in securities through the medium of any such member," §15(c)(2)

---

[7] The Commission's rule is still numbered 8c-1.

authorizes the Commission by rule to "define, and prescribe means reasonably designed to prevent, such acts and practices as are fraudulent [or] deceptive" in connection with transactions effected by *any* broker or dealer *otherwise than on an exchange.* The Commission, therefore, covered all situations by adopting two identical sets of rules, one under each section.[8]

In 1966, in the light of the development of centralized systems for the handling and delivery of securities through the use of automated procedures, the Commission added paragraph (g) to each rule to provide that the hypothecation of customers' securities held by a clearing corporation (or other subsidiary organization of an exchange or of the NASD) or by a custodian bank pursuant to a central system in which the customers' securities are commingled with others does not of itself constitute a prohibited commingling.[9]

Even apart from statute, a broker is guilty of a conversion when, without his customer's consent, he hypothecates his customer's securities for loans in excess of the customer's indebtedness to him or commingles his securities with those of the broker or other customers.[10] And there may be legislation or blue sky rules[11] in a particular state. The New York General Business Law contains a provision that is in some respects more strict than §8(b) of the

---

[8] Rules 8c-1, 15c2-1. For a general description of these rules, see Sec. Ex. Act Rel. 2690 (1940), reprinted in 2 Loss 1193-99.

[9] Sec. Ex. Act Rel. 7896 (1966). For the exemption to be applicable, the custodian, in general, must agree to deliver the securities that it holds as directed by the system and not to assert any claim, right, or lien against the securities; the system must have safeguards for the handling, transfer, and delivery of securities; it must provide fidelity bond coverage of employees and agents of the clearing corporation or other subsidiary organization; and it must contain provision for periodic examination by independent public accountants. The exemption applies only after the Commission finds this agreement and these safeguards and provisions, as well as any amendments of them, to be adequate for the protection of investors. Ibid.

[10] See Lefever, Stockbrokers' Rehypothecation of Customers' Securities As Constituting Conversion in Pennsylvania, 13 Temp. L. Q. 312 (1939); Turner v. Schwarz, 140 Md. 465, 117 Atl. 904 (1922); Sproul v. Sloan, 241 Pa. 284, 88 Atl. 501 (1913); but see Stein v. Broder, 8 N. J. Misc. 357, 150 Atl. 194 (Sup. Ct. 1930), aff'd per curiam, 107 N. J. L. 536, 154 Atl. 768 (1931). Of course, when an insolvent broker or dealer, in connection with his customers' buy orders, accepts their fully paid securities for safekeeping with the intention of converting them to his own use — or accepts their securities as collateral for margin loans with the intention of selling (or hypothecating) the securities for more than the balances due from those customers and converting the proceeds to his own use — he commits a fraud. SEC v. Lawson, 24 F. Supp. 360 (D. Md. 1938).

[11] See Cal. Ad. Code, Tit. 10, c. 3, Rules 260, 216.8, CCH Blue Sky L. Rep. ¶ 12,189.

1934 Act and in other respects less strict. Whereas Clause (1) of §8(b) does not attach to a hypothecation when there is no commingling, New York makes it a felony to pledge or dispose of a security under any circumstances unless the broker has a lien on the security or some special property in it or obtains the customer's consent. Again, whereas Clause (3) of §8(b) speaks in terms of the aggregate indebtedness of all customers and makes the customer's consent irrelevant, the comparable New York provision prohibits the hypothecation of a *particular* customer's securities for more than the amount of the broker's lien on those *particular* securities *unless the customer consents.*[12]

e.   Inspection

Section 17(b) subjects all the records of registered brokers, dealers, municipal dealers, and transfer agents, as well as the self-regulatory organizations, to "reasonable periodic, special, or other examinations" by the Commission and the bank regulators, as the case may be.[13] Although the Commission has never had the facilities to inspect all these persons at fixed intervals, even with the increased selectivity permitted by the increasing cooperation among the SEC, the NASD, the exchanges, and the states, the inspection program is one of the most important implements in the detection and prevention of violations not only of the record-keeping and capital rules but also of the 1933 and 1934 Acts and the Commission's rules generally by broker-dealers.

Broker-dealer inspections are conducted as a matter of routine by accountants in the Commission's Regional Offices. Sometimes they are limited to particular phases of a firm's operation, such as

---

[12] N. Y. Gen. Bus. Law §339-e, which replaced N. Y. Penal Law §956 as of September 1, 1967. Although this provision is less strict than §8(b)(3) in that the customer can consent, it is stricter in that under §8(b)(3), theoretically, a broker-dealer owed $100,000 in margin accounts by all customers could hypothecate one customer's securities for that sum even though that one customer owed a much lesser amount. For an application of the former §956, see, e. g., People v. Atwater, 229 N. Y. 303, 128 N. E. 196 (1920); see also In re Salmon Weed & Co., Inc., 53 F. 2d 335 (2d Cir. 1931), where the court, influenced by that provision, held that a broker's unauthorized pledge of a customer's securities for a greater amount than the original loan was a conversion *ipso facto* without any tender or demand on the customer's part, and therefore limited the broker's claim against the customer's estate in bankruptcy to the difference between the customer's debt in his margin account and the damages for conversion.

[13] This extends also to "securities information processors." See p. 767 infra.

its financial condition or its method of handling particular accounts. They are made on a surprise basis. And they are of three kinds: (1) routine inspections, mostly of "SECO" broker-dealers; (2) inspections for cause, which are usually limited to the subject matter of a customer's complaint; and (3) oversight inspections of self-regulatory organization members, which include a review of the latest inspection by the self-regulatory organization with a view to determining whether its inspection program is thorough and effective.

These inspections are designed not only to ferret out violations but also to educate those inspected in the legal requirements. In addition, they provide information that is useful in determining the need for new regulations or amendments to existing rules. Accordingly, most of the infractions that are discovered result in corrective measures on the basis of purely informal cautioning by the Commission's Regional Offices.

A number of provisions are directed to the multiregulator and multimembership problems:

(1) The Commission and the appropriate bank regulator are to consult with respect to their inspections of municipal dealers, transfer agents, and clearing agencies that are banks with a view to avoiding unnecessary duplication of regulation.[14]

(2) With respect to a member of more than one self-regulatory organization, the Commission, by rule or order, may relieve any of the self-regulatory organizations in question of any responsibility to inspect or receive reports or carry out other specified regulatory functions. And it may also allocate rulemaking authority when it is shared by two or more self-regulatory organizations.[15]

(3) A Commission rule implements the former authority.[16] Another rule invites the self-regulatory organizations to propose plans for allocating regulatory responsibilities.[17] Any any lacuna in an effective plan will be filled by Commission direction.[18]

One's failure to permit an authorized inspection is a violation of law that may activate the usual disciplinary, injunctive, and criminal sanctions. And it has been held in mandatory injunction

---

[14] §§ 17(b), 17(c)(3).

[15] § 17(d)(1).

[16] Rule 17d-1, adopted by Sec. Ex. Act Rel. 12,532, 9 SEC Dock. 450 (1976).

[17] Rule 17d-2, adopted by Sec. Ex. Act Rel. 12,935, 10 SEC Dock. 807 (1976). See Sec. Ex. Act Rel. 15,191, 15 SEC Dock. 1163 (1978), *amended*, Sec. Ex. Act Rel. 15,723, 17 SEC Dock. 262 (1979) (plan filed by NASD in conjunction with four regional exchanges).

[18] Rule 17d-2(g).

actions that the inspection power does not constitute an unreasonable search and seizure within the Fourth Amendment and that, since a registered broker-dealer's books and records are held subject to the Commission's examination, even an individual registrant may not refuse to make his books and records available to the Commission on the ground that their production might tend to incriminate him.[19]

2. SHORT SALES

a. Pre-SEC Legal Status of Short Sales

The 1934 report of the Senate investigation described the mechanics of the modern short sale:

> Short selling is a device whereby the speculator sells stock which he does not own, anticipating that the price will decline and that he will thereby be enabled to "cover," or make delivery of the stock sold, by purchasing it at the lesser price. If the decline materializes, the short seller realizes as a profit the differential between the sales price and the lower purchase or covering price.
>
> An order is given to a broker to sell the stock short, and the order is executed on the floor of the exchange and recorded in precisely the same manner as any other order to sell. The purchaser is altogether unaware whether he is buying from a short seller or an actual owner of stocks. The seller is required to make delivery of the stocks he has sold within the period limited by the rules of the exchange. Since he has no shares to deliver, he must obtain them somewhere. The usual practice is for the broker executing the sale to borrow the stock on his customer's behalf. Usually, it is borrowed from another broker. There must be deposited with the lender of the stock the market value of the stock loaned, and the amount of this deposit varies with changes

---

[19] United States v. Kaufman, 429 F. 2d 240, 247 (2d Cir. 1970), *cert. denied* sub nom. Burns v. United States, Florea v. United States, Garber v. United States, and Kaufman v. United States, 400 U. S. 925; see also SEC v. Olsen, 243 F. Supp. 338, 339 (S. D. N. Y. 1965), *contempt adjudication aff'd,* 354 F. 2d 166 (2d Cir. 1965) (Inv. Adv. Act). In Marshall v. Barlow's, Inc., 436 U. S. 307 (1978), the Court held that an inspection without a warrant under §8(a) of the Occupational Safety and Health Act of 1970, 29 U. S. C. §657(a), was an unreasonable search and seizure. But it referred to certain industries, like liquor and firearms, with "such a history of government oversight that no reasonable expectation of privacy * * * could exist for a proprietor over the stock of such an enterprise." 436 U. S. at 313. And it left the question to be decided statute by statute, emphasizing that "we base today's opinion on the facts and law concerning OSHA." 436 U. S. at 322.

in the price of the security. If the market price rises, the deposit must be increased; and, conversely, if the market price drops, the borrower of the stock may request the return of the difference between the amount which he has deposited and the then market value of the stock. In brief, the lender is entitled at all times to have on deposit a sum equivalent to the market value of the stock. The broker uses the borrowed stock to make delivery to the person who has purchased from his customer, the short seller. Later, when the short seller covers, his broker purchases the stock in the market and delivers it to the lender. When the borrowed stock is returned, the lender repays the sum which is on deposit with him and the transaction is closed.

Where the stock borrowed is in demand, a premium is exacted by the lender for the loan of the stock. This premium at times may be substantial. * * *

In a "flat loan," the stock is loaned without the payment of interest or premium. A loan that is "flat" in the first instance may change to a loan on interest or a loan on premium when there is a change in rate.

Where a lender is also a broker, he generally lends the securities of his customers who have authorized him to do so. In the absence of agreement to the contrary, customers whose securities are loaned receive no part of any premium paid for the loan — that is retained by their broker. Nor do they participate in the interest earned on the funds deposited with their broker when he loans their stock — that also he keeps.[20]

Daniel Drew, one of the nineteenth century financial buccaneers, was the author of the jingle:

[20] Stock Exchange Practices, Report of Com. on Banking & Currency, S. Rep. No. 1455, 73d Cong., 2d Sess. (1934) 50-51. Speculation is only one of the motivations for short selling. Among the nonspeculative kinds of short selling are the so-called technical short sale (for example, by arbitragers, specialists, and odd-lot dealers), the hedging short sale, the short sale for tax purposes, and the sale "against the box." 2 SEC, Report of Special Study of Securities Markets, H. R. Doc. No. 95, 88th Cong., 1st Sess. (1963) 247, 249-51.
· The Senate report had this to say about the last device: "A type of sale not technically a short sale, but similar in nature, is a sale 'against the box.' In such a transaction, the seller owns and possesses stock which he can deliver but which for some reason he prefers not to deliver. This is a device which can be employed by corporate officials and insiders who desire to sell their corporation's stock short without disclosing such short selling. Like the ordinary short seller, he borrows stock for the purpose of making delivery. It is contended by stock-exchange authorities that a sale 'against the box' is not a short sale, since the customer need not buy the stock back but may make delivery from the securities in his box. It is plain, however, that when a person initially makes a sale 'against the box' but subsequently changes his mind, there is nothing to prevent him from covering in the open market. In such case he is indistinguishable from any other short seller." Stock Exchange Practices, supra, at 52.

> He that sells what isn't his'n,
> Must buy it back, or go to prison.[21]

This bit of doggerel expresses the feeling — which seems to have been shared by legislators in different ages and different lands — that the very idea of a person's selling something he does not own, in the hope of buying it back later at a lower price, is essentially immoral. The result is that short selling has been a favorite whipping boy, both when it has deserved to be and when it has not.

More than three centuries ago the Dutch first banned short selling and then subjected it to special taxation, but both schemes were ignored and in time the laws were repealed. Napoleon attacked the practice in 1802 by requiring actual delivery of securities and making short sales of public securities criminal, but these regulations were not too strictly enforced and in 1885 the French law was changed.[22] On June 17, 1864, in the closing days of the Civil War, Congress prohibited short sales of gold. In those days gold was traded on the New York Stock Exchange like a commodity because the large amounts of paper money had driven it out of circulation. But the law was repealed on July 2 after a two-week increase in the price of 100 gold dollars from about 200 paper dollars to almost 300.[23] Germany enacted a stringent Exchange Law in 1896. This act, among other things, prohibited all future dealings in grain and in mining and industrial stocks and permitted such dealings in other securities only between persons who entered their names on an "Exchange Register."[24] The statute had been favored by the agrarians on the theory that short selling was responsible for the low agricultural prices, and the act was designed to stop speculation by the general public. But the law was full of loopholes and was substantially amended in 1908.[25]

In England Sir John Barnard's "act to prevent the infamous

---

[21] See B. White, The Book of Daniel Drew (1910) 180.

[22] See J. Flynn, Securities Speculation (1934) 266-70; J. Meeker, Short Selling (1932) 205-07, 217-21; Stevens, The Utility of Speculation in Modern Commerce, 7 Pol. Sci. Q. 419, 419-20 (1892).

[23] 13 Stat. 132, 344 (1864); J. Meeker, Short Selling (1932) 232-34; J. Eames, The New York Stock Exchange (1894) c. 24, New York Gold Exchange.

[24] Börsengesetz, RGB (1896) Nr. 15, Art. 4, §50.

[25] Börsengesetz, RGB (1908) Nr. 27. The 1908 law remained on the books until the Nazi regime. See U. S. Treasury Dept., Office of the General Counsel, Germany — Preliminary Report on Selected Financial Laws, Decrees and Regulations — Corporate Securities, Dividends and Profits (1944). See generally J. Meeker, German Regulation of Stock Exchanges 1896-1908, 15 Stock Exchange Practices, Hearings before Senate Com. on Banking & Currency, 73d Cong., 2d Sess. (1934) 7159-65.

practice of stock-jobbing," passed in 1734, voided puts and calls, as well as all contracts to sell "public securities" when the seller did not have possession or legal or beneficial ownership, and subjected persons participating in such transactions to fine.[26] But as early as 1838 short sales were held to be legal.[27] Then the act was repealed in 1860.[28] And in 1893 a law, which is still on the books, was passed specifically authorizing short sales.[29]

Essentially this same legislative pattern has been repeated in many of the American states. For example, a New York statute of 1813 prohibited short sales of stock and United States or state bonds.[30] This act was modified in 1830[31] and repealed in 1858 in favor of a provision (now in the General Obligation Law) that specifically authorizes short sales.[32] Today the courts' touchstone in distinguishing between gambling contracts on the one hand and short sales of securities (or commodity futures contracts or contracts to sell securities "when issued") on the other hand is whether there was an intent to deliver when the contract was made rather than merely to adjust price differences later.[33]

This was the status of the short sale when in early 1932 the Senate resolved to determine to what extent the "bear raiders" were preventing recovery.[34] The Banking and Currency Committee found in its 1934 report:

---

[26] 7 Geo. 2, c. 8, §VIII (1734).

[27] Hibblewhite v. McMorine, 5 M. & W. 462, 151 Eng. Reprint 195 (Ex. 1838), cited with approval in Clews v. Jamieson, 182 U. S. 461, 489 et seq. (1901), infra n. 33.

[28] 23 Vict., c. 28 (1860).

[29] "The goods which form the subject of a contract of sale may be either existing goods, owned or possessed by the seller, or goods to be manufactured or acquired by the seller after the making of the contract of sale, in this Act called 'future goods.'" Sale of Goods Act 1893, 56 & 57 Vict., c. 71, §5(1).

[30] 2 L. 1813, p. 187, §18.

[31] 1 Rev. Stat. (2d ed. 1836) *710, §6.

[32] L. 1858, c. 134, modified by L. 1897, c. 417, §22, later Pers. Prop. Law §§33(1), now Gen. Oblig. Law §5-1101; see also UCC §2-105(2).

[33] Hurd v. Taylor, 181 N. Y. 231, 73 N. E. 977 (1905); cf. Clews v. Jamieson, 182 U. S. 461, 489 et seq. (1901) (sale of securities for future delivery, with a dictum on short sales).

[34] President Hoover is said to have been convinced that the stock market situation was primarily due to the "bear raids" of short sellers, who were canceling out his measures for halting the panic, and in March 1932 the Senate passed a resolution calling for an investigation by its Banking and Currency Committee. Nor was Hoover alone. "It is of more than passing interest," Mr. John T. Flynn observed at the time, "that the blaze of popular wrath against the Exchange flamed up not when people found themselves stripped of their life's savings in the disorderly declines of 1929 and 1930, but later in 1931 when the notion got about that the decline was the work of a group of wicked bear raiders — professional speculators — who by selling short were driving prices lower and preventing recovery." J. Flynn, Se-

Few subjects relating to exchange practices have been characterized by greater differences of opinion that that of short selling. The proponents of short selling contend that it is a necessary feature of an open market for securities; that in a crisis short sellers

are useful in maintaining an orderly market; and that their activities serve as a cushion to break the force of a decline in the price of stocks. Its opponents assert that short selling unsettles the market, forces liquidation, depresses prices, accelerates declines, and has no economic value or justification.[35]

Apparently finding it impossible to discover where the truth lay between the extreme views that had been expressed, Congress in §10(a) simply placed the practice of short selling in registered securities under the plenary rulemaking authority of the Commission.[36]

b. SEC Short-Selling Rules

Effective in 1938 — and as since amended partly in response to the evolving national market system — there are three short selling rules:

---

curity Speculation (1934) 216. At any rate, it was the 1932 Senate resolution — bolstered by a second resolution very early in the Roosevelt Administration containing a new set of teeth with a harder bite — that led to the first securities statutes. S. Res. 56, 73d Cong., 1st Sess. (1933); see also S. Res. 97, 73d Cong., 1st Sess. (1933). Both are set out in Stock Exchange Practices, Report of Senate Com. on Banking & Currency, S. Rep. No. 1455, 73d Cong., 2d Sess. (1934) 2-3. For a popular account of the investigation, see F. Pecora, Wall Street under Oath (1939).

[35] Stock Exchange Practices, Report of Senate Com. on Banking & Currency, S. Rep. No. 1455, 73d Cong., 2d Sess. (1934) 50.

[36] The same section applies to the use or employment of any "stop-loss order" in connection with a registered security. "A stop-loss order is an order to buy or sell a stated amount of a security at the market if and when a transaction occurs at a designated price. The purpose of such an order may be to limit the loss on an open commitment; to safeguard a profit on an open commitment; or to insure the making of a new commitment when a specified price level is reached." SEC, Report on the Feasibility and Advisability of the Complete Segregation of the Functions of Dealer and Broker (1936) 26. But the Commission has never implemented that portion of §10(a) by rules.

The SEC Acts contain three other provisions on short selling by certain persons. Section 16(c) of the Exchange Act and §30(f) of the Investment Company Act, which prohibit short sales by certain types of corporate insiders, have already been noticed. See pp. 605 n. 4, 607 supra. In addition, §12 (a)(3) of the Investment Company Act gives the Commission rulemaking power (which it has never exercised) to regulate short sales of any securities by registered investment companies except in connection with underwritings in which they participate.

Rule 3b-3 defines "short sale":

> The term "short sale" means any sale of a security which the seller does not own or any sale which is consummated by the delivery of a security borrowed by, or for the account of, the seller. A person shall be deemed to own a security if (1) he or his agent has title to it; or (2) he has purchased, or has entered into an unconditional contract, binding on both parties thereto, to purchase it but has not yet received it; or (3) he owns a security convertible into or exchangeable for it and has tendered such security for conversion or exchange; or (4) he has an option to purchase or acquire it and has exercised such option; or (5) he has rights or warrants to subscribe to it and has exercised such rights or warrants: Provided, however, That a person shall be deemed to own securities only to the extent that he has a net long position in such securities.

Rule 10a-1, subject to a number of exceptions of a technical sort, prohibits a short sale (1) *below* the last sale price or (2) *at* the last sale price unless that price is above the next preceding different price; and each exchange may elect whether short sales are to be governed by this "tick test" in terms of its own market or any market in the composite "transaction reporting system."[37] In other words, after sales at $49\frac{7}{8}$ and 50 an indefinite number of short sales may be effected at 50; but, after sales at $49\frac{7}{8}$ and $49\frac{3}{4}$, the minimum price at which a short sale may be effected is $49\frac{7}{8}$.[38]

The third rule, Rule 10a-2, has to do with covering transactions. If on the due date of delivery of a security sold pursuant to an order marked "long" the member has not received the security from the customer, he must cover the open position unless he knows or has been informed by the seller either (1) that the security is in transit to him, or (2) that the seller owns the security, that it is then impracticable to deliver it and that it will be delivered as soon as is possible without undue inconvenience or expense.[39]

Beginning in 1975 the Commission repeatedly questioned whether the great increase in sophistication of the regulatory

---

[37] Both of the New York exchanges have elected the second alternative.

[38] Every sale order must be marked "long" or "short." Rule 10a-1(b) to (d); see Naftalin & Co., Inc. v. Merrill Lynch, Pierce, Fenner & Smith, Inc., 469 F. 2d 1166, 1172 n. 5 (8th Cir. 1972).

[39] See Edwards & Hanly v. Wells Fargo Securities Clearance Corp., 602 F. 2d 478, 486 (2d Cir. 1979), *cert. denied*, 444 U. S. 1045. The rule does not in so many words require that the position be covered. It prohibits delivery with a borrowed security or failure to deliver on the due date. This leaves no alternative but covering.

framework since 1938, together with the evolution of a central market system, might not permit detection of destructive short selling by the Commission or the self-regulatory organizations without complex federal regulation of each short sale.[40] In 1977 the Commission held a public investigation and rulemaking proceeding on the question.[41] But in 1980 the Commission announced an apparent consensus among those who commented that the "tick test" was working well and should not be modified.[42]

These rules seem pretty well to have taken the caffein out of the short sale. Nevertheless, Representative Sabath, inveighing against the evils of short selling, introduced a bill in May 1947 that would have levied a 5 percent tax on all short sales of stocks or commodities — thus completing the circle begun by his Dutch predecessors of three centuries ago.[43]

3. Credit Regulation

a. The Statutory Credit Provisions and Their Philosophy [§7]

Section 7(a) directs the Board of Governors of the Federal Reserve System to prescribe rules from time to time "with respect to the amount of credit that may be initially extended and subsequently maintained" on any nonexempted security.

Section 7(c) makes it unlawful for an exchange member, broker, or dealer, "directly or indirectly, to extend or maintain credit or arrange for the extension or maintenance of credit to or for any customer" on any nonexempted security in contravention of the Board's rules. It is unlawful likewise for any member, broker, or dealer to extend or maintain credit, or arrange for its extension or maintenance, on any collateral *other than* securities, or without collateral at all, except insofar as the Board's rules may permit (A) the maintenance for a limited period of credit initially extended in conformity with its rules and (B) the extension or maintenance of credit for some purpose other than purchasing or carrying securities; with these limited exemptions, unregistered securities

---

[40] Sec. Ex. Act Rel. 11,276, 6 SEC Dock. 378, 381 n. 4 (1975); see also Sec. Ex. Act Rel. 11,468, 7 SEC Dock. 150, 154 (1975); Sec. Ex. Act Rel. 12,384, 9 SEC Dock. 495, 496 (1976).

[41] Sec. Ex. Act Rel. 13,091, 11 SEC Dock. 1229 (1976).

[42] Sec. Ex. Act Rel. 17,347, 21 SEC Dock. 781 (1980).

[43] H. R. 3593, 80th Cong., 1st Sess. (1947). No hearings were held.

have no loan value. Acting primarily under §7(c), the Board adopted Regulation T.[44]

Section 7(d) authorizes the Board to adopt similar rules governing the extension or maintenance of credit by any person not covered by §7(c) when the purpose of the credit is to purchase or carry a security. But it exempts, among other things, not only a loan on an exempted security but also "a loan by a bank on a security other than an equity security." Under this section the Board adopted Regulation U, applicable only to banks, and (in 1968) Regulation G, applicable to certain lenders not covered by Regulation T or U.

The Act and its legislative history indicate that the credit provisions rest on three separate philosophies, which are not altogether consistent:

(1) The statute itself speaks in terms of "preventing the excessive use of credit for the purchase or carrying of securities." So does the House report:

> The main purpose [of the credit provisions] is to give a Government credit agency an effective method of reducing the aggregate amount of the nation's credit resources which can be directed by speculation into the stock market and out of other more desirable uses of commerce and industry — to prevent a recurrence of the pre-cash situation where funds which would otherwise have been available at normal interest rates for uses of local commerce, industry, and agriculture, were drained by far higher rates into security loans and the New York call market.[45]

---

[44] Section 7 as a whole does not apply to exempted securities. Here as elsewhere in the Act it is the SEC rather than the Board that has the authority to define "exempted securities." §3(a)(12), supra p. 476. The Commission has exempted from the §7(c) prohibition against extension of credit on unregistered securities (1) all the securities exempted from registration by its rules under §12(a) except Rule 12a-4 on short-term warrants and (2) securities traded on an exempted exchange. Rules 7c2-1, 12a-1 to 12a-3, 12a-5. These two categories of securities are treated, in effect, as if they were registered for purposes of §7(c). Apart from §7, however, the New York Stock Exchange imposes its own margin requirements (see p. 730 infra) of 5 percent of principal amount on positions in Government bonds and 15 percent of principal amount or 25 percent of market (whichever is lower) on positions in other exempted securities (for the most part state and municipal bonds), unless in either case the Exchange reduces the requirement on written application with respect to a particular issue. N. Y. Stock Ex. Rule 431(c)(2), CCH N. Y. Stock Ex. Guide ¶2431.

[45] H. R. Rep. No. 1383, 73d Cong., 2d Sess. (1934) 8; see Naftalin & Co., Inc. v. Merrill Lynch, Pierce, Fenner & Smith, Inc., 469 F. 2d 1166, 1180 (8th Cir. 1972) (§7 "is more concerned with the regulation of macro-economic conditions").

(2) The report of the Senate Banking and Currency Committee's investigation, on the other hand, says that the margin provisions are also intended "to protect the margin purchaser by making it impossible for him to buy securities on too thin a margin.[46] As Chairman Rayburn of the House Commerce Committee put it in language no less forceful for its mixed metaphor: "A reasonably high margin requirement is essential so that a person cannot get in the market on a shoe string one day and be one of the sheared lambs when he wakes up the next morning."[47]

(3) At the same time, Congress apparently had in mind also that the Board's powers would be used to prevent undue market fluctuations and help stabilize the economy generally, because it directed the Board to adopt for its initial rules a formula based on the nature of past price movements of the collateral.

b. The Federal Reserve Formulas and Percentages

In the early and most recent years, at least, the chief emphasis seems to have been placed on this third philosophy. Although there is no statutory requirement that the margin be the same for lenders of all types, the Board has never differentiated. Since November 1974 the margin requirement has stood at 50 percent.[48] But it has oscillated between 40 percent and, for a period of more than a year beginning in January 1946, 100 percent.[49] "While it was recognized," Board Chairman Eccles stated shortly after that "dry" interval, "that margin requirements would have only a minor influence in combatting general inflation, the Board nevertheless felt that it should do what it could to curb inflationary developments brought about by speculative activity in the stock markets."[50]

[46] Stock Exchange Practices, Report of Senate Com. on Banking & Currency, S. Rep. No. 1455, 73d Cong., 2d Sess. (1934) 11. The House report refers to this as "a by-product of the main purpose." H. R. Rep. No. 1383, 73d Cong., 2d Sess. (1934) 8.

[47] 78 Cong. Rec. 7700 (1934).

[48] This means that one who buy 100 shares of a security at $100 must put up either $5000 in cash or $10,000 of other securities eligible for margin, which at 50 percent of their market value equals the required $5000 deposit.

[49] The regulations do not prescribe margin figures. Rather they prescribe a "loan value" for securities in terms of a percentage of their "market value." A "loan value" of 30 percent would mean a margin requirement of 70 percent.

[50] Eccles, Readjustment of Margin Requirements, 33 Fed. Res. Bul. 149, 149-50 (1947). Professor Friend concluded in 1982: "The empirical evidence

c.   Extension of Credit by Brokers and Dealers [Reg. T]

Regulation T reflects the fact that purchases of securities, like purchases of any merchandise, may be effected either for cash or on credit. A customer who buys securities for cash pays the broker or dealer outright the full amount of the purchase price. On the other hand, a customer who buys on credit pays only part of the purchase price in cash and receives an extension of credit from the broker or dealer for the unpaid balance; usually the broker or dealer in turn uses the customer's securities so purchased as collateral for bank loans to finance the balance of the purchase price, as we have seen in our examination of the SEC's rehypothecation rules.[51] Under Regulation T purchases for cash are usually made in "special cash accounts" (there are a number of other special accounts), and credit purchases are made in "general" or "margin" accounts. The usual credit purchases are treated in §3 of the regulation, cash purchases in §4(c).

Section 3(a) starts with the premise that "All financial relations between a customer and a creditor * * * shall be included in and be deemed part of the customer's general account with the creditor," except that "relations which section 4 permits to be included in any special account provided for by that section may be included in the appropriate special account * * * ." Section 3(b) of the regulation goes on to provide, in substance, that the required margin or down payment in a general account must be deposited by the customer "as promptly as possible" and in any event before the expiration of seven full business days following the date of the transaction. When this is not done, the broker or dealer is required by §3(e), before the expiration of the seven-day period, to effect sufficient liquidating transactions (beginning with any nonexempted margin securities[52] in the account) to bring the

---

on the impact of margin regulation on market efficiency is conflicting * * * ." Friend, Economic and Equity Aspects of Securities Regulation (Rodney L. White Center for Financial Research, Wharton School, U. Pa., Working Paper No. 7-82, 1982) 34-35.

[51] See p. 707 supra. On the technique, the justification, and the economic function of margin trading, see Twentieth Century Fund, Inc., The Security Markets (1935) c. 9. For an economic analysis of the claim that speculation aids in directing the flow of savings into those industries in which the need for additional funds is greatest, see id., c. 10. For a comprehensive discussion of security credit generally, see J. Bogen and H. Krooss, Security Credit: Its Economic Role and Regulation (1960).

[52] "Margin security" is defined to mean "any registered security, OTC margin stock, OTC margin bond, or any security issued by an open-end investment company or unit investment trust registered under" the 1940 Act. An "OTC margin stock" (or "OTC stock") is any over-the-counter

account into compliance with Regulation T, unless he obtains an extension from an appropriate exchange committee.

A special cash account may be used, under §4(c)(1), to effect *"bona fide* cash transactions in securities" if (i) in the case of a *purchase* by a customer "funds sufficient for the purpose are already held in the account or the purchase * * * is in reliance upon an agreement accepted by the creditor in good faith that the customer will promptly make full cash payment for the security and that the customer does not contemplate selling the security prior to making such payment," and (ii) in the case of a *sale* by a customer "the security is held in the account or the creditor is informed that the customer or his principal owns the security and the * * * sale is in reliance upon an agreement accepted by the creditor in good faith that the security is to be promptly deposited in the account.[53]

Normally, if full cash payment is not obtained within seven full business days after the date of purchase, §4(c)(2) requires the creditor "promptly" to cancel or otherwise liquidate the transaction. But that is simply an outside period. The privilege of using a special cash account is conditioned on acceptance "in good faith" of the customer's agreement that he will "promptly make full cash payment." And that does not give the broker or dealer the privilege of automatically delaying collection for seven business days.

One of the other special accounts is a "special miscellaneous account," which is used (*inter alia*) for extensions of credit "without collateral or on any collateral whatever for any purpose other than purchasing or carrying or trading in securities."[54] But every extension of credit on a nonexempted margin security is considered to be for the purpose of purchasing or carrying or trading in securities "unless the creditor has accepted in good faith a written

---

stock that the Board "has determined to have the degree of national investor interest, the depth and breadth of market, the availability of information respecting the stock and its issuer, and the character and permanence of the issuer to warrant subjecting such stock to the requirements of" Regulation T. And an "OTC margin bond" is an over-the-counter debt security that meets three requirements: (1) at least $25 million principal amount is outstanding; (2) the issue was registered under the 1933 Act and the insuer either files reports under the 1934 Act or is an insurance company within §12(g)(2)(G) of the 1934 Act; (3) the lending broker or dealer "has a reasonable basis for believing that the issuer is not in default on interest or principal payments." Reg. T, §2(e), (f), (i). There are several hundred "OTC margin stocks" on the list that the Board publishes from time to time. See CCH Fed. Sec. L. Rep. ¶22,210.

[53] Clause (ii) reflects the fact that Regulation T applies the same 50 percent margin requirement to short sales.

[54] Reg. T, §4(f)(8).

statement to the contrary in conformity with the requirements of Form F. R. T-4 executed by the customer and executed and accepted in good faith by the creditor prior to such extension"; "good faith" means that the creditor "must (1) be alert to the circumstances surrounding the extension of credit and (2) if he has any information which would cause a prudent man not to accept the statement without inquiry, have investigated and be satisfied that the customer's statement is truhful."[55]

Although §7(a) of the Act directs the Board to require the *maintenance* of certain margins as well as their initial deposit, no margin calls are required after the initial deposit, no matter how much the market falls. Regulation T, however, specifically saves the right of the broker or dealer to call for additional collateral of any description for his own protection, as well as the right of the exchanges to adopt more stringent rules on both initial extension and maintenance, and the exchanges do have maintenance requirements, as we shall see.[56]

d.   Extension of Credit by Banks [Reg. U]

Section 7(d) of the Act and Regulation U are more restricted in scope than §7(c) and Regulation T, although the gap was narrowed by the amendment of Regulation U concurrently with the adoption of Regulation G in early 1968 and then by the amendment of §7 itself in mid-1968 together with subsequent amendments of the regulations:

(1) Although §7(d) authorizes the Board to regulate extensions of credit "by any person not subject to subsection (c)" as long as he lends "in the ordinary course of his business," the credit provisions of Regulation U have always applied only to banks.[57]

(2) Although §7(d) extends to *any* bank loan for the purpose of purchasing or carrying *any* security, except a loan "on a security other than an equity security," Regulation U applies only to extensions of credit on "margin stock" for the purpose of purchasing or carrying "margin stock";[58] and that term is defined to mean any exchange-traded stock, an "OTC margin stock," a debt security convertible into, or carrying a right to purchase, a margin

[55] Id., §7(c); see Naftalin & Co., Inc. v. Merrill Lynch, Pierce, Fenner & Smith, Inc., 469 F. 2d 1166, 1175 (8th Cir. 1972); SEC v. Packer, Wilbur & Co., Inc., 498 F. 2d 978, 981 n. 1 (2d Cir. 1974).

[56] See p. 730 infra.

[57] With respect to foreign banks, see p. 682 supra, p. 726 infra.

[58] Reg. U, §3(m).

stock, any such right itself, and most investment company securities.[59] Any collateral other than "stock" has whatever loan value the bank determines in good faith.[60]

(3) Until 1968, §7(c) gave no loan value whatever to unregistered securities and §7(d), by contrast, was silent on the question. The 1934 legislative hearings reveal several reasons for the distinction between brokers and banks so far as the eligibility of unregistered securities for credit is concerned. On the one hand, brokers were prohibited from extending credit on unregistered securities because, their market value being usually indefinite, the lenders could otherwise evade the margin restrictions with respect to registered securities by extending credit on a package of registered and unregistered securities and overvaluing the latter. On the other hand, it was thought that banks (which in any event were subject to an additional check by virtue of periodic bank examinations) would handle loans on unregistered securities as a purely commercial matter, so that they would be less apt to engage in similar practices.[61]

As of July 29, 1968, on the recommendation of the SEC's "Special Study,"[62] and with everybody's blessing, §§7(a), 7(c), and 7(d) were amended to delete all the restrictions to "registered" securities. And the Board's regulations have been appropriately

---

[59] Reg. U, §3(v). "OTC margin stock" is defined in §3(d) of Regulation U as in §2(e) of Regulation T, supra n. 52. And the simple term "stock" is defined to include a voting trust certificate, a security convertible into "stock" or carrying a right to purchase "stock," such a right itself, and any similar security that the SEC considers by rule should be treated like an equity security. Reg. U, §3(l).

Until March 31, 1982, Regulation U applied more broadly to extensions of credit on *any* stock for the purpose of purchasing or carrying "margin stock." The reason for the pre-1982 limitation to loans collateralized by stock of some kind was to avoid subjecting banks to the administrative burden of determining the purpose of all their loans regardless of collateral, particularly since it was assumed that most persons who finance their stock purchases at the bank tend in fact to pledge stock as collateral. See Solomon and Hart, Recent Developments in the Regulation of Securities Credit, in Practising Law Institute, Second Annual Institute on Securities Regulation (1971) 167, 174.

[60] Reg. U, §§1(a), 3(s). This means, the Board has said, that the maximum loan value of any such collateral "should be the amount which the bank would customarily lend on such collateral if that were the only collateral for the loan." 24 Fed. Res. Bul. 1042 (1938).

[61] 15 Stock Exchange Practices, Hearings before Senate Com. on Banking & Currency, 73d Cong., 2d Sess. (1934) 6473-74; Stock Exchange Regulation, Hearing before House Com. on Int. & For. Commerce on H. R. 7852 and H. R. 8720, 73d Cong., 2d Sess. (1934) 92, 687; see also 4 SEC, Report of Special Study of Securities Markets, H. R. Doc. No. 95, 88th Cong., 1st Sess. (1963) 18-19.

[62] 4 id. at 22-23, 38-39.

accommodated to certain over-the-counter securities, as we have seen.[63] Nevertheless, even when the purpose of a bank loan is to purchase or carry a registered security or an "OTC margin stock," Regulation U still allows the same loan value for *all* stocks — a discrimination between brokers and banks that may be of no great consequence when the margin requirement is very high (that is to say, when the loan value is very low), but one that becomes more important in times of lower margin requirements.

(4) Section 7(d), unlike §7(c), gives the Board an exemptive authority, which it has used — although the Board has achieved much the same result under Regulation T through the "special miscellaneous account."

(5) Banks' stock-collateralized loans, in the nature of things, may be made for purposes altogether unrelated to the purchasing or carrying of securities — so-called non-purpose loans. To make sure that Regulation U is complied with unless the loan is clearly "non-purpose," the bank must obtain, and retain in its records for three years after repayment, a statement executed on the Board's Form U-1 by both the borrower and a duly authorized officer of the bank before the credit is extended (except that this requirement does not apply in connection with routine loans to brokers and dealers, in view of their regulation by the SEC, as well as certain exempted loans). The statement must affirmatively describe the purpose of the loan, and it must be accepted by the officer in good faith.[64]

So far as the "carrying" as distinct from the "purchasing" part of §7(d) of the act is concerned, Regulation U provides: "Credit to enable the customer to reduce or retire indebtedness which was originally incurred to purchase a margin stock is for the purpose of 'carrying' such a security."[65]

e.   Extension of Credit by Persons Other Than Brokers, Dealers, or Banks [Reg. G]

The "Special Study" confirmed the existence of a group of unregulated moneylenders (or "factors," as they are sometimes

---

[63] See nn. 52, 59 supra.

[64] Reg. U, §3(a); see Serzysko v. Chase Manhattan Bank, 290 F. Supp. 74 (S. D. N. Y. 1968), *aff'd per curiam*, 409 F. 2d 1360 (2d Cir. 1969), *cert. denied*, 396 U. S. 904.

[65] Reg. U, §3(b)(2); Serzysko v. Chase Manhattan Bank, 290 F. Supp. 74, 83 (S. D. N. Y. 1968), *aff'd per curiam*, 409 F. 2d 1360 (2d Cir. 1969), *cert. denied*, 396 U. S. 904; see Solomon and Hart, Simplicity v. Effectiveness: Trade-Offs in Regulating Credit to "Carry" Securities, 25 Mercer L. Rev. 415, esp. at 418 (1974).

called) that financed the purchase or carrying of securities, either intermittently or regularly.[66] As early as 1959 the Board codified a 1946 interpretation[67] by adopting §3(q) of Regulation U. That section, as it now stands, applies Regulation U to credit extended to any customer that is not subject to Regulation T or U and that is engaged, "principally, or as one of the customer's important activities," in the business of extending credit (which is to say, relending) for the purpose of purchasing or carrying margin stocks.[68] In the case of a so-called "q lender," the loan is subject to the regular margin restrictions, whether or not it is secured by "stock" and whatever its stated purpose might be. A number of factors who had been actively engaged in making loans for this purpose were forced to withdraw from the securities loan business when §3(q) dried up their source of financing. But the "Special Study" found that §3(q) "itself does not appear to have played an appreciable role in restricting bank loans to unregulated lenders except those that are well known and confine their activities to lending on securities."[69]

Finally the Board hit the problem head on by adopting Regulation G, effective March 11, 1968. Unlike the two older regulations, this one necessarily begins with a registration requirement. As the regulation now reads, every person who "in the ordinary course of his business" and during any calendar quarter extends or arranges for the extension of $100,000 or more of credit secured to any extent by "margin securities,"[70] or who has $500,000 or more of such credit outstanding at any time during the quarter, must register within thirty days after the end of the quarter, unless he is already subject to Regulation T or U.[71] If either of these tests is met, *registration* is required even though the particular loans

---

[66] 4 SEC, Report of Special Study of Securities Markets, H. R. Doc. No. 95, 88th Cong., 1st Sess. (1963) 5-6.

[67] 32 Fed. Res. Bul. 874 (1946).

[68] See 45 Fed. Res. Bul. 485 (1959); Cooper v. North Jersey Trust Co. of Ridgewood, N. J., Inc., 226 F. Supp. 972, 976 (S. D. N. Y. 1964).

[69] 4 SEC, Report of Special Study of Securities Markets, H. R. Doc. No. 95, 88th Cong., 1st Sess. (1963) 30.

[70] The Regulation G definition of "margin security" (§2(d)) is substantially like the Regulation U definition of "margin stock" (§3(v), supra pp. 722-23).

[71] Reg. G, §1(a). "Any person so registered who has not, during the preceding 6 calendar months, extended or arranged for the extension or maintenance of and has not had more than $200,000 of credit outstanding at any time during such period, secured directly or indirectly, in whole or in part, by collateral that includes any margin securities, may apply for termination of such registration by filing Federal Reserve Form G-2 with the Federal Reserve Bank of the district in which the principal office of such person is located." Registration is terminated when the application is approved by the Board. Id., §1(b).

thereafter made have nothing to do with securities and hence will not be subject to the *margin requirements* of the regulation. It should be noted, however, that the $500,000 test applies only to the extension, not to the arranging, of credit.

Lenders under Regulation G, like banks under Regulation U, are subject to whatever margin and retention requirements the Board sets from time to time, and thus far it has specified the same figures as for Regulations T and U.[72]

f.   Obtaining of Credit by Persons Other Than Brokers or Dealers [Reg. X]

Until 1971 nothing in the 1934 Act affected *borrowers* other than brokers or dealers.[73] And, particularly when domestic credit was tight, borrowers went to foreign banks. Although arguably a foreign bank (at least one not present in and regulated in the United States) is not a "bank,"[74] and therefore *could* be a "broker" or "dealer" whose *lending* would be subject to Regulation T,[75] principles of territoriality would preclude applicability of the regulation.[76] Indeed, Regulation U specifically exempts "Any credit extended outside the United States."[77]

This foreign gap was substantially narrowed in 1970, when Congress added §7(f) to the 1934 Act in order to make it unlawful for any "United States person" (as defined), or any foreign person controlled by or acting for or with a United States person, to "obtain, receive, or enjoy" credit from *any* lender *anywhere* "for the purpose of (A) purchasing or carrying United States securities [as defined], or (B) purchasing or carrying within the United States of any other securities," if the loan would have been prohibited had it occurred in a lender's place of business in the United States.[78] The Board has implemented §7(f) by adopting Regulation X.

---

[72] Id., §§1(c), 1(d), 1(j)(1).

[73] With respect to brokers and dealers, see p. 727 infra.

[74] See p. 682 supra.

[75] United States v. Weisscredit Banca Commerciale e d'Investimenti, 325 F. Supp. 1384, 1390-92 (S. D. N. Y. 1971).

[76] Metro-Goldwyn-Mayer, Inc. v. Transamerica Corp., 303 F. Supp. 1354, 1357-58 (S. D. N. Y. 1969). The court relied not only on §30(b) of the 1934 Act — to the effect that (subject to rulemaking authority that the SEC has never exercised) the Act does not apply to any person "insofar as he transacts a business in securities without the jurisdiction of the United States" — but also, with respect to Regulation G, on the absence of a Federal Reserve district in which the foreign bank might register. See p. 67 supra.

[77] Reg. U, §2(i).

[78] 84 Stat. 1124 (1970).

Despite all this, bills introduced in June 1981 would further approach the limits of territoriality by extending §7(f) beyond any "United States person" to *any* person.[79] The limitation of one of these bills to tender offer (and §13(d)) situations reflects the origin of the proposed extension of §7(f) in the fear of foreign takeovers of American industry.

g.   Broker-Dealer Borrowing [§8(a)]

Almost inevitably, once a broker or dealer becomes a lender he must also "a borrower be." The Board's authority in §7(c) over the *lending* activities of brokers and dealers is complemented by its authority in §8(a) over their *borrowing* activities. Insofar as their borrowing is collateralized by securities of customers — whether the same margin customers to whom the brokers or dealers extend credit or customers whose fully paid securities the brokers or dealers are holding in safekeeping — §8(a) is also the reverse side of the coin of which the obverse is the Commission's hypothecation rules.

Section 8(a) makes it unlawful for any exchange member, or any broker or dealer who is registered or does business through a member, to borrow "in the ordinary course of business as a broker or dealer" on any nonexempted registered security except (1) from or through a member bank of the Federal Reserve System, (2) from a nonmember bank that has filed with the Board an agreement to comply with all the provisions of the Exchange Act, the Federal Reserve Act, and the Banking Act of 1933 that are applicable to member banks and that relate to the use of credit to finance transactions in securities,[80] or (3) in accordance with whatever rules the Board prescribes to permit loans between such brokers and dealers "or to permit loans to meet emergency needs." The Board has implemented Clause (3) of this section by adopting §5 of Regulation T, which in substance permits one broker or dealer to borrow from another on the same terms on which Regulation T permits the second broker or dealer to lend.[81]

---

[79] H. R. 4145, 97th Cong., and H. R. Rep. No. 97-258 (1981).

[80] The Board may terminate any such agreement, after notice and opportunity for hearing, for the bank's failure to comply with the provisions of the agreement or of the designated statutes. Willful violation of the agreement subjects the bank to the penalties provided for violations of rules prescribed under the Exchange Act. And for this one purpose §8(a) gives the Board the same powers to investigate and sue for injunction or mandamus as the Commission has generally under §21.

[81] Reg. T, §§5(a)(3), 5(c).

h. Arranging for Others to Extend Credit

Both §7(c) and §7(d) of the statute give the Board rulemaking authority not only with respect to extending credit but also with respect to *arranging* for the extension of credit. And §7(a) of Regulation T has long provided, in substance and with exceptions, that a broker or dealer may not arrange for credit to be given a customer except on the same conditions on which he could himself extend the credit; as amended effective February 15, 1982, this section excludes credit that results from "investment banking services" (as defined). But, apart from the 1959 adoption of §3(q) of Regulation U with respect to bank loans to significant re-lenders,[82] Regulation U contained no similar provision on "arranging" until the amendments of early 1968. The SEC's "Special Study" found evidence that United States banks did in fact arrange loans with foreign banks for their domestic customers.[83] And in 1968 provisions similar to §7(a) of Regulation T were accordingly inserted in both Regulations U and G.[84]

There has been a fair amount of litigation on what constitutes "arranging."[85]

i. Unconventional Extensions of Credit

There is space here only to note the inevitable clash between a technical set of retail securities credit regulations and the emergence of many types of unconventional but widely marketed securities, not to mention the financing needs connected with the corporate acquisition movement.[86] For example:

(1) The Board has ruled that Regulation T does not apply to a dealer's extension of credit to a corporation in connection with the retirement of its own stock.[87]

(2) The Board's staff, on the other hand, has taken the position

[82] See p. 725 supra.

[83] 4 SEC, Report of Special Study of Securities Markets, H. R. Doc. No. 95, 88th Cong., 1st Sess. (1963) 31.

[84] Reg. U, §3(u); Reg. G, §4(e).

[85] Sutro Bros. & Co., 41 SEC 443, 456 (1963); see also, e. g., Pearlstein v. Scudder & German, 429 F. 2d 1136, 1140-41 (2d Cir. 1970), *cert. denied*, 401 U. S. 1013; Shull v. Dain, Kalman & Quail, Inc., 561 F. 2d 152, 160-61 (8th Cir. 1977).

[86] See Hart and Homer, Some Credit Aspects of Unconventional Securities, 25 Mercer L. Rev. 395 (1974); The Impact of the Federal Reserve Margin Regulations on Acquisition Financing, A Program by the [American Bar Association] Committee on Developments and Business Financing, 35 Bus. Law. 517 (1980).

[87] 48 Fed. Res. Bul. 1589 (1962).

that a private placement of a debt issue to finance the purchase of securities is an extension of credit, distinguishing a *public* offering only by a pragmatic reference to custom and concern about damage to the bond market.[88]

(3) In the Board's view, the installment sale of various tax-shelter programs (typically in the form of limited partnership interests relating to oil and gas exploration or real estate syndication or cattle) is an "arranging" within Regulation T.[89]

(4) This may be equally true with respect to tender offers. The question ultimately turns on the facts of each case.[90]

(5) The SEC has adopted an exemptive rule, on certain conditions, for a broker's or dealer's arranging credit on an "investment contract security involving the direct ownership of specified residential real property."[91]

j. Enforcement

Although the promulgation of margin rules is the function of the Board, their enforcement is assigned to the SEC along with all the other provisions of the Exchange Act. All the statutory sanctions (administrative, injunctive, and criminal) apply without qualification to violations of §§7 and 8(a) and of the Board's credit regulations.[92]

Regulation T is enforced primarily through the Commission's routine inspections of registered brokers and dealers and by the exchanges' and NASD's inspection and disciplining of their members.

The Commission in practice leaves the policing of Regulation U to the federal and state bank examining authorities under an arrangement whereby substantial violations are to be brought to the Commission's attention. But even with respect to banks any injunctive proceedings must be brought in the Commission's name under §21(e).

---

[88] See Karmel, The Investment Banker and the Credit Regulations, 45 N. Y. U. L. Rev. 59, 74 (1970).

[89] 58 Fed. Res. Bul. 398 (1972).

[90] Shull v. Dain, Kalman & Quail, Inc., 561 F. 2d 152, 161, *cert. denied,* 434 U. S. 1086 (8th Cir. 1977); see generally Schwartz and Kelley, Bank Financing of Corporate Acquisitions — The Cash Tender Offer, 88 Banking L. J. 99 (1971).

[91] Rule 3a12-5; see generally Hart, Securities Regulation of Real Estate Developments — Financing Arrangement Considered As an Extension of Credit, 35 Ohio St. L. J. 300 (1974).

[92] In a criminal prosecution based in part on Regulation T, the constitu-

The matter of implied civil liability of violating lender to borrower, as well as enforceability of a violating lender's contract, is considered in the chapter on civil liability.

k.   Margin Requirements of the Exchanges and the NASD

The margin rules of the exchanges and the NASD themselves are subject, like all their rules, to the jurisdiction of the SEC, not the Board.[93] But the Commission has never used this indirect margin authority, perhaps because the exchanges' rules go further than the Board's. For example:

(1) The most significant difference is a strict maintenance requirement, which on the New York Stock Exchange is currently (with some exceptions) 25 percent of all securities "long" in the account.[94]

An exchange member must comply, of course, with the margin requirements of both his exchange and the Board. For purposes of illustrating the interrelation of the two requirements, let us assume the present "T" margin requirement of 50 percent. Let us assume further that a New York Stock Exchange member buys 100 shares of stock for a customer when the market is 100. The customer deposits $5000 in cash or margin securities with a market value of $10,000[95] (or an appropriate combination of cash and securities) in order to meet the Board's 50 percent initial margin requirement. The market ultimately falls to $66\frac{2}{3}$, so that the stock that was bought is worth $6666.67. The member is not required to call for additional margin, although he may wish to do so for his own protection,[96] because the customer still has an equity in the account of $1666.67 ($6666.67, the current market value, minus

---

tionality of §7 of the Act and the validity of the regulation were sustained on appeal. United States v. McDermott, 131 F. 2d 313 (7th Cir. 1942), *cert. denied*, 318 U. S. 765. But see United States v. Van de Carr, 343 F. Supp. 993 (C. D. Cal. 1972), infra, text at n. 104 (directed verdict under Reg. U).

[93] Sec. Ex. Act §§19(b)(1)-(3), 19(c).

[94] N. Y. Stock Ex. Rule 431(b)-(d), CCH N. Y. Stock Ex. Guide ¶2431. The maintenance margin for securities "short" in the account varies with the market price of the stock; and it is different for bonds. With respect to exempted securities, see n. 44 supra.

[95] See n. 48 supra.

[96] It is said that most firms have "house" maintenance requirements of their own that are usually higher than the Stock Exchange margin, and that vary from account to account depending on the kind of securities held as collateral and other factors. Solomon and Hart, Recent Developments in the Regulation of Securities Credit, 20 J. Pub. L. 172-73 (1971).

the debt of $5000), which is 25 percent of the current market value ($6666.67). The market then falls to 65, giving the shares a value of $6500. No matter how much the market declines, Regulation T does not require any margin calls if there are no withdrawals. But at this point the customer's equity is only $1500, and it has to be brought up to $1625 (25 percent of the new market value) in order to comply with the Exchange's maintenance requirement. This may be done by depositing either $125 in cash or securities in such an amount ($166.67) that the equity in the account ($1666.67) will be 25 percent of the market value of all the securities in the account ($6666.67).

(2) The New York Stock Exchange also has an *initial* margin rule that requires the deposit of cash equal to the cost of the security, or cash or securities reflecting an equity in the account of at least $2000. And withdrawals of cash or securities are not permitted from any account that has a debit balance, short position, or commitments unless the equity will be at least $2000 or the amount specified in the maintenance requirement, whichever is greater.[97]

(3) "Substantial additional margin must be required in all cases where the securities carried are subject to unusually rapid or violent changes in value, or do not have an active market on a recognized exchange, or where the amount carried is such that it cannot be liquidated promptly."[98]

The NASD has a set of more or less similar rules, from which members of the leading exchanges are exempted.[99]

1. Extension of Credit on New Issues [§11(d)(1)]

The Exchange Act contains one other credit provision in §11 (d)(1). That section is not a part of the scheme of credit control by the Board of Governors of the Federal Reserve System. It is part of the treatment of the general problem of segregation of the functions of broker and dealer.[100] As the House committee described the section, it

> strikes at one of the greatest potential evils inherent in the combination of the broker and dealer function in the same person,

---

[97] Rule 431(a), CCH N. Y. Stock Ex. Guide ¶2431.
[98] Rule 431(d)(1).
[99] Rules of Fair Practice, Art. III, §30 and App. A, CCH NASD Manual ¶¶2180, 2180A.
[100] See 2 Loss c. 7D.

by assuring that he will not induce his customers to buy on credit securities which he has undertaken to distribute to the public.[101]

The section does this by making it unlawful, in substance, for a person who is *both* a broker *and* a dealer to extend, maintain, or arrange for credit "to or for a customer on any security (other than an exempted security) which was a part of a new issue in the distribution of which he participated as a member of a selling syndicate or group within thirty days prior to such transaction."[102]

Unfortunately, §11(d)(1) — however laudable its purpose — has been one of the most troublesome provisions of the 1934 Act to construe. As is apparent from its language, it raises many of the interpretative problems with which the Commission and the public have had to struggle under the prospectus provision of the 1933 Act, along with some peculiar difficulties of its own. And the Code deletes it, both because it has long since lost its broker-dealer-segregation motif and "because any *raison d'être* that survives is the avoidance of 'share-pushing' by persons engaged in distributions, and the Commission is given ample authority to attack that problem both by direct rule * * * and by using its enhanced rulemaking authority with reference to exchanges and the NASD."[103]

m.   Proposals for Change

The margin regulations — and it must be emphasized that what has been presented here is a condensed and simplified version with many qualifications omitted — are not among the most happily drafted in the securities regulatory structure. In a 1972 case the court wondered whether anybody "could ever be an 'expert' in the maze of conflicting, contradictory and confusing regulations issued by the Federal Reserve Board, enforced by the Securities and Exchange Commission, and attempted to be used here as bases for this criminal prosecution."[104]

---

[101] H. R. Rep. No. 1383, 73d Cong., 2d Sess. (1934) 22; see also S. Rep. No. 792, 73d Cong., 2d Sess. (1934) 12. As the House committee put it when the section was amended in 1954: "The apparent purpose was to provide that new issues would be initially placed with investors rather than with speculators." H. R. Rep. No. 1542, 83d Cong., 2d Sess. (1954) 15.

[102] See A. J. White & Co. v. SEC, 556 F. 2d 619, 623-24 (1st Cir. 1977), *cert. denied*, 434 U. S. 969.

[103] 1 Code 417.

[104] United States v. Van de Carr, 343 F. Supp. 993, 1011 n. 28 (C. D. Cal. 1972).

The Board has been engaged for some time in a "general over-haul of its margin regulations aimed at bringing them up to date with current circumstances in the securities markets, reducing regulatory burden, and simplifying and clarifying the language."[105] And in late 1982 it announced a more ambitious staff study, in cooperation with the staffs of the SEC and the CFTC, because of the changes since 1934 in the structure of financial markets and the development of markets for financial futures and options, which operate under a different framework from the cash markets on which they are based.[106]

The Code[107] assays a "major overhaul of the credit provisions * * * designed to facilitate understanding of a technical area rather than to make significant changes of substance."[108] Toward this end the Code's Reporter enjoyed the expert and enthusiastic assistance of key members of the Board's staff.

E.   INVESTMENT ADVISERS

1.   REGISTRATION

The emergence of investment advisers as an independent oc-cupation or profession did not occur until after the First World War. But the brief supplemental report on investment advisers that the Commission filed an incident of its investment trust study[1] found sufficient evidence of abuse by the fringe operators in this new field to persuade the Senate Banking and Currency Com-mittee to state in 1940:

> Not only must the public be protected from the frauds and misrepresentations of unscrupulous tipsters and touts, but the bona fide investment counsel must be safeguarded against the stigma of the activities of these individuals. Virtually no limita-tions or restrictions exist with respect to the honesty and integrity of individuals who may solicit funds to be controlled, managed, and supervised. Persons who may have been convicted or en-joined by courts because of perpetration of securities fraud are

[105] Fed. Res. rel. (Jan. 18, 1982).
[106] Fed. Res. rel. (Oct. 21, 1982).
[107] §917.
[108] 1 Code 414.

C. 8E [1] SEC, Investment Counsel, Investment Management, Investment Supervisory, and Investment Advisory Services (1939).

able to assume the role of investment advisers. Individuals assuming to act as investment advisers at present can enter profit-sharing contracts which are nothing more than "heads I win, tails you lose" arrangements. Contracts with investment advisers which are of a personal nature may be assigned and the control of funds of investors may be transferred to others without the knowledge of consent of the client.[2]

The result was the enactment of the Investment Advisers Act of 1940 as Title II of the bill of which Title I was the Investment Company Act.[3] For twenty years this statute was little more than a continuing census of the Nation's investment advisers. But it was substantially tightened by a series of amendments in 1960, fifteen years after the Commission had first urged such action in a special report to Congress,[4] and was again amended in the Investment Company Amendments Act of 1970 and the Securities Acts Amendments of 1975.

The 1975 amendments were designed essentially to conform the registration and disciplinary *procedures* more closely to those concurrently prescribed in the same legislation for broker-dealers.[5] But there are still differences, notably (1) provision for the filing of a registration application by "any person who presently contemplates becoming an investment adviser," (2) specification of the contents of the application for registration as an adviser, whereas the contents of the broker-dealer application are left entirely to the Commission, and (3) the absence of any prescribed qualifications or financial responsibility provisions for registration as an adviser.[6] Otherwise what has been said with respect to broker-dealer registration and disciplinary procedures applies equally here.

2. DEFINITION OF "INVESTMENT ADVISER"

The critical definition, of course, is that of "investment adviser":

---

[2] S. Rep. No. 1775, 76th Cong., 3d Sess. (1940) 21-22.

[3] For an exhaustive study of the statute, see T. Frankel, The Regulation of Money Managers: The Investment Company Act and the Investment Advisers Act (4 vols. 1978-80). On a broader front — covering also the Employee Retirement and Income Security Act (ERISA), pension plans, and bank and insurance company activities — see H. Bines, The Law of Investment Management (1978).

[4] SEC, Protection of Clients' Securities and Funds in Custody of Investment Advisers (1945), summarized in Inv. Adv. Act Rel. 39 (1945).

[5] See pp. 699-701 supra.

[6] Inv. Adv. Act §203(c), (e), (f), (h). The registration application is filed on Form ADV. And there is no *pendente lite* suspension provision. See c. 8C n. 58 supra.

"Investment adviser" means any person who, for compensation, engages in the business of advising others, either directly or through publications or writings, as to the value of securities or as to the advisability of investing in, purchasing, or selling securities, or who, for compensation and as part of a regular business, issues or promulgates analyses or reports concerning securities; but does not include (A) a bank, or any bank holding company as defined in the Bank Holding Company Act of 1956 which is not an investment company; (B) any lawyer, accountant, engineer, or teacher whose performance of such services is solely incidental to the practice of his profession; (C) any broker or dealer whose performance of such services is solely incidental to the conduct of his business as a broker or dealer and who receives no special compensation therefor; (D) the publisher of any bona fide newspaper, news magazine or business or financial publication of general and regular circulation; (E) any person whose advice, analyses, or reports relate to no securities other than securities which are direct obligations of or obligations guaranteed as to principal or interest by the United States, or securities issued or guaranteed by corporations in which the United States has a direct or indirect interest which shall have been designated by the Secretary of the Treasury, pursuant to section 3(a)(12) of the Securities Exchange Act of 1934, as exempted securities for the purposes of that Act; or (F) such other persons not within the intent of this paragraph, as the Commission may designate by rules and regulations or order.[7]

a. In General

This definition is broad enough to cover every person who for compensation gives advice as to securities, from the highest grade investment counselor who renders personalized service to the publisher of the lowliest tipster sheet. Quite clearly the definition does not cover a person who merely advises issuers with respect to a tender offer[8] or the value of their own securities generally; for there is nothing to indicate that Congress intended that the Advisers Act should regulate investment banking functions. It is equally clear, on the other hand, that the reports referred to in the definition do not necessarily have to analyze specific securities; it is enough that the person advises with respect to the desirability of investing in the securities markets rather than another medium like commodities or gold or real estate. Whether a professional *appraiser* is an investment adviser depends on whether

---

[7] §202(a)(11).

[8] Goldman, Sachs & Co. v. Hydrometals, Inc., CCH Fed. Sec. L. Rep. ¶96,534 (N. Y. Sup. Ct. 1978).

he performs the purely ministerial functions of checking the various financial services to determine market prices, or whether he actually makes an independent judgment of value by examining the financial reports of issuers or preparing comparative charts or the like.

This much said, a considerable gray area survives the exclusions in Clauses (A)-(F).

Query:

(1) What about persons who provide advisory services as a component of other financially related services — for example, financial or pension consultants or sports or entertainment representatives, as distinct from the lawyers and brokers and others whose advisory services are equally incidental but who are specifically excluded by Clauses (B) and (C)?[9]

(2) Should a person who is engaged in the business of finding advisers for others be considered to be an adviser himself on the theory that he is advising his clients to invest in the securities recommended by the adviser he selects? Possibly, though the reasoning requires a bit of a stretch.[10]

(3) When a limited partnership is organized for the purpose of investing in securities — a so-called hedge fund that provides a pass-through tax shelter and would be an investment company except for the exclusion in §3(c)(1) of the Investment Company Act for issuers that have fewer than a hundred security holders and do not make a public offering — is the general partner an investment adviser to the limited partners? The Second Circuit has said yes, citing (1) the limited partners' reliance on monthly reports in determining whether or not to withdraw their funds and (2) the fact that the general partners' compensation depended in part on profit and capital gains.[11] But suppose those two factors or at least the second is absent and the general partner limits himself to the day-to-day management of the firm, relying on an outside adviser who either (a) recommends or (b) is given authority to decide what and when to buy and sell. Indeed, even without an outside adviser — which should be a relatively easy case

---

[9] In Zinn v. Parrish, 644 F. 2d 360 (7th Cir. 1981), the isolated screening of stock recommendations as agent for a football player was considered incidental to the agent's principal duty of negotiating football contracts. See generally Inv. Adv. Act Rel. 770, 23 SEC Dock. 556, 559 (1981).

[10] Id. at 559.

[11] Abrahamson v. Fleschner, 568 F. 2d 862, 869-70 (2d Cir. 1977), *cert. denied,* 436 U. S. 913; see Hacker and Rotunda, SEC Registration of Private Investment Partnerships after Abrahamson v. Fleschner, 78 Colum. L. Rev. 1471 (1978).

— it has not been suggested that the president of an internally managed *corporate* investment company should be considered to be an investment adviser to his stockholder "clients." In the case of a trust, it has been held that the trustee does not advise the trust corpus but acts as principal; that is to say, the trustee himself embodies the trust.[12] A further complication, and a question apparently left open by the Second Circuit: if the general partner *is* an adviser, does he have a single client, the firm, in which event he could come within the §203(b)(3) exemption in terms of fewer than fifteen clients,[13] or is each limited partner a client?

(4) In parent-subsidiary situations in which the adviser subsidiary is undercapitalized, or dependent on the parent's personnel or office facilities or research data for the practical ability to render advice, is the question of the parent's status as an adviser to be determined by the usual veil-piercing factors? Or does §208(d) — to the effect that it is unlawful for any person to do "indirectly, or through or by any other person," anything it would be unlawful for him to do directly — sharpen the veil-piercing dagger?[14] Does such a provision add anything anyway under modern concepts of statutory construction?

b.   What Constitutes a "Business"

What has been said with reference to the term "business" as used in the definitions of "broker" and "dealer" under the Exchange Act applies equally here.[15] But there is one significant point peculiar to the definition of "investment adviser": Registration is not required simply because one is the author or publisher of a book, pamphlet, or article that "does not contain recommendations, reports, analyses, or other advisory information relating to specific securities or issuers" and is not one of a series intended to be supplemented.[16]

c.   Exclusions

(i)   *Certain professional persons:* Of course, a lawyer or accountant or engineer or a teacher of any kind *can* be an investment

[12] Selzer v. Bank of Bermuda, Ltd., 385 F. Supp. 415, 420 (S. D. N. Y. 1974).
[13] See p. 741 infra.
[14] See Inv. Adv. Act Rel. 353 (1972).
[15] See p. 678 supra.
[16] Inv. Adv. Act Rel. 563, 11 SEC Dock. 1500 (1977). The staff there abandoned the further condition that the publication not contain any "formulae or guidelines."

adviser if the advice he renders is not solely incidental to the practice of his profession. Much of what will be said in a moment with reference to the exclusion of certain brokers and dealers by Clause (C) is equally applicable here. Arguably, however, it is not essential that every advisory client of the lawyer be a legal client as well if the lawyer does not hold himself out to the public as an investment adviser and is first and foremost a lawyer whose advisory services are "solely incidental" to his law practice generally.

(ii) *Publishers:* It is sometimes a close question whether an individual who writes advisory material for a newspaper or other periodical is an employee or an independent contractor. However, the spirit of Clause (D) would seem to cover even the author of a syndicated financial column.[17] In the absence of a comparable exemption for radio and television stations, there is some question whether the stations, or the producers of the programs, may not come within the definition if they broadcast programs of investment advice. The fact that their compensation comes from the sponsor rather than the listeners is not necessarily decisive.[18]

This area is complicated by First Amendment considerations, particularly since the Supreme Court's recent recognition of the availability of some degree of constitutional protection for commercial speech.[19] When the New York Attorney General had earlier sought, under the substantially similar language in the Martin Act,[20] to examine the books and papers of a corporation that was registered with the SEC as an investment adviser and that had published a book by one Darvas, a professional dancer, entitled How I Made $2,000,000 in the Stock Market, he had prevailed in the Court of Appeals without any discussion of free speech.[21] And the Second Circuit, in similarly allowing the SEC to investigate a daily publication that reprinted broker-dealers' market letters, had held that the "bona fide" phrase in Clause (D) should not be construed as if the sole issue was the number of "the usual indicia of a newspaper." Rather, the phrase refers to

---

[17] See Loomis, The Securities Exchange Act of 1934 and the Investment Advisers Act of 1940, 28 Geo. Wash. L. Rev. 214, 245 n. 97 (1959).

[18] Ibid. On the Code's clarification of Clause (D), see §202(78)(B)(iv)-(v); 1 Code 116-17.

[19] Virginia State Board of Pharmacy v. Virginia Citizens Consumer Council, 425 U. S. 748 (1976); see Schoeman, Subscription Advisers, Blue Sky Registration and the First Amendment, 33 Bus. Law 249 (1977).

[20] N. Y. Gen. Bus. Law, Art. 23-A, §359-eee(a).

[21] Matter of Attorney-General of the State of N. Y. (Darvas), 10 N. Y. 2d 108, 176 N. E. 2d 402 (1961), *cert. denied,* 368 U. S. 947.

"those publications which seem to deviate from customary newspaper activities to such an extent that there is a likelihood that the wrongdoing which the Act was designed to prevent has occurred." And the court thought it was "not necessary to enlarge the category of 'bona fide' newspapers into an exclusion for all publications which could conceivably be brought within the term 'typical newspaper' in order to avoid the 'seeds of a constitutional controversy' * * * ."[22]

(iii) *Brokers and dealers:* Two related questions are presented under Clause (C): the meaning of "solely incidental" and what constitutes "special compensation."

So far as the first phrase is concerned, it is the administrative view that a broker or dealer whose business consists *almost exclusively* of managing discretionary accounts is an investment adviser.[23]

With respect to the meaning of "special compensation," the Commission's General Counsel early stated:

Clause (C) of Section 202(a)(11) amounts to a recognition that brokers and dealers commonly give a certain amount of advice to their customers in the course of their regular business, and that it would be inappropriate to bring them within the scope of the Investment Advisers Act merely because of this aspect of their business. On the other hand, that portion of clause (C) which refers to "special compensation" amounts to an equally clear recognition that a broker or dealer who is specially compensated for the rendition of advice should be considered an investment adviser and not be excluded from the purview of the Act merely because he is also engaged in effecting market transactions in securities. It is well known that many brokers and dealers have investment advisory departments which furnish investment advice for compensation in the same manner as does an investment adviser who operates solely in an advisory capacity. The essential distinction to be borne in mind in considering borderline cases * * * is the distinction between compensation for advice itself and compensation for services of another character to which advice is merely incidental.[24]

[22] SEC v. Wall St. Transcript Corp., 422 F. 2d 1371, 1378-79 (2d Cir. 1970), *cert. denied,* 398 U. S. 958; see also SEC v. C. R. Richmond & Co., 565 F. 2d 1101, 1107 (9th Cir. 1977); SEC v. Wall St. Transcript Corp., 454 F. Supp. 559 (S. D. N. Y. 1978) (the exclusion applied under Second Circuit's test); Lowe Management Corp., Inv. Adv. Act Rel. 759, 22 SEC Dock. 1093, 1096 n. 6 (1981).

[23] Inv. Adv. Act Rel. 640, 15 SEC Dock. 1211, 1212 (1978).

[24] Op. Gen. Counsel, Inv. Adv. Act Rel. 2 (1940); see also Inv. Adv. Act Rel. 626, 14 SEC Dock. 946 (1978).

This approach is equally applicable in principle to dealers as well as brokers, except that, since dealers do not ordinarily disclose their profits or spreads, it is more difficult as a practical matter to determine whether the profit or spread in a particular case is greater because of the amount of incidental investment advice rendered. Similar problems have resulted from the "unbundling" of rates and the discounting that followed the abolition of fixed stock exchange commissions in 1975. It would be fatal, not surprisingly, for a firm to make two general fee schedules available whose difference is attributable primarily to the presence or absence of investment advice. But the staff does not consider that there is "special compensation" merely because, for example, a "full service" firm charges higher rates than a "discount" firm, or a firm negotiates different fees with different clients for similar transactions.[25]

Frequently brokers and dealers distribute to their customers reports or analyses concerning specific securities or securities of certain types. It is understood to be the administrative construction that a broker or dealer does not receive "special compensation" for such pamphlets when he charges no more than the cost of *printing* and *distributing* them. Manifestly, however, there would be nothing left of the "no special compensation" restriction if a broker or dealer could charge any of the cost of *preparing* the pamphlet and still avoid registration as an investment adviser. When a broker or dealer distributes a pamphlet prepared *by another person,* he may likewise charge not more than the cost of the pamphlet to him and the postage.

When a broker or dealer thus acts as a conduit for the distribution of reports or analyses prepared by others and charges *more* than the cost and postage, the question whether it is he who "issues or promulgates" the analyses or reports within the meaning of the definition depends on other considerations. If the identity of the author is disclosed and the broker or dealer does not adopt the analyses or reports as his own by adding his own name — for example, when a broker or dealer merely distributes the Standard and Poor's reports on specific securities to his customers — he would not seem to be a person who "issues or promulgates" the reports. On the other hand, when the reports, although prepared by a third person, are issued under the sole name of a broker or dealer, he would seem to come within the definition. When he

---

[25] Id. at 950-51.

merely adds his own name to that of the author, there is room for argument.[26]

(iv) *Commission's power to exclude:* A single rule under Clause (F) excludes persons who merely advise their employer-sponsored employee benefit plans (as defined in the Employee Retirement Income Security Act) in the course of their regular employment.[27] But there have been a number of orders excluding, typically, professional trustees[28] and family corporations rendering advice solely to their stockholders.[29]

3. EXEMPTIONS

Apart from a plenary exemptive authority by rule or order in §206A, which was inserted in the 1970 amendments, §203(b) contains three exemptions from the registration requirement:

(1) any investment adviser all of whose clients are residents of the State within which such investment adviser maintains his or its principal office and place of business, and who does not furnish advice or issue analyses or reports with respect to securities listed or admitted to unlisted trading privileges on any national securities exchange;

(2) any investment adviser whose only clients are insurance companies; or

(3) any investment adviser who during the course of the preceding twelve months has had fewer than fifteen clients and who neither holds himself out generally to the public as an investment adviser nor acts as an investment adviser to any [registered investment company or "business development company" within §54 of the Investment Company Act]. * * *

The only problems of any substance are raised by the third clause: The maximum of fourteen applies to the total number of clients during the past twelve months rather than the number at any one time. On the other hand, the term "clients" refers

[26] Whether the *author* of reports must register depends on (1) whether he is an employee or independent contractor, and (2) the exemption granted by §203(b)(3) (infra p. 741).

[27] "Person" includes also a company controlled by or under common control with the employer, and "employer" includes also a company in any control relationship with a person. Rule 202-1, adopted by Inv. Adv. Act Rel. 503, 9 SEC Dock. 234 (1976).

[28] Augustus P. Loring, Jr., 11 SEC 885 (1942).

[29] Pitcairn Co., 29 SEC 186 (1949).

presumably to paying clients, so that a broker or dealer who renders advice to his customers generally and hence is excluded from the definition of "investment adviser" can charge a few customers for his advice and still come within this exemption.

So far as the second condition of the exemption is concerned, the important consideration, as with respect to the 1933 Act exemption for transactions "not involving any public offering," is the number of persons whom the adviser is willing to accept as clients rather than the number of actual clients. In other words, an adviser with only one client, or none at all, may not describe himself as an investment adviser in his letterheads or literature or list himself in the classified section of the telephone book. Under the language of the exemption, it is difficult for a person "to start from scratch" and build up to a maximum of fourteen clients without holding himself out generally to the public as an investment adviser. He would have to restrict himself to a small predetermined group of persons and demonstrate an unwillingness to accept other clients. As a practical matter, this exemption is used for the most part by persons who, for compensation, advise members of their families or close friends.

4.   REGULATORY PROVISIONS

a.   Recordkeeping, Reports, and Inspection

The 1960 amendments supplied the original statute's lack of any provision comparable to §17(a) of the 1934 Act, which gives the Commission authority to inspect the books and records of registered brokers and dealers, to prescribe what books and records shall be kept, and to require the filing of reports.[30] The rules prescribe certain records and reports.[31] And a so-called brochure rule requires advisers (with certain exceptions) to deliver a specified "disclosure statement" with respect to their background and business practices to every client or prospective client initially, and thereafter to offer annually in writing to deliver a current disclosure statement on request without charge.[32]

A visitatorial power has always raised more delicate questions with respect to those investment advisers who do personalized

---

[30] See pp. 703-04, 709-11 supra.

[31] Rules 204-1, 204-2.

[32] Rule 204-3; for staff interpretations of the statement, see Inv. Adv. Act Rel. 767, 23 SEC Dock. 156, 157-59 (1981).

counseling than with respect to broker-dealers because of "the personal details of a client's life which the adviser keeps on file to assist management of a portfolio."[33] Even the original statute prohibited the Commission from making public the facts ascertained during an *investigation* — or, indeed, the fact that an investigation was being conducted — except in a subpoena-enforcement or injunctive proceeding or a public hearing under the statute or in the event of a resolution or request from either House of Congress.[34] And this provision was extended by the 1960 amendments so that it applies equally to examinations under the new visitatorial power and also prohibits the members and employees of the Commission from disclosing, except to each other or with the Commission's approval, any information obtained as the result of an examination or investigation. The staff is thus "under a duty of nondisclosure similar to that of a bank examiner."[35]

b.   Profit-Sharing [§205(1)]

Investment advisers compensate themselves in a number of ways. Those who for the most part give continuous advice on the basis of the individual needs of each client generally charge a fixed fee or a fee computed at a certain percentage of the aggregate value of the assets managed. Some scale their rates according to the size of the fund supervised. And those whose services consist only of uniform publications charge fixed subscription prices. With one exception, any basis of compensation may be used as long as it is not so vague as to amount to a fraudulent practice. That exception is a prohibition against compensation based on "a share of capital gains upon or capital appreciation of the funds or any portion of the funds of the client"; and that exception is itself subject to several exceptions, which were enlarged in the 1970 amendments and again in the Small Business Investment Incentive Act of 1980 to permit certain performance or incentive fees in advisory contracts with investment companies and "business development companies."[36]

The purpose was "to prohibit arrangements for contingent compensation to investment advisers based on profit-sharing arrangements with clients which encourage advisers to take undue

---

[33] S. Rep. No. 1760, 86th Cong., 2d Sess. (1960) 6.
[34] §210(b).
[35] S. Rep. No. 1760, 86th Cong., 2d Sess. (1960) 7.
[36] §205(1); Rules 205-1, 205-2; see Inv. Co. Act Rel. 7130 (1972) ("Survey of Investment Company Incentive Fee Arrangements").

risks with the funds of clients"[37] — or, as the Senate committee put it, arrangements of the "heads I win, tails you lose" variety.[38] It seems clear from this statement of legislative purpose that the prohibition cannot be evaded by any "satisfaction or your money back" arrangements, or by means of purported gratuities that bear any relation to the amount of capital gains or appreciation.[39]

c. Assignment of Advisory Contracts [§205(2)]

Section 205 prohibits any advisory contract that "fails to provide, in substance, that no assignment of such contract shall be made by the investment adviser without the consent of the other party to the contract." And the statute contains a broad definition of "assignment" to include "any direct or indirect transfer or hypothecation of an investment advisory contract by the assignor or of a controlling block of the assignor's outstanding voting securities by a security holder of the assignor."[40]

Section 205(2) obviously rules out any indefinite consent to future assignments when the contract is entered into; otherwise the section could easily be rendered nugatory. Moreover, it has been the administrative policy to resolve any doubts in favor of the client in view of the "delicate fiduciary nature of an investment advisory relationship."[41] In a sense, §205(2) merges into §206, the general fraud provision.[42] For example, if a new partnership were formed and the name of a former partner were retained in the firm after he had dropped out, a careful explanation should be

---

[37] H. R. Rep. No. 2639, 76th Cong., 3d Sess. (1940) 29.

[38] S. Rep. No. 1775, 76th Cong., 3d Sess. (1940) 22.

[39] Inv. Adv. Act Rel. 721, 20 SEC Dock. 89, 90-91 n. 13 (1980).

[40] §202(a)(1); to the same effect, see Inv. Co. Act §2(a)(4), construed in Willheim v. Murchison, 342 F. 2d 33 (2d Cir. 1965), cert. denied, 382 U. S. 840. The definition goes on to provide that, "if the investment adviser is a partnership, no assignment of an investment advisory contract shall be deemed to result from the death or withdrawal of a minority of the members of the investment adviser having only a minority interest in the business of the investment adviser, or from the admission to the investment adviser of one or more members who, after such admission, shall be only a minority of the members and shall have only a minority interest in the business." On the other hand, §205(2) is supplemented by §205(3), which requires the advisory contract "to provide, in substance, that the investment adviser, if a partnership, will notify the other party to the contract of any change in the membership of such partnership within a reasonable time after such change."

[41] See SEC v. Capital Gains Research Bureau, Inc., 375 U. S. 180, 191 n. 38 (1963).

[42] See p. 977 infra.

made to each client. Again, whether or not fee-splitting amounts to a partial assignment of the contract, it would seem to be a fraudulent and deceptive practice for the adviser to fail to disclose the fact that anyone other than an employee shares in his fee or furnishes advice that he automatically passes on to his client.

d. Use of the Title "Investment Counsel" [§208(c)]

At the urging of the branch of the industry that renders continuous investment advice on a personalized basis, there was inserted in the Act after the introduction of the original bill a provision, §208(c), that, as amended in 1960, makes it unlawful for any registered investment adviser to "represent that he is an investment counsel or to use the name 'investment counsel' as descriptive of his business unless (1) his or its principal business consists of acting as investment adviser and (2) a substantial part of his or its business consists of rendering investment supervisory services."[43] The term "investment supervisory services" is defined to mean "the giving of continuous advice as to the investment of funds on the basis of the individual needs of each client."[44] The criterion for the use of the descriptive term "investment counsel" is thus the continuity and personalized nature of the advice rather than how conservative or speculative it is.

5. Proposals for Change

The Advisers Act is no exception to the gales of change that seem to be blowing — from one direction or another — in the SEC field generally.

The Code attacks the most serious defect that remains in the statute: the absence of any educational or other qualifications for registration as an investment adviser. Registrations have become effective for "booking agents, dress designers in Hollywood, dentists and real estate people, physicians, physicists, hotel managers, salesmen of floor wax, [and] a manager of a surgical supply

---

[43] There is also a complementary provision in §210(c) that protects "any investment adviser engaged in rendering investment supervisory services" against disclosure to the Commission of "the identity, investments, or affairs of any client" except as necessary or appropriate in a particular proceeding or investigation to enforce the statute.

[44] §202(a)(13).

house."[45] It is not even certain that the Commission could do anything about professed astrologers, one or two of whom have registered in the past.[46]

Borrowing from §15(b)(7) of the Exchange Act as amended in 1975, §703(e) of the Code simply extends the broker-dealer qualification provisions to investment advisers, the commentary stating:

> As a matter of principle, it is difficult to understand why broker-dealers and their associates should be subjected to certain qualifications while investment advisers and their associates — whose occupation "can cause havoc unless engaged in by those with appropriate background and standards"[47] — are permitted to hold themselves out as experts without regard to education, training

[45] See Schenker, The S. E. C. Looks at Investment Advisers, 3 Inv. Counsel Annual 6, 11 (1941); see also 7 SEC Ann. Rep. 34 (1941). Mr. Schenker, who was Chief Counsel of the Investment Trust Study and the first Director of the Commission's former Investment Company Division, told also of one flowery application — withdrawn after investigation — that turned out to have been filed by a convict who was doing a "bit" in a Wisconsin jail for assault with intent to rob and murder and wanted to use his registration as an investment adviser in an attempt to persuade the parole board that he had a business he could go into as soon as he was released. Schenker, supra, at 14. Murder is not a disqualification under §203(e)(2), though burglary would be!

The report of the "Special Study" tells the story, simultaneously hilarious and hair-raising, of the new publication entitled The Trading Floor that appeared on several newsstands in downtown New York City on May 21, 1962, selling for $.50 and advertised as a daily investment advisory service that would recommend eleven new stocks in each issue. The publisher and entire staff turned out to be a nineteen-year-old who had held seven different jobs during the eighteen months after he had dropped out of college. His "major source" of information was two cousins who he said were "fanatically interested in the stock market and * * * send away for all this free advice." One cousin was a twenty-year-old college student and the other a fourteen-year-old high school freshman. The mastermind's mother helped him collate and staple the pages after he had run them off on a mimeograph machine in the kitchen of their Brooklyn apartment. It is perhaps anticlimactic to add that his registration was withdrawn. 1 SEC, Report of Special Study of Securities Markets, H. R. Doc. No. 95, 88th Cong., 1st Sess. (1963) 147-48.

[46] A 1966 news story quoted a Washington seeress whose predictions on the basis of "psychic information" had been widely publicized as saying: "So many people have come to me in the past two weeks that I just can't count them. I can help many of these people. It depends on the psychic atmosphere and whether God really wants them to know." Wall St. J., May 16, 1966, p. 1, col. 4. But what of the sun spot theorists? The same story quotes the chairman of the advisory committee of an investment counsel firm as saying that because of a historical pattern in sun spots "an important stock market peak may lie some one to four years hence," and a research partner of a New York Stock Exchange member firm as saying: "I believe the market reacts to atmospheric or cosmic influences, but I've never seen any theory refined enough to accurately predict the stock market."

[47] Citing Marketlines, Inc. v. SEC, 384 F. 2d 264, 267 (2d Cir. 1967), cert. denied, 390 U. S. 947.

or experience. And the Commission is understood to have evidence of the practical need for covering investment advisers. Arguments of avoidance of duplicate federal and state regulation are equally applicable with respect to brokers and dealers.[48]

Section 705 conveys a similar grant of across-the-board rulemaking authority with respect to financial responsibility safeguards. It does not follow, of course, that the Commission would in fact impose the same qualifications or financial responsibility safeguards with respect to broker-dealers and advisers. It is "also quite possible that an applicant will meet the qualifications for one type of registration but not those for another, or conceivably (for example) that he will meet the possibly lesser qualifications for investment advisers that have subscribers rather than clients without meeting the qualifications for broker-dealer registration. By way of further example, the Commission might want to develop different tests (or additional test questions) for different kinds of broker-dealers (in oil royalties, variable annuities, etc.)."[49]

The Code also suggests several less major, but significant, reforms:

(1) Section 703 greatly simplifies existing law by providing a unified registration procedure — as §1809 provides a single disciplinary procedure — for (a) brokers and dealers, (b) municipal brokers and dealers, and (c) investment advisers. "The Commission presumably will develop a form in several parts, so that a particular applicant will be able to complete any or all of them."[50]

(2) Advisory contracts must be in writing.[51]

(3) The intrastate exemption is deleted, as it is with respect to broker-dealers.

(4) Section 914(c), complemented by §202(95) and the rule making authority in §915(b), reflects a novel approach to the "mini-account," that is to say, the investment management services that many investment advisers (and some broker-dealers, banks, and bank affiliates) have developed in recent years for persons with as little as $5000 or even $1000 to invest. Whereas today this evolving investment medium is in a state of limbo because of the necessity of an all-or-nothing approach — either full registration under the Securities and Investment Company Acts or no regulation at all apart from the fraud provisions, which are themselves applicable only if there is a "security" — the Code

[48] 1 Code 330, Comment (1).
[49] 1 Code 326; see §703(e)(2)(A).
[50] 1 Code 326.
[51] §919(a)(1).

offers a new approach by way of regulation of the investment advisers (including for this purpose banks).[52]

Code reforms aside, the Commission in 1980 requested comment with respect to the issues it should consider in the course of a study of the Advisers Act, including the possibility of establishing one or more self-regulatory organizations and application of the "SECO" concept.[53]

F. A NATIONAL MARKET SYSTEM

When Congress, in connection with the Securities Acts Amendments of 1975, directed the Commission in the new §11A of the 1934 Act "to use its authority * * * to facilitate the establishment of a national market system for securities."[1] it bestowed on that agency a role that, wanted or not, was clearly unwonted: that of coaxer, encourager, prodder, midwife, what have you, toward the *industry's* development of the disparate exchange and over-the-counter markets into some sort of unelucidated "national market system."

The article by Professor Poser that follows paints a picture of the stage *circa* late 1981 in the evolutionary process; and major developments in the year or so since are reflected in bracketed footnotes. Professor Poser is not only dubious of the endeavor's desirability but also critical of a certain wishywashiness in the Commission's handling of its task. Perhaps, therefore, one proposition on which he and all the post-1975 Commissioners would agree is that in the American economy one does not tamper lightly with the guts of the New York Stock Exchange.

Be that as it may, this essay is reprinted here not because the present writer necessarily agrees with everything its author says,[2] but because, critique aside, it is an excellent exposition of a technical, complex, and vital subject by one whose experience, as

---

[52] See 1 Code 396-407; cf. Small Account Investment Management Services, Report of the Advisory Committee on Investment Management Services for Individual Investors (1973), reprinted in Fixed Rates and Institutional Membership, Hearings on S. 470 and S. 488 before Subcom. on Securities of Senate Com. on Banking, Housing & Urban Affairs, 93d Cong., 1st Sess. (1973) 474, 476-77.

[53] Inv. Adv. Act Rel. 717, 19 SEC Dock. 1195 (1980).

C. 8F [1] §11A(a)(2).

[2] For a decidedly more favorable appraisal, see J. Seligman, The Transformation of Wall Street (1982) c. 12 *passim.*

both key SEC official and Executive Vice President of the American Stock Exchange before his happy ascent to Academe, uniquely qualifies him to tell the story.

POSER, RESTRUCTURING THE STOCK MARKETS: A CRITICAL LOOK AT THE SEC'S NATIONAL MARKET SYSTEM, PARTS II-VI
56 New York University Law Review 881 (1981)[a]

* * *

II. DEVELOPMENTS LEADING TO THE NMS PROPOSAL

The proposal for a national market system came out of a particular background of regulations, relationships, and events. The proposal itself, as well as the difficulties of implementing it, can be understood only against that background. Until the early 1970's, the markets operated under a regulatory structure effectively imposed by the NYSE and acquiesced in by the SEC. As one writer has suggested, that structure rested on three "fundamental principles . . . (i) fixed commission rates for securities transactions; (ii) limitation of membership to persons engaged in the securities business; and (iii) a requirement that all transactions (with certain exceptions) by members of an exchange be executed on that exchange."[50]

The NYSE commission rate rule required that members charge their customers minimum commissions according to a fixed scale, which was based on the price of the stock purchased or sold. To protect the rule from circumvention, rebates of commissions to customers and sharing of commissions with nonmembers were prohibited, but rebates and sharing of commissions with other members were permitted. Since the minimum commission rate applied to each round lot (in most cases, 100 shares) purchased or sold, a member could not give customers the benefit of a volume discount on larger transactions. Thus, the commission on a 1,000-share transaction was exactly ten times the commission on a 100-share transaction, even though the cost of executing the larger

---

[a] ED.: Copyright 1981 by the New York University Law Review and reprinted with the permission of the editors and of Professor Poser. The first part of this article is set out supra pp. 667-76.

[50] Harman, The Evolution of the National Market System — An Overview, 33 Bus. Law. 2275, 2277 (1978).

transaction was normally much less than ten times as great. The other stock exchanges developed commission rate schedules that were for the most part identical to that of the NYSE.

The limitation of NYSE membership to persons engaged primarily in the securities business effectively prevented institutional investors, such as mutual funds, pension funds, and insurance companies, from avoiding the fixed minimum commission rate by becoming stock exchange members themselves or establishing a broker-dealer affiliate that became a member, in order to buy and sell securities for their own portfolios. The requirement (known as the "off-board trading" rule) that members execute their transactions in listed securities on the exchange[54] prevented members from trading in the third market, or from becoming third market dealers themselves. In 1941, however, the SEC held invalid an NYSE rule that would have forbidden its members from executing transactions in dually traded securities on a regional stock exchange.[55]

In the 1960's, these restrictions came under considerable legal and economic pressure. In 1963, the U. S. Supreme Court held in *Silver* v. *New York Stock Exchange* that stock exchanges may be subject to the antitrust laws.[56] The Court noted that the Exchange Act contains no express exemption from the antitrust laws and held that an exemption would be implied "only if necessary to make the Securities Exchange Act work, and even then only to the minimum extent necessary."[57] In determining whether a particular stock exchange action is exempted from antitrust coverage, the Court will examine whether the SEC has power to review such action and, if it does have review power, whether the SEC has actually exercised oversight.[58] Thus, the NYSE's ability to with-

---

[54] [N. Y. Stock Ex. Rule 394, rescinded Mar. 31, 1976, and replaced by Rule 390, CCH N. Y. Stock Ex. Guide ¶2390.]

[55] In re Rules of the New York Stock Exchange, 10 SEC 270, 292 (1941) (Multiple Trading Case).

[56] 373 U. S. 341, 364-65 (1963).

[57] Id. at 357.

[58] Gordon v. New York Stock Exch., 422 U. S. 659, 682-91 (1975): "Only if the SEC is actively and aggressively exercising its powers of review and approval can we be sure that fixed commission rates are being monitored in the manner which Congress intended." Id. at 692 (Douglas, J., concurring).

It is unclear, however, that *actual* SEC oversight is a precondition to antitrust immunity. In United States v. National Ass'n of Sec. Dealers, 422 U. S. 694 (1975), the Court stated that the allegedly anticompetitive practices of the NASD were

> among the kinds of restrictions Congress contemplated when it enacted that section. And this conclusion necessarily leads to a determination that they are immune from liability under the Sherman Act, for we see

stand an antitrust attack would depend on the SEC's oversight role. Though the facts of *Silver* did not involve exchange rules relating to commission rates, membership, or off-board trading, it was not difficult to see that the decision raised the possibility that these rules might be subject to antitrust attack by the government or private litigants.[59]

Silver furnished the legal setting for the collapse of the NYSE's market system; economic developments in the securities markets brought on the actual collapse. During the 1960's the volume of securities transactions increased enormously. Average daily volume on the NYSE grew from three million shares in 1960 to 11.4 million shares in 1969. Along with the growth in total volume, the proportion of volume attributable to institutional investors also grew rapidly, increasing from about thirty-three percent of public share volume on the NYSE in 1960 to about sixty percent in 1971. This increase in institutional investment was caused by the growth of institutions that invested in equity securities and by a movement of institutional portfolios away from fixed income securities and into equities. Furthermore, as institutions became larger, so did their portfolio transactions. For example, between 1960 and 1971, the average size of mutual fund orders on the NYSE increased from 550 to 4,206 shares. Transactions of 10,000 shares or more, which composed only 3.1% of total NYSE volume in 1965, rose to 14.1% in 1969.[64]

The increase in institutional business placed pressures on the inflexible NYSE minimum commission rate, which permitted no volume discounts and no rebates to nonmembers. Managers of institutional portfolios found ways of using the "fat" (i. e., the excess over the cost plus a reasonable profit) in the commissions

---

no way to reconcile the Commission's power to authorize these restrictions with the competing mandate of the antitrust laws.

Id. at 721-22. Additionally, even if actual SEC oversight *is* a precondition to antitrust immunity, unexercised SEC power to regulate may influence the outcome of an antitrust attack. "[W]ithin the area of supervised self-regulation contemplated by the Securities Exchange Act, *per se* concepts are generally displaced and the courts are to examine whether the particular restraint, even though it would be a *per se* violation if performed by others, was reasonable." Jacobi v. Bache & Co., 520 F. 2d 1231, 1238 (2d Cir. 1975), *cert. denied*, 423 U. S. 1053 (1976).

[59] See Gordon v. New York Stock Exch., 422 U. S. 659 (1975); Thill Sec. Corp. v. New York Stock Exch., 433 F. 2d 264 (7th Cir. 1970), *cert. denied*, 401 U. S. 994 (1971); Kaplan v. Lehman Bros., 371 F. 2d 409 (7th Cir.), *cert. denied*, 389 U. S. 954 (1967) (Warren, C. J., dissenting from denial of certiorari).

[64] * * * By October 1981, this figure had risen to 34.4%, Wall St. J., Nov. 9, 1981, at 6, col. 4.

on large transactions for the benefit of the institution or for their own benefit. For example, the manager of a mutual fund would direct the broker executing a portfolio transaction to share the commissions with other broker-dealers who had sold mutual fund shares or provided research or other services to the fund or its manager. If the transaction was executed on the NYSE, the rules of that exchange required such sharing (or "give-up") of commissions to be limited to NYSE members; if, on the other hand, it was executed on a regional exchange, give-ups could be made to members of that exchange. To attract institutional business, several regional exchanges also amended their rules to permit give-ups to any broker-dealer registered with the SEC, whether or not he was an exchange member.

The opportunity for making give-ups provided by the fixed commission rate caused a certain amount of institutional business in NYSE-listed stocks to be executed on regional exchanges. In most instances, this business did not go to the regionals because the regionals were offering a better price than that available on the NYSE. In many instances, in fact, the price of a transaction often was fixed even before it was taken to the regional exchange. Brokerage firms that were members of both the NYSE and of the major regional exchanges negotiated transactions on behalf of their institutional customers over the telephone, as in the over-the-counter market. However, the off-board trading rule of the NYSE required these prearranged transactions to be brought to the floor of an exchange and executed there. In some cases, these large transactions were executed on a regional exchange rather than on the NYSE to provide greater opportunity for making give-ups.

The third market also owed a substantial portion of its activity to the minimum commission rate. To avoid paying the fixed rate, managers of institutional portfolios would deal directly with non-member market makers in the over-the-counter market. Typically, the market maker would buy from, or sell to, the institution at a price slightly more favorable to the institution than the NYSE price, taking into account the commission that would have been paid on the transaction if it had been executed on the NYSE.

Thus, as a result of the NYSE commission rate structure, the regionals and the third market gained business at the expense of the NYSE. A 1973 report by a Senate subcommittee noted "a steady growth" of activity in these secondary markets. It stated that in 1971, more than seventeen percent of the volume in common stocks listed on the NYSE represented transactions in other markets (ten percent on regionals and seven percent in the third market), and that the percentages were considerably higher for the most actively traded stocks.

This "market fragmentation," resulting from a combination of fixed commission rates and the "institutionalization" of the markets, has been given as a primary reason for establishing a national market system. Nevertheless, the extent of the fragmentation should not be overstated. In 1961, before the process of institutionalization of the securities markets was fully under way, the NYSE accounted for 65.65% of share volume on all stock exchanges, the Amex 25.84%, and the four major regional exchanges a total of 6.79%. In 1971, the year that a national market system was first proposed, the NYSE accounted for 71.34%, the Amex 18.42%, and the four regional exchanges 9.58%. Thus, the NYSE actually gained a larger portion of total exchange volume during this period, at the expense of the Amex. Since Amex stocks are generally more speculative than those on the NYSE, the shift appears to have been the result of a decrease in the speculative climate of the market between 1961 and 1971. Although the percentage of regional volume increased by forty-one percent (from 6.79% to 9.58%), the relationship between NYSE volume and regional volume did not change markedly.

In 1968, the SEC commenced public investigatory hearings into the stock exchange commission rate structure.[76] After the hearings had provided a full airing of commission give-ups and related practices, the Commission came to the conclusion that "fixed charges [on institutional size orders] are neither necessary nor appropriate" and should be replaced with competitive rates.[77] In late 1970, using the leverage over the stock exchanges that had been provided by the Silver decision (i. e., fear of antitrust attack if the SEC's protective umbrella of regulatory oversight were removed), the SEC began phasing out the fixed commission rate,[78] first by prohibiting any minimum commission to be charged on portions of orders in excess of $500,000. By May 1, 1975, all commission rates paid by public customers became subject to negotiation.[79]

---

[76] SEC Exch. Act Release No. 8324 (1968), [1967-1969 Transfer Binder] Fed. Sec. L. Rep. (CCH) ¶77,557.

[77] SEC Exch. Act Release No. 9007 (1970), [1970-1971 Transfer Binder] Fed. Sec. L. Rep. (CCH) ¶77,918, at 80,047; see SEC Exch. Act Release No. 11,203, 40 Fed. Reg. 7394, 7397 (1975).

[78] SEC Exch. Act Release No. 9079 (1971), [1970-1971 Transfer Binder] Fed. Sec. L. Rep. (CCH) ¶77,955 at 80,124; SEC Exch. Act Release No. 9007 (1970), [1970-1971 Transfer Binder] Fed. Sec. L. Rep. (CCH) ¶77,918 at 80,047.

[79] Minimum commission rates paid by exchange members were not elimi-

III. The Proposal for a National Market System

A. THE SEC PROPOSAL

The SEC proposal to link the markets in a national market system, made in 1971, represented a reversal of past policy. Until 1975, when Congress mandated creation of the NMS, the SEC's authority over the structure of the securities markets was limited to control over the granting of unlisted trading privileges and to review power over stock exchange rules in certain specified areas. Where it did exercise such authority, its policy was to favor separate but competing markets.[82] Thus, the SEC facilitated dual trading of NYSE- and Amex-listed securities by freely granting unlisted trading privileges to the regional exchanges, and by forcing the NYSE to permit its member firms to trade NYSE-listed securities on the regionals.[84]

In view of the significance of the NMS proposal, it was made surprisingly casually. In March 1971, the Commission transmitted to Congress a report on its study of institutional investors. In the letter of transmittal, but not in the report itself, the Commission proposed that a national market system be established. The Commission stated:

> A major goal and ideal of the securities markets and the securities industry has been the creation of a strong central market system for securities of national importance, in which all buying and selling interest in these securities could participate and be represented under a competitive regime. This goal has not as yet been attained.[86]

This language is curious, since the concept of a central market system, far from having been a "major goal and ideal," had never before been proposed or, so far as published documents disclose, even considered by the Commission. Be that as it may, the SEC pointed out that the "combination of fixed minimum commission rates and barriers to access"[88] had been the principal cause of "the

---

nated until May 1, 1976. SEC Exch. Act Release No. 12,396, 41 Fed. Reg. 19,270-74 (1976) (NYSE rule change to eliminate minimum commission rates paid by exchange members); see SEC Exch. Act Release No. 11,203, 40 Fed. Reg. 7394 (1975) (adopting Rule 19b-3), 17 C. F. R. 240.19b-3 (1981)).

[82] SEC Exch. Act Release No. 9484, Statement on the Future Structure of the Securities Markets, 37 Fed. Reg. 5286, 5286-87 (1972) (hereinafter Market Structure Statement).

[84] See text accompanying note 55 supra.

[86] [8 SEC, Institutional Investor Study Report, H. R. Doc. No. 92-64 (1971) xxiv.]

[88] [Id. at xxii.]

accelerating growth of institutional trading on the regional stock exchanges and in the third market."[89] It stated further that the ability of market makers (including specialists, block positioners, and third market makers) to offset temporary imbalances in supply and demand ultimately "is impeded if the market maker's opportunity to participate in the total volume of trading is limited by rules which artificially restrict its exposure to that volume."[90] In addition, individual investors should have an opportunity to participate in trades with institutional investors, since "advantageous discounts and premiums . . . often result from such trading."[91] Finally, the Commission noted that "modern communication and data processing facilities [now make it] possible to preserve geographically separated trading markets while at the same time tying them together on a national basis."[92]

On its face, the NMS proposal seems logical and straightforward. After all, why not use modern technology to link the markets and thereby improve their quality, enhance competition, and secure better executions of investors' transactions? Laudable as these goals are, the SEC might have been more cautious in proposing so monumental a change in the structure of the markets, particularly since less drastic steps might have served just as well. The perceived need for a national market system was based on the fragmentation of the markets, a phenomenon caused by the diversion of institutional trading away from the primary exchanges to the regional exchanges and the third market. In turn, this market fragmentation was caused primarily by the NYSE fixed commission rate structure and by barriers to access to the NYSE. At the time the SEC made the proposal, however, the Commission had determined that fixed commission rates should be repealed at least on large transactions, and had taken the first step toward replacing them with negotiated rates.

In view of this situation, it is surprising that the Commission did not consider the possibility that the effect of repealing fixed rates would be to enable the NYSE to recapture the institutional business that was switching to the regional exchanges and the third market, and that this might make irrelevant the national market system proposal. In this case, the NYSE would for all practical purposes be the national market. After the repeal of mandatory fixed, nongraduated commission rates, the NYSE rules barring

[89] Id.
[90] Id.
[91] Id. at xxiii.
[92] Id.

institutional investors from membership would have little practical importance, since once the institutions would be able to negotiate the commissions they would pay, their economic incentive to become exchange members would disappear. One commentator observed in 1978, perhaps with a certain degree of exaggeration:

> What was not as well understood in the early 1970s as it is today was that these issues are interdependent. For example, fully negotiated commission rates tend to make institutional access an academic question; price competition for institutional business among exchange members effectively removes the *raison d'etre* for the third market; and direct competition between upstairs firms[b] and the specialists renders the regional exchanges obsolete and the desire to "link all market centers" a proposal without a constituency.[95]

In 1971, it could be predicted that repeal of the restrictive NYSE rules that for many years had dictated the structure of the markets would, paradoxically, concentrate even more business on the NYSE. One can surmise that an important reason behind the SEC's advocacy of a national market system at that time was precisely its desire to avoid such a result. To the extent that the NYSE was an *auction* (or agency) market providing a place for customers' buy and sell orders to be executed against each other in an auction-type trading process, it made sense to concentrate all trading on one exchange, since this would maximize the opportunity for buy and sell orders to meet and would tend to increase the liquidity of the markets. But to a certain extent the NYSE was a *dealer* market, in which customers' orders were executed against the bids and offers of the specialist. Since the NYSE had no competing specialists, concentration of trading on the NYSE would strengthen the monopoly of the unitary NYSE specialist and eliminate such dealer competition as was provided by the regional exchanges and the third market. In 1963, the Commission had stated that the benefits of competition by the regional exchanges in dually traded stocks "outweigh[ed] any possible effects on the depth of the existing markets."[97] The NMS proposal appears to have been based on the view that linking the markets would preserve and extend this competition.

---

[b] ED.: Large brokerage firms executing buy and sell orders in their own offices.

[95] Harman, supra note 50, at 2300. * * *

[97] [2 SEC, Report of Special Study of Securities Markets, H. R. Doc. No. 95, 88th Cong., 1st Sess. (1963) 951.]

Once the NMS proposal had been made, it gained almost unanimous public approval, although differences soon surfaced as to what should be the essential contours of the system. Even before receiving its legislative mandate to establish a national market system, and notwithstanding its questionable authority to do so, the SEC began taking steps in 1972 to implement its plan: it issued reports, proposed and adopted rules, and appointed advisory committees. By the time Congress acted on the proposal, plans for a national market system were well under way.

B. THE LEGISLATION

In June 1975, after studying the securities markets for four years, Congress enacted the Securities Acts Amendments of 1975. This legislation had its genesis in the operational and financial crisis that beset the securities industry in 1969 and 1970 and caused the demise of more than 100 broker-dealers, including several of the largest and oldest Wall Street firms. Despite the fact that Congress' initial focus was on the financial responsibility and "back-office" efficiency of the securities industry, congressional scrutiny soon broadened to encompass the structure of the markets and the manner in which they were regulated. Congress adopted the SEC's proposal for a national market system and gave the SEC broad powers to implement the proposal.

1. Section 11A

The legislative mandate to establish an NMS is embodied in section 11A of the Exchange Act, which states that the "securities markets are an important national asset which must be preserved and strengthened," and set forth five qualities that the markets should have:

> (i) economically efficient execution of . . . transactions; (ii) fair competition among [brokers, dealers, and markets]; (iii) the availability to brokers, dealers, and investors of information with respect to quotations [and transactions]; (iv) the practicability of brokers executing investors' orders in the best market; and (v) an opportunity, consistent with [efficiency and best execution], for investors' orders to be executed without the participation of a dealer.[e]

Congress found that these goals would be achieved by the "linking of all markets for qualified securities through communication and

---

[e] ED.: Brackets are in the original.

data processing facilities." Having made these preliminary findings, Congress directed the Commission "to use its authority under this title to facilitate the establishment of a national market
system for securities."

Since the statute neither defines the term "national market system" nor identifies the elements that would compose it, the five
qualities of markets set forth above are the closest that the legislators came to explaining the concept of the NMS. It is useful,
therefore, to take a closer look at these statutory objectives.

a. *Economically Efficient Execution of Transactions* — To
economists, " 'efficiency' means exploiting economic resources in
such a way that 'value' — human satisfaction *as measured by aggregate consumer willingness to pay* for goods and services — is
maximized."[113] Applied to the securities markets, "economically
efficient execution of transactions" presumably refers to reducing
the costs of executing orders. The lower the transaction costs, the
greater the trading volume, and the easier it will be for securities
to gravitate to those investors who value them most. Thus, the
"value" to society will be maximized.

In modern high-volume markets, automation provides the most
significant reduction of transaction costs, and it is the availability
of automation that makes establishment of an NMS feasible.
However, the desirability of using automation should not be confused with the desirability of establishing an NMS. Whether or
not an NMS is built, automation can and should be used to reduce
transaction costs and to enable the markets to function smoothly.
In fact, in recent years, the individual stock exchanges, the NASD,
and brokerage firms have applied automated systems advan-
tageously to such matters as the dissemination of quotations, the
routing of orders from firms to exchange floors, the execution
of orders, the clearance and settlement of transactions, and the
keeping of records. But simply because automation makes possible the development of an NMS, it does not necessarily follow
that an NMS will reduce transaction costs or achieve the goal of
"economically efficient execution of securities transactions." It is
possible that the costs of developing and operating an NMS may
be greater than any saving that can be achieved by investors
through executions at more favorable prices.

---

[113] R. Posner, Economic Analysis of Law 10 (2d ed. 1977) (emphasis in
original). Economic efficiency may, however, have several possible meanings.
See Coleman, Efficiency, Exchange, and Auction: Philosophic Aspects of the
Economic Approach of Law, 68 Calif. L. Rev. 221, 222-23 (1980).

b. *Fair Competition Among Broker-Dealers and Among Markets* — Congress' view that an NMS would "enhance competition"[117] was apparently based on a belief that linking the markets would enable regional exchange specialists and third market makers to compete effectively with primary market specialists. The Commission took this position despite its findings in its 1971 Institutional Investor Study Report that "[t]here is little evidence that a better price is frequently provided by the regional specialists,"[119] and that the "primary reason for the execution of [institutional-size transactions] in the third market appears to be the saving in transactions charge"[120] (a saving that would disappear with the end of fixed commission rates). Indeed, the repeal of the NYSE's restrictive rules, notably the fixed minimum commission rate, brought to the securities markets a substantial measure of competition among broker-dealers. Thus, it is questionable whether the goal of "fair competition" could have best been achieved by mandating the establishment of an NMS, rather than by simply repealing these restrictions.

Given the fact that the secondary markets do not engage in price competition with the primary markets to any substantial extent, the view that linking the markets in an NMS will "enhance competition" does not take into account how the securities markets actually work, but is based, rather, on an optimistic prediction of how they *might* work if an NMS were established. Nevertheless, the central point that has guided the Commission's efforts to establish the NMS is that "fair competition" is stifled because regional exchange specialists and third market makers do not have "effective access" to the flow of orders on the floor of the NYSE.[121] In the Commission's view, if such access were provided by the NMS, "fair competition" would ensue. In 1979, for example, the Commission stated:

> If market makers in a particular market center have reasonable expectations that they will receive a greater amount of order flow if they make markets which are consistently better in terms of price, depth, or ease of execution, the Commission believes they will be more likely to compete aggressively — thereby providing a better and more efficient market.[122]

---

[117] [Sec. Ex. Act §11(a)(1)(D).]
[119] 4 Institutional Investor Study, supra note [86], at 1822.
[120] Id. at 1824.
[121] See id. at 1861, 1956.
[122] SEC Exch. Act Release No. 15,671, Development of a National Market System, 17 SEC Docket 24, 35 (1979) (hereinafter 1979 Status Report).

Regional specialists and third market makers did not have access to order flow because of the procedures employed by brokerage firms in routing their customers' orders. Most retail brokerage firms routinely send the great preponderance of their small- and medium-sized orders to the primary exchanges. The order-routing systems of the larger firms channeled small retail (i. e., noninstitutional) orders to the primary market automatically. As a result, regional specialists and third market makers, having no opportunity to execute these orders against their own bids and offers, were unwilling to disseminate competitive price quotations. Presumably, if facilities were developed as part of an NMS that would enable customers' orders to be routed to the market providing the best quotation, then regional specialists and third market makers would begin to publish competing bids and offers.

The validity of this hypothesis is subject to debate. The difficulties that the Commission has recently encountered in its attempts to encourage market maker competition — despite the existence of market linkages and a rule requiring publication of competing quotations — seem to indicate that the Commission's "order flow" theory is questionable. It is noteworthy that in 1971, the Justice Department, which has invariably encouraged intermaket competition, conceded that price competition between primary market and regional exchange specialists was limited in nature not because regional exchange specialists did not have access to the order flow, but rather because they were not sufficiently capitalized.[125]

The question of how much weight should be given to the goal of "fair competition" is a peculiarly difficult one. Many regulations designed to protect investors will restrict competition to some degree; and, conversely, increases in competition may conflict with the other objectives set forth in the statute. Furthermore, the potential conflict between competition and regulatory control is particularly likely to arise in the context of establishing a national market system. The linking of markets necessarily contemplates a degree of cooperation among the markets, as well as the establishment of uniform practices and rules; these concomitants of market linkage may inhibit the development of strong competition.

The legislative history of the 1975 amendments makes clear that the Commission is required to strike a balance between "fair

---

125 * * * Of course, order flow and capital may be related, since a specialist to whom a substantial amount of order flow is directed may be in a better position to attract capital.

competition" and the other objectives of the Act. The Senate Committee on Banking, Housing and Urban Affairs stated when it reported out the bill:

> This explicit obligation to balance, against other regulatory criteria and considerations, the competitive implications of self-regulatory and Commission action should not be viewed as requiring the Commission to justify that such actions be the least anti-competitive manner of achieving a regulatory objective. Rather, the Commission's obligation is to weigh competitive impact in reaching regulatory conclusions.[127]

c. *The Availability to Brokers and Investors of Information with Respect to Quotations and Transactions* — In formulating its plans for the national market system, Congress regarded the provision of "access to accurate, up-to-the-second information" concerning completed transactions and quotations as "the heart" of the system.[128] In fact, the establishment of facilities to provide public dissemination of such market information has been the least controversial and consequently the most readily implemented of the goals of the NMS. The objective has been to display "information as to the prices at which transactions in particular securities are taking place (i. e., last sale reports) and the prices at which . . . traders have expressed their willingness to buy or sell (i. e., quotations)."[129] This information is to be shown for each dually traded stock in a single format, in such a way that the information provided by one market is no easier to view, or to recall by means of interrogation devices, than that provided by any other market.[130] Of course, the value to brokers and investors of such displays of information is no better than the validity of the information disseminated. As will be seen, the quotation information disseminated has in some instances been of questionable value.

d. *The Practicability of Brokers Executing Investors' Orders in the Best Market* — "Best execution" of investors' orders is a key concept of the national market system.[132] * * *

---

[127] Senate Report, *supra* note 4, at 13, [1975] U. S. Code Cong. & Ad. News at 191; Bradford Nat'l Clearing Corp. v. SEC, 590 F. 2d 1085, 1105-06 (D. C. Cir. 1978). * * *

[128] Senate Report, *supra* note 4, at 9, [1975] U. S. Code Cong. & Ad. News at 187; see Bradford Nat'l Clearing Corp. v. SEC, 590 F. 2d at 1094.

[129] [S. Rep. No. 75, 95th Cong., 1st Sess.] at 9, [1975] U. S. Code Cong. & Ad. News at 187.

[130] SEC Exch. Act Release No. 14,416, Development of a National Market System, 14 SEC Docket 31, 42 (1978) (hereinafter 1978 Status Report).

[132] The term "best execution" refers to the duty of an agent or other

The common law of agency requires agents, as fiduciaries, "to be loyal to the principal's interests and to use reasonable care to obtain terms which best satisfy the manifested purposes of the principal."[134] An agent, including a stockbroker, must exercise reasonable discretion to obtain the best price available, and he is normally expected to act in accordance with the customs of his business.[135] In the securities markets, brokerage firms customarily send small "retail" orders in dually traded stocks to the primary market, even though it is possible that at any given time a better execution might be available on a regional exchange or in the third market. Their reasons for following this practice include the additional costs of checking several markets before executing an order (which might exceed any saving from obtaining a better price), the possibility that a secondary market quotation will not be reliable (i. e., the specialist or market maker may not be willing to deal at his quoted price), and the possibility that the broker will "miss the market" on the primary exchange while trying to obtain a better execution elsewhere. Large institutional orders, on the other hand, are generally negotiated by "block positioning" firms, even though the orders may subsequently be executed on an exchange. These transactions are committed to the expertise and resources of block positioning firms precisely because their complex nature necessitates special handling to ensure their "best execution."

In view of these practices for negotiating and executing broker-age orders in dually traded stocks, and given the fact that the regional exchanges have not provided price competition to any substantial degree, "best execution" does not appear to have been a problem for investors. In fact, the congressional and SEC hearings that provided the basis for the 1975 amendments did not lead to any finding that investors were not receiving the best available execution of their orders. Although certain well-identified problems of investor protection have beset the securities markets during the past two decades and have given rise to remedial legislation and regulatory reform, the lack of "best execution" of investors' orders has not been one of these problems. Consequently, a trouble-some question concerning the national market system proposed

fiduciary to obtain for a customer the best price discoverable in effecting securities transactions in the exercise of reasonable diligence. See Opper v. Hancock Sec. Corp., 250 F. Supp. 668, 676 (S. D. N. Y.), aff'd, 367 F. 2d 157 (2d Cir. 1966); In re Arleen W. Hughes, 27 S. E. C. 629, 636 (1948), aff'd, 174 F. 2d 969 (D. C. Cir. 1949).

[134] Restatement (Second) of Agency §424 (1958).

[135] Id. Comment b; see Harman, supra note 50, at 2296-97.

must be raised: Is a restructuring of the markets justified in order to solve this nonexistent or at most marginal problem? If facilities are established for routing orders to the market providing the best execution, it is possible that price competition will develop, and that it will then be feasible to hold brokers to a stricter "best execution" requirement. However, the experience thus far with the Quote Rule and the Intermarket Trading System provides little support for this view.[d]

e. *An Opportunity for Investors' Orders to be Executed Without the Participation of a Dealer* — The final goal set forth in the statute is to provide an opportunity, consistent with the goals of economically efficient execution of transactions and "best execution," for investors' orders to be executed without the participation of a dealer. For reasons alluded to earlier, this goal is implicit in the very notion of a *centralized* NMS.

In 1973, the SEC proposed that all trading in the national market system be subject to two basic rules. First, an "auction trading" rule would require that limit price orders of public customers be satisfied before any transaction in the same security is effected anywhere in the system at a less favorable price to the other party. Second, a "public preference" rule would provide that public orders have price priority over the bids and offers of specialists and market makers. Thus, a professional dealer could not operate in the system unless he were willing to buy at a price higher, or sell at a price lower, than any available public bid or offer. The Senate committee report on the bill indicated approval of these two rules but pointed out that the goal of "protecting" investors' orders throughout the system against trading on another exchange could not be achieved until a "mechanism" was devised "by which all buying and selling interested [*sic*] in a given security can be centralized and thus assure public investors best execution."[e] The attempts that have been made to achieve protection of public limit orders throughout the system are discussed below.

2. *Other Provisions Pertinent to the NMS*

To fulfill its mandate of facilitating the establishment of a national market system, the SEC was authorized by the statute to create advisory committees and employ experts; to require the self-regulatory organizations to act jointly in planning, developing, operating, or regulating a national market system; and to

---

[d] See pp. 769-76 infra.
[e] ED.: The "*sic*" is in the original.

conduct studies and make recommendations to Congress from time to time as to the need for modifications of the scheme of self-regulation so as to adapt it to a national market system. Furthermore, the SEC was directed to use its broad rulemaking authority under the Securities Exchange Act to establish and regulate an NMS.

Section 11A also provided for the registration and regulation of "securities information processors," those persons engaged in the business of (a) collecting, processing, or preparing for the distribution or publication of information with respect to securities quotations or transactions, or (b) distributing or publishing such information (whether by means of a ticker tape, a communications network, a terminal display device, or otherwise) on a current and continuing basis.[153]

The 1975 amendments also dealt with the three rules of the NYSE on which the structure of the markets had previously rested. First, subject to minor exceptions, fixed commission rates were abolished by the statute,[155] even though the SEC had itself eliminated them by a rule that became effective one month before the legislation was enacted.[156] Second, stock exchange membership was thrown open to any qualified broker-dealer, but the stock exchanges were permitted to continue to limit the size of their memberships.[157] However, the legislation prohibited exchange members from effecting transactions on the exchanges for their own accounts, for the accounts of associated persons, or for accounts for which they exercised investment discretion, subject to certain stated exemptions and to any further exemptions that the SEC may make by rule.[158] Third, Congress dealt with the off-board trading question by directing the SEC to review all stock

---

[153] * * * §3(a)(22)(A), 15 U. S. C. §78c(a)(22)(A) (1976). Only those fitting the definition of "exclusive processor," id. §3(a)(22)(B), 15 U. S. C. §78c(a)(22)(B) (1976), must automatically register to lawfully use the mails or any means of interstate commerce in their information processing activities. All other information processors are exempt from the registration requirement "unless the Commission, by rule or order, finds that the registration of such securities information processor is necessary or appropriate in the public interest, for the protection of investors, or for the achievement of the purposes of this section." Id. §11A(b)(1), 15 U. S. C. §78k-1(b)(1) (1976). [For an explanation and the Code's simplification, see 1 Code 194-96.]

[155] [§6(e).]

[156] SEC Exch. Act Release No. 11,203, 40 Fed. Reg. 7394 (1975), adopted SEC rule 19b-3, 17 C. F. R. §240.19b-3 (1981), which made fixed rates illegal after May 1, 1975. The statute was enacted on June 4, 1975 and by its own terms, * * * §6(e)(1) * * * took effect the same day.

[157] [§6(c).]

[158] [§11(a).]

exchange rules "which limit or condition the ability of members to effect transactions in securities otherwise than on such exchanges" and to take prompt steps "to amend any such rule imposing a burden on competition which does not appear to the Commission to be necessary or appropriate in furtherance of the purposes of this chapter."[160] Thus, unlike the issues of commission rates and membership, the issue of off-board trading was left to the SEC to resolve.

The 1975 legislative amendments also included a number of other provisions relating to the national market system. In adopting any new rules, the stock exchanges[161] and the NASD[162] are required to consider whether such rules would "remove impediments to and perfect the mechanism of a free and open market and a national market system."[163] Furthermore, both the SEC and the self-regulatory organizations are prohibited from adopting any rule that imposes a burden on competition not necessary or appropriate to further the purposes of the Exchange Act.[165]

* * * f

IV. THE ELEMENTS OF THE NMS

Although the basic concept of the NMS is a relatively simple one — consisting of a linkage of the markets that would enable customers to receive the best available execution of their orders and market makers and specialists to compete — the actual development of the system has turned out to be a complex task requiring numerous intricate and difficult decisions. In its efforts to implement the NMS, the SEC has identified six major "elements," some of which are facilities that can be regarded as components of the NMS, and others that are changes in the regulations governing the securities markets. These elements are (1) a system for public reporting of completed transactions on a consolidated basis (consolidated tape), (2) a composite system for the collection and display of bid and asked quotations (composite quotation

---

[160] [§11A(c)(4)(A).]
[161] [§6(b)(5).]
[162] [§15A(b)(6).]
[163] [§6(b)(5).]
[165] [§§23(a)(2), 6(b)(8), 15A(b)(9).]
f ED.: The omitted paragraph refers to the SEC's authority with respect to the self-regulatory organizations' rules and disciplinary action, as well as the direction to the Commission to facilitate a national clearance and settlement system. See pp. 693-95, 698, 701-03 supra.

system), (3) systems for transmitting orders to buy and sell securities and reports of completed transactions from one market to another (market linkage systems), (4) elimination of restrictions on the ability of exchange members to effect over-the-counter transactions in listed securities (off-board trading rules), (5) nationwide protection of limit price orders against inferior execution in another market, and (6) rules defining the securities that are qualified to be traded in the NMS.

A. THE CONSOLIDATED TAPE

Since the late nineteenth century, the ticker tape has been a symbol and central feature of the stock market. The disclosure of volume and prices of completed stock exchange transactions within moments after their execution benefits investors by providing them with up-to-date market information and also gives the securities industry a valuable tool for selling securities. Long before the NMS was proposed, the NYSE and Amex had developed procedures for rapid collection of transaction data on their trading floors, for processing these data, and for transmitting them over leased wires to subscribers throughout the country on ticker tapes. The regional exchanges either had no ticker tapes or their ticker tapes were not widely followed.

In February 1972, one year after first proposing that an NMS be established, the SEC identified as an element of the NMS, "a nationwide disclosure or market information system to make universally available price and volume in all markets." Shortly thereafter, the Commission proposed and subsequently adopted[177] a rule requiring that every national securities exchange and the NASD file with the SEC a plan for the collection, processing, and dissemination of reports of completed transactions in securities admitted to trading on an exchange. The rule also provided that, after a certain date, no exchange or association could make available such reports on a current and continuing basis except pursuant to a plan declared effective by the Commission.

In early 1973, in an effort of intermarket cooperation that was to establish a pattern for the implementation of other NMS elements,[180] five of the principal stock exchanges and the NASD filed

---

[177] [Rule 17a-15, subsequently designated Rule 11Aa3-1.]

[180] In early 1981 the SEC adopted rule 11A3-2, 17 C. F. R. §240.11Aa3-2 (1981), which established procedures and requirements for joint industry plans in connection with planning, developing, operating, or regulating the NMS

a joint plan with the SEC.[181] The plan called for two ticker networks: Network A would disseminate price and volume information concerning transactions in all NYSE-listed stocks, whether executed on the NYSE, on a regional exchange, or in the third market. Network B would disseminate comparable information concerning all Amex-listed stocks, as well as certain stocks listed only on one or more of the participating regional exchanges. The plan was to be administered by an unincorporated association called the Consolidated Tape Association (CTA).

In addition to providing the last-sale information for the two ticker tapes represented by Networks A and B, the plan contemplated making the information available through interrogation devices provided to subscribers by securities information processors. Thus, investors and market professionals would be able to obtain the last-sale price of any stock covered by the system, regardless of the market in which the transaction was executed. After the plan became effective, this information was disseminated over high-speed transmission lines. Interrogation devices that receive data over these lines remain current in periods of high trading volume, notwithstanding delays in the low-speed lines that transmit data to the ticker tapes. Owing to unanticipated technical problems, the consolidated tape did not go into full operation until April 30, 1976, more than four years after the SEC first proposed it. A year later, the Commission was able to report that the system was working smoothly, "substantially free of reporting disruption due to system failure."[185]

The impact of the consolidated tape is limited, since this facility only provides a record of the prices at which transactions were effected in the past, rather than an indication of present trading interests (i. e., the prices at which future transactions may be effected). Nevertheless, the ability of brokers and investors to see primary exchange, regional exchange, and third market transactions on a single tape may be useful to investors "in indicating general trends and temporary price disparities between market centers" at any particular time.[187] Most important, perhaps, the consolidated tape represented the first solid step in the development of the NMS.

---

or any of its facilities. SEC Exch. Act Release No. 17,580, 46 Fed. Reg. 15,866 (1981).

[181] See SEC Exch. Act Release No. 15,250, 15 SEC Docket 1355, 1356 (1978).

[185] [1976-1977] SEC Ann. Rep. 10.

[187] [1974-1975] SEC Ann. Rep. 13.

B. THE COMPOSITE QUOTATION SYSTEM

In its 1972 Statement on the Future Structure of the Markets, the SEC identified a composite quotation system (CQS) as an element of the NMS, and for several years thereafter continued to regard the CQS as a "cornerstone" of the system. The central concept of a CQS is that the bids and offers of competing specialists and market makers would be displayed in a format that would enable a broker representing a customer's order to ascertain the highest bid and the lowest offer. Thus, the broker would be in a position to seek out and obtain the best available execution of the customer's order at any given time. This concept is based, of course, on the premise that regional specialists and third market makers will compete with each other and with the primary market (NYSE or Amex) specialist by disseminating competing quotations. As stated above, the SEC had found that such competition among markets as existed was closely related to the fixed minimum commission rate, which was in the process of being abolished. Nevertheless, the Commission believed that meaningful price competition would develop once the CQS and other elements of the NMS were in operation.

The history of the CQS proposal has been one of false starts and changes of direction. In March 1972, the Commission proposed a rule that would have required the exchanges to make specialists' quotations, and the NASD to make third market makers' quotations, available to vendors of market information on a current and continuing basis.[194] Two years later, having taken no further action, the SEC revised the proposal to require the reporting of quotations pursuant to a plan to be filed by the exchanges and the NASD.[195] The proposal was never adopted, and in March 1975 the Commission took a new approach: it requested the stock exchanges to eliminate all restrictions on access to quotation information disseminated by any quotation vendor, the supposition being that competition would develop if such restrictions were removed.[196] Although each exchange subsequently reported to the SEC that it had taken the action requested or that it did not have any restrictions on the dissemination of quotations, competition in quotations nevertheless did not develop.[197] Despite the efforts

---

[194] SEC Exch. Act Release No. 9529, 37 Fed. Reg. 5760 (1972) (proposing rule 17a-14).

[195] SEC Exch. Act Release No. 10,969, 5 SEC Docket 735 (1974).

[196] SEC Exch. Act Release No. 11,288, 6 SEC Docket 425 (1975).

[197] SEC Exch. Act Release No. 11,406, 6 SEC Docket 859 (1975).

of several vendors to develop a composite quotation service, the Commission found that "the lack of reliable quotations from the various markets was hampering private and self-regulatory efforts to establish a viable composite quotation system, the absence of which in turn was impeding development of a national market system."[198]

In July 1976, the SEC returned to its earlier approach. It published for comment a new proposed rule (the Quote Rule) that would require the exchanges and the NASD to collect quotations from their specialists and market makers for reported securities (i. e., securities covered by the consolidated tape), and to make these quotations available to quotation vendors.[199] The rule required every exchange member and third market maker promptly to communicate bids and offers to the exchange or the NASD. Publishing quotations in "size" (i. e., in multiples of a 100-share unit of trading) was optional, but quotations were required to be for at least one unit of trading. Subject to certain exceptions, quotations were required to be "firm": that is, a specialist or third market maker was required to execute any order presented to him at a price at least as favorable as his published bid or offer in any amount up to his published quotation size. In June 1977, the SEC amended the proposed Quote Rule to require the exchanges to make available to vendors a single quotation for each reported security, reflecting the highest bid and lowest offer communicated at the "post" on the exchange floor where the security was traded.[203] That quotation would not necessarily be the quotation of a specialist, but would reflect the buying and selling interest of all brokers and dealers.

The Quote Rule was adopted in January 1978 and finally became effective on August 1, 1978. At the time of the rule's adoption, the Commission expressed its belief that, "for the first time, relatively reliable and comprehensive information as to prices and sizes of quotations for all reported securities from all markets, whether on exchanges or over-the-counter, will be made available to market professionals and the public."[206] In February

---

[198] [1975-1976] SEC Ann. Rep. 7.

[199] SEC Exch. Act Release No. 12,670, 41 Fed. Reg. 32,856, 32,856 (proposed rule 11Ac1-1 * * *).

[203] [1976-1977] SEC Ann. Rep. 8; SEC Exch. Act Release No. 13,626, 42 Fed. Reg. 32,418, 32,418 (1977) (amending proposed rule 11Ac1-1).

[206] [Sec. Ex. Act Rel. 14,416, Development of a National Market System, 14 SEC Dock. 31, 38 (1978) ("Status Report").]

1981, however, the SEC announced that its hopes for the Quote Rule had not been fully realized.[207] The Commission stated that

> [w]hile certain regional exchange specialists do actively compete for order flow by disseminating competitive quotations in a limited number of actively traded ITS [Intermarket Trading System[208]] stocks, regional exchanges (and their specialists), by and large, prefer to continue to use other methods to compete with the primary exchanges for order flow. These methods include reductions in charges for execution or clearing services and guarantees * * * against transactions occurring on the primary exchanges at equal or superior prices.[209]

A major problem noted by the Commission was the unreliability of quotations disseminated by regional exchange specialists. This problem arose in connection with Autoquote — a computer system developed by the regional exchanges for the specific purpose of complying with the Quote Rule — which disseminates quotations automatically in response to quotation changes on the primary exchanges. The SEC noted that "certain regional exchange specialists" failed "to consistently honor their automatically generated quotations,"[210] while others disseminated quotations that were uncompetitive with the primary market or that had unusually large spreads.[211]

Third market makers, according to the Commission, did not use Autoquote to comply with the Quote Rule, but instead disseminated quotations manually. "[I]n order to avoid the costs associated with constantly monitoring and updating their quotations, certain third market makers disseminate quotations on an extremely infrequent basis during the trading day . . . ."[212] Consequently, third market quotations tend not to give an accurate indication of the prices at which a third market maker is willing to deal. Faced with the failure of the Quote Rule to achieve the results expected of it, the Commission proposed to amend the rule to "permit regional exchange specialists and third market makers to disseminate quotations on a voluntary, rather than mandatory, basis."[213] The Commission believed that if regional exchange specialists and third market makers were permitted to issue quota-

---

[207] SEC Exch. Act Release No. 17,583, 46 Fed. Reg. 15,713, 15,715 (1981) (proposed amendment to rule 11Ac1-1, 17 C. F. R. §240.11Ac1-1 (1981)).
[208] See text accompanying notes 220-32 infra.
[209] SEC Exch. Act Release No. 17,583, 46 Fed. Reg. at 15,715.
[210] Id. at 15,716.
[211] Id.
[212] Id. at 15,717.
[213] Id.

tions only in those stocks in which they were interested in actively competing with the primary exchanges, "the information disseminated to the public should more accurately reflect the interest of regional exchange specialists or third market makers in attracting order flow."[214] Although the Commission was undoubtedly correct in its belief, the new proposal represents a substantial lowering of its sights insofar as the potential for intermarket price competition is concerned.[g]

The unsatisfactory results of the efforts to create a CQS necessarily raise the question whether it is feasible to induce regional specialists and third market makers to publish accurate and reliable competing quotations. If it is not feasible, the value to the investing public of developing a complex system for routing orders among market centers remains questionable. It is of course possible that under the Commission's "order flow" hypothesis,[215] price competition among markets will blossom once facilities have been established for giving all markets equal access to order flow. The Catch-22 in this hypothesis is that on the one hand, the development of a facility that would route orders automatically to the market displaying the best quotation would be worthless unless one could be assured that it would produce meaningful price competition; on the other hand, a regional exchange specialist or third market maker has little incentive to publish competing quotations under the existing system, since the primary market specialist, to whom the bulk of the customers' orders are channeled, can retain the business simply by adjusting his own quotations to match the prices of any competing quotations. In any event, the admittedly limited experience with the Quote Rule provides little basis for confidence that a system of competing quotations will come into existence.

C. MARKET LINKAGE SYSTEMS

The consolidated tape and the CQS are means for ascertaining the market in which a broker can obtain the best available execution of his customer's order. In order to obtain "best execution," however, there must be an effective means to transmit the order to the best market. In theory, a broker could route each order he

---

[214] Id. at 15,718.

[g] ED.: The Commission adopted substantially its 1981 voluntary dissemination proposal in Sec. Ex. Act Rel. 18,482, 24 SEC Dock. 876 (1982).

[215] 1978 Status Report, supra note [206], at 39; see text accompanying notes 121-24 supra.

receives to the best market on an order-by-order basis. For large firms that handle thousands of customers' orders daily, the only way to accomplish this is by use of a computerized system that routes orders automatically to the market with the highest bid or lowest offer at any particular time. In early 1978, the SEC requested the exchanges and the NASD to combine their efforts to implement by September 30 of that year such a "common message switch," which it described as "a single system for the prompt and efficient routing of orders for qualified securities directly from brokers' and dealers' offices to any qualified market."[216] The principal stock exchanges and several brokerage firms opposed the SEC proposal on the ground that it would eliminate broker discretion by forcing automatic routing of all orders on the basis of machine-displayed quotations.[217] These commentators argued that in deciding to which market to route an order, a broker must consider factors other than price, including the size of the order, the costs of execution and clearing, the reliability of the displayed quotation, and the possibility of obtaining an execution at a price more favorable than that of the displayed quotation.[218]

Faced with these objections, the Commission did not press its request that a common message switch be developed, but at the same time it did not withdraw the request. Instead, it quietly placed it on the back burner. It is likely that the Commission's decision to defer consideration of the common message switch was based less on its assessment of the objections raised by the stock exchanges than on the practical conclusion that without the willing cooperation of the stock exchanges, implementation of the common message switch would be extremely difficult. Furthermore, it is understandable that the stock exchanges would oppose the common message switch, since such a facility would, in effect, bypass the stock exchanges by placing the switching mechanism that would form the heart of the NMS in a "neutral" central computer.

Faces with this dilemma, the Commission chose to support the development by the NYSE and five other exchanges of a linkage of the stock exchange floors. This facility, known as the Intermarket Trading System (ITS), has a more limited capability than the

---

[216] 1978 Status Report, supra note [206], at 39 & n. 46.
[217] 1979 Status Report, supra note 122, at 35.
[218] Id. An execution at a price better than the displayed quotation might be obtained, for example, if a member in the exchange trading "crowd" is willing to buy or sell at a more favorable price than that announced by the specialist.

common message switch, but it has the practical advantage of stock exchange sponsorship.[220] ITS is a facility by which orders held by a broker or specialist on the floor of one exchange can be transmitted electronically to another exchange displaying a better quotation (higher bid or lower offer) than that displayed at the originating exchange.[221] Since its inception in 1978, the Commission has regarded ITS as a key element of the NMS.

ITS began operations in April 1978 with a linkage between the NYSE and Phlx in eleven dually traded stocks. Within a few months, linkage was extended to Amex, BSE, MSE, and PSE. The number of stocks included in the system has increased steadily, reaching 871 in November 1980. Of these, 750 stocks were listed on the NYSE, 124 on the Amex; three were listed on both the

---

[220] ITS was developed jointly by the Amex, BSE, NYSE, PSE, and Phlx. See Directorate of Economic and Policy Analysis, SEC, A Monitoring Report on the Operation of the Intermarket Trading System 1 & n. 2 (1981) (hereinafter ITS Monitoring Report); 1979 Status Report, supra note 122 at 27 n. 10.

[221] The SEC has described ITS as follows:

The primary function of the ITS is to link the various market centers by routing messages between them so that participants in one market center can communicate with participants in other market centers in order to purchase or sell stock. . . . The ITS enables brokers and specialists who are physically present in one market center to transmit electronically their own orders or their customers' orders in an ITS Stock to another market center. This is accomplished by the entry of a "commitment to trade" into a computer terminal located on the floor of a participating exchange.

A commitment to trade identifies the destination market center, provides the necessary clearing data, specifies whether the commitment is a buy or sell, and indicates the number of shares involved and the price at which the security is to be executed . . . .

An order, i. e., a "commitment to trade," initiated by an originating market center by entry into a computer terminal is delivered or queued for delivery to the destination market center's output terminal in a matter of seconds . . . . Assuming . . . that the commitment is transmitted correctly, the broker or specialist at the destination market then has the following options: the commitment can be allowed to expire; the commitment can be cancelled; the commitment can be accepted; or an administrative message can be sent.

A commitment to trade entered into the system is a firm obligation for a fixed period of time on the part of its originator to buy or sell the specified security. If a commitment to trade is accepted by a broker or specialist at the receiving market center, a short message is entered into the system and the system quickly reports an execution back to the originating market center. If a commitment is not accepted during the designated time-period the commitment is automatically cancelled. A commitment to trade may also be manually rejected within the designated time-period. In that event, the cancellation is reported back to the originating market.

ITS Monitoring Report, supra note 220, at 5-8 (citations omitted).

NYSE and Amex. ITS trading volume has expanded, increasing from 20.7 million shares in November 1979, when 643 stocks were in the system, to 38.4 million shares in November 1980.[226]

Despite its growth, ITS cannot be regarded as a significant factor in the markets. In November 1980, ITS facilitated only 4.2% of total share volume and 6.6% of the total number of trades in the 871 ITS stocks.[227] Furthermore, ITS does not appear to have improved the quality of the markets. In a report issued in early 1981 the SEC staff stated: "it cannot be concluded that the ITS caused the spreads in the primary market either to narrow or to widen."[228] Stated another way, the earlier prediction that the NMS would increase the liquidity of the markets has not thus far been borne out. In large part, this failure was due to the fact, referred to earlier, that regional exchange specialists and third market makers did not publish reliable competing quotations. The Commission described the problem succinctly:

> To a significant extent, the effectiveness of any international link-age system is dependent on the quality and reliability of the market information disseminated. Unless market participants are confident that the displayed quotation information is accurate and timely, they may be unwilling to send commitments through the ITS for fear of missing the market on their own exchange.[229]

In one respect, however, ITS has achieved a degree of success. The SEC staff report stated that ITS was being used by brokers and dealers physically present on an exchange floor to seek out prices on another exchange that were better than the displayed quotations and that more than ten percent of ITS executions represented successful attempts to "reach through" the published quotations.[230] It is not clear, however, whether this finding repre-

---

226 Id. at 10.

227 [Id. at 11. A later report shows that by year-end 1981 the number of stocks in the system reached 921, about 90 percent of them listed on the New York Stock Exchange; and that the number of ITS trades grew by 28 percent and ITS share volume by 37 percent in 1981 (while there was an actual decrease in composite trading, and an increase of only 12 percent in composite share volume, in ITS stocks). SEC Directorate of Economic and Policy Analysis, A Report on the Operation of the Intermarket Trading System: 1978-1981 (1982) i ("1982 Report").]

228 Id. at 38. [This was confirmed in the 1982 Report (at 40).]

229 SEC Exch. Act Release No. 16,214, 18 SEC Docket 467, 470 (1979).

230 ITS Monitoring Report, supra note 220, at 32-35. The SEC defines "reach-throughs" as "attempts by brokers or dealers in one market center to reach prices more favorable than those reflected in the existing quotes of destination market centers." Id. at 32. The report also noted a low incidence of "trade-throughs" (i. e., executions at one ITS market center when another market center is offering a better price). Id. at 35-36. In April 1981 the SEC

sents customers obtaining better executions of their orders than those available in the originating market, or regional exchange specialists sending orders for their own account through ITS to the primary markets to trade there without buying an NYSE or Amex seat.

The use made of ITS by the various stock exchanges is enlightening. The NYSE participated in about ninety percent of all ITS trades, sixty percent as executing market center and thirty percent as originating market center, indicating that the regional exchanges do the great majority of their ITS trading with the NYSE, rather than with each other or with the Amex.[231] Moreover, the net effect of ITS has been to channel securities business from the regional exchanges to the NYSE. At least partially as a result of this, the NYSE's share of all share volume in securities listed on that exchange increased from 85.71% in 1977, the year before ITS began operations, to 87.76% in 1980.[232] It would indeed be ironic if the NMS, which was intended to increase competition among the markets, should instead become an instrument for consolidation of the monopolistic position of the NYSE specialist.

Concurrently with ITS, an experiment was begun with the use of a fully automated, electronic trading system. This is the National Securities Trading System (NSTS) of the Cincinnati Stock Exchange (CSE), a small regional stock exchange. NSTS is an electronic communications network that enables CSE members to enter orders for themselves or their customers without leaving their offices. Orders entered are stored in a computer, and buy orders are automatically matched with sell orders. The computer is programmed to assign priority to orders based on the price and time of entry, with public orders receiving priority over those of members.[233]

---

approved rule proposals of the six ITS exchanges and the CSE prohibiting trade-throughs. SEC Exch. Act Release No. 17,704, 22 SEC Docket 709, 711 (1981). [Data in the 1982 Report (at iii) suggest that the 10 percent figure in the test grew to about one-third.]

[231] ITS Monitoring Report, supra note 220, at 13-21.

[232] NYSE, Fact Book 1981, at 14 (26th ed. 1981).

[233] [See SEC, Directorate of Economic and Policy Analysis, A Report on the Operation of the Cincinnati Stock Exchange National Securities Trading System 1978-1982 (1982) i:

As of August 1982, there were 12 "upstairs" firms participating in the NSTS. Of these 12 firms, 10 were approved dealers, who participate in the NSTS by entering agency and dealer quotations through terminals located in their respective trading rooms, while two upstairs firms participated in the system in an agency capacity.

NSTS began operations in June 1978 with thirty-eight stocks, and by the end of 1980 there were forty-nine stocks in the system. The system has been used only to a limited extent: ninety-seven percent of the NSTS share volume in 1980 was accounted for by five participating firms; one firm, Merrill Lynch, Pierce, Fenner & Smith, accounted for about seventy-five percent of this volume. Despite efforts by the SEC to encourage brokerage firms to participate in the experiment, during 1980 NSTS accounted for only 1.8% of the composite share volume in the stocks listed in the system.

The SEC has stated correctly that the limited use that has been made of NSTS thus far has made it difficult to evaluate the effects of trading through an electronic facility of this type. It should be noted, however, that NSTS does not represent a "linking of all markets" as contemplated by the 1975 legislation. It is, rather, a totally new market whose affiliation with an existing stock exchange is purely fortuitous, being necessary to enable NYSE and Amex members to participate in the system without violating the off-board trading rules of those exchanges.

Furthermore, although a fully automated market is technically feasible, it should be kept in mind that automation does not itself create a market. In the overwhelming majority of stocks, public buying and selling is often insufficient to ensure that the order of a willing buyer can always be matched with that of a willing seller. For that reason, markets are created or their quality is improved by professional dealers (specialists or market makers) who put their own capital at risk and thereby supply liquidity to the markets. It is not clear, however, that professional dealers will be willing to participate in a fully automated system. If they are not, technology will not create a liquid market.

D. NATIONWIDE PROTECTION OF LIMIT ORDERS

As a basic feature of the stock exchanges' auction-type procedure, limit orders entrusted to a specialist are "protected" against an execution at an inferior price. Although each of the major stock exchanges has rules or practices that ensure such protection,

---

A specialist on the floor of an exchange linked to the NSTS can also directly enter bids and offers into the system in any stock traded in the NSTS ("NSTS Stock") for which the specialist is registered. At the present time, only specialists on the floor of the Boston Stock Exchange ("BSE") can participate in this manner, since the BSE is the only exchange with NSTS terminals on its floor.]

a limit order left with the specialist on one exchange is not protected against executions at an equal or inferior price on another exchange. In fact, one reason that some block transactions in dually listed securities are executed on a regional exchange may be that the executing brokers (who may be representing both sides of the transaction) or the institutional customers wish to avoid having to satisfy limit orders on the book of the primary market specialist. Thus, customers' orders left on the specialist's book in one market (usually the NYSE or Amex) are not executed when a block transaction is executed at an equal or inferior price on another market (usually a regional exchange).

Early in its implementation of the NMS, the SEC identified nationwide protection of limit orders as an objective of the system. The "auction trading" rule proposed by the Commission in 1973 was intended to ensure "best execution" of customers' orders[242] by extending protection of limit orders to the entire system. However, realization of this objective has been elusive. In part, the difficulties have been due to technical problems associated with disseminating and displaying public limit order information from each market. In part, too, they are doubtless due to "political" problems arising from the fact that implicit in a central electronic facility for storing and executing limit orders is the assumption that exchange specialists would no longer control the execution of orders on their separate limit order books. Since the income derived from executing these orders constitutes a substantial portion of the revenues received by specialists, opposition to such a "consolidated limit order book" (CLOB) was to be expected.

In large part, however, the delays that have been encountered in implementing nationwide protection of limit orders have been due to indecisiveness on the part of the SEC. In 1978, the Commission requested the stock exchange and the NASD to take joint action promptly to develop a central file for limit orders that would not only protect limit orders against executions at an inferior price, but would also give priority to orders entered into CLOB, based on the time of entry.[245] Although the Commission attempted to reassure the stock exchanges that its proposal should not be "interpreted as a decision to force all auction trading into an electronic system with automatic execution capabilities,"[246] it is difficult to see how it could be interpreted any other way. In fact, the self-regulatory organizations asserted that the absolute

---

[242] [See text at n. 42 supra.]
[245] 1978 Status Report, supra note [206], at 40-41 & n. 54. * * *
[246] [Id. at 41.]

time priority proposed to be afforded public limit orders entered in CLOB "would eventually lead to the elimination of exchange trading floors by inexorably forcing all trading into a fully automated trading system."[247] To protect their customers' orders adequately, brokers would be impelled to enter their customers' orders into the system. The CLOB would thus act like a vacuum cleaner, swallowing up the order flow and depriving the exchanges of their business and function. In addition, the exchanges had vividly before them the NSTS experiment, the only example of a fully automated execution facility, and one that operated under the same priority rules that the SEC had just proposed for the entire market.

Faced with strong opposition to its proposal, the SEC retreated. In 1979 the Commission stated its "first priority" — "the achievement of nation-wide *price* protection for public limit orders against executions at inferior prices."[248] Thus, the Commission returned to the concept of protecting limit orders against executions at inferior prices, and simultaneously dropped the proposal that public orders should receive priority on the basis of the time of entry into the system. The Commission requested the self-regulatory organizations to develop a joint plan of price protection for all public limit orders, to be implemented on a pilot basis by the end of 1980.[249] Such a plan was to be based on proposals made by the NYSE and the MSE, proposals that envisioned expanding ITS to provide intermarket price protection.

Under the plan, known as the Limit Order Information System (LOIS), limit orders entered from all exchanges participating in ITS at various price levels would be displayed on the floor of each participating exchange. This plan, although supported by five of the ITS participants, did not receive the approval of the Pacific Stock Exchange, which objected to the high cost of developing LOIS. In late 1981, almost one year after the deadline established by the SEC, it does not appear likely that LOIS will be implemented.

*   *   *

The SEC's unsuccessful pursuit of intermarket price protection for limit orders highlights securities regulation at its worst. * * *

*   *   *

[247] 1979 Status Report, supra note 122, at 29.
[248] Id. at 28 (emphasis supplied).
[249] Id. at 31.

E. ELIMINATION OF OFF-BOARD TRADING RESTRICTIONS

Off-board (i. e., over-the-counter) trading in listed stocks has emerged as the most controversial and important issue affecting the structure of the markets and the NMS. For many years, the NYSE and Amex have restricted the transactions their members can execute in stocks listed on the over-the-counter market.[253] This restriction prevented the members of these exchanges from engaging in a number of activities:

1. They could not, acting as agents for customers, execute transactions in a listed stock over-the-counter with third market makers or with any other brokers or dealers.

2. They could not, acting as agents for both the buying and selling customers, execute such transactions in their own offices ("in-house agency crosses").

3. They could not, acting as principals, execute such transactions over-the-counter with other brokers or dealers. Thus, they could not act as third market makers themselves.

Over the years, the impact of the off-board trading rules and the SEC's and industry's perceptions of them have changed as the structure of the markets has changed. During the 1960's, a few third market makers, dealing directly with institutional investors and nonmember broker-dealers, were able to compete with the primary market specialists largely because, not being members of the exchanges, they were not bound by the fixed minimum commission rate. During that period, the off-board trading rules were seen as having two principal effects: first, the rules protected the minimum commission rate by requiring members who wished to trade with a third market maker to execute the transaction on the exchange floor and to charge the third market maker the full nonmember commission. In effect, the NYSE and Amex regarded the third market maker as a customer of the member firm. Second, the rules potentially prevented exchange members from fulfilling their agency duty to execute their customers' orders in the best possible market.[255]

---

[253] [1978] 2 NYSE Guide (CCH) 3651 (rule 390) (formerly rule 394); [1981] 2 Am. Stock Ex. Guide (CCH) 2419 (rule 5).

[255] The controversy over off-board trading came to a head after enactment of the Securities Acts Amendments of 1964 * * * . These amendments added §12(g) to the Exchange Act, which extended the continuous disclosure requirements of §13 * * * to a large number of issuers whose equity securities were traded over-the-counter. * * * As a result, a number of large OTC companies that had not previously chosen to list their shares because of the lesser disclosure requirements for OTC companies decided to list on the NYSE. Nonmember broker-dealers that specialized in making markets in

The termination of fixed rates effectively ended the third market as a significant factor in the securities markets. Over-the-counter trading in NYSE stocks, which had amounted to seven percent of total volume in these stocks in 1971, fell to two percent by 1980. Nevertheless, the problem of off-board trading did not disappear along with fixed rates; instead, the restrictions acquired a new significance, which did not become fully clear until after enactment of the 1975 legislation.

The 1975 legislation treated off-board trading rules differently from the other restrictive exchange rules — specifically, fixed commission rates and membership rules. For all practical purposes, the statute eliminated the latter two types of restrictions,[258] but the resolution of the off-board trading issue was left to the discretion of the SEC. The Commission was directed to undertake a two-step procedure: first, it was to review the rules to determine their "effects on competition"; and second, it was to determine whether any burdens on competition imposed by the rules were "necessary or appropriate in furtherance of the purposes of" the Exchange Act.[259] The difference between the legislative treatment of off-board trading rules and the other anticompetitive exchange rules was due to Congress' recognition that the auction markets benefited from a rule requiring execution of all orders on an exchange floor, and that this benefit might not be outweighed by the anticompetitive impact of the rule. In fact, the off-board trading rules pose a sharp conflict between two of the explicit statutory objectives of the NMS. The objective of "fair competition" requires that as few restrictions as possible be placed on the ability of broker-dealers to act as market makers or to choose the markets in which their customers' and their own orders are to be executed. On the other hand, the objective of facilitating the execution of investors' orders without the participation of a dealer requires that all investors' orders be executed at one central location, where auction-type procedures provide the greatest opportunity for matching investors' buy and sell orders.

The balancing of objectives that the statute directed the Commission to perform in deciding whether to retain the off-board trading rules was similar to the balancing required for all stock exchange rules. There was, however, one important difference:

---

these stocks found themselves in the position of third market makers, since NYSE members were prohibited from dealing with them by rule 394, the NYSE off-board trading rule. * * *

[258] [§§6(d), 6(e).]
[259] [§11A(c)(4)(A).]

Congress insisted that the issue of off-board trading be speedily resolved. Unlike the requirements imposed on other exchange rules, the statute mandated a tight timetable for the Commission's consideration of off-board trading rules. It required the Commission to submit to Congress a report giving the results of the Commission's initial review of the rules within ninety days after enactment of the 1975 amendments. Moreover, it required the Commission to conclude a proceeding to amend any rule imposing an unjustified burden on competition within ninety days of the date of publication of notice of its commencement.

If Congress expected swift resolution of the issue, it was to be disappointed. Even in 1981, more than six years after enactment of the amendments, it is still not clear whether the stock exchanges are to be permitted to retain any off-board restrictions and, if not, how soon the remaining restrictions are to be eliminated. In fairness to the Commission, the delays have been due in part to changes in market structure that could not easily have been predicted and partly to the difficulty of coordinating repeal of the off-board trading rules with the development of the NMS. Nevertheless, a House subcommittee's charge that the Commission has approached its task of building the NMS with "timidity and apparent purposelessness"[268] is not entirely inapplicable to its record with respect to the closely related issue of off-board trading restrictions.

On September 2, 1975, exactly ninety days after enactment of the legislation, the SEC submitted a report to Congress in which it concluded that off-board trading rules did indeed impose burdens on competition.[269] The Commission found that off-board trading rules disadvantaged third market makers in competing with exchange specialists for agency orders entrusted to exchange members for execution.[270] With respect to principal orders, the Commission found that these rules prevented exchange members other than specialists from competing with specialists and third market makers in making markets in listed securities.[271]

Three months later, the Commission adopted rule 19c-1, which

[268] Subcomm. on Oversight and Investigations of the House Comm. on Interstate and Foreign Commerce, 96th Cong., 2d Sess., National Market System: Five Year Status Report at III (Comm. Print 1980).

[269] SEC Exch. Act Release No. 11,628, 40 Fed. Reg. 41,808, 41,808 (1975) (proposing rule 19c-3 * * * .

[270] Id. at 41,812. At the same time, the Commission published for comment a proposed rule 19c-1, and announced the commencement of a rulemaking proceeding. Id. at 41,816-17.

[271] Id. at 41,812.

required the exchanges, by March 31, 1976, to eliminate all restrictions on exchange members' execution of agency transactions (i. e., transactions for customers) in the third market.[272] Exchange rules restricting the ability of members to execute off-board transactions as principal, or to execute in-house agency crosses, were not affected by the rule. The Commission stated, however, that it would reconsider, no later than March 1, 1977, whether off-board trading rules applicable to these types of transactions should be eliminated. The Commission expected that by then it would be in a better position to measure the progress that had been made in developing the NMS. The Commission's view was that any fragmenting effect of permitting exchange members to make markets in listed stocks in their own offices would be reduced or eliminated once all the markets were linked in an NMS and, more particularly, once there was nationwide protection for limit orders.

Despite its self-imposed deadline of March 1, 1977, the Commission took no further action until June 27, 1977, when it stated that "because [remaining] restrictions represent burdens on competition which do not appear necessary or appropriate in furtherance of the purposes of the Act, it must now establish a firm date for elimination of those restrictions."[275] Accordingly, the Commission simultaneously proposed rule 19c-2, which would eliminate restrictions on principal transactions and in-house agency crosses as of January 1, 1978. The Commission acknowledged that elimination of these restrictions might be accompanied by adverse effects on the markets, including increased fragmentation of customers' orders, reduced protection of limit orders, and increased opportunity for "overreaching" by retail firms (i. e., executing customers' orders as principal at prices less favorable than those that could have been obtained had the firm acted as agent). Nevertheless, the Commission stated that neither the inevitability of these effects, nor their potential severity, had been sufficiently demonstrated. The Commission further noted that efforts by the securities industry to link the markets had been disappointing. Therefore, elimination of the remaining rules should not be deferred in the hope that the private sector would, "without further economic or regulatory compulsion, subordinate what [it] believes to be [its] separate and private interests and work collectively . . . to achieve . . . market linkage."[278] Thus, the Commission was using the threat of repeal of off-board trading rules to

---

[272] SEC Exch. Act Release No. 11,942 * * *.
[275] SEC Exch. Act Release No. 13,662, 42 Fed. Reg. 33,510, 33,515 (1977) (proposing rule 19c-2 * * *).
[278] Id. at 33,514.

coerce the securities industry to *cooperate* in the development of a market linkage system, at the very time that the industry was supposed to be developing more intensive intermarket *competition*.

January 1, 1978 passed, but the off-board trading rules were not eliminated. Later that month, the Commission stated that it was deferring further consideration of proposed rule 19c-2 "until the Commission has had an opportunity to evaluate industry and self-regulatory organizations [*sic*] responses to the national market system initiatives."[280] The Commission followed this with the rather weak statement that it did "not wish its determination to defer consideration of proposed Rule 19c-2 at this time to be perceived as indicating that the Commission is willing to postpone removal of off-board trading restrictions indefinitely."

It was not until 1980 that the SEC took the first step toward resolving this controversial issue. How this came about illustrates the changes in the structure of the markets that had occurred since (and as a result of) the elimination of fixed commission rates. In March 1977, the Amex filed with the Commission two proposed amendments to its standards for original listing of securities.[282] The intent of the amendments was to make eligible for listing the shares of certain foreign companies with broad worldwide (but not U. S.) share distribution and certain large domestic companies with no history of earnings. The SEC staff indicated informally to the Amex that the proposed rules would be approved, but only if the exchange made its off-board restrictions inapplicable to any companies that might be listed under the new provisions. When the Amex refused to comply with this condition, the SEC commenced a proceeding under the statute to determine whether the two proposals should be disapproved, on the ground that their effect would be to broaden the reach of the exchange's off-board trading restrictions by making it possible for the exchange to list new categories of stocks.[284] The proceeding attracted little attention at the time, and in December 1978 the SEC approved the proposed rule changes, stating that it was neither necessary nor appropriate to attempt a final resolution of the issue of off-board trading rules in the confines of a special proceeding relating only to the Amex.[285]

Upon the Commission's approval of the Amex rules, the securities industry apparently woke up to the potential impact of the decision. Several broker-dealer firms, including some of the largest

---

[280] 1978 Status Report, supra note 130, at 41. [The "*sic*" is in the original.]
[282] SEC Exch. Act Release No. 13,391, 11 SEC Docket 2090 (1977).
[284] SEC Exch. Act Release No. 13,542, 12 SEC Docket 429, 429-30 (1977).
[285] SEC Exch. Act Release No. 15,376, 16 SEC Docket 333, 338 (1978).

and most influential members of the NYSE and Amex, objected strenuously and publicly to the Commission's action. These firms conducted profitable businesses as market makers in OTC stocks, operations that they would have to terminate as to any stocks that might be listed on the Amex under the new listing standards. Previously, the NYSE and Amex had led the resistance to any relaxation of off-board trading restrictions, and it may be surmised that the SEC's reluctance to repeal these restrictions was in large part due to this resistance. Now it became clear that the exchanges did not have the support of a substantial portion of their own memberships, at least as to extending the restrictions to stocks not already covered by them. Traditional loyalty to the exchanges was outweighed by hard business realities.

This episode made clear the fact that, since the repeal of fixed commission rates, the interests of many large brokerage firms no longer coincided with those of the exchanges of which they were members. Fixed rates had provided the economic community of interest that united the stock exchanges with their memberships. Under the new regime of negotiated rates, the large member firms, whose business was with the public, had functionally become customers of the specialists and other floor members, with whom the member firms negotiated to obtain the lowest possible commission rate. If they could handle the business in listed stocks more profitably in their own offices, they would do so. Insofar as off-board trading restrictions were concerned, although most exchange member firms would not press for repeal, they would resist any extension of the restrictions.

Once the Commission found that the stock exchange community did not fully support the off-board trading rules, it acted swiftly. On April 26, 1979, the SEC published for comment proposed rule 19c-3, which would preclude application of off-board trading restrictions to stocks that became listed on an exchange after that date, or that were traded on an exchange on that date but did not remain listed thereafter.[287] The SEC took the position that many of the arguments raised in support of off-board trading restrictions "may not be applicable to or warrant extension of these rules to securities which are currently traded exclusively over-the-counter."[288] This contention, however, is not very persuasive, since the dangers of market fragmentation, lack of limit order protection, and "overreaching" cited by the Commission in June 1977 would seem to be equally present regardless of whether all listed stocks

[287] SEC Exch. Act Release No. 15,769, 44 Fed. Reg. 26,688 (1979) * * * .
[288] Id. at 26,689 (quoting 1979 Status Report, supra note 122, at 37).

or only some of them were freed from off-board restrictions. Somewhat more persuasively, the Commission argued that the limited experiment of rule 19c-3 would "not appear to involve the potential for the kind of dramatic and radical effects on the existing exchange markets which have been predicted"[289] with respect to total repeal of the off-board trading rules. The Commission stated:

> Since most firms currently providing continuous over-the-counter markets with respect to securities traded exclusively over-the-counter are exchange members, when a security becomes exchange traded for the first time, the pre-existing over-the-counter market for that security is seriously impaired, if not, as a practical matter, extinguished. This situation is to be contrasted with the consequences of adopting proposed Rule 19c-2, which would permit over-the-counter trading by these same exchange members in securities now confined, to a significant degree, to exchange trading.[290]

In June 1980, the SEC adopted rule 19c-3[291] and simultaneously withdrew rule 19c-2.[292] In addition, the Commission announced that it did not contemplate taking any further steps "in the near future" toward repeal of off-board trading restrictions.[293]

Adoption of rule 19c-3 has had little effect on the trading patterns in the stocks affected by the rule. In early 1981, the Commission reported that the "great preponderance of trading in 19c-3 Securities occurs on the primary stock exchanges," although there was significant third market volume in a few such stocks.[294] It is

[289] Id. at 26,690.

[290] Id.

[291] SEC Exch. Act Release No. 16,888, 45 Fed. Reg. 41,125, 41,125 (1980) * * * .

[292] SEC Exch. Act Release No. 16,889, 45 Fed. Reg. 41,156 (1980) * * * .

[293] Id. at 41,157. * * *

[294] SEC Exch. Act Release No. 17,516, 21 SEC Docket 1519, 1527-28 (1981). A report issued by the SEC in August 1981 confirmed these findings. * * * Directorate of Economic and Policy Analysis and Division of Market Regulation, SEC, A Monitoring Report on the Operation and Effects of Rule 19c-3 Under the Securities Exchange Act of 1934, at 6-7 (1981) (hereinafter 19c-3 Monitoring Report). * * *

The SEC report also noted that exchange members who acted as market makers in 19c-3 common stocks executed 58% of their flow in their own offices, sent 39% to the primary market for execution, and sent three percent to other OTC market makers. Id. at 15. Most brokerage firms that were not market makers continued to send their retail orders to the primary market. Id. at 17. Contrary to the Commission's expectations which it had expressed when it adopted rule 19c-3, see SEC Exch. Act Release No. 16,888, 45 Fed. Reg. 41,125, 41,126-27 (1980), the rule did not improve the quality of the primary market. On the other hand, contrary to the predictions of the opponents of rule 19c-3, it had not adversely affected the quality of the market either. 19c-3 Monitoring Report, supra, at 19-20 * * * . The Commission apparent that despite the protests made by certain large brokerage firms to the extension of off-board restrictions to new classes of Amex-listed stocks, most of these firms are not willing to continue making markets in the newly listed stocks in which they had made markets before listing. Although the reasons for this are not entirely clear, it may be that for most brokerage firms the most economically efficient method of executing brokerage orders in most stocks is to send them to a stock exchange.

The Commission has taken the position, however, that the failure of rule 19c-3 to provide the benefits that the Commission expected of it was due to the lack of a linkage between the exchanges and over-the-counter markets.[296] In 1979, the NASD announced plans to enhance its NASDAQ system by developing a "computer assisted execution system" (CAES), which would enable brokers to obtain automatic execution of orders against the quotations published by OTC market makers.[297] The NASD also proposed that an Automated Interface (AI) be developed between CAES and ITS "to permit automated execution of commitments sent from participating exchanges and to permit market makers participating in the enhanced NASDAQ to efficiently route commitments to exchange markets for execution there."[298] In April 1981, the Commission, stating that "the immediate implementation of the Automated Interface is a critical event in the development of a national market system," issued an order requiring the six ITS participating exchanges and the NASD to act jointly in planning, developing, and operating the AI. Under the order, the AI would become operational on a pilot basis by March 1, 1982 and fully operational by September 1, 1982.[h]

The history of the Commission's concern with off-board trading

---

stated, however, "that it will not be possible to draw any significant conclusions from rule 19c-3 trading until greater experience is obtained with respect to the enhanced NASDAQ System and that System is linked to the ITS." 19c-3 Monitoring Report, supra, at 5 * * * .

[296] SEC Exch. Act Release No. 17,516, 21 SEC Docket 1519, 1527-28 (1981).

[297] Id. at 1522. As noted above, the NASDAQ system does not provide for automatic execution of orders. See note 47 supra. CAES began operation on a pilot basis on February 20, 1981. Thus far, it has attracted only limited trading interest. 19c-3 Monitoring Report, supra note 294, at 41. See generally SEC Exch. Act Release No. 17,601, 22 SEC Docket 331 (1981).

[298] SEC Exch. Act Release No. 17,516, 21 SEC Docket 1519, 1522 (1981).

[h] Ed.: Sec. Ex. Act Rel. 17,744, 22 SEC Dock. 845 (1981); see also Sec. Ex. Act Rel. 18,536, 24 SEC Dock. 1079 (1982) (status report). And the pilot marriage was somewhat forcibly consummated in May 1982, after the Commission on its own motion had adopted appropriate amendments to the ITS plan in the absence of complete agreement between plan participants and the NASD. Sec. Ex. Act Rel. 18,713, 25 SEC Dock. 243 (1982).]

restrictions has been presented in considerable detail because it is the central unresolved matter relating to the future structure of the markets under the 1975 legislative amendments. The matter raises a number of difficult issues of market structure and investor protection, any detailed discussion of which is beyond the scope of this Article. These issues include the following: (1) repeal of off-board trading restrictions may result in large retail firms' "internalizing" their order flow, i. e., "withholding . . . retail orders from other market centers for the purpose of executing them 'in-house' as principal, without exposing those orders to buying and selling interest in those other market centers";[301] (2) since the largest retail firms have the largest flow of orders and therefore the greatest opportunity to match customers' buy and sell orders in their own offices, such firms will have an advantage as market makers, with the result that elimination of the restrictions is likely to accelerate the tendency toward concentration in the securities industry; (3) the diversion of customers' orders from the primary exchanges will reduce the opportunity for buy and sell orders to meet without the participation of a dealer and may reduce the liquidity of the markets; (4) execution of orders by firms as principals with their own customers in their own offices rather than as agents on an exchange floor increases the possibility of unfair dealing and makes effective surveillance of the markets by the SEC and the self-regulatory organizations more difficult; and (5) more generally, competition between the exchanges and their own members may result in a weakening of the exchanges' function as price setting mechanisms, a result that seems to be neither in the interest of investors nor contemplated by the statute. On the other hand, since the large member firms constitute the best-capitalized group of potential competitors with the primary market specialists, it may well be that repeal of the off-board trading rules is the only way in which effective competition can be introduced into the market making process in listed stocks.

Faced with this dilemma, the Commission has faltered. It has

---

[301] SEC Exch. Act Release No. 16,888, 20 SEC Docket 334, 340 n. 31 (1980). See also Parker, Off Board Trading Restrictions, 13 Rev. Sec. Reg. 919 (1980). [In May 1982 the Commission, emphasizing that it had not determined whether any "anti-internalization measure is necessitated by present conditions or by implementation of the interface between the ITS and OTC markets," invited comment on that question and on alternative rule proposals submitted by the New York Stock Exchange and the Securities Industry Association. Sec. Ex. Act Rel. 18,738, 25 SEC Dock. 358, 361 (1982). And at year-end 1982 the Commission substituted a revised proposal. Sec. Ex. Act Rel. 19,372, 26 SEC Dock. 1549 (1982).]

not developed the economic data that might indicate the appropriate course to take. Instead, it has tried to placate both the proponents of repeal of the restrictions and the proponents of the status quo, all the while obscuring its indecision in verbiage. Each time its regulatory policies have failed to produce price competition among markets, it has justified the failure with the assertion that one *additional* regulatory action will produce a successful resolution of the conflicting goals of market making competition and liquid, auction-type markets. Whether the Automated Interface between the OTC markets, represented by CAES, and the exchanges, represented by ITS, will bring success to the Commission's efforts remains to be seen.

F. QUALIFIED SECURITIES

Section 11A contemplates that the NMS will include only "qualified" securities[304] and directs the Commission to designate by rule "the securities or classes of securities qualified for trading in the national market system from among securities other than exempted securities."[305] The term "securities" embraces a number of types of instruments traded in the public markets, and the legislative history of section 11A makes clear that it was the intention of Congress that all publicly traded securities, other than "exempted securities," be eligible to be qualified for trading in the NMS. However, all of the studies and hearings on which the legislation was based, and the subsequent efforts by the SEC to implement the NMS, have been concerned almost exclusively with common stocks.

Both Congress and the SEC expressed the view that participation in the NMS should be limited to those equity securities whose characteristics of size, earnings history, breadth of ownership, and investor interest make them "suitable" for auction-market trading. Presumably, any stock having the requisite characteristics is traded by public investors in sufficient volume so that buy and sell orders may be executed against each other without the constant participation of a dealer. Although exchange-listed stocks generally are regarded as having these characteristics to a greater extent than stocks that are traded exclusively over-the-counter, not all listed stocks are suitable for auction-market trading. Conversely, there are many OTC stocks, some of which meet exchange listing requirements, that are suitable. These stocks are not listed

---

[304] [§11A(a)(1)(D).]
[305] [§11A(a)(2).]

on an exchange because the companies' managements have chosen not to seek a listing.

In June 1979 the SEC proposed a rule governing qualification of securities for the NMS.[313] The rule was a masterpiece of both complexity and irrelevance. It proposed two different sets of standards for determining whether a stock was to be qualified. Each set of standards related to (i) assets and earning power of the issuer, and (ii) distribution of the security, (iii) market activity, and (iv) multiple-market interest in the stock. Stocks meeting the first, higher set of standards would be designated "Tier 1" stocks, and would be automatically qualified. Those meeting the second, less stringent set of standards would be designated "Tier 2" stocks, and would be qualified upon application by the issuer or by two or more market centers or prospective market centers provided that they were designated "national market system securities" under a "designation plan" filed with the Commission by the various self-regulatory organizations.

To make the rule proposal even more complex, the Commission set forth three alternative sets of standards for Tier 1 and for Tier 2 stocks. The Commission estimated that under the most stringent of the alternative standards for Tier 1 status, only 295 NYSE stocks, fifteen Amex stocks, and forty-nine NASDAQ-reported stocks would be qualified; under the least stringent of the Tier 1 standards, 868 NYSE stocks, seventy-two Amex stocks, and 319 NASDAQ-reported stocks would be qualified. Even under the least stringent of the three sets of alternative Tier 2 standards, only 180 Amex stocks, or approximately seventeen percent of all Amex listings, would be eligible to be included in the NMS.

The proposed rule was little more than an exercise in draftsmanship, however, since absolutely nothing rested on the qualification of an NYSE or Amex stock as a national market system security; the Commission intended that all NYSE and Amex stocks would continue to be included in the consolidated tape, the composite quotation system, and any other NMS facilities that might be developed. Furthermore, all NYSE and Amex stocks, whether or not qualified, would be subject to any additional NMS rules that the SEC might adopt, such as rules relating to off-board trading. The only possible effect of the proposed rule on listed companies would be to give public investors the impression that stocks failing to qualify for the NMS were somehow of lower quality than those that qualified.

---

[313] SEC Exch. Act Release No. 15,926, 44 Fed. Reg. 36,912 (1979) (proposing rule 11Aa2-1).

In February 1981, the SEC adopted the qualification rule in a substantially modified form.[320] The basic structure of the rule, with its two tiers of securities, remains; but the rule applies only to stocks traded exclusively over-the-counter. Securities admitted to trading on a stock exchange are, at least for the present, not affected by the rule. The Commission postponed consideration of the largely academic question "whether exchange traded securities should be designated as NMS Securities and which securities should be so designated."

The immediate effect of the rule is to designate automatically approximately forty OTC securities as NMS securities based on their qualifying as Tier 1 stocks. Another group of approximately 454 securities will become eligible as Tier 2 stocks, which will be included in the NMS only if they are designated as NMS securities by their issuers. The Commission will also require any OTC stocks designated as NMS securities to be included in a real-time disclosure system.[325] Thus, much the same market information will be available for exchange-traded stocks as for OTC stocks included in the NMS. The rule will become effective on March 1, 1982.

One curious aspect of the inclusion of OTC securities in the NMS is that the Commission stated that it will not at this time grant unlisted trading privileges to any exchange that wishes to admit any of these OTC/NMS securities to trading.[327] This position leads to two anomalous results: first, OTC/NMS stocks will be part of the national market system but will not be traded on any exchange within the system; and second, although rule 19c-3 now permits exchange members to make third markets in any stocks that were admitted to listing on a stock exchange since April 26, 1979, stock exchange specialists will be precluded from making exchange markets in any OTC stocks included in the NMS.

Thus, at present, the decision as to whether and to what extent

---

[320] [Sec. Ex. Act Rel. 17,549, 22 SEC Dock. 22 (1981).]

[325] At the same time that it adopted rule 11Aa2-1, the Commission amended paragraphs (b)(1) and (b)(4)(i) of its consolidated tape rule, rule 11Aa3-1, 17 C. F. R. §240.11Aa3-1 (1981), to incorporate the real-time disclosure requirement. SEC Exch. Act Release No. 17,549, 46 Fed. Reg. 13,992, 14,006 (1981). It is not required, however, that OTC-NMS securities be reported through the consolidated system. Id. at 13,997, nn. 34-35 and 66-67.

*   *   *

[327] Id. at 14,003-04.

an eligible stock is traded in the NMS rests largely with the issuer. By seeking an exchange listing, issuers of Tier 1 OTC stocks will be able to open up market making to competition from exchange specialists. Issuers of Tier 2 OTC stocks will have even more control over trading in their securities. First, they will have the option of designating their stocks as NMS securities. If they choose to go only this far, their stocks will not be traded on any exchange. And second, they will have the option of being listed on one or more exchanges, provided that their stocks and their companies meet the relevant listing requirements. If this second option is exercised, their stocks will be traded on any exchange with which they are listed, on any exchange that obtains unlisted trading privileges in the stocks, and in the OTC market, as well as in the NMS. This is a peculiar result, in view of the Commission's statement in its release proposing the rule that it "does not believe that issuers should be permitted to veto designation of its [*sic*] securities as national market system securities"[329] and considering the Senate committee's conclusion that "there is little or no justification for an issuer to deprive securities holders of the advantages of exchange trading."[330] Presumably, the Commission's decision to give issuers a de facto veto with respect to Tier 2 stocks and not to permit unlisted trading in any OTC/NMS stocks owes more to political compromise than to thoughtful analysis.

V.   The Role of the SEC

*   *   *

In view of the fact that the SEC has generally been regarded as among the most effective of the federal regulatory agencies, its procrastination and lack of direction in dealing with the NMS require an explanation. Such an explanation can be found in the nature of the role that the agency has been required to play. Establishing an NMS has involved the Commission in activities that are very different from its usual operations. For the first time, the Commission has been called upon to perform a promotional, or developmental, function — one that, in the words of ex-SEC Commissioner Roberta S. Karmel, is "designed to benefit or foster private business growth or development which Congress has de-

---

[329] SEC Exch. Act Release No. 15,926, 44 Fed. Reg. 36,912, 36,916 (1979) (proposing rule 11Aa2-1). [The "*sic*" is in the original.]

[330] Senate Report, supra note [129], at 19, [1975] U. S. Code Cong. & Ad. News at 197.

termined is in the public welfare."[340] Furthermore, the Commission is now faced with the problems of making decisions that directly affect the relative positions of competing entities.

Historically, the Commission's administration of the Exchange Act has focused on ensuring that issuers of securities disclose adequate information to the public and enforcing prohibition against fraudulent and manipulative practices. The Commission has not been, and has not considered itself to be, an "economic" regulator, such as the Federal Communications Commission or the Civil Aeronautics Board among others, whose duties include allocating valuable franchises among competitors. * * *

* * *

VI.   COMPETITION AMONG SPECIALISTS AND MARKET MAKERS

As stated earlier, Congress believed when it mandated an NMS that such a system would enhance competition by enabling regional exchange specialists and third market makers to compete effectively with primary market specialists. Thus, the NMS was intended to do more than merely link the markets to enable customers and their brokers to *find* the best available execution of dually traded stocks. Since there was little price competition among markets, a system that was designed only to increase the ability of a broker to satisfy his "best execution" obligation would have been of minor importance or interest. Rather, the NMS was envisioned as an instrument for the *creation of* better prices through competition among specialists and market makers. It would not only ensure that investors receive the most favorable execution of their transactions, but also would improve the liquidity of the markets.

The primary market specialist's obligation to offset temporary imbalances in supply and demand is embodied in NYSE and Amex rules,[366] which are enforced by these exchanges and subject to SEC oversight.[367] In 1963, the SEC's Special Study found that, although the system appeared "to be serving its purposes satisfactorily,"[368] there was a "gulf so wide" between the market conduct of different NYSE specialists "as to threaten the image of

---

[340] R. Karmel, The SEC as a Developmental Agency 3 (Sept. 24, 1978) (speech by ex-SEC Commissioner to National Securities Traders Association).

[366] NYSE rule 104, [1980] 2 NYSE Guide (CCH) ¶2703-3 to -5; Amex rule 170, [1978] 2 Am. Stock Ex. Guide (CCH) ¶2470-71.

[367] SEC rule 11b-1, 17 C. F. R. §240.11b-1 (1981).

[368] Special Study, supra note [97], at 167.

the Exchange as a marketplace whose specialist system assures strength in all markets."[369] Accordingly, the Commission and the exchanges tightened the regulations governing the conduct of specialists, particularly with regard to their dealings for their own accounts.[370] In its 1971 Institutional Investor Study Report, the SEC again emphasized that there were "important differences among NYSE specialist units in the extent to which they participate in depth to reduce temporary price fluctuations,"[371] and furthermore that "[t]he performance of those NYSE specialist units that do participate in great depth indicates that some NYSE specialist units could reduce the frequency of large temporary price fluctuations in their specialty stocks by similar participation."[372]

These findings were used by the Senate Subcommittee on Securities in its 1973 Securities Industry Study to support its own position that "as the present time institutional trading is characterized by such substantial imbalances that the specialist system as a whole is unable to offset them."[373] The Senate subcommittee criticized the effectiveness of the NYSE regulation of its specialists and concluded

> that regulation and exhortation of a single market-maker will not be adequate to provide stability and continuity in the markets for listed securities. To assure markets adequate to serve individual and institutional investors, encouragement must be given to all groups of market-makers to make simultaneous competing markets in each security within the new central system.[374]

This key recommendation was carried forward as a central purpose of the legislative mandate to establish an NMS. Yet it was made in the face of experience that at the very least should have cast strong doubt on the feasibility of sustaining competition among market makers over a period of time, either in a single market or in multiple markets. In the first place, the earlier system of competing specialists disappeared from the NYSE in 1967. The SEC's Special Study of the Securities Markets, commenting on the specialist competition that still remained in 1963, called it "unsatisfactory for several reasons."[376] These included confusion

---

[369] Id. at 162.
[370] See [1963-1964] SEC Ann. Rep. 3-4.
[371] 4 Institutional Investor Study, supra note [86], at 1959.
[372] Id.
[373] [Securities Industry Study, Com. Print, Subcom. on Securities, Senate Com. on Banking, Housing & Urban Affairs, 93d Cong., 1st Sess. (1973) 108.]
[374] Id. at 125-26.
[376] Special Study, supra note [97], at 62.

on the part of brokerage firms as to who was quoting the market in active stocks, the practice of the firms not to shop for the best service but to give each competitor half of their brokerage business, and the difficulty of allocating market making responsibility among the competing specialists. In addition, there doubtless was a natural tendency by competing specialists who stood next to each other all day on the floor of the exchange to cooperate with each other in handling the business rather than to compete.

Even in the OTC market, in which competing market makers are not in close physical proximity but deal with each other over the telephone, there was an "appearance of competition [among market makers] that may not always accord with reality."[379] Although the Special Study did not seek to determine the prevalence of noncompetitive practices in the OTC markets, it pointed out that competition was minimal or nonexistent in the many stocks that have one or two market makers, and that even "the appearance of several dealers' active interest in a security may not be a reliable indication of a competitive market . . . "[380] In some instances, most of the dealers making markets in a security were in fact appearing on behalf of one market maker; in others, various cooperative practices among market makers restrained actual competition.[381]

The practical difficulty of achieving competition among market makers in a multiple market context is increased by the brokerage firms' practice of sending their orders for listed stocks to the primary market. This practice, based on considerations of operating efficiency and maximum opportunity to obtain a favorable execution price, serves to perpetuate a particular exchange as the primary market. In the markets for listed stocks, the practice of sending orders routinely to the primary market may be the result of longstanding habit. The NYSE and Amex are the traditional primary markets, and the tradition may be hard to change, particularly since a broker may believe that there is greater safety from liability to his customer for failing to meet his "best execution" obligation if he sends his orders to the primary market. However, the "primary market" practice is also employed in the

---

379 Id. at 577.

380 Id. at 661.

381 Id. at 661-62. It should be noted, however, that the introduction of NASDAQ in 1971, by greatly facilitating the dissemination of OTC quotations, may have enhanced price competition among OTC market makers. See note 47 supra.

market for listed options, a relatively new market that lacks the traditions of the stock markets.[383]

The listed options markets began in 1973 when the Chicago Board Options Exchange (CBOE) was organized for that purpose. Subsequently, markets in options opened at the Amex, the Phlx, and the PSE. These exchanges trade options to buy stocks (calls) and options to sell stocks (puts) on terms standardized as to exercise prices and dates of expiration. Almost all of the underlying stocks for the options are listed on the NYSE, but no options are listed or traded on the NYSE.[1] The CBOE has consistently traded a larger number of options and greater volume than any of the other exchanges trading options, but it has never achieved the dominance that the NYSE enjoys in listed stocks.

Since the options markets began operations, twenty-two classes of options have been traded simultaneously on more than one exchange.[384] Owing to the tendency of brokerage firms automatically to route the bulk of their orders in any option class to the exchange with the highest volume of activity in that class, virtually all retail order flow in dually traded options has been routed to a single exchange, which has quickly become the primary market for the options class. For this reason, the Commission has stated that expansion of multiple trading of options may actually *impede* "fair competition" among markets, and for the past few years it has not permitted any additional options to be dually traded.

Thus, the experience with competing specialists and market makers on the NYSE, the OTC market, and the listed options markets offers little encouragement to those who believe that market making competition will improve the liquidity of the markets. Furthermore, the recent experience with those elements of the incipient NMS that are in operation provides little reason to expect that the regional exchange specialists or the third market will become meaningful competitors. If competition is to develop, it is more likely to come from the large, well-capitalized retail member firms of the NYSE, which would be permitted to make markets and execute orders as principals with their own customers

---

[383] 3 House Comm. on Interstate and Foreign Commerce, 96th Cong., 1st Sess., Report of the Special Study of the Options Markets to SEC 853 (Comm. Print 1979) (noting primary market phenomenon in options markets) * * * For a description of the options markets, see [id.] at 1-72.

[1] The New York Stock Exchange now trades options on various stock indexes. See c. 3K n. 36 supra.

[384] SEC Exch. Act Release No. 16,701, 19 SEC Docket 998, 1004 n. 34 (1980).

if the off-board trading restrictions are lifted. The limited experiment of rule 19c-3, however, does not indicate that these firms wish to compete with the primary market specialists in more than a handful of active issues.

Moreover, even assuming that these firms are willing and able to compete, it is not clear that the end result will be beneficial to the markets or to investors. Unlike other potential competitors, these firms collectively control the flow of orders from the investing public. Their decision to compete actively with the primary market specialist by executing orders in their own offices has the potential to divert the bulk of order flow away from the exchange floors and thus to destroy the specialist system and perhaps the exchanges themselves. Such a result would hardly seem to constitute "fair competition." At best, encouragement of market maker competition by the larger member firms would single out the goal of competition to the exclusion of the other statutory goals, an intention disclaimed by Congress.

What conclusions can be drawn? First and foremost, it appears that contrary to the hope of Congress and the SEC, market making competition is likely to play only a limited role in the NMS. Some regional exchange specialists and third market makers do disseminate reliable competing quotes, and it is possible that more will do so. They should certainly have an opportunity to compete. More meaningful competition is likely to come from the larger NYSE member firms; yet to the extent that the off-board trading rules are repealed, exchange members dealing as principals with their own customers should be under an obligation to expose their customers' orders to the trading process not only in order to protect customers against "overreaching," but also to maximize liquidity and assure "fair competition" among market makers and compliance with auction-trading procedures.

It seems unlikely, however, that market making competition will provide the markets with substantial additional liquidity as trading volume continues to increase and financial institutions account for an even greater share of that volume. Furthermore, the specialist system, regardless of how well it is regulated, suffers from a basic defect: it requires a private entrepreneur to perform a public function. The specialist is required to buy and sell stocks for his own account to add to the liquidity of the market. Yet, since he cannot stay in business unless his operation is profitable, it is not always in his interest to perform his specialist function properly. Moreover, since the specialist uses his own capital, he may not always possess the means to perform this function properly. In fact, a telling finding of the SEC's Institutional Investor Study was that the NYSE specialist system has been unable to meet the demands for capital imposed by the institutionalization of the markets.

In view of the capital needs and potential conflict of interest of the specialist, the SEC and the exchanges should give consideration to rebuilding the specialist system on a broader base. Under such a plan, exchanges themselves would provide the capital necessary to offset temporary imbalances between supply and demand. This capital would be raised from the exchange memberships generally, and the profits or losses arising from performance of the specialist function, less a fee or salary paid to the exchange member or employee actually performing the specialist function, as well as other costs of operation, would accrue to the memberships generally. Capital would be used in the markets on the basis of need, in view of market conditions, rather than on the basis of whether the particular specialist to whom a stock is allocated is willing and able to commit his capital to the trading function.

This notion of "institutionalization" of the specialist function has been employed with success in the past, although only on a limited and temporary basis. On the Amex in the mid-1960's, when a particular specialist was unable to handle an extremely active and volatile stock, a consortium of large member firms contributed one million dollars of capital, with the approval of the exchange, to handle the stock, using professional specialists to conduct the day-to-day business on behalf of the consortium. A similar episode occurred in the late 1970's in an active Amex option. In both instances, the consortiums were disbanded and normal specialist activity was resumed as soon as the crisis had passed. Such a pattern, made a permanent feature of the stock markets and broadened to include the entire stock exchange community rather than just a few members, might provide an answer to the need for additional market liquidity.

CONCLUSION

The failures, frustrations, and waste of resources that have been encountered over the past ten years in the attempt to link the stock markets in a national market system have two principal causes. First, the SEC is ill-equipped by its traditional regulatory orientation, its lawyer-dominated staff, and the limited authority provided to it by Congress to take the lead effectively in a restructuring of the stock markets. It is questionable, moreover, whether this is an appropriate role for a government agency to play. The agency has demonstrated little ability or foresight as a planner in this area. The Commission's involvement, first in proposing to Congress and then in attempting to implement an NMS, has served neither to further the public interest nor to protect investors.

Second, the basic premise of the NMS proposal — that market makers trading in the same security will engage in price competition with each other if they have equal access to order flow — is open to serious question. Although this premise cannot be conclusively proved invalid, it is not supported by the experience of the securities markets, either during the course of the implementation of the NMS, or in earlier years.

It is the conclusion of this writer that Congress and the SEC should reconsider the desirability of a project that has already cost millions of dollars of government and private resources, that has involved the SEC in activities for which it has little capacity, and that is based on an unproved and probably invalid presumption. Ten years of floundering is enough. Section 11A should be repealed and other avenues of improving the quality of the securities markets should be pursued.

CHAPTER 9

"FRAUD" AND MANIPULATION

A. COMMON LAW AND SEC "FRAUD"

1. The Weapons in the Federal Arsenal

Before the Securities Act of 1933 there was no way for the federal government to deal with securities frauds except by criminal prosecution for violating the mail fraud statute[1] or for conspiring to violate it,[2] or by the Postmaster General's administratively entering a so-called "fraud order" whereby all mail directed to the respondent or his agent was returned to the sender.[3]

All these remedies remain.[4] And they are used. Indeed, the

C. 9A [1] "Whoever, having devised or intending to devise any scheme or artifice to defraud, or for obtaining money or property by means of false or fraudulent pretenses, representations, or promises, * * * for the purpose of executing such scheme or artifice or attempting so to do, places in any post office or authorized depository for mail matter, any matter or thing whatever to be sent or delivered by the Postal Service, or takes or receives therefrom, any such matter or thing, or knowingly causes to be delivered by mail according to the direction thereon, or at the place at which it is directed to be delivered by the person to whom it is addressed, any such matter or thing, shall be fined not more than $1,000 or imprisoned not more than five years, or both." 18 U. S. C. §1341. See generally Comment, Survey of the Law of Mail Fraud, [1975] U. Ill. L. F. 237. There is a parallel statute on fraud by interstate or foreign "wire, radio, or television communications." 18 U. S. C. §1343.

[2] 18 U. S. C. §371.

[3] As the statute now reads, "Upon evidence satisfactory to the Postal Service that any person is engaged in conducting a scheme or device for obtaining money or property through the mails by means of false representations," the Service may also forbid the payment of any money order or postal note made out to the person and return the money. 39 U. S. C. §3005(a). The constitutionality of the statute has been sustained. Donaldson v. Read Magazine, Inc., 333 U. S. 178 (1948); Public Clearing House v. Coyne, 194 U. S. 497 (1904); Lynch v. Blount, 330 F. Supp. 689 (S. D. N. Y. 1971), aff'd per curiam, 404 U. S. 1007 (1972) (notwithstanding the 1968 amendment that made it unnecessary to show scienter or intent to defraud).

[4] In Edwards v. United States, 312 U. S. 473, 483-84 (1941), the Court held

mail fraud statute has been applied to certain breaches of fiduciary duty, as by an agent's obtaining secret profits.[5] But the 1933 Act, aside from requiring the registration of new offerings and certain secondary distributions under §5, included a general antifraud provision (§17(a)) and a limited sort of antitouting provision (§17(b)). Section 17(a) creates three separate offenses:

> It shall be unlawful for any person in the offer or sale of any securities by the use of any means or instruments of transportation or communication in interstate commerce or by the use of the mails, directly or indirectly —
>
> > (1) to employ any device, scheme, or artifice to defraud, or
> > (2) to obtain money or property by means of any untrue statement of a material fact or any omission to state a material fact necessary in order to make the statements made, in the light of the circumstances under which they were made, not misleading, or

---

that §17(a) of the 1933 Act had not repealed the mail fraud statute with respect to securities.

    Still another statute will bear watching: Chapter 96 of the Criminal Code, 18 U. S. C. §§1961-68, entitled Racketeer Influenced and Corrupt Organizations ("RICO"), which was adopted as Title IX of the Organized Crime Control Act of 1970, 84 Stat. 922 (1970). The RICO statute makes it unlawful, *inter alia*, for "any person through a pattern of racketeering activity * * * to acquire or maintain, directly or indirectly, any interest in or control of any enterprise which is engaged in, or the activities of which affect, interstate or foreign commerce." 18 U. S. C. §1962(b). It defines "pattern of racketeering activity" to require "at least two acts of racketeering activity, one of which occurred after the effective date of this chapter and the last of which occurred within ten years (excluding any period of imprisonment) after the commission of a prior act of racketeering activity"; and "racketeering activity" is defined to include "fraud in the sale of securities." 18 U. S. C. §1961.

    How the last phrase got into the definition — whose fourth category couples it with bankruptcy fraud and "the felonious manufacture * * * or * * * dealing in narcotic or other dangerous drugs" — is no more clear than what "fraud" means in this context. The closest reference in the legislative history is (in the testimony of J. Edgar Hoover) to "thefts of securities from brokerage houses," in a number of which "Close associates and relatives of La Cosa Nostra figures are known to be involved." S. Rep. No. 617, 91st Cong., 1st Sess. (1969) 77; see also 39 SEC Ann. Rep. 89 (1973).

    See generally United States v. Turkett, 452 U. S. 576 (1981); Atkinson, "Racketeer Influenced and Corrupt Organizations," 18 U. S. C. §§1961-68: Broadest of the Federal Criminal Statutes, 69 J. Crim. L. & Criminology 2 (1978).

    [5] United States v. Buckner, 108 F. 2d 921, 926 (2d Cir. 1940), *cert. denied,* 309 U. S. 669 (scheme by protective committee to defraud bondholders in course of supposed efforts to secure favorable legislation by Philippine Government); United States v. Groves, 122 F. 2d 87 (2d Cir. 1941), *cert. denied,* 314 U. S. 670 (officer's secret profit on purchase of company's stock and resale to company); United States v. Bryza, 522 F. 2d 414 (7th Cir. 1975), *cert. denied,* 426 U. S. 912 (buying agent's accepting kickbacks from suppliers); cf. United

(3) to engage in any transaction, practice, or course of business which operates or would operate as a fraud or deceit upon the purchaser.[6]

This section marked an advance over the mail fraud statute in a number of respects: (1) It is specifically tailored to the securities field. (2) The 1933 Act affords the civil remedy of injunction, thus making it possible to nip certain types of fraud in the bud rather than to rely exclusively on criminal prosecution after the deed.[7] (3) Clause (2) does not refer to "fraud" as such but speaks in terms of material misstatements and half-truths. The entire section, however, refers to fraud or misrepresentation "in the offer or sale of any securities." It is perhaps arguable that this does not limit the application of the section to cases of fraud by *sellers* as distinct from fraud by *buyers* of securities — that it was intended merely to make it clear that §17(a), in contrast to the mail fraud statute, is restricted to the securities field. But the Commission has never sought to apply §17(a) except against fraudulent *sellers*.[8]

States v. Bush, 522 F. 2d 641 (7th Cir. 1975), *cert. denied*, 424 U. S. 977 (city employee's failure to disclose his interest in a company to which the city awarded a contract); United States v. Newman, 664 F. 2d 12, 19-20 (2d Cir. 1981); but cf. Epstein v. United States, 174 F. 2d 754, 767-68 (6th Cir. 1949) (whether a breach of trust is an active fraud depends upon what the particular breach consists of, and it is not enough to show that directors of Company *A* profited from other companies that sold commodities to *A* and that they did not disclose the relationship, there being no proof of overreaching). These are not securities cases, but there is no reason why the principle should not apply in a securities context.

[6] Since the three clauses of §17(a) are in the disjunctive, United States v. Naftalin, 441 U. S. 768, 774 (1979), the Government or the Commission need not prove a violation of all three, United States v. Strand, 617 F. 2d 571 (10th Cir. 1980), *cert. denied*, 449 U. S. 841, and an indictment that charges all three in separate counts in not duplicitous, United States v. Amick, 439 F. 2d 351, 359 (7th Cir. 1971), *cert. denied*, 404 U. S. 823. But this is not to say that there may be three convictions for a single offense pleaded under all three clauses. United States v. Greenberg, 30 F. R. D. 164, 169-70 (S. D. N. Y. 1962).

Moreover, mail fraud and §17(a) counts are commonly joined in the same indictment, and this is permissible. United States v. Tallant, 547 F. 2d 1291, 1299 (5th Cir. 1977), *cert. denied*, 434 U. S. 889. But under the majority view consecutive sentences are improper when the convictions arose out of a single fact pattern. United States v. Reed, 639 F. 2d 896, 903-06 (2d Cir. 1981), and cases cited; see also Code §1821(a)(7).

[7] §20(b). Section 17(a) does not itself create a crime any more than §5 does. But, apart from the injunctive remedy, any person who "willfully" violates *any* provision of the 1933 Act commits a crime under §24, in addition to subjecting himself or itself to administrative disciplinary proceedings under the 1934 Act if he or it is registered with the Commission in certain capacities or is an associate of a person so registered. See pp. 699-701 supra. The 1934 Act (see §§32(a), 21(e)) and the other statutes follow the same pattern.

[8] This includes the "man bite dog" case of the *customer* who defrauds his

In 1934 the Securities Exchange Act added two relevant provisions, §§9(a)(4) and 10(b). The former, part of the §9 attack on market *manipulation,* makes it unlawful for any "dealer or broker, or other person selling or offering for sale or purchasing or offering to purchase the security, to make, regarding any security registered on a national securities exchange, for the purpose of inducing the purchase or sale of such security, any statement which was at the time and in the light of the circumstances under which it was made, false or misleading with respect to any material fact, and which he knew or had reasonable ground to believe was so false or misleading." Section 9(a)(4) is self-operative but limited to registered securities. Section 10(b), on the other hand, is an omnibus section that is not so limited but is not self-operative either:

> · It shall be unlawful for any person, directly or indirectly, by the use of any means or instrumentality of interstate commerce or of the mails, or of any facility of any national securities exchange —
>
> *   *   *
>
> (b) To use or employ, in connection with the purchase or sale of any security registered on a national securities exchange or any security not so registered, any manipulative or deceptive device or contrivance in contravention of such rules and regulations as the Commission may prescribe as necessary or appropriate in the public interest or for the protection of investors.

The potentialities of §10(b) — and the most illustrious of its progeny, Rule 10b-5, which we shall examine at some depth — were not appreciated for some years, as we shall see. But the Commission has developed a gaggle of other rules under §10(b): Rules 10b-1, 10b-2, 10b-3, 10b-6, and 10b-18, on manipulation;[9] 10b-4 and 10b-13, on short tendering and buying "alongside" a tender offer;[10] 10b-7 and 10b-8, on market stabilization;[11] 10b-9, which imposes certain restrictions on "all-or-none" offerings; 10b-10, the

---

broker by selling short with no intention to deliver if the market goes up; for the purposes of the Act go beyond the protection of investors to the achieving of "a high standard of business ethics * * * *in every facet of the securities industry."* United States v. Naftalin, 441 U. S. 768, 775 (1979), quoting from SEC v. Capital Gains Research Bureau, Inc., 375 U. S. 180, 186-87 (1963) (the ellipsis and italics are the Court's).

[9] See c. 9D infra.

[10] See p. 576, 588 supra.

[11] See p. 1000 infra.

confirmation rule;[12] 10b-16, on disclosure of credit terms in margin transactions;[13] and 10b-17, on untimely announcements of record dates for dividends and other specified events.

In 1936 the Exchange Act was amended by adding what is the present §15(c)(1), then §15(c). As amended in 1975, that section provides that

> No broker or dealer shall make use of the mails or of any means or instrumentality of interstate commerce to effect any transaction in, or to induce the purchase or sale of, any security (other than commercial paper, bankers' acceptance, or commercial bills) otherwise than on a national securities exchange of which it is a member by means of any manipulative, deceptive, or other fraudulent device or contrivance.

There is a similar prohibition with respect to municipal dealers so far as municipal securities are concerned, except that there is no reference to exchange trading because it is virtually non-existent. And the section concludes:

> The Commission shall, for the purposes of this paragraph, by rules and regulations define such devices or contrivances as are manipulative, deceptive, or otherwise fraudulent.

This section differs in substance from §10(b) in a number of respects: (1) Although it directs the Commission to adopt rules of definition, the first portion of the section is literally self-operative, whereas §10(b) is not operative in the absence of specific rules. (2) It is limited to over-the-counter transactions, whereas §10(b) is not. (3) It is limited to transactions by brokers or dealers (or, since 1975, municipal dealers). However, like §10(b) and unlike §17(a), it covers fraud in the purchase as well as the sale of securities.

There are eight rules, all of them in form definitions of the term "manipulative, deceptive, or other fraudulent device or contrivance" as used in §15(c)(1) of the Act. Rule 15c1-1 simply defines "customer" and "completion of the transaction" as used in this series of rules. And Rule 15c1-2 is a general antifraud provision that is modeled on Clauses (2) and (3) of §17(a) of the 1933

---

[12] See p. 804 n. 17 infra.

[13] This reflects the exemption of brokers' margin loans from the disclosure requirement of the Truth in Lending Act, 15 U. S. C. §1603(2), on the legislative assumption that the Commission would adopt an appropriate rule. Sec. Ex. Act Rel. 8773 (1969); see Liang v. Dean Witter & Co., Inc., 540 F. 2d 1107, 1110-11 (D. C. Cir. 1976). "Regardless of whether there is a private cause of action under Rule 10b-16, * * * nothing in that provision * * * operates to preclude a claim under Rule 10b-5." Steinberg v. Shearson Hayden Stone, Inc., 546 F. Supp. 699, 700 (D. Del. 1982).

Act, except that the portion comparable to Clause (2) applies only when the "statement or omission is made with knowledge or reasonable grounds to believe that it is untrue or misleading."[14] The other six rules are particularizations of Rule 15c1-2,[15] although the Commission was careful to provide in that rule that they are not exhaustive.[16]

Rule 15c1-3, in substance, prohibits a broker-dealer from representing that his registration indicates that the Commission has passed on his financial standing or conduct or the merits of any security or transaction.

Rules 15c1-5 and 15c1-6[17] are complementary. The former requires any broker or dealer "controlled by, controlling, or under common control with, the issuer of any security" to disclose the existence of control to his customer before entering into any purchase or sale contract. Rule 15c1-6 requires a *broker* who is acting for a customer or for both sides, as well as a *dealer* who is to receive a fee from a customer for rendering advice, to give his customer written notification, at or before the completion of the transaction, whenever he "is participating or is otherwise financially interested" in "the primary or secondary distribution" of the security being bought or sold.

Rule 15c1-7 contains two requirements in connection with discretionary accounts. Immediately after effecting any transaction with or for a discretionary account, the broker or dealer must make a record of the customer's name, the name, amount, and price of the security, and the date and time of the transaction. And trans-

---

[14] In full text:

(a) The term "manipulative, deceptive, or other fraudulent device or contrivance," as used in section 15(c)(1) of the Act, is hereby defined to include any act, practice, or course of business which operates or would operate as a fraud or deceit upon any person.
(b) The term "manipulative, deceptive, or other fraudulent device or contrivance," as used in section 15(c)(1) of the Act, is hereby defined to include any untrue statement of a material fact and any omission to state a material fact necessary in order to make the statements made, in the light of the circumstances under which they are made, not misleading, which statement or omission is made with knowledge or reasonable grounds to believe that it is untrue or misleading.

[15] William I. Hay, 19 SEC 397, 408 n. 15 (1945).
[16] "The scope of this rule shall not be limited by any specific definitions of the term 'manipulative, deceptive, or other fraudulent device or contrivance' contained in other rules adopted pursuant to section 15(c)(1) of the act." Rule 15c1-2(c).
[17] The former Rule 15c1-4 was a confirmation rule, which in the late 1970s gave way to Rule 10b-10 because §15(c)(1) is limited to over-the-counter transactions. Sec. Ex. Act Rel. 13,508, 12 SEC Dock. 299 (1977).

actions may not be "excessive in size or frequency in view of the financial resources and character" of the account. The latter prohibition is directed at the "churning" of customers' accounts. Here again, however, this rule is but a partial particularization of Rule 15c1-2. Even though Rule 15c1-7 applies only when the broker or dealer has been "vested" with discretionary power, the Commission has repeatedly held that the "churning" of customers' accounts may violate Rule 15c1-2, as well as §17(a)(3) of the 1933 Act, "whenever the broker or dealer is in a position to determine the volume and frequency of transactions by reason of the customer's willingness to follow the suggestions of the broker or dealer and he abuses the customer's confidence by over-trading."[18]

Rule 15c1-8, in effect, prohibits purported "market offerings" (as distinct from "fixed price offerings") unless the broker or dealer knows or has reasonable ground to believe that a market exists other than that made or controlled by him or a related person. It is noteworthy that Rules 15c1-7 and 15c1-8, alone among the broker-dealer fraud rules under §15(c)(1), go beyond the disclosure philosophy. This is particularly evident in the case of Rule 15c1-7.

Rule 15c1-9 prohibits the use of any *pro forma* financial statement — that is, a statement "purporting to give effect to the receipt and application of any part of the proceeds from the sale or exchange of securities" — unless the underlying assumptions are clearly set forth as part of the caption of the statement.

As part of the Maloney Act amendment that added §15A in 1938,[19] Congress enacted the present §15(c)(2), which is similar to §15(c)(1) except that (1) it does not apply to an "exempted security," (2) it covers "fictitious quotations" as well as fraudulent, deceptive, or manipulative practices, and (3) it directs the Commission by rule to "prescribe means reasonably designed to prevent" such practices and quotations as well as to define them.

---

[18] Norris & Hirshberg, Inc., 21 SEC 865, 890 (1946), *aff'd* sub nom. Norris & Hirshberg, Inc. v. SEC, 177 F. 2d 228 (D. C. Cir. 1949); see also, e.g., Russell L. Irish, 42 SEC 735 (1965), *aff'd* sub nom. Irish v. SEC, 367 F. 2d 637 (9th Cir. 1966), *cert. denied,* 386 U. S. 911; Hecht v. Harris, Upham & Co., 430 F. 2d 1202, 1206-07 (9th Cir. 1970); Fey v. Walston & Co., Inc., 493 F. 2d 1036 (7th Cir. 1974); Carras v. Burns, 516 F. 2d 251 (4th Cir. 1975); Miley v. Oppenheimer & Co., Inc., 637 F. 2d 318 (5th Cir. 1981). But "the excessive trading element of a churning case is not established unless the frequency of the trades was unrelated to the customer's objectives." Follansbee v. Davis, Skaggs & Co., Inc., 681 F. 2d 673, 676 (9th Cir. 1982). On methods of computing turnover, as well as measuring damages in private actions, see Note, Churning by Securities Dealers, 80 Harv. L. Rev. 869, 875-76, 883-85 (1967); see also Code §§1606, 1717.

[19] See p. 689 supra.

Like §15(c)(1), §15(c)(2) has a first sentence that on its face is self-operative; and a proscription of "fictitious quotations" would seem specific enough even for a criminal prosecution without the emendation afforded by rules. Nevertheless, the Commission, in arguing to the Supreme Court that §206(4) of the Investment Advisers Act, which was modeled on §15(c)(2), was not self-operative, stated that the Commission had "for many years interpreted" §15(c)(2) that way.[20] And the Commission has seldom if ever instituted any action under either §15(c)(1) or §15(c)(2) without pleading a specific rule, of which there are now seven under §15(c)(2). Three of them we have already noticed: Rule 15c2-1, on hypothecation of customers' securities;[21] 15c2-8, on delivery of preliminary and final prospectuses;[22] and Rule 15c2-11, which, in effect, prohibits quotations without specified information.[23] The other four rules are 15c2-3, a postwar rule that prohibits trading in German securities without validation; 15c2-4, on handling the proceeds of non-firm-commitment underwritings;[24] 15c2-5, which calls for certain credit and other information going beyond the prospectus in connection with the joint selling of mutual fund shares and life insurance; and 15c2-7, on the identification of quotations submitted to an inter-dealer quotation system.

With §10(b) non-self-operative, the combination of §17(a) of the 1933 Act and §§9(a)(4), 15(c)(1) and 15(c)(2) of the 1934 Act did not cover fraud in the *purchase* of securities by persons *other than* (1) brokers and dealers acting over the counter or (2) persons buying registered securities for the purpose of inducing their purchase by others. This was a serious gap, because an issuer itself, or an officer or director or principal stockholder, could buy in its securities by fraudulent practices without being touched by federal authority except for criminal prosecution under the mail or wire fraud statute or the entry of a mail fraud order. In the revision program of 1941 the Commission and the securities industry jointly suggested an amendment to extend §17(a) to the purchase

---

[20] Petition for Cert., p. 19, SEC v. Capital Gains Research Bureau, Inc., 375 U. S. 180 (1963).

[21] See p. 708 n. 8 supra.

[22] See p. 133 supra.

[23] See p. 333 n. d supra.

[24] See Eastside Church of Christ v. National Plan, Inc., 391 F. 2d 357, 361 (5th Cir. 1968), *cert. denied* sub nom. Church of Christ v. National Plan, Inc., 393 U. S. 913, *judgment for plaintiff on remand aff'd* sub nom. McGregor Blvd. Church of Christ v. Walling, 428 F. 2d 401 (5th Cir. 1970); United States v. Koss, 506 F. 2d 1103, 1110 (2d Cir. 1974), *cert. denied,* 421 U. S. 911. Cf. Rule 10b-9, supra p. 802.

as well as the sale of securities.[25] When this program fell casualty to Pearl Harbor, the Commission in May 1942 hit upon a solution to this problem that from hindsight appears exceedingly simple and obvious. Acting under §10(b), which had been in the Exchange Act from the beginning, the Commission adopted Rule 10b-5 (originally designated X-10B-5), which merely borrows the language of §17(a), except for the reference in Clause (2) to *obtaining money or property by means of* an untrue statement or half-truth, and applies it "in connection with the purchase or sale of any security":

> It shall be unlawful for any person, directly or indirectly, by the use of any means or instrumentality of interstate commerce, or of the mails, or of any facility of any national securities exchange,
>
> (1) to employ any device, scheme, or artifice to defraud,
>
> (2) to make any untrue statement of a material fact or to omit to state a material fact necessary in order to make the statements made, in the light of the circumstances under which they were made, not misleading, or
>
> (3) to engage in any act, practice, or course of business which operates or would operate as a fraud or deceit upon any person,
>
> in connection with the purchase or sale of any security.[26]

Aside from these provisions and rules relating to purchases or sales, there are a number of others that are more specialized: We have already noticed Rule 14a-9, the proxy fraud rule, together with its analogue, Rule 14c-6, when an "information statement" is used.[27] We have noticed also §§14(e) and 13(e) of the 1934 Act, with respect to tender offers and issuer repurchases.[28] In addition, §17(j) of the Investment Company Act, on the model of the rulemaking provision in §15(c)(2) of the Exchange Act, authorizes the Commission to "define, and prescribe means reasonably designed

[25] Investment Bankers Assn. et al., Report on the Conferences with the SEC and Its Staff on Proposals for Amending the Securities Act of 1933 and the Securities Exchange Act of 1934 (1941) 167.

[26] In one respect §10(b) and the rule may be *narrower* than §17(a), which reads "in the *offer or* sale" — an incident of the 1954 amendment of §5 to permit offers during the waiting period (see pp. 99-101) — in contrast with the "sale" of Rule 10b-5. See Blue Chip Stamps v. Manor Drug Stores, 421 U. S. 723, 732-34 (1975), set out infra p. 904, at pp. 907-08.

The rule has been held not to be unconstitutionally vague. United States v. Persky, 520 F. 2d 283, 287 (2d Cir. 1975); see also Speed v. Transamerica Corp., 99 F. Supp. 808, 831-32 (D. Del. 1951) (rejecting arguments of vagueness and delegation as "shop worn").

[27] See pp. 541, 561 supra.

[28] See pp. 574, 578. On the rules under these sections, see pp. 585-88 supra.

to prevent, * * * fraudulent, deceptive or manipulative acts" by persons in specified relationships to registered investment companies in connection with their portfolio securities;[29] and §206 of the Advisers Act is a cross, so far as investment advisers are concerned, between the language of 1933 Act §17(a)(1) and (3) and 1934 Act §10(b), with the addition of rulemaking authority along the lines of 1934 Act §15(c)(2).[30]

This cacophony — which characterizes not only the substantive language but also the jurisdictional references to use of the mails or interstate commerce[31] — has resulted in much wasteful litigation. Virtually every proceeding, public or private, is based alternatively on as many of these provisions and rules as may be applicable, for fear of missing a pearl here or there. Accordingly, the integration of all these "fraud" provisions into basically a single section is one of the major reforms proposed by the Code. In the words of the commentary:

> Sections 202(61) and 202(96) define "fraudulent act" and "misrepresentation" basically in the language of the respective portions of S17(a) — which was borrowed in Rule 10b-5 — but with special provision in §202(96)(B) for estimates and projections. These definitions, together with the definitions of "fact" and "material" in §§202(55) and 202(92), make it possible in a single brief section (§1602(a)) to cover all of today's fraud provisions with respect to purchases, sales, proxy solicitations, tender requests and investment advice. There is a limited duty to correct (§1602(b)). These provisions are self-operative. But §1614(a) gives the Commission rulemaking authority (along the lines, for example, of X15(c)(2)) not only to define, but also to "prescribe means reasonably designed to prevent," conduct in violation of Part XVI ("Fraud, Misrepresentation, and Manipulation") generally.[32]

2. THE RELATION BETWEEN SEC "FRAUD" CONCEPTS AND COMMON LAW DECEIT

Statutes build on the common law and, especially when statutes are new, judges and lawyers who are trained in the common law

---

[29] These rules may require registered investment companies and their investment advisers and principal underwriters to adopt codes of ethics. And Rule 17j-1, *inter alia*, has implemented that authority.

[30] The rules under §206 are described infra pp. 977-79.

[31] Ink has been spilled over the difference, if any, between the "in interstate commerce" of 1933 Act §17(a) and the "of interstate commerce" of 1934 Act §10(b). See p. 98 supra.

[32] 1 Code xlv.

are apt to look to it for guidance. This is not the place for a detailed discussion of the common law tort action of deceit,[33] or of its criminal analogue in the false pretenses statutes that go back to George II.[34] At the same time, it is impossible to describe the statutory fraud concepts that have developed under the securities laws without some brief summary of what has gone before — a summary that, because of its generalization and the great number of common law jurisdictions, must be taken *cum grano salis*.

The hornbook "elements" of deceit — which, it must be remembered, was not consciously or especially molded for the flotation of securities — are six in number: There must be (1) a false representation of (2) a material (3) fact; (4) the defendant must know of the falsity (this kind of knowledge is called scienter) but make the statement nevertheless for the purpose of inducing the plaintiff to rely on it; and (5) the plaintiff must justifiably rely on it and (6) suffer damage as a consequence. The enumeration of these elements suggests the questions that have arisen and that in large measure carry over to the SEC Acts:

(1) It would seem to be a relatively simple matter to determine whether a representation is true or false. But what of ambiguous statements — those that are true in one sense but false in another? And what of statements that are literally true but convey a different impression to the average person? Or half-truths — statements that are true as far as they go but are misleading because of the absence of pertinent qualifications? Or an omission to make any express representation at all when there is an implied representation of fair dealing or when a fiduciary relationship imposes an affirmative duty to speak?

(2) A fact is material if "a reasonable man would attach importance to its existence or nonexistence in determining his choice of action in the transaction in question."[35] But there is still ample room for argument on the facts of particular cases and typically the question will be for the fact finder.

(3) What is a statement of fact as distinguished from an expression of opinion — for example, a statement of value or mere "puffing"? Or as distinguished from a statement of law — for example,

---

[33] See Restatement (Second) of Torts, Div. 4, Deceit, esp. c. 22, Misrepresentation and Nondisclosure Causing Pecuniary Loss; Green, Deceit, 16 Va. L. Rev. 749 (1930).

[34] 30 Geo. 2, c. 24 (1757); see Note, The Crime of False Pretenses in the Context of Commercial Credit Transactions, 65 Yale L. J. 887 (1956).

[35] Restatement (Second) of Torts §538(2)(a); see Shores v. Sklar, 647 F. 2d 462, 468 (5th Cir. *en banc* 1981), *cert. denied*, 103 S. Ct. 722.

[36] See Kripke, Rule 10b-5 Liability and "Material" "Facts," 46 N. Y. U. L. Rev. 1061, 1070-75 (1972).

that a corporation is empowered to do certain things? Or as distinguished from a forecast or promise — for example, that certain dividends will be earned or that the proceeds of an issue of securities will be applied to certain purposes?[36]

(4) The fourth element, scienter, has been stated above in its most rigorous aspect. But it has been variously defined to mean everything from knowing falsity with an implication of *mens rea,* through the various gradations of recklessness, down to such non-action as is virtually equivalent to negligence or even liability without fault (and were better treated as creating a distinct species of liability not based on intent).[37]

(5) There is always the question whether the plaintiff relied on the false representation complained of or on something quite unrelated — perhaps a tip from a third person.[38]

(6) Finally there are all the questions of causation in which the law of torts abounds.[39]

In effect, the charge of deceit (as least in those jurisdictions that have not substantially watered down the concept of scienter) is an accusation of thievery. In 1889 the House of Lords was so concerned with its implications that it could not bring itself to hold that gentlemen respected in the business community could be guilty of deceit because of a false statement in a prospectus however unreasonable their belief in the statement's truth.[40] The

[37] "Where a party innocently misrepresents a material fact by mistake * * * such representation will support an action for fraud." Stein v. Treger, 182 F. 2d 696, 699 (D. C. Cir. 1950), and cases cited; see also, e. g., Mears v. Accomac Banking Co., Inc., 160 Va. 311, 321, 168 S. E. 740, 743 (1933). It is said that a majority of the states now permit actions on the basis of negligent or sometimes innocent misrepresentation. See Prosser, Handbook of the Law of Torts (4th ed. 1971) 699-714. "There has * * * been a growing recognition by common-law courts that the doctrines of fraud and deceit which developed around transactions involving land and other tangible items of wealth are ill-suited to the sale of such intangibles as advice and securities, and that accordingly, the doctrines must be adapted to the merchandise in issue." SEC v. Capital Gains Research Bureau, Inc., 375 U. S. 180, 194 (1963). For The American Law Institute's view, see Restatement (Second) of Torts §526.

[38] On the concept of *justifiable* reliance, see p. 1127 infra. In List v. Fashion Park, Inc., 340 F. 2d 457, 462 (2d Cir. 1965), cert. denied sub nom. List v. Lerner, 382 U. S. 811, a case under Rule 10b-5, the court contrasted materiality and reliance by stating that reliance requires that the *individual plaintiff* must have acted upon the fact misrepresented, whereas materiality requires that a *reasonable person* would have so acted. The court added, however, that care must be taken to distinguish the requirement that a reasonable person would have *believed* the fact misrepresented, since there is a marked trend away from that common law requirement.

[39] See 1 Code 61-62, Comment (5).

[40] Derry v. Peek, 14 A. C. 337 (1889).

immediate reaction of Parliament was to pass the Directors' Liability Act of 1890, as we shall see when we come to the chapter on Civil Liability. But in the last sixty years the courts in both England and the United States have considerably softened the common law of deceit — the degree of liberalization varying, of course, with the jurisdiction. Thus, apart from the watering down of the scienter concept, there is ample precedent for holding that false statements on legal matters are actionable. And at this point it is almost obligatory to quote Lord Bowen's observation that "The state of a man's mind is as much a fact as the state of his digestion."[41]

Perhaps nowhere is this liberalization more noticeable than it is with respect to what constitutes a false representation. It is now quite clear that a half-truth is as bad as an outright lie. Thus, in 1932 a British court sent Lord Kylsant to prison because his steamship line had issued a prospectus that had *truthfully* stated its average net income for the past ten years and its dividends for the past seventeen, but had deliberately *concealed* the fact that its earnings during the first three of the ten years had been greatly augmented by World War I as compared with the seven lean years that followed.[42] This was a criminal prosecution rather than a deceit action. The Larceny Act of 1861, under which it was brought, made it a misdemeanor for a director to make "any written statement or account which he shall know to be false in any material particular" with intent to induce any person to advance property to his company.[43] It is not surprising, therefore, that the same view should prevail in common law deceit. In 1941, for example, the Supreme Court of the United States, applying Iowa law in a deceit case involving an allegedly misleading prospectus, approved the view of The American Law Institute to the effect (in the Court's paraphrase) that "a statement of a half truth is as much a misrepresentation as if the facts stated were untrue."[44] A lay Englishman managed to capture the thought very well:

---

[41] Edgington v. Fitzmaurice, 29 Ch. D. 459, 483 (1885). The Restatement of Torts (Second) has it that "One who fraudulently makes a misrepresentation of fact, opinion, intention or law for the purpose of inducing another to act or refrain from action in reliance upon it, is subject to liability to the other in deceit for pecuniary loss caused to him by his justifiable reliance upon the misrepresentation." §525; see esp. Comment d; see also id., §§539, 544, 545.

[42] Rex v. Kylsant, 23 Cr. App. R. 83, [1932] 1 K. B. 442.

[43] 24 & 25 Vict., c. 96, §84.

[44] Equitable Life Ins. Co. of Iowa v. Halsey, Stuart & Co., 312 U. S. 410, 424-26 (1941).

That a lie which is half a truth is ever the blackest of lies,
That a lie which is all a lie may be met and fought with outright.
But a lie which is part a truth is a harder matter to fight.[45]

At the same time there is still no common law liability in deceit for complete nondisclosure as distinguished from a half-truth, unless the one party to a business transaction "by concealment or other action intentionally prevents the other from acquiring material information,"[46] or the one party is under a duty to the other to exercise reasonable care to disclose the matter in question "because of a fiduciary or other similar relation of trust and confidence between them."[47] So far as a fiduciary is concerned, however, the courts have posed

> an affirmative duty of "utmost good faith, and full and fair disclosure of all material facts," as well as an affirmative obligation "to employ reasonable care to avoid misleading" his clients.[48]

Now there are superimposed on this common law background the several antifraud provisions of the SEC statutes. It is obvious from the language that some of the basic problems are the same — what is false, what is a fact, what is material. Because of the legislative background it seems reasonable to assume at the very least that the most liberal common law views on these questions should govern under the statutes.[49] The antifraud provisions are part of a statutory scheme that resulted from a finding that securities are "intricate merchandise"[50] and a congressional determination

---

45 Tennyson, The Grandmother, Stanza 8.
46 Restatement (Second) of Torts §550.
47 Id., §551(2)(a).
48 SEC v. Capital Gains Research Bureau, Inc., 375 U. S. 180, 194 (1963). Indeed, fraud in equity rather than law

> properly includes all acts, omissions and concealments which involve a breach of legal or equitable duty, trust, or confidence, justly reposed, and are injurious to another, or by which an undue and unconscientious advantage is taken of another.

Id. at 194, quoting Moore v. Crawford, 130 U. S. 122, 128 (1888), which in turn quoted 1 Story, Equity Jurisprudence (13th ed. 1886) §187.
49 See Burger, C. J., in Chiarella v. United States, 445 U. S. 222, 228 n. 10 (1980); see also SEC v. Capital Gains Research Bureau, Inc., 375 U. S. 180, 195 (1963): "Congress intended the Investment Advisers Act of 1940 to be construed like other securities legislation "enacted for the purpose of avoiding frauds,' not technically and restrictively, but rather flexibly to effectuate its remedial purposes." In thus indulging in the game of labels, however, Justice Goldberg overlooked the more realistic approach of a distinguished predecessor. See Jackson, J., in SEC v. C. M. Joiner Leasing Corp., 320 U. S. 344, 350-53 (1943), set out supra p. 186, at pp. 188-90.
50 H. R. Rep. No. 85, 73d Cong., 1st Sess. (1933) 8.

that the public interest demanded legislation that would recognize the gross inequality of bargaining power between the professional securities firm and the average investor. "The essential objective of securities legislation is to protect those who do not know market conditions from the overreachings of those who do."[51]

The fact is that the courts have repeatedly said that the fraud provisions in the SEC Acts, as well as the mail fraud statute, are not limited to circumstances that would give rise to a common law action for deceit.[52] How much further the statutes go is difficult to say definitely. The courts have traditionally refused, whether at common law deceit or under securities laws, to define fraud with specificity. Were any hard and fast rule to be laid down as to what constitutes fraud under the blue sky law, the Oregon court has said, "a certain class of gentlemen of the 'J. Rufus Wallingford' type — 'they toil not neither do they spin' — would lie awake nights endeavoring to conceive some devious and shadowy way of evading the law. It is more advisable to deal with each case as it arises."[53] Nevertheless certain propositions are reasonably clear. Whether to this extent the SEC acts go beyond common law fraud depends upon the particular common law jurisdiction:

(1) It has been the law under the mail fraud statute ever since a Supreme Court decision in 1896[54] that "to promise what one does not mean to perform or to declare an opinion as to future events which one does not hold is a fraud."[55] On this approach the Commission regards valuations, geological reports, and the like, although they may be expressions of opinion, as based on implied representations that appropriate standards have been followed;

---

[51] Charles Hughes & Co., Inc. v. SEC, 139 F. 2d 434, 437 (2d Cir. 1943), *cert. denied,* 321 U. S. 786; see also Hall v. Geiger-Jones Co., 242 U. S. 539, 552 (1917).

[52] See, e. g., Charles Hughes & Co., Inc. v. SEC, 139 F. 2d 434, 437 (2d Cir. 1943), *cert. denied,* 321 U. S. 786; Harris v. American Investment Co., 523 F. 2d 220, 224 (8th Cir. 1975), *cert. denied,* 423 U. S. 1054. Under the mail fraud statute, see, e. g., United States v. Groves, 122 F. 2d 87, 90 (2d Cir. 1941), *cert. denied,* 314 U. S. 670.

[53] State v. Whiteaker, 118 Ore. 656, 661, 247 Pac. 1077, 1079 (1926). It was on this approach that §401(d) of the Uniform Securities Act was drafted to provide merely that " 'Fraud,' 'deceit,' and 'defraud' are not limited to common-law deceit." See Loss, Commentary on the Uniform Securities Act (1976) 93-94.

[54] Durland v. United States, 161 U. S. 306, 313-14 (1896). The mail fraud statute has since been amended to cover "false promises" specifically.

[55] E. g., United States v. Grayson, 166 F. 2d 863, 866 (2d Cir. 1948); Burns v. Paddock, 503 F. 2d 18, 23 (7th Cir. 1974); but cf. Marx & Co., Inc. v. Diners' Club, Inc., 550 F. 2d 505, 514-15 (2d Cir. 1977), *cert. denied,* 434 U. S. 861 (the general nature of predictions about a possible takeover precluded their being representations of fact).

hence a failure to observe those standards by one who is held out as an expert involves a misrepresentation of fact.[56] An accountant's report is likewise regarded as a material fact.[57] And estimates or statements of prospects are regarded as involving misrepresentations of fact if they are lacking in foundation.[58] The same thing may be true with respect to a misstatement of a point of law.[59]

All this is to say that there is no longer much room for judicial predilection in drawing the line between misrepresentation and "puffing"; for the "puffing" concept in the securities context has all but gone the way of the dodo. One still sees occasional characterizations of loose talk as "puffing."[60] But it is not the kind of rhetoric that is likely to appeal, at least to the Commission, which has said:

> The concept of "puffing" is derived from the doctrine of *caveat emptor* and arises primarily in the sale of tangibles where it appears that examination by the purchaser may offset exaggerated statements and expressions of opinion by the salesman. It can have little application to the merchandising of securities.[61]

The judge put it all very succinctly in a common law deceit case involving the sale of insurance when he said: " 'Buyer beware' lingers now only in the argument of the lawyers."[62]

---

[56] E. g., Haddam Distillers Corp., 1 SEC 37, 42 (1934); Intermountain Petroleum, Inc., 38 SEC 538, 544 (1958).

[57] Cornucopia Gold Mines, 1 SEC 364, 367 (1936).

[58] E. g., American Kid Co., 1 SEC 694, 699 (1936); Marx v. Computer Sciences Corp., 507 F. 2d 485 (9th Cir. 1974). The Commission's former antipathy to forecasts *per se* (see pp. 163-65 supra) applied only with respect to prospectuses and proxy statements. The text statement here presumably applies today to forecasts in those media as it has always applied to forecasts in other media.

[59] Byron v. United States, 273 Fed. 769, 772-73 (9th Cir. 1921), *cert. denied,* 257 U. S. 653 (mail fraud statute).

[60] E. g., in Campo v. Shearson Hayden Stone, Inc., CCH Fed. Sec. L. Rep. ¶97,517 at 97,726 (S. D. N. Y. 1980), the court considered a statement that the plaintiff "could make a lot of money if he invested in options" to be, "at worst, an example of brokers' 'puffing' which does not rise to the level of an actionable wrong under the federal securities laws." On "puffing" in proxy contests, see p. 543 supra.

[61] B. Fennekohl & Co., 41 SEC 210, 216 (1962). As the Commission put it with commendable restraint in another proceeding:

> In his testimony Pollock [an employee of the broker-dealer] characterized himself as a "sales promotionist." He went on to define this term as follows: "Have you watched TV programs, sir? Do they huff, do they puff? This is sales promotion." It is clear to us that Pollock completely misconceived the role of a writer of securities sales literature.

Fred L. Carvalho, 41 SEC 620, 622 n. 2 (1963).

[62] Knox v. Anderson, 159 F. Supp. 795, 806 (D. Hawaii 1958), *aff'd sub*

(2) We have already noticed the Supreme Court's 1976 definition of materiality in the context of Rule 14a-9, the proxy fraud rule, as a fact with respect to which "there is a substantial likelihood that a reasonable shareholder would consider it important in deciding how to vote,"[63] and we have observed that that definition has been followed in other contexts.[64] Nevertheless, the learning of some of the earlier cases under Rule 10b-5 presumably survives by way of indicating what sort of evidence will satisfy the Supreme Court's test:

(a) In the *Texas Gulf Sulphur* case, where the question was whether inside buyers should have disclosed that preliminary drilling for copper and other minerals had produced one or more rich cores, a majority of the Second Circuit *en banc* emphasized that the test of materiality assumed a *reasonable* man, not merely a "prudent" or "conservative" investor.[65]

(b) Presumably by way of extrapolation of the basic "reasonable man" test, a number of opinions have described as "material" those facts "which in reasonable and objective contemplation might affect the value of the corporation's stock or securities."[66] And that means market value when there is a market.[67]

(c) Precedent in the securities field also mirrors the common law view that a matter is material if "the maker of the representation

---

nom. Anderson v. Knox, 297 F. 2d 702 (9th Cir. 1961), *cert. denied,* 370 U. S. 915.

[63] TSC Industries, Inc. v. Northway, Inc., 426 U. S. 438, 449 (1976), set out supra p. 544, at p. 549.

[64] See p. 550 supra.

[65] SEC v. Texas Gulf Sulphur Co., 401 F. 2d 833, 849 (2d Cir. 1968), *cert. denied* sub nom. Coates v. SEC and Kline v. SEC, 394 U. S. 976 ("speculators and chartists * * * are also 'reasonable' investors"); Lehigh Valley Trust Co. v. Central National Bank of Jacksonville, 409 F. 2d 989, 992-93 (5th Cir. 1969) (transaction between banks); Carroll v. First National Bank of Lincolnwood, 413 F. 2d 353, 357 (7th Cir. 1969), *cert. denied,* 396 U. S. 1003 (brokers are protected); Wheat v. Hall, 535 F. 2d 874, 876 (5th Cir. 1976).

[66] E. g., Kohler v. Kohler Co., 319 F. 2d 634, 642 (7th Cir. 1963).

[67] The Code defines "material" in the Supreme Court's language, but, with respect to an "insider's" *failure* to disclose as distinct from a misstatement or half-truth, coins a new phrase, "fact of special significance"; and a fact is "of special significance" if "(A) in addition to being material it would be likely on being made generally available to affect the market price of a security to a significant extent, or (B) a reasonable person would consider it especially important under the circumstances in determining his course of action in the light of such factors as the degree of its specificity, the extent of its difference from information generally available previously, and its nature and reliability." §§202(56), 202(92)(A). See p. 819 infra. However, the version of the Code approved by the Commission requires the plaintiff to plead and prove only materiality, affording a *defense* (except in SEC injunctive and disciplinary actions) of *lack* of special significance.

knows or has reason to know that its recipient regards or is likely to regard the matter as important * * * although a reasonable man would not so regard it."[68] For the securities laws "were enacted for the very purpose of protecting those who lack business acumen."[69] Hence "the monumental credulity of the victim is no shield for the accused."[70] But this is not to say that omissions to state material facts are justified by the investor's being a person of financial sophistication.[71]

(d) The mere fact that otherwise material negotiations (as for a patent-licensing contract) have not yet been consummated does not preclude a finding of materiality.[72]

(e) Thus far there has been a good deal of speculation but no square decision on the question whether failure to disclose the insider's identity is itself a violation of the rule. Invariably nondisclosure of identity has been accompanied by a failure to reveal

---

[68] Restatement (Second) of Torts §538(2)(b); cf. Code §202(92)(B).

[69] United States v. Monjar, 47 F. Supp. 421, 425 (D. Del. 1942), *aff'd*, 147 F. 2d 916 (3d Cir. 1944), *cert. denied*, 325 U. S. 859; Norris & Hirshberg, Inc. v. SEC, 177 F. 2d 228, 233 (D. C. Cir. 1949) ("the investing and usually naive public").

[70] Deaver v. United States, 155 F. 2d 740, 744-45 (D. C. Cir. 1946), *cert. denied*, 329 U. S. 766 (mail fraud statute).

[71] Rogen v. Ilikon Corp., 361 F. 2d 260, 266 (1st Cir. 1966). That is "only one factor to be considered in determining the overall reasonableness of [the plaintiff's] reliance * * * ." Nye v. Blyth Eastman Dillon & Co., 588 F. 2d 1189, 1197 (8th Cir. 1978). "The securities laws were not enacted to protect sophisticated businessmen from their own errors of judgment." Hirsch v. duPont, 553 F. 2d 750, 763 (2d Cir. 1977); see also IIT v. Vencap, Ltd., 519 F. 2d 1001, 1011-12 (2d Cir. 1975).

The Commission tried a pseudo-mathematical formula in Raymond L. Dirks, Sec. Ex. Act Rel. 17,480, 21 SEC Dock. 1401, 1408 n. 32 (1981), citing cases, *aff'd sub nom.* Dirks v. SEC, 681 F. 2d 824, 842-44 (D. C. Cir. 1982), *cert. granted*, 103 S. Ct. 371:

> The probability-magnitude test weighs the likelihood that an event will occur against its magnitude if it should occur. The market impact test weighs the actual impact on the market of disclosure of the information in question. These tests are, however, merely serviceable objective methods for making the factual determination mandated by [TSC Industries, Inc. v. Northway, Inc., 426 U. S. 438 (1976)], and they have been regularly employed since *Texas Gulf Sulphur. Northway* did not disapprove these tests, and courts have continued to use them.

[72] Rogen v. Ilikon Corp., 361 F. 2d 260, 266-67 (1st Cir. 1966), *rev'g* 250 F. Supp. 112, 116 (D. Mass. 1966); SEC v. Shapiro, 494 F. 2d 1301, 1306 (2d Cir. 1974); SEC v. Geon Industries, Inc., 531 F. 2d 39, 47-48 (2d Cir. 1976); SEC v. Mize, 615 F. 2d 1046, 1054-55 (5th Cir. 1980), *cert. denied*, 449 U. S. 901; but cf. Harnett v. Ryan Hanes, Inc., 496 F. 2d 832, 838 (3d Cir. 1974) (drawing the line at "inchoate ideas, musings as it were"). For a good analysis of materiality from the "gleam in the eye" stage to consummation, see Fleischer, in Symposium, Insider Trading in Stocks, 21 Bus. Law. 1009, 1017 (1966).

other material facts. All that can be safely said in the present state of the law, therefore, is that an insider cannot be certain that failure to disclose his identity will *not* be considered a violation of Rule 10b-5, or at the very least will not be more likely to lead the courts to find a violation when the nondisclosure of identity is considered in connection with all the other circumstances.

(3) Clause (2) of §17(a) of the 1933 Act, as well as the comparable clauses in Rules 10b-5 and 15c1-2, is specifically aimed at half-truths.[73] But those provisions are still limited to half-truths as distinct from complete omissions to disclose anything. They do not require the seller "to state every fact about stock offered that a prospective purchaser might like to know or that might, if known, tend to influence his decision."[74] In the next sections of this chapter we shall notice the development of special fraud doctrines based on *implied* representations in certain circumstances. But otherwise Clause (2) of §17(a), with its requirement that some statement be made, may not go so far in some cases as Clauses (1) and (3), under which a scheme to defraud may perhaps more readily be based upon silence when there is a duty to speak.[75]

(4) There is another respect in which Clause (2) of §17(a) is narrower than Clauses (1) and (3). It is a specific element of the offense under Clause (2) that the seller actually "obtain money or property by means of" the false statement or half-truth.[76] By contrast, Clause (3) refers to a transaction, practice, or course of business that operates "or would operate" as a fraud or deceit upon the purchaser. And it is clear that the establishment of a "scheme * * * to defraud" under Clause (1) is not dependent on proof that any victim suffered actual loss. In other words, it is irrelevant whether the scheme succeeded or failed.[77]

(5) The extent to which the SEC "fraud" provisions require scienter — and what it means when it is required — are considered in connection with the Rule 10b-5 saga, to which we now turn.

[73] Hughes v. SEC, 174 F. 2d 969, 976 (D. C. Cir. 1949); Myzel v. Fields, 386 F. 2d 718, 733 (8th Cir. 1967), *cert. denied*, 390 U. S. 951.

[74] Otis & Co. v. SEC, 106 F. 2d 579, 582 (6th Cir. 1939). On the duty to correct statements that are discovered to be misleading or that are rendered misleading by subsequent events, see 2 Code 650-55.

[75] E. g., List v. Fashion Park, Inc., 340 F. 2d 457, 462 (2d Cir. 1965), *cert. denied* sub nom. List v. Lerner, 382 U. S. 811. See p. 900 infra.

[76] This is not true of the second clause of Rule 10b-5, which omits the words, "to obtain money or property by means of," that appear in Clause (2) of §17(a).

[77] United States v. Amick, 439 F. 2d 351, 366 (7th Cir. 1971), *cert. denied*, 404 U. S. 823; United States v. Pollack, 534 F. 2d 964, 971 (D. C. Cir. 1976), *cert. denied*, 429 U. S. 924.

B. CORPORATE "INSIDERS"

1. INSIDERS' PURCHASES AT COMMON LAW

Rule 10b-5, like §17(a) of the Securities Act, is not limited to corporate insiders — however that term may be defined. The rule may be invoked whenever any person, insider or outsider, indulges in fraudulent practices, misstatements, or half-truths in connection with the purchase or sale of securities. However, it is in the application of Rule 10b-5 to *purchases* by *corporate insiders* that most of the special problems have arisen. The typical pattern is a purchase by a corporate insider, or by the issuer itself, without disclosure of relevant financial data or other information that indicates that the security is worth considerably more than it appears to be worth on the basis of market value or whatever information may be available to the seller. We start with another obeisance to the common law and then examine the changes that have been produced by Rule 10b-5.

The courts are divided on the common law duty of disclosure owed by an officer or director in purchasing the stock of his corporation. Under the view that is usually described as the "majority" or "strict" rule ("loose" might be a better characterization), officers and directors have a fiduciary obligation only *to the corporation* and to the stockholders in their dealings *with or on behalf of the corporation;* hence as individuals they may trade in the securities of the corporation without any affirmative obligation of disclosure as long as there is no misrepresentation or half-truth or active concealment by word or deed.[1] Under the so-called minority or fiduciary rule — which is followed in a few of the more agrarian states and approved by most commentators — corporate insiders

---

C. 9B [1] A leading case for this view is Carpenter v. Danforth, 52 Barb. 581 (N. Y. Sup. Ct. 1868). This is also the English view. Percival v. Wright, [1902] 2 Ch. 421. But there is said to be "more judicial authority than is generally realized" for a development in England similar to the American development at common law whereby additional facts may convert a director into a quasi-trustee for the stockholders. See Gower, Investor Protection in the U. S. A., 15 Mod. L. Rev. 446, 452-53 (1952), citing Allen v. Hyatt, 30 T. L. R. 444 (P. C. 1914). And Parliament finally criminalized insider trading in some detail in the Companies Act 1980, 28 & 29 Eliz. 2, c. 22, §§68-75. But Percival v. Wright, which has had a remarkable career for a *nisi prius* case, remains unreversed despite repeated legislative proposals going back at least to the Jenkins Report of 1962. Board of Trade, Report of the Company Law Amendment Committee, Cmd. 1749 (1962) §§86-89, 99(b). Indeed, its principle is reflected in the 1980 Companies Act. 28 & 29 Eliz. 2, c. 22, §46(2). The only case to question *Percival*, anywhere in the Commonwealth apparently, is Coleman v. Myers, [1977] 2 N. Z. L. R. 297.

are held to fiduciary standards in their dealings with stockholders and hence must make full disclosure of all material facts.[2] And a number of jurisdictions take an in-between position, imposing liability for nondisclosure by insiders through application of the so-called "special circumstances" doctrine enunciated by the Supreme Court in 1909 in *Strong* v. *Repide*. The Court there held that a controlling stockholder and general manager of a corporation was guilty of fraud in purchasing the holdings of a minority stockholder without disclosure of the then current status of negotiations for the sale of the corporation's property because, on a consideration of all the factors and particularly the insider's position and consequent special knowledge of the company, "it became the duty of the defendant, acting in good faith to state the facts before making the purchase."[3]

This is the dialectic — which, of course, an advocate can never afford to ignore. In actual results the old "majority" rule has substantially merged into the "special circumstances" doctrine,[4] which in turn is scarcely distinguishable from the so-called minority rule. Although one does not begin in the "majority" or "special circumstances" jurisdictions with the premise that insiders are fiduciaries, the "special circumstances" doctrine is manifestly based on the existence of a relationship between director and stockholder that is different from the relationship between arm's-length traders. In *Strong* v. *Repide* the "special circumstances" were found in the fact that the defendant had been entrusted with the negotiations to sell the corporate assets; but certainly if he had not been a director he never would have had an affirmative duty to make disclosure. In other jurisdictions, similarly, the "special circumstances" are commonly no more substantial. Thus, the Michigan court described them in 1925 as any "fact or condition enhancing the value of the stock, known by the officer or officers, not known by the stockholder, and not to be ascertained by an inspection of the books."[5]

---

[2] Oliver v. Oliver, 118 Ga. 362, 45 S. E. 232 (1903); Stewart v. Harris, 69 Kan. 498, 77 Pac. 277 (1904); Jacobson v. Yaschik, 249 S. C. 577, 584-85, 155 S. E. 2d 601, 605 (1967).

[3] Strong v. Repide, 213 U. S. 419, 431 (1909). Since this case came up from the Philippines, the Supreme Court was applying civil law, but it indicated that the common law rule was the same. Under Erie v. Tompkins, of course, this opinion is no longer binding on the federal courts in diversity cases.

[4] See Arlinghaus v. Ritenour, 622 F. 2d 629, 636 (2d Cir. 1980), *cert. denied,* 449 U. S. 1013, and New York cases cited.

[5] Buckley v. Buckley, 230 Mich. 504, 508, 202 N. W. 955, 956 (1925).

An Illinois case indicates that there may be a greater common law duty to disclose when an insider buys for the account of the issuer than when he buys

It seems fair to conclude from all this that the so-called majority view is gradually giving way to the generally growing feeling of responsibility of corporate insiders — the development of a status of "trusteeship" in a nontechnical sense. Very likely a more pronounced evolution of the common law toward the "minority" view was aborted by the onslaught of Rule 10b-5, as so often happens when legislation comes on the scene.

2.   INTRODUCTION TO RULE 10b-5

The 10b-5 story tempts the pen. For it is difficult to think of another instance in the entire *corpus juris* in which the interaction of the legislative, administrative rulemaking, and judicial processes has produced so much from so little. What is more remarkable is that the whole development was unplanned. Like the British Empire, which Eamon de Valera called "A domain created in a moment of world absent-mindedness,"[6] it just happened. One has his choice of figures of speech: Justice Rehnquist's "judicial oak which has grown from little more than a legislative acorn";[7] Professor Painter's reference to the medieval alchemist's "universal solvent" that was so potent it dissolved every container employed to hold it;[8] the present writer's occasional reference to the rule as "a horse of dubious pedigree but very fleet of foot."

We have already noticed the gap left by §17(a) of the 1933 Act and §§9(a)(4), 15(c)(1), and 15(c)(2) of the 1934 Act: fraud in a *purchase* unless effected (1) by a *broker or dealer over the counter* or (2) by any person buying a *registered* security for the purpose of inducing its purchase by others. We have noticed also the abortive 1941 attempt to extend §17(a) to the purchase side and the 1942 resort to §10(b) by the adoption of Rule 10b-5.

---

for his own account. In sustaining a complaint that alleged constructive fraud, the court relied on both Strong v. Repide, 213 U. S. 419 (1909), and Oliver v. Oliver, 118 Ga. 362, 45 S. E. 232 (1903), supra nn. 2, 3, and distinguished various Illinois cases on the ground that they had involved purchases by officers *for their own accounts.* Whatever the position of a director when he acts in his individual capacity with a stockholder, the court held, he occupies the position of a trustee for each individual stockholder when he acts *for the company.* Northern Trust Co. v. Essaness Theatres Corp., 348 Ill. App. 134, 108 N. E. 2d 493 (1952). *Contra:* Gladstone v. Murray Co., 314 Mass. 584, 50 N. E. 2d 958 (1943).

[6] E. Brussell (ed.), Dictionary of Quotable Definitions (1970) 59.

[7] Blue Chip Stamps v. Manor Drug Stores, 421 U. S. 723, 737 (1975).

[8] Painter, The Use of Rule 10b-5 in Derivative Actions, in V. Nordin (ed.), Emerging Federal Securities Law: Potential Liability (1969) c. 3 at 37.

Section 10(b) itself has been characterized by the Supreme Court as a "catch-all."[9] If that is not perfectly obvious from the provision's juxtaposition in the statute — following, as it does, a number of provisions in §§9 and 10(a) designed to curb or regulate such practices as market manipulation, trading in puts and calls, short selling, and "stop loss orders" — one need only refer to the Administration's spokesman's apt characterization of the somewhat broader version that was §9(c) of the original 1934 bills: "Subsection (c) says, 'Thou shalt not devise any other cunning devices.' "[10]

As for the adoption of the rule, the present writer recalls very well the account given by Mr. Milton V. Freeman, for many years a distinguished member of the District of Columbia Bar, because the writer was "at the creation" as his junior:

> It was one day in the year 1943, I believe, I was sitting in my office in the S. E. C. building in Philadelphia and I received a call from Jim Treanor who was then the Director of the Trading and Exchange Division. He said, "I have just been on the telephone with Paul Rowen," who was then the S. E. C. Regional Administrator in Boston, "and he has told me about the president of some company in Boston who is going around buying up the stock of his company from his own shareholders at $4.00 a share, and he has been telling them that the company is doing very badly, whereas, in fact, the earnings are going to be quadrupled and will be $2.00 a share for this coming year. Is there anything we can do about it?" So he came upstairs and I called in my secretary and I looked at Section 10(b) and I looked at Section 17, and I put them together, and the only discussion we had there was where "in connection with the purchase or sale" should be, and we decided it should be at the end.
>
> We called the Commission and we got on the calendar, and I don't remember whether we got there that morning or after lunch. We passed a piece of paper around to all the commissioners. All the commissioners read the rule and they tossed it on the table, indicating approval. Nobody said anything except Sumner Pike who said, "Well," he said, "we are against fraud, aren't we?" That is how it happened.[11]

Here is the administrative rulemaking process reacting to the legislative process. The Commission got what it wanted: a handle for investigating and obtaining injunctive relief against insiders

---

[9] Ernst & Ernst v. Hochfelder, 425 U. S. 185, 203 (1976).

[10] Thomas G. Corcoran in Stock Exchange Regulation, Hearings before House Com. on Int. & For. Commerce, 73d Cong., 2d Sess. (1934) 115.

[11] Am. B. Assn., Section of Corp., Banking & Bus. Law, Conference on Codification of the Federal Securities Laws, 22 Bus. Law. 793, 921-23, esp. at 922 (1967).

who were buying their companies' stock. The writer can vouch that nobody at the Commission table gave any indication that he was remotely thinking of civil liability.[12] That was the function of the Third Branch, aided and abetted, to be sure, by the Commission's frequent appearances as *amicus curiae*. And the courts have responded with such gusto that there are now two multivolume treatises devoted primarily to Rule 10b-5.[13]

Although the volume of private litigation has thus dwarfed the proceedings initiated by the Commission, we leave most questions that are unique to private actions (for example, reliance and causation) to the next chapter, on Civil Liability. In this chapter the existence of a private right of action for violation of the rule is assumed, and we include private cases basically for their learning on the substantive law.

That law, of course, is federal: the "federal common law" of which Judge Friendly and others have spoken as forming a penumbra around every federal statute.[14] In theory the courts are merely construing a statute and rule. But, when the statute and rule are, like §10(b) and Rule 10b-5, virtually as vague as the Due Process Clause, the law is surely as much judge-made as is the classic common law of the states. *Erie* is of no consequence. Precedents under state law have whatever weight the federal courts want to give them. Indeed, when the state courts do have to interpret the SEC statutes and rules — although the 1934 Act, alone of the series, gives the federal courts exclusive jurisdiction — *they* must look to the *federal* law: a process that some writers have called *"reverse Erie."*[15]

---

[12] See id. at 922.

[13] A. Bromberg and L. Lowenfels, Securities Fraud and Commodities Fraud (1979); A. Jacobs, Litigation and Practice under Rule 10b-5 (2d ed. 1981); see also 3 Loss 1445-74, 1757-97; 6 id. 3556-3647, 3864-3925; W. Painter, The Federal Securities Code and Corporate Disclosure (1979) cc. 3-8.

[14] Friendly, In Praise of *Erie* — and of the New Federal Common Law, 19 Record A. B. C. N. Y. 64 (1964), reprinted with minor changes, 39 N. Y. U. L. Rev. 383 (1964); see also Friendly, The Gap in Lawmaking — Judges Who Can't and Legislators Who Won't, 63 Colum. L. Rev. 787 (1963); Note, Exceptions to Erie v. Tompkins: The Survival of Federal Common Law, 59 Harv. L. Rev. 966 (1946). In McClure v. Borne Chemical Co., 292 F. 2d 824, 834 (3d Cir. 1961), *cert. denied*, 368 U. S. 939, Judge Biggs said: "It can be fairly said that the Exchange Act, of which sections 10(b) and 29(b) are parts, constitute far-reaching federal substantive corporation law." See also Rekant v. Dresser, 425 F. 2d 872, 879-80 (5th Cir. 1970). But cf. Burks v. Lasker, 441 U. S. 471, 478 (1979) ("Congress has never indicated that the entire corpus of state corporation law is to be replaced simply because plaintiff's cause of action is based upon" the Investment Company Act); Texas Industries, Inc. v. Radcliff Materials, Inc., 451 U. S. 630, 640-47 (1981).

[15] Cf. Local 174, Teamsters, Chauffeurs, Warehousemen & Helpers of Amer-

It is this emancipation from state law that undoubtedly accounts for "the 10b-5 revolution." For most judges in the second half of the twentieth century seem to view the "majority" rule at common law — a rule that holds a director to the standard of a fiduciary when he is dealing with the corporation, which is only a *persona ficta*, a ghost, but not when he is dealing with the flesh-and-blood persons who are his constituents — as a monument to the ability of lawyers and judges to hypnotize themselves with their own fictions.

We shall notice something of a counterrevolution as the Supreme Court belatedly awoke in the 1970s to the rapid growth of the oak tree under the tender nursing of the lower courts. But close analysis reveals that those cases are not cataclysmic. One may still cry, *"Viva la revolución!"*

3. "DISCLOSE OR ABSTAIN"

It does not seem too much to say today that the "minority" or "trusteeship" view at common law has become, thanks to Rule 10b-5, the law of the land. Two early cases set the pattern:

The first judicial pronouncement on the rule (apart from a passing reference by the Second Circuit)[16] came in *Kardon v. National Gypsum Company,* a case in which a father and son sued two brothers for an accounting of profits allegedly resulting from the defendants' purchase of the plaintiffs' stock in violation of the rule. These four persons were the sole stockholders, officers, and directors, and they had owned the outstanding stock in equal portions. The plaintiffs charged a conspiracy between the defendants and a third company to which the defendants had sold the bulk of the corporate assets pursuant to an agreement made prior to their purchase of the plaintiffs' stock. There was some dispute whether the defendants had expressly stated in purchasing the shares that there was no agreement to sell the corporate assets. Judge Kirkpatrick found for the plaintiffs on the question of fact but held that they were entitled to an accounting in any event.[17]

---

ica v. Lucas Flour Co., 369 U. S. 95, 102 (1962) (state court must apply federal law under Labor Management Relations Act §301(a)); International Union, United Automobile, Aerospace & Agricultural Implement Workers of America v. Hoosier Cardinal Corp., 383 U. S. 696 (1966).

[16] Baird v. Franklin, 141 F. 2d 238, 244 (2d Cir. 1944), *cert. denied,* 323 U. S. 737.

[17] Kardon v. National Gypsum Co., 73 F. Supp. 798 (E. D. Pa. 1947).

At about the same time Judge Leahy decided *Speed* v. *Transamerica Corporation*.[18] Transamerica, as majority stockholder of Axton-Fisher Tobacco Company, had inside information that the cash realization value of Axton-Fisher's large tobacco inventory was far greater than the "average cost" book value set forth in its published financial statements, which did not reveal the enormous increase in the market value of the tobacco. This information was not made available to the minority stockholders. Intending to capture the enhanced value of this inventory by merging, dissolving, or liquidating the company, Transamerica purchased most of the minority-held stock directly from its holders. The price it paid was in excess of the current market but far below the redemption or liquidating value of the shares. It then caused Axton-Fisher to sell some of its tobacco, distribute the rest to its stockholders by means of warehouse receipts, and dissolve. These were the facts that Judge Leahy ultimately found.

First, one Geller, who had sold his stock to Transamerica, brought a common law deceit action against Transamerica based on diversity of citizenship. Finding that both Delaware and Kentucky, the charter state, followed the so-called majority view, Judge Leahy granted summary judgment for the defendant on the ground that it had not been guilty of misrepresentation or active concealment and had been under no duty to say anything about the appreciation of the tobacco inventory.[19]

Then one Speed and others brought a similar action based also on Rule 10b-5, and the court held that the complaint alleged a violation of the rule.[20] This was in 1947. Four years and twenty-three briefs later, Judge Leahy found for the plaintiffs in an exhaustive opinion in which he stated:

> The rule is clear. It is unlawful for an insider, such as a majority stockholder, to purchase the stock of minority stockholders without disclosing material facts affecting the value of the stock, known to the majority stockholder by virtue of his inside position but not known to the selling minority stockholders, which information would have affected the judgment of the sellers.[21]

---

[18] 71 F. Supp. 457 (D. Del. 1947).

[19] Geller v. Transamerica Corp., 53 F. Supp. 625 (D. Del. 1943), *aff'd per curiam*, 151 F. 2d 534 (3d Cir. 1945), *petition for leave to file bill of review based on discovery of new matter denied*, 63 F. Supp. 248 (D. Del. 1945).

[20] Speed v. Transamerica Corp., 71 F. Supp. 457 (D. Del. 1947).

[21] Id., 99 F. Supp. 808, 828-29 (D. Del. 1951), *reaff'd on later motions*, 100 F. Supp. 461, 463 (D. Del. 1951), 103 F. Supp. 47 (D. Del. 1952), *opinion on damages*, 135 F. Supp. 176 (D. Del. 1955), *modified*, 235 F. 2d 369 (3d Cir. 1956).

Here, then, is proof positive of the utility of Rule 10b-5. For it enabled Speed to stay in court, and ultimately to obtain a very substantial judgment, whereas Geller's common law action arising out of the same purchase had been dismissed.[22]

But *is* the rule clear? One may applaud the result as an overdue reform in American corporation law while conceding that there is a good deal of *ipse dixit* in the cases so far as the underlying basis of the affirmative duty to disclose is concerned. Judge Kirkpatrick in *Kardon* said simply:

> Under any reasonably liberal construction, these provisions [§10 (b) and Rule 10b-5] apply to directors and officers who, in purchasing the stock of the corporation from others, fail to disclose a fact coming to their knowledge by reason of their position, which would materially affect the judgment of the other party to the transaction.[23]

And Judge Leahy in *Transamerica* went on to say only this:

> The duty of disclosure stems from the necessity of preventing a corporate insider from utilizing his position to take unfair advantage of the uninformed minority stockholders. It is an attempt to provide some degree of equalization of bargaining position in order that the minority may exercise an informed judgment in any such transaction. Some courts have called this a fiduciary duty while others state it is a duty imposed by the "special circumstances." One of the primary purposes of the Securities Exchange Act of 1934 was to outlaw the use of inside information by corporate officers and principal stockholders for their own financial advantage to the detriment of uninformed public security holders.[24]

---

[22] The force of this contrast is not weakened by the fact that Judge Leahy in his opinion on the merits, purporting (not too convincingly) to distinguish the *Geller* case, reinstated the common law deceit count on which he had originally granted summary judgment to the defendant. Speed v. Transamerica Corp., 99 F. Supp. 808, 828 (D. Del. 1951), supra n. 21. For the dismissal of Geller's action would have been the last chapter if Speed had not joined a count under the rule in his suit. Nor can the teaching of *Kardon* and *Speed* be wished away on the ground that neither went to appeal and the *Kardon* language with respect to nondisclosure was *obiter* to boot. For there are now square appellate holdings to the effect that "total nondisclosure" (that is to say, the absence of any significant communication bearing on value except for offer and acceptance) can violate Rule 10b-5. SEC v. Texas Gulf Sulphur Co., 401 F. 2d 833 (2d Cir. 1968), *cert. denied* sub nom. Coates v. SEC and Kline v. SEC, 394 U. S. 976; List v. Fashion Park, Inc., 340 F. 2d 457, 461-62 (2d Cir. 1965), *cert. denied* sub nom. List v. Lerner, 382 U. S. 811. See also Chiarella v. United States, 445 U. S. 222, 226-30 (1980), set out infra p. 853; cf. Affiliated Ute Citizens of Utah v. United States, 406 U. S. 128 (1972), infra p. 1129.

[23] 73 F. Supp. at 800.

[24] 99 F. Supp. at 828-29; see also Kohler v. Kohler Co., 319 F. 2d 634, 638

Indeed, Judge Leahy reacted with some impatience to the defendant's attempt to pin the plaintiff down among the three clauses of the rule. Though relying primarily on Clauses (1) and (3), he emphasized that the three clauses "are mutually supporting and not mutually exclusive," so that an insider's breach of his disclosure obligation "can be viewed as a violation of all three subparagraphs."[25]

After thirty-five years and more of building, there is little one can add to the underpinnings. Nevertheless there are three mutually supporting theories:

(1) At least when the insider's identity is not hidden, and in the absence of countervailing representations, Clause (2) of the rule may be invoked on the basis of an implied representation flowing from the insider's fiduciary obligation,[26] or at any rate from the "special circumstances" that satisfied the Supreme Court in pre-*Erie* and pre-SEC days, that the insider has performed his duty and has not withheld any material inside information.

(2) On the analogy of certain developments in the field of broker-dealer fraud concepts that will be examined later in this chapter,[27] the insider's offer to buy at a fixed price might be considered to constitute an implied representation, again under Clause (2), that within reasonable limits the stated price represents the insider's judgment of the value of the security.[28]

(3) Since §10(b) is part of a statute designed to raise the morals of the marketplace, and in view of the consensus that the SEC

(7th Cir. 1963); SEC v. Texas Gulf Sulphur Co., 401 F. 2d 833, 848 (2d Cir. 1968), *cert. denied* sub nom. Coates v. SEC and Kline v. SEC, 394 U. S. 976.

[25] 99 F. Supp. at 829. On the mutually supporting nature of the three clauses, see also Cady, Roberts & Co., 40 SEC 907, 913 (1961), set out infra p. 851, at p. 855; List v. Fashion Park, Inc., 240 F. 2d 457, 462 (2d Cir. 1965), *cert. denied* sub nom. List v. Lerner, 382 U. S. 811.

[26] See Connelly v. Balkwill, 174 F. Supp. 49, 59 (N. D. Ohio 1959), *aff'd per curiam,* 279 F. 2d 685 (6th Cir. 1960). This theory wears a bit thin (1) as applied to *debt* securities, or (2) even with respect to stock when the insider *sells* to one not already a stockholder. It begs the question, of course, to observe that §10(b) and the rule apply universally. But they do, for what it is worth. Moreover, the Supreme Court has said, in a bankruptcy context, that a majority stockholder is bound by the "fiduciary standards of conduct which he owes the corporation, its stockholders *and creditors*" (italics supplied). Pepper v. Litton, 308 U. S. 295, 311 (1939). And the securities cases reflect judicial impatience with any buyer-seller distinction so far as duty to disclose is concerned. SEC v. Murphy, 626 F. 2d 633, 652 n. 23 (9th Cir. 1980); cf. Gratz v. Claughton, 187 F. 2d 46, 49 (2d Cir. 1951), *cert. denied,* 341 U. S. 920.

[27] See pp. 946-58 infra.

[28] Judge Leahy did find in *Transamerica:* "In making an offer of 33⅓% above the current market price, defendant impliedly represented that the price offered was a fair price at that time." 99 Supp. at 843.

fraud provisions are not limited to common law deceit,[29] perhaps the most honest approach is to say simply that the insider's action may be considered a scheme to defraud by misleading or over-reaching, or an act, practice, or course of business that would so operate to defraud public security holders.[30]

Whatever the theory, one cannot cavil with the results of the relatively small number of nondisclosure cases that have survived defendants' motions for summary judgment and subsequent settlement negotiations to go to final judgment for the plaintiffs on the merits: for example, a contract to sell the company's assets;[31] a several-fold increase in basic inventory value;[32] a rich ore strike;[33] a plan by the buyers to sell shares at a much higher price;[34] large installment land sales.[35] Indeed, all these cases could fit quite readily under a "special circumstances" approach if that rubric were to mark the limits of the 10b-5 disclosure obligation. As the Second Circuit has stated, "An insider's duty to disclose information or his duty to abstain from dealing in his company's securities arises only in 'those situations which are essentially extraordinary in nature and which are reasonably certain to have a substantial effect on the market price of the security if [the extraordinary situation is] disclosed.' "[36]

Note the statement of the duty in the alternative: "to disclose * * * or * * * abstain." In end result, since conflict is inevitable between the director's 10b-5 duty to the other party to the transaction to disclose material facts and the common law duty he

---

[29] See p. 813.

[30] " * * * the Act is violated when directors with inside information purchase stock without full disclosure. Such conduct constitutes engaging in an 'act, practice, or course of business which * * * would operate as a fraud.' " Kardon v. National Gypsum Co., 83 F. Supp. 613, 614 (E. D. Pa. 1947) (the ellipsis is the court's).

[31] Kardon v. National Gypsum Co., 73 F. Supp. 798, 800 (E. D. Pa. 1947), supra p. 823.

[32] Speed v. Transamerica Corp., 99 F. Supp. 808 (D. Del. 1951), supra p. 824 and n. 21.

[33] SEC v. Texas Gulf Sulphur Co., 401 F. 2d 833 (2d Cir. 1968), *cert. denied* sub nom. Coates v. SEC and Kline v. SEC, 394 U. S. 976.

[34] Ross v. Licht, 263 F. Supp. 395, 409 (S. D. N. Y. 1967).

[35] Baumel v. Rosen, 283 F. Supp. 128 (D. Md. 1968), *rev'd on other grounds,* 412 F. 2d 571 (4th Cir. 1969), *cert. denied,* 396 U. S. 1037.

[36] SEC v. Texas Gulf Sulphur Co., 401 F. 2d 833, 848 (2d Cir. 1968), *cert. denied* sub nom. Coates v. SEC and Kline v. SEC, 394 U. S. 976, quoting from Fleischer, Securities Trading and Corporate Information Practices: The Implications of the Texas Gulf Sulphur Proceeding, 51 Va. L. Rev. 1271, 1289 (1965) (brackets are the court's). It is on this theory that the Code defines "fact of special significance" as one that is a bit more than "material." See c. 9A, n. 61 supra.

will often have to the company *not* to make premature disclosure, the director has no viable alternative but to abstain.[37]

There is no insoluble conflict between federal and state law here — no occasion for invocation of the Supremacy Clause. If your duty to the company requires you not to make premature disclosure of negotiations or other material information that Rule 10b-5 requires you to disclose when you trade, just don't trade. After all, there is nothing in Holy Writ that requires the insider to buy or sell. And it would be a strange rule of fiduciary conduct that yielded to a plea of conflict of interest, especially a conflict so readily avoidable. When the issuer itself wants to buy or sell its own securities, it has a choice: desist or disclose. But, when the buyer or seller is an insider rather than the company itself, the *only* solution is not to trade on inside information. For it is neither his role nor his responsibility to disseminate corporate information to the public; that is a corporate function.

The leading exchanges have played a significant role in alleviating the problem by expecting their listed companies to "release quickly * * * any news or information which might reasonably be expected to materially affect the market for [the] securities" and to "act promptly to dispel unfounded rumors which result in unusual market activity or price variations."[38] In 1965 the New York Stock Exchange went so far as to recommend a series of quite stringent guidelines that might be followed by insiders to avoid any conflict-of-interest criticism when they want to buy or sell.[39] But there is no escaping the conclusion that a person who may want to trade — especially if he is a broker-dealer — has to think twice before becoming a director or other insider.[40]

Are insiders safe, then, if they simply refrain from trading when there is material information undisclosed? Or might they be held to have violated the rule by causing the company not to release material information that, if available, would presumably have affected the market price? Short of a Supreme Court holding, there is no doubt that a company and its responsible insiders can violate the rule by disseminating *false* information, whether in a report or a press release or a director's speech or in any other way, even though neither the company nor any insider does any

---

[37] Oliver v. Oliver, 118 Ga. 362, 368, 45 S. E. 232, 234 (1903); Cady, Roberts & Co., 40 SEC 907, 911 (1961); Rogen v. Ilikon Corp., 361 F. 2d 260, 268 (1st Cir. 1966); SEC v. Texas Gulf Sulphur Co., 401 F. 2d 833, 848 (2d Cir. 1968), *cert. denied* sub nom. Coates v. SEC and Kline v. SEC, 394 U. S. 976.

[38] N. Y. Stock Ex. Company Manual A-18.

[39] N. Y. Stock Ex., The Corporate Director and the Investing Public (1965) 12-13; N. Y. Stock Ex. Company Manual A-25 to A-27.

[40] Compare the discussion of the "Chinese wall," infra pp. 843-51.

trading. In the *Texas Gulf Sulphur* case, which involved a misleadingly unfavorable press release with respect to a tremendous ore strike in Ontario, the Second Circuit, concluding that "It does not appear to be unfair to impose upon corporate management a duty to ascertain the truth of any statements the corporation releases to its shareholders or to the investing public at large," held that the rule "is violated whenever assertions are made * * * in a manner reasonably calculated to influence the investing public, e. g., by means of the financial media * * * , if such assertions are false or misleading or are so incomplete as to mislead irrespective of whether the issuance of the release was motivated by corporate officials for ulterior purposes."[41] But both the Commission[42] and the courts[43] have recognized the propriety of *temporarily withholding* material information from the market when there are good business reasons, so long as neither the issuer nor insiders trade.

Whether there is a *greater* duty to disclose to the marketplace by way of correcting an earlier statement that has become misleading in a material respect presents a harder question. The Commission "believes that, depending on the circumstances, there is a duty to correct statements made in any filing * * * if the statements either have become inaccurate by virtue of subsequent events, or are later discovered to have been false and misleading from the outset, and the issuer knows or should know that persons are continuing to rely on all or any material portion of the statement."[44] Moreover, the cases, though by no means conclusive, point to a general duty to correct.[45]

[41] SEC v. Texas Gulf Sulphur Co., 258 F. Supp. 262, 293 (S. D. N. Y. 1966), *aff'd in part and rev'd in part*, 401 F. 2d 833, 861-63 (2d Cir. 1968), *cert. denied* sub nom. Coates v. SEC and Kine v. SEC, 394 U. S. 976. The court made one concession: "that if corporate management demonstrates that it was diligent in ascertaining that the information it published was the whole truth and that such diligently obtained information was disseminated in good faith, Rule 10b-5 would not have been violated." 401 F. 2d at 862. See the discussion of scienter, infra p. 870.

[42] Investors Management Co., Inc., 44 SEC 633, 646 (1971); see Ferber (SEC Solicitor), Duties of Disclosure of Corporate Insiders, 34 U. Mo. Kan. City L. Rev. 222, 223 (1966).

[43] Dolgow v. Anderson, 438 F. 2d 825, 829 (2d Cir. 1970); cf. Financial Industrial Fund, Inc. v. McDonnell Douglas Corp., 474 F. 2d 514 (10th Cir. 1973), *cert. denied*, 414 U. S. 874 (judgment against issuer *rev'd*).

[44] Sec. Act Rel. 6084, 17 SEC Dock. 1048, 1054 (1979); see also Sec. Ex. Act Rel. 8995 (1970) (a company that has complied with the reporting requirements "still has an obligation to make full and prompt announcement of facts regarding the company's financial condition"). Cf. c. 7D n. 80 supra. The duty is, if anything, more acute since the advent of "shelf registration" and integrated disclosure (supra pp. 140-54).

[45] See SEC v. Shattuck Denn Mining Corp., 297 F. Supp. 470, 475-76

4. WHO IS AN "INSIDER"?

When Congress specifically addressed itself to inside trading in §16, it spoke of directors, officers, and 10+ percent beneficial owners. In the §10(b) area, where there is no evidence that Congress was thinking of insiders specifically, we do not have any comparable prepackaging. It has, therefore, been up to the courts to decide precisely what persons should have an affirmative obligation to disclose; and that group one loosely calls "insiders."

In connection with its codification of a good deal of the 10b-5 jurisprudence, §1603(b) of the Code defines "insider" in a manner thought to represent existing case law:

> For purposes of section 1603, "insider" means (1) the issuer, (2) a director or officer of, or a person controlling, controlled by, or under common control with, the issuer, (3) a person who, by virtue of his relationship or former relationship to the issuer, knows a material fact about the issuer or the security in question that is not generally available, or (4) a person who learns such a fact from a person within section 1603(b) (including a person within section 1603(b)(4)) with knowledge that the person from whom he learns the fact is such a person, unless the Commission or a court finds that it would be inequitable, on consideration of the circumstances and the purposes of this Code (including the deterrent effect of liability), to treat the person within section 1603(b)(4) as if he were within section 1603(b)(1), (2), or (3).

More specifically:

First: "Certainly directors and officers are insiders."[46]

Second: Controlling persons are almost invariably directors except when they are corporations. But, when they are not, there is

---

(S. D. N. Y. 1968) (failure to correct press release); Butler Aviation Int'l, Inc. v. Comprehensive Designers, Inc., 425 F. 2d 842, 843 (2d Cir. 1970) *semble* (same); Thomas v. Duralite Co., 386 F. Supp. 698, 715 (D. N. J. 1974), *aff'd as to liability and rev'd and remanded as to damages,* 524 F. 2d 577 (3d Cir. 1975); Ross v. A. H. Robins Co., Inc., 465 F. Supp. 904, 908 (S. D. N. Y. 1979), *rev'd on other grounds,* 607 F. 2d 545 (2d Cir. 1979), *cert. denied,* 446 U. S. 946 (failure to correct prospectus and annual reports to stockholders); cf. Fischer v. Kletz, 266 F. Supp. 180, 189-94 (S. D. N. Y. 1967) (accountant's failure to disclose later discovered falsity of financial statements certified for inclusion in annual report filed with SEC); United States v. Natelli, 527 F. 2d 311, 319 (2d Cir. 1975), *cert. denied,* 425 U. S. 934; Hirsch v. du Pont, 553 F. 2d 750, 761 (2d Cir. 1977) (dictum); Sharp v. Coopers & Lybrand, 83 F. R. D. 343, 346-47 (E. D. Pa. 1979).

[46] Ross v. Licht, 263 F. Supp. 395, 409 (S. D. N. Y. 1967). And "There appears to be no valid reason why the duty to make full disclosure should be any less stringent upon the issuing corporation itself than upon an officer or director buying for his own account." Kohler v. Kohler Co., 208 F. Supp. 808, 820 (E. D. Wis. 1962), *aff'd,* 319 F. 2d 634, 638 (7th Cir. 1963).

no reason to treat them any differently from directors or officers.[47]

Third: In *Texas Gulf Sulphur* Judge Bonsal agreed that the "insider" concept extends for purposes of Rule 10b-5 to any employees "who are in possession of material undisclosed information obtained in the course of their employment."[48] And the Eighth Circuit has approved an instruction that "An insider is a person who because of his position or intimate association with a corporation has greater knowledge of the financial affairs of the corporation."[49] This should be broad enough to cover the outside consultant, such as a law firm and *its* employees.[50]

Fourth: Whatever duty of disclosure Rule 10b-5 imposes on any of the persons so far mentioned could be readily bypassed if the same duty were not held to devolve at least on their spouses, members of their immediate families, and family trusts.[51]

Fifth: The courts having come this far on the "slippery slope," they could hardly ignore the friend or acquaintance who is given information from an insider that he knows to be nonpublic — in short, the "tippee."[52] The first published opinion was one issued by the Commission itself in 1961:

IN THE MATTER OF CADY, ROBERTS & CO.
Securities and Exchange Commission, 1961
40 SEC 907

By CARY, Chairman.

This is a case of first impression and one of signal importance in

---

[47] Speed v. Transamerica Corp., 71 F. Supp. 457 (D. Del. 1947) (on motion for summary judgment), 99 F. Supp. 808 (D. Del. 1951) (on the merits); Cochran v. Channing Corp., 211 F. Supp. 239, 242 (S. D. N. Y. 1962); Kohler v. Kohler Co., 319 F. 2d 634, 637-38 (7th Cir. 1963) (court found no violation on the facts); Schoenbaum v. Firstbrook, 268 F. Supp. 385, 395 n. 5 (S. D. N. Y. 1967) (dictum), *modified on other grounds en banc,* 405 F. 2d 215 (2d Cir. 1968), *cert. denied* sub nom. Manley v. Schoenbaum, 395 U. S. 906; see also Kuehnert v. Texstar Corp., 286 F. Supp. 340, 344 (S. D. Tex. 1968), *aff'd,* 412 F. 2d 700 (5th Cir. 1969) ("major stockholders").

[48] SEC v. Texas Gulf Sulphur Co., 258 F. Supp. 262, 279 (S. D. N. Y. 1966), *aff'd in part and rev'd in part,* 401 F. 2d 833 (2d Cir. 1968), *cert. denied* sub nom. Coates v. SEC and Kline v. SEC, 394 U. S. 976.

[49] Myzel v. Fields, 386 F. 2d 718, 739 (8th Cir. 1967), *cert. denied,* 390 U. S. 951; see also Cady, Roberts & Co., 40 SEC 907, 912 (1961), infra p. 831.

[50] See Sec. Ex. Act Rel. 13,437, 11 SEC Dock. 2231 (1977).

[51] In *Texas Gulf Sulphur* the Court of Appeals treated sales made in the names of insiders' wives as having been made by the insiders, noting simply that any other treatment would be "unrealistic." 401 F. 2d at 841 n. 4.

[52] "Professor Louis Loss invented the convenient term 'tippee' for those who receive tips from insiders. In his * * * Securities Regulation in the

our administration of the Federal securities acts. It involves a selling broker who executes a solicited order and sells for discretionary accounts (including that of his wife) upon an exchange. The crucial question is what are the duties of such a broker after receiving nonpublic information as to a company's dividend action from a director who is employed by the same brokerage firm.

* * * The respondents [Cady, Roberts & Co. ("registrant") and Gintel (a partner)] have submitted an offer of settlement which essentially provides that the facts stipulated by respondents shall constitute the record in these proceedings for the purposes of determining the occurrence of a willful violation of the designated antifraud provisions [§17(a) of the 1933 Act and Rule 10b-5] * * * .

*   *   *

On the morning of November 25, the Curtiss-Wright directors, including J. Cheever Cowdin ("Cowdin"), then a registered representative of registrant, met to consider, among other things, the declaration of a quarterly dividend. The company had paid a dividend, although not earned, of $.625 per share for each of the first three quarters of 1959. The Curtiss-Wright board, * * * approved a dividend for the fourth quarter at the reduced rate of $.375 per share. At approximately 11:00 A. M., the board authorized transmission of information of this action by telegram to the New York Stock Exchange. The Secretary of Curtiss-Wright immediately left the meeting room to arrange for this communication. There was a short delay in the transmission of the telegram because of a typing problem and the telegram, although transmitted to Western Union at 11:12 A. M., was not delivered to the Exchange until 12:29 P. M. It had been customary for the company also to advise the Dow Jones News Ticker Service of any dividend action. However, apparently through some mistake or inadvertence, the Wall Street Journal was not given the news until approximately 11:45 A. M., and the announcement did not appear on the Dow Jones ticker tape until 11:48 A. M.

Sometime after the dividend decision, there was a recess of the Curtiss-Wright directors' meeting, during which Cowdin telephoned registrant's office and left a message for Gintel that the

---

USA, Professor Loss in 1969 said: 'Having some respect for the English language, he does pray his readers, for at least a decent interval, not to join elements of the press in dropping the quotation marks' (vol. vi, p. 3561). Perhaps the decent interval can now be regarded as having elapsed." A. Johnson, The City Take-Over Code (1980) 156 n. 1.

dividend had been cut. Upon receiving this information, Gintel entered two sell orders for execution on the Exchange, one to sell 2,000 shares of Curtiss-Wright stock for 10 accounts, and the other to sell short 5,000 shares for 11 accounts. Four hundred of the 5,000 shares were sold for three of Cowdin's customers. According to Cowdin, pursuant to directions from his clients, he had given instructions to Gintel to take profits on these 400 shares if the stock took a "run-up." These orders were executed at 11:15 and 11:18 A. M. at 40¼ and 40⅜, respectively.

When the dividend announcement appeared on the Dow Jones tape at 11:48 A. M., the Exchange was compelled to suspend trading in Curtiss-Wright because of the large number of sell orders. Trading in Curtiss-Wright stock was resumed at 1:59 P. M. at 36½ ranged during the balance of the day between 34⅛ and 37, and closed at 34⅞.

Violation of Anti-Fraud Provisions

So many times that citation is unnecessary, we have indicated that the purchase and sale of securities is a field in special need of regulation for the protection of investors. To this end one of the major purposes of the securities acts is the prevention of fraud, manipulation or deception in connection with securities transactions. Consistent with this objective, Section 17(a) of the Securities Act, Section 10(b) of the Exchange Act and Rule 10b-5, issued under that Section, are broad remedial provisions aimed at reaching misleading or deceptive activities, whether or not they are precisely and technically sufficient to sustain a common law action for fraud and deceit. Indeed, despite the decline in importance of a "Federal rule" in the light of *Erie R. Co.* v. *Tompkins,* the securities acts may be said to have generated a wholly new and far-reaching body of Federal corporation law.[10]

Section 17(a) and Rule 10b-5 * * * are not intended as a specification of particular acts or practices which constitute fraud, but rather are designed to encompass the infinite variety of devices by which undue advantage may be taken of investors and others.[12]

---

[10] As was stated in McClure v. Borne Chemical Co., Inc., 292 F. 2d 824, 834 (C. A. 3, 1961):

   * * * It can be said fairly that the Exchange Act, of which Sections 10(b) and 29(b) are parts, constitutes far reaching Federal substantive corporation law.

[12] It might be said of fraud that age cannot wither, nor custom stale its infinite variety.

Section 17 and Rule 10b-5 apply to securities transactions by "any person." Misrepresentations will lie within their ambit, no matter who the speaker may be. An affirmative duty to disclose material information has been traditionally imposed on corporate "insiders," particularly officers, directors, or controlling stockholders. We, and the courts have consistently held that insiders must disclose material facts which are known to them by virtue of their position but which are not known to persons with whom they deal and which, if known, would affect their investment judgment. Failure to make disclosure in these circumstances constitutes a violation of the anti-fraud provisions. If, on the other hand, disclosure prior to effecting a purchase or sale would be improper or unrealistic under the circumstances, we believe the alternative is to forego the transaction.

The ingredients are here and we accordingly find that Gintel willfully violated Sections 17(a) and 10(b) and Rule 10b-5. We also find a similar violation by the registrant, since the actions of Gintel, a member of registrant, in the course of his employment are to be regarded as actions of registrant itself. It was obvious that a reduction in the quarterly dividend by the Board of Directors was a material fact which could be expected to have an adverse impact on the market price of the company's stock. The rapidity with which Gintel acted upon receipt of the information confirms his own recognition of that conclusion.

We have already noted that the anti-fraud provisions are phrased in terms of "any person" and that a special obligation has been traditionally required of corporate insiders, e. g., officers, directors and controlling stockholders. These three groups, however, do not exhaust the classes of persons upon whom there is such an obligation. Analytically, the obligation rests on two principal elements; first, the existence of a relationship giving access, directly or indirectly, to information intended to be available only for a corporate purpose and not for the personal benefit of anyone, and second, the inherent unfairness involved where a party takes advantage of such information knowing it is unavailable to those with whom he is dealing. In considering these elements under the broad language of the anti-fraud provisions we are not to be circumscribed by fine distinctions and rigid classifications. Thus our task here is to identify those persons who are in a special relationship with a company and privy to its internal affairs, and thereby suffer correlative duties in trading in its securities. Intimacy demands restraint lest the uninformed be exploited.

The facts here impose on Gintel the responsibilities of those commonly referred to as "insiders." He received the information prior to its public release from a director of Curtiss-Wright, Cowdin, who was associated with the registrant. Cowdin's relationship to the company clearly prohibited him from selling the securities affected by the information without disclosure. By logical sequence, it should prohibit Gintel, a partner of registrant.[17] This prohibition extends not only over his own account, but to selling for discretionary accounts and soliciting and executing other orders. In somewhat analogous circumstances, we have charged a broker-dealer who effects securities transactions for an insider and who knows that the insider possesses non-public material information with the affirmative duty to make appropriate disclosures or dissociate himself from the transaction.[18]

The three main subdivisions of Section 17 and Rule 10b-5 have been considered to be mutually supporting rather than mutually exclusive. Thus, a breach of duty of disclosure may be viewed as a device or scheme, an implied misrepresentation, and an act or practice, violative of all three subdivisions.[19] Respondents argue that only clause (3) may be applicable here. We hold that, in these circumstances, Gintel's conduct at least violated clause (3) as a practice which operated as a fraud or deceit upon the purchasers. Therefore, we need not decide the scope of clauses (1) and (2).

We cannot accept respondents' contention that an insider's responsibility is limited to existing stockholders and that he has no special duties when sales of securities are made to non-stockholders. This approach is too narrow. It ignores the plight of the buying public — wholly unprotected from the misuse of special information.

Neither the statutes nor Rule 10b-5 establishes artificial walls of responsibility. Section 17 of the Securities Act explicitly states that it shall be unlawful for any person in the offer or sale of securities to do certain prescribed acts. Although the primary function of Rule 10b-5 was to extend a remedy to a defrauded seller, the courts and this Commission have held that it is also applicable to

---

[17] See 3 Loss, Securities Regulation 1450-1 (2d ed., 1961). Cf. Restatement, Restitution, Section 201(2) (1937). Although Cowdin may have had reason to believe that news of the dividend action had already been made public when he called registrant's office, there is no question that Gintel knew when he received the message that the information was not yet public and was received from a director.

[18] Hughes & Treat, 22 S. E. C. 623, 626 (1946); Fry v. Schumaker, 83 F. Supp. 476, 478 (E. D. Pa. 1947). Cf. William I. Hay, 19 S. E. C. 397, 406-09 (1945); R. D. Bayly & Co., 19 S. E. C. 773, 784 (1945); Alexander Smith, 22 S. E. C. 13, 18 (1946).

[19] Speed v. Transamerica Corp., 99 F. Supp. 808, 829 (D. Del. 1951).

a defrauded buyer. There is no valid reason why persons who *purchase* stock from an officer, director or other person having the responsibilities of an "insider" should not have the same protection afforded by disclosure of special information as persons who *sell* stock to them. Whatever distinctions may have existed at common law based on the view that an officer or director may stand in a fiduciary relationship to existing stockholders from whom he purchases but not to members of the public to whom he sells, it is clearly not appropriate to introduce these into the broader anti-fraud concepts embodied in the securities acts.[23]

Respondents further assert that they made no express representations and did not in any way manipulate the market, and urge that in a transaction on an exchange there is no further duty such as may be required in a "face-to-face" transaction.[24] We reject this suggestion. It would be anomalous indeed if the protection afforded by the anti-fraud provisions were withdrawn from transactions effected on exchanges, primary markets for securities transactions. If purchasers on an exchange had available material information known by a selling insider, we may assume that their investment judgment would be affected and their decision whether to buy might accordingly be modified. Consequently, any sales by the insider must await disclosure of the information.

*   *   *

Respondents argue that any requirement that a broker-dealer in exchange transactions make disclosure of "adverse factors dis-

[23] As Judge Learned Hand has stated in the context of Section 16(b) of the Exchange Act:

> For many years a grave omission in our corporation law had been its indifference to dealings of directors or other corporate officers in the shares of their companies. When they bought shares they came literally within the conventional prohibitions of the law of trusts; yet the decisions were strangely slack in so deciding. When they sold shares, it could indeed be argued that they were not dealing with a beneficiary, but with one whom his purchase made a beneficiary. That should not, however, have obscured the fact that the director or officer assumed a fiduciary relation to the buyer by the very sale; for it would be a sorry distinction to allow him to use the advantage of his position to induce the buyer into the position of a beneficiary although he was forbidden to do so once the buyer had become one.

Gratz v. Claughton, 187 F. 2d 46, 49 (C. A. 2, 1951), *cert. denied,* 341 U. S. 920 (1951). [See also Chiarella v. United States, 445 U. S. 222, 227 n. 8 (1980), set out infra p. 853, at p. 854 n. 8.]

[24] It is interesting to note that earlier attacks on the applicability of Rule 10b-5 rested on the contention that it applied only to exchange transactions

closed by his analysis" would create uncertainty and confusion as to the duties of those who are constantly acquiring and analyzing information about companies in which they or their clients are interested. Furthermore, it is claimed, substantial practical difficulties would be presented as to the manner of making disclosures.

There should be no quandary on the facts here presented. While there may be a question as to the materiality and significance of some corporate facts and as to the necessity of their disclosure under particular circumstances, that is not this case. Corporate dividend action of the kind involved here is clearly recognizable as having a direct effect on the market value of securities and the judgment of investors. Moreover, knowledge of this action was not arrived at as a result of perceptive analysis of generally known facts, but was obtained from a director (and associate) during the time when respondents should have known that the board of directors of the issuer was taking steps to make the information publicly available but before it was actually announced.

Furthermore, the New York Stock Exchange has recognized that prompt disclosure of important corporate developments, including specifically dividend action, is essential for the benefit of stockholders and the investing public and has established explicit requirements and recommended procedures for the immediate public release of dividend information by issuers whose securities are listed on the Exchange. The practical problems envisaged by respondents in effecting appropriate disclosures in connection with transactions on the Exchange are easily avoided where, as here, all the registered broker-dealer need do is to keep out of the market until the established procedures for public release of the information are carried out instead of hastening to execute transactions in advance of, and in frustration of, the objectives of the release.

Finally, we do not accept respondents' contention that Gintel was merely carrying out a program of liquidating the holdings in his discretionary accounts — determined and embarked upon prior to his receipt of the dividend information. In this connection, it is further alleged that he had a fiduciary duty to these accounts to continue the sales, which overrode any obligations to unsolicited purchasers on the Exchange.

The record does not support the contention that Gintel's sales were merely a continuance of his prior schedule of liquidation.

---

or other transactions on an organized security market. The courts have rejected these attempts to narrow the broad applicability of the rule. *Matheson v. Armbrust*, 284 F. 2d 670 (C. A. 9, 1960), *cert. denied*, 365 U. S. 870 (1961); *Fratt v. Robinson*, 203 F. 2d 627 (C. A. 9, 1953).

* * * Moreover, while Gintel undoubtedly occupied a fiduciary relationship to his customers, this relationship could not justify any actions by him contrary to law.[31] Even if we assume the existence of conflicting fiduciary obligations, there can be no doubt which is primary here. On these facts, clients may not expect of a broker the benefits of his inside information at the expense of the public generally. * * *

THE PUBLIC INTEREST

All the surrounding circumstances and the state of mind of the participants may be taken into consideration in determining what sanctions should appropriately be imposed here.

It is clear that Gintel's conduct was willful in that he knew what he was doing. However, there is no evidence of a preconceived plan whereby Cowdin was to "leak" advance information of the dividend reduction so that Gintel could use it to advantage before the public announcement; on the contrary, the evidence points to the conclusion that Cowdin probably assumed, without thinking about it, that the dividend action was already a matter of public information and further that he called registrant's office to find out the effect of the dividend news upon the market. The record, moreover, indicates that Gintel's conduct was a spontaneous reaction to the dividend news, that he intended primarily to benefit existing clients of Cady, Roberts & Co. and that he acted on the spur of the moment and so quickly as to preclude the possibility of review by registrant or of his own more deliberate consideration of his responsibilities under the securities acts.

* * * Under all the circumstances we conclude that the public interest and the protection of investors will be adequately and appropriately served if Gintel is suspended from the New York Stock Exchange for 20 days and if no sanction is imposed against the registrant. Accordingly, we accept respondents' offer of settlement.

*   *   *

31 "But to say that a man is a fiduciary only begins analysis; it gives direction to further inquiry, to which is he a fiduciary? What obligation does he owe as a fiduciary?" S. E. C. v. Chenery Corporation, 318 U. S. 80, 85-86 (1943). In the circumstances, Gintel's relationship to his customers was such that he would have a duty not to take a position adverse to them, not to take secret profits at their expense, not to misrepresent facts to them, and in general to place their interests ahead of his own.

Judicial recognition of the tippee concept was not long in following.[53] Indeed, there is nothing radical about it. So long as the concept is limited to one who knew, or at least should reasonably have inferred, that he was being given an inside tip, treating him as if he stood in the shoes of the tipper does no violence to common law tradition. "Where a fiduciary in violation of his duty to the beneficiary communicates confidential information to a third person, the third person, if he had notice of the violation of duty, holds upon a constructive trust for the beneficiary any profit which he makes through the use of such information."[54] And persons who knowingly join with a fiduciary in transactions constituting a breach of his duty become jointly and separately liable for the profits.[55]

But, if "tippees" are to be held liable, the next question is *which* "tippees." There are many variables. There is a scale running from the director of Corporation *X* who gives a tip to his good friend in a similar position with Corporation *Y* — perhaps on an express or implied "I'll scratch your back and you scratch mine" basis — to the director who feels in an expansive mood while he is having a manicure. There is the studied eavesdropper, or the briber, or perhaps in this day and age the wiretapper, or the representative of the news media who upon hearing an important announcement from a company calls his broker before he calls his office, versus the barber or the taxi driver or the caddy who by chance overhears a bit of corporate news. There is the direct as against the indirect tippee — the tippee's tippee, in a progres-

[53] E. g., Ross v. Licht, 263 F. Supp. 395, 410 (S. D. N. Y. 1967). Indeed, it has been suggested that "Tipping because it involves a more widespread imbalance of information presents an even greater threat to the integrity of the marketplace than simple insider trading." Fridrich v. Bradford, 542 F. 2d 307, 327 n. 12 (6th Cir. 1976) (concurring opinion), *cert. denied,* 429 U. S. 1053.

The courts have also applied the *in pari delicto* doctrine to tippees who have complained of being duped by *false* tips; perhaps they should be called "dupees." Kuehnert v. Texstar Corp., 286 F. Supp. 340, 345 (S. D. Tex. 1968), *aff'd,* 412 F. 2d 700 (5th Cir. 1969) (the *in pari delicto* point was conceded on appeal); Tarasi v. Pittsburgh National Bank, 555 F. 2d 1152 (3d Cir. 1977).

On the quite independent question whether the *in pari delicto* doctrine should apply at all to actions under Rule 10b-5 — or, for that matter, under the SEC statutes generally — see p. 1196 infra.

[54] Restatement of Restitution §201(2). On the notice point, cf. SEC v. Monarch Fund, 608 F. 2d 938 (2d Cir. 1979). Of course, "Realistically, it may be hard to envision a tippee inquiring of the donor goose as to where she came upon the golden eggs and whether they have been offered to everyone. To question the goose may render her barren in the future." Note, Scienter and Rule 10b-5, 69 Colum. L. Rev. 1057, 1071 (1969).

[55] Jackson v. Smith, 254 U. S. 586, 588-89 (1921); Irving Trust Co. v. Deutsch, 73 F. 2d 121, 123, 125 (2d Cir. 1934), *cert. denied,* 294 U. S. 708.

sion that can go on indefinitely. There is what might be called the specific tip as opposed to the general tip. Obviously, to take these last two classifications alone, (1) a director's statement to his best friend that his corporation is about to consummate a merger that should double the price of the stock stands at the opposite extreme from (2) the case of the stranger to the corporation who is told by his secretary that she was told by the corporation's geologist that if she had any extra cash it might not be a bad idea to buy some of the stock; and in between there are many gradations.

Under any reasonable view of the tippee concept, a person who picks up private information in the course of business negotiations with a corporation — perhaps negotiations to buy the corporation's assets or the management's stock — should normally be treated like a tippee of the second corporation as long as that information remains private.[56] So, too, a broker who buys on behalf of an insider and who has knowledge of inside information would seem to be under the same obligation to disclose as the insider who purchases directly.[57] And, of course, a dealer who is himself a director or officer or controlling person of the issuer of the securities in which he trades has an insider's obligation to make full disclosure of material facts.[58] Since these facts may sometimes concern secret processes or plans which the legitimate business interests of the corporation dictate should not be disclosed, a broker or dealer who becomes a corporate insider must assume the risk that his duty to the corporation may sometimes prevent him from making a market in its securities. This has long been the case under common law agency principles, presumably, so far as concerns an insider-broker's acting as *agent* for a customer in the purchase or sale of his corporation's securities.[59]

There is also the matter of pricking out a line between the financial analyst who draws correct inferences solely on the basis of his shrewd analytical powers and his colleague whose analysis is reinforced by a visit to the corporation's plant. Presumably even an insider is under no obligation to give the ordinary investor the

[56] Van Alstyne, Noel & Co., 43 SEC 1080 (1969); SEC v. Shapiro, 494 F. 2d 1301 (2d Cir. 1974) ("corporate marriage broker").
[57] List v. Fashion Park, Inc., 340 F. 2d 457, 461 (2d Cir. 1965), *cert. denied* sub nom. List v. Lerner, 382 U. S. 811; Myzel v. Fields, 386 F. 2d 718, 739 (8th Cir. 1967), *cert. denied,* 390 U. S. 957.
[58] Freeman v. Decio, 584 F. 2d 186, 200 (7th Cir. 1978).
[59] Black v. Shearson, Hammill & Co., 266 Cal. App. 2d 362, 368, 72 Cal. Rptr. 157, 161 (1968).

benefit of his superior financial analysis.[60] "Even though a shrewd guess by an insider is often worth fifty accounting statements, it would be highly unfair to make him publicize his guess and then to hold him responsible if it turns out to be wrong."[61] Nevertheless, a broker or other person who has determined through his own financial analysis that "A security is ripe for purchase or sale may find that receipt of certain information regarding that security will bar him from taking action without disclosure, even though the inside information serves only to confirm an independently reached decision."[62] Consequently, prudent corporate counsel will advise the officers not to speak at financial analyst societies' luncheons unless the press is present, or to grant exclusive press interviews unless the newspaper or other news medium has a sufficient circulation to make it reasonable to consider that publication has been achieved.[63]

[60] Kohler v. Kohler Co., 208 F. Supp. 808, 827 (E. D. Wis. 1962), *aff'd on other grounds,* 319 F. 2d 634 (7th Cir. 1963); Arber v. Essex Wire Corp., 490 F. 2d 414, 421 (6th Cir. 1974), *cert. denied,* 419 U. S. 830; Feldman v. Simkins Industries, Inc., 679 F. 2d 1299, 1304 (9th Cir. 1982).

[61] Comment, The Prospects for Rule X-10B-5: An Emerging Remedy for Defrauded Investors, 59 Yale L. J. 1120, 1148 (1950).

[62] Note, Broker Silence and Rule 10b-5: Expanding the Duty to Disclose, 71 Yale L. J. 736, 745 (1962). "Securities analysts can be an important source of information for the public, supplementing an often overtaxed SEC enforcement staff and the press. There is some danger that the threat of liability under Rule 10b-5 may dampen the zeal of analysts in ferreting out the truth about corporate practices." But "Securities analysts associated with registered broker-dealers must respect the disclose-or-refrain obligations of their corporate sources, and they must stop short of transferring the losses from a fraud to those least able to avoid them." Dirks v. SEC, 681 F. 2d 824, 829, 846 (D. C. Cir. 1982), *cert. granted,* 103 S. Ct. 371.

[63] "Whenever managers and analysts meet elsewhere than in public, there is a risk that the analysts will emerge with knowledge of material information which is not publicly available." Elkind v. Liggett & Myers, Inc., 635 F. 2d 156, 165 (2d Cir. 1980).

When information becomes generally available is, of course, a separate question. Certainly not the moment a release is handed to the press. "Before insiders may act upon material information, such information must have been effectively disclosed in a manner sufficient to insure its availability to the investing public." SEC v. Texas Gulf Sulphur Co., 401 F. 2d 833, 854 (2d Cir. 1968), *cert. denied* sub nom. Coates v. SEC and Kline v. SEC, 394 U. S. 976. In that case both courts expressed the hope that the Commission would use its expertise in order to adopt a rule that would "provide some predictability of certainty for the business community." 401 F. 2d at 854 n. 18; 258 F. Supp. at 289. But the Commission has not done so. And unofficial rules of thumb have run from "waiting for the morning newspaper to carry the information" or "for fifteen minutes after the tape runs" [2 A. Bromberg and L. Lowenfels, Securities Fraud and Commodities Fraud (1979) 190.3, quoted in Billard v. Rockwell Int'l Corp., 526 F. Supp. 218, 220 (S. D. N. Y. 1981)] to twenty-four hours after publication of a release in a national medium or forty-eight hours

That is to say, types of tippees aside, it is now quite clear that Rule 10b-5 falls on the nontrading tipper as well as the trading tippee. In *Texas Gulf Sulphur* the Commission, faced with a choice of seeking injunctive and restitutional relief[64] against certain tippees, who were not insiders but who *had* been unjustly enriched, or against their tippers, who had not received any direct benefit from the tippees' purchases but who *were* insiders, the Commission apparently decided that the tipper was the more likely prospect for the first sally into court. And it won a ruling that one of the defendants had violated by tipping.[65]

---

when publication is not so widespread [American Stock Exchange Disclosure Policies (1970) 16-17]. The Code provides: "A fact is 'generally available' one week (or any other period prescribed by Commission rule) after it is disclosed by means of a filing or press release or in any other manner reasonably designed to bring it to the attention of the investing public. Otherwise the burden of proving that a fact is 'generally available' is on the person who so asserts." §202(64).

But what if the news item is not significant enough for what has been called the Wall Street Journal's policy of "selective revelation"? This leaves the insider in something like the position of a principal who seeks to protect himself against the apparent authority of a discharged agent. One does the best he can. If there are local newspapers or appropriate trade publications, he might consider paid advertisements or a letter to stockholders or distribution of a release to dealers known to have an interest in the security. See American Stock Exchange Disclosure Policies (1970) 13; Report of the Industrial Issuers Advisory Committee to the SEC (1972) ¶17. But in the last analysis the burden here is on the insider.

In any event, whatever may be the effective moment of disclosure, the critical time to which it is related is not when the insider's order is executed but when it is placed. "Otherwise, insiders would be able to 'beat the news' * * * by requesting in advance that their orders be executed immediately after the dissemination of a major news release but before outsiders could act on the release." SEC v. Texas Gulf Sulphur Co., 401 F. 2d at 853 n. 17. It follows, on the other hand, that knowledge acquired *after* the parties are committed to each other does not affect the bargain. Radiation Dynamics, Inc. v. Goldmuntz, 464 F. 2d 876, 890-91 (2d Cir. 1972); Sundstrand Corp. v. Sun Chemical Corp., 553 F. 2d 1033, 1050 (7th Cir. 1977, *cert. denied*, 434 U. S. 875; but cf. Goodman v. Epstein, 582 F. 2d 388, 412-13 (7th Cir. 1978), *cert. denied*, 440 U. S. 939 (a series of potential investment decisions).

[64] This case is also a bellwether with respect to the Commission's practice of seeking various kinds of restitution or disgorgement of profits. SEC v. Texas Gulf Sulphur Co., 446 F. 2d 1301 (2d Cir. 1971), *cert. denied*, 404 U. S. 1005, *on remand*, 331 F. Supp. 671 (S. D. N. Y. 1971); SEC v. Manor Nursing Centers, Inc., 458 F. 2d 1082, 1103-06 (2d Cir. 1972), *on remand*, CCH Fed. Sec. L. Rep. ¶93,359 (S. D. N. Y. 1972); SEC v. Shapiro, 494 F. 2d 1301, 1309 (2d Cir. 1974). The theory is deterrence rather than compensation. And the relief is ancillary to the court's equity jurisdiction. See pp. 1176-78 infra.

[65] SEC v. Texas Gulf Sulphur Co., 401 F. 2d 833, 852 (2d Cir. 1968), *cert. denied* sub nom. Coates v. SEC and Kline v. SEC, 394 U. S. 976; cf. Mosser v. Darrow, 341 U. S. 267 (1951); see 2 Code 666, Comment (6). Nice questions arise if the "tipper" is to be held for the "tippee's" gains. For example:

(1) Would the corporation itself then be liable to a market seller because

Having held the "tippee" to be a violator of Rule 10b-5 in *Cady, Roberts & Co.* and having persuaded the Second Circuit in *Texas Gulf Sulphur* that the "tipper" had violated as well, the Commission next brought an administrative proceeding against the Merrill Lynch firm in which it combined both these theories. The firm and certain of its personnel having consented to various suspensions and censures, the Commission found that the firm had disclosed to twelve institutional and other large customers certain nonpublic information, obtained in connection with its proposed underwriting of a debenture offering, concerning a precipitate drop in the earnings of Douglas Aircraft Co., Inc.; that some of those customers had thereafter sold Douglas stock, either long or short, before public disclosure of the information; and that during that period the broker-dealer had effected purchases of Douglas stock on behalf of other customers without telling them what it had told the twelve large customers.[66] The same incident resulted in a Second Circuit decision that held Merrill Lynch liable as tipper to persons who had bought Douglas stock in the market during the same period.[67]

In accepting Merrill Lynch's offer of settlement of the administrative proceeding, the Commission, with appropriate words of caution and a reminder that prompt public dissemination was the

---

it had done nothing to prevent its directors and other insiders from taking advantage of inside information? We have already noticed a suggestion that a director who knows that *another* director is buying securities on the basis of confidential information may incur a liability for failure to prevent his colleague's action, since a trustee has an obligation to prevent a co-trustee from violating their joint trust. See p. 665 supra.

(2) If both tipper and tippee are liable, will there be contribution? Or will the two be treated as joint tortfeasors with neither in a superior position? See p. 1198 infra.

[66] Merrill Lynch, Pierce, Fenner & Smith, Inc., 43 SEC 933 (1968); see also Investors Management Co., Inc., 44 SEC 633 (1971) (proceeding against the sellers in the same case).

[67] Shapiro v. Merrill Lynch, Pierce, Fenner & Smith, Inc., 495 F. 2d 228 (2d Cir. 1974); see also State Teachers Retirement Board v. Fluor Corp., 654 F. 2d 843, 854-55 (2d Cir. 1981). The question of liability to *whom* and for *how much* is considered in the next chapter. See p. 1132 infra. In Dirks v. SEC, 681 F. 2d 824 (D. C. Cir. 1982), *cert. granted*, 103 S. Ct. 371, the court held that a broker-dealer's analyst-employee who had passed on bearish information that he had received as tippee had violated Rule 10b-5 as aider and abettor of *his* tippees' illegal sales. *Query:* Doesn't the aiding and abetting run in the other direction — from tippee (the secondary violator) to tipper (the primary violator in his fiduciary capacity)? In Chiarella v. United States, 445 U. S. 222, 230 n. 12 (1980), the Court stated: "The tippee's obligation has been viewed as arising from his role as a participant after the fact in the insider's breach of a fiduciary duty." See also cases cited supra nn. 65-67; United States v. Newman, 664 F. 2d 12 (2d Cir. 1981), infra n. 78.

best preventive, took into account the firm's erection of what has come to be known as a "Chinese wall" between its underwriting division and its retail personnel.[68] And the custom has spread among not only multiservice securities houses but also commercial banks, which face the same problem when their loan departments obtain inside information of value to their trust departments. But how effective is the "wall"? In the first place, particularly in the case of smaller banks whose lending and trust officers are in continual contact, will juries be convinced that the "wall" is not porous? And, even if a securities firm's "wall" is found to be air-tight, that very quality will inevitably result in its salesmen's innocently "bulling" to "widows and orphans" stock that they would not touch if they knew what the underwriting personnel knew. Surely it cannot be assumed that agency law would not attribute the underwriting personnel's knowledge to the firm — how else can a corporation or other firm "know" *anything?* — and the *firm* is thus selling stock (the salesmen being only its agents) with respect to which the *firm* as tippee has material information of a "bearish" nature. A firm that followed the Merrill Lynch model soon learned that these are not academic questions:

SLADE v. SHEARSON, HAMMILL & CO., INC.
United States Court of Appeals, Second Circuit, 1974
577 F. 2d 398

Before MOORE, OAKES and GURFEIN, Circuit Judges.
OAKES, Circuit Judge.

Is an investment banker/securities broker who receives adverse material nonpublic information about an investment banking client precluded from soliciting customers for that client's securities on the basis of public information which (because of its possession of inside information) it knows to be false or misleading?

This intriguing question, "certified" to us under the provisions of 28 U. S. C. §1292(b) has been briefed not only by the opposing parties but by three amici curiae, each of which has taken a different position in response not only to the "certified" question but to related questions. The case itself has tremendous implications both for the securities industry and the investing public, as it involves questions some resolutions of which Judge Carter recognized in his Memorandum Opinion of March 18, 1974, could make it

---

[68] Merrill Lynch, Pierce, Fenner & Smith, Inc., 43 SEC 933, 938 (1968). See also Rule 14e-3(b)(2)(ii), infra p. 868.

"exceedingly difficult for any [brokerage firm] to function as an investment banker for a company and at the same time function as a broker-dealer in that company's securities."[a] And, too, a decision in this case might possibly even have impacts in the banking business where bank trust departments are effectuating transactions in securities of companies with which the bank has a commercial banking relationship. See generally Herman & Safanda, The Commercial Bank Trust Department and the "Wall," 14 B. C. Ind. & Comm. L. Rev. 21 (1972).

*   *   *

* * * this is precisely the kind of case in which the implications are so considerable and the issues so complex that in the proper exercise of judicial restraint, an abstract answer to an abstract

---

[a] ED.: Judge Carter denied the defendant's motion for partial summary judgment, stating:

> It is, of course, true that an investment banker may not reveal inside information obtained pursuant to a confidential investment banking relationship, to its retail customers through its brokerage organization. However, defendant contends that an investment banker, once it receives adverse inside information, also may not *prevent* its brokerage organization from soliciting customers on the basis of public information which (because of its possession of inside information) it knows to be false or misleading. Defendant's reliance on In re Merrill Lynch, Pierce, Fenner & Smith, Inc., [43 SEC 933 (1948)], is misplaced, inasmuch as *Merrill Lynch* stands for no more than the proposition that a banker who receives inside information from an investment banking client cannot reveal same "to favored customers."

*   *   *

> Defendant Shearson is no doubt troubled by the realization that among the consequences of applying the rule enunciated in *Texas Gulf Sulphur* to transactions such as the one here at issue is that an investment banker/broker-dealer who possesses adverse inside information about a security in which it is dealing is disadvantaged vis-a-vis other broker-dealers who do not possess such information, and hence are not disabled from soliciting purchasers. It must be remembered, however, that Shearson voluntarily entered into a fiduciary relationship with Tidal Marine, as a consequence of which it received confidential information. Shearson also voluntarily entered into fiduciary relationships with its customers. It cannot recognize its duty to the former while ignoring its obligation to the latter. Having assumed fiduciary responsibilities, Shearson is required to incur whatever commercial disadvantage fulfillment of those obligations entails.

CCH Fed. Sec. L. Rep. ¶94,329 at 95,131-32 (S. D. N. Y. 1974); cf. Black v. Shearson, Hammill & Co., Inc., 266 Cal. App. 2d 362, 368, 72 Cal. Rptr. 157, 161 (1968).

question is the least desirable of *judicial* solutions. Thus, we decline to answer the question certified or to make any other decision on the law of this case, and we remand for further action of the district court, in no way expressing approval or disapproval of Judge Carter's order below or his memorandum of opinion in connection therewith.

It would perhaps be sufficient for us to stop with what we have said, but in the light of the grant of permission for the interlocutory appeal we wish to spell out a little further exactly what is involved so that our rather unusual order of remand may be better understood.

This case involves two separate consolidated class actions brought by purchasers of the stock of Tidal Marine International Corp. (Tidal Marine) under the antifraud provisions of * * * Rule 10b-5 * * * . The actions complain that Shearson, Hammill & Co., Inc. (Shearson), was an investment banker to Tidal Marine and that it came into possession of material adverse information about Tidal Marine and nevertheless promoted the sale of Tidal Marine stock to brokerage customers including the assorted plaintiffs.

Shearson has a Corporate Finance Department which performs its investment banking functions and a Retail Sales Organization which handles its broker-dealer transactions for the firm's public customers. Shearson claims that according to its internal policies and procedures the corporate finance department is prohibited from releasing any information about one of its investment banking clients to the retail sales organization and the firm's public customers until the information is made publicly available by the company. The retail sales organization is administered separately from the investment banking department and Shearson's claim is that its "investment executives" or security salesmen are permitted to "solicit" purchases and sales of securities on the basis of their own analysis of public available information including the securities of concerns for which Shearson is acting as investment banker.

Shearson claims that its policy prohibited the "recommendation" of securities issued by investment banking clients and that the firm never "recommended" Tidal Marine and did not put it on its "master buy" list. Shearson claims that its sales of Tidal stock by its retail sales organization to various customers, including the plaintiff-appellees, were purely on the basis of favorable public information. Shearson further claims that its investment banking department did not come into the possession of material adverse information about Tidal until May of 1972, several weeks after the last of plaintiff-appellees' purchases, and that pursuant both to its policy of nondisclosure and in conformity with its fiduciary relationship to its investment banking customer, Tidal, Shearson did not disclose this information either to the general public or to its customers or to its own retail sales force by virtue of its internal policy which includes the maintenance of a so-called "Chinese wall" between its investment banking department and its sales department, the policy thereby prohibiting the interdepartmental flow of information. In any event, Shearson's claim is that upon advice to Tidal that Shearson would be required to disclose the adverse information — a shortage of cash following upon damages to Tidal's fleet of ships that were not covered by insurance — Tidal finally made a public disclosure of the cash shortage, together with its negotiations with its lenders and its decline in unaudited earnings, following which Shearson terminated its investment banking relationship.

The plaintiff-appellees, on the other hand, assert that Shearson either knew or was chargeable with knowledge of adverse facts about Tidal *prior* to the purchases of securities by plaintiff-appellees and that, as opposed to a strict "Chinese wall" erected to prevent the retail sales department from knowing what the investment banking department knew, there were at least four instances of the transmission of bullish information concerning Tidal from Shearson's investment banking department to its retail salesmen: these instances included wires touting the stock and referring to the expansion of Tidal fleet and net income, economies of size, its successful maintenance of its vessels and its ability to secure borrowings. Beyond this plaintiff-appellees claim that Shearson's policy required its salesmen to use the content of the wires when they discussed Tidal with their customers. And the plaintiff-appellees take issue with the "recommendation"/"solicitation" distinction proposed by Shearson, contending that Shearson violated its own policy not to recommend securities by permitting its salesmen to solicit their purchase on the strength of the favorable information transmitted from Shearson's investment banking department. Finally, plaintiff-appellees suggest that there is an even further conflict of interest on the part of Shearson in that it was also acting as the principal market maker in Tidal stock. Plaintiff-appellees argue that Shearson thus had a motive to continue recommending Tidal stock while concealing unfavorable information.

There are, then, at least three separate factual issues which are unresolved; thus, to answer the legal questions presented would requires an exposition sufficiently broad to cover the various factual ramifications that may occur, an exposition which we are not prepared to give. The first of these is whether the material adverse information was received before or after the last of the plaintiff-appellees' purchases. The certified question assumes that at the time the transactions in question took place Shearson *knew* the material inside information, but if Shearson's contention is correct its liability might well be nonexistent and the entire question certified would be postponed until further litigation. Secondly, while Shearson claims that there was a solid "Chinese wall," that is to say, an effective separation of its two departments, which might in a given instance call for one answer to the legal questions raised, the appellants claim that in this case there was no effective separation of departments, and that misleading favorable information was given the retail sales department by the investment banking department, possibly to protect Shearson's position as the principal market maker for Tidal's stock. This claim, if substantiated, would put a different complexion on the case and might in a given situation call for plain and simple application of basic principles of fraud.

Lastly, the extent to which there is a difference between "solicitation" and "recommendation" in connection with the purchase of securities may have a bearing. Salomon Brothers, like the plaintiff-appellees, argues that the facts of this case present a situation where the transaction was not merely "solicited" but was affirmatively "recommanded" and argues that the "mere solicitation" of transactions in circumstances where no recommendation is made should not be prohibited where there is an effective "Chinese wall." The Securities Exchange Commission believes that if the situation implies an "affirmative representation," the solicitation should be prohibited but that this would presumably not be the case in "block trading" or "market making" transactions not involving express or implied opinions or representations. The amicus brief of Paine, Webber, Jackson & Curtis, Inc. (Paine, Webber), suggests that Salomon is not significantly engaged in the business of "recommending" securities to its customers so that if only "recommendation" were prohibited, but "solicitation" were not, Salomon, which acts as a principal for its own account and not simply as a broker for others, would be competitively favored over such firms as Paine, Webber. That is to say, Paine, Webber argues that there is no legitimate basis either in law or in policy for the suggested distinction between "recommendation" and "solicitation," one that is put forth interestingly enough both by the defendant-appellant Shearson on the one hand and Salomon Brothers on the other hand.

The parties and amici have as much difficulty spelling out the legal questions that are here involved and which it is suggested we answer in the abstract. Shearson contends that the federal securities laws and particularly *SEC* v. *Texas Gulf Sulphur,* 401 F. 2d 833, 847-48 (2d Cir. 1968), *cert. denied,* 394 U. S. 976 (1969), precluded it from using nonpublic information for the benefit of its own customers and that the district court's decision on the motion for partial summary judgment applies to facts materially different from the case at hand. The plaintiff-appellees assert that Shearson's excuse that the inside information rule forbade it from ordering its salesmen to desist from a selling campaign which is mulcting its own customers is a perversion of the rule and permits fraud on the public. The SEC, pointing out that the case involves at least two important principles, first that persons who have been given material undisclosed information may not take advantage of it in the market, and, second, that brokers must treat their customers fairly, apparently looks favorably upon the erection of a proper "Chinese wall," see *Merrill Lynch, Pierce, Fenner & Smith, Inc.* [43 SEC 933 (1968)]. But cf. *Van Alstyne Noel & Co.,* 33 SEC 311, 321 (1952); and see *Cady Roberts & Co.,* 40 SEC 907 (1961). But the Commission expresses concern with extending *Texas Gulf* so as to make a rule which would preclude a brokerage firm from having any transactions with or on behalf of customers in the securities of the companies with which it has investment banking relationships. The SEC suggests that through the use of a device such as a "restricted list" issued inside the company, outstanding recommendations could be withdrawn and further recommendations prevented.

Salomon, which seconds the SEC with regard to the use of restricted lists, further argues that in any event the sales department of a brokerage firm may not affirmatively recommend and promote the purchase of a security based upon public information known to the investment banking department to be false. The SEC's position is disputed, however, by Paine, Webber which suggests that it is misleading in its simplicity and would have drastic and far-reaching consequences for the securities industry. According to Paine, Webber the Commission's proposal ignores the critically important "research" function of an investment banking firm and fails to recognize that since the function of an investment banker is to underwrite an offering of securities it must necessarily "recommend" the securities being underwritten and, indeed, may well have an obligation to "serve as a sponsor in the trading market" for the issue being underwritten.

Thus, it is plain that what we have here is not one legal question that has been certified, but a complexity of interlocking questions the answers to which may vastly affect the operations of one of the most important financial businesses in the country, the securities business, as well as the investment public being protected and the various enterprises whose securities are being underwritten and traded. Inside information problems can arise in the context of a multiplicity of various functions performed by brokerage firms and in a multiplicity of factual contexts. These differing contexts may well involve different considerations and may require different solutions.

It would be the height of judicial folly, we think, to attempt on an indeterminate factual record to make an abstract exposition that would adequately cover the various contexts and reach the proper overall results, however desirable this might be for the guidance of the business or however judicially challenging such an exposition might be. It is altogether possible that some of the questions may not be reached for some time to come or may follow from previous case by case determinations. It may well be that some of the solutions to the questions asked may be reached in entirely different decision making bodies than the courts. Meanwhile, fully appreciating the importance of this court's decisions to the world of commerce, we have determined to proceed on a case to case basis and, as we have indicated above, to await in this case full findings of fact and a consequent narrowing of the issues.

Case remanded in accordance with opinion; costs to neither party.

At the moment, in short, the problem defies clear solution. The Commission's suggestion of a "restricted list" is bound to create rumors: Customer gives A, a representative of Firm X, an order to buy. A says, "Sorry, that security is on our restricted list." "Why?" "I can't say." "But Firm Y next door is trading the stock." "Sorry, I can't explain." Nevertheless, many multiservice firms use a restricted list as a supplement to a "wall" in order to avoid any appearance of impropriety. "For example," an officer of one of these firms has said, "it does not make good sense to issue a sell recommendation, even innocently, about the stock of an issuer for which you are about to launch a tender offer."[69]

[69] Harmon, The Chinese Wall, in Practising Law Institute, Twelfth Annual Institute on Securities Regulation (1981) c. 24 at 426. Another prob-

A determined effort to draft for the Code a "Chinese wall" provision that would preclude liability in certain instances floundered on the difficulties here expounded. But, in connection with a provision to the effect that questions of imputation of an agent's knowledge to his principal should be governed by federal common law, the Code directs the courts and the Commission to consider, when it is the fact, that the principal has established either a wall or (as some firms have done) procedures "reasonably designed * * * to prevent transactions in and recommendations concerning securities of the [particular] issuer."[70] This reliance on the common law technique to prick out a line was preferred over some sort of "safe harbor" approach, because "it gives the courts sufficient flexibility to consider, in developing the law in this area, not only the particular factual configuration but also the type, purpose and 'morality' of the specific procedures that have been adopted."[71]

5. THE "QUASI-INSIDER" CONCEPT

All the cases, real and hypothetical, so far discussed fall within the classic pattern of insider-*cum*-tippee. Now consider:

(1) A law clerk to a Supreme Court Justice, knowing that an opinion will be coming down within a week to the effect that the antitrust laws do not require General Motors to split up, buys.

(2) A large institution enters an order to buy 10,000 shares of *X* stock on the New York Stock Exchange without revealing that it intends to buy up to 5 percent over the next few weeks.

(3) The president of company *A,* which uses widgets in its own manufacturing, buys heavily into Company *B,* a widget manufacturer with which he has had no previous relationship, after deciding to give Company *B* a large order for widgets.

These three cases are similar to each other, as well as to the cases previously discussed, in that each buyer has a significant advantage. They are also similar to each other but different from the cases previously discussed, in that none of the buyers is either an insider of the *issuer* or such an insider's tippee.[72] It would be

---

lem with relying solely on a "wall" is that Rule 10b-6 (infra p. 1001) prohibits purchases during a distribution without regard to whether market personnel have knowledge of the distribution. See generally Lipton and Mazur, The Chinese Wall Solution to the Conflict Problems of Securities Firms, 50 N. Y. U. L. Rev. 459 (1975).

[70] §202(86)(C)(ii).

[71] 1 Code 149.

[72] Cases of this type are sometimes characterized as involving "market information." This is a confusing phrase as so used, because "there is no reason

convenient to have a new category of "quasi-insider" that would cover the first case (which everybody instinctively wants to cover),[73] but not the second (which produces a smile from anybody with the slightest understanding of what a market is), while looking to the common law process for the third (which is the classic undistributed middle).[74]

The Code's answer — apart from extending the Commission's rulemaking power to *prevent* fraudulent practices from §15(c)(2) of the 1934 Act and §206(4) of the Advisers Act[75] to the Code's fraud part generally — is not to attempt to extend §1603, the affirmative disclosure provision, beyond insiders (including tippees) on some theory of "market egalitarianism." Instead the Code invites the courts to fall back on the more general §1602(a)(1), which basically repeats Rule 10b-5, "to the extent that a sufficiently egregious or shocking or offensive case of trading while silent *cannot* be rationalized on an 'insider' analysis."[76]

This "quasi-insider" idea met with the Second Circuit's favor. But the Supreme Court (considering, of course, the *existing* statutory structure) reversed. The case produced five opinions:

---

in either principle or the case law to distinguish * * * between material information that is intrinsic to the company (for example, a major mineral discovery) and market information that will not affect the company's assets or earning power (for example, information received by the president from a large brokerage firm's analyst who has interviewed him to the effect that the firm is about to publish a favorable report on the company together with a 'buy' recommendation)." 2 Code 657. See generally Fleischer, Mundheim and Murphy, An Initial Inquiry into the Responsibility to Disclose Market Information, 121 U. Pa. L. Rev. 798 (1973).

[73] Cf. Blyth & Co., Inc., 43 SEC 1037 (1969) (traders in broker-dealer's Government bond department got advance information from Federal Reserve Bank employee of terms of new Government issues).

[74] The first hypothetical case (inside government information) and the third (the two-company situation) were covered in so many words when the British Companies Act 1980 criminalized insider trading. 28 & 29 Eliz. 2, c. 22. §§68(2), 69. But this sort of particularization invites argument by negative implication when novel schemes come along. And at the purely criminal level there are other statutes available in this country. See United States v. Peltz, 433 F. 2d 48 (2d Cir. 1970), *cert. denied*, 401 U. S. 955 (conspiracy to defraud the Government by trading on basis of information about proposed litigation obtained from an SEC employee); United States v. Keane, 522 F. 2d 534, 544-51 (7th Cir. 1975), *cert. denied*, 424 U. S. 976 (mail fraud statute).

[75] See p. 805 supra; p. 927 infra.

[76] 2 Code 663. Professor Brudney has advanced another theory: that there should be a universal ban on trading by persons who obtain material, nonpublic information through "unerodable informational advantages" — which is to say, advantages that normally arise because of a person's position giving access to information not legally available to public investors however diligent. Brudney, Insiders, Outsiders and Informational Advantages under the Federal Securities Laws, 93 Harv. L. Rev. 322 (1979).

CHIARELLA v. UNITED STATES
Supreme Court of the United States, 1980
445 U. S. 222

MR. JUSTICE POWELL delivered the opinion of the Court.

The question in this case is whether a person who learns from the confidential documents of one corporation that it is planning an attempt to secure control of a second corporation violates §10(b) of the Securities Exchange Act of 1934 if he fails to disclose the impending takeover before trading in the target company's securities.

I

Petitioner is a printer by trade. In 1975 and 1976, he worked as a "markup man" in the New York composing room of Pandick Press, a financial printer. Among documents that petitioner handled were five announcements of corporate takeover bids. When these documents were delivered to the printer, the identities of the acquiring and target corporations were concealed by blank spaces or false names. The true names were sent to the printer on the night of the final printing.

The petitioner, however, was able to deduce the names of the target companies before the final printing from other information contained in the documents. Without disclosing his knowledge, petitioner purchased stock in the target companies and sold the shares immediately after the takeover attempts were made public. By this method, petitioner realized a gain of slightly more than $30,000 in the course of 14 months. Subsequently, the Securities and Exchange Commission (Commission or SEC) began an investigation of his trading activities. In May 1977, petitioner entered into a consent decree with the Commission in which he agreed to return his profits to the sellers of the shares. On the same day, he was discharged by Pandick Press.

In January 1978, petitioner was indicted on 17 counts of violating §10(b) of the Securities Exchange Act of 1934 (1934 Act) and SEC Rule 10b-5.[3] After petitioner unsuccessfully moved to dismiss the indictment, he was brought to trial and convicted on all counts.

The Court of Appeals for the Second Circuit affirmed petitioner's conviction. 588 F. 2d 1358 (1978). We granted certiorari, 441 U. S. 942 (1979), and we now reverse.

---

[3] * * * Petitioner was charged with 17 counts of violating the Act because he had received 17 letters confirming purchase of shares.

II

[Justice Powell here sets out §10(b) and Rule 10b-5(a) and (c).][5]

The case concerns the legal effect of the petitioner's silence. The District Court's charge permitted the jury to convict the petitioner if it found that he willfully failed to inform sellers of target company securities that he knew of a forthcoming takeover bid that would make their shares more valuable. In order to decide whether silence in such circumstances violates §10(b), it is necessary to review the language and legislative history of that statute as well as its interpretation by the Commission and the federal courts.

Although the starting point of our inquiry is the language of the statute, *Ernst & Ernst* v. *Hochfelder*, 425 U. S. 185, 197 (1976), §10(b) does not state whether silence may constitute a manipulative device. Section 10(b) was designed as a catchall clause to prevent fraudulent practices. 425 U. S., at 202, 206. But neither the legislative history nor the statute itself affords specific guidance for the resolution of this case. When Rule 10b-5 was promulgated in 1942, the SEC did not discuss the possibility that failure to provide information might run afoul of §10(b).

The SEC took an important step in the development of §10(b) when it held that a broker-dealer and his firm violated that section by selling securities on the basis of undisclosed information obtained from a director of the issuer corporation who was also a registered representative of the brokerage firm. In *Cady, Roberts & Co.*, 40 S. E. C. 907 (1961), the Commission decided that a corporate insider must abstain from trading in the shares of his corporation unless he has first disclosed all material inside information known to him. * * * The Commission emphasized that the duty arose from (i) the existence of a relationship affording access to inside information intended to be available only for a corporate purpose, and (ii) the unfairness of allowing a corporate insider to take advantage of that information by trading without disclosure. Id., at 912, and n. 15.[8]

---

[5] Only Rules 10b-5(a) and (c) are at issue here. * * * The portion of the indictment based on [Rule 10b-5(b)] was dismissed because the petitioner made no statements at all in connection with the purchase of stock.

[8] In *Cady, Roberts*, the broker-dealer was liable under §10(b) because it received nonpublic information from a corporate insider of the issuer. Since the insider could not use the information, neither could the partners in the brokerage firm with which he was associated. The transaction in *Cady, Roberts* involved sale of stock to persons who previously may not have been shareholders in the corporation. 40 S. E. C., at 913, and n. 21. The Commission embraced the reasoning of Judge Learned Hand that "the director

That the relationship between a corporate insider and the stock-holders of his corporation gives rise to a disclosure obligation is not a novel twist of the law. At common law, misrepresentation made for the purpose of inducing reliance upon the false statement is fraudulent. But one who fails to disclose material information prior to the consummation of a transaction commits fraud only when he is under a duty to do so. And the duty to disclose arises when one party has information "that the other [party] is entitled to know because of a fiduciary or other similar relation of trust and confidence between them."[9] In its *Cady, Roberts* decision, the Commission recognized a relationship of trust and confidence between the shareholders of a corporation and those insiders who have obtained confidential information by reason of their position with that corporation.[10] This relationship gives rise to a duty to disclose because of the "necessity of preventing a corporate insider from * * * tak[ing] unfair advantages of the uninformed minor-ity stockholders." *Speed* v. *Transamerica Corp.,* 99 F. Supp. 808, 829 (Del. 1951).

The federal courts have found violations of §10(b) where corpo-rate insiders used undisclosed information for their own benefit. E. g., *SEC* v. *Texas Gulf Sulphur Co.,* 401 F. 2d 833 (C. A. 2 1968), *cert. denied,* 404 U. S. 1005 (1971). The cases also have empha-sized, in accordance with the common-law rule, that "[t]he party

---

or officer assumed a fiduciary relation to the buyer by the very sale; for it would be a sorry distinction to allow him to use the advantage of his position to induce the buyer into the position of a beneficiary although he was for-bidden to do so once the buyer had become one." Id., at 914, n. 23, quoting Gratz v. Claughton, 187 F. 2d 46, 49 (C. A. 2), *cert. denied,* 341 U. S. 920 (1951).

[9] Restatement (Second) of Torts §551(2)(a) (1976). See James & Gray, Misrepresentation — Part II, 37 Md. L. Rev. 488, 523-527 (1978). As regards securities transactions, the American Law Institute recognizes that "silence when there is a duty to * * * speak may be a fraudulent act." ALI, Federal Securities Code §262 (b) (Prop. Off. Draft 1978).

[10] See 3 W. Fletcher, Cyclopedia of the Law of Private Corporations §838 (rev. 1975) (hereinafter Fletcher); 3A Fletcher, §§1168.2, 1171, 1174; 3 L. Loss, Securities Regulation 1446-1448 (2d ed. 1961); 6 id., at 3557-3558 (1969 Supp.). * * *

The dissent of Mr. Justice Blackmun suggests that the "special facts" doctrine may be applied to find that silence constitutes fraud where one party has superior information to another. Post, at 247-248. This Court has never so held. In Strong v. Repide, 213 U. S. 419, 431-434 (1909), this Court applied the special-facts doctrine to conclude that a corporate insider had a duty to disclose to a shareholder. In that case, the majority share-holder of a corporation secretly purchased the stock of another shareholder without revealing that the corporation, under the insider's direction, was about to sell corporate assets at a price that would greatly enhance the value of the stock. The decision in Strong v. Repide was premised upon the fiduciary duty between the corporate insider and the shareholder. See Pepper v. Litton, 308 U. S. 295, 307, n. 15 (1939).

charged with failing to disclose market information must be under a duty to disclose it." *Frigitemp Corp.* v. *Financial Dynamics Fund, Inc.,* 524 F. 2d 275, 282 (C. A. 2 1975). Accordingly, a purchaser of stock who has no duty to a prospectus seller because he is neither an insider nor a fiduciary has been held to have no obligation to reveal material facts. See *General Time Corp.* v. *Talley Industries, Inc.,* 403 F. 2d 159, 164 (C. A. 2 1968), *cert. denied,* 393 U. S. 1026 (1969).

This Court followed the same approach in *Affiliated Ute Citizens* v. *United States,* 406 U. S. 128 (1972). A group of American Indians formed a corporation to manage joint assets derived from tribal holdings. The corporation issued stock to its Indian shareholders and designated a local bank as its transfer agent. Because of the speculative nature of the corporate assets and the difficulty of ascertaining the true value of a share, the corporation requested the bank to stress to its stockholders the importance of retaining the stock. Id., at 146. Two of the bank's assistant managers aided the shareholders in disposing of stock which the managers knew was traded in two separate markets — a primary market of Indians selling to non-Indians through the bank and a resale market consisting entirely of non-Indians. Indian sellers charged that the assistant managers had violated §10(b) and Rule 10b-5 by failing to inform them of the higher prices prevailing in the resale market. The Court recognized that no duty of disclosure would exist if the bank merely had acted as a transfer agent. But the bank also had assumed a duty to act on behalf of the shareholders, and the Indian sellers had relied upon its personnel when they sold their stock. 406 U. S., at 152. Because these officers of the bank were charged with a responsibility to the shareholders, they could not act as market makers inducing the Indians to sell their stock without disclosing the existence of the more favorable non-Indian market. Id., at 152-153.

Thus, administrative and judicial interpretations have established that silence in connection with the purchase or sale of securities may operate as a fraud actionable under §10(b) despite the absence of statutory language or legislative history specifically addressing the legality of nondisclosure. But such liability is premised upon a duty to disclose arising from a relationship of trust and confidence between parties to a transaction. Application of a duty to disclose prior to trading guarantees that corporate insiders, who have an obligation to place the shareholder's welfare before their own, will not benefit personally through fraudulent use of material, nonpublic information.[12]

[12]"Tippees" of corporate insiders have been held liable under §10(b)

III

In this case, the petitioner was convicted of violating §10(b) although he was not a corporate insider and he received no confidential information from the target company. Moreover, the "market information" upon which he relied did not concern the earning power or operations of the target company, but only the plans of the acquiring company.[13] Petitioner's use of that information was not a fraud under §10(b) unless he was subject to an affirmative duty to disclose it before trading. In this case, the jury instructions failed to specify any such duty. In effect, the trial court instructed the jury that petitioner owed a duty to everyone; to all sellers, indeed, to the market as a whole. The jury simply was told to decide whether petitioner used material nonpublic information at a time when "he knew other people trading in the securities market did not have access to the same information." Record 677.

The Court of Appeals affirmed the conviction by holding that "[a]*nyone* — corporate insider or not — who regularly receives material nonpublic information may not use that information to trade in securities without incurring an affirmative duty to disclose." 588 F. 2d, at 1365 (emphasis in original). Although the court said that its test would include only persons who regularly receive material, nonpublic information, id., at 1366, its rationale for that limitation is unrelated to the existence of a duty to disclose.[14] The Court of Appeals, like the trial court, failed to identify a relationship between petitioner and the sellers that could

---

because they have a duty not to profit from the use of inside information that they know is confidential and know or should know came from a corporate insider, Shapiro v. Merrill Lynch, Pierce, Fenner & Smith, Inc., 495 F. 2d 228, 237-238 (C. A. 2 1974). The tippee's obligation has been viewed as arising from his role as a participant after the fact in the insider's breach of a fiduciary duty. * * *

[13] See Fleischer, Mundheim, & Murphy, An Initial Inquiry into the Responsibility to Disclose Market Information, 121 U. Pa. L. Rev. 798, 799 (1973).

[14] The Court of Appeals said that its "regular access to market information" test would create a workable rule embracing "those who occupy * * * strategic places in the market mechanism." 588 F. 2d, at 1365. These considerations are insufficient to support a duty to disclose. A duty arises from the relationship between parties, see nn. 9 and 10, supra, and accompanying text, and not merely from one's ability to acquire information because of his position in the market.

The Court of Appeals also suggested that the acquiring corporation itself would not be a "market insider" because a tender offeror creates, rather than receives, information and takes a substantial economic risk that its offer will be unsuccessful. 588 F. 2d, at 1366-1367. Again, the Court of Appeals departed from the analysis appropriate to recognition of a duty. The Court of Appeals for the Second Circuit previously held, in a manner consistent with our analysis here, that a tender offeror does not violate give rise to a duty. Its decision thus rested solely upon its belief that the federal securities laws have "created a system providing equal access to information necessary for reasoned and intelligent investment decisions." Id., at 1362. The use by anyone of material information not generally available is fraudulent, this theory suggests, because such information gives certain buyers or sellers an unfair advantage over less informed buyers and sellers.

This reasoning suffers from two defects. First, not every instance of financial unfairness constitutes fraudulent activity under §10(b). See *Santa Fe Industries, Inc.* v. *Green,* 430 U. S. 462, 474-477 (1977).ª Second, the element required to make silence fraudulent — a duty to disclose — is absent in this case. No duty could arise from petitioner's relationship with the sellers of the target company's securities, for petitioner had no prior dealings with them. He was not their agent, he was not a fiduciary, he was not a person in whom the sellers had placed their trust and confidence. He was, in fact, a complete stranger who dealt with the sellers only through impersonal market transactions.

We cannot affirm petitioner's conviction without recognizing a general duty between all participants in market transactions to forgo actions based on material, nonpublic information. Formulation of such a broad duty, which departs radically from the established doctrine that duty arises from a specific relationship between two parties, see n. 9, *supra,* should not be undertaken absent some explicit evidence of congressional intent.

As we have seen, no such evidence emerges from the language or legislative history of §10(b). Moreover, neither the Congress nor the Commission ever has adopted a parity-of-information rule. Instead the problems caused by misuse of market information have been addressed by detailed and sophisticated regulation that recognizes when use of market information may not harm operation of the securities markets. For example, the Williams Act[15] limits but does not completely prohibit a tender offeror's purchases of target

---

§10(b) when it makes preannouncement purchases precisely because there is no relationship between the offeror and the seller:

> We know of no rule of law * * * that a purchaser of stock, who was not an "insider" and had no fiduciary relation to a prospective seller, had any obligation to reveal circumstances that might raise a seller's demands and thus abort the sale. General Time Corp. v. Talley Industries, Inc., 403 F. 2d 159, 164 (1968), *cert. denied,* 393 U. S. 1026 (1969).

ª ED.: This case is set out infra p. 928.

[15] Title 15 U. S. C. §78m(d)(1) (1976 ed., Supp. II) permits a tender offeror to purchase 5% of the target company's stock prior to disclosure of its plan for acquisition.

corporation stock before public announcement of the offer. Congress' careful action in this and other areas[16] contrasts, and is in some tension, with the broad rule of liability we are asked to adopt in this case.

Indeed, the theory upon which the petitioner was convicted is at odds with the Commission's view of §10(b) as applied to activity that has the same effect on sellers as the petitioner's purchases. "Warehousing" takes place when a corporation gives advance notice of its intention to launch a tender offer to institutional investors who then are able to purchase stock in the target company before the tender offer is made public and the price of shares rises.[17] In this case, as in warehousing, a buyer of securities purchases stock in a target corporation on the basis of market information which is unknown to the seller. In both of these situations, the seller's behavior presumably would be altered if he had the nonpublic information. Significantly, however, the Commission has acted to bar warehousing under its authority to regulate tender offers[18] after recognizing that action under §10(b) would rest on a "somewhat different theory" than that previously used to regulate insider trading as fraudulent activity.[19]

We see no basis for applying such a new and different theory of liability in this case. As we have emphasized before, the 1934 Act cannot be read " 'more broadly than its language and the statutory scheme reasonably permit.' " *Touche Ross & Co.* v. *Redington*, 442 U. S. 560, 578 (1979), quoting *SEC* v. *Sloan*, 436 U. S. 103,

[16] Section 11 of the 1934 Act generally forbids a member of a national securities exchange from effecting any transaction on the exchange for its own account. 15 U. S. C. §78k(a)(1). But Congress has specifically exempted specialists from this prohibition — broker-dealers who execute orders for customers trading in a specific corporation's stock, while at the same time buying and selling that corporation's stock on their own behalf. §11(a)(1)(A), 15 U. S. C. §78k(a)(1)(A); see S. Rep. No. 94-75, p. 99 (1975); Securities and Exchange Commission, Report of Special Study of Securities Markets, H. R. Doc. No. 95, 88th Cong., 1st Sess., pt. 2, pp. 57-58, 76 (1963). See generally S. Robbins, The Securities Markets 191-193 (1966). The exception is based upon Congress' recognition that specialists contribute to a fair and orderly marketplace at the same time they exploit the informational advantage that comes from their possession of buy and sell orders. H. R. Doc. No. 95, supra, at 78-80. Similar concerns with the functioning of the market prompted Congress to exempt market makers, block positioners, registered odd-lot dealers, bona fide arbitrageurs, and risk arbitrageurs from §11's general prohibition on member trading. 15 U. S. C. §§78k(a)(1)(A)-(D); see S. Rep. No. 94-75, supra, at 99. See also Securities Exchange Act Release No. 34-9950, 38 Fed. Reg. 3902, 3918 (1973).

[17] Fleischer, Mundheim, & Murphy, supra n. 13, at 811-812.

[18] SEC Proposed Rule §240.14e-3, 44 Fed. Reg. 70352-70355, 70359 (1979).

[19] 1 SEC Institutional Investor Study Report, H. R. Doc. No. 92-64, pt. 1, p. xxxii (1971).

116 (1978). Section 10(b) is aptly described as a catchall provision, but what it catches must be fraud. When an allegation of fraud is based upon nondisclosure, there can be no fraud absent a duty to speak. We hold that a duty to disclose under §10(b) does not arise from the mere possession of nonpublic market information. The contrary result is without support in the legislative history of §10(b) and would be inconsistent with the careful plan that Congress has enacted for regulation of the securities markets. Cf. *Sante Fe Industries, Inc. v. Green*, 430 U. S., at 479.

IV

In its brief to this Court, the United States offers an alternative theory to support petitioner's conviction. It argues that petitioner breached a duty to the acquiring corporation when he acted upon information that he obtained by virtue of his position as an employee of a printer employed by the corporation. The breach of this duty is said to support a conviction under §10(b) for fraud perpetrated upon both the acquiring corporation and the sellers.

We need not decide whether this theory has merit for it was not submitted to the jury. The jury was told, in the language of Rule 10b-5, that it could convict the petitioner if it concluded that he either (i) employed a device, scheme, or artifice to defraud or (ii) engage in an act, practice, or course of business which operated or would operate as a fraud or deceit upon any person. Record 681. The trial judge stated that a "scheme to defraud" is a plan to obtain money by trick or deceit and that "a failure by Chiarella to disclose material, non-public information in connection with his purchase of stock would constitute deceit." Id., at 683. Accordingly, the jury was instructed that the petitioner employed a scheme to defraud if he "did not disclose * * * material nonpublic information in connection with the purchases of the stock." Id., at 685-686.

Alternatively, the jury was instructed that it could convict if "Chiarella's alleged conduct of having purchased securities without disclosing material, non-public information would have or did have the effect of operating as a fraud upon a seller." Id., at 686. The judge earlier had stated that fraud "embraces all the means which human ingenuity can devise and which are resorted to by one individual to gain an advantage over another by false misrepresentation, suggestions or by suppression of the truth." Id., at 683.

The jury instructions demonstrate that petitioner was convicted merely because of his failure to disclose material, non-public information to sellers from whom he bought the stock of target corporations. The jury was not instructed on the nature of elements of a duty owed by petitioner to anyone other than the sellers. Because we cannot affirm a criminal conviction on the basis of a theory not presented to the jury, *Rewis* v. *United States,* 401 U. S. 808, 814 (1971), see *Dunn* v. *United States,* 442 U. S. 100, 106 (1979), we will not speculate upon whether such a duty exists, whether it has been breached, or whether such a breach constitutes a violation of §10(b).[21]

The judgment of the Court of Appeals is reversed.

MR. JUSTICE STEVENS, concurring.

* * * I agree with the Court's determination that petitioner owed no duty of disclosure to the sellers, that his conviction rested on the erroneous premise that he did owe them such a duty, and that the judgment of the Court of Appeals must therefore be reversed.

* * *

I write simply to emphasize the fact that we have not necessarily placed any stamp of approval on what this petitioner did, nor have we held that similar actions must be considered lawful in the future. Rather, we have merely held that petitioner's criminal conviction cannot rest on the theory that he breached a duty he did not owe.

I join the Court's opinion.

MR. JUSTICE BRENNAN, concurring in the judgment.

---

[21] The dissent of The Chief Justice relies upon a single phrase from the jury instructions, which states that the petitioner held a "confidential position" at Pandick Press, to argue that the jury was properly instructed on the theory "that a person who has misappropriated nonpublic information has an absolute duty to disclose that information or to refrain from trading." Post, at 240. The few words upon which this thesis is based do not explain to the jury the nature and scope of the petitioner's duty to his employer, the nature and scope of petitioner's duty, if any, to the acquiring corporation, or the elements of the tort of misappropriation. Nor do the jury instructions suggest that a "confidential position" is a necessary element of the offense for which petitioner was charged. Thus, we do not believe that a "misappropriation" theory was included in the jury instructions.

The conviction would have to be reversed even if the jury had been instructed that it could convict the petitioner either (1) because of his failure to disclose material, nonpublic information to sellers or (2) because of a breach of a duty to the acquiring corporation. We may not uphold a criminal conviction if it is impossible to ascertain whether the defendant has been punished for noncriminal conduct. United States v. Gallagher, 576 F. 2d 1028, 1046 (C. A. 3 1978); see Leary v. United States, 395 U. S. 6, 31-32 (1969); Stromberg v. California, 283 U. S. 359, 369-370 (1931).

[Justice Brennan agreed with Part I of the Chief Justice's dissent — to the effect that "a person violates §10(b) whenever he improperly obtains or converts to his own benefit nonpublic information which he then uses in connection with the purchase or sale of securities" — but concurred in the judgment because he could "find no instruction suggesting that one element of the offense was the improper conversion or misappropriation of that nonpublic information."]

MR. CHIEF JUSTICE BURGER, dissenting.

I believe that the jury instructions in this case properly charged a violation of §10(b) and Rule 10b-5, and I would affirm the conviction.

I

As a general rule, neither party to an arm's-length business transaction has an obligation to disclose information to the other unless the parties stand in some confidential or fiduciary relation. See W. Prosser, Law of Torts §106 (2d ed. 1955). This rule permits a businessman to capitalize on his experience and skill in securing and evaluating relevant information; it provides incentive for hard work, careful analysis, and astute forecasting. But the policies that underlie the rule also should limit its scope. In particular, the rule should give way when an informational advantage is obtained, not by superior experience, foresight, or industry, but by some unlawful means. One commentator has written:

> [T]he way in which the buyer acquires the information which he conceals from the vendor should be a material circumstance. The information might have been acquired as the result of his bringing to bear a superior knowledge, intelligence, skill or technical judgment; it might have been acquired by mere chance; or it might have been acquired by means of some tortious action on his part. . . . *Any time information is acquired by an illegal act it would seem that there should be a duty to disclose that information.* Keeton, Fraud — Concealment and Non-Disclosure, 15 Texas L. Rev. 1, 25-26 (1930) (emphasis added).

I would read §10(b) and Rule 10b-5 to encompass and build on this principle: to mean that a person who has misappropriated nonpublic information has an absolute duty to disclose that information or to refrain from trading.

The language of §10(b) and of Rule 10b-5 plainly support such a reading. By their terms, these provisions reach *any* person engaged in *any* fraudulent scheme. This broad language negates the suggestion that congressional concern was limited to trading by "corporate insiders" or to deceptive practices related to "corporate information."[1] * * *

The history of the statute and of the Rule also supports this reading. The antifraud provisions were designed in large measure "to assure that dealing in securities is fair and without undue preferences or advantages among investors." H. R. Conf. Rep. No. 94-229, p. 91 (1975). These provisions prohibit "those manipulative and deceptive practices which have been demonstrated to fulfill no useful function." S. Rep. No. 792, 73d Cong., 2d Sess., 6 (1934). An investor who purchases securities on the basis of misappropriated nonpublic information possesses just such an "undue" trading advantage; his conduct quite clearly serves no useful function except his own enrichment at the expense of others.

This interpretation of §10(b) and Rule 10b-5 is in no sense novel. It follows naturally from legal principles enunciated by the Securities and Exchange Commission in its seminal *Cady, Roberts* decision. 40 S. E. C. 907 (1961). There, the Commission relied upon two factors to impose a duty to disclose on corporate insiders: (1) " . . . access . . . to information intended to be available only for a corporate purpose *and not for the personal benefit of anyone*" (emphasis added); and (2) the unfairness inherent in trading on such information when it is inaccessible to those with whom one is dealing. Both of these factors are present whenever a party gains an informational advantage by unlawful means. Indeed, in *In re Blyth & Co.*, 43 S. E. C. 1037 (1969), the commission applied its *Cady, Roberts* decision in just such a context. In that case a broker-dealer had traded in Government securities on the basis of confidential Treasury Department information which it received from a Federal Reserve Bank employee. The Commission ruled that the trading was "improper use of inside information" violative of §10(b) and Rule 10b-5. 43 S. E. C. at

---

[1] Academic writing in recent years has distinguished between "corporate information" — information which comes from within the corporation and reflects on expected earnings or assets — and "market information." See, e. g., Fleischer, Mundheim, & Murphy, An Initial Inquiry into the Responsibility to Disclose Market Information, 121 U. Pa. L. Rev. 798, 799 (1973). It is clear that §10(b) and Rule 10b-5 by their terms and by their history make no such distinction. See Brudney, Insiders, Outsiders, and Informational Advantages under the Federal Securities Laws, 93 Harv. L. Rev. 322, 329-333 (1979).

1040. It did not hesitate to extend *Cady, Roberts* to reach a "tippee" of a Government insider.[3]

Finally, it bears emphasis that this reading of §10b and Rule 10b-5 would not threaten legitimate business practices. So read, the antifraud provisions would not impose a duty on a tender offeror to disclose its acquisition plans during the period in which it "tests the water" prior to purchasing a full 5% of the target company's stock. Nor would it proscribe "warehousing." See generally SEC, Institutional Investor Study Report, H. R. Doc. No. 92-64, pt. 4, p. 2273 (1971). Likewise, market specialists would not be subject to a disclose-or-refrain requirement in the performance of their everyday market functions. In each of these instances, trading is accomplished on the basis of material, nonpublic information, but the information has not been unlawfully converted for personal gain.

II

The Court's opinion, as I read it, leaves open the question whether §10(b) and Rule 10b-5 prohibit trading on misappropriated nonpublic information. Instead, the Court apparently concludes that this theory of the case was not submitted to the jury. In the Court's view, the instructions given the jury were premised on the erroneous notion that the mere failure to disclose nonpublic information, however acquired, is a deceptive practice. And because of this premise, the jury was not instructed that the means by which Chiarella acquired his informational advantage — by violating a duty owed to the acquiring companies — was an element of the offense. See ante at 236.

The Court's reading of the District Court's charge is unduly restrictive. Fairly read as a whole and in the context of the trial, the instructions required the jury to find that Chiarella obtained his trading advantage by misappropriating the property of his employer's customers. * * *

In any event, even assuming the instructions were deficient in

---

[3] This interpretation of the antifraud provisions also finds support in the recently proposed Federal Securities Code prepared by the American Law Institute under the direction of Professor Louis Loss. The ALI Code would construe the antifraud provisions to cover a class of "quasi-insiders," including a judge's law clerk who trades on information in an unpublished opinion or a Government employee who trades on a secret report. See ALI Federal Securities Code §1603, comment 3(d), pp. 538-539 (Prop. Off. Draft 1978). These quasi-insiders share the characteristic that their informational advantage is obtained by conversion and not by legitimate economic activity that society seeks to encourage.

not charging misappropriation with sufficient precision, on this record any error was harmless beyond a reasonable doubt. Here, Chiarella, himself, testified that he obtained his informational advantage by decoding confidential material entrusted to his employer by its customers. * * *

In sum, the evidence shows beyond all doubt that Chiarella, working literally in the shadows of the warning signs in the printshop, misappropriated — stole to put it bluntly — valuable nonpublic information entrusted to him in the utmost confidence. He then exploited his ill-gotten informational advantage by purchasing securities in the market. In my view, such conduct plainly violates §10(b) and Rule 10b-5. Accordingly, I would affirm the judgment of the Court of Appeals.

MR. JUSTICE BLACKMUN, with whom MR. JUSTICE MARSHALL joins, dissenting.

Although I agree with much of what is said in Part I of the dissenting opinion of The Chief Justice, *ante*, p. 239, I write separately because, in my view, it is unnecessary to rest petitioner's conviction on a "misappropriation" theory. The fact that petitioner Chiarella purloined, or, to use The Chief Justice's word, *ante*, at 245, "stole," information concerning pending tender offers certainly is the most dramatic evidence that petitioner was guilty of fraud. * * * But I also would find petitioner's conduct fraudulent within the meaning of * * * Rule 10b-5, * * * even if he had obtained the blessing of his employer's principals before embarking on his profiteering scheme. Indeed, I think petitioner's brand of manipulative trading, with or without such approval, lies close to the heart of what the securities laws are intended to prohibit.

The Court continues to pursue a course, charted in certain recent decisions, designed to transform §10(b) from an intentionally elastic "catchall" provision to one that catches relatively little of the misbehavior that all too often makes investment in securities a needlessly risky business for the uninitiated investor. [Citations omitted.] Such confinement in this case is now achieved by imposition of a requirement of a "special relationship" akin to fiduciary duty before the statute gives rise to a duty to disclose or to abstain from trading upon material, nonpublic information. The Court admits that this conclusion finds no mandate in the language of the statute or its legislative history. *Ante*, at 226. Yet the Court fails even to attempt a justification of its ruling in terms of the purposes of the securities laws, or to square that ruling with the long-standing but now much abused principle that the federal securities laws are to be construed flexibly rather than with narrow technicality. [Citations omitted.]

I, of course, agree with the Court that a relationship of trust can establish a duty to disclose under §10(b) and Rule 10b-5. But I do not agree that a failure to disclose violates the Rule only when the responsibilities of a relationship of that kind have been breached. As applied to this case, the Court's approach unduly minimizes the importance of petitioner's *access* to confidential information that the honest investor, no matter how diligently he tried, could not legally obtain. In doing so, it further advances an interpretation of §10(b) and Rule 10b-5 that stops short of their full implications. Although the Court draws support for its position from certain precedent, I find its decision neither fully consistent with developments in the common law of fraud, nor fully in step with administrative and judicial application of Rule 10b-5 to "insider" trading.

The common law of actionable misrepresentation long has treated the possession of "special facts" as a key ingredient in the duty to disclose. See *Strong* v. *Repide,* 213 U. S. 419, 431-433 (1909); 1 F. Harper & F. James, Law of Torts §7.14 (1956). Traditionally, this factor has been prominent in cases involving confidential or fiduciary relations, where one party's inferiority of knowledge and dependence upon fair treatment is a matter of legal definition, as well as in cases where one party is on notice that the other is "acting under a mistaken belief with respect to a material fact." *Frigitemp Corp.* v. *Financial Dynamics Fund, Inc.,* 524 F. 2d 275, 283 (C. A. 2 1975); see also Restatement of Torts §551 (1938). Even at common law, however, there has been a trend away from strict adherence to the harsh maxim *caveat emptor* and toward a more flexible, less formalistic understanding of the duty to disclose. See, e. g., Keeton, Fraud — Concealment and Non-disclosure, 15 Texas L. Rev. 1, 31 (1936). Steps have been taken toward application of the "special facts" doctrine in a broader array of contexts where one party's superior knowledge of essential facts renders a transaction without disclosure inherently unfair. [Citations omitted.]

By its narrow construction of §10(b) and Rule 10b-5, the Court places the federal securities laws in the rearguard of this movement, a position opposite to the expectations of Congress at the time the securities laws were enacted. * * *

Indeed, the importance of access to "special facts" has been a recurrent theme in administrative and judicial application of Rule 10b-5 to insider trading. Both the SEC and the courts have stressed the insider's misuse of secret knowledge as the gravamen of illegal conduct. The Court, I think, unduly minimizes this aspect of prior decisions.

*   *   *

* * * Although I am not sure I fully accept the "market insider" category created by the Court of Appeals, I would hold that persons having access to confidential material information that is not legally available to others generally are prohibited by Rule 10b-5 from engaging in schemes to exploit their structural informational advantage through trading in affected securities. * * *

Whatever the outer limits of the Rule, petitioner Chiarella's case fits neatly near the center of its analytical framework. He occupied a relationship to the takeover companies giving him intimate access to concededly material information that was sedulously guarded from public access. The information, in the words of *Cady, Roberts & Co.,* 40 S. E. C., at 912, was "intended to be available only for a corporate purpose and not for the personal benefit of anyone." Petitioner, moreover, knew that the information was unavailable to those with whom he dealt. And he took full, virtually riskless advantage of this artificial information gap by selling the stocks shortly after each takeover bid was announced. By any reasonable definition, his trading was "inherent[ly] unfai[r]." Ibid. This misuse of confidential information was clearly placed before the jury. Petitioner's conviction, therefore, should be upheld, and I dissent from the Court's upsetting that conviction.

Perhaps the most significant aspect of these several opinions is that they all accept the affirmative obligation of insiders to disclose material facts when they trade. True, everything positive that was said about Rule 10b-5 was technically *obiter* in view of the ultimate conclusion of lack of violation. But it cannot be without significance that the majority opinion seems to bless even the extension of the principle to sellers "to persons who previously may not have been shareholders.[77] Beyond this:

(1) The Commission — not unexpectedly, and with significant judicial success — is pressing the misappropriation or breach-of-fiduciary-duty-to-a-third-person theory, which was approved by four Justices (the three dissenters and Justice Brennan) and left open by the others.[78]

[77] 455 U. S. at 227 n. 8, supra.
[78] See Sec. Ex. Act Rel. 17,120, 20 SEC Dock. 1241, 1245 (1980). In United

(2) Without waiting for a judicial test of that theory, the Commission resorted to its rulemaking authority in §14(e)[79] to get at *tender offerors'* tippees who buy *target companies'* stock. Once a person "has taken a substantial step or steps to commence" a tender offer, Rule 14e-3 prohibits any such tippee from trading in target securities until "a reasonable time" after public disclosure of any material information he may have with respect to the tender offer and the source of that information.[80] But an exception is made for a non-natural person that shows that (1) the individuals within the organization that made the investment decision did not in fact know the information in question *and* (2) the organization

> had implemented one or a combination of policies and procedures, reasonable under the circumstances, taking into consideration the nature of the person's business, to ensure that individual(s) making investment decision(s) would not violate [the rule], which policies and procedures may include, but are not limited to, (i) those which restrict any purchase, sale and causing any purchase and sale of any such security or (ii) those which prevent such individual(s) from knowing such information.[81]

Clause (ii), of course, refers to the "Chinese wall." And Clause (i) contemplates restricted lists. The Commission cautioned:

> Depending on the circumstances, it may be appropriate to advise customers of its [the organization's] use of the Chinese Wall, because the institution would not be using all information that it

---

States v. Newman, 664 F. 2d 12 (2d Cir. 1981), where employees of investment banking firms allegedly tipped Newman (the only person before the court) and other co-conspirators with respect to proposed mergers and acquisitions, the court reversed the dismissal of an indictment on the ground that Newman had aided and abetted the employees' duty of loyalty to their employers, thus defrauding not only the investment banking firms but *their* clients. "Had appellant used similar deceptive practices to mulct [the firms] of cash or securities," the court stated, "it could hardly be argued that those [firms] had not been defrauded." 664 F. 2d at 17. See also People v. Florentine, 456 N. Y. S. 2d 638 (N. Y. C. Cr. Ct. 1982) (the first criminal prosecution under N. Y. Martin Act §352-c for insider trading). But it does not follow that such a duty "transmutes itself into a duty to support a private action." Moss v. Morgan Stanley, Inc., CCH Fed. Sec. L. Rep. ¶99,045 (S. D. N. Y. 1983).

[79] See p. 574 supra.

[80] Rule 14e-3(a). Examples of a "substantial step" presumably include such actions as a board resolution or the arranging of financing or the preparation of tender offer material, or possibly an offeror's purchase of 5 percent of a target's stock after negotiations have broken off but before a public tender offer is announced. The prohibition applies also to tippees from the target companies whose stock they trade. Ibid. And the rule prohibits *tipping per se.* Rule 14e-3(d). The first is a classic 10b-5 situation in any event.

[81] Rule 14e-3(b).

had received to the benefit of a particular customer. There is also a danger that the Chinese Wall may not be fully effective in all instances and that information may pass through the wall. In that regard, other informal procedures are often used in conjunction with and to supplement the Chinese Wall at times when the institution has material, nonpublic information but before the information is appropriate for public release or to cause placement of the security on a strict list. This "watch list" procedure enables the institution to monitor trading activity to determine whether any leaks in the Chinese Wall have occurred.[82]

Presumably this use of the rulemaking authority in §14(e) to make a potential felon out of not only the prospective tender offeror's president but also his personal secretary who buys target stock, while leaving the prospective tender offeror itself free to buy before any announcement is made, finds its explanation in the "free 5 percent" provision in §13(d).[83] There is an inherent anomaly, however, that goes beyond Rule 14e-3 to the Commission-advocated misappropriation theory under Rule 10b-5: The president of Company *B* who buys Company *A* stock without disclosing his intention to cause *B* to give a huge order for widgets to *A* is safe so far as Rule 10b-5 is concerned, thanks to *Chiarella*. But, once more, his poor secretary had better watch out; for the secretary's purchase of *A* stock would violate a fiduciary duty owed to his or her "boss."

(3) *Query* whether *Chiarella* leaves anything of "scalping" cases like *Zweig* v. *Hearst Corp.*,[84] where Rule 10b-5 was applied with respect to a newspaper columnist's practice of buying shares of companies that he expected to discuss favorably. The court analyzed the case in terms of the defendant's failure to disclose his ownership. But it did cite the Supreme Court's decision in *SEC* v. *Capital Gains Research Bureau, Inc.*,[85] where the "scalper" was an investment adviser who made recommendations in monthly reports to subscribers. To be sure, an investment adviser — even the publisher of a tipster sheet — is a fiduciary. But more important, arguably, is the language of the underlying statute in

---

[82] Sec. Ex. Act Rel. 17,120, 20 SEC Dock. 1241, 1252 (1980).

[83] See p. 573 supra.

[84] 594 F. 2d 1261 (9th Cir. 1979). See Note, The First Amendment and "Scalping" by a Financial Columnist: May a Newspaper Article Be Commercial Speech?, 57 Ind. L. J. 131 (1981).

[85] 375 U. S. 180 (1963). In Santa Fe Industries, Inc. v. Green, 430 U. S. 462, 471 n. 11 (1977), set out infra p. 928, where the Court was talking not of scienter but of the relationship of nondisclosure to "fraud," it observed that the references in *Capital Gains* to fraud in the "equitable" sense of the term were premised on the recognition that Congress intended the Advisers Act to establish federal fiduciary standards for advisers. See also Aaron v. SEC, 446 U. S. 680, 691-95 (1980), set out infra p. 887.

the *Capital Gains* case: §206 of the Advisers Act contains "fraud" language comparable to Clauses (1) and (3) of Rule 10b-5 but no prohibition of misstatements or half-truths along the lines of Clause (2). A *Zweig* type of case might, therefore, have a better chance of surviving *Chiarella* if it were analyzed in terms of a fraudulent "act" or "scheme" rather than a failure to disclose.[86]

(4) It has been suggested that the wrong associated with insider trading has to do with "self-dealing and breach of fiduciary duty toward the corporation or shareholders and clients as a group, rather than with misrepresentation or deception of individual investors," and that the Court in *Chiarella* "appears simply to be playing games with [common law misrepresentation] doctrine in order to limit liability without articulating the reasons why liability should be limited in just that way."[87]

6. SCIENTER

Whatever scienter may mean in common law deceit,[88] it has been held that intent is essential to a "scheme to defraud" under §17(a)(1) of the 1933 Act, as it is under the mail and wire fraud statutes.[89] But "The law is settled that no amount of honest belief that the enterprises would ultimately make money for the stockholders can excuse or justify false representations" in the sale of securities.[90] This kind of "good faith" argument — which Lord Chief Justice Hewart analogized to "the excuse of the office boy who takes a half-crown from the till because he has a good thing for the Grand National"[91] — is quite different from the defense of good faith in the sense that the defendant had reasonable ground to believe that his statements were true.[92]

---

[86] On fraud by deed, see 2 Code 661-62; pp. 900-02 infra.

[87] Anderson, Fraud, Fiduciaries, and Insider Trading, 10 Hofstra L. Rev. 341, 373, 376 (1982); see also Brudney, Insiders, Outsiders and Informational Advantages under the Federal Securities Laws, 93 Harv. L. Rev. 322 (1979); Dooley, Enforcement of Insider Trading Restrictions, 66 Va. L. Rev. 1 (1980).

[88] See p. 809 supra.

[89] Troutman v. United States, 100 F. 2d 628, 632 (10th Cir. 1938), *cert. denied*, 306 U. S. 649; Rice v. United States, 149 F. 2d 601 (10th Cir. 1945).

[90] Foshay v. United States, 68 F. 2d 205, 210 (8th Cir. 1933), *cert. denied*, 291 U. S. 674, and cases cited (mail fraud statute); Frank v. United States, 220 F. 2d 559, 564 (10th Cir. 1955) (also §17(a)); United States v. Painter, 314 F. 2d 939, 943 (4th Cir. 1963), *cert. denied*, 374 U. S. 831 (mail and wire fraud statutes); United States v. Diamond, 430 F. 2d 688, 691 (5th Cir. 1970) (mail fraud statute).

[91] Rex v. Bishirgian, [1936] 1 All E. R. 586, 594 (C. C. A.).

[92] Frank v. United States, 220 F. 2d 559, 564-65 (10th Cir. 1955).

Moreover, intent (or scienter) being subjective, it must often "be inferred from a series of seemingly isolated acts and instances which have been * * * aptly designated as badges of fraud."[93] It has been inferred also "where the lack of knowledge consists of ignorance of facts which any ordinary person under similar circumstances should have known."[94] In short, intent to defraud in the context of §17(a)(1) and the mail and wire fraud statutes has taken on a coloration of recklessness.[95]

These softening precedents as to intent and scienter were made primarily in the context of criminal prosecutions under §17(a) or the mail fraud statute or both. So far as criminal prosecutions under §17(a) are concerned, the element of willfulness alone in §24, the penal provision, presumably requires (whatever it may mean in other contexts) knowledge of the falsity (or recklessness with respect to the truth of the matter) if nothing else. But the rationale of these holdings should apply with at least equal force to injunction actions or other civil cases based on Clause (1) of §17(a) or its counterparts in the fraud rules.[96]

This leaves the question — to which we turn next — of the applicability of this learning to *civil* actions under §17(a) generally, as well as Rule 10b-5 and the other fraud provisions.

ERNST & ERNST v. HOCHFELDER
Supreme Court of the United States, 1976
425 U. S. 185

Mr. Justice Powell delivered the opinion of the Court.

The issue in this case is whether an action for civil damages may lie under §10(b) of the Securities Exchange Act of 1934 (1934

---

[93] Nassan v. United States, 126 F. 2d 613, 615 (4th Cir. 1942) (mail fraud statute); see also Deaver v. United States, 155 F. 2d 740, 744 (D. C. Cir. 1946), *cert. denied*, 329 U. S. 766 (same); Walters v. United States, 256 F. 2d 840, 841 (9th Cir. 1958), *cert. denied*, 358 U. S. 833; United States v. Vandersee, 279 F. 2d 176, 179 (3d Cir. 1960), *cert. denied*, 364 U. S. 943.

[94] Stone v. United States, 113 F. 2d 70, 75 (6th Cir. 1940); see also Irwin v. United States, 338 F. 2d 770, 774 (9th Cir. 1964), *cert. denied*, 381 U. S. 911 (mail fraud statute); United States v. Meyer, 359 F. 2d 837, 839 (7th Cir. 1966), *cert. denied*, 385 U. S. 837; United States v. Seasholtz, 435 F. 2d 4, 8 (10th Cir. 1970) (mail fraud statute).

[95] See United States v. Henderson, 446 F. 2d 960, 966 (8th Cir. 1971), *cert. denied*, 401 U. S. 991 ("reckless disregard" of the facts); United States v. Mackay, 491 F. 2d 616, 623 (10th Cir. 1973), *cert. denied*, 416 U. S. 972, 419 U. S. 1047 (mail fraud statute); United States v. Boyer, 694 F. 2d 58 (3d Cir. 1982).

[96] SEC v. Glass Marine Industries, Inc., 208 F. Supp. 727, 742-43 (D. Del. 1962).

Act), 48 Stat. 891, 15 U. S. C. §78j(b), and Securities and Exchange Commission Rule 10b-5, 17 C. F. R. §240.10b-5 (1975), in the absence of an allegation of intent to deceive, manipulate, or defraud on the part of the defendant.

I

Petitioner, Ernst & Ernst, is an accounting firm. From 1946 through 1967 it was retained by First Securities Company of Chicago (First Securities), a small brokerage firm and member of the Midwest Stock Exchange and of the National Association of Securities Dealers, to perform periodic audits of the firm's books and records. In connection with these audits Ernst & Ernst prepared for filing with the Securities and Exchange Commission (Commission) the annual reports required of First Securities under §17(a) of the 1934 Act, 15 U. S. C. §78q(a). It also prepared for First Securities responses to the financial questionnaires of the Midwest Stock Exchange (Exchange).

Respondents were customers of First Securities who invested in a fraudulent securities scheme perpetrated by Leston B. Nay, president of the firm and owner of 92% of its stock. Nay induced the respondents to invest funds in "escrow" accounts that he represented would yield a high rate of return. Respondents did so from 1942 through 1966, with the majority of the transactions occurring in the 1950's. In fact, there were no escrow accounts as Nay converted respondents' funds to his own use immediately upon receipt. These transactions were not in the customary form of dealings between First Securities and its customers. The respondents drew their personal checks payable to Nay or a designated bank for his account. No such escrow accounts were reflected on the books and records of First Securities, and none was shown on its periodic accounting to respondents in connection with their other investments. Nor were they included in First Securities' filings with the Commission or the Exchange.

This fraud came to light in 1968 when Nay committed suicide, leaving a note that described First Securities as bankrupt and the escrow accounts as "spurious." Respondents subsequently filed this action for damages against Ernst & Ernst in the United States District Court for the Northern District of Illinois under §10(b) of the 1934 Act. The complaint charged that Nay's escrow scheme violated §10(b) and Commission Rule 10b-5, and that Ernst & Ernst had "aided and abetted" Nay's violations by its "failure" to conduct proper audits of First Securities. As revealed through discovery, respondents' cause of action rested on a theory of negligent nonfeasance. The premise was that Ernst & Ernst had failed to utilize "appropriate auditing procedures" in its audits of First Securities, thereby failing to discover internal practices of the firm said to prevent an effective audit. The practice principally relied on was Nay's rule that only he could open mail addressed to him at First Securities or addressed to First Securities to his attention, even if it arrived in his absence. Respondents contended that if Ernst & Ernst had conducted a proper audit, it would have discovered this "mail rule." The existence of the rule then would have been disclosed in reports to the Exchange and to the Commission by Ernst & Ernst as an irregular procedure that prevented an effective audit. This would have led to an invesigation of Nay that would have revealed the fraudulent scheme. Respondents specifically disclaimed the existence of fraud or intentional misconduct on the part of Ernst & Ernst.[5]

After extensive discovery the District Court granted Ernst & Ernst's motion for summary judgment and dismissed the action. The court rejected Ernst & Ernst's contention that a cause of action for aiding and abetting a securities fraud could not be maintained under §10(b) and Rule 10b-5 merely on allegations of negligence. It concluded, however, that there was no genuine issue of material fact with respect to whether Ernst & Ernst had conducted its audits in accordance with generally accepted auditing standards.

The Court of Appeals for the Seventh Circuit reversed and remanded, holding that one who breaches a duty of inquiry and disclosure owed another is liable in damages for aiding and abetting a third party's violation of Rule 10b-5 if the fraud would have been discovered or prevented but for the breach. 503 F. 2d 1100 (1974). The court reasoned that Ernst & Ernst had a common-law and statutory duty of inquiry into the adequacy of First Securities' internal control system because it had contracted to audit First Securities and to prepare for filing with the Commission the annual report of First Securities' financial condition required under §17 of the 1934 Act and Rule 17a-5. The court further reasoned that respondents were beneficiaries of the statutory duty to inquire and the related duty to disclose any material irregularities that were discovered. 503 F. 2d, at 1105-1111. The court concluded that there were genuine issues of fact as to whether Ernst & Ernst's

---

[5] In their response to interrogatories in the District Court respondents conceded that they did "not accuse Ernst & Ernst of deliberate, intentional fraud," merely with "inexcusable negligence." App. 81.

failure to discover and comment upon Nay's mail rule constituted a breach of its duties of inquiry and disclosure, id., at 1111, and whether inquiry and disclosure would have led to the discovery or prevention of Nay's fraud. Id., at 1115.

We granted certiorari to resolve the question whether a private cause of action for damages will lie under §10(b) and Rule 10b-5 in the absence of any allegation of "scienter" — intent to deceive, manipulate, or defraud.[12] 421 U. S. 909 (1975). We conclude that it will not and therefore we reverse.

II

Federal regulation of transactions in securities emerged as part of the aftermath of the market crash in 1929. The Securities Act of 1933 (1933 Act), 48 Stat. 74, as amended, 15 U. S. C. §77a et seq., was designed to provide investors with full disclosure of material information concerning public offerings of securities in commerce, to protect investors against fraud and, through the imposition of specified civil liabilities, to promote ethical standards of honesty and fair dealing. See H. R. Rep. No. 85, 73d Cong., 1st Sess., 1-5 (1933). The 1934 Act was intended principally to protect investors against manipulation of stock prices through regulation of transactions upon securities exchanges and in over-the-counter markets, and to impose regular reporting requirements on companies whose stock is listed on national securities exchanges. See S. Rep. No. 792, 73d Cong., 2d Sess., 1-5 (1934). Although the Acts contain numerous carefully drawn express civil remedies and criminal penalties, Congress recognized that efficient

---

12 Although the verbal formulations of the standard to be applied have varied, several Courts of Appeals have held in substance that negligence alone is sufficient for civil liability under §10(b) and Rule 10b-5. Other Courts of Appeals have held that some type of scienter — i. e., intent to defraud, reckless disregard for the truth, or knowing use of some practice to defraud — is necessary in such an action. But few of the decisions announcing that some form of negligence suffices for civil liability under §10(b) and Rule 10b-5 actually have involved only negligent conduct. [Citations in this paragraph are omitted.]

In this opinion the term "scienter" refers to a mental state embracing intent to deceive, manipulate or defraud. In certain areas of the law recklessness is considered to be a form of intentional conduct for purposes of imposing liability for some act. We need not address here the question whether, in some circumstances, reckless behavior is sufficient for civil liability under §10(b) and Rule 10b-5.

Since this case concerns an action for damages we also need not consider the question whether scienter is a necessary element in an action for injunctive relief under §10(b) and Rule 10b-5. Cf. SEC v. Capital Gains Research Bureau, 375 U. S. 180 (1963).

regulation of securities trading could not be accomplished under a rigid statutory program. As part of the 1934 Act Congress created the Commission, which is provided with an arsenal of flexible enforcement powers. See, e. g., 1933 Act §§8, 19, 20, 15 U. S. C. §§77h, 77s, 77t; 1934 Act §§9, 19, 21, 15 U. S. C. §§78i, 78s, 78u.

[Justice Powell here quotes §10(b) and Rule 10b-5.]

Although §10(b) does not by its terms create an express civil remedy for its violation, and there is no indication that Congress, or the Commission when adopting Rule 10b-5, contemplated such a remedy, the existence of a private cause of action for violations of the statute and the Rule is now well established. *Blue Chip Stamps* v. *Manor Drug Stores,* 421 U. S. 723, 730 (1975); *Affiliated Ute Citizens* v. *United States,* 406 U. S. 128, 150-154 (1972); *Superintendent of Insurance* v. *Bankers Life & Cas. Co.,* 404 U. S. 6, 13 n. 9 (1971). During the 30-year period since a private cause of action was first implied under §10(b) and Rule 10b-5, a substantial body of case law and commentary has developed as to its elements. Courts and commentators long have differed with regard to whether scienter is a necessary element of such a cause of action, or whether negligent conduct alone is sufficient.[17] In addressing this question, we turn first to the language of §10(b), for "[t]he starting point in every case involving construction of a statute is the language itself." *Blue Chip Stamps,* supra, at 756 (Powell, J., concurring); see *FTC* v. *Bunte Bros., Inc.,* 312 U. S. 349, 350 (1941).

A

Section 10(b) makes unlawful the use or employment of "any manipulative or deceptive device or contrivance" in contravention of Commission rules. The words "manipulative or deceptive" used in conjunction with "device or contrivance" strongly suggest that §10(b) was intended to proscribe knowing or intentional misconduct. See *SEC* v. *Texas Gulf Sulphur Co.,* 401 F. 2d 833, 868 (C. A. 2 1968) (Friendly, J., concurring), *cert. denied* sub nom. *Coates* v. *SEC,* 394 U. S. 976 (1969); Loss, Summary Remarks, 30 Bus. Law. 163, 165 (Special Issue 1975). See also *Kohn* v.

---

17 * * * Compare, e. g., Comment, Scienter and Rule 10b-5, 69 Col. L. Rev. 1057, 1080-1081 (1969); Note, Negligent Misrepresentations under Rule 10b-5, 32 U. Chi. L. Rev. 824, 839-844 (1965); Note, Securities Acts, 82 Harv. L. Rev. 938, 947 (1969); Note, Civil Liability Under Section 10B and Rule 10B-5: A Suggestion for Replacing the Doctrine of Privity, 74 Yale L. J. 658, 682-689 (1965), with, e. g., 3 L. Loss, Securities Regulation 1766 (2d ed. 1961); 6 id., at 3883-3885 (1969).

American Metal Climax, Inc., 458 F. 2d 255, 280 (C. A. 3 1972)
(Adams, J., concurring and dissenting).

In its *amicus curiae* brief, however, the Commission contends
that nothing in the language "manipulative or deceptive device or
contrivance" limits its operation to knowing or intentional practices.[18] In support of its view, the Commission cites the overall
congressional purpose in the 1933 and 1934 Acts to protect
investors against false and deceptive practices that might injure
them. See *Affiliated Ute Citizens* v. *United States*, supra, at 151;
Superintendent of Insurance v. *Bankers Life & Cas. Co.*, supra, at
11-12; *J. I. Case Co.* v. *Borak*, 377 U. S. 426, 432-433 (1964). See
also *SEC* v. *Capital Gains Res. Bur.*, 375 U. S. 180, 195 (1963).
The Commission then reasons that since the "effect" upon investors of given conduct is the same regardless of whether the conduct
is negligent or intentional, Congress must have intended to bar all
such practices and not just those done knowingly or intentionally.
The logic of this effect-oriented approach would impose liability
for wholly faultless conduct where such conduct results in harm to
investors, a result the Commission would be unlikely to support.
But apart from where its logic might lead, the Commission would
add a gloss to the operative language of the statute quite different
from its commonly accepted meaning. See, e. g., *Addison* v. *Holly
Hill Fruit Products, Inc.*, 322 U. S. 607, 617-618 (1944).[19] The

---

[18] The Commission would not permit recovery upon proof of negligence
in all cases. In order to harmonize civil liability under §10(b) with the express
civil remedies contained in the 1933 and 1934 Acts, the Commission would
limit the circumstances in which civil liability could be imposed for negligent
violation of Rule 10b-5 to situations in which (i) the defendant knew or
reasonably could foresee that the plaintiff would rely on his conduct, (ii) the
plaintiff did in fact so rely, and (iii) the amount of the plaintiff's damages
caused by the defendant's conduct was definite and ascertainable. Brief for
SEC as Amicus Curiae 23-33. The Commission concludes that the present
record does not establish these conditions since Ernst & Ernst could not
reasonably have foreseen that the financial statements of First Securities
would induce respondents to invest in the escrow accounts, respondents in
fact did not rely on Ernst & Ernst's audits, and the amount of respondents'
damages was unascertainable. Id., at 33-36. Respondents accept the Commission's basic analysis of the operative language of the statute and Rule,
but reject these additional requirements for recovery for negligent violations.

[19] "To let general words draw nourishment from their purpose is one
thing. To draw on some unexpressed spirit outside the bounds of the normal
meaning of words is quite another. * * * After all, legislation when not
expressed in technical terms is addressed to the common run of men and is
therefore to be understood according to the sense of the thing, as the
ordinary man has a right to rely on ordinary words addressed to him."
Addison v. Holly Hill Fruit Products, Inc., 322 U. S., at 617-618. See Frankfurter, Some Reflections on the Reading of Statutes, 47 Col. L. Rev. 527,
536-537 (1947).

argument simply ignores the use of the words "manipulative," "device," and "contrivance" — terms that make unmistakable a congressional intent to proscribe a type of conduct quite different from negligence.[20] Use of the word "manipulative" is especially significant. It is and was virtually a term of art when used in connection with securities markets. It connotes intentional or willful conduct designed to deceive or defraud investors by controlling or artificially affecting the price of securities.[21]

In addition to relying upon the Commission's argument with respect to the operative language of the statute, respondents contend that since we are dealing with "remedial legislation," *Tcherepnin* v. *Knight,* 389 U. S. 332, 336 (1967), it must be construed " 'not technically and restrictively, but flexibly to effectuate its remedial purposes.' " *Affiliated Ute Citizens* v. *United States,* 406 U. S. at 151, quoting *SEC* v. *Capital Gains Research Bureau,* supra, at 195. They argue that the "remedial purposes" of the Act demand a construction of §10(b) that embraces negligence as a standard of liability. But in seeking to accomplish its broad remedial goals, Congress did not adopt uniformly a negligence standard even as to express civil remedies. In some circumstances and with respect to certain classes of defendants, Congress did create express liability predicated upon a failure to exercise reasonable care. E. g., 1933 Act §11(b)(3)(B), 48 Stat. 82, as amended, 15 U. S. C. §77k(b)(3)(B) (liability of "experts," such as accountants, for misleading statements in portions of registration statements for which they are responsible). But in other situations good faith is an absolute defense. 1934 Act §18, 48 Stat. 897, as amended, 15 U. S. C. §78r (misleading statements in any document filed pursuant to the 1934 Act). And in still other circumstances Congress created express liability regardless of the defendant's fault, 1933 Act §11(a), 15 U. S. C. §77k(a) (issuer liability for misleading statements in the registration statement).

---

[20] Webster's International Dictionary (2d ed. 1934) defines "device" as "[t]hat which is devised, or formed by design; a contrivance; an invention; project; scheme; often, a scheme to deceive; a stratagem; an artifice," and "contrivance" in pertinent part as "[a] thing contrived or used in contriving; a scheme, plan, or artifice." In turn, "contrive" in pertinent part is defined as "[t]o devise; to plan; to plot * * * [t]o fabricate * * * design; invent * * * to scheme * * * ." The Commission also ignores the use of the terms "[t]o use or employ," language that is supportive of the view that Congress did not intend §10(b) to embrace negligent conduct.

[21] Webster's International Dictionary, supra, defines "manipulate" as "to manage or treat artfully or fraudulently; as to *manipulate* accounts * * * . 4. *Exchanges.* To force (prices) up or down, as by matched orders, wash sales, fictitious reports * * * ; to rig."

It is thus evident that Congress fashioned standards of fault in the express civil remedies in the 1933 and 1934 Acts on a particularized basis. Ascertainment of congressional intent with respect to the standard of liability created by a particular section of the Acts must therefore rest primarily on the language of that section. Where, as here, we deal with a judicially implied liability, the statutory language certainly is no less important. In view of the language of §10(b), which so clearly connotes intentional misconduct, and mindful that the language of a statute controls when sufficiently clear in its context, *United States* v. *Oregon,* 366 U. S. 643, 648 (1961); *Packard Motor Car Co.* v. *NLRB,* 330 U. S. 485, 492 (1947), further inquiry may be unnecessary. We turn now, nevertheless, to the legislative history of the 1934 Act to ascertain whether there is support for the meaning attributed to §10(b) by the Commission and respondents.

B

Although the extensive legislative history of the 1934 Act is bereft of any explicit explanation of Congress' intent, we think the relevant portions of that history support our conclusion that §10 (b) was addressed to practices that involve some element of scienter and cannot be read to impose liability for negligent conduct alone.

*   *   *

* * * The most relevant exposition of the provision that was to become §10(b) was by Thomas G. Corcoran, a spokesman for the drafters. Corcoran indicated:

> Subsection (c) [§9(c) of H. R. 7852 — later §10(b)][a] says, "Thou shalt not devise any other cunning devices."

*   *   *

> Of course subsection (c) is a catch-all clause to prevent manipulative devices. I do not think there is any objection to that kind of clause. The Commission should have the authority to deal with new manipulative devices. Hearings on H. R. 7852 and H. R. 8720 before the House Committee on Interstate and Foreign Commerce, 73d Cong., 2d Sess., 115 (1934).

This brief explanation of §10(b) by a spokesman for its drafters is significant. The section was described rightly as a "catchall"

---

[a] ED.: The bracketed material in this paragraph is Justice Powell's.

clause to enable the Commission "to deal with new manipulative [or cunning] devices." It is difficult to believe that any lawyer, legislative draftsman, or legislator would use these words if the intent was to create liability for merely negligent acts or omissions. Neither the legislative history nor the briefs supporting respondents identify any usage or authority for construing "manipulative [or cunning] devices" to include negligence.

*   *   *

c

The 1933 and 1934 Acts constitute interrelated components of the federal regulatory scheme governing transactions in securities. See *Blue Chip Stamps,* 421 U. S., at 727-730. As the Court indicated in *SEC* v. *National Securities, Inc.,* 393 U. S. 453, 466 (1969), "the interdependence of the various sections of the securities laws is certainly a relevant factor in any interpretation of the language Congress has chosen. . . . " Recognizing this, respondents and the Commission contrast §10(b) with other sections of the Acts to support their contention that civil liability may be imposed upon proof of negligent conduct. We think they misconceive the significance of the other provisions of the Acts.

The Commission argues that Congress has been explicit in requiring willful conduct when that was the standard of fault intended, citing §9 of the 1934 Act, 48 Stat. 889, 15 U. S. C. §78i, which generally proscribes manipulation of securities prices. * * *

The structure of the Acts does not support the Commission's argument. In each instance that Congress created express civil liability in favor of purchasers or sellers of securities it clearly specified whether recovery was to be premised on knowing or intentional conduct, negligence, or entirely innocent mistake. * * * The express recognition of a cause of action premised on negligent behavior in §11 stands in sharp contrast to the language of §10(b), and significantly undercuts the Commission's argument.

We also consider it significant that each of the express civil remedies in the 1933 Act allowing recovery for negligent conduct, see §§11, 12(2), 15, 15 U. S. C. §§77k, 77*l*(2), 77*o*, is subject to significant procedural restrictions not applicable under §10(b). Section 11(e) of the 1933 Act, for example, authorizes the court to require a plaintiff bringing a suit under §11, §12(2), or §15 thereof to post a bond for costs, including attorneys' fees, and in specified circumstances to assess costs at the conclusion of the litigation. Section 13 specifies a statute of limitations of one year from the time the violation was or should have been discovered, in no event to exceed three years from the time of offer or sale, applicable to actions brought under §11, §12(2), or §15. These restrictions, significantly, were imposed by amendments to the 1933 Act adopted as part of the 1934 Act. * * * We think these procedural limitations indicate that the judicially created private damages remedy under §10(b) — which has no comparable restrictions[29] — cannot be extended, consistently with the intent of Congress, to actions premised on negligent wrongdoing. Such extension would allow causes of action covered by §§11, 12(2), and 15 to be brought instead under §10(b) and thereby nullify the effectiveness of the carefully drawn procedural restrictions on these express actions. See, e. g., *Fischman v. Raytheon Mfg. Co.*, 188 F. 2d 783, 786-787 (C. A. 2 1951); *SEC v. Texas Gulf Sulphur Co.*, 401 F. 2d at 867-868 (Friendly, J., concurring); *Rosenberg v. Globe Aircraft Corp.*, 80 F. Supp. 123, 124 (E. D. Pa. 1948); 3 Loss, supra, n. 17, at 1787-1788; R. Jennings & H. Marsh, Securities Regulation 1070-1074 (3d ed. 1972). We would be unwilling to bring about this result absent substantial support in the legislative history, and there is none.[31]

D

We have addressed to this point, primarily the language and history of §10(b). The Commission contends, however, that subsections (b) and (c) of Rule 10b-5 are cast in language which — if standing alone — could encompass both intentional and negligent behavior. These subsections respectively provide that it is unlawful "[t]o make any untrue statement of a material fact or to omit to state a material fact necessary in order to make the statements made, in the light of the circumstances under which they were made, not misleading . . . " and "[t]o engage in any act, practice, or course of business which operates or would operate as a

---

[29] Since no statute of limitations is provided for civil actions under §10(b), the law of limitations of the forum State is followed as in other cases of judically implied remedies. See Holmberg v. Armbrecht, 327 U. S. 392, 395 (1946), and cases cited therein. Although it is not always certain which state statute of limitations should be followed, such statutes of limitations usually are longer than the period provided under §13. 3 Loss, supra, n. 17, at 1773-1774. * * *

[31] Section 18 of the 1934 Act creates a private cause of action against persons, such as accountants, who "make or cause to be made" materially misleading statements in reports or other documents filed with the Commission. 15 U. S. C. §78r. We need not consider the question whether a cause of action may be maintained under §10(b) on the basis of actions that would constitute a violation of §18. * * *

fraud or deceit upon any person. . . . " Viewed in isolation the language of subsection (b), and arguably that of subsection (c), could be read as proscribing, respectively, any type of material misstatement or omission, and any course of conduct, that has the effect of defrauding investors, whether the wrongdoing was intentional or not.

We note first that such a reading cannot be harmonized with the administrative history of the Rule, a history making clear that when the Commission adopted the Rule it was intended to apply only to activities that involved scienter.[32] More importantly, Rule 10b-5 was adopted pursuant to authority granted the Commission under §10(b). The rulemaking power granted to an administrative agency charged with the administration of a federal statute is not the power to make law. Rather, it is " 'the power to adopt regulations to carry into effect the will of Congress as expressed by the statute.' " *Dixon* v. *United States,* 381 U. S. 68, 74 (1965), quoting *Manhattan General Equipment Co.* v. *Commissioner,* 297 U. S. 129, 134 (1936). Thus, despite the broad view of the Rule advanced by the Commission in this case, its scope cannot exceed the power granted the Commission by Congress under §10(b). For the reasons stated above, we think the Commission's original interpretation of Rule 10b-5 was compelled by the language and history of §10(b) and related sections of the Acts. See, e. g., *Gerstle* v. *Gamble-Skogmo, Inc.,* 479 F. 2d 1281, 1299 (C. A. 2 1973); *Lanza* v. *Drexel & Co.,* 479 F. 2d 1277, 1304-1305 (C. A. 2 1973); *SEC* v. *Texas Gulf Sulphur Co.,* 401 F. 2d, at 868 (Friendly, J., concurring); 3 Loss, supra, n. 17, at 1766; 6 id., at 3883-3885. When a statute speaks so specifically in terms of manipulation and deception, and of implementing devices and contrivances — the commonly understood terminology of intentional wrongdoing — and

---

[32] Apparently the Rule was a hastily drafted response to a situation clearly involving intentional misconduct. * * * [See p. 821 supra.] There is no indication in the administrative history of the Rule that any of the subsections was intended to proscribe conduct not involving scienter. Indeed the Commission's release issued contemporaneously with the Rule explained:

> The Securities and Exchange Commission today announced the adoption of a rule prohibiting fraud by any person in connection with the purchase of securities. The previously existing rules against fraud in the purchase of securities applied only to brokers and dealers. The new rule closes a loophole in the protections against fraud administered by the Commission by prohibiting individuals or companies from buying securities if they engage in fraud in their purchase. SEC Release No. 3230 (May 21, 1942).

That same year, in its Annual Report, the Commission again stated that the purpose of the Rule was to protect investors against "fraud" * * * .

when its history reflects no more expansive intent, we are quite unwilling to extend the scope of the statute to negligent conduct.[33]

III

Recognizing that §10(b) and Rule 10b-5 might be held to require proof of more than negligent nonfeasance by Ernst & Ernst as a precondition to the imposition of civil liability, respondents further contend that the case should be remanded for trial under whatever standard is adopted. Throughout the lengthy history of this case respondents have proceeded on a theory of liability premised on negligence, specifically disclaiming that Ernst & Ernst had engaged in fraud or intentional misconduct. In these circumstances, we think it inappropriate to remand the action for further proceedings.

The judgment of the Court of Appeals is reversed.

MR. JUSTICE STEVENS took no part in the consideration or decision of this case.

---

[33] As we find the language and history of §10(b) dispositive of the appropriate standard of liability, there is no occasion to examine the additional considerations of "policy," set forth by the parties, that may have influenced the lawmakers in their formulation of the statute. We do note that the standard urged by respondents would significantly broaden the class of plaintiffs who may seek to impose liability upon accountants and other experts who perform services or express opinions with respect to matters under the Acts. Last Term, in *Blue Chip Stamps*, 421 U. S., at 747-748, the Court pertinently observed:

> While much of the devolpment of the law of deceit has been the elimination of artificial barriers to recovery on just claims, we are not the first court to express concern that the inexorable broadening of the class of plaintiff who may sue in this area of the law will ultimately result in more harm than good. In Ultramares Corp. v. Touche, 255 N. Y. 170, 174 N. E. 441 (1931), Chief Judge Cardozo observed with respect to a liability in an indeterminate amount for an indeterminate time to an indeterminate class:
>
> > "The hazards of a business conducted on these terms are so extreme as to enkindle doubt whether a flaw may not exist in the implication of a duty that exposes to these consequences." Id., at 179-180, 174 N. E., at 444.

This case, on its facts, illustrates the extreme reach of the standard urged by respondents. As investors in transactions initiated by Nay, not First Securities, they were not foreseeable users of the financial statements prepared by Ernst & Ernst. Respondents conceded that they did not rely on either these financial statements or Ernst & Ernst's certificates of opinion. * * * The class of persons eligible to benefit from such a standard, though small in this case, could be numbered in the thousands in other cases. Acceptance of respondents' view would extend to new frontiers the "hazards" of rendering expert advice under the Acts, raising serious policy questions not yet addressed by Congress.

Mr. Justice Blackmun, with whom Mr. Justice Brennan joins, dissenting.

Once again — see *Blue Chip Stamps* v. *Manor Drug Stores,* 421 U. S. 723, 730 (1975)[b] — the Court interprets §10(b) of the Securities Exchange Act of 1934, 15 U. S. C. §78j(b), and the Securities and Exchange Commission's Rule 10b-5, 17 C. F. R. §240.10b-5 (1975), restrictively and narrowly and thereby stultifies recovery for the victim. This time the Court does so by confining the statute and the Rule to situations where the defendant has "scienter," that is, the "intent to deceive, manipulate, or defraud." Sheer negligence, the Court says, is not within the reach of the statute and the Rule, and was not contemplated when the great reforms of 1933, 1934, and 1942 were effectuated by Congress and the Commission.

Perhaps the Court is right, but I doubt it. The Government and the Commission doubt it too, as is evidenced by the thrust of the brief filed by the Solicitor General on behalf of the Commission as *amicus curiae*. The Court's opinion, to be sure, has a certain technical consistency about it. It seems to me, however, that an investor can be victimized just as much by negligent conduct as by positive deception, and that it is not logical to drive a wedge between the two, saying that Congress clearly intended the one but certainly not the other.

No one questions the fact that the respondents here were the victims of an intentional securities fraud practiced by Leston B. Nay. What is at issue, of course, is the petitioner accountant firm's involvement and that firm's responsibility under Rule 10b-5. The language of the Rule [Justice Blackmun here quotes Clauses (b) and (c)] seems to me, clearly and succinctly, to prohibit negligent as well as intentional conduct of the kind proscribed, to extend beyond common-law fraud, and to apply to negligent omission and commission. This is consistent with Congress' intent, repeatedly recognized by the Court, that securities legislation enacted for the purpose of avoiding frauds be construed "not technically and restrictively, but flexibly to effectuate its remedial purposes." *SEC* v. *Capital Gains Research Bureau,* 375 U. S. 180, 195 (1963); *Superintendent of Insurance* v. *Bankers Life & Cas. Co.,* 404 U. S. 6, 12 (1971); *Affiliated Ute Citizens* v. *United States,* 406 U. S. 128, 151 (1972).

On motion for summary judgment, therefore, the respondents' allegations, in my view, were sufficient, and the District Court's

---

[b] Ed.: This case is set out infra p. 904.

dismissal of the action was improper to the extent that the dismissal rested on the proposition that suit could not be maintained under §10(b) and Rule 10b-5 for mere negligence. * * *

The critical importance of the auditing accountant's role in insuring full disclosure cannot be overestimated. The SEC has emphasized that in certifying statements the accountant's duty "is to safeguard the public interest, not that of his client." *In re Touche, Niven, Bailey & Smart,* 37 S. E. C. 629, 670-671 (1957). "In our complex society the accountant's certificate and the lawyer's opinion can be instruments for inflicting pecuniary loss more potent than the chisel or the crowbar." *United States* v. *Benjamin,* 328 F. 2d 854, 863 (C. A. 2), *cert. denied* sub nom. *Howard* v. *United States,* 377 U. S. 953 (1964). In this light, the initial inquiry into whether Ernst & Ernst's preparation and certification of the financial statements of First Securities Company of Chicago were negligent, because of the failure to perceive Nay's extraordinary mail rule, and in other alleged respects, and thus whether Rule 10b-5 was violated, should not be thwarted.

But the Court today decides that it is to be thwarted, and so once again it rests with Congress to rephrase and to re-enact, if investor victims, such as these, are ever to have relief under the federal securities laws that I thought had been enacted for their broad, needed, and deserving benefit.

————————

The majority opinion in *Ernst & Ernst* is puzzling, and it leaves as many questions as it answers:

(1) Insofar as it construes the "manipulative or deceptive device or contrivance" of §10(b) as requiring that some sort of scienter element be read into Rule 10b-5, the opinion is profoundly correct. The western Circuits that read Clause (2) literally as requiring only proof of a misstatement or a half-truth were not sufficiently sensitive to the fact that they were dealing with a *rule,* which must be construed against the enabling provision of the statute.[97] Consequently, just as the courts will construe a *statute* if at all possible so as to avoid holding it *unconstitutional,* they should construe a *rule* if at all possible so as to avoid holding it *ultra vires.* With respect, it is no answer to say, as Justice Blackmun did following the SEC's contention as *amicus curiae,* that "an investor can be victimized just as much by negligent conduct as by positive deception."[98] A pedestrian fatally hit by a negligent driver is just as

———

[97] See, e. g., Ellis v. Carter, 291 F. 2d 270 (9th Cir. 1961).

[98] 425 U. S. at 216, supra p. 883 (Blackmun, J.); id. at 198, supra p. 876 (description of SEC's reasoning by Powell, J.).

dead as if the driver had been roaring drunk, but that does not convict the negligent driver of manslaughter.

(2) It is necessary, therefore, that "some sort of watered-down scienter element" be read into Clause (2).[99] But why — in construing a fraud provision that was designed to *raise* the standards of securities trading, and that the courts have repeatedly interpreted as not limited to circumstances that would amount to common law deceit[100] — did the majority opinion reach back in history to the strictest common law definition: not merely knowing falsity but "intent to deceive, manipulate, or defraud"?[101]

(3) What is even more strange is that the Court did not have to define scienter at all. All it had to hold was that *negligence* did *not* suffice; for negligence is all that was alleged.[102] Indeed, one might persuasively argue that the *ratio decidendi* is even more limited: that, whatever may be the degree of culpability contemplated by Rule 10b-5 with respect to a *primary* violator, an accounting firm is not *secondarily* liable for mere negligence.[103] Therefore, as law students are taught to read cases, all the talk about the meaning of scienter is interesting but *obiter* — although it is easier for an academic than for a lower court judge to say that in the face of the majority opinion as a whole.

(4) What has just been said *is* reflected to an extent in a footnote — the famous note 12, with its invitation to the lower federal courts to consider whether "recklessness" might not suffice "in some circumstances" after all.[104] That leaves the question of inter-

---

[99] 3 Loss 1766; 6 id. 3884.

[100] See p. 809 supra.

[101] In common law deceit, as the Supreme Court stated *obiter* in SEC v. Capital Gains Research Bureau, Inc., 375 U. S. 180, 192 n. 39 (1963), an action for injunction under §206 of the Investment Advisers Act, "the intent which must be established need not be an intent to cause injury to the client"; all that is required is proof that the defendant intended action in reliance on the truth of the misrepresentation. That is to say, intent to *cause harm* is of no importance at common law except with respect to the issue of punitive damages; the intent to deceive or mislead or convey a false impression that is implicit in the scienter concept goes simply to the matter of belief, or absence of belief, that the representation is true. Prosser, Law of Torts 700 (4th ed. 1971).

[102] See Aaron v. SEC, 446 U. S. 680, 690 (1980), infra p. 887; United States v. Chiarella, 588 F. 2d 1358, 1370-71 (2d Cir. 1978), *rev'd on other grounds* sub nom. Chiarella v. United States, 445 U. S. 222 (1980).

[103] See SEC v. Coffey, 493 F. 2d 1304, 1315-16 (6th Cir. 1974), *cert. denied,* 420 U. S. 908; cf. Code §1724(b). In Robinson v. Heilman, 563 F. 2d 1304, 1308 (9th Cir. 1977), the court held that *Hochfelder* was equally applicable to a direct participant — though, "the closer the relationship of the person charged to the corporation and the greater his participation in the transactions attacked, the easier it will be to prove the requisite scienter."

[104] The invitation has been accepted. Coleco Industries, Inc. v. Berman, 567 F. 2d 569, 574 (3d Cir. 1977); Rolf v. Eastman Dillon & Co., Inc., 570

preting "reckless." Several Circuits have followed the rather strict approach taken by the Seventh Circuit in 1977: "In view of the Supreme Court's analysis in *Hochfelder* of the statutory scheme of implied private remedies and express remedies, the definition of 'reckless behavior' should not be a liberal one lest any discernible distinction between 'scienter' and 'negligence' be obliterated for these purposes. We believe 'reckless' in these circumstances comes closer to being a lesser form of intent than merely a greater degree of ordinary negligence."[105]

At the same time, there is authority that *Hochfelder* did not "establish a standard of specific intent to defraud"[106] unless there is a fiduciary relationship;[107] that the plaintiff need not prove knowledge of *illegality*;[108] and that recklessness connotes "carelessness approaching indifference"[109] (one might say "negligence plus" rather than the Seventh Circuit's "intent minus").

About all that can be said with confidence is that "the standard falls somewhere between intent and negligence."[110]

(5) *Query* whether the reference in Rule 15c1-2(b) to a "statement or omission [that] is made with knowledge or reasonable grounds to believe that it is untrue or misleading" adequately reflects — phrased as it is in the alternative — the §15(c)(1) test in terms of "any manipulative, deceptive, or other fraudulent device or contrivance."

F. 2d 38, 46 (2d Cir. 1978) (at least when defendant owed a fiduciary duty); McLean v. Alexander, 599 F. 2d 1190, 1197 (5th Cir. 1979); Hackbart v. Holmes, 675 F. 2d 1114 (9th Cir. 1982); Dirks v. SEC, 681 F. 2d 824, 844 (D. C. Cir. 1982), *cert. granted,* 103 S. Ct. 371 ("the overwhelming rule in the Courts of Appeals").

[105] Sanders v. John Nuveen & Co., Inc., 554 F. 2d 790, 793 (7th Cir. 1977); see also Pegasus Fund, Inc. v. Laraneta, 617 F. 2d 1335, 1340-41 (9th Cir. 1980); Broad v. Rockwell Int'l Corp., 614 F. 2d 418, 440 (5th Cir. *en banc* 1981); G. A. Thompson & Co. v. Partridge, 636 F. 2d 945, 961 (5th Cir. 1981) ("severe recklessness"); but cf. Sunstrand Corp v. Sun Chemical Corp., 553 F. 2d 1033, 1044 (7th Cir., 1977), *cert. denied,* 434 U. S. 875 (in holding that reckless *nondisclosure* suffices, court considered it "highly inappropriate to construe the Rule 10b-5 remedy to be more restrictive in substantive scope than its common law analogs").

[106] United States v. Chiarella, 588 F. 2d 1358, 1370 (2d Cir. 1978), *rev'd on other grounds* sub nom. Chiarella v. United States, 445 U. S. 222 (1980).

[107] Edwards & Hanly v. Wells Fargo Securities Clearance Corp., 602 F. 2d 478, 485 (2d Cir. 1979).

[108] Arthur Lipper Corp. v. SEC, 547 F. 2d 171, 180-81 (2d Cir. 1976), *rehearing en banc denied,* 551 F. 2d 915 (2d Cir. 1977); SEC v. Falstaff Brewing Corp., 629 F. 2d 62, 76-77 (D. C. Cir. 1980).

[109] Hoffman v. Estabrook & Co., Inc., 587 F. 2d 509, 516 (1st Cir. 1978); see also Bell v. Cameron Meadows Land Co., 669 F. 2d 1278, 1282-83 (9th Cir. 1982).

[110] Mansbach v. Prescott, Ball & Turben, 598 F. 2d 1017, 1025 n. 36 (6th Cir. 1979).

(6) For a while the Commission fought a rearguard action in reliance on *Hochfelder's* expressly leaving the scienter question open in injunctive actions.[111] Then came:

AARON v. SECURITIES AND EXCHANGE COMMISSION
Supreme Court of the United States, 1980
446 U. S. 680

MR. JUSTICE STEWART delivered the opinion of the Court.

The issue in this case is whether the Securities and Exchange Commission (Commission) is required to establish scienter as an element of a civil enforcement action to enjoin violations of §17(a) of the Securities Act of 1933 (1933 Act), §10(b) of the Securities Exchange Act of 1934 (1934 Act), and Commission Rule 10b-5 promulgated under that section of the 1934 Act.

I

When the events giving rise to this enforcement proceeding occurred, the petitioner was a managerial employee at E. L. Aaron & Co. (the firm), a registered broker-dealer with its principal office in New York City. Among other responsibilities at the firm, the petitioner was charged with supervising the sales made by its registered representatives and maintaining the so-called "due diligence" files for those securities in which the firm served as a market maker. One such security was the common stock of Lawn-A-Mat Chemical & Equipment Corp. (Lawn-A-Mat), a company engaged in the business of selling lawn-care franchises and supplying its franchisees with products and equipment.

Between November 1974 and September 1975, two registered representatives of the firm, Norman Schreiber and Donald Jacobson, conducted a sales campaign in which they repeatedly made false and misleading statements in an effort to solicit orders for the purchase of Lawn-A-Mat common stock. * * *

* * *

In February 1976, the Commission filed a complaint in the District Court for the Southern District of New York against the

---

There is authority that failure to profit personally from the fraudulent scheme (corrupt payments abroad) does not preclude scienter. Cramer v. General Telephone & Electronics Corp., 582 F. 2d 259, 273 (3d Cir. 1978). There is also contrasting authority that investment of one's own money tends to negative scienter since it "belies any known or obvious danger." Hoffman v. Estabrook & Co., Inc., 587 F. 2d 509, 517 (1st Cir. 1978).

[111] 425 U. S. at 193 n. 12.

petitioner and seven other defendants in connection with the offer and sale of Lawn-A-Mat common stock. In seeking preliminary and final injunctive relief pursuant to §20(b) of the 1933 Act and §21(d) of the 1934 Act, the Commission alleged that the petitioner had violated and aided and abetted violations of three provisions — §17(a) of the 1933 Act, §10(b) of the 1934 Act, and Commission Rule 10b-5 promulgated under that section of the 1934 Act. The gravamen of the charges against the petitioner was that he knew or had reason to know that the employees under his supervision were engaged in fraudulent practices, but failed to take adequate steps to prevent those practices from continuing. Before commencement of the trial, all the defendants except the petitioner consented to the entry of permanent injunctions against them.

[The District Court concluded that the petitioner had acted with scienter and entered an injunction.]

The Court of Appeals for the Second Circuit affirmed the judgment. 605 F. 2d 612. Declining to reach the question whether the petitioner's conduct would support a finding of scienter, the Court of Appeals held instead that when the Commission is seeking injunctive relief, "proof of negligence alone will suffice" to establish a violation of §17(a), §10(b), and Rule 10b-5. Id., at 619. With regard to §10(b) and Rule 10b-5, the Court of Appeals noted that this Court's opinion in *Ernst & Ernst* v. *Hochfelder*, 425 U. S. 185, which held that an allegation of scienter is necessary to state a private cause of action for damages under §10(b) and Rule 10b-5, had expressly reserved the question whether scienter must be alleged in a suit for injunctive relief brought by the Commission. Id., at 194, n. 12. The conclusion of the Court of Appeals that the scienter requirement of *Hochfelder* does not apply to Commission enforcement proceedings was said to find support in the language of §10(b), the legislative history of the 1934 Act, the relationship between §10(b) and the overall enforcement scheme of the securities laws, and the "compelling distinctions between private damage actions and government injunction actions."[3] For

[3] The Court of Appeals observed that its previous decisions had required scienter in private damages actions under §10(b) even before this Court's decision in the *Hochfelder* case, but also had "uniformly * * * held that the language and history of the section [did] not require a showing of scienter in an injunction enforcement action brought by the Commission." 605 F. 2d, at 620-621. This distinction had been premised on the fact that the two types of suits under §10(b) advance different goals: actions for damages are designed to provide compensation to individual investors, whereas suits for injunctive relief serve to provide maximum protection for the investing public. In the present case, the Court of Appeals, relying on its reasoning in previous cases, concluded that "[i]n view of the policy considerations underlying the securities acts, * * * the increased effectiveness of

its holding that scienter is not a necessary element in a Commission injunctive action to enforce §17(a), the Court of Appeals relied on its earlier decision in *SEC* v. *Coven*, 581 F. 2d 1020. There that court had noted that the language of §17(a) contains nothing to suggest a requirement of intent and that, in enacting §17(a), Congress had considered a scienter requirement, but instead "opted for liability without willfulness, intent to defraud, or the like." Id., at 1027-1028.[4] Finally, the Court of Appeals affirmed the District Court's holding that, under all the facts and circumstances of this case, the Commission was entitled to injunctive relief. 605 F. 2d, at 623-624.

We granted certiorari to resolve the conflict in the federal courts as to whether the Commission is required to establish scienter — an intent on the part of the defendant to deceive, manipulate, or defraud[5] — as an element of a Commission enforcement action to enjoin violations of §17(a), §10(b), and Rule 10b-5. 444 U. S. 914.

II

[Justice Stewart here sets out §17(a), §10(b), and Rule 10b-5.]

The civil enforcement mechanism for these provisions consists of both express and implied remedies. One express remedy is a suit by the Commission for injunctive relief [under §20(b) of the 1933 Act or §21(d) of the 1934 Act].

Another facet of civil enforcement is a private cause of action for money damages. This remedy, unlike the Commission injunctive action, is not expressly authorized by statute, but rather has been judicially implied. See *Ernst & Ernst* v. *Hochfelder*, 425 U. S., at 196-197. Although this Court has repeatedly assumed the existence of an implied cause of action under §10(b) and Rule 10b-5, see *Ernst & Ernst* v. *Hochfelder*, supra; *Blue Chip Stamps* v. *Manor Drug Stores*, 421 U. S. 723, 730; *Affiliated Ute Citizens* v. *United States*, 406 U. S. 128, 150-154; *Superintendent of Insurance* v. *Bankers Life & Cas. Co.*, 404 U. S. 6, 13, n. 9, it has not had occasion to address the question whether a private cause of action

---

government enforcement actions predicated on a showing of negligence alone outweigh[s] the danger of potential harm to those enjoined from violating the securities laws." Id., at 621.

[4] Neither the District Court nor the Court of Appeals gave any indication of which subsection or subsections of §17(a) of the 1933 Act the petitioner had violated.

[5] The term "scienter" is used throughout this opinion, as it was in Ernst & Ernst v. Hochfelder, 425 U. S. 185, 194, n. 12, to refer to "a mental state embracing intent to deceive, manipulate, or defraud." We have no occasion here to address the question, reserved in *Hochfelder*, ibid., whether, under some circumstances, scienter may also include reckless behavior.

exists under §17(a). See *Blue Chip Stamps* v. *Manor Drug Stores,* supra, at 733, n. 6.

The issue here is whether the Commission in seeking injunctive relief either under §20(b) for violations of §17(a), or under §21(d) for violations of §10(b) or Rule 10b-5, is required to establish scienter. Resolution of that issue could depend upon (1) the substantive provisions of §17(a), §10(b), and Rule 10b-5, or (2) the statutory provisions authorizing injunctive relief "upon a proper showing," §20(b) and §21(d). We turn to an examination of each to determine the extent to which they may require proof of scienter.

A

*   *   *

In our view, the rationale of *Hochfelder* ineluctably leads to the conclusion that scienter is an element of a violation of §10(b) and Rule 10b-5, regardless of the identity of the plaintiff or the nature of the relief sought. Two of the three factors relied upon in *Hochfelder* — the language of §10(b) and its legislative history — are applicable whenever a violation of §10(b) or Rule 10b-5 is alleged, whether in a private cause of action for damages or in a Commission injunctive action under §21(d). In fact, since *Hochfelder* involved an implied cause of action that was not within the contemplation of the Congress that enacted §10(b), id., at 196, it would be quite anomalous in a case like the present one, involving as it does the express remedy Congress created for §10(b) violations, not to attach at least as much significance to the fact that the statutory language and its legislative history support a scienter requirement.

The Commission argues that *Hochfelder*, which involved a private cause of action for damages, is not a proper guide in construing §10(b) in the present context of a Commission enforcement action for injunctive relief. We are urged instead to look to *SEC* v. *Capital Gains Research Bureau,* 375 U. S. 180. That case involved a suit by the Commission for injunctive relief to enforce the prohibition in §206(2) of the Investment Advisers Act of 1940, 15 U. S. C. §80b-6, against any act or practice of an investment adviser that "operates as a fraud or deceit upon any client or prospective client." The injunction sought in *Capital Gains* was to compel disclosure of a practice known as "scalping," whereby an investment adviser purchases shares of a given security for his own account shortly before recommending the security to investors as a long-term investment, and then promptly sells the shares at a profit upon the rise in their market value following the recommendation.

The issue in *Capital Gains* was whether in an action for injunctive relief for violations of §206(2) the Commission must prove that the defendant acted with an intent to defraud. The Court held that a showing of intent was not required. This conclusion rested upon the fact that the legislative history revealed that the "Investment Advisers Act of 1940 . . . reflects a congressional recognition 'of the delicate fiduciary nature of an investment advisory relationship,' as well as a congressional intent to eliminate, or at least to expose, all conflicts of interest which might incline an investment adviser — consciously or unconsciously — to render advice which was not disinterested." 375 U. S., at 191-192 (footnote omitted). To require proof of intent, the Court reasoned, would run counter to the expressed intent of Congress.

The Court added that its conclusion was "not in derogation of the common law of fraud." Id., at 192. Although recognizing that intent to defraud was a necessary element at common law to recover money damages for fraud in an arm's-length transaction, the Court emphasized that the Commission's action was not a suit for damages, but rather a suit for an injunction in which the relief sought was the "mild prophylactic" of requiring a fiduciary to disclose his transactions in stocks he was recommending to his clients. Id., at 193. The Court observed that it was not necessary in a suit for "equitable or prophylactic relief" to establish intent, for "[f]raud has a broader meaning in equity [than at law] and intention to defraud or to misrepresent is not a necessary element." Ibid., quoting W. De Funiak, Handbook of Modern Equity 235 (2d ed. 1956). Moreover, it was not necessary, the Court said, in a suit against a fiduciary such as an investment adviser, to establish all the elements of fraud that would be required in a suit against a party to an arm's-length transaction. Finally, the Court took cognizance of a "growing recognition by common-law courts that the doctrines of fraud and deceit which develop around transactions involving land and other tangible items of wealth are ill-suited to the sale of such intangibles as advice and securities, and that, accordingly, the doctrines must be adapted to the merchandise in issue." 375 U. S., at 194. Unwilling to assume that Congress was unaware of these developments at common law, the Court concluded that they "reinforce[d]" its holding that Congress had not sought to require a showing of intent in actions to enjoin violations of §206(2). Id., at 195.

The Commission argues that the emphasis in *Capital Gains*

upon the distinction between fraud at law and in equity should guide a construction of §10(b) in this suit for injunctive relief. We cannot, however, draw such guidance from *Capital Gains* for several reasons. First, wholly apart from its discussion of the judicial treatment of "fraud" at law and in equity, the Court in *Capital Gains* found strong support in the legislative history for its conclusion that the Commission need not demonstrate intent to enjoin practices in violation of §206(2). By contrast, as the Court in *Hochfelder* noted, the legislative history of §10(b) points towards a scienter requirement. Second, it is quite clear that the language in question in *Capital Gains*, "any . . . practice . . . which *operates* as a fraud or deceit," (emphasis added) focuses not on the intent of the investment adviser, but rather on the effect of a particular practice.[a] Again, by contrast, the Court in *Hochfelder* found that the language of §10(b) — particularly the terms "manipulative," "device," and "contrivance," — clearly refers to "knowing or intentional misconduct." Finally, insofar as *Capital Gains* involved a statutory provision regulating the special fiduciary relationship between an investment adviser and his client, the Court there was dealing with a situation in which intent to defraud would not have been required even in a common-law action for money damages. Section 10(b), unlike the provision at issue in *Capital Gains*, applies with equal force to both fiduciary and nonfiduciary transactions in securities. It is our view, in sum, that the controlling precedent here is not *Capital Gains*, but rather *Hochfelder*. Accordingly, we conclude that scienter is a necessary element of a violation of §10(b) and Rule 10b-5.

B

In determining whether proof of scienter is a necessary element of a violation of §17(a), there is less precedential authority in this Court to guide us. But the controlling principles are well settled. Though cognizant that "Congress intended securities legislation enacted for the purpose of avoiding frauds to be construed 'not technically and restrictively, but flexibly to effectuate its remedial purposes,'" *Affiliated Ute Citizens* v. *United States*, 406 U. S., at 151, quoting *SEC* v. *Capital Gains Research Bureau*, 375 U. S., at 195, the Court has also noted that "generalized references to the 'remedial purposes'" of the securities laws "will not justify reading a provision 'more broadly than its language and the statutory

---

[a] ED.: This, of course, is also the language of the third clause of §17(a) and Rule 10b-5.

scheme reasonably permit.' "   *Touche Ross & Co.* v. *Redington,* 442 U. S. 560, 578, quoting, *SEC* v. *Sloan,* 436 U. S. 103, 116. Thus, if the language of a provision of the securities laws is sufficiently clear in its context and not at odds with the legislative history, it is unnecessary "to examine the additional considerations of 'policy' . . . that may have influenced the lawmakers in their formulation of the statute." *Ernst & Ernst* v. *Hochfelder,* 425 U. S., at 214, n. 33.

The language of §17(a) strongly suggests that Congress contemplated a scienter requirement under §17(a)(1), but not under §17(a)(2) or §17(a)(3). The language of §17(a)(1), which makes it unlawful "to employ any device, scheme, or artifice to defraud," plainly evinces an intent on the part of Congress to proscribe only knowing or intentional misconduct. Even if it be assumed that the term "defraud" is ambiguous, given its varied meanings at law and in equity, the terms "device," "scheme," and "artifice" all connote knowing or intentional practices. Indeed, the term "device," which also appears in §10(b), figured prominently in the Court's conclusion in *Hochfelder* that the plain meaning of §10 (b) embraces a scienter requirement. Id., at 199.

By contrast, the language of §17(a)(2), which prohibits any person from obtaining money or property "by means of any untrue statement of a material fact or any omission to state a material fact," is devoid of any suggestion whatsoever of a scienter requirement. As a well-known commentator has noted, "[t]here is nothing on the face of Clause (2) itself which smacks of scienter or intent to defraud." 3 L. Loss, Securities Regulation 1442 (2d ed. 1961). In fact, this Court in *Hochfelder* pointed out that the similar language of Rule 10b-5(b) "could be read as proscribing . . . any type of material misstatement or omission . . . that has the effect of defrauding investors, whether the wrongdoing was intentional or not." 425 U. S., at 212.

Finally, the language of §17(a)(3), under which it is unlawful for any person "to engage in any transaction, practice, or course of business which *operates* or *would operate* as a fraud or deceit," (emphasis added) quite plainly focuses upon the *effect* of particular conduct on members of the investing public, rather than upon the culpability of the person responsible. This reading follows directly from *Capital Gains,* which attributed to a similarly worded provision in §206(2) of the Investment Advisers Act of 1940 a meaning that does not require a "showing [of] deliberate dishonesty as a condition precedent to protecting investors." 375 U. S., at 200.

It is our view, in sum, that the language of §17(a) requires scienter under §17(a)(1), but not under §17(a)(2) or §17(a)(3). Although the parties have urged the Court to adopt a uniform culpability requirement for the three subparagraphs of §17(a), the language of the section is simply not amenable to such an interpretation. This is not the first time that this Court has had occasion to emphasize the distinctions among the three subparagraphs of §17(a). In *United States* v. *Naftalin,* 441 U. S. 768, 774, the Court noted that each subparagraph of §17(a) "proscribes a distinct category of misconduct. Each succeeding prohibition is meant to cover additional kinds of illegalities — not to narrow the reach of the prior sections." (Footnote omitted.) Indeed, since Congress drafted §17(a) in such a manner as to compel the conclusion that scienter is required under one subparagraph but not under the other two, it would take a very clear expression in the legislative history of congressional intent to the contrary to justify the conclusion that the statute does not mean what it so plainly seems to say.

We find no such expression of congressional intent in the legislative history. * * *

＊   ＊   ＊

* * * It seems clear, therefore, that the legislative history, albeit ambiguous, may be read in a manner entirely consistent with the plain meaning of §17(a).[18] In the absence of a conflict between reasonably plain meaning and legislative history, the words of the statute must prevail.[19]

C

There remains to be determined whether the provisions authorizing injunctive relief, §20(b) of the 1933 Act and §21(d) of the

[18] The Commission, in further support of its view that scienter is not required under any of the subparagraphs of §17(a), points out that §17(a) was patterned upon New York's Martin Act, N. Y. Gen. Bus. Law §§352-353 (Consol. 1921), and that the New York Court of Appeals had construed the Martin Act as not requiring a showing of scienter as a predicate for injunctive relief by the New York Attorney General. People v. Federated Radio Corp., 244 N. Y. 33, 154 N. E. 655 (1926). But, in the absence of any indication that Congress was even aware of the *Federated Radio* decision, much less that it approved of that decision, it cannot fairly be inferred that Congress intended not only to adopt the language of the Martin Act, but also a state judicial interpretation of that statute at odds with the plain meaning of the language Congress enacted as §17(a)(1).

[19] Since the language and legislative history of §17(a) are dispositive, we

1934 Act, modify the substantive provisions at issue in this case so far as scienter is concerned.

The language and legislative history of §20(b) and §21(d) both indicate that Congress intended neither to add to nor to detract from the requisite showing of scienter under the substantive provisions at issue. Sections 20(b) and 21(d) provide that the Commission may seek injunctive relief whenever it appears that a person "is engaged or [is] about to engage in any acts or practices" constituting a violation of the 1933 or 1934 Act or regulations promulgated thereunder and that, "upon a proper showing," a district court shall grant the injunction. The elements of "a proper showing" thus include, at a minimum, proof that a person is engaged in or is about to engage in a substantive violation of either one of the Acts or of the regulations promulgated thereunder. Accordingly, when scienter is an element of the substantive violation sought to be enjoined, it must be proved before an injunction may issue. But with respect to those provisions such as §17(a)(2) and §17(a)(3), which may be violated even in the absence of scienter, nothing on the face of §20(b) or §21(d) purports to impose an independent requirement of scienter. And there is nothing in the legislative history of either provision to suggest a contrary legislative intent.

This is not to say, however, that scienter has no bearing at all on whether a district court should enjoin a person violating or about to violate §17(a)(2) or §17(a)(3). In cases where the Commission is seeking to enjoin a person "*about* to engage in any acts or practices which . . . *will* constitute" a violation of those provisions, the Commission must establish a sufficient evidentiary predicate to show that such future violation may occur. See *SEC* v. *Commonwealth Chemical Securities, Inc.,* 574 F. 2d 90, 98-100 (C. A. 2 1978) (Friendly, J.); 3 L. Loss, Securities Regulation, at 1976. An important factor in this regard is the degree of intentional wrongdoing evident in a defendant's past conduct. See *SEC* v. *Wills,* 472 F. Supp. 1250, 1273-1275 (D. C. 1978). Moreover, as the Commission recognizes, a district court may consider scienter or lack of it as one of the aggravating or mitigating factors to be taken into account in exercising its equitable discretion in deciding whether or not to grant injunctive relief. And the proper exercise of equitable discretion is necessary to ensure a "nice adjustment and reconciliation between the public interest and private needs." *Hecht Co.* v. *Bowles,* 321 U. S. 321, 329.

---

have no occasion to address the "policy" arguments advanced by the parties. See *Ernst & Ernst* v. *Hochfelder,* 425 U. S., at 214, n. 33.

III

For the reasons stated in this opinion, we hold that the Commission is required to establish scienter as an element of a civil enforcement action to enjoin violations of §17(a)(1) of the 1933 Act, §10(b) of the 1934 Act, and Rule 10b-5 promulgated under that section of the 1934 Act. We further hold that the Commission need not establish scienter as an element of an action to enjoin violations of §17(a)(2) and §17(a)(3) of the 1933 Act. The Court of Appeals affirmed the issuance of the injunction in this case in the misapprehension that it was not necessary to find scienter in order to suport an injunction under any of the provisions in question. Accordingly, the judgment of the Court of Appeals is vacated, and the case is remanded to that court for further proceedings consistent with this opinion.

It is so ordered.

Mr. Chief Justice Burger, concurring.

I join the opinion of the Court and write separately to make three points:

(1) No matter what mental state §10(b) and §17(a) were to require, it is clear that the District Court was correct here in entering an injunction against petitioner. * * * The District Court's findings (a) that petitioner "intentionally failed" to terminate the fraud and (b) that his conduct was reasonably likely to repeat itself find abundant support in the record. In my view, the Court of Appeals could well have affirmed on that ground alone.

(2) I agree that §10(b) and §17(a)(1) require scienter but that §17(a)(2) and §17(a)(3) do not. I recognize, of course, that this holding "drives a wedge between [sellers and buyers]ᵇ and says that henceforth only the seller's negligent misrepresentations may be enjoined." Post, at 715 (Blackmun, J., dissenting). But it is not this Court that "drives a wedge"; Congress has done that. The Court's holding is compelled in large measure by *Ernst & Ernst* v. *Hochfelder*, 425 U. S. 185 (1976), and gives effect to congressional intent as manifested in the language of the statutes and their histories. If, as intimated, the result is "bad" public policy, that is the concern of Congress where changes can be made.

(3) It bears mention that this dispute, though pressed vigorously by both sides, may be much ado about nothing. This is so because of the requirement in injunctive proceedings of a showing that "there is a reasonable likelihood that the wrong will be repeated."

ᵇ Ed.: The bracketed material is the Chief Justice's.

SEC v. *Manor Nursing Centers, Inc.,* 458 F. 2d 1082, 1100 (C. A. 2 1975). Accord, *SEC* v. *Keller Corp.,* 323 F. 2d 397, 402 (C. A. 7 1963). To make such a showing, it will almost always be necessary for the Commission to demonstrate that the defendant's past sins have been the result of more than negligence. Because the Commission must show some likelihood of a future violation, defendants whose past actions have been in good faith are not likely to be enjoined. See opinion of the Court, ante, at 701. That is as it should be. An injunction is a drastic remedy, not a mild prophylactic, and should not be obtained against one acting in good faith.

MR. JUSTICE BLACKMUN, with whom MR. JUSTICE BRENNAN and MR. JUSTICE MARSHALL join, concurring in part and dissenting in part.

* * * I am of the view that [none of the provisions in question] requires the Commission to prove scienter before it can obtain equitable protection against deceptive practices in securities trading. * * *

*   *   *

Today's decision requires the Commission to prove scienter in many, if not most, situations before it is able to obtain an injunction. This holding unnecessarily undercuts the Commission's authority to police the marketplace. * * * I believe that there are sound reasons for distinguishing between private damages actions and public enforcement actions under these statutes, and for applying a scienter standard, if one must be applied anywhere, only in the former class of cases.

I

In keeping with the reasoning of *Hochfelder,* the Court places much emphasis upon statutory language and its assertedly plain meaning. The words "device, scheme, or artifice to defraud" in §17(a)(1), and the words "manipulative or deceptive device or contrivance" in §10(b), are said to connote "knowing or intentional misconduct." Ante, at 690, 696. And this connotation, it is said, implicitly incorporates the requirement of scienter traditionally applicable in the common law of fraud. But there are at least two specific responses to this wooden analysis. First, it is quite unclear that the words themselves call for so restrictive a definition. Second, as the Court recognized in *SEC* v. *Capital Gains Research*

Bureau, 375 U. S. 180 (1963), the common-law requirement of scienter generally observed in actions for fraud at law was often dispensed with in actions brought before chancery.

* * *

II

Although I disagree with the Court's textual exegesis and its assessment of history, I believe its most serious error may be a failure to appreciate the structural interrelationship among equitable remedies in the 1933 and 1934 Acts, and to accord that interrelationship proper weight in determining the substantive reach of the Commission's enforcement powers under §17(a) and §10(b).

* * *

* * * As the reported cases illustrate, injunctions against negligent dissemination of misinformation play an essential role in preserving market integrity and preventing serious financial loss. [Citations omitted.][8]

* * *

(1) The fragmentized result in *Aaron* reflects the fragmentization of the fraud provisions as they stand. The case is, therefore, eloquent testimony to the necessity of the integration that would be effected by the Code.[112]

(2) Meanwhile the Commission, of course, will simply plead under Clauses (2) and (3) of §17(a), as it normally has done anyhow. More significant is the non-scienter "out" afforded private plaintiffs if buyers should be given access to §17(a) at all in view of their express (and in some respects more limited) rights of action under §§11 and 12(2). It is a very substantial "if" in this writer's view. Nevertheless, the weight of judicial authority permits private actions under §17(a).[113]

---

[8] In recognition of the importance to the investing public of the Commission's authority to prevent negligent misstatements, the proposed Federal Securities Code drafted by the American Law Institute provides the Commission with power to obtain injunctions preventing deception and misrepresentation without proof of scienter. ALI, Federal Securities Code §§262(d), 297(a), 1602(a), 1819(a)(3), 1819(a)(4) (Prop. Off. Draft 1978). * * *

[112] See p. 808 supra.

[113] See pp. 1148-49 infra.

(3) Any tightening of federal fraud law bespeaks closer attention to the state blue sky laws. That is particularly true with respect to scienter. First of all, insofar as an action under state law is considered to require scienter, the state courts (or the federal courts in applying state law) might well give the term a more modern reading than it received in *Hochfelder,* especially if the common law of deceit in the particular state incorporates a relatively relaxed construction of the term.[114] Secondly, §101 of the Uniform Securities Act is a virtual carbon copy of Rule 10b-5 except that it is, of course a statute like §17(a), without the limiting language of §10(b), not a rule. And, although §410(h) forecloses private actions for violation of §101,[115] a number of states have adopted the Uniform Act without that aspect of §410(h).[116] In those states, under the Supreme Court's reasoning in *Aaron,* Clause (2) of §101 should not require scienter at all.[117]

(4) On the one hand, a literal reading of §17(a)(2) and (3) does not require even negligence; at least under §17(a)(2), any misstatement of a material fact would do, however innocent. On the other hand, it cannot be assumed that *Aaron* dispenses with scienter under §17(a)(2) and (3) so far as liability on an aider and abettor or a conspiracy basis is concerned.[118]

(5) *Query:* Should a court consider disgorgement of profits by way of ancillary relief in an injunctive action[119] in which there is no proof of scienter?

(6) Finally, to go back to *Hochfelder* as well as *Aaron,* to what extent does their teaching carry over to the more specialized fraud sections and rules?

So far as Rule 14a-9 is concerned, §14(a) has none of the limiting language of §10(b). Even so, the Sixth Circuit, in an opinion reminiscent of the Cardozo prose that has indoctrinated generations of torts students,[120] held that scienter had to be shown in

[114] See p. 810 supra.

[115] See 3 Loss 1649 n. 100; Loss, Commentary on the Uniform Securities Act (1976) 8.

[116] See 6 Loss 3798 n. 100.

[117] Kittilson v. Ford, 93 Wash. 2d 223, 608 P. 2d 264 (1980); cf. Pottern v. Bache Halsey Stuart, Inc., 41 Colo. App. 451, 589 P. 2d 1378 (1978), where the court held that a previous judgment for the defendant under Rule 10b-5 was not *res judicata* with respect to an action under Colorado's equivalent of §12(2) because that section did not require scienter.

[118] The point was queried in Pharo v. Smith, 621 F. 2d 656, 674 (5th Cir. 1980).

[119] See p. 842 n. 64 supra.

[120] Ultramares Corp. v. Touche, 255 N. Y. 170, 174 N. E. 441 (1931). That case's limitation of accountants' liability for negligence to their clients has been weakened in recent years, at least with respect to members of a

order to recover against accountants.[121] But the Third Circuit has applied a negligence standard in a case involving "outside" directors.[122]

What then about 1934 Act §15(c)(1) and (2), with respect to over-the-counter broker-dealer fraud, 1934 Act §§14(e) and 13(e), with respect to tender offers and issuer repurchases, and Advisers Act §206? None of those sections echoes the second clause of §17 (a). Instead the 1934 Act sections follow basically the §10(b) formula, and §206 does so as an *alternative* to the language of the *first* and *third* clauses of §17(a). We consider in the next chapter whether private actions may be based at all on certain of these sections or.[123] But to whatever extent there may be private plaintiffs, and in any event so far as SEC injunctive actions are concerned, presumably *Hochfelder* and *Aaron* apply with respect to the 1934 Act sections;[124] and there is lower court authority applying *Aaron* to §206(1) (modeled on Clause (1) of §17(a)) but not to §206(2) (modeled on Clause (3)).[125]

7. Violation of Rule 10b-5 by Nonverbal Acts

Although the second clause's misstatement and half-truth language, without any "fraud" or "deceit" terminology, makes that clause broader *prima facie* than the first and third clauses even apart from the question of scienter, the Supreme Court observed a decade ago that the first and third clauses were not restricted by the language of the second, and that the defendants' *activities* (indeed, their silence under circumstances giving them a duty to

---

class whose reliance is foreseen. See Restatement (Second) of Torts §552; Fiflis, Current Problems of Accountants' Responsibilities to Third Parties, 28 Vand. L. Rev. 31, esp. at 101-13 (1975).

[121] Adams v. Standard Knitting Mills, Inc., 623 F. 2d 422 (6th Cir. 1980); see also Gerstle v. Gamble-Skogmo, Inc., 478 F. 2d 1281, 1300-01 (2d Cir. 1973) (pre-*Hochfelder* dictum).

[122] Gould v. American-Hawaiian Steamship Co., 535 F. 2d 761 (3d Cir. 1976); but see Gerstle v. Gamble-Skogmo, Inc., 478 F. 2d 1281, 1300-01 (2d Cir. 1973) (dictum).

[123] See pp. 1090-98, 1105-06, 1123-25 infra.

[124] In Lowenschuss v. Kane, 520 F. 2d 255, 268 n. 10 (2d Cir. 1975), the Second Circuit, which applied a recklessness type of scienter requirement under Rule 10b-5 in those pre-*Hochfelder* days, referred to the culpability standard of §14(e) as "unsettled" in the light of the three opinions by the panel (two of whom were the same) that had sat in Chris-Craft Industries, Inc. v. Piper Aircraft Corp., 480 F. 2d 341 (2d Cir. 1973), *cert. denied*, 414 U. S. 910.

[125] SEC v. National Executive Planners, Ltd., 503 F. Supp. 1066, 1074 (M. D. N. C. 1980).

speak) "disclose, within the very language of one or the other of
those [clauses], a 'course of business' or a 'device, scheme or artifice' that operated as a fraud upon the * * * sellers."[126] That is
to say, "deception [under Rule 10b-5] may take the form of nonverbal acts."[127]

Indeed, when liability under Rule 10b-5 is based on nondisclosure rather than a false statement or a half-truth, it comes close to
a matter of semantics (or a lawyer might prefer to say the advocate's
choice of rhetoric) whether to say that liability is grounded philosophically on silence that certain activity of the insider makes
misleading or on that activity itself. At any rate, there is no dearth
of cases.[128] Sometimes the two themes are intertwined, as in a case
where the "defendants not only failed to disclose a material fact
(the true reason for the cut in the dividend rate) but were themselves responsible for its very existence."[129]

Essentially under this heading, there are several "man bite dog"
cases in which customers were held to have defrauded their brokers — notably a recent criminal case in the Supreme Court involving a short-selling customer who had no intent to deliver if the
market went up.[130] It follows, moreover, that the fraud need not
relate to the investment value of the securities.[131] Thus, where a
widow had been induced by the defendant and his co-conspirators

[126] Affiliated Ute Citizens of Utah v. United States, 406 U. S. 128, 153
(1972).
[127] O'Neill v. Maytag, 339 F. 2d 764, 768 (2d Cir. 1964) (dictum).
[128] E. g., Herbert L. Honohan, 13 SEC 754, 755, 757-58 (1943) (in tender
of non-listed bonds to sinking funds, broker-dealer submitted bids based
on inside information purchased from employee of corporate trustee); Richard
K. Fudge, 30 SEC 334 (1949) (partner and employee of broker-dealer firm
defrauded holders of assessable shares by inducing prospective bidders to
refrain from entering competitive bids at public delinquent assessment
sale); Kavit v. A. L. Stamm & Co., CCH Fed. Sec. L. Rep. ¶91,915 (S. D. N. Y.
1967) (broker-dealer's unauthorized short sale); for additional cases, see 2
Code 661-62; Pittsburgh Terminal Corp. v. Baltimore & Ohio R. R. Co., 680
F. 2d 933, 941-42 (3d Cir. 1982); cf. also pp. 995-98 infra (over-the-counter
manipulation); p. 805 infra ("churning").
[129] Cochran v. Channing Corp., 211 F. Supp. 239, 243 (S. D. N. Y. 1962).
[130] United States v. Naftalin, 441 U. S. 768 (1979); see also A. T. Brod &
Co. v. Perlow, 375 F. 2d 393 (2d Cir. 1967) (customers entered purchase or
sale orders with the intention of defaulting in payment or delivery if the
market went down or up, as the case might be, before the settlement date);
Walling v. Beverly Enterprises, Inc., 476 F. 2d 393 (9th Cir. 1973) (entering
into a reorganization agreement without unconditional intent to perform
it); Mansbach v. Prescott, Ball & Turben, 598 F. 2d 1017, 1026-27 (6th Cir.
1979) (improper executions by broker as well as refusal to return customer's
fully paid bonds).
[131] Id. at 1026; Cooper v. North Jersey Trust Co. of Ridgewood, N. J.,
Inc., 226 F. Supp. 972, 978 (S. D. N. Y. 1964); Glickman v. Schweickart &
Co., 242 F. Supp. 670, 674 (S. D. N. Y. 1965).

to sell certain securities and other property worth $124,000 in
return for a deed to 125 acres of land represented to be worth
$150,000 but afterward discovered to be worth only $12,500, the
Ninth Circuit not only applied Rule 10b-5 to fraud with respect
to the value of the consideration given for the security rather than
the value of the security itself, but also exercised pendent jurisdiction over the entire scheme on a finding that there was a single
cause of action involving a single fraudulent scheme to defraud
the plaintiff of her property, non-securities as well as securities.[132]

8.   SCOPE OF RULE 10b-5

a.   The Rule's Universality

In its first case involving a private action under Rule 10b-5, the
Supreme Court "read §10(b) to mean that Congress meant to bar
deceptive devices and contrivances in the purchase or sale of securities whether conducted in the organized markets or [as in that
case] face-to-face."[133]

So far as face-to-face transactions are concerned, the seminal
Kardon case was on its facts as extreme as any case could be in this
respect: although the two plaintiffs and two defendants were the
sole stockholders, and all four were directors, Judge Kirkpatrick
stated that he could not agree "that two men who have acquired
ownership of the stock of a corporation are not investors merely
because they own half of the total issue."[134]

So far as market transactions are concerned, there are problems
— to be considered in the next chapter, with respect to civil liability — of determining who are eligible plaintiffs and fixing their

---

[132] Errion v. Connell, 236 F. 2d 447 (9th Cir. 1956).

[133] Superintendent of Ins. of the State of N. Y. v. Bankers Life & Casualty
Co., 404 U. S. 6, 12 (1971).

[134] Kardon v. National Gypsum Co., 69 F. Supp. 512, 514 (E. D. Pa. 1946);
to the same effect, see also, e. g., SEC v. Texas Gulf Sulphur Co., 401 F. 2d
833, 848 (2d Cir. 1968), *cert. denied* sub nom. Coates v. SEC and Kline
v. SEC, 394 U. S. 976; Spector v. L Q Motor Inns, Inc., 517 F. 2d 278 (5th
Cir. 1975) (transfer of eighteen shares as part of a divorce settlement). But
see Judge Posner's concurring opinion in Trecker v. Scag, 679 F. 2d 703, 710-11
(7th Cir. 1982): while conceding that an incidental intrastate telephone call
created federal jurisdiction over "a spat between two shareholders of a closely
held corporation," he suggested that "perhaps we should not have jurisdiction" that displaces "state substantive law and state court jurisdiction in an
area remote from any federal concern that might arise from federal regulation of the securities markets," a result that "could not have been foreseen
by the framers of the Securities Exchange Act."

damages, particularly when insiders have traded in silence. But those problems are not insuperable, as we shall see. And, of course, it "would be anomalous indeed if the protection afforded by the antifraud provisions were withdrawn from transactions affected on exchanges, primary markets for securities transactions."[135] Moreover, in principle, it would be an odd rule of fiduciary conduct that permitted an insider to avoid his affirmative disclosure obligation by hiding behind the mask of the stock exchange. Surely an insider could not escape that obligation by trading off-board through an agent for an undisclosed principal.[136] And what is a stock exchange if not an aggregation of agents trading for undisclosed principals?[137]

The plaintiff does, of course, have to prove that the prohibited conduct was effected, in the language of §10(b), "by the use of any means or instrumentality of interstate commerce or of the mails, or of any national securities exchange." But it is "well established" that "the jurisdictional hook need not be large to fish for securities law violations."[138]

b.   "In Connection with a Purchase or Sale"

The requirement of both section and rule that the prohibited conduct be "in connection with the purchase or sale of any security" is not the least difficult aspect of the 10b-5 complex to tie down. A good deal of the difficulty is traceable to Justice Douglas's reference in the first Supreme Court case (involving an incredibly complicated fraud in which an insurance company was bought with its own assets) to the plaintiff's having "suffered an injury as a result of deceptive practices touching its sale of securities as an investor"[139] — although there is no reason to believe that the

---

[135] Cady, Roberts & Co., 40 SEC 907, 914 (1961).

[136] See Strong v. Repide, 213 U. S. 419 (1909), supra n. 3.

[137] More precisely the principals are *partially* disclosed; for (specialists aside) they know that their brokers are not buying or selling for their own accounts.

[138] Lawrence v. SEC, 398 F. 2d 276, 278 (1st Cir. 1968); SEC v. United Financial Group, Inc., 474 F. 2d 354, 356-57 (9th Cir. 1973); see 3 and 6 Loss c. 9F; p. 98 supra. There are nevertheless limitations. See United States v. Maze, 414 U. S. 395 (1974). The Code's solution is drastic but simple, reflecting a later constitutional milieu than that of the thirties. Section 1902 "schematically collects all of the Code's references to the mails or 'Federal commerce' (a new term defined to include both interstate and foreign commerce), eliminating a great deal of unnecessary verbiage in the process. That is to say, §1902 aside, the Code reads as if there were no problem of federal power at all." 1 Code lv.

[139] Superintendent of Ins. of the State of N. Y. v. Bankers Life & Casualty Co., 404 U. S. 6, 12-13 (1971).

Justice's use of "touching" was anything more than his variation of "in connection with" as a matter of literary style. Certain things, however, are reasonably clear.

First: As stated in the Code's commentary:

> No change is intended in the interpretation of "in connection with." For example, nothing in the Code is inconsistent with any of the learning (though uncodified) of *Superintendent of Insurance* v. *Bankers Life & Casualty Co.,* 404 U. S. 6 (1971): (A) that "the fact that creditors of the defrauded corporate buyer or seller of securities may be the ultimate victims does not warrant disregard of the corporate entity" (404 U. S. at 12); and (B) that misappropriation of the proceeds of a sale of securities may be a fraudulent act creating liability for the misappropriator if "the seller was duped into believing that it, the seller, would receive the proceeds" (404 U. S. at 9), even though the sale is for full value and the misappropriator is neither a buyer nor a seller.

Second: A fraud is not "in connection with" a purchase or sale if the purchaser or seller was aware of the facts when he bought or sold.[140]

Third: The rule may be violated by feeding misinformation into the marketplace, or even withholding information too long, without any buying or selling. This we have already noticed.[141]

Fourth: The plaintiff, however, does have to be a buyer or seller:

BLUE CHIP STAMPS v. MANOR DRUG STORES
Supreme Court of the United States, 1975
421 U. S. 723

MR. JUSTICE REHNQUIST delivered the opinion of the Court. This case requires us to consider whether the offerees of a stock

---

[140] Shivers v. AMERCO, 670 F. 2d 826, 829-30 (9th Cir. 1982).

[141] See pp. 828-29 supra. In Heit v. Weitzen, 402 F. 2d 909 (2d Cir. 1968), the court held that the "in connection with" clause was satisfied by complaints in two related actions by market buyers against the same issuer and its directors (together with the issuer's controlling stockholder and auditor in one of the cases) alleging the dissemination of financial statements that had overstated the issuer's net assets and past and prospective income because of the failure to disclose substantial, recoverable overcharges by the issuer on governmental contracts. Although the judge below had considered the alleged scheme as directed primarily toward the Government notwithstanding the possibility of an incidental market impact, the appellate court held that the "ulterior motive" was irrelevant as long as the false information had been circulated to a large segment of the investing public, and that it was of no consequence that none of the defendants had been engaged in buying or selling.

offering, made pursuant to an antitrust consent decree and registered under the Securities Act of 1933, 48 Stat. 74, as amended, 15 U. S. C. §77a et seq. (1933 Act), may maintain a private cause of action for money damages where they allege that the offeror has violated the provisions of Rule 10b-5 of the Securities and Exchange Commission, but where they have neither purchased nor sold any of the offered shares. See *Birnbaum* v. *Newport Steel Corp.*, 193 F. 2d 461 (C. A. 2), *cert. denied,* 343 U. S. 956 (1952).[a]

I

In 1963 the United States filed a civil antitrust action against Blue Chip Stamp Co. (Old Blue Chip), a company in the business of providing trading stamps to retailers, and nine retailers who owned 90% of its shares. In 1967 the action was terminated by the entry of a consent decree. *United States* v. *Blue Chip Stamp Co.,* 272 F. Supp. 432 (C. D. Cal.), *aff'd* sub nom. *Thrifty Shoppers Scrip Co.* v. *United States,* 389 U. S. 580 (1968). The decree contemplated a plan of reorganization whereby Old Blue Chip was to be merged into a newly formed corporation, Blue Chip Stamps (New Blue Chip). The holdings of the majority shareholders of Old Blue Chip were to be reduced, and New Blue Chip, one of the petitioners here, was required under the plan to offer a substantial number of its shares of common stock to retailers who had used the stamp service in the past but who were not shareholders in the old company. Under the terms of the plan, the offering to nonshareholder users was to be proportional to past stamp usage and the shares were to be offered in units consisting of common stock and debentures.

The reorganization plan was carried out, the offering was registered with the SEC as required by the 1933 Act, and a prospectus was distributed to all offerees as required by §5 of that Act, 15 U. S. C. §77e. Somewhat more than 50% of the offered units were actually purchased. In 1970, two years after the offering, respondent, a former user of the stamp service and therefore an offeree of the 1968 offering, filed this suit in the United States District Court for the Central District of California. Defendants below and petitioners here are Old and New Blue Chip, eight of the nine

---

[a] ED.: In *Birnbaum* the Second Circuit held that a sale of control without giving noncontrolling stockholders an opportunity to sell their shares on the same favorable basis did not violate Rule 10b-5.

majority shareholders of Old Blue Chip, and the directors of New Blue Chip (collectively called Blue Chip).

Respondent's complaint alleged, *inter alia,* that the prospectus prepared and distributed by Blue Chip in connection with the offering was materially misleading in its overly pessimistic appraisal of Blue Chip's status and future prospects. It alleged that Blue Chip intentionally made the prospectus overly pessimistic in order to discourage respondent and other members of the allegedly large class whom it represents from accepting what was intended to be a bargain offer, so that the rejected shares might later be offered to the public at a higher price. The complaint alleged that class members because of and in reliance on the false and misleading prospectus failed to purchase the offered units. Respondent therefore sought on behalf of the alleged class some $21,400,000 in damages representing the lost opportunity to purchase the units; the right to purchase the previously rejected units at the 1968 price; and in addition, it sought some $25,000,000 in exemplary damages.

The only portion of the litigation thus initiated which is before us is whether respondent may base its action on Rule 10b-5 of the Securities and Exchange Commission without having either bought or sold the securities described in the allegedly misleading prospectus. * * *

II

* * *

Despite the contrast between the provisions of Rule 10b-5 and the numerous carefully drawn express civil remedies provided in the Acts of both 1933 and 1934, it was held in 1946 by the United States District Court for the Eastern District of Pennsylvania that there was an implied private right of action under the Rule. *Kardon* v. *National Gypsum Co.,* 69 F. Supp. 512. This Court had no occasion to deal with the subject until 25 years later, and at that time we confirmed with virtually no discussion the overwhelming consensus of the District Courts and Courts of Appeals that such a cause of action did exist. *Superintendent of Insurance* v. *Bankers Life & Cas. Co.,* 404 U. S. 6, 13 n. 9 (1971); *Affiliated Ute Citizens* v. *United States,* 406 U. S. 128, 150-154 (1972). Such a conclusion was, of course, entirely consistent with the Court's recognition in *J. I. Case Co.* v. *Borak,* 377 U. S. 426, 432 (1964), that private enforcement of Commission rules may "[provide] a necessary supplement to Commission action."

Within a few years after the seminal *Kardon* decision, the Court of Appeals for the Second Circuit concluded that the plaintiff class for purposes of a private damage action under §10(b) and Rule 10b-5 was limited to actual purchasers and sellers of securities. *Birnbaum* v. *Newport Steel Corp.,* supra.

The Court of Appeals [for the Ninth Circuit] in this case did not repudiate *Birnbaum;* indeed, another panel of that court (in an opinion by Judge Ely) had but a short time earlier affirmed the rule of that case. *Mount Clemens Industries, Inc.* v. *Bell,* 464 F. 2d 339 (1972). But in this case a majority of the Court of Appeals found that the facts warranted an exception to the *Birnbaum* rule. For the reasons hereinafter stated, we are of the opinion that *Birnbaum* was rightly decided, and that it bars respondent from maintaining this suit under Rule 10b-5.

III

The panel which decided *Birnbaum* consisted of Chief Judge Swan and Judges Learned Hand and Augustus Hand: the opinion was written by the last named. Since both §10(b) and Rule 10b-5 proscribed only fraud "in connection with the purchase or sale" of securities, and since the history of §10(b) revealed no congressional intention to extend a private civil remedy for money damages to other than defrauded purchasers or sellers of securities, in contrast to the express civil remedy provided by §16(b) of the 1934 Act, the court concluded that the plaintiff class in a Rule 10b-5 action was limited to actual purchasers and sellers. 193 F. 2d, at 463-464.

Just as this Court had no occasion to consider the validity of the *Kardon* holding that there was a private cause of action under Rule 10b-5 until 20-odd years later, nearly the same period of time has gone by between the *Birnbaum* decision and our consideration of the case now before us. As with *Kardon,* virtually all lower federal courts facing the issue in the hundreds of reported cases presenting this question over the past quarter century have reaffirmed *Birnbaum*'s conclusion that the plaintiff class for purposes of §10(b) and Rule 10b-5 private damage actions is limited to purchasers and sellers of securities. See 6 L. Loss, Securities Regulation 3617 (1969). [Case citations omitted.]

In 1957 and again in 1959, the Securities and Exchange Commission sought from Congress amendment of §10(b) to change its wording from "in connection with the purchase or sale of any security" to "in connection with the purchase or sale of, *or any attempt to purchase or sell,* any security." 103 Cong. Rec. 11636

(1937) (emphasis added); SEC Legislation, Hearings on S. 1178-1182 before a Subcommittee of the Senate Committee on Banking & Currency, 86 Cong., 1st Sess., 367-368 (1959); S. 2545, 85th Cong., 1st Sess. (1957); S. 1179, 86th Cong., 1st Sess. (1959). In the words of a memorandum submitted by the Commission to a congressional committee, the purpose of the proposed change was "to make section 10(b) also applicable to manipulative activities in connection with any attempt to purchase or sell any security." Hearings on S. 1178-1182, supra, at 331. Opposition to the amendment was based on fears of the extension of civil liability under §10(b) that it would cause. Id., at 368. Neither change was adopted by Congress.

The longstanding acceptance by the courts, coupled with Congress' failure to reject *Birnbaum*'s reasonable interpretation of the wording of §10(b), wording which is directed toward injury suffered "in connection with the purchase or sale" of securities, argues significantly in favor of acceptance of the *Birnbaum* rule by this Court. *Blau* v. *Lehman*, 368 U. S. 403, 413 (1962).

Available evidence from the texts of the 1933 and 1934 Acts as to the congressional scheme in this regard, though not conclusive, supports the result reached by the *Birnbaum* court. The wording of §10(b) directed at fraud "in connection with the purchase or sale" of securities stands in contrast with the parallel antifraud provision of the 1933 Act, §17(a), as amended, 68 Stat. 686, 15 U. S. C. §77q,[6] reaching fraud "in the offer or sale" of securities. Cf. §5 of the 1933 Act, 15 U. S. C. §77e. When Congress wished to provide a remedy to those who neither purchase nor sell securities, it had little trouble in doing so expressly. Cf. §16(b) of the 1934 Act, 15 U. S. C. §78p(b).

Section 28(a) of the 1934 Act, 15 U. S. C. §78bb(a), which limits recovery in any private damages action brought under the 1934 Act to "actual damages," likewise provides some support for the purchaser-seller rule. See, e. g., Bromberg §8.8, p. 21. While the damages suffered by purchasers and sellers pursuing a §10(b) cause of action may on occasion be difficult to ascertain, *Affiliated Ute Citizens* v. *United States,* 406 U. S., at 155, in the main such purchasers and sellers at least seek to base recovery on a demonstrable

___

[6] * * * We express, of course, no opinion on whether §17(a) in light of the express civil remedies of the 1933 Act gives rise to an implied cause of action. Compare Greater Iowa Corp. v. McLendon, 378 F. 2d 783, 788-791 (C. A. 8 1967), with Fischman v. Raytheon Mfg. Co., 188 F. 2d 783, 787 (C. A. 2 1951). See, e. g., SEC v. Texas Gulf Sulphur Co., 401 F. 2d 833, 867 (C. A. 2 1968) (Friendly, J., concurring), *cert. denied* sub nom. Coates v. SEC, 394 U. S. 976 (1969); 3 L. Loss, Securities Regulation 1785 (2d ed. 1961).

number of shares traded. In contrast, a putative plaintiff, who neither purchases nor sells securities but sues instead for intangible economic injury such as loss of a noncontractual opportunity to buy or sell, is more likely to be seeking a largely conjectural and speculative recovery in which the number of shares involved will depend on the plaintiff's subjective hypothesis. Cf. *Estate Counseling Service, Inc.* v. *Merrill Lynch, Pierce, Fenner & Smith, Inc.*, 303 F. 2d 527, 533 (C. A. 10 1962); *Levine* v. *Seilon, Inc.*, 439 F. 2d 328, 335 (C. A. 2 1971); *Wolf* v. *Frank*, 477 F. 2d 467, 478 (C. A. 5 1973).

One of the justifications advanced for implication of a cause of action under §10(b) lies in §29(b) of the 1934 Act, 15 U. S. C. §78cc(b), providing that a contract made in violation of any provision of the 1934 Act is voidable at the option of the deceived party. See, e. g., *Kardon* v. *National Gypsum Co.*, 69 F. Supp., at 514; *Slavin* v. *Germantown Fire Insurance Co.*, 174 F. 2d 799, 815 (C. A. 3 1949); *Fischman* v. *Raytheon Mfg. Co.*, 188 F. 2d 783, 787 n. 4 (C. A. 2 1951); Bromberg §2.4(1)(b). But that justification is absent when there is no actual purchase or sale of securities, or a contract to purchase or sell, affected or tainted by a violation of §10(b). Cf. *Mount Clemens Industries, Inc.* v. *Bell*, supra.

The principal express nonderivative private civil remedies, created by Congress contemporaneously with the passage of §10(b), for violations of various provisions of the 1933 and 1934 Acts are by their terms expressly limited to purchasers or sellers of securities. Thus §11(a) of the 1933 Act confines the cause of action it grants to "any person acquiring such security" while the remedy granted by §12 of that Act is limited to the "person purchasing such security." Section 9 of the 1934 Act, prohibiting a variety of fraudulent and manipulative devices, limits the express civil remedy provided for its violation to "any person who shall purchase or sell any security" in a transaction affected by a violation of the provision. Section 18 of the 1934 Act, prohibiting false or misleading statements in reports or other documents required to be filed by the 1934 Act, limits the express remedy provided for its violation to "any person . . . who . . . shall have purchased or sold a security at a price which was affected by such statement. . . ." It would indeed be anomalous to impute to Congress an intention to expand the plaintiff class for a judicially implied cause of action beyond the bounds it delineated for comparable express causes of action.[8]

[8] * * * Rule 10b-5 was adopted in order to close "a loophole in the protections against fraud * * * by prohibiting individuals or companies from

Having said all this, we would by no means be understood as suggesting that we are able to divine from the language of §10(b) the express "intent of Congress" as to the contours of a private cause of action under Rule 10b-5. When we deal with private actions under Rule 10b-5, we deal with a judicial oak which has grown from little more than a legislative acorn. Such growth may be quite consistent with the congressional enactment and with the role of the federal judiciary in interpreting it, see *J. I. Case* v. *Borak,* supra, but it would be disingenuous to suggest that either Congress in 1934 or the Securities and Exchange Commission in 1942 foreordained the present state of the law with respect to Rule 10b-5. It is therefore proper that we consider, in addition to the factors already discussed, what may be described as policy considerations when we come to flesh out the portions of the law with respect to which neither the congressional enactment nor the administrative regulations offer conclusive guidance.

Three principal classes of potential plaintiffs are presently barred by the *Birnbaum* rule. First are potential purchasers of shares, either in a new offering or on the Nation's post-distribution trading markets, who allege that they decided not to purchase because of an unduly gloomy representation or the omission of favorable material which made the issuer appear to be a less favorable investment vehicle than it actually was. Second are actual shareholders in the issuer who allege that they decided not to sell their shares because of an unduly rosy representation or a failure to disclose unfavorable material. Third are shareholders, creditors, and perhaps others related to an issuer who suffered loss in the value of their investment due to corporate or insider activities in connection with the purchase or sale of securities which violate Rule 10b-5. It has been held that shareholder members of the second and third of these classes may frequently be able to circumvent the *Birnbaum* limitation through bringing a derivative action on behalf of the corporate issuer if the latter is itself a purchaser or seller of securities. See, e. g., *Schoenbaum* v. *Firstbrook,* 405 F. 2d 215, 219 (C. A. 2 1968), *cert. denied* sub nom. *Manley* v. *Schoenbaum,* 395 U. S. 906 (1969). But the first of these classes, of which respondent is a member, cannot claim the benefit of such a rule.

A great majority of the many commentators on the issue before us have taken the view that the *Birnbaum* limitation on the plaintiff class in a Rule 10b-5 action for damages is an arbitrary restric-

_____

buying securities if they engage in fraud in their purchase." See SEC Release No. 3230 (May 21, 1942) * * * tion which unreasonably prevents some deserving plaintiffs from recovering damages which have in fact been caused by violations of Rule 10b-5. See, e. g., Lowenfels, The Demise of the *Birnbaum* Doctrine: A New Era for Rule 10b-5, 54 Va. L. Rev. 268 (1968). The Securities and Exchange Commission has filed an *amicus* brief in this case espousing that same view. We have no doubt that this is indeed a disadvantage of the *Birnbaum* rule,[9] and if it had no countervailing advantages it would be undesirable as a matter of policy, however much it might be supported by precedent and legislative history. But we are of the opinion that there are countervailing advantages to the *Birnbaum* rule, purely as a matter of policy, although those advantages are more difficult to articulate than is the disadvantage.

There has been widespread recognition that litigation under Rule 10b-5 presents a danger of vexatiousness different in degree and in kind from that which accompanies litigation in general. This fact was recognized by Judge Browning in his opinion for the majority of the Court of Appeals in this case, 492 F. 2d, at 141, and by Judge Hufstedler in her dissenting opinion when she said:

> The purchaser-seller rule has maintained the balances built into the congressional scheme by permitting damage actions to be brought only by those persons whose active participation in the marketing transaction promises enforcement of the statute without undue risk of abuse of the litigation process and without distorting the securities market. Id., at 147.

Judge Friendly in commenting on another aspect of Rule 10b-5 litigation has referred to the possibility that unduly expansive imposition of civil liability "will lead to large judgments, payable in the last analysis by innocent investors, for the benefit of speculators and their lawyers. . . . " *SEC* v. *Texas Gulf Sulphur Co.,* 401 F. 2d 833, 867 (C. A. 2 1968) (concurring opinion). See

---

[9] Obviously this disadvantage is attenuated to the extent that remedies are available to nonpurchasers and nonsellers under state law. Cf. §28 of the 1934 Act, 15 U. S. C. §78bb. See Iroquois Industries, Inc. v. Syracuse China Corp., 417 F. 2d 963, 969 (C. A. 2 1969), *cert. denied,* 399 U. S. 909 (1970). Thus, for example, in *Birnbaum* itself, while the plaintiffs found themselves without federal remedies, the conduct alleged as the gravamen of the federal complaint later provided the basis for recovery in a cause of action based on state law. See 3 L. Loss, Securities Regulation 1469 (2d ed. 1961 [citing Perlman v. Feldman, 219 F. 2d 173 (2d Cir. 1955), *cert. denied,* 349 U. S. 952]. And in the immediate case, respondent has filed a state-court class action held in abeyance pending the outcome of this suit. Manor Drug Stores v. Blue Chip Stamps, No. C-5652 (Superior Court, County of Los Angeles, Cal.).

also Boone & McGowan, Standing to Sue under SEC Rule 10b-5, 49 Tex. L. Rev. 617, 648-649 (1971).

We believe that the concern expressed for the danger of vexatious litigation which could result from a widely expanded class of plaintiffs under Rule 10b-5 is founded in something more substantial than the common complaint of the many defendants who would prefer avoiding lawsuits entirely to either settling them or trying them. These concerns have two largely separate grounds.

The first of these concerns is that in the field of federal securities laws governing disclosure of information even a complaint which by objective standards may have very little chance of success at trial has a settlement value to the plaintiff out of any proportion to its prospect of success at trial so long as he may prevent the suit from being resolved against him by dismissal or summary judgment. The very pendency of the lawsuit may frustrate or delay normal business activity of the defendant which is totally unrelated to the lawsuit. See, e. g., Sargent, The SEC and the Individual Investor: Restoring His Confidence in the Market, 60 Va. L. Rev. 553, 562-572 (1974); Dooley, The Effects of Civil Liability on Investment Banking and the New Issues Market, 58 Va. L. Rev. 776, 822-843 (1972).

Congress itself recognized the potential for nuisance or "strike" suits in this type of litigation, and in Title II of the 1934 Act amended §11 of the 1933 Act to provide that:

> In any suit under this or any other section of this title the court may, in its discretion, require an undertaking for the payment of the costs of such suit, including reasonable attorney's fees. . . . §206(d), 48 Stat. 881, 908.

Senator Fletcher, Chairman of the Senate Banking and Finance Committee, in introducing Title II of the 1934 Act on the floor of the Senate, stated in explaining the amendment to §11(e): "This amendment is the most important of all." 78 Cong. Rec. 8669. Among its purposes was to provide "a defense against blackmail suits." Ibid.

Where Congress in those sections of the 1933 Act which expressly conferred a private cause of action for damages, adopted a provision uniformly regarded as designed to deter "strike" or nuisance actions, *Cohen* v. *Beneficial Loan Corp.*, 337 U. S. 541, 548-549 (1949), that fact alone justifies our consideration of such potential in determining the limits of the class of plaintiffs who may sue in an action wholly implied from the language of the 1934 Act.

The potential for possible abuse of the liberal discovery provisions of the Federal Rules of Civil Procedure may likewise exist in this type of case to a greater extent than they do in other litigation. The prospect of extensive deposition of the defendant's officers and associates and the concomitant opportunity for extensive discovery of business documents, is a common occurrence in this and similar types of litigation. To the extent that this process eventually produces relevant evidence which is useful in determining the merits of the claims asserted by the parties, it bears the imprimatur of those Rules and of the many cases liberally interpreting them. But to the extent that it permits a plaintiff with a largely groundless claim to simply take up the time of a number of other people, with the right to do so representing an *in terrorem* increment of the settlement value, rather than a reasonably founded hope that the process will reveal relevant evidence, it is a social cost rather than a benefit. Yet to broadly expand the class of plaintiffs who may sue under Rule 10b-5 would appear to encourage the least appealing aspect of the use of the discovery rules.

Without the *Birnbaum* rule, an action under Rule 10b-5 will turn largely on which oral version of a series of occurrences the jury may decide to credit, and therefore no matter how improbable the allegations of the plaintiff, the case will be virtually impossible to dispose of prior to trial other than by settlement. In the words of Judge Hufstedler's dissenting opinion in the Court of Appeals:

> The great ease with which plaintiff can allege the requirements for the majority's standing rule and the greater difficulty that plaintiffs are going to have proving the allegations suggests that the majority's rule will allow a relatively high proportion of "bad" cases into court. The risk of strike suits is particularly high in such cases; although they are difficult to prove at trial, they are even more difficult to dispose of before trial. 492 F. 2d, at 147 n. 9.

The *Birnbaum* rule, on the other hand, permits exclusion prior to trial of those plaintiffs who were not themselves purchasers or sellers of the stock in question. The fact of purchase of stock and the fact of sale of stock are generally matters which are verifiable by documentation, and do not depend upon oral recollection, so that failure to qualify under the *Birnbaum* rule is a matter that can normally be established by the defendant either on a motion to dismiss or on a motion for summary judgment.

Obviously there is no general legal principle that courts in fashioning substantive law should do so in a manner which makes it easier, rather than more difficult, for a defendant to obtain a summary judgment. But in this type of litigation, where the mere existence of an unresolved lawsuit has settlement value to the plaintiff not only because of the possibility that he may prevail on the merits, an entirely legitimate component of settlement value, but because of the threat of extensive discovery and disruption of normal business activities which may accompany a lawsuit which is groundless in any event, but cannot be proved so before trial, such a factor is not to be totally dismissed. The *Birnbaum* rule undoubtedly excludes plaintiffs who have in fact been damaged by violations of Rule 10b-5, and to that extent it is undesirable. But it also separates in a readily demonstrable manner the group of plaintiffs who actually purchased or actually sold, and whose version of the facts is therefore more likely to be believed by the trier of fact, from the vastly larger world of potential plaintiffs who might successfully allege a claim but could seldom succeed in proving it. And this fact is one of its advantages.

The second ground for fear of vexatious litigation is based on the concern that, given the generalized contours of liability, the abolition of the *Birnbaum* rule would throw open to the trier of fact many rather hazy issues of historical fact the proof of which depended almost entirely on oral testimony. We in no way disparage the worth and frequent high value of oral testimony when we say that dangers of its abuse appear to exist in this type of action to a peculiarly high degree. * * *

* * *

In considering the policy underlying the *Birnbaum* rule, it is not inappropriate to advert briefly to the tort of misrepresentation and deceit, to which a claim under Rule 10b-5 certainly has some relationship. Originally under the common law of England such an action was not available to one other than a party to a business transaction. That limitation was eliminated in *Pasley* v. *Freeman*, 3 T. R. 51, 100 Eng. Rep. 450 (1789). Under the earlier law the misrepresentation was generally required to be one of fact, rather than opinion, but that requirement, too, was gradually relaxed. Lord Bowen's famous comment in *Edgington* v. *Fitzmaurice*, [1882] L. R. 29 Ch. Div. 459, 483, that "the state of a man's mind is as much a fact as the state of his digestion," suggests that this distinction, too, may have been somewhat arbitrary. And it has long been established in the ordinary case of deceit that a misrepresentation which leads to a refusal to purchase or to sell is actionable in just the same way as a misrepresentation which leads to the consummation of a purchase or sale. *Butler* v. *Watkins,* 13 Wall. 456 (1872). These aspects of the evolution of the tort of deceit and misrepresentation suggest a direction away from rules such as *Birnbaum.*

But the typical fact situation in which the classic tort of misrepresentation and deceit evolved was light years away from the world of commercial transactions to which Rule 10b-5 is applicable. The plaintiff in *Butler,* supra, for example, claimed that he had held off the market a patented machine for tying cotton bales which he had developed by reason of the fraudulent representations of the defendant. But the report of the case leaves no doubt that the plaintiff and defendant met with one another in New Orleans, that one presented a draft agreement to the other, and that letters were exchanged relating to that agreement. Although the claim to damages was based on an allegedly fraudulently induced decision not to put the machines on the market, the plaintiff and the defendant had concededly been engaged in the course of business dealings with one another, and would presumably have recognized one another on the street had they met.

In today's universe of transactions governed by the 1934 Act, privity of dealing or even personal contact between potential defendant and potential plaintiff is the exception and not the rule. The stock of issuers is listed on financial exchanges utilized by tens of millions of investors, and corporate representations reach a potential audience, encompassing not only the diligent few who peruse filed corporate reports or the sizable number of subscribers to financial journals, but the readership of the Nation's daily newspapers. Obviously neither the fact that issuers or other potential defendants under Rule 10b-5 reach a large number of potential investors, or the fact that they are required by law to make their disclosures conform to certain standards, should in any way absolve them from liability for misconduct which is proscribed by Rule 10b-5.

But in the absence of the *Birnbaum* rule, it would be sufficient for a plaintiff to prove that he had failed to purchase or sell stock by reason of a defendant's violation of Rule 10b-5. The manner in which the defendant's violation caused the plaintiff to fail to act could be as a result of the reading of a prospectus, as respondent claims here, but it could just as easily come as a result of a claimed reading of information contained in the financial pages of a local newspaper. Plaintiff's proof would not be that he purchased or sold stock, a fact which would be capable of documentary verification in most situations, but instead that he decided *not* to purchase or sell stock. Plaintiff's entire testimony could be dependent upon uncorroborated oral evidence of many of the crucial elements of his claim, and still be sufficient to go to the jury. The jury would not even have the benefit of weighing the plaintiff's version against the defendant's version, since the elements to which the plaintiff would testify would be in many cases totally unknown and unknowable to the defendant. The very real risk in permitting those in respondent's position to sue under Rule 10b-5 is that the door will be open to recovery of substantial damages on the part of one who offers only his own testimony to prove that he ever consulted a prospectus of the issuer, that he paid any attention to it, or that the representations contained in it damaged him. The virtue of the *Birnbaum* rule, simply stated, in this situation, is that it limits the class of plaintiffs to those who have at least dealt in the security to which the prospectus, representation, or omission relates. And their dealing in the security, whether by way of purchase or sale, will generally be an objectively demonstrable fact in an area of the law otherwise very much dependent upon oral testimony. In the absence of the *Birnbaum* doctrine, bystanders to the securities marketing process could await developments on the sidelines without risk, claiming that inaccuracies in disclosure caused nonselling in a falling market and that unduly pessimistic predictions by the issuer followed by a rising market caused them to allow retrospectively golden opportunities to pass.

While much of the development of the law of deceit has been the elimination of artificial barriers to recovery on just claims, we are not the first court to express concern that the inexorable broadening of the class of plaintiff who may sue in this area of the law will ultimately result in more harm than good. In *Ultramares Corp. v. Touche,* 255 N. Y. 170, 174 N. E. 441 (1931), Chief Judge Cardozo observed with respect to "a liability in an indeterminate amount for an indeterminate time to an indeterminate class":

> The hazards of a business conducted on these terms are so extreme as to enkindle doubt whether a flaw may not exist in the implication of a duty that exposes to these consequences. Id., at 179-180, 174 N. E., at 444.

*   *   *

* * * We are dealing with a private cause of action which has been judicially found to exist, and which will have to be judicially delimited one way or another unless and until Congress addresses the question. Given the peculiar blend of legislative, administrative, and judicial history which now surrounds Rule 10b-5, we believe that practical factors to which we have adverted, and to which other courts have referred, are entitled to a good deal of weight.

Thus we conclude that what may be called considerations of policy, which we are free to weigh in deciding this case, are by no means entirely on one side of the scale. Taken together with the precedential suport for the *Birnbaum* rule over a period of more than 20 years, and the consistency of that rule with what we can glean from the intent of Congress, they lead us to conclude that it is a sound rule and should be followed.

IV

The majority of the Court of Appeals in this case expressed no disagreement with the general proposition that one asserting a claim for damages based on the violation of Rule 10b-5 must be either a purchaser or seller of securities. However, it noted that prior cases have held that persons owning contractual rights to buy or sell securities are not excluded by the *Birnbaum* rule. Relying on these cases, it concluded that respondent's status as an offeree pursuant to the terms of the consent decree served the same function, for purposes of delimiting the class of plaintiffs, as is normally performed by the requirement of a contractual relationship. 492 F. 2d, at 142.

*   *   *

A contract to purchase or sell securities is expressly defined by §3(a) of the 1934 Act, 15 U. S. C. §78c(a), as a purchase or sale of securities for the purposes of that Act. Unlike respondent, which had no contractual right or duty to purchase Blue Chip's securities, the holders of puts, calls, options, and other contractual rights or duties to purchase or sell securities have been recognized as "purchasers" or "sellers" of securities for purposes of Rule 10b-5, not because of a judicial conclusion that they were similarly situated to "purchasers" or "sellers," but because the definitional provisions of the 1934 Act themselves grant them such a status.

Even if we were to accept the notion that the *Birnbaum* rule could be circumvented on a case-by-case basis through particularized judicial inquiry into the facts surrounding a complaint, this respondent and the members of its alleged class would be unlikely candidates for such a judicially created exception. While the *Birnbaum* rule has been flexibly interpreted by lower federal courts,[14]

[14] Our decision in SEC v. National Securities, Inc., 393 U. S. 453 (1969),

we have been unable to locate a single decided case from any court in the 20-odd years of litigation since the *Birnbaum* decision which would support the right of persons who were in the position of respondent here to bring a private suit under Rule 10b-5. Respondent was not only not a buyer or seller of any security but it was not even a shareholder of the corporate petitioners.

As indicated, the 1934 Act, under which respondent seeks to assert a cause of action, is general in scope but chiefly concerned with the regulation of post-distribution trading on the Nation's stock exchanges and securities trading markets. The 1933 Act is a far narrower statute chiefly concerned with disclosure and fraud in connection with offerings of securities — primarily, as here, initial distributions of newly issued stock from corporate issuers. 1 L. Loss, Securities Regulation 130-131 (2d ed. 1961). Respondent, who derives no entitlement from the antitrust consent decree and does not otherwise possess any contractual rights relating to the offered stock, stands in the same position as any other disappointed offeree of a stock offering registered under the 1933 Act who claims that an overly pessimistic prospectus, prepared and distributed as required by §§5 and 10 of the 1933 Act, has caused it to allow its opportunity to purchase to pass.

There is strong evidence that application of the *Birnbaum* rule to preclude suit by the disappointed offeree of a registered 1933 Act offering under Rule 10b-5 furthers the intention of Congress as expressed in the 1933 Act.[15] * * *

Sections 11 and 12 of the 1933 Act provide express civil remedies for misrepresentations and omissions in registration statements and prospectuses filed under the Act, as here charged, but restrict recovery to the offering price of shares actually purchased: * * * And in Title II of the 1934 Act, 48 Stat. 905-908, the same Act adopting §10(b), Congress amended §11 of the 1933 Act to limit still further the express civil remedy it conferred. * * * The additional congressional restrictions, contained in Title II of the 1934 Act, on the already limited express civil remedies pro-

---

established that the purchaser-seller rule imposes no limitation on the standing of the SEC to bring actions for injunctive relief under §10(b) and Rule 10b-5.

[15] Blue Chip did not here present the question of whether an implied action under §10(b) of the 1934 Act and Rule 10b-5 will lie for actions made a violation of the 1933 Act and the subject of express civil remedies under the 1933 Act. We therefore have no occasion to pass on this issue. Compare Rosenberg v. Globe Aircraft Corp., 80 F. Supp. 123 (E. D. Pa. 1948), with Thiele v. Shields, 131 F. Supp. 416 (S. D. N. Y. 1955). Cf. 3 L. Loss, Securities Regulation 1787-1791 (2d ed. 1961); 6 L. Loss, Securities Regulation 3915-3917 (1969); Bromberg §2.4(2).

vided by the 1933 Act for misrepresentations or omissions in a registration statement or prospectus reflected congressional concern over the impact of even these limited remedies on the new issues market. 78 Cong. Rec. 8668-8669 (1934). * * * There is thus ample evidence that Congress did not intend to extend a private cause of action for money damages to the nonpurchasing offeree of a stock offering registered under the 1933 Act for loss of the opportunity to purchase due to an overly pessimistic prospectus.

Beyond the difficulties evident in an extension of standing to this respondent, we do not believe that the *Birnbaum* rule is merely a shorthand judgment on the nature of a particular plaintiff's proof. As a purely practical matter, it is doubtless true that respondent and the members of its class, as offerees and recipients of the prospectus of New Blue Chip, are a smaller class of potential plaintiffs than would be all those who might conceivably assert that they obtained information violative of Rule 10b-5 and attributable to the issuer in the financial pages of their local newspaper. And since respondent likewise had a prior connection with some of petitioners as a result of using the trading stamps marketed by Old Blue Chip, and was intended to benefit from the provisions of the consent decree, there is doubtless more likelihood that its managers read and were damaged by the allegedly misleading statements in the prospectus than there would be in a case filed by a complete stranger to the corporation.

But respondent and the members of its class are neither "purchasers" nor "sellers," as those terms are defined in the 1934 Act, and therefore to the extent that their claim of standing to sue were recognized, it would mean that the lesser practical difficulties of corroborating at least some elements of their proof would be regarded as sufficient to avoid the *Birnbaum* rule. While we have noted that these practical difficulties, particularly in the case of a complete stranger to the corporation, support the retention of that rule, they are by no means the only factor which does so. The general adoption of the rule by other federal courts in the 25 years since it was announced, and the consistency of the rule with the statutes involved and their legislative history, are likewise bases for retaining the rule. Were we to agree with the Court of Appeals in this case, we would leave the *Birnbaum* rule open to endless case-by-case erosion depending on whether a particular group of plaintiffs was thought by the court in which the issue was being litigated to be sufficiently more discrete than the world of potential purchasers at large to justify an exception. We do not believe that such a shifting and highly fact-oriented disposition of the issue of who may bring a damages claim for violation of Rule 10b-5 is a satisfactory basis for a rule of liability imposed on the conduct of business transactions. Nor is it as consistent as a straightforward application of the *Birnbaum* rule with the other factors which support the retention of that rule. We therefore hold that respondent was not entitled to sue for violation of Rule 10b-5, and the judgment of the Court of Appeals is reversed.

MR. JUSTICE POWELL, with whom MR. JUSTICE STEWART and MR. JUSTICE MARSHALL join, concurring.

*   *   *

* * * If an issue of statutory construction is to be decided on the basis of assuring a *federal* remedy — in addition to state remedies — for every perceived fraud, at least we should strike a balance between the opportunities for fraud presented by the contending views. It may well be conceded that *Birnbaum* does allow some fraud to go unremedied under the federal securities Acts. But the construction advocated by the dissent could result in wider opportunities for fraud. As the Court's opinion makes plain, abandoning the *Birnbaum* construction in favor of the rule urged by the dissent would invite any person who failed to purchase a newly offered security that subsequently enjoyed substantial market appreciation to file a claim alleging that the offering prospectus understated the company's potential. The number of possible plaintiffs with respect to a public offering would be virtually unlimited. As noted above (at 758 n. 2), an honest offeror could be confronted with subjective claims by plaintiffs who had neither purchased its securities nor seriously considered the investment. It frequently would be impossible to refute a plaintiff's assertion that he relied on the prospectus, or even that he made a decision not to buy the offered securities. A rule allowing this type of open-ended litigation would itself be an invitation to fraud.[5]

---

[5] The dissent also charges that we are callous toward the "investing public" — a term it does not define. It would have been more accurate, perhaps, to have spoken of the noninvesting public, because the Court's decision does not abandon the investing public. The great majority of registered issues of securities are offered by established corporations that have shares outstanding and held by members of the investing public. The types of suits that the dissent would encourage could result in large damage claims, costly litigation, generous settlements to avoid such cost, and often — where the litigation runs its course — in large verdicts. The shareholders of the defendant corporations — the "investing public" — would ultimately bear the burden of this litigation, including the fraudulent suits that would not be screened out by the dissent's bare requirement of a "logical nexus between the alleged fraud and the sale or purchase of a security."

MR. JUSTICE BLACKMUN, with whom MR. JUSTICE DOUGLAS and MR. JUSTICE BRENNAN join, dissenting.

Today the Court graves into stone *Birnbaum*'s arbitrary principle of standing. For this task the Court, unfortunately, chooses to utilize three blunt chisels: (1) reliance on the legislative history of the 1933 and 1934 Securities Acts, conceded as inconclusive in this particular context; (2) acceptance as precedent of two decades of lower court decisions following a doctrine, never before examined here, that was pronounced by a justifiably esteemed panel of that Court of Appeals regarded as the "Mother Court" in this area of the law, but under entirely different circumstances; and (3) resort to utter pragmaticality and a conjectural assertion of "policy considerations" deemed to arise in distinguishing the meritorious Rule 10b-5 suit from the meretricious one. * * *

* * *

* * * the greater portion of the Court's opinion is devoted to its discussion of the "danger of vexatiousness," ante, at 739, that accompanies litigation under Rule 10b-5 and that is said to be "different in degree and in kind from that which accompanies litigation in general." Ibid. It speaks of harm from the "very pendency of the lawsuit," ante, at 740, something like the recognized dilemma of the physician sued for malpractice; of the "disruption of normal business activities which may accompany a lawsuit," ante, at 743; and of "proof . . . which depend[s] almost entirely on oral testimony," ibid., as if all these were unknown to lawsuits taking place in America's courthouses every day. In turning to, and being influenced by, these "policy considerations," ante, at 737, or these "considerations of policy," ante, at 749, the Court, in my view, unfortunately mires itself in speculation and conjecture not usually seen in its opinions. * * *

* * *

* * * Sensible standards of proof and of demonstrable damages would evolve and serve to protect the worthy and shut out the frivolous.

Blue Chip was not the apocalypse that some in the Commission and the academic world believed it was, at least initially. For one thing, *Birnbaum* had reigned virtually supreme at the appellate level for twenty-three years.[142] The cascade of 10b-5 litigation during that period confirmed the utility of the buy-sell requirement as *some* means to keep the little rule from taking over a large slice of the corporation law universe. And there is no gainsaying that a grant of standing to a plaintiff who had not changed his position would be, in most factual configurations if not that in *Birnbaum* or *Blue Chip,* an invitation to perjury.

What is disturbing to many is not the holding but the tone of the majority opinion as a possible harbinger of the demise or crippling of Rule 10b-5. Is a majority of the Court determined drastically to roll back the whole development of a "federal corporation law"?[143] Or will *Blue Chip* and later 10b-5 cases turn out to be simply another example of the pendulum phenomenon that has characterized so much legal doctrine?

Current history is hard to write. We have already noticed the Court's strict scienter approach in *Hochfelder* and *Aaron.* And we shall soon consider the Court's unwillingness to expand the rule's "fraud" concept in another sense.[144] But all these cases together leave the rule intact for fraudulent acts or statements known to be false (or probably false statements made with reckless disregard as to truth or falsity) in connection with *any* purchase or sale of *any* security by *any* person to *any* person — not to mention cases of insiders' silence. And that is no small thing.

Meanwhile *Blue Chip* puts heavy weight on what constitutes a "sale" or "purchase" within the meaning of the rule. The lower courts in the period between *Birnbaum* and *Blue Chip,* while almost uniformly following the Second Circuit — and principally the Second Circuit itself — did put a high gloss on those critical terms. How much of that gloss still shines?

(1) Our analysis in Chapter 4A of the term "sale" in §2(3) of the 1933 Act cannot be applied blindly in the 10b-5 context, because, as we have noticed elsewhere,[145] §§3(a)(13) and 3(a)(14) of the 1934 Act do not really define "purchase" and "sale." But we have noticed also that there is authority for looking to the 1933

---

[142] The only discordant voice in the appellate courts was Eason v. General Motors Acceptance Corp., 490 F. 2d 654 (7th Cir. 1973), *cert. denied,* 416 U. S. 960.

[143] The Second Circuit has recently referred to Justice Rehnquist's language with reference to the settlement value of 10b-5 complaints in construing the requirement in Rule 9(b) of the Federal Rules of Civil Procdure that fraud be pleaded with particularity. Decker v. Massey-Ferguson, Ltd., 681 F. 2d 111, 114 (2d Cir. 1982).

[144] Santa Fe Industries, Inc. v. Green, 430 U. S. 462 (1977), set out infra p. 928.

[145] See p. 655 supra.

Act definition in construing the 1934 Act on an *in pari materia* approach.[146]

(2) In stockholders' derivative actions it is the corporation, not the plaintiff, that must have bought or sold.[147]

(3) As long as *somebody* bought or sold, *Blue Chip* should not affect criminal or SEC injunctive actions.

(4) The Second Circuit did not apply its own *Birnbaum* ruling in private injunctive actions — as where stockholders complained that insiders had manipulated the market and kept dividends down in order to force the other stockholders to sell out cheaply, although the plaintiffs themselves had not sold.[148] *Query* whether the Supreme Court will be more amenable to recognizing such an exception from *Blue Chip* in injunctive actions than it was in *Aaron* with respect to an exception from the scienter requirement of *Hochfelder*. Arguably the context here goes only to standing, not to violation as in the scienter context.

(5) It is quite well established that, although one does not ordinarily speak of an *issuance* of stock as a "sale" because there is nothing to be sold until the issuance has occurred, an issuance does involve a "sale" or "purchase" for purposes of Rule 10b-5.[149] This, as we shall see, opens up a good deal of the corporate mis-management area to federal law as long as the other elements of Rule 10b-5 are present;[150] for many, if not most, derivative actions involve a security transaction to which the corporation is a party.

(6) The "forced seller" in a "short-form merger" is a "seller" under the rule.[151] And this is true *a fortiori* with respect to an ordinary merger in which the stockholders have a vote; on this point there is Supreme Court precedent antedating *Blue Chip*.[152]

---

[146] See pp. 655-56 supra.

[147] Herpich v. Wallace, 430 F. 2d 792 (5th Cir. 1970) (a company is a "purchaser" entitled to damages for harmful acts already committed in furtherance of a merger plan not yet consummated).

[148] Mutual Shares Corp. v. Genesco, Inc., 384 F. 2d 540 (2d Cir. 1967) (stockholders complained that *others* had been forced to sell out cheaply by insiders' having manipulated the market and kept dividends down); see also Kahan v. Rosenstiel, 424 F. 2d 161 (3d Cir. 1970).

[149] Hooper v. Mountain States Securities Corp., 282 F. 2d 195 (5th Cir. 1960); Ruckle v. Roto American Corp., 339 F. 2d 24 (2d Cir. 1964); Rochelle v. Marine Midland Grace Trust Co. of N. Y., 535 F. 2d 523, 527-28 (9th Cir. 1976) (debentures).

[150] See pp. 925-44 infra.

[151] Vine v. Beneficial Finance Co., Inc., 374 F. 2d 627 (2d Cir. 1967).

[152] SEC v. National Securities, Inc., 393 U. S. 453 (1969). But cf. Rathborne v. Rathborne, 683 F. 2d 914 (5th Cir. 1982) (parent corporation's transfer of assets to a newly organized and wholly owned subsidiary in exchange for subsidiary's stock was a mere "transfer between corporate pockets"). See

This means that Rule 10b-5 is available to attack proxy literature for a merger when Rule 14a-9, the proxy fraud rule, is unavailable because the security is not registered.[153]

(7) In connection with the 1933 Act we have noticed the uncertainty whether a liquidating dividend payable in securities is a "sale."[154] In the 10b-5 context, the Fifth Circuit has applied the "forced sale" concept to liquidations on the theory that the nature of the shareholder's investment "has been fundamentally changed from an interest in a going enterprise into a right solely to a payment of money for his shares."[155] The same court has reaffirmed this view since *Blue Chip*, concluding that "The forced seller doctrine does not undermine the policy objectives of" that case.[156] On the other hand, just *before Blue Chip* the Fifth Circuit, again, *rejected* a contention that the issuance of new shares in a refinancing plan had so diluted the plaintiffs' position as to make them "forced sellers."[157]

(8) A redemption of convertible debentures in order to prevent conversions and dilution of voting control has been held to be a "purchase." As a result of the redemption, the Second Circuit *en banc* stated, the controlling stockholder "was acquiring the bondholders' rights to obtain common stock by conversion and thereby reducing the outstanding rights to interests in the equity securities of the corporation to the same extent as though it had purchased common shares on the open market."[158] In any event,

---

generally Annot., "Forced Seller" for Purposes of Maintenance of Civil Action under §10(b) * * * and SEC Rule 10b-5, 59 A. L. R. Fed. 10 (1982).

153 "The fact that there may well be some overlap is neither unusual nor unfortunate." SEC v. National Securities, Inc., 393 U. S. 453, 468 (1969).

154 See pp. 269-77 supra.

155 Dudley v. Southeastern Factor & Finance Corp., 446 F. 2d 303 (5th Cir. 1971), *cert. denied* sub nom. McDaniel v. Dudley, 404 U. S. 858. So, too, with respect to the liquidation of a limited partnership. Feldberg v. O'Connell, 338 F. Supp. 744 (D. Mass. 1972). But cf. Rathborne v. Rathborne, 683 F. 2d 914 (5th Cir. 1982) (parent corporation's *pro rata* distribution of stock of newly issued subsidiary was not the kind of fundamental change in the nature of stockholder's investment as to make him a "purchaser").

156 Alley v. Miramon, 614 F. 2d 1372, 1385-86 (5th Cir. 1980); but cf. Arnesen v. Shawmut County Bank, N. A., 504 F. Supp. 1077 (D. Mass. 1980) (Supreme Court's "policy to confine Rule 10b-5 within manageable limits" dictates a narrow interpretation of the "forced seller" doctrine as inapplicable in the absence of a formal liquidation even though a bank's foreclosure left minority shareholders with valueless stock in a company that had ceased its active existence). In Falls v. Fickling, 621 F. 2d 1362 (5th Cir. 1980), the court applied the "forced seller" doctrine to a person whose stock had been bought at a sheriff's sale.

157 Sargent v. Genesco, Inc., 492 F. 2d 750, 765 (5th Cir. 1974).

158 Drachman v. Harvey, 453 F. 2d 722, 737 n. 2 (2d Cir. *en banc* 1972). The court distinguished SEC v. Sterling Precision Corp., 393 F. 2d 214, 217-18

there can be no doubt that persons who do convert are both sellers and purchasers.[159]

(9) Quite clearly a pledgor is a "seller" and a pledgee is a "purchaser."[160]

(10) In 1965 the Southern District of New York sustained a complaint that alleged that the plaintiffs had been induced to defer market sales by the fraudulent representations of a broker-dealer and ultimately had sold at a greater loss.[161] Quite clearly this case of the *frustrated* seller does *not* survive *Blue Chip*.[162]

(11) There are quite a few cases of agent's liability to principal or vice versa, or trustee's liability to beneficiary.[163] Those cases are hostile to *Blue Chip*'s literal language. But, arguably, they are not inconsistent with its philosophy; for "the principal-agent (or similar) relationship affords at least as close a nexus as does the buyer-seller relationship."[164] On that basis, the Code, while not challenging *Blue Chip* otherwise,[165] provides:

> When an agent buys or sells a security for his principal, or a director or controlling person of a company buys or sells a security for the account or benefit of the company, or any other fiduciary buys or sells a security for the account or benefit of his beneficiary, both persons are buyers or sellers * * * .[166]

c. Corporate Mismanagement: The "New Fraud" Theory and Its Demise

Two seemingly self-evident, but not readily reconcilable, propositions have been repeated in judicial utterances: (1) Congress "did

---

(2d Cir. 1968), supra c. 7E n. 96, on the ground that "sale" had a broader meaning in the Exchange Act than in the Investment Company Act.

[159] See p. 263 supra. In our analysis of the 1933 Act we have noticed cases where the *pledgor* violated §5 or 17(a). See pp. 265, 283 supra. In Dopp v. Franklin National Bank, 374 F. Supp. 904 (S. D. N. Y. 1974), the pledgor alleged that the defendant *pledgee* had violated Rule 10b-5 by promising the plaintiff a right of first refusal without disclosing negotiations to sell to others.

[160] Rubin v. United States, 449 U. S. 424 (1981), set out supra p. 265.

[161] Stockwell v. Reynolds & Co., 252 F. Supp. 215 (S. D. N. Y. 1965).

[162] This is made explicit by Code §1722(b) so far as private actions (as distinct from SEC injunctive or administrative or criminal proceedings) are concerned.

[163] See the collection of cases in 2 Code 735-36; on beneficiary *versus* trustee, see also James v. Gerber Products Co., 483 F. 2d 944 (6th Cir. 1973).

[164] 2 Code 736.

[165] See 2 Code 659-60, Comment (3)(a).

[166] §1709(d).

not seek to regulate transactions which constitute no more than internal corporate mismanagement."[167] (2) The mere fact that the sale or purchase transaction "was part of a broader scheme of corporate mismanagement" does not preclude an action under Rule 10b-5.[168]

It fell to the Second Circuit's lot to explore these outer frontiers of the rule in a series of parries and thrusts that ultimately produced another visit from the Supreme Court. The story is best told chronologically:

In *Ruckle*,[169] a 1964 case, a director who represented more than half the voting stock, but somehow had let control evade or escape him, brought a derivative action against his six fellow directors, who constituted the corporation's officers, alleging that they had sought to perpetuate their control, among other ways, by having the board approve the issuance of some 75,000 treasury shares that were to be resold to the president or voted as he directed. The plaintiff alleged that the defendants had withheld the latest financial statements from the board, had arbitrarily ascribed a $3 value to the shares, and had approved several transactions involving the stock without disclosing pertinent facts to the entire board. Reversing a dismissal, the court held that it was possible under Rule 10b-5 for a corporation to be defrauded by a majority of its directors "or even the entire board."[170]

Only a few weeks later, in *O'Neill*,[171] the court distinguished *Ruckle*. *O'Neill* was a derivative action by a National Airlines stockholder against all nine of the National directors and Pan American complaining that the two companies had eliminated their cross-ownership (as ordered by the Civil Aeronautics Board) at an unfavorable ratio that cost National $1 million on the basis of market prices. The plaintiff's theory was that the National directors had caused National to pay a premium in order to get rid

---

[167] Superintendent of Ins. of the State of N. Y. v. Bankers Life & Casualty Co., 404 U. S. 6, 12 (1971); see also Birnbaum v. Newport Steel Corp., 193 F. 2d 461, 464 (2d Cir. 1952) (using the phrase, "*fraudulent* mismanagement").

[168] Herpich v. Wallace, 430 F. 2d 792, 808 (5th Cir. 1970); Schlick v. Penn-Dixie Cement Corp., 507 F. 2d 374, 380 (2d Cir. 1974).

[169] Ruckle v. Roto American Corp., 339 F. 2d 24 (2d Cir. 1964).

[170] To the effect that there is no conceptual difficulty in carrying through with the fiction that a corporation is a separate "person" that can be defrauded by a majority or even all of its directors, see also Condon v. Richardson, 411 F. 2d 489, 491-92 (7th Cir. 1969); Shell v. Hensley, 430 F. 2d 819 (5th Cir. 1970); Goldberg v. Meridor, 567 F. 2d 209, 215 (2d Cir. 1977), *cert. denied*, 434 U. S. 1069, set out infra p. 939.

[171] O'Neill v. Maytag, 339 F. 2d 764 (2d Cir. 1964).

of a Pan American threat to their control. The panel split. The two who sat in both cases, Judges Lumbard and Marshall, distinguished *Ruckle* because of the allegation there of the withholding of the company's most recent financial statement. Judge Hays, the only judge who had *not* sat in *Ruckle,* dissented without opinion.

The next case, *Schoenbaum,*[172] culminated in a rehearing *en banc.* A derivative complaint on behalf of Banff Oil against all its directors and a company called Aquitaine alleged that Aquitaine, after winning control of Banff through a tender offer, had put three directors on its eight-person board, which had then caused Banff to sell stock to Aquitaine at a market price that did not reflect an oil strike on Banff's properties. The court denied the defendants' motion for summary judgment by a vote of seven to three. Judge Hays, for the majority, said simply that Aquitaine had "exercised a controlling influence over the issuance to it of treasury shares of Banff for a wholly inadequate consideration," and that this violated the third clause of the rule — to which he added that "Aquitaine and the directors of Banff were guilty of deceiving the stockholders of Banff (other than Aquitaine)."[173] The opinion cited *Ruckle* but not *O'Neill.*

The case could be rationalized on the basis of the parent buyer's nondisclosure of the oil strike to "the corporation" as represented by the stockholders in the absence of a disinterested majority of directors.[174] And it was later so read.[175] On the other hand, since the majority opinion was *not* specifically analyzed in terms of failure to disclose the inadequate consideration, some commentators found in *Schoenbaum* a "new fraud" theory of Rule 10b-5: that inadequate (some said "grossly unfair") price coupled with con-

---

[172]Schoenbaum v. Firstbrook, 405 F. 2d 215 (2d Cir. *en banc* 1968), *cert. denied* sub nom. Manley v. Schoenbaum, 395 U. S. 906.

[173]405 F. 2d at 219-20.

[174]See Pappas v. Moss, 393 F. 2d 865, 869 (3d Cir. 1968). Should the procedure of a stockholder vote be too clumsy, the answer — as in the case of the insider whose duty to the corporation requires him to remain silent with respect to facts that he would have to disclose under Rule 10b-5 if he bought or sold in the market (see p. 827 supra) — is that there is no compulsion on the directors to go through with the particular transaction. And, even if the interested directors own or can influence the holders of enough shares to obtain ratification regardless of disclosure, it still does not follow that disclosure is nugatory; for, apart from the fact that the very requirement of disclosure may counter directors' overacquisitive instincts, it may prompt a derivative action for an injunction, which is in fact what was done in both *Ruckle* and *O'Neill* after the facts had come to light. See p. 943 infra.

[175]Popkin v. Bishop, 464 F. 2d 714 (2d Cir. 1972).

trolling influence was enough to establish a violation regardless of disclosure.[176]

Usually there will be little if any difference in end result, whichever theory is followed; for to say that an insider may not buy from (or sell to) his company at an unfair price without disclosing the unfairness to an *independent* board (or, in the absence of an independent board, to the *stockholders,* typically by means of a proxy statement cleared by the SEC) is to say as a practical matter that he may not buy (or sell). In any event, the next Second Circuit case resulted in the demise of a doctrine that probably never was:

SANTA FE INDUSTRIES, INC. v. GREEN
Supreme Court of the United States, 1977
430 U. S. 462

MR. JUSTICE WHITE delivered the opinion of the Court.

The issue in this case involves the reach and coverage of §10(b) of the Securities Exchange Act of 1934 and Rule 10b-5 thereunder in the context of a Delaware short-form merger transaction used by the majority stockholder of a corporation to eliminate the minority interest.

I

In 1936, petitioner Santa Fe Industries, Inc. (Santa Fe), acquired control of 60% of the stock of Kirby Lumber Corp. (Kirby), a Delaware corporation. Through a series of purchases over the succeeding years, Santa Fe increased its control of Kirby's stock to 95%; the purchase prices during the period 1968-1973 ranged from $65 to $92.50 per share. In 1974, wishing to acquire 100% ownership of Kirby, Santa Fe availed itself of §253 of the Delaware Corporation Law, known as the "short-form merger" statute. Section 253 permits a parent corporation owning at least 90% of the stock of a subsidiary to merge with that subsidiary, upon approval by the parent's board of directors, and to make payment in cash for the shares of the minority stockholders. The statute does not require the consent of, or advance notice to, the minority stockholders. However, notice of the merger must be given within 10 days after its effective date, and any stockholder who is dissatis-

---

[176] See, e. g., Note, The Controlling Influence Standard in Rule 10b-5 Corporate Mismanagement Cases, 86 Harv. L. Rev. 1007 (1973).

fied with the terms of the merger may petition the Delaware Court of Chancery for a decree ordering the surviving corporation to pay him the fair value of his shares, as determined by a court-appointed appraiser subject to review by the court. Del. Code Ann., Tit. 8, §§253, 262 (1975 ed. and Supp. 1976).

Sante Fe obtained independent appraisals of the physical assets of Kirby — land, timber, buildings, and machinery — and of Kirby's oil, gas, and mineral interests. These appraisals, together with other financial information, were submitted to Morgan Stanley & Co. (Morgan Stanley), an investment banking firm retained to appraise the fair market value of Kirby stock. Kirby's physical assets were appraised at $320 million (amounting to $640 for each of the 500,000 shares); Kirby's stock was valued by Morgan Stanley at $125 per share. Under the terms of the merger, minority stockholders were offered $150 per share.

The provisions of the short-form merger statute were fully complied with. The minority stockholders of Kirby were notified the day after the merger became effective and were advised of their right to obtain an appraisal in Delaware court if dissatisfied with the offer of $150 per share. They also received an information statement containing, in addition to the relevant financial data about Kirby, the appraisals of the value of Kirby's assets and the Morgan Stanley appraisal concluding that the fair market value of the stock was $125 per share.

Respondents, minority stockholders of Kirby, objected to the terms of the merger, but did not pursue their appraisal remedy in the Delaware Court of Chancery. Instead, they brought this action in federal court on behalf of the corporation and other minority stockholders, seeking to set aside the merger or to recover what they claimed to be the fair value of their shares. The amended complaint asserted that, based on the fair market value of Kirby's physical assets as revealed by the appraisal included in the information statement sent to minority shareholders, Kirby's stock was worth at least $772 per share. The complaint alleged further that the merger took place without prior notice to minority stockholders; that the purpose of the merger was to appropriate the difference between the "conceded pro rata value of the physical assets," App. 103a, and the offer of $150 per share — to "freez[e] out the minority stockholders at a wholly inadequate price," id., at 100a; and that Santa Fe, knowing the appraised value of the physical assets, obtained a "fraudulent appraisal" of the stock from Morgan Stanley and offered $25 above that appraisal "in order to lull the minority stockholders into erroneously believing that [Santa Fe was] generous." Id., at 103a. This course of conduct was alleged to be "a violation of Rule 10b-5 because defendants employed a 'device, scheme, or artifice to defraud' and engaged in an 'act, practice or course of business which operates or would operate as a fraud or deceit upon any person, in connection with the purchase or sale of any security.'" Ibid. Morgan Stanley assertedly participated in the fraud as an accessory by submitting its appraisal of $125 per share although knowing the appraised value of the physical assets.

The District Court dismissed the complaint for failure to state a claim upon which relief could be granted. 391 F. Supp. 849 (S. D. N. Y. 1975). As the District Court understood the complaint, respondents' case rested on two distinct grounds. First, federal law was assertedly violated because the merger was for the sole purpose of eliminating the minority from the company, therefore lacking any justifiable business purpose, and because the merger was undertaken without prior notice to the minority shareholders. Second, the low valuation placed on the shares in the cash-exchange offer was itself said to be a fraud actionable under Rule 10b-5. In rejecting the first ground for recovery, the District Court reasoned that Delaware law required neither a business purpose for a short-form merger nor prior notice to the minority shareholders who the statute contemplated would be removed from the company, and that Rule 10b-5 did not override these provisions of state corporate law by independently placing a duty on the majority not to merge without prior notice and without a justifiable business purpose.

As for the claim that actionable fraud inhered in the allegedly gross undervaluation of the minority shares, the District Court observed that respondents valued their shares at a minimum of $772 per share, "basing this figure on the *pro rata* value of Kirby's physical assets." Id., at 853. Accepting this valuation for purposes of the motion to dismiss, the District Court further noted that, as revealed by the complaint, the physical asset appraisal, along with other information relevant to Morgan Stanley's valuation of the shares, had been included with the information statement sent to respondents within the time required by state law. It thought that if "full and fair disclosure is made, transactions eliminating minority interests are beyond the purview of Rule 10b-5," and concluded that the "complaint fail[ed] to allege an omission, misstatement or fraudulent course of conduct that would have impeded a shareholder's judgment of the value of the offer." Id., at 854. The complaint therefore failed to state a claim and was dismissed.

A divided Court of Appeals for the Second Circuit reversed.

533 F. 2d 1283 (1976). It first agreed that there was a double aspect to the case: first, the claim that gross undervaluation of the minority stock itself violated Rule 10b-5; and second, that "without any misrepresentation or failure to disclose relevant facts, the merger itself constitutes a violation of Rule 10b-5" because it was accomplished without any corporate purpose without prior notice to the minority stockholders. Id., at 1285. As to the first aspect of the case, the Court of Appeals did not disturb the District Court's conclusion that the complaint did not allege a material misrepresentation or nondisclosure with respect to the value of the stock; and the court declined to rule that a claim of gross undervaluation itself would suffice to make out a Rule 10b-5 case. With respect to the second aspect of the case, however, the court fundamentally disagreed with the District Court as to the reach and coverage of Rule 10b-5. The Court of Appeals' view was that, although the Rule plainly reached material misrepresentations and nondisclosures in connection with the purchase or sale of securities, neither misrepresentation nor nondisclosure was a necessary element of a Rule 10b-5 action; the Rule reached "breaches of fiduciary duty by a majority against minority shareholders without any charge of misrepresentation or lack of disclosure." Id., at 1287.[8] The court went on to hold that the complaint, taken as a whole, stated a cause of action under the Rule:

> We hold that a complaint alleges a claim under Rule 10b-5 when it charges, in connection with a Delaware short-form merger, that the majority has committed a breach of its fiduciary duty to deal fairly with minority shareholders by effecting the merger without any justifiable business purpose. The minority shareholders are given no prior notice of the merger, thus having no opportunity to apply for injunctive relief, and the proposed price to be paid is substantially lower than the appraised value reflected in the Information Statement. Id., at 1291.

See also id., at 1289.

We granted the petition for certiorari challenging this holding because of the importance of the issue involved to the administration of the federal securities laws. 429 U. S. 814 (1976). We reverse.

---

[8] The court concluded its discussion thus: "Whether full disclosure has been made is not the crucial inquiry since it is the merger and the undervaluation which constituted the fraud, and not whether or not the majority determines to lay bare their real motives. If there is no valid corporate purpose for the merger, then even the most brazen disclosure of that fact to the minority shareholders in no way mitigates the fraudulent conduct." 533 F. 2d, at 1292.

II

*   *   *

* * * The court below construed the term "fraud" in Rule 10b-5 by adverting to the use of the term in several of this Court's decisions in contexts other than the 1934 Act and the related Securities Act of 1933, 15 U. S. C. §77a et seq.[11] The Court of Appeals' approach to the interpretation of Rule 10b-5 is inconsistent with that taken by the Court last Term in *Ernst & Ernst* v. *Hochfelder,* 425 U. S. 185 (1976).

Ernst & Ernst makes clear that in deciding whether a complaint states a cause of action for "fraud" under Rule 10b-5, "we turn first to the language of §10(b), for '[t]he starting point in every case involving construction of a statute is the language itself.' " Id., at 197, quoting *Blue Chip Stamps* v. *Manor Drug Stores,* 421 U. S. 723, 756 (1975) (Powell, J., concurring). In holding that a cause of action under Rule 10b-5 does not lie for mere negligence, the Court began with the principle that "[a]scertainment of congressional intent with respect to the standard of liability created by a particular section of the[1933 and 1934] Acts must . . . rest primarily on the language of that section," 425 U. S., at 200, and then focused on the statutory language of §10(b) — "[t]he words 'manipulative or deceptive' used in conjunction with 'device or contrivance.' " Id., at 197. The same language and the same principle apply to this case.

To the extent that the Court of Appeals would rely on the use of the term "fraud" in Rule 10b-5 to bring within the ambit of the Rule all breaches of fiduciary duty in connection with a securities transaction, its interpretation would, like the interpretation re-

---

[11] The Court of Appeals quoted passages from Pepper v. Litton, 308 U. S. 295, 306, 311 (1939) (where this Court upheld the disallowance of a bankruptcy claim of a controlling stockholder who violated his fiduciary obligation to the other stockholders), and from 1 J. Story, Equity Jurisprudence §187 (1853); the court also cited cases that quoted the passage from Mr. Justice Story's treatise — Moore v. Crawford, 130 U. S. 122, 128 (1889) (a diversity suit to compel execution of a deed held in constructive trust), and SEC v. Capital Gains Research Bureau, 375 U. S. 180, 194 (1963) (Investment Advisers Act of 1940 prohibits, as a "fraud or deceit upon any client," a registered investment adviser's failure to disclose to his clients his own financial interest in his recommendations). Although *Capital Gains* involved a federal securities statute, the Court's references to fraud in the "equitable" sense of the term were premised on its recognition that Congress intended the Investment Advisers Act to establish federal fiduciary standards for investment advisers. See *id.,* at 191-192, 194. Moreover, the fraud that the SEC sought to enjoin in *Capital Gains* was, in fact, a nondisclosure.

jected by the Court in *Ernst & Ernst,* "add a gloss to the operative language of the statute quite different from its commonly accepted meaning." Id., at 199. But, as the Court there held, the language of the statute must control the interpretation of the Rule:

> Rule 10b-5 was adopted pursuant to authority granted the [Securities and Exchange] Commission under §10(b). The rulemaking power granted to an administrative agency charged with the administration of a federal statute is not the power to make law. Rather, it is "the power to adopt regulations to carry into effect the will of Congress as expressed by the statute." . . . [The scope of the Rule] cannot exceed the power granted the Commission by Congress under §10(b). Id., at 212-214.[12]

The language of §10(b) gives no indication that Congress meant to prohibit any conduct not involving manipulation or deception. Nor have we been cited to any evidence in the legislative history that would support a departure from the language of the statute. "When a statute speaks so specifically in terms of manipulation and deception, . . . and when its history reflects no more expansive intent, we are quite unwilling to extend the scope of the statute . . . ." Id., at 214. Thus the claim of fraud and fiduciary breach in this complaint states a cause of action under any part of Rule 10b-5 only if the conduct alleged can be fairly viewed as "manipulative or deceptive" within the meaning of the statute.

III

It is our judgment that the transaction, if carried out as alleged in the complaint, was neither deceptive nor manipulative and therefore did not violate either §10(b) of the Act or Rule 10b-5.

As we have indicated, the case comes to us on the premise that

---

[12] The case for adhering to the language of the statute is even stronger here than in *Ernst & Ernst,* where the interpretation of Rule 10b-5 rejected by the Court was strongly urged by the Commission. See also Piper v. Chris-Craft Industries, Inc., ante, p. 1, and Blue Chip Stamps v. Manor Drug Stores, 421 U. S. 723 (1975) (rejecting interpretations of Rule 10b-5 urged by the SEC as *amicus curiae*). By contrast, the Commission apparently has not concluded that Rule 10b-5 should be used to reach "going private" transactions where the majority stockholder eliminates the minority at an allegedly unfair price. See SEC Securities Act Release No. 5567 (Feb. 6, 1975), CCH Fed. Sec. L. Rep. ¶80,104 (proposing Rules 13e-3A and 13e-3B dealing with "going private" transactions, pursuant to six sections of the 1934 Act including §10(b), but stating that the Commission "has reached no conclusions with respect to the proposed rules"). [See p. 585 supra.] Because we are concerned here only with §10(b), we intimate no view as to the Commission's authority to promulgate such rules under other sections of the Act.

the complaint failed to allege a material misrepresentation or material failure to disclose. The finding of the District Court, undisturbed by the Court of Appeals, was that there was no "omission" or "misstatement" in the information statement accompanying the notice of merger. On the basis of the information provided, minority shareholders could either accept the price offered or reject it and seek an appraisal in the Delaware Court of Chancery. Their choice was fairly presented, and they were furnished with all relevant information on which to base their decision.[14]

We therefore find inapposite the cases relied upon by respondents and the court below, in which the breaches of fiduciary duty held violative of Rule 10b-5 included some element of deception.[15] Those cases forcefully reflect the principle that "[§]10(b) must be read flexibly, not technically and restrictively" and that the statute provides a cause of action for any plaintiff who "suffer[s] an injury as a result of deceptive practices touching its sale [or purchase] of

[14] In addition to their principal argument that the complaint alleges a fraud under clauses (a) and (c) of Rule 10b-5, respondents also argue that the complaint alleges nondisclosure and misrepresentation in violation of clause (b) of the Rule. Their major contention in this respect is that the majority stockholder's failure to give the minority advance notice of the merger was a material nondisclosure, even though the Delaware short-form merger statute does not require such notice. Brief for Respondents 27. But respondents do not indicate how they might have acted differently had they had prior notice of the merger. Indeed, they accept the conclusion of both courts below that under Delaware law they could not have enjoined the merger because an appraisal proceeding is their sole remedy in the Delaware courts for any alleged unfairness in the terms of the merger. Thus, the failure to give advance notice was not a material nondisclosure within the meaning of the statute or the Rule. Cf. TSC Industries, Inc. v. Northway, Inc., 426 U. S. 438 (1976).

[15] The decisions of this Court relied upon by respondents all involved deceptive conduct as part of the Rule 10b-5 violation alleged. Affiliated Ute Citizens v. United States, 406 U. S. 128 (1972) (misstatements of material fact used by bank employees in position of market maker to acquire stock at less than fair value); Superintendent of Insurance v. Bankers Life & Cas. Co., 404 U. S. 6, 9 (1971) ("seller [of bonds] was duped into believing that it, the seller, would receive the proceeds"). Cf. SEC v. Capital Gains Research Bureau, 375 U. S. 180 (1963) (injunction under Investment Advisers Act of 1940 to compel registered investment adviser to disclose to his clients his own financial interest in his recommendations).

We have been cited to a large number of cases in the Courts of Appeals, all of which involved an element of deception as part of the fiduciary misconduct held to violate Rule 10b-5. E. g., Schoenbaum v. Firstbrook, 405 F. 2d 215, 220 (C. A. 2 1968) (en banc), cert. denied sub nom. Manley v. Schoenbaum, 395 U. S. 906 (1969) (majority stockholder and board of directors "were guilty of deceiving" the minority stockholders) * * * . See Recent Cases, 89 Harv. L. Rev. 1917, 1926 (1976) (stating that no appellate decision before that of the Court of Appeals in this case and in Marshel v. AFW Fabric Corp., 533 F. 2d 1277 (C. A. 2), vacated and remanded for a determination of mootness, 429 U. S. 881 (1976), "had permitted a 10b-5 claim without some element of misrepresentation or nondisclosure") (footnote omitted).

securities . . . ." *Superintendent of Insurance* v. *Bankers Life & Cas. Co.,* 404 U. S. 6, 12-13 (1971). But the cases do not support the proposition, adopted by the Court of Appeals below and urged by respondents here, that a breach of fiduciary duty by majority stockholders, without any deception, misrepresentation, or non-disclosure, violates the statute and the Rule.

It is also readily apparent that the conduct alleged in the complaint was not "manipulative" within the meaning of the statute. "Manipulation" is "virtually a term of art when used in connection with securities markets." *Ernst & Ernst,* 425 U. S., at 199. The term refers generally to practices, such as wash sales, matched orders, or rigged prices, that are intended to mislead investors by artificially affecting market activity. See, e. g., §9 of the 1934 Act, 15 U. S. C. §78i (prohibiting specific manipulative practices); *Ernst & Ernst,* supra, at 195, 199 n. 21, 205; *Piper* v. *Chris-Craft Industries, Inc.,* ante, at 43 (Rule 10b-6, also promulgated under §10(b), is "an antimanipulative provision designed to protect the orderliness of the securities market during distributions of stock" and "to prevent stimulative trading by an issuer in its own securities in order to create an unnatural and unwarranted appearance of market activity"); 2 A. Bromberg, Securities Law: Fraud §7.3 (1975); 3 L. Loss, Securities Regulation 1541-1570 (2d ed. 1961); 6 id., at 3755-3763 (Supp. 1969). Section 10(b)'s general prohibition of practices deemed by the SEC to be "manipulative" — in this technical sense of artificially affecting market activity in order to mislead investors — is fully consistent with the fundamental purpose of the 1934 Act " 'to substitute a philosophy of full disclosure for the philosophy of *caveat emptor* . . . .' " *Affiliated Ute Citizens* v. *United States,* 406 U. S. 128, 151 (1972), quoting *SEC* v. *Capital Gains Research Bureau,* 375 U. S. 180, 186 (1963). Indeed, nondisclosure is usually essential to the success of a manipulative scheme. 3 Loss, supra, at 1565. No doubt Congress meant to prohibit the full range of ingenious devices that might be used to manipulate securities prices. But we do not think it would have chosen this "term of art" if it had meant to bring within the scope of §10(b) instances of corporate mismanagement such as this, in which the essence of the complaint is that shareholders were treated unfairly by a fiduciary.

IV

The language of the statute is, we think, "sufficiently clear in its context" to be dispositive here, *Ernst & Ernst,* supra, at 201; but even if it were not, there are additional considerations that weigh heavily against permitting a cause of action under Rule 10b-5 for the breach of corporate fiduciary duty alleged in this complaint. Congress did not expressly provide a private cause of action for violations of §10(b). Although we have recognized an implied cause of action under that section in some circumstances, *Superintendent of Insurance* v. *Bankers Life & Cas. Co.,* supra, at 13 n. 9, we have also recognized that a private cause of action under the antifraud provisions of the Securities Exchange Act should not be implied where it is "unnecessary to ensure the fulfillment of Congress' purposes" in adopting the Act. *Piper* v. *Chris-Craft Industries,* ante, at 41. Cf. *J. I. Case Co.* v. *Borak,* 377 U. S. 426, 431-433 (1964). As we noted earlier, supra, this page, the Court repeatedly has described the "fundamental purpose" of the Act as implementing a "philosophy of full disclosure"; once full and fair disclosure has occurred, the fairness of the terms of the transaction is at most a tangential concern of the statute. Cf. *Mills* v. *Electric Auto-Lite Co.,* 396 U. S. 375, 381-385 (1970). As in *Cort* v. *Ash,* 422 U. S. 66, 80 (1975), we are reluctant to recognize a cause of action here to serve what is "at best a subsidiary purpose" of the federal legislation.

A second factor in determining whether Congress intended to create a federal cause of action in these circumstances in "whether 'the cause of action [is] one traditionally relegated to state law . . . .'" *Piper* v. *Chris-Craft Industries, Inc.,* ante, at 40, quoting *Cort* v. *Ash,* supra, at 78. The Delaware Legislature has supplied minority shareholders with a cause of action in the Delaware Court of Chancery to recover the fair value of shares allegedly undervalued in a short-form merger. See supra, at 465-466. Of course, the existence of a particular state-law remedy is not dispositive of the question whether Congress meant to provide a similar federal remedy, but as in *Cort* and *Piper,* we conclude that "it is entirely appropriate in this instance to relegate respondent and others in his situation to whatever remedy is created by state law." 422 U. S., at 84; ante, at 41.

The reasoning behind a holding that the complaint in this case alleged fraud under Rule 10b-5 could not be easily contained. It is difficult to imagine how a court could distinguish, for purposes of Rule 10b-5 fraud, between a majority stockholder's use of a short-form merger to eliminate the minority at an unfair price and the use of some other device, such as a long-form merger, tender offer, or liquidation, to achieve the same result; or indeed how a court could distinguish the alleged abuses in these going private transactions from other types of fiduciary self-dealing involving transactions in securities. The result would be to bring within the Rule a wide variety of corporate conduct traditionally left to state regulation. In addition to posing a "danger of vexatious litigation which could result from a widely expanded class of plaintiffs under Rule 10b-5," *Blue Chip Stamps* v. *Manor Drug Stores,* 421 U. S., at 740, this extension of the federal securities laws would overlap and quite possibly interfere with state corporate law. Federal courts applying a "federal fiduciary principle" under Rule 10b-5 could be expected to depart from state fiduciary standards at least to the extent necessary to ensure uniformity within the federal system.[16] Absent a clear indication of congressional intent, we are reluctant to federalize the substantial portion of the law of corporations that deals with transactions in securities, particularly where established state policies of corporate regulation would be overridden. As the Court stated in *Cort* v. *Ash,* supra: "Corporations are creatures of state law, and investors commit their funds to corporate directors on the understanding that, except where federal law *expressly* requires certain responsibilities of directors with respect to stockholders, state law will govern the internal affairs of the corporation." 422 U. S., at 84 (emphasis added).

We thus adhere to the position that "Congress by §10(b) did not seek to regulate transactions which constitute no more than internal corporate mismanagement." *Superintendent of Insurance* v. *Bankers Life & Cas. Co.,* 404 U. S., at 12. There may well be a need for uniform federal fiduciary standards to govern mergers such as that challenged in this complaint. But those standards should not be supplied by judicial extension of §10(b) and Rule 10b-5 to "cover the corporate universe."

The judgment of the Court of Appeals is reversed, and the case is remanded for further proceedings consistent with this opinion.

So ordered.

MR. JUSTICE BRENNAN dissents and would affirm for substantially the reasons stated in the majority and concurring opinions in the Court of Appeals, 533 F. 2d 1283 (C. A. 2 1976).

---

[16] For example, some States apparently require a "valid corporate purpose" for the elimination of the minority interest through a short-form merger, whereas other States do not. * * * Thus to the extent that Rule 10b-5 is interpreted to require a valid corporate purpose for elimination of minority shareholders as well as a fair price for their shares, it would impose a stricter standard of fiduciary duty than that required by the law of some States.

MR. JUSTICE BLACKMUN, concurring in part.

Like Mr. Justice Stevens, I refrain from joining Part IV of the Court's opinion. I, too, regard that part as unnecessary for the decision in the instant case and, indeed, as exacerbating the concerns I expressed in my dissents in *Blue Chip Stamps* v. *Manor Drug Stores*, 421 U. S. 723, 761 (1975), and in *Ernst & Ernst* v. *Hochfelder*, 425 U. S. 185, 215 (1976). I, however, join the remainder of the Court's opinion and its judgment.

MR. JUSTICE STEVENS, concurring in part.

For the reasons stated by Mr. Justice Blackmun in his dissenting opinion in *Blue Chip Stamps* v. *Manor Drug Stores*, 421 U. S. 723, 761, and those stated in my dissent in *Piper* v. *Chris-Craft Industries*, ante, p. 53, I believe both of those cases were incorrectly decided. I foresee some danger that Part IV of the Court's opinion in this case may incorrectly be read as extending the holdings of those cases. Moreover, the entire discussion in Part IV is unnecessary to the decision of this case. Accordingly, I join only Parts I, II, and III of the Court's opinion. I would also add further emphasis to the fact that the controlling stockholders in this case did not breach any duty owed to the minority shareholders because (a) there was complete disclosure of the relevant facts, and (b) the minority are entitled to receive the fair value of their shares. The facts alleged in the complaint do not constitute "fraud" within the meaning of Rule 10b-5.

The Supreme Court's reversal was no surprise — indeed, the Second Circuit denied a rehearing *en banc* because it was "confident" that a grant of *certiorari* was "inevitable"[177] — for this time the panel that sat dispelled "any lingering doubt" that in its view it was sufficient to allege that the "majority has committed a breach of its fiduciary duty to deal fairly with minority shareholders by effecting [a Delaware short-form] merger without any justifiable business purpose."[178] As Judge Moore remarked, this would "override and nullify" the short-form merger statutes of three-quarters of the states.[179] He might have gone further and said that the majority opinion came "very close to holding that the Delaware law is a device to defraud."[180] Oddly enough, the venerable Judge

---

[177] Green v. Santa Fe Industries, Inc., 533 F. 2d 1309 (2d Cir. 1976).

[178] Id., 533 F. 2d 1283, 1287, 1291 (2d Cir. 1976).

[179] 533 F. 2d at 1299.

[180] Dyer, An Essay on Federalism in Private Actions under Rule 10b-5, [1976] Utah L. Rev. 7, 9.

Medina, writing in his ninetieth year, did not mention his bitter "what is the world coming to?" dissent in *Schoenbaum,* in which he had viewed the majority opinion as "nothing short of a standing invitation to blackmail and distortion."[181]

In any event, the Supreme Court's decision was not the last word. Six months later a sharply divided panel of the Second Circuit concluded that *Santa Fe* did not overrule *Schoenbaum:*

GOLDBERG v. MERIDOR
United States Court of Appeals, Second Circuit, 1977
567 F. 2d 209

Before FRIENDLY, TIMBERS and MESKILL, Circuit Judges.
FRIENDLY, Circuit Judge.

[A derivative action on behalf of UGO charged that its parent, Maritimecor, had caused it to issue shares to the parent for all its assets and liabilities in an unfair transaction and on the basis of nondisclosure or misleading disclosure of material facts that were known to all the directors.]

*   *   *

The problem with the application of §10(b) and Rule 10b-5 to derivative actions has lain in the degree to which the knowledge of officers and directors must be attributed to the corporation, thereby negating the element of deception. * * *

* * * [There is no requirement that there be] one virtuous or ignorant lamb among the directors in order for liability to arise under §10(b) or Rule 10b-5 on a deception theory as to securities transactions with a controlling stockholder.

* * * *Schoenbaum* has been generally applauded by commentators, even though it may sometimes have been read to mean more than it does or than is needed to call for a reversal here. * * * It likewise is viewed with approval — indeed seemingly would be adopted — by §§1303 and 1402(c) of the proposed ALI Federal Securities Code, Tent. Draft No. 2 (March 1973) and revised comments in Reporter's Revision of Text of Tentative Drafts Nos. 1-3, pp. 104-06 (Oct. 1, 1974), see also §§234D(c) and 1301.[a] It has also found favor in other circuits. * * *

---

[181] 405 F. 2d at 221.
[a] ED.: These excerpts became Code §§202(56), 202(61)(E), 202(64), 202 (86)(B), 1602, 1603, and 2 Code 661-62.

Schoenbaum, then, can rest solidly on the now widely recognized ground that there is deception of the corporation (in effect, of its minority shareholders) when the corporation is influenced by its controlling shareholder to engage in a transaction adverse to the corporation's interests (in effect, the minority shareholders' interests) and there is nondisclosure or misleading disclosures as to the material facts of the transaction. Assuming that, in light of the decision in *Green,* the existence of "controlling influence" and "wholly inadequate consideration" — an aspect of the *Schoenbaum* decision that perhaps attracted more attention, see 405 F. 2d at 219-20 — can no longer alone form the basis for Rule 10b-5 liability, we do not read *Green* as ruling that no action lies under Rule 10b-5 when a controlling corporation causes a partly owned subsidiary to sell its securities to the parent in a fraudulent transaction and fails to make a disclosure or, as can be alleged here, makes a misleading disclosure. The Supreme Court noted in *Green* that the court of appeals "did not disturb the District Court's conclusion that the complaint did not allege a material misrepresentation or nondisclosure with respect to the value of the stock" of Kirby; the Court's quarrel was with this court's holding that "neither misrepresentation nor nondisclosure was a necessary element of a Rule 10b-5 action," 430 U. S. at 470, and that a breach of fiduciary duty would alone suffice, see fn. 8. It was because "the complaint failed to allege a material misrepresentation or material failure to disclose" that the Court found "inapposite the cases [including *Schoenbaum*] relied upon by respondents and the court below, in which the breaches of fiduciary duty held violative of Rule 10b-5 included some element of deception," 430 U. S. at 475, see fn. 15. While appellant is wrong in saying that the Court "approved" these cases, there is no indication that the Court would have casually overturned such an impressive and unanimous body of decisions by courts of appeals. To the contrary, the Court used rather benign language about them, saying that they "forcefully reflect the principle that [s]ection 10(b) must be read flexibly not restrictively' and that the statute provides a cause of action for any plaintiff who 'suffer[s] an injury as a result of deceptive practices touching its sale [or purchase] of securities . . . ,' " citing the *Superintendent of Insurance* case, supra, 404 U. S. at 12-13. Mr. Justice White simply distinguished these cases as not supporting the position we had taken in *Green,* namely, "that a breach of fiduciary duty by majority stockholders, *without any deception, misrepresentation, or nondisclosure,* violates the statute and the Rule." (Emphasis supplied.)

Here the complaint alleged "deceit . . . upon UGO's minority shareholders" and, if amendment had been allowed as it should have been, would have alleged misrepresentation as to the UGO-Maritimecor transaction at least in the sense of failure to state material facts "necessary in order to make the statements made, in the light of the circumstances under which they were made, not misleading," Rule 10b-5(b).[8] The nub of the matter is that the conduct attacked in *Green* did not violate the " 'fundamental purpose' of the Act as implementing a 'philosophy of full disclosure,' " 430 U. S. at 478; the conduct here attacked does.

Defendants contend that even if all this is true, the failure to make a public disclosure or even the making of a misleading disclosure would have no effect, since no action by stockholders to approve the UGO-Maritimecor transaction was required. Along the same lines our brother Meskill invoking the opinion in *Green,* 430 U. S. at 474 n. 14, contends that the defendants' acts were not material since plaintiff has failed adequately to allege what would have been done had he known the truth.

* * * When, as in a derivative action, the deception is alleged to have been practiced on the corporation, even though all the directors were parties to it, the test [of materiality] must be whether the facts that were not disclosed or were misleadingly disclosed to the shareholders "would have assumed actual significance in the deliberations" of reasonable and disinterested directors or created "a substantial likelihood" that such directors would have considered the "total mix" of information available to have been "significantly altered." That was the basis for liability in *Schoenbaum;* it was likely that a reasonable director of Banff, knowing the facts as to the oil discovery that had been withheld from minority shareholders, would not have voted to issue the shares to Aquitaine at a price below their true value. * * *

Beyond this Goldberg and other minority shareholders would not have been without remedy if the alleged facts had been disclosed. The doubts entertained by our brother as to the existence of injunctive remedies in New York * * * are unfounded. * * *

The availability of injunctive relief if the defendants had not lulled the minority stockholders of UGO into security by a deceptive disclosure, as they allegedly did, is in sharp contrast to *Green,* where the disclosure following the merger transaction was

---

[8] We do not mean to suggest that §10(b) or Rule 10b-5 requires insiders to characterize conflict of interest transactions with pejorative nouns or adjectives. However, if Maritimecor was in the parlous financial condition alleged in the opposing affidavit of plaintiff's counsel, a disclosure of the acquisition of Maritimecor that omitted these facts would be seriously misleading.

full and fair, and, as to the pre-merger period, respondents accepted "the conclusion of both courts below that under Delaware law they could not have enjoined the merger because an appraisal proceeding is their sole remedy in the Delaware courts for any alleged unfairness in the terms of the merger," fn. 14. * * *

* * *

The order dismissing the complaint is reversed and the case is remanded to the district court for further proceedings, including amendment of the complaint, consistent with this opinion.

MESKILL, Circuit Judge concurring in part and dissenting in part:

* * *

* * * The primary role of the states in these matters has been emphasized in a number of recent opinions of the Supreme Court. * * *

Those who breach their fiduciary duties seldom disclose their intentions ahead of time. Yet under the majority's reasoning the failure to inform stockholders of a proposed defalcation gives rise to a cause of action under 10b-5. Thus, the majority has neatly undone the holdings of *Green, Piper*[b] and *Cort*[c] by creating a federal cause of action for a breach of fiduciary duty that will apply in all cases, save for those rare instances where the fiduciary denounces himself in advance.

* * *

(1) *Query:* Is the last paragraph of Judge Meskill's opinion here reproduced a fair characterization of the majority opinion? Judge Friendly did limit the holding to cases of "nondisclosure or misleading disclosures as to *the material facts* of the transaction" (italics supplied).[182] And other appellate courts have read *Goldberg* as requiring more than mere nondisclosure of impure motive or culpability.[183]

[b] ED.: Piper v. Chris-Craft Industries, Inc., 430 U. S. 1 (1977).
[c] ED.: Cort v. Ash, 422 U. S. 66 (1975), set out infra p. 1065.
[182] 567 F. 2d at 217, supra p. 940.
[183] Alabama Farm Bureau Mutual Casualty Co., Inc. v. American Fidelity

(2) The *Goldberg* case has attracted a following. But there is disagreement whether its reference to the "availability of injunctive relief if the defendants had not lulled the minority stockholders of UGO into security by a deceptive disclosure"[184] requires proof than an action for injunction under state law would have been won,[185] or merely that such an action was "available" and that the facts shown make out a prima facie case for relief,[186] or that there was a "reasonable probability" of success.[187] The first and third of those views require a trial within a trial.

(3) The Seventh Circuit seems to have brought fairness back in (with the burden of going forward on the defendant) as a limitation on the *Goldberg* rule when there *is* nondisclosure.[188]

(4) *Goldberg* does produce an anomaly with its rationale that a state law remedy for breach of fiduciary duty, far from foreclosing a 10b-5 action, is precisely the foundation for a theory of deception in that inadequate disclosure lulls stockholders into foregoing their state law remedies. As Judge Aldisert put it in a dissenting opinion: "Thus, rather than aiding plaintiffs under federal law who have no state remedy, the majority's formulation provides federal relief to plaintiffs who have state remedies, but denies federal relief to plaintiffs who have no state remedy!"[189]

Life Ins. Co., 606 F. 2d 602, 610 (5th Cir. 1979); Panter v. Marshall Field & Co., 646 F. 2d 271, 291 (7th Cir. 1981).

[184] 567 F. 2d at 220, supra p. 941.

[185] Kidwell *ex rel.* Penfold v. Merkle, 597 F. 2d 1277, 1294 (9th Cir. 1979). The Ninth Circuit also thought that the proper inquiry on the materiality question was what would have been considered significant by a reasonable shareholder, not by a reasonable director as stated in *Goldberg*. Id. at 1293 w. 10.

[186] Alabama Farm Bureau Mutual Casualty Co., Inc. v. American Fidelity Life Ins. Co., 606 F. 2d 602, 614 (5th Cir. 1979).

[187] Healey v. Catalyst Recovery of Pa., Inc., 616 F. 2d 641, 648 (3d Cir. 1980). On these several approaches, see Comment, Causation in Rule 10b-5 Actions for Corporate Mismanagement, 48 U. Chi. L. Rev. 936 (1981).

[188] Wright v. Heizer Corp., 560 F. 2d 236, 255-56 (7th Cir. 1977). For another limitation on *Goldberg*, see Abbey v. Control Data Corp., 603 F. 2d 724, 731 (8th Cir. 1979), where the court, citing *Santa Fe*, stated: "Illegal foreign payments clearly involve state law questions of breach of fiduciary duties. They should not be dealt with under the general disclosure provisions of the federal securities laws where it is apparent, as here, that the nondisclosure of such payments had little, if any, impact on the plaintiff's dealings in the corporation's stock."

[189] Healey v. Catalyst Recovery of Pa., Inc., 616 F. 2d 641, 658 (3d Cir. 1980). Arthur Borden of the New York Bar has coined the phrase "sue fact doctrine" to describe the group of cases stemming from *Goldberg*, a doctrine that he calls "judicial casuistry": "The 'sue fact' doctrine holds that Rule 10b-5 requires the disclosure not only of information relevant to an *investment decision* but also information relevant to a *decision to sue* under state law, whenever such law provides a remedy to the shareholder. * * * A 'sue fact'

(5) We have already observed that Rule 10b-5 may be violated through nonverbal acts by reference to the first and third clauses, which in some respects are broader than the second.[190] Although the Code endorses *Santa Fe,* its commentary does say that "it may be assumed that there is a grey area in which 'unfairness' if gross enough may merge into 'fraud.' "[191]

(6) The *Santa Fe* limitation has been applied to §14(e) and Rule 14a-9 (with respect to tender offers and proxy solicitations) because of their similarity of purpose to Rule 10b-5.[192]

(7) Urged on perhaps by Professor Cary's "race to the bottom" criticism of the Delaware Supreme Court,[193] that court and other state courts have reacted to *Santa Fe's* reminder that questions of fairness, business purpose and breach of fiduciary duty in "squeeze-out" mergers are matters of state law.[194]

9. Relation to §16(b)

Query: Since both §16(b) and Rule 10b-5 apply to trading by corporate insiders, does either have to yield to the other because of the possibility of double liability? Suppose, for example, that an insider purchases a listed equity security without disclosing secret information and sells within six months at a handsome profit. Is he liable both to the seller under Rule 10b-5 (or by way of common law deceit) and to the corporation under §16(b)? The question has not arisen. But it would seem strange if the seller's rights could be cut off at any time within six months by a second transaction with which he had nothing to do — a trans-

---

is, in general, a fact which is material to a sue decision. A 'sue decision' is a decision by a shareholder whether or not to institute a representative or derivative suit alleging a state-law cause of action." Borden, "Sue Fact" Rule Mandates Disclosure to Avoid Litigation in State Courts, in H. Schlagman and N. Hirsch (eds.), SEC '82 (L. J. Seminars-Press 1982) 201, 204, 206.

[190] See p. 900 supra.

[191] 2 Code 662.

[192] Golub v. PPD Corp., 576 F. 2d 759 (8th Cir. 1978); see also In re Sunshine Mining Co. Securities Litigation, 496 F. Supp. 9, 11 (S. D. N. Y. 1979).

[193] Cary, Federalism and Corporate Law: Reflections upon Delaware, 83 Yale L. J. 663 (1974).

[194] Singer v. Magnavox Co., 380 A. 2d 969 (Del. 1977); see also Bryan v. Brock & Blevins Co., Inc., 490 F. 2d 563 (5th Cir. 1974) (Georgia law); Perl v. IU Int'l Corp., 61 Hawaii 622, 639-40, 607 P. 2d 1036, 1046 (1980); Berkowitz v. Power/Mate Corp., 135 N. J. Super. 36, 342 A. 2d 566 (1975). For a summary of later Delaware cases, see Nathan and Sternberg, State Law Implications in Going Private Transactions, 2 Legal Notes & Viewpoints, No. 2, p. 31 (1982).

action effected by the very party responsible for his loss. Indeed, the insider buyer who had violated 10b-5 would in effect get a rebate on his purchase price by sharing indirectly as a stockholder in the recovery pursuant to §16(b).[195]

The insider who had paid the seller first, by way of judgment or settlement, might be in a better position to defend against a §16(b) action on the ground that the payment had destroyed his profit.[196] On the other hand, it might be argued that there is no reason to read the word "profit" in §16(b) to mean net after deduction of losses in a lawsuit, since this would, in effect, confine §16(b) to *innocent* transactions.[197] There is no absolute rule of law precluding double liability. In *Diamond* v. *Oreamuno,* the common law action that has been set out in connection with our examination of §16(b), the New York Court of Appeals was not "deterred, in formulating a State remedy, by the defendants' claim of possible double liability."[198] Indeed, if an insider tried hard enough to put his neck in a noose, one could conjure up the horror of *treble* liability: (1) to his company under §16(b), (2) to his sellers for misrepresentation or nondisclosure having a "bearish" effect, and (3) to his *buyers* for misrepresentation (or nondisclosure if he was under a duty to disclose) having a "bullish" effect.

The Code erects appropriate safeguards against double liability:[199]

> The profit under section 1714(a) [the Code's §16(b)] is reduced by the amount of any damages, interest, and costs (not including the defendant's attorneys' fees) paid by the defendant to sellers or buyers in the transactions in question pursuant to (1) a judgment on a claim under section 1703(a) or (b) [the Code's 10b-5]

---

[195] But cf. Schur v. Salzman, 50 A. D. 2d 784, 377 N. Y. S. 2d 82 (1st Dept. 1975), where a §16(b) payment was credited against damages in a later derivative action against the same defendant for profits resulting from his sell-out in breach of his fiduciary duty.

[196] *Query* whether this approach might be carried so far as to give the insider an action to recover what he had paid the company under §16(b) to the extent of what he later paid the seller or buyer. *Query* also whether, if the company should make such a repayment voluntarily, another action would lie under §16(b), or perhaps a derivative action against the directors generally for waste of corporate assets.

[197] Baumel v. Rosen, 283 F. Supp. 128, 145 (D. Md. 1968), *aff'd in part and rev'd in part on other grounds,* 412 F. 2d 571 (4th Cir. 1969), *cert. denied,* 396 U. S. 1039.

[198] 24 N. Y. 2d 494, 504, 248 N. E. 2d 910, 915 (1969), set out supra p. 657, at p. 663; cf. McCandless v. Furlaud, 296 U. S. 140, 167 (1935). The interpleader suggestion made in *Diamond* presents jurisdictional problems.

[199] §1714(i).

or a comparable claim under State or foreign law, or (2) settlement of such a claim if the defendant proves that the settlement was not collusive. If the defendant makes any such payment after he has paid the profit under section 1714(a) to the issuer, he may recover the amount of the payment in an action against the issuer, but in no event more than the net amount received by the issuer after payment by it (or out of the amount paid by the section 1714(a) defendant) of all costs (including the fees of the attorneys for both the issuer and any security holder claimant under section 1714(b) and reasonable costs of investigating the defendant's claim).

C. BROKERS, DEALERS, AND INVESTMENT ADVISERS

Section 17(a) of the 1933 Act, Rule 10b-5 and §9(a)(4) of the 1934 Act, as well as the proxy and tender offer fraud provisions (Rule 14a-9 and §14(e)), apply to broker-dealers along with everybody else.[1] But over-the-counter brokers-dealers, as we have already noticed, are subject *in addition* to §15(c)(1) and (2) of the 1934 Act and a batch of rules under those provisions.[2] Moreover, a number of special fraud concepts have been developed in connection with brokers and dealers.

1. THE "SHINGLE" THEORY

CHARLES HUGHES & CO., INC. v. SECURITIES AND EXCHANGE COMMISSION
United States Court of Appeals, Second Circuit, 1943
139 F. 2d 434, *cert. denied,* 321 U. S. 786

Before AUGUSTUS N. HAND, CHASE, and CLARK, Circuit Judges. CLARK, Circuit Judge.

C. 9C [1] Recently, indeed, an appellate court, in holding that a broker-dealer-employed analyst who was both tippee and tipper had violated Rule 10b-5 as aider and abettor of *his* tippees' trading, stated that the analyst had obligations to the SEC and the public "completely independent" of any acquired under the 10b-5 doctrine with respect to tipping, because the 1934 Act subjects registered broker-dealers and their associates "to myriad duties not imposed on corporate officers or other members of the general public." Dirks v. SEC, 681 F. 2d 824, 840 (D. C. Cir. 1982), *cert. granted,* 103 S. Ct. 371.

[2] See pp. 803-06 supra. Although those provisions are limited to brokers and dealers, presumably an employee or other person may violate them as an accessory and hence become a principal under the federal aider and abettor

This is a petition, pursuant to §25(a) of the Securities Exchange Act of 1934, 15 U. S. C. A. §78y(a), to review an order of the Securities and Exchange Commission, entered July 19, 1943, under §15(b) of that Act, 15 U. S. C. A. §78o(b), in which petitioner's registration as a broker and dealer was revoked. The order developed from a proceeding which was instituted by the Commission to determine whether or not petitioner had willfully violated [§17(a) of the 1933 Act and §15(c)(1) of the 1934 Act]. * * *

Petitioner was incorporated on April 9, 1940, under the laws of New York, and maintains its principal office and place of business in New York City. It is engaged in over-the-counter trading in securities as a broker and dealer, being registered as such with the Commission under the 1934 statute cited above. The dealings which resulted in the revocation were continued sales of securities to customers at prices very substantially over those prevailing in the over-the-counter market, without disclosure of the mark-up to the customers. The Commission concluded that such practices constituted fraud and deceit upon the customers in violation of §17(a) of the Securities Act, §15(c)(1) of the Securities Exchange Act, and its own Rule X-15C1-2 [now 15c1-2].

* * *

Petitioner's dealings which are here in question were carried out by various of its customers' men. The customers were almost entirely single women or widows who knew little or nothing about securities or the devices of Wall Street. An outline of the sales plan used with Mrs. Stella Furbeck gives a representative picture of how petitioner worked. Stillman, a Hughes & Co. agent, having her name as a prospect, called Mrs. Furbeck on the telephone and told her of a "wonderful" stock that she should buy. She replied that she was not interested. The next day he called again, and he persisted in his calls until she finally relented and made a purchase.

---

statute. 18 U. S. C. §2. Apparently there have been no criminal prosecutions against persons other than brokers or dealers under §15(c)(1); for it is simpler to rely on Rule 10b-5 on the purchase side and §17(a) on the sale side. But the Commission has found officers and salesmen guilty of violating §15(c)(1) in administrative proceedings. E. g., Richard K. Fudge, 30 SEC 334, 338 n. 11 (1949); Naftalin & Co., Inc., 41 SEC 823, 832 (1964). It has also used the aider and abettor statute as a basis for injunction. E. g., SEC v. Barraco, 438 F. 2d 97 (10th Cir. 1971). But cf. Gilbert v. Bagley, 492 F. Supp. 714, 732 (M. D. N. C. 1980) (private action). These administrative and injunctive practices of the Commission were codified in 1960 with respect to the Advisers Act. §§203(e)(5), 209(e). And §§1809(a)-(b) and 2006(c) of the Code extend that codification to the Exchange Act.

From that time on, he and a co-employee of his, one Armstrong, worked their way so completely into her confidence that she virtually placed complete control of her securities portfolio in their hands. Every few days one or the other would have another "marvelous" buy — one that was definitely "beyond the usual" — and she would add it to her collection, selling a more reputable security in order to finance the transaction.

The prices which Mrs. Furbeck and other customers paid for the securities purchased in this manner ranged from 16.1 to 40.9 per cent over market value. In addition, most of the transactions involved little or no risk for petitioner, because an order was usually confirmed before it bought the securities that it was selling. There is conflict in the record as to whether Stillman and Armstrong made any direct representations to Mrs. Furbeck of the relation of the price paid to market value. She claims that every time she made a purchase it was directly induced by the statement that the price would be under that current in the over-the-counter market, while they deny such statements completely. It is unchallenged, however, that at no time did either Stillman or Armstrong reveal the true market price of any security to Mrs. Furbeck or the fact that petitioner's profits averaged around twenty-five per cent. Similar evidence as to other customers all amply furnished the "substantial evidence" required by the statute to make conclusive the Commission's finding of a course of business by petitioner to sell at excessive mark-up prices without disclosure of market values to its customers. [Citations omitted.]

Petitioner challenges the order on three grounds: (1) that §15 (c)(1) of the Securities Exchange Act is unconstitutional because of an unconstitutional delegation of legislative power and that S. E. C. Rule X-15C1-2 is invalid for vagueness, indefiniteness, and uncertainty, (2) that no violation of §17(a) of the Securities Act was proved, and (3) that the Commission did not offer substantial evidence to establish the actual market price of the securities involved. We think none of them are to be sustained.

The objections to §15(c)(1) of the Securities Exchange Act and to S. E. C. Rule X-15C1-2 are insubstantial. The standard for determining the acts prohibited by §15(c)(1) is set up in the statute itself, and is more than adequate. The fact that the devices must be "manipulative, deceptive, or otherwise fraudulent" makes certainly for far more definiteness than such a standard as was approved by the *Supreme Court in Buttfield* v. *Stranahan*, 192 U. S. 470, and in numerous other cases. See, also, *Smolowe* v. *Delendo Corp.*, 2 Cir., 136 F. 2d 231, 240, *certiorari denied* 64 S. Ct. 56.

As for Rule X-15C1-2, its words are almost identical with those of §17(a) of the Securities Act, a section which has already been sustained as against the claim of vagueness. *Coplin* v. *United States,* 9 Cir., 88 F. 2d 652, *certiorari denied* 301 U. S. 703. This similarity makes the first claim of error appear frivolous, indeed, since no allegation is made that §17(a) of the Securities Act is invalid and since the revocation can be based on the violation of that section alone.

There is evidence in the record to show a threefold violation of §17(a) of the Securities Act, *viz.,* the obtaining of money "by means of any untrue statement of a material fact"; the "omission to state a material fact" necessary to make statements actually made not misleading; and the engaging in a course of business which operates "as a fraud or deceit upon the purchaser." It is true that the only specific evidence of false statements of a material fact is that of Mrs. Furbeck that the sales price was under the market price, and, as we have noted, these statements were denied by the salesmen. Although the Commission has neglected to make any finding of fact on this point, we need not remand for a specific finding resolving this conflict, for we feel that petitioner's mark-up policy operated as a fraud and deceit upon the purchasers, as well as constituting an omission to state a material fact.

An over-the-counter firm which actively solicits customers and then sells them securities at prices as far above the market as were those which petitioner charged here must be deemed to commit a fraud. It holds itself out as competent to advise in the premises, and it should disclose the market price if sales are to be made substantially above that level. Even considering petitioner as a principal in a simple vendor-purchaser transaction (and there is doubt whether, in several instances at least, petitioner was actually not acting as broker-agent for the purchasers, in which case all undisclosed profits would be forfeited), it was still under a special duty, in view of its expert knowledge and proffered advice, not to take advantage of its customers' ignorance of market conditions. The key to the success of all of petitioner's dealings was the confidence in itself which it managed to instill in the customers. Once that confidence was established, the failure to reveal the mark-up pocketed by the firm was both an omission to state a material fact and a fraudulent device. When nothing was said about market price, the natural implication in the untutored minds of the purchasers was that the price asked was close to the market. The law of fraud knows no difference between express representation on the one hand and implied misrepresentation or concealment on the other. *Strong* v. *Repide,* 213 U. S. 419, 430; *United States* v. *Brown,* 2 Cir., 79 F. 2d 321, *certiorari denied* 296 U. S. 650. "The best element of business has long since decided that honesty should govern competitive enterprises, and that the rule of caveat emptor should not be relied upon to reward fraud and deception." *Federal Trade Commission* v. *Standard Education Society,* 302 U. S. 112, 116.

We need not stop to decide, however, how far common-law fraud was shown. For the business of selling investment securities has been considered one peculiarly in need of regulation for the protection of the investor. "The business of trading in securities is one in which opportunities for dishonesty are of constant recurrence and ever present. It engages acute, active minds, trained to quick apprehension, decision and action." *Archer* v. *Securities and Exchange Commission,* 8 Cir., 133 F. 2d 795, 803, *certiorari denied* 319 U. S. 767. The well-known "blue sky laws" of 43 states have in fact proved inadequate, so that in 1933 Congress after the most extensive investigations started on a program of regulation, of which this is one of the fruits. In its interpretation of §17(a) of the Securities Act, the Commission has consistently held that a dealer cannot charge prices not reasonably related to the prevailing market price without disclosing that fact. See, among others, *Duker & Duker,* 6 S. E. C. 386; *Jansen and Co.,* 6 S. E. C. 391; *W. K. Archer & Co.,* SEA Release No. 3253; *Theodore T. Golden,* SEA Release No. 3404; *Guranty Underwriters, Inc.,* SEA Release No. 3481. Had we been in doubt on the matter we should have given weight to these rulings as a consistent and contemporaneous construction of a statute by an administrative body. *United States* v. *American Trucking Associations, Inc.,* 310 U. S. 534; *Gray* v. *Powell,* 314 U. S. 402. As we have hitherto said of "the peculiar function" of the Commission: "One of the principal reasons for the creation of such a bureau is to secure the benefit of special knowledge acquired through continuous experience in a difficult and complicated field. Its interpretation of the act should control unless plainly erroneous." *Securities and Exchange Commission* v. *Associated Gas & Electric Co.,* 2 Cir., 99 F. 2d 795, 798. But we are not content to rest on so colorless an interpretation of this important legislation.

The essential objective of securities legislation is to protect those who do not know market conditions from the overreachings of those who do. Such protection will mean little if it stops short of the point of ultimate consequence, namely, the price charged for the securities. Indeed, it is the purpose of all legislation for the prevention of fraud in the sale of securities to preclude the sale of "securities which are in fact worthless, or worth substantially less than the asking price." *People* v. *Federated Radio Corp.,* 244 N. Y. 33, 40, 154 N. E. 655, 658. If after several years of experience under this highly publicized legislation we should find that the public cannot rely upon a commission-licensed broker not to charge unsuspecting investors 25 per cent more than a market price easily ascertainable by insiders, we should leave such legislation little more than a snare and a delusion. We think the Commission has correctly interpreted its responsibilities to stop such abusive practices in the sale of securities.

Petitioner's final contention is that the actual market price of the securities was never satisfactorily proved. We agree, however, with the Commission that the evidence of the quotations published in the National Daily Quotation Sheets, a recognized service giving "daily market indications," as petitioner stipulated, and the prices paid concurrently by petitioner itself sufficiently indicated prevailing market price in the absence of evidence to the contrary.

Order affirmed.

This has nothing to do with any agency obligation. The theory is that even a dealer at arm's length impliedly represents when he hangs out his shingle that he will deal fairly with the public. It is an element of that implied representation, the theory goes, that his prices will bear some reasonable relation to the current market unless he discloses to the contrary. Therefore, charging a price that does not bear such a relation is a breach of the dealer's implied representation and works a fraud on the customer. Just as the doctrine is not an aspect of agency or brokerage law, it has nothing to do with limiting the amount of the dealer's profit — except, of course, when his own purchase is substantially contemporaneous with his sale. If a dealer buys a security at $10 and holds onto it until the market hits $20, he is perfectly free to take his profit of 100 percent and a bit more. Conversely, if he buys a security at $10 and is unlucky enough to stay with it until the market falls to $5, it is fraudulent for him without disclosure to sell it at a price not reasonably related to the current market of $5 notwithstanding that he will suffer a loss.

Of course, just as the "abstain or disclose" principle under Rule 10b-5 normally means "abstain," so here. For who will trade with a dealer that states he will charge (or pay) a price that is unreasonable in relation to current market? Furthermore, the theory suffers

more than a little from question-begging. If I am allowed to state
the major premise of my syllogism, I shall march inexorably to the
conclusion I want. And Judge Clark got carried away a bit when
he stated in a later case that the broker-dealer "implicitly *warrants*
the soundness of statements of stock value."[3] For the theory clearly
does not extend to non-negligent errors of fact, much less of
analysis or opinion. Quite the contrary, the scienter requirement
of Rule 10b-5 presumably extends to the shingle theory whether
the plaintiff relies on that rule or on Rule 15c1-2.[4]

By now — one may add "happily" — the shingle theory not
only is unchallenged but has been considerably refined.

Thus, the Commission has made it clear that a violation exists
when unreasonable prices are charged in individual transactions;
that in computing mark-ups on sales to customers the dealer may
not deduct self-imposed losses sustained in purchases from them
as part of the scheme to induce the switching of securities and
maintain customers' confidence; and that a dealer may not "avoid
the onus which attaches to the practice of gouging customers in
individual transactions by pointing to the over-all percentage of
profits he has extracted."[5] Nor is a violation precluded by the
existence of large selling expenses[6] or the fact that the customer's
financial position was improved.[7] Not surprisingly, the Commission has applied the same approach in the slightly different context
of failure to disclose lower market transactions when affecting a
distribution of securities, whether under a Securities Act registration statement[8] or under a prospectus for an unregistered offering.[9]

---

[3] Kahn v. SEC, 297 F. 2d 112, 115 (2d Cir. 1961) (concurring opinion,
italics supplied); see also SEC v. N. A. R. & D. Corp., 424 F. 2d 63, 84 (2d
Cir. 1970).

[4] See pp. 803-04 supra.

[5] Trost & Co., Inc., 12 SEC 531, 535 (1942); Maryland Securities Co., Inc.,
41 SEC 836, 838 (1964) (NASD case). Because many of the Commission's
opinions by way of review of NASD disciplinary orders for violation of the
NASD's own philosophy on reasonable spreads (infra p. 970) are equally
appropriate in the present context, some of those cases will be cited here
with a "cf." and the distinguishing signal, "NASD case."

[6] Morris Luster, 36 SEC 298, 300 (1955).

[7] E. H. Rollins & Sons, Inc., 18 SEC 347, 371 (1945). One can go on:
Evidence of sales by other dealers at comparable prices is not a defense; at
most it creates a conflict in the evidence. Associated Securities Corp. v. SEC,
293 F. 2d 738, 741 (10th Cir. 1961). It is no defense that in sales to employees
of the issuer the price was specified by them. Wesco & Co., 43 SEC 8, 9 n. 3
(1966) (NASD case). Nor is it a defense that a sale is short, with whatever
risk that entails. Investment Service Co., 41 SEC 188, 196 (1962), aff'd sub
nom. Barnett v. United States, 319 F. 2d 340 (8th Cir. 1963).

[8] Cristina Copper Mines, Inc., 33 SEC 397, 401-02 (1952). This was a
stop-order opinion under the 1933 Act, so that it did not even involve a
broker-dealer respondent.

[9] Indiana State Securities Corp., 38 SEC 118 (1957). An underwriter im-

Moreover, the potentialities of the "shingle" theory are not necessarily exhausted by using it as a basis for an implied representation of pricing reasonably related to the market. Since a dealer impliedly represents that he will execute only authorized transactions on behalf of customers, the effecting of unauthorized transactions violates the fraud provisions.[10] Since trade custom requires a dealer to consummate transactions with customers promptly unless there is a clear understanding or indication to the contrary, it is a fraud to fail to disclose to customers whose orders and payments are accepted that the dealer has no intention of filling their orders promptly but intends to use their funds in his other business activities.[11] Since a selling dealer impliedly represents that the buyer will have clear title to securities he buys for cash, it is fraudulent not to state that the securities were pledged without authority from the customer.[12] Since a dealer impliedly represents that he is able to meet his obligations as they mature, it is fraudulent for him to accept customers' funds or securities while insolvent; on this basis the Commission almost routinely shuts down broker-dealers that are discovered (usually through a routine inspection) to be insolvent or undercapitalized[13] by moving for a preliminary injunction (sometimes an *ex parte* restraining order) under the fraud provisions and asking the court to appoint a receiver by way of ancillary relief.[14] It is likewise an

---

pliedly represents "that he has met the standards of his profession in his investigation of the issuer." Sanders v. John Nuveen & Co., Inc., 524 F. 2d 1064, 1070 (7th Cir. 1975). So, too, a dealer who recommends the purchase of mutual fund shares violates the fraud provisions if he fails to disclose that substantial savings in sales load would be available through the purchase of additional shares or the combination of purchases to equal or exceed the break-point amount. Russell L. Irish, 42 SEC 735, 740-42 (1965), *aff'd* sub nom. Irish v. SEC, 367 F. 2d 637 (9th Cir. 1966), *cert. denied*, 386 U. S. 911. And cf. United States v. Bronson, 145 F. 2d 939 (2d Cir. 1944), where the court confirmed the conviction of a mining promoter under §17(a) and the mail fraud statute for distributing treasury stock on the market without disclosing that the price exceeded the net return to the corporate treasury plus a fair commission.

[10] First Anchorage Corp., 34 SEC 299 (1952).

[11] Ned J. Bowman Co., 39 SEC 879, 883 (1960); DeMarco v. Edens, 390 F. 2d 836, 840 (2d Cir. 1968) (§12(2) judgment on ground of underwriter's failure to disclose that it would neither remit proceeds to issuer nor deliver stock to plaintiffs); cf. Investment Service Co., 41 SEC 188, 197-98 (1962), *aff'd* sub nom. Barnett v. United States, 319 F. 2d 340, 344-45 (8th Cir. 1963) (it is a fraud to accept an order to sell "at the earliest possible date" and to fail to execute it with due diligence, other sales having been effected at a higher price after receipt of the first order); Sec. Ex. Act Rel. 8363 (1968).

[12] Richard A. Sebastian, 38 SEC 865, 868-69 (1959).

[13] See Rule 15c3-1, supra p. 704.

[14] E. g., SEC v. Alan F. Hughes, Inc., 461 F. 2d 974, 981-83 (2d Cir. 1972);

incident of the representation of fair dealing that the dealer will disclose any substantial long or short position or other bias that may affect his recommendations.[15] And an oil royalty dealer impliedly represents that his selling price is reasonably related not only to the current wholesale price — as is true of dealers in securities generally — but also to reasonable estimates of the oil recoverable from the tract underlying the royalty interest.[16]

Notwithstanding all this, it does not detract from the landmark character of the *Hughes* opinion to say that it does not answer all the questions posed by the "shingle" theory:

First: Although the court considered the Hughes firm "as a principal in a simple vendor-purchaser transaction," it referred to its "special duty, in view of its expert knowledge and proffered advice, not to take advantage of its customers' ignorance of market conditions."[17] In most of the cases there has been some similar

---

Tcherepnin v. Franz, 485 F. 2d 1251, 1256 (7th Cir. 1973), *cert. denied* sub nom. McGurren v. Ittelson, 415 U. S. 918; SEC v. Bartlett, 422 F. 2d 475 (8th Cir. 1970); SEC v. Investors Security Corp., 560 F. 2d 561, 567 (3d Cir. 1977); SEC v. Wencke, 577 F. 2d 619, 623 (9th Cir. 1978), *cert. denied,* 439 U. S. 964. In SEC v. Heritage Trust Co., 402 F. Supp. 744 (D. Ariz. 1975), the court at first denied a receivership, whereupon the company issued a newsletter stating: "GOOD NEWS — WE WON — WE BEAT THE S. E. C. ! ! * * * ." Thereupon, on renewal of the motion, the court found that "The purpose and content of that newsletter was a blatant attempt to mislead defendants' investors," and appointed a receiver. Id. at 753.

The Code expressly authorizes ancillary relief, including "a receivership of the defendant or the defendant's assets," whether in a Commission or a private action and "whether or not the court grants the principal relief requested." §1819(l)(1). Since the Securities Investor Protection Act of 1970 (supra p. 41), however, it has been the Commission's practice to move for appointment of a temporary receiver until the SIPC applies for appointment of a liquidating trustee. E. g., SEC v. Baron & Co., Inc., Litig. Rel. 5250 (D. N. J. 1971).

[15]See p. 965 infra. In Chasins v. Smith, Barney & Co., 438 F. 2d 1167 (2d Cir. 1970), the court, without specific mention of the shingle theory, held that a dealer's failure to disclose a conflict resulting from his status as a marketmaker had violated Rule 10b-5. Although the opinion was rewritten to tie it down to the circumstances of the case, the Supreme Court in Affiliated Ute Citizens of Utah v. United States, 406 U. S. 128, 153 (1972), held, without express qualification, that the first and third clauses of Rule 10b-5 required marketmakers' status to be disclosed in connection with "sales their activities produced." Disclosure of marketmaker status by a broker-dealer acting for his own account with respect to an equity security is now required by the confirmation rule. Rule 10b-10(a)(5)(ii).

[16]SEC v. LeDone, Litig. Rel. 394 (S. D. N. Y. 1947) (consent injunction); but cf. United States v. Grayson, 166 F. 2d 863 (2d Cir. 1948) (difficulties of proof); Klein v. SEC, 224 F. 2d 861 (2d Cir. 1955) (*inter alia,* NASD's failure to object to 50 percent mark-ups after an earlier inspection created an interpretation on which the firm reasonably relied).

[17]139 F. 2d at 437, supra p. 949.

element of advice and of disparity in the degree of knowledge of market conditions possesed by dealer and customer. But the Commission has indicated "that the fundamental principle underlying these cases is that any person, regardless of his knowledge of the matter or his access to market information, is entitled to rely on the implied representation, made by a registered dealer in securities, that customers will be treated fairly."[18] And it would seem that the doctrine should likewise apply regardless of the amount of solicitation or advice on the part of the dealer. For the doctrine is founded on the supreme importance of market value in the purchase and sale of securities — intangibles that have no intrinsic use value.[19] The doctrine thus has an affinity to the holdings that it is a fraud for a dealer to sell without disclosing that he has manipulated the market or otherwise dominated it.[20]

Second: How does one ascertain the market that is so important in the pricing of transactions when there are no published quotations? The *Hughes* case, where quotations *were* available, looked also to the dealer's own substantially contemporaneous cost. And gradually, as the concept of substantially contemporaneous cost has been refined, it has come to be preferred even when current, independent asked prices are available.[21] Of course, if there is no market and the dealer has held the security for some time before

---

[18] United Securities Corp., 15 SEC 719, 727 (1944).

[19] The Supreme Court has referred to securities as "the equivalent of money." Geddes v. Anaconda Copper Mining Co., 254 U. S. 590, 598 (1921). Indeed, intrinsic or other value will be generally considered in the case of securities only when there is no market value. Cf. Virginia v. West Virginia, 238 U. S. 202, 212-13 (1915) (establishing value in deceit action).

[20] On manipulation, see c. 9D infra. On market domination, see Norris & Hirshberg, Inc., 21 SEC 865, 874-82 (1946), *aff'd* sub nom. Norris & Hirshberg, Inc. v. SEC, 177 F. 2d 228 (D. C. Cir. 1949). Cf. the cases, supra n. 15, on disclosure of "marketmaker" status under certain circumstances.

[21] Managed Investment Programs, 37 SEC 783, 786 (1957) (NASD case); J. A. Winston & Co., 42 SEC 62, 68-69 (1964). This will not work, however, in the case of a marketmaker. For a marketmaker typically buys from other dealers at or around its bid and sells to other dealers at or around its offering price, so that using its cost as a basis for computing markups might compel it to charge retail prices that are less than its wholesale offering prices, and that would impair market liquidity by deterring marketmakers from taking the risk of maintaining a market. Normally, therefore, a marketmaker's markups are computed on the basis of its actual contemporaneous sales to other dealers or its contemporaneous offering prices. On the other hand, when the marketmaker dominates the market, using its own offering prices would give it unrestricted latitude; and so in that situation the Commission uses either (1) contemporaneous prices charged by that or other marketmakers in actual sales to other dealers or (2) contemporaneous and representative asked quotations of other marketmakers. Peter J. Kirsch, Sec. Ex. Act Rel. 19,005, 25 SEC Dock. 1242, 1246-47 (1982).

selling it, there is nothing for the *Hughes* doctrine to operate on. But many (probably most) over-the-counter dealers do not carry any substantial inventory, whether for lack of capital or to avoid risk. Typically the dealer buys a security for his own account only after he has obtained an order from a customer.

Third: It is customary for dealers in the over-the-counter market to take lower spreads on the purchase side than they do on the sale side. Indeed, in shifting a customer from one security into another they frequently act as agent in disposing of the old security for the customer and as principal in selling him the new. Nevertheless, if a dealer should *purchase* a security from a customer at a price not reasonably related to the current market (or, in the absence of a market, at a price not reasonably related to the price received by the dealer on substantially contemporaneous resale), his failure to disclose that fact would clearly violate the *Hughes* doctrine.[22]

Fourth: This leaves the most critical question of all — precisely what spread is reasonable in relation to whatever base is used. The Commission has carefully refrained from fixing any arbitrary standards, presumably for fear that the maximum spread would tend to become the minimum in all cases. It is necessary to consider the entire business conduct of a particular firm rather than one or a half-dozen isolated transactions or even (as we have seen) the *average* mark-up.[23] Percentages are particularly unreliable when the gross dollar amount of a particular transaction is relatively small. Nevertheless, the mark-up may be excessive even with securities selling at very low unit prices.[24] And, despite the uncertainty, the Commission's application of the *Hughes* doctrine has apparently eliminated the more shocking mark-ups.

In this endeavor the Commission's work has been supplemented by the NASD in what is a good example of the alliance of law and ethics that it was the purpose of §15A to encourage. The NASD has always had a rule to the effect that a member trading as principal with a customer "shall buy or sell at a price which is fair, taking into consideration all relevant circumstances, including market conditions with respect to [the] security at the time of the transaction, the expense involved, and the fact that he is entitled to a profit."[25] In a 1943 survey the Association found that 47 per-

---

[22] Associated Securities Corp., 40 SEC 10, 14-17 (1960) *stay denied* sub nom. Associated Securities Corp. v. SEC, 283 F. 2d 773 (10th Cir. 1960).
[23] See p. 952, text at n. 5 supra.
[24] J. A. Winston & Co., Inc., 42 SEC 62, 69 (1964).
[25] NASD Rules of Fair Practice, Art. III, §4, CCH NASD Manual D-6.

cent of its members' over-the-counter transactions had been effected at a gross spread over the current market of not more than 3 percent and 71 percent of the transactions at a gross spread of not more than 5 percent.[26] As a result, the Board of Governors adopted an interpretation of its basic rule against unethical conduct:

> It shall be deemed conduct inconsistent with just and equitable principles of trade for a member to enter into any transaction with a customer in any security at any price not reasonably related to the current market price of the security.[27]

This is in substance the *Hughes* doctrine, except that it is stated without reference to disclosure. Disclosure will not always obviate a violation of rules of ethics. Nevertheless, the Commission has held, the degree of disclosure made must be considered along with all other pertinent circumstances in judging the reasonableness of the mark-ups and the ethics of the transactions.[28] In short, "there is no hard and fast '5 percent rule.' "[29]

The shingle theory is an area in which the Code makes one of its most significant contributions. Disavowing any "intention to enlarge the Commission's rulemaking authority with respect to brokers and dealers beyond the 'fraud' rubric of the 'shingle' theory," the commentary speaks, rather, of a design "to avoid the artificiality of that theory — however nobly it may have served its purpose in an earlier day — and to relieve both the Commission and the securities industry of the 'fraud' opprobrium that is necessarily attached to every practice that is today proscribed by the 'shingle' concept."[30] This the Code does by carving out "a degree

---

[26] The trend since has been steadily downward.

[27] CCH NASD Manual ¶2154, esp. at 2056. The Commission rejected a contention that this interpretation, with its accompanying instructions, amounted to a 5 percent "rule" that was illegal because it had neither been submitted to a vote of the membership nor been filed with the Commission; and it found that there were adequate safeguards in the statute against improper use of the policy thus established. National Assn. of Securities Dealers, Inc., 17 SEC 459 (1944). There is also a judicial holding that "The statement of the 5% policy establishes sufficient guidelines" to overcome a due process argument. Handley Investment Co. v. SEC, 354 F. 2d 64, 66 (10th Cir. 1965).

[28] Herrick, Waddell & Co., Inc., 25 SEC 437 (1947).

[29] Samuel B. Franklin & Co. v. SEC, 290 F. 2d 719, 725 (9th Cir. 1961), *cert. denied*, 368 U. S. 889.

Municipal bonds are exempted from §15A and therefore from the NASD's rules. But they have always been subject to the statutory fraud provisions and the shingle theory. Crosby & Elkin, Inc., Sec. Ex. Act Rel. 17,709, 22 SEC Dock. 722, 775 (1981).

[30] 1 Code 391.

of misconduct that is more than 'unethical,' so that it is within the proper sphere of direct regulation rather than self-regulation, but less than 'fraudulent,' "[31] and dealing with that subject matter in Part IX, Market Regulation, rather than Part XVI, Fraud, Misrepresentation, and Manipulation.

The net effect is a three-way approach: (1) §913, which makes certain of the most common manifestations of the shingle theory (prompt execution, disclosure of control, unauthorized executions, and unreasonable spreads) unlawful without regard to rules; (2) §915(a), which specifies a number of additional practices but is not self-executing; and (3) §915(b), whose rulemaking authority extends to both §913 and §915(a) as well as "any similar conduct that constitutes unfair dealing * * * ."

2.   "Now I'm a Principal, Now I'm an Agent"

a.   Disclosure Required of a Dealer Occupying a Fiduciary Position

Concurrently with the development of the "shingle" theory that culminated in the Second Circuit's opinion in the *Hughes* case, the Commission began exploring the status of a broker-dealer who, although purporting to act as principal rather than agent, places himself in a position of trust and confidence with his customer.[32] Such a broker-dealer, the Commission declared, is under a much stricter obligation than merely to refrain from taking excessive mark-ups over the current market. His duty as a fiduciary selling his own property to his principal, or buying from his principal for his own account, is to make a scrupulously full disclosure of every element of his adverse interest in the transaction. Like the "shingle" theory, this doctrine culminated in a Commission opinion[33] that was sustained on judicial review. Oddly, the broker-dealer here, too, was named Hughes.[34]

---

[31] Ibid.

[32] Allender Co., Inc., 9 SEC 1043, esp. at 1053-55 (1941); William J. Stelmack Corp., 11 SEC 601, esp. at 617-21 (1942); Lawrence R. Leeby, 13 SEC 499, 505-09 (1943).

[33] Arleen W. Hughes, 27 SEC 629 and 952 (1948).

[34] Stranger still, both firms were operated by women. And, if one is interested in statistical probabilities, still another coincidence might be noted: both opinions were written by judges named Clark.

HUGHES v. SECURITIES AND EXCHANGE COMMISSION

United States Court of Appeals, District of Columbia Circuit, 1949
174 F. 2d 969

Before CLARK, PRETTYMAN, and PROCTOR, Circuit Judges.
CLARK, Circuit Judge.

The case is before this court on petition of Arleen W. Hughes, doing business as E. W. Hughes & Company, to review and set aside an order of respondent Securities and Exchange Commission revoking her registration as a broker and dealer.

[Arleen Hughes registered with the Commission both as a broker-dealer and as an investment adviser. Each of her clients signed a "Memorandum of Agreement" specifying that she was to act in all transactions as both investment adviser and principal except as otherwise agreed. The contract included an elaborate schedule of rates and charges applicable to each transaction, and it specified maximum spreads which would be added to a so-called base price when the firm sold securities to a client or bought them from a client. There was no allegation of unreasonable spreads.]

*   *   *

There was filed in this court, prior to oral argument of the case and pursuant to order of this court, a brief on behalf of 120 of petitioner's 175 clients, who call themselves amici curiae. That brief purports to speak for a majority of the clients themselves. It argues that the clients have at all times had full knowledge and understanding of the Memorandum of Agreement and the capacity in which petitioner dealt with her clients and that the action of the Commission deprives the clients "of the right to continue to do business with Petitioner under a contractual relationship which they fully understand, and which has afforded them a high degree of investment protection, financial gain and security and financial peace of mind, * * * " Therefore, amici urge reversal of the order of revocation. Assuming arguendo the truth of the unverified statements in the amici brief, many of which are based on matters outside the record in the instant case, such statements do not constitute grounds for overturning the decision of the Commission in this case. If the Commission's decision that petitioner had wilfully violated specified anti-fraud sections of pertinent statutes and regulations is legally correct and supported by substantial evidence of record, it is immaterial whether or not a majority, or even all, of petitioner's clients understood completely the nature of their dealings with petitioner and were satisfied with, and had profited by, petitioner's method of doing business with them. Therefore, we will give no further consideration to the claims of amici for it is our understanding that the Commission is by statute empowered, and, in fact, is required to revoke a broker-dealer registration where there has been wilful violation of statute and where such revocation is in the public interest. This is true whether or not the clients of the broker-dealer happen to have knowledge of, completely understand, or condone and profit by the acts of the broker-dealer which constitute wilful violation of statute. Assuming the existence of both of the above-stated prerequisites for revocation, the revocation is proper even if one, or none, of the particular clients here involved has been misled or has suffered injury.

*   *   *

[After quoting §§17(a), 10(b), and 15(c)(1) together with Rules 10b-5 and 15c1-2, and referring to the "substantial evidence" rule of judicial review under §25(a) of the Exchange Act, Judge Clark continued:]

The charted course is clear. In this case the Commission has expressly found that petitioner has wilfully violated the above-quoted anti-fraud sections of the two Acts. The Commission also expressly found that the revocation of petitioner's registration is in the public interest. If those two express findings have substantial evidentiary support in the record before us, we cannot set aside the order of revocation. Such support does exist in this record.

In the vast majority of transactions between this petitioner and her clients, petitioner concededly acted as a fiduciary. The record shows clearly that, except for a few isolated instances, petitioner acted simultaneously in the dual capacity of investment adviser and of broker and dealer. In such capacity, conflicting interests must necessarily arise. When they arise, the law has consistently stepped in to provide safeguards in the form of prescribed and stringent standards of conduct on the part of the fiduciary. More than 100 years ago the Supreme Court set forth this principle as follows:

> In this conflict of interest, the law wisely interposes. It acts not on the possibility, that, in some cases, the sense of that duty may prevail over the motives of self-interest, but it provides against the probability in many cases, and the danger in all cases, that the

dictates of self-interest will exercise a predominant influence, and supersede that of duty.[12]

But the Commission in this case did not, and we in turn do not, base the validity of the revocation order upon common law principles of fraud or deceit. Section 17(a) of the Securities Act of 1933, Sections 10(b) and 15(c)(1) of the Securities Exchange Act of 1934, and Commission-made rules thereunder, all quoted supra, in prohibitory language, set out the statutory prescription as to the conduct of the business of a broker and dealer in securities. If any one of these statutes or rules has been wilfully violated by petitioner and revocation is found to be in the public interest, the respondent, by virtue of Section 15(b), supra, has authority to revoke.

It cannot now be doubted that, as respondent points out, the securities field, by its nature, requires specialized and unique legal treatment. This is recognized by the very statutes and regulations here under consideration as well as by recent federal and state court decisions. Thus in the *Archer* case it was said:

> The business of trading in securities is one in which opportunities for dishonesty are of constant recurrence and ever present. It engages acute, active minds, trained to quick apprehension, decision and action. The Congress has seen fit to regulate this business. Though such regulation must be done in strict subordination to constitutional and lawful safeguards of individual rights, it is to be enforced notwithstanding the frauds to be suppressed may take on more subtle and involved forms than those in which dishonesty manifests itself in cruder and less specialized activities.[14]

The acts of petitioner which constitute violations of the antifraud sections of statutes and of regulations thereunder are acts of omission in that petitioner failed to fully disclose the nature and extent of her adverse interest. The Commission found that petitioner failed to disclose to her clients (1) the best price at which the securities could be purchased for the clients in the open market in the exercise of due diligence and (2) the cost to petitioner of the securities sold by her to her clients. In no less than three places in the above-quoted statutes and regulations we find that, "any omission to state a material fact necessary in order to make the statements made, in the light of the circumstances under which

---

[12] [Michoud v. Girod, 4 How. 503, 555 (U. S. 1846).] * * *

[14] [Archer v. SEC, 133 F. 2d 795, 803 (8th Cir. 1943), *cert. denied*, 319 U. S. 767.] * * *

they were made, not misleading," is expressly made unlawful. These quoted words as they appear in the statute can only mean that Congress forbid not only the telling of purposeful falsity but also the telling of half-truths and the failure to tell the "whole truth." These statutory words were obviously designed to protect the investing public as a whole whether the individual investors be suspicious or unsuspecting. The best price currently obtainable in the open market and the cost to registrant are both material facts within the meaning of the above-quoted language and they are both factors without which informed consent to a fiduciary's acting in a dual and conflicting role is impossible.

Petitioner strongly urges that she has fully and completely fulfilled any disclosure requirement by the insertion in the Memorandum of Agreement (entered into with each of her clients since 1943) of the clause that the "Company, when acting as investment adviser, shall act as Principal in every such transaction, except as otherwise agreed," and that, in any event, petitioner has always stood ready to provide any further information which her clients desired. The cause inserted in the Memorandum of Agreement does not even approach the minimum disclosure requirements. In the first place, it is certainly doubtful whether petitioner's clients either knew of or understood the legal effect of the technical language inserted in fine print in the printed document which each client signed when he or she first became a client of petitioner. Secondly, even assuming, as urged by amici, that *all* of petitioner's clients are persons of more than average experience and intelligence with regard to the conceded intricacies of securities transactions, an assumption which is at best dubious in view of the present record, their full knowledge that petitioner either sold them securities she then owned or bought securities in her own name and then resold them to the clients cannot be considered sufficient knowledge to enable the clients to give their informed consent. When Mrs. Hughes took the witness stand in the proceedings below she categorically denied that she ever disclosed to her clients either the price she paid for a security, its market price, or any bid and ask prices for the security. She thereafter stated: "If at any time one of my clients wants to ask anything, why, of course, I will answer them and they all know that." Based upon petitioner's own testimony then, the Commission's finding that her disclosure was inadequate was reasonable and correct and supported by substantial evidence of record. It is not enough that one who acts as an admitted fiduciary proclaim that he or she stands ever ready to divulge material facts to the ones whose interests she is being paid to protect. Some knowledge is prerequisite to intelligent questioning. This is particularly true in the securities field. Readiness and willingness to disclose are not equivalent to disclosure. The statutes and rules discussed above make it unlawful to omit to state material facts irrespective of alleged (or proven) willingness or readiness to supply that which has been omitted.

*   *   *

Affirmed.[a]

The teaching, of course, is considerably older: "No man can serve two masters * * * ."[35] And it applies equally to any person who stands in a fiduciary relation toward another, whether he be trustee, executor, administrator, lawyer, officer, director, investment adviser, or broker.[36] The law has always looked with such suspicion upon a fiduciary's dealing with his beneficiary for his own account without scrupulously fair disclosure of his adverse interest that it permits the beneficiary at any time to set aside the transaction without proving actual abuse or damage.[37]

What the *Arleen Hughes* case does is to say that such conduct amounts to a violation of the fraud provisions of the securities laws.[38] More than that, the opinion spells out precisely what disclosure is required in this type of case.

First, there must be a clear statement of the fiduciary's capacity and his actual cost (or, in the case of a purchase from a client, the

[a] ED.: See also Chasins v. Smith, Barney & Co., Inc., 438 F. 2d 1167 (2d Cir. 1970); but cf. Avern Trust v. Clarke, 415 F. 2d 1238, 1239-40 (7th Cir. 1969), *cert. denied*, 397 U. S. 963.

[35] Matt. 6:24; see Tisdale v. Tisdale, 2 Sneed 596, 608, 64 Am. Dec. 775, 783 (Tenn. 1855). This maxim, the Supreme Court has observed, "is especially pertinent if one of the masters happens to be economic self-interest." United States v. Mississippi Valley Generating Co., 364 U. S. 520, 549 (1961); see also SEC v. Capital Gains Research Bureau, Inc., 375 U. S. 180, 196 n. 50 (1963).

[36] Hotchkiss v. Fischer, 136 Kan. 530, 537, 16 P. 2d 531, 534 (1932); Tate v. Williamson, L. R. 1 Eq. 528, 537 (1866), *aff'd*, L. R. 2 Ch. 55 (1866); G. Bower, The Law Relating to Actionable Non-disclosure (1915) §§320, 408; 3 J. Pomeroy, Equity Jurisprudence (5th ed. 1941) §956a.

[37] Robertson v. Chapman, 152 U. S. 673, 681 (1894).

[38] Compare the mail fraud cases cited supra c. 9A n. 5. The same point had earlier been made in Op. Dir. Trading & Ex. Div., Sec. Ex. Act Rel. 3653, Inv. Adv. Act Rel. 40 (1945). That opinion was qualified by the Commission thirty years later, as we shall see (infra p. 982). But the story is best told chronologically.

fiduciary's resale price when known). This much the law has traditionally required of a fiduciary on pain of having the transaction
set aside.[39] In addition, however, the Commission's opinion recognized the obvious fact that in the securities field there is another
criterion of adverse interest that is usually a good deal more significant. That criterion is the current market price — the best available bid or offer, as the case may be, that the fiduciary is able to
discover in the exercise of reasonable diligence.[40] Of course, it is
not essential to disclose the best available market price unless it
is more favorable than the price at which the fiduciary proposes to
buy from or sell to his client. Furthermore, disclosure of cost and
market will normally be the same when the fiduciary effects an
approximately contemporaneous transaction with another dealer
to offset a transaction with a client. However, when the fiduciary
has held a security in inventory for some time before selling it to
a client, the fiduciary's cost, although still significant, is of secondary importance, and disclosure of cost alone without disclosure of
current market may be positively misleading. Suppose, for example, that the fiduciary paid 50 for a security in inventory and is
charging the client 20, but the current market is 10; disclosure of
cost alone would indicate that the client is getting a bargain,
whereas in fact he is being cheated.

The Commission also spelled out in some detail how the required disclosure of capacity and market might be made. The
nature and extent of disclosure with respect to capacity will vary
with the particular client involved. In some cases use of the term
"principal" itself may suffice. In others a more detailed explanation will be required. In all cases, however, the burden is on the
firm that acts as fiduciary to make certain that the client understands that the firm is selling its own securities. In disclosing

---

[39] Old Dominion Copper Mining & Smelting Co. v. Bigelow, 188 Mass.
315, 320-21, 74 N. E. 653, 658 (1905), *aff'd on other grounds,* 225 U. S. 111
(1912); Norris v. Beyer, 124 N. J. Eq. 284, 286-87, 1 A. 2d 460, 461 (1938);
Allender Co., Inc., 9 SEC 1043, 1054 (1941).

[40] The fact situations that have been dealt with by the courts have related
for the most part to unique properties rather than properties having a readily
ascertainable market value, and generally relief has been based on failure
to disclose the fact that the fiduciary was selling for his own account or to
disclose the amount of his cost or profit. However, even in these situations
the courts have recognized that the fiduciary is under a duty to obtain or
dispose of the property for his principal at the best price discoverable in the
exercise of reasonable diligence. Doyen v. Bauer, 211 Minn. 140, 147, 300
N. W. 451, 455 (1941); Berkeley Sulphur Springs v. Liberty, 10 N. J. Misc.
1067, 1069, 162 Atl. 191, 192 (Ch. 1932); Van Dusen v. Bigelow, 13 N. D.
277, 283, 100 N. W. 723, 724-25 (1904); Ridgeway v. McGuire, 176 Ore. 428,
433, 158 P. 2d 893, 895-96 (1945).

market price, when it is more favorable than cost, the firm must make certain that the quotations it furnishes to clients are reliable and truly indicative of the current market.

All this, of course, is aside from the duty the agent always has to disclose to his principal all facts "which he should realize have or are likely to have a bearing upon the desirability of the transaction from the viewpoint of the principal."[41] It is understood to be the administrative construction, for example, that one incident of this duty is that a broker or investment adviser who solicits or recommends purchases or sales must disclose the existence (though not necessarily the amount) of any long or short position of the firm, or any partner, officer, director or member of their immediate families, or any employee assuming responsibility for the recommendation, if the position is substantial in relation to the total resources and holdings of the firm or any such individual.[42] Any other bias of the firm or of any such individual must likewise be disclosed. And, on the theory of an implied representation of fair dealing, the same duty is considered to apply even to a *dealer* who does any recommending or soliciting. Again, a broker, as well as a dealer who recommends or solicits purchases or sales, must be careful to avoid conflicts of interest between different classes of customers. All this is under penalty of violating the fraud provisions.[43]

---

[41] Restatement (Second) of Agency §390, Comment a. The obligation of fair dealing is not diminished because a statutory prospectus or offering circular has been or is to be delivered, since the information in those documents furnishes background against which the salesman's representations may be tested. J. P. Howell & Co., Inc., 43 SEC 325, 329 (1967), *aff'd sub nom.* Vanasco v. SEC, 395 F. 2d 349 (2d Cir. 1968).

[42] Brennan v. Midwestern United Life Ins. Co., 286 F. Supp. 702, 707 (N. D. Ind. 1968), *aff'd on other grounds,* 417 F. 2d 147 (7th Cir. 1969), *cert. denied,* 397 U. S. 989; see CCH N. Y. Stock Ex. Guide ¶2474A.10; CCH Am. Stock Ex. Guide ¶9495.10.

[43] A *broker* owes a fiduciary duty to his customer despite the presence of an investment adviser. Rolf v. Blyth, Eastman Dillon & Co., Inc., 570 F. 2d 38, 45 n. 10 (2d Cir. 1978), *cert. denied,* 439 U. S. 1039.

The common law recognizes that an agent who deals with his principal on his own account in regard to the subject matter of his employment may be excused from his disclosure obligation when the principal has manifested that he either knows all material facts in connection with the transaction or does not care to know them. Restatement (Second) of Agency §390 and Comment b; see also id., §389, Comments b, d. Presumably, however, at least so far as the antifraud provisions of the securities laws are concerned, any sort of waiver or "advance ratification" on the part of a fiduciary's client will be construed very strictly, particularly in the case of a relatively unsophisticated investor. Section 14 of the 1933 Act and §29(a) of the 1934 Act provide that any waiver of compliance with any provision of the statute or of the Commission's rules is "void." At the very least these sections indicate a congressional feeling that by and large the professional broker-dealer and

b. Determination of Fiduciary Status

Unfortunately there is no touchstone for determining when a dealer assumes the obligation of a fiduciary. Sometimes, as in the *Arleen Hughes* case itself, the answer is easy: A firm that is registered as an investment adviser, and that admittedly renders investment advice with respect to the same transactions in which it purports to act as principal, can hardly deny its fiduciary status. Nor can a firm that is specifically vested with discretionary authority.[44] But take a broker-dealer firm that simply buys and sells securities as principal, rendering the incidental investment advice that is well-nigh universal in the industry and without which it could hardly operate. The Commission emphasized in the *Arleen Hughes* case that "it is not intended that the disclosure requirements, which we have found applicable to registrant, be imposed upon broker-dealers who render investment advice merely as an incident to their broker-dealer activities unless they have by a course of conduct placed themselves in a position of trust and confidence as to their customers."[45] When, then, does a firm cross the line from the first *Hughes* doctrine to the second?

The fact that the firm confirms as principal is not conclusive as

---

the investor do not bargain on a par with each other. Cf. id., §390, Comment a: "If the principal has limited business experience, an agent cannot properly fail to give such information merely because the principal says he does not care for it; the agent's duty of fair dealing is satisfied only if he reasonably believes that the principal understands the implications of the transaction."

For a legal-sociological analysis of various mechanisms for resolving what sociologists would call the broker's status-set and role-set conflicts, see Levin and Evan, Professionalism and the Stockbroker, 21 Bus. Law 337 (1966). These mechanisms are said to be segregation of statuses, regulatory and self-regulatory structures, and professionalization.

[44] Norris & Hirshberg, Inc., 21 SEC 865, 883-85 (1946), *aff'd sub nom.* Norris & Hirshberg, Inc. v. SEC, 177 F. 2d 228 (D. C. Cir. 1949). Discretionary authority is basically inconsistent with the firm's buying or selling for its own account; for it no longer has a genuinely discretionary power in so far as it obtains the customer's informed consent to each transaction. Rule 15c1-7, supra p. 804, prohibits excessive trading by any "broker or dealer * * * with or for any customer's account" as to which he has discretionary power. But the Commission has denied that this language contemplates that a dealer may hold discretionary power and trade for his own account. "The rule is intended to be broad in coverage and to include excessive activity even by a dealer — whether he has procured adequate consent to act as a dealer or is violating his duties. The attempt to make of Rule [15c1-7] a license to permit fiduciaries to violate their duties is utterly beyond the purpose and spirit of that rule." Norris & Hirshberg, Inc., supra, at 885.

[45] 27 SEC at 639. Cf. Inv. Adv. Act §202 (a)(11)(C), supra p. 739.

to the relationship of the parties.[46] Nor, on the other hand, does the absence of inventory when the firm solicits a customer to buy establish an agency relationship. In a 1946 opinion, in which the language was not too happily chosen, the Commission did indicate that in such circumstances a firm would normally be considered an agent.[47] There was no disputing the firm's capacity in the particular case. One customer was a ninety-year-old widow, and the other was a spinster ten years her junior. However, there was considerable furor about the Commission's broad language. Taken literally, it would have put a very substantial segment of the over-the-counter industry on an agency basis in view of the practice of many firms to sell before they buy. The fact is, of course, that a securities dealer, like any other type of merchant, does not become an agent for his customer *merely* because he tries to sell merchandise that he does not own at the time.[48] And the Commission

---

[46] Twomey v. Mitchum, Jones & Templeton, Inc., 262 Cal. App. 2d 690, 715, 69 Cal. Rptr. 222, 240 (1968); Birch v. Arnold & Sears, Inc., 288 Mass. 125, 192 N. E. 591 (1934); Porter v. Wormser, 94 N. Y. 431, 447 (1884); Norris & Hirshberg, Inc. v. SEC, 177 F. 2d 228, 233 n. 16 (D. C. Cir. 1949) *semble;* Allender Co., Inc., 9 SEC 1043, 1054-55 (1941); J. Logan & Co., 41 SEC 88, 98-99 (1962), *aff'd per curiam* sub nom. Hersh v. SEC, 325 F. 2d 147 (9th Cir. 1963), *cert. denied,* 377 U. S. 937.

It is not improper for a broker-dealer to act on one occasion as agent for a customer and on another occasion as principal, as long as the relationship is agreed to by the customer at or before the completion of each transaction. G. Alex Hope, 7 SEC 1082, 1083 (1940). But an agent must make a clean break with his principal if he wants to shift to a principal-and-principal basis in future dealings, and it is his burden to prove that he brought the change "to the attention of his principal in such a manner as to avoid all chance of misunderstanding." Smokeless Fuel Co. v. Western United Corp., 19 F. 2d 834, 836 (4th Cir. 1927). When the relationship from the start has been that of *broker* and customer, the mere sending of a confirmation reading "We confirm purchase from you" does not change the relationship to one of *dealer* and customer. Hence, when a broker buys in for his own account securities pledged as collateral by a customer, he is guilty of conversion and the transaction is voidable at the customer's option, unless the broker sustains the burden of proving that the customer knew and consented to the broker's purchase for his own account. Johnson v. Winslow, 155 Misc. 170, 279 N. Y. Supp. 147 (Sup. Ct. 1935), *aff'd per curiam,* 246 App. Div. 800, 285 N. Y. Supp. 1075 (1st Dept. 1936), *aff'd per curiam,* 272 N. Y. 467, 3 N. E. 2d 872 (1936). For a discussion of what constitutes adequate disclosure of capacity in the confirmation, see Bates and Douglas, Secondary Distribution of Securities — Problems Suggested by Kinney v. Glenny, 41 Yale L. J. 949, 985-94 (1932).

[47] Oxford Co., Inc., 21 SEC 681, 692-93 (1946).

[48] See Douglas and Bates, Stock "Brokers" As Agents and Dealers, 43 Yale L. J. 46, 60-61 (1933); Bates and Douglas, Secondary Distribution of Securities — Problems Suggested by Kinney v. Glenny, 41 Yale L. J. 949, 980-81 (1932). For a summary of the legal relationship between customer and broker and the standards of behavior whose violation gives rise to rights and duties *inter se,* see id. at 964-72.

soon made it clear that it had no intention of establishing such a rule of thumb.[49] But disclosure of spread in these riskless transactions is now required with respect to equity securities by the confirmation rule (unless the broker-dealer is acting as a market-maker), the theory being that they are in many respects equivalent to agency transactions.[50]

The determination of a broker-dealer's capacity in a particular transaction must depend on all the circumstances, including the degree of sophistication of the parties and the course of conduct between them.[51] The law must operate on the habits of people. Typically there is no express meeting of the minds as to the nature of the relationship. The two *Hughes* doctrines really blur into each other, to the point where a finding of fraud is occasionally based on violation of the two doctrines in the alternative. Indeed, the Commission in recent years seems to have deemphasized *Hughes II,* incorporating a good deal of it into *Hughes I*[52] — which may not be the wisest policy, as the author has had occasion to say elsewhere in suggesting that

> the Commission would be likely to find firmer ground under its collective feet if it were to talk in terms of *Hughes II* when the circumstances warranted — and to take the relatively small step of extending the "reasonable basis" and "suitability" doctrines [infra pp. 968-77] to agents, including manufactured agents of the *Hughes II* type — rather than attempting to construe the statutory fraud provisions as imposing a greater fiduciary obligation on principals than the common law imposes on agents.[53]

3.   DUTY TO INVESTIGATE AND THE DOCTRINE OF SUITABILITY

More recently, in an evolution from ethical precept to law that is still far from complete, the Commission (with some help from

[49] See the present writer's address before the Stock Brokers' Associates of Chicago and the former Chicago Stock Exchange, in his then capacity as Chief Counsel to the Commission's Division of Trading and Exchanges, The SEC and the Broker-Dealer, Mar. 16, 1948, reprinted with annotations in 1 Vand. L. Rev. 516, 529-30 (1948). The *Oxford* case was ignored by the Commission in the *Arleen Hughes* case, although about half the transactions there represented solicited, non-position trading.

[50] Rule 10b-10(a)(5)(i).

[51] In Value Line Fund, Inc. v. Marcus, CCH Fed. Sec. L. Rep. ¶91,523 at 94,967-68, 94,973 (S. D. N. Y. 1965), the court held that a firm acting as principal in form might be an agent in substance, at least for purposes of finding the privity between the firm's selling principal and the buyer that is required by §12 of the 1933 Act.

[52] Contrast Russell L. Irish, 42 SEC 735 (1965), *aff'd* sub nom. Irish v. SEC, 367 F. 2d 637 (9th Cir. 1966), *cert. denied,* 386 U. S. 911, with Mason, Moran & Co., 35 SEC 84 (1953).

[53] Loss, Book Rev., 18 J. Legal Ed. 238, 241-42 (1965).

the courts) has been refining its "shingle" and "fair dealing" concepts into something that approaches a "suitability" requirement — an obligation on the part of the dealer to recommend only securities that are suitable to the needs of the particular customer.

The development began as an attack on the evils of high-pressure selling, mainly via the long-distance telephone — which is to say, the "boiler room," so called because of the high pressure generated in the selling effort. The term has appeared in the judicial literature for at least four decades.[54] And Judge Friendly has given us a colorful description of a typical "boiler room" operation:

> The process would begin by sending to persons on various occupational lists, "such as doctors, plumbers, anything you want," which Kimball owned or would purchase, "teaser letters" describing the bright financial future afforded by low-priced stocks. These were followed by sales literature touting some particular stock. Next would come a telephone call from a salesman called an "opener," who "would try and sell the prospect as much or as little as he could." This would be followed by more mail relating the "good news about the company," and then by the knock-out blow, a call from a "high-pressure salesman," colorfully characterized as a "loader," who would "try and increase the purchase of the stock."[55]

In the Commission's view, "boiler rooms" fell under the ban of the fraud provisions on alternative theories: (1) because those provisions "contemplate at the least, that recommendations of a security made to proposed purchasers shall have a reasonable basis and that they shall be accompanied by disclosure of known or easily ascertainable facts bearing upon the justification for the representation"[56] and (2) because of *failure* to *disclose* to custom

---

[54] United States v. Rollnick, 91 F. 2d 911, 915 (2d Cir. 1937).

[55] United States v. Ross, 321 F. 2d 61, 64 (2d Cir. 1963), *cert. denied,* 375 U. S. 894; see also J. Logan & Co., 41 SEC 88, 89-91 (1962), *aff'd sub nom.* Hersh v. SEC, 325 F. 2d 147 (9th Cir. 1963), *cert. denied,* 377 U. S. 937.

[56] Best Securities, Inc., 39 SEC 931, 933-34 (1960); see also Mac Robbins & Co., Inc., 41 SEC 116, 119 (1962), *aff'd sub nom.* Berko v. SEC, 316 F. 2d 137 (2d Cir. 1963); Green v. Jonhop, Inc., 358 F. Supp. 413, 419 (D. Ore. 1973). Neither "blind faith in the issuer's self-serving assurances" nor the defendant's own investment and loss are a defense. Richard C. Spangler, Inc., 46 SEC 238 (1976). But a broker who has neither solicited the order nor recommended the security "has a minimal duty, if any at all, to investigate the purchase and disclose material facts to a customer." Canizaro v. Kohlmeyer & Co., 370 F. Supp. 282, 289 (E. D. La. 1974), *aff'd per curiam,* 512 F. 2d 484 (5th Cir. 1975). And when the Commission published a proposed "boiler room" rule in 1962 — which it withdrew as unnecessary three years later — it inserted an exemption for "isolated transactions not a part of any concentrated sales effort by the broker-dealer." Sec. Ex. Act Rels. 6885 (1962), 7517 (1965).

ers "the lack of adequate financial information or caution them as to the risk involved in purchasing the stock without such information."[57]

So far as salesmen are concerned, they may not rely blindly on information furnished by the broker-dealer by whom they are employed, or by the issuer, especially if the broker-dealer has an underwriter's responsibility and more especially in the case of a promotional issue.[58] In a pair of "boiler room" cases involving two salesmen who were held to be causes of the revocation of their employer's registration as a broker-dealer, the Second Circuit, after initially remanding to the Commission for further findings,[59] ultimately added its *imprimatur* to the Commission's statement:

> Whatever may be a salesman's obligation of inquiry, or his right to rely on information provided by his employer, where securities of an established issuer are being recommended to customers by a broker-dealer who is not engaged in misleading and deceptive high-pressure selling practices, * * * there can be little, if any, justification for a claim of reliance on literature furnished by an employer who is engaged in a fraudulent sales campaign.[60]

Meanwhile the NASD had always had a rule on its books, dating from the Investment Bankers Code of NRA days:

> In recommending to a customer the purchase, sale, or exchange of any security, a member shall have reasonable grounds for believing that the recommendation is suitable for such customer upon the basis of the facts, if any, disclosed by such customer as to his other security holdings and as to his financial situation and needs.[61]

---

[57] B. Fennekohl & Co., 41 SEC 210, 215, 217 (1962). See also Sec. Act Rel. 4445 (1962). "Where public information concerning the company is not available from the Commission or standard research sources, the extent of inquiry required to reasonably assure the broker or dealer that the proposed transaction complies with applicable legal requirements will be correspondingly greater." Sec. Act Rel. 5168 (1971). And an unseasoned company needs more investigation that one that is well established. Merrill Lynch, Pierce, Fenner & Smith, Inc., Sec. Ex. Act Rel. 14,149, 13 SEC Dock. 646 (1977). In general, see Brudney, Origins and Limited Applicability of the "Reasonable Basis" or "Know Your Merchandise" Doctrine, in Practising Law Institute, Fourth Annual Institute on Securities Regulation (1973) c. 9.

[58] Hanly v. SEC, 415 F. 2d 589, 595-97 (2d Cir. 1969) (review of administrative proceeding); SEC v. N. A. R. & D. Corp., 424 F. 2d 63, 84 (2d Cir. 1970) (injunction); Franklin Savings Bank v. Levy, 551 F. 2d 521, 527 (2d Cir. 1977) (§12(2) defense).

[59] Kahn v. SEC, 297 F. 2d 112 (2d Cir. 1961); Berko v. SEC, 297 F. 2d 116 (2d Cir. 1961).

[60] Mac Robbins & Co., Inc., 41 SEC 116, 128-29 (1962), *aff'd* sub nom. Berko v. SEC, 316 F. 2d 137, 142-43 (2d Cir. 1963).

[61] Rules of Fair Practice, Art. III, §2, CCH NASD Manual ¶2152.

And the New York Stock Exchange's "know your customer" rule[62] — which has been called "the eleventh commandment of Wall Street"[63] — is being pulled in the same direction, although its requirement of "due diligence to learn the essential facts relative to every customer [and] every order" seems more designed to protect the member firm than the customer.[64]

In the *Greenberg* case in 1960, where the broker-dealer had not raised (or at least had not stressed) before the NASD the restriction of the duty under the language of the rule to cases where the relevant facts have been disclosed to the broker by the customer, the Commission in effect read that limitation out of the rule:

> The clear purpose of the Rule would be defeated if it were construed as permitting a broker or dealer to engage in a practice of recommending low price speculative securities to unknown customers — a practice which by its nature involves a high probability that the recommendation will not be suitable to at least some of the persons solicited — without any knowledge of or attempt to obtain information concerning the customer's other security holdings, his financial situation, and his needs so as to be in a position to judge the suitability of the recommendation.[65]

The NASD's interpretation, on the other hand, gives effect to the words "if any" by not requiring the broker-dealer "to assume any responsibility until the customer objectively demonstrates his reliance on the superior skill and knowledge of the broker-dealer by supplying him with financial information about himself."[66] And the Special Study's recommendation that "Greater emphasis should be given by the Commission and the self-regulatory bodies

---

[62] Rule 405, CCH N. Y. Stock Ex. Guide ¶2405; see also Am. Stock Ex. Rule 411, CCH Am. Stock Ex. Guide ¶943.

[63] Surgil v. Kidder, Peabody & Co., Inc., 63 Misc. 2d 473, 477, 311 N. Y. S. 2d 157, 162 (Civ. Ct. 1970), *rev'd on other grounds*, 69 Misc. 2d 213, 329 N. Y. S. 2d 993 (Sup. Ct. 1971).

[64] See N. Y. Stock Ex. M. F. Educ. Circ. 234 (1968): "An important purpose of this rule is to protect the firm against loss or rule violation due to unethical actions of customers."

[65] Gerald M. Greenberg, 40 SEC 133, 137-38 (1960).

[66] Mundheim, Professional Responsibilities of Broker-Dealers: The Suitability Doctrine, [1965] Duke L. J. 445, 458; see 1 SEC, Report of Special Study of Securities Markets, H. R. Doc. No. 95, 88th Cong., 1st Sess. (1963) 311-12; Parsons v. Hornblower & Weeks-Hemphill Noyes, 447 F. Supp. 482, 495 (M. D. N. C. 1977), *aff'd per curiam*, 571 F. 2d 203 (4th Cir. 1978).

to the concept of 'suitability' of particular securities for particular customers"[67] received a cold reception from the industry.[68]

Since the early 1960s all concerned have been living with a compromise. The NASD in 1964 adopted a set of guidelines on "Fair Dealing with Customers."[69] And a year earlier the New York Stock Exchange — whose members normally, of course, have the fiduciary obligation that the law imposes on an agent — adopted certain "guideposts" for *written* communications with the public, one of which has to do with recommendations:

> A recommendation (even though not labeled as a recommendation) must have a basis which can be substantiated as reasonable.
> When recommending the purchase, sale, or switch of specific securities, supporting information should be provided or offered.[70]

This compromise, however, goes more to the "duty to investigate" or "know your merchandise" concept than to "know your customer" or "suitability." And it could not have ended the controversy over whether the dealer should have an affirmative obligation to *seek out* the information relevant to a determination of suitability. For, as long as the NASD has a suitability rule, §15 (b)(9) of the Act presumably gives the Commission itself an obligation to adopt a suitability rule of its own for those broker-dealers that are not members of the NASD. And since 1967 the Commission's Rule 15b10-3 has required every nonmember broker or dealer (or associated person) who recommends to a customer the purchase, sale, or exchange of a security to

> have reasonable grounds to believe that the recommendation is not unsuitable for such customer on the basis of information furnished by such customer after reasonable inquiry concerning the customer's investment objectives, financial situation and needs, and any other information known by such broker or dealer or associated person.[71]

[67] 1 SEC, Report of Special Study of Securities Markets, H. R. Doc. No. 95, 88th Cong., 1st Sess. (1963) 329.

[68] 1 Investor Protection, Hearings before Subcom. of House Com. on Int. & For. Commerce on H. R. 6789, H. R. 6793, S. 1642, 88th Cong., 1st Sess. (1963) 394, 471; 2 id. 686, 690 (1963-64).

[69] CCH NASD Manual ¶2152.

[70] CCH N. Y. Stock Ex. Guide ¶2474A.10(1); see also N. Y. Stock Ex. P. R. & R. I. Circ. 5 (1964) 2 (what is a "reasonable" basis for a recommendation is a matter of interpretation dependent on the circumstances, but the usual primary or secondary research sources would normally be considered reasonable).

[71] This is supplemented by a requirement in the recordkeeping rule that a record be made (presumably whether or not the particular recommendation is acted upon) of

Thus, in the "SECO" area the suitability concept not only has taken a form that goes beyond the NASD rule — as the NASD recognized in opposing the Commission's proposed rule, wondering perhaps whether it could long hold out itself if the Commission were to codify *Greenberg*.[72] In addition — and more significantly from the point of view of sanctions, including presumably implied private actions if they are recognized[73] — suitability in the "SECO" area has hardened into law as distinct from ethical precept.

Apart from Rule 15b10-3, it does not follow, of course, that a broker-dealer's effecting a transaction on the basis of an unsuitable recommendation is a violation of the general fraud rules, at least outside (1) the "boiler room" context, where by hypothesis the relationship to customers is such that there can be no basis for believing that *any* recommendation is suitable or unsuitable and (2) perhaps the situation where the broker-dealer is acting as agent or pseudo-agent, though even the law of agency does not impose a duty under all circumstances to make affirmative inquiry as required by Rule 15b10-3. Nevertheless, there are enough cases (though there is still a paucity of square holdings) to indicate that a subtle shift from ethics to law may be in process.[74] And this is

---

the customer's occupation, marital status, investment objectives, other information concerning the customer's financial situation and needs which the broker or dealer or the associated person considered in making the recommendation, and the signature of the broker or dealer or associated person who made the recommendation to the customer.

Rule 15b10-6(a)(1)(B); see also Rule 15b10-6(c).

[72] NASD News, Mar. 1967, p. 4.

[73] See pp. 1157-62 infra.

[74] A number of Commission decisions point in that direction, albeit by way of dictum or under extraordinary circumstances. Herbert R. May, 27 SEC 814, 824 (1948); Ramey Kelly Corp., 39 SEC 756, 759 (1960); Powell & McGowan, Inc., 41 SEC 933, 935 (1964).

In SEC v. Rabinowitz, Litig. Rel. 2444 (D. Ariz. 1962), a "spread" case in which the Commission got a preliminary injunction, it pleaded partly on a theory of "contravention of high standards of commerical honor and just and equitable principles of trade."

In Merrill Lynch, Pierce, Fenner & Smith, Inc. v. Bocock, 247 F. Supp. 373, 376-77 (S. D. Tex. 1965), apparently a common law case involving a short sale, the court cited the NASD rule in support of its conclusion that the plaintiff was a "suitable person."

By 1967, after citing "boiler room" cases and others indiscriminately with respect to the duty to make reasonable inquiry, the Commission was able to say flatly that, when the record clearly established a scheme to defraud in the sale of a speculative security by means of a high-pressure campaign involving the recurring use of the same basic fraudulent representations and predictions, the legal principles were the same whether or not there was a specific finding of the existence of a "boiler-room." James De Mammos, 43 SEC 333, 337 (1967), *aff'd sub nom.* De Mammos v. SEC, 2d Cir., Dock. No. 31,469, Oct. 13, 1967.

In Hecht v. Harris, Upham & Co., 283 F. Supp. 417, 428-31 (N. D. Cal.

apart from the extent to which the suitability idea is already reflected in the SEC structure — going back to the Supreme Court's
"self-fending" concept in the *Ralston Purina* case, which finds expression also in Rule 506(b)(2)(ii), the private offering rule.[75]

Finally — and oddly — it was a common law deceit action
involving the sale of insurance rather than securities that gave the
Commission the greatest aid and comfort. In a case coming up
from Hawaii, the Ninth Circuit held that an insurance agent who

---

1968), *aff'd on this point and modified on other grounds,* 430 F. 2d 1202 (9th
Cir. 1970), the court's finding of estoppel on the part of the plaintiff — a
widow who was "neither as 'dumb' in matters of brokerage accounts as plaintiff's counsel contends or as plaintiff, herself, made herself appear to be on
the stand, nor * * * as smart, experienced, or informed as defendants' counsel
would make her out to be" — made it unnecessary for the court to decide
whether there might be liability for violation of the "suitability" rule of the
NASD and the "know your customer" rule of the New York Stock Exchange.
But the court thought that those rules "may in any event be considered as
expressions of the industry itself concerning what constitutes proper conduct,
the violation of which under certain circumstances may amount to fraud."
283 F. Supp. at 433.

In Twomey v. Mitchum, Jones & Templeton, Inc., 262 Cal. App. 2d 690,
721-22, 69 Cal. Rptr. 222, 244 (1968), a common law action, the court stated
in following certain guidelines that had been suggested for the NASD:

> It may be asserted that the proposed guidelines are merely ethical
> standards and should not be a predicate for civil liability. Good ethics
> should not be ignored by the law. It would be inconsistent to suggest
> that a person should be defrocked as a member of his calling, and yet
> not be liable for the injury which resulted from his acts or omissions.

In Plunkett v. Dominick & Dominick, Inc., 414 F. Supp. 885, 896 (D. Conn.
1976), the court without elucidation referred to the NASD suitability rule as
imposing duties "identical to what is at least imposed at common law."

In Michael Batterman, 46 SEC 304 (1976), a consent case, the Commission
expressed its particular concern with respect to the suitability of option transactions for particular customers.

In Delporte v. Shearson, Hammill & Co., Inc., 548 F. 2d 1149 (5th Cir.
1977), the court found a margin account to be unsuitable, but the plaintiff's
signature on the margin agreement was forged.

Perhaps most significantly, in Clark v. John Lamula Investors, Inc., 583 F.
2d 594 (2d Cir. 1978), the court held that, under the circumstances, violation
of the NASD rule coupled with the scienter finding required by *Hochfelder*
amounted to a violation of Rule 10b-5. Although the charge to the jury was
limited to "the circumstances," proof of scienter in this context should normally present no great obstacle.

The uniform limited offering exemption adopted in 1982 by the North
American Securities Administrators Association contains a "reasonable inquiry" suitability condition, but with a presumption of suitability if the
investment does not exceed 20 percent of the investor's net worth. It is not
stated whether the presumption is rebuttable. CCH Blue Sky L. Rep. ¶5294A,
§D1.

[75]See p. 373 supra; on the concept as applied in various special situations
(e. g., Rule 15c2-5, supra p. 806), see Roach, The Suitability Obligations of
Brokers: Present Law and the Proposed Federal Securities Code, 29 Hastings
L. J. 1067, 1073-1119 (1978).

had induced the plaintiff to purchase excessive amounts of bank-financed insurance was liable because of his false representation that what he was selling "was a suitable program for plaintiff and his family and fitted his needs."[76]

This evaluation (whether planned or not) has not gone unchallenged:

At common law even a business *agent* (let alone a dealer acting as principal) "represents that he has the knowledge which is standard for the profession in which he is employed; there is, however, no representation that his knowledge is complete and accurate."[77] Moreover, there is the question of how much investigation and actual knowledge will satisfy the obligation once it is imposed. For the duty (as the Commission sees it) to inquire into the financial resources of the customer goes beyond the implied warranty of fitness for a particular purpose that is imposed by §2-315 of the Uniform Commercial Code when the seller of goods has reason to know the particular purpose for which the goods are acquired and the buyer relies on the seller's skill or judgment in selecting or furnishing goods that are suitable for the purpose. Will the broker-dealer be held to the standard of "a prudent man in the management of his own property" as under §11 of the 1933 Act? "From a practical standpoint, the broker-dealer trading in an issue or participating in the sale of a small number of shares, as distinguished from being engaged in a major distribution of such securities, could not afford to make an investigation of the type required to be made by a principal underwriter of an issuer."[78]

On the other hand, the common law does not set the outer limits of the SEC fraud provisions.[79] And the suitability doctrine has been well rationalized by Dean Mundheim in terms of "risk threshold":

A suitability doctrine imposes a responsibility on the broker-dealer to take the risk threshold of his customers into account when he recommends or sells securities to them. * * * The

---

[76] Anderson v. Knox, 297 F. 2d 702, 705 (9th Cir. 1961), *cert. denied*, 370 U. S. 915; cf. Steadman v. McConnell, 149 Cal. App. 2d 334, 308 P. 2d 361 (1957); Hardt v. Brink, 192 F. Supp. 879 (W. D. Wash. 1961). It has been claimed that the *Anderson* case has not in fact been followed. Leatherberry, Remedies for the Buyer or Beneficiary of an Unsuitable Life Insurance Plan, 32 Rutgers L. Rev. 431, 447 (1979).

[77] Restatement (Second) of Agency §10, Comment c; see also id., §379, which speaks simply of the care and skill that are "standard in the locality for the kind of work which [the agent] is employed to perform."

[78] Kennedy, in Symposium, Current Problems of Securities Underwriters and Dealers, 18 Bus. Law. 27, 76-77 (1962).

[79] See p. 813 supra.

broker-dealer may discharge his responsibility under the suitability doctrine by informing the customer of the risk aspects of the
transaction in a way which will enable the customer, in light of
his individual capabilities, to relate these risks to his risk threshold
and thus make his own determination of suitability. If under these
circumstances the customer wishes to purchase the security, the
broker-dealer can sell it to him even though he does not think it
is within the customer's risk threshold.

*   *   *

If the customer refuses to furnish the broker-dealer with information sufficient to determine the customer's risk threshold, the
broker-dealer should not be required to prevent the customer
from purchasing securities which are beyond his risk threshold.[80]

As for the question of what constitutes a recommendation, the only
time when the broker-dealer is clearly relieved of a suitability
duty is when his only relationship with the customer is that of
an order clerk; in the intermediate cases between the order clerk
situation, where reliance is clearly absent, and the recommendation
to an inexperienced customer, where reliance is clearly present,
there should be (Dean Mundheim suggests) a presumption of reliance, which, however, the broker-dealer should be free to rebut.[81]
He also proposes an NASD guideline on suitability that would
suggest ways to handle some of the common but troublesome
cases — like the "sweet trusting widow" who turns out to be "a
greedy old lady."[82]

In this state of affairs the Code's solution, while preserving the
existing self-regulatory organization and "SECO" strictures, is to
make it unlawful for a broker or dealer (or a municipal broker or
dealer), but only if in contravention of a Commission rule,

to recommend a transaction in a security unless he reasonably
believes that it is not unsuitable for the customer on the basis of

---

[80] Mundheim, Professional Responsibilities of Broker-Dealers: The Suitability Doctrine, [1965] Duke L. J. 445, 449-50.

[81] Id. at 450, 472-73.

[82] Id. at 472-79. For an analysis of the great many variations that go into a
determination of suitability, see Bines, Setting Investment Objectives: The
Suitability Doctrine — Part II, 4 Sec. Reg. L. J. 418 (1977). For an examination of the economists' "portfolio concept" of risk suitability and a suggestion
of a way of using that theoretical model to provide additional substantive
content to the legal standards, see Cohen, The Suitability Rule and Economic
Theory, 80 Yale L. J. 1604 (1971); but cf. Note, The Regulation of Risky
Investments, 83 Harv. L. Rev. 603, 624 (1970): "The law conceives of risk
as the risk of capital loss associated with particular securities rather than with
the portfolio as a whole."

(A) information furnished by the customer on reasonable inquiry with respect to his investment objectives, financial situation, and needs, and (B) any other information known by the broker, dealer, municipal broker, or municipal dealer.[83]

4. FRAUD BY INVESTMENT ADVISERS

Section 206 of the Investment Advisers Act makes it unlawful for any investment adviser, by use of the mails or interstate facilities, directly or indirectly "(1) to employ any device, scheme, or artifice to defraud any client or prospective client; (2) to engage in any transaction, practice, or course of business which operates as a fraud or deceit upon any client or prospective client; * * * [or] (4) to engage in any act, practice, or course of business which is fraudulent, deceptive, or manipulative," with rulemaking authority under Clause (4), as in §15(c)(2) of the 1934 Act, to "define, and prescribe means reasonably designed to prevent, such acts, practices, and courses of business as are fraudulent, deceptive, or manipulative."[84]

The first two clauses are modeled on Clauses (1) and (3) of the 1933 Act; the substantive portion of the fourth clause is modeled on §10(b) of the 1934 Act; and the rulemaking authority is modeled on §15(c)(2) of the 1934 Act.[85] Consequently, everything that has been said thus far in this chapter applies with equal force to investment advisers *mutatis mutandis*. In other words, Arleen Hughes's course of business violated §206(1) and (2) of the Advisers Act as well as the fraud provisions of the 1933 and 1934 Acts.[86] Section 206, however, can be violated without a securities transaction;[87] indeed, when there is a securities transaction, §206 is hardly needed.

There are three rules under §206(4):

[83] §9 15(a)(3).

[84] On §206(3), see p. 981 infra. Section 206(4), together with the rulemaking authority, was added in 1960.

[85] See p. 805 supra.

[86] The Commission's proceeding was based solely on the 1933 and 1934 Acts, because it then had no power to proceed against a person's registration either as a broker-dealer or as an investment adviser for violation of §206 of the Advisers Act.

[87] Ronald B. Donati, Inc., Inv. Adv. Act Rels. 666, 683, 16 SEC Dock. 1081 (1979), 17 SEC Dock. 1215 (1979) (respondent consented to a finding that it had violated §206 by persuading its clients to guarantee its bank loans and ultimately to post their securities as collateral without disclosing its deteriorating financial condition and other outstanding loans).

The first, Rule 206(4)-1, is an advertising rule, which defines "advertisement" to include any communication, addressed to more than one person,

> which offers (1) any analysis, report, or publication concerning securities, or which is to be used in making any determination as to when to buy or sell any security, or which security to buy or sell, or (2) any graph, chart, formula or other device to be used in making any determination as to when to buy or sell any security, or which security to buy or sell, or (3) any other investment advisory service with regard to securities.

This definition has been considered broad enough to cover advisory material, as well as so-called Progress Reports, designed to induce subscriptions.[88]

In announcing the adoption of the rule, the Commission stated that

> it should be borne in mind that investment advisers are professionals and should adhere to a stricter standard of conduct than that applicable to merchants, securities are "intricate merchandise," and clients or prospective clients of investment advisers are frequently unskilled and unsophisticated in investment matters.[89]

Accordingly, the cases stress that advisers' conduct "must be measured from the viewpoint of a person unskilled and unsophisticated in investment matters";[90] that advertisements may be "deceptive and misleading in their over-all effect even though it might be argued that, when narrowly and literally read, no single statement of a material fact was false";[91] and that brochures must not overstate "the amounts and probabilities of gains" and understate "the risks and speculative elements involved."[92]

Rule 206(4)-2 requires advisers who have custody or possession of funds or securities of clients to segregate their securities, hold them in safekeeping, and set up a separate trust account in a bank

---

[88] SEC v. C. R. Richmond & Co., 565 F. 2d 1101, 1105 (9th Cir. 1977); Spear & Staff, Inc., 42 SEC 549, 555-56 (1965).

[89] Inv. Adv. Act Rel. 121 (1961); see also Inv. Adv. Act Rels. 113 (1961) (original proposal), 119 (1961) (amended proposal); Stanford Investment Management, Inc., 43 SEC 864, 867 (1968), and cases cited.

[90] SEC v. C. R. Richmond & Co., 565 F. 2d 1101, 1104-05 (9th Cir. 1977).

[91] Spear & Staff, Inc., 42 SEC 549, 553 (1965).

[92] Stanford Investment Management, Inc., 43 SEC 864 (1968); see also T. J. Holt & Co., Inc., Inv. Adv. Act Rel. 254 (1969). In general, see Marketlines, Inc., 43 SEC 267, 268-70 (1967), aff'd sub nom. Marketlines, Inc. v. SEC, 384 F. 2d 264 (2d Cir. 1967), cert. denied, 390 U. S. 947; Paul K. Peers, Inc., 42 SEC 539 (1965).

for the funds belonging to each client. Among other conditions in the rule, the adviser must send each client, at least quarterly, an itemized statement of the funds and securities in his custody or possession and all debits, credits and transactions in the account during the period; and at least once each calendar year the funds and securities must be verified by an independent public accountant in a surprise examination.

Rule 206(4)-3 prohibits cash payments for the solicitation of clients except under specified circumstances and conditions.[93]

The great case under the Advisers Act is *SEC* v. *Capital Gains Research Bureau, Inc.,* decided by the Supreme Court in 1963.[94] In six instances the advisory firm took a long position in a listed stock on the New York Stock Exchange shortly before sending its approximately 5000 subscribers one of its "Special Recommendations" or "Special Bulletins" containing a financial analysis of the particular company without disclosing the firm's position or intention. In each case there was a small market rise and the firm within a few days sold its stock at a profit. There was also one instance of a short position followed by converse activity. The practice is known on Wall Street as "scalping." In a broad opinion (perhaps unduly broad in some of its language) Justice Goldberg stated for the Court (only Justice Harlan dissenting):

(1) "The Investment Advisers Act of 1940 * * * reflects a congressional recognition 'of the delicate fiduciary nature of an investment advisory relationship,' as well as a congressional intent to eliminate, or at least to expose, all conflicts of interest which might incline an investment adviser — consciously or unconsciously — to render advice which was not disinterested. It would defeat the manifest purpose of the Investment Advisers Act of 1940 for us to hold, therefore, that Congress, in empowering the courts to enjoin any practice which operates 'as a fraud or deceit,' intended to require proof of intent to injure and actual injury to clients."[95]

(2) This conclusion is not in derogation of the common law of fraud. "Even in a damage suit between parties to an arms-length transaction, the intent which must be established need not be an intent to cause injury to the client, as the courts below seem to have assumed."[96]

---

[93] The Commission cautioned in adopting the rule that it should not be taken as an indication that it was proper to use clients' *brokerage* to pay referral fees. Inv. Adv. Act Rel. 688, 17 SEC Dock. 1293, 1294 n. 4 (1979).
[94] 375 U. S. 180 (1963).
[95] Id. at 191-92.
[96] Id. at 192 n. 39.

(3) The content of common law fraud has not remained static, and it also has a broader meaning in equity than at law in that an intention to defraud or misrepresent is not a necessary element in equity.[97]

(4) "We cannot assume that Congress, in enacting legislation to prevent fraudulent practices by investment advisers, was unaware of these developments in the common law of fraud. Thus, even if we were to agree with the courts below that Congress had intended, in effect, to codify the common law of fraud in the Investment Advisers Act of 1940, it would be logical to conclude that Congress codified the common law 'remedially' as the courts had adapted it to the prevention of fraudulent securities transactions by fiduciaries, not 'technically' as it has traditionally been applied in damage suits between parties to arms-length transactions involving land and ordinary chattels."[98]

(5) The legislative history indicates that the omission of something like Clause (2) of §17(a) of the 1933 Act "does not seem significant."[99] Clause (2) was included in §17(a), part of a statute that was the first experiment in federal securities regulation, "out of an abundance of caution."[100] "It soon became clear, however, that the courts, aware of the previously outlined developments in the common law of fraud, were merging the proscription against nondisclosure into the general proscription against fraud, treating the former, in effect, as one variety of the latter."[101] In 1940 Congress presumably "deemed a specific proscription against nondisclosure surplusage."[102]

(6) The legislative history of the 1960 amendment of §206 that gave the Commission authority to adopt rules defining and designed to prevent fraudulent practices offers no indication "that Congress intended such rules to substitute for the 'general and flexible' antifraud provisions which have long been considered necessary to control 'the versatile inventions of fraud-doers.' "[103]

(7) The argument that the advice was "honest" in the sense that it was believed to be sound is but another way of putting the rejected argument that the elements of technical common law fraud — particularly intent — must be established before an injunction requiring disclosure may be ordered. The Advisers Act

[97] Id. at 193-94.
[98] Id. at 195.
[99] Id. at 197.
[100] Id. at 198.
[101] Ibid.
[102] Id. at 199.
[103] Ibid.

was "directed not only at dishonor but also at conduct that tempts dishonor."[104]

Query how much of this will turn out to survive *Aaron*, the 1980 decision that requires scienter in an injunction action under Rule 10b-5.[105] The Court there distinguished *Capital Gains* on the basis essentially of "the delicate fiduciary nature of an investment advisory relationship" and the disparate legislative history of §§10(b) and 206. But, once more, the question is how much to make of the difference in *tone* between the two opinions.

It remains to consider §206(3), which makes it unlawful for an adviser,

> acting as principal for his own account, knowingly to sell any security to or purchase any security from a client, or acting as broker for a person other than such client, knowingly to effect any sale or purchase of any security for the account of such client, without disclosing to such client in writing before the completion of such transaction the capacity in which he is acting and obtaining the consent of the client to such transaction.[106]

In the *Arleen Hughes* case the Commission by way of dictum adopted the same position that had been previously announced in a staff opinion, to the effect that the written disclosure must be made and the consent obtained "before the completion of each transaction of purchase or sale."[107] The Commission added the thought that this provision, apart from requiring that the disclosure be made in writing, was merely declaratory of the common law. The opinions of the Commission and the court also demonstrate that Clause (3) does not define the full measure of the disclosure obligation of an adviser who seeks to trade with his own clients. Therefore, when §206(3) goes on to provide that it does not apply "to

---

[104] Id. at 200, quoting from United States v. Mississippi Valley Generating Co., 364 U. S. 520, 549 (1961). Dishonor in this field, nevertheless, is a virus that defies immunization. The Special Study found evidence of "scalping" among both brokers and investment advisers. 1 SEC, Report of Special Study of Securities Markets, H. R. Doc. No. 95, 88th Cong., 1st Sess. (1963) 372.

The matter of "scalping" aside, the Commission has also made it clear that Clauses (1) and (2) of §206 are violated by the dissemination of unverified tips, since advisers have at least as great a duty as broker-dealers to use a high degree of care in order to ensure accurate and adequate representations with respect to securities they discuss in printed advisory material. Anne C. Robin, 41 SEC 634, 637 (1963).

[105] Aaron v. SEC, 446 U. S. 680 (1980), set out supra p. 887.

[106] Written *consent*, though advisable, is not required.

[107] Arleen W. Hughes, 27 SEC 629, 641 n. 17 (1948), aff'd on *other grounds* sub nom. Hughes v. SEC, 174 F. 2d 969 (D. C. Cir. 1949); Op. Dir. Trading & Ex. Div., Inv. Adv. Act Rel. 40 (1945).

any transaction with a customer of a broker or dealer if such broker or dealer is not acting as an investment adviser in relation to such transaction," it does not exclude the applicability of the other three clauses and of the fraud provisions in the 1933 and 1934 Acts.[108]

In 1975 the Commission adopted an exemptive rule, 206(3)-1, in recognition of the fact that the abolition of fixed stock exchange commissions created a §206(3) problem for broker-dealers who "unbundled" their advisory services. The rule exempts advisers who are registered broker-dealers with respect to the providing "of certain impersonal investment advisory services as to which the benefits of the Section 206(3) protections, because of the nature of the relationship between the investment adviser and the client in those situations, are far outweighed by the administrative difficulties and the costs involved in compliance with Section 206(3)."[109] In that connection the Commission recalled that §206(3) did not exclude any other fraud provision that might be applicable, but it modified the 1945 staff opinion[110] that had preceded the *Arleen Hughes* case "in light of the investment advisory business as it has evolved to the present time" by stating that the duty to disclose any particular facts (including cost and market) "will depend both upon the materiality of such facts in each situation and upon the degree of the client's trust and confidence in and reliance on the investment adviser with respect to the transaction."[111]

D.   THE "FREE MARKET" CONCEPT

1.   A CLASSIC PORTRAIT OF MARKET MANIPULATION

Related to the field of fraud — but not altogether a part of it as a matter of legal analysis — is the matter of market manipulation. The practice is probably as old as the securities markets.[1]

---

[108] Ibid.

[109] Inv. Adv. Act Rel. 470, 7 SEC Dock. 686 (1975).

[110] Op. Dir. Trading & Ex. Div., Inv. Adv. Act Rel. 40 (1945), supra nn. 38, 107.

[111] Inv. Adv. Act Rel. 470, 7 SEC Dock. 686, 687 (1975); Note to Rule 206(3)-1.

C. 9D [1] In 1903 it was estimated that roughly a third of all the trading on the New York Stock Exchange represented manipulation, a third represented members' floor trading, and a third represented actual buying and selling by pools and public. S. Pratt, The Work of Wall Street (1903) 48.

And — perhaps because the tragedy involved in some of the notorious market pools has been mixed with an element of drama
— there is a substantial literature on the classic manipulation
techniques.[2] The practices of the typical "bull" pools of the years
before the SEC have been described in this "simplified composite
picture":

COMMENT, MARKET MANIPULATION AND THE SECURITIES EXCHANGE ACT

46 Yale Law Journal 624, 626-28 (1937)

* * * The group first secures an option to purchase at a price
higher than the then market quotation a large block of a stock
which possesses actual or potential market appeal[12] and an easily
controllable floating supply. It is the task of the pool manager and
operator to raise the market price above the option price, and,
if the supply on the market remains constant,[14] this can be accomplished only by increasing the demand. The most effective
manner of inducing others to purchase is to have a favorable
ticker tape record which indicates to prospective purchasers that
others consider the security to be underpriced. The manager
opens a number of accounts with various brokers and, fortified by
a knowledge of the condition of the market obtained from the
book of a specialist, enters both buying and selling orders with
a preponderance of the former so that the price is made to rise

[2] See, e. g., Twentieth Century Fund, Inc., The Security Markets (1935)
c. 13; Stock Exchange Practices, Report of Com. on Banking & Currency, S.
Rep. No. 1455, 73d Cong., 2d Sess. (1934) 30-55; J. Flynn, Security Speculation
(1934) cc. 5, 6.

[12] Since the success of the manipulative venture depends on the ability of
the operator to induce the public to purchase the security, the probabilities of
a profitable outcome are enhanced if the stock is one which may easily be
played up to the trader's imagination. Thus, the radio securities in 1929, the
liquor stocks in 1933, and the aircraft securities in 1934 all lent themselves to
manipulation. * * * [As a matter of fact, a pool that operated in Libbey-
Owens-Ford Glass Co. in June 1933 was materially aided by a popular delusion
that the company made glass bottles, so that the stock was a Repeal stock.
Actually the company made no bottles at all. It was confused with Owens-
Illinois Glass Co. See Stock Exchange Practices, Report of Com. on Banking
& Currency, S. Rep. No. 1455, 73d Cong., 2d Sess. (1934) 36-37.]

[14] In actual practice the supply is diminished. The operator may drive
down the price to touch off stop-loss orders and cause weak holders of the
stock to sell, thereby enabling him to purchase more readily. He also contracts
with large holders of the stock in order that their holdings may be kept off
the market for a suitable period of time. Thus, supply is decreased as well as
demand stimulated, and the pool attains its mark-up in price by attacking
both sides of the market.

slowly upon an increasing volume of transactions. In the cruder form of operation many of these transactions will be washed sales in which the operator is both buyer and seller of the same stock; in others known as matched orders he enters orders to sell with the knowledge that some confederate is concomitantly entering orders to purchase the same amount of stock at the same price. As the price slowly rises, a complex publicity apparatus is set into motion to aid the stimulation of demand: The directors of the corporation whose stock is being manipulated, who may be members of the pool, issue favorable, but not wholly true, statements concerning the corporation's prospects; brokers, likewise interested in the operations, advise customers through market letters and customers' men to purchase the stock; subsidized tipster sheets and financial columnists in the daily papers tell glowingly of the corporation's future; "chisellers," "touts," and "wire-pluggers" are employed to disseminate false rumors of increased earnings or impending merger. As the market price passes the option price, the operator exercises his option and, increasing his sales over purchases, carefully unloads upon the public the optioned stock as well as that acquired in the process of marking up the price. But the operator does not necessarily rest with this gain. If he is able to distribute his holdings, he may sell short, and the stock, priced at an uneconomically high level and bereft of the pool's support, declines precipitately. As it approaches its normal quotation the pool covers its short position, thereby profiting both from the rise which it has engineered and the inevitable reaction.

2. MANIPULATION BEFORE THE SEC

It is of the essence of the economic function of a securities exchange that it be a free market — free of the artificiality of manipulation (the laying of hands on the scales) as it is free of the unfairness of insider trading (playing cards with a marked deck). If the Americans are well ahead of the British in the unceasing struggle against insider trading, the British took the lead in the largely successful fight against manipulation.[3]

The first English manipulation case was *Rex* v. *de Berenger*, decided by the King's Bench in 1814. The Allies were hoping

---

[3] In general, see Berle, Liability for Stock Market Manipulation, 31 Colum. L. Rev. 264 (1931); Berle, Stock Market Manipulation, 38 Colum. L. Rev. 393 (1938); Comment, Regulation of Stock Market Manipulation, 56 Yale L. J. 509 (1947).

for a speedy end to the war. Many rumors were current, mostly favorable. As each gained credence stocks rose, only to fall when confirmation failed. On the morning of February 21, 1814, a man dressed in a military uniform arrived in Winchester from Dover, scattering French gold among the postillions. He had let it be known on the way that he bore glorious news: Napoleon had been killed and the Allies were at Paris. Shortly afterwards two other men dressed as French Loyalist officers arrived with similar tidings, to disappear forthwith. Stocks immediately rose and, of couse, fell again when this rumor proved to be as unfounded as the others. This time, however, the Stock Exchange investigated with success. The first traveler, who had called himself du Bourg, turned out to be de Berenger, a Prussian subject who had sought employment as an instructor of sharpshooters from Admiral Sir Alexander Cochrane. It was at the house of the Admiral's nephew that de Berenger had alighted upon arriving in Winchester. The younger Cochrane was a gallant naval captain who had made a fortune under the prize system and had gone into the stock market. As the market rose with the rumor of Napoleon's death, he and a number of friends sold their holdings and made large profits. The Stock Exchange was determined to prosecute, and Cochrane, de Berenger and seven others were convicted of a conspiracy to raise the price of public Government funds and other Government securities without just cause and with intent to injure the public who might buy such securities on February 21.

Moving in arrest of judgment, the defendants argued that a conspiracy to raise the price of Government funds was not a crime in the absence of some collateral object giving it a criminal character, "as if it had been shewn that on that day the defendants were possessed of certain shares in the funds, and intended to sell them, and thereby, by raising the price, to cheat the particular persons who should become purchasers; or if the indictment had alleged that it was the day on which the commissioners for reducing the national debt were wont to purchase, and that the defendants did it with intent to enhance the price of such purchases."[4] As a matter of fact, it was argued, "the higher the price of the public funds, the better for the country, because the higher the state of public credit."[5] But a unanimous court overruled these objections. It was not necessary to show either that the Government as such had been injured or that the defendants had benefited. Both the means

[4] Rex v. de Berenger, 3 Maule & S. 67, 70, 105 Eng. Reprint 536, 537 (K. B. 1814).
[5] Ibid.

used and the object sought were wrong. The essence of the matter is that the public has a right that a natural market should not be tampered with. As Lord Ellenborough put it:

A public mischief is stated as the object of this conspiracy; the conspiracy is by false rumours to raise the price of the public funds and securities; and the crime lies in the act of conspiracy and combination to effect that purpose, and would have been complete although it had not been pursued to its consequences, or the parties had not been able to carry it into effect. The purpose itself is mischievous, it strikes at the price of a vendible commodity in the market, and if it gives it a fictitious price, by means of false rumours, it is a fraud levelled against all the public, for it is against all such as may possibly have any thing to do with the funds on that particular day. It seems to me also not to be necessary to specify the persons, who became purchasers of stock, as the persons to be affected by the conspiracy, for the defendants could not, except by a spirit of prophecy, divine who would be the purchasers on a subsequent day. The excuse is, that it was impossible they should have known, and if it were possible, the multitude would be an excuse in point of law. But the statement is wholly unnecessary, the conspiracy being complete independantly [*sic*] of any persons being purchasers. I have no doubt it must be so considered in law according to the cases.[6]

Thus there became established in Great Britain, as a matter of criminal law, the concept of a free and open public market.[7] And near the end of the century that concept was applied to a case of manipulation by means of trading alone, without the dis-

[6] 3 Maule & S. at 72-73, 105 Eng. Reprint at 538. For an interesting account of this case, with emphasis upon Lord Cochrane's part in it, see F. Birkenhead, Famous Trials of History (2d ed. 1926) 193-204. Some of the background facts related in the text are found in this account rather than in the court's opinion. For the latest of several reviews of the case — which concludes, unlike several earlier biographies of Cochrane, that he was clearly guilty — see H. Cecil, A Matter of Speculation: The Case of Lord Cochrane (1965). Guilty or not, Cochrane — who served a term in prison, was forced to leave the Navy, and saw his banner of the Order of the Bath unscrewed from its place in Westminster Abbey to be literally kicked out of the Chapel and down the steps — was not only reelected post-haste to the House of Commons, where he made fierce attacks on the judge in his case, Lord Ellenborough, but also lived to help liberate Chile, Peru and Brazil, to receive a "free pardon" in 1832 from William IV, to be restored to the Navy List in the rank he would have held if he had never left it, and to be considered for employment in the Crimean War when he was nearly eighty. Appropriately enough, he was also buried in the Abbey (though, lest the matter be overdone, without a public funeral). See also W. Tute, Cochrane: A Life of Admiral the Earl of Dundonald (1965).

[7] See also Regina v. Aspinall, 1 Q. B. D. 730 (1876), aff'd, 2 Q. B. D. 48 (C. A. 1876).

semination of false rumors. "I can see no substantial distinction," Lord Lopes said in *Scott* v. *Brown*, "between false rumours and false and fictitious acts."[8]

The pre-SEC cases in the United States followed much the same trend, although in some respects they did not go so far and in other respects they went further. As in England, the cases arose in three contexts — criminal prosecution, litigation between manipulators, and litigation between investor and manipulator.

The criminal attack on manipulation came under the mail fraud statute and special state legislation, primarily in New York. In 1933 Judge Woolsey in the Southern District of New York wholeheartedly adopted the open market theory in overruling a demurrer to an indictment under the mail fraud and conspiracy statutes. The defendants bribed customers' men to tout the stock, "washed" the stock among ninety-one accounts, and put out false statements with respect to the company's earnings. Without regard to this evidence of conventional fraud, Judge Woolsey, after reviewing the English law beginning with the *de Berenger* case,

---

[8] Scott v. Brown, Doering, McNab & Co., [1892] 2 Q. B. 724, 730, 61 L. J. (N. S.) 738, 741 (C. A.). That case was an unsuccessful rescission action against a broker who had agreed to buy certain shares on the Exchange for the plaintiff with the sole purpose, as the court found, of creating trading on the Exchange at a "premium" in order to mislead the public as to the market and to induce public buying. Sir Frederick Pollock referred to the case as a modern version of the "well-known legal legend * * * of a highwayman coming into equity for an account against his partner." 9 L. Q. Rev. 105 (1893). But Scott v. Brown contains a dictum to the effect that a third person induced to buy from the manipulators at an unfair price may sue any or all of them for damages. [1892] 2 Q. B. at 734, 61 L. J. (N. S.) at 743. This is supported by the cases to the extent that the plaintiffs have been able to work out a contract or trust relationship with the defendants. E. g., Barry v. Croskey, 2 J. & H. 1, 70 Eng. Reprint 945 (Ch. 1861). Otherwise, however, the British courts have been reluctant to adopt the free market concept. As a result, plaintiffs purchasing on the open market have been unable to surmount the hurdles of reliance and privity, as is so often the case in common law deceit actions. E. g., Salaman v. Warner, 64 L. T. R. (N. S.) 598, 7 T. L. R. 431 (Q. B. 1891), aff'd, 65 L. T. R. (N. S.) 132, 7 T. L. R. 484 (C. A. 1891). On the English cases generally, see Moore and Wiseman, Market Manipulation and the Exchange Act, 2 U. Chi. L. Rev. 46, 57-65 (1934).

Interesting analogies, whose influence may be noticed in the common law manipulation cases, are afforded by the early English statutory crimes (borrowed from the Roman law) of engrossing, regrating, and forestalling. 5 & 6 Edw. 6, c. 14 (1551-52). Engrossing resembled the modern practice of cornering the supply. Forestalling consisted of intercepting the seller on his way to the market and buying his wares to keep them off the market. Regrating was the process of producing an artificial scarcity by buying up goods in the market and reselling them in or near the same market. See 3 Wharton, Criminal Law and Procedure (1957) c. 45, esp. §1193; Mason, Monopoly in Law and Economics, 47 Yale L. J. 34, 38-39 (1937).

held squarely that the manipulative trading itself was fraudulent.[9] The Second Circuit, in affirming the conviction that followed, sustained the indictment on the narrow ground of the allegations concerning touting, wash sales, and false statements. Consequently, the court held that it "need not enter into a general discussion of the lawfulness of stock 'pools,' as the judge did below."[10] At the same time, it did not overrule the District Court's holding to the effect that interference with a free and open market by manipulative trading is itself fraudulent. And substantially the same results have been reached under various provisions formerly in the New York Penal Law and now in the General Business Law.[11]

So far as litigation between manipulators is concerned, before the mid-1930s there was no American case of manipulation by trading alone, like *Scott* v. *Brown*. The courts refused to enforce contracts in the extreme cases of corners,[12] or contracts to effect fictitious transactions[13] or for the touting of securities.[14] But otherwise neither the defendants nor the courts seem to have raised the question of illegality or public policy in litigation between pool members.[15] Then in the late 1930s two courts — perhaps influenced by the passage of the SEC statutes, although both cases were decided at common law — went even further than *Scott* v. *Brown* in that they refused to enforce contracts for "stabilization" or "pegging," which (as we shall see) is a relatively benign form of manipulation.[16]

In the context of litigation between a third party and one of the manipulators, the American cases have followed much the same pattern as the British. Contracts of sale between manipulators and innocent persons have been held voidable upon proof of manipu-

---

[9] United States v. Brown, 5 F. Supp. 81, 85 (S. D. N. Y. 1933).

[10] Id., 79 F. 2d 321, 323 (2d Cir. 1935), *cert. denied* sub nom. McCarthy v. United States, 296 U. S. 650; see also Harris v. United States, 48 F. 2d 771 (9th Cir. 1931); Goddard v. United States, 86 F. 2d 884 (10th Cir. 1936).

[11] N. Y. Gen. Bus. Law §§339 to 339-b. For references to similar statutes in a number of other states that have stock exchanges, see Moore and Wiseman, Market Manipulation and the Exchange Act, 2 U. Chi. L. Rev. 46, 66 n. 85 (1934).

[12] Sampson v. Shaw, 101 Mass. 145 (1869). A corner is a purchase of more than the available supply of a security (or commodity) with the intention of forcing settlement from short sellers at the purchaser's figure.

[13] Livermore v. Bushnell, 5 Hun 285 (N. Y. App. Div., 1st Dept. 1875).

[14] Ridgely v. Keene, 134 App. Div. 647, 119 N. Y. Supp. 451 (2d Dept. 1909).

[15] For a collection of such cases, see Moore and Wiseman, Market Manipulation and the Exchange Act, 2 U. Chi. L. Rev. 46, 69-70 (1934).

[16] Harper v. Crenshaw, 82 F. 2d 845 (D. C. Cir. 1936), *cert. denied,* 298 U. S. 685; Bigelow v. Oglesby, 302 Ill. App. 27, 36, 23 N. E. 2d 378, 382 (1939).

lation.[17] However, the right of an open market purchaser to recover against market manipulators seems to be quite a different matter.[18]

3. Manipulation of the Exchange Markets under the SEC Statutes

As in the general field of fraud, the supervention of the SEC statutes in no sense derogates from the body of common and statutory law that has been developed independently of those Acts. The function of the SEC statutes has been to give a greater degree of definiteness to the concept of manipulation and to supply an enforcement and preventive mechanism. The problem of manipulation was attacked by Congress in a number of ways — by specific prohibitions, by giving the Commission rulemaking authority in certain areas, and by a general prohibition against any trading for a manipulative purpose. As we shall see, the statutory scheme is a blend of fraud theories and the open market concept developed in the English and American cases.

First of all, there are the basic fraud provisions — §17(a) of the 1933 Act and §§10(b) and 15(c)(1) and (2) of the 1934 Act — which, like the mail fraud statute, have been used in the attack on certain types of manipulative practices. In fact, §§10(b), 15(c)(1), and 15(c)(2) use the *word* "manipulative," which, the Supreme Court has said *obiter*, is "virtually a term of art" reflecting Congress' intention "to prohibit the full range of ingenious devices that might be used to manipulate securities prices."[19] Moreover, some of the rules under these sections have a distinctly antimanipulative flavor — for example, Rule 15c1-8, which prohibits broker-dealers in certain circumstances from offering securities at a price represented as being related to the market price unless an independent market exists.[20]

---

[17] Willcox v. Harriman Securities Corp., 10 F. Supp. 532 (S. D. N. Y. 1933); Singleton v. Harriman, 152 Misc. 323, 272 N. Y. Supp. 905 (Sup. Ct. 1933), *aff'd per curiam,* 241 App. Div. 857, 271 N. Y. Supp. 996 (1st Dept. 1934); Scherer v. Zacks, [1952] 4 D. L. R. 503, [1952] O. W. N. 341 (Ont. High Ct.). On the other hand, the courts have held buyers to their contracts when they *knew* that their sellers were rigging the market or when they were *in pari delicto.* In re B. Solomon & Co., 268 Fed. 108 (2d Cir. 1920); Bacciocco v. Transamerica Corp., 2 Cal. App. 2d 595, 38 P. 2d 417 (1934).

[18] See Moore and Wiseman, Market Manipulation and the Exchange Act, 2 U. Chi. L. Rev. 46, 70-72 (1934).

[19] Santa Fe Industries, Inc. v. Green, 430 U. S. 462, 477 (1977), set out *supra* p. 928, at p. 935.

[20] See also Rules 10b-2, 10b-6, *infra* p. 1001.

Next, Congress in §9 of the Exchange Act outlawed a series of specific manipulative practices. Section 9(a)(1) prohibits wash sales and matched orders[21] when the purpose is to create "a false or misleading appearance of active trading in any security registered on a national securities exchange, or a false or misleading appearance with respect to the market for any such security."[22] And §9(a)(3)-(5) contains a series of prohibitions against manipulation of the market (again in registered securities) by false statements, rumors, or paid touts.[23]

In addition, §§9(b) and 9(c) give the Commission rulemaking authority with respect to the acquisition, endorsement, and guarantee of any put, call, or other option or privilege, as well as the effecting of transactions in connection with which any such option or privilege is outstanding. We have already noted the manipulation-prone history of these instruments in considering whether they are "securities."[24] A 1959-61 staff report[25] discussed, *inter alia,* the Put and Call Brokers and Dealers Association, organized in 1934 to represent the interests of put and call broker-dealers during the legislative hearings. That report found: "The attitude of the Association has always been that it will police its members and it has been most willing to adopt recommendations made from

[21] See p. 984 supra.

[22] The specific purpose requirement has been given a stringent reading. Harold T. White, 3 SEC 466, 510 (1938); Southern Brokerage Co. v. Cannarsa, 405 S. W. 2d 457, 461-62 (Tex. Civ. App. 1966), *cert. denied,* 386 U. S. 1004. Thus, there is nothing illegal about the sale and immediate repurchase of a security in order to establish a capital gain and obtain the benefit of a higher cost base for tax purposes. Again, the mere "crossing" of orders is not itself illegal. "Where a broker has both an order to buy and an order to sell at the same price, the transaction can be consummated by the crossing of these orders in accordance with the protective provisions of the exchange rules." Michael J. Meehan, 2 SEC 588, 606 (1937).

[23] Although all of §9 is limited to securities registered on a national securities exchange, it is not altogether correct to speak of §9 as coextensive with manipulation of the exchange markets. On the one hand, it applies to over-the-counter manipulation of registered securities — that is, those that are either listed or admitted to unlisted trading privileges. Charles C. Wright, 3 SEC 190, 213 (1938), *rev'd on other grounds* sub nom. Wright v. SEC, 112 F. 2d 89 (2d Cir. 1940), *order reinstated on remand,* 12 SEC 100 (1942), *aff'd* sub nom. Wright v. SEC, 134 F. 2d 733 (2d Cir. 1943). On the other hand, §9 does not apply to exempted securities even when they are traded on an exchange. §9(f); on the definition of "exempted securities," §3(a)(12), see p. 476 supra. There the attack on manipulation is made on the same basis as it is with respect to securities that are traded solely in the over-the-counter market.

[24] See p. 251 supra.

[25] SEC, Div. of Trading & Exchanges, Report on Put and Call Options (1961).

time to time by the Commission's staff."[26] Whether on that account or because the other antimanipulative weapons have worked well enough so that there would be no point in needlessly hampering the legitimate use of options, there are no rules of an antimanipulative nature in effect under §9.[27] This, of course, does not preclude a violation of §9(a) when transactions in connection with an option are involved.[28] Moreover, there are various exchange rules governing options.[29]

It is too early to say whether the revolution in this field with the creation of the Chicago Board Options Exchange in 1974 will give rise to new problems of manipulation. One of the concerns expressed by the Commission in initiating the study that led to the 1978 report[30] related to "the ability of self-regulatory organizations to detect price manipulations of options and their underlying securities."[31]

Finally, these specific provisions in §9 are complemented by §9(e), a provision on civil liability that will be considered in the next chapter, and a general provision in §9(a)(2), which has led the attack on manipulation of the exchange markets:

> It shall be unlawful for any person, directly or indirectly, by the use of the mails or any means or instrumentality of interstate commerce, or of any facility of any national securities exchange, or for any member of a national securities exchange * * * [i] to effect, alone or with one or more other persons, a series of transactions in any security registered on a national securities exchange [ii] creating actual or apparent active trading in such security or raising or depressing the price of such security, [iii] for the purpose of inducing the purchase or sale of such security by others.

[26] Id. at 100.

[27] The Commission did adopt a Rule 9b-1 in 1973 to require the filing by exchanges of plans regulating transactions in options. Sec. Ex. Act Rel. 10,552, 3 SEC Dock. 224 (1973). But after the 1975 statutory amendments the Commission repealed the rule because its procedures were largely duplicated by the new §19(b) and Rule 19b-4, with respect to the filing of self-regulatory organizations' rule changes generally. Sec. Ex. Act Rel. 11,604, 7 SEC Dock. 652, 655 (1975). On the altogether different Rule 9b-1 adopted in 1982 — basically a disclosure rule of the 1933 Act type — see pp. 252-53 supra.

[28] Harold T. White, 3 SEC 466, 535-37 (1938).

[29] See, e. g., N. Y. Stock Ex. Rules 77, 96, 102, 105, 424, CCH N. Y. Stock Ex. Guide ¶¶2077, 2096, 2102, 2105, 2424.

[30] Report of the Special Study of the Options Markets to the Securities and Exchange Commission, House Com. Print 96-IFC3, 96th Cong., 1st Sess. (1978).

[31] Sec. Ex. Act Rel. 14,056, 13 SEC Dock. 366, 372 (1977). See J. Newman & Co., Sec. Ex. Act Rel. 14,384, 13 SEC Dock. 1401 (1978) (option manipulation case); cf. Shultz v. SEC, 614 F. 2d 561 (7th Cir. 1980) (circular trading by CBOE marketmaker in violation of exchange rules).

The object of §9(a)(2) — which the Commission has termed "the very heart of the act"[32] — is to outlaw not only pool operations, but "every other device used to persuade the public that activity in a security is the reflection of a genuine demand instead of a mirage."[33] This accounts for the general language of the section. And the bracketed numbers here added indicate the three elements that must be proved.

(i) One who initiates a transaction "effects" it even though he acts as agent for another;[34] and the phrase, "alone or with one or more other persons," embraces considerably more than the idea of a common plan or conspiracy. The word "series" is satisfied by as few as three purchases;[35] perhaps even two would suffice. And the Commission has held that the term "transactions" has a broader meaning than "purchases or sales" — that in an auction market the mere placing of bids, even though they are not met by sellers, "may be as effective an influence on price as a completed sale," since the result would normally be to force other bidders to raise their bids.[36]

(ii) So far as the type of prohibited activity is concerned, there do not seem to be any reported cases without a price change, but it is clear that the creation of trading and changing the price are alternative requirements.[37] It seems apparent, moreover, that, when §9(a)(2) talks of "raising or depressing the prices * * * for the purpose of inducing the purchase or sale of such security by others," it means raising the price for the purpose of inducing purchases or depressing the price for the purpose of inducing sales;[38] and this is made explicit in the Code.[39] Even a small price change suffices.[40] And the price of a security may be raised without

---

[32] SEC, Report on Proposals for Amendments to the Securities Act of 1933 and the Securities Exchange Act of 1934, H. R. Com. Print, Com. on Int. & For. Commerce, 77th Cong., 1st Sess. (1941) 50.

[33] Stock Exchange Practices, Report of Com. on Banking & Currency, S. Rep. No. 1455, 73d Cong., 2d Sess. (1934) 54. Both these quotations were repeated in Crane Co. v. Westinghouse Air Brake Co., 419 F. 2d 787, 794 (2d Cir. 1969), *cert. denied*, 400 U. S. 822.

[34] S. Rep. No. 792, 73d Cong., 2d Sess. (1934) 17; Op. Gen. Counsel, Sec. Ex. Act Rel. 605 (1936); Michael J. Meehan, 2 SEC 588, 605, 616 (1937) (transactions for discretionary account).

[35] Kidder, Peabody & Co., 18 SEC 559, 568 (1945).

[36] Id. at 568-70; Gob Shops of America, Inc., 39 SEC 92, 101 (1959). The Code is express that bids and offers are "transactions" for purposes of the manipulation provisions. §1611.

[37] United States v. Stein, 456 F. 2d 844, 850 (2d Cir. 1972).

[38] For an instance of the latter practice (a "bear raid"), see Financial Investments Corp., Sec. Ex. Act Rel. 10,834, 4 SEC Dock. 354 (1974).

[39] §1609(c); but cf. §1710(e) and comment.

[40] Kidder, Peabody & Co., 18 SEC 559, 571 (1945) (½ point on a $50 stock);

raising the bid. *Following* the market too closely on a rise with either purchases or bids may be just as instrumental in creating a price rise. The obvious effect of promptly putting a new floor under the market each time it goes up as the result of an independent purchase or bid is to exhaust the supply of securities that may be offered at lower levels and thus to force others to raise their bids.[41]

(iii) Most of the litigation under §9(a)(2), not surprisingly, has involved the troublesome requirement of showing a purpose to *induce others* to buy or sell.[42]

The dictum in *Rex* v. *de Berenger* that "raising or lowering the price of the public funds is not per se a crime"[43] finds expression in the legislative reports underlying the Exchange Act. "If a person is merely trying to acquire a large block of stock for investment, or desires to dispose of a big holding," the House report says, "his knowledge that in doing so he will affect the market price does not make his action unlawful."[44]

For the rest, the precise theoretical definition of "purpose" — whether there is any distinction between "purpose" and "intent" in the criminal sense — may be left to the metaphysicians.[45] It is more fruitful to consider what evidence has sufficed to prove purpose in specific cases under §9(a)(2). "Since it is impossible to probe into the depths of a man's mind," the Commission has said, "it is necessary in the usual case (that is, absent an admission) that the finding of manipulative purpose be based on inferences drawn from circumstantial evidence."[46] In short, a *motive* to manipulate,

---

United States v. Stein, 456 F. 2d 844, 846 (2d Cir. 1972), *cert. denied,* 408 U. S. 922.

[41] Sec. Ex. Act Rel. 17,222, 21 SEC Dock. 212, 230 n. 65 (1980).

[42] The Code, as amended after discussions with the Commission, substitutes "for the purpose of raising or depressing the price." §1609(c).

[43] 3 Maule & S. 67, 74, 105 Eng. Reprint 536, 539 (K. B. 1814).

[44] H. R. Rep. No. 1383, 73d Cong., 2d Sess. (1934) 20; Frigitemp Corp. v. Financial Dynamics Fund, 524 F. 2d 275, 277 n. 1 (2d Cir. 1975); Alabama Farm Bureau Mutual Casualty Co., Inc. v. American Fidelity Life Ins. Co., 606 F. 2d 602, 615 n. 12 (5th Cir. 1979).

[45] See Cook, Act, Intention, and Motive in the Criminal Law, 26 Yale L. J. 645 (1917). At the hearings, the terms were said to be synonymous. See 15 Stock Exchange Practices, Hearings before Senate Com. on Banking & Currency, 73d Cong., 2d Sess. (1934) 6510.

[46] Federal Corp., 25 SEC 227, 230 (1947). In the oft quoted language of United States v. Allis, 73 Fed. 165, 171 (C. C. E. D. Kan. 1893): "The intent with which an act is done is often more clearly and conclusively shown by the act itself than by any words or explanations of the actor. Thus, if you found a stranger leading your horse, saddled and bridled, from your barn, in the night, without your permission, and he should explain to you that he did not intend to steal him, but was simply leading him out for exercise, you would undoubtedly infer his intent from his act rather than from his words."

when joined with the requisite series of transactions, *prima facie* establishes the manipulative *purpose* and shifts to the accused the burden of going forward with the evidence.[47]

The motive might be an option to purchase a substantial amount of the security at a price above the current market,[48] or a desire to obtain more than the current market price for a block of stock that the manipulator plans to distribute either as owner or as best-efforts underwriter[49] or that is left in an underwriter's hands after a "sticky" offering,[50] or to get rid of a "white elephant,"[51] or to make more attractive a security pledged as collateral for a bank loan that the borrower is being pressed to repay or reduce,[52] or to further[53] or defeat[54] a tender offer.

The *evidence* of purpose might be an option to buy successive blocks at stepped-up rates,[55] or the pattern of trading.[56] Again, the series of purchases may be coupled with devices of one sort or another to reduce or "dry up" the overhanging supply of the security (such as agreements with large holders to withhold their securities from the market),[57] or the sending out of misleadingly "bullish" literature,[58] or paying touts to recommend the security,[59] or guaranteeing purchasers against loss,[60] or arranging for the

[47] Alabama Farm Bureau Mutual Casualty Co., Inc. v. American Fidelity Life Ins. Co., 606 F. 2d 602, 616 (5th Cir. 1979).

[48] Charles C. Wright, 3 SEC 190, 206 (1938), *rev'd on other grounds sub nom.* Wright v. SEC, 112 F. 2d 89 (2d Cir. 1940), *order reinstated on remand,* 12 SEC 100 (1942), *aff'd sub nom.* Wright v. SEC, 134 F. 2d 733 (2d Cir. 1943).

[49] Federal Corp., 25 SEC 227 (1947).

[50] Halsey, Stuart & Co., Inc., 30 SEC 106, 109, 112-14, 124 (1949).

[51] R. J. Koeppe & Co. v. SEC, 95 F. 2d 550 (7th Cir. 1938).

[52] Op. Gen. Counsel, Sec. Ex. Act Rel. 3056 (1941).

[53] Davis v. Pennzoil Co., 438 Pa. 194, 207-08, 264 A. 2d 597, 603 (1970) (by increasing the price of the offeror's stock).

[54] Crane Co. v. Westinghouse Air Brake Co., 419 F. 2d 787, 792-99 (2d Cir. 1969), *cert. denied,* 400 U. S. 822 (by increasing the price of the target's stock).

[55] United States v. Minuse, 114 F. 2d 36 (2d Cir. 1940).

[56] R. J. Koeppe & Co. v. SEC, 95 F. 2d 550, 552 (7th Cir. 1938) (frequently effecting the opening and closing transactions of the day); United States v. Minuse, 114 F. 2d 36 (2d Cir. 1940) (wash sales and matched orders); F. S. Johns & Co., Inc., 43 SEC 124, 136 n. 14 (1966), *aff'd sub nom.* Dlugash v. SEC, 373 F. 2d 107, 109 (2d Cir. 1967), and *per curiam* sub nom. Winkler v. SEC, 377 F. 2d 517 (2d Cir. 1967) ("reaching" for the security by bidding more than necessary); Crane Co. v. Westinghouse Air Brake Co., 419 F. 2d 787, 793-95 (2d Cir. 1969), *cert. denied,* 400 U. S. 822 ("painting the tape" by buying virtually all the shares traded on a given day, or buying on the exchange so as to establish a "print" on the tape and selling for the most part over the counter so as to minimize publicity and also reduce the "floating supply").

[57] Aurelius F. DeFelice, 29 SEC 595 (1949).

[58] United States v. Minuse, 114 F. 2d 36 (2d Cir. 1940).

[59] Ibid.

[60] Ibid.

issuer to declare a dividend at a critical juncture in the manipulation.[61]

Immediate resale of the shares purchased by the manipulator is not an indispensable element of the offense,[62] but it is "of great *evidentiary weight* in determining the *purpose* with which the buying was undertaken."[63] Indeed, the Commission has held that, in the absence of a satisfactory explanation, an inference of manipulative purpose arises from the mere fact that "one who has purchased stock in a series of transactions and raised its price disposes of the stock before the true effect of his purchases has been dissipated by other market factors."[64] For this reason, the Commission's General Counsel has advised that a person who effects a series of transactions raising the price of a security for the *bona fide* purpose of acquiring a supply that he will be able to dispose of at a profit if a further increase materializes *from other causes* should take care, before making any sales either on or off the exchange, "to permit a sufficient period of time to elapse from [the] time of his last purchase to make sure that the effect of his purchases on the market will have been dissipated, and the market will have found a level (whether above, below, or at, his last purchase price) which is its own independent level, created by outside factors of supply and demand and unaffected by his own activities."[65] It is impossible to tell in advance how much time will be required for the effect of a buyer's purchases to be dissipated. The answer will depend, among other things, on the character of the market, the length of time during which the buying activities continued, their pattern, the extent of the market rise, and the size of the floating supply. The period may be weeks or months. If the purchases dried up virtually the entire supply, it is difficult to say when a resale may be effected without creating an inference that the purchases had a manipulative purpose.

4. MANIPULATION OF THE OVER-THE-COUNTER MARKET UNDER THE SEC STATUTES

The field of manipulation is no exception to the pre-1964 lopsidedness of the Exchange Act so far as the specificity of regulation

[61] Collins v. United States, 157 F. 2d 409 (9th Cir. 1946).
[62] Federal Corp., 25 SEC 227, 231 (1947).
[63] Op. Gen. Counsel, Sec. Ex. Act Rel. 3056 (1941).
[64] Thornton & Co., 28 SEC 208, 223 (1948), *aff'd per curiam* sub nom. Thornton v. SEC, 171 F. 2d 702 (2d Cir. 1948).
[65] Op. Gen. Counsel, Sec. Ex. Act Rel. 3056 (1941).

of the exchange and over-the-counter markets is concerned. In
contrast to the relatively elaborate structure of §9 that Congress
erected to deal with manipulation of the market for securities
registered on exchanges, the only statutory bases for dealing with
the manipulation of unregistered securities are the general antifraud provisions of the 1934 Act — which specifically refer, as we
have noticed, to "manipulative" as well as "deceptive" practices —
together with §17 of the 1933 Act. Nevertheless, consistently with
the legislative intention that the Commission should use its administrative powers to place the regulation of the two markets on a
par so far as practicable, it has managed to put over-the-counter
manipulation beyond substantially the same pale as manipulation
of the exchange markets.

In the *Barrett* case, the first over-the-counter manipulation
proceeding, the Commission concluded, after a reference to §9
(a)(2):

> We think that there is no reasonable distinction in this respect
> between manipulation of over-the-counter prices and manipula-
> tion of prices on a national securities exchange, and that both are
> condemned as fraudulent by the Securities Exchange Act and, in
> fact, were fraudulent at common law. * * * We believe that the
> Securities Exchange Act contemplates that Section 15(c)(1) affords
> to the over-the-counter market at least as great a degree of pro-
> tection against manipulation or attempted control as is afforded
> to the exchange market by Section 9(a).[66]

Even when §9 applies, it has been repeatedly held both by the
Commission and by the courts that there is a violation of the antifraud provisions when securities are in fact sold at manipulated
prices without *disclosure* of the manipulation.[67] So, too. in the

----

[66] Barrett & Co., 9 SEC 319, 328 (1941); see also SEC v. Management Dynamics, Inc., 515 F. 2d 801, 810 (2d Cir. 1975).

Rule 10b-5 and §15(c)(1) are *broader* than §9 in the sense that they contain
no purpose requirement. And, of course, the first and third clauses of both
the rule and §17(a) must not be overlooked in this context. United States v.
Charnay, 537 F. 2d 341 (9th Cir. 1976), *cert. denied*, 429 U. S. 1000.

[67] Coplin v. United States, 88 F. 2d 652, 661-64 (9th Cir. 1973), *cert. denied*,
301 U. S. 703; Thornton & Co., 28 SEC 208, 224 (1948), *aff'd per curiam* sub
nom. Thornton v. SEC, 171 F. 2d 702 (2d Cir. 1948); Carroll v. United States,
326 F. 2d 72, 76-77 (9th Cir. 1963); United States v. Hayutin, 398 F. 2d 944,
949 (2d Cir. 1968), *cert. denied*, 393 U. S. 961; Davis v. Pennzoil Co., 438 Pa.
194, 208, 264 A. 2d 597, 604 (1970). Most of these cases involved offerings
represented to be "at the market." See Rule 15c1-8, supra p. 805. But the
Commission has held that "The market price level prior to and during the
commencement of a secondary [or presumably primary] distribution is an
extremely important fact to prospective purchasers, whether the offering be
at a fixed price or at the market." Kidder, Peabody & Co., 18 SEC 559, 571
(1945).

Barrett case the Commission did not rely solely on the pseudo-
9(a)(2) application of §15(c)(1). It fortified its holding with a
reference to its long line of decisions to the effect that,

> when a security is sold "at the market," the failure to disclose to
> purchasers the fact that the market price has been artificially in-
> flated by the sellers' manipulation is an omission to state a ma-
> terial fact and constitutes a fraud on the purchasers.[68]

Whereas this application of the antifraud provisions is essentially ancillary to §9(a)(2) in the exchange cases, it is perhaps more
proper in the over-the-counter cases, where there is no specific
9(a)(2) language, to take the further step of proving nondisclosure
and thus bring the manipulation more nearly within the conventional fraud theories. Since nondisclosure of a manipulation is
usually, if not invariably, essential to its success,[69] this is of little
practical consequence. The fact is that in the more recent cases
the Commission has been deemphasizing the 9(a)(2) approach,
although it has never been abandoned.[70]

Although a few large-scale manipulations were detected in the
early years of the Commission's history, the Commission was able
by 1950 to express the belief that manipulation was no longer "an
appreciable factor in our markets."[71] Eleven years later the
Chairman referred to "evidences of a substantial amount of
manipulation."[72] And in April 1967 the American Stock Exchange
announced that, in cooperation with the SEC and the United
States Attorney's office, it was conducting an investigation of trading into certain listed stocks "which may have been influenced by
alleged manipulative activities." There were rumors of under-
world involvement, with "talk of entrapment employing prosti-
tutes and incriminating photographs."[73] It does seem fair to say,
however, that in recent years attempts to manipulate have become
more subtle and complex. And, in large measure, whatever success
the Commission has had in this field has been due to the continual

---

[68] Barrett & Co., 9 SEC 319, 329 (1941).
[69] See Santa Fe Industries, Inc. v. Green, 430 U. S. 462, 477 (1977) (dictum).
[70] E. g., Gob Shops of America, Inc., 39 SEC 92, 98, 101 (1959). The manipulation section of the Code applies universally. §1609; 2 Code 674, Comment
(2).
[71] 16 SEC Ann. Rep. 37 (1950).
[72] Securities Markets Investigation, Hearings before Subcom. of House
Com. on Int. & For. Commerce on H. J. Res. 438, 87th Cong., 1st Sess. (1961)
33.
[73] Wall St. J., Apr. 24, 1967, p. 32, col. 1.

improvement in its procedures (as well as the exchanges') for the systematic surveillance of the markets.

5. STABILIZATION

There is one further provision in §9, which acts as a limitation on §9(a)(2) in that it excludes certain types of manipulation ("any series of transactions for the purchase and/or sale of any security registered on a national securities exchange for the purpose of pegging, fixing, or stabilizing the price of such security") from the general prohibition and subjects them to the Commission's rule-making authority.

Stabilization, which is a generic term, has been described by the Commission as "that process whereby the market price of a security is pegged or fixed for the limited purpose of preventing or retarding a decline in contemplation of or during a public offering of securities."[74] The sudden glut tends to destabilize the market. So usually the syndicate managers reserve the right to stabilize on behalf of syndicate members and during the life of the syndicate. Not infrequently the agreement among underwriters limits the maximum position resulting from stabilizing purchases to a fixed percentage of the amount of securities being offered. When the security is traded on an exchange, a bid for a stated amount of the security is normally placed with the specialist, and it is followed by additional bids for stated amounts if necessary. The result is that the market price of the security is supported or stabilized by absorbing, to the extent of the amounts specified in the bids, all sell orders that meet the bids and are not taken up by others. Moreover, the general publicity given to stabilizing purchases on the ticker tape and in the other reporting media — where they are never distinguished from nonstabilizing purchases — has a secondary stabilizing effect in that nobody is likely to sell in the over-the-counter market or on another exchange at a price materially less than the last reported price on the exchange on which the stabilization is being conducted. When the security to be stabilized is not traded on an exchange, one or more bids are normally placed with various dealers known to be active in the security.[75]

---

[74] Sec. Ex. Act Rel. 4163 (1948).

[75] Since the word "manipulative" as used in §§10(b) and 15(c)(1) has never had any precise meaning, it seems obvious that those sections incorporate the policy, reflected in §9(a)(6), of leaving it largely to the Commission to distin-

In either case, if the selling pressure gets too heavy to permit the constant "pegging" of the market, the syndicate bid is usually dropped to successively lower levels or it may have to be withdrawn altogether. For the same reason, stabilization cannot be used as a practical matter to stem a market or economic trend of any real significance. On the other hand, in the case of a particularly successful issue, stabilization is unnecessary because the market usually takes care of itself. Thus, as the Commission has observed, "stabilizing is regarded as necessary only in the case of issues which are neither notable successes nor notable failures."[76]

The statute itself recognizes, by placing the provision on stabilization in a section labeled "Prohibition against Manipulation of Security Prices," that stabilization is a form of manipulation. Indeed, it would hardly lie in the mouth of a person who is stabilizing the price of a security as a means of facilitating its distribution to deny that his transactions are "for the purpose of inducing the purchase * * * of such security by others." But Congress found that the evidence as to the value of stabilizing operations was "far from conclusive."[77] And so it authorized the Commission, as the Senate committee put it, "to prescribe such rules as may be necessary or appropriate to protect investors and the public from the vicious and unsocial aspects of these practices."[78] The Commission thus inherited the problem that the English courts had tackled forty years earlier.[79]

In the early years the Commission proceeded in a gingerly fashion. For people do not relish even benign tumors. In a 1940 "Statement of the SEC on the Regulation of Pegging, Fixing and Stabilizing of Security Prices," Commissioner Healey, who favored outright prohibition of stabilization as an interference with free

---

guish between stabilization and unlawful manipulation in the over-the-counter market.

[76] Sec. Ex. Act Rel. 2446 (1940).

[77] H. R. Rep. No. 1383, 73d Cong., 2d Sess. (1934) 10; see also id. at 21.

[78] Stock Exchange Practices, Report of Com. on Banking & Currency, S. Rep. No. 1455, 73d Cong., 2d Sess. (1934) 55.

[79] Six years after Scott v. Brown, supra p. 987, one of the judges who had sat in that case distinguished it and enforced a contract by which jobbers on the Exchange had made a market at a "fair price" while the defendant had distributed a block of stock. Sanderson & Levi v. British Westralian Mine & Share Corp., 43 Sol. J. 45 (Q. B. 1898), aff'd, London Times, July 19, 1899, p. 4, col. 1 (C. A.), reprinted in United States v. Brown, 5 F. Supp. 81, 90 n. 1 (S. D. N. Y. 1933), aff'd, 79 F. 2d 321 (2d Cir. 1935), cert. denied sub nom. McCarthy v. United States, 296 U. S. 650; see also Masterson v. Pergament, 203 F. 2d 315, 335 (6th Cir. 1953), cert. denied, 346 U. S. 832. But cf. the *Harper* and *Bigelow* cases, supra n. 16.

markets, rejected the argument of necessity: "This is about equivalent to saying the distributor cannot induce the public to buy unless he is allowed to fool the public. The reasoning employed would almost justify taking the public's money by force if the corporation needing it had a maturity to meet."[80] And the majority seemed not too comfortable in recognizing that stabilization "is now an integral part of the American system of fixed price security distribution" that is essential for the purpose of "preserving the ready flow of capital into industry" — that "in the field of stabilizing it is faced with an existing condition, not a theory."[81]

In this state of affairs the Commission gradually developed an "SEC common law" of stabilization (Chairman Demmler called it a "folklore") through informal and unpublished rulings of its staff, to the point where the jumble was codified into Rule 10b-7 in 1955.[82] One's expectation of complexity in an area of this sort is not disappointed on an examination of the rule. But its core is a command that "no person shall (i) begin to stabilize a security at a price higher than the highest current independent bid price for such security or (ii) raise the price at which he is stabilizing" or (iii) stabilize at a price above the current distribution price.[83] There is also a series of exemptions "to provide for unusual siutations which may fall within the literal language of a rule but can be demonstrated not to be comprehended within its purpose,"[84] together with reporting and disclosure requirements.[85]

---

[80] Sec. Ex. Act Rel. 2446 (1940).
[81] Demmler, How Shall We Amend the SEC Acts?, 178 Com. & Fin. Chron. 2381, 2438 (1953).
[82] Sec. Ex. Act Rel. 5194 (1955). The Commission concurrently adopted Rule 10b-6, which will be considered in the next section (infra p. 1002), and Rule 10b-8, with specific reference to rights offerings. These rules were adopted under §10(b) because of the limitations of §9(a)(6) to registered securities.
Those who looked the gift horse in the mouth thought at first that they saw a risk that the promulgation of anything more than perhaps a statement of policy on the subject would destroy in large measure the elasticity of the informal system of control with which they had learned to live. See Foshay, Market Activities of Participants in Securities Distributions, 45 Va. L. Rev. 907, 919 (1959).
[83] Rule 10b-7(j)(1)(i) and (6). On Rule 10b-7 generally, see Klein, Stabilizing Securities Prices, 5 Sec. Reg. L. J. 13 (1977); Williams, Current Developments under Exchange Act Rule 10b-7, in Practising Law Institute, Ninth Annual Institute on Securities Regulation (1979) c. 14.
[84] Sec. Ex. Act Rel. 5194 (1955). In practice, the stabilizing bid is entered at a price below the current market in order to avoid potential short sellers' bombarding the bid. N. Y. Stock Ex. letter, Oct. 11, 1974, attached to Sec. Ex. Act Rel. 11,051, 5 SEC Dock. 277, 283 (1974).
[85] Rule 10b-7(k) and (l); see also Rule 17a-2; Reg. S-K, Item 502(d).

6. PROHIBITION OF TRADING DURING DISTRIBUTION
[RULE 10b-6]

By 1943 the administrative view had become sufficiently established to warrant publication of a release to the effect that the limitations on stabilization could not be avoided by an underwriter's effecting purchases through its "trading" department, even though that department operated independently of the firm's retail distributing organization.[86] And the general doctrine limiting the trading activity of underwriters was codified into Rule 10b-6 as a complement to the stabilization rule in 1955.

The rule prohibits any person who is participating in a "distribution," whether acting alone or with others, from bidding for, or buying for any account in which he has a beneficial interest (or attempting to induce any other person to buy), any security that is the subject of the distribution, or any security of the same class and series, or any right to purchase any such security.[87] When the three rules are viewed together, Rule 10b-6 is the central rule that prohibits *all* bidding or purchasing subject to a series of exemptions.[88] "Where the rule applies, its prohibition is absolute."[89]

---

[86] Op. Dir. Trading & Ex. Div., Sec. Ex. Act Rel. 3505 (1943); see also Op. Gen. Counsel, Sec. Ex. Act Rel. 3056 (1941); Halsey, Stuart & Co., Inc., 30 SEC 106, 123-25 (1949); S. T. Jackson & Co., Inc., Sec. Ex. Act Rel. 4459 (1950) 30, n. 51.

[87] See also the much older Rule 10b-2, which in general prohibits a person who is interested in a distribution from paying compensation to a second person for soliciting a third person to buy the security on an exchange. The concept underlying these overlapping rules — "that buying (or inducing purchases) during a distribution is manipulation *per se* without regard to any sort of purpose requirement as in X9(a)(2)" (2 Code 677) — was considered sufficiently basic to warrant statutory codification into a single §1609(d). See generally 2 Code 677-81; Lewis, Overview of Rules 10b-2 and 10b-6, in Practising Law Institute, The 10b Series of Rules (Corp. Prac. Tr. Ser. 21, 1975) c. 9 at 279-80.

[88] Two of the exemptions are for transactions permitted by Rules 10b-7 and 10b-8. At the same time, those two rules are not *merely* exemptions from Rule 10b-6. In form, they contain their own prohibitions with their own exemptions. Consequently, a transaction that is not permitted by Rule 10b-7 or 10b-8 violates one or the other of those rules and, as a result of the destruction of the exemptions from Rule 10b-6, the latter rule as well. Goldstein v. Regal Crest, Inc., 62 F. R. D. 571, 575 (E. D. Pa. 1974).

Another significant exemption applies when the distribution is to the employees or shareholders of an issuer or subsidiary pursuant to a "bonus, profit-sharing, pension, retirement, thrift, savings, incentive, stock purchase, stock ownership, stock appreciation, stock option, dividend reinvestment or similar plan." Rule 10b-6(c)(4).

[89] Jaffee & Co. v. SEC, 446 F. 2d 387, 391 (2d Cir. 1971). *Query* whether this manipulation *per se* approach, with its corollary that the defendant need

A key question, obviously, goes to the meaning of "distribution" in this context:

> The term "distribution" as used in Rule 10b-6 is to be interpreted in the light of the rule's purposes as covering offerings of such a nature or magnitude as to require restrictions upon open market purchases by participants in order to prevent manipulative practices. For these purposes a distribution is to be distinguished from ordinary trading transactions and other normal conduct of a securities business upon the basis of the magnitude of the offering and particularly upon the basis of the selling efforts and selling methods utilized.[90]

On the one hand, the term is not limited to its meaning in §2(11) of the 1933 Act, the definition of "underwriter"; for one thing, the absence of control is irrelevant.[91] On the other hand, not every distribution that is registerable under the 1933 Act comes within Rule 10b-6. In 1975 the Commission overruled its earlier view to the contrary,[92] stating that it could result in unnecessary disruption of the trading markets, particularly when a specialist or other marketmaker had acquired registered shares in the performance of his normal functions.[93] It has also been said — a point reminiscent of some of the 1933 Act exemptions — that, at least under certain

not be shown to have "actually intended to defraud the marketplace through his purchases" (ibid.) — survives the scienter requirement (supra p. 870). With respect to Rule 10b-16 (supra c. 9A n. 13), on disclosure of credit terms in margin transactions, it has been argued *against* the scienter requirement that, since Congress created a private right of action without scienter under the Truth in Lending Act and exempted broker-dealers in contemplation of "substantially similar" requirements to be imposed by Commission rule, it must have anticipated an analogous remedy. Haynes v. Anderson & Strudwick, Inc., 508 F. Supp. 1303, 1321 (E. D. Va. 1981); Saunders v. Oppenheimer Government Securities, Inc., CCH Fed. Sec. L. Rep. ¶98,318 (D. Ore. 1981). *Contra:* Furer v. Paine, Webber, Jackson & Curtis, Inc., CCH Fed. Sec. L. Rep. ¶98,701 at 93,495 (C. D. Cal. 1982); cf. SEC v. Mick Stack Associates, Inc., 675 F. 2d 1148, 1150 n. 1 (10th Cir. 1982) (Rule 10b-13, supra p. 588).

[90] Bruns, Nordeman & Co., 40 SEC 652, 660 (1961); see also Schraufnagel v. Broadwall Securities Corp., CCH Fed. Sec. L. Rep. ¶91,827 at 95,849 (S. D. N. Y. 1966).

[91] SEC v. American Beryllium & Oil Corp., 303 F. Supp. 912, 916 (S. D. N. Y. 1969).

[92] Jaffee & Co., Sec. Ex. Act Rel. 8866 (1970), *aff'd in relevant part and vacated on other grounds* sub nom. Jaffee & Co. v. SEC, 446 F. 2d 387 (2d Cir. 1961).

[93] Collins Securities Corp., Sec. Ex. Act Rel. 11,766, 8 SEC Dock. 250, 256 (1975), *remanded on other grounds* sub nom. Collins Securities Corp. v. SEC, 562 F. 2d 820 (D. C. Cir. 1977). In Oppenheimer & Co., Inc., Sec. Ex. Act Rel. 16,817, 20 SEC Dock. 58, 59 n. 7 (1980), the Commission stated that *Collins* did not alter the definition in *Bruns*, supra, text at n. 90.

circumstances, a distribution cannot be considered complete "until the shares came to rest in the hands of public investors."[94]

For the rest, there are provisions on when the trading prohibition begins and when it ends; and the answers vary depending on whether the person that wants to trade is an issuer or other distributor, an underwriter or "prospective underwriter," a broker or dealer, or another participant in the distibution.

The rule is specific that

> The distribution of a security (1) which is immediately exchangeable for or convertible into another security, or (2) which entitles the holder thereof immediately to acquire another security, shall be deemed to include a distribution of such other security within the meaning of this rule.

One effect of Clause (2) is, at least arguably, to prevent an exchange tender offeror from buying the target's securities for which the offeror's securities are exchangeable. But the substantial codification of this interpretation by the adoption of Rule 10b-13 in 1969[96] makes its validity "of secondary importance."[97] And, as part of the deregulatory mood that in late 1982 produced a safe harbor rule numbered 10b-18,[98] the Commission concurrently exempted purchases during what it called a "technical" distribution:[99] that is to say,

> bids for or purchases of any security of an issuer, any security of the same class and series as such security, or any security immediately convertible into, or exchangeable or exerciseable for, any such security solely because the issuer or a subsidiary of such issuer *has outstanding* securities which are immediately convertible into, or exchangeable or exerciseable for, such security (italics supplied).[100]

---

[94] Mayo & Co., Inc., 41 SEC 944, 947 (1964); R. A. Holman & Co., Inc. v. SEC, 366 F. 2d 446, 449 (2d Cir. 1966), *amended on rehearing*, 377 F. 2d 665 (2d Cir. 1967), *cert. denied*, 389 U. S. 991.

[95] Rule 10b-6(b).

[96] Sec. Ex. Act Rel. 8595 (1969).

[97] Piper v. Chris-Craft Industries, Inc., 430 U. S. 1, 43 n. 30 (1977). The 10b-6 provisions may extend to one or two situations not covered by 10b-13. See Goolrick, Purchases on the Market of Target Company Stock, 26 Bus. Law. 457, 467-71 (1970); Wheat, Trading Activity in Exchange Offers: Some Possible Pitfalls, in Practising Law Institute, Second Annual Institute on Securities Regulation (1971) 291.

[98] See p. 1004 infra.

[99] Sec. Ex. Act Rel. 19,244, 26 SEC Dock. 868, 876 (1982).

[100] Rule 10b-6(f).

The rule, it bears repeating, is complex.[101] The Code attempts a degree of simplification by stating only the basic principles with respect to stabilization and trading during a distribution.[102] With specific reference to the meaning of "distribution," the Commission is authorized to define the term by rule "in light of such factors as size (absolute or relative) of the offering, number of sellers and buyers, selling method, characteristics of the market used, and compensation"; and the principle of Rule 10b-13 is put into statutory language along with the 1982 exemption.[103] But this inevitably leaves fairly substantial interstices to be filled in by a second-generation rule.[104]

7. THE SAFE HARBOR [RULE 10b-18]

SECURITIES EXCHANGE ACT RELEASE NO. 19,244: PURCHASES OF CERTAIN EQUITY SECURITIES BY THE ISSUER AND OTHERS; ADOPTION OF SAFE HARBOR
Securities and Exchange Commission, 1982
26 SEC Dock. 868

The Commission has considered on several occasions since 1967 the issue of whether to regulate an issuer's repurchases of its own securities. The predicates for this effort have been twofold: first, investors and particularly the issuer's shareholders should be able to rely on a market that is set by independent market forces and not influenced in any manipulative manner by the issuer or persons closely related to the issuer. Second, since the general language of the anti-manipulative provisions of the federal securities laws offers little guidance with respect to the scope of permissible issuer market behavior, certainty with respect to the potential lia-

---

[101] On the further complications created by Rule 415, the "shelf registration" rule (supra pp. 140-47), see Sec. Ex. Act Rel. 18,528, 24 SEC Dock. 1444 (1982) (proposed amendments); Sec. Ex. Act Rel. 18,666, 25 SEC Dock. 124 (1982) (staff interpretations of the proposed amendments); Ferrara and Sweeney, Shelf Registrations under SEC Temporary Rule 415, 5 Corp. L. Rev. 308, 315-21 (1982). The pending amendments, among other things, would supply a definition of "distribution" that "would, in broad terms, codify the current case law," and would in general apply equally to "shelf registrations," so that many shelf-registered offerings would be likely to constitute 10b-6 distributions. Sec. Ex. Act Rel. 18,528, 24 SEC Dock. at 1448, 1450.

[102] §§1609(c)-(d), 1610.

[103] §1609(d)(3); see also §1610(c).

[104] For a more detailed discussion of the entire manipulation-stabilization area — which has not erupted with the same rigor as most of the SEC volcanoes in the past fifteen years — see 3 and 6 Loss c. 10A-B.

bilities for issuers engaged in repurchase programs has seemed desirable.

The most recent phase of this proceeding is proposed Rule 13e-2 which was published for public comment on October 17, 1980.[2] This rule would have imposed disclosure requirements and substantive purchasing limitations on an issuer's repurchases of its common and preferred stock. These restrictions, which generally would have limited the time, price, and volume of purchases, also would have been imposed on certain persons whose purchases could be deemed to be attributable to the issuer. In addition, the issuer, its affiliates, and certain other persons would have been subject to a general antifraud provision in connection with their purchases of the issuer's common and preferred stock.

The Commission has recognized that issuer repurchase programs are seldom undertaken with improper intent, may frequently be of substantial economic benefit to investors, and, that, in any event, undue restriction of these programs is not in the interest of investors, issuers, or the marketplace. Issuers generally engage in repurchase programs for legitimate business reasons and any rule in this area must not be overly intrusive. Accordingly, the Commission has endeavored to achieve an appropriate balance between the goals described above and the need to avoid complex and costly restrictions that impinge on the operation of issuer repurchase programs.

In light of these considerations, and based on the extensive public files developed in this proceeding, the Commission has determined that it is not necessary to adopt a mandatory rule to regulate issuer repurchases. Accordingly, the Commission has today withdrawn proposed Rule 13e-2, and, as discussed in this release, is amending Rule 10b-6 to eliminate most issuer repurchase regulation under that rule. In lieu of direct regulation under Rule 10b-6 and proposed Rule 13e-2, the Commission has determined that a safe harbor is the appropriate regulatory approach to offer guidance concerning the applicability of the anti-manipulative provisions of Rule 10b-5 and Section 9(a)(2) to issuer repurchase programs. New Rule 10b-18 reflects this determination.

The Commission wishes to stress, however, that the safe harbor is not mandatory nor the exclusive means of effecting issuer purchases without manipulating the market. As a safe harbor, new Rule 10b-18 will provide clarity and certainty for issuers and broker-dealers who assist issuers in their repurchase programs.

[2][Sec. Ex. Act Rel. 17,222, 21 SEC Dock. 212 (1980).]

If an issuer effects its repurchases in compliance with the conditions of the rule, it will avoid what might otherwise be substantial and unpredictable risks of liability under the general anti-manipulative provisions of the federal securities laws.[5] * * *

The Commission emphasizes that no affirmative inference should be drawn that bids for or purchases of an issuer's stock by persons to which the safe harbor is not explicitly available, or with respect to securities other than the issuer's common stock, should be made in accordance with the safe harbor. The safe harbor is not intended to define the appropriate limits to be observed by those persons not covered by the safe harbor nor the appropriate limits to be observed by anyone when purchasing securities other than common stock. In addition, the safe harbor is not the exclusive means by which issuers and their affiliated purchasers may effect purchases of the issuer's stock in the marketplace. Given the greatly varying characteristics of the markets for the stock of different issuers, there may be circumstances under which an issuer could effect repurchases outside of the guidelines that would not raise manipulative concerns. This is especially the case in the context of the uniform volume guidelines, which cannot easily reflect those varying market characteristics. * * * In order to make it clear that Rule 10b-18 is not the exclusive means to effect issuer repurchases, paragraph (c) of the rule provides that no presumption shall arise that an issuer or affiliated purchaser has violated Section 9(a)(2) or Rule 10b-5 if the purchases do not meet the conditions of paragraph (b).

* * *

The rule applies only to "a purchase of common stock of an issuer by or for the issuer or any affiliated purchaser of the issuer" (a term defined in terms of control) subject to a number of exceptions. The conditions go to the use of a single broker or dealer and the timing, price, and volume of purchases.

---

[5] Paragraph (b) of the rule provides that any issuer and its affiliated purchasers could not be held liable under the antimanipulative provisions of Section 9(a)(2) of the Act or Rule 10b-5 under the Act solely by reason of the number of brokers or dealers used, and the time, price, and amount of bids for or purchases of common stock of the issuer, if such bids or purchases are effected in compliance with all of the conditions of paragraph (b) of the rule. Of course, Rule 10b-18 is not a safe harbor from violations of Rule 10b-5 which may occur in the course of an issuer repurchase program but which do not entail manipulation. * * *

CHAPTER 10

CIVIL LIABILITY

Persons injured in securities transactions are frequently able to choose among (and under modern alternative pleading to combine) a substantial number of private rights of action. They may be grouped into three categories — (A) actions at common law or in equity, (B) actions, express and implied, under the state blue sky laws, and (C) actions, express and implied, under the federal securities statutes. About two-thirds of the blue sky laws specifically save the nonstatutory rights and remedies;[1] and (the tender offer area aside)[2] there is no question of supersedure so far as the SEC statutes are concerned, because the 1933, 1934, and 1939 Acts specifically save all other rights and remedies and there is no reason to assume a federal-state conflict so far as the other statutes are concerned.[3]

A. COMMON LAW AND EQUITABLE LIABILITIES

The remedies at common law and in equity are breach of warranty, rescission (both by way of an affirmative action seeking restitution and by way of defense to an action on the contract) and the tort action of deceit. The last of these has already been considered to some extent in the discussion of the "substantive

---

C. 10   [1] See Unif. Sec. Act §410(h).

[2] See pp. 601-03 supra.

[3] "The ultimate effectiveness of the federal remedies, when the defendants are not prone to settle, may depend in large measure on the applicability of the class action device." 3 Loss 1819. This statement has been repeatedly quoted by the courts. E. g., Esplin v. Hirschi, 402 F. 2d 94, 101 (10th Cir. 1968), cert. denied, 394 U. S. 928; Green v. Wolf Corp., 406 F. 2d 291, 295 (2d Cir. 1968), cert. denied, 395 U. S. 977; Blackie v. Barrack, 524 F. 2d 891, 903 (9th Cir. 1975), cert. denied, 429 U. S. 816. And there have been many class actions under the SEC statutes, mostly involving Rule 10b-5. But the intricacies of the class action must be left to the writers on civil procedure.

law" of fraud.[1] Suffice it here to include a brief synopsis of those remedies, subject to a strong *caveat* by reason of the necessary generalization, and to consider a few matters (such as the question of the measure of recovery) that are more appropriate here.[2]

1. BREACH OF WARRANTY

Breach of warranty is the most limited of all nonstatutory remedies in the securities field. The Uniform Commercial Code is explicit that the term "goods" in Article 2 (Sales) does not include "investment securities and things in action."[3] Moreover, Article 8 (Investment Securities) provides that "A person by transferring a certificated security to a purchaser for value warrants only that: (a) his transfer is effective and rightful; (b) the security is genuine and has not been materially altered; and (c) he knows no fact which might impair the validity of the security."[4] Consequently the only warranties implied from the mere sale are a warranty of title and a warranty that the stock or bond is a general security of the kind it purports to be on its face; there is no implied warranty of quality or value.

To make matters even worse, a plaintiff relying on this remedy may find that the parol evidence rule (if otherwise applicable in the particular jurisdiction) will be invoked against him to exclude consideration of any promises, and probably representations as well, not contained in the written contract (if there is a written contract that may be considered an "integration" of the parties' previous negotiations). The parol evidence rule is not applicable to deceit actions, or to rescission actions based on the promisor's conscious falsity.[5] But the hapless plaintiff at common law who pursues his remedy in deceit may avoid the parol evidence pitfall only to run into the scienter hurdle.[6]

2. RESCISSION (INCLUDING DEFENSE TO ACTION ON CONTRACT)

Although all the common law and equitable remedies reveal, to a greater or lesser degree, the fact that they were not developed

---

C. 10A [1] See pp. 808-12 supra.

[2] For a synthesis of the various remedies for misrepresentation, see Prosser, Handbook of the Law of Torts (4th ed. 1971) c. 18 and §105.

[3] §2-105(1); but cf. Agar v. Orda, 264 N. Y. 248, 191 N. E. 479 (1934), discussed in UCC — Official Text (9th ed. 1978) 41.

[4] §8-306(2).

[5] 9 Wigmore, Evidence (Chadbourn ed. 1981) §§2423, 2439.

[6] Cabot v. Christie, 42 Vt. 121, 1 Am. Rep. 313 (1869).

with particular reference to the idiosyncrasies of securities trading, rescission (legal and equitable insofar as there may still be vestiges of the historical distinction)[7] is the simplest of the nonstatutory remedies when it is available. This includes the defensive employment of the law of rescission in resisting a seller's action for breach of contract, as well as its use by the buyer offensively in an action for restitution. And the principles are the same whether it is the buyer or the seller who is the person offended, although most of the cases (understandably enough) involve rescission actions by the buyer for return of the purchase price, or actions by the seller for breach of contract. For convenience, therefore, the discussion here will proceed (unless otherwise stated) from the point of view of the buyer alone.

The elements of rescission, in a nutshell, are "misrepresentation" of a "material" "fact" on which the buyer justifiably "relied." The buyer need not show any causal connection between the misrepresentation and his damage; indeed, he need not even show that he has been damaged. Nor is the knowledge or intent of the seller relevant. However, unless the buyer can prove that the misrepresentation was intentional, he must worry about what is "material" and also, perhaps, about whether the court will regard it as equitable to grant restitution when the security has suffered a severe depreciation in market value.[8] In any event, whether the misstatement was intentional, negligent or altogether innocent, there is the problem of distinguishing between a statement of "fact" on the one hand and an expression of "opinion" or a "forecast" or a statement of "law" or "value" on the other. Moreover, the buyer, though escaping the obstacles of causation and scienter that he faces in a deceit action, meets rescission's own prerequisites of "privity" between the parties and ability to restore the seller to the *status quo*.[9] Problem children of the latter element are the difficulties of "tender," "laches," "waiver," and "ratification."

Rescission or cancellation is not the only remedy that equity has to give in cases of fraud — or what is paradoxically labeled "equitable fraud," that is, such conduct as will support an equitable

---

[7] For a summary of the historical distinction, see Prosser, Handbook of the Law of Torts (4th ed. 1971) §94, §105 at 687-88.

[8] The law is not clear on this point. See Restatement of Restitution §69, esp. the caveat, and §142, esp. the caveat and Comment c.

[9] The better rule is that, in the case of fungibles like securities, the buyer need not restore the identical pieces of paper but may substitute a like amount of other pieces. Id. §66(4) and Comment e. There is a certain amount of flexibility here. "Courts have recognized that the restoration need not be exact for rescission to be proper." Harman v. Diversified Medical Investments Corp., 524 F. 2d 361, 364 (10th Cir. 1975).

rescission suit.[10] In a proper case the plaintiff may also obtain reformation, specific performance of the bargain as represented or a receivership, or he may have a constructive trust declared or be awarded any other appropriate relief within the comprehensive powers of equity to grant.[11]

3. Deceit

Deceit has the same elements as rescission so far as misrepresentation of a material fact and reliance are concerned.[12] In addition, the buyer must prove causation (that he suffered damage as a consequence of his reliance on the misrepresentation) and scienter. The latter element, as we have seen, has been variously defined.[13] Ever since 1789 there has been no absolute requirement of privity as there is in rescission.[14] It is thus possible to hold third parties in a deceit action — but only if the plaintiff is one to whom, or to influence whom, the third party made the representation.[15] There is always the question, too, whether the defendant (a director or officer, for example) actively participated in the making of the representation by his corporation.[16]

4. Measure of Damages

In rescission there is no problem of computing damages. Either the plaintiff can restore the defendant to the *status quo ante* or

---

[10] See People v. Federated Radio Corp., 244 N. Y. 33, 154 N. E. 655 (1926).

[11] 3 Pomeroy, Equity Jurisprudence (5th ed. 1941) §910; Deckert v. Independence Shares Corp., 311 U. S. 282 (1940).

[12] On "justifiable" reliance in the deceit context and its relation to contributory negligence, which the better reasoned cases have rejected as a defense applicable to intentional deceit, see Prosser, Handbook of the Law of Torts (4th ed. 1971) 715-18; see also Restatement (Second) of Torts §§540-41.

[13] See p. 810 supra.

[14] Pasley v. Freeman, 3 D. & E. (3 Term. Rep.) 51, 100 Eng. Reprint 450 (K. B. 1789).

[15] Restatement (Second) of Torts §531; cf. also id. §533 (representation made through a third person). Thus, when the directors of a corporation make a false statement in a prospectus published to induce subscriptions to its bonds, the representation is made to every purchaser of bonds, but not to persons who in reliance on the prospectus buy the corporation's *stock*, whether in the open market or from the corporation itself or even from one of the directors. Id. §531, Comment d. Cf. Peek v. Gurney, L. R. 6 H. L. 377, 403 (1873).

[16] See Note, The Liability of Directors and Officers for Misrepresentation in the Sale of Securities, 34 Colum. L. Rev. 1090 (1934).

he has no action of rescission at all (or no rescission-based defense to an action on the contract).

In an action for breach of warranty the recognized measure of damages is the so-called loss-of-bargain rule. That rule is codified in the Uniform Commercial Code as "the difference at the time and place of acceptance between the value of the goods accepted and the value they would have had if they had been as warranted, unless special circumstances show proximate damages of a different amount"[17] — in short, value as warranted minus value at delivery. The theory is that the plaintiff should not only be made whole, as he would if he got the difference between actual purchase price and value at delivery, but should have the benefit he bargained for.

A majority of the states apply the same loss-of-bargain or warranty measure of damages in deceit.[18] However, the English courts and some of the states have followed the so-called tort measure or out-of-pocket rule, under which the buyer is limited to the difference between the purchase price and the value at the time of delivery.[19] Whereas the "warranty rule" gives the buyer the benefit of his bargain, the "tort rule" is intended merely to make him whole.[20]

[17] §2-714(2).

[18] Prosser, Handbook of the Law of Torts (4th ed. 1971) 734; see Spencer Companies, Inc. v. Armonk Industries, Inc., 489 F. 2d 704, 706 (1st Cir. 1973).

[19] Peek v. Derry, L. R. 37 Ch. Div. 541 (C. A. 1887), *rev'd on other grounds* sub. nom. Derry v. Peek, 14 A. C. 337 (1889); Reno v. Bull, 226 N. Y. 546, 124 N. E. 144 (1919) (corporate stock). This was also the pre-*Erie* federal rule. Smith v. Bolles, 132 U. S. 125 (1889) (mining corporation stock); Sigafus v. Porter, 179 U. S. 116 (1900).

[20] The American Law Institute initially favored the tort rule (§549), but the Restatement (Second) of Torts allows benefit-of-the-bargain damages if they are "proved with reasonable certainty":

> (1) The recipient of a fraudulent misrepresentation is entitled to recover as damages in an action of deceit against the maker the pecuniary loss to him of which the misrepresentation is a legal cause, including
> (a) the difference between the value of what he has received in the transaction and its purchase price or other value given for it; and
> (b) pecuniary loss suffered otherwise as a consequence of the recipient's reliance upon the misrepresentation.
> (2) The recipient of a fraudulent misrepresentation in a business transaction is also entitled to recover additional damages sufficient to give him the benefit of his contract with the maker, if these damages are proved with reasonable certainty.

However, the tort measure "must of necessity be adopted where the defendant is a third party who has made no contract with the plaintiff." Prosser, Handbook of the Law of Torts (4th ed. 1971) 734. And a further complication is presented when in a warranty-rule jurisdiction the value-if-the-warranty-were-true is hard to prove, so that the court is induced to look to

Actually few states have applied either rule consistently. And the usual statements of the measures of damages need a good deal of tailoring for securities cases. For example, the New York Court of Appeals, which had apparently wedded itself to the tort measure in *Reno* v. *Bull*,[21] found it necessary to obtain at least a limited divorce a few short years later when it was confronted with a case involving a bond that the defendant brokerage firm had recommended, and that he had been informed was being purchased, as an *investment*. In such circumstances, the court held, the value of the bond need not be determined by the market at the time of the purchase; for that would result in *no* damages. Instead, the value at the time of purchase could be determined in the light of the subsequent history of the issuer, an oil company that because of its unsound financial condition was unable to withstand a period of distress and was forced into liquidation. Hence damages were computed at $980 per bond (the price paid), with interest from the date of payment, less the trivial amount of $5.85 received on liquidation, less the interest received by the plaintiff.[22] Substantially this rule appears to have been adopted in the Restatement (Second) of Torts. That is, when there is a widespread belief in misrepresentations similar to those made to the plaintiff, as often happens in the case of sales of securities, value is determined after the discovery of the fraud, when the price ceases to be fictitious.[23]

B. BLUE SKY LAWS

Blue sky civil liability — which shows signs of a revival in the wake of the recent restriction of the 10b-5 remedy[1] — comes in a

---

the price paid as some evidence of it. Morrell v. Wiley, 119 Conn. 578, 178 Atl. 121 (1935). When that is done, both rules reach the same result.

[21] 226 N. Y. 546, 124 N. E. 144 (1919).

[22] Hotaling v. A. B. Leach & Co., Inc., 247 N. Y. 84, 159 N. E. 870 (1928). See 1 Harper and James, The Law of Torts (1956) 598-603; Note, Measure of Damages in Action for Fraud in the Sale of Corporate Securities, 23 Minn. L. Rev. 205 (1939).

[23] §549, Comment c. This comment is further qualified when the plaintiff has sold before anyone has discovered the falsity. There his loss is the difference between the price paid and the price received on resale. When the plaintiff discovers the falsity sometime after the general public, the value is fixed by the market price at the time of his own discovery. Still another qualification: one who retains securities in reliance on a particular representation cannot recover any loss that was in no way due to the falsity of that representation but was caused by some subsequent unrelated event. Ibid. In short, "causation" survives this distillation of the measure-of-damages formula.

C. 10B   [1] For example:

    (1) Section 415 of the Uniform Securities Act provides that "This act shall

variety of shapes and sizes, and not infrequently two or more provisions are found in a single jurisdiction:

(1) Consistently with the aim of furthering federal-state coordination as well as uniformity, the draftsmen of the Uniform Securities Act closely modeled §410(a) on §12 of the Securities Act of 1933.[2] Thus, §410(a)(1) imposes civil liability on a person who offers or sells a security in violation of specified registration and other provisions, and §410(a)(2) imposes civil liability for sales by means of fraud or misrepresentation. Much of the analysis of §410(a) can accordingly be left for the subsequent discussion of §12.

At the same time, the remainder of §410, in light of the experience under the state statutes and §12, incorporates a number of features that are not found in the federal statute: a detailed specification of those *prima facie* liable under §410(b) along with the seller;[3] specific provisions on prejudgment tender and on survivability on both sides; a ban on the enforceability of any illegal contract; and, in addition to a flat two-year statute of limitations running from the contract of sale, a bar against suit

---

be so construed as to effectuate its general purpose to make uniform the law of those states which enact it and to coordinate the interpretation and administration of this act with the related federal regulation." See, e. g., Shermer v. Baker, 2 Wash. App. 845, 848, 472 P. 2d 589, 592 (1970); Lane v. Midwest Bancshares Corp., 337 F. Supp. 1200, 1209 (E. D. Ark. 1972). But that section merely expresses "a general statement of legislative policy," not a requirement. Draftsmen's commentary to §415, in Loss, Commentary on the Uniform Securities Act (1976) 165.

(2) We have already noticed the possibility of a weaker scienter requirement at the state level than under Rule 10b-5, or perhaps none at all. See p. 810 supra.

(3) Section 410(b) of the Uniform Act (infra n. 3) and comparable provisions elsewhere may enable a plaintiff to reach additional defendants.

(4) Attorneys' fees might be more readily awarded. See Melton v. Unterreiner, 575 F. 2d 204, 209 (8th Cir. 1978) (Missouri law).

(5) The punitive damages that are foreclosed under the Securities Exchange Act of 1934, at least (see p. 1139 infra), might be available in some states.

(6) See People v. Florentino, 456 N. Y. S. 2d 638 (N. Y. C. Cr. Ct. 1982), supra c. 9B n. 78.

[2] See pp. 1017-29 infra. In a princely gesture toward federal-state coordination, Florida, a nonuniform state, has simply incorporated the federal remedies "for the purchase or seller of securities." Fla. Stat. (1981) §517.241(3).

[3] The list includes "Every person who directly or indirectly controls a seller liable under subsection (a), every partner, officer, or director of such a seller, every person occupying a similar status or performing similar functions, every employee of such a seller who materially aids in the sale, and every broker-dealer or agent who materially aids in the sale." With respect to the activities that might bring a lawyer within this kind of language, see Black & Co., Inc. v. Nova-Tech, Inc., 333 F. Supp. 468 (D. Ore. 1971); Adams v. American Western Securities, Inc., 265 Ore. 514, 510 P. 2d 838 (1973); Annot., Attorney's Preparation of Legal Document Incident to Sale of Securities As

(1) if the buyer received a written offer, before suit and at a time when he owned the security, to refund the consideration paid together with interest at six percent per year from the date of payment, less the amount of any income received on the security, and he failed to accept the offer within thirty days of its receipt, or (2) if the buyer received such an offer before suit and at a time when he did not own the security, unless he rejected the offer in writing within thirty days of its receipt.

The Uniform Act forecloses implied actions, although that provision has been deleted in some states.[4]

(2) The typical pattern before the Uniform Act was — and it still is in the nonuniform states — some sort of provision voiding all or specified types of illegal contracts, almost universally with a specific right of rescission in favor of the buyer and usually with an enumeration of the persons liable as well as specification of the measure of recovery.

(3) The Uniform Act followed the existing pattern in authorizing the administrator by rule (a) to require registered broker-dealers (as well as their agents) and investment advisers to post surety bonds in amounts up to $10,000 and (b) to determine the conditions of the bonds.[5] A bond must provide for suit thereon with respect to causes of action under §410 and, if the administrator requires by rule or order, with respect to nonstatutory actions. In addition, a few nonuniform states, in an elusive search for risk-less investment, require surety bonds in connection with *the registration of securities*.[6]

(4) The only states with no civil liability provisions of any type (not even broker-dealer bonding requirements) are New York and Rhode Island. With rare exceptions, however, the courts generally, on one basis or another, have recognized implied rights of action for rescission of illegal sales. Indeed, some of the best known of the early blue sky cases were decisions to the effect that sales made in violation of the statutes were either "void" or "voidable," without benefit of statutory declaration to that effect.[7]

Paradoxically one of the few cases in modern times to reject an

---

Rendering Him Liable under State Securities Regulation Statutes, 62 A. L. R. 3d 252 (1975).

[4] §410(h); see 1 and 4 Loss c. 1B n. 100. One result of the deletion is the possibility of an implied action for violation of §101, which substantially repeats Rule 10b-5 and thus covers fraud in connection with the purchase as well as the sale of a security.

[5] §202(e).

[6] E. g., Ga. Code §10-5-6(b).

[7] E. g., Kneeland v. Emerton, 280 Mass. 371, 183 N. E. 155 (1932); Drees v. Minnesota Petroleum Co., 189 Minn. 608, 250 N. W. 563 (1933); Pennicard v. Coe, 124 Ore. 423, 263 Pac. 920 (1928).

implied rescission remedy was in Rhode Island.[8] In New York it has been held that the dealer's failure to file the required "state notice" does not afford a basis for rescission, because the purpose of that provision is merely to inform the Attorney General so that he may properly enforce the antifraud provisions by way of injunction or criminal prosecution.[9] But this did not prevent the recognition of a private action under §51 of the New York Insurance Law, with respect to the unlicensed public sale of insurance company securities.[10] And the lower courts have recognized actions under one of the blue sky fraud sections as well as the section on registration of real estate securities.[11]

C. SEC CIVIL LIABILITY: AN INTRODUCTION

Superimposed on this array of liabilities at common law and under the state legislation are the civil liabilities under the six SEC statutes of 1933-40. Apparently concluding that the older liabilities were a good deal richer in quantity than in quality, Congress inserted one or more specific liability provisions in each of the Acts except the Advisers Act, especially the first two. And the courts have also implied additional liabilities under certain provisions of the SEC statutes.

As a Court of Appeals put it in an early case,[1]

> The purpose of the civil liability provisions of the first Act was to broaden the law of deceit. In that branch of the law of torts there had raged one of those controversies that delight lawyers and disgust laymen. It had its inception in the famous case of *Derry* v. *Peek*[2] and stemmed from a 19th Century English

---

[8] Coastal Finance Corp. v. Coastal Finance Corp. of North Providence, 387 A. 2d 1373, 1378 (R. I. 1978) (very little discussion). Cf. Penn-Allen Broadcasting Co. v. Traylor, 389 Pa. 490, 497, 133 A. 2d 528, 532 (1957), decided before Pennsylvania's adoption of the Uniform Act, where the court enforced an issuer's contract against a subscriber's defense that the plaintiff had improperly received an exemption as a "dealer."

[9] Sajor v. Ampol, Inc., 275 N. Y. 125, 9 N. E. 2d 803 (1937).

[10] See p. 17 supra.

[11] Gen. Bus. L., §§352-c, 352-e; Lupardo v. I. N. M. Industries Corp., 36 F. R. D. 438, 439 (S. D. N. Y. 1965); Barnes v. Peat, Marwick, Mitchell & Co., 69 Misc. 2d 1068, 1072, 332 N. Y. S. 2d 281, 285 (Sup. Ct. 1972), *stayed pending federal action*, 42 A. D. 2d 15, 344 N. Y. S. 2d 645 (1st Dept. 1973).

On the tender requirement, ratification and related defenses, and officers' and directors' liability (express and implied), see 3 Loss 1672-82; 6 id. 3817-20.

C. 10C [1] Rosenberg v. Hano, 121 F. 2d 818, 819 (3d Cir. 1941).

[2] 14 A. C. 337 (1889), supra p. 1011.

Court's conservative reluctance to believe ill of the tycoons of its day.

The effects of that classic case can be seen most vividly in §11 of the 1933 Act, which was modeled on provisions of the English Companies Act derived from the Directors' Liability Act, 1890, an act passed by Parliament within a year after the House of Lords in *Derry* had demonstrated the impotence of the common law deceit action in the realm of securities.[3] Section 11, particularly, is thus a good deal closer to the English law, with its similar disclosure philosophy, than it is to the blue sky statutes in this country. This makes available a body of relatively close judicial precedent — not only in the British courts but also in the courts of Commonwealth countries whose prospectus provisions were likewise borrowed from England's — which should not be overlooked by the American practitioner.

There are three civil liability provisions in the 1933 Act. Section 11 subjects the issuer of *registered* securities and numerous other classes of persons to liability for damages when the registration statement is materially misleading or defective. Section 12(1) imposes liability for rescission or damages upon anyone who offers or sells a security in violation of the registration or prospectus provisions of §5. Section 12(2) imposes liability for rescission or damages upon anyone who offers or sells any security, *whether or not registered or exempt from registration,* by means of a material misstatement. In addition, §15 imposes liability on any person who "controls" a person liable under §11 or §12, subject to a special defense of innocence. A statute of limitations is prescribed in §13. Section 22 gives the state and federal courts concurrent jurisdiction over "all suits in equity and actions at law brought to enforce any liability or duty created by" the Act[4] and gives

---

[3] 53 & 54 Vict., c. 64. That statute was later incorporated in the Companies Act, and it was from the Companies Act, 1929, that the draftsmen of the 1933 Act borrowed it. 19 & 20 Geo. 5, c. 23, §37. The successor provision now in effect is in the Companies Act, 1948, 11 & 12 Geo. 6, c. 38, §43.

[4] This is true of all the SEC statutes except the 1934 Act (which has given rise to most of the private actions) and, since December 1970, §36(b)(5) of the Investment Company Act (infra p. 1162). Since there is no explanation in the legislative history for singling out those areas, and the exclusive jurisdiction gives rise to serious problems (of jurisdiction, *res judicata,* and collateral estoppel) when the proxy rules, for example, are urged by way of defense or replication in state court proceedings (see 2 Loss 977-1001; 5 id. 2950-58), the Code, with a few exceptions, provides for concurrent jurisdiction, but without the non-removal provisions found in the 1933 and other Acts. §1822(a); see 2 Code 942-44; for the venue and worldwide service provisions, see §1822 (b)-(i).

private plaintiffs the same privileges of wide choice of venue and nationwide (really worldwide) service of process in the federal courts that the Commission enjoys in its own actions.

Writing about these provisions in 1933 — with remarkable foresight as it turned out — Professor Shulman concluded: "Once the policy questions as to the objectives of the Act are answered, there is little in the civil liability provisions which, in a less scientific and less systematic manner, could not or would not have been quietly developed over a period of years by courts on the basis of their own common-law precedents."[5] Certainly events have allayed the fears expressed by some well-informed persons at the time that the new liabilities would constitute an undue threat to free investment.[6]

First we shall consider the specific liabilities by categories. Then we shall look at the development of the implied liabilities. And, finally, we shall discuss a number of matters — such as secondary liability, ancillary relief, the class action device, *in pari delicto* and related defenses, indemnification, security for costs, and the like — that are common to several or all of these liabilities.

D. VIOLATION OF REGISTRATION OR PROSPECTUS PROVISIONS OF THE 1933 ACT [§12(1)]

1. ELEMENTS OF THE ACTION

Section 12(1) can afford to be brief when it provides that "Any person who offers or sells a security in violation of section 5 shall be liable to the person purchasing such security from him," because the liability is virtually absolute.[1] The theory, of course, is deterrence, not restitution. The plaintiff need allege and prove only (1) that the defendant was a seller;[2] (2) that the mails or some means of transportation or communication in interstate commerce

[5] Shulman, Civil Liability and the Securities Act, 43 Yale L. J. 227, 253 (1933).

[6] See Douglas and Bates, The Federal Securities Act of 1933, 43 Yale L. J. 171 (1933); Dean, The Federal Securities Act: I, 8 Fortune 50 (Aug. 1933); Seligman, Amend the Securities Act, 153 Atl. Monthly 370 (Mar. 1934); Ballantine, Amending the Federal Securities Act, 20 A. B. A. J. 85 (1934).

C. 10D [1] White Lighting Co. v. Wolfson, 68 Cal. 2d 336, 355, 438 P. 2d 345, 356-57 (1968); Swenson v. Engelstad, 626 F. 2d 421, 424 n. 5 (5th Cir. 1980). [2] The built-in privity requirement is discussed infra p. 1188 as part of the general problem of secondary liability.

was used, not just in connection with the offering of the security generally but in the offer or sale to the particular plaintiff;[3] (3) that the defendant failed to comply with either the registration or the prospectus requirement;[4] (4) that the action is not barred by the statute of limitations; and (5) that adequate tender was made when the plaintiff is seeking rescission.

The only defense then available to the defendant is to allege and prove that the particular security or transaction was exempt from §5. The seller's intent and his knowledge of the violation, though they may be relevant to an administrative or criminal proceeding or perhaps even a Commission action for injunction based on the violation, are entirely irrelevant in an action under §12(1).[5] Nor is *ultra vires* a defense for a corporation.[6] And, when there are separate transactions, there is no reason why the plaintiff cannot choose to rescind only those that have been unprofitable.[7]

2. Illegal Offer

What if an illegal offer is followed by a legal sale? Suppose, in other words, that the seller either "beats the gun" in violation of §5(c) or makes a preeffective or posteffective offer in violation of §5(b)(1), but the actual *sale* is made after the effective date and a proper prospectus accompanies or precedes the confirmation or the security (whichever is sent first) in full compliance with §5(b).

---

[3] Aid Auto Stores, Inc. v. Cannon, 525 F. 2d 468, 470 (2d Cir. 1975).

[4] On burden of going forward, see pp. 299-301 supra.

[5] Wonneman v. Stratford Securities Co., CCH Fed. Sec. L. Rep. ¶91,034 at 93,459 (S. D. N. Y. 1961) (even if president and sole stockholder of defendant company believed in good faith on the basis of an opinion of counsel that the securities were exempt, "that does not negative the knowledge he admittedly had of the facts giving rise to the liability of [the company] * * * and thus, does not absolve him from liability"); Hill York Corp. v. American Int'l Franchises, Inc., 448 F. 2d 680, 694 n. 19 (5th Cir. 1971); Smith v. Manausa, 385 F. Supp. 443, 451 (E. D. Ky. 1974), *modified and aff'd on other grounds,* 535 F. 2d 353 (6th Cir. 1976) (advice of counsel is no defense); SEC v. Holschuh, 694 F. 2d 130, 137 n. 10 (7th Cir. 1982) (court in injunctive action held good faith was "not relevant to whether there has been a primary violation of the registration requirements," but did not consider its bearing on equity to enjoin). Even "reliance upon a statement made by the corporation commissioner to the effect that no permit was necessary" has been held no defense under the California statute. Boss v. Silent Drama Syndicate, 82 Cal. App. 109, 113, 255 Pac. 225, 227 (1927); but cf. Bartlett v. Suburban Estates, Inc., 12 Cal. 2d 527, 86 P. 2d 117 (1939).

[6] Stadia Oil & Uranium Co. v. Wheelis, 251 F. 2d 269, 276 (10th Cir. 1957).

[7] Piantes v. Hayden-Stone, Inc., 30 Utah 2d 110, 112, 514 P. 2d 529, 530 (1973), *cert. denied,* 415 U. S. 995 (Utah Uniform Securities Act).

Of course, the offeree can have no recourse if he does not buy, whatever action may be taken against the offeror for the violation by way of public enforcement. But what if he does buy?

Whatever doubt there may once have been as to the applicability of §12(1) to illegal offers was resolved when the original definition of "sale" was split into separate definitions of "sale" and "offer" in 1954, with the incidental amendment of §12(1) to refer to any person "who offers or sell a security in violation of section 5" so as "to preserve the effect of the present law" by not excluding the newly permissible preeffective offers from liabilities under §12.[8] Although the result "may appear to be harsh," Congress "made altogether clear that an offeror of a security who had failed to follow one of the allowed paths could not achieve absolution simply by returning to the road of virtue before receiving payment."[9] And the authority under the state statutes preponderates in the same direction.[10] But the Code follows the minority view in order to make a sale possible in such a case without giving the buyer a put.[11]

3.   ILLEGAL DELIVERY

Section 5 has separate subdivisions directed to offers and sales on the one hand and to deliveries after sale on the other. Section 12(1), however, makes no specific reference to delivery; it imposes liability in so many words only upon a person who "offers or sells" in violation of §5. Suppose, then, that a person does not violate §5(a)(1) or §5(b)(1) or §5(c) because he makes no use of the mails or interstate facilities in *offering* or *selling* the securities, but he does violate §5(a)(2) or §5(b)(2) because he uses the mails to *deliver* an unregistered security, or a registered security not accompanied or preceded by a statutory prospectus. Is such a person liable under §12(1)?

Before this question came to be squarely litigated, the Second Circuit said by way of dictum, in an action under §12(2), that "we

---

[8] S. Rep. No. 1036 at 18 and H. R. Rep. No. 1542 at 26, 83d Cong., 2d Sess. (1954).

[9] Diskin v. Lomasney & Co., 452 F. 2d 871, 876 (2d Cir. 1971), set out *supra* p. 107, at p. 110.

[10] E. g., United Bank & Trust Co. v. Joyner, 40 Ariz. 229, 11 P. 2d 829 (1932); California Western Holding Co. v. Merrill, 7 Cal. App. 2d 131, 46 P. 2d 175 (1935). *Contra:* Bauer v. Bond & Goodwin, Inc., 285 Mass. 117, 118 N. E. 708 (1934).

[11] §1702(a)(1); 2 Code 692, Comment (7).

cannot doubt that the liability [under §12(1)] was intended to embrace all transactions made unlawful by section 5." The court thought it was "inconceivable" that Congress intended to impose civil liability on a person who violated the one half of §5 but not on a person who violated the other half.[12] So far as the contrast in the language of §§5 and 12(1) is concerned, the court merely pointed out that §2 itself makes the statutory definitions applicable "unless the context otherwise requires." The court held that §2(3), with its reference to any "disposition" of a security, defined the term "sale" broadly enough to include a delivery after sale, and Judge Swan concluded: "In section 5 where the draftsman differentiated between use of the mails to sell and use of the mails for delivery after sale, the context requires a narrower definition of the term 'sell,' but there is nothing in section 12 to require the definition to be so narrowed."[13]

Under this view, in short, §12(1) is construed as if it referred to "any person who violates section 5." This was obviously the statutory purpose. There are now several square holdings to that effect.[14] And the Code extends to "a person who sells or confirms a sale of a security, delivers a security after sale, or accepts payment for a security in violation of" the registration and prospectus provision.[15]

4. MEASURE OF DAMAGES

It seems clear in statutory context that, when the plaintiff in §12 no longer owns the security, damages are to be measured so as to result in the substantial equivalent of rescission — namely, the difference between the purchase price and the plaintiff's resale price, plus interest, and less any income or return of capital (with interest) that the plaintiff received on the security.[16] Obviously,

---

[12] Schillner v. H. Vaughan Clarke & Co., 134 F. 2d 875, 878 (2d Cir. 1943), infra p. 1027. This was before the 1954 amendments, when there were only §§5(a) and 5(b).

[13] Ibid.

[14] Dupler v. Simmons, 163 F. Supp. 535, 540-42 (D. Wyo. 1958), *appeal dismissed by stipulation* sub nom. Simmons v. Dupler, 268 F. 2d 217 (10th Cir. 1959); Repass v. Rees, 174 F. Supp. 898, 903 (D. Colo. 1959); Value Line Fund, Inc. v. Marcus, CCH Fed. Sec. L. Rep. ¶91,523 at 94,969 (S. D. N. Y. 1965) (use of mails to confirm); Nicewarner v. Bleavins, 244 F. Supp. 261, 265 (D. Colo. 1965) (use of mails to correct error in royalty instrument).

[15] §1702(a)(1).

[16] Cady v. Murphy, 113 F. 2d 988, 991 (1st Cir. 1940), *cert. denied*, 311 U. S. 705; Code §1702(d)(1). In Foster v. Financial Technology, Inc., 517 F. 2d

too, the plaintiff is entitled to restoration of the entire purchase price without deduction for the defendant's selling commission.[17] And the rate of interest is determined not by reference to local statutes but in accordance with the equitable considerations of the particular case.[18]

E. MISSTATEMENT OR OMISSION IN SALE OF SECURITIES

1. GENERALLY [§12(2)]

a. Elements of the Action

Since §12(2) is not too happily drafted, it is best not to attempt a paraphrase:

> Any person who offers or sells a security (whether or not exempted by the provisions of section 3, other than paragraph (2) of subsection (a) thereof), by the use of any means or instruments of transportation or communication in interstate commerce or of the mails, by means of a prospectus or oral communication, which includes an untrue statement of a material fact or omits to state a material fact necessary in order to make the statements, in the light of the circumstances under which they were made, not misleading (the purchaser not knowing of such untruth or omission), and who shall not sustain the burden of proof that he did not know, and in the exercise of reasonable care could not have known, of such untruth or omission, shall be liable to the person purchasing such security from him, who may sue either at law or in equity in any court of competent jurisdiction, to recover the consideration paid for such security with interest thereon, less the amount of any income received thereon, upon the tender of such security, or for damages if he no longer owns the security.

To start with what is clearest, the section applies to all sales of securities, whether or not registered and whether or not the particular security or transaction is exempted from §5,[1] with one

---

1068, 1071 (9th Cir. 1975), the court held that forbearance to institute an action on a franchise matter constituted consideration in a bilateral contract for the sale of securities and that its reasonable value was recoverable.

[17] Stadia Oil & Uranium Co. v. Wheelis, 251 F. 2d 269, 276 (10th Cir. 1957).

[18] Johns Hopkins University v. Hutton, 297 F. Supp. 1165, 1229 (D. Md. 1968), *aff'd in part and rev'd in part on other grounds*, 422 F. 2d 1124 (4th Cir. 1970).

C. 10E [1] Although the first parenthetical phrase of §12(2) refers only to exception: securities exempted under §3(a)(2), which in substance are those of the federal, state and local governments, banks, and interests in certain bank common trust funds and tax-exempt plans. When the seller is the issuer itself or an underwriter and the security is registered, there is some overlap between §§12(2) and 11.[2] But, so far as the ultimate investor is concerned in the orthodox distribution, §12(2) is vital even when there is registration; for the ordinary dealer, whether or not a member of the selling group, is not covered by §11.

Section 12(2) can perhaps best be analyzed and evaluated by comparing it with common law (or equitable) rescission, from which it was adapted; if the differences between rescission and deceit are kept in mind,[3] the comparison will indicate the contrasts between §12(2) and deceit as well. It must be remembered, of course, that the buyer's meat is the seller's poison.

Rescission and §12(2) are *substantially the same* in that both require the buyer to prove a "misrepresentation" of "fact."[4] It may be assumed that the common law concern over the distinction between what is "fact" on the one hand and forecast or promise or opinion or law on the other is substantially carried over. There is every reason in the general policy of the Act, of course, for applying the most progressive common law view on those questions. There is even more reason, in view of the express reference to omissions, to expunge any lingering distinction between outright lies and half-truths. And the Second Circuit has held that "the standards of disclosure required of a registered company are equally applicable [under §12(2)] to the prospectus of an unregistered company";[5] that the court "need not find that the prospectus

---

securities exempted by §3 and not to transactions exempted by §4, this is a mere happenstance of drafting. The introductory clause of §3 creates an exemption from "the provisions of this title" "Except as hereinafter expressly provided," whereas the introductory clause of §4 exempts only from "The provisions of section 5." See Hill York Corp. v. American Int'l Franchises, Inc., 448 F. 2d 680, 695 (5th Cir. 1971).

[2] The purchaser of a registered security, whether from the issuer directly or from an underwriter or dealer, presumably cannot rescind the transaction under §12(2) and at the same time retain his status as a security holder in order to sue for damages under §11. In re Gap Stores Securities Litigation, 79 F. R. D. 283, 307 (N. D. Cal. 1978). But "it is reasonable to assume that the plaintiff may pursue both remedies to judgment, electing his choice at the last possible moment." Ibid.

[3] See pp. 1008-10 supra.

[4] *Query:* Is the parol evidence rule an obstacle in making such proof? We have seen that in common law deceit actions, as well as rescission actions based on the seller's conscious falsity, the rule presents no obstacle. See p. 1008 supra. But §12(2) covers negligent as well as intentional misstatements.

[5] Dale v. Rosenfeld, 229 F. 2d 855, 857 (2d Cir. 1956); DeMarco v. Edens, 390 F. 2d 836, 840-41 (2d Cir. 1968).

contained untrue statements" if it was "misleading"; and that "Availability elsewhere of truthful information cannot excuse untruths or misleading omissions in the prospectus."[6] At the same time, §12(2) does not impose liability for omissions *per se* — although here again the section presumably goes at least as far as the common law in imposing an affirmative duty to speak in special situations, as when the seller occupies a fiduciary relationship to the buyer; in such cases the "statements" referred to in the section take the form (as we have seen) of implied representations flowing from the special circumstances.[7]

The *advantages* that §12(2) affords the buyer as compared with common law rescission are several:

(1) He does not have to prove "reliance" on the misstatement or omission; he must show only that he did not know of it, which

---

[6] Dale v. Rosenfeld, 229 F. 2d 855, 858 (2d Cir. 1956).

A California state court has held in an action under §12(2) that an issuer offering securities in California impliedly represents that a permit has been obtained under the California blue sky law, and that the omission to state that a permit has not been obtained creates a liability under §12(2). Leven v. Legarra, Los Angeles Daily J., Dec. 23, 1949, p. 1, col. 3 (Cal. Super. Ct.), *aff'd without reference to federal law,* 103 Cal. App. 2d 319, 229 P. 2d 383 (1951). This holding apparently goes back to Mary Pickford Co. v. Bayly Bros., Inc., 12 Cal. 2d 501, 519, 86 P. 2d 102, 111 (1939), where the court stated, referring to the Corporate Securities Act: "Whenever, therefore, an issuer or underwriter of securities offers them for sale to the public, he impliedly represents that the applicable provisions of law have been complied with. The falsity of that representation may give rise to an action either for breach of warranty or for fraud depending upon the culpability of the seller in the particular transaction." See also Elzarian v. Wiser, 216 Cal. App. 506, 31 Cal. Rptr. 126 (1963) (violation of terms of permit); Korber v. Lehman, 41 Misc. 2d 568, 569-70, 245 N. Y. S. 2d 830, 831-32 (Sup. Ct. 1963) (§12(2)); Pennebaker v. Kimble, 126 Ore. 317, 325, 269 Pac. 981, 983-84 (1928).

These cases, if they are sound, create an interesting bridge between the state and federal statutes. In effect, any buyer who has a state cause of action for failure to comply with the state statute automatically has a federal cause of action under §12(2) (if the mails or facilities of interstate commerce are used) unless the seller expressly states that the security has not been qualified under the state statute. But is this not too facile? On the same reasoning why does not the implied representation go also to registration under the federal act? If so, almost every 12(1) action can be transformed into a 12(2) action. Although normally a private plaintiff would be foolish to prefer §12(2) over §12(1), the same logic would seem to transform every violation of the registration or prospectus provisions of §5 (when the seller did not disclose the violation) into a violation of the fraud provisions of §17(a). That somehow goes against the grain. See Rotstein v. Reynolds & Co., 359 F. Supp. 109 (N. D. Ill. 1973); Ingenito v. Bermec Corp., 376 F. Supp. 1154, 1176-77 (S. D. N. Y. 1974); cf. Thiele v. Davidson, 440 F. Supp. 585, 589 (M. D. Fla. 1977), *aff'd mem.,* 612 F. 2d 578 (5th Cir. 1980).

The phenomenon is reminiscent of the equally questionable movement in the other direction — from §12(2) to §12(1) — on the theory that a defective prospectus is no §10 prospectus at all. See p. 118 supra.

[7] See pp. 946-58 supra.

is presumably a lesser burden.[8] The common law rule that contributory negligence is no defense[9] carries over to §12(2).[10] And the plaintiff, however sophisticated, has no duty to investigate beyond applying his general knowledge.[11]

Inevitably, to be sure, some element of reliance (which is subjective) is inherent in the concept of materiality (which is an objective, "reasonably prudent person" concept).[12] But, especially since Congress left §12(2) alone when it amended §11 in 1934 to require proof of reliance in some circumstances, that element should not be permitted to come in the back door by way of a definition of materiality.

This legislative history also argues against reading something like a reliance (or causation) requirement into the statutory reference to a sale "by means of" a misleading prospectus or oral communication.[13] At the same time, that phrase presumably

---

[8] Johns Hopkins University v. Hutton, 422 F. 2d 1124, 1129-30 (4th Cir. 1970); Gilbert v. Nixon, 429 F. 2d 348, 356-57 (10th Cir. 1970); Hill York Corp. v. American Int'l Franchises, Inc., 448 F. 2d 680, 695 (5th Cir. 1971); Alton Box Board Co. v. Goldman, Sachs & Co., 560 F. 2d 916, 919 n. 3 (8th Cir. 1977); Wigand v. Flo-Tek, Inc., 609 F. 2d 1028, 1034 (2d Cir. 1979).

[9] See p. 1010 n. 12 supra.

[10] American Bank & Trust Co. in Monroe v. Joste, 323 F. Supp. 843, 847 (W. D. La. 1970).

[11] Hill York Corp. v. American Int'l Franchises, Inc., 448 F. 2d 680, 696 (5th Cir. 1971); Wigand v. Flo-Tek, Inc., 609 F. 2d 1028, 1034 (2d Cir. 1979); Sanders v. John Nuveen & Co. ["Sanders IV"], 619 F. 2d 1222, 1229 (7th Cir. 1980), *cert. denied,* 450 U. S. 1005. Compare the discussion (infra p. 1127) of the plaintiff's duty under Rule 10b-5. Compare also the rule in common law deceit, to the effect that the recipient of a fraudulent misrepresentation "is justified in relying upon its truth, although he might have ascertained the falsity of the representation had he made an investigation," unless "he knows that it is false or its falsity is obvious to him." Restatement (Second) of Torts §§540-41.

[12] Gilbert v. Nixon, 429 F. 2d 348, 356-57 (10th Cir. 1970).

[13] In Sanders v. John Nuveen & Co. ("Sanders IV"), 619 F. 2d 1222, 1225 (7th Cir. 1980), *cert. denied,* 450 U. S. 1005, the court held that the "by means of" language did not require proof that the plaintiff had ever received the misleading prospectus; that the causal connection contemplated by §12(2) was an open-market theory (cf. p. 1130 infra with respect to Rule 10b-5); and that "Thus, it is enough that the seller sold by means of a misleading prospectus securities of which those purchased by the plaintiff were a part." The court expressed some concern about the application of its open-market theory to the extent that §12(2) covered oral communications, since "Spoken words lack continuing vitality and are unlikely to affect the general market price of a security," but left that problem for another day. Id. at 1227; cf. Jackson v. Oppenheim, 533 F. 2d 826, 830 n. 8 (2d Cir. 1976). To the effect that proof of causation is not necessary, see also Hill York Corp. v. American Int'l Franchises, Inc., 448 F. 2d 680, 696 (5th Cir. 1971). But cf. Alton Box Board Co. v. Goldman, Sachs & Co., 560 F. 2d 916, 924 (8th Cir. 1977), where the court held that, although the plaintiff need not prove reliance, "some causal relationship between the misleading representation and the sale must be

saves the seller who uses a misleading "preliminary prospectus" during the waiting period from being liable under §12(2) to the buyer who saw only the corrected final prospectus. The case of the buyer who saw the misleading "preliminary prospectus" is more difficult, because the 1954 addition of the words "offers or," as an incident of the split of the original definition of "sale" into separate definitions of "sale" and "offer," must be given some meaning. Yet it does not seem necessary to follow here the categorical §12(1) approach that grounds liability on an illegal offer followed by a legal sale.[14] In §12(1) there is no alternative to that reading except to disregard both the addition of the words "offers or" in 1954 and the general realization that there is often no other effective sanction for "beating the gun." But it is possible in §12 (2) to give meaning to both phrases — "offers or" and "by means of" — by grounding liability on the use of a misleading prospectus or other document that was corrected before the sale *unless it is clear that the correction was brought to the buyer's attention before he bought.* If this analysis is correct — and this is another area of SEC law that is *terra incognita* — it indicates the advisability of emphasizing the correction, perhaps to the extent of sending a separate letter along with the final prospectus.

(2) The second respect in which the buyer is better off under §12(2) than in a common law rescission action is that, if he is not in a position to tender the security for rescission because he no longer owns it, he may obtain damages. Indeed, whereas from the point of view of the common law tender requirement the buyer may weaken his position by reselling, there is if anything the reverse question under §12(2) whether the buyer may not be under a *duty* to resell in order to mitigate damages after he learns of the misstatement or omission.

(3) Section 12(2) permits the buyer to pierce the privity requirement that normally prevails in common law rescission to the extent of reaching (as we shall see) controlling persons under §15, "sellers" who are agents rather than principals, and others who participate in the sale more or less in the criminal aider and abettor sense.[15]

(4) The final advantage that §12(2) affords the buyer is the right to sue in a federal court, without at the same time losing ac-

shown"; the court went on to hold, however, that that had been established as a matter of law from the defendant's failure to investigate the creditworthiness of the Penn Central notes that it had sold. Ibid.

[14] See pp. 1018-19 supra.

[15] See pp. 1179-89 infra.

cess to his local state court. He may pick his forum with due regard to strategic, geographical and other considerations. If he picks the federal court, he has a broad choice of venue, with the privilege of nationwide service of process, and he need not comply with the usual $10,000 requirement, and the defendant cannot remove.

So far the buyer has both his common law cake and his statutory icing. But the icing may be too rich for his blood:

(1) The most important concession that §12(2) makes to the *seller* is to give him a defense, which he does not have in common law rescission, if he can "sustain the burden of proof that he did not know, and in the exercise of reasonable care could not have known, of such untruth or omission." Obviously having in mind common law deceit with its scienter element rather than rescission, the House Committee report on the bill that became the Securities Act justified this "shift in the burden of proof[16] as both just and necessary, inasmuch as the knowledge of the seller as to any flaw in his selling statements or the failure of the seller to exercise reasonable care are matters in regard to which the seller may readily testify, but in regard to which the buyer is seldom in a position to give convincing proof."[17]

(2) Since this defense in effect limits §12(2) to *intentional* or *negligent* misstatements or omissions, and since the buyer need not prove the materiality of *intentional* misstatements in order to obtain restitution in the absence of statute, the reference in §12(2) to materiality is another respect in which the buyer who can prove an intentional misstatement or omission is given no favor by the statutory action.

(3) Again, the buyer is faced with a much shorter statute of limitations under §12(2) than in a nonstatutory action, where all he may have to worry about is laches and in any event the local statute of limitations usually is considerably longer.

(4) Finally, the dependence of §12(2) on use of the mails or interstate facilities has on occasion been the buyer's nemesis and relegated him to his common law or state statutory remedies.[18]

---

[16] Wilko v. Swan, 346 U. S. 427, 431 (1953) (dictum).

[17] H. R. Rep. No. 85, 73d Cong., 1st Sess. (1933) 9, 23-24.

[18] Another problem has been raised but never decided. Section 12(2) refers to anyone who offers or sells a security "by means of a prospectus or oral communication." Section 2(10)(a) provides that in certain circumstances supplementary selling literature accompanying or following the statutory prospectus "shall not be deemed a prospectus." What, then, if the seller uses the statutory prospectus, which tells the truth and the whole truth, but sends supplementary literature containing a pack of lies along with or after the official

b. Use of the Mails or Interstate Facilities

We have noticed the question under §12(1) whether there is liability when the mails are used only in making delivery.[19] A similar question has arisen under §12(2). More precisely, the question there is whether the mails must be used in making the misrepresentation or whether it suffices to prove an oral misrepresentation (not made by interstate telephone) and use of the mails or interstate facilities in making delivery or in some other aspect of the transaction.

In the case in the Second Circuit that we have already noticed because of the court's arguing by analogy to §12(1), there was an oral misrepresentation followed by the mailing of the securities from Philadelphia to Rome, New York. The court took the broad view, reasoning partly from the premise that the word "sells" must have the same meaning in both parts of §12 and that (as we have already seen) it must be taken to include "delivers" if §12(1) is not to be limited to violations of only one part of §5. The narrow construction, the court thought, was not "the inevitable, or even the most natural, meaning of the statutory language" of §12(2). That construction "would render the phrase 'oral communication' of most limited application because the section would then reach only interstate telephone calls or conversations where the parties might be talking across a state line."[20]

---

prospectus? The question has not been litigated. Although a Victorian court might have considered itself helpless, it seems hard to believe that many judges today would so exalt a "drafting bug" over the clear legislative intention as to deny recovery. The obvious escape, once more, is that §2 defines various terms, including "prospectus," "unless the context otherwise requires." In §12(2) the context most certainly requires that supplementary selling literature be considered a "prospectus." Some support for this construction is found in the 1954 amendment of §2(10)(a). See c. 2B, n. 44 supra. Actually it would have been better to amend §12(2) itself than to insert the parenthetical language in §2(10)(a); for the latter solution invites an *expressio unius* argument to the effect that supplementary literature *other than* a §10(b) summary prospectus is *not* a "prospectus" for purposes of §12(2). Even so, however, the clearly manifested statutory purpose in §12(2) should prevail over an argument drawn purely from the words of the statute. See Code §1703(a)-(b). Section 410(a)(2) of the Uniform Securities Act avoids the question by referring simply to any person who "offers or sells a security by means of any untrue statement * * * ."

[19] See p. 1019 supra.

[20] Schillner v. H. Vaughan Clarke & Co., 134 F. 2d 875, 877 (2d Cir. 1943).

This view has been followed[21] except in the Seventh Circuit.[22] And, although §12(2) is not a model of draftsmanship, the language seems to favor the Second Circuit's view. More important, there is no justification in the background of the statute for assuming that Congress regarded the jurisdictional language of §12(2) as anything more than a constitutional necessity.[23] As we have seen, it is perfectly clear that a violation of the mail fraud statute and of §17(a) and the other SEC fraud provisions can be made out without showing that the mails were used in making the misrepresentation. It seems odd, as the Eighth Circuit observed, to withhold civil liability under §12(2) for a fraud that could put the defendant in jail under §17(a) or the mail fraud statute.[24]

The broadest reading of §12(2), however, requires — as with §12(1)[25] — *some* use of the mails or interstate facilities in connection with the sale *to the particular plaintiff*.[26]

c. Defense of Reasonable Care

The statutory defense requires the defendant to prove "that he did not know, and in the exercise of reasonable care could not have known," of the untruth or omission.[27] There is not much

---

[21] Blackwell v. Bentsen, 203 F. 2d 690 (5th Cir. 1953), *cert. dismissed,* 347 U. S. 925 (1954); Creswell-Keith, Inc. v. Willingham, 264 F. 2d 76, 82 (8th Cir. 1959) (mails were used only in *buyer's* remittances of checks to defendant's creditors as part of the purchase price); cf. Fratt v. Robinson, 203 F. 2d 627, 633-34 n. 20 (9th Cir. 1953) (distinguishing the question under Rule 10b-5, the court referred to *Schillner,* supra n. 20, as having "the best reasoning in support").

[22] Kemper v. Lohnes, 173 F. 2d 44, 46 (7th Cir. 1949).

[23] Creswell-Keith, Inc. v. Willingham, 264 F. 2d 76, 80 (8th Cir. 1959).

[24] Ibid.; see p. 98 supra.

[25] See pp. 1017-18 supra.

[26] Larson v. Tony's Investments, Inc., CCH Fed. Sec. L. Rep. ¶92,578 at 98,648 (M. D. Ala. 1970); Franklin Savings Bank v. Levy, 406 F. Supp. 40, 42 (S. D. N. Y. 1975), *rev'd on other grounds,* 551 F. 2d 521 (2d Cir. 1977). Thus there is no reason to suppose that a buyer who receives a prospectus without use of the mails may rescind because another buyer (with respect to whom the mails *were* used) failed to receive one. See Schneider and Zall, Section 12(1) and the Imperfect Exempt Transaction: The Proposed I & I Defense, 28 Bus. Law. 1011, 1021 (1973).

[27] For an analysis of the various "due care" locutions under the existing statutes and the Code, together with a table that charts the Code's provisions with their respective sources (if any) in existing law, see 1 Code 134-49. The locution in §1703(f), successor to §12(2), requires the defendant to prove merely that "he reasonably did not believe that there was a misrepresentation." And §202(131) defines "reasonably" to require "reasonable care," adding that "the questions whether reasonable care requires an investigation

law on how this defense may be established. The Second Circuit, speaking *obiter,* has said that the defendant must show that he "could not have known" of the omission, not merely that "he had used reasonable care" to avoid or correct it: "It is true that in some cases evidence of steps taken to avoid or correct an omission in a communication would negate reasonable knowledge that an omission existed. * * * But reasonable effort to extinguish ignorance does not necessarily prove reasonable unawareness of continued ignorance."[28] Presumably one may rely on SEC filings at least while they are relatively fresh. The key word is "reasonable."

2. MISSTATEMENT OR OMISSION IN REGISTRATION STATEMENT [§11]

a. Elements of the Action

Section 11 was the *bête noire* that was going to stifle legitimate financing — and that did not produce a substantial recovery for

---

or inquiry and, if so, its extent are left to construction in context and in the light of the circumstances." All this is subject to §1704(g):

> In determining what constitutes reasonable investigation and reasonable ground for belief * * * , the standard of reasonableness is that required of a prudent man under the circumstances in the conduct of his own affairs. Relevant circumstances include, with respect to a defendant other than the registrant, (1) the type of registrant, (2) the type of defendant, (3) when the defendant is an officer, the office held, (4) when the defendant is an officer, director, or proposed director, (A) the presence or absence of another relationship to the registrant, and (B) reasonable reliance on officers (or other officers when the defendant is an officer), employees, and other whose duties would reasonably be expected to give them knowledge of the particular facts (in light of the functions and responsibilities of the particular defendant with respect to the registrant and the filing), (5) when the defendant is an underwriter, the type of underwriting arrangement and the role of the particular defendant as an underwriter, and (6) whether, with respect to a fact or document incorporated by reference, the particular defendant had any responsibility for the fact or document at the time of the filing from which it was incorporated.

[28] Jackson v. Oppenheim, 533 F. 2d 826, 829 n. 7 (2d Cir. 1976). For additional treatments of the defense, see Murphy v. Cady, 30 F. Supp. 466, 468-69 (D. Me. 1939), *aff'd on other grounds* sub nom. Cady v. Murphy, 113 F. 2d 988 (1st Cir. 1940), *cert. denied,* 311 U. S. 705; First Trust & Savings Bank of Zanesville, Ohio v. Fidelity-Philadelphia Trust Co., 214 F. 2d 320 (3d Cir. 1954), *cert. denied,* 348 U. S. 856; DeMarco v. Edens, 390 F. 2d 836, 841-43 (2d Cir. 1968); Gilbert v. Nixon, 429 F. 2d 348 (10th Cir. 1970).

Query Sanders v. John Nuveen & Co., 524 F. 2d 1064 (7th Cir. 1975), *on later appeal,* 619 F. 2d 1222 (7th Cir. 1980), where the court equated an under-thirty years. But before we examine the scant litigation history we must have a look at the elements of the action.[29]

(i) *Plaintiffs:* Suit may be brought by any person who acquired a *registered* security, whether in the process of distribution or in the open market. All he must prove is that "any part of the registration statement, when such part became effective, contained an untrue statement of a material fact or omitted to state a material fact required to be stated therein or necessary to make the statements therein not misleading."[30] The plaintiff is spared any concern about reliance (at least insofar as it is divorced from materiality) unless he bought after the issuer had made generally available to its security holders an earnings statement covering a period of at least a year beginning after the effective date; but even then "reliance may be established without proof of the reading of the registration statement by such person."[31] And, instead of the plaintiff's having to prove causation, damages are reduced to the extent that the *defendant* proves that they did not result from his misconduct[32] — what might be called "comparative causation with a reverse twist."[33]

---

writer's §12(2) duty of care in the sale of §3(a)(3)-exempted commercial paper to an underwriter's duty with respect to a false registration statement under §11 (infra p. 1033). Indeed, the court referred to the defendant's failure to verify the audited financial statements or to review the auditor's work papers — steps that are not required even by §11(b)(3)(C) (infra p. 1034).

With respect to measure of damages, what has been said under §12(1) (supra p. 1020) applies equally to §12(2). With respect to privity, see p. 1031 infra.

[29] Section 11 was made less harsh in a number of respects concurrently with the passage of the 1934 Act. On the political background of the 1934 amendments, see M. Parrish, Securities Regulation and the New Deal (1970) 186-98.

[30] §11(a). Since the "preliminary prospectus" under Rule 430 is not part of an effective registration statement, deficiencies in it cannot give rise to §11 liability if they are corrected before the effective date. The expanded "tombstone ad" under Rule 134 is not filed as part of the registration statement at all. And §10(b) specifically excludes the "summary prospectus" under Rule 431 from §11 liability.

[31] §11(a), last ¶. This limited reliance requirement was added in 1934. Commentators had pointed out that the shift of the burden of proof to the defendant filled a long-felt need particularly during the early life of the security, when the registration statement is an important conditioner of the market; but after a substantial time, they observed, there is less justification for so weighting the scales in the investor's favor, because the information in the registration statement then becomes outmoded and discounted by many other factors. See Douglas and Bates, The Federal Securities Act of 1933, 43 Yale L. J. 171, 176 (1933); H. R. Rep. No. 1838, 73d Cong., 2d Sess. (1934) 41.

[32] §11(e).

[33] See Collins v. Signetics Corp., 605 F. 2d 110, 114 (3d Cir. 1979). In Feit v. Leasco Data Processing Equipment Corp., 332 F. Supp. 544, 586

(ii) *Defendants:* There is a wide variety of potential defendants:[34] (1) every person who signed the registration statement, which is to say under §6(a), the issuer itself, "its principal executive officer or officers, its principal financial officer, its comptroller or principal accounting officer," and in the case of a foreign or territorial issuer "its duly authorized representative in the United States"; (2) every person who was a director (or person performing similar functions) of the issuer or a partner in the issuer "at the time of the filing of the part of the registration statement with respect to which his liability is asserted"; (3) every person who with his consent was named in the statement as about to assume any such position;[35] (4) every accountant, engineer, appraiser or other expert named in the statement with his consent, but only to the extent of liability concerning any part of the statement or any related report or valuation prepared or certified by him; and (5) every underwriter.[36] In addition, §15 reaches anyone whom the plaintiff can show to be in control of any of these persons.[37]

(iii) *Defenses:* The issuer's liability is absolute with but one exception: it has the defense, available to all defendants, of showing that the plaintiff knew of the untruth or omission at the time of his acquisition of the security.[38] For other defendants an elabo-

---

(E. D. N. Y. 1971), the court took judicial notice of "the very drastic general decline in the stock market in 1969" and adjusted the damage figure accordingly. Cf. Rolf v. Blyth, Eastman Dillon & Co., Inc., 637 F. 2d 77, 84 (2d Cir. 1980), *on remand,* CCH Fed. Sec. L. Rep. ¶98,201 at 91,414-15 (S. D. N. Y. 1981) (Rule 10b-5).

[34] §11(a)(1)-(5).

[35] If any person who has not signed the registration statement is named in it as about to become a director, his written consent must be filed with the registration statement unless the registrant files a verified statement giving the reasons for omitting such a consent and establishing that obtaining it "is impracticable or involves undue hardship on the registrant." Rule 438.

[36] "If any person becomes an underwriter with respect to the security after the part of the registration statement with respect to which his liability is asserted has become effective, then for the purposes of [his liability] such part of the registration statement shall be considered as having become effective with respect to such person as of the time when he became an underwriter." §11(d).

[37] See p. 1179 infra. Even when a registration statement is filed in connection with a secondary distribution by a person in a control relationship with the issuer, that person is not liable under §11 directly. He is liable only under §15, since he need not sign the registration statement.

[38] *Query* the impact of this strict liability of the issuer on the status of stockholder plaintiffs under §11 (or §12(2) or Rule 10b-5) vis-à-vis creditors of the issuer (who may or may not be holders of debt securities with their own rights under §11) when the issuer is insolvent. (It is very likely on account of this problem that the issuer is not held at all under the English Companies Act.) The cases are in disarray:

(1) For the *parity* point of view, see, e. g., SEC v. Insurance Investors

rate series of reasonable care *defenses* is substituted for scienter:[39]

Trust Co., CCH Fed. Sec. L. Rep. ¶93,259 at 91,553 (W. D. Ky. 1971), where the court weighed (a) the interests of tradesmen, who must hear "the beating of the distant drum" that warns them to "take cash and let the credit go," against (b) the adoption by Congress of protective statutes "designed to make whole, if possible, the fleeced unwary." Cf. Oppenheimer v. Harriman National Bank & Trust Co., 301 U. S. 206, 213-15 (1937), where the Court held that a claim by a stockholder who had rescinded a sale to him of the bank's own stock on account of fraud was entitled to rank on a parity with the claims of other unsecured creditors in the receivership. The Commission cited this case in arguing that stockholders to whom stock of a Chapter X debtor had been sold in alleged violation of the 1933 and 1934 Acts had claims against the debtor on which they should participate on a parity with general, unsecured creditors. See TMT Trailer Ferry, Inc., Corp. Reorg. Rel. 226 (1965) 13-15. But the court in confirming a plan of reorganization held that these claims had been filed too late to be considered on the merits. Protective Committee for Independent Stockholders of TMT Trailer Ferry, Inc. v. Anderson, 364 F. 2d 936 (5th Cir. 1966), *rev'd on other grounds*, 390 U. S. 414 (1968). This position of the Commission is not a little anomalous in view of its traditional espousal of the absolute priority rule when it is wearing its reorganization hat.

(2) For an even stronger pro-investor view, which gives the rescinding stockholder *priority* to the extent that he can trace the consideration he paid for the securities into an identifiable *res* in the issuer's possession, see, e. g., In re Rhine, 241 F. Supp. 86 (D. Colo. 1965).

(3) At the other extreme is subordination. See, e. g., Federal Deposit Ins. Corp. v. American Bank Trust Shares, Inc., 412 F. Supp. 302, 308 (D. S. C. 1976), *vacated on other grounds*, 558 F. 2d 711 (4th Cir. 1977); In the Matter of Stirling Homex Corp., 579 F. 2d 206 (2d Cir. 1978); cf. In re Racine Auto Tire Co., 290 Fed. 939 (7th Cir. 1923) (estoppel approach with respect to blue sky claim); In re American Aluminum Metal Products Co., 15 F. 2d 234, 235 (S. D. Cal. 1926) (same).

See generally Slain and Kripke, The Interface between Securities Regulation and Bankruptcy — Allocating the Risk of Illegal Securities Issuance between Securityholders and the Issuer's Creditors, 48 N. Y. U. L. Rev. 261 (1973); Huff, the Defrauded Investor in Chapter X Reorganizations: Absolute Priority v. Rule 10b-5, 50 Am. Bankr. L. J. 197 (1976).

The Code addresses this problem by providing that the Code does not affect the courts' powers with respect to the treatment of Code claimants "in relation to one or more classes of other creditors or security holders." §1903 (d)(2)(B). As stated in the comment (2 Code 958):

> This reflects the Bankruptcy Reform Act, 11 U. S. C. §510(c)(1), which authorizes the court, "under principles of equitable subordination, [to] subordinate * * * all or part of an allowed claim to all or part of another allowed claim * * * ." * * *

The effect of §1903(d)(2) is to make it clear that nothing in the Code prevents the courts from using their traditional equity powers to do whatever is appropriate so far as subordination is concerned, not merely with respect to the issuer under §1704 but with respect to *any* involvent defendant under the Code *generally.*

[39] For an analysis of the subtle distinctions between these defenses and the due care defense in §12(2), see Folk, Civil Liabilities under the Federal Securities Acts: The *BarChris* Case — Part II — The Broader Implications, 55 Va. L. Rev. 199, 207-16 (1969).

(A) The defendant might establish that before the effective date of the part of the registration statement in question, or upon becoming aware of its effectiveness, he had taken appropriate steps to sever all his described connections with the issuer and had advised the issuer and the Commission that he had taken such action and would not be responsible for that part of the statement and (when it was the fact) had given reasonable public notice that that part of the statement had become effective without his knowledge.[40]

(B) A nonexpert defendant (which is to say a director, officer, or underwriter), as well as an expert sued on his "expertized" portion of the registration statement, might establish that "he had, after reasonable investigation, reasonable ground to believe and did believe, at the time such part of the registration statement became effective," that it was true and complete.[41] And the standard of reasonableness was changed in 1934 — largely for psychological reasons, so it seems — from "that required of a person occupying a fiduciary relationship" to "that required of a prudent man in the management of his own property."[42]

This is substantially the standard adopted in the Restatement (Second) of Trusts[43] and applied under the English Companies Act; the English courts recognize that a director may rely on clerks and other competent persons for information concerning the business,[44] but do not regard reliance on the statements of promoters or approval of the prospectus by other directors as a defense.[45] Indeed, even under the original "fiduciary" standard, the conference report on the bill that became the Securities Act recognized that a fiduciary need not "individually perform every duty imposed upon him," but may delegate to others "the performance of acts which it is unreasonable to require that the fiduciary shall personally perform," especially "where the character of the acts involves professional skill or facilities not possessed by the fiduciary himself."[46]

---

[40] §11(b)(1)-(2).
[41] §11(b)(3)(A)-(B).
[42] §11(c).
[43] §174.
[44] Stevens v. Hoare, 20 T. L. R. 407 (Ch. 1904) (Directors' Liability Act, 1890).
[45] Adams v. Thrift, [1915] 2 Ch. 21 (C. A.); see also Bundle v. Davies, [1932] N. Z. L. R. 1097, 1099 (Sup. Ct.). Both *Stevens*, supra n. 44, and *Adams* were cited approvingly in Lanza v. Drexel & Co., 479 F. 2d 1277, 1297 (2d Cir. *en banc, obiter*, 1973). And *Adams* was followed in Escott v. BarChris Construction Corp., 283 F. Supp. 643, 688 (S. D. N. Y. 1968).
[46] H. R. Rep. No. 152, 73d Cong., 1st Sess. (1933) 26.

(C) A nonexpert defendant sued on an "expertized" portion of the registration statement has a somewhat readier, double-negative defense: that "he had no reasonable ground to believe and did not believe, at the time such part of the registration statement became effective, that the statements therein were untrue or that there was an omission to state a material fact required to be stated therein or necessary to make the statements therein not misleading * * * ."[47]

b. "Expertising"

To what extent may officers, directors and underwriters legitimately mitigate their burden of due care under §11 by relying on experts? Certainly not to the extent of all or substantially all of the registration statement. Section 7, as implemented by the Commission's rules, requires the manually signed consent of any expert named as having prepared or certified any part of the registration statement or a report or valuation for use in connection with the registration statement.[48] This whole machinery obviously was intended for such parts of the registration statement as the financial data, appraisers' valuations, engineers' reports, the opinion of counsel as to the legality of the issue, and the like. The Commission will not permit the central data in the registration statement — the description of the business, the promotional history, the underwriting arrangements and so on — to be "expertized."[49] In fact, the Commission has indicated that even when an expert may be properly employed — indeed, is essential, as in the case of independently prepared financial statements — management may not

---

[47] §11(b)(3)(C).

[48] Rules 436-37.

[49] As Judge McLean put it in Escott v. BarChris Construction Corp., 283 F. Supp. 643, 683 (S. D. N. Y. 1968):

> To say that the entire registration statement is expertised because some lawyer prepared it would be an unreasonable construction of the statute. Neither the lawyer for the company nor the lawyer for the underwriters is an expert within the meaning of Section 11.

Although a lawyer normally prepares the bulk of the registration statement, he is an "expert" only with respect to his required opinion on the legality of the issue. But lawyers' opinions sometimes cover a variety of other questions. See A. Jacobs, Opinion Letters in Securities Matters (1980). On lawyers' liability as *lawyers* under §11 and Rule 10b-5, see Small, An Attorney's Responsibilities under Federal and State Securities Laws: Private Counselor or Public Servant?, 61 Calif. L. Rev. 1189 (1973); Cheek, Counsel Named in a Prospectus, 6 Rev. Sec. Reg. 939 (1973).

rely blindly on the expert's work; for "The fundamental and primary responsibility for the accuracy of information filed with the Commission and disseminated among the investors rests upon management."[50]

In *Escott v. BarChris Construction Corp.*, the court sitting without a jury, although it concluded (1) that one of the outside directors believed that certain figures that had been audited by a national accounting firm were correct because he had confidence in the firm and had no reasonable ground to believe otherwise, and (2) that a young lawyer who had become secretary and a director could likewise rely on those figures, found also (3) that the corporation's treasurer and chief financial officer, who had reason to believe that those same figures were incorrect, "could not shut his eyes to the facts and rely on [the accounting firm] for that portion," and (4) that the controller, a relatively minor figure in the company, had nevertheless failed to establish his defense because he was familiar with the issuer's books as its financial officer.[51]

c.   Comparison with Common Law Actions and §12(2)

How does this elaborate structure of §11 compare with the common law actions and §12(2)?

So far as proving a "misstatement" of a "material" "fact" is concerned, they would all seem to be alike. The novel aspect of materiality under §11 is that, no matter whether the plaintiff purchased a day or a year after the effective date of the particular part of the registration statement complained of, materiality is reckoned as of that one date.[52]

[50] Interstate Hosiery Mills, Inc., 4 SEC 706, 721 (1939); United States v. Erickson, 601 F. 2d 296, 305 (7th Cir. 1979), *cert. denied*, 444 U. S. 979. The English courts have taken a similar view in denying company officials the defense that statements in the prospectus were phrased or omitted under legal advice. Shepheard v. Broome, [1904] A. C. 342, 347, *aff'g* Broome v. Speak, [1903] 1 Ch. 586 (C. A.); but see Adams v. Thrift, [1915] 2 Ch. 21, 24 (C. A.). In general, see Hawes and Sherrard, Reliance on Advice of Counsel As a Defense in Corporate and Securities Cases, 62 Va. L. Rev. 1, 112-22 (1976). The Code leaves the matter to judicial development. See 2 Code 694, Comment (1).

[51] 283 F. Supp. 643, 685-87 (S. D. N. Y. 1968).

[52] This creates a problem of currency for the accountant's audit figures. In Escott v. BarChris Construction Corp., 283 F. Supp. 643, 697-704 (S. D. N. Y. 1968), the court held that the purpose of a so-called "S-1 review" after the date of the balance sheet was to ascertain whether any material change had occurred in the issuer's financial position that should be disclosed in order to prevent the balance sheet figures from being misleading; that this did not amount to a complete audit; that the accountant's *program* for the

Reliance, which is required in both common law actions but not as such under §12(2), is back in §11 subject to the one-year provision; and causation, which is an element of deceit but not of §12(2), is likewise back in §11 to the extent that *lack* of causation is at least a partial affirmative defense. Anyway, neither reliance nor causation is entirely banished as long as materiality is in issue; much of this is dialectic. Whereas §12(2) requires the *purchaser* to prove that he did *not* know of the particular untruth or omission, §11 makes the purchaser's knowledge a matter of affirmative defense. One searches vainly for the rationale of this kind of distinction.[53]

Scienter, the hobgoblin of both common law deceit and Rule 10b-5, is foreign to the vocabulary of §11 just as in the case of common law rescission and §12(2). Although the parties must conjure with the substitute concepts of reasonable investigation and reasonable ground for belief, the new standards sound more in negligence than in fraud. The requirement of reasonable investigation and reasonable ground to believe, the House Committee said, "throws upon originators of securities a duty of competence as well as innocence which the history of recent spectacular failures overwhelmingly justifies."[54] This is not to say that all participants in the process of distribution were intended to be held to the identical burden of investigation. The House Committee recognized that "The duty of care to discover varies in its demands upon participants in security distribution with the importance of their place in the scheme of distribution and with the degree of protection that the public has a right to expect."[55] But it was recognized also, and intended, that there would be a minimum duty of investigation upon all directors that would "have a direct tendency to preclude persons from acting as nominal directors while shirking their duty to know and guide the affairs of the corporation" and "result in persons retiring from many boards and confining their efforts to a few boards where they will actually direct."[56]

---

review conformed to generally accepted auditing standards, but that the actual review had not; that there were enough danger signals in the materials that the accountant had examined to require some further investigation on his part; and that the accountant had not sustained the defense under §11(b). The court held also that the plaintiffs could not take advantage of any undertakings or representations in the accountant's "comfort letter" to the underwriters, 283 F. Supp. at 698.

[53] The Code puts the burden on the defendant in the successors to both provisions. §§1703(e), 1704(e); see 2 Code 710, Comment (1) to §1704(e).

[54] H. R. Rep. No. 85, 73d Cong., 1st Sess. (1933) 9.

[55] Ibid.

[56] S. Rep. No. 47, 73d Cong., 1st Sess. (1933) 5.

Not surprisingly, the chief executive officer and the other "inside" (management) directors have a greater burden than "outside" directors,[57] to the point where Judge Weinstein was "led to the conclusion that liability will lie in practically all cases of misrepresentation."[58] But the extent to which participating underwriters may rely on the principal underwriters to make a reasonable investigation is still not altogether clear. It has been suggested that participating underwriters may delegate their duties to the managing underwriter as long as he himself makes an appropriate investigation.[59] On the other hand, a Commission release would require each participant to "satisfy himself that the managing underwriter makes the kind of investigation the participant would have performed if he were the manager."[60]

In practice, the principal underwriters traditionally arranged sometime during the waiting period for a "due diligence meeting" attended by representatives of the issuer, its counsel, the underwriters and their counsel, the accountant, and any other experts. Everybody was thus afforded an opportunity to exercise "due diligence" by asking questions.[61] But the practice is in a state of

[57] Escott v. BarChris Construction Corp., 283 F. Supp. 643, 684 (S. D. N. Y. 1968).

[58] Feit v. Leasco Data Processing Equipment Corp., 332 F. Supp. 544, 578 (E. D. N. Y. 1971). A lawyer-director may be so deeply involved in a particular case as to become an insider. Id. at 576.

[59] Folk, Civil Liabilities under the Federal Securities Acts: The *BarChris* Case, Part I — Section 11 of the Securities Act of 1933, 55 Va. L. Rev. 1, 56-58 (1969).

[60] Sec. Act Rel. 5275 (1972) 12; see In re Gap Stores Securities Litigation, 79 F. R. D. 283, 299-302 (N. D. Cal. 1978). The question was left open in Escott v. BarChris Construction Corp., 283 F. Supp. 643, 697 n. 26 (S. D. N. Y. 1968), because the lead underwriter itself had failed to establish its due diligence. Contrast Competitive Associates, Inc. v. International Health Sciences, Inc., CCH Fed. Sec. L. Rep. ¶94,966 at 97,337 (S. D. N. Y. 1975), where the lead underwriter's successful defense "inured to the benefit of all the underwriters," though some were not present at the "due diligence meeting." One of the circumstances going to the question of reasonable investigation under the Code is "the type of underwriting arrangement [and] the role of the particular defendant as an underwriter." §1704(g)(6), borrowed in Rule 176(g), supra p. 152. This clause is "designed to permit discrimination, for example, * * * between ordinary and 'technical' underwriters, and between managing underwriters and members of the underwriting group. At the same time, Clause (6) is not intended entirely to relieve conventional underwriters other than managing underwriters of the duty to investigate regardless of obstacles that the issuer may put in the way of their access." 2 Code 714. Underwriters, it has been said, "must play devil's advocate." Feit v. Leasco Data Processing Equipment Corp., 332 F. Supp. 544, 582 (E. D. N. Y. 1971).

[61] In general, see Symposium, Current Problems of Securities Underwriters and Dealers, 18 Bus. Law. 27, 37-42 (1962), with a checklist for underwriters' investigation at 90-91. Of course, the "due diligence" meeting must not be used to whip up the interest of salesmen or there is likely to be a violation of

flux. We have noticed the exacerbation of the general due diligence problem with the trend toward incorporation by reference from 1934 Act filings, as well as the Commission's borrowing of the Code's solution.[62] And new practices will also have to evolve in the light of the new "shelf rule."[63]

Unlike §12, §11 presents no problem of use of the mails or the channels of interstate commerce. Constitutionality is afforded by conditioning registration on the use of those instrumentalities.

It is in its assault on the citadel of privity that §11 marks its greatest departure from precedent. In the first place, §11 increases the number of potential plaintiffs by considerably broadening the common law exception to the extent that it permits the ultimate investor to sue both the issuer and the underwriter notwithstanding a chain of title from issuer to underwriter to dealer to investor, and gives the same right of action even to a buyer in the open market, all without the plaintiff's proving that the misrepresentation was addressed to or intended to influence *him*.[64] In the second place, the section increases the number of potential *defendants* insofar as it covers officers, directors, and experts.

On the latter score the "revolutionary" change that Chief Judge Cardozo (as he then was) referred to in the famous *Ultramares* case[65] has now been "wrought by legislation" as he said it would

---

§5. For this reason, the managing underwriter would be wise to screen attendance so as to limit the audience to underwriters.

[62] See pp. 152-53 supra; Greene, Determining the Responsibility of Underwriters Distributing Securities within an Integrated Disclosure System, 56 Notre Dame Law. 755 (1981); Committee on Federal Regulation of Securities, Am. B. Ass'n, Current Issues and Developments in the Duties and Liabilities of Underwriters and Securities Dealers, 33 Bus. Law. 335, esp. at 350 (1977) (for an approach varying with the circumstances).

[63] Rule 415, supra p. 142. It should be significant in this respect that the Commission has said that a court would not expect the accountant's investigation in connection with a short-form registration of a seasoned company to be the same as would be reasonable in connection with an initial public offering. Sec. Act Rel. 6383, 24 SEC Dock. 1262, 1296 n. 101 (1982).

[64] The open-market buyer, however, must be able to trace his particular securities to the registration statement when it covered additional securities of an outstanding class. This is a nonsensical, but unavoidable, result of a statutory scheme that registers not *classes* but *units* of securities. Barnes v. Osofsky, 373 F. 2d 269 (2d Cir. 1967). The Code achieves the *pro rata* treatment of all holders of the class that the court there considered itself powerless to order. §1704(c); see 2 Code 693, Comment (2).

[65] Ultramares Corp. v. Touche, 255 N. Y. 170, 187, 174 N. E. 441, 447 (1931). The common law has not stood still since. E. g., Haddon View Investment Co. v. Coopers & Lybrand, 70 Ohio St. 2d 154, 436 N. E. 2d 212 (1982); see Fiflis, Current Problems of Accountants' Responsibilities to Third Parties, 28 Vand. L. Rev. 31, esp. at 102-13 (1975). "Is the 'public' in 'public accountant,' " he asks, 'still akin to the 'public' in 'public stenographer'?" Id. at 105.

have to be. Section 11 goes as far in protecting purchasers of securities as the New York Court of Appeals there refused to go at common law in protecting creditors who had relied on a certified balance sheet negligently prepared by accountants for an insolvent borrower. Indeed, it goes further in putting the burden on the accountant (or other expert) to show affirmatively that he made a reasonable investigation and had reasonable ground to believe and did believe that the "expertized" statements were true and that there was no omission of a material fact.

Section 11 had originally referred to damages, without definition, as a substitute for rescission. Obviously, in that context, it meant what it does today in §12: the difference between purchase price and resale price (with interest) less any income or return of capital received by the buyer on the security. As amended in 1934, however, §11(e) incorporates a modified "tort measure" of damages — in the main, purchase price less value at the time of *suit* rather than *delivery*. Section 11(g) limits the amount that may be recovered to the price at which the security was offered to the public;[66] this primarily limits the plaintiff who purchased in the open market rather than in the course of the distribution. When the security has been disposed of in the open market before suit, the measure of damages is purchase price less resale price (with no mention of interest or of deducting income received on the security as in §12). If the market goes up *pending suit* and the security is disposed of before judgment, the defendant gets the benefit of the increase over the value at the time of suit; but, if the market goes *down* and the security is disposed of pending suit, the plaintiff still gets only the difference between the purchase price and the value at the time of suit. In other words, it is to the plaintiff's advantage not to hold the security after filing suit if he wants to be sure of being made whole.[67]

---

[66] See also §§11(e), 1st parenthetical clause.

[67] An underwriter who does not receive preferential treatment over other underwriters has his aggregate liability limited, so far as all suits brought against him under §11 are concerned, to the total offering price of that part of the issue underwritten by him and actually distributed; otherwise, at least in theory, the aggregate liability is unlimited, since an indefinite number of successive purchasers can recover their trading losses (limited only by the provision that the plaintiff's purchase price cannot exceed the public offering price of the security) unless the defendant proves that they were not due to the misstatement or omission complained of. On the other hand, since the preferential treatment must come "from the issuer" under §11(e) in order for the underwriter to be liable *in solido,* the clause is routinely evaded by having the managing underwriter's extra fee come from the members of the underwriting group. For that reason, and because extending the preferential language to cover that practice would create a severe problem under the capital

d. Litigation History

The 30,000 registration statements filed during the first thirty-five years of the SEC's history resulted in two adjudicated recoveries together with six reported decisions approving settlements of class actions.[68] The first substantial recovery did not come until 1963, in *Cherner v. Transitron Electronic Corp.*, and that case taxed the resources of the judicial process.[69] An allegation that the registration statement falsely disavowed any patent claims resulted in a pretrial settlement of $5.3 million, which was approved in January 1963. The court appointed a special master, together with an electronic data processing corporation as assistant special master, and the court was not able to approve the master's final report until November 1965 and to discharge him finally until October 1968. More than 33,000 claims were approved by the master, for total "recognized losses" of $42.7 million within the meaning of the settlement agreement. The settlement fund, which had been paid in Treasury bills, earned income of about $330,000, which more than paid the total counsel fees of some $275,000. But total administration costs came to some $860,000, leaving just under $4.5 million for distribution. Ultimately claimants got 10.51 percent of their recognized losses. A total of 1777 claims were disapproved, including 143 after hearing.[70]

In terms of leading cases that went to judgment on the merits, *Cherner* was followed by *Escott v. BarChris Construction Co.* in

---

rules, the clause in question is deleted in the Code. See 2 Code 730, comment.

This clause was one reason for the transition from joint to several underwriting. Assume an issue offered to the public for $1 million and underwritten equally by ten firms. The value of the securities has declined by $500,000 by the time a misstatement is discovered in the registration statement. If the underwriting was joint, each firm is liable for the entire $500,000, subject to its right of contribution (see p. 1198 infra). If the underwriting was several, on the other hand, each firm's initial liability is only $100,000, which is the amount of his underwriting participation. Note, however, that even when the underwriting is several each firm's maximum liability initially is not merely 10 percent of the *total liability* or $50,000. It will work out that way after contribution if all the underwriters are sufficiently solvent, but initially each firm is liable up to $100,000 to any one or more plaintiffs, whether or not they can trace title back to that firm.

For a good analysis of the measure of damages, see Feit v. Leasco Data Processing Equipment Corp., 332 F. Supp. 544, 584-88 (E. D. N. Y. 1971). On indemnification and contribution, see p. 1198 infra.

[68] 6 Loss 3826.

[69] 221 F. Supp. 48 (D. Mass. 1963).

[70] Id., Civ. No. 61-857-W, Report of Special Master with Respect to Proposed Final Distribution, D. Mass., Oct. 1, 1965; see Transitron: One for the Books, 67 Fortune 191 (Mar. 1963).

1968,[71] the first considered opinion on the several defenses, and *Feit v. Leasco Data Processing Equipment Corp.* in 1971.[72] The two opinions (54 and 39 pages, respectively) are far too long, and properly too detailed, to be set out here. But both cases have been so liberally cited in the footnotes that what has already been said, together with what is about to follow, should suffice here.

In *BarChris* Judge McLean concluded that the defense had not been established by any of the defendants: the chief executive officer, the president, the vice president, the treasurer and chief financial officer, the controller, a young lawyer who had become secretary and a director, two outside directors, a lawyer-director who had prepared the registration statement, the underwriters, and the accountants. [73]

In the process, the court held that the liability of *officers* and *directors* did not depend on whether or not they had read the registration statement or, if they had, whether or not in view of their very limited education they had understood what they had read; that an officer who must have known that the registration statement was untrue in part "was not entitled to sit back and place the blame on the lawyers for not advising him about it";[74] that §11 imposed liability in the first instance on a director, no matter how new he was, so that his general reliance on the assurance of the principal officers in answer to his general inquiries in the nature of a credit check did not establish the defense of reasonable diligence; that the issuer's lawyer, though sued as a director rather than for malpractice in his professional capacity, nevertheless had to establish more in the way of reasonable investigation than could fairly be expected of a director who had had no connection with the writing of the registration statement; and that, although this did not require the lawyer-director to make an independent audit of the figures supplied to him by his client, it was not unreasonable to require him to check matters easily verifiable by way of testing oral information against the original written record.

With respect to the *underwriter* defendants, the court held that they were just as responsible for false statements as the company so far as the Securities Act was concerned, particularly because prospective investors rely on the reputation of the underwriters; that, consequently, it was no more sufficient than in the case of the

---

[71] 283 F. Supp. 643 (S. D. N. Y. 1968).
[72] 332 F. Supp. 544 (E. D. N. Y. 1971).
[73] With respect to the accountants, see n. 52 supra.
[74] 283 F. Supp. at 685.

lawyer who had prepared the registration statement merely to ask questions, to obtain answers that would be thought satisfactory if true, and to let it go at that, without seeking to ascertain from the records whether the answers were in fact true and complete; that, even if it were assumed *arguendo* that a *director* might rely on information furnished to him by the officers without independently verifying it, the *underwriters* could not be so trusting with respect to information received from the issuer's officers, whose position was in a sense adverse to their own; that otherwise the inclusion of underwriters in §11 would afford investors no additional protection; that the underwriters must "make some reasonable attempt to verify the data submitted to them" instead of relying solely on the issuer's officers or counsel; and that the principal underwriter was bound by its own counsel's failure to make a reasonable investigation.[75]

The surprising thing about *BarChris* — where just about everything that could go wrong did go wrong with a bowling alley manufacturer after the bowling bubble had deflated — is the very surprise on the part of elements of the securities Bar at discovering that §11 meant what Congress had said thirty-five years before. More than a thousand lawyers, accountants and investment bankers flocked from all over the country to the Waldorf-Astoria in New York, which had to turn even more away for lack of space, to attend a two-day "National Institute" on the *BarChris* case sponsored by the American Bar Association's Section of Corporation, Banking and Business Law.[76] The present writer was hard put to it to find words of wisdom to utter as the keynote speaker:[77]

> I don't find anything new in the opinion, in principle. Let me run through it quickly.
>
> We are told at page 40 that a prospectus can be literally true and yet false by implication. Well, there is nothing new about that. That's true even in common law deceit.
>
> Then a few pages later, around page 43, there is some talk about what "material" means. I shall have a little more to say about that a little later, but I do want to point out, by way of negativing some of the shockwaves from this opinion, that the judge made almost as many negative findings as he did affirmative findings on what was material in the particular case.
>
> At page 47 we learn that we cannot "expertise," if I may use a bastard word, the whole registration statement. Certainly we

[75] Id. at 692-97.
[76] 24 Bus. Law. 523 (1969).
[77] Loss, The Opinion, 24 Bus. Law. 527 (1969).

lawyers ought to breathe a sigh of relief about that, because you know who would be the "experts."

We then read something about the defenses that are applicable to the signers of the registration statement and the directors, and we are told that they must investigate. We are told that they must not rely blindly on others. In the case of the president and the executive vice president and the vice president in this case, and the treasurer and the comptroller, it seems to me a plaintiff could not have wanted a case that was more open and shut on the facts as they were painted by the judge. Anyway, these are findings of fact on a very long record, so I see nothing startling in those pages.

At page 52 there are some references to the young lawyer who was house counsel. Well, he found himself in a tough position. I might say I have often doubted the wisdom of law firms' making young lawyers secretaries, or assistant secretaries, of corporate clients.

Then we have some learning at pages 53 to 56 about the outside directors who were held liable. There the court goes all the way back to an English opinion, *Adams* v. *Thrift,* [1915] 1 Ch. 557, *aff'd,* [1915] 2 Ch. 21, which held that a director who knew nothing about the prospectus and who had not even read it, but who had simply relied on the statement of the managing director that it was "all right," was liable for its untrue statements.

Next we are told at page 66 that the underwriter is just as liable as the issuer, subject to the underwriter's statutory defense, and that the underwriter can no more rely solely on the issuer's officers and counsel than can the outside directors. Surely, there is nothing new in that, as a matter of principle, to anybody who has ever looked at Section 11.

As far as accountants are concerned, I agree entirely with what Mr. Sommers says in his outline, that virtually all the instances of lack of due diligence that the court found involved simple mistake rather than errors in judgment. And, anyway, here again there were findings both ways, findings of fact on a very long record.

We are told at page 77 that, so far as the S-1 review is concerned, the accountant must not disregard danger signals. Again, there is nothing startling there.

To back up a few pages to around 56 — the case of Mr. Grant, the lawyer who was a director and who did most of the work on the registration statement — that case is to me a bit stickier. But first I must emphasize, as the court did, that he was not liable as a lawyer. He was held liable as a director. I find it hard to quarrel with the holding at page 57 that, so far as the non-expertised portion of the registration statement is concerned, the director who is a lawyer and who did most of the work on the registration statement has a somewhat greater burden by way of establishing his defense than the other directors. * * * To me it is one of the most interesting aspects in the case, perhaps because it strikes closest to home.

Here again, I have often wondered, I must say, why it is that lawyers are so anxious to be directors. It has always seemed to me that there are many reasons why a lawyer should not want to be a director. Surely as general counsel he can attend the board meetings without being a director. Insofar as he is a director, he has to some extent a fool for a client — he becomes that much more emotionally attached to his client — and it may just possibly be that this case will persuade some lawyers that it is the better part of valor not to become a director of a corporate client. If this gentleman had not been a director, any liability he might have had would have been purely of the common law variety for malpractice. It would not have been a Section 11 liability at all. It is, of course, a matter of taste; I don't suggest remotely that there is anything unprofessional about a lawyer's being a director.

Be that as it may — again I must acknowledge that I haven't read the record, and we must bear in mind that this case has not been appealed but, I take it, has been settled — surely every experienced lawyer knows how essential it is to cross-examine his own witnesses severely, quite apart from the SEC field. *A fortiori* that is true in the context of Section 11. And, although it is easy to be a Monday morning quarterback, a lawyer hardly makes a reasonable investigation, whether he is acting for the issuer or for the underwriter, if he doesn't read the basic agreements, like the factoring agreement in this case, or if he doesn't follow up on absent minutes, as the court found was not done in this case. So, here again, I see nothing in principle to be excited about.

In general, I simply don't see anything to quarrel with as a matter of principle. The press and a good part of the Bar in this country tend not infrequently to discover profound truths a few decades after they have been writ large in our statute book. It has been thirty-five years since Congress determined in this country that directors are supposed to direct so far as registration statements are concerned. What would have been really surprising, I suggest to you, would have been a contrary decision. It is a little bit like imagining the consequences of the Supreme Court's having decided *Brown* v. *Board of Education* the *other* way ten years ago.

We must remember that the basic philosophy of the '33 and '34 Acts — I emphasize the word "philosophy" — is that as nearly as possible everybody should be on a par in trading in a security. We know that it is not possible, but that is the guiding spirit of this legislation. * * *

You may quarrel, if you like, with that philosophy. But there is no doubt that that is the philosophy of the statute. So I suggest to you, gentlemen, that the real question in the case and the *raison d'être* of this institute are not questions of principle. They are practical questions: What do you do as counsel for the company, as counsel for the underwriter, as counsel for the accountants, and so on, in the light of this opinion and in the light of Section 11 generally?

Since on that score I would defer to most of the people in this room, let me now take the broader look that I earlier said I would like to take and get away from the opinion as such, which others are going to discuss for the next two days.

First, though, I do want to negative any suggestion that the opinion answers all the legal questions under Section 11 — and I don't think one can fairly criticize the court for not answering questions that in the context of the case simply were not raised.

One question that one could speculate about is this: Does the court's treatment of the lawyer-director indicate that perhaps inside directors generally will be held to a higher standard under Section 11 than outside directors? Section 11 makes no distinction between one director and another. But I suppose that, if the director who happens as a lawyer to prepare the registration statement is held to a higher standard of care (or, rather, is given a tougher defense to have to prove) than the other directors and if you have a large board, and three non-lawyer members are delegated to be primarily responsible for working with counsel, who is not himself a director, one could argue (I am not saying that it is right, but one could argue) that those three directors are held to a higher standard because they were delegated the primary responsibility for working with counsel who was preparing the registration.

We all know what the contrary argument would be. It would be based on the fact that Section 11 doesn't distinguish between one director and another. That would have been the argument, I suppose, if *BarChris* had gone up on appeal.

Nevertheless, if *BarChris* is right, I suggest that perhaps there are distinctions between inside directors and outside directors. I suppose, on the same assumption, it might be argued that the ordinary director is entitled to rely more on outside counsel than on one who is himself a director. If that is so, it may be not only that the lawyer himself, in the light of *BarChris*, will now have an extra motivation not to go on the board, but also that the other directors will prefer to have registrations prepared by lawyers who are not themselves directors, so that, if they are sued, they will be able to say, "Well, we didn't rely on a fellow director. We relied on a lawyer. This is a complicated matter. And what would you have us do, particularly those of us who are outside directors? What are we supposed to do?"

Indeed, what *should* an outside director do? I have heard

some people criticize *BarChris* for not telling us what an outsider should have to do. Well, it doesn't tell us. But, of course, all the court had to decide in this particular case was that what the directors did was not enough. We don't know what would be enough in another case.

Well, there are many other questions that one could talk about. But to me the really surprising thing about *BarChris* is that it took so long for it to come along — that it took so long generally for Section 11 to get off the ground. * * *

So far as the *Feit* case is concerned — a case that grew out of an exchange tender offer for the stock of an insurance company without adequate disclosure in the registration statement of the substantial possibility of the issuer's gaining control of some $100 million of assets not required for operating the target company — perhaps Judge Weinstein's scholarly opinion will be best remembered for teaching non-insurance lawyers the meaning of "surplus surplus": that "portion of surplus not required in insurance operations."[78]

F.　VOIDABILITY PROVISIONS

Is violation of one of the statutes or rules a defense to an action by the violator on the contract? We have already met this question under the blue sky laws.[1] At least when the defendant himself could bring a rescission action on any basis, there should be little doubt of an affirmative answer under §29(b) of the Exchange Act and its counterparts in the Holding Company, Investment Company, and Investment Advisers Acts. Those sections provide — subject to the apparently congenital disability in these closely related statutes to draft any two comparable provisions quite the same — that every contract made in violation of the statute or any rule thereunder, as well as every contract whose performance would involve such a violation, is "void" as regards the rights of (1) any violator and (2) any person, not a party to the contract, who acquires any right thereunder with actual knowledge of the facts resulting in the violation.[2]

[78]Feit v. Leasco Data Processing Equipment Corp., 332 F. Supp. 544, 550 (E. D. N. Y. 1971).

C. 10F　[1]See pp. 1013-14 supra.
[2]Holding Co. Act §26(b); Inv. Co. Act §47(b); Inv. Adv. Act §215(b); see Goldenberg v. Bache & Co., 270 F. 2d 675, 681 (5th Cir. 1959); but cf. Cameron v. Outdoor Resorts of America, Inc., 608 F. 2d 187, 195 (5th Cir. 1979), *modified on other grounds*, 611 F. 2d 105 (5th Cir. 1980) (assignee of investment contract who had taken from the seller in good faith and without knowledge

Indeed, this should be so even under the Securities Act, which contains no provision comparable to §29(b) of the Exchange Act. There would be little point in giving the seller an action on his contract only to have the buyer put things *in statu quo ante* by counterclaiming or bringing his own action under §11 or §12.[3] And, as is generally held under the blue sky laws,[4] expiration of the statute of limitations for an action by the buyer should not be a bar to his asserting the violation defensively.[5]

It by no means follows, however, that *all* contracts involving a violation of these statutes (at least the Securities Act) are unenforceable. The Supreme Court spoke to this point in *A. C. Frost & Co. v. Coeur d'Alene Mines Corp.*, decided in 1941.[6] But the case did not involve an attempt to enforce an illegal sale contract against a reluctant buyer. Quite the contrary, an underwriter's assignee sued an issuer for breach of an option contract on treasury shares given by the issuer to the plaintiff's assignor. After some of the optioned shares had been sold by the issuer for the plaintiff's account (as authorized by a modification of the contract), the issuer repudiated the contract because the shares had not been registered. Reversing the Idaho court, the Supreme Court stated through Justice McReynolds:

> No provision of the Act declares that in the absence of registration, contracts in contemplation of or having relation to a public offering shall be void. * * *
>
> Although the challenged contract bears no evidence of criminality and is fair upon its face, we are asked to apply a sanction beyond that specified [in §12(1)] by declaring it null and void because of relationship to a public offering. The basis for this demand is a supposed federal public policy which requires such annulment in order to secure observance, effectuate the legislative purpose and prevent noxious consequences.
>
> Courts have often added a sanction to those prescribed for an

---

of Rule 10b-5 violation could foreclose on buyers' defaulted mortgage notes). The Investment Company Act was amended in 1980 to go over to the Code model (§1722(c)) in terms of which course "would produce a more equitable result."

[3] See Garfield v. Strain, 320 F. 2d 116, 119 (10th Cir. 1963).

[4] Mechanics Loan & Savings Co. v. Mathers, 185 Ga. 501, 195 S. E. 429 (1938); Midwest Management Corp. v. Stephens, 291 N. W. 2d 896, 905-06 (Iowa 1980); Zehring v. Foster, 184 Kan. 599, 399 P. 2d 331 (1959).

[5] Cf. United States v. Western Pacific R. R. Co., 352 U. S. 59, 72-73 (1956). A contrary argument might be based on the federal rule (see p. 1166 infra) that, when the very statute that creates the cause of action also contains a limitation period, the statute of limitations not only bars the remedy but also destroys the liability. See Lamb v. Young, 250 Ore. 228, 441 P. 2d 616 (1968) (blue sky law).

[6] 312 U. S. 38 (1941).

offense created by statute where the circumstances fairly indicated this would further the essential purpose of the enactment; but we think where the contrary definitely appears — actual hindrance indeed of that purpose — no such addition is permissible. The latter situation is beyond the reason which supports the doctrine now relied upon.

Here the clear legislative purpose was protection of innocent purchasers of securities. They are given definite remedies inconsistent with the idea that every contract having relation to sales of unregistered shares is absolutely void; and to accept the conclusion reached by the supreme court below would probably seriously hinder rather than aid the real purpose of the statute.

*   *   *

The rule that contracts in contravention of public policy are not enforceable came under discussion in *Steele* v. *Drummond,* 275 U. S. 199 and *Twin City Co.* v. *Harding Glass Co.,* 283 U. S. 353, 356, 357. In the latter the opinion declares, the principle "should be applied with caution and only in cases plainly within the reasons on which that doctrine rests. It is only because of the dominant public interest that one who, like respondent, has had the benefit of performance by the other party will be permitted to avoid his own promise."

The protean basis underlying this doctrine has often been stated thus — No one can lawfully do that which tends to injure the public or is detrimental to the public good. If it definitely appears that enforcement of a contract will not be followed by injurious results, generally, at least, what the parties have agreed to ought not to be struck down.[7]

If this is a hard case that made bad law, the Commission must share the blame. For it advocated the result reached, and Justice McReynolds quoted from its brief as *amicus curiae:*

It is obvious that the purposes of the Act would be defeated by any judicial doctrine which prevented the issuing corporation from recovering from the underwriter, and putting to the intended use in its business, the money invested by the public in the issuer. And it would be anomalous to rest such an injury to the investors upon the fact that the transactions in which the securities were distributed violated the Act, which was designed to

---

[7] Id. at 41-44 (1941); see also Judson v. Buckley, 130 F. 2d 174, 179-80 (2d Cir. 1942), *cert. denied,* 317 U. S. 679; Wood v. Reznik, 248 F. 2d 549, 552 (7th Cir. 1957) (recovery of broker's commission for effecting an illegal sale); Fuller v. Dilbert, 244 F. Supp. 196, 213-14 (S. D. N. Y. 1965), *aff'd per curiam* sub nom. Righter v. Dilbert, 358 F. 2d 305 (2d Cir. 1966); cf. Mathers Fund, Inc. v. Colwell Co., 564 F. 2d 780 (7th Cir. 1977).

protect those investors. Compare Sections 11 and 12 which, by implication, permit a purchaser to affirm a sale in violation of the Act. It can scarcely be assumed that any court would render such an unfortunate decision. Yet this would be the logical consequence of applying literally the broad language used by the Supreme Court of Idaho in stating the proposition that the courts will not lend their aid to the parties to a contract that is prohibited by law or is against public policy.

It appears to us to be entirely immaterial whether in such a case, the agreement is labelled "void" or the parties are held to be "in pari delicto." There, labels, as often is the case, merely state the conclusion reached, but do not aid in solution of the problem. The ultimate issue is whether the result in the particular case would effectuate or frustrate the purposes of the Act.[8]

The Commission showed insufficient faith in the Supreme Court's ability to distinguish when necessary in subsequent cases. The result reached in the *Frost* case was hardly required in order to protect future issuers against doublecrossing underwriters in the hypothetical situation posed by the Commission. Indeed, enforcement of the contract would not be essential in order to avoid doing violence to the public interest even in the Commission's hypothetical case; for the buyers would clearly have an action against the underwriter under §12(2), and probably nonstatutory remedies as well. One cannot quarrel with the Court's rejection of a formalistic determination whether to enforce contracts made in violation of the act. But, granted that there should be an inquiry in each case to decide whether enforcement or nonenforcement of the contract would better promote the purposes of the statute, why encourage violations by enforcing illegal contracts between two guilty parties when no public interest is involved? Only a year after the *Frost* case the Commission again filed a brief as *amicus curiae* in which it stated that on the facts of the *Frost* case it would recommend nonenforcement.[9]

The question did not arise again until 1952, when the Second Circuit decided *Kaiser-Frazer Corp.* v. *Otis & Co.* This was an issuer's action for breach of an underwriting agreement. Agreeing with the underwriter's defense that the registration statement contained false and misleading statements, the court held that the contract was illegal and unenforceable. "We cannot blind ourselves," Judge Clark said, "to the fact that the sale of this stock by

---

[8] A. C. Frost & Co. v. Coeur d'Alene Mines Corp., 312 U. S. 38, 43 n. 2 (1941).

[9] Judson v. Buckley, 130 F. 2d 174, 179-80 (2d Cir. 1942), *cert. denied*, 317 U. S. 679.

Kaiser-Frazer, though, insofar as the particular contract was concerned, [it] was a sale only to the underwriters, was but the initial step in the public offering of the securities which would necessarily follow. The prospectus, which has been found to have been misleading, formed an integral part of the contract and the public sale of the stock by the underwriter was to be made and could only have been made in reliance on that prospectus."[10]

The court's conclusion seems unexceptionable enough if the materiality of the misstatement is assumed. Indeed, since it was a condition of the contract that the registration statement be accurate, the court did not have to reach the question of illegality except in determining compliance with the condition. But the failure to mention the *Frost* case, together with the Supreme Court's denial of *certiorari* notwithstanding the argument in the petition directed to the *Frost* case, leaves the law here in something less than a satisfactory state. It is understood, for example, that, for a while at least after the *Kaiser-Frazer* opinion, some law firms qualified their opinions to their underwriting clients with respect to the enforceability of the usual indemnity and warranty clauses against the issuer. Their fear was that, when an underwriter had been held accountable in damages to a purchaser under §11 because of his failure to sustain the burden of proof under that section, his rights under those clauses might not be recognized if it were shown later that the registration statement contained a material misstatement or omitted to state a material fact, even though the underwriter had completed the distribution and paid for the securities in full and there was no evidence of his having joined with the issuer in intentionally or knowingly perpetrating the misrepresentation.

The *Kaiser-Frazer* case seems distinguishable in this context under the doctrine that a lawful bargain is not invalidated by a collateral or remote bargain or act that is illegal.[11] This is an area of the law in which so much depends on the public policy underlying the particular statute, as well as the question of who is suing whom for what, that generalization from holdings in other statutory contexts is risky. With that caveat, however, it is worth pointing out that the Supreme Court seems to have followed the "remote act" doctrine under the antitrust laws:

> As a defense to an action based on contract, the plea of illegality based on violation of the Sherman Act has not met with

[10] 195 F. 2d 838, 844 (2d Cir. 1952), *cert. denied*, 344 U. S. 856.
[11] 6 Corbin, Contracts (1951) §1529; Restatement (Second) of Contracts §184.

much favor in this Court. This has been notably the case where the plea has been made by a purchaser in an action to recover from him the agreed price of goods sold. * * *

* * *

* * * Past the point where the judgment of the Court would itself be enforcing the precise conduct made unlawful by the Act, the courts are to be guided by the overriding general policy, as Mr. Justice Holmes put it, "of preventing people from getting other people's property for nothing when they purport to be buying it."[12]

One may hazard the guess that, when a seller sues a buyer for breach of an executory contract whose enforcement would violate §5 or §17 of the Securities Act, *Kaiser-Frazer* rather than *Frost* will carry the day.[13] On the other hand, when the seller has already delivered the securities in violation of §5, or after a sale that violates §5 or §17(a), the court may be expected to be somewhat concerned about the general policy that was so pungently expressed by Justice Holmes.[14]

In this state of affairs, the Code conditions enforceability, as well as denial of rescission of a consummated contract, on a showing that such action "would produce a more equitable result" and "would not be inconsistent with the purposes of" the Code.[15]

One proposition that is quite clear is that, although state law governs in general the rights and duties of sellers and purchasers of goods, "the effect of illegality under a federal statute is a matter of federal law * * * even in diversity actions in the federal courts after" *Erie.*[16]

---

[12] Kelly v. Kosuga, 358 U. S. 516, 518, 520-21 (1959), quoting from dissenting opinion in Continental Wall Paper Co. v. Louis Voigt & Sons Co., 212 U. S. 227, 271 (1909); see also Lyons v. Westinghouse Electric Corp., 222 F. 2d 184, 187-88 (2d Cir. 1955), *cert. denied* sub nom. Walsh v. Lyons, 350 U. S. 825.

[13] See General Life of Mo. Investment Co. v. Shamburger, 546 F. 2d 774, 783-85 (8th Cir. 1976); Byrnes v. Faulkner, Dawkins & Sullivan, 550 F. 2d 1303, 1313 (2d Cir. 1977).

[14] Cf. Bankers Life & Casualty Co. v. Bellanca Corp., 288 F. 2d 784 (7th Cir. 1961), *cert. denied,* 368 U. S. 827; Goldman v. Bank of the Commonwealth, 467 F. 2d 439, 447 (6th Cir. 1972); Occidental Life Ins. Co. of N. C. v. Pat Ryan & Associates, Inc., 496 F. 2d 1255, 1266-67 (4th Cir. 1974), *cert. denied,* 419 U. S. 1023.

[15] §1722(c).

[16] Kelly v. Kosuga, 358 U. S. 516, 519 (1959) (antitrust case); General Life of Mo. Investment Co. v. Shamburger, 546 F. 2d 774, 783 n. 15 (8th Cir. 1976). *Contra:* Bankers Life & Casualty Co. v. Bellanca Corp., 288 F. 2d 784 (7th Cir. 1961), *cert. denied,* 368 U. S. 827.

G. MISCELLANEOUS STATUTORY LIABILITIES

First: The voidability provisions in all six Acts except those of 1933 and 1939 have their offensive as well as their defensive side, in that they are one of the bases of the implied liabilities that we discuss in the next subchapter. In that sense implied actions are really semi-express.

Second: We have already examined the provisions on recapture of short-term trading in §16(b) of the 1934 Act together with §17(b) of the 1935 Act and §30(f) of the Investment Company Act.[1]

Third: Under §9(e) of the 1934 Act any person "who willfully participates in any act or transaction" in violation of the remainder of §9, the manipulation section,[2] is liable "to any person who shall purchase or sell any security at a price which was affected by such act or transaction" for "the damages sustained as a result of any such act or transaction." There is a contribution provision comparable to that in §11(f) of the 1933 Act,[3] except that it is not expressly limited to situations where the plaintiff in contribution was not guilty of fraud and the defendant in contribution was.

It is small wonder that §9(e) has been a dead letter so far as producing recoveries is concerned. For, aside from its ignoring privity of contract between plaintiff and defendant as does §11 of the 1933 Act, it is no bargain:

(1) Although §9(e), apart from some of the substantive provisions in §9(a)-(d), does not require proof of scienter and does not specifically refer to "reliance," it does not shift the burden on causation to the defendant as §11(e) does. Quite the contrary, §9(e) contains a causation requirement that may be stricter than the burden the plaintiff would face in a common law deceit action based on the defendant's manipulation:[4] It is not only that damages are limited to those "sustained as a result" of the manipulation; the plaintiff must also show that he bought or sold "at a price which was affected by" the manipulation. Presumably this language does not import anything analogous to the "comparative negligence" rule. In other words, once the plaintiff shows that he has bought or sold "at a price which was affected by" the illegal activity, it is at least arguable that the damages he has "sustained as a result" of that activity do not have to be prorated according to the extent to which the price was affected by that activity as

C. 11G   [1] See p. 606 supra.
    [2] See p. 990 supra.
    [3] See p. 1198 supra.
    [4] On manipulation at common law, see pp. 984-89 supra.

distinct from the extent to which it may have been affected by ordinary market movements — a fanciful subject for speculation at best. But even this is by no means certain. And except in the cruder cases of manipulation — which are not apt to recur as long as the SEC walks its beat — it may be no mean trick to demonstrate, in addition to the *fact* of the wash sales or other illegal activity, that that activity affected the price at which the plaintiff bought or sold. With all the factors that determine stock market prices, the plaintiff will be particularly hard put to sustain this burden if he bought or sold some months after the manipulation complained of, when its lingering effects may have become intermingled with many other market determinants.

(2) Apart from this double-barreled problem of causation, the plaintiff must prove also that the defendant "willfully" participated in the manipulation. Ordinarily, on the assumption that there is any proof that the defendant participated at all in the manipulation, this requirement should not cause much trouble in view of the loose way the courts have interpreted "willfully" even in criminal cases and in broker-dealer revocation proceedings under the 1934 Act.[5] But it is some indication of the legislative approach to §9(e) that it is the only civil liability provision in any of the six statutes that contains the "willfully" requirement.

(3) The only apparent advantage that §9(e) offers in comparison with §§11 and 12(2) of the Securities Act — aside from the privity requirement in §12(2) — is that there is no express reference to the plaintiff's knowledge of the manipulation. Because actual cases if they ever arise will most likely present infinite factual variations, there is not much point in speculating whether this apparent advantage is a thing of substance.

(4) There is no measure of damages specified in §9(e), or anywhere else in the 1934 Act, and the question has not yet been litigated. Presumably the answer will be found in the "tort measure" traditionally favored by the federal courts.[6]

---

[5] See p. 699 n. 55 supra.

[6] A few of the cases under §9(e) are worth mention.

In Rosenberg v. Hano, 121 F. 2d 818 (3d Cir. 1941), the plaintiff was an elderly and semi-retired lawyer who spent some of his leisure time in the customers' room of the defendant brokerage firm. On the representation, allegedly, of a customers' man that a certain whiskey stock was going to advance 15 points as the result of a deal made with the editor of a tipster sheet, the plaintiff bought 100 shares. When the stock declined, as the court put it, "our 'investor' fled for protection and restitution to the legislation designed, as he thought, for such as he." "In his eagerness," the court added, "he does not seem to have given much thought to either its philosophy or its terms."

The Code's successor to §9(e), among other reforms, applies the "price affected by the violation" requirement only if the plaintiff bought or sold "more than thirty days after the date of the last act constituting part of the violation" (which seems fair enough), and contains a measure of damages that treats causation as a *pro rata* defense along the lines of §11(e).[7]

Fourth: Section 18 of the 1934 Act (together with its satellites in §16(a) of the 1935 Act and §323(a) of the 1939 Act) is a very much attenuated §11. It imposes liability on any person who makes or causes to be made in any application or report or document filed under the 1934 Act or any rule under that Act — and there are many such papers — any statement that "was at the time and in the light of the circumstances under which it was made false or misleading with respect to any material fact."[8] The Second Circuit has construed this section as applicable to any document filed with a national securities exchange, even though it is not filed also with the Commission.[9] There is the same double-barreled causation requirement as in §9(e): the liability runs to anyone who buys or sells "at a price which was affected by such statement" and it is for "damages caused by" reliance on the statement.[10] For

---

Id. at 819. The court held that the plaintiff's remedy, if any, was under §12(2) of the 1933 Act, as to which the statute of limitations had run.

In Fischman v. Raytheon Mfg. Co., 188 F. 2d 783, 788 (2d Cir. 1951), the court held that common stockholders, whose cause of action under §11 of the 1933 Act had been dismissed because the registration statement on which they claimed to have relied covered only the issuer's preferred stock, should be permitted to amend (if they could) by alleging facts showing that the defendants had deliberately used the registration statement for the purpose of fraudulently inducing the purchase of common stock sold by the defendants, in violation of §9(a)(4) of the 1934 Act.

In In re Penn Central Securities Litigation, 347 F. Supp. 1327, 1343 (E. D. Pa. 1972), *modified on other grounds*, 357 F. Supp. 869 (E. D. Pa. 1973), *aff'd on other grounds*, 494 F. 2d 528 (3d Cir. 1974), the court held that the plaintiff must be a buyer or seller, not a mere holder.

In Crane Co. v. American Standard, Inc., 603 F. 2d 244, 251-53 (2d Cir. 1979), the court held that a tender offeror's claim for loss of an opportunity to control the target was not within the scope of §9(e), since the price at which offeror's stock in the target was sold was not "affected by the alleged manipulation."

[7] §1710.

[8] A specific reference to omissions in this section was removed in conference "as surplusage in view of the fact that a statement obviously may be misleading because of a material omission." H. R. Rep. No. 1838, 73d Cong., 2d Sess. (1934) 36; cf. id. at 32 (§9(a)(4)).

[9] Fischman v. Raytheon Mfg. Co., 188 F. 2d 783, 788 (2d Cir. 1951), supra n. 6. The court held that the plaintiffs should be permitted to amend so as to allege (if they could) that the registration statement or prospectus had been filed with a national securities exchange, in which event §18(a) would apply.

[10] See Hoover v. Allen, 241 F. Supp. 213, 223-25 (S. D. N. Y. 1965).

good measure, there is a specific reliance requirement, together with a requirement that the plaintiff not know the statement is false or misleading when he buys or sells; and there is not even a provision, as in §11 of the 1933 Act, that reliance may be established without proof of the plaintiff's reading of the particular document. The capstone is a provision letting the defendant off if he proves "that he acted in good faith and had no knowledge that such statement was false or misleading." Aside from the shift in the burden of proof to the defendant, this seems to be first cousin to scienter. And there is a contribution provision as in §9(e).

Except for avoiding any question that the person making the false statement or causing it to be made can be sued by the buyer or seller notwithstanding the absence of privity between them, it is hard to see what advantage §18 gives the investor that he does not have in common law deceit, where (if he has a right of action at all) he might at least be able to avoid proving, under traditional concepts of causation and reliance, that he had bought or sold at a price affected by the false statement. At common law, whether a particular document filed with a government agency is intended for the public at large is a question of construction of the particular statute.[11]

The Code, after a section on false registration statements and offering statements that reflects §11, blends §18 and aspects of the jurisprudence under Rule 10b-5 into a section on civil liability for other false filings.[12]

---

[11] Restatement (Second) of Torts §536.

[12] §§1704-05, infra pp. 1151-52. For the sake of completeness:

Section 305(d) of the 1939 Act makes §§11 and 12 of the 1933 Act and §323 of the 1939 Act itself (the provision modeled on §18 of the 1934 Act) inapplicable to "statements in or omissions from any analysis" of indenture provisions required by the 1939 Act. Section 309(d) of the 1939 Act withholds liability on the part of a trustee under a qualified indenture on account of its failure to comply with the statute. See also Trust Ind. Act §305(a), last sentence.

There are also two fidelity bond rules: for registered management investment companies against larceny and embezzlement by officers and employees with access to securities or funds (Inv. Co. Act Rule 17g-1), and for "SECO" broker-dealers who are members of the Securities Investor Protection Corporation and have employees (Sec. Ex. Act Rule 15b10-11).

Finally, §33 of the Investment Company Act requires that, whenever certain actions have been settled with court approval or final judgment has been entered on the merits, every registered investment company that was a party to the action, as well as every "affiliated person" who was a defendant, shall within thirty days transmit copies of the record to the Commission for its use in connection with any report or study that it may make of lawsuits of investment companies or companies generally.

Fifth: Lurking in the wings — and perhaps panting with antici-pation of a career to rival Rule 10b-5's — is "RICO" (the chapter of the Criminal Code on Racketeer Influenced and Corrupt Or-ganizations), whose criminal aspect has already been noticed.[13] Any person who proves injury "in his business or property" by reason of a violation may obtain treble damages and costs (includ-ing a reasonable attorney's fee).[14] And the District Courts may enter divestiture orders, dissolve or reorganize an enterprise, and impose "reasonable restrictions on the future activities of any person."[15] This statute may prove particularly useful when the plaintiff anticipates difficulty in establishing a "sale" of a "secu-rity." Time will tell.[16]

H. IMPLIED LIABILITIES

1. THEORY AND SCOPE: SEVEN DECADES OF SUPREME COURT HISTORY

Until a number of recent Supreme Court cases, most of this rich structure of express liabilities, especially in the 1933 and 1934 Acts, was quite overshadowed by the wide recognition of implied liabilities. After a historical exegesis of theory and scope cul-minating in those cases — not all of them involving the SEC statutes by any means — we shall try to ascertain the present status of the most important implied liabilities in the light of the Su-preme Court's teaching.

---

[13] Crim. Code c. 96, 18 U. S. C. §§1961-68, supra c. 9A n. 4.

[14] Id. §1964(c).

[15] Id. §1964(a).

[16] Compare Spencer Companies, Inc. v. Agency Rent-A-Car, Inc., CCH Fed. Sec. L. Rep. ¶98,361 (D. Mass. 1981) (allegations that an acquiring company filed a series of misleading statements in violation of Sec. Ex. Act §13(d) stated a "pattern of racketeering activity"), with Adair v. Hunt Int'l Resources Corp., 526 F. Supp. 736, 746-48 (N. D. Ill. 1981) (land buyers' claim against developers for treble damages for securities fraud in context of real estate transactions did not state a cause of action where developers were not involved with organized crime).

In general, see Long, Treble Damages for Violations of the Federal Secu-rities Laws: A Suggested Analysis and Application of the RICO Civil Cause of Action, 85 Dick. L. Rev. 201 (1981); Note, Civil RICO: The Temptation and Impropriety of Judicial Restrictions, 45 Harv. L. Rev. 1101 (1982). For collections of cases, see Hanna Mining Co. v. Norcen Energy Resources, Ltd., CCH Fed. Sec. L. Rep. ¶98,742 (N. D. Ohio 1982), and Mauriber v. Shearson/ American Express, Inc., 546 F. Supp. 391, 396-97 (S. D. N. Y. 1982), where the court held that the plaintiff need not allege "competitive injury" or "racke-teering activity."

The idea of implying civil liabilities from the violation of statutes is an old one. Lord Campbell applied the doctrine 130 years ago in construing an 1844 statute that subjected shipowners who did not keep certain medicines aboard to a penalty of £20 for each default, to be paid in part to any common informer bringing an action and for the rest to the Seaman's Hospital Society.[1] Although the court sustained a demurrer to an injured seaman's first count, which pleaded (without reference to the statute) what would today be called unseaworthiness in admiralty law, a second count that alleged noncompliance with the statute was held to give the plaintiff an action; for "in every case, where a statute enacts, or prohibits a thing for the benefit of a person, he shall have a remedy * * * for the recompence of a wrong done to him contrary to the said law."[2]

The text writers on the law of torts tend to discuss the doctrine in terms of negligence cases: Since the "reasonably prudent man" of the law of negligence — who, of course, is presumed to know the law — does not commit crimes, his violating the speed limit when he hits a pedestrian is negligence *per se,* or at least, in a substantial minority of American courts, "evidence of negligence."[3]

C. 10H [1] 7 & 8 Vict., c. 112, §18.

[2] Couch v. Steel, 3 E. & B. 402, 411, 118 Eng. Reprint 1193, 1196 (Q. B. 1854), cited in Texas & Pacific Ry. Co. v. Rigsby, 241 U. S. 33, 40 (1916), and in Greater Iowa Corp. v. McLendon, 378 F. 2d 783, 789-90 (8th Cir. 1967). *Couch* is the last, not the first, of a line of English tort cases going back at least to the beginning of the eighteenth century. H. Street, The Law of Torts (6th ed. 1976) 265 n. 4. Indeed, the lineage may be much more ancient. Lord Campbell described the Statute of Westminster 2, 13 Ed. 1, c. 50 (1385), as giving "a remedy by action on the case to all who are aggrieved by the neglect of any duty created by statute." 3 E. & B. at 411, 118 Eng. Reprint at 1196. It may be that looseness has been bred, as Dean Thayer said (Thayer, Public Wrong and Private Action, 27 Harv. L. Rev. 317, 331 (1914)), by Lord Campbell's unqualified quotation of the statement in Comyns' Digest that "in every Case, where a Statute enacts, or prohibits a Thing for the Benefit of a Person, he shall have a Remedy upon the same Statute for the Thing enacted for his Advantage, or for the Recompence of a Wrong done to him contrary to the said Law." 1 Com. Dig. 248 (1762). But, if it be assumed that Lord Campbell was a poor historian, his error seems to have been legitimated by time, at least (as we shall soon see) by many American courts as well as The American Law Institute. *Communis error facit jus.*

Oddly enough, although the English-invented doctrine has flowered in America, it has been considerably qualified by the English courts except with respect to industrial welfare legislation. See Williams, The Effect of Penal Legislation in the Law of Tort, 23 Mod. L. Rev. 233 (1960). However, it is worthy of note that the civil law is said to impose liability much more broadly than the common law. See Newman, Breach of Statute As the Basis of Responsibility in the Civil Law, 27 Can. B. Rev. 782, esp. at 797-802 (1949).

[3] In general, see Harper and James, The Law of Torts (1956) §17.6. For

The doctrine, however, is not limited to negligence cases.[4] The Restatement (Second) of Torts puts it this way:

> When a legislative provision protects a class of persons by proscribing or requiring certain conduct but does not provide a civil remedy for the violation, the court may, if it determines that the remedy is appropriate in furtherance of the purpose of the legislation and needed to assure the effectiveness of the provision, accord to an injured member of the class a right of action, using a suitable existing tort action or a new cause of action analogous to an existing tort action.[5]

The Supreme Court's decisions in the past twenty years have gone through several stages, not marked by clear boundaries. The first — which might be called the "ebullient stage" — was marked by a case involving Rule 14a-9, the proxy fraud rule under the 1934 Act, and it was the first implication of a private action by the Supreme Court under the SEC statutes:

---

a number of different philosophical approaches, see Thayer, Public Wrong and Private Action, 27 Harv. L. Rev. 317, 320 (1914); Lowndes, Civil Liability Created by Criminal Legislation, 16 Minn. L. Rev. 361, 369 (1932); Morris, The Role of Criminal Statutes in Negligence Actions, 49 Colum. L. Rev. 21 (1949).

In 1916 the Supreme Court recognized an action by an intrastate railroad employee for violation of the Safety Appliance Acts, although only *interstate* employees were given an express right of action:

> A disregard of the command of the statute is a wrongful act, and where it results in damage to one of the class for whose especial benefit the statute was enacted, the right to recover the damages from the party in default is implied, according to a doctrine of the common law * * * . This is but an application of the maxim, *Ubi jus ibi remedium.*

Texas & Pacific Ry. Co. v. Rigsby, 241 U. S. 33, 39-40 (1916); but cf. Moore v. Chesapeake & Ohio Ry. Co., 291 U. S. 205 (1934).

[4] See Tunstall v. Brotherhood of Locomotive Firemen & Enginemen, 323 U. S. 210, 213 (1944) (injunction and damage action against a labor union "which is derived from the duty imposed by the Railway Labor Act" on the union to represent all employees in the craft regardless of race); Reitmeister v. Reitmeister, 162 F. 2d 691, 694 (2d Cir. 1947) (wiretapping provision of Communications Act of 1944); Fitzgerald v. Pan American World Airways, Inc., 229 F. 2d 499, 501 (2d Cir. 1956) (statute prohibiting discrimination by air carriers). In the last of these cases the court relied on two of its own decisions under the SEC statutes. Goldstein v. Groesbeck, 142 F. 2d 422 (2d Cir. 1944), *cert. denied,* 323 U. S. 727 (1935 Act); Fischman v. Raytheon Mfg. Co., 188 F. 2d 783 (2d Cir. 1951); see also Baird v. Franklin, 141 F. 2d 238, 244-45 (2d Cir. 1944), *cert. denied,* 323 U. S. 737 (Sec. Ex. Act §6(b), requiring exchanges to discipline members for unethical conduct).

[5] §874A; see also §§285(a), 286-88C.

J. I. CASE CO. v. BORAK
Supreme Court of the United States, 1964
377 U. S. 426

MR. JUSTICE CLARK delivered the opinion of the Court.

This is a civil action brought by respondent, a stockholder of petitioner J. I. Case Company, charging deprivation of the pre-emptive rights of respondent and other shareholders by reason of a merger between Case and the American Tractor Corporation. It is alleged that the merger was effected through the circulation of a false and misleading proxy statement by those proposing the merger. The complaint was in two counts, the first based on diversity and claiming a breach of the directors' fiduciary duty to the stockholders. The second count alleged a violation of §14(a) of the Securities Exchange Act of 1934 with reference to the proxy solicitation material. The trial court held that as to this count it had no power to redress the alleged violations of the Act but was limited solely to the granting of declaratory relief thereon under §27 of the Act. The court held Wis. Stat., 1961, §180.405(4), which requires posting security for expenses in derivative actions, applicable to both counts, except that portion of Count 2 requesting declaratory relief. It ordered the respondent to furnish a bond in the amount of $75,000 thereunder and, upon his failure to do so, dismissed the complaint, save that part of Count 2 seeking a declaratory judgment. On interlocutory appeal the Court of Appeals reversed on both counts, holding that the District Court had the power to grant remedial relief and that the Wisconsin statute was not applicable. 317 F. 2d 838. We granted certiorari. 375 U. S. 901. We consider only the question of whether §27 of the Act authorizes a federal cause of action for rescission or damages to a corporate stockholder with respect to a consummated merger which was authorized pursuant to the use of a proxy statement alleged to contain false and misleading statements violative of §14(a) of the Act. * * *

I

Respondent, the owner of 2,000 shares of common stock of Case acquired prior to the merger, brought this suit based on diversity jurisdiction seeking to enjoin a proposed merger between Case and the American Tractor Corporation (ATC) on various grounds, including breach of the fiduciary duties of the Case directors, self-dealing among the management of Case and ATC and misrepresentations contained in the material circulated to obtain proxies. The injunction was denied and the merger was thereafter consummated. Subsequently successive amended complaints were filed and the case was heard on the aforesaid two-count complaint. The claims pertinent to the asserted violation of the Securities Exchange Act were predicated on diversity jurisdiction as well as on §27 of the Act. They alleged: that petitioners, or their predecessors, solicited or permitted their names to be used in the solicitation of proxies of Case stockholders for use at a special stockholders' meeting at which the proposed merger with ATC was to be voted upon; that the proxy solicitation material so circulated was false and misleading in violation of §14(a) of the Act and Rule 14a-9 which the Commission had promulgated thereunder; that the merger was approved at the meeting by a small margin of votes and was thereafter consummated; that the merger would not have been approved but for the false and misleading statements in the proxy solicitation material; and that Case stockholders were damaged thereby. The respondent sought judgment holding the merger void and damages for himself and all other stockholders similarly situated, as well as such further relief "as equity shall require." * * *

II

It appears clear that private parties have a right under §27 to bring suit for violation of §14(a) of the Act. Indeed, this section specifically grants the appropriate District Courts jurisdiction over "all suits in equity and actions at law brought to enforce any liability or duty created" under the Act. The petitioners make no concessions, however, emphasizing that Congress made no specific reference to a private right of action in §14(a); that, in any event, the right would not extend to derivative suits and should be limited to prospective relief only. In addition, some of the petitioners argue that the merger can be dissolved only if it was fraudulent or non-beneficial, issues upon which the proxy material would not bear. But the causal relationship of the proxy material and the merger are questions of fact to be resolved at trial, not here. We therefore do not discuss this point further.

III

While the respondent contends that his Count 2 claim is not a derivative one, we need not embrace that view, for we believe that a right of action exists as to both derivative and direct causes.

The purpose of §14(a) is to prevent management or others from obtaining authorization for corporate action by means of deceptive or inadequate disclosure in proxy solicitation. The section stemmed from the congressional belief that "[f]air corporate suffrage is an important right that should attach to every equity security bought on a public exchange." H. R. Rep. No. 1383, 73d Cong., 2d Sess., 13. It was intended to "control the conditions under which proxies may be solicited with a view to preventing the recurrence of abuses which * * * [had] frustrated the free exercise of the voting rights of stockholders." Id., at 14. "Too often proxies are solicited without explanation to the stockholder of the real nature of the questions for which authority to cast his vote is sought." S. Rep. No. 792, 73d Cong., 2d Sess., 12. These broad remedial purposes are evidenced in the language of the section * * * . While this language makes no specific reference to a private right of action, among its chief purposes is "the protection of investors," which certainly implies the availability of judicial relief where necessary to achieve that result.

The injury which a stockholder suffers from corporate action pursuant to a deceptive proxy solicitation ordinarily flows from the damage done the corporation, rather than from the damage inflicted directly upon the stockholder. The damage suffered results not from the deceit practiced on him alone but rather from the deceit practiced on the stockholders as a group. To hold that derivative actions are not within the sweep of the section would therefore be tantamount to a denial of private relief. Private enforcement of the proxy rules provides a necessary supplement to Commission action. As in antitrust treble damage litigation, the possibility of civil damages or injunctive relief serves as a most effective weapon in the enforcement of the proxy requirements. The Commission advises that it examines over 2,000 proxy statements annually and each of them must necessarily be expedited. Time does not permit an independent examination of the facts set out in the proxy material and this results in the Commission's acceptance of the representations contained therein at their face value, unless contrary to other material on file with it. Indeed, on the allegations of respondent's complaint, the proxy material failed to disclose alleged unlawful market manipulation of the stock of ATC, and this unlawful manipulation would not have been apparent to the Commission until after the merger.

We, therefore, believe that under the circumstances here it is the duty of the courts to be alert to provide such remedies as are necessary to make effective the congressional purpose. As was said in *Sola Electric Co.* v. *Jefferson Electric Co.*, 317 U. S. 173, 176 (1942):

> When a federal statute condemns an act as unlawful, the extent and nature of the legal consequences of the condemnation, though left by the statute to judicial determination, are nevertheless federal questions, the answers to which are to be derived from the statute and the federal policy which it has adopted.

See also *Tunstall* v. *Brotherhood of Locomotive Firemen & Enginemen,* 323 U. S. 210, 213 (1944); *Deitrick* v. *Greaney,* 309 U. S. 190, 201 (1940). It is for the federal courts "to adjust their remedies so as to grant the necessary relief" where federally secured rights are invaded. "And it is also well settled that where legal rights have been invaded, and a federal statute provides for a general right to sue for such invasion, federal courts may use any available remedy to make good the wrong done." *Bell* v. *Hood,* 327 U. S. 678, 684 (1946). Section 27 grants the District Courts jurisdiction "of all suits in equity and actions at law brought to enforce any liability or duty created by this title. . . ." In passing on almost identical language found in the Securities Act of 1933, the Court found the words entirely sufficient to fashion a remedy to rescind a fraudulent sale, secure restitution and even to enforce the right to restitution against a third party holding assets of the vendor. *Deckert* v. *Independence Shares Corp.,* 311 U. S. 282 (1940). This significant language was used:

> The power *to enforce* implies the power to make effective the right of recovery afforded by the Act. And the power to make the right of recovery effective implies the power to utilize any of the procedures or actions normally available to the litigant according to the exigencies of the particular case. At 288.

See also *Porter* v. *Warner Holding Co.,* 328 U. S. 395 (1946); *Mitchell* v. *Robert DeMario Jewelry, Inc.,* 361 U. S. 288 (1960); *Schine Chain Theatres, Inc.* v. *United States,* 334 U. S. 110 (1948).

Nor do we find merit in the contention that such remedies are limited to prospective relief. This was the position taken in *Dann* v. *Studebaker-Packard Corp.,* 288 F. 2d 201, where it was held that the "preponderance of questions of state law which would have to be interpreted and applied in order to grant the relief sought . . . is so great that the federal question involved . . . is really negligible in comparison." At 214. But we believe that the overriding federal law applicable here would, where the facts required, control the appropriateness of redress despite the provisions of state corporation law, for it "is not uncommon for federal

courts to fashion federal law where federal rights are concerned."
Textile Workers v. *Lincoln Mills,* 353 U. S. 448, 457 (1957). In
addition, the fact that questions of state law must be decided does
not change the character of the right; it remains federal. As Chief
Justice Marshall said in *Osborn* v. *Bank of the United States,* 9
Wheat. 783 (1824):

> If this were sufficient to withdraw a case from the jurisdiction
> of the federal Courts, almost every case, although involving the
> construction of a law, would be withdrawn. . . . At 819-820.

Moreover, if federal jurisdiction were limited to the granting
of declaratory relief, victims of deceptive proxy statements would
be obliged to go into state courts for remedial relief. And if the
law of the State happened to attach no responsibility to the use of
misleading proxy statements, the whole purpose of the section
might be frustrated. Furthermore, the hurdles that the victim
might face (such as separate suits, as contemplated by *Dann* v.
Studebaker-Packard Corp., supra, security for expenses statutes,
bringing in all parties necessary for complete relief, etc.) might
well prove insuperable to effective relief.

IV

Our finding that federal courts have the power to grant all
necessary remedial relief is not to be construed as any indication
of what we believe to be the necessary and appropriate relief in
this case. We are concerned here only with a determination that
federal jurisdiction for this purpose does exist. Whatever remedy
is necessary must await the trial on the merits.

The other contentions of the petitioners are denied.

Affirmed.

The result is eminently sound. But the opinion disappointed:

(1) To consider it "clear" without discussion that a private action under the proxy rules *is* one "brought to enforce any liability
or duty created by" the Act within the meaning of §27 is to beg
the question. For §27 simply confers jurisdiction on the District
Courts to hear actions created expressly or by implication elsewhere in the statute.[6]

(2) The treble damage actions that the opinion refers to as

---

[6] See Touche Ross & Co. v. Redington, 442 U. S. 560, 577 (1979), set out
infra p. 1081, at p. 1088.

"a most effective weapon" are, of course, expressly provided for in the antitrust laws.

(3) All that the *Deckert* case stands for — as well as the other restitution or divestiture cases that are cited in the opinion — is that historic equity jurisprudence gives the federal courts very broad authority to grant relief that is ancillary to an action expressly created.

In short, the Court reached the right result not for the wrong reason but for no reason at all. It would have been much easier to write an opinion in terms of the tort doctrine. Yet, inexplicably, the Court did not so much as mention that concept. This, with respect, is the opinion's greatest fault. For, if the Court really meant to hold that aid to enforcement was itself an independent basis of civil liability — as some commentators assumed — the implications not only for the extension of implied liability, but also for the type of proof required in contrast to a tort-based rationale, were considerable. On this account alone it was fairly predictable that the Court one day would have to rationalize *Borak* in more traditional terms. As Justice Harlan put it in his concurring opinion just six years later in a case in which the Court implied an action for violation of the Fourth Amendment by a federal agent acting under color of authority:

> * * * the exercise of judicial power involved in *Borak* simply cannot be justified in terms of *statutory construction* * * * ; nor did the *Borak* Court purport to do so. * * * The notion of "implying" a remedy, therefore, as applied to cases like *Borak*, can only refer to a process whereby the federal judiciary exercises a choice among *traditionally available* judicial remedies according to reasons related to the substantive social policy embodied in an act of positive law.[7]

A few months later the Court finally decided a case under the then twenty-eight-year-old Rule 10b-5.[8] By that time Justice Douglas was able to content the Court with the statement: "It is now established that a private right of action is implied under §10(b)."[9] In sum, whereas *Borak* gave us an opinion without a workable

[7] Bivens v. Six Unknown Named Agents of the Federal Bureau of Narcotics, 403 U. S. 388, 402 n. 4 (1971); see also Wyandotte Transportation Co. v. United States, 389 U. S. 191, 201-08 (1967), where Justice Fortas cited the Restatement (Second) of Torts.

[8] The earlier case of Tcherepnin v. Knight, 389 U. S. 332 (1967), though brought under Rule 10b-5, came to the Court only on the question whether a "security" was involved.

[9] Superintendent of Ins. of the State of N. Y. v. Bankers Life & Casualty Co., 404 U. S. 6, 13 n. 9 (1971).

ratio decidendi, the 10b-5 case gave us a decision without an opinion. So much for the Court's "ebullient" stage!

What might be called the "back to orthodoxy" stage that was heralded by the Harlan concurring opinion soon evolved into what might be called the "shift of presumption" stage. Indeed, in the very Fourth Amendment case in which Justice Harlan concurred, Chief Justice Burger dissented, stating: "Legislation is the business of the Congress, and it has the facilities and competence for that task — as we do not."[10] This was followed by cases in which the Court rejected private actions to enjoin the discontinuance of passenger service under the "Amtrak" Act[11] and to compel the Securities Investor Protection Corporation to take action against a financially troubled broker-dealer under the Securities Investor Protection Act.[12] There were also other skirmishes, all leading to a unanimous opinion that seemed designed as a definitive guide to Bench and Bar:

CORT v. ASH
Supreme Court of the United States, 1975
422 U. S. 66

MR. JUSTICE BRENNAN delivered the opinion of the Court.

There are other questions, but the principal issue presented for decision is whether a private cause of action for damages against corporate directors is to be implied in favor of a corporate stockholder under 18 U. S. C. §610, a criminal statute prohibiting corporations from making "a contribution or expenditure in connection with an election at which Presidential and Vice Presidential electors . . . are to be voted for." We conclude that implication of such a federal cause of action is not suggested by the legislative context of §610 or required to accomplish Congress' purposes in enacting the statute. * * *

[Ash, a stockholder of Bethlehem Steel Corp., brought an action, on behalf of himself and derivatively, against Cort for an injunction and damages. After noting that the statute expressly vested the Federal Election Commission with "primary jurisdiction" so far as injunctive relief was concerned, Justice Brennan continued:]

---

[10] Bivens v. Six Unknown Named Agents of the Federal Bureau of Narcotics, 403 U. S. 388, 412 (1971).

[11] 45 U. S. C. §547; National R. R. Passenger Corp. v. National Assn. of R. R. Passengers, 414 U. S. 453 (1974).

[12] Securities Investor Protection Corp. v. Barbour, 421 U. S. 412 (1975).

III

* * * we turn next to the holding of the Court of Appeals that "a private cause action . . . by a stockholder to secure . . . derivative damage relief [is] proper to remedy violation of §610." We hold that such relief is not available with regard to a 1972 violation under §610 itself, but rather is available, if at all, under Delaware law governing corporations.

In determining whether a private remedy is implicit in a statute not expressly providing one, several factors are relevant. First, is the plaintiff "one of the class for whose *especial* benefit the statute was enacted," *Texas & Pacific R. Co.* v. *Rigsby*, 241 U. S. 33, 39 (1916) (emphasis supplied) — that is, does the statute create a federal right in favor of the plaintiff? Second, is there any indication of legislative intent, explicit or implicit, either to create such a remedy or to deny one? See, e. g., *National Railroad Passenger Corp.* v. *National Assn. of Railroad Passengers*, 414 U. S. 453, 458, 460 (1974) (*Amtrak*). Third, is it consistent with the underlying purposes of the legislative scheme to imply such a remedy for the plaintiff? See, e. g., *Amtrak,* supra; *Securities Investor Protection Corp.* v. *Barbour*, 421 U. S. 412, 423 (1975); *Calhoon* v. *Harvey*, 379 U. S. 134 (1964). And finally, is the cause of action one traditionally relegated to state law, in an area basically the concern of the States, so that it would be inappropriate to infer a cause of action based solely on federal law? See *Wheeldin* v. *Wheeler*, 373 U. S. 647, 652 (1963); cf. *J. I. Case Co.* v. *Borak*, 377 U. S. 426, 434 (1964); *Bivens* v. *Six Unknown Federal Narcotics Agents*, 403 U. S. 388, 394-395 (1971); id., at 400 (Harlan, J., concurring in judgment).

The dissenting judge in the Court of Appeals and petitioners here suggest that where a statute provides a penal remedy alone, it cannot be regarded as creating a right in any particular class of people. "Every criminal statute is designed to protect some individual, public, or social interest. . . . To find an implied civil cause of action for the plaintiff in this case is to find an implied civil right of action for every individual, social, or public interest which might be invaded by violation of any criminal statute. To do this is to conclude that Congress intended to enact a civil code companion to the criminal code." 496 F. 2d at 428-429 (Aldisert, J., dissenting). Cf. *Nashville Milk Co.* v. *Carnation Co.*, 355 U. S. 373, 377 (1958).

Clearly, provision of a criminal penalty does not necessarily *preclude* implication of a private cause of action for damages. *Wyandotte Transportation Co.* v. *United States*, 389 U. S. 191,

201-202 (1967); see also *J. I. Case Co.* v. *Borak,* supra; *Texas &
Pacific R. Co.* v. *Rigsby,* supra. However, in *Wyandotte, Borak,*
and *Rigsby,* there was at least a statutory basis for inferring that
a civil cause of action of some sort lay in favor of someone.[11]
Here, there was nothing more than a bare criminal statute, with
absolutely no indication that civil enforcement of any kind was
available to anyone.

We need not, however, go so far as to say that in this circumstance a bare criminal statute can *never* be deemed sufficiently
protective of some special group so as to give rise to a private
cause of action by a member of that group. For the intent to protect corporate shareholders particularly was at best a subsidiary
purpose of §610, and the other relevant factors all either are not
helpful or militate against implying a private cause of action.

First, §610 is derived from the Act of January 26, 1907, which
"seems to have been motivated by two considerations. First, the
necessity for destroying the influence over elections which corporations exercised through financial contribution. Second, the feeling
that corporate officials had no moral right to use corporate funds
for contribution to political parties without the consent of the
stockholders." *United States* v. *CIO,* 335 U. S. 106, 113 (1948).
See 40 Cong. Rec. 96 (1905) (Annual Message of President Theodore Roosevelt). Respondent bases his derivative action on the
second purpose, claiming that the intent to protect stockholders
from use of their invested funds for political purposes demonstrates that the statute set up a federal right in shareholders not
to have corporate funds used for this purpose.

However, the legislative history of the 1907 Act, recited at
length in *United States* v. *Auto Workers,* 352 U. S. 567 (1957),
demonstrates that the protection of ordinary stockholders was at
best a secondary concern. * * * [T]he legislation was primarily
concerned with corporations as a source of aggregated wealth and
therefore of possible corrupting influence, and not directly with

---

11   *   *   *

In *Borak,* §27 of the Securities Exchange Act of 1934 specifically granted
jurisdiction to the district courts over civil actions to "enforce any liability
or duty created by this title or the rules and regulations thereunder," and
there seemed to be no dispute over the fact that at least a private suit for
declaratory relief was authorized; the question was whether a derivative suit
for rescission and damages was also available. 377 U. S., at 430-431. Further
it was clear that the Securities and Exchange Commission could sue to enjoin
violations of §14(a) of the Act, the section involved in *Borak.* See §21 of the
Act, 15 U. S. C. §78u.
                      *   *   *

the internal relations between the corporations and their stockholders. In contrast, in those situations in which we have inferred a federal private cause of action not expressly provided, there has generally been a clearly articulated federal right in the plaintiff, e. g., *Bivens* v. *Six Unknown Federal Narcotics Agents,* supra, or a pervasive legislative scheme governing the relationship between the plaintiff class and the defendant class in a particular regard, e. g., *J. I. Case Co.* v. *Borak,* supra.

Second, there is no indication whatever in the legislative history of §610 which suggests a congressional intention to vest in corporate shareholders a federal right to damages for violation of §610. True, in situations in which it is clear that federal law has granted a class of persons certain rights, it is not necessary to show an intention to *create* a private cause of action, although an explicit purpose to *deny* such cause of action would be controlling. But where, as here, it is at least dubious whether Congress intended to vest in the plaintiff class rights broader than those provided by state regulation of corporations, the fact that there is no suggestion at all that §610 may give rise to a suit for damages or, indeed, to any civil cause of action, reinforces the conclusion that the expectation, if any, was that the relationship between corporations and their stockholders would continue to be entrusted entirely to state law.

Third, while "it is the duty of the courts to be alert to provide such remedies as are necessary to make effective the congressional purpose," *J. I. Case Co.* v. *Borak,* 377 U. S. at 433, in this instance the remedy sought would not aid the primary congressional goal. Recovery of derivative damages by the corporation for violation of §610 would not cure the influence which the use of corporate funds in the first instance may have had on a federal election. Rather, such a remedy would only permit directors in effect to "borrow" corporate funds for a time; the later compelled repayment might well not deter the initial violation, and would certainly not decrease the impact of the use of such funds upon an election already past.

Fourth, and finally, for reasons already intimated, it is entirely appropriate in this instance to relegate respondent and others in his situation to whatever remedy is created by state law. In addition to the *ultra vires* action pressed here, * * * the use of corporate funds in violation of federal law may, under the law of some States, give rise to a cause of action for breach of fiduciary duty. See, e. g., *Miller* v. *American Telephone & Telegraph Co.,*

507 F. 2d 759 (C. A. 3 1974). Corporations are creatures of state law, and investors commit their funds to corporate directors on the understanding that, except where federal law expressly requires certain responsibilities of directors with respect to stockholders, state law will govern the internal affairs of the corporation. If, for example, state law permits corporations to use corporate funds as contributions in state elections, see *Miller,* supra, at 763 n. 4, shareholders are on notice that their funds may be so used and have no recourse under any federal statute. We are necessarily reluctant to imply a federal right to recover funds used in violation of a federal statute where the laws governing the corporation may put a shareholder on notice that there may be no such recovery.

In *Borak,* supra, we said: "[If] the law of the State happened to attach no responsibility to the use of misleading proxy statements, the whole purpose of [§14(a) of the Securities Exchange Act of 1934] might be frustrated." 377 U. S. at 434-435. Here, committing respondent to state-provided remedies would have no such effect. In *Borak,* the statute involved was clearly an intrusion of federal law into the internal affairs of corporations; to the extent that state law differed or impeded suit, the congressional intent could be compromised in state-created causes of action. In this case, Congress was concerned, not with regulating corporations as such, but with dulling their impact upon federal elections. As we have seen, the existence or nonexistence of a derivative cause of action for damages would not aid or hinder this primary goal.

Because injunctive relief is not presently available * * * , and because implication of a federal right of damages on behalf of a corporation under §610 would intrude into an area traditionally committed to state law without aiding the main purpose of §610, we reverse.

Two years later the Court relied largely on its *Cort* v. *Ash* analysis to reject an implied action for damages under §14(e) of the 1934 Act[13] and Rule 10b-6[14] by Chris-Craft Industries, Inc., the loser of two competing tender offerors for the stock of Piper Aircraft Corporation, against the winner, Bangor Punta Corporation:

* * *

[13] See p. 589 supra.
[14] See p. 1001 supra.

PIPER v. CHRIS-CRAFT INDUSTRIES, INC.
Supreme Court of the United States, 1977
430 U. S. 1

MR. CHIEF JUSTICE BURGER delivered the opinion of the Court.

*   *   *

IV

Our analysis begins, of course, with the statute itself. Section 14(e), like §10(b), makes no provision whatever for a private cause of action, such as those explicitly provided in other sections of the 1933 and 1934 Acts. E. g., §§11, 12, 15 of the 1933 Act, 15 U. S. C. §§77k, 77*l*, 77o; §§9, 16, 18, 20 of the 1934 Act, 15 U. S. C. §§78i, 78p, 78r, 78t. This Court has nonetheless held that in some circumstances a private cause of action can be implied with respect to the 1934 Act's antifraud provisions, even though the relevant provisions are silent as to remedies. *J. I. Case Co.* v. *Borak,* 377 U. S. 426 (1964) (§14(a)); *Superintendent of Ins.* v. *Bankers Life & Cas. Co.,* 404 U. S. 6, 13 n. 9 (1971) (§10(b)).

The reasoning of these holdings is that, where congressional purposes are likely to be undermined absent private enforcement, private remedies may be implied in favor of the particular class intended to be protected by the statute. For example, in *J. I. Case Co.* v. *Borak,* supra, recognizing an implied right of action in favor of a shareholder complaining of a misleading proxy solicitation, the Court concluded as to such a shareholder's right:

> While [§14(a)] makes no specific reference to a private right of action, among its chief purposes is *"the protection of investors,"* which certainly implies the availability of judicial relief *where necessary to achieve that result.* 377 U. S., at 432. (Emphasis supplied.)

Indeed, the Court in *Borak* carefully noted that because of practical limitations upon the SEC's enforcement capabilities, "[p]rivate enforcement . . . provides *a necessary supplement to Commission action." Ibid.* (Emphasis added.) Similarly, the Court's opinion in *Blue Chip Stamps* v. *Manor Drug Stores,* 421 U. S. 723, 730 (1975), in reaffirming the availability of a private right of action under §10(b), specifically alluded to the language in *Borak* concerning the *necessity* for supplemental private remedies without which congressional protection of shareholders would be defeated. See also *Rondeau* v. *Mosinee Paper Corp.*, 422 U. S. 49, 62 (1975).[a]

Against this background we must consider whether §14(e), which is entirely silent as to private remedies, permits this Court to read into the statute a damages remedy for unsuccessful tender offerors. To resolve that question we turn to the legislative history to discern the congressional purpose underlying the specific statutory prohibition in §14(e). Once we identify the legislative purpose, we must then determine whether the creation by judicial interpretation of the implied cause of action asserted by Chris-Craft is necessary to effectuate Congress' goals.

A

* * *

The legislative history * * * shows that Congress was intent upon regulating takeover bidders, theretofore operating covertly, in order to protect the shareholders of target companies. * * *

* * *

The sponsors of this legislation were plainly sensitive to the suggestion that the measure would favor one side or the other in control contests; however, they made it clear that the legislation was designed solely to get needed information to the investor, the constant focal point of the committee hearings. * * *

Accordingly, the congressional policy of "evenhandedness" is non-probative of the quite disparate proposition that the Williams Act was intended to confer rights for money damages upon an injured takeover bidder.

* * *

The legislative history * * * shows that the sole purpose of the Williams Act was the protection of investors who are confronted with a tender offer. * * * We find no hint in the legislative history, on which respondent so heavily relies, that Congress contemplated a private cause of action for damages by one of sev-

---

[a] ED.: This case (set out supra p. 591, at p. 597) held that not every violation of §13(d) (supra pp. 577-78) automatically justified an injunction — that is to say, the chancellor must always "balance the equities" — without consideration of the plaintiff's standing.

eral contending offerors against a successful bidder or by a losing contender against the target corporation.

*   *   *

B

Our conclusion as to the legislative history is confirmed by the analysis in *Cort v. Ash,* 422 U. S. 66 (1975). There, the Court identified four factors as "relevant" in determining whether a private remedy is implicit in a statute not expressly providing one. The first is whether the plaintiff is " 'one of the class for whose *especial* benefit the statute was enacted . . . .' " Id. at 78. (Emphasis in original.) As previously indicated, examination of the statute and its genesis shows that Chris-Craft is not an intended beneficiary of the Williams Act, and surely is not one "for whose *especial* benefit the statute was enacted." Ibid. To the contrary, Chris-Craft is a member of the class whose activities Congress intended to regulate for the protection and benefit of an entirely distinct class, shareholder-offerees. As a party whose previously unregulated conduct was purposefully brought under federal control by the statute, Chris-Craft can scarcely lay claim to the status of "beneficiary" whom Congress considered in need of protection.

Second, in *Cort v. Ash* we inquired whether there was "any indication of legislative intent, explicit or implicit, either to create such a remedy or to deny one." Ibid. Although the historical materials are barren of any express intent to deny a damages remedy to tender offerors as a class, there is, as we have noted, no indication that Congress intended to create a damages remedy in favor of the loser in a contest for control. Fairly read, we think the legislative documents evince the narrow intent to curb the unregulated activities of tender offerors. The expression of this purpose, which pervades the legislative history, negates the claim that tender offerors were intended to have additional weapons in the form of an implied cause of action for damages, particularly if a private damages action confers no advantage on the expressly protected class of shareholder-offerees, a matter we discuss later. Infra, at 39.

Chris-Craft argues, however, that Congress intended standing under §14(e) to encompass tender offerors since the statute, unlike §10(b), does not contain the limiting language, "in connection with the purchase or sale" of securities. Instead, in §14(e), Congress broadly proscribed fraudulent activities "in connection with any tender offer . . . or any solicitation . . . in opposition to or in favor of any such offer. . . ."

The omission of the purchaser-seller requirement does not mean, however, that Chris-Craft has standing to sue for damages under §14(e) in its capacity as a takeover bidder. It may well be that Congress desired to protect, among others, shareholder-offerees who decided not to tender their stock due to fraudulent misrepresentations by person opposed to a takeover attempt. See generally 1 A. Bromberg, Securities Law: Fraud §6.3 (1021), p. 122.17 (1969). See also Senate Report 2; House Report 3. These shareholders, who might not enjoy the protection of §10(b) under *Blue Chip Stamps* v. *Manor Drug Stores,* 421 U. S. 723 (1975), could perhaps state a claim under §14(e), even though they did not tender their securities. But increased protection, if any, conferred upon the class of shareholders-offerees by the elimination of the purchaser-seller restriction can scarcely be interpreted as giving protection to the entirely separate and unrelated class of persons whose conduct the statute is designed to regulate.

Third, *Cort* v. *Ash* tells us that we must ascertain whether it is "consistent with the underlying purposes of the legislative scheme to imply such a remedy for the plaintiff." 422 U. S., at 78. We conclude that it is not. As a disclosure mechanism aimed especially at protecting shareholders of target corporations, the Williams Act cannot consistently be interpreted as conferring a monetary remedy upon regulated parties, particularly where the award would not redound to the direct benefit of the protected class. * * *

Nor can we agree that an ever-present threat of damages against a successful contestant in a battle for control will provide significant additional protection for shareholders in general. The deterrent value, if any, of such awards can never be ascertained with precision. More likely, however, is the prospect that shareholders may be prejudiced because some tender offers may never be made if there is a possibility of massive damages claims for what courts subsequently hold to be an actionable violation of §14(e). * * *

*　　*　　*

Fourth, under the *Cort* v. *Ash* analysis, we must decide whether "the cause of action [is] one traditionally relegated to state law. . . ." 422 U. S., at 78. Despite the pervasiveness of federal securities regulation, the Court of Appeals concluded in these cases that Chris-Craft's complaint would give rise to a cause of action under common-law principles of interference with a prospective commercial advantage. Although Congress is, of course, free to create a remedial scheme in favor of contestants in tender offers, we conclude, as we did in *Cort* v. *Ash,* that "it is entirely appropriate in this instance to relegate [the offeror-bidder] and others in [that] situation to whatever remedy is created by state law," id., at 84, at least to the extent that the offeror seeks damages for having been wrongfully denied a "fair opportunity" to compete for control of another corporation.

c

What we have said thus far suggests that, unlike *J. I. Case Co.* v. *Borak,* supra, judicially creating a damages action in favor of Chris-Craft is unnecessary to ensure the fulfillment of Congress' purposes in adopting the Williams Act. Even though the SEC operates in this context under the same practical restraints recognized by the Court in *Borak,* institutional limitations alone do not lead to the conclusion that any party interested in a tender offer should have a cause of action for damages against a competing bidder. First, as Judge Friendly observed in *Electronic Specialty Co.* v. *International Controls Corp.,* 409 F. 2d 937, 947 (C. A. 2 1969), in corporate control contests the stage of preliminary injunctive relief, rather than post-contest lawsuits, "is the time when relief can best be given." Furthermore, awarding damages to parties other than the protected class of shareholders has only a remote, if any, bearing upon implementing the congressional policy of protecting shareholders who must decide whether to tender or retain their stock.[28] Indeed, as we suggested earlier, a damages award of this nature may well be inconsistent with the interests of many members of the protected class and of only indirect value to shareholders who accepted the exchange offer of the defeated takeover contestant.

We therefore conclude that Chris-Craft, as a defeated tender offeror, has no implied cause of action for damages under §14(e).

V

In addition to its holding under §14(e), the Court of Appeals held that Bangor was liable for damages under Rule 10b-6 be-

---

[28] Our holding is a limited one. Whether shareholder-offerees, the class protected by §14(e), have an implied cause of action under §14(e) is not before us, and we intimate no view on the matter. Nor is the target corporation's standing to sue in issue in this case. We hold only that a tender offeror, suing in its capacity as a takeover bidder, does not have standing to sue for damages under the Williams Act.

cause of its off-exchange cash purchases of Piper stock in May 1969. * * *

Rule 10b-6 is an antimanipulative provision designed to protect the orderliness of the securities market during distributions of stock. The Rule in essence prohibits issuers whose stock is in the process of distribution from market tampering by purchasing either the stock or rights to purchase the stock until the distribution has been completed. The purpose of the Rule is to prevent stimulative trading by an issuer in its own securities in order to create an unnatural and unwarranted appearance of market activity. See generally E. Aranow & H. Einhorn, Tender Offers for Corporate Control 131 (1973). Here, the Court of Appeals held, and its holding is unchallenged, that the cash purchases of Piper stock during the pendency of Bangor's exchange offer constituted purchases of "right[s] to purchase" Bangor stock within the meaning of Rule 10b-6.

*   *   *

Although we reserve judgment on the broader standing issues arising under Rule 10b-6, we hold that, in the context of these cases, Chris-Craft is without standing to sue for damages on account of Bangor's alleged Rule 10b-6 violations. Our holding is based upon one critical factor: As the parties themselves have framed the issues for resolution in this litigation, Chris-Craft is clearly outside the express concern of Rule 10b-6. At no time has Chris-Craft complained of or even suggested that the price which it paid for Piper shares was influenced by Bangor's Rule 10b-6 violations. Indeed, Chris-Craft does not assert standing as a *Piper shareholder;* on the contrary, it claims damages because, in its view of the case, it lost the opportunity to gain control of Piper by virtue of Bangor's Rule 10b-6 violations. Assuming the correctness of this theory, the fact remains that Rule 10b-6 is not directed at or concerned with contests for corporate control. This technical rule is focused narrowly upon a precise goal — maintaining an orderly market for the distribution of securities free from artificial or manipulative influences. Thus, as the issues have been framed, Chris-Craft did not come to the courts in the posture of a hoodwinked investor victimized by market manipulation; its complaint, as we noted, is that it lost a chance to gain control of a corporation, a claim beyond the bounds of the specific concern of Rule 10b-6.

Our conclusion in this respect is buttressed by the close relationship of Rule 10b-6 with §9 of the 1934 Act, 15 U. S. C. §78i. Section 9, among other things, prohibits transactions by issuers in their own securities, if forbidden by SEC regulations, even though the transactions are designed to stabilize the market for the issuer's stock. §78i(a)(6). The SEC suggests in its *amicus* brief that Rule 10b-6 was promulgated pursuant to the Commission's authority under §9(a)(6), as well as under §10(b) of the 1934 Act. It contends that, in view of this bifurcated statutory origin, Chris-Craft need only be a purchaser of Piper stock to have standing under Rule 10b-6, since §9 requires only that an aggrieved party have purchased or sold "any security" affected by the violation. 15 U. S. C. §78i(e). Under this view, Chris-Craft's failure to purchase Bangor Punta stock is irrelevant, since its purchases of Piper shares satisfied the "any security" requirement of §9.

Unlike §10(b), however, §9 provides an express cause of action for persons injured by unlawful market activities. 15 U. S. C. §78i(e). Yet, that cause of action is framed specifically in favor of "any person who shall purchase or sell any security *at a price which was affected by such act or transaction. . . .*" Ibid. (Emphasis supplied.) Congress therefore focused in §9 upon the amount actually paid by an investor for stock that had been the subject of manipulative activity. This is not, as we have seen, the gravamen of Chris-Craft's complaint. It seeks no recovery for an improper premium exacted for Piper stock; rather it desires compensation for its lost opportunity to control Piper. We therefore conclude that, on its claimed basis for relief, Chris-Craft cannot avail itself of Rule 10b-6.

*   *   *

Accordingly, the judgment of the Court of Appeals is reversed.

MR. JUSTICE BLACKMUN, concurring in the judgment.

I concur in the judgment. For the reasons set out in Mr. Justice Stevens' dissenting opinion, post, p. 53, I am willing to begin with the premise that respondent Chris-Craft had "standing" in the sense that it possessed an implied right to sue under §14(e) of the Securities Exchange Act of 1934, 15 U. S. C. §78n(e). Unlike the dissenters, however, I do not conclude, from this, that the Court of Appeals' judgment as to liability is to be affirmed. Since I am of the opinion that respondent failed to prove that petitioners' violations of the securities laws caused its injury, I agree with the Court that the judgment below should be reversed.

* * *

MR. JUSTICE STEVENS, with whom MR. JUSTICE BRENNAN joins, dissenting.

* * *

No one seriously questions the premise that Congress implicitly created a private right of action when it enacted §14(e) in 1968.[4] * * *

I

Shareholders of a target corporation may be injured by a fraudulent tender offer in two quite different ways. They may exchange their shares for an inadequate consideration in reliance on the misrepresentation. Or they may retain their shares and be harmed by the fact that other shareholders were induced to surrender control to unworthy newcomers. The legislative history of §14(e) persuades me that Congress intended to protect the shareholders from both of these potential harms. Since Chris-Craft claims to have suffered the latter type of harm, it has asserted a cause of action created by the statute.

Section 14(e) was patterned after §14(a), which regulates proxy contests. It is clear that a shareholder may recover in a suit under

---

[4] Although originally one might have argued that the private remedies created by the Securities Acts are limited to those expressly described in the legislation itself, history has foreclosed any such argument today. The statutes originally enacted in 1933 and 1934 have been amended so often with full congressional awareness of the judicial interpretation of Rule 10b-5 as implicitly creating a private remedy that we must now assume that Congress intended to create rights for the specific beneficiaries of the legislation as well as duties to be policed by the SEC. This case therefore does not present the same kind of issue discussed in Cort v. Ash, 422 U. S. 66, namely, *whether* the statute created an implied private remedy. Rather, the question presented here is *who* may invoke that remedy. Nevertheless, it is noteworthy that none of the factors identified in the *Cort* opinion militates against implying a private cause of action in favor of Chris-Craft. Indeed, it is beyond dispute that here, as in J. I. Case Co. v. Borak, 377 U. S. 426, 431-433, the asserted private remedy would unquestionably aid the "primary goal" of the statute. See *Cort,* supra, at 85.

§14(a) even though he was not himself deceived by the misrepresentation. I do not understand why §14(e) should receive any narrower construction.[9] * * *

II

Even if we disregard Chris-Craft's stock ownership in Piper and focus only on its status as a tender offeror, it remains clear to me that its legal rights were invaded by the defendants' violation of §14(e). This conclusion is compelled by (a) a fair evaluaation of the legislative purpose in the light of the rationale of *J. I. Case Co.* v. *Borak,* 377 U. S. 426; and (b) respect for the opinions of the Securities and Exchange Commission and the numerous federal judges who have recognized that §14(e) is little more than a restatement of Rule 10b-5 unless it has broadened the class of potential litigants who may challenge defective cash tender offers to include rival contestants for control as well as shareholders.

A

* * *

In both proxy and tender offer contests, the remedy which will most effectively deter violations of the statute is unquestionably the private damages action. * * *

If a private remedy must be implied to ensure full compliance with the statute, the remedy must be available to the litigants who are most vitally interested in effective enforcement. * * *

The potential litigants who have the most to gain from enforcement of the statute — and the most to lose if its provisions can be ignored with impunity — are plainly the rival contestants. * * *

* * * I find ample evidence of congressional interest in fair competition between outsiders and insiders in making and op-

---

[9] The tender offer is just one species of solicitation that either an incumbent or an outside group may use in a contest for control of a corporation. Power to direct the destiny of the corporation may be obtained by acquiring proxies for a majority of the shares, by acquiring the shares themselves, or more typically by a combination of proxies and actual purchases. Section 14 broadly prohibits fraudulent solicitations, not merely to protect the individual shareholder from casting a misguided vote or from making an ill-advised sale, but more importantly to protect the corporate entity as a whole from the consequences of a vital decision procured by fraud.

posing tender offers to shareholders of the target company. That evidence persuades me that both contenders are included within the class of persons protected by §14(e).

*   *   *

III

Petitioners view *Cort* v. *Ash,* 422 U. S. 66, as foreclosing standing in this case because tender offerors do not belong to the "especial class" Congress intended to benefit. I am convinced, however, that the controlling authority is not *Cort,* but *J. I. Case Co.* v. *Borak,* supra. * * *

*   *   *

Two years after *Piper,* a non-SEC case (*Cannon* v. *University of Chicago*) that came out the other way on a *Cort* analysis shattered the unanimity of the *Cort* Court. Six Justices implied a private right of action under §901(a) of Title IX of the Education Amendments of 1972, which prohibits discrimination on the basis of sex under any education program receiving federal assistance.

With respect to the second *Cort* factor, Justice Stevens for the majority recognized that the legislative history of a statute that does not expressly create or deny a private right of action will typically be silent or ambiguous. "Therefore, in situations such as the present one 'in which it is clear that federal law has granted a class of persons certain rights, it is not necessary to show an intention to *create* a private right of action, although an explicit purpose to *deny* such cause of action would be controlling.' "[15] Here, the opinion continued, the drafters of Title IX explicitly assumed that it would be interpreted to grant a private right of action as Title VI (with respect to race) had been during the preceding eight years. Even so: "When Congress intends private litigants to have a cause of action to support their statutory rights, the far better course is for it to specify as much when it creates those rights."[16]

Justice Rehnquist, though joining the Stevens opinion, was much more pointed in a concurring opinion in which Justice

---

[15] 441 U. S. 677, 694 (1979), quoting from Cort v. Ash, 422 U. S. 66, 82 (1975).

[16] 441 U. S. at 717.

Stewart joined: After expressing his agreement with the view of the Stevens opinion that Congress intended to lean on the courts with respect to civil rights actions, Justice Rehnquist stated: "It seems to me that the factors to which I have here briefly adverted apprise the lawmaking branch of the Federal Government that the ball, so to speak, may well now be in its court. Not only is it 'far better' for Congress to so specify when it intends private litigants to have a cause of action, but for this very reason this Court in the future should be extremely reluctant to imply a cause of action absent such specificity on the part of the Legislative Branch."[17]

This attack on *Cort's* four-part analysis was as nothing compared with the dissenting opinion of Justice Powell. Whereas Justices White and Blackmun also dissented, questioning the minor premise of the syllogism as it were, Justice Powell squarely attacked the major premise, concluding that *Cort* was an unconstitutional encroachment on the separation of powers:

> * * * as mounting evidence from the courts below suggests, and the decision of the Court today demonstrates, the mode of analysis we have applied in the recent past cannot be squared with the doctrine of the separation of powers. The time has come to reappraise our standards for the judicial implication of private causes of action.

> *   *   *

> In recent history, the Court has tended to stray from the Art. III and separation-of-power principle of limited jurisdiction. This, I believe, is evident from a review of the more or less haphazard line of cases that led to our decision in *Cort* v. *Ash,* 422 U. S. 66 (1975). The "four factor" analysis of that case is an open invitation to federal courts to legislate causes of action not authorized by Congress. It is an analysis not faithful to constitutional principles and should be rejected. Absent the most compelling evidence of affirmative congressional intent, a federal court should not infer a private cause of action.

> *   *   *

> * * * In the four years since we decided *Cort,* no less than 20 decisions by the Courts of Appeals have implied private actions from federal statutes. [Citations omitted.] It defies reason

[17] Id. at 718.

to believe that in each of these statutes Congress absentmindedly forgot to mention an intended private action. * * * [18]

Here, then, are several members of the Court who seem to be denigrating three of the four *Cort* factors in favor of the second, which goes to legislative intent. And the two SEC cases that follow indicate that, although *Cort* may yet have a long "half-life," its four-factor analysis is already passé.

TOUCHE ROSS & CO. v. REDINGTON
Supreme Court of the United States, 1979
442 U. S. 560

MR. JUSTICE REHNQUIST delivered the opinion of the Court.

Once again, we are called upon to decide whether a private remedy is implicit in a statute not expressly providing one. During this Term alone, we have been asked to undertake this task no fewer than five times in cases in which we have granted certiorari. Here we decide whether customers of securities brokerage firms that are required to file certain financial reports with regulatory authorities by §17(a) of the Securities Exchange Act of 1934 (1934 Act), 48 Stat. 897, as amended, 15 U. S. C. §78q(a), have an implied cause of action for damages under §17(a) against accountants who audit such reports, based on misstatements contained in the reports.

I

Petitioner Touche Ross & Co. is a firm of certified public accountants. Weis Securities, Inc. (Weis), a securities brokerage firm registered as a broker-dealer with the Securities and Exchange Commission (Commission) and a member of the New York Stock Exchange (Exchange), retained Touche Ross to serve as Weis' independent certified public accountant from 1969 to 1973. In this capacity, Touche Ross conducted audits of Weis' books and records and prepared for filing with the Commission the annual reports of financial condition required by §17(a) of the 1934 Act, 15 U. S. C. §79q(a), and the rules and regulations adopted thereunder. 17 CFR §240.17a-5 (1972). Touche Ross also prepared for Weis responses to financial questionnaires required by the Exchange of its member firms.

---

[18] Id. at 730, 731, 741-42.

This case arises out of the insolvency and liquidation of Weis. In 1973, the Commission and the Exchange learned of Weis' precarious financial condition and of possible violations of the 1934 Act by Weis and its officers. In May 1973, the Commission sought and was granted an injunction barring Weis and five of its officers from conducting business in violation of the 1934 Act.[4] At the same time, the Securities Investor Protection Corporation (SIPC), pursuant to statutory authority, applied in the United States District Court for the Southern District of New York for a decree adjudging that Weis' customers were in need of the protection afforded by the Securities Investor Protection Act of 1970 (SIPA), 84 Stat. 1636, 15 U. S. C. §78aaa et seq. The District Court granted the requested decree and appointed respondent Redington (Trustee) to act as trustee in the liquidation of the Weis business under SIPA.

During the liquidation, Weis' cash and securities on hand appeared to be insufficient to make whole those customers who had left assets or deposits with Weis. Accordingly, pursuant to SIPA, SIPC advanced the Trustee $14 million to satisfy, up to specified statutory limits, the claims of the approximately 34,000 Weis customers and certain other creditors of Weis. Despite the advance of $14 million by SIPC, there apparently remain several million dollars of unsatisfied customer claims.

In 1976, SIPC and the Trustee filed this action for damages against Touche Ross in the District Court for the Southern District of New York. The "common allegations" of the complaint, which at this stage of the case we must accept as true, aver that certain of Weis' officers conspired to conceal substantial operating losses during its 1972 fiscal year by falsifying financial reports required to be filed with regulatory authorities pursuant to §17(a) of the 1934 Act. App. 8. SIPC and the Trustee seek to impose liability upon Touche Ross by reason of its allegedly improper audit and certification of the 1972 Weis financial statements and preparation of answers to the Exchange financial questionnaire. Id., at 15-19. The complaint alleges that because of its improper conduct, Touche Ross breached duties that it owed SIPC, the Trustee, and others under the common law, §17(a) and the regulations thereunder, and that Touche Ross' alleged dereliction prevented Weis' true financial condition from becoming known

---

[4] Some months later, several of Weis' officers were indicted, in part, for a conspiracy to violate and a number of substantive violations of the record-keeping and reporting regulations adopted by the Commission under §17(a). * * *

until it was too late to take remedial action to forestall liquidation or to lessen the adverse financial consequences of such a liquidation to the Weis customers. App. 8-9. The Trustee seeks to recover $51 million on behalf of Weis in its own right and on behalf of the customers of Weis whose property the Trustee was unable to return. SIPC claims $14 million, either as subrogee of Weis' customers whose claims it has paid under SIPA or in its own right. The federal claims are based on §17(a) of the 1934 Act; the complaint also alleges several state common-law causes of action based on accountants' negligence, breach of contract, and breach of warranty.

The District Court dismissed the complaint, holding that no claim for relief was stated because no private cause of action could be implied from §17(a). 428 F. Supp. 483 (S. D. N. Y. 1977). A divided panel of the Second Cicuit reversed. 592 F. 2d 617 (1978). The court first found that §17(a) imposes a duty on accountants. 592 F. 2d, at 621. It next concluded, based on the factors set forth in *Cort* v. *Ash*, 422 U. S. 66, 78 (1975), that an accountant's breach of his §17(a) duty gives rise to an implied private right of action for damages in favor of a broker-dealer's customers, even though it acknowledged that the "legislative history of the section is mute on the issue." 592 F. 2d, at 622. The court held that SIPC and the Trustee could assert this implied cause of action on behalf of the Weis customers. We granted certiorari, 439 U. S. 979 (1978), and we now reverse.

II

The question of the existence of a statutory cause of action is, of course, one of statutory construction. *Cannon* v. *University of Chicago*, 441 U. S. 677, 688 (1979); see *National Railroad Passenger Corp.* v. *National Association of Railroad Passengers*, 414 U. S. 453, 458 (1974) (hereinafter *Amtrak*). SIPC's argument in favor of implication of a private right of action based on tort principles, therefore, is entirely misplaced. Brief for Respondent SIPC 22-23. As we recently have emphasized, "the fact that a federal statute has been violated and some person harmed does not automatically give rise to a private cause of action in favor of that person." *Cannon* v. *University of Chicago, supra*, at 688. Instead, our task is limited solely to determining whether Congress intended to create the private right of action asserted by SIPC and the Trustee. And as with any case involving the interpretation of a statute, our analysis must begin with the language of the statute itself. *Cannon v. University of Chicago,* supra, at 689; *Teamsters v. Daniel,* 439 U. S. 551, 558 (1979); *Santa Fe Industries, Inc. v. Green,* 430 U. S. 462, 472 (1977); *Piper v. Chris-Craft Industries, Inc.,* 430 U. S. 1, 24 (1977); *Ernst & Ernst v. Hochfelder,* 425 U. S. 185, 197 (1976).

* * * In terms, §17(a) simply requires broker-dealers and others to keep such records and file such reports as the Commission may prescribe. It does not, by its terms, purport to create a private cause of action in favor of anyone. It is true that in the past our cases have held that in certain circumstances a private right of action may be implied in a statute not expressly providing one. But in those cases finding such implied private remedies, the statute in question at least prohibited certain conduct or created federal rights in favor of private parties. E. g., *Cannon v. University of Chicago,* supra (20 U. S. C. §1681); *Superintendent of Insurance v. Bankers Life & Cas. Co.,* 404 U. S. 6 (1971) (15 U. S. C. §78j(b)); *J. I. Case Co. v. Borak,* 377 U. S. 426 (1964) (15 U. S. C. §78n(a)).ᵃ By contrast, §17(a) neither confers rights on private parties nor proscribes any conduct as unlawful.

The intent of §17(a) is evident from its face. Section 17(a) is like provisions in countless other statutes that simply require certain regulated businesses to keep records and file periodic reports to enable the relevant governmental authorities to perform their regulatory functions. The reports and records provide the regulatory authorities with the necessary information to oversee compliance with and enforce the various statutes and regulations with which they are concerned. In this case, the §17(a) reports, along with inspections and other information, enable the Commission and the Exchange to ensure compliance with the "net capital rule," the principal regulatory tool by which the Commission and the Exchange monitor the financial health of brokerage firms and protect customers from the risks involved in leaving their cash and securities with broker-dealers.[10] The information

---

ᵃ ED.: Some citations are omitted.

10   *   *   *

A number of provisions of the 1934 Act provide the Commission with the authority needed to enforce the reporting requirements of §17(a) and the rules adopted thereunder. E. g., §15(b)(4), 15 U. S. C. §78o(b)(4) (authorizes institution of administrative proceedings and imposition of sanctions against brokers for, *inter alia,* materially misleading statements in reports or applications required to be filed with the Commission); §21, 15 U. S. C. §78u (allows Commission to investigate and enjoin violations and to refer violations to the Attorney General for possible prosecution); §32, 15 U. S. C. §78ff (authorizes criminal sanctions for violations of statute and rules and for materially miscontained in the §17(a) reports is intended to provide the Commission, the Exchange, and other authorities with a sufficiently early warning to enable them to take appropriate action to protect investors before the financial collapse of the particular broker-dealer involved. But §17(a) does not by any stretch of its language purport to confer private damages rights or, indeed, any remedy in the event the regulatory authorities are unsuccessful in achieving their objectives and the broker becomes insolvent before corrective steps can be taken. By its terms, §17(a) is forward-looking, not retrospective; it seeks to forestall insolvency, not to provide recompense after it has occurred. In short, there is no basis in the language of §17(a) for inferring that a civil cause of action for damages lay in favor of anyone. *Cort v. Ash,* 422 U. S., at 79.

As the Court of Appeals recognized, the legislative history of the 1934 Act is entirely silent on the question whether a private right of action for damages should or should not be available under §17(a) in the circumstances of this case. 592 F. 2d, at 622. SIPC and the Trustee nevertheless argue that because Congress did not express an intent to deny a private cause of action under §17(a), this Court should infer one. But implying a private right of action on the basis of congressional silence is a hazardous enterprise, at best. See *Santa Clara Pueblo* v. *Martinez,* 436 U. S. 49, 64 (1978). And where, as here, the plain language of the provision weighs against implication of a private remedy, the fact that there is no suggestion whatsoever in the legislative history that §17(a) may give rise to suits for damages reinforces our decision not to find such a right of action implicit within the section. See *Cort v. Ash,* supra, at 82-84; cf. *Securities Investor Protection Corp.* v. *Barbour,* 421 U. S. 412 (1975); *Amtrak,* 414 U. S. 453 (1974); *T. I. M. E. Inc.* v. *United States,* 359 U. S. 464 (1959).

Further justification for our decision not to imply the private remedy that SIPC and the Trustee seek to establish may be found in the statutory scheme of which §17(a) is a part. First, §17(a) is flanked by provisions of the 1934 Act that explicitly grant private causes of action. §16(b), 15 U. S. C. §78p(b); §18(a), 15 U. S. C. §78r(a). Section 9(e) of the 1934 Act also expressly provides a private right of action. 15 U. S. C. §78i(e). See also §20, 15 U. S. C. §78t. Obviously, then, when Congress wished to provide a private damages remedy, it knew how to do so and

---

leading statements in reports or documents required to be filed by the statute or rules); see n. 4, supra.

did so expressly. *Blue Chip Stamps* v. *Manor Drug Stores,* 421 U. S. 723, 734 (1975); see *Amtrak,* supra, at 458; *T. I. M. E. Inc.* v. *United States,* supra, at 471.

Second, §18(a) creates a private cause of action against persons, such as accountants, who "make or cause to be made" materially misleading statements in any reports or other documents filed with the Commission, although the cause of action is limited to persons who, in reliance on the statements, purchased or sold a security whose price was affected by the statements. 15 U. S. C. §78r(a); see *Ernst & Ernst* v. *Hochfelder,* 425 U. S., at 211 n. 31; *Blue Chip Stamps* v. *Manor Drug Stores,* supra, at 736. Since SIPC and the Trustee do not allege that the Weis customers purchased or sold securities in reliance on the §17(a) reports at issue, they cannot sue Touche Ross under §18(a).[13] Instead, their claim is that the Weis customers did not get the enforcement action they would have received if the §17(a) reports had been accurate. SIPC and the Trustee argue that §18(a) cannot provide the exclusive remedy for misstatements made in §17(a) reports because the cause of action created by §18(a) is expressly limited to purchasers and sellers. They assert that Congress could not have intended in §18(a) to deprive customers, such as those whom they seek to represent, of a cause of action for misstatements contained in §17(a) reports.

There is evidence to support the view that §18(a) was intended to provide the exclusive remedy for misstatements contained in any reports filed with the Commission, including those filed pursuant to §17(a). Certainly, SIPC and the Trustee have pointed to no evidence of a legislative intent to except §17(a) reports from §18(a)'s purview. Cf. *Securities Investor Protection Corp.,* 421 U. S., at 419-420; *Amtrak,* 414 U. S., at 458. But we need not decide whether Congress expressly intended §18(a) to provide the exclusive remedy for misstatements contained in

---

[13] In another action arising out of the Weis financial collapse, the District Court has sustained a §18(a) claim against Touche Ross by a bank that allegedly purchased securities of Weis in reliance upon the §17(a) reports involved in this case. Exchange National Bank v. Touche Ross & Co., 75 Civ. 916 (S. D. N. Y.); see 592 F. 2d, at 631 n. 5 (Mulligan, J., dissenting). And in a case related to the instant case, the customers of Weis brought a class action against Touche Ross under §18(a), claiming, *inter alia,* that Touche Ross violated Commission Rule 17a-5, 17 C. F. R. §240.17a-5 (1972). The District Court in that case dismissed the complaint on the ground that the plaintiffs did not meet the purchaser-seller requirement of §18(a) and thus could not maintain an action under that section. Rich v. Touche Ross & Co., 415 F. Supp. 95, 102-104 (S. D. N. Y. 1976). We express no view as to the correctness of either of these rulings.

§17(a) reports. For where the principal express civil remedy for misstatements in reports created by Congress contemporaneously with the passage of §17(a) is by its terms limited to purchasers and sellers of securities, we are extremely reluctant to imply a cause of action in §17(a) that is significantly broader than the remedy that Congress chose to provide. *Blue Chip Stamps* v. *Manor Drug Stores,* supra, at 735-736; see *Ernst & Ernst* v. *Hochfelder,* supra, at 210; *Securities Investor Protection Corp.* v. *Barbour,* supra, at 421-423; *Amtrak,* supra, at 458; cf. *T. I. M. E. Inc.* v. *United States,* 359 U. S., at 471.

SIPC and the Trustee urge, and the Court of Appeals agreed, that the analysis should not stop here. Relying on the factors set forth in *Cort* v. *Ash,* 422 U. S., at 78, they assert that we also must consider whether an implied private remedy is necessary to "effectuate the purpose of the section" and whether the cause of action is one traditionally relegated to state law. SIPC and the Trustee contend that implication of a private remedy is essential to the goals of §17(a) and that enforcement of §17(a) is properly a matter of federal, not state, concern. Brief for Respondent Redington 30-35; Brief for Respondent SIPC 42-52. We need not reach the merits of the arguments concerning the "necessity" of implying a private remedy and the proper forum for enforcement of the rights asserted by SIPC and the Trustee, for we believe such inquiries have little relevance to the decision of this case. It is true that in *Cort* v. *Ash,* the Court set forth four factors that it considered "relevant" in determining whether a private remedy is implicit in a statute not expressly providing one. But the Court did not decide that each of these factors is entitled to equal weight. The central inquiry remains whether Congress intended to create, either expressly or by implication, a private cause of action. Indeed, the first three factors discussed in *Cort* — the language and focus of the statute, its legislative history, and its purpose, see 422 U. S., at 78 — are ones traditionally relied upon in determining legislative intent. Here, the statute by its terms grants no private rights to any identifiable class and proscribes no conduct as unlawful. And the parties as well as the Court of Appeals agree that the legislative history of the 1934 Act simply does not speak to the issue of private remedies under §17(a). At least in such a case as this, the inquiry ends there: The question whether Congress, either expressly or by implication, intended to create a private right of action, has been definitely answered in the negative.

Finally, SIPA and the Trustee argue that our decision in *J. I.*

Case Co. v. *Borak,* 377 U. S. 426 (1964), requires implication of a private cause of action under §17(a). In *Borak,* the Court found in §14(a) of the 1934 Act, 15 U. S. C. §78n(a), an implied cause of action for damages in favor of shareholders for losses resulting from deceptive proxy solicitations in violation of §14(a). SIPC and the Trustee emphasize language in *Borak* that discusses the remedial purposes of the 1934 Act and §27 of the Act, which, *inter alia,* grants to federal district courts the exclusive jurisdiction of violations of the Act and suits to enforce any liability or duty created by the Act or the rules and regulations thereunder. They argue that Touche Ross has breached its duties under §17(a) and the rules adopted thereunder and that in view of §27 and of the remedial purposes of the 1934 Act, federal courts should provide a damages remedy for the breach.

The reliance of SIPC and the Trustee on §27 is misplaced. Section 27 grants jurisdiction to the federal courts and provides for venue and service of process. It creates no cause of action of its own force and effect; it imposes no liabilities. The source of plaintiffs' rights must be found, if at all, in the substantive provisions of the 1934 Act which they seek to enforce, not in the jurisdictional provision. See *Securities Investor Protection Corp.* v. *Barbour,* 421 U. S., at 424. The Court in *Borak* found a private cause of action implicit in §14(a). See *Cannon* v. *University of Chicago,* 441 U. S., at 690-693, n. 13; *Piper* v. *Chris-Craft Industries, Inc.,* 430 U. S., at 25; *Allen* v. *State Board of Elections,* 393 U. S., at 557. We do not now question the actual holding of that case, but we decline to read the opinion so broadly that virtually every provision of the securities Acts gives rise to an implied private cause of action. E. g., *Piper* v. *Chris-Craft Industries, Inc.,* supra.[19]

---

[19] We also have found implicit within §10(b) of the 1934 Act a private cause of action for damages. See Superintendent of Insurance v. Bankers Life & Cas. Co., 404 U. S. 6, 13 n. 9 (1971). But we recently have stated that in *Superintendent* this Court simply explicitly acquiesced in the 25-year-old acceptance by the lower federal courts of an implied action under §10(b). Cannon v. University of Chicago, 441 U. S., at 690-693, n. 13; see Ernst & Ernst v. Hochfelder, supra, at 196; Blue Chip Stamps v. Manor Drug Stores, 421 U. S. 723, 730 (1975). There is no similar history of longstanding lower-court interpretation in this case. Indeed, only one other court in the 45-year history of the 1934 Act has held that a private cause of action for damages is available under §17(a). Hawkins v. Merrill, Lynch, Pierce, Fenner & Beane, 85 F. Supp. 104, 124 (W. D. Ark. 1949). In *Hawkins,* a national brokerage firm was held liable for damages under §17(a) to a defalcating correspondent's customers for improperly advising the correspondent, who was found to be controlled by the national firm, to describe its business in such a way as to avoid filing certified financial statements with the Commission under §17(a). Citing Kardon

The invocation of the "remedial purposes" of the 1934 Act is similarly unavailing. Only last Term, we emphasized that generalized references to the "remedial purposes" of the 1934 Act will not justify reading a provision "more broadly than its language and the statutory scheme reasonably permit." *SEC* v. *Sloan,* 436 U. S. 103, 116 (1978); see *Ernst & Ernst* v. *Hochfelder,* 425 U. S., at 200. Certainly, the mere fact that §17(a) was designed to provide protection for brokers' customers does not require the implication of a private damages action in their behalf. *Cannon* v. *University of Chicago,* supra, at 688, and n. 9; *Securities Investor Protection Corp.* v. *Barbour,* supra, at 421. To the extent our analysis in today's decision differs from that of the Court in *Borak,* it suffices to say that in a series of cases since *Borak* we have adhered to a stricter standard for the implication of private causes of action, and we follow that stricter standard today. *Cannon* v. *University of Chicago,* supra, at 688-709. The ultimate question is one of congressional intent, not one of whether this Court thinks that it can improve upon the statutory scheme that Congress enacted into law.

III

SIPC and the Trustee contend that the result we reach sanctions injustice. But even if that were the case, the argument is made in the wrong forum, for we are not at liberty to legislate. If there is to be a federal damages remedy under these circumstances, Congress must provide it. "[I]t is not for us to fill any *hiatus* Congress has left in this area." *Wheeldin* v. *Wheeler,* 373 U. S. 647, 652 (1963). Obviously, nothing we have said prevents Congress from creating a private right of action on behalf of brokerage firm customers for losses arising from misstatements contained in §17(a) reports. But if Congress intends those customers to have such a federal right of action, it is well aware of how it may effectuate that intent.

The judgment of the Court of Appeals is reversed, and the case is remanded for further proceedings consistent with this opinion.

It is so ordered.

MR. JUSTICE POWELL took no part in the consideration or decision of this case.

---

v. *National Gypsum Co.,* 69 F. Supp. 612 (E. D. Pa. 1946), the District Court simply stated that violation of any of the provisions of the 1934 Act would give rise to a civil suit for damages on the part of the one injured, and that the defendants did not contend to the contrary. 85 F. Supp., at 121.

MR. JUSTICE BRENNAN, concurring.

* * * Although analyses of the several factors outlined in *Cort*
v. *Ash,* 422 U. S. 66 (1975), may often overlap, I agree that when,
as here, a statute clearly does not "create a federal right in favor
of the plaintiff," id., at 78, i. e., when the plaintiff is not " 'one
of the class for whose *especial* benefit the statute was enacted,' "
ibid., quoting *Texas & Pacific R. Co.* v. *Rigsby,* 241 U. S. 33, 39
(1916), and when there is also in the legislative history no "indication of legislative intent, explicit or implicit, . . . to create such
a remedy," 422 U. S., at 78, the remaining two *Cort* factors cannot by themselves be a basis for implying a right of action.

MR. JUSTICE MARSHALL, dissenting.

*   *   *

* * * [S]traightforward application of the four *Cort* factors
compels affirmance of the judgment below. Because the Court mis-
applies this precedent and disregards the evident purpose of §17,
I respectfully dissent.

Note the correction of *Borak's* erroneous reading of §27, the
jurisdictional provision, as creating a cause of action of its own
force and effect.

Note also the relegation of three of the four *Cort* factors — a
process begun in *Cannon* — to a negative role. Apparently they
may not, even as a troika, carry the day unless "Congress intended
to create, either expressly or by implication, a private cause of
action." We shall have a bit more to say about legislative intent
after we examine the next case, with its surprise ending:

TRANSAMERICA MORTGAGE ADVISORS, INC. v. LEWIS
Supreme Court of the United States, 1979
444 U. S. 11

MR. JUSTICE STEWART delivered the opinion of the Court.

The Investment Advisers Act of 1940, 15 U. S. C. §80b-1 et seq.,
was enacted to deal with abuses that Congress had found to exist
in the investment advisers industry. The questiton in this case is
whether that Act creates a private cause of action for damages or
other relief in favor of persons aggrieved by those who allegedly
have violated it.

The respondent, a shareholder of petitioner Mortgage Trust of America (Trust), brought this suit in a Federal District Court as a derivative action on behalf of the Trust and as a class action on behalf of the Trust's shareholders. Named as defendants were the Trust, several individual trustees, the Trust's investment adviser, Transamerica Mortgage Advisors, Inc. (TAMA), and two corporations affiliated with TAMA, Land Capital, Inc. (Land Capital), and Transamerica Corp. (Transamerica), all of which are petitioners in this case.[1]

The respondent's complaint alleged that the petitioners in the course of advising or managing the Trust had been guilty of various frauds and breaches of fiduciary duty. The complaint set out three causes of action, each said to arise under the Investment Advisers Act of 1940. The first alleged that the advisory contract between TAMA and the Trust was unlawful because TAMA and Transamerica were not registered under the Act and because the contract had provided for grossly excessive compensation. The second alleged that the petitioners breached their fiduciary duty to the Trust by causing it to purchase securities of inferior quality from Land Capital. The third alleged that the petitioners had missappropriated profitable investment opportunities for the benefit of other companies affiliated with Transamerica. The complaint sought injunctive relief to restrain further performance of the advisory contract, rescission of the contract, restitution of fees and other considerations paid by the Trust, an accounting of illegal profits, and an award of damages.

The trial court ruled that the Investment Advisers Act confers no private right of action, and accordingly dismissed the complaint. The Court of Appeals [for the Ninth Circuit] reversed, *Lewis* v. *Transamerica Corp.,* 575 F. 2d 237, holding that "implication of a private right of action for injunctive relief and damages under the Advisers Act in favor of appropriate plaintiffs is necessary to achieve the goals of Congress in enacting the legislation."

---

[1] Hereinafter "the petitioners" refers to the petitioners other than the Trust. The Trust is a real estate investment trust within the meaning of §§856-858 of the Internal Revenue Code of 1954, 26 U. S. C. §§856-858. TAMA, in addition to advising the Trust, managed its day-to-day operations. Transamerica is the sponsor of the Trust and the parent of Land Capital. Land Capital is the parent of TAMA, through a subsidiary, and sold the Trust its initial portfolio of investments. Several of the individual trustees were at the time of suit affiliated with TAMA, Transamerica, or other subsidiaries of Transamerica.

Id., at 239.[4] We granted certiorari to consider the important federal question presented. 439 U. S. 952.

The Investment Advisers Act nowhere expressly provides for a private cause of action. The only provision of the Act that authorizes any suits to enforce the duties or obligations created by it is §209, which permits the Securities and Exchange Commission (Commission) to bring suit in a federal district court to enjoin violations of the Act or the rules promulgated under it. The argument is made, however, that the clients of investment advisers were the intended beneficiaries of the Act and that courts should therefore imply a private cause of action in their favor. See *Cannon* v. *University of Chicago,* 441 U. S. 677, 689; *Cort* v. *Ash,* 422 U. S. 66, 78; *J. I. Case Co.* v. *Borak,* 377 U. S. 426, 432.

The question whether a statute creates a cause of action, either expressly or by implication, is basically a matter of statutory construction. *Touche Ross & Co.* v. *Redington,* 442 U. S. 560, 568; *Cannon* v. *University of Chicago,* supra, at 688; see *National Railroad Passenger Corp.* v. *National Association of Railroad Passengers,* 414 U. S. 453, 458 *(Amtrak).* While some opinions of the Court have placed considerable emphasis upon the desirability of implying private rights of action in order to provide remedies thought to effectuate the purposes of a given statute, e. g., *J. I. Case Co.* v. *Borak,* supra, what must ultimately be determined is whether Congress intended to create the private remedy asserted, as our recent decisions have made clear. *Touche Ross & Co.* v. *Redington,* supra, at 568; *Cannon* v. *University of Chicago,* supra, at 688. We accept this as the appropriate inquiry to be made in resolving the issues presented by the case before us.

Accordingly, we begin with the language of the statute itself. *Touche Ross & Co.* v. *Redington,* supra, at 568; *Cannon* v. *University of Chicago,* supra, at 689; *Santa Fe Industries, Inc.* v. *Green,* 430 U. S. 462, 472; *Piper* v. *Chris-Craft Industries, Inc.,* 430 U. S. 1, 24. It is asserted that the creation of a private right of action can fairly be inferred from the language of two sections of the Act. The first is §206, which broadly proscribes fraudulent practices by investment advisers, making it unlawful for any investment adviser "to employ any device, scheme, or artifice to

---

4　　　　　　　*　　*　　*

The Court of Appeals in this case followed the Courts of Appeals for the Fifth and Second Circuits, which also have held that private causes of action may be maintained under the Act. See Wilson v. First Houston Investment Corp., 566 F. 2d 1235 (C. A. 5 1978); Abrahamson v. Fleschner, 568 F. 2d 862 (C. A. 2, 1977).

defraud . . . [or] to engage in any transaction, practice, or course of business which operates as a fraud or deceit upon any client or prospective client," or to engage in specified transactions with clients without making required disclosures. The second is §215, which provides that contracts whose formation or performance would violate the Act "shall be void . . . as regards the rights of" the violator and knowing successors in interest.

It is apparent that the two sections were intended to benefit the clients of investment advisers, and, in the case of §215, the parties to advisory contracts as well. As we have previously recognized, §206 establishes "federal fiduciary standards" to govern the conduct of investment advisers, *Santa Fe Industries, Inc. v. Green,* supra, at 471, n.11; *Burks v. Lasker,* 441 U. S. 471, 481-482, n. 10; *SEC v. Capital Gains Research Bureau, Inc.,* 375 U. S. 180, 191-192. Indeed, the Act's legislative history leaves no doubt that Congress intended to impose enforceable fiduciary obligations. See H. R. Rep. No. 2639, 76th Cong., 3d Sess., 28 (1940); S. Rep. No. 1775, 76th Cong., 3d Sess., 21 (1940); SEC, Report on Investment Trusts and Investment Companies (Investment Counsel and Investment Advisory Services), H. R. Doc. No. 477, 76th Cong., 2d Sess., 27-30 (1939). But whether Congress intended additionally that these provisions would be enforced through private litigation is a different question.

On this question the legislative history of the Act is entirely silent — a state of affairs not surprising when it is remembered that the Act concededly does not explicitly provide any private remedies whatever. See *Cannon v. University of Chicago,* supra, at 694. But while the absence of anything in the legislative history that indicates an intention to confer any private right of action is hardly helpful to the respondent, it does not automatically undermine his position. This Court has held that the failure of Congress expressly to consider a private remedy is not inevitably inconsistent with an intent on its part to make such a remedy available. *Cannon v. University of Chicago,* supra, at 694. Such an intent may appear implicitly in the language or structure of the statute, or in the circumstances of its enactment.

In the case of §215, we conclude that the statutory language itself fairly implies a right to specific and limited relief in a federal court. By declaring certain contracts void, §215 by its terms necessarily contemplates that the issue of voidness under its criteria may be litigated somewhere. At the very least Congress must have assumed that §215 could be raised defensively in private litigation to preclude the enforcement of an investment advisers contract. But the legal consequences of voidness are typically not so limited. A person with the power to avoid a contract ordinarily may resort to a court to have the contract rescinded and to obtain restitution of consideration paid. See *Deckert* v. *Independence Corp.*, 311 U. S. 282, 289; S. Williston, Contracts §1525 (3d ed. 1970); J. Pomeroy, Equity Jurisprudence §§881 and 1092 (4th ed. 1918). And this Court has previously recognized that a comparable provision, §29(b) of the Securities Exchange Act of 1934, 15 U. S. C. §78cc(b), confers a "right to rescind" a contract void under the criteria of the statute. *Mills* v. *Electric Auto-Lite Co.*, 396 U. S. 375, 388. Moreover, the federal courts in general have viewed such language as implying an equitable cause of action for rescission or similar relief. E. g., *Kardon* v. *National Gypsum Co.*, 69 F. Supp. 512, 514 (E. D. Pa. 1946); see 3 L. Loss, Securities Regulation 1758-1759 (2d ed. 1961). Cf. *Blue Chip Stamps* v. *Manor Drug Stores*, 421 U. S. 723, 735.

For these reasons we conclude that when Congress declared in §215 that certain contracts are void, it intended that the customary legal incidents of voidness would follow, including the availability of a suit for rescission or for an injunction against continued operation of the contract, and for restitution.[8] Accordingly, we hold that the Court of Appeals was correct in ruling that the respondent may maintain an action on behalf of the Trust seeking to void the investment adviser's contract.[9]

We view quite differently, however, the respondent's claims for damages and other monetary relief under §206. Unlike §215, §206 simply proscribes certain conduct, and does not in terms create or alter any civil liabilities. If monetary liability to a private plaintiff is to be found, it must be read into the Act. Yet it is an elemental canon of statutory construction that where a statute expressly provides a particular remedy or remedies, a court must be chary of reading others into it. "When a statute limits a thing to be done in a particular mode, it includes the negative of any other mode." *Botany Mills* v. *United States*, 278 U. S. 282, 289. See *Amtrak*, 414 U. S., at 458; *Securities Investor Protection Corp.* v. *Barbour*, 421 U. S. 412, 419; *T. I. M. E., Inc.* v. *United States*,

---

[8] One possibility, of course, is that Congress intended that claims under §215 would be raised only in state court. But we decline to adopt such an anomalous construction without some indication that Congress in fact wished to remit the litigation of a federal right to the state courts.

[9] Jurisdiction of such suits would exist under §214, 15 U. S. C. §80b-14, which, though referring in terms only to "suits in equity to enjoin any violation," would equally sustain actions where simple declaratory relief or rescission is sought.

359 U. S. 464, 471. Congress expressly provided both judicial and administrative means for enforcing compliance with §206. First, under §217, 15 U. S. C. §80b-17, willful violations of the Act are criminal offenses, punishable by fine or imprisonment, or both. Second, §209 authorizes the Commission to bring civil actions in federal courts to enjoin compliance with the Act, including, of course, §206. Third, the Commission is authorized by §203 to impose various administrative sanctions on persons who violate the Act, including §206. In view of these express provisions for enforcing the duties imposed by §206, it is highly improbable that "Congress absentmindedly forgot to mention an intended private action." *Cannon* v. *University of Chicago,* 441 U. S., at 742 (Powell, J., dissenting).

Even settled rules of statutory construction could yield, of course, to persuasive evidence of a contrary legislative intent. *Securities Investor Protection Corp.* v. *Barbour,* supra, at 419; *Amtrak,* supra, at 458. But what evidence of intent exists in this case, circumstantial though it be, weighs against the implication of a private right of action for a monetary award in a case such as this. Under each of the securities laws that preceded the Act here in question, and under the Investment Company Act of 1940 which was enacted as companion legislation, Congress expressly authorized private suits for damages in prescribed circumstances. For example, Congress provided an express damages remedy for misrepresentations contained in an underwriter's registration statement in §11(a) of the Securities Act of 1933, and for certain materially misleading statements in §18(a) of the Securities Exchange Act of 1934. "Obviously, then, when Congress wished to provide a private damages remedy, it knew how to do so and did so expressly." *Touche Ross & Co.* v. *Redington,* 442 U. S., at 572. *Blue Chip Stamps* v. *Manor Drug Stores,* supra, at 734; see *Amtrak,* supra, at 458; *T. I. M. E., Inc.* v. *United States,* supra, at 471. The fact that it enacted no analogous provisions in the legislation here at issue strongly suggests that Congress was simply unwilling to impose any potential monetary liability to a private suitor. See *Abrahamson* v. *Fleschner,* 568 F. 2d 862, 883 (C. A. 2 1977) (Gurfein, J., concurring and dissenting).

*   *   *

Relying on the factors identified in *Cort* v. *Ash,* 422 U. S. 66, the respondent and the Commission, as *amicus curiae,* argue that our inquiry in this case cannot stop with the intent of Congress, but must consider the utility of a private remedy, and the fact that it may be one not traditionally relegated to state law. We rejected the same contentions last Term in *Touche Ross & Co.* v. *Redington* * * * . * * *

The statute in *Touche Ross* by its terms neither granted private rights to the members of any identifiable class, nor proscribed any conduct as unlawful. *Touche Ross & Co.* v. *Redington*, 442 U. S., at 576. In those circumstances it was evident to the Court that no private remedy was available. Section 206 of the Act here involved concededly was intended to protect the victims of the fraudulent practices it prohibited. But the mere fact that the statute was designed to protect advisers' clients does not require the implication of a private cause of action for damages on their behalf. *Touche Ross & Co.* v. *Redington*, supra, at 578; *Cannon* v. *University of Chicago*, 441 U. S., at 690-693; *Securities Investor Protection Corp.* v. *Barbour*, 421 U. S., at 421. The dispositive question remains whether Congress intended to create any such remedy. Having answered that question in the negative, our inquiry is at an end.

For the reasons stated in this opinion, we hold that there exists a limited private remedy under the Investment Advisers Act of 1940 to void an investment advisers contract, but that the Act confers no other private causes of action, legal or equitable.[14] Accordingly, the judgment of the Court of Appeals is affirmed in part and reversed in part, and the case is remanded to that court for further proceedings consistent with this opinion.

It is so ordered.

MR. JUSTICE POWELL, concurring.

I join the Court's opinion, which I view as compatible with my dissent in *Cannon* v. *University of Chicago*, 441 U. S. 677, 730 (1979). Ante, at 19-21.

MR. JUSTICE WHITE, with whom MR. JUSTICE BRENNAN, MR. JUSTICE MARSHALL, and MR. JUSTICE STEVENS join, dissenting.

The Court today holds that private rights of action under the

[14] Where rescission is awarded, the rescinding party may of course have restitution of the consideration given under the contract, less any value conferred by the other party. See 5 A. Corbin, Contracts §1114 (1964). Restitution would not, however, include compensation for any diminution in the value of the rescinding party's investment alleged to have resulted from the adviser's action or inaction. Such relief could provide by indirection the equivalent of a private damages remedy that we have concluded Congress did not confer.

Investment Advisers Act of 1940 (Act) are limited to actions for rescission of investment advisers contracts. In reaching this decision, the Court departs from established principles governing the implication of private rights of action by confusing the inquiry into the existence of a right of action with the question of available relief. By holding that damages are unavailable to victims of violations of the Act, the Court rejects the conclusion of every United States Court of Appeals that has considered the question. *Abrahamson* v. *Fleschner,* 568 F. 2d 862 (C. A. 2 1977); *Wilson* v. *First Houston Investment Corp.,* 566 F. 2d 1235 (C. A. 5 1978); *Lewis* v. *Transamerica Corp.,* 575 F. 2d 237 (C. A. 9 1978). The Court's decision cannot be reconciled with our decisions recognizing implied private actions for damages under securities laws with substantially the same language as the Act.[1] By resurrecting distinctions between legal and equitable relief, the Court reaches a result that, as all parties to this litigation agree, can only be considered anomalous.

I

This Court has long recognized that private rights of action do not require express statutory authorization. *Texas & Pacific R. Co.* v. *Rigsby,* 241 U. S. 33 (1916); *Tunstall* v. *Locomotive Firemen & Enginemen,* 323 U. S. 210 (1944). The preferred approach for determining whether a private right of action should be implied from a federal statute was outlined in *Cort* v. *Ash,* 422 U. S. 66, 78 (1975). See *Cannon* v. *University of Chicago,* 441 U. S. 677 (1979). Four factors were thought relevant; and although subsequent decisions have indicated that the implication of a private right of action "is limited solely to determining whether Congress intended to create the private right of action," *Touche Ross & Co.* v. *Redington,* 442 U. S. 560, 568 (1979), these four factors are "the criteria through which this intent could be discerned." *Davis* v. *Passman,* 442 U. S. 228, 241 (1979). Proper

---

[1] The provisions of §206 of the Investment Advisers Act of 1940, 15 U. S. C. §80b-6, are substantially similar to §10(b) of the Securities Exchange Act of 1934, 15 U. S. C. §78j(b), and Rule 10b-5, 17 C. F. R. §240.10b-5 (1979), both of which have been held to create private rights of action for which damages may be recovered. Superintendent of Insurance v. Bankers Life & Cas. Co., 404 U. S. 6, 13, n. 9 (1971); Blue Chip Stamps v. Manor Drug Stores, 421 U. S. 723, 730 (1975). The provisions of §215(b) of the Act, 15 U. S. C. §80b-15(b), are substantially similar to other provisions in the Securities Exchange Act of 1934 [§29(b)], 15 U. S. C. §78cc(b).

application of the factors outlined in *Cort* clearly indicates that §206 of the Act, 15 U. S. C. §80b-6, creates a private right of action.

*   *   *

III

*   *   *

The Court's conclusion that §215, but not §206, creates an implied private right of action ignores the relationship of §215 to the substantive provisions of the Act contained in §206. Like the jurisdictional provisions of a statute, §215 "creates no cause of action of its own force and effect; it imposes no liabilities." *Touche Ross & Co.* v. *Redington,* supra, at 577. Section 215 merely specifies one consequence of a violation of the substantive prohibitions of §206. The practical necessity of a private action to enforce this particular consequence of a §206 violation suggests that Congress contemplated the use of private actions to redress violations of §206. It also indicates that Congress did not intend the powers given to the SEC to be the exclusive means for enforcement of the Act.

The Court's holding that private litigants are restricted to actions for contract rescission confuses the question whether a cause of action exists with the question of the nature of relief available in such an action. * * *

*   *   *

VI

Each of the *Cort* factors points toward implication of a private cause of action in favor of clients defrauded by investment advisers in violation of the Act. The Act was enacted for the special benefit of clients of investment advisers, and there is no indication of any legislative intent to deny such a cause of action, which would be consistent with the legislative scheme governing an area not traditionally relegated to state law. Under these circumstances an implied private right of action for damages should be recognized.

———————

There have been other Supreme Court cases[19] — notably:

[19] E. g., Davis v. Passman, 442 U. S. 228 (1979) (*Cort* analysis does not

MERRILL LYNCH, PIERCE, FENNER & SMITH, INC.
v. CURRAN
Supreme Court of the United States, 1982
102 S. Ct. 1825

[One of four cases, reported together, involved an action by an investor in commodity futures contracts against his futures commission merchant (broker) for violation of an antifraud provision of the Commodity Exchange Act, and the other three involved actions by speculators in futures contracts against the New York Mercantile Exchange and its officials and against futures commission merchants, claiming damages resulting from unlawful price manipulation that allegedly could have been prevented by the Exchange's enforcement of its own rules.]

Justice Stevens delivered the opinion of the Court.

*   *   *

Our approach to the task of determining whether Congress intended to authorize a private cause of action has changed significantly, much as the quality and quantity of federal legislation has undergone significant change. When federal statutes were less comprehensive, the Court applied a relatively simple test to determine the availability of an implied private remedy. If a statute was enacted for the benefit of a special class, the judiciary normally recognized a remedy for members of that class. *Texas & Pacific R. Co. v. Rigsby,* 241 U. S. 33 (1916). Under this approach, fed-

---

apply to actions based directly on the Constitution, in this case an allegation of sex-based discrimination by a Congressman in violation of the Fifth Amendment); Carlson v. Green, 446 U. S. 14 (1980) (Court extended *Bivens,* supra p. 1064, to Eighth Amendment's proscription of cruel and unusual punishment); Kissinger v. Reporters Committee for Freedom of the Press, 445 U. S. 136 (1980) (no action under Federal Records Act of 1950, as supplemented by Records Disposal Act, or Freedom of Information Act); Universities Research Assn. v. Coutu, 450 U. S. 754 (1981) (no employee action for back wages under Davis-Bacon Act, with respect to federal construction contracts); Northwest Airlines, Inc. v. Transport Workers Union of America, 451 U. S. 77 (1981), infra p. 1205 (no statutory or federal common law allows federal courts to fashion contribution among violators of Equal Pay Act of 1963 and Title VII of Civil Rights Act of 1964); California v. Sierra Club, 451 U. S. 287 (1981) (no action for violation of requirement in §10 of Rivers and Harbors Appropriations Act of 1899 that any obstruction to navigable capacity be authorized by Congress); Texas Industries, Inc. v. Radcliff Materials, Inc., 451 U. S. 630 (1981), infra p. 1206 (no statutory or federal common law allows federal courts to fashion contribution among antitrust violators); Middlesex County Sewerage Authority v. National Sea Clammers Assn., 453 U. S. 1 (1981) (no action for violation of Federal Water Pollution Control Act and Marine Protection, Research, and Sanctuaries Act of 1972).

eral courts, following a common-law tradition, regarded the denial of a remedy as the exception rather than the rule.

Because the *Rigsby* approach prevailed throughout most of our history, there is no merit to the argument advanced by petitioners that the judicial recognition of an implied private remedy violates the separation of powers doctrine. * * *

During the years prior to 1975, the Court occasionally refused to recognize an implied remedy, either because the statute in question was a general regulatory prohibition enacted for the benefit of the public at large, or because there was evidence that Congress intended an express remedy to provide the exclusive method of enforcement. While the *Rigsby* approach prevailed, however, congressional silence or ambiguity was an insufficient reason for the denial of a remedy for a member of the class a statute was enacted to protect.

In 1975 the Court unanimously decided to modify its approach to the question whether a federal statute includes a private right of action. In *Cort* v. *Ash,* 422 U. S. 66 (1975), the Court confronted a claim that a private litigant could recover damages for violation of a criminal statute that had never before been thought to include a private remedy. In rejecting that claim the Court outlined criteria that primarily focused on the intent of Congress in enacting the statute under review. The increased complexity of federal legislation and the increased volume of federal litigation strongly supported the desirability of a more careful scrutiny of legislative intent than *Rigsby* had required. * * * The key to this case is our understanding of the intent of Congress in 1974 when it comprehensively reexamined and strengthened the federal regulation of futures trading.

*   *   *

Prior to the comprehensive amendments to the CEA enacted in 1974, the federal courts routinely and consistently had recognized an implied private cause of action on behalf of plaintiffs seeking to enforce and to collect damages for violation of provisions of the CEA or rules and regulations promulgated pursuant to the statute. The routine recognition of a private remedy under the CEA prior to our decision in *Cort* v. *Ash* was comparable to the routine acceptance of an analogous remedy under the Securities Exchange Act of 1934. * * *a

*   *   *

a ED.: This theme is repeated in Herman & MacLean v. Huddleston, 103 S. Ct. 683, 689 set out infra p. 1141, at pp. 1145-46.

* * * A review of the legislative history of the statute persuasively indicates that preservation of the remedy was indeed what Congress actually intended.

*   *   *

In view of our construction of the intent of the legislature there is no need for us to "trudge through all four of the factors when the dispositive question of legislative intent has been resolved." See *California* v. *Sierra Club,* 451 U. S., at 302 (Rehnquist, J., concurring in the judgment). We hold that the private cause of action under the CEA that was previously available to investors survived the 1974 amendments.

*   *   *

JUSTICE POWELL, with whom THE CHIEF JUSTICE, JUSTICE REHNQUIST, and JUSTICE O'CONNOR join, dissenting.

The Court today holds that Congress intended the federal courts to recognize implied causes of action under five separate provisions of the Commodity Exchange Act (CEA), 7 U. S. C. §1 et seq. The decision rests on two theories. First, the Court relies on fewer than a dozen cases in which the lower federal courts *erroneously* upheld private rights of action in the years prior to the 1974 Amendments to the CEA. Reasoning that these mistaken decisions constituted "the law" in 1974, the Court holds that Congress must be assumed to have endorsed this path of error when it *failed to amend* certain sections of the CEA in that year. This theory is incompatible with our constitutional separation of powers, and in my view it is without support in logic or in law. * * *

*   *   *

* * * Fewer than a dozen district courts wrongly create a remedy in damages under the CEA; Congress fails to correct the error; and congressional silence binds this Court to follow the erroneous decisions of the district courts and courts of appeals. * * *

*   *   *

The Court's holding today may reflect its view of desirable policy. If so, this view is doubly mistaken.

First, modern federal regulatory statutes tend to be exceedingly complex. Especially in this context, courts should recognize that intricate policy calculations are necessary to decide when new enforcement measures are desirable additions to a particular regulatory structure. Judicial creation of private rights of action is as likely to disrupt as to assist the functioning of the regulatory schemes developed by Congress. See, e. g., *University Research Assn., Inc.* v. *Coutu,* 450 U. S. 754, 782-784 (1981).

Today's decision also is disquieting because of its implicit view of the judicial role in the creation of federal law. The Court propounds a test that taxes the legislative branch with a duty to respond to opinions of the lower federal courts. The penalty for silence is the risk of having those erroneous judicial opinions imputed to Congress itself — on the basis of its presumptive knowledge of "the contemporary legal context." Ante, at — . Despite the Court's allusion to the lawmaking powers of courts at common law, see ante, at — , this view is inconsistent with the theory and structure of our constitutional government.

For reasons that I have expressed before, I remain convinced that "we should not condone the implication of any private right of action from a federal statute absent the most compelling evidence that Congress in fact intended such an action to exist." *Cannon* v. *University of Chicago,* supra, 441 U. S., at 749 (Powell, J., dissenting).[17] Here the evidence falls far short of this constitutionally appropriate standard.

Accordingly, I respectfully dissent.

With one subsequent SEC case, *Herman & MacLean* v. *Huddleston*[20] — which is set out later because it involved the question whether the established right of action under Rule 10b-5 applied in the face of an express remedy for the same conduct under §11 of the 1933 Act — all the Supreme Court cases that are directly in point under the SEC statutes have been set out or referred to here, as well as the most significant non-SEC cases. *Query* where all this leaves the matter of implied liability under the securities legislation:

[17] There can be little doubt that failure to adhere to this standard will encourage the discovery of private causes of action of which Congress never dreamed. The escalating recourse to damages suits has placed a severe and growing burden on the lower federal courts. My research — accomplished mostly through a computer search of cases in the federal reporters — indicates that in the past decade there have been at least 243 reported circuit court opinions and 515 district court opinions dealing with the existence of implied causes of action under various federal statutes. It is time federal courts discontinued the speculative creation of damages liability where the legislative branch has chosen to remain silent.

[20] 103 S. Ct. 683 (1983), set out infra p. 1141.

(1) It seems fairly clear that *Cort,* though still used, has been weakened, at least to the extent that the third and fourth factors (consistency with the statutory scheme and impact on state law) are irrelevant unless the second factor (legislative intent) — together perhaps with the first (whether the plaintiff is a member of a class meant to be especially benefited)[21] — points to an affirmative conclusion.

(2) It is difficult to quarrel with legislative intent as the ultimate determinant. After all, that criterion — perhaps better phrased more objectively as statutory purpose — is the key to all statutory construction. The trouble is that, in the ordinary case in which a statute makes no mention of a civil remedy, "the obvious conclusion can only be that when the legislature said nothing about it, they either did not have the civil suit in mind at all, or deliberately omitted to provide for it."[22] But that assumption concedes too much. History, after all, has vindicated Lord Coke and not James I.[23] Legislative intention in the literal, lay sense is one thing, and the growth of the common law (including the *Erie*-resistant "federal common law" that surrounds federal statutes) by the interaction of judges' decisions upon legislation is another.[24] The statutory tort doctrine, more or less as expounded in the Restatement,[25] is now an accepted part of American law. Consequently, if the silence of the statute does not justify the conclusion that the legislature affirmatively "intended" that there should be a private remedy, neither does it justify the conclusion that Congress had the contrary "intention." There is no need, as Dean Thayer wrote almost seventy years ago, for the court to try to discover "supposed legislative intent." "The legislature is to be credited with meaning just what it said — that the conduct forbidden is an offense against the public, and that the offender shall suffer certain specified penalties for his offense.

---

[21] California v. Sierra Club, 451 U. S. 287, 297 (1981).

[22] Prosser, Handbook of the Law of Torts (4th ed. 1971) 191.

[23] "Then the King said, that he thought the Law was founded upon reason, and that he and others had reason, as well as the Judges: To which it was answered by me, that * * * causes which concerne the life, or inheritance, or goods, or fortunes of his Subjects; they are not to be decided by naturall reason, but by the artificial reason and judgment of Law, which Law is an act which requires long study and experience * * * ." Prohibitions del Roy, 12 Rep. 63, 64-65 (1608).

[24] The theme has been developed in a number of well-known essays. Landis, Statutes and the Sources of Law, in Harv. Legal Essays (1934) 213; Pound, Common Law and Legislation, 21 Harv. L. Rev. 383 (1908); Stone, The Common Law in the United States, 50 Harv. L. Rev. 4, esp. at 12-16 (1936).

[25] See p. 1058 supra.

Whether his offense shall have any other legal consequence has not been passed on one way or the other as a question of legislative intent, but is left to be determined by the rules of law."[26]

All this is to say (now that the Supreme Court has spoken) that, although legislative intent is currently "the name of the game," the statutory tort doctrine (the first *Cort* factor) should be considered along with legislative intent, or at least as a significant factor in determining legislative intent. That is where a majority of the Court now seems to be, with the other two *Cort* factors ignored except as brakes on the first two.

(3) Suppose Congress wants civil liability but prefers to delegate the job of working out the nuances to the courts. For example, both of the legislative reports on the Small Business Investment Incentive Act of 1980,[27] emphasized the value of private rights of action as a necessary adjunct to the SEC's enforcement efforts as well as providing a compensatory function, and made it plain that the courts were expected to recognize private rights of action under the legislation, since they "would be consistent with and further Congress' intent in enacting [the particular] provision, and * * * such actions would not improperly occupy an area traditionally the concern of state law."[28] So, even under Justice Powell's constitutional view a formula exists for affording judicial flexibility without at the same time offending Article III. That view — which (with respect) is weakened by its ignoring the statutory tort doctrine's roots in the common law well before 1789[29] — seems to have picked up three more Justices.[30]

---

[26] Thayer, Public Wrong and Private Action, 27 Harv. L. Rev. 317, 320 (1914).

[27] See p. 338 supra.

[28] H. R. Rep. No. 96-1341 at 28-29 and S. Rep. No. 96-958 at 14 (1980). The Code's approach, after codifying today's express liabilities as well as those most often implied, is this (1 Code xlvii):

> So far as implying further liabilities is concerned, the Code proceeds on the basis that it would be both impracticable and undesirable to make everything express and foreclose further judicial inventiveness. At the same time, the recent series of Supreme Court decisions on the implication of private rights of action (see Comment (3) to §1716) counsels against too ready dependence on the implication alternative. Consequently, §1722(a) authorizes the courts to recognize private actions not expressly included in the Code, but only if (*inter alia*) they are not inconsistent with the conditions and restrictions in the express actions and the plaintiff satisfies the court that "under the circumstances the type of remedy sought is not disproportionate to the alleged violation."

[29] See p. 1057 supra; Merrill Lynch, Pierce, Fenner & Smith, Inc. v. Curran, 102 S. Ct. 1825, 1837-38 (1982), set out supra p. 1099, at p. 1100.

[30] Id. at 1848.

(4) The Latin maxims resist burial. Justice White complained in his dissenting opinion in the case under the Advisers Act:

> The Court concludes that because the Act expressly provides for SEC enforcement proceedings, Congress must not have intended to create private rights of action. This application of the oft-criticized maxim *expressio unius est exclusio alterius* ignores our rejection of it in *Cort v. Ash,* 422 U. S., at 82-83, n. 14, in the absence of specific support in the legislative history for the proposition that express statutory remedies are to be exclusive.[31]

However convenient a role maxims play by way of affording "the verbal tools of accepted rhetoric for use in court,"[32] they are no more than a substitute for legal reasoning, worthy perhaps of being sprinkled throughout an opinion as a chef sprinkles spice after his culinary creation has been completed. Maxims not only tyrannize, as Justice Jackson observed. They also are self-defeating: in this very context of determining when to imply civil liability from violation of a criminal statute, a comment in the Restatement (Second) of Torts puts it:

> Resort is sometimes made to maxims of statutory construction. Here, as in other instances, however, these maxims point in opposite directions and therefore prove to be inconclusive. One maxim is *Ubi ius ibi remedium,* suggesting that if the legislation created a right it must have been intended to create an adequate remedy to enforce that right. Opposed to this is the maxim, *Expressio unius exclusio alterius est,* suggesting that if the legislation called for a criminal penalty the civil liability must have intentionally been omitted, or if one section calls for civil liability and another does not it must have been intended that there would be no civil liability under the second section.[33]

Four years after *Transamerica* Justice Marshall echoed this thought for a unanimous Court — dare one say finally? — when he said in *Herman & MacLean,* recalling Justice Jackson's response to argument from maxims in the *Joiner* case,[34] "We also reject application of the maxim of statutory construction, *expressio unius est exclusio alterius.*"[35]

(5) The Advisers Act case makes it crystal clear that the voidability provisions in the 1934, 1935, and 1940 Acts may be used by

---

[31] Transamerica Mortgage Advisors, Inc. v. Lewis, 444 U. S. 11, 29 n. 6.
[32] Ballantine, Corporations (rev. ed. 1946) 313, quoting Llewellyn.
[33] §874A, Comment c.
[34] SEC v. C. M. Joiner Leasing Co., 320 U. S. 344, 350 (1943), set out supra p. 186.
[35] 103 S. Ct. at 690 n. 23, set out infra p. 1146, n. 23.

the innocent party offensively to achieve rescission, not merely defensively to avoid enforcement of the contract. This is at least three-quarters for a loaf, and one whose aroma seems pleasing to all nine Justices. Indeed, it is arguable even in the face of *Transamerica* that §29(b) of the 1934 Act makes the *whole* loaf available — damages as well as rescission — because it alone of the four voidability provisions contains a statute of limitations, inserted in 1936 along with the enactment of what is now §15(c)(1), with respect to the voiding of any contract for violation of that section "in any action maintained in reliance on" §29(b).[36] In any event, it should not be overlooked that rescission, or a rescission measure of damages, is all that §12 of the 1933 Act allows. And, although the voidability provisions *ex hypothesi* require a contract, their restitution rationale makes causation irrelevant.[37] It may be too much to say that the Advisers Act and Commodity Exchange Act cases and *Herman & MacLean* herald what might be called a new "Lazarus stage." But surely the last chapter in the history of the Court's struggle with implied liabilities is yet to be written.

(6) The *approach* of *Borak* does seem quite dead, except perhaps in cases based on civil rights legislation or directly on the Constitution.[38] But the *holding* of *Borak* was "grandfathered" in by *Touche Ross & Co. v. Redington.*[39] So were the 10b-5 cases, although the proxy rules could readily have been distinguished as displacing virtually no state law.[40] At the same time, a majority of the Court was unwilling to extend *Borak's* holding to the closely related form of corporate warfare by tender offer rather than by proxy, at least when the plaintiff is outside looking in. And, as we saw in the last chapter, the Court has been narrowing Rule 10b-5 as a matter of substantive coverage.[41]

---

[36] See, e. g., Geismar v. Bond & Goodwin, Inc., 40 F. Supp. 876 (S. D. N. Y. 1941). The courts divided on the question whether the statute of limitations applied to damage as well as rescission actions. *Yes:* Newburger, Loeb & Co., Inc. v. Gross, 365 F. Supp. 1364, 1372 (S. D. N. Y. 1973). *No:* Douglass v. Glenn E. Hinton Investments, Inc., 440 F. 2d 912 (9th Cir. 1971).

[37] Regional Properties, Inc. v. Financial & Real Estate Consulting Co., 678 F. 2d 552, 559 (5th Cir. 1982). The court held also that §29(b) of the 1934 Act could be invoked by persons other than investors. Id. at 561.

[38] *Borak* was cited in Cannon v. University of Chicago, 441 U. S. 677, 711 (1979) and Herman & MacLean v. Huddleston, 103 S. Ct. 683, 686 n. 9, set out infra p. 1142 n. 9.

[39] 442 U. S. 560, 577 (1979).

[40] " * * * a private right of action under Section 10(b) of the 1934 Act and Rule 10b-5 has been consistently recognized for more than 35 years. The existence of this implied remedy is simply beyond peradventure." Herman & MacLean v. Huddleston, 103 S. Ct. 683, 687 (1983), set out infra p. 1141, at p. 1142.

[41] The Code, in a section that parallels the civil liability section on proxy

(7) Certainly the old talk about implying a private right of action "unless the legislation evidences a contrary intention"[42] is no longer justified. The lower courts have "got the message": that the burden of the argument now goes the other way. Nevertheless, there has been some foot-dragging. For example, the District of Columbia Circuit, in applying the *Cort* tests to conclude that nothing in §11 or 12(2) of the 1933 Act or §18 of the 1934 Act precluded resort to Rule 10b-5, stated:

> If Congress had spoken plainly enough, the task would be simple. The quest, therefore, is not necessarily for evidence that Congress specifically intended to imply a private right of action, but rather for indications whether Congress meant to deny such a remedy. This was the thrust of *Transamerica*.[43]

Judge Friendly probably captured the present state of affairs best in his opinion in one of the commodity cases that the Supreme Court recently affirmed, when he said that *Cort* should be read "in light of the later *caveat* in *Touche Ross & Co.* v. *Redington*, 442 U. S. 560, 575 (1979), that the basic inquiry is always to plumb the intent of Congress, that the *Cort* factors are simply inquiries helpful in that endeavor, and that satisfaction of one or more of the *Cort* factors will not alone carry the day."[44] To this he later added, with reference to "the recent triad" of *Cannon*, *Redington*, and *Transamerica*:

---

violations (§1713(a), supra c. 7D n. 136), authorizes the court, in an action by "the issuer of a security that is the subject of a tender offer (or a proposed tender offer) or whose acquisition requires a filing under section 605(b) [today's §13(d)], a holder of such a security (or of another security whose interests are adversely affected), a person who has tendered a security pursuant to a tender offer, or a person who has made or proposes to make a tender offer," to "(1) enjoin a violation or further violation, (2) require compliance, (3) enjoin the voting of securities acquired in violation or the consummation of action authorized by their having been voted, (4) set aside action so consummated, (5) award damages against the violator for any loss caused by his violation, or (6) grant other appropriate relief (preliminary or final), including a combination of the types of relief set forth in section 1713(b)."

[42] Brown v. Bullock, 194 F. Supp. 207, 224 (S. D. N. Y. 1961), *aff'd en banc*, 294 F. 2d 415 (2d Cir. 1961) (Inv. Co. Act). It is interesting, in view of the English history (supra p. 572), that The Law Commission (as well as The Scottish Law Commission) recommended in 1969 a statutory declaration that "the breach of an obligation is intended to be actionable at the suit of any person who by reason of that breach suffers or apprehends damage, unless a contrary intention is expressly stated." The Interpretation of Statutes, Law Com. No. 21 and Scot. Law Com. No. 11 (1969) ¶38.

[43] Wachovia Bank & Trust Co. v. National Student Marketing Corp., 650 F. 2d 342, 352 (D. C. Cir. 1980), *cert. denied* sub nom. Peat, Marwick, Mitchell & Co. v. Wachovia Bank & Trust Co., 452 U. S. 954.

[44] Leist v. Simplot, 638 F. 2d 283, 302 n. 20 (2d Cir. 1980), *aff'd* sub nom. Merrill Lynch, Pierce, Fenner & Smith, Inc. v. Curran, 102 S. Ct. 1825 (1982).

We do think, however, that the rumors about the death of the implied cause of action which have been circulating in the wake of these decisions — an attitude strongly reflected in the dissent — are exaggerated, at least as far as previously enacted statutes are concerned, and that the effect of the decisions is simply to emphasize that the ultimate touchstone is congressional intent and not judicial notions of what would constitute wise policy.[45]

We must now examine those civil liabilities that were most commonly applied before the recent Supreme Court cases and try to ascertain their present status in the light of those cases.

2.   PROXY RULES

An earlier chapter has explored the quantum of relief available on a showing of violation of the proxy rules, since there is no reason to suppose that the answer turns (except for the possibility of awarding damages to a private plaintiff) on whether the plaintiff is a private person or the Commission itself.[46] We examine here a number of questions that arise only in private actions.

a.   Standing

Since *Borak* it is clear that the corporation itself has standing to sue, which means that stockholders may also sue derivatively. This view is consistent with the administrative approach of neutrality in proxy contests — a position firmly grounded on legislative history. The Senate report on the bill that became the 1934 Act is more specific here than it is on most of the statutory provisions:

> It is contemplated that the rules and regulations promulgated by the Commission will protect investors from promiscuous solicitation of their proxies, on the one hand, by irresponsible outsiders seeking to wrest control of a corporation away from honest and conscientious corporation officials; and, on the other hand, by unscrupulous corporate officials seeking to retain control of the management by concealing and distorting facts.[47]

---

[45] 638 F. 2d at 316.

[46] See pp. 562-67 supra. With respect to scienter, see pp. 899-900 supra.

[47] S. Rep. No. 1455, 73d Cong., 2d Sess. (1934) 77; see also Studebaker Corp. v. Gittlin, 360 F. 2d 692, 695 (2d Cir. 1966); Greater Iowa Corp. v. McLendon, 378 F. 2d 783, 795 (8th Cir. 1967). *Contra:* Cook United, Inc. v. Stockholders Protective Committee of Cook United, Inc., CCH Fed. Sec. L. Rep. ¶96,875 at 95,578 n. 1 (S. D. N. Y. 1979).

It is less clear whether a stockholder has standing to sue non-derivatively when he has not himself given a proxy to the defendant. In most of the cases (including *Borak*) it can be inferred from the very hostility between the parties that the plaintiff did not give a proxy to anybody in the defendant's camp. And the private right of action is based not on any concept of the proxy attorney's violation of a fiduciary obligation to his principal, but on the premise that either side in a contested solicitation has a legitimate interest, in view of the statutory purpose, to cry "Foul" against the other.[48] So the answer should be "Yes."

b.　Causation

Borak's admonition that "the causal relationship of the proxy material and the merger are questions of fact to be resolved at trial,"[49] together with the lower court cases on causation in the immediate wake of *Borak,* led the present writer to say that it was "apparent that causation has now become the critical question in this area."[50] But a second proxy case that the Supreme Court decided within months after he made that statement proved him a false prophet:

MILLS v. ELECTRIC AUTO-LITE CO.
Supreme Court of the United States, 1970
396 U. S. 375

Mr. Justice Harlan delivered the opinion of the Court.

This case requires us to consider a basic aspect of the implied private right of action for violation of §14(a) of the Securities Exchange Act of 1934, recognized by this Court in *J. I. Case Co. v. Borak*, 377 U. S. 426 (1964). As in *Borak* the asserted wrong is that a corporate merger was accomplished through the use of a proxy statement that was materially false or misleading. The question with which we deal is what causal relationship must be

---

[48] See Dann v. Studebaker-Packard Corp., 288 F. 2d 201, 209-11 (6th Cir. 1961); Union Pacific R. R. Co. v. Chicago & North Western Ry. Co., 226 F. Supp. 400 (N. D. Ill. 1964); Clayton v. Skelly Oil Co., CCH Fed. Sec. L. Rep. ¶96,269 at 92, 747-48 (S. D. N. Y. 1977); Lynch v. Fulks, CCH Fed. Sec. L. Rep. ¶97,831 (D. Kan. 1980). *Contra:* Gaines v. Haughton, 645 F. 2d 761, 773-74 (9th Cir. 1981), *cert. denied,* 454 U. S. 1145; cf. Textron, Inc. v. American Woolen Co., 122 F. Supp. 305, 307-10 (D. Mass. 1954).

[49] J. I. Case Co. v. Borak, 377 U. S. 426, 431 (1964), set out supra p. 1059, at p. 1060.

[50] 5 Loss 2933.

shown between such a statement and the merger to establish a cause of action based on the violation of the Act.

I

Petitioners were shareholders of the Electric Auto-Lite Company until 1963, when it was merged into Mergenthaler Linotype Company. They brought suit on the day before the shareholders' meeting at which the vote was to take place on the merger, against Auto-Lite, Mergenthaler, and a third company, American Manufacturing Company, Inc. The complaint sought an injunction against the voting by Auto-Lite's management of all proxies obtained by means of an allegedly misleading proxy solicitation; however, it did not seek a temporary restraining order, and the voting went ahead as scheduled the following day. Several months later petitioners filed an amended complaint, seeking to have the merger set aside and to obtain such other relief as might be proper.

In Count II of the amended complaint, which is the only count before us, petitioners predicated jurisdiction on §27 of the 1934 Act, 15 U. S. C. §78aa. They alleged that the proxy statement sent out by the Auto-Lite management to solicit shareholders' votes in favor of the merger was misleading, in violation of §14(a) of the Act and SEC Rule 14a-9 thereunder. (17 C. F. R. §240.14a-9.) Petitioners recited that before the merger Merganthaler owned over 50% of the outstanding shares of Auto-Lite common stock, and had been in control of Auto-Lite for two years. American Manufacturing in turn owned about one-third of the outstanding shares of Mergenthaler, and for two years had been in voting control of Mergenthaler and, through it, of Auto-Lite. Petitioners charged that in light of these circumstances the proxy statement was misleading in that it told Auto-Lite shareholders that their board of directors recommended approval of the merger without also informing them that all 11 of Auto-Lite's directors were nominees of Mergenthaler and were under the "control and domination of Mergenthaler." Petitioners asserted the right to complain of this alleged violation both derivatively on behalf of Auto-Lite and as representatives of the class of all its minority shareholders.

On petitioners' motion for summary judgment with respect to Count II, the District Court for the Northern District of Illinois ruled as a matter of law that the claimed defect in the proxy statement was, in light of the circumstances in which the statement was made, a material omission. The District Court concluded, from its reading of the *Borak* opinion, that it had to hold a hearing on the issue whether there was "a causal connection between the finding that there had been a violation of the disclosure requirements of §14(a) and the alleged injury to the plaintiffs" before it could consider what remedies would be appropriate. (Unreported opinion dated February 14, 1966.)

After holding such a hearing, the court found that under the terms of the merger agreement, an affirmative vote of two-thirds of the Auto-Lite shares was required for approval of the merger, and that the respondent companies owned and controlled about 54% of the outstanding shares. Therefore, to obtain authorization of the merger, respondents had to secure the approval of a substantial number of the minority shareholders. At the stockholders' meeting, approximately 950,000 shares, out of 1,160,000 shares outstanding, were voted in favor of the merger. This included 317,000 votes obtained by proxy from the minority shareholders, votes that were "necessary and indispensable to the approval of the merger." The District Court concluded that a causal relationship had thus been shown, and it granted an interlocutory judgment in favor of petitioners on the issue of liability, referring the case to a master for consideration of appropriate relief. (Unreported findings and conclusions dated Sept. 26, 1967; opinion reported at 281 F. Supp. 826 (1967).)

The District Court made the certification required by 28 U. S. C. §1292(b), and respondents took an interlocutory appeal to the Court of Appeals for the Seventh Circuit. That court affirmed the District Court's conclusion that the proxy statement was materially deficient, but reversed on the question of causation. The court acknowledged that, if an injunction had been sought a sufficient time before the stockholders' meeting, "corrective measures would have been appropriate." 403 F. 2d 429, 435 (1968). However, since this suit was brought too late for preventive action, the courts had to determine "whether the misleading statement and omission caused the submission of sufficient proxies," as a prerequisite to a determination of liability under the Act. If the respondents could show, "by a preponderance of probabilities, that the merger would have received a sufficient vote even if the proxy statement had not been misleading in the respect found," petitioners would be entitled to no relief of any kind. Id., at 436.

The Court of Appeals acknowledged that this test corresponds to the common-law fraud test of whether the injured party relied on the misrepresentation. However, rightly concluding that "[r]eliance by thousands of individuals, as here, can scarcely be inquired into" (id., at 436 n. 10), the court ruled that the issue was to be determined by proof of the fairness of the terms of the merger. If respondents could show that the merger had merit and was fair to the minority shareholders, the trial court would be justified in concluding that a sufficient number of shareholders would have approved the merger had there been no deficiency in the proxy statement. In that case respondents would be entitled to a judgment in their favor.

Claiming that the Court of Appeals has construed this Court's decision in *Borak* in a manner that frustrates the statute's policy of enforcement through private litigation, the petitioners then sought review in this Court. We granted certiorari, 394 U. S. 971 (1969), believing that resolution of this basic issue should be made at this stage of the litigation and not postponed until after a trial under the Court of Appeals' decision.

II

* * * The decision below, by permitting all liability to be foreclosed on the basis of a finding that the merger was fair, would allow the stockholders to be bypassed, at least where the only legal challenge to the merger is a suit for retrospective relief after the meeting has been held. A judicial appraisal of the merger's merits could be substituted for the actual and informed vote of the stockholders.

The result would be to insulate from private redress an entire category of proxy violations — those relating to matters other than the terms of the merger. Even outrageous misrepresentations in a proxy solicitation, if they did not relate to the terms of the transaction, would give rise to no cause of action under §14(a). Particularly if carried over to enforcement actions by the Securities and Exchange Commission itself, such a result would subvert the congressional purpose of ensuring full and fair disclosure to shareholders.

Further, recognition of the fairness of the merger as a complete defense would confront small shareholders with an additional obstacle to making a successful challenge to a proposal recommended through a defective proxy statement. The risk that they would be unable to rebut the corporation's evidence of the fairness of the proposal, and thus to establish their cause of action, would be bound to discourage such shareholders from the private enforcement of the proxy rules that "provides a necessary supplement to Commission action." *J. I. Case Co.* v. *Borak,* 337 U. S., at 432.[5]

Such a frustration of the congressional policy is not required by anything in the wording of the statute or in our opinion in the *Borak* case. Section 14(a) declares it "unlawful" to solicit proxies in contravention of Commission rules, and SEC Rule 14a-9 prohibits solicitations "containing any statement which . . . is false or misleading with respect to any material fact, or which omits to state any material fact necessary in order to make the statements therein not false or misleading. . . ." Use of a solicitation that is materially misleading is itself a violation of law, as the Court of Appeals recognized in stating that injunctive relief would be available to remedy such a defect if sought prior to the stockholders' meeting. In *Borak,* which came to this Court on a dismissal of the complaint, the Court limited its inquiry to whether a violation of §14(a) gives rise to "a federal cause of action for rescission or damages," 377 U. S., at 428. Referring to the argument made by petitioners there "that the merger can be dissolved only if it was fraudulent or non-beneficial, issues upon which the proxy material would not bear" the Court stated: "But the causal relationship of the proxy material and the merger are questions of fact to be resolved at trial, not here. We therefore do not discuss this point further." *Id.,* at 431. In the present case there has been a hearing specifically directed to the causation problem. The question before the Court is whether the facts found on the basis of that hearing are sufficient in law to establish petitioners' cause of action, and we conclude that they are.

Where the misstatement or omission in a proxy statement has

---

[5] The Court of Appeals' ruling that "causation" may be negated by proof of the fairness of the merger also rests on a dubious behavioral assumption. There is no justification for presuming that the shareholders of every corporation are willing to accept any and every fair merger offer put before them; yet such a presumption is implicit in the opinion of the Court of Appeals. That court gave no indication of what evidence petitioners might adduce, once respondents had established that the merger proposal was equitable, in order to show that the shareholders would nevertheless have rejected it if the solicitation had not been misleading. Proof of actual reliance by thousands of individuals would, as the court acknowledged, not be feasible, see R. Jennings & H. Marsh, Securities Regulation, Cases and Materials 1001 (2d ed. 1968); and reliance on the *nondisclosure* of a fact is a particularly difficult matter to define or prove, see 3 L. Loss, Securities Regulation 1766 (2d ed. 1961). In practice, therefore, the objective fairness of the proposal would seemingly be determinative of liability. But, in view of the many other factors that might lead shareholders to prefer their current position to that of owners of a larger, combined enterprise, it is pure conjecture to assume that the fairness of the proposal will always be determinative of their vote. Cf. *Wirtz* v. *Hotel, Motel & Club Employees Union,* 391 U. S. 492, 508 (1968).

been shown to be "material," as it was found to be here, that determination itself indubitably embodies a conclusion that the defect was of such a character that it might have been considered important by a reasonable shareholder who was in the process of deciding how to vote.[6] This requirement that the defect have a significant *propensity* to affect the voting process is found in the express terms of Rule 14a-9, and it adequately serves the purpose of ensuring that a cause of action cannot be established by proof of a defect so trivial, or so unrelated to the transaction for which approval is sought, that correction of the defect or imposition of liability would not further the interests protected by §14(a).

There is no need to supplement this requirement, as did the Court of Appeals, with a requirement of proof of whether the defect actually had a decisive effect on the voting. Where there has been a finding of materiality, a shareholder has made a sufficient showing of causal relationship between the violation and the injury for which he seeks redress if, as here, he proves that the proxy solicitation itself, rather than the particular defect in the solicitation materials, was an essential link in the accomplishment of the transaction. This objective test will avoid the impracticalities of determining how many votes were affected, and, by resolving doubts in favor of those the statute is designed to protect, will effectuate the congressional policy of ensuring that the shareholders are able to make an informed choice when they are consulted on corporate transactions. Cf. *Union Pac. R. Co.* v. *Chicago & N. W. R. Co.*, 226 F. Supp. 400, 411 (D. C. N. D. Ill. 1964); 2 L. Loss, Securities Regulation 962 n. 411 (2d ed. 1961); 5 id., at 2929-2930 (Supp. 1969).[7]

---

[6] Cf. List v. Fashion Park, Inc., 340 F. 2d 457, 462 (C. A. 2d Cir. 1965); General Time Corp. v. Talley Industries, Inc., 403 F. 2d 159, 162 (C. A. 2d Cir. 1968); Restatement (Second) of Torts §538(2)(a) (Tent. Draft No. 10, 1964); 2 L. Loss, Securities Regulation 917 (2d ed. 1961); 6 id., at 3534 (Supp. 1969).

In this case, where the misleading aspect of the solicitation involved failure to reveal a serious conflict of interest on the part of the directors, the Court of Appeals concluded that the crucial question in determining materiality was "whether the minority shareholders were sufficiently alerted to the board's relationship to their adversary to be on their guard." 403 F. 2d, at 434. An adequate disclosure of this relationship would have warned the stockholders to give more careful scrutiny to the terms of the merger than they might to one recommended by an entirely disinterested board. Thus, the failure to make such a disclosure was found to be a material defect "as a matter of law," thwarting the informed decision at which the statute aims, regardless of whether the terms of the merger were such that a reasonable stockholder would have approved the transaction after more careful analysis. See also Swanson v. American Consumer Industries, Inc., 415 F. 2d 1326 (C. A. 7th Cir. 1969).

[7] We need not decide in this case whether causation could be shown where

III

Our conclusion that petitioners have established their case by showing that proxies necessary to approval of the merger were obtained by means of a materially misleading solicitation implies nothing about the form of relief to which they may be entitled. We held in *Borak* that upon finding a violation the courts were "to be alert to provide such remedies as are necessary to make effective the congressional purpose," noting specifically that such remedies are not to be limited to prospective relief. 377 U. S., at 433, 434. In devising retrospective relief for violation of the proxy rules, the federal courts should consider the same factors that would govern the relief granted for any similar illegality or fraud. One important factor may be the fairness of the terms of the merger. Possible forms of relief will include setting aside the merger or granting other equitable relief, but, as the Court of Appeals below noted, nothing in the statutory policy "requires the court to unscramble a corporate transaction merely because a violation occurred." 403 F. 2d, at 436. In selecting a remedy the lower courts should exercise " 'the sound discretion which guides the determinations of courts of equity,' " keeping in mind the role of equity as "the instrument for nice adjustment and reconciliation between the public interest and private needs as well as between competing private claims." *Hecht Co.* v. *Bowles,* 321 U. S. 321, 329-330 (1944), quoting from *Meredith* v. *Winter Haven,* 320 U. S. 228, 235 (1943).

We do not read §29(b) of the Act, which declares contracts made in violation of the Act or a rule thereunder "void . . . as regards the rights of" the violator and knowing successors in interest, as requiring that the merger be set aside simply because

---

the management controls a sufficient number of shares to approve the transaction without any votes from the minority. Even in that situation, if the management finds it necessary for legal or practical reasons to solicit proxies from minority shareholders, at least one court has held that the proxy solicitation might be sufficiently related to the merger to satisfy the causation requirement, see Laurenzano v. Einbender, 264 F. Supp. 356 (D. C. E. D. N. Y. 1966); cf. Swanson v. American Consumer Industries, Inc., 415 F. 2d 1326, 1331-1332 (C. A. 7th Cir. 1969); Eagle v. Horvath, 241 F. Supp. 341, 344 (D. C. S. D. N. Y. 1965); Globus, Inc. v. Jaroff, 271 F. Supp. 378, 381 (D. C. S. D. N. Y. 1967); Comment, Shareholders' Derivative Suit to Enforce a Corporate Right of Action Against Directors Under SEC Rule 10b-5, 114 U. Pa. L. Rev. 578, 582 (1966). But see Hoover v. Allen, 241 F. Supp. 213, 231-232 (D. C. S. D. N. Y. 1965); Barnett v. Anaconda Co., 238 F. Supp. 766, 770-774 (D. C. S. D. N. Y. 1965); Robbins v. Banner Industries, Inc., 285 F. Supp. 758, 762-763 (D. C. S. D. N. Y. 1966). See generally 5 L. Loss, Securities Regulation 2933-2938 (Supp. 1969).

the merger agreement is a "void" contract. This language establishes that the guilty party is precluded from enforcing the contract against an unwilling innocent party, but it does not compel the conclusion that the contract is a nullity, creating no enforceable rights even in a party innocent of the violation. The lower federal courts have read §29(b), which has counterparts in the Holding Company Act, the Investment Company Act, and the Investment Advisers Act, as rendering the contract merely voidable at the option of the innocent party. [Citations omitted.] See also 5 Loss, supra at 2925-2926 (Supp. 1969); 6 id., at 3866. This interpretation is eminently sensible. The interests of the victim are sufficiently protected by giving him the right to rescind; to regard the contract as void where he has not invoked that right would only create the possibility of hardships to him or others without necessarily advancing the statutory policy of disclosure.

The United States, as *amicus curiae,* points out that as representatives of the minority shareholders, petitioners are not parties to the merger agreement and thus do not enjoy a statutory right under §29(b) to set it aside.[11] Furthermore, while they do have a derivative right to invoke Auto-Lite's status as a party to the agreement, a determination of what relief should be granted in Auto-Lite's name must hinge on whether setting aside the merger would be in the best interests of the shareholders as a whole. In short, in the context of a suit such as this one, §29(b) leaves the matter of relief where it would be under *Borak* without specific statutory language — the merger should be set aside only if a court of equity concludes, from all the circumstances, that it would be equitable to do so. Cf. *SEC* v. *National Securities, Inc.,* 393 U. S. 453, 456, 463-464 (1969).

Monetary relief will, of course, also be a possibility. Where the defect in the proxy solicitation relates to the specific terms of the merger, the district court might appropriately order an accounting to ensure that the shareholders receive the value that was represented as coming to them. On the other hand, where, as here, the misleading aspect of the solicitation did not relate to terms of the merger, monetary relief might be afforded to the shareholders only if the merger resulted in a reduction of the

11 If petitioners had submitted their own proxies in favor of the merger in response to the unlawful solicitation, as it does not appear they did, the language of §29(b) would seem to give them, as innocent parties to that transaction, a right to rescind their proxies. But it is clear in this case, where petitioners' combined holdings are only 600 shares, that such rescission would not affect the authorization of the merger.

earnings or earnings potential of their holdings. In short, damages should be recoverable only to the extent that they can be shown. If commingling of the assets and operations of the merged companies makes it impossible to establish direct injury from the merger, relief might be predicated on a determination of the fairness of the terms of the merger at the time it was approved. These questions, of course, are for decision in the first instance by the District Court on remand, and our singling out of some of the possibilities is not intended to exclude others.

IV

Although the question of relief must await further proceedings in the District Court, our conclusion that petitioners have established their cause of action indicates that the Court of Appeals should have affirmed the partial summary judgment on the issue of liability. The result would have been not only that respondents, rather than petitioners, would have borne the costs of the appeal, but also, we think, that petitioners would have been entitled to an interim award of litigation expenses and reasonable attorneys' fees. Cf. *Highway Truck Drivers Local 107* v. *Cohen,* 220 F. Supp. 735 (D. C. E. D. Pa. 1963). We agree with the position taken by petitioners, and by the United States as *amicus,* that petitioners, who have established a violation of the securities laws by their corporation and its officials, should be reimbursed by the corporation or its survivor for the costs of establishing the violation.

*   *   *

For the foregoing reasons we conclude that the judgment of the Court of Appeals should be vacated and the case remanded to that court for further proceedings consistent with this opinion.
It is so ordered.[a]
MR. JUSTICE BLACK, concurring in part and dissenting in part.

*   *   *

Query:
(1) Does materiality subsume causation always or only sometimes? In a merger case decided a few weeks *before Mills,* the

---

[a] The balance of this opinion, with reference to attorneys' fees, is excerpted infra p. 1210.

Seventh Circuit held that a second proxy statement that was admittedly fair and complete had remedied any deficiencies in the original proxy statement.[51] And the Ninth Circuit has held that *Mills'* materiality-causation equation "is logically limited to situations in which shareholder approval was sought (and fraudulently secured) for a transaction requiring such approval, typically so-called 'fundamental corporate changes.' "[52] By contrast, directors' failure to disclose alleged misconduct (in that case questionable foreign payments) was not "the legal cause of the pecuniary loss to the corporation, if any," so long as there was no underlying transaction that required shareholder approval and the case was not one of self-dealing or fraud against the corporation.[53]

(2) A number of courts have written in these cases in terms of "a showing of both *loss causation* — that the misrepresentations or omissions caused the economic harm — and *transaction causation* — that the violations in question caused the [shareholder] to engage in the transaction in question."[54] With all the confusion already inherent in the more traditional terms, "causation in fact" or "but for" causation (which is really reliance) and "legal cause,"[55] does adding two new terms advance the discourse?

[51] Schy v. Susquehanna Corp., 419 F. 2d 1112, 1117 (7th Cir. 1970), *cert. denied,* 400 U. S. 826.

[52] Gaines v. Haughton, 645 F. 2d 761, 775 (9th Cir. 1981), *cert. denied,* 454 U. S. 1145.

[53] 645 F. 2d at 775; see also Weisberg v. Coastal States Gas Corp., 609 F. 2d 650 (2d Cir. 1979), *cert. denied,* 445 U. S. 951. There is authority, too, that the *Mills* equation does not apply to an omission to include information affirmatively required by Rule 14a-3 if the omission does not violate Rule 14a-9. Ash v. GAF Corp., 546 F. Supp. 89 (E. D. Pa. 1982), and cases cited.

[54] Schlick v. Penn-Dixie Cement Corp., 507 F. 2d 374, 380 (2d Cir. 1974), *cert. denied,* 421 U. S. 976.

[55] See 1 Code 57-63, comments to §202(19), which defines causation in traditional terms: "A loss is 'caused' by specified conduct to the extent that (A) the conduct was a substantial factor in producing the loss, and (B) the loss was of a kind that might reasonably have been expected to occur as a result of the conduct." The commentary has this to say:

§202(19)(A): This is the language of "causation in fact" that Restatement (Second) of Torts §546 uses in stating the general rule on causation in deceit. As applied to the *fact* of causation alone, according to Prosser, no better test has been devised. Prosser, Torts 240, 248 (4th ed. 1971). The language makes it plain, for example, that, if the defendant's misrepresentation was a "substantial factor" in inducing the plaintiff to buy, the defendant is not absolved merely because other factors — for example, the plaintiff's having recently received a large inheritance or his having been counseled to diversify his portfolio — contributed to the result.

§202(19)(B): To repeat, it does not follow that "but for" causation (as defined in "substantial factor" terms) should always establish liabil-

Are both new terms subsumed within "causation in fact," so as to leave room for the policy and foreseeability arguments traditionally associated with "causation at law"? Or are "transaction" and "loss" causation synonymous, respectively, with "causation in fact" and "legal causation"? If so, why bother? If not, what is the difference? Judge Frankel, while he thought that the new labels "may prove eventually to be useful," was "not convinced at this time that the Circuit ought to be committed to their employment or to their still uncertain implications."[56]

(3) Whatever one calls the first step in the causation chain — why not simply "reliance"? — *Mills* is clear that, once the plaintiff has shown materiality, he "has made a sufficient showing of causal relationship between the violation and the injury for which he seeks redress if, as here, he proves that the proxy solicitation itself, rather than the particular defect in the solicitation materials, was an essential link in the accomplishment of the transaction."[57]

(4) What about the question, which *Mills* left open, whether causation could be shown when the management itself controls enough shares to approve the transaction?[58] A substantial number of cases now say it makes no difference.[59] The usual arguments are that the minority stockholders will be in a better position to protect their interests with full disclosure and that an unfavorable minority vote might influence the majority to modify or reconsider the transaction in question. In a case where the stockholders had no appraisal rights under state law because the stock was listed on the New York Stock Exchange, the court advanced two additional considerations: (1) the *market* would be informed; and (2) even "a rapacious controlling management" might modify the terms of the merger because it would not want to "hang its

---

ity. For "but for" is at most a rule of exclusion: if it is not satisfied, clearly there can be no causation, but, even if it *is* satisfied, policy considerations other than factual causation may preclude liability. See id. at 238-39. These are the considerations subsumed under the question-begging but useful term, "legal cause," which §202(19)(B) defines in the reasonable expectancy language of Restatement (Second) of Torts §548A — a test that, realistically, must be viewed as a general caveat that "but for" is not necessarily enough. * * *

[56] Schlick v. Penn-Dixie Cement Corp., 507 F. 2d 374, 384 (2d Cir. 1974, concurring opinion), *cert. denied,* 421 U. S. 976.

[57] 396 U. S. at 385, supra p. 1114.

[58] 396 U. S. at 385 n. 7, supra p. 1114 n. 7.

[59] E. g., Cole v. Schenley Industries, Inc., 563 F. 2d 35, 40 (2d Cir. 1977); Popkin v. Bishop, 464 F. 2d 714, 720 (2d Cir. 1972) (Rule 10b-5); Selk v. St. Paul Ammonia Products, Inc., 597 F. 2d 635, 638 (8th Cir. 1979) (dictum).

dirty linen out on the line and thereby expose itself to suit or Securities Commission or other action — in terms of reputation and future take-overs."[60]

c.   Interrelation with State Law

In a unitary system of government we would be at the end of our problem. But, of course, the SEC proxy rules are superimposed on the state law governing proxies and shareholder meetings. The fact is, as a former Chairman of the Commission has written, that "The stuff of these controversies [under the SEC rules] is the sort of thing which courts have been adjudicating since corporate elections began. The injury to the complainant, real or fancied, may, and usually does, include substantive matters unrelated to the proxy rule violation."[61] In this the proxy rules are not atypical. We have it from a scholar who was a keen student of the federal courts that "legal problems repeatedly fail to come wrapped up in neat packages marked 'all-federal' or 'all-state.'"[62]

Since this is so, nobody will quarrel with the proposition that, ideally, whichever court adjudicates a controversy about a corporate election, or a merger or stock option plan or other extraordinary transaction that requires a vote of stockholders, should adjudicate the whole controversy, in both its state and its federal elements. This raises difficult problems concerning the relationship between federal and state courts. And the problems are only aggravated, not created, by the provision in §27 of the 1934 Act — the only such general provision in any of the SEC statutes — giving the United States District Courts "exclusive jurisdiction of violations of this title or the rules and regulations thereunder, and

---

[60] Schlick v. Penn-Dixie Cement Corp., 507 F. 2d 374, 384 (2d Cir. 1974), *cert. denied,* 421 U. S. 976. We shall have more to say about causation generally when we get to Rule 10b-5. See p. 1126 infra.

[61] Demmler, Private Suits Based on Violation of the Proxy Rules, 20 U. Pitt. L. Rev. 587, 591 (1959).

[62] Hart, The Relations between State and Federal Law, 54 Colum. L. Rev. 489, 498 (1954). It is characteristic of federal law that it "is generally interstitial in its nature. * * * Federal legislation * * * builds upon legal relationships established by the states, altering or supplanting them only so far as necessary for the special purpose. Congress acts, in short, against the background of the total *corpus juris* of the states in much the way that a state legislature acts against the background of the common law, assumed to govern unless changed by legislation." Hart and Wechsler, The Federal Courts and the Federal System (2d ed. 1973) 470-71.

of all suits in equity and actions at law brought to enforce any liability or duty created by this title or the rules and regulations thereunder."

There are many grounds on which either side may wish to enjoin or attack an election, or on which a stockholder may wish to enjoin or attack something like a merger or a stock option plan. Some of these grounds raise questions purely of state law: for example, proxies that have been forged, otherwise improperly signed, given by persons who are not stockholders of record, or revoked by later proxies. Other grounds raise questions purely of federal law: for example, soliciting orally without furnishing a proxy statement, or soliciting too early, or perhaps an opposition group's soliciting somewhat more than ten persons without filing a proxy statement at all. And at least one ground — probably the most important — raises questions of both federal and state law: soliciting on the basis of misleading or inadequate information.

Suppose, first, that a plaintiff with allegations in two or more of these three categories, or even the third alone, brings his action in a state court. He may be attacking an election in the traditional manner of a proceeding in the nature of *quo warranto,* or under a special statute,[63] or he may be seeking injunctive relief in equity (or perhaps a mandamus) before or during the meeting. In any event, he is met with the *defense* that *he,* the *plaintiff,* has violated the proxy rules and hence should be denied relief, whether as a matter of federal law that the state court must honor under the Supremacy Clause or as a matter of the state law relating to unclean hands. Still another plaintiff might base his case on state law but answer a defense of stockholder ratification, or anticipate the defense and include a replication-type allegation in his initial pleading, by claiming that the ratification is ineffective because of violation of the proxy rules. *Can* the state court decide the questions of violations and its effect? *Must* it? And is the *decision* of the highest state court reviewable by the Supreme Court of the United States if the court refuses to consider those questions? Or for error in interpreting the rules, or determining the effect of a violation, or both, if the court does consider those questions? Indeed, is a state court complaint that pleads a violation of the SEC rules removable to the federal court in the first place?

Suppose now that the plaintiff in our hypothetical case walks across the street to the federal court. Take first the simpler case in which there is diversity of citizenship. If the charter state has

[63] E. g., Del. Code, Tit. 8, §225.

a special statute on review of elections, as in Delaware, is that statute within the "equitable remedial rights doctrine," in which event it cannot be applied by a federal court? Or is it essentially "substantive" within *Erie?* Or might it be both? Indeed, did the remedial rights doctrine survive the *Erie* holocaust in the first place — not to mention the merger of law and equity in the Federal Rules of Civil Procedure? If it did, and a statute on review of elections exists in the charter state, is it necessary to decide whether the statute is "substantive" or "remedial"? Or is the remedy supplied by the historic equity jurisdiction of the federal courts? Does not this last question have to be faced in any event if the charter states does *not* have a statute of the Delaware type, since the plaintiff certainly cannot rely on the state *quo warranto* remedy in the federal court and there is no independent federal *quo warranto* jurisdiction?[64] Suppose next that there is no diversity of citizenship. On the assumption that the complaint states a non-frivolous claim under the proxy rules, will the federal court have "pendent jurisdiction" to consider those elements of the action that are based on state law? Will that be so even if the federal law count, say, is based on solicitation without delivery of a proxy statement and the state law count is based on forged proxies, so that there is no common evidence? If so, what of the defendant who has been brought into court through extraterritorial service of process under §27? And what of the purely federal-law plaintiff who is met with a state-law counterclaim?

If the plaintiff is to be faced with all these difficult questions when he chooses to bring the federal elements of his action into a state court or the state elements into a federal court, is his solution to bring two separate actions? Apart from the general undesirability of splitting causes of action, and the very practical problem that arises if neither the federal aspects of the action nor the state aspects, standing alone, affect enough votes to alter the outcome, this course immediately raises questions of *res judicata* or, at any rate, collateral estoppel.

These are problems so complex that one could wish that "judicial federalism" in the United States had developed along simpler lines. But the problems are there. They cannot be wished away. And they are anything but purely theoretical. Unfortunately, space limitations here preclude more than references to discussions elsewhere.[65]

[64] See p. 566 supra.
[65] There has not been too much movement here since Loss, The SEC Proxy Rules and State Law, 73 Harv. L. Rev. 1249 (1960), reprinted with

One basic point should be made, however, if only because a very important court in the corporate world, the Supreme Court of Delaware, overlooked it.[66] It is this: Even if it be assumed that §27 precludes a state court from entertaining an action insofar as relief is sought on the basis of alleged violation of the proxy rules, nothing in that section prevents a state court from considering questions under the proxy rules that are introduced by way of defense, and failure to do so would violate the Supremacy Clause.[67]

3. TENDER OFFERS

We have already visited the matter of available relief for violation of the tender offer provisions, usually §14(e), since that question is not peculiar to private actions.[68] And much of what has just been said with respect to litigation under the proxy rules applies here *mutatis mutandis*.[69] The big question here is what implied liability, if any, survives *Piper*, where the Court expressly reserved its views on (1) whether either the target or its stockhold-

---

insubstantial changes in 2 Loss 973-1019 and supplemented in 5 *id.* 2949-80. For more general surveys, see Note, Problems of Parallel State and Federal Remedies, 71 Harv. L. Rev. 513 (1958); Note, Exclusive Jurisdiction of the Federal Courts in Private Civil Actions, 70 Harv. L. Rev. 509 (1957). On a more fundamental level, no lawyer should approach this maze without reading Professor Hart's penetrating essay, The Relations between State and Federal Law, 54 Colum. L. Rev. 489 (1954).

[66] Standard Power & Light Corp. v. Investment Associates, Inc., 29 Del. Ch. 593, 606, 51 A. 2d 572, 579 (1947). But cf. Columbian Fuel Corp. v. Superior Court, 52 Del. 365, 374, 378, 158 A. 2d 478, 483, 485 (1960), *aff'd sub nom.* Pan American Petroleum Corp. v. Superior Court, 366 U. S. 656 (1961).

[67] See Pratt v. Paris Gas Light & Coke Co., 168 U. S. 255 (1897) (defense going to the validity of a patent); Lear, Inc. v. Adkins, 395 U. S. 653, 675-76 (1969) (state court jurisdiction assumed); Aetna State Bank v. Altheimer, 430 F. 2d 750, 754, 756 (7th Cir. 1970); Shareholders Management Co. v. Gregory, 449 F. 2d 326 (9th Cir. 1971); Birenbaum v. Bache & Co., 555 S. W. 2d 513, 514-15 (Tex. Civ. App. 1977).

So, too, when questions under the proxy rules are raised by way of replication. A stockholder, for example, brings a derivative action under state law seeking to enjoin the consummation of an executive stock option plan as a waste of corporate assets. The defendants plead shareholder ratification. The plaintiff — either in replication or, anticipating the defense, in his complaint — argues that the ratification is ineffective because of fraud or inadequate disclosure in soliciting proxies. See Eliasberg v. Standard Oil Co., 23 N. J. Super. 431, 92 A. 2d 862 (Ch. 1952), *aff'd per curiam,* 12 N. J. 467, 97 A 2d 437 (1953); cf. American Well Works Co. v. Layne & Bowler Co., 241 U. S. 257, 259-60 (1916).

[68] See pp. 600-01 supra.

[69] With respect to scienter, see pp. 899-900 supra.

ers had standing and (2) whether a *tender offeror* might obtain injunctive relief as distinct from damages.[70]

Several Circuits — one of them *since Piper* — have permitted *injunctive* actions by target companies.[71] The First Circuit, in a *pre-Piper* case, recognized target actions for damages as well.[72] The Second Circuit, in the first appellate opinion under the tender offer provisions, permitted *nontendering stockholders* to join the target company as plaintiffs;[73] stockholders who have tendered do not need §14(e), because they are classic sellers within Rule 10b-5. On the other hand, there is authority that target stockholders may not sue *their own company* for chilling the offer by misrepresenting the offeror's intentions, because the very fact that no offer was ever made precluded the required proof of reliance on misrepresentations made by target management.[74]

These holdings are presumably weakened to the extent that they rely, explicitly or implicitly, on the two-way standing in the proxy cases. But the *Piper* Court, despite its disclaimer, almost invites target company or target stockholder actions when it observes that the preliminary injunctive stage is the time when relief can best be given;[75] for *somebody* must be the plaintiff. And, if the target or its stockholders or both may sue for injunctive relief, why not for damages as well? The Court's refusal to distinguish SEC injunctive actions and damage actions for purposes of the 10b-5 scienter requirement[76] furnishes some analogy, although the question there goes to substance rather than standing. Finally, there is

---

[70] Piper v. Chris-Craft Industries, Inc., 430 U. S. 1, 42 n. 28, 47 n. 33 (1977), set out supra p. 1070, at p. 1074 n. 28.

[71] Electronic Specialty Co. v. International Controls Corp., 409 F. 2d 937 (2d Cir. 1969); Gulf & Western Industries, Inc. v. Great Atlantic & Pacific Tea Co., Inc., 476 F. 2d 687 (2d Cir. 1973); Smallwood v. Pearl Brewing Co., 489 F. 2d 579, 596 (5th Cir. 1974), *cert. denied,* 419 U. S. 873; Marathon Oil Co. v. Mobil Corp., 669 F. 2d 378 (6th Cir. 1981). In recent years, however, the courts have been more sensitive to the fact that "a delay of several days or a week to require an offeror to cure its disclosure defects could result in the temporary or even permanent lost opportunity to acquire the target company." Martin-Marietta Corp. v. Bendix Corp., 547 F. Supp. 533, 539-40 (D. Md. 1982).

[72] H. K. Porter Co. v. Nicholson File Co., 482 F. 2d 421 (1st Cir. 1973).

[73] Electronic Specialty Co. v. International Controls Corp., 409 F. 2d 937 (2d Cir. 1969).

[74] Lewis v. McGraw, 619 F. 2d 192 (2d Cir. 1980), *cert. denied,* 449 U. S. 951; Panter v. Marshall Field & Co., 646 F. 2d 271 (7th Cir. 1981), *cert. denied,* 454 U. S. 1092; but cf. Lowenschuss v. Kane, 520 F. 2d 255 (2d Cir. 1975). *Panter* held also that there was no right of action on behalf of stockholders who had decided *not* to sell in the *market.*

[75] 430 U. S. at 42, set out supra p. 1074.

[76] See p. 887 supra.

District Court authority distinguishing *Piper* to permit the *offeror* to sue a competitor for *injunctive relief.*[77]

So far as §13(d) is concerned, again there is appellate authority — some of it *post-Piper* — granting injunctive relief to the company and its stockholders.[78] On the other hand, some courts have rejected actions not only for damages[79] but also, since *Piper,* for injunctive relief.[80] Damage actions for false filings under §13(d) raise the question whether the exclusive remedy is not under §18.[81]

4. RULE 10b-5

The Supreme Court is clearly disinclined to question implied liability for violation of Rule 10b-5, extending not merely to contractual rescission under §29(b) but to damages as well.[82] On that assumption a plaintiff's counsel who is not of the *cognoscenti* might conclude that all he needs to prove is (1) some use of the mails or interstate commerce and (2) an untrue statement of a material fact (or some activity within the first or third clause of the rule) in connection with (3) a purchase or sale of a security. But, if it is "cricket" for the federal courts to invent new torts or tort-like actions, it seems fair enough for them to invent reasonable restrictions on the new actions as common law judges a long time ago invented doctrines like materiality and scienter and reliance and causation in order to pressure a sense of balance.

---

[77] Humana, Inc. v. American Medicorp, Inc., 445 F. Supp. 613 (S. D. N. Y. 1978).

[78] GAF Corp. v. Milstein, 453 F. 2d 709, 720-21 (2d Cir. 1971), *cert. denied,* 406 U. S. 910; Mosinee Paper Corp. v. Rondeau, 500 F. 2d 1011 (7th Cir. 1974), *rev'd on other grounds* sub nom. Rondeau v. Mosinee Paper Corp., 422 U. S. 49 (1975) (without considering question of private right of action, court ordered injunction, which Supreme Court reversed for lack of irreparable injury); Chromalloy American Corp. v. Sun Chemical Corp., 611 F. 2d 240 (8th Cir. 1979) (relief granted without discussion of standing); Dan River, Inc. v. Unitex, Ltd., 624 F. 2d 1216 (4th Cir. 1980), *cert. denied,* 449 U. S. 1101.

[79] E. g., Myers v. American Leisure Time Enterprises, Inc., 402 F. Supp. 213 (S. D. N. Y. 1975), *aff'd without opinion,* 538 F. 2d 312 (2d Cir. 1976); see Note, Private Rights of Action for Damages under Section 13(d), 32 Stan. L. Rev. 581 (1980).

[80] E. g., Leff v. CIP Corp., 540 F. Supp. 857 (S. D. Ohio 1982), citing cases both ways.

[81] See p. 1163 infra.

[82] See Herman & MacLean v. Huddleston, 103 S. Ct. 683, 687 (1983), set out infra p. 1141, at p. 1142.

We have already gone into materiality and scienter, and we have also noticed that there is no privity requirement in private actions under Rule 10b-5.[83] We here examine reliance and causation and explore the measure of relief that is available to the successful plaintiff.

a. Reliance and Causation

As the Second Circuit put it in 1965, imposition of a reliance requirement is reasonable in a private action under Rule 10b-5, since the aim of the rule "is to qualify, as between insiders and outsiders, the doctrine of *caveat emptor* — not to establish a scheme of investors' insurance."[84] Although abandonment of the reliance requirement would facilitate outsiders' proof of insiders' fraud and thus advance the purpose of the rule, that is "an inadequate reason for reading out of the rule so basic an element of tort law as the principle of causation in fact."[85] Civil actions differ from administrative proceedings under the rule, whose aim is to deter misconduct by insiders rather than to compensate their victims. There the fact that no harm actually results from the misconduct, because of the peculiar circumstances of the particular outsiders involved, is ordinarily irrelevant to the preventive purpose.

When the plaintiff rests his 10b-5 case on §29(b), it is arguable that reliance is no more an element of recovery than it is when an action is based on §12(2) of the 1933 Act or (normally) §11. But it cannot be assumed that the courts will not imply a reliance requirement in either event. Reliance is, of course, an element of traditional rescission for fraud.

Many cases have simply *assumed* that reliance is an element of

---

[83] See pp. 544-50, 870, 904 supra.

[84] List v. Fashion Park, Inc., 340 F. 2d 457, 463 (2d Cir. 1965), *cert. denied* sub nom. List v. Lerner, 382 U. S. 811.

[85] Ibid.; see also, e. g., Janigan v. Taylor, 344 F. 2d 781, 785-86 (1st Cir. 1965), *cert. denied*, 382 U. S. 879; Britt v. Cyril Bath Co., 417 F. 2d 433, 436 (6th Cir. 1969); Dopp v. Franklin National Bank, 461 F. 2d 873, 880 (2d Cir. 1972); Landy v. Federal Deposit Ins. Corp., 486 F. 2d 139, 170 (3d Cir. 1973), *cert. denied*, 416 U. S. 960; Clegg v. Conk, 507 F. 2d 1351 (10th Cir. 1974), *cert. denied*, 422 U. S. 1007; Harris v. American Investment Co., 523 F. 2d 220, 229 n. 7 (8th Cir. 1975), *cert. denied*, 423 U. S. 1054; Kiernan v. Homeland, Inc., 611 F. 2d 785 (9th Cir. 1980).

a private action.[86] And there is no difficulty in conceptualizing reliance on an insider's *silence*. The test is not whether the plaintiff consciously had in mind the negative of the fact concealed but "whether the plaintiff would have been influenced to act differently than he did if the defendant had disclosed to him the undisclosed fact."[87]

On the other hand, "it is not necessary that plaintiff have relied *exclusively* upon the defendants."[88] And the Second Circuit has foregone proof of reliance "in the limited instance when no volitional act is required and the result of a forced sale is exactly that intended by the wrongdoer."[89]

We have seen that the concept of *justifiable* reliance is in disfavor even with respect to common law deceit.[90] But, quite apart from the fact that the concept of materiality supplies something of the objective element,[91] the courts have shown a tendency to impose *some* sort of duty on the *plaintiff* — whether by speaking of *justifiable* reliance or by considering the plaintiff's due care to be an element of a violation of Rule 10b-5 (or, at least, lack of due care to be an affirmative defense).[92] Since a 10b-5 plaintiff must prove scienter, it would be odd to subject him to a greater duty of care than at common law, where "contributory negligence is not a defense to an intentional tort case of fraud."[93] At the

[86]E. g., Reed v. Riddle Airlines, 266 F. 2d 314, 319 (5th Cir. 1959); Texas Continental Life Ins. Co. v. Dunne, 307 F. 2d 242 (6th Cir. 1962).

[87]List v. Fashion Park, Inc., 340 F. 2d 457, 463 (2d Cir. 1965), *cert. denied* sub nom. List v. Lerner, 382 U. S. 811; cf. Stier v. Smith, 473 F. 2d 1205 (5th Cir. 1973).

[88]Kohler v. Kohler Co., 208 F. Supp. 808, 824 (E. D. Wis. 1962), *aff'd on other grounds,* 319 F. 2d 634 (7th Cir. 1963) (italics supplied); see also cases cited supra c. 9A n. 71.

[89]Vine v. Beneficial Finance Co., Inc., 374 F. 2d 627, 635 (2d Cir. 1967), *cert. denied,* 389 U. S. 970; see also Mader v. Armel, 402 F. 2d 158, 162 (6th Cir. 1968), *cert. denied* sub nom. Young v. Mader, 394 U. S. 930.

[90]See c. 10A n. 12 supra.

[91]See List v. Fashion Park, Inc., 340 F. 2d 457, 462 (2d Cir. 1965), *cert. denied* sub nom. List v. Lerner, 382 U. S. 811. On the blurring of subjective reliance and objective materiality, see Titan Group, Inc. v. Faggen, 513 F. 2d 234, 239 (2d Cir. 1975), *cert. denied,* 423 U. S. 840; Thomas v. Duralite Co., Inc., 524 F. 2d 577, 584 (3d Cir. 1975).

[92]See Wheeler, Plaintiff's Duty of Due Care under Rule 10b-5: An Implied Defense to an Implied Remedy, 70 Nw. U. L. Rev. 561 (1975).

[93]Holdsworth v. Strong, 545 F. 2d 687, 694 (10th Cir. 1976), *cert. denied,* 430 U. S. 955; see also Dupuy v. Dupuy, 551 F. 2d 1005, 1018 (5th Cir. 1977), *cert. denied,* 434 U. S. 911; Sundstrand Corp. v. Sun Chemical Corp., 553 F. 2d 1033, 1048 (7th Cir. 1977), *cert. denied,* 434 U. S. 875; cf. Carroll v. First National Bank of Lincolnwood, 413 F. 2d 353, 358 (7th Cir. 1969), *cert. denied,* 396 U. S. 1003 (Rule 10b-5).

same time, "a plaintiff may not reasonably or justifiably rely on a misrepresentation where its falsity is palpable."[94] This mirrors the common law,[95] and is reflected in the Code.[96]

As with respect to reliance (causation in fact), the concept of legal causation is so integral a part of the law of torts generally that the courts have generally assumed the requirement in actions under Rule 10b-5.[97] But the cases do not agree on what the concept means.[98] Some speak in the "but for" terms of "causation in fact": "But for your misstatement," says the plaintiff, "I would not have bought."[99] Other cases, however, seem closer to requiring "legal cause."[100] And in most cases there is no indication one way or the other.

Whereas the courts traditionally require proof of *reliance* in fraud cases whether the basis of the action is tort or restitution, the concept of *legal cause* is foreign to the law of restitution. In any event, the private action under §29(b), as we have seen,[101] is more express than implied. And there is authority that reliance may be dispersed with under that section.[102]

This was essentially the state of the 10b-5 law with respect to reliance and causation in 1972, when the Supreme Court, in *Affiliated Ute Citizens of Utah* v. *United States*,[103] applied to Rule 10b-5 what it had said two years earlier with respect to Rule 14a-9 in the *Mills* case:[104]

---

[94]Holdsworth v. Strong, 545 F. 2d 687, 694 (10th Cir. 1976), *cert. denied,* 430 U. S. 955.

[95]See 2 Code 700-01.

[96]§§1703(e), 1704(e), 1705(e), 1707(e).

[97]E. g., Vine v. Beneficial Finance Co., Inc., 374 F. 2d 627, 635 (2d Cir. 1967), *cert. denied,* 389 U. S. 970; Mutual Shares Corp. v. Genesco, Inc., 384 F. 2d 540, 546 (2d Cir. 1967); Britt v. Cyril Bath Co., 417 F. 2d 433, 435-36 (6th Cir. 1969).

[98]See n. 51 supra.

[99]E. g., Vine v. Beneficial Finance Co., Inc., 374 F. 2d 627, 635 (2d Cir. 1967), *cert. denied,* 389 U. S. 970; Chasins v. Smith, Barney & Co., Inc., 438 F. 2d 1167, 1172 (2d Cir. 1971) (defendant's failure to disclose that it was a marketmaker); Gottreich v. San Francisco Investment Corp., 552 F. 2d 866 (9th Cir. 1977).

[100]See pp. 131-32 infra.

[101]See p. 1052 supra.

[102]Eastside Church of Christ v. National Plan, Inc., 391 F. 2d 357, 361-62 (5th Cir. 1968), *cert. denied* sub nom. Church of Christ v. National Plan, Inc., 393 U. S. 913; Regional Properties, Inc. v. Financial & Real Estate Consulting Co., 678 F. 2d 552, 558-59 (5th Cir. 1982).

[103]406 U. S. 128 (1972).

[104]Mills v. Electric Auto-Lite Co., 396 U. S. 375, 384-85 (1970), set out supra p. 1109, at pp. 1113-14.

Under the circumstances of this case, involving primarily a failure to disclose, positive proof of reliance is not a prerequisite to recovery. All that is necessary is that the facts withheld be material in the sense that a reasonable investor might have considered them important in the making of his decision. See *Mills v. Electric Auto-Lite Co.,* 396 U. S. 375, 384 (1970); *SEC v. Texas Gulf Sulphur Co.,* 401 F. 2d 833, 849 (C. A. 2 1968), *cert. denied* sub nom. *Coates v. SEC,* 394 U. S. 976 (1969); 6 L. Loss, Securities Regulation 3876-3880 (1969 Supp. to 2d ed. of Vol. 3); A. Bromberg, Securities Law, Fraud — SEC Rule 10b-5, §§2.6 and 8.6 (1967). This obligation to disclose and this withholding of a material fact establish the requisite element of causation in fact.[105]

It has been suggested that "the rationale for a presumption of causation in fact [which is to say, reliance] in cases like *Affiliated Ute,* in which no positive statements exist," is that "reliance as a practical matter is impossible to prove."[106] Certainly the holding — which is not limited to face-to-face transactions[107] — has an important effect on class actions.[108] But the holding is a bit soft around the edges.

First, although the holding is limited to "omissions" (nondisclosure) as distinct from "misrepresentations,"[109] the line between the two is fuzzy[110] and "The labels by themselves * * * are of little help."[111] The *Ute* presumption has been applied to half-truths[112] (which analytically are closer to lies than to nondisclosure) and also to cases involving both misrepresentations and omissions.[113]

[105] 406 U. S. at 153-54.

[106] Wilson v. Comtech Telecommunications Corp., 648 F. 2d 88, 93 (2d Cir. 1981).

[107] Shapiro v. Merrill Lynch, Pierce, Fenner & Smith, Inc., 495 F. 2d 228, 240 (2d Cir. 1974).

[108] See Cameron v. E. M. Adams & Co., 547 F. 2d 473, 477 (9th Cir. 1976).

[109] Titan Group, Inc. v. Faggen, 513 F. 2d 234 (2d Cir. 1975), *cert. denied,* 423 U. S. 840; Chelsea Associates v. Rapanos, 527 F. 2d 1266, 1271 (6th Cir. 1975); Holdsworth v. Strong, 545 F. 2d 687 (10th Cir. 1976); Vervaecke v. Chiles, Heider & Co., Inc., 578 F. 2d 713, 717 (8th Cir. 1978).

[110] Blackie v. Barrack, 524 F. 2d 891, 906 (9th Cir. 1975), *cert. denied,* 429 U. S. 816; Little v. First Cal. Co., 532 F. 2d 1302, 1304 n. 4 (9th Cir. 1976).

[111] Wilson v. Comtech Telecommunications Corp., 648 F. 2d 88, 93 (2d Cir. 1981).

[112] Chris-Craft Industries, Inc. v. Piper Aircraft, Inc., 480 F. 2d 341 (2d Cir. 1973), *cert. denied,* 414 U. S. 910; Herbst v. International Telephone & Telegraph Corp., 495 F. 2d 1308 (2d Cir. 1974).

[113] Sharp v. Coopers & Lybrand, 649 F. 2d 175, 188 (3d Cir. 1981), *cert. denied,* 455 U. S. 938; Austin v. Loftsgaarden, 675 F. 2d 168, 178 n. 21 (8th Cir. 1982).

Secondly, as with Rule 14a-9 and the *Mills* case, *Ute* by no means forecloses all consideration of reliance. Although the plaintiff need not prove reliance in "omission" cases, the courts have held that lack of reliance is a defense. In short, the effect of *Ute* is simply a shift in the burden of going forward on the reliance issue.[114] And, the Fifth Circuit *en banc* has held, the plaintiff's admission that he did not read or otherwise rely on the offering circular is enough to rebut the presumption.[115]

The court, however, limited this last holding — and the *Ute* presumption itself — to the *second* clause of Rule 10b-5, so that the plaintiff's not having read the offering circular did not defeat his claim of a fraudulent scheme to market bonds that was so pervasive that without it the bonds would never have entered the marketplace. The central purposes of the SEC statutes go far beyond disclosure to include "the promotion of free and honest markets." And it would have availed the plaintiff nothing to have read the circular. For the theory

> is not that he bought inferior bonds, but that the Bonds he bought were fraudulently marketed. The securities laws allow an investor to rely on the integrity of the market to the extent that the securities it offers to him for purchase are entitled to be in the market place.[116]

This is a variation on the so-called "fraud on the market" theory, which is based on the feeding of false information into the marketplace.[117] The variation works not only to defeat rebuttal of the

---

[114] Rochez Bros., Inc. v. Rhoades, 491 F. 2d 402, 410 (3d Cir. 1973); Carras v. Burns, 516 F. 2d 251, 257 (4th Cir. 1975); Chelsea Associates v. Rapanos, 527 F. 2d 1266, 1271 (6th Cir. 1975); Sundstrand Corp. v. Sun Chemical Corp., 553 F. 2d 1033, 1048 (7th Cir. 1977); St. Louis Union Trust Co. v. Merrill Lynch, Pierce, Fenner & Smith, Inc., 562 F. 2d 1040 (8th Cir. 1977), *cert. denied*, 435 U. S. 925; Rifkin v. Crow, 574 F. 2d 256 (5th Cir. 1978); cf. Simon v. Merrill Lynch, Pierce, Fenner & Smith, Inc., 482 F. 2d 880 (5th Cir. 1973) (court distinguished *Ute* where plaintiff had made his own investment decisions and relied on no way on defendant's recommendations); Vohs v. Dickson, 495 F. 2d 607 (5th Cir. 1974).

[115] Shores v. Sklar, 647 F. 2d 462, 468 (5th Cir. *en banc* 1981), *cert. denied*, 103 S. Ct. 722.

[116] Id. at 470-71. The vote was 12 to 10, an elaborate dissent complaining that the majority was establishing "a new theory of recovery" under Rule 10b-5 that would effectively dispense with the reliance requirement, "at least where the security offered can be shown to be not 'entitled to be marketed.'" Id. at 486.

[117] Blackie v. Barrack, 524 F. 2d 891, 906 (9th Cir. 1975), *cert. denied*, 429 U. S. 816; Panzirer v. Wolf, 663 F. 2d 365 (2d Cir. 1981); see Note, The Fraud-on-the-Market Theory, 95 Harv. L. Rev. 1143 (1982) (the efficient market hypothesis is the most persuasive rationale for the theory); Rapp, Rule 10b-5 and "Fraud-on-the-Market" — Heavy Seas Meet Tranquil Shores, 39 Wash. & Lee L. Rev. 861 (1982).

reliance presumption in "omission" cases but also to establish reliance as part of the plaintiff's case when he complains of a "misrepresentation." Although this approach nominally allows the defendant to rebut the plaintiff's imputed reliance, it is hard to conceive of how that might be done in an open market situation.[118]

A fortiori the *Ute* case does not affect considerations of *legal* causation. For neither *Ute* nor its predecessor, *Mills*, presented questions of "intervening" or multiple causes. Thus, when the market declines after the published rectification of a false earnings statement that was used in the sale of an electronics stock, the misrepresentation is not the "legal cause" of the buyer's loss, or at any rate not the *sole* legal cause, to the extent that a subsequent event that had no connection with or relation to the misrepresentation caused a market drop — for example, the suicide of the corporation's president, or a softening of the market in all electronics stocks, or a political assassination or invasion in some part of the world.

In one case the Second Circuit referred to the "clear instructions on causation" below to the effect that the "misleading statement or omission played a substantial part in bringing about or causing the damage suffered by [the plaintiff] and that the damage was either a direct result or a reasonably foreseeable result of the misleading statement."[119] And in another case the same court, after calculating 10b-5 damages as the difference in the value of a mismanaged portfolio between the time the defendant broker began to aid and abet the adviser's fraud and the time of revocation of the adviser's trading authorization, reduced the resultant figure by the average percentage decline of the markets as a whole based on a common index such as Dow Jones or the Standard & Poor's

---

[118] Little v. First Cal. Co., 532 F. 2d 1302, 1304 n. 3 (9th Cir. 1976). It has been suggested further:

> Acceptance of the logic of the fraud on the market theory * * * leads to the conclusion that there is no need in a securities fraud case for separate inquiries into materiality, reliance, causation, and damages. These inquiries are necessary in a face-to-face transaction where each party must make a subjective valuation of information provided by the other party, but irrelevant in open market transactions where the market price transmits all relevant information. The relevant inquiry in open-market transactions should be whether the market price was in fact artificially affected by false information.

Fischel, Use of Modern Finance Theory in Securities Fraud Cases, 38 Bus. Law. 1, 13 (1982).

[119] Globus v. Law Research Service, Inc., 418 F. 2d 1276, 1291 (2d Cir. 1969), *cert. denied,* 397 U. S. 913.

500.[120] The Ninth Circuit, on the other hand, in sustaining a claim that the misrepresentations caused the plaintiffs to make and hold investments in a declining market, met the defendants' argument that there was a general decline in stock prices by stating simply that the plaintiffs "relied on the misrepresentations; thus causation is adequately alleged."[121]

b.   Relief Available[122]

The Code authorizes the court, within certain restrictions, to vary the prescribed measure of damages or definition of rescission on a showing that a different result "would be plainly more appropriate on consideration of such factors as the plaintiff's loss, the defendant's profit, and the deterrent effect of the particular type of liability."[123] By way of justifying that provision, the commentary states that

> there has been so much variegation in the cases that it is tempting to conclude that "there is no law of damages under Rule 10b-5" — that the courts have taken an *ad hoc* approach and that, broadly using the common law out-of-pocket measure as an initial reference point, the appellate courts have exercised the discretion traditionally left to the trial courts in finding damages appropriate to the facts of the case.[124]

First of all, like the plaintiff at common law in the case of a contract allegedly induced by fraud — and unlike the §12(2) plaintiff, who is restricted to rescission or a rescission measure of damages — the seller who proves a violation of Rule 10b-5 has the

---

[120] Rolf v. Blyth Eastman Dillon & Co., Inc., 570 F. 2d 38, 49 (2d Cir. 1978); see also Sundstrand Corp. v. Sun Chemical Corp., 553 F. 2d 1033, 1050 (7th Cir. 1977), *cert. denied*, 434 U. S. 875.

[121] Gottreich v. San Francisco Investment Corp., 552 F. 2d 866 (9th Cir. 1977).

[122] For the sake of simplicity, the plaintiff normally will be considered to be a seller rather than a buyer.

[123] §1723(e).

[124] 2 Code 789, quoting from Note, Measurement of Damages in Private Actions under Rule 10b-5, [1968] Wash. U. L. Q. 165, 179; see also Note, Insiders' Liability under Rule 10b-5 for the Illegal Purchase of Actively Traded Securities, 78 Yale L. J. 864, 875-91 (1969); John R. Lewis, Inc. v. Newman, 446 F. 2d 800, 805 (5th Cir. 1971) ("federal courts may use any available remedy to make good the wrong done"); Nye v. Blyth Eastman Dillon & Co., 588 F. 2d 1189, 1198 (8th Cir. 1978), quoting from Garnatz v. Stifel, Nicolaus & Co., Inc., 559 F. 2d 1357, 1360 (8th Cir. 1977), *cert. denied*, 435 U. S. 951 (court's "function is to fashion the remedy best suited to the harm").

choice of undoing the bargain (when events since the transaction have not made rescission impossible) or holding the defendant to the bargain by requiring him to pay damages.[125] If the securities are still in existence and the plaintiff elects rescission, the defendant may presumably return the securities (together with any dividends or interest that he may have received on them) upon the plaintiff's repaying the amount the defendant originally paid him for them; or, since securities of the same class are fungible, the defendant should be permitted to pay the plaintiff the cash equivalent, at least when the securities are readily obtainable in the market.[126] In the latter event, the market price of the securities will presumably be computed as of the date of judgment.

Whether it is to the plaintiff's advantage to seek rescission or damages will naturally depend on the market action since the date of the transaction. If the plaintiff can prove that the security was worth 80 when he sold it to the defendant at 50, but the market when suit is brought has fallen to 40, obviously he will ask for damages rather than rescission.[127]

In the usual situation damages have been computed in accordance with the tort or out-of-pocket measure applied by the federal courts in common law fraud cases before *Erie*.[128] Normally that measure may be expected to yield the difference between the value

[125] Estate Counseling Service, Inc. v. Merrill Lynch, Pierce, Fenner & Smith, Inc., 303 F. 2d 527, 531 (10th Cir. 1962); Rogen v. Ilikon Corp., 361 F. 2d 260, 268-69 (1st Cir. 1966); Myzel v. Fields, 386 F. 2d 718, 740-49 (8th Cir. 1967), *cert. denied,* 389 U. S. 951; Sackett v. Beaman, 399 F. 2d 884, 891 (9th Cir. 1968). The plaintiff who seeks rescission need not prove damages with the degree of particularity required in an action for damages. All he must establish is his injury. Holdsworth v. Strong, 545 F. 2d 687, 697 (10th Cir. *en banc* 1976).

[126] Baumel v. Rosen, 283 F. Supp. 128, 148 (D. Md. 1968), *aff'd in part and rev'd in part on other grounds,* 412 F. 2d 571 (4th Cir. 1969), *cert. denied,* 396 U. S. 1037; cf. Strong v. Repide, 213 U. S. 419, 421-22 (1909).

[127] The plaintiff's election is not absolute. An unequivocal demand for recission will preclude a later action for damages under Rule 10b-5. Estate Counseling Service, Inc. v. Merrill Lynch, Pierce, Fenner & Smith, Inc., 303 F. 2d 527, 531-32 (10th Cir. 1962). And, "Where parties have the right to rescind, they cannot delay the exercise of that right to determine whether avoidance or affirmance will be more profitable to them." Id. at 532; Chiodo v. General Waterworks Corp., 380 F. 2d 860, 867 (10th Cir. 1967), *cert. denied,* 389 U. S. 1004; Johns Hopkins University v. Hutton, 488 F. 2d 912, 915 n. 12 (4th Cir. 1973); see also Restatement of Restitution §64. That is to say, the plaintiff cannot play the market at the defendant's expense. But cf. Myzel v. Fields, 386 F. 2d 718, 740-41 (8th Cir. 1967), *cert. denied,* 389 U. S. 951 ("rescissional damages"); Rogen v. Ilikon Corp., 361 F. 2d 260, 269 (1st Cir. 1966).

[128] Affiliated Ute Citizens of Utah v. United States, 406 U. S. 128, 154-55 (1972).

of the security (not necessarily market value at the time of the defendant's purchase but presumably value at that time as judged in the light of the issuer's subsequent history) and the price paid the plaintiff for it (or the value of anything that the defendant may have given in exchange). In the case of a close corporation, or when the market is thin, the court is not restricted to actual sales prices but may draw reasonable inferences.[129]

So much for the rule. Enter now the voracious exceptions:

(1) If the defendant buyer's profit on resale is greater than the tort measure, the plaintiff is entitled to the profit.[130] Once it is found that the defendant acquired the property by fraud and that the profit was the proximate consequence of the fraud, whether foreseeable or not, "it is more appropriate to give the defrauded party the benefit even of windfalls than to let the fraudulent party keep them.[131] The damages ceiling imposed by §28(a) in terms of "actual damages on account of the act complained of" does not foreclose a windfall recovery based on the defendant's benefit rather than the plaintiff's loss.[132]

(2) Although some courts have assumed that §28(a) *would* preclude the warranty measure of damages[133] that is the majority rule in common law deceit actions,[134] the Second Circuit has held that the "actual damages" of §28(a) could include benefit-of-the-bargain

[129] Id. at 155; see also Holmes v. Bateson, 583 F. 2d 542, 563 (1st Cir. 1978); Glick v. Campagna, 613 F. 2d 31, 37 (3d Cir. 1979).

[130] Affiliated Ute Citizens of Utah v. United States, 406 U. S. 128, 155 (1972).

[131] Janigan v. Taylor, 344 F. 2d 781, 786 (1st Cir. 1965), *cert. denied,* 382 U. S. 879; see also Gould v. American-Hawaiian Steamship Co., 535 F. 2d 761, 782 (3d Cir. 1976); but cf. Levine v. Seilon, Inc., 439 F. 2d 328, 334 (2d Cir. 1971); Simon v. New Haven Board & Carton Co., Inc., 516 F. 2d 303, 306 (2d Cir. 1975). There is authority for reducing the defendant's recoverable profit to reflect his own post-fraud efforts. Thomas v. Duralite Co., Inc., 524 F. 2d 577, 586 (3d Cir. 1975); but cf. Rochez Bros., Inc. v. Rhoades, 491 F. 2d 402, 412 (3d Cir. 1973). Moreover, pointing to the Code, a split court sitting *en banc* held that the profit should be measured (as much by way of disgorgement in an SEC injunction action as in a private action) by the price "a reasonable time after public dissemination of the inside information." SEC v. MacDonald, — F. 2d — , — (1st Cir. 1983).

[132] Myzel v. Fields, 386 F. 2d 718, 748-49 (8th Cir. 1967), *cert. denied,* 389 U. S. 951. The courts have granted recovery also of fraudulent windfall profits reaped by fraudulent *sellers,* although they are harder to prove. Zeller v. Bogue Electric Mfg. Corp., 476 F. 2d 795, 801-03 (2d Cir. 1973), *cert. denied,* 414 U. S. 908; Ohio Drill & Tool Co. v. Johnson, 498 F. 2d 186, 190 (6th Cir. 1974); Hackbart v. Holmes, 675 F. 2d 1114, 1122 (10th Cir. 1982); but cf. Occidental Life Ins. Co. of N. C. v. Pat Ryan & Associates, Inc., 496 F. 2d 1255, 1265 (4th Cir. 1974), *cert. denied,* 419 U. S. 1023.

[133] Estate Counseling Service, Inc. v. Merrill Lynch, Pierce, Fenner & Smith, Inc., 303 F. 2d 527, 533 (10th Cir. 1972); Kohler v. Kohler Co., 208 F. Supp. 808, 825 (E. D. Wis. 1962), *aff'd on other grounds,* 319 F. 2d 634 (7th Cir. 1963).

[134] See p. 1133 supra.

damages "when they can be established with reasonable certainty."[135] "Since the price paid by the successful offeror in a tender offer contest often exceeds the fair market value of the securities surrendered by the shareholders, defrauded shareholders of a target company would hardly ever, under the out-of-pocket measure of damages, have redress."[136]

(3) Consequential damages (which are "actual damages") are recoverable on top of everything else — for example, the plaintiff's cost of investigating the transaction before he entered into it.[137] And rescission does not preclude consequential damages for pre-rescission losses.[138] But "A plaintiff seeking consequential damages for fraud, at common law or under federal securities legislation, must establish the causal nexus with a good deal of certainty," varying "somewhat inversely with the depth of the fraud."[139] Under the familiar principle of mitigation of damages, a plaintiff cannot recover for his own failure to take reasonable steps to avoid further harm; at a point where a reasonable man would have taken protective action, the chain of causation is broken.[140]

(4) Presumably §28(a) does not exclude the so-called "highest intermediate value" rule of damages when it would be appropriate. That is to say, the seller who can prove that "he probably would have made a sale while the [security] was at its highest point in value" within a reasonable time after the defendant's purchase in violation of Rule 10b-5 might well argue that that is the basis for measuring what his "actual damages" are.[141]

---

[135] Osofsky v. Zipf, 645 F. 2d 107, 114 (2d Cir. 1981).

[136] Ibid.

[137] Esplin v. Hirschi, 402 F. 2d 94, 105 (10th Cir. 1968), *cert. denied,* 394 U. S. 928; Madigan, Inc. v. Goodman, 498 F. 2d 233, 238-39 (7th Cir. 1974); see also Bowman & Bourdon, Inc. v. Rohr, 296 F. Supp. 847, 852 (D. Mass. 1969), *aff'd per curiam,* 417 F. 2d 780 (1st Cir. 1969); McLean v. Alexander, 449 F. Supp. 1251, 1268-70 (D. Del. 1978), *rev'd on other grounds,* 599 F. 2d 1190 (3d Cir. 1979).

[138] Foster v. Financial Technology, Inc., 517 F. 2d 1068, 1072 (9th Cir. 1975).

[139] Zeller v. Bogue Electric Mfg. Corp., 476 F. 2d 795, 803 (2d Cir. 1973), *cert. denied,* 414 U. S. 908; see also Chris-Craft Industries, Inc. v. Piper Aircraft Corp., 516 F. 2d 172, 191 (2d Cir. 1975), *rev'd on other grounds* sub nom. Piper v. Chris-Craft Industries, Inc., 430 U. S. 1 (1977).

[140] Foster v. Financial Technology, Inc., 517 F. 2d 1068, 1072 (9th Cir. 1975).

[141] See Restatement of Restitution §151, Comment c; Code §1723(e), Comment (1); cf. Fridrich v. Bradford, CCH Fed. Sec. L. Rep. ¶94,723 at 96,407 (M. D. Tenn. 1974), *rev'd on other grounds,* 542 F. 2d 307 (6th Cir. 1976), *cert. denied,* 429 U. S. 1053; but cf. Gerstle v. Gamble-Skogmo, Inc., 478 F. 2d 1281, 1305-06 (2d Cir. 1973).

(5) In appropriate circumstances the plaintiff may obtain an accounting for profits.[142]

(6) The courts have granted "rescissory" (or "rescissional" or "restitutional") damages in various factual configurations,[143] sometimes doing their best to reconstruct the scenario as it would have been if everybody had acted properly.[144]

(7) So far we have not conjured with the complications created by the anonymity of market trading, where tracing shares to determine which were the subject of insiders' transactions would be (a) impossible and (b) in any event a lottery. If an insider buys 100 shares on the basis of a false press release or without *any* disclosure of "bullish" information — or if an insider who is responsible for a false press release does not trade at all — to whom is he liable for how much? If the *Texas Gulf Sulphur* defendants had been held liable to all those who had sold in the market during the five-month period between the mineral discovery and its truthful disclosure, Dean Ruder calculated that restitution damages would have exceeded $300 million.[145]

In *Shapiro* v. *Merrill Lynch,* the Second Circuit held that the defendant tippers were liable to all who had bought in the market "during the same period" when the tippees had sold. But, because the case had come up on an interlocutory appeal from an order denying the defendants' motion for judgment on the pleadings, the court was able to leave to the District Court on remand "the appropriate form of relief to be granted, including the proper measure of damages."[146]

---

[142] Kardon v. National Gypsum Co., 73 F. Supp. 798, 801-02 (E. D. Pa. 1947); Glick v. Campagna, 613 F. 2d 31 (3d Cir. 1979) (with rescission).

[143] Myzel v. Fields, 386 F. 2d 718, 740-41 (8th Cir. 1967), *cert. denied,* 389 U. S. 951; Chasins v. Smith, Barney & Co., Inc., 438 F. 2d 1167, 1173 (2d Cir. 1971); Garnatz v. Stifel, Nicolaus & Co., Inc., 559 F. 2d 1357 (8th Cir. 1977), *cert. denied,* 435 U. S. 951; Rolf v. Blyth Eastman Dillon & Co., Inc., 570 F. 2d 38, 49 (2d Cir. 1978) ("gross economic loss on a portfolio-wide basis during a relevant period of time"); Austin v. Loftsgaarden, 675 F. 2d 168, 181 (8th Cir. 1982).

[144] Speed v. Transamerica Corp., 135 F. Supp. 176, 186-94 (D. Del. 1955), *modified on another point and aff'd,* 235 F. 2d 369 (3d Cir. 1956); Opper v. Hancock Securities Corp., 250 F. Supp. 668, 676 (S. D. N. Y. 1966), *aff'd per curiam,* 367 F. 2d 157 (2d Cir. 1966); Gottlieb v. Sandia American Corp., 304 F. Supp. 980, 989-92 (E. D. Pa. 1969), *aff'd on this point and rev'd in part on other grounds,* 452 F. 2d 510 (3d Cir. 1971), *cert. denied* sub nom. Wechsler v. Gottlieb, 404 U. S. 938; John R. Lewis, Inc. v. Newman, 446 F. 2d 800, 805 (5th Cir. 1971); cf. Bird v. Ferry, 497 F. 2d 112 (5th Cir. 1974); Alley v. Miramon, 614 F. 2d 1372, 1387 (5th Cir. 1980).

[145] Ruder, Texas Gulf Sulphur — The Second Round, 63 Nw U. L. Rev. 423, 428-29 (1968).

[146] Shapiro v. Merrill Lynch Pierce, Fenner & Smith, Inc., 495 F. 2d 228, 241 (2d Cir. 1974).

Several years later, in a case in which the defendants had not sold on the same day on which the insiders had bought, or even in the same month, and with no proof that the defendants' trading activities had had any impact on the market price, a majority of a Sixth Circuit panel disagreed with *Shapiro* and limited the *Ute* presumption of "causation" essentially to face-to-face transactions, so as to conclude that there was simply no "causation."[147] Judge Celebrezze, concurring in the result, would have allowed recovery by any plaintiffs (there were none) who had sold concurrently with any defendants' purchases.

The Second Circuit later followed Judge Celebrezze's approach:

In *Shapiro*, 495 F. 2d at 237, this court held insider sellers subject to a duty to disclose only to those who purchased the stock "during the same period" as the insiders' sales. To be sure, the district court on remand interpreted this language to refer to the period of time from the defendants' trades to the public disclosure of the insider information, *Shapiro* v. *Merrill Lynch, Pierce, Fenner & Smith, Inc.*, [1975-1976 Transfer Binder] Fed. Sec. L. Rep. (CCH) ¶95,377, at 98,878 (S. D. N. Y. 1975), but the entire period in that case was only four days. To extend the period of liability well beyond the time of the insider's trading simply because disclosure was never made could make the insider liable to all the world. See *Shapiro*, 495 F. 2d at 239; *Globus* v. *Law Research Service, Inc.*, 418 F. 2d 1276, 1292 (2d Cir. 1969), *cert. denied*, 397 U. S. 913 (1970). Any duty of disclosure is owed only to those investors trading contemporaneously with the insider; non-contemporaneous traders do not require the protection of the "disclosure or abstain" rule because they do not suffer the disadvantage of trading with someone who has superior access to information. See *Fridrich* v. *Bradford*, 542 F. 2d 307, 326 (6th Cir. 1976) (Celebrezze, J., concurring), *cert. denied*, 429 U. S. 1053 (1977). * * * Because, in the instant case, Wilson purchased his Comtech stock approximately one month after appellees' sales, he did not trade contemporaneously with the insiders and he has no standing to sue on this claim.[148]

When there *is* standing under this test, the Second Circuit's rule is

(1) to allow any uninformed investor, where a reasonable investor would either have delayed his purchase or not purchased at all if he had had the benefit of the tipped information, to recover

---

[147]Fridrich v. Bradford, 542 F. 2d 307 (6th Cir. 1976), *cert. denied*, 429 U. S. 1053.

[148]Wilson v. Comtech Telecommunications Corp., 648 F. 2d 88, 94-95 (2d Cir. 1981).

any post-purchase decline in market value of his shares up to a reasonable time after he learns of the tipped information or after there is a public disclosure of it but (2) limit his recovery to the amount gained by the tippee as a result of his selling at the earlier date rather than delaying his sale until the parties could trade on an equal informational basis. * * * Should the intervening buyers, because of the volume and price of their purchases, claim more than the tippee's gain, their recovery (limited to that gain) would be shared *pro rata*.[149]

The court referred to this "disgorgement measure" as having "in substance been recommended by the Code."[150]

---

[149] Elkind v. Liggett & Myers, Inc., 635 F. 2d 156, 172 (2d Cir. 1980).

[150] Ibid.; Code §§1603, 1703(b), 1708(b), 1711(j). The Code differs in several respects. For example, (1) it cuts off standing not when the insider or tippee stops trading as in *Elkind* but when the information in question becomes generally available as in *Shapiro,* and (2) it imposes arbitrary monetary ceilings in addition to a ceiling in terms of the defendant's profit. For a summary description of the Code scheme, see 1 Code xlix-l:

(10) *Face-to-face versus market transactions:* Today S12(1) and 12(2) (not to mention Rule 10b-5) ignore the very real differences between face-to-face transactions and purchases in an organized market, where the tracing of certificates from seller to buyer (or vice versa), if mechanically possible at all, produces an altogether fortuitous result. The successor provisions, §§1702-03, treat the two types of transactions separately, so that, if a transaction is effected in a manner that would make the matching of buyers and sellers substantially fortuitous, all persons who buy or sell on a given day are treated alike (§§1702(b), 1703(b)).

(11) *Limitation and proration of recovery in market transactions:* If this is not to subject the defendant to greater total liability with respect to market transactions than with respect to face-to-face transactions (as it should not) and if the race is not to go to the swift, there must be machinery for prorating the recovery among all those persons who are entitled to it. Section 1711 does this by extending the authority of the Judicial Panel on Multidistrict Litigation beyond the pretrial stage so as to select a single forum for consolidated discovery and trial of all related actions.

The unavoidable price of thus considering plaintiffs of a given class to be fungible, as it were, and then prorating the total recovery among them is that there will be less recovery per plaintiff. Indeed, the provision contemplates that some or all of the recovery may go to the issuer, or to SIPC when the issuer is itself a defendant, to the extent that the expense of allocation is not worth the candle. * * *

The same proration procedure solves two other problems. First, it cures today's unavoidable but nonsensical result under S11 whereby, when a registration statement covers additional securities of an outstanding class, recovery goes only to those persons who can prove that they got registered certificates. [See p. 1038 n. 64 supra.] Secondly, the proration machinery is essential to the concept of an arbitrary limitation on damages per defendant (which is itself essential), in actions under §1704 that are based on a false registration statement (in the Code sense) or annual report, or actions under §1705 (false filings generally)

(8) Finally, on top of whatever monetary award is made, prejudgment interest may be awarded in the discretion of the court.[151] And in appropriate circumstances all the ancillary remedies are available that equity traditionally recognizes. But it is clear that punitive or exemplary damages are precluded by the limitation in §28(a) to "actual damages."[152] It is clear, too, from the holdings to that effect, that §28(a) is not limited to the *express* liability provisions. But note:

(a) What about actions under §12(2), or (if they are permitted)[153] §17(a) of the 1933 Act, which has no provision comparable to §28(a)?[154]

---

or §1707 (false publicity), in all of which there is no built-in governor of maximum liability as there is in terms of the amount of securities sold under an offering statement. That arbitrary limitation is whichever is the greatest of (A) [$200,000], (B) one percent (to a maximum of [$2 million]) of gross income in the defendant's last fiscal year if the defendant is a "company," or (C) the defendant's profit; but there is *no* limitation when the plaintiff proves knowledge of falsity [or omission], nor does it apply with respect to the registrant to the extent that an offering statement covers a primary offering, or with respect to an underwriter (§1708(c)(2); see also §1710(d)).

[151] *Granted, or remanded after denial:* E. g., Wessel v. Buhler, 437 F. 2d 279, 284 (9th Cir. 1971); Mitchell v. Texas Gulf Sulphur Co., 446 F. 2d 90, 106 (10th Cir. 1971), *cert. denied,* 404 U. S. 1004; Chris-Craft Industries, Inc. v. Piper Aircraft Corp., 516 F. 2d 172, 190 (2d Cir. 1975), *rev'd on other grounds* sub nom. Piper v. Chris-Craft Industries, Inc., 430 U. S. 1 (1977); Thomas v. Duralite Co., 524 F. 2d 577, 589 (3d Cir. 1975); Holmes v. Bateson, 583 F. 2d 542, 564 (1st Cir. 1978); Rolf v. Blyth, Eastman Dillon & Co., Inc., 637 F. 2d 77, 87 (2d Cir. 1980) ("compensatory," "customary in cases involving a breach of fiduciary duties," and "governed by fundamental considerations of fairness," even though defendant did not have the use of plaintiffs' money during the relevant period).

Denied, or remanded after grant: E. g., Norte & Co. v. Huffines, 416 F. 2d 1189, 1191-92 (2d Cir. 1969), *cert. denied* sub nom. Muscat v. Norte, 397 U. S. 989; Wolf v. Frank, 477 F. 2d 467, 479 (5th Cir. 1973), *cert. denied,* 414 U. S. 975; White v. Abrams, 495 F. 2d 724, 736 (9th Cir. 1974); cf. Occidental Life Ins. Co. of N. C. v. Pat Ryan & Associates, Inc., 496 F. 2d 1255, 1269 (4th Cir. 1974), *cert. denied,* 419 U. S. 1023.

With respect to the rate when interest is granted, see, e. g., Sanders v. John Nuveen & Co., Inc. ("Sanders II"), 524 F. 2d 1064, 1075-76 (7th Cir. 1975). In Madigan, Inc. v. Goodman, 498 F. 2d 233, 240 (7th Cir. 1974), the court held that plaintiffs who sought more than the market rate "must prove with a good deal of certainty that they would have made a particular alternative investment that would have produced a higher return."

[152] Green v. Wolf Corp., 406 F. 2d 291, 302-03 (2d Cir. 1968), *cert. denied,* 395 U. S. 977; Myzel v. Fields, 386 F. 2d 718, 748 (8th Cir. 1967), *cert. denied,* 390 U. S. 951; Richardson v. MacArthur, 451 F. 2d 35, 43 (10th Cir. 1971); Byrnes v. Faulkner, Dawkins & Sullivan, 550 F. 2d 1303, 1313 (2d Cir. 1977); Osofsky v. Zipf, 645 F. 2d 107, 111 (2d Cir. 1981) (even apart from §28(a)).

See c. 10J n. 7, 2d ¶ infra.

[153] See pp. 1348-50 infra.

[154] The only other SEC statute with a comparable provision is the Trust

(b) The very nonavailability of punitive damages, at least under Rule 10b-5, is an additional reason for adding a common law deceit count by way of pendent jurisdiction (or diversity jurisdiction when it exists). Will that stratagem work?[155] If there is substantial doubt, would the plaintiff with a good common law deceit case do better to forego a statutory action altogether, or would he be met with an argument that §28(a) applies to any action that *might* have been brought under the 1934 Act?[156]

(c) For "common law deceit" in the last paragraph, substitute "blue sky law."[157]

(d) Damages for mental distress are a species of "actual damages."[158] And they have been awarded not only in purely common law deceit cases[159] but also pursuant to pendent claims notwith-

---

Indenture Act. §323(b). And the courts are divided under both §§12(2) and 17(a):

Punitive damages *permitted* under §12(2): Nagel v. Prescott & Co., 36 F. R. D. 445, 449 (N. D. Ohio 1964). *Contra:* Hill York Corp. v. American Int'l Franchises, Inc., 448 F. 2d 680, 697 (5th Cir. 1971); Salonin v. Spyro-Dynamics Corp., CCH Fed. Sec. L. Rep. ¶94,506 at 95,770 (S. D. N. Y. 1974).

Permitted under §17(a): Larson v. Tony's Investments, Inc., CCH Fed. Sec. L. Rep. ¶92,324 at 97,532 (M. D. Ala. 1968) (dictum); Klein v. Spear, Leeds & Kellogg, 306 F. Supp. 743, 751 (S. D. N. Y. 1969). *Contra:* deHaas v. Empire Petroleum Co., 435 F. 2d 1223, 1229-32 (10th Cir. 1970); Schaefer v. First National Bank of Lincolnwood, 326 F. Supp. 1186, 1193 (N. D. Ill. 1970), *aff'd in part and rev'd in part on other grounds,* 509 F. 2d 1287 (7th Cir. 1975), *cert. denied,* 425 U. S. 943; Globus v. Law Research Service, Inc., 418 F. 2d 1276, 1283-87 (2d Cir. 1969), *cert. denied,* 397 U. S. 913 (the two statutes are *in pari materia*); Burkhart v. Allson Realty Trust, 363 F. Supp. 1286, 1290 (N. D. Ill. 1973).

[155] Apparently it will. Young v. Taylor, 466 F. 2d 1329, 1337-38 (10th Cir. 1972); Flaks v. Koegel, 504 F. 2d 702, 706-07 (2d Cir. 1974); Nye v. Blyth Eastman Dillon & Co., 588 F. 2d 1189, 1200 (8th Cir. 1978); Miley v. Oppenheimer & Co., 637 F. 2d 318, 330 (5th Cir. 1981).

[156] In Schaefer v. First National Bank of Lincolnwood, 326 F. Supp. 1186, 1193 (N. D. Ill. 1970), *aff'd in part and rev'd in part on other grounds,* 509 F. 2d 1287 (7th Cir. 1972), *cert. denied,* 425 U. S. 943, the court found the conclusion "unavoidable that common law damage rules permitting recovery in excess of actual damages have not been saved."

[157] Punitive damages have been allowed. Allied Steel & Tractor Products, Inc. v. First National City Bank of N. Y., 54 F. R. D. 256 (N. D. Ohio 1971); Bateman v. Petro Atlas, Inc., CCH Blue Sky L. Rep. ¶71,463 at 68,522 (S. D. Tex. 1977) (court applied provision in Texas blue sky law that permits punitive damages up to twice the actual damages when the representation or omission is proven to have been willfully made).

[158] Greitzer v. United States National Bank, 326 F. Supp. 762 (S. D. Cal. 1971).

[159] Malandris v. Merrill Lynch, Pierce, Fenner & Smith, Inc., 447 F. Supp. 543 (D. Colo. 1977); cf. Anderson v. Knox, 297 F. 2d 702, 728-31 (9th Cir. 1961), *cert. denied,* 370 U. S. 915 (sale of unsuitable insurance policy).

standing argument addressed to §28(a),[160] though not in 10b-5 actions themselves.[161]

c.   Actions by Buyers [Herein Also of §17(a)]

May *buyers,* for whom Congress legislated specifically in §§11 and 12(2) of the 1933 Act, forego those express rights of action in favor of Rule 10b-5, and thus make an "end run" around the conditions and limitations of the express actions such as the short statute of limitations in §13 of the 1933 Act? Indeed, may buyers resort to an implied right of action under §17(a) of the 1933 Act?

HERMAN & MACLEAN v. HUDDLESTON
Supreme Court of the United States, 1983
103 S. Ct. 683

JUSTICE MARSHALL delivered the opinion of the Court.

These consolidated cases raise two unresolved questions concerning Section 10(b) of the Securities Exchange Act of 1934, 15 U. S. C. §78j(b). The first is whether purchasers of registered securities who allege they were defrauded by misrepresentations in a registration statement may maintain an action under Section 10(b) notwithstanding the express remedy for misstatements and omissions in registration statements provided by Section 11 of the Securities Act of 1933, 15 U. S. C. §77k. The second question is whether persons seeking recovery under Section 10(b) must prove their cause of action by clear and convincing evidence rather than by a preponderance of the evidence.[a]

I

In 1969 Texas International Speedway, Inc. ("TIS"), filed a registration statement and prospectus with the Securities and Exchange Commission offering a total of $4,398,900 in securities to

---

[160] Ryan v. Foster & Marshall, Inc., 556 F. 2d 460, 464 (9th Cir. 1977); Martin v. Howard, Weil, Labouisse, Friedricks, Inc., 487 F. Supp. 503, 508 (E. D. La. 1980).

[161] Greitzer v. United States National Bank, 326 F. Supp. 762 (S. D. Cal. 1971), supra n. 154; Emmons v. Merrill Lynch, Pierce, Fenner & Smith, Inc., 532 F. Supp. 480, 485 (S. D. Ohio 1982).

[a] ED.: On this second part of the opinion, which is not set out, see p. 700 n. 56 supra.

the public. * * * the corporation filed a petition for bankruptcy on November 30, 1970.

* * * [2] Plaintiffs sued most of the participants in the offering, including the accounting firm, Herman & MacLean, which had issued an opinion concerning certain financial statements and a pro forma balance sheet that were contained in the registration statement and prospectus. * * * The court * * * entered judgment for the plaintiffs.

*   *   *

II

The Securities Act of 1933 and the Securities Exchange Act of 1934 "constitute interrelated components of the federal regulatory scheme governing transactions in securities." *Ernst & Ernst* v. *Hochfelder*, 425 U. S. 185, 206 (1976). The Acts created several express private rights of action,[8] one of which is contained in Section 11 of the 1933 Act. In addition to the private actions created explicitly by the 1933 and 1934 Acts, federal courts have implied private remedies under other provisions of the two laws.[9] Most significantly for present purposes, a private right of action under Section 10(b) of the 1934 Act and Rule 10b-5 has been consistently recognized for more than 35 years.[10] The existence of this implied remedy is simply beyond peradventure.

---

[2] Plaintiffs also alleged violations of, inter alia, Section 17(a) of the Securities Act of 1933, 15 U. S. C. §77q(a). We have previously reserved decision on whether Section 17(a) affords a private remedy, International Brotherhood of Teamsters v. Daniel, 439 U. S. 551, 557, n. 9 (1979), and we do so once again. Plaintiffs have abandoned their Section 17(a) claim, Brief, at 4, n. 6, and the Court of Appeals did not address the existence of a separate cause of action under Section 17(a). Accordingly, there is no need for us to decide the issue.

[8] Securities Act, §§11, 12, 15, 15 U. S. C. §§77k, 77*l*, 77o; Securities Exchange Act, §§9, 16, 18, 15 U. S. C. §§78i, 78p, 78r.

[9] See, e. g., J. I. Case Co. v. Borak, 377 U. S. 426 (1964) (Section 14(a) of the Securities Exchange Act); Dan River, Inc. v. Unitex Ltd., 624 F. 2d 1216 (C. A. 4 1980), cert. denied, 449 U. S. 1101 (1981) (Section 13[d] of the Securities Exchange Act); Kirshner v. United States, 603 F. 2d 234, 241 (C. A. 2 1978), *cert. denied,* 442 U. S. 909 (1979) (Section 17(a) of the Securities Act). * * *

[10] The right of action was first recognized in Kardon v. National Gypsum Co., 69 F. Supp. 512 (E. D. Pa 1946). By 1961, four courts of appeals and several district courts in other circuits had recognized the existence of a private remedy under Section 10(b) and Rule 10b-5, and only one district court decision had reached a contrary conclusion. See III L. Loss, Securities Regulation 1763-1764 and nn. 260-263 (2d ed. 1961) (collecting cases). By 1969, the existence of a private cause of action had been recognized by ten of the

The issue in this case is whether a party should be barred from invoking this established remedy for fraud because the allegedly fraudulent conduct would apparently also provide the basis for a damage action under Section 11 of the 1933 Act.[11] The resolution of this issue turns on the fact that the two provisions involve distinct causes of action and were intended to address different types of wrongdoing.

Section 11 of the 1933 Act allows purchasers of a registered security to sue certain enumerated parties in a registered offering when false or misleading information is included in a registration statement. The section was designed to assure compliance with the disclosure provisions of the Act by imposing a stringent standard of liability on the parties who play a direct role in a registered offering. If a plaintiff purchased a security issued pursuant to a registration statement, he need only show a material misstatement or omission to establish his *prima facie* case. Liability against the issuer of a security is virtually absolute, even for innocent misstatements. Other defendants bear the burden of demonstrating due diligence. See 15 U. S. C. §77k(b).

Although limited in scope, Section 11 places a relatively minimal burden on a plaintiff. In contrast, Section 10(b) is a "catchall" antifraud provision, but it requires a plaintiff to carry a heavier burden to establish a cause of action. While a Section 11 action must be brought by a purchaser of a registered security, must be based on misstatements or omissions in a registration statement, and can only be brought against certain parties, a Section 10(b) action can be brought by a purchaser or seller of *"any* security" against *"any* person" who has used *"any* manipulative or deceptive device or contrivance" in connection with the purchase or

---

eleven courts of appeals. See VI L. Loss, Securities Regulation 3871-3873 (2d ed. Supp. 1969) (collecting cases). When the question whether an implied cause of action can be brought under Section 10(b) and Rule 10b-5 was first considered in this Court, we confirmed the existence of such a cause of action without extended discussion. See Superintendent of Insurance v. Bankers Life & Cas. Co., 404 U. S. 6, 13, n. 9 (1971). We have since repeatedly reaffirmed that "the existence of a private cause of action for violations of the statute and the Rule is now well established." Ernst & Ernst v. Hochfelder, supra, 425 U. S., at 196 (citing prior cases).

[11] The Court of Appeals noted that the plaintiffs "apparently did have a Section 11 remedy." 640 F. 2d, at 541, n. 5. While accurate as to the two other defendants, this conclusion may be open to question with respect to Herman & MacLean. Accountants are liable under Section 11 only for those matters which purport to have been prepared or certified by them. 15 U. S. C. 77k(a)(4). Herman & MacLean contends that it did not "expertise" at least some of the materials that were the subject of the lawsuit, Tr. of Oral Arg. at 6-8, which if true could preclude a Section 11 remedy with respect to these materials.

sale of a security. 15 U. S. C. §78j (emphasis added). However, a Section 10(b) plaintiff carries a heavier burden than a Section 11 plaintiff. Most significantly, he must prove that the defendant acted with scienter, i. e., with intent to deceive, manipulate, or defraud.

Since Section 11 and Section 10(b) address different types of wrongdoing, we see no reason to carve out an exception to Section 10(b) for fraud occurring in a registration statement just because the same conduct may also be actionable under Section 11.[17] Exempting such conduct from liability under Section 10(b) would conflict with the basic purpose of the 1933 Act: to provide greater protection to purchasers of registered securities. It would be anomalous indeed if the special protection afforded to purchasers in a registered offering by the 1933 Act were deemed to deprive such purchasers of the protections against manipulation and deception that Section 10(b) makes available to all persons who deal in securities.

While some conduct actionable under Section 11 may also be actionable under Section 10(b), it is hardly a novel proposition that the Securities Exchange Act and the Securities Act "prohibit some of the same conduct." *United States* v. *Naftalin,* 441 U. S. 768, 778 (1979) (applying Section 17(a) of the 1933 Act to conduct also prohibited by Section 10(b) of the 1934 Act in an action by the SEC). " 'The fact that there may well be some overlap is neither unusual nor unfortunate.' " Ibid., quoting *SEC* v. *National Securities, Inc.,* 393 U. S. 453, 468 (1969). In savings clauses included in the 1933 and 1934 Acts, Congress rejected the notion that the express remedies of the securities laws would preempt all other rights of action. Section 16 of the 1933 Act states unequivocally that "[t]he rights and remedies provided by this subchapter shall be in addition to any and all other rights and remedies that may exist at law or in equity." 15 U. S. C. §77p. Section 28(a) of the 1934 Act contains a parallel provision. 15 U. S. C. §78bb(a). These provisions confirm that the remedies in each Act were to be supplemented by "any and all" additional remedies.

This conclusion is reinforced by our reasoning in *Ernst & Ernst* v. *Hochfelder,* supra, which held that actions under Section 10(b) require proof of scienter and do not encompass negligent conduct. In so holding, we noted that each of the express civil remedies in the 1933 Act allowing recovery for negligent conduct is subject to

_____
[17] Cf. Mills v. Electric Auto-Lite, 396 U. S. 375, 390-391 (1970) (existence of express provisions for recovery of attorneys' fees in §§9(e) and 18(a) of 1934 Act does not preclude award of attorneys' fees under §14(a) of the Act).

procedural restrictions not applicable to a Section 10(b) action.[18] 425 U. S., at 208-210. We emphasized that extension of Section 10(b) to negligent conduct would have allowed causes of action for negligence under the express remedies to be brought instead under Section 10(b), "thereby nullify[ing] the effectiveness of the carefully drawn procedural restrictions on these express actions." Id., at 210 (footnote omitted). In reasoning that scienter should be required in Section 10(b) actions in order to avoid circumvention of the procedural restrictions surrounding the express remedies, we necessarily assumed that the express remedies were not exclusive. Otherwise there would have been no danger of nullification. Conversely, because the added burden of proving scienter attaches to suits under Section 10(b), invocation of the Section 10(b) remedy will not "nullify" the procedural restrictions that apply to the express remedies.

This cumulative construction of the remedies under the 1933 and 1934 Acts is also supported by the fact that, when Congress comprehensively revised the securities laws in 1975, a consistent line of judicial decisions had permitted plaintiffs to sue under Section 10(b) regardless of the availability of express remedies. In 1975 Congress enacted the "most substantial and significant revision of this country's Federal securities laws since the passage of the Securities Exchange Act in 1934." See Securities Acts Amendments of 1975, Pub. L. No. 94-29, 89 Stat. 97. When Congress acted, federal courts had consistently and routinely permitted a plaintiff to proceed under Section 10(b) even where express remedies under Section 11 or other provisions were available.[21] In

---

[18] For example, a plaintiff in a Section 11 action may be required to post a bond for costs, 15 U. S. C. §77k(e), and the statute of limitations is only one year, §77m. In contrast, Section 10(b) contains no provision requiring plaintiffs to post security for costs. Also, courts look to the most analogous statute of limitations of the forum state, which is usually longer than the period provided for Section 11 actions. See Ernst & Ernst v. Hochfelder, supra, 425 U. S., at 210, n. 29.

[21] [Citations omitted.] Two early district court decisions had refused to recognize an action under Rule 10b-5 in the face of overlap with Section 11. Rosenberg v. Globe Aircraft Corp., 80 F. Supp. 123 (E. D. Pa. 1948); Montague v. Electronic Corp. of America, 76 F. Supp. 933 (S. D. N. Y. 1948). The latter case was not subsequently followed in the Southern District, e. g., Osborne v. Mallory, 86 F. Supp. 869 (S. D. N. Y. 1949), and it has no precedential value in light of the Second Circuit's decision in Fischman v. Ratheon Mfg. Co., supra. The *Rosenberg* decision stood alone at the time of the 1975 amendments, and even that decision had not been followed in the district in which it was decided, Premier Industries, Inc. v. Delaware Valley Financial Corp., 185 F. Supp. 694 (E. D. Pa. 1960), or elsewhere within the same circuit, Dauphin Corp. v. Redwall Corp., 201 F. Supp. 466 (D. Del. 1962). Since the 1975 amendments, the lower courts have continued to recognize that an im-

light of this well-established judicial interpretation, Congress' decision to leave Section 10(b) intact suggests that Congress ratified the cumulative nature of the Section 10(b) action. See *Merrill Lynch, Pierce, Fenner & Smith, Inc.* v. *Curran,* — U. S. —, — (1982); *Lorillard* v. *Pons,* 434 U. S. 575, 580-581 (1978).

A cumulative construction of the securities laws also furthers their broad remedial purposes. In enacting the 1934 Act, Congress stated that its purpose was "to impose requirements necessary to make [securities] regulation and control reasonably complete and effective." 15 U. S. C. §78b. In furtherance of that objective, Section 10(b) makes it unlawful to use "*any* manipulative or deceptive device or contrivance" in connection with the purchase or sale of any security. The effectiveness of the broad proscription against fraud in Section 10(b) would be undermined if its scope were restricted by the existence of an express remedy under Section 11.[22] Yet we have repeatedly recognized that securities laws combating fraud should be construed "not technically and restrictively, but flexibly to effectuate [their] remedial purposes." *SEC* v. *Capital Gains Research Bureau,* 375 U. S. 180, 195 (1963). Accord: *Superintendent of Insurance* v. *Bankers Life & Cas. Co.,* 404 U. S. 6, 12 (1971); *Affiliated Ute Citizens* v. *United States,* 406 U. S. 128, 151 (1972). We therefore reject an interpretation of the securities laws that displaces an action under Section 10(b).[23]

Accordingly, we hold that the availability of an express remedy under Section 11 of the 1933 Act does not preclude defrauded purchasers of registered securities from maintaining an action un-

---

plied cause of action under Section 10(b) can be brought regardless of whether express remedies are available. [Citations omitted.]

[22] Moreover, certain individuals who play a part in preparing the registration statement generally cannot be reached by a Section 11 action. These include corporate officers other than those specified in 15 U. S. C. §77k(a), lawyers not acting as "experts," and accountants with respect to parts of a registration statement which they are not named as having prepared or certified. If, as Herman & MacLean argues, purchasers in registered offerings were required to rely solely on Section 11, they would have no recourse against such individuals even if the excluded parties engaged in fraudulent conduct while participating in the registration statement. The exempted individuals would be immune from federal liability for fraudulent conduct even though Section 10(b) extends to "any person" who engages in fraud in connection with a purchase or sale of securities.

[23] We also reject application of the maxim of statutory construction, *expressio unius est exclusio alterius.* See H. Hart & A. Sacks, The Legal Process: Basic Problems in the Making and Application of Law 1173-1174 (tent. ed. 1958); Note, Implying Civil Remedies from Federal Regulatory Statutes, 77 Harv. L. Rev. 285, 290-291 (1963). As we stated in SEC v. Joiner Corp., 320 U. S. 344, 350-351 (1943), such canons "long have been subordinated to the doctrine that courts will construe the details of an act in conformity with its

der Section 10(b) of the 1934 Act. To this extent the judgment of the court of appeals is affirmed.

*   *   *

IV

The judgment of the Court of Appeals is affirmed in part [on the §11 point] and reversed in part [on the clear and convincing evidence point, here omitted] and otherwise remanded for proceedings consistent with this opinion.

It is so ordered.

JUSTICE POWELL took no part in the consideration or decision of these cases.

---

1. Clearly buyers and sellers should be treated alike, as they are in the Code. But the very first case that allowed a seller to sue his buyer for violation of Rule 10b-5 gave birth to a dilemma that soon made itself felt under present law. On the one hand, since §10(b) applies equally to sellers and buyers, may a buyer waive his express remedy under §11 or 12(2) of the 1933 Act and claim an implied remedy under Rule 10b-5 in order to avoid the short statute of limitations in §13 of the 1933 Act and the risk of having to pay his opponents' counsel fees as well as to post advance security for costs pursuant to §11(e)? The two statutes have been repeatedly held to be *in pari materia*.[162] And "special provisions prevail over general ones which, in the absence of the special provisions, would control."[163] On the other hand, is the cultivated pearl that is Rule 10b-5 to be limited to the seller, a relative stepchild of Congress, while the buyer, its favorite child, is relegated to whatever gleanings he can find in §11 or 12(2)?

Judge Jerome Frank's solution was to allow the buyer to escape the strictures of §11 but only at the cost of proving fraud (scienter)

---

dominating general purpose." See generally Silver v. New York Stock Exchange, 373 U. S. 341, 357 (1963) (favoring "an analysis which reconciles the operation of both statutory schemes with one another rather than holding one completely ousted"). We believe the maxim cannot properly be applied to a situation where the remedies redress different misconduct and where the remedial purposes of the Acts would be undermined by a presumption of exclusivity.

[162] E. g., Axelrod & Co. v. Kordich, Victor & Neufeld, 451 F. 2d 838, 843 (2d Cir. 1971).

[163] Missouri v. Ross, 299 U. S. 72, 76 (1936).

under Rule 10b-5.[164] And that is essentially the rationale of *Herman & MacLean.*

2. *Query:* The only exempted securities to which §12(2) applies by its terms are those specified in §3(a)(2): municipals, banks, and interests in certain tax-exempt plans. Will buyers of those securities be permitted to escape that exemption by resorting to Rule 10b-5?[165]

3. Will §17(a) of the 1933 Act support a private right of action? Justice Marshall's opinion, as we have seen, was able to avoid that question.[166] If *anything* in the 1933 Act can be stated categorically, the answer should be no. In November 1933 Commissioner Landis of the Federal Trade Commission, who had played a prominent part in the drafting of the statute, stated in an address:

> The suggestion has been made on occasion that civil liabilities arise also from a violation of Section 17, the first subsection of which makes unlawful the circulation of falsehoods and untruths in connection with the sale of a security in interstate commerce or through the mails. But a reading of this section in the light of the entire Act leaves no doubt but that violations of its provisions give rise only to a liability to be restrained by injunctive action or, if wilfully done, to a liability to be punished criminally.[167]

The following passage has been frequently quoted by the lower courts:

> It is one thing to imply a private right of action under §10(b) or the other provisions of the 1934 act, because the specific liabilities created by §§9(e), 16(b) and 18 do not cover all the variegated actitivites with which that act is concerned. But it is quite another thing to add an implied remedy under §17(a) of the 1933 act to the detailed remedies specifically created by §§11 and 12. The 1933 act is a much narrower statute. It deals only with disclosure and fraud *in the sale* of securities. It has but two important substantive provisions, §§5 and 17(a). Noncompliance with §5 results in civil liability under §12(1). Faulty compliance results

---

[164] Fischman v. Raytheon Mfg. Co., 188 F. 2d 783, 786-88 (2d Cir. 1951).

[165] See 3 Loss 1788-89.

[166] 103 S. Ct. at 685 n. 2, set out supra p. 1141, at p. 1142 n. 2.

[167] Landis, Liability Sections of Securities Act, 18 Am. Accountant 330, 331 (1933). See also Douglas and Bates, The Federal Securities Act of 1933, 43 Yale L. J. 171, 181-82 (1933), where the authors queried "whether the making of an act unlawful by the Act gives to purchasers an action of rescission on the grounds of illegality," but stated that it seemed clear by negative implication from §§11 and 12 that §17 probably does not enlarge the civil remedies of purchasers.

in liability under §11. And §17(a) has its counterpart in §12(2). It all makes a rather neat pattern. Within the area of §§5 and 17(a), §§11 and 12 (unlike §§9(e), 16(b) and 18 of the 1934 act) are all-embracing. This is not to say that the remedies afforded by §§11 and 12 are complete. But the very restrictions contained in those sections and the differences between them — for example, the fact that §11 but not §12 imposes liability on certain persons connected with the issuer without regard to their participation in the offering and the fact that §12(2) does not go so far in relation to §17(a) as §12(1) goes in relation to §5 — make it seem the less justifiable to permit plaintiffs to circumvent the limitations of §12 by resort to §17(a). Particularly is this so in view of the fact that §11, together with the statute of limitations in §13, was actually tightened in the 1934 amendments to the Securities Act.[168]

Judge Friendly, in his concurring opinion in *Texas Gulf Sulphur*, took the position that §17 was not intended to be the basis of any private actions; that, on the other hand, there seemed little practical point in denying a private action under §17 once it was established that a buyer had an action under Rule 10b-5, "with the important proviso that fraud, as distinct from mere negligence, must be alleged"; and that to go further "would totally undermine the carefully framed limitations imposed on the buyer's right to recover granted by §12(2) of the 1933 Act."[169]

Finally, in 1979, on a background of conflict of authority, the Second Circuit concluded, with no analysis, that "the language of §17 is broad enough to imply a private right of action."[170]

---

[168] 3 Loss 1785; see, e. g., Dyer v. Eastern Trust & Banking Co., 336 F. Supp. 890, 904-05 (D. Me. 1971); Hill v. Der, 521 F. Supp. 1370, 1373-78 (D. Del. 1981). It is noteworthy, too, that §15 imposes liability on persons who control those liable under §11 or 12, without mention of §17.

[169] SEC v. Texas Gulf Sulphur Co., 401 F. 2d 833, 867-68 (2d Cir. 1968), *cert. denied* sub nom. Coates v. SEC and Kline v. SEC, 394 U. S. 976. And this view was widely followed. E. g., Sanders v. John Nuveen & Co., Inc., 554 F. 2d 790, 795-96 (7th Cir. 1977).

[170] Kirshner v. United States, 603 F. 2d 234, 241 (2d Cir. 1978); see also Newman v. Prior, 518 F. 2d 97, 99 (4th Cir. 1975); Daniel v. International Brotherhood of Teamsters, 561 F. 2d 1223, 1245 (7th Cir. 1977), *rev'd on other grounds* sub nom. International Brotherhood of Teamsters v. Daniel, 439 U. S. 551 (1979); Huddleston v. Herman & MacLean, 640 F. 2d 534, 540-41 (5th Cir. 1981), *vacated on other grounds* sub nom. Herman & MacLean v. Huddleston, 103 S. Ct. 683 (1983); Stephenson v. Calpine Conifers II, Ltd., 652 F. 2d 808 (9th Cir. 1981); Berger v. Bishop Investment Corp., 695 F. 2d 302 (8th Cir. 1982).
There seems to be only one appellate holding *contra*. Landry v. All American Assurance Co., 688 F. 2d 381, 389-91 (5th Cir. 1982); see also, e. g., Architectural League of N. Y. v. Bartos, 404 F. Supp. 304, 313 (S. D. N. Y. 1975); McFarland v. Memorex Corp., 493 F. Supp. 631, 649-53 (N. D. Cal. 1980);

It would be wrong to assume that §17(a) adds nothing to Rule 10b-5: Arguably §17(a), like Rule 10b-5, is not limited to §12's rescission measure of damages;[171] indeed, there is no bar to punitive damages as there is under the 1934 Act.[172] The plaintiff is guaranteed access to a state court if he prefers it.[173] And — most importantly — the scienter that is required under Rule 10b-5 because of the "deceptive" language of §10(b) is not required under §17(a)(2) or (3).[174] This is perhaps the best reason for restricting §17(a) to public proceedings. For, unless the courts are willing to write §12(2)'s due care defense into §17(a), the result would seem to be the strict liability for misstatements that Congress imposed in only one case — the issuer when sued under §11.

All this led to the statement in a 1974 case (and the confusion is certainly no less today): "It is the necessity of dealing with such issues, which cannot be resolved satisfactorily, that reflects the need for prompt enactment of the proposed federal securities code."[175]

4. What of §11's pale sister, §18 of the 1934 Act?[176] That section has been held not to preclude 10b-5 actions for false filings.[177] But implied actions — to the extent they are allowed at all under the tender offer provisions, §§13(d), 13(e), 14(d), and 14(e) — might meet a roadblock under §18 on the ground that none of them requires scienter as Rule 10b-5 does.[178] The Second Circuit has concluded that liability for negligent misstatements or omissions in violation of Rule 14a-9, the proxy fraud rule, is not inconsistent with §18, because §14(a) is specifically directed at proxy regulation and most documents within §18 are not distributed to stockholders for the purpose of inducing action.[179] But the Su-

---

Manchester Bank v. Connecticut Bank & Trust Co., 497 F. Supp. 1304, 1314 (D. N. H. 1980); Kaufman v. Magid, 539 F. Supp. 1088, 1097-98 (D. Mass. 1982).

[171] Dorfman v. First Boston Corp., 336 F. Supp. 1089, 1096 (E. D. Pa. 1972).

[172] See p. 1139 supra.

[173] Compare Sec. Act §22(a) with Sec. Ex. Act §27.

[174] Aaron v. SEC, 446 U. S. 680 (1980), set out supra p. 887.

[175] Crowell v. Pittsburgh & Lake Erie R. R., 373 F. Supp. 1303, 1310 (E. D. Pa. 1974).

[176] See p. 1054 supra.

[177] Ross v. A. H. Robins Co., Inc., 607 F. 2d 545 (2d Cir. 1979); Wachovia Bank & Trust Co. v. National Student Marketing Corp., 650 F. 2d 342, 356-57 (D. D. C. 1980).

[178] Would-be §13(d) plaintiffs must also meet §18's purchaser or seller requirement. Myers v. American Leisure Time Enterprises, Inc., 402 F. Supp. 213 (S. D. N. Y. 1975), aff'd without opinion, 538 F. 2d 312 (2d Cir. 1976); W. A. Krueger Co. v. Kirkpatrick, Pettis, Smith, Polian, Inc., 466 F. Supp. 800, 803 (D. Neb. 1979).

[179] Gerstle v. Gamble-Skogmo, Inc., 478 F. 2d 1281, 1299 n. 18 (2d Cir. 1973).

preme Court, as we have seen, has taken a narrower view of implied actions with respect to tender offers than with respect to proxy solicitations.[180]

As Justice Marshall said in *Herman & MacLean,* "it is hardly a novel proposition that the Securities Exchange Act and the Securities Act 'prohibit some of the same conduct.' "[181] In the *Naftalin* case,[182] there cited, the Court applied §17(a) of the 1933 Act to "ordinary market trading" despite the contention that that was the province of Rule 10b-5 and that §17(a) should be limited to distributions. In the *National Securities* case,[183] also cited by Justice Marshall, the Court applied Rule 10b-5 to a merger of two insurance companies notwithstanding the inapplicability of the proxy rules because the companies did not then have any registered securities. Similarly, since it has long been clear that §17(a) did not *pro tanto* repeal the mail fraud statute,[184] dismissal of a §17(a) count for failure to allege a "security" surely would not prevent a mail fraud conviction for the same transaction. And it has been held that Rule 10b-5 can stand independently of the express civil liability provision in §9(e) of the 1934 Act for market manipulation in violation of §9(a)-(c).[185]

5. The clash between §11 and Rule 10b-5 produced the only bad split among the persons who produced the Code. With the Code's shift from securities to company registration and continuous reporting, some thought it would be anomalous to retain the Code's §11 successor, §1704, for the basic company registration statement and the occasional offering statement (today's registration statement) while the field annual report (the "10-K"), which would be the Code's central disclosure document, would be subject only to the milder 10b-5 type of liability under Code §1705. Others objected to the necessity of practicing §11-type "due diligence" every year. The upshot was that the Institute took no position on the question, and that the version of the Code that survived the subsequent negotiations with the Commission is a compromise that retains §11's multiple defendants, with the burden of going forward on them, but changes the defense from today's elaborate scheme based essentially on a negligence standard

---

[180] See pp. 1069-79 supra.

[181] 103 S. Ct. at 688, set out supra p. 1141, at p. 1144.

[182] United States v. Naftalin, 441 U. S. 768, 778 (1979).

[183] SEC v. National Securities, Inc., 393 U. S. 453, 468 (1969).

[184] Edwards v. United States, 312 U. S. 473, 483-84 (1941).

[185] Schaefer v. First National Bank of Lincolnwood, 509 F. 2d 1287, 1292 (7th Cir. 1975), *cert. denied,* 425 U. S. 943. Chemetron Corp. v. Business Funds, Inc., 682 F. 2d 1149 (5th Cir. 1982), which held to the contrary, was vacated and remanded, — S. Ct. — (1983), "for further consideration in light of Herman & MacLean v. Huddleston."

to proof of *lack of scienter*,[186] and adds a new provision that simply makes it unlawful (without any civil liability) for a director to sign a filed annual report without "a reasonable investigation of its contents."[187]

5. Margin Rules

FEDERAL SECURITIES CODE §1716 WITH COMMENTS

SEC. 1716. (a) *Excessive Credit.* — A lender or other person who violates a rule under section 918 [successor to 1934 Act §§7, 8] limiting the amount of permissible credit is liable to the borrower for (1) the interest paid (including any amount charged by way of discount), and (2) in the court's discretion on consideration of the circumstances (including the conduct of the parties and the amounts involved) and the purposes of this Code (including the deterrent effect of liability), an additional amount not in excess of the sum of (A) twice the interest paid or accrued (including any amount charged by way of discount), and (B) the difference between any trading losses of the borrower and any trading losses that he would have suffered in the absence of the violation.

(b) *Nonpayment or Failure to Deposit Collateral.* — A lender or other person who violates a rule under section 918 requiring securities to be sold for nonpayment or failure to deposit collateral is liable to the borrower for the difference between the amount that would have been received if they had been timely sold and any lesser amount received on their late sale, except to the extent that that amount is determined to be excessive on consideration of the circumstances and purposes specified in section 1716(a)(2).

*   *   *

COMMENT

(1) There is something about the idea of allowing recovery to a customer who would have enjoyed greater profits as a result of the excessive credit he received if the market had moved in his favor

---

[186] See 2 Code 703-18; 2 id. (2d Supp. 1981) 75-78.
[187] §2003(c)(4).

— or who complains that the broker should have sold him out promptly when he did not pay in time — that causes the judicial gorge to rise. See *Pearlstein* v. *Scudder & German ("Pearlstein I"),* 429 F. 2d 1136, 1145, 1149 (2d Cir. 1970) (dissenting opinion of Friendly, J.), *cert. denied,* 401 U. S. 1013; *Serzysko* v. *Chase Manhattan Bank,* CCH Fed. Sec. L. Rep. ¶91,676 at 95,481 (S. D. N. Y. 1966), *on the merits,* 290 F. Supp. 74, 78 (S. D. N. Y. 1968), *aff'd per curiam,* 409 F. 2d 1360 (2d Cir. 1969), *cert. denied,* 396 U. S. 404;[a] * * * *Goldman* v. *Bank of the Commonwealth,* 467 F. 2d 439, 447 (6th Cir. 1972) * * * . Indeed, the legislative purpose of X7 was by no means confined to the protection of margin speculators. See Friendly, J., in *Pearlstein I,* supra, at 1147-48; see also [pp. 717-19 supra].

(2) Nevertheless, as the Second Circuit stated *obiter* in *Junger* v. *Hertz, Neumark & Warner,* 426 F. 2d 805, 806 (1970), *cert. denied,* 400 U. S. 880, "It has long been settled that a person for whom a broker [or presumably a bank or, under Reg. G, anybody else] has unlawfully arranged credit has a private right of action," whether in tort or under X29(b). And the 1970's produced a number of square appellate holdings. *Pearlstein I,* supra Comment (1) (broker's failure to sell customer out on his nonpayment in a special account); *Goldman,* supra Comment (1) (overextension of credit by bank); see also *Landry* v. *Hemphill, Noyes & Co.,* 473 F. 2d 365, 370 (1st Cir. 1973), *cert. denied,* 414 U. S. 1002; *Spoon* v. *Walston & Co.,* 478 F. 2d 246 (6th Cir. 1973), *aff'g per curiam* 345 F. Supp. 518 (E. D. Mich. 1972); *Grove* v. *First National Bank of Herminie,* 489 F. 2d 512 (3d Cir. 1973); *McCormick* v. *Esposito,* 500 F. 2d 620, 623 (5th Cir. 1974), *cert. denied,* 420 U. S. 912; cf. In the Matter of *Naftalin & Co., Inc.* v. *Merrill Lynch, Pierce, Fenner & Smith, Inc.,* 469 F. 2d 1166 (8th Cir. 1972). And even Judge Friendly conceded in *Pearlstein I* that "it may be proper in some instances to impose civil liability in furtherance of the subsidiary purpose of X7(c), protection of the innocent 'lamb' attracted to speculation by the possibility of large profits with low capital investment." 429 F. 2d at 1148.

[a] ED.: Judge Murphy introduced his opinion by stating:

Mr. John Q. Public would indeed be surprised to learn that one can borrow a few hundred thousand dollars from a bank in order to play the stock market, give the bank the stock he purchased as collateral for the loan and if the market went down and your collateral was sold you could sue the bank for having loaned you the money in violation of law — but that is what Edward Serzysko did in this case.

CCH ¶91,676 at 95,481.

(3) All this, however, as the court observed in *Stern* v. *Merrill Lynch, Pierce, Fenner & Smith, Inc.*, 603 F. 2d 1073 (4th Cir. 1979), predated both the 1970 enactment of X7(f), which for the first time made it unlawful to *borrow* in violation of Federal Reserve rules,[b] and the Supreme Court's teaching in *Cort* v. *Ash,* 422 U. S. 66 (1975), together with a bevy of other cases concerning the judicial implication of private rights of action. [Citations omitted.]

(4) The more recent holdings under the margin rules are predominantly in the negative. In addition to the *Stern* case, supra Comment (3), see *Utah State University of Agriculture & Applied Science* v. *Bear, Stearns & Co.*, 549 F. 2d 164, 170 (10th Cir. 1977), cert. denied, 434 U. S. 890; * * * *Pearlstein* v. *Scudder & German* ("*Pearlstein II*"), 527 F. 2d 1141, 1145, n. 3 (2d Cir. 1975) (dictum);[c] Comment, *Civil Liability for Margin Violations — The Effect of Section 7(f) and Regulation X,* 43 Ford L. Rev. 93 (1964). But there is [a relatively small amount of] authority the other way. *Neill* v. *David A. Noyes & Co.*, 416 F. Supp. 78, 80 (N. D. Ill. 1976); *Palmer* v. *Thomson & McKinnon Auchincloss, Inc.*, 427 F. Supp. 915 (D. Conn. 1977);[d] cf. *McNeal* v. *Paine, Webber, Jackson & Curtis, Inc.*, 429 F. Supp. 359, 363-65 (N. D. Ga. 1977);[e] see Solomon and Hart, *Recent Developments in the Regulation of Securities Credit*, 20 J. Pub. L. 167, 209 (1971); Note, *Regulation X and Investor-Lender Margin Violation Disputes*, 57 Minn. L. Rev. 208 (1972). Significantly, in *Stern,* supra Comment (3), Judge Butzner dissented, citing the Code and stating that the legislative history disclosed "a dual intent on the part of the Congress to regulate credit and to protect investors." 603 F. 2d at 1099.

(5) A number of cases have also put in issue the *in pari delicto* doctrine, which the courts have refused to apply [*Pearlstein I,* supra Comment (1), at 1141, Friendly, J., dissenting at 1148] except perhaps in cases approaching conspiracy [*Moscarelli* v. *Stamm,* 288 F. Supp. 453, 459 (E. D. N. Y. 1968)] or fraud by the borrower [*Goldman* v. *Bank of the Commonwealth,* supra Comment (1), at 446)] or, more recently, under the influence of X7(f) [*Bell* v. *J. D. Winer & Co., Inc.*, 392 F. Supp. 646, 654 (S. D. N. Y. 1975); *Lantz* v. *Wedbush, Noble, Cooke, Inc.*, 418 F. Supp. 653 (D. Alaska

---

[b] Ed.: See pp. 726-27 supra.

[c] Ed.: See also Gilman v. Federal Deposit Ins. Corp., 660 F. 2d 688 (6th Cir. 1981); Walck v. American Stock Exchange, Inc., 687 F. 2d 778, 788-89 (3d Cir. 1982).

[d] Ed.: See also Panayotopoulas v. Chemical Bank, 464 F. Supp. 199 (S. D. N. Y. 1979).

[e] Ed.: *Rev'd on other grounds,* 598 F. 2d 888 (5th Cir. 1979).

1976)]. As a District Judge put it after stating that he was "disturbed by the entire transaction," involving as it did a "knowledgeable" short seller and a lawbreaking broker:

> To allow the broker to plead contributory negligence or causation by the customer as the reason for a violation would remove the very heart of the legislation, for in every case of a violation the dealer could be heard to assert participation. * * *
>
> The Court will not entertain a cacophony of blame on the part of the brokers and customers — each blaming the other for not meeting the requirements — the ultimate responsibility must be placed somewhere and Congress has indicated that it is with the brokers or dealers.

Avery v. *Merrill Lynch, Pierce, Fenner & Smith, Inc.,* 328 F. Supp. 677, 680-81 (D. D. C. 1971).

(6) In any event, this is a code, not a restatement. And all things considered — the importance of deterrence, the discretion that §1716 gives the courts with respect to damages (see Comment (9)), and the flexibility with respect to *in pari delicto* under §1725(d)[f] — the Code opts for liability as expressed in §1716.

(7) So far as *types of violations* are concerned, it would not be practicable to try to codify them all, especially since the highly technical Regs. T, U, G and X are ever changing. The two subsections of §1716 cover the two types of violation that have figured in all or most of the cases. Others are referred to the residual liability provisions in §1722(a).[g]

*   *   *

(9) *Measure of damages:* (a) There is not much question under §1716(b). Cf. In the Matter of *Naftalin & Co., Inc.* v. *Merrill Lynch, Pierce, Fenner & Smith, Inc.,* 469 F. 2d 1166, 1182 (8th Cir. 1972). So far as §1716(a) is concerned, some cases have gone so far as to allow recovery of the margin deposit and cancellation of the note. *Grove* v. *First National Bank of Herminie,* 489 F. 2d 512 (3d Cir. 1973); *Caldwell* v. *Genesco Employees Credit Assn.,* 393 F. Supp. 741, 747-48 (M. D. Tenn. 1975); and see cases cited in 5 Loss 3309. When one considers the highly technical nature of some of the regulatory provisions and the sometimes huge credits involved, the result is apt to be Draconian.

---

[f] ED.: See pp. 1197-98 infra.
[g] ED.: See p. 1104 n. 28 supra.

The suggested solution in §1716(a) affords essential leeway — from mere recovery of interest, which is a matter of right, to recovery of that amount trebled plus trading losses attributable to the violation — to take care of such variables as the degree of the *plaintiff's* guilt (see Comment (5)) and the amounts involved. Cf. the *Goldman, Landry, Spoon, and Grove cases,* supra Comment (2); *Pearlstein II,* supra Comment (4). Moreover, §1722(d) saves the lender's right to recover the principal amount of the loan, subject to setoff with respect to the amount of his liability under §1716.

*   *   *

(10) *Causation:* Causation (see §202(19)) is not a factor except implicitly in §1716(a)(2)(B). With that exception, violation of the credit regulations is more like violation of a filing requirement than fraud. At the same time, §1716(a)(2)(B) reflects the judicial assumption that causation is a factor in the recovery of *trading losses.* In addition to the cases cited in 5 Loss 3308, esp. *Meisel* v. *North Jersey Trust Co.,* 218 F. Supp. 274 (S. D. N. Y. 1963), see the dictum in *Junger,* supra Comment (2), 426 F. 2d at 805, 806, n. 1; *Pearlstein* v. *Scudder & German,* 346 F. Supp. 443, 453 (S. D. N. Y. 1972), *rev'd on other grounds, Pearlstein II,* 527 F. 2d 1141 (2d Cir. 1975); *Landry* v. *Hemphill, Noyes & Co.,* supra Comment (2), at 370-71. Indeed, without §1716(a)(2)(B) one cannot be certain, under the "apparently indivisible injury" concept of the law of torts, that a court would even offset trading losses that would have been suffered in the absence of a violation. See 5 Loss 3309, quoting from Prosser, *Torts* 255 (3d ed. 1964) [(4th ed. 1971) 321].

If, as seems likely, an implied tort action does not survive the dual barriers imposed by §7(f) and the recent Supreme Court opinions, other possibilities remain. Section 29(b) — applied by the Supreme Court in *Transamerica*[188] — makes rescission (as distinct from damages) available both offensively[189] and defensively.[190]

---

[188] Transamerica Mortgage Advisors, Inc. v. Lewis, 444 U. S. 11 (1979), set out supra p. 411.

[189] First Ala. Bancshares, Inc. v. Lowder, CCH Fed. Sec. L. Rep. ¶98,015 at 91,251-52 (N. D. Ala. 1981) (dictum). This assumes privity of contract between plaintiff and defendant. In Natkin v. Exchange National Bank of Chicago, 342 F. 2d 675 (7th Cir. 1965), plaintiffs who delivered stock to one who used it as collateral in a loan transaction with a bank that allegedly violated Regulation U stated no cause of action against the bank on the basis of its wrongful conversion of the stock.

[190] Goldenberg v. Bache & Co., 270 F. 2d 675, 681 (5th Cir. 1959) (broker's

And a violation of the Federal Reserve rules is apt to entail a violation also of the margin rules, and perhaps other rules, of the particular stock exchange. On the assumption that neither a federal tort action nor an action under §29(b) would lie on the basis of the exchange rules themselves,[191] the borrower might bring an action *ex contractu* under state law "based on the contract between stockbroker and customer as affected by the federal statute and regulations."[192] That is to say, the usages of the marketplace — which should certainly include the federal margin rules along with the rules and customs of the exchange — are an implied term of the contract[193] even if the contract establishing the margin account does not expressly provide (as it typically does) that the contract is subject to all applicable federal, state, and exchange rules.

6.   SELF-REGULATORY ORGANIZATION RULES

FEDERAL SECURITIES CODE §1721 WITH COMMENTS

SEC. 1721. (a) *Determination of Rules to Which Section Applies.* — A member of or participant in a self-regulatory organization who violates a rule of the organization, or a broker, dealer, municipal broker, or municipal dealer within section 905(c) [successor to Sec. Ex. Act §15(b)(9)][a] who violates a rule prescribed under that section, is liable to his customer for any loss caused by the violation if —

(1) the rule violated has been determined by Commission rule to be within section 1721; or

(2) a court, except with respect to those rules determined by Commission rule not to be within section 1721, decides that a private right of action under this Code should be recognized in

---

counterclaim); In the Matter of Naftalin & Co., Inc. v. Merrill Lynch, Pierce, Fenner & Smith, Inc., 469 F. 2d 1166, 1180-82 (8th Cir. 1972); Johnson, Lane, Space, Smith & Co., Inc. v. Lenny, 129 Ga. App. 55, 198 S. E. 2d 923 (1973); Staley v. Salvesen, 35 Pa. D. & C. 2d 318, 321 (C. P. 1963).

[191] See p. 1157 infra.

[192] Goldenberg v. Bache & Co., 270 F. 2d 675, 680 (5th Cir. 1959). But the Fifth Circuit later declined to permit use of the exchange rules "by a knowing beneficiary [of the rules] as a dagger against his perhaps too lenient broker." McCormick v. Esposito, 500 F. 2d 620, 628 (5th Cir. 1974), *cert. denied,* 420 U. S. 912; see also Gordon v. duPont Glore Forgan, Inc., 487 F. 2d 1260 (5th Cir. 1973), *cert. denied,* 417 U. S. 946.

[193] See p. 1190 n. 154 infra.

[a] ED.: This is the "SECO" provision. See p. 693 supra.

accordance with the principles of common law and equity, applied as a matter of Federal jurisprudence, and the standards of section 1722(a).[b]

(b) *Commission's Rulemaking Authority.* — The rules of the Commission may designate either specific self-regulatory organization (or section 905(c)) rules or categories of such rules that are or are not within section 1721.

(c) *Criteria to Guide Commission.* — Among the criteria that the Commission shall consider in exercising its authority under section 1721 are (1) whether the particular self-regulatory organization rule was required by the Commission to be adopted, amended, or supplemented, (2) whether the particular rule is substantially a substitute for or parallel to a rule of the Commission (other than a section 905(c) rule), (3) whether the particular rule is designed for the special benefit of a class of persons to which a potential plaintiff belongs against the kind of harm alleged, and (4) the risk, in the case of a self-regulatory organization rule, that the imposition of liability under section 1721 will discourage the organization from full performance of its intended role.

(d) *Nonretroactivity.* — No rule change adopted by the Commission under section 1721 after a violation has occurred affects an action based on that violation.

*   *   *

COMMENT

(1) Not long after the Second Circuit (per Friendly, J.) left the door ajar in *Colonial Realty Corp.* v. *Bache & Co.,* 358 F. 2d 178 (1966), *cert. denied,* 385 U. S. 817, the Seventh Circuit flung it wide open in recognizing (at least *obiter*) an action for violation of NYSE Rule 405, the "know your customer" rule, which it assumed was a rule required by X6. *Buttrey* v. *Merrill Lynch, Pierce, Fenner & Smith, Inc.,* 410 F. 2d 135 (1969), *cert. denied,* 396 U. S. 838; see also *Avern Trust* v. *Clarke,* 415 F. 2d 1238, 1242 (7th Cir. 1969), *cert. denied,* 387 U. S. 963 (dictum on NASD "suitability" rule); *SEC* v. *First Securities Co. of Chicago,* 463 F. 2d 981, 988 (7th Cir. 1972), *cert. denied* sub nom. *McKy* v.

---

[b] ED.: This section has to do with the courts' recognition of private actions not otherwise created by the Code. See p. 1104 n. 28 supra.

Hochfelder, 409 U. S. 880 (NASD rule requiring members' supervision of their representatives); *Landy* v. *FDIC,* 486 F. 2d 139, 164-67 (3d Cir. 1973), *cert. denied,* 416 U. S. 960 (dictum *re* NYSE Rule 405); *Van Gemert* v. *Boeing Co.,* 520 F. 2d 1373 (2d Cir. 1975), *cert. denied,* 423 U. S. 947 (violation of NYSE listing agreement and section of Company Manual); *Hughes* v. *Dempsey-Tegeler & Co., Inc.,* 534 F. 2d 156, 173 (9th Cir. 1976), *cert. denied,* 429 U. S. 896 (NYSE Constitution, Art. XIII, requiring suspension of member firm in unsafe condition, and Rule 325, the debt-capital ratio rule); *Sacks* v. *Reynolds Securities, Inc.,* 593 F. 2d 1234, 1241-42 (D. C. Cir. 1978) (NYSE Rule 412 *re* transfer of accounts to another firm).

Contra: Carras v. *Burns,* 516 F. 2d 251, 260 (4th Cir. 1975) (exchange margin maintenance rules were designed primarily to protect solvency of members); *Hayden* v. *Walston & Co., Inc.,* 528 F. 2d 901 (9th Cir. 1975) (NASD rule requiring registration of representatives);[c] cf. *Sanders* v. *John Nuveen & Co., Inc.,* 554 F. 2d 790, 796-97 (7th Cir. 1977) (in holding that NASD rule requiring members' suspension of their representatives did not support a private action without a finding of fraud, court was "mindful of the admonition in *Colonial* [supra] against adopting a simplistic all-or-nothing approach in deciding whether a private civil damage action exists"); *Utah State University of Agriculture & Applied Science* v. *Bear, Stearns & Co.,* 549 F. 2d 164, 167-69 (10th Cir. 1977), *cert. denied,* 434 U. S. 890 (something "tantamount to fraud" must be shown for NASD suitability rule and NYSE "know your customer" rule to give rise to a private action);[d] *Shull* v. *Dain, Kalman & Quail, Inc.,* 561 F. 2d 152 (8th Cir. 1977), *cert. denied,* 434 U. S. 1086 (no action for breach of Chicago Mercantile Exchange rule without finding of fraud); Walck v. American Stock Exchange, Inc., 687 F. 2d 778, 788 (3d Cir. 1982) ("no basis for an inference that the Exchanges in their quasi-legislative capacity intended to subject *themselves* [italics supplied] to damages for non-enforcement").

(2) Nobody has suggested foreclosing *all* federal actions under

[c] ED.: See also Jablon v. Dean Witter & Co., 614 F. 2d 671 (9th Cir. 1980); State Teachers Retirement Board v. Fluor Corp., 654 F. 2d 843, 852-53 (2d Cir. 1981) (NYSE Company Manual section requiring immediate announcement of unusual market activity).

[d] ED.: In Clark v. John Lamula Investors, Inc., 583 F. 2d 594 (2d Cir. 1978), the court held that unsuitability plus intent to defraud violated Rule 10b-5, so that it was not necessary to decide whether there was an action based on the rules *per se.*

self-regulatory organization rules, if only because of the sometimes fortuitous choice of quasi-legislator as between one of those bodies and the SEC; the readiest example, cited by Judge Friendly himself (358 F. 2d at 182, n. 4), is the NYSE rule on the voting of "street name" stock, which apparently caused the Commission to terminate a rulemaking proceeding of its own under X14(b). On the other hand, Judge Friendly also drew attention to the consequences of too ready a recognition of federal actions in terms of (a) saddling the federal courts with garden-variety customer-broker suits, (b) the outlawing of enforced arbitration under *Wilko v. Swan,* 346 U. S. 427 (1953),[e] and (c) the ousting of state courts because of the exclusive federal jurisdiction of X27. With respect to the last of these points, §1822(a) makes jurisdiction concurrent so far as most private actions, including all those under §1721, are concerned; and, with respect to the second, §1725(b)(3)(B) exempts agreements to arbitrate disputes arising under most self-regulatory organization rules from the antiwaiver provision in §1725(a).

* * *

(4) There is a basic anomaly inherent in this area of civil liability in that the courts are not used to recognizing actions based on violations of rules of ethics that constitute neither illegal conduct nor breach of contract.

(5) Where does all this point? Leaving everything to the courts would be too uncertain; and the situation would not be much improved by giving the Commission (as some have suggested) an advisory and intervention function along the lines of what used to be Chapter X of the Bankruptcy Act. Leaving it all to Commission rule might invite excessive coverage, at least during a few experimental years. Instead §1721 is an amalgam of most of the approaches here described:

(a) The Commission may either include or exclude by rule; and under §1721(b) it may (and is likely to) designate categories rather than individual exchange or association rules.

(b) Commission rules are binding on the courts, whether those rules are inclusionary or exclusionary.

(c) The courts under §1721(a)(2), which incorporates the standards of §1722(a), may recognize additional self-regulatory rules

[e] ED.: See p. 1192 infra.

that have been neither included nor excluded by Commission rule.

(d) When the Commission has not acted, §1721(a)(2) is not merely an invitation to the courts to consider applicable self-regulatory rules in measuring a member's duty in a common law [or SEC fraud] action. This they are free to do today. See *Cash* v. *Frederick & Co., Inc.*, 57 F. R. D. 71, 78 (E. D. Wis. 1972); *Piper, Jaffray & Hopwood, Inc.* v. *Ladin*, 399 F. Supp. 292, 298 (S. D. Iowa 1975); *Lange* v. *H. Hentz & Co.*, 418 F. Supp. 1376, 1383-84 (N. D. Tex. 1976).[f] By contrast, the jurisdiction under §1721(a)(2) is as truly federal as it is under §1721(a)(1), and it is "federal common law" that is referred to. This means (i) that a federal court may act without diversity or pendent jurisdiction, and (ii) that a state court, exercising its concurrent jurisdiction under §1822 (a)(2), likewise must apply federal law (which is to say, this is one of the manifestations of "reverse *Erie*"). Cf. Labor Management Relations Act §301, 29 U. S. C. §185(a), as construed in *Textile Workers Union of America* v. *Lincoln Mills of Alabama*, 353 U. S. 448 (1957).

* * *

(8) Section 1721(a) specifies only damages. The courts will have to decide under §1722(a)[g] — as well as §1819(l), which gives them "the authority of a court of equity to grant appropriate ancillary or other relief" in *any* action — whether, for example, to enjoin (or even, under the teaching in *J. I. Case Co.* v. *Borak*, 377 U. S. 426 (1964), undo) a merger approved by proxies obtained in violation of the New York Stock Exchange's "street name" rules. Cf. *Walsh & Levine* v. *Peoria & Eastern Ry. Co.*, 222 F. Supp. 516 (S. D. N. Y. 1963), described in 5 Loss 2870-71.

* * *

(12) §1721(c): The criteria do not include the availability of an action under state law, because in the Code's context that criterion runs in both directions: On the one hand, why needlessly

---

[f] ED.: See also the *Utah State University* and *Shull* cases, supra p. 1159, Comment (1); Mercury Investment Co. v. A. G. Edwards & Sons, 295 F. Supp. 1160 (S. D. Tex. 1969); Miley v. Oppenheimer & Co., 637 F. 2d 318, 333 (5th Cir. 1981) (violation of NYSE and NASD suitability rules as one factor in detemining whether account had been churned); Petrites v. J. C. Bradford & Co., 646 F. 2d 1033, 1034 n. 1 (5th Cir. 1981). And see p. 1157, text at n. 179 supra.

[g] ED.: See n. b supra.

add a federal action? On the other hand, the very availability of a nonstatutory action might be thought to bespeak uniform federal coverage in a Code that regulates the conduct of brokers and dealers.

*　　*　　*

7. INVESTMENT COMPANY ACT

Quite apart from restitutional possibilities under the voidability provision in §47(b) of the Investment Company Act,[194] liability has repeatedly been implied for violation of various provisions of that statute.[195] These holdings extended even to the original §36, which made nothing unlawful but simply authorized the appropriate District Court, at the instance of the Commission, to enjoin an investment company officer, director, or adviser (among others) from continuing to act in any of those capacities on a finding of "gross misconduct or gross abuse of trust."[196] The Second Circuit has held that this liability survives both (1) the 1970 addition of a §36(b),[197] which creates an express private right of action for a "breach of fiduciary duty" with respect to compensation,[198] and (2) *Transamerica's* denial of damages (as distinct from rescission under §47(b)) for violation of the Advisers Act.[199] But questions of individual standing remain.[200]

---

[194] See, e. g., Esplin v. Hirschi, 402 F. 2d 94, 103-04 (10th Cir. 1968), *cert. denied*, 394 U. S. 928. In Brown v. Bullock, 194 F. Supp. 207, 231-32 (S. D. N. Y. 1961), *aff'd*, 294 F. 2d 415 (2d Cir. 1961), §47(b) was applied to a "proxy contract." See also Mills v. Electric Auto-Lite Co., 396 U. S. 375, 387 (1970) (dictum).

[195] E. g., Taussig v. Wellington Fund, Inc., 313 F. 2d 472, 476 (3d Cir. 1963), *cert. denied*, 374 U. S. 806; Levitt v. Johnson, 334 F. 2d 815 (1st Cir. 1964), *cert. denied*, 379 U. S. 961. The only authority *contra* is Brouk v. Managed Funds, Inc., 286 F. 2d 901 (8th Cir. 1961), *vacated pursuant to a settlement*, 369 U. S. 424 (1962); and the Eighth Circuit in Greater Iowa Corp. v. McLendon, 378 F. 2d 783 (8th Cir. 1967), stated *obiter* that *Brouk* was probably inconsistent with *Borak*, set out supra p. 1059.

[196] E. g., Moses v. Burgin, 445 F. 2d 369, 373 (1st Cir. 1971), *cert. denied* sub nom. Johnson v. Moses, 404 U. S. 994.

[197] Tannenbaum v. Zeller, 552 F. 2d 402, 417 (2d Cir. 1977), *cert. denied* sub nom. F. Eberstadt & Co. v. Tannenbaum, 434 U. S. 934. The original §36 became §36(a), which now refers to "a breach of fiduciary duty involving personal misconduct."

[198] See Galfand v. Chestnutt, 545 F. 2d 807 (2d Cir. 1976); Grossman v. Johnson, 674 F. 2d 115 (1st Cir. 1982), *cert. denied* sub nom. Grossman v. Fidelity Municipal Bond Fund, Inc., 103 S. Ct. 85.

[199] Transamerica Mortgage Advisors, Inc. v. Lewis, 444 U. S. 11 (1979), set out supra p. 1090; see also S. Rep. No. 91-184 (1969) 16; H. R. Rep. No. 91-1382 (1969) 38.

[200] In General Time Corp. v. American Investors Fund, Inc., 283 F. Supp.

8. MISCELLANEOUS IMPLIED LIABILITIES

We have noticed the principal areas of implied liability under the SEC statutes. But other provisions have given rise to civil liability on one theory or another. [201] For example, the Fifth Circuit has twice applied §29(b) of the 1934 Act to broker-dealers doing business without registration in violation of §15(a). [202] And we have earlier noticed the recent cases under the Trust Indenture Act. [203] On the other hand, except apparently for only one 1963 case, [204] the courts have concluded that implication of a private action under §13(a) of the 1934 Act for false reports is precluded by §18(a). [205]

400, 401-02 (S. D. N. Y. 1968), *aff'd sub nom.* General Time Corp. v. Talley Industries, Inc., 403 F. 2d 159 (2d Cir. 1968), *cert. denied,* 393 U. S. 1026, the court held that a company that was the subject of a takeover bid by an investment company had no standing to assert violations of §§17(d) and 13(a)(3) of the Investment Company Act. As Judge Bryan there noticed (id. at 402 n. 4), there was an earlier case in which the court issued a preliminary injunction, at the instance of a corporation threatened with a takeover bid, against the defendant's violation of the registration provision of the Investment Company Act, but the question of standing was assumed without discussion. Natco Corp. v. Great Lakes Industries, Inc., 214 F. Supp. 185 (W. D. Pa. 1962), *remanded for dismissal, apparently pursuant to settlement,* CCH Fed. Sec. L. Rep. ¶91,236 (3d Cir. 1963). The appellate court in *General Time* expressly disavowed passing on the point. 403 F. 2d at 164. But the same panel soon acknowledged in a related appeal that its earlier decision "would better have been placed" on Judge Bryan's conclusion. SEC v. General Time Corp., 407 F. 2d 65, 71 (2d Cir. 1968), *cert. denied,* 393 U. S. 1026; see also Greater Iowa Corp. v. McLendon, 378 F. 2d 783 (8th Cir. 1967); Herpich v. Wallace, 430 F. 2d 792 (5th Cir. 1970) (no standing in stockholder of *portfolio* company); but cf. Independent Investor Protective League v. SEC, 495 F. 2d 311 (2d Cir. 1974) *(non sequitur* that *only* investors in an investment company have standing).

[201] For a comprehensive list of cases both recognizing and rejecting implied liabilities, see 2 Code 775-79.

[202] Eastside Church of Christ v. National Plan, Inc., 391 F. 2d 357 (5th Cir. 1968), *cert. denied* sub nom. Church of Christ v. National Plan. Inc., 393 U. S. 913, *judgment for plaintiff on remand aff'd* sub nom. McGregor Blvd. Church of Christ v. Walling, 428 F. 2d 401 (5th Cir. 1970); Regional Properties, Inc. v. Financial & Real Estate Consulting Co., 678 F. 2d 552 (5th Cir. 1982); see also Davis v. Avco Corp., 371 F. Supp. 782, 789 (N. D. Ohio 1974).

[203] See c. 1D n. 41 supra.

[204] Kroese v. Crawford, CCH Fed. Sec. L. Rep. ¶91,262 (S. D. N. Y. 1963).

[205] See 2 Code 776; cf. p. 1150 supra. In Westinghouse Credit Corp. v. Bader & Dufty, 627 F. 2d 221, 224 (10th Cir. 1980), the court held that one company had no standing to seek an injunction against another company's offering certain securities unless they were registered under §5 of the 1933 Act and §13(a) reports were filed simply because the plaintiff wanted to use the information to defend a state court action brought by the second company; for the reporting requirements were designed to protect the investing public. In ScienTex Corp. v. Kay, 689 F. 2d 879 (9th Cir. 1982), the court rejected an

All these affirmative cases, particularly those decided before the recent Supreme Court decisions, must be reassessed in the light of those holdings.[206]

I. STATUTES OF LIMITATIONS

1. EXPRESS LIABILITIES

a. The Prescribed Periods

Section 13 of the 1933 Act provides a double-barreled statute of limitations for all three civil liability provisions in that statute. With respect to §12(1) it is one year after the alleged violation of §5 and three years after the security was "bona fide offered to the public." Presumably this means *first* offered to the public. And neither period is tolled pending discovery of the alleged violation.[1] But the statute does not begin to run until whichever of the defendant's activities — offer, sale, or delivery by use of the mails or interstate commerce — occurred last.[2]

For §12(2) the period is "one year after the discovery of the untrue statement or the omission, or after such discovery should have been made by the exercise of reasonable diligence," and three years after the sale. And the statute of limitations for §11 follows the 12(2) formula with respect to the one-year period and the 12(1) formula with respect to the three-year period: one year after discovery, with the same "reasonable diligence" test, and three years after the security was "bona fide offered to the public."[3]

---

implied mandatory injunction action to require the filing of ownership reports under §16(a) of the 1934 Act.

[206] See Walck v. American Stock Exchange, Inc., 687 F. 2d 778, 786-88 (3d Cir. 1982), where the court rejected the holding in Baird v. Franklin, 141 F. 2d 238 (2d Cir. 1944), *cert. denied*, 323 U. S. 737, of an exchange's implied liability for violation of §6(b) of the 1934 Act (as it stood before the 1975 amendments) in failing to enforce its own rules.

C. 10I [1] Cook v. Avien, Inc., 573 F. 2d 685, 691 (1st Cir. 1978) (one-year period). *Query* the holding in Hoglund v. Covington County Bank, CCH Fed. Sec. L. Rep. ¶95,910 (M. D. Ala. 1977), that fraudulent concealment does toll the one-year period.

[2] Doran v. Petroleum Management Corp., 576 F. 2d 91 (5th Cir. 1978).

[3] The respective periods in §11 were two and ten years instead of one and three in the original statute; they were cut down in the 1934 amendments. As a result, it is literally possible for the statute to expire before the purchaser acquires the security in the case of a very slow offering that may still be going on after three years! When §24(e) of the Investment Company Act was

The standard under the one-year clauses is objective, requiring reasonable diligence on the part of the buyer.[4] And, as with §12(1), the three-year cutoffs are absolute,[5] although there are estoppel possibilities.[6] None of the SEC statutes contains a provision, common to many of the blue sky laws, permitting the seller substantially to reduce the limitation period by making a rescission offer.[7]

In §§9(e) and 18(c) of the 1934 Act (with respect to manipulation and false filings) the periods are (1) one year after discovery of "the facts constituting the violation" in the case of §9(e) or "the cause of action" in the case of §18(c) and (2) three years after the violation or the accrual of the cause of action. The statute of limitations in §29(b) for actions under §15(c)(1), we have already noticed, is similar to that for §9(e).[8] Although none of the three sections refers, as does §13 of the 1933 Act, to when "such discovery should have been made by the exercise of reasonable diligence," the Fifth Circuit ignored the contrast between the two statutes in reading a "reasonable diligence" requirement into the one-year discovery clause of §29(b).[9]

---

amended in 1954 to permit the registration of additional securities of open-end investment companies to be effected by amending an earlier registration statement instead of filing a new one, and to require the filing of their supplemental prospectuses as posteffective amendments, it was provided in that section that for purposes of §13 "no such security shall be deemed to have been bona fide offered to the public prior to the effective date of the latest amendment filed pursuant to this subsection." S. Rep. No. 1036 at 21 and H. R. Rep. No. 1542 at 31, 83d Cong., 2d Sess. (1954). And we have noticed the Commission's perhaps dubious use of the undertaking technique in "shelf" registrations in an attempt to postpone the starting date of the limitations period from the effective date of the registration statement to the effective date of the posteffective amendment. See p. 144 supra; cf. First Multifund for Daily Income, Inc. v. United States, 602 F. 2d 332, 335-36 (Ct. Cl. 1979), *cert. denied*, 445 U. S. 916. For the Code's solution, see 2 Code 812, Comment (3)(b)(ii).

[4] Johns Hopkins University v. Hutton, 422 F. 2d 1124, 1130 (4th Cir. 1970).

[5] Summer v. Land & Leisure, Inc., 664 F. 2d 965, 968 (5th Cir. 1981); SEC v. Seaboard Corp. (Admiralty Fund v. Hugh Johnson & Co., Inc.), 677 F. 2d 1301, 1308 (9th Cir. 1982); cf. Walck v. American Stock Exchange, Inc., 687 F. 2d 778, 791-92 (3d Cir. 1982) (Sec. Ex. Act §9(e), infra p. 1165); Aldrich v. McCulloch Properties, Inc., 627 F. 2d 1036, 1042 (10th Cir. 1980) (Interstate Land Sales Full Disclosure Act).

[6] Katz v. Amos Treat & Co., 411 F. 2d 1046, 1055 (2d Cir. 1969).

[7] See pp. 1013-14 supra.

[8] See p. 1106 supra. With respect to the statute of limitations in §16(b), see p. 612 supra.

[9] Goldenberg v. Bache & Co., 270 F. 2d 675, 681 (5th Cir. 1959).

b. Burden of Proof

It is the general rule in the federal courts that, when the very statute that creates the cause of action also contains a limitation period, the statute of limitations not only bars the remedy but also destroys the liability, and therefore the plaintiff must plead and prove facts showing that he is within the statute.[10] This view has been consistently followed under the Securities Act.[11] So far as satisfying the burden is concerned, the facts in the decided cases are, of course, highly variegated.[12]

c. Laches

Does the doctrine of laches have any place with respect to the express liabilities? If the buyer discovers an untruth or §5 violation shortly after his purchase, may he wait until almost a full year has expired before tendering the security to the seller or reselling it on the market? This question lends itself to better discussion at a later point, after an analysis of the limitations problems with respect to the implied liabilities.

2. IMPLIED LIABILITIES

There is by hypothesis no statute of limitations for rights of action that have been invented by the courts; for there is no federal statute of limitations for civil actions generally. But "statutes of repose" are so basic an element of our jurisprudence — criminal as well as civil — that it would be unthinkable to be able to sue

---

[10] Cook v. Avien, Inc., 573 F. 2d 685, 695 (1st Cir. 1978). A limitation of this kind, moreover, must be applied in actions brought in state courts whether the state statute be longer or shorter. Brennan, J., concurring in McAllister v. Magnolia Petroleum Co., 357 U. S. 221, 228 (1958), and cases cited. Presumably state courts are equally bound to apply the federal rule of burden of proof even though the state rule puts the burden on the defendant. See C. Wright and A. Miller, Federal Practice and Procedure (1979) §§1270-74.

[11] Pennsylvania Co. for Insurances on Lives & Granting Annuities v. Deckert, 123 F. 2d 979, 985 (3d Cir. 1941); Chambliss v. Coca-Cola Bottling Corp., 274 F. Supp. 401, 408 (E. D. Tenn. 1967), *aff'd per curiam,* 414 F. 2d 256 (6th Cir. 1969), *cert. denied,* 397 U. S. 916; Johns Hopkins University v. Hutton, 488 F. 2d 912, 915 n. 12 (4th Cir. 1973), *cert. denied,* 416 U. S. 916.

[12] E. g., Dale v. Rosenfeld, 229 F. 2d 855 (2d Cir. 1956); MacClain v. Bules, 275 F. 2d 431, 437 (8th Cir. 1960); Hoffman v. Estabrook & Co., Inc., 587 F. 2d 509, 518-19 (1st Cir. 1978).

under Rule 10b-5, for example, without limit of time. In this state of affairs resort must be had to a number of basic propositions that have been laid down by the Supreme Court:

(1) In federally created actions *at law* "the silence of Congress has been interpreted to mean that it is federal policy to adopt the local law of limitation."[13] This rule is followed even though it often makes the result vary depending upon the state in which the action is brought, and even though, especially under a statute like the 1934 Act that provides for a broad choice of venue and nationwide service of process, it permits the plaintiff a considerable amount of forum-shopping.[14]

(2) But an action for fraud cannot be barred, regardless of the local statute of limitations, as long as the plaintiff remains in ignorance of the fraud "without any fault or want of diligence or care on his part," "though there be no special circumstances or efforts on the part of the party committing the fraud to conceal it from the knowledge of the other party." "This equitable doctrine is read into every federal statute of limitation."[15]

(3) When suit is based on "a federally-created right * * * for which the *sole* remedy is *in equity*," the traditional equitable doctrine of laches alone governs the question whether the action is timely.[16] On the other hand, the federal equity doctrine does *not* prevail over the state statute of limitations even in equitable actions "when the jurisdiction of the federal court is concurrent

[13] Holmberg v. Armbrecht, 327 U. S. 392, 395 (1946), and cases cited; for SEC cases, see, e. g., Ernst & Ernst v. Hochfelder, 425 U. S. 185, 210 n. 29 (1976), set out supra p. 871, at p. 880 (dictum); Klein v. Bower, 421 F. 2d 338, 343 (2d Cir. 1970); Roberts v. Magnetic Metals Co., 611 F. 2d 450, 452 (3d Cir. 1979).
This includes any local "borrowing" statute. See, e. g., N. Y. CPLR §202 (applicable when the cause of action accrued outside the state and plaintiff is a nonresident); Sack v. Low, 478 F. 2d 360, 365 (2d Cir. 1973); Arneil v. Ramsey, 550 F. 2d 774, 779-80 (2d Cir. 1977); Industrial Consultants, Inc. v. H. S. Equities, Inc., 646 F. 2d 746, 747 (2d Cir. 1981), *cert. denied,* 454 U. S. 838; Brodsky, Statutes of Limitations, 12 Rev. Sec. Reg. 909 (1979).

[14] H. L. Green Co., Inc. v. MacMahon, 312 F. 2d 650, 652 n. 3 (2d Cir. 1962, *leave to file pet. for cert. denied* sub nom. H. L. Green Co. v. United States Court of Appeals for the Second Circuit, 372 U. S. 928. However, although the distinction between a traditional limitation on the time for bringing suit and a time limitation on the right created may have some utility in certain areas of the law — for example, in conflict-of-laws cases when the choice is between the forum and the jurisdiction under whose laws the cause of action arose — that distinction should not be considered in determining the choice of statutes of limitations in Rule 10b-5 actions or the like. Berry Petroleum Co. v. Adams & Peck, 518 F. 2d 402, 407 (2d Cir. 1975).

[15] Holmberg v. Armbrecht, 327 U. S. 392, 397 (1946).

[16] Id. at 395 (italics are supplied).

with that of law, or the suit is brought in aid of a legal right."[17]

This reference to state law makes for a great amount of utterly wasteful litigation. Since there are fifty-two jurisdictions and at least two statutes of limitations to choose from in each jurisdiction (for example, one for action based on fraud, another in the blue sky law, and often a third residual statute) and five or six commonly implied actions under the SEC statutes (Rules 10b-5 and 14a-9, §14(e) of the 1934 Act, §36(a) of the Investment Company Act, and various rules of the self-regulatory organizations, not to mention rescission actions under the Investment Advisers Act pursuant to the *Transamerica* case), there are *at least* 500-odd possible answers (52 x 2 x 5). That is to say, if the Second Circuit today decides that New York's statute of limitations for fraud cases governs in a 10b-5 action, and tomorrow a 10b-5 case comes up from Connecticut, the court might decide that Connecticut's blue sky period is closer to 10b-5. And, if the next day a case comes to the Second Circuit from New York again, but it is a proxy case, the court will have to start afresh once more. The *reductio ad absurdum* is marked by a 1977 case in which the District Court, properly holding that the statutes of limitations that would have governed the original actions continued to govern after their transfer to another forum by the Judicial Panel on Multidistrict Litigation, had to determine which state statute applied to each class of plaintiffs in a number of class actions.[18]

The Code, of course, supplies a series of limitations for all actions, express or "implied."[19] Meanwhile, with the 1933 and 1934 Acts so closely related, why not look to *their* statutes of limitations by way of analogy rather than to a variant state law? Would it not be eminently more consistent with the overall statutory scheme to look to what Congress itself did when it was thinking

---

[17] Russell v. Todd, 309 U. S. 280, 289 (1940) (dictum); Cope v. Anderson, 331 U. S. 461, 463-64 (1947); International Union, United Automobile Workers of America v. Hoosier Cardinal Corp., 383 U. S. 696, 703-05 (1966); see also Myzel v. Fields, 386 F. 2d 718, 742 (8th Cir. 1967), *cert. denied,* 389 U. S. 951 (fact that original prayer was for rescission or damages in alternative would not change applicability of state limitations statute as opposed to laches); Morgan v. Koch, 419 F. 2d 993, 996 (7th Cir. 1969).

[18] In re Clinton Oil Co. Securities Litigation, CCH Fed. Sec. L. Rep. ¶96,015 at 91,566-67 (D. Kan. 1977).

[19] §1727. The basic formula is that of §13 of the 1933 Act, but with an absolute cutoff of five years rather than three in recognition of the absence of *any* absolute cutoff with respect to implied actions today. See p. 1167, text at n. 15 supra. There is also a provision that permits a violator to cut short the statute of limitations and cut off his contingent liability if he is willing to forego any defense on the merits. §1727(g); see text at n. 7 supra.

specifically of private actions in securities cases rather than to a grab-bag of more or less analogous state statutes?

Two District Courts have turned back arguments directed to §13 by saying simply that that section does not apply to actions under §17(a) of the 1933 Act or Rule 10b-5, missing the point, of course, that the *state* statutes do not apply by their terms either but are simply applied *by analogy when there is no analogous statute of limitations at the federal level.*[20] And quite a few courts have looked wistfully to what the Fifth Circuit has considered "the logically appealing course of applying the period of limitations applicable to a similar cause of action expressly provided in the federal securities laws," while concluding that the rule of looking to state law was too definitely established.[21] Thus Judge Pollack, despite his own view that "Common sense and logic dictate" looking to the periods in the 1933 and 1934 Acts, was deterred by Judge Learned Hand's caution thirty years earlier that it was not "desirable for a lower court to embrace the exhilarating opportunity of anticipating a doctrine which may be in the womb of time, but whose birth is distant."[22]

The Supreme Court has yet to speak in the SEC context. But there are utterances in other contexts negating any idea that a state limitations period is to be "mechanically applied * * * simply because a limitations period is absent from the federal statute." "State legislatures," the Court stated, "do not devise their limitations periods with national interests in mind, and it is the duty of the federal courts to assure that the importation of state law will not frustrate or interfere with the implementation of national policies. * * * State limitations periods will not be borrowed if their application would be inconsistent with the underlying policies of the federal statute."[23] The federal courts

[20] Premier Industries, Inc. v. Delaware Valley Financial Corp., 185 F. Supp. 694 (E. D. Pa. 1960); Hendricks v. Flato Realty Investments, CCH Fed. Sec. L. Rep. ¶92,290 at 97,389 (S. D. Tex. 1968).

[21] McNeal v. Paine, Webber, Jackson & Curtis, Inc., 598 F. 2d 888, 892 (5th Cir. 1979); see also, e. g., Nickels v. Koehler Management Corp., 541 F. 2d 611, 614-15 (6th Cir. 1976), *cert. denied,* 429 U. S. 1074; Roberts v. Magnetic Metals Co., 611 F. 2d 450, 452 (3d Cir. 1979).

[22] Spector Motor Service, Inc. v. Walsh, 139 F. 2d 809, 823 (2d Cir. 1944) (L. Hand, J., dissenting); Mittendorf v. J. R. Williston & Beane, Inc., 372 F. Supp. 821, 830 n. 4 (S. D. N. Y. 1974).

[23] Occidental Life Ins. Co. v. Equal Employment Opportunity Commission, 432 U. S. 355, 367 (1977); see also McAllister v. Magnolia Petroleum Co., 357 U. S. 221 (1958) (a court may not apply a shorter period to a judicially created action for unseaworthiness than Congress prescribed for Jones Act negligence); International Union, United Automobile Workers of America v. Hoosier Cardinal Corp., 383 U. S. 696, 707 n. 9 (1966) ("an unusually

would not be engaging in a "drastic sort of judicial legislation" as they would be if they were to devise a uniform time limitation;[24] they would simply be deciding that the federal statutes afforded a better analogy than a reference to state law. And, for what it is worth, the commentators seem to be of one view.[25]

As it is, fitting Rule 10b-5 into the existing doctrinal framework (the other implied liabilities will be ignored here for the sake of simplicity and also because Rule 10b-5 has been by far the most prolific breeder of litigation) is not easy:

(1) Can there ever be occasion under Rule 10b-5 to forgo state limitation law entirely in favor of the federal laches doctrine? Normally not. The typical action for damages is nothing more than a modified form of common law deceit. Even when the plaintiff seeks equitable rescission because the legal remedy is inadequate, the fact remains that alternative remedies do exist at law for violation of the rule. And, even in the case of a stockholder's derivative action on behalf of a corporation injured by a violation of the rule, it is only the derivative *remedy,* not the underlying "legal right," that is equitable.

(2) The Supreme Court has held that "the characterization of [the] action for the purpose of selecting the appropriate state limitations provision is ultimately a question of federal law," although "there is no reason to reject the characterization that state law would impose unless that characterization is unreasonable or otherwise inconsistent with national labor policy."[26] And Judge

---

short or long limitations period" under state law would raise questions). See esp. Justice Brennan's concurring opinion in *McAllister,* supra, to the effect that in Cope v. Anderson, supra n. 17, "The state statutes were chosen by default." 357 U. S. at 228-29.

[24] International Union, United Automobile Workers of America v. Hoosier Cardinal Corp., 383 U. S. 696, 703 (1966).

[25] See Schulman, Statutes of Limitation in 10b-5 Actions: Complication Added to Confusion, 13 Wayne L. Rev. 635 (1967); Israels, Book Rev., 77 Yale L. J. 1585, 1591-92 (1968); Martin, Statutes of Limitations in 10b-5 Actions: Which State Statute Is Applicable?, 29 Bus. Law. 443, 455 n. 91 (1974); Bromberg, Curing Securities Violations: Rescission Offers and Other Techniques, 1 J. Corp. L. 1, 9-10 (1975).

There *is* some precedent for considering the relatively brief federal periods in comparison with state law, as well as the absolute federal cutoffs, as one reason for preferring the shorter state blue sky period over the longer fraud period. Hitchcock v. deBruyne, 377 F. Supp. 1403, 1407 (D. Conn. 1974); Newman v. Prior, 518 F. 2d 97, 100 (4th Cir. 1975); Mooney v. Tallant, 397 F. Supp. 680, 683-84 (N. D. Ga. 1975). But there is also authority favoring the longer fraud period as preferable in carrying out the federal policy. United Cal. Bank v. Salik, 481 F. 2d 1012 (9th Cir. 1973), *cert. denied,* 414 U. S. 1004; Berry Petroleum Co. v. Adams & Peck, 518 F. 2d 402, 409 (2d Cir. 1975).

[26] International Union, United Automobile Workers of America v. Hoosier Cardinal Corp., 383 U. S. 696, 706 (1966).

Friendly has said for the Second Circuit, in an action under the Clayton Act, that the court "looks first to federal law to determine the nature of the claim and then to state court interpretations of the statutory catalogue to see where the claim fits into the state scheme."[27]

(3) On the conflict-of-laws question of *which* state's limitation statute governs, that of the forum or that of the state where all the operative events occurred, it is not clear whether the choice of law should be made in accordance with *Erie* concepts or by operation of a different, federal conflict-of-laws rule.[28]

(4) With respect to the ultimate question of deciding which state statute of limitations is most nearly analogous to Rule 10b-5, the early cases rather uniformly followed (as have some recent ones) the period for actions grounded on "fraud,"[29] but more recent cases (with some exceptions) tend to favor the blue sky period.[30] The courts have worried a good deal about matching up Rule 10b-5 and the blue sky law with respect to scienter, which some Circuits did not require before the *Hochfelder* case.[31] In

---

[27] Moviecolor, Ltd. v. Eastman Kodak Co., 288 F. 2d 80, 83 (2d Cir. 1961), *cert. denied,* 368 U. S. 821.

[28] See International Union, United Automobile Workers of America v. Hoosier Cardinal Corp., 383 U. S. 696, 705 n. 8 (1966); Hart and Wechsler, The Federal Courts and the Federal System (2d ed. 1973) 829. There are several 10b-5 cases in which the Ninth Circuit looked to the *lex loci delicti* without discussion of the choice of law. Fratt v. Robinson, 203 F. 2d 627, 634 (9th Cir. 1953); Errion v. Connell, 236 F. 2d 447, 455 (9th Cir. 1956); Turner v. Lundquist, 377 F. 2d 44, 46 (9th Cir. 1967); see also Hooper v. Mountain State Securities Corp., 282 F. 2d 195, 205 (5th Cir. 1960).

[29] E. g., Fratt v. Robinson, 203 F. 2d 627, 635 (9th Cir. 1953); Aldrich v. McCulloch Properties, Inc., 627 F. 2d 1036, 1041 (10th Cir. 1980); Wood v. Combustion Engineering, Inc., 643 F. 2d 339 (5th Cir. 1981) (applying Texas' two-year fraud statute rather than its three-year blue sky statute, court did not "follow the practice of several other Circuits of making an inquiry into which state limitations period, independent of consideration of the substantive provisions of the corresponding state statute, best effectuates the purposes of Rule 10b-5"); Robuck v. Dean Witter & Co., Inc., 649 F. 2d 641, 644 (9th Cir. 1980); Sharp v. Coopers & Lybrand, 649 F. 2d 175, 191-92 (3d Cir. 1981), *cert. denied,* 455 U. S. 938.

[30] E. g., Berry Petroleum Co. v. Adams & Peck, 518 F. 2d 402 (2d Cir. 1975); Morris v. Stifel, Nicolaus & Co., Inc., 600 F. 2d 139 (8th Cir. 1979); Cahill v. Ernst & Ernst, 625 F. 2d 151 (7th Cir. 1980); Wachovia Bank & Trust Co. v. National Student Marketing Corp., 650 F. 2d 342, 346-48 (D. C. Cir. 1980), *cert. denied* sub nom. Peat, Marwick, Mitchell & Co. v. Wachovia Bank & Trust Co., 452 U. S. 954; White v. Sanders, 650 F. 2d 627 (5th Cir. 1981); Hern v. Stafford, 663 F. 2d 669 (6th Cir. 1981); Gurley v. Documation, Inc., 674 F. 2d 253, 258 (4th Cir. 1982). For further collections of cases both ways, see Hill v. Der, 521 F. Supp. 1370, 1379-84 (D. Del. 1981); Block and Barton, Statute of Limitations in Private Actions under Section 10(b) — A Proposal for Achieving Uniformity, 7 Sec. Reg. L. J. 374 (1980).

[31] See, e. g., Charney v. Thomas, 372 F. 2d 97 (6th Cir. 1967).

result, at least when the fraud period is applied, it is almost invariably longer than the federal period would be.[32]

(5) Even when the period of limitation has been determined, a surprising number of collateral issues may require decision before it can be said that a particular action is or is not barred: for example, when the action under Rule 10b-5 accrues,[33] when an action is deemed to be commenced, whether an amendment to a complaint relates back, when the period of limitation is tolled, and the impact of changes in venue. Some of these questions seem rather uniformly to be referred to federal law, others to state law, and often the question of choice of law is either left in doubt or ignored.[34]

(6) With respect to the express rights of action in the SEC statutes, we have seen that the plaintiff has the burden of bringing himself within the particular statute of limitations.[35] But the case here is different. To be sure, Rule 8(c) of the Federal Rules of Civil Procedure, which makes the statute of limitations a matter of affirmative defense, covers only the matter of *pleading*, so that the *burden of proof* is referred to state law in diversity cases.[36] In federal question cases, however, where there is no reason to refer to state law except to find a limitation period, it seems more appropriate to look to federal rather than state law in order to place the burden. And, when the right of action is judicially created, placing the burden of going forward on the defendant not only seems to follow by negative implication from the federal rule that puts the burden on the plaintiff when the very statute that creates the cause of action also contains a limitation period but also seems more consistent with Rule 8(c) than otherwise.[37]

---

[32] See Ernst & Ernst v. Hochfelder, 425 U. S. 185, 210 n. 29 (1976), set out supra p. 871, at p. 880 n. 29.

[33] See generally Moviecolor, Ltd. v. Eastman Kodak Co., 288 F. 2d 80, 83 (2d Cir. 1961), *cert. denied,* 368 U. S. 821; see also Sackett v. Beaman, 399 F. 2d 884, 891 (9th Cir. 1968); Norte & Co. v. Krock, CCH Fed. Sec. L. Rep. ¶92,295 at 94,409 (S. D. N. Y. 1968); Parrent v. Midwest Rug Mills, Inc., 455 F. 2d 123, 128 (7th Cir. 1972); Jennings v. Boenning & Co., 523 F. 2d 889 (3d Cir. *per curiam* 1975); Stull v. Bayard, 561 F. 2d 429 (2d Cir. 1977), *cert. denied,* 434 U. S. 1035; Vigman v. Community National Bank & Trust Co., 635 F. 2d 455, 458-59 (5th Cir. 1981).

[34] See Developments in the Law: Statutes of Limitations, 63 Harv. L. Rev. 1177, 1266-67 (1950); Blume and George, Limitations and the Federal Courts, 49 Mich. L. Rev. 937, 950-62 (1951); Note, Federal Statutes without Limitations Provisions, 53 Colum. L. Rev. 68, 71-72 (1953).

[35] See p. 1165 supra.

[36] Cf. Palmer v. Hoffman, 318 U. S. 109, 117 (1943) (contributory negligence).

[37] *Contra:* In Mooney v. Vitolo, CCH Fed. Sec. L. Rep. ¶92,116 at 96,549 (S. D. N. Y. 1967), the court, without discussion, directed that an amended

(7) When there is a federal statute of limitations that is silent on the point, it is always tolled while a reasonably diligent plaintiff remains in ignorance of any *fraud* that is an element of the cause of action.[38] This is true at law as it is in equity.[39] Moreover, although most state courts follow the same view,[40] the federal courts will apply the tolling doctrine in any event.[41] This is doctrinally sound. For, "when considering federal questions, federal courts should not be bound by the state's interpretation of the statute, as they are in diversity cases, but should adhere only to the period of time provided by the statute, since only that portion of federal law is lacking."[42]

(8) What constitutes reasonable diligence on the plaintiff's part is itself a federal question.[43] The plaintiff need not show active concealment.[44] When there *is* active concealment, it tolls the statute of limitations in some courts until *actual* discovery by the plaintiff.[45] But, when there is no active concealment or the particular court does not recognize that doctrine, the plaintiff may not sit on his hands. He "must have exercised reasonable care and

---

complaint should "affirmatively plead facts which show that the statute of limitations has not run."

[38] Holmberg v. Armbrecht, 327 U. S. 392, 395, 397 (1946), supra n. 15.

[39] Bailey v. Glover, 21 Wall. 342 (U. S. 1874); Tobacco & Allied Stocks, Inc. v. Transamerica Corp., 244 F. 2d 902, 103 (3d Cir. 1957); Morgan v. Koch, 419 F. 2d 993, 997 (7th Cir. 1969). There is no similar doctrine that tolls the statute of limitations pending an SEC investigation, because private and enforcement proceedings under the SEC statutes are quite independent. Corson v. First Jersey Securities, Inc., 537 F. Supp. 1263, 1267 (D. N. J. 1982).

[40] See Dawson, Undiscovered Fraud and Statutes of Limitation, 31 Mich. L. Rev. 591 (1933); Errion v. Connell, 236 F. 2d 447, 455 (9th Cir. 1956); Vance v. National Realty Trust, CCH Fed. Sec. L. Rep. ¶95,004 (D. C. Cir. 1975); IIT v. Cornfeld, 619 F. 2d 909, 928-29 (2d Cir. 1980).

[41] Janigan v. Taylor, 344 F. 2d 781, 784 (1st Cir. 1965), *cert. denied,* 382 U. S. 879; Saylor v. Lindsley, 391 F. 2d 965, 970 (2d Cir. 1968); Vanderboom v. Sexton, 422 F. 2d 1233, 1240 (8th Cir. 1970); Aboussie v. Aboussie, 441 F. 2d 150, 156 (5th Cir. 1971), *rehearing on other grounds,* 446 F. 2d 56 (5th Cir. 1971); Schaefer v. First National Bank of Lincolnwood, 509 F. 2d 1287, 1298 (7th Cir. 1975), *cert. denied,* 425 U. S. 943; Newman v. Prior, 518 F. 2d 97, 100 (4th Cir. 1975); Hilton v. Mamaw, 522 F. 2d 588, 602 (9th Cir. 1975); State of Ohio v. Peterson, Lowry, Rall, Barber & Ross, 651 F. 2d 687, 691 (10th Cir. 1981), *cert. denied,* 454 U. S. 895.

[42] 70 Harv. L. Rev. 566, 568 (1957); Wolf v. Frank, 477 F. 2d 467, 475 (5th Cir. 1973), *cert. denied,* 414 U. S. 975.

[43] Tobacco & Allied Stocks, Inc. v. Transamerica Corp., 143 F. Supp. 323, 329 (D. Del. 1956), *aff'd on other grounds,* 244 F. 2d 902 (3d Cir. 1957); Trecker v. Scag, 679 F. 2d 703, 706 (7th Cir. 1982).

[44] Bailey v. Glover, 21 Wall. 342, 348 (U. S. 1874).

[45] Tomera v. Galt, 511 F. 2d 504, 510 (7th Cir. 1975); see also Sperry v. Barggren, 523 F. 2d 708 (7th Cir. 1975). *Contra:* State of Ohio v. Peterson, Lowry, Rall, Barber & Ross, 651 F. 2d 687, 694 (10th Cir. 1981), *cert. denied,* 454 U. S. 895; Campbell v. Upjohn Co., 676 F. 2d 1122, 1126-28 (6th Cir. 1982).

diligence in seeking to learn the facts which would disclose fraud."[46] The burden here is on the plaintiff once the defendant pleads the statute of limitations.[47] And the question is for the jury.[48] But the plaintiff is likely to satisfy the burden when (a) he shows his own lack of knowledge under §12(2) or whatever conduct is required of him under Rule 10b-5[49] or (b) he pleads the fraud with the particularity required by Rule 9(b) of the Federal Rules of Civil Procedure.[50]

(9) If the federal doctrine that *protects* the reasonably careful but unsuspecting plaintiff is read into the state statute of limitations, may a federal court under Rule 10b-5 also *bar* the plaintiff *before* the expiration of the statutory period if he was not reasonably diligent or, worse, if he is shown to have acquired actual knowledge of the fraud shortly after the transaction but to have waited several years before bringing suit? When a state statute of limitations applies to equitable as well as legal actions, it is clear that laches may still bar the federal plaintiff *in equity* before the expiration of the state statute[51] — at least when the state statute does not provide otherwise for the state courts and perhaps, since laches is a matter of federal equity jurisprudence,[52] even when it does.[53]

The fact remains, however, that laches is an equitable, not a legal, doctrine. Therefore, although a *federal* statute of limita-

---

[46] Morgan v. Koch, 419 F. 2d 993, 997 (7th Cir. 1969); see also deHaas v. Empire Petroleum Co., 435 F. 2d 1223, 1226 (10th Cir. 1970); Occidental Life Ins. Co. of N. C. v. Pat Ryan Associates, Inc., 496 F. 2d 1255, 1268 (4th Cir. 1974), *cert. denied,* 419 U. S. 1023; Berry Petroleum Co. v. Adams & Peck, 518 F. 2d 402, 410 (2d Cir. 1975); Goldstandt v. Bear, Stearns & Co., 522 F. 2d 1265 (7th Cir. 1975); Koke v. Stifel, Nicolaus & Co., Inc., 620 F. 2d 1340 (8th Cir. 1980).

[47] Cook v. Avien, Inc., 573 F. 2d 685, 695 (1st Cir. 1978).

[48] Johns Hopkins University v. Hutton, 422 F. 2d 1124, 1131 (4th Cir. 1970), *reconsidered after remand,* 488 F. 2d 912 (4th Cir. 1973), *cert. denied,* 416 U. S. 916.

[49] See pp. 1023-24, 1127 supra.

[50] Schaefer v. First National Bank of Lincolnwood, 509 F. 2d 1287, 1297 (7th Cir. 1975), *cert. denied,* 425 U. S. 943.

[51] Patterson v. Hewitt, 195 U. S. 309, 319 (1904); see Russell v. Todd, 309 U. S. 280, 288 n. 1 (1940); 2 Pomeroy, Equity Jurisprudence (5th ed. 1941) §419b.

[52] See text at n. 42 supra.

[53] Royal Air Properties, Inc. v. Smith, 312 F. 2d 210, 214 (9th Cir. 1962) (10b-5 action seeking a *legal* remedy); see also e. g., Tobacco & Allied Stocks, Inc. v. Transamerica Corp., 143 F. Supp. 323, 327-28 (D. Del. 1956), *aff'd on other grounds,* 244 F. 2d 902 (3d Cir. 1957); Gordon v. Burr, 366 F. Supp. 156, 170-71 (S. D. N. Y. 1973), *aff'd in part and rev'd in part on other grounds,* 506 F. 2d 1080 (2d Cir. 1976).

tions will be extended to *protect* the reasonably diligent plaintiff suing on a fraud theory even in an action at *law* (unless the particular statute provides otherwise), it does not follow that a plaintiff who seeks a *legal* remedy on a federal cause of action within the period specified in the applicable statute of limitations, whether federal or state, should be barred under any circumstances short of the expiration of the statutory period.[54] The discovery doctrine at law was devised by the federal courts to protect victims of fraud, and the logical symmetry of using that exception *against* a plaintiff suing at law within the statutory period is only superficial.[55]

---

[54]Stevens v. Abbott, Proctor & Paine, 288 F. Supp. 836, 845 (E. D. Va. 1968); Norte & Co. v. Krock, CCH Fed. Sec. L. Rep. ¶92,295 at 94,410 (S. D. N. Y. 1968). Moreover, the doctrine of laches is not applicable merely because an action under Rule 10b-5 or the proxy rules is brought derivatively. Ibid.

[55]Cf. Myzel v. Fields, 386 F. 2d 718, 742 (8th Cir. 1967), *cert. denied,* 389 U. S. 951, supra n. 17. In Jennings v. Boenning & Co., 352 F. Supp. 1000, 1006 (E. D. Pa. 1972), *rev'd on other grounds,* 482 F. 2d 1128 (3d Cir. 1973), *cert. denied,* 414 U. S. 1025, the court said that "the equitable doctrine of laches should be subordinated to the strong principles of public policy embodied in the Securities laws."

A limitations question that is not directly relevant to Rule 10b-5, because it arises under the statutes of limitations governing the express actions, has been left for discussion here in the light of the federal-state analysis that has just been made: *If* laches may bar a plaintiff suing on a federal cause of action in equity before expiration of the appropriate state limitation period to which reference is made, might it have the same effect on a cause of action that is governed by a *federal* statute of limitations like §13 of the 1933 Act or §16(b), §9(e), §18(c), or §29(b) of the 1934 Act?

It need hardly be mentioned that the question must be approached as one of federal statutory construction. And the short answer Dean Shulman gave it in 1933 seems sound: "there being nothing in the section to the contrary, the buyer may do what he pleases so long as he brings suit within" the stipulated period. Shulman, Civil Liability and the Securities Act, 43 Yale L. J. 227, 246-47 (1933). It is one thing for a court of equity to apply the traditional doctrine of laches to an action whose outside limitation period is referred to state law. But we have seen that that is explained by simply not referring to state law beyond the point of necessity. That is to say, when Congress has not bothered to write its own limitation period, there is normally no evidence of a statutory purpose to exclude so basic an equitable doctrine as laches. But when Congress does prescribe a specific and relatively short statute of limitations for a federal action as it has done in the sections here specified — especially when it has rather uniformly provided that the action may be enforced "at law or in equity" as it has done in §12 of the 1933 Act and §§9(e), 16(b), and 18(a) of the 1934 Act — there is a strong inference that the prescribed limitation period is not to be cut short, whether in an action sounding in fraud or, *a fortiori,* in an action under §12(1) of the 1933 Act for violation of §5. See Straley v. Universal Uranium & Milling Corp., 289 F. 2d 370 (9th Cir. 1961).

J. MISCELLANEOUS ASPECTS OF CIVIL LIABILITY UNDER THE SEC STATUTES

There are a number of aspects of civil liability that are common to several or all of the federal actions:

1. ANCILLARY RELIEF

The Supreme Court early held that a plaintiff under §12(2) of the 1933 Act was not limited to a money judgment but could have the ancillary remedies traditionally available in a court of equity. The plaintiffs alleged fraud in the sale of unit trust installment certificates. The Court was unanimous:

> We think the Securities Act does not restrict purchasers seeking relief under its provisions to a money judgment. On the contrary, the Act as a whole indicates an intention to establish a statutory right which the litigant may enforce in designated courts by such legal or equitable actions or procedures as would normally be available to him. Undoubtedly any suit to establish the civil liability imposed by the Act must ultimately seek recovery of the consideration paid less income received or damages if the claimant no longer owns the security. §12(2). But §12(2) states the legal consequences of conduct proscribed by the Act; it does not purport to state the form of action or procedure the claimant is to employ.
>
> Moreover, in Section 22(a) specified courts are given jurisdiction "of all suits in equity and actions at law brought *to enforce* any liability or duty created by this subchapter." The power *to enforce* implies the power to make effective the right of recovery afforded by the Act. And the power to make the right of recovery effective implies the power to utilize any of the procedures or actions normally available to the litigant according to the exigencies of the particular case. If petitioners' bill states a cause of action when tested by the customary rules governing suits of such character, the Securities Act authorizes maintenance of the suit, providing the bill contains the allegations the Act requires. That it does not authorize the bill in so many words is no more significant than the fact that it does not in terms authorize execution to issue on a judgment recovered under §12(2).
>
> We are of the opinion that the bill states a cause for equitable relief. There are allegations that [the issuer] is insolvent, that its business is practically halted, that it is threatened with many law suits, that its assets are endangered, and that preferences to creditors are probable. There are prayers for an accounting,

appointment of a receiver, an injunction *pendente lite,* and for return of petitioners' payments. * * *

The principle objects of the suit are rescission * * * and restitution * * * . That a suit to rescind a contract induced by fraud and to recover the consideration paid may be maintained in equity, at least where there are circumstances making the legal remedy inadequate, is well established. * * *

*   *   *

We hold that the injunction was a reasonable measure to preserve the status quo pending final determination of the questions raised by the bill. * * *[1]

Everything the Court said applies equally in principle to §§11 and 12(1) of the 1933 Act as well as all the other civil liabilities, express and implied, under the SEC statutes. A District Court followed this case in a §12(1) action in which holders of voting trust certificates issued without registration were granted restoration of the stock deposited.[2] The Eighth Circuit, relying simply on Rule 54(c) of the Federal Rules of Civil Procedure,[3] held in an action under §12(1) that the trial court had acted properly in (1) giving the plaintiffs a lien on certain property in the defendant's hands to ensure payment of the judgment; (2) giving the defendant who was a selling agent of the corporate defendant a similar lien if he should pay any part of the judgment, by way of ensuring his indemnification by his principal under the law of agency; and (3) impressing a trust for the plaintiffs' benefit upon the funds paid by them for drilling expenses.[4]

Injunctive relief has been regularly approved in private actions

---

C. 10J [1] Deckert v. Independence Shares Corp., 311 U. S. 282, 287-90 (1940), *on remand,* 39 F. Supp. 592 (E. D. Pa. 1941), *rev'd on other grounds* sub nom. Pennsylvania Co. for Insurances on Lives & Granting Annuities v. Deckert, 123 F. 2d 979 (3d Cir. 1941); cf. United States v. E. I. du Pont de Nemours & Co., 366 U. S. 316, 323 (1961) (broad equity powers to fashion effective remedies in injunction suits under antitrust statutes).

[2] Corporation Trust Co. v. Logan, 52 F. Supp. 999 (D. Del. 1943); see also Kinsey v. Knapp, 154 F. Supp. 263 (E. D. Mich. 1957), *rev'd on other grounds* sub nom. Knapp v. Kinsey, 249 F. 2d 797 (6th Cir. 1957), *leave to file petition for cert. denied,* 356 U. S. 935.

[3] "Except as to a party against whom a judgment is entered by default, every final judgment shall grant the relief to which the party in whose favor it is rendered is entitled, even if the party has not demanded such relief in his pleadings."

[4] Whittaker v. Wall, 226 F. 2d 868, 872-73 (8th Cir. 1955) 64; cf. Speed v. Transamerica Corp., 135 F. Supp. 176, 187 (D. Del. 1955), *modified on other grounds and aff'd,* 235 F. 2d 369 (3d Cir. 1956).

implied under Rule 10b-5, §14(e) (the tender offer fraud provision), and the Investment Company Act. We have also seen how far the courts have gone and might go in preventing violators of the proxy rules from enjoying the fruits of their illegality.[5] And we have noticed the appointment of receivers for insolvent or undercapitalized broker-dealers.[6] Perhaps the most dramatic use of the courts' ancillary jurisdiction has been in their ordering restitution or disgorgement of profits in SEC injunctive actions.[7]

---

[5] See pp. 562-67 supra.

[6] See p. 953 supra. There is also precedent

for appointing a "custodian" [Adelman v. CGS Scientific Corp., 332 F. Supp. 137, 147 (E. D. Pa. 1971)] or "special agent" to see to compliance with the reporting requirements [SEC v. Beisinger Industries Corp., 552 F. 2d 15 (1st Cir. 1977)] or "special fiscal agent" [Braasch v. Muscat, CCH Fed. Sec. L. Rep. ¶92,148 (S. D. N. Y. 1968), *vacated per curiam on other grounds*, 398 F. 2d 1022 (2d Cir. 1968); SEC v. Philip S. Budin & Co., Inc., CCH Fed. Sec. L. Rep. ¶93,088 (D. N. J. 1971)] or "escrow agent" [SEC v. Bennett & Co., 207 F. Supp. 919, 924-25 (D. N. J. 1962)] or "special counsel" [United States v. Handler, CCH Fed. Sec. L. Rep. ¶96,519 at 94,023-24 (C. D. Cal. 1978)] or a "trustee" to oversee restitution [SEC v. Manor Nursing Centers, Inc., 458 F. 2d 1082, 1103-06 (2d Cir. 1972)]. See also SEC v. Vesco, 571 F. 2d 129 (2d Cir. 1978); Malhas v. Shinn, 597 F. 2d 28 (2d Cir. 1979).

2 Code 929-30, Comment (2).

[7] See p. 842 n. 64 supra; Farrand, Ancillary Remedies in SEC Civil Enforcement Suits, 89 Harv. L. Rev. 1779 (1976); Mathews, Recent Trends in SEC Requested Ancillary Relief in SEC Level Injunctive Actions, 31 Bus. Law. 1323 (1976); Comment, Equitable Remedies in SEC Enforcement Actions, 123 U. Pa. L. Rev. 1188 (1975); SEC Civil Injunctive Actions, Program of the Committee on Federal Regulation of Securities, 30 Bus. Law. 1303 (1975). All this is aside from the many consent injunctions in recent years that have provided for the appointment of directors [see Note, The SEC and Court-Appointed Directors: Time to Tailor the Director to Fit the Suit, 60 Wash. U. L. Q. 507 (1982)] or special counsel [see p. 1208 infra]. In SEC v. Data Access Systems, Inc., CCH Fed. Sec. L. Rep. ¶98,779 (D. N. J. 1982), where a consent judgment permitted the defendants to seek the court's leave to refuse to implement specific recommendations of a "special agent," the court held that it would review recommendations only under a "clearly erroneous" test.

In late 1982 the Commission, recognizing "that current remedies do not provide sufficient deterrence" against insider trading notwithstanding its stepped up efforts in recent years "to combat this threat to the securities markets," recommended enactment of an Insider Trading Sanctions Act that would empower the Commission, along with or instead of a prayer for disgorgement, to seek the defendant's payment into the United States Treasury of an amount of money up to three times the profit gained through the illicit transactions. The new statutory provision would apply to any transaction "(i) on or through the facilities of a national securities exchange or from or through a broker or dealer, and (ii) which is not part of a public offering by an issuer or securities other than standardized options." And the Commission would have rulemaking authority to exempt "any class of persons or transactions." SEC memorandum, CCH Fed. Sec. L. Rep. ¶83,259 (Sept. 27, 1982).

2.   SECONDARY LIABILITY

a.   Controlling Persons

The 1933 and 1934 Acts provide, in somewhat different language, that anyone who "controls" a person liable thereunder is equally liable, subject to a special defense that varies in the two statutes.[8] In effect, Congress has repealed limited liability *prima facie* so far as persons in control of corporations are concerned. So far as the meaning of "controls" is concerned, there is by now a fair amount of case law specifically directed to the concept of "control" in connection with civil liability. And, for the rest, we

---

Query: Is it fair for individual defendants to be thus pitted against the Government so far as private damages are concerned? Is it "cricket" to deprive defendants of a jury trial? And should the Commission be able, in effect, to obtain private relief without having to prove the reliance or causation that a private plaintiff would have to establish? See Katz and Nerheim, Injunctive Proceedings and Ancillary Remedies under Federal Securities Statutes, in Practising Law Institute, The 10b Series of Rules (Corp. Prac. Tr. Ser. 21, 1975) 203-04. These questions must be considered in the light particularly of the availability of the class action.

The Code provides:

> In a civil action created by or based on a violation of this Code, whether or not brought by the Commission and whether or not the court grants the principal relief requested, the court has the authority of a court of equity to grant appropriate ancillary or other relief, including an injunction, an accounting, a receivership of the defendant or the defendant's assets, disgorgement of profits, restitution, and limitation of the defendant's activities.

But, in order to prevent abuse of the injunctive route to evade restrictions that would apply to private actions, the court, in exercising its discretion whether to order restitution, must consider whether fraud or deception was intended although such a finding is not necessary for an injunction *per se.* §1819(l)(1).

[8] Sec. Act §15; Sec. Ex. Act §20(a). The two formulas are reflected in somewhat different language in the Code, which saves a controlling person from liability

> if he proves (A) that he reasonably did not believe that the controlled person's conduct was unlawful or a breach of duty, or involved a fraudulent or manipulative act, a misrepresentation, or nondisclosure of a fact of special significance by an insider (as defined in section 1603(b)), or (B) in the case of section 1714 [Sec. Ex. Act §16(b)], that he acted in good faith and did not induce the transactions in question.

§1724(a)(2). The Code also reflects, for what they are worth, the provisions in the Exchange, Holding Company and Investment Company Acts that make it unlawful for any person to do indirectly, or cause to be done through another person, what he may not do directly. Sec. Ex. Act §20(b); Holding Co. Act §27(a); Inv. Co. Act §48(a); Inv. Adv. Act §208(d); Code §2006(a).

are relegated, in the absence of a statutory definition in the 1933 or 1934 Act, to the many considerations discussed in the chapter on control.[9]

For example the partners of a New York broker-dealer firm were held liable, on a jury's finding of control, for a new California broker-dealer corporation's violations of Rule 10b-5 and the margin rules under §7 of the Exchange Act. The California corporation's president was a close friend of several of the partners of the New York firm, and two-thirds of the capital was provided by wives and relatives of those partners. The New York firm paid for a direct wire between the two offices. But it customarily paid for direct wires to its out-of-town correspondents. And neither its partners nor their wives and relatives ever interfered with the management of the California corporation.[10]

A number of propositions are reasonably clear:

(1) The control sections apply only to a person who was in control at the time the liability of the controlled person accrued, and not to a person who obtained control thereafter.[11]

(2) The defenses require some supervisory procedures and perhaps other precautionary measures, depending on the circumstances.[12] Thus, a newspaper publisher does not have the same duty to supervise a financial columnist[13] that a broker-dealer has to supervise its employees.[14]

---

[9] C. 6 supra.

[10] Smith v. Bear, 237 F. 2d 79, 82 (2d Cir. 1956); see also, e. g., Hawkins v. Merrill Lynch, Pierce, Fenner & Beane, 95 F. Supp. 104, 123 (W. D. Ark. 1949) (nationwide brokerage firm *held* liable for Arkansas wire correspondent's violation of Rule 10b-5 and provisions on confirmations and financial reports); DeMarco v. Edens, CCH Fed. Sec. L. Rep. ¶91,856 at 95,934-36 (S. D. N. Y. 1966), *aff'd,* 390 F. 2d 836 (2d Cir. 1968); Myzel v. Fields, 386 F. 2d 718, 738-39 (8th Cir. 1967), *cert. denied,* 389 U. S. 951 (a controlling person who induced the conduct that violated Rule 10b-5 was liable even without knowledge of the specific wrongdoing if he was the intended beneficiary of the stock purchase); SEC v. First Securities Co. of Chicago, 463 F. 2d 981 (7th Cir. 1972), *cert. denied* sub nom. McKy v. Hochfelder, 409 U. S. 880 (broker-dealer corporation controlled its president); Hughes v. Dempsey-Tegeler & Co., Inc., CCH Fed. Sec. L. Rep. ¶94,133 at 94,550-51 (C. D. Cal. 1973), *aff'd on other grounds,* 534 F. 2d 156 (9th Cir. 1976), *cert. denied,* 429 U. S. 896 (stock exchange, in view of its directions to an undercapitalized member, controlled the member, but had the statutory defenses).

[11] Wittenberg v. Continental Real Estate Partners, Ltd., 478 F. Supp. 504 (D. Mass. 1979), *aff'd per curiam,* 625 F. 2d 5 (1st Cir. 1980); Code §1724(a); 2 Code 792, Comment (1).

[12] Richardson v. MacArthur, 451 F. 2d 35, 42 (10th Cir. 1971).

[13] Zweig v. Hearst Corp., 521 F. 2d 1129, 1132-35 (9th Cir. 1975), *cert. denied,* 423 U. S. 1025.

[14] Lorenz v. Watson, 258 F. Supp. 724, 732 (E. D. Pa. 1966); Henricksen v. Henricksen, 640 F. 2d 880, 888 (7th Cir. 1981), *cert. denied* sub nom. Smith

(3) It is not necessary to join the allegedly controlled person.[15]

(4) Neither §15 nor §20(a) provides for contribution among controlling persons.[16]

(5) Sections 15 and 20(a) do not affect actions for injunction or disciplinary proceedings.[17]

(6) One who controls an aider and abettor[18] is covered, though twice removed from the person primarily liable.[19] On the other hand, one cannot aid and abet a violation of one of the control provisions, because they are not substantive provisions that proscribe specified conduct.[20]

Less clear is the question — on which the Circuits are split — whether the control provisions are exclusive or whether principals are liable for the acts of their agents on common law agency concepts of *respondeat superior* without the statutory defenses. The Code follows the majority view, which recognizes common law liability, so that the defenses are available only when the defendant controls as a holding company or in some other nonagency way.[21]

Barney, Harris Upham & Co. v. Henricksen, 454 U. S. 1097; but cf. Sennott v. Rodman & Renshaw, 474 F. 2d 32, 39, 40 n. 5 (7th Cir. 1973), *cert. denied,* 414 U. S. 926 (broker-dealer firm's duty to control its partners, agents, and past employees extended only to their transactions involving the firm, and it could not have exercised bad faith with respect to transactions of which it had no knowledge).

[15] DeMarco v. Edens, 390 F. 2d 836, 840 (2d Cir. 1968); Kemmerer v. Weaver, 445 F. 2d 76, 78 (7th Cir. 1971).

[16] Shea v. Unger, CCH Fed. Sec. L. Rep. ¶91,558 (S. D. N. Y. 1965).

[17] SEC v. Coffey, 493 F. 2d 1304, 1318 (6th Cir. 1974), *cert. denied,* 420 U. S. 908; but cf. SEC v. Management Dynamics, Inc., 515 F. 2d 801, 812-13 (2d Cir. 1975). See 2 Code 792, Comment (2).

[18] See pp. 1186-87 infra.

[19] Edwards & Hanly v. Wells Fargo Securities Clearance Corp., 458 F. Supp. 1110, 1126-27 (S. D. N. Y. 1978), *rev'd on other grounds,* 602 F. 2d 478 (2d Cir. 1979), *cert. denied,* 444 U. S. 1045.

[20] In re Investors Funding Corp. of N. Y. Securities Litigation, 523 F. Supp. 533, 543 (S. D. N. Y. 1980).

[21] §1724(a). In addition to the three appellate decisions that way and the two *contra* that are cited in 2 Code 792-93, Comment (3)(b), see the following cases that decidedly strengthen the majority view: Reyos v. United States, 431 F. 2d 1337, 1346-47 (10th Cir. 1970), *aff'd on this point and rev'd on other grounds* sub nom. Affiliated Ute Citizens of Utah v. United States, 406 U. S. 128, 154 (1972); Marbury Management, Inc. v. Kohn, 629 F. 2d 705, 712-17 (2d Cir. 1980), *cert. denied* sub nom. Wooder, Walker & Co. v. Marbury Management, Inc., 449 U. S. 1011; Paul F. Newton & Co. v. Texas Commerce Bank, 630 F. 2d 1111, 1118-19 (5th Cir. 1980); Henricksen v. Henricksen, 640 F. 2d 880, 888 (7th Cir. 1981), *cert. denied* sub nom. Smith Barney, Harris Upham & Co. v. Henricksen, 454 U. S. 1097; cf. Sharp v. Coopers & Lybrand, 649 F. 2d 175, 181-84 (3d Cir. 1981), *cert. denied,* 455 U. S. 938 (judgment against accounting firm was limited to the facts in recognition of the important services performed by accountants "in evaluating, synthesizing, and explicating complex financial data").

The commentary observes that the control provisions were aimed at the "dummy director" problem:

> There is no reason to assume that Congress contemplated a *lesser* liability than the law of agency would impose in the typical employer-employee case. Such liability may be based not only (i) on the *principal's* conduct in (for example) intentionally causing the agent's acts or failing properly to supervise [Restatement (Second) of Agency §§212-14] but also (ii) on vicarious concepts when the principal himself is quite innocent (id. §§257-58).[22]

Finally, one can only *query* whether the scienter holding of *Hochfelder* in 10b-5 actions carries over to the controlling person if it is established that the controlled person acted with scienter. The question of secondary liability based on either §20(a) or *respondeat superior,* which is a vicarious, deeper pocket sort of liability, seems different from the question of secondary liability based on aiding and abetting, where the required degree of fault is greater, if anything, than it is with respect to the person primarily liable.[23] Sections 15 and 20(a), of course, have their own defenses. The Fifth Circuit has given the §20(a) defense a recklessness reading in the light of *Hochfelder.*[24] But other Circuits, without using "scienter" language, have required the plaintiff to show not only control but also culpable participation in the allegedly illegal activities.[25]

b.   Agents, Participants, and Aiders and Abettors

Brokers or other agents of the seller — persons who are not sellers in the mystical sense of passing "title" — are normally held accountable under §17(a) of the 1933 Act, which literally applies to "any person" who engages in fraudulent or misleading practices "in the sale of any securities." By contrast, §12 specifies that "Any person who sells * * * shall be liable to the person purchasing * * * from him." Even so it is now quite clear that a broker for the seller is a "person who sells."[26] So, just as logically,

---

In any event, the control provisions do not preclude "piercing the corporate veil" when that conclusion is justified under principles of corporation law. Kersh v. General Council of the Assemblies of God, 535 F. Supp. 494, 496-98 (N. D. Cal. 1982); 2 Code 793, Comment (3)(c).

[22] 2 Code 793, Comment (3)(b).

[23] See pp. 1186-87 infra.

[24] G. A. Thompson & Co. v. Partridge, 636 F. 2d 945 (5th Cir. 1981).

[25] Christoffel v. E. F. Hutton & Co., 588 F. 2d 665, 668 (9th Cir. 1978), and cases cited.

[26] Cady v. Murphy, 113 F. 2d 988 (1st Cir. 1940), *cert. denied,* 311 U. S. 705;

is a broker who represents both sides.[27] And, since the term "offer" is defined to include the "solicitation of an offer to buy a security," it has been held that even a broker who represents the buyer alone "sells" to his customer within the meaning of §12(2) so as to be accountable for any false statements made in soliciting the customer's buy order.[28] In principle this applies equally to render liable under §12(1) a broker who solicits a buy order in violation of §5. At the same time, when the broker represents the buyer alone and executes a purely *unsolicited* order, it is difficult to see how he could be considered one who "sells" even within the meaning of the Securities Act.[29]

There is nothing basically incongruous about forcing a broker for either seller or buyer to assume ownership of the securities for the first time. When rescission is based on a contract theory — mistake, or breach of contract — only the party to the contract is liable. But, when it is predicated on fraud, privity is not essential. "To avoid unjust enrichment, general equitable principles indicate the preferability of the purchaser pursuing first the seller, rather than his partner in the fraud. However, as between the innocent purchaser and the wrongdoer who, though not a privy to the fraudulent contract, nonetheless induced the victim to make the purchase, equity requires the wrongdoer to restore the victim to the status quo."[30] Besides, it would be a strange construction that permitted the buyer to recover damages if he had resold the security, but not rescission; he could easily avoid such a rule in any event by reselling just before suit, and (conversely) the broker upon whom the security is forced by rescission can resell it if there

---

Schillner v. H. Vaughan Clarke & Co., 134 F. 2d 875, 879 (2d Cir. 1943); First Trust & Savings Bank of Zanesville, Ohio v. Fidelity-Philadelphia Trust Co., 214 F. 2d 320, 324 (3d Cir. 1954), *cert. denied,* 348 U. S. 856; White Lighting Co. v. Wolfson, 68 Cal. 2d 336, 355, 356 and n. 13, 438 P. 2d 345, 357 and n. 13 (1968); Lawler v. Gilliam, 569 F. 2d 1283, 1287-88 (4th Cir. 1978); cf. Brown v. Cole, 155 Tex. 624, 629, 291 S. W. 2d 704, 708 (1956) (state act).

[27] Cady v. Murphy, 113 F. 2d 988 (1st Cir. 1940), *cert. denied,* 311 U. S. 705; DeMarco v. Edens, 390 F. 2d 836, 844-45 (2d Cir. 1968) (dictum).

[28] Murphy v. Cady, 30 F. Supp. 466, 469 (D. Me. 1939), *aff'd on other grounds* sub nom. Cady v. Murphy, 113 F. 2d 988 (1st Cir. 1940), *cert. denied,* 311 U. S. 705; Boehm v. Granger, 181 Misc. 680, 42 N. Y. S. 2d 246 (Sup. Ct. 1943), *aff'd per curiam,* 268 App. Div. 855, 50 N. Y. S. 2d 845 (1st Dept. 1944); Smith v. Smith, 424 S. W. 2d 244 (Tex. Civ. App. 1968) (state act); Katz v. Amos Treat & Co., 411 F. 2d 1046, 1052-53 (2d Cir. 1969); see also SEC v. Chinese Consolidated Benevolent Assn., 120 F. 2d 738, 740 (2d Cir. 1941), *cert. denied,* 314 U. S. 618.

[29] Katz v. Amos Treat & Co., 411 F. 2d 1046, 1053 (2d Cir. 1969). This is apart from the fact that, so far as §12(1) is concerned, an unsolicited brokerage order would normally be exempted from §5 by §4(4).

[30] Gordon v. Burr, 506 F. 2d 1080, 1085 (2d Cir. 1974).

is a market, take his loss, and (selling cost aside) be no worse off than if he had paid damages.[31]

If a broker may be liable under §12, it is hard to distinguish the case of an officer or director or employee or other non-broker agent of the seller who actively participates in the sale.[32]

There are, to be sure, a number of obstacles to the application of §12: When Congress provided in §11 for the liability of various persons connected with an issuer filing a registration statement, it set up an elaborate scheme of defenses in lieu of the scienter element in common law deceit. It also inserted a contribution provision in §11, as well as in the sections of the 1934 Act that contemplate multiple defendants.

On the other hand, there would still be a distinction under §12 between the liability of the seller proper and the liability of other persons, in that the seller proper would have the burden under the statute of proving his innocence but the plaintiff obviously would have the burden of proving that the other persons had participated in an unlawful sale,[33] a burden that (at least under §12(2) as distinguished from §12(1)) would almost inevitably involve proof by the plaintiff of some sort of scienter on their part. In other words, there would still be a marked contrast between §§11 and 12 in this regard: officers and directors of a corporate seller would in no event be liable automatically under §12(2) subject only to the privilege of somehow purging themselves.[34]

The Second Circuit *en banc* drew a similar contrast between §11 and Rule 10b-5 in holding that an outside (nonmanagement) director has no 10b-5 "duty to convey" — that is, "to insure that all material, adverse information is conveyed to prospective purchasers" of the corporation's stock. His 10b-5 liability "can thus only be secondary, such as that of an aider and abettor, a conspirator, or a substantial participant in fraud perpetrated by others." Without such participation the plaintiff must prove scienter in the sense of "actual knowledge * * * [or] a willful, deliberate, or reckless disregard for the truth that is the equivalent

---

[31] This assumes a rescission measure rather than a deceit or warranty measure of damages. See p. 1136 supra.

[32] In re Caesars Palace Securities Litigation, 360 F. Supp. 366, 383 (S. D. N. Y. 1973).

[33] Id. at 380 (determination of sufficiency of the participation must await discovery).

[34] As for §12(1), the court stated in Katz v. Amos Treat & Co., 411 F. 2d 1046, 1053 (2d Cir. 1969), that that section was not "intended to embrace a corporate officer or director merely because he has knowledge of a sale of unregistered stock and plays * * * a minor role in facilitating it."

of knowledge."[35] Although the Second Circuit had earlier read Rule 10b-5 as requiring scienter even with respect to one alleged to be a *primary* violator, it is quite clear from the opinion that the court would have required no less of the plaintiff under §12(2).[36]

Indeed, even though recklessness may suffice to constitute scienter as applied to the principal defendant, some of the 10b-5 decisions speak in terms of "knowledge" on the part of the person liable secondarily.[37] This is consistent with the common law of torts, which makes a person liable for harm resulting to a third person from the tortious conduct of another only (insofar as is here relevant) if he "knows that the other's conduct constitutes a breach of duty and gives substantial assistance or encouragement to the other so to conduct himself."[38]

A number of tests have been suggested for what constitutes sufficient participation to come within §12:

In a 1953 case the Commission argued successfully as *amicus curiae,* on the analogy of the brokers' liability cases, that any person who lent *substantial assistance* to a wrongful sale should be liable under §12(2) — for example, a defendant who was the driver of a sightseeing tour around the citrus groves in which investment contracts were being sold and who allegedly made fraudulent representations to induce persons to buy.[39]

---

[35] Lanza v. Drexel & Co., 479 F. 2d 1277, 1289, 1305 (2d Cir. *en banc* 1973). The offering was private, so that §11 did not apply.

[36] See esp. id. at 1298; see also Aid Auto Stores, Inc. v. Cannon, 525 F. 2d 468, 470-71 (2d Cir. *per curiam* 1975) (both §12(2) and Rule 10b-5 require "knowledge" of the principal defendant's breach of trust).

But cf. Sanders v. John Nuveen & Co., 619 F. 2d 1222 (7th Cir. 1980), supra p. 1029 n. 28, which equated an underwriter's duty under §12(2) in the sale of commercial paper exempted under §3(a)(3) to its duty under §11. The Seventh Circuit's reading is the harder to understand in view of the opinion's reference to the underwriter's failure to verify the audited statements or to review the auditor's work papers — conduct not required to make out even the double-negative defense in §11(b)(3)(C). See p. 1034 supra.

[37] See Zabriskie v. Lewis, 507 F. 2d 546, 554 (10th Cir. 1974); Woodward v. Metro Bank of Dallas, 522 F. 2d 84, 94-100 (5th Cir. 1975); Rochez Bros., Inc. v. Rhoades, 527 F. 2d 880, 886-87 (3d Cir. 1975); Hirsch v. du Pont, 553 F. 2d 750, 759 (2d Cir. 1977); Edwards & Hanly v. Wells Fargo Securities Clearance Corp., 602 F. 2d 478, 485 (2d Cir. 1979), *cert. denied,* 444 U. S. 1045 ("something closer to an actual intent to aid in the fraud"). But there is authority, at least in SEC injunctive actions, that "liability predicated on aiding and abetting may be founded on less than actual knowledge and participation in the activity proscribed by" Rule 10b-5. SEC v. First Securities Co. of Chicago, 463 F. 2d 981, 987 (7th Cir. 1972), *cert. denied* sub nom. McKy v. Hochfelder, 409 U. S. 880; SEC v. Spectrum, Ltd., 489 F. 2d 535, 541 (2d Cir. 1973).

[38] Restatement (Second) of Torts §876(b).

[39] SEC brief as *amicus curiae,* Blackwell v. Bentsen, 203 F. 2d 690 (5th Cir. 1953), *cert. dismissed,* 347 U. S. 925.

In a 1964 case the court thought that liability under §12(1) "must lie somewhere between the narrow view, which holds only the party to the sale, and the too-liberal view, which would hold all who remotely participated in the events leading up to the transaction." On analogy from the law of negligence, the court thought the test should be whether the injuries to the plaintiff flowed "directly and proximately from the actions of [the] particular defendant." But "The hunter who seduces the prey and leads it to the trap he has set is no less guilty than the hunter whose hand springs the snare." On this approach the court held the defendant (Roger) who had made the initial contact with the plaintiffs and convinced them to invest, as well as the defendant (vice-president of the defendant corporation) who had assisted Roger and "represented the symbol of authority which Roger said he lacked," and the president, who had signed the agreement.[40]

In 1977, however, the Eighth Circuit rejected the proximate cause test as failing to focus on implementing statutory policy. Toward that end, one factor to be considered, the court thought, was whether the defendant was in a unique position to ask relevant questions, to require material information, or to disclose his findings.[41]

At the other extreme, a number of cases, some expressly influenced by the Supreme Court's recent approach to implied actions, reject *any* secondary liability under §12 except as provided in §15.[42]

Everything thus far said about holding participants under §12(2) should apply *a fortiori* to Rule 10b-5, because it does not in so many words refer to seller's liability to buyer as does §12. And there are in fact more cases under Rule 10b-5. But the opinions speak in terms of "aiding and abetting"[43] rather than "participa-

---

[40] Lennerth v. Mendenhall, 234 F. Supp. 59, 65 (N. D. Ohio 1964). To the same effect, see Lawler v. Gilliam, 569 F. 2d 1283, 1287-88 (4th Cir. 1978). (§12(1)); Junker v. Crory, 650 F. 2d 1349, 1360 (5th Cir. 1981), and cases cited.

[41] Wasson v. SEC, 558 F. 2d 879, 885-86 (8th Cir. 1977).

[42] In re Equity Funding Corp. of America Securities Litigation, 416 F. Supp. 161, 181 (C. D. Cal. 1976); McFarland v. Memorex Corp., 493 F. Supp. 631, 647 (N. D. Cal. 1980); Benoay v. Decker, 517 F. Supp. 490, 494 (E. D. Mich. 1981); SEC v. Seaboard Corp. (Admiralty Fund v. Hugh Johnson & Co., Inc.), 677 F. 2d 1301, 1311 n. 12 (9th Cir. 1982).

[43] E. g., Brennan v. Midwestern United Life Ins. Co., 417 F. 2d 147, 151-54 (7th Cir. 1969), *cert. denied,* 397 U. S. 989; Rolf v. Blyth, Eastman Dillon & Co., Inc., 570 F. 2d 38, 44-48 (2d Cir. 1978); Monsen v. Consolidated Dressed Beef Co., Inc., 479 F. 2d 793 (3d Cir. 1978), *cert. denied* sub nom. First Pa. Bank, N. A. v. Monsen, 439 U. S. 930 (also §12(1) and (2)); see also Errion v. Connell, 236 F. 2d 447 (9th Cir. 1956); but cf. Landy v. FDIC, 486 F. 2d 139, 162-64 (3d Cir. 1973), *cert. denied,* 416 U. S. 960.

tion," perhaps because §12(2) at least (as distinguished from §12(1)) is not based on a *violation* of anything but merely imposes civil liability for false statements. It is on aider and abettor concepts, for example, that a non-broker-dealer can violate §15(c)(1) of the 1934 Act, which applies only to brokers and dealers.[44] Some of the 10b-5 cases — including the very first — speak also in terms of conspiracy.[45]

All this is encapsulated in the Code as follows:

> An agent or other person who knowingly causes or gives substantial assistance to conduct by another person (herein a "principal") giving rise to liability under this Code (* * * except for section 1714 [successor to §16(b)]) with knowledge that the conduct is unlawful or a breach of duty, or involves a fraudulent or manipulative act, a misrepresentation, or nondisclosure of a material fact by an insider (as defined in section 1603(b) [successor to Rule 10b-5]), is liable as a principal. A person may cause or give substantial assistance to conduct by inaction or silence when he has a duty to act or speak.[46]

The concept of assisting another person's wrong has its roots in the law of torts as well as the criminal law. Restatement (Second) of Torts §876(b), supra p. 1185, text at n. 38.

All this is not to say that an accounting firm might not be liable as a principal violator. Chemical Bank v. Arthur Andersen & Co., 552 F. Supp. 439, 454-55 (S. D. N. Y. 1982), and cases cited.

[44] The Commission has found officers and salesmen guilty of violating §15(c) in disciplinary proceedings. E. g., Nees v. SEC, 414 F. 2d 211, 219 (9th Cir. 1969); Luckhurst & Co., Inc., 40 SEC 539, 540 (1961). And it has also used the aider and abettor statute, Cr. Code §2, 18 U. S. C. §2, as a basis for injunction. E. g., SEC v. Barraco, 438 F. 2d 97 (10th Cir. 1971).

[45] In the *Kardon* case Judge Kirkpatrick used conspiracy language to sustain the complaint as against the company with which the defendants had negotiated a sale of assets. Kardon v. National Gypsum Co., 69 F. Supp. 512, 514-15 (E. D. Pa. 1946), *on the merits,* 73 F. Supp. 798 (E. D. Pa. 1947), *on requests for additional findings,* 83 F. Supp. 613 (E. D. Pa. 1947), supra p. 823. See also, e. g., Texas Continental Life Ins. Co. v. Dunne, 307 F. 2d 242, 249 (6th Cir. 1962); Dasho v. Susquehanna Corp., 380 F. 2d 262, 267 n. 2 (7th Cir. 1967), *cert. denied* sub nom. Bard v. Dasho, 389 U. S. 977; Shell v. Hensley, 430 F. 2d 819, 827 n. 13 (5th Cir. 1970); Ferguson v. OmniMedia, Inc., 469 F. 2d 194, 197 (1st Cir. 1972); Ruder, Multiple Defendants in Securities Law Fraud Cases: Aiding and Abetting, Conspiracy, *In Pari Delicto,* Indemnification, and Contribution, 120 U. Pa. L. Rev. 597, 620-44 (1972).

[46] §1724(b)(1); see William R. Carter, Sec. Ex. Act Rel. 17,597, 22 SEC Dock. 292, 315-16 (1981), set out infra p. 1243, at pp. 1249-51. The second sentence, which was added in the course of the discussions with the SEC, reflects the case law, which is by no means uniform. See, e. g., SEC v. Coffey, 493 F. 2d 1304, 1317 (6th Cir. 1974) (dictum), and cases cited; Kerbs v. Fall River Industries, Inc., 502 F. 2d 731, 740 (10th Cir. 1974); Hochfelder v. Midwest Stock Exchange, 503 F. 2d 364, 374-75 (7th Cir. 1974), *cert. denied,* 419 U. S. 875; Woodward v. Metro Bank of Dallas, 522 F. 2d 84, 94-100 (5th Cir. 1975), and cases cited; IIT v. Cornfeld, 619 F. 2d 909, 925-27 (2d Cir. 1980); see also

Liability in these cases is several, not joint.[47] When the broker is the innocent party as between himself and the selling principal, presumably he has a right to be indemnified by the principal under common law agency concepts. Such a right over would seem to lie under §12 or Rule 10b-5 itself when the broker represented only the buyer, so that the broker was in effect a principal vis-à-vis the seller.[48]

Subject to the exceptions involving controlling persons, agents, and participants — the last of which may sometimes permit Z to sue X as well as Y even though X sold to Y, who sold to Z, if Z can prove that X participated to the required degree in Y's violation of §5 or Y's fraud — it seems quite clear that §12 contemplates only an action by a buyer against *his immediate seller*.[49] That is to say, in the case of the typical firm-commitment underwriting, the ultimate investor can recover only from the dealer who sold to him. But the dealer in turn can recover over against the underwriter, and the latter (with some caveat by reason of the "preliminary negotiations" clause of §2(3)) against the issuer; and each defendant can bring in his predecessor in the chain of distribution as a third-party defendant under the Federal Rules of Civil Procedure. Moreover, in the case of "best-efforts" distributions in which the distributors act as the issuer's agents, so that title passes from the issuer directly to the ultimate investor, the investor can proceed under §12 against the issuer, the underwriters, the broker-

---

Brennan v. Midwestern United Life Ins. Co., 417 F. 2d 147, 154-55 (7th Cir. 1969), *cert. denied,* 397 U. S. 989; cf. Walck v. American Stock Exchange, Inc., 687 F. 2d 778, 791, (3d Cir. 1982) (only if defendant *"consciously* intended to assist in the perpetration of a wrongful act"). *Contra:* Wessel v. Buhler, 437 F. 2d 279, 283 (10th Cir. 1971).

In general, see Note, The Private Action against a Securities Fraud Aider and Abettor: Silent and Inactive Conduct, 29 Vand. L. Rev. 1233 (1976). On lawyers as aiders and abettors, see SEC v. National Student Marketing Corp., 457 F. Supp. 682 (D. D. C. 1978), set out infra p. 1217; William R. Carter, Sec. Ex. Act Rel. 17,597, 22 SEC Dock. 292 (1981), set out infra p. 1243. For a suggestion that the implication of secondary liability is no longer viable since the recent Supreme Court decisions on implied liabilities, see Fischel, Secondary Liability under Section 10(b) of the Securities Act of 1934 [*sic*], 69 Calif. L. Rev. 80 (1981).

[47] Stadia Oil & Uranium Co. v. Wheelis, 251 F. 2d 269, 276 (10th Cir. 1957).

[48] Cf. American Bank & Trust Co. v. Barad Shaff Securities Corp., 335 F. Supp. 1276, 1279-80 (S. D. N. Y. 1972) (bank that bought stock for a customer who subsequently defaulted can recover from seller under §12(1)).

[49] Surowitz v. Hilton Hotels Corp., 342 F. 2d 596, 603 (7th Cir. 1965), *rev'd on other grounds,* 383 U. S. 363 (1966); Wolf v. Frank, 477 F. 2d 467, 478 (5th Cir. 1973), *cert. denied,* 414 U. S. 975; Collins v. Signetics Corp., 605 F. 2d 111, 113-14 (3d Cir. 1979).

dealer, and the salesman with whom he dealt; for they are all "sellers."[50]

3. NONWAIVER PROVISIONS (HEREIN OF ARBITRATION)

In England before the Companies Act of 1900 the courts honored stipulations that bound the purchasers to waive the statutory liabilities as long as the stipulations were not too "tricky."[51] Since the turn of the century, however, this ready means of evasion has been unavailable in England, and here again Congress profited from the English experience.[52]

All six SEC statutes specify that any condition, stipulation, or provision binding any person to waive compliance with any provision of the Act or any rule of the Commission "shall be void."[53] Except in the case of the 1933 and 1934 Acts, this extends also to any *order* of the Commission. The provision in the 1934 Act refers, in addition, to "any rule of an exchange required" by that Act. Presumably this covers those disciplinary rules that all exchanges are required by §6(b) to adopt as a condition of registration, as well as any exchange rules altered or supplemented by the Commission pursuant to §19(c).[54]

---

[50] DeMarco v. Edens, CCH Fed. Sec. L. Rep. ¶91,856 at 95,934 (S. D. N. Y. 1966), *aff'd on other grounds,* 390 F. 2d 836 (2d Cir. 1968).

[51] Greenwood v. Leather Shod Wheel Co., [1900] 1 Ch. 421 (C. A.); Cackett v. Keswick, [1902] 2 Ch. 456 (C. A.). Under the blue sky laws, the courts worry about "virtual nullification." Foreman v. Holsman, 10 Ill. 2d 551, 553-54, 141 N. E. 2d 31, 32 (1957); Irving v. Bankers' Mortgage Co., 169 Miss. 890, 151 So. 740 (1934); 6 Corbin, Contracts (1951) 982-83; more generally, see id. §§1515-16; but cf. DePolo v. Greig, 338 Mich. 703, 707, 62 N. W. 2d 441, 442 (1954) (extenuating circumstances leading to estoppel as well as waiver). In any event, of course, a waiver will be disregarded if it was obtained by fraud. Lolkus v. Vander Wilt, 258 Iowa 1074, 141 N. W. 2d 600 (1966).

[52] Companies Act, 1948, 11 & 12 Geo. 6, c. 38, §§38(2), 47(5), 417(2).

[53] Sec. Act §14; Sec. Ex. Act §29(a); Holding Co. Act §26(a); Trust Ind. Act §327; Inv. Co. Act §47(a); Inv. Adv. Act §215(a); see also Unif. Sec. Act §410(g). See Stonehill v. Security National Bank, 68 F. R. D. 24, 33 (S. D. N. Y. 1975) (provision in loan guarantee allowing bank to recover on the guarantee even though the loan violated Regulation U); Annot., Construction and Application of §14 of Securities Act of 1933 and §29(a) of Securities Exchange Act of 1934, Voiding Waiver of Compliance with Statutory Provisions or Rules or Regulations, 26 A. L. R. Fed. 495 (1976).

[54] Brown v. Gilligan, Will & Co., 287 F. Supp. 766, 773 n. 13 (S. D. N. Y. 1968); but cf. Rospigliosi v. Clogher, 46 So. 2d 170 (Fla. 1950), *cert. denied,* 340 U. S. 853, where the court enforced a member firm's contract made in violation of an exchange rule prohibiting a registered employee from having

In view of these provisions, as well as the repeated holdings apart from the SEC statutes that a "hedge clause" or legend disclaiming liability has little if any legal effect as protection against civil liability for either intentional or negligent misstatements in the sale of securities,[55] the Commission's General Counsel in a

---

an interest in a customer's account, because it had not been shown that this was a rule "required by the act."

The Florida court's result seems open to some question entirely apart from the nonwaiver provision of the Exchange Act. A customer is usually held to the established customs and usages of the market when he sends an order to a broker established in that market, even if the customer is ignorant of those usages. Bibb v. Allen, 149 U. S. 481, 489-90 (1893); Hawkins v. Merrill Lynch, Pierce, Fenner & Beane, 85 F. Supp. 104, 121 (W. D. Ark. 1949); Samuels v. Oliver, 130 Ill. 73, 22 N. E. 499 (1889); White v. Merrill Lynch, Pierce, Fenner & Smith, Inc., 90 N. J. Super. 565, 218 A. 2d 655 (1966); Lynch v. Maw, 3 Utah 2d 271, 282 P. 2d 841 (1955); see C. Meyer, The Law of Stockbrokers and Stock Exchanges and of Commodity Brokers and Commodity Exchanges (1931) 157-63; Annot., Regulations, Rules, Custom, or Usage of Stock or Produce Exchange or of Stock or Produce Broker as Affecting Customers, 79 A. L. R. 592 (1932). But cf. Gordon v. Diffenderfer, 317 Pa. 425, 430, 177 Atl. 21, 23 (1935); Mercury Investment Co. v. A. G. Edwards & Sons, 295 F. Supp. 1160, 1163 (S. D. Tex. 1969).

In practice, although the *Rospigliosi* opinion is silent on the point, the rules and customs of the exchange are usually made a part of the broker's contract with the customer. Clews v. Jamieson, 182 U. S. 461, 481-82 (1901); American Cotton Mills v. Monier, 61 F. 2d 852, 854 (4th Cir. 1932).

If a customer is thus held to the usages of the exchange when they work to his disadvantage, should he not also benefit from usage and rules that are either expressly or impliedly a part of his contract? There is no indication in the *Rospigliosi* opinion that this argument was considered by the court. It was held merely that the record did not establish that the plaintiff employee had come into court with unclean hands. The case generally was perhaps colored by the fact that it arose in the context of a suit for divorce of an alleged common law marriage between the plaintiff and his customer, although the court did not disturb the denial of a divorce on the ground that there had been no marriage.

In any event, it does not follow, of course, that *every* violation of an exchange rule should make a member's contract unenforceable against his customer, since this is not true even of a *contract* that is illegal. See p. 1047 supra.

[55] Equitable Life Ins. Co. of Iowa v. Halsey, Stuart & Co., 312 U. S. 410, 419 (1941); Wolfe v. A. E. Kusterer & Co., 269 Mich. 424, 431, 257 N. W. 729, 731 (1934); People v. Federated Radio Corp., 244 N. Y. 33, 41, 154 N. E. 655, 658 (1926). In Wilko v. Swan, 346 U. S. 427, 433-34 (1953), there was agreement as to the invalidity under §14 of the provision in a margin agreement purporting to relieve the broker-dealer of liability for any "representation or advice by you or your employees or agents regarding the purchase or sale of any property." See also the opinion below, 201 F. 2d 439, 442-43 (2d Cir. 1953).

The Restatement (Second) of Agency permits innocent principals to contract themselves out of liability for deceit, though not for rescission, because of an agent's unauthorized fraud. §§259, 260. But as to fraud see id. §166, comment e, illus.: "The P company employs A to sell its shares, instructing A not to make any representations except those contained in the prospectus.

published opinion questioned "whether the result, if not the purpose, of such a legend is to create in the mind of the investor a belief that he has given up legal rights and is foreclosed from a remedy which he might otherwise have either at common law or under the SEC statutes." Consequently, he ruled, "the anti-fraud provisions of the SEC statutes are violated by the employment of any legend, hedge clause or other provision which is likely to lead an investor to believe that he has in any way waived any right of action he may have."[56] The opinion concluded that the type of legend in common use by brokers, dealers, and investment advisers — which states, in effect, that the information is obtained from specified sources and is believed to be reliable but that its accuracy is not guaranteed — is not objectionable if the representations as to the source of the information and the belief in its reliability are true.[57] That is to say, the facts may make such a hedge clause misleading in suggesting the employment of objective, careful procedures totally at variance with the deception engaged in by the firm issuing the market letter.[58]

There is authority that an acceleration clause in a purchase money note is not necessarily void,[59] but that a contractual provision for something in the nature of liquidated damages is.[60] And it should not be overlooked that the statutory provisions void waivers by *agreement* of some kind, so that they do not automatically preclude waiver (or estoppel or ratification) by *conduct*[61]

The prospectus states nothing as to the assets of the company, the number of shareholders, or the company affiliations. *A* knowingly makes untruthful statements concerning the assets of the company upon which *T* relies, and then contracts with *T* by a written contract in which it is stated that *A* is not authorized to make statements except those in the prospectus. It may be found that, from the known habit of stock salesmen and the necessity of making statements concerning the assets of the company, the *P* company intended that *A* should make such statements; if so, an action for deceit will lie against the principal." And the reporter's notes to §260 refer specifically to "the cases involving exculpatory clauses in prospectuses and contracts involving the purchase of shares of stock." 3 id. 417.

[56] See Meason v. Gilbert, 236 Ga. 862, 863, 226 S. E. 2d 49, 50 (1976) (state act).

[57] Op. Gen. Counsel, Sec. Act Rel. 3411 (1951); see also the present writer's letter as Chief Counsel, Div. of Trading & Ex., SEC, reprinted in 13 Inv. Dealers' Digest 30 (Mar. 17, 1947).

[58] Heft, Kahn & Infante, Inc., 41 SEC 379, 389 (1963); Linder, Bilotti & Co., Inc., 42 SEC 407, 408 (1964).

[59] Titan Group, Inc. v. Faggen, 513 F. 2d 234, 239 (2d Cir. 1975), *cert. denied,* 423 U. S. 840.

[60] Special Transportation Services, Inc. v. Balto, 325 F. Supp. 1185 (D. Minn. 1971).

[61] See p. 1196 infra.

or settlements of *existing* controversies.[62] At the same time, their very presence should help the person asserting a violation as against arguments directed by his adversary to ratification or estoppel as well as waiver by conduct.[63]

The most litigated question in this area is the effect of the nonwaiver provisions on arbitration:

In 1953 the Supreme Court had to decide whether the nonwaiver provision in §14 of the 1933 Act invalidated a provision in a customer's margin agreement that any controversy between him and the securities firm should be determined by arbitration under the New York Arbitration Law. The United States Arbitration Act provides that the court shall stay the trial of any action "upon being satisfied that the issue involved * * * is referable to arbitration" under a written arbitration agreement.[64] The customer sued the firm under §12(2). There was thus presented a neat conflict between two socially desirable policies — arbitration with its advantages of speed and economy, and protection of the rights of investors against persons with superior bargaining power. The District Court resolved this conflict in favor of the Securities Act, the Second Circuit reversed with one judge dissenting, and the Supreme Court again reversed by a vote of seven to two.[65]

---

[62] Goodman v. Epstein, 582 F. 2d 388, 402-04 (7th Cir. 1978) (a release is valid only with respect to ripened claims of which the releasing party had knowledge or that he could have discovered on reasonable inquiry); but cf. Royal Air Properties, Inc. v. Smith, 333 F. 2d 568, 571 (9th Cir. 1964), infra n. 63. Of course, the enforcement of post-controversy arbitration agreements (see n. 69 infra) argues *a fortiori* for the inapplicability of the nonwaiver provisions to settlement agreements.

[63] "Since under this section the corporation cannot be estopped by an express waiver, an implied waiver must likewise be void." Jefferson Lake Sulphur Co. v. Walet, 104 F. Supp. 20, 23-24 (E. D. La. 1952), *aff'd sub nom.* Walet v. Jefferson Lake Sulphur Co., 202 F. 2d 433, 435 (5th Cir. 1953), *cert. denied,* 346 U. S. 820; see also Kaiser-Frazer Corp. v. Otis & Co., 195 F. 2d 838, 843-44 n. 8 (2d Cir. 1952), *cert. denied,* 344 U. S. 856; Can-Am Petroleum Co. v. Beck, 331 F. 2d 371 (10th Cir. 1964); Rogen v. Ilikon Corp., 361 F. 2d 260, 268 (1st Cir. 1966) (court used §29(a) to void a contractual acknowledgement of nonreliance); Meyers v. C & M Petroleum Producers, Inc., 476 F. 2d 427, 429 (5th Cir. 1973), *cert. denied,* 414 U. S. 829; Fox v. Kane-Miller Corp., 398 F. Supp. 609, 624 (D. Md. 1975), *aff'd on other grounds,* 542 F. 2d 915 (4th Cir. 1976).

In Royal Air Properties, Inc. v. Smith, 333 F. 2d 568, 571 (9th Cir. 1964), the court, without mentioning §29(a), emphasized that waiver, as "the voluntary or intentional relinquishment of a known right," required full knowledge of a right rather than merely enough facts to put the plaintiff on inquiry. "To hold one to diligence in discovering his rights is reasonable in the case of laches and estoppel, where another has acted in the interim to his detriment," but not in the case of waiver, which is "unilaterally accomplished." Id. at 571.

[64] §3, 9 U. S. C. §3.

[65] Wilko v. Swan, 107 F. Supp. 75 (S. D. N. Y. 1952), *rev'd,* 201 F. 2d 439 (2d Cir. 1953), *rev'd,* 346 U. S. 427 (1953).

The Court concluded that the right to select the judicial forum was the kind of "provision" that could not be waived under §14, because "it is clear that the Securities Act was drafted with an eye to the disadvantages under which buyers labor."[66] The case did not involve a determination of "the quality of a commodity or the amount of money due under a contract," the Court said, but required "subjective findings on the purpose and knowledge of an alleged violator of the Act."[67]

This eminently sensible decision has spawned a number of equally sensible exceptions, which are substantially reflected in the Code:

SEC. 1725. (a) *Waivers Void.* — A purported waiver of compliance with this Code (as defined in section 202(24))[68] or a rule of recovery under this Code is void * * * .

(b) *Arbitration.* — Section 1725(a) does not affect —

(1) a good faith settlement of, or agreement to arbitrate, an existing dispute;[69]

(2) action taken pursuant to a rule of the Municipal Board under section 1103(a)(8)[70] or by any other self-regulatory organization to settle disputes between its members or participants;[71] or

(3) an advance agreement —

(A) by a member of or participant in a self-regulatory organization to arbitrate any dispute;[72]

---

[66] Id. at 435.

[67] Id. at 435-36. The *Wilko* case has been followed under the blue sky laws. Sandefer v. Reynolds Securities, Inc., 44 Colo. App. 343, 618 P. 2d 690 (1980); Shearson, Hammill & Co. v. Vouis, 247 So. 2d 733 (Fla. App. 1971); Kiehne v. Purdy, 309 N. W. 2d 60 (Minn. 1981); State *ex rel.* Geil v. Corcoran, 623 S. W. 2d 555 (Mo. App. 1981).

[68] This definition covers the rules of the self-regulatory organizations.

[69] See Moran v. Paine, Webber, Jackson & Curtis, 422 Pa. 66, 220 A. 2d 624 (1966); Moran v. Paine, Webber, Jackson & Curtis, 389 F. 2d 242 (3d Cir. 1968); Murtagh v. University Computing Co., 490 F. 2d 810, 816 (5th Cir. 1974), *cert. denied,* 419 U. S. 835.

[70] This section authorizes the Board to provide for the binding arbitration of disputes relating to transactions in municipal securities so far as municipal brokers or dealers or their associates are concerned.

[71] This provision reflects §28(b)(1) and (2) of the 1934 Act, as amended in 1975 to add Clause (2) with respect to municipals. On the binding effect of arbitration agreements between members, see In re Revenue Properties Litigation Cases, 451 F. 2d 310 (1st Cir. 1971); Coenen v. R. W. Pressprich & Co., Inc., 453 F. 2d 1209 (2d Cir. 1972), *cert. denied,* 406 U. S. 949; Tullis v. Kohlmeyer & Co., 551 F. 2d 632 (5th Cir. 1977); but cf. Allegaert v. Perot, 548 F. 2d 432 (2d Cir. 1977), *cert. denied,* 432 U. S. 910. On the advantages of arbitration between members, see Legg, Mason & Co., Inc. v. Mackall & Coe, Inc., 351 F. Supp. 1367 (D. D. C. 1972).

[72] On the binding effect of a member-*customer* agreement on the *member,*

(B) by any person to arbitrate a dispute arising under a rule of a self-regulatory organization (other than the Municipal Board), unless a violation of the rule is (i) a violation of this Code, or (ii) actionable under section 1721(a);[73] or

(C) between any persons if a court determines, on consideration of their financial and legal sophistication and the relationship between them, that the purposes of this Code do not require the application of section 1725(a).[74]

A few points remain:

---

see Axelrod & Co. v. Kordich, Victor & Neufeld, 451 F. 2d 838 (2d Cir. 1971). Such an advance agreement is usually reflected in the rules of the self-regulatory organizations. The Commission has expressed concern about the use of arbitration clauses in broker-dealer-customer agreements that purport to bind the *customer* to arbitrate all future disputes. If their meaning, effect and enforceability are not specified, the Commission cautioned, this practice may be "inconsistent with just and equitable principles of trade" and also raise serious questions under the antifraud provisions. Sec. Ex. Act Rel. 15,984, 17 SEC Dock. 1167 (1979).

Section 28(b)(3), which was §28(b)(2) before the 1975 amendments inserted the present §28(b)(2) with respect to arbitration rules of the Municipal Board, is not clear when it saves "the binding effect * * * of any action described in paragraph (1) or (2) on any person who has agreed to be bound thereby." In the words of the Code commentary:

> If X28(b)(2) [this should read X28(b)(3)] is meant to enforce a non-member's agreement to arbitrate an existing dispute, it is covered by §1725(b)(1). If it is meant to enforce a nonmember's agreement to arbitrate a *future* dispute — and the courts have given no more validity to agreements to arbitrate future disputes with respect to Rule 10b-5 than with respect to the 1933 Act [see Merrill Lynch, Pierce, Fenner & Smith, Inc. v. Moore, 590 F. 2d 823 (10th Cir. 1978)] — X28(b)(2) is out of harmony with the law as it has developed.

2 Code 804, Comment (3)(b); the case citation is in the original. At any rate, the language of §1725(b)(3)(A) is designed to be broad enough to replace Clause (3) as well as Clause (1) of §28(b). Ibid.

More generally, although one or two cases have applied §28(b) to the 1933 Act on an *in pari materia* approach (Brown v. Gilligan, Will & Co., 287 F. Supp. 766 (S. D. N. Y. 1968); Axelrod & Co. v. Kordich, Victor & Neufeld, 451 F. 2d 838, 843 (2d Cir. 1971)), most cases under the 1934 Act achieve parity between the two statutes by simply ignoring §28(b). E. g., Greater Continental Corp. v. Schechter, 422 F. 2d 1100, 1103-04 (2d Cir. 1970).

[73] This provision makes it plain that even nonmembers are bound by agreements to arbitrate rule disputes that are not actionable under the Code and do not involve illegal conduct under the Code.

[74] "This recognizes Scherk v. Alberto-Culver Co., 417 U. S. 506 (1974), which involved a sale of a business (later challenged under Rule 10b-5) pursuant to a contract in which the parties had bargained for arbitration under the rules of the International Chamber of Commerce in Paris. But the provision is not limited to cases with the international aspect that saved the arbitration in that particular case. The typical case that may commend itself to the court is that of two more or less equally sophisticated institutions." 2 Code 804, Comment (4).

(1) The *Wilko* holding applies fully to implied actions.[75]

(2) Depending on the circumstances, the plaintiff's becoming an exchange member after a controversy has arisen may[76] or may not[77] bind the plaintiff to arbitration.

(3) The *Wilko* case does not affect a common law action just because a security is involved.[78] But what if the same controversy involves questions that under *Wilko* are not arbitrable as well as questions that standing alone would be arbitrable? Are the federal securities claims "the very core of the action"?[79] Or, as the same court put it in another case, are they "the rather small tail to a much larger dog"?[80] In the middle, the courts exercise their discretion,[81] sometimes deciding even the arbitrable claims[82] and sometimes splitting them off.[83] There is also authority, depending again on the circumstances, for the court's *staying* arbitration pending a judicial resolution of just the SEC issues, however "intertwined,"[84] as well as the court's staying its own proceedings so that arbitration of the non-SEC issues can proceed first.[85]

(4) Suppose a broker's customer submits to arbitration, loses and *then* argues *Wilko*. Too late. As the Court observed in *Wilko,* judicial power to vacate an award is limited by the Arbitration Act.[86] Although "manifest disregard" of the law as distinct from error in its interpretation is theoretically subject to judicial review,

[75] Ayres v. Merrill Lynch, Pierce, Fenner & Smith, Inc., 538 F. 2d 532, 536-37 (3d Cir. 1976), *cert. denied,* 429 U. S. 1010; Weissbuch v. Merrill Lynch, Pierce, Fenner & Smith, Inc., 558 F. 2d 831 (7th Cir. 1977).

[76] Coenen v. Pressprich & Co., Inc., 453 F. 2d 1209 (2d Cir. 1972), *cert. denied,* 406 U. S. 949.

[77] Laupheimer v. McDonnell & Co., Inc., 500 F. 2d 21 (2d Cir. 1974); De Lancie v. Birr, Wilson & Co., 648 F. 2d 1255 (9th Cir. 1981).

[78] Barbi v. W. E. Hutton & Co., 53 A. D. 2d 562, 384 N. Y. S. 2d 828 (1st Dept. 1976).

[79] Sawyer v. Raymond, James & Associates, Inc., 642 F. 2d 791, 793 (5th Cir. 1981).

[80] Sibley v. Tandy Corp., 543 F. 2d 540, 543 (5th Cir. 1976), *cert. denied,* 434 U. S. 824.

[81] See Mansbach v. Prescott, Ball & Turben, 598 F. 2d 1017, 1030-31 (6th Cir. 1979).

[82] E. g., Shapiro v. Jaslow, 320 F. Supp. 598 (S. D. N. Y. 1970); Laurence v. Corwin, 79 A. D. 2d 840, 427 N. Y. S. 2d 865 (2d Dept. 1980); Miley v. Oppenheimer & Co., 637 F. 2d 318, 334-36 (5th Cir. 1981); Sandefer v. District Court, — Colo. — , 635 P. 2d 547 (1981); Cunningham v. Dean Witter Reynolds, 550 F. Supp. 578 (E. D. Cal. 1982).

[83] E. g., Macchiavelli v. Shearson, Hammill & Co., Inc., 384 F. Supp. 21, 31 (E. D. Cal. 1974); Davend Corp. v. Michael, CCH Fed. Sec. L. Rep. ¶95,540 (S. D. N. Y. 1976).

[84] Dickinson v. Heinold Securities, Inc., 661 F. 2d 638, 644 (7th Cir. 1981).

[85] Greater Continental Corp. v. Schechter, 422 F. 2d 1100, 1103-04 (2d Cir. 1970); Kavit v. A. L. Stamm & Co., 491 F. 2d 1176, 1178 n. 2 (2d Cir. 1974).

[86] 9 U. S. C. §10.

how is a court to be made aware that the arbitrators *ignored* the applicable law instead of *misapplying* it? For expedition, the very purpose of arbitration, dictates that awards may be made without a statement of reasons or a complete record.[87]

4. In Pari Delicto, Estoppel, and Related Defenses

We have already touched on laches[88] and on waiver by conduct.[89] The blue sky cases on those defenses and their siblings — ratification, estoppel, *in pari delicto,* and (in equity) unclean hands — are too numerous to mention. Unfortunately they are also too variegated to permit generalization.[90] But they constitute a research resource beyond the blue sky area itself because of their precedential value with respect to the federal statutes.

At the federal level we have also examined the attitude of the courts toward the *in pari delicto* defense in the context of the credit provisions.[91] In 10b-5 cases they have entertained the defense,[92] as they have in proxy cases.[93] And the cases are mixed

---

[87] On this paragraph of the text generally, see Wilko v. Swan, 346 U. S. 427, 436-37 (1953); Sobel v. Hertz, Warner & Co., 469 F. 2d 1211 (2d Cir. 1972), *rev'g* 338 F. Supp. 287 (S. D. N. Y. 1971), where Judge Pollack, in remanding to the arbitrators for a statement of reasons, sought to differentiate controversies based on statutory duties as under §12(2) or Rule 10b-5 from ordinary commercial problems.

[88] See pp. 1174-75 supra.

[89] See pp. 1191-92 supra.

[90] See 3 Loss 1676-80; 6 id. 3818-19.

[91] See p. 1154 supra.

[92] Royal Air Properties, Inc. v. Smith, 312 F. 2d 210, 213 (9th Cir. 1962); Kuehnert v. Texstar Corp., 412 F. 2d 700 (5th Cir. 1969), supra p. 839 n. 53 (tippee v. tipper); James v. DuBreuil, 500 F. 2d 155 (5th Cir. 1974); Tarasi v. Pittsburgh National Bank, 555 F. 2d 1152 (3d Cir. 1977), *cert. denied,* 434 U. S. 965; cf. Bosse v. Crowell Collier & MacMillan, 565 F. 2d 602, 611 n. 15 (9th Cir. 1977) (laches); but cf. Mallis v. Bankers Trust Co., 615 F. 2d 68 (2d Cir. 1980), *cert. denied,* 449 U. S. 1123 (containing a review of the cases). Of course, *establishing* estoppel or one of the related defenses may be another matter. Royal Air Properties, Inc. v. Smith, 333 F. 2d 568 (9th Cir. 1964).

[93] Gaudiosi v. Mellon, 269 F. 2d 873 (3d Cir. 1959), *cert. denied,* 361 U. S. 902; Walsh & Levine v. Peoria & Eastern Ry. Co., 222 F. Supp. 516 (S. D. N. Y. 1963); Dunning v. Rafton, CCH Fed. Sec. L. Rep. ¶91,660 at 95,438-39 (N. D. Cal. 1965); Studebaker Corp. v. Allied Products Corp., 256 F. Supp. 173, 192 (W. D. Mich. 1966).

See also Wolfson v. Baker, 623 F. 2d 1074, 1081-82 (5th Cir. 1980), *cert. denied,* 450 U. S. 966 (New York Stock Exchange "know your customer" rule); Regional Properties, Inc. v. Financial & Real Estate Consulting Co., 678 F. 2d 552, 562 (5th Cir. 1982) (Sec. Ex. Act §15(a)).

under both §§12(1)[94] and 12(2)[95] as they are under the blue sky laws. When the doctrine *is* considered, one must remember an elementary bit of Latin translation sometimes overlooked — that *pari delicto* means *equal* fault.[96] As the Fifth Circuit put it, the fault of the parties must be "mutual, simultaneous, and relatively equal."[97]

The unanswerable question is whether the cases that allow the *in pari delicto* defense are out of spirit with the Supreme Court's holding in *Perma Life Mufflers, Inc.* v. *International Parts Corp.* that "the doctrine of *in pari delicto,* with its complex scope, contents, and effects is not to be recognized as a defense to an antitrust action," and its reminder that it had "often indicated the inappropriateness of invoking broad common-law barriers to relief where a private suit serves important public purposes."[98] The *Kuehnert* case,[99] where the doctrine was applied to bar a tippee's recovery from his tipper for alleged violation of Rule 10b-5, has been criticized in the light of this holding.[100]

The Code innovates here:

---

[94] The doctrine was held inapplicable in Lawler v. Gilliam, 569 F. 2d 1283, 1291-94 (4th Cir. 1978). When it *is* applied, there is no reason to believe that the plaintiff's mere knowledge of the violation places him *in pari delicto*. For a dictum to this effect with reference to §12(2) — which should apply *a fortiori* to §12(1) — see Rosenberg v. Hano, 121 F. 2d 818, 822 (3d Cir. 1941): "The mere fact that the plaintiff knew of the defendant's illegal actions and intended to profit upon them is not enough to place him *in pari delicto*." At the other extreme, a plaintiff will not be allowed to attack his own investment representation. Value Line Fund, Inc. v. Marcus, CCH Fed. Sec. L. Rep. ¶ 91,523 at 94,971 (S. D. N. Y. 1965). And there are cases holding the doctrine applicable to §12(1) but finding that the plaintiffs were not *in pari delicto* in point of fact. Can-Am Petroleum Co. v. Beck, 331 F. 2d 371 (10th Cir. 1964); Belhumeur v. Dawson, 229 F. Supp. 78, 86-87 (D. Mont. 1964). It has been held, too, that the defenses of estoppel and waiver by conduct are available to a §12(1) defendant. Straley v. Universal Uranium & Milling Corp., 289 F. 2d 370, 373-74 (9th Cir. 1961); Katz v. Amos Treat & Co., 411 F. 2d 1046, 1054-55 (2d Cir. 1969); Henderson v. Hayden, Stone, Inc., 461 F. 2d 1069, 1072 (5th Cir. 1972). *Query:* Is this consistent with strict liability?

[95] See Rosenberg v. Hano, 121 F. 2d 818, 822 (3d Cir. 1941), supra n. 94; Dale v. Rosenfeld, 229 F. 2d 855, 859 (2d Cir. 1956) (doctrine not established on the facts).

[96] Carpenter v. Hall, 311 F. Supp. 1099, 1106 (S. D. Tex. 1970).

[97] James v. DuBreuil, 500 F. 2d 155, 160 (5th Cir. 1974).

[98] 392 U. S. 134, 138, 140 (1968).

[99] See p. 839 n. 53 supra.

[100] Nathanson v. Weis, Voisin, Cannon, Inc., 325 F. Supp. 50 (S. D. N. Y. 1971); Moholt v. Dean Witter Reynolds, Inc., 478 F. Supp. 451 (D. D. C. 1979); cf. Woolf v. S. D. Cohn & Co., 515 F. 2d 591, 602-05 (5th Cir. 1975), *rehearing denied,* 521 F. 2d 225 (5th Cir. 1975), *remanded on other grounds* sub nom. S. D. Cohn & Co. v. Woolf, 426 U. S. 944 (1976).

In a private action created by or based on a violation of this
Code * * * , the defense of in pari delicto is valid only to the
extent (which may be complete) that the court determines appropriate on consideration of (1) the deterrent effect of the particular type of liability, (2) the financial and legal sophistication of
the parties, and (3) their relative responsibility for the loss incurred.[101]

5. INDEMNIFICATION, CONTRIBUTION, AND INSURANCE

The SEC statutes are silent on indemnification except for provisions in the Trust Indenture and Investment Company Acts.[102]
Those civil liability provisions of the 1933 and 1934 Acts that
contemplate more than one defendant do contain provisions on
contribution. Section 11(f) of the 1933 Act provides:

All or any one or more of the persons specified in subsection
(a)[103] shall be jointly and severally liable, and every person who

---

[101] §1724(d). The reference to unclean hands was deleted from the approved draft at the Commission's suggestion on the ground that the second
and third factors are not adapted to that defense, which has been involved
in relatively few SEC cases. Lawler v. Gilliam, 569 F. 2d 1283, 1294 (4th Cir.
1978); Wolf v. Frank, 477 F. 2d 467, 474 (5th Cir. 1973), *cert. denied*, 414
U. S. 975; Bertoglio v. Texas Int'l Co., 488 F. Supp. 630, 662 (D. Del. 1980),
and cases cited. The result is to leave unclean hands, as estoppel and ratification are left, to development as a matter of "federal common law."

In general, see Comment, Rule 10b-5: The *In Pari Delicto* and Unclean
Hands Defenses, 58 Calif. L. Rev. 1149 (1970); Annot., *In Pari Delicto* as
Defense in Private Action for Violation of Securities Act or Securities Ex-
change Act, 26 A. L. R. Fed. 682 (1976).

[102] Section 315(d)(2) of the former statute permits the indenture to contain
provisions protecting the trustee "from liability for any error of judgment
made in good faith by a responsible officer * * * unless it shall be proved
that such trustee was negligent in ascertaining the pertinent facts." Section
17(h) of the Investment Company Act nullifies all exculpatory clauses that
purport to protect any director or officer against liability to the company or
its security holders "by reason of willful misfeasance, bad faith, gross negligence or reckless disregard of the duties involved in the conduct of his office."
And §17(i) contains similar language with respect to investment advisers of
registered investment companies or their principal underwriters. The Commission has interpreted these provisions to prohibit indemnification for expenses and the amount of any judgment handed down against the specified
categories of persons. In cases of settlement it has taken the position that
indemnity may be offered only when the reasonable expenses of prosecution
of a case to judgment would exceed the amount paid in settlement. 7 SEC
Ann. Rep. 16 (1941), quoted in Inv. Co. Act Rel. 7221 (1972). See also Brown
v. Bullock, 194 F. Supp. 207, 237-38 (S. D. N. Y. 1961), *aff'd en banc on other
grounds*, 294 F. 2d 415 (2d Cir. 1961); Chabot v. Empire Trust Co., 301 F.
2d 458, 461 (2d Cir. 1962); SEC v. Continental Growth Fund, Inc., CCH Fed.
Sec. L. Rep. ¶91,437 (S. D. N. Y. 1964).

[103] Although this does not literally cover controlling persons liable under
§15, they nevertheless fall within the scope of §11(f) because §15 specifies

becomes liable to make any payment under this section may recover contribution as in cases of contract from any person who, if sued separately, would have been liable to make the same payment, unless the person who has become liable was, and the other was not, guilty of fraudulent misrepresentation.

In the 1934 Act §§9(e) (manipulation) and 18(b) (false filings) contain the same language except for the absence of the introductory reference to joint and several liability and the "unless" clause at the end. But, of course, the 1934 Act is silent, by hypothesis, with respect to contribution in the *implied* actions under Rule 10b-5 and other provisions.

Section 11(f) was taken almost bodily from the English Companies Act.[104] And its obvious purpose was to avoid the historic policy against contribution among joint tortfeasors, aside from the specific exception in the section. With that exception, the section presumably contemplates contribution *pro rata* as in contract rather than on a fault basis as in tort.[105]

The issues that have proved much more serious in the administration of the 1933 Act relate to indemnification rather than contribution — to the question whether liability *inter se* may be governed by express contract. We have already noticed the Commission's use of its acceleration authority to enforce its anti-indemnification policy so far as §11 is concerned.[106] The Commission's codification of that policy in Regulation S-K[107] is carefully phrased to preserve the two exceptions that the Commission has traditionally followed:

(1) No objection is made to an agreement by a *controlling stockholder* in a secondary (or partially secondary) distribution to indemnify the issuer and its directors, officers, and experts. Since the offering is made solely for the benefit of the controlling stockholder, Congress could not have intended to foreclose his reimbursing the issuer (and indirectly the minority stockholders) for

---

the same *prima facie* liability as §11. Laventhol, Krekstein, Horwath & Horwath v. Horwitch, 637 F. 2d 672 (9th Cir. 1980), *cert. denied* sub nom. Frank v. United States Trust Co., 452 U. S. 963.

[104] 19 & 20 Geo. 5, c. 23, §37(3) (1929).

[105] See Douglas and Bates, The Federal Securities Act of 1933, 43 Yale L. J. 171, 178-81 (1933); on contribution in general, see 1 Harper and James, The Law of Torts (1956) §10.2; 2 Williston, Contracts (2d ed. 1959) §345.

[106] See pp. 133-34 supra. Indemnification provisions come to the Commission's attention also under the proxy rules when a company with a security registered under the Exchange Act (or a company subject to the Holding Company or Investment Company Act) seeks stockholder approval of an agreement or bylaw or charter amendment on indemnification.

[107] Item 512(i); see also Item 702.

any liability or expense the issuer might suffer by reason of §11, although it is arguable that the issuer's directors, officers, and experts should no more be relieved of their statutory duties in secondary than in primary distributions.

(2) It is common practice for the issuer and *underwriters* to enter into cross-indemnification agreements whereby (a) the underwriters agree to indemnify the issuer, its directors, and those officers signing the registration statement with respect to any information furnished by the underwriters expressly for the registration statement, and (b) the issuer agrees to indemnify the underwriters and their controlling persons as to everything else. The Commission grants acceleration in such cases as long as the "Johnson & Johnson formula"[108] is applied to any person who happens to be both (a) a director, officer, or controlling person of the issuer and (b) an underwriter or a partner or controlling person of an underwriter. In the case of secondary distributions, the formula would seem to apply in such interlocking situations when the *issuer* indemnifies the underwriters, but there should be no concern when the indemnification is provided by the selling stockholder. This special treatment of underwriters apparently has a historical explanation in the fears expressed during the early days of the Act that underwriters would be unwilling to assume the full risks of §11, with attendant danger to the country's economic recovery.[109]

There is a further anomaly in that the Commission has not raised similar objection to *insurance* against §11 liability, regardless of who bears the cost. This position was formalized in 1982 as Rule 461(c). Presumably the explanation lies in the insurance company's furnishing another pocket for plaintiffs.[110]

---

[108] See c. 2C n. 17 supra.

[109] Professor Berle later wrote that the Reconstruction Finance Corporation was "erected into a huge capital banking institution" and that, "In effect, we broke the capital strike." Berle, Prologue to Federal Securities Law Symposium, 15 N. Y. L. F. 213, 214 (1969).

The Commission's failure to apply the formula to underwriters' indemnification does not assure that the particular indemnification will be honored. Cf. Globus v. Law Research Service, Inc. [*Globus I*], 418 F. 2d 1276 (2d Cir. 1969), *cert. denied,* 397 U. S. 913, set out infra p. 1201. On the other hand, a "technical" underwriter is in a different position from the investment banker, since his opportunity to participate in the preparation of the registration statement, or even to check its accuracy, may be virtually nil. See Cohen, in Symposium. The *BarChris* Case: Prospectus Liability, 24 Bus. Law. 523, 551-52 (1969).

[110] By way of recognizing the anti-indemnification provision in §17(h) of the Investment Company Act (supra n. 102), the rule's nonacceleration policy does extend to insurance of a director or officer of a registered investment

The Commission's view of §11 does not interfere, of course, with the issuer's reimbursing officers or directors who have been *successful* in defending §11 actions, with or without a prior agreement to do so, at least when they have won an adjudication on the merits.[111] The provisions for joint and several liability of all persons liable, and for contribution, militate in favor of such reimbursement; for a vigorous defense by any officers or directors who are sued will tend to reduce the chance that the issuer itself will be held liable. But (*pace* settlements) it is prudent not to place any reliance on indemnification against an adjudicated liability under §11. The *in terrorem* purpose of individual liability is reinforced by the antiwaiver provision in §14. What little case law there is under §11 (it must be remembered that there is relatively little case law under §11 altogether) supports the Commission's view.[112] And consider, both under Rule 10b-5 *per se* and for its analogical value under §11:

GLOBUS v. LAW RESEARCH SERVICE, INC.
[GLOBUS I]
United States Court of Appeals, Second Circuit, 1969
418 F. 2d 1276, *cert. denied,* 397 U. S. 913

Before WATERMAN, SMITH and KAUFMAN, Circuit Judges.
KAUFMAN, Circuit Judge.
This tortuous litigation raises at least two issues of great importance: are punitive damages available in private actions based on §17(a) of the Securities Act of 1933, 15 U. S. C. §77q(a); and, may an underwriter be indemnified by an issuer for liabilities arising out of misstatements in an offering circular of which the underwriter had actual knowledge? We hold that punitive damages

---

company or a "business development company" (see p. 336 infra) against "willful misfeasance, bad faith, gross negligence or reckless disregard of the duties involved in the conduct of his or her office" if the cost is borne by any person other than the insured.

[111] Galdi v. Berg, 359 F. Supp. 698 (D. Del. 1973); Goldstein v. Alodex Corp., 409 F. Supp. 1201 (E. D. Pa. 1976); cf. Koch Industries, Inc. v. Vosko, 494 F. 2d 713, 725 (10th Cir. 1974); Collins v. Fitzwater, 277 Ore. 401, 560 P. 2d 1074 (1977) (state act).

[112] In Laventhal, Krekstein, Horwath & Horwath v. Horwitch, 637 F. 2d 672, 676 (9th Cir. 1980), the court held, with little discussion except for citation of a 10b-5 case, that indemnification under §11 "would undermine the statutory purpose of assuring diligent performance of duty and deterring negligence." See Gould v. American Hawaiian Steamship Co., 387 F. Supp. 163, 168 n. 11 (D. Del. 1974), *vacated and remanded on other grounds,* 535 F. 2d 761 (3d Cir. 1976).

may not be recovered under §17(a) and that an underwriter may not be indemnified in a case such as this.

The plaintiffs-appellees, purchasers of the stock of Law Research Services, Inc. (LRS), initiated this action against LRS, its president Ellias C. Hoppenfeld, and the underwriter of LRS's public stock offer, Blair & Co., Granbery Marache, Inc. (Blair). They contended that the appellants violated §17(a) of the Securities Act of 1933, §10(b) of the Securities Exchange Act of 1934, 15 U. S. C. §78j(b), and also committed common law fraud. The essence of their charge is that the offering circular prepared in connection with LRS's offer to sell 100,000 shares of its stock to the public under Regulation A of the Securities and Exchange Commission was misleading since it prominently featured an attractive contract between LRS and the Sperry Rand Corp. (Sperry Rand) while failing to refer to a dispute between the two companies which had led Sperry Rand to terminate some of its services to LRS and in turn caused LRS to file suit against Sperry Rand. Moreover, the plaintiffs contended that Blair's actions violated §12(2) of the 1933 Act, 15 U. S. C. §77l (2), and §15(c) of the 1934 Act, 15 U. S. C. §78o-c.

Judge Mansfield presided over a ten-day trial of these claims, to a jury in the Southern District of New York. The jury returned a verdict in favor of Blair, LRS and Hoppenfeld on the common law fraud claim but also decided that all three had violated both the Securities Act of 1933 and the Securities Exchange Act of 1934. Accordingly, the jury awarded compensatory damages to all plaintiffs totaling $32,591.14 and punitive damages against Hoppenfeld in the amount of $26,812.06 and Blair in the amount of $13,000, based on the violation of §17(a) of the 1933 Act.

The jury was also called upon to deal with a cross-claim asserted by Blair against LRS, which rested on an indemnity clause included in the underwriting agreement, and against Hoppenfeld and a third-party defendant, Paul Wiener, Secretary-Treasurer of LRS, sounding in tort. At the same time, LRS and Hoppenfeld asserted a cross-claim against Blair, grounded on the same indemnity agreement. On all these cross-claims, the jury found for Blair.

Blair and Hoppenfeld then moved unsuccessfully to have Judge Mansfield set aside the award of punitive damages. LRS, Hoppenfeld and Wiener, however, moved successfully to set aside the verdict on the cross-claims for indemnity and the entry of judgment, pursuant to Fed. R. Civ. P. 50(b). Judge Mansfield's careful and thorough opinion of July 19, 1968 is reported at 287 F.

Supp. 188. In sum therefore, LRS, Hoppenfeld and Blair appeal from the award of damages to appellees and Blair appeals from the Judgment on the cross-claims and third-party action.

* * *

III. INDEMNITY

Judge Mansfield * * * granted the motion of LRS and Hoppenfeld to set aside the jury's verdict on the cross-claims granting indemnification to Blair. He thus struck down the indemnity agreement between the issuer and the underwriter, at least as it applied to the facts before us. Blair's cross-claim against LRS was based on a provision which compelled LRS to indemnify the underwriter for any loss arising out of an untrue statement of a material fact in the offering circular, except that Blair was not to obtain indemnification by reason of any wilful misfeasance, bad faith or gross negligence in the performance of its duties or by reason of its reckless disregard of its obligations under the agreement. Its claim against Hoppenfeld and Wiener, who did not sign the indemnification agreement in their personal capacities rests on the theory that they were "active" wrongdoers while Blair was merely a "passive" joint tortfeasor.

The jury, by awarding compensatory and punitive damages to the plaintiffs under sections 17(a) and 10(b), necessarily found in light of the judge's charge, that Blair had actual knowledge of the material misstatements. [Citations omitted.] Accordingly the court had ample basis to find Blair not deserving of recovery under the indemnity agreement itself. See 44 N. Y. U. L. Rev. 226, 227 (1969). But it chose instead the broader ground that where there is actual knowledge of the misstatement by the underwriter and wanton indifference by Blair to its obligations, "it would be against the public policy embodied in the federal securities legislation to permit Blair and Co. * * * to enforce its indemnification agreement." 287 F. Supp. at 199. Thus it is important to emphasize at the outset that at this time we consider only the case where the underwriter has committed a sin graver than ordinary negligence.

Given this state of the record, we concur in Judge Mansfield's ruling that to tolerate indemnity under these circumstances would encourage flaunting the policy of the common law and the Securities Act. It is well established that one cannot insure himself against his own reckless, wilful or criminal misconduct. See *Kansas City Operating Co.* v. *Durwood,* 278 F. 2d 354 (8th Cir.

1960); cf. *Holman* v. *Johnson*, 1 Cowper 341, 343, 98 Eng. Rep. 1120, 1121; Prosser, Torts, §48 (3d ed. 1964). See also 6 Loss at 3980.

Although the 1933 Act does not deal expressly with the question before us, provisions in that Act confirm our conclusion that Blair should not be entitled to indemnity from LRS. See generally Note, Indemnification of Underwriters and §11 of the Securities Act of 1933, 72 Yale L. J. 406. For example, §11 of the Act, 15 U. S. C. §77k, makes underwriters jointly liable with directors, experts and signers of the registration statement.[16] And, the SEC has announced its view that indemnification of directors, officers and controlling persons for liabilities arising under the 1933 Act is against the public policy of the Act. 17 C. F. R. §230.460. If we follow the syllogism through to its conclusion, underwriters should be treated equally with controlling persons and hence prohibited from obtaining idemnity from the issuer. See 72 Yale, supra, at 411. But see 3 Loss supra, at 1834 (1961).

Civil liability under section 11 and similar provisions was designed not so much to compensate the defrauded purchaser as to promote enforcement of the Act and to deter negligence by providing a penalty for those who fail in their duties. And Congress intended to impose a "high standard of trusteeship" on underwriters. Kroll, supra, at 687. Thus, what Professor Loss terms the *"in terrorem* effect" of civil liability, 3 Loss, supra, at 1831, might well be thwarted if underwriters were free to pass their liability on to the issuer. Underwriters who knew they could be indemnified simply by showing that the issuer was "more liable" than they (a process not too difficult when the issuer is inevitably closer to the facts) would have a tendency to be lax in their independent investigations. Cf. *New York Central RR* v. *Lockwood,* 84 U. S. (17 Wall.) 357, 377-378 (1873). Cases upholding indemnity for negligence in other fields are not necessarily apposite. The goal in such cases is to compensate the injured party. But the Securities Act is more concerned with prevention than cure.

Finally, it has been suggested that indemnification of the underwriter by the issuer is particularly suspect. Although in form the underwriter is reimbursed by the issuer, the recovery ultimately comes out of the pockets of the issuer's stockholders. Many of these stockholders may be the very purchasers to whom the underwriter should have been initially liable. The 1933 Act prohibits agreements with purchasers which purport to exempt individuals from liability arising under the Act. 15 U. S. C.

---

[16]§16 applies to full registrations. LRS's issue was under Regulation A.

§77n; see 82 Harv. L. Rev., supra, at 958. The situation before us is at least reminiscent of the evil this section was designed to avoid. But see Note, Indemnification of Underwriters, supra, 72 Yale L. J. at 408.

To turn briefly to the question of the cross-claim against Hoppenfeld and the third-party claim against Wiener, similar reasoning supports Judge Mansfield's decision to grant judgment n. o. v. Blair may have been less active than Hoppenfeld, but since it had actual knowledge of the omitted facts and failed to take corrective action, it would be incongruous to permit it to recover over. Compare *Burns* v. *Cunard SS Co.,* 404 F. 2d 60 (2d Cir. 1968), *cert. denied,* 393 U. S. 1117.

*   *   *

There are also *negligence* cases not arising under §11 in which indemnification has been denied.[113] The *Globus* court later approved *contribution*.[114] But there is a question whether these contribution cases survive recent Supreme Court decisions under the Equal Pay Act together with Title VII of the Civil Rights Act of 1964 in one case[115] and §4 of the Clayton Act in another.[116]

Compare 44 N. Y. U. L. Rev. at 229 n. 34 with Kroll, Some Reflections on Indemnification Provisions & S. E. C. Liability Insurance in The Light of *BarChris* and *Globus,* 24 Bus. L. 685 (1969).

[113] Gould v. American-Hawaiian Steamship Co., 387 F. Supp. 163, 168-72 (D. Del. 1974), *vacated and remanded on other grounds,* 535 F. 2d 761 (3d Cir. 1976) (Rule 14a-9, the proxy fraud rule); Odette v. Shearson, Hammill & Co., Inc., 394 F. Supp. 946, 956-57 (S. D. N. Y. 1975) (§12(2)).

[114] Globus, Inc. v. Law Research Service, Inc. [*Globus II*], 318 F. Supp. 955 (S. D. N. Y. 1970), *aff'd per curiam,* 442 F. 2d 1346 (2d Cir. 1971), *cert. denied* sub nom. Law Research Service, Inc. v. Blair & Co., 404 U. S. 941; see also deHaas v. Empire Petroleum Co., 286 F. Supp. 809, 815-16 (D. Colo. 1968), *aff'd on this point,* 435 F. 2d 1223 (10th Cir. 1970); Gould v. American-Hawaiian Steamship Co., 387 F. Supp. 163, 168-72 (D. Del. 1974), *remanded on other grounds,* 535 F. 2d 761 (3d Cir. 1976). With respect to the holdings in both *Globus* cases, see also Heizer Corp. v. Ross, 601 F. 2d 330 (7th Cir. 1979); Stowell v. Ted S. Finkel Investment Services, Inc., 641 F. 2d 323 (5th Cir. 1981). On the complications created by partial settlements, see Laventhol, Krekstein, Horwath & Horwath v. Horwitch, 637 F. 2d 672 (9th Cir. 1980), *cert. denied* sub nom. Frank v. United States Trust Co., 452 U. S. 963; Adamski, Contribution and Settlement in Multiparty Actions under Rule 10b-5, 66 Iowa L. Rev. 533 (1981). For a comprehensive discussion of contribution and indemnification under Rule 10b-5 in historical terms, see McLean v. Alexander, 449 F. Supp. 1251, 1265-68 (D. Del. 1978), *rev'd on other grounds,* 599 F. 2d 1190 (3d Cir. 1979). In general, see J. Bishop, The Law of Corporate Officers and Directors: Indemnification and Insurance (1981).

[115] 29 U. S. C. §206(d); Tit. VII, §703, 42 U. S. C. §2000e-2; Northwest Airlines, Inc. v. Transport Workers Union, 451 U. S. 77 (1981).

[116] 15 U. S. C. §15; Texas Industries, Inc. v. Radcliff Materials, Inc., 451 U. S. 630 (1981).

Concluding that "a right to contribution may arise in either of two ways: first, through the affirmative creation of a right of action by Congress, either expressly or by clear implication; or, second, through the power of federal courts to fashion a federal common law of contribution,"[117] the Court refused to take the second route.

As Judge Friendly later said,[118] the Supreme Court "left open the question whether federal courts could properly provide for contribution when an implied right of action was found to exist under the securities laws." For the statutes before the Supreme Court "expressly created the private damage actions and failed to provide for contribution, although §11(f) of the Securities Act of 1933 and §18(b) of the Securities Exchange Act demonstrated that Congress knew how to do this when it wished." But one cannot ignore the *contra* argument that the contribution provisions in §§11(f) and 18(b) apply only for purposes of those sections, just as one does not apply the provisions on attorneys' fees in §11(e) of the 1933 Act and §§9(e) and 18(a) of the 1934 Act to actions under Rule 10b-5. So *query*.[119]

Under the Federal Rules of Civil Procedure anyone sued under §11 or one of the implied liabilities can bring in as third-party defendants those who may be liable to him by way of contribution or indemnification.[120] Under the broad provisions of §22(a) of the 1933 Act and §27 of the 1934 Act there will frequently (perhaps usually) be no problem of venue or personal service; indeed, even if it be assumed that the defendant's third-party complaint is based not on one of the 1934 Act's contribution provisions but on a contract of indemnification (or presumably a common law right of indemnification), such a complaint is ancillary to the principal cause of action created by §11 or implied under the 1934 Act, so that no independent basis of jurisdiction over the subject matter is required.[121] It has been held also that

---

[117] 451 U. S. at 638; see also 451 U. S. at 90-91.

[118] Fogel v. Chestnutt, 668 F. 2d 100, 119 n. 17 (2d Cir. 1981).

[119] In Noonan v. Granville-Smith, 532 F. Supp. 1007 (S. D. N. Y. 1982), *certificate of interlocutory appeal,* 535 F. Supp. 335 (S. D. N. Y. 1982), the court held that the Second Circuit's contribution holdings did survive.

[120] F. R. Civ. P. 14(a).

[121] Miller v. Hano, 8 F. R. D. 67, 71 (E. D. Pa. 1947) (third-party complaint under §11(f) by underwriters against officers and directors); Lyons v. Marrud, Inc., 46 F. R. D. 451 (S. D. N. Y. 1968) (third-party complaint under §11(f) by underwriters against selling stockholders). The majority rule is the same with respect to venue. Lyons v. Marrud, CCH Fed. Sec. L. Rep. ¶92,307 at 97,455 (S. D. N. Y. 1968); Black & Co., Inc. v. Nova Tech, Inc., 333 F. Supp. 468, 473 (D. Ore. 1971).

a §11 defendant's third-party complaint based on indemnification and breach of warranty and apparently contribution is not governed by the statute of limitations in the Securities Act.[122]

The Code is considerably more detailed than the present statutes:

So far as *indemnification* is concerned, it precludes nonacceleration solely because of the terms of an indemnification (or contribution) provision.[123] Instead (with the traditional exceptions for underwriters or the expenses of a successful defense, where the validity of indemnification is left to whatever may be the proper admixture of state and federal common law) the Code gives the Commission rulemaking authority to permit indemnification against Code liability generally "on consideration of such factors as the gains, losses, and conduct of the indemnitor and the indemnitee and the deterrent effect of the particular type of liability."[124] The same factors govern a court's determination "as a matter of Federal jurisprudence" when there is no rule.[125] The Commission may bring an action or intervene in any action to prevent unauthorized indemnification (or contribution).[126] And it may by rule require the filing of every pleading or motion that seeks indemnification.[127]

So far as *contribution* is concerned, the Code prefers the flexibility of today's British statute,[128] on which all three clauses of the following §1724(f)(2) are modeled:

To the extent consistent with section 1724(e)[129] —

(1) two or more persons liable in an action created by or based on a violation of this Code * * * may allocate liability among themselves by contract made either before or after liability is imposed; and

(2) to the extent that there is no such contract, and on consideration of the relative responsibility of each person for the loss incurred, the judgment in an action for contribution may —

(A) order any such person to pay to any other such person

---

[122] Metzger v. Breeze Corporations, Inc., 37 F. Supp. 693 (D. N. J. 1941); Lyons v. Marrud, Inc., CCH Fed. Sec. L. Rep. ¶92,307 at 97,456 (S. D. N. Y. 1968).

[123] §2003(b)(2).

[124] §1724(e).

[125] §1724(e)(3).

[126] §1819(k).

[127] §1728(a).

[128] Civil Liability (Contribution) Act 1978, 25 & 26 Eliz. 2, c. 47.

[129] This "reflects the fact, which is recognized by §1724(f)(2)(B), that contribution-indemnification is a continuum." 2 Code 801, Comment (1).

as much as is determined to be just and equitable by way of contribution;

(B) order that the contribution of any such person amount to a complete indemnity; or

(C) determine that any such person is not liable to make contribution,

except that no such person may be ordered to pay more under section 1724(f) than what his maximum liability would have been if he had been a defendant in the action giving rise to the action for contribution.[130]

Insurance is made enforceable by the Code "without regard to (A) any State law to the contrary, or (B) the identity of the person who pays the premium."[131] "Since insurance companies presumably will not insure against liability for egregious conduct, and since any statutory limitation on the kind of conduct that is insurable would invite litigation with respect to the scope of the insurance coverage, the effect of this section is that there is simply no limitation as a matter of either federal or state law. At the same time, nothing here overrides any limitation on the authority to write specified kinds of insurance as a matter of state insurance regulation. That is to say, the provision does not apply unless the insurance is in fact written."[132]

6. ATTORNEYS' FEES AND SECURITY FOR COSTS

If an officer's or director's right to look to the issuer for reimbursement of his litigation expenses is not altogether clear, what are his chances of being awarded his costs at the expense of the plaintiff in the principal action — or, better yet from his point of view, being secured against his costs in advance by the plaintiff's posting a surety bond?

In the absence of some statutory provision or rule of court, no advance security for costs may be required.[133] Under Rule 54(d) of the Federal Rules of Civil Procedure, costs are "allowed as of

---

[130]The "except" clause "is designed to assure against piercing the various limitations of liability." Id. at 802, Comment (4); see p. 1138 n. 150 supra.

[131]§1724(e)(5).

[132]2 Code 800-01, Comment (7).

[133]McClure v. Borne Chemical Co., Inc., 292 F. 2d 824, 836-37 (3d Cir. 1961), *cert. denied*, 368 U. S. 939. There may, however, be a *contractual* condition of security for costs. See Chabot v. Empire Trust Co., 301 F. 2d 458 (2d Cir. 1962). And F. R. Civ. P. 65(c) requires security from an applicant for a temporary restraining order or preliminary injunction.

course to the prevailing party unless the court otherwise directs."[134] But costs normally do not include attorneys' fees when there is no specific statutory provision or rule.[135] To this last proposition the courts have developed a number of exceptions:

(1) Under the "common fund" theory a plaintiff who has established a fund under the control of the court, classically in a stockholder's derivative or a class action, may recover his counsel fees from the fund.[136]

---

[134] The trial court has broad discretion with respect to the items of costs to be allowed. Fey v. Walston & Co., Inc. 493 F. 2d 1036, 1056 (7th Cir. 1974) (10b-5 churning case).

See also 28 U. S. C. §1912 (a Court of Appeals or the Supreme Court, when affirming a judgment, may give the prevailing party "just damages for his delay, and single or double costs"); F. R. App. P. 38 (to the same effect on a determination that an appeal is frivolous); Oscar Gruss & Son v. Lumbermens Mutual Casualty Co., 422 F. 2d 1278, 1285 (2d Cir. 1970).

The statutes in New York (Bus. Corp. Law §627) and a number of other states on security for costs in stockholders' derivative actions apply under the *Erie* doctrine to diversity cases in the federal courts. Cohen v. Beneficial Industrial Loan Corp., 337 U. S. 541 (1949). But those statutes, whether in the forum state or the state of incorporation, do not apply in federal question cases. McClure v. Borne Chemical Co., Inc., 292 F. 2d 824, 829-35 (3d Cir. 1961), *cert. denied,* 368 U. S. 939 (Rule 10b-5). Counts based on pendent jurisdiction are another matter unless amended out of the complaint. Lowey v. Vanderbilt, CCH Fed. Sec. L. Rep. ¶93,135 (S. D. N. Y. 1971). When a complaint is based on both federal and state law, "there should be no exaction of a joint undertaking covering all causes of action, but the requirement should be limited to those causes of action as to which the statute authorizes a bond." Fischman v. Raytheon Mfg. Co., 188 F. 2d 783, 789 (2d Cir. 1951); cf. Phelps v. Burnham, 327 F. 2d 812 (2d Cir. 1964); Lerman v. Tenney, 425 F. 2d 236 (2d Cir. 1970).

The inapplicability of state statutes on security to actions under the SEC statutes does not preclude application of the local court rules that exist (without limitation to stockholders' derivative actions) in some federal courts. But those rules are limited to "costs," which, as distinct from "expenses," usually involve a relatively small initial outlay. McClure v. Borne Chemical Co., supra, 292 F. 2d at 835; see, e. g., Leighton v. Paramount Pictures, Inc., 340 F. 2d 859, 861 (2d Cir. 1965), *cert. denied,* 381 U. S. 925 (court required $2000 bond of a "habitual *pro se* litigant whose claims were often conclusory and lacking in legal merit"); Competitive Associates, Inc. v. International Health Sciences, Inc., CCH Fed. Sec. L. Rep. ¶93,632 at 92,871-73 (S. D. N. Y. 1972) (court pretermitted question of propriety of costs under §11(e) by acting under local court rule).

[135] Alyeska Pipeline Service Co. v. Wilderness Society, 421 U. S. 240 (1975). This "American rule" is "unknown in the rest of the world." Ehrenzweig, Reimbursement of Counsel Fees and the Great Society, 54 Calif. L. Rev. 792, 793 (1966). And Professor Dawson concludes: "No adequate historical explanation for the American departure has ever been advanced, and in any event, the reasons commonly given — the spirit of individualism in frontier societies, the conception in earlier times of lawsuits as sporting contests, and the widespread hostility toward lawyers — are not persuasive now." Dawson, Lawyers and Involuntary Clients: Attorney Fees from Funds, 87 Harv. L. Rev. 1597, 1598 (1974).

[136] Trustees v. Greenough, 105 U. S. 527, 532 (1882).

(2) This gradually developed into a broader "common benefit" theory. As the Supreme Court put it in a case we have encountered in connection with enforcement of the proxy rules:

MILLS v. ELECTRIC AUTO-LITE CO.
Supreme Court of the United States, 1970
396 U. S. 375

Mr. Justice Harlan delivered the opinion of the court.
[The facts and the earlier parts of the opinion are set out supra p. 1109.]

* * *

* * * the specific provisions in §§9(e) and 18(a) should not be read as denying to the courts the power to award counsel fees in suits under other sections of the Act when circumstances make such an award appropriate, any more than the express creation by those sections of private liabilities negates the possibility of an implied right of action under §14(a). * * *

While the general American rule is that attorneys' fees are not ordinarily recoverable as costs, both the courts and Congress have developed exceptions to this rule for situations in which overriding considerations indicate the need for such recovery. A primary judge-created exception has been to award expenses where a plaintiff has successfully maintained a suit, usually on behalf of a class, that benefits a group of others in the same manner as himself. * * * This suit presents such a situation. The dissemination of misleading proxy solicitations was a "deceit practiced on the stockholders as a group," *J. I. Case Co.* v. *Borak*, 377 U. S., at 432, and the expenses of petitioners' lawsuit have been incurred for the benefit of the corporation and the other shareholders.

The fact that this suit has not yet produced, and may never produce, a monetary recovery from which the fees could be paid does not preclude an award based on this rationale. * * *

Other cases have departed further from the traditional metes and bounds of the doctrine, to permit reimbursement in cases where the litigation has conferred a substantial benefit on the members of an ascertainable class, and where the court's jurisdiction over the subject matter of the suit makes possible an award that will operate to spread the costs proportionately among them. This development has been most pronounced in shareholders' derivative actions, where the courts increasingly have recognized that the expenses incurred by one shareholder in the vindication of a corporate right of action can be spread among all shareholders through an award against the corporation, regardless of whether an actual money recovery has been obtained in the corporation's favor. For example, awards have been sustained in suits by stockholders complaining that shares of their corporation had been issued wrongfully for an inadequate consideration. * * *

In many of these instances the benefit conferred is capable of expression in monetary terms, if only by estimating the increase in market value of the shares attributable to the successful litigation. However, an increasing number of lower courts have acknowledged that a corporation may receive a "substantial benefit" from a derivative suit, justifying an award of counsel fees, regardless of whether the benefit is pecuniary in nature. * * *

*   *   *

MR. JUSTICE BLACK, concurring in part and dissenting in part. * * * The courts are interpreters, not creators, of legal rights to recover and if there is a need for recovery of attorneys' fees to effectuate the policies of the Act here involved, that need should in my judgment be met by Congress, not by this Court.

———————

Five years after *Mills*[137] the Supreme Court held in the *Alyeska*

---

[137] With the majority opinion see also Sprague v. Ticonic National Bank, 307 U. S. 161 (1939); Hall v. Cole, 412 U. S. 1 (1973); Wolf v. Frank, 477 F. 2d 467, 480 (5th Cir. 1973), *cert. denied,* 414 U. S. 975 (Rule 10b-5); Ramey v. Cincinnati Enquirer, Inc., 508 F. 2d 1188, 1194-96 (6th Cir. 1974), *cert. denied,* 422 U. S. 1048 (Rule 10b-5 and §14(a)); Kopet v. Esquire Realty Co., 523 F. 2d 1005 (2d Cir. 1975) (award in a §12(1) action apart from §11(e), infra p. 1212).

But cf. Gerstle v. Gamble-Skogmo, Inc., 478 F. 2d 1281, 1308-10 (2d Cir. 1973) (court refused to extend *Mills* so as to charge counsel fees to defendant even when a fund *was* recovered); Isaacs Bros. v. Hibernia Bank, 481 F. 2d 1168, 1170 (9th Cir. 1973) (no substantial class benefit); Grace v. Ludwig, 484 F. 2d 1262, 1267-70 (2d Cir. 1973), *cert. denied,* 416 U. S. 905 (no fee for intervention in SEC proceeding under 1940 Act on behalf of minority stockholders); Wechsler v. Southeastern Properties, Inc., 506 F. 2d 631 (2d Cir. 1974) (private action based on a state proceeding); SEC v. Capital Counsellors, Inc., 512 F. 2d 654 (2d Cir. 1975) (unsuccessfully resisting a broker-dealer receivership); Bender v. Crown, 551 F. 2d 169 (7th Cir. 1977); Silberman v. Bogle, 683 F. 2d 62 (3d Cir. 1982).

See generally Dawson, Lawyers and Involuntary Clients in Public Interest Litigation, 88 Harv. L. Rev. 849, 867-70 (1975).

The result in *Mills* on remand was anticlimactic: the District Court found

Pipeline case[138] that there was no inherent authority under federal law to award fees on any "private attorney general" theory — which the *Mills* case seemed to approach when it shifted from "common benefit" language to talk of "corporate therapeutics" that "furnish a benefit to *all* shareholders."[139] But the Court cited *Mills* with approval.[140]

(3) It "has long been established that even under the American common-law rule attorney's fees may be awarded against a party who has proceeded in bad faith."[141] But the courts are split on two important questions: whether the presence of a claim that is at least colorable precludes a finding of bad faith,[142] and whether pre-litigation conduct (acts forming the basis of the lawsuit as distinct from conduct during the litigation) may supply the necessary "bad faith."[143]

So far as the *express* liabilities are concerned, Congress did supply variant provisions on costs, including counsel fees:

In 1934 the fear of "strike suits"[144] led Congress to amend §11(e) of the Securities Act to provide both for security and for the award of counsel fees:

> In any suit under this or any other section of this title the court may, in its discretion, require an undertaking for the payment of

---

the exchange to be unfair and awarded damages that with prejudgment interest came to almost $2 million but the Court of Appeals reversed. Mills v. Electric Auto-Lite Co., 552 F. 2d 1239 (7th Cir. 1977), *cert. denied*, 434 U. S. 922.

138 Alyeska Pipeline Service Co. v. Wilderness Society, 421 U. S. 240, 262 (1975).

139 396 U. S. at 396 (italics are supplied).

140 421 U. S. at 258.

141 Christiansburg Garment Co. v. Equal Employment Opportunity Commission, 434 U. S. 412, 419 (1978); see also Hall v. Cole, 412 U. S. 1, 5 (1973) (action "in bad faith, vexatiously, wantonly, or for oppressive reasons"); Alyeska Pipeline Service Co. v. Wilderness Society, 421 U. S. 240, 258-59 (1975); Kahan v. Rosenstiel, 424 F. 2d 161, 167 (3d Cir. 1970), *cert. denied* sub nom. Glen Alden Corp. v. Kahan, 398 U. S. 950 (10b-5 case involving "a willful and persistent 'defiance of the law' ").

142 *Yes:* Browning Debenture Holders Committee v. DASA Corp., 560 F. 2d 1078, 1088 (2d Cir. 1977). *Contra:* Lipsig v. National Student Marketing Corp., 663 F. 2d 178, 182 (D. C. Cir. 1980).

143 *Yes:* Adams v. Standard Knitting Mills, Inc., CCH Fed. Sec. L. Rep. ¶95,713 (E. D. Tenn. 1976); cf. Tse Zung Yao v. W. E. Hutton & Co., CCH Fed. Sec. L. Rep. ¶96,039 (S. D. N. Y. 1977) (but not in 10b-5 cases). *Contra:* Straub v. Vaisman & Co., Inc., 540 F. 2d 591, 599 (3d Cir. 1976) (award of fees on basis of underlying acts would amount to punitive damages); Huddleston v. Herman & McLean, 640 F. 2d 534, 559-60 (5th Cir. 1981), *aff'd in part and rev'd in part on other grounds* sub nom. Herman & MacLean v. Huddleston, 103 S. Ct. 683 (1983).

144 See Linchuck v. Cooper, 43 F. R. D. 382, 384 (S. D. N. Y. 1967).

the costs of such suit, including reasonable attorney's fees, and if judgment shall be rendered against a party litigant, upon the motion of the other party litigant, such costs may be assessed in favor of such party litigant (whether or not such undertaking has been required) if the court believes the suit or the defense to have been without merit, in an amount sufficient to reimburse him for the reasonable expenses incurred by him, in connection with such suit, such costs to be taxed in the manner usually provided for taxing of costs in the court in which the suit was heard.[145]

Abbreviated versions of the same provision appear in §9(e) of the Exchange Act, the section creating civil liability for manipulation, as well as §18 of that Act and the similar sections in the Holding Company and Trust Indenture Acts creating civil liabilities for false statements filed with the Commission, but not in the provisions on recovery of insiders' short-term trading profits or the voidability provisions like §29(b) of the Exchange Act. The language of §§9(e) and 18(a) of the Exchange Act (the latter of which is incorporated by reference into §16(a) of the Holding Company Act) is simply this:

> In any such suit the court may, in its discretion, require an undertaking for the payment of the costs of such suit, and assess reasonable costs, including reasonable attorneys' fees, against either party litigant.

The Senate Committee stated in its report on the 1934 bill that "bad faith" was the intended test.[146] But the specific reference to the "merit" of the action that Congress wrote into §11 of the Securities Act by amendment in 1934 simultaneously with the passage of the Exchange Act was omitted from the latter statute, only to reappear in strengthened form in §323(a) of the Trust Indenture Act. That section adds to the language of §18(a) of the Exchange Act the clause: "having due regard to the merits and good faith of the suit or defense."[147]

---

[145] See Douglas and Bates, The Federal Securities Act of 1933, 43 Yale L. J. 171, 210, 215 (1933).

[146] S. Rep. No. 792, 73d Cong., 2d Sess. (1934) 17-18. But the cases attack the "bad faith" rubric with varying prose. Jackson v. Oppenheim, 533 F. 2d 826, 831 (2d Cir. 1976) (whether claim is "frivolous or brought in bad faith"); Driscoll v. Oppenheimer & Co., Inc., 500 F. Supp. 174 (N. D. Ill. 1980) ("a colorable basis" for claims precludes "bad faith"); Weil v. Investment/Indicators, Research & Management, Inc., 647 F. 2d 18, 22 (9th Cir. 1981) (whether claim "borders on the frivolous"); Junker v. Crory, 650 F. 2d 1349, 1364 n. 20 (5th Cir. 1981) (whether defense was "without merit").

[147] Cf. Trust Ind. Act §315(e); Browning Debenture Holders' Committee v. DASA Corp., 560 F. 2d 1078, 1088 (2d Cir. 1977), *on remand,* 81 F. R. D.

A number of observations on this kaleidoscope:

(1) On the one hand, the courts' creation of implied actions has not persuaded them to imply a right to counsel fees by analogy to the express provisions on fees.[148] On the other hand, the presence of §§9(e) and 18(a) has not prevented the award of fees under §16(b).[149] But there, of course, the analogy is to the production of a fund in a stockholder's derivative action.[150]

(2) The desire to escape the double danger of paying counsel fees and posting security was yet another reason for buyers with complaints to rush to Rule 10b-5 in the face of their express remedies under §§11 and 12(2).[151]

(3) *Query* whether §11(e) applies to actions under §17(a) on the assumption that such actions are possible.[152]

(4) Although §11(e) contains no standards with respect to requiring security and the 1934 Act provisions contain no standards at all, the courts have applied a basically "bad faith" standard throughout.[153]

(5) All the provisions, though even-handed so far as assessment of costs is concerned, favor defendants in that they cannot be required to post security regardless of how *mala fide* their defense may be.

(6) Perhaps because of the readiness with which the plaintiff's motives are attacked, at least in the case of stockholders' suits,[154] the judicial attitude toward requiring plaintiffs to post security for costs under these statutory provisions seems to be on the chary

---

407 (S. D. N. Y. 1978). Presumably all these provisions yield in the case of "a person who makes affidavit that he is unable to pay * * * costs or give security therefor." 28 U. S. C. §1915(a).

[148] McClure v. Borne Chemical Co., Inc., 292 F. 2d 824, 836-37 (3d Cir. 1961), *cert. denied*, 368 U. S. 939; Van Alen v. Dominick & Dominick, 560 F. 2d 547, 553-54 (2d Cir. 1977).

[149] Mills v. Electric Auto-Lite Co., 396 U. S. 375, 390-91 (1970), set out *supra* p. 1210, at p. 1210.

[150] See Smolowe v. Delendo Corp., 136 F. 2d 231, 241 (2d Cir. 1963), *cert. denied*, 320 U. S. 751.

[151] In 10b-5 and other implied liability cases the defendant (and, of course, the plaintiff if he wins) should not overlook the possibility of getting counsel fees under the blue sky law (the Uniform Securities Act is silent) or some other state statute. Compare Young v. Taylor, 466 F. 2d 1329, 1338 (10th Cir. 1972), with Hail v. Heyman-Christiansen, Inc., 536 F. 2d 908 (10th Cir. 1976).

[152] See pp. 1148-50 *supra*. The court apparently *assumed* an affirmative answer in Klein v. Shields & Co., 470 F. 2d 1344, 1347-48 (2d Cir. 1972); see also Ruebe v. Pharmacodynamics, Inc., 348 F. Supp. 900, 916 (E. D. Pa. 1972).

[153] See n. 146 *supra*.

[154] See McClure v. Borne Chemical Co., Inc., 292 F. 2d 824, 837 n. 13 (3d Cir. 1961), *cert. denied*, 368 U. S. 939.

side.[155] On the analogy of the summary judgment procedure under Rule 56 of the Federal Rules of Civil Procedure, there must be a substantial showing.[156] The small amount of the plaintiff's holdings does not establish bad faith *per se*.[157] And the mere failure to present sufficient evidence to support the claims made does not itself warrant a determination of frivolousness.[158]

On the other side of the coin, plaintiffs have been ordered to post security on a variety of grounds: the "large amount of work necessary in the defense of the actions by the numerous defendants," when considered together with the filing of defendants' affidavits containing "such detailed facts as tend strongly to refute the allegations in the amended complaints as to the untrue statements and omissions in the Registration Statement";[159] the fact that the plaintiff's affidavits "do not dispel the notion that they knew of the alleged misleading statements and the like long before they presently assert";[160] naming three defendants as co-conspirators on the basis solely of hearsay and rumor;[161] and the small value of the plaintiff's shares ($800) in relation to the potential damages ($5 million), when considered together with the plaintiff's apparent attempt to reargue matters already decided in a prior litigation that had caused the defendant much expense.[162] There is also precedent for assessing substantial costs against a *defendant* whose defense was without merit and not made in good faith.[163]

---

[155] Ibid.; see also, e. g., Can-Am Petroleum Co. v. Beck, 331 F. 2d 371, 374 (10th Cir. 1964); Oil & Gas Income, Inc., v. Woods Exploration & Producing Co., Inc., 362 F. 2d 309 (5th Cir. 1966), *on later appeal* sub nom. Oil & Gas Income, Inc. v. Trotter, 395 F. 2d 753 (5th Cir. 1968); Klein v. Shields & Co., 470 F. 2d 1344, 1348 (2d Cir. 1972); Rucker v. Lousiana Co., Inc., 496 F. 2d 850, 853 (8th Cir. 1974); Nemeroff v. Abelson, 620 F. 2d 339 (2d Cir. 1980).

[156] Stella v. Kaiser, 83 F. Supp. 431 (S. D. N. Y. 1949).

[157] Ibid.

[158] Aid Auto Stores, Inc. v. Cannon, 525 F. 2d 468, 471 (2d Cir. *per curiam* 1975).

[159] Montague v. Electronic Corp. of America, 76 F. Supp. 933, 936 (S. D. N. Y. 1948).

[160] Fischman v. Raytheon Mfg. Co., 9 F. R. D. 707, 711 (S. D. N. Y. 1949). But on appeal the court held that the bond requirement was premature: "Passing the question whether the judge's 'feeling' and 'notion' about the knowledge of the preferred stockholders sufficed to show a lack of 'merit,' we think that, as amendment of the complaint was permitted, consideration of whether a bond should be exacted must be postponed until the amended complaint has been filed." Id., 188 F. 2d 783, 788-89 (2d Cir. 1951).

[161] Miller v. Schweikart, 413 F. Supp. 1059 (S. D. N. Y. 1976).

[162] Dabney v. Alleghany Corp., 164 F. Supp. 28, 33 (S. D. N. Y. 1958).

[163] Stadia Oil & Uranium Co. v. Wheelis, 251 F. 2d 269, 277 (10th Cir. 1957).

The Code's provision on costs applies to all actions "created or based on a violation of" the Code (including any that might be implied under the Code's standards); extends equally to plaintiffs and defendants with respect to security as well as assessment of costs; and applies "on a finding that the action or defenses (as the case may be) are frivolous, vexatious, or brought or advanced in bad faith."[164]

---

[164]§1723(d).

CHAPTER 11

THE SEC LAWYER

In varying degrees the Commission and the securities Bar have been rubbing each other on a number of fronts in recent years:

A. THE SEC LAWYER'S ROLE

The question whether a lawyer may have a duty not only to resign but also to "turn his client in" when he is aware of the client's intention to commit an illegal act became the subject of a *cause célèbre* (with inconclusive results) in the 1970s:

SECURITIES AND EXCHANGE COMMISSION v.
NATIONAL STUDENT MARKETING CORP.
United States District Court for the District of Columbia, 1978
457 F. Supp. 682

PARKER, District Judge.

This opinion covers the final act in a civil proceeding brought by the Securities and Exchange Commission (Commission or SEC) seeking injunctive sanctions against numerous defendants as a result of their participation in alleged securities laws violations relating to the National Student Marketing Corporation (NSMC) securities fraud scheme. The original defendants included the corporation and certain of its officers and directors; the accounting firm of Peat, Marwick, Mitchell & Co. (Peat Marwick) and two of its partners; several officers and directors of Interstate National Corporation (Interstate); the law firm of White & Case and one of its partners; and the law firm of Lord, Bissell & Brook (LBB) and two of its partners. The majority of these defendants are not now before the Court. As discovery progressed during the pre-trial stages of this litigation, NSMC and other principal defendants consented to the entry of final judgments of permanent injunction or otherwise reached a resolution of the charges against them.[a] The only defendants remaining are Lord, Bissell & Brook; its two partners, Max E. Meyer and Louis F. Schauer; and Cameron Brown, a former president and director of Interstate, and presently a director of and consultant to NSMC.

The focal point of the Commission's charges against these defendants is the corporate merger of Interstate with NSMC on October 31, 1969. The principal question presented is whether the defendants violated or aided and abetted the violation of the anti-fraud provisions of the federal securities laws in two instances: (1) consummation of the NSMC merger; and (2) the immediately following sale of newly acquired NSMC stock by former Interstate principals, including certain of the defendants. These transactions are alleged to have occurred despite the prior receipt by the defendants of information which revealed that NSMC's interim financial statements, used in securing shareholder approval of the merger and available to the investing public generally, were grossly inaccurate and failed to show the true condition of the corporation. The information was included in a comfort letter prepared by NSMC's accounts [*sic:* accountants]. The Commission contends that these violations demonstrate a reasonable likelihood of future misconduct by the defendants, thereby justifying the requested permanent injunctive relief.

The matter was tried without a jury. After reviewing the extensive record in this case, the Court concludes, for the reasons stated below, that while each of the defendants violated the securities laws in specific instances, the Commission has not fulfilled its obligation of demonstrating a reasonable likelihood that they will do so in the future. Accordingly, the Commission's request for injunctive relief must be denied.

*　　*　　*

I. BACKGROUND

A. THE COMPANIES

National Student Marketing Corporation was incorporated in

C. 11A　[a] ED.: In SEC v. National Student Marketing Corp., Litig. Rel. 7902, 12 SEC Dock. 336 (D. D. C. 1977), Epley, the White & Case partner, consented to a permanent injunction that required him to comply with applicable procedures of his firm, and he also agreed not to practice before the Commission for 180 days. The firm was not enjoined, but it stipulated that it would comply with the SEC laws in any future representation of NSMC and undertook to adopt and maintain procedures in connection with its representation of clients in matters affecting the SEC statutes.

the District of Columbia in 1966. The company enjoyed early prosperity; it grew rapidly and experienced a steady increase in assets, sales and earnings. * * * White & Case served as its outside legal counsel, with Marion J. Epley, III, as the partner immediately in charge of the firm's representation. Peat Marwick served as its outside accountant.

Interstate National Corporation, a Nevada corporation, was an insurance holding company. Its principal assets were several wholly-owned subsidiary insurance companies. The company's common stock was traded on the over-the-counter market and owned by approximately 1200 shareholders. Cameron Brown was president, chief executive officer, principal shareholder and a director of the company. Other Interstate principals and directors included Robert P. Tate, chairman of the board; William J. Bach, general counsel; Paul E. Allison, secretary; Louis W. Biegler; and Max E. Meyer. Between board meetings, all management authority was delegated to an executive committee composed of Brown, Tate, Bach, Allison and Biegler. Max E. Meyer, a director and shareholder, was a partner in the Chicago law firm of Lord, Bissell & Brook, which had long represented Interstate and served as its outside legal counsel in all matters relating to the merger of the corporation with NSMC. Meyer, a personal friend and legal advisor to Cameron Brown, served as the contact partner for the Interstate account and was otherwise in overall charge of his firm's representation. Another partner of the firm, Louis F. Schauer, was also involved in the merger transaction due to his experience in corporate and securities law. Peat Marwick served as Interstate's outside accountant during the period in question.

B.   THE MERGER NEGOTIATIONS

National Student Marketing Corporation developed a reputation for having a unique and successful marketing network for selling its own and other products to college and high school students. Commencing in 1969, it undertook a highly active program to acquire companies specializing in selling goods and services to students. It was in this connection that NSMC first approached representatives of Interstate.

Initially, NSMC discussed the possibility of acquiring an Interstate subsidiary that specialized in selling insurance to students. After Interstate indicated an unwillingness to dispose of a single subsidiary, NSMC expressed interest in acquiring its entire insurance holding company operation. Cortes W. Randell, NSMC's president and chief executive officer, proposed a merger of the two corporations, offering one share of NSMC stock for every two shares of Interstate stock.

On June 10, 1969, NSMC representatives, including Randell and James F. Joy, a senior vice president and finance committee member, were invited before the Interstate directors to make a presentation concerning the proposed merger. The directors were provided with NSMC's 1968 annual report and its financial report for the first half of 1969. Randell discussed the company's acquisition program, reviewed several pending corporate acquisition commitments, and made certain earnings predictions for the fiscal year ending August 31, 1969. He also increased the earlier offer to two shares of NSMC common for every three shares of Interstate common. When certain Interstate directors expressed a desire to sell a portion of the NSMC stock which they expected to acquire in the merger, Randell responded that a registered public offering was planned for the fall of 1969, at which time the former Interstate shareholders could sell up to 25 percent of their shares.[6] Very few questions were asked by Randell or Joy about the business and financial affairs of Interstate, an aspect of the meeting which surprised several of Interstate's representatives.

This meeting resulted in an agreement in principle for the merger. Essentially identical press releases were then issued by the companies, announcing the agreed upon stock exchange ratio, the estimated value of the transaction as $37 million based on the current market value of NSMC stock, and the fact that the transaction represented approximately a 100 percent premium for the Interstate shares based on their market value at the time. Representations were also made in the releases as to NSMC's earnings for the first six months of fiscal 1969, which ended February 28, 1969.

*   *   *

The Agreement also provided several conditions precedent to the obligations of the two corporations to consummate the merger. One required the receipt by NSMC of an opinion letter from Interstate's counsel LBB to the effect, *inter alia*, that Interstate had taken all actions and procedures required of it by law and that all transactions in connection with the merger had been duly and

---

[6] Because of an accounting method in use in 1969, a company was permitted to "pool" the earnings of an acquired company with the earnings of the parent as though the companies had always operated together. However, in order for NSMC to take advantage of this retroactive pooling, no more than 25 percent of the shares received in the merger exchange could be sold during the first year.

validly taken, to the best knowledge of counsel, in full compliance with applicable law; a similar opinion letter was required to be delivered from NSMC's counsel to Interstate. Another condition was the receipt by each company of a "comfort letter" from the other's independent public accountants. Each letter was required to state: (1) that the accountants had no reason to believe that the unaudited interim financial statements for the company in question were not prepared in accordance with accounting principles and practices consistent with those used in the previous year-end audited financials; (2) that they had no reason to believe that any material adjustments in those financials were required in order fairly to present the results of operations of the company; and (3) that the company had experienced no material adverse change in its financial position or results of operations from the period covered by its interim financial statement up to five business days prior to the effective date of the merger. Although setting forth these specific conditions to consummation of the merger, the final paragraph of the Agreement also provided that:

> Anything herein to the contrary notwithstanding and notwithstanding any stockholder vote of approval of this Agreement and the merger provided herein, this Agreement may be terminated and abandoned by mutual consent of the Boards of Directors of NSMC and Interstate at any time prior to the Effective Date and the Board of Directors of any party may waive any of the conditions to the obligations of such party under this Agreement.

*   *   *

Both NSMC and Interstate utilized proxy statements and notices of special stockholder meetings to secure shareholder approval of the proposed merger. Interstate's materials included a copy of the Merger Agreement and NSMC's Proxy Statement; the latter contained NSMC's financial statements for the fiscal year ended August 31, 1968, and the nine-month interim financial statement for the period ending May 31, 1969. Interstate shareholders were urged to study the NSMC Proxy Statement. * * *

In mid-October, Peat Marwick began drafting the comfort letter concerning NSMC's unaudited interim financials for the nine-month period ended May 31, 1969. As issued by NSMC, those financials had reflected a profit of approximately $700,000.

Soon after beginning work on the comfort letter, Peat Marwick representatives determined that certain adjustments were required

1222 THE SEC LAWYER [Ch. 11A

with respect to the interim financials. Specifically, the accountants proposed that a $500,000 adjustment to deferred costs, a $300,000 write-off of unbilled receivables, and an $84,000 adjustment to paid-in capital be made retroactive to May 31 and be reflected in the comfort letter delivered to Interstate. Such adjustments would have caused NSMC to show a loss for the nine-month period ended May 31, 1969, and the company as it existed on May 31 would have broken even for fiscal 1969. Although Peat Marwick discussed the proposed adjustments with representatives of NSMC, neither the accountants nor NSMC informed Interstate of the adjustments prior to the closing. A draft of the comfort letter, with the adjustments, was completed on October 30 and on the next day, the morning of the closing, it was discussed among senior partners of Peat Marwick.

C. THE CLOSING AND RECEIPT OF THE COMFORT LETTER

The closing meeting for the merger was scheduled at 2 P. M. on Friday, October 31, at the New York offices of White & Case. Brown, Meyer and Schauer were present in addition to Interstate directors Bach, Allison and Tate. The representatives of NSMC included Randell, Joy, John G. Davies, their attorney Epley and other White & Case associates.

Although Schauer had had an opportunity to review most of the merger documents at White & Case on the previous day, the comfort letter had not been delivered. When he arrived at White & Case on the morning of the merger, the letter was still not available, but he was informed by a representative of the firm that it was expected to arrive at any moment.

The meeting proceeded. When the letter had not arrived by approximately 2:15 P.M., Epley telephoned Peat Marwick's Washington office to inquire about it. Anthony M. Natelli, the partner in charge, thereupon dictated in Epley's secretary a letter which provided in part:

> [N]othing has come to our attention which caused us to believe that:
>
> 1. The National Student Marketing Corporation's unaudited consolidated financial statements as of and for the nine months ended May 31, 1969:
>
> * * *
>
> b. Would require any material adjustments for a fair and reasonable presentation of the information shown except with

respect to consolidated financial statements of National Student Marketing Corporation and consolidated subsidiaries as they existed at May 31, 1969 and for the nine months then ended, our examination in connection with the year ended August 31, 1969 which is still in process, disclosed the following significant adjustments which in our opinion should be reflected retroactive to May 31, 1969:

1.   In adjusting the amortization of deferred costs at May 31, 1969, to eliminate therefrom all costs for programs substantially completed or which commenced 12 months or more prior, an adjustment of $500,000 was required. Upon analysis of the retroactive effect of this adjustment, it appears that the entire amount could be determined applicable to the period prior to May 31, 1969.

2.   In August 1969 management wrote off receivables in amounts of $300,000. It appears that the uncollectibility of these receivables could have been determined at May 31, 1969 and such charge off should have been reflected as of that date.

3.   Acquisition costs in the amount of $84,000 for proposed acquisitions which the Company decided not to pursue were transferred from additional paid-in capital to general and administrative expenses. In our opinion, these should have been so transferred as of May 31, 1969.

*   *   *

Epley delivered one copy of the typed letter to the conference room where the closing was taking place. Epley then returned to his office.

Schauer was the first to read the unsigned letter. He then handed it to Cameron Brown, advising him to read it. Although there is some dispute as to which of the Interstate representatives actually read the letter, at least Brown and Meyer did so after Schauer. They asked Randell and Joy a number of questions relating to the nature and effect of the adjustments. The NSMC officers gave assurances that the adjustments would have no significant effect on the predicted year-end earnings of NSMC and that a substantial portion of the $500,000 adjustments to deferred costs would be recovered. Moreover, they indicated that NSMC's year-end audit for fiscal 1969 had been completed by Peat Marwick, would be published in a couple of weeks, and would demonstrate that NSMC itself had made each of the adjustments for its fourth quarter. The comfort letter, they explained, simply determined that those adjustments should be reflected in the third quarter ended May 31, 1969, rather than the final quarter of NSMC's fiscal year. Randell and Joy indicated that while NSMC disagreed with what they felt was a tightening up of its accounting practices, everything requested by Peat Marwick to "clean up" its books had been undertaken.

At the conclusion of this discussion, certain of the Interstate representatives, including at least Brown, Schauer and Meyer, conferred privately to consider their alternatives in light of the apparent nonconformity of the comfort letter with the requirements of the Merger Agreement. Although they considered the letter a serious matter and the adjustments as significant and important, they were nonetheless under some pressure to determine a course of action promptly since there was a 4 p.m. filing deadline if the closing were to be consummated as scheduled on October 31. Among the alternatives considered were: (1) delaying or postponing the closing, either to secure more information or to resolicit the shareholders with corrected financials; (2) closing the merger; or (3) calling it off completely.

The consensus of the directors was that there was no need to delay the closing. The comfort letter contained all relevant information and in light of the explanations given by Randell and Joy, they already had sufficient information upon which to make a decision. Any delay for the purpose of resoliciting the shareholders was considered impractical because it would require the use of year-end figures instead of the stale nine-month interim financials. Such a requirement would make it impossible to resolicit shareholder approval before the merger upset date of November 28, 1969, and would cause either the complete abandonment of the merger or its renegotiation on terms possibly far less favorable to Interstate. The director also recognized that delay or abandonment of the merger would result in a decline in the stock of both companies, thereby harming the shareholders and possibly subjecting the directors to lawsuits based on their failure to close the merger. The Interstate representatives decided to proceed with the closing. They did, however, solicit and receive further assurances from the NSMC representatives that the stated adjustments were the only ones to be made to the company's financial statements and that 1969 earnings would be as predicted. When asked by Brown whether the closing could proceed on the basis of an unsigned comfort letter, Meyer responded that if a White & Case partner assured them that this was in fact the comfort letter and that a signed copy would be forthcoming from Peat Marwick, they could close. Epley gave this assurance. Meyer then announced that Interstate was prepared to proceed, the closing was consummated, and a previously arranged telephone call was made which resulted in the filing of the Articles of Merger at the Office of the Recorder of Deeds of the District of Columbia. * * * The closing was solemnized with a toast of warm champagne.

Unknown to the Interstate group, several telephone conversations relating to the substance of the comfort letter occurred on the afternoon of the closing between Peat Marwick representatives and Epley. The accountants were concerned with the propriety of proceeding with the closing in light of the adjustments to NSMC's nine-month financials. One such conversation occurred after Epley delivered the unsigned letter to the Interstate participants but before the merger had been consummated. At that time Epley was told that an additional paragraph would be added in order to characterize the adjustments. The paragraph recited that with the noted adjustments properly made, NSMC's unaudited consolidated statement for the nine-month period would not reflect a profit as had been indicated but rather a net loss, and the consolidated operations of NSMC as they existed on May 31, 1969, would show a break-even as to net earnings for the year ended August 31, 1969. Epley had the additional paragraph typed out, but failed to inform or disclose this change to Interstate. In a second conversation, after the closing was completed and the Interstate representatives had departed, Epley was informed of still another proposed addition, namely, a paragraph urging resolicitation of both companies' shareholders and disclosure of NSMC's corrected nine-month financials prior to closing. To this, he responded that the deal was closed and the letter was not needed. Peat Marwick nonetheless advised Epley that the letter would be delivered and that its counsel was considering whether further action should be taken by the firm.

The final written draft of the comfort letter arrived at White & Case late that afternoon. Peat Marwick believed that Interstate had been informed and was aware of the conversations between its representatives and Epley and of its concern about the adjustments. Because of this belief and especially since the merger had been closed without benefit of the completed letter, Peat Marwick's counsel perceived no obligation to do anything further about the merger. Nonetheless, a signed copy of the final letter was sent to each board member of the two companies, presumably in an effort to underline the accountants' concern about consummation of the merger without shareholder resolicitation.

The signed comfort letter was delivered to the Interstate offices on Monday, November 3. It was first seen and read by Donald Jeffers, Interstate's chief financial officer. He had not been present at the October 31 closing or informed of the adjustments to the interim financials. Concerned, he contacted Brown immediately and read the letter to him. Since a meeting with other Interstate principals was scheduled for the next morning the letter was added to the other matters to be discussed.

The signed letter was virtually identical to the unsigned version delivered at the closing, except for the addition of the following two paragraphs:

> Your attention is called, however, to the fact that if the afore-mentioned adjustments had been made at May 31, 1969 the un-audited consolidated statement of earnings of National Student Marketing Corporation would have shown a net loss of approximately $80,000. It is presently estimated that the consolidated operations of the company as it existed at May 31, 1969 will be approximately a break-even as to net earnings for the year ended August 31, 1969.
>
> In view of the above mentioned facts, we believe the companies should consider submitting corrected interim unaudited financial information to the shareholders prior to proceeding with the closing.

The only other change was the reduction in the write-off to receivables from $300,000 to $200,000, making total negative adjustments to NSMC's nine-month financials in the amount of $784,000.

At the meeting the following day, the matter was fully discussed by the former Interstate principals. * * *

On that afternoon, Schauer contacted Epley by telephone. Epley stated that he had not known of the additional paragraphs until after the closing. He added that in any case the additions did not expand upon the contents of the earlier unsigned letter; the "break-even" paragraph simply reflected the results of an arithmetic computation of the effects of the adjustments, and the "resolicitation" paragraph was gratuitous and a matter for lawyers, not accountants. While Schauer disagreed, Epley again responded that the additional paragraphs made no difference and that NSMC regarded the deal as closed.

Brown and Jeffers fared no better with Peat Marwick. That company's representative, Cormick L. Breslin, met briefly with several Interstate representatives on November 4. He could give no information concerning the matter other than that he had not seen a similar letter before and thought it was rather unusual. Later, when contacted again by Brown, Breslin stated that the letter would have to speak for itself and his company would provide no additional information, comment or advice.

Over the next several days the Interstate directors continued their discussion of the matter, consulting frequently with their counsel, Meyer and Schauer. As they viewed it, the available options were to attempt to undo the merger, either permanently or until the shareholders could be resolicited, or to leave things as they were. The attorneys indicated that rescission would be impractical, if not impossible, since Interstate no longer existed and NSMC had indicated that it would oppose any effort to undo the merger. Meanwhile, the market value of NSMC stock continued to increase, and the directors noted that any action on their part to undo the merger would most likely adversely affect its price. By the end of the week, the decision was made to abstain from any action. Thereafter, Brown issued a memorandum to all Interstate employees announcing completion of the merger. No effort was ever made by any of the defendants to disclose the contents of the comfort letter to the former shareholders of Interstate, the SEC or to the public in general.

D. THE STOCK SALES

Early in the negotiations the principal Interstate shareholders understood that they would be able to sell a portion of the NSMC stock received in the merger through a public offering planned for the fall of 1969. Various shareholders, including Brown, Tate, Allison, Bach and Meyer, intended to profit by this opportunity and sell up to 25 percent of their newly acquired stock. The opportunity did not materialize, however, because within several days of the merger the NSMC operating committee decided to postpone the registration. Brown was advised that the shareholders could still sell up to 25 percent of their shares in a private placement under SEC Rule 133.[b] If they so decided, he was urged to have all use the same broker to avoid upsetting the market for the stock.

Brown then contacted Henry Meers, a personal friend and a partner in the White Weld brokerage firm, advised him of their desire to sell and inquired as to whether he could handle the transaction. * * *

Two matters of significance to the stock sales occurred on the day of the closing. First, certain of the Interstate principals, including Brown, were informed that the amount of NSMC shares they could sell following the merger was limited due to a restriction on

---

[b] ED.: On this former "no sale rule" with respect to mergers and the like, see p. 316 supra.

their Interstate stock. As a result, Brown was limited to selling only about seven percent of his newly acquired NSMC stock instead of the 25 percent previously planned. * * *

White Weld began processing the sales on the afternoon of October 31. It subsequently sold a total of 59,500 shares of NSMC stock. The gross received was slightly less than $3 million. * * * White Weld was never informed of the comfort letter adjustments before it undertook the sale as agents for the Interstate principals.

*   *   *

II. THE PRESENT ACTION

*   *   *

The Commission charges Brown and Meyer with responsibility for proceeding with the merger of Interstate and NSMC. Since shareholder approval of the merger was secured in part on the basis of the nine-month financials which the comfort letter indicated were inaccurate, the SEC contends that Brown and Meyer should have refused to close until the shareholders could be resolicited with corrected financials. The Commission also charges the two directors with effecting the sale of NSMC stock following the merger, without first disclosing the information contained in the comfort letter. * * *

Numerous charges, all of which appear to allege secondary liability, are leveled against the attorney defendants. Schauer is charged with "participating in the merger between Interstate and NSMC," apparently referring to his failure to interfere with the closing of the merger after receipt of the comfort letter. Such inaction, when alleged to facilitate a transaction, falls under the rubric of aiding and abetting. See *Kerbs* v. *Fall River Industries, Inc.,* 502 F. 2d 731, 739-40 (10th Cir. 1974). Both Schauer and Meyer are charged with issuing false opinions in connection with the merger and stock sales, thereby facilitating each transaction, and with acquiescence in the merger after learning the contents of the signed comfort letter. The Commission contends that the attorneys should have refused to issue the opinions in view of the adjustments revealed by the unsigned comfort letter, and after receipt of the signed version, they should have withdrawn their opinion with regard to the merger and demanded resolicitation of the Interstate shareholders. If the Interstate directors refused, the attorneys should have withdrawn from the representation and informed the shareholders or the Commission. * * *

Since any liability of the alleged aiders and abettors depends on a finding of a primary violation of the antifraud provisions, the Court will first address the issues relating to the Commission's charges against the principals. * * *

III. Past Violations

*   *   *

* * * the Court finds that Brown and Meyer violated §10(b), Rule 10b-5, and §17(a) through their participation in the closing of the Interstate/NSMC merger and through their sales of NSMC stock immediately following the merger, in each instance without first disclosing the material information contained in the unsigned comfort letter.

IV. Aiding and Abetting

*   *   *

The Commission's allegations of aiding and abetting by the defendants * * * seem to fall into four basic categories: (1) the failure of the attorney defendants to take any action to interfere in the consummation of the merger; (2) the issuance by the attorneys of an opinion with respect to the merger; (3) the attorneys' subsequent failure to withdraw that opinion and inform the Interstate shareholders or the SEC of the inaccuracy of the nine-month financials; and (4) the issuance by the attorneys and Brown of an opinion and letter, respectively, concerning the validity of the stock sales under Rule 133. The SEC's position is that the defendants acted or failed to act with an awareness of the fraudulent conduct by the principals, and thereby substantially assisted the two violations. The Court concurs with regard to the attorneys' failure to interfere with the closing, but must conclude that the remaining actions or inaction alleged to constitute aiding and abetting did not substantially facilitate either the merger or the stock sales.

As noted, the first element of aiding and abetting liability has been established by the finding that Brown and Meyer committed primary violations of the securities laws. Support for the second element, that the defendants were generally aware of the fraudulent activity, is provided by the previous discussion concerning scienter. * * *

The final requirement for aiding and abetting liability is that the conduct provide knowing, substantial assistance to the violation. In addressing this issue, the Court will consider each of the SEC's allegations separately. The major problem arising with regard to the Commission's contention that the attorneys failed to interfere in the closing of the merger is whether inaction or silence constitutes substantial assistance. While there is no definitive answer to this question, courts have been willing to consider inaction as a form of substantial assistance when the accused aider and abettor had a duty to disclose. * * *

Upon receipt of the unsigned comfort letter, it became clear that the merger had been approved by the Interstate shareholders on the basis of materially misleading information. In view of the obvious materiality of the information, especially to attorneys learned in securities law, the attorneys' responsibilities to their corporate client required them to take steps to ensure that the information would be disclosed to the shareholders. However, it is unnecessary to determine the precise extent of their obligations here, since it is undisputed that they took no steps whatsoever to delay the closing pending disclosure to and resolicitation of the Interstate shareholders. But, at the very least, they were required to speak out at the closing concerning the obvious materiality of the information and the concomitant requirement that the merger not be closed until the adjustments were disclosed and approval of the merger was again obtained from the Interstate shareholders. Their silence was not only a breach of this duty to speak, but in addition lent the appearance of legitimacy to the closing * * * . The combination of these factors clearly provided substantial assistance to the closing of the merger.

Contrary to the attorney defendants' contention, imposition of such a duty will not require lawyers to go beyond their accepted role in securities transactions, nor will it compel them to "err on the side of conservatism, . . . thereby inhibiting clients' business judgments and candid attorney-client communications." Courts will not lightly overrule an attorney's determination of materiality and the need for disclosure. However, where, as here, the significance of the information clearly removes any doubt concerning the materiality of the information, attorneys cannot rest on asserted "business judgments" as justification for their failure to make a legal decision pursuant to their fiduciary responsibilities to client shareholders.

*   *   *

The SEC's contention with regard to counsel's alleged acquiescence in the merger transaction raises significant questions concerning the responsibility of counsel. The basis for the charge appears to be counsel's failure, after the merger, to withdraw their opinion, to demand resolicitation of the shareholders, to advise their clients concerning rights of rescission of the merger, and ultimately, to inform the Interstate shareholders or the SEC of the completion of the merger based on materially false and misleading financial statements. The defendants counter with the argument that their actions following the merger are not subject to the coverage of the securities laws.

The filing of the complaint in this proceeding generated significant interest and an almost overwhelming amount of comment within the legal profession on the scope of a securities lawyer's obligation to his client and to the investing public.[73] The very initiation of this action, therefore, has provided a necessary and worthwhile impetus for the profession's recognition and assessment of its responsibilities in this area. The Court's examination, however, must be more limited. Although the complaint alleges varying instances of misconduct on the part of several attorneys and firms, the Court must narrow its focus to the present defendants and the charges against them.

Meyer, Schauer and Lord, Bissell & Brook are, in essence, here charged with failing to take any action to "undo" the merger. The Court has already concluded that counsel had a duty to the Interstate shareholders to delay the closing of the merger pending disclosure and resolicitation with corrected financials, and that the breach of that duty constituted a violation of the antifraud provisions through aiding and abetting the merger transaction. * * *

* * *

Thus, the Court finds that the attorney defendants aided and abetted the violation of §10(b), Rule 10b-5, and §17(a) through their participation in the closing of the merger.

V. Appropriateness of Injunctive Relief

Although the Commission has proved past violations by the defendants, that does not end the Court's inquiry. Proof of a past

---

[73] For an extensive listing of articles dealing with the issue, see Hoffman, On Learning of a Corporate Client's Crime or Fraud — the Lawyer's Dilemma, 33 Bus. Law. 1389, 1404-05 n. 38 (1978).

violation is not a prerequisite to the grant of injunctive relief, see *United States* v. *W. T. Grant Co.*, 345 U. S. 629, 633 (1953), nor by itself necessarily sufficient to justify such relief, see *SEC* v. *Bausch & Lomb, Inc.*, 565 F. 2d 8 (2d Cir. 1977); *SEC* v. *Management Dynamics, Inc.*, 515 F. 2d 801, 807 (2d Cir. 1975), but it may, in combination with other factors, warrant an inference of future misconduct by the charged party, *SEC* v. *Manor Nursing Centers, Inc.*, 458 F. 2d 1082, 1100 (2d Cir. 1972). The crucial question, though, remains not whether a violation has occurred, but whether there exists a reasonable likelihood of future illegal conduct by the defendant, "something more than the mere possibility which serves to keep the case alive." *United States* v. *W. T. Grant Co.*, supra. Thus, the SEC must "go beyond the mere facts of past violations and demonstrate a realistic likelihood of recurrence." *SEC* v. *Commonwealth Chemical Securities, Inc.*, 574 F. 2d 90, 100 (2d Cir. 1978).

The factors which are relevant to such a showing have been previously stated by this Court:

> The character of the past violations, the effectiveness of the discontinuance and the bona fides of the expressed intent to comply are considered. The number and duration of past wrongs, the time which has elapsed since the last violation, the opportunity to commit further illegal acts, the novelty of the violation, and the harmful impact of the injunction on the defendant are objective factors which the courts have examined. Subjective inquiries into the wilfulness or bad faith in a defendant's prior conduct and the sincerity of his representations not to violate the law are also pertinent.

SEC v. *National Student Marketing Corp.*, 360 F. Supp. 284, 297 (D. D. C. 1973). * * * The Court must assess these factors and determine, under the "totality of circumstances," "[w]hether the inference that the defendant is likely to repeat the wrong is properly drawn . . . ." *SEC* v. *Mangement Dynamics, Inc.*, supra. Exercising the broad discretion accorded it in making this determination, *SEC* v. *Universal Major Industries Corp.*, 546 F. 2d at 1048; *SEC* v. *National Student Marketing Corp.*, supra, the Court concludes that in this instance injunctive relief is not warranted.

The Commission has not demonstrated that the defendants engaged in the type of repeated and persistent misconduct which usually justifies the issuance of injunctive relief. * * * Instead, it has shown violations which principally occurred within a period of a few hours at the closing of the merger in 1969. The Commission has not charged, or even suggested, that the defendants were involved in similar misconduct either before or after the events involved in this proceeding. Thus, the violations proved by the SEC appear to be part of an isolated incident, unlikely to recur and insufficient to warrant an injunction. * * * The Commission appears to agree, for in the six years since the filing of this action, it has made no attempt to obtain interlocutory injunctive relief against these defendants. Such inaction argues strongly against the need for injunctive relief. * * *

Further, it is difficult to characterize the violations presented here as either "willful, blatant, and often completely outrageous," *SEC* v. *Manor Nursing Centers, Inc.,* 458 F. 2d at 1101, or as the "garden variety fraud" urged by the Commission, SEC Post-Trial Brief at 129. There is no evidence to suggest that these defendants knew about the comfort letter adjustments prior to the receipt of the unsigned comfort letter at the closing; and after receiving the letter, the defendants were under some pressure to determine a course of action, either to proceed with the transactions as scheduled or to abort both the merger and stock sales. Although it has now been found that they unlawfully and with scienter decided to proceed, their actions in this regard hardly resemble the deliberate and well-planned fraudulent scheme frequently found in securities fraud cases.

Finally, the Commission asserts that an injunction is necessary because the professional occupations of the defendants provide significant opportunities for further involvement in securities transactions. It notes that Brown holds positions as a director and as a consultant with NSMC, and that Meyer, Schauer and LBB continue to be involved in various corporate activities, including securities transactions, as part of their legal practice. While these opportunities distinguish the present defendants from those who, because they completely lack such opportunities, should not be subject to the threat of an injunction, see *SEC* v. *National Student Marketing Corp.,* 360 F. Supp. at 300, they do not alone justify relief. In fact, various circumstances indicate that this factor is not as one-sided as the Commission suggests. Although Brown retains his positions with NSMC, he is in effect virtually retired; the likelihood of his being involved in a securities transaction, other than as an investor, seems quite small. See *SEC* v. *Parklane Hosiery Co.,* supra. While the attorney defendants are more likely to be so involved, that fact is countered somewhat by their professional responsibilities as attorneys and officers of the court to conform their conduct to the dictates of the law. The Court is confident that they will take appropriate steps to ensure that their professional conduct in the future comports with the law.

After considering the "totality of circumstances" presented here, the Court concludes that the Securities and Exchange Commission has not fulfilled its statutory obligation to make a "proper showing" that injunctive relief is necessary to prevent further violations by these defendants. Accordingly, judgment will be entered for the defendants and the complaint will be dismissed.

As Judge Parker indicated, the *NSM* case gave commentators a field day.[1] And its pendency produced a strong reaction from the organized Bar:

STATEMENT OF POLICY ADOPTED BY THE AMERICAN BAR ASSOCIATION REGARDING RESPONSIBILITIES AND LIABILITIES OF LAWYERS IN ADVISING WITH RESPECT TO THE COMPLIANCE BY CLIENTS WITH LAWS ADMINISTERED BY THE SECURITIES AND EXCHANGE COMMISSION
31 Bus. Law. 543 (1975)[a]

As previously noted, the Committee on Counsel Responsibility and Liability of the Section of Corporation, Banking and Business Law of the American Bar Association has been examining the responsibilities and liabilities of lawyers engaged in securities law matters. The Committee (the membership of which in addition to members of this Section also includes liaison representatives from the other ABA Sections and Committees noted below) prepared the following Statement of Policy and related Report. The Statement of Policy was adopted by the ABA House of Delegates on August 12, 1975 pursuant to recommendation by the Council of

---

[1] 457 F. Supp. at 714 n. 73; see, e. g., S. Goldberg (Ed.), Expanding Responsibilities under the Securities Laws (conference co-chaired by J. Flom and L. Loss 1973); for a critique of the Commission's view, see Lipman, The SEC's Reluctant Police Force: A New Role for Lawyers, 49 N. Y. U. L. Rev. 437 (1974); for a pungent criticism by a civil libertarian, see Freedman, A Civil Libertarian Looks at Securities Regulation, 35 Ohio St. L. J. 280, esp. at 285 (1974) (the SEC Bar is already a "wholly-owned subsidiary" of the Commission); see also the reference in Am. B. Foundation, Annotated Code of Professional Responsibility (1979) 321-26.

[a] Ed.: Copyright 1979 by the American Bar Association and reprinted with the permission of the Association and its Section of Corporation, Banking, and Business Law.

the Section. The specifics of how the Code of Professional Responsibility speaks to the question of disclosure by lawyers in the SEC context is examined in the Report which appeared in the July, 1975 issue of The Business Lawyer.[b] It is recognized that the principles involved have broader application.

*   *   *

AMERICAN BAR ASSOCIATION

REPORT TO THE HOUSE OF DELEGATES

SECTION OF CORPORATION, BANKING AND BUSINESS LAW
RECOMMENDATION

The Section of Corporation, Banking and Business Law recommends adoption of the following resolution:

BE IT RESOLVED, that this Association adopts the following Statement of Policy regarding responsibilities and liabilities of lawyers in advising with respect to the compliance by clients with laws administered by the Securities and Exchange Commission ("SEC"):

1. The confidentiality of lawyer-client consultations and advice and the fiduciary loyalty of the lawyer to the client, as prescribed in the American Bar Association's Code of Professional Responsibility ("CPR"), are vital to the basic function of the lawyer as legal counselor because they enable and encourage clients to consult legal counsel freely, with assurance that counsel will respect the confidentiality of the client's communications and will advise independently and in the client's best interest without conflicting loyalties or obligations.

2. This vital confidentiality of consultation and advice would be destroyed or seriously impaired if it is accepted as a general principle that lawyers must inform the SEC or others regarding confidential information received by lawyers from their clients even though such action would not be permitted or required by the CPR. Any such compelled disclosure would seriously and adversely affect the lawyers' function as counselor, and may seriously and adversely affect the ability of lawyers as advocates to represent and defend their clients' interests.

3. In light of the foregoing considerations, it must be recognized that a lawyer cannot, consistently with his essential role as

[b] ED.: The Code of Professional Responsibility and the Responsibility of Lawyers Engaged in Securities Law Practice — A Report by the Committee on Counsel Responsibility and Liability, 30 Bus. Law. 1289 (1975).

legal adviser, be regarded as a source of information concerning possible wrong-doing by clients. Accordingly, any principle of law which, except as permitted or required by the CPR, permits or obliges a lawyer to disclose to the SEC otherwise confidential information, should be established only by statute after full and careful consideration of the public interests involved, and should be resisted unless clearly mandated by law.

4.   Lawyers have an obligation under the CPR to advise clients, to the best of their ability, concerning the need for or advisability of public disclosure of a broad range of events and circumstances, including the obligation of the client to make appropriate disclosures as required by various laws and regulations administered by the SEC. In appropriate circumstances, a lawyer may be permitted or required by the Disciplinary Rules under the CPR to resign his engagement if his advice concerning disclosures is disregarded by the client and, if the conduct of a client clearly establishes his prospective commission of a crime or the past or prospective perpetration of a fraud in the course of the lawyer's representation, even to make the disclosures himself. However, the lawyer has neither the obligation nor the right to make disclosure when any reasonable doubt exists concerning the client's obligation of disclosure, i. e., the client's failure to meet his obligation is not clearly established, except to the extent that the lawyer should consider appropriate action, as required or permitted by the CPR, in cases where the lawyer's opinion is expected to be relied on by third parties and the opinion is discovered to be not correct, whether because it is based on erroneous information or otherwise.

5.   Fulfillment by attorneys of their obligations to clients under the CPR best serves the public interest of assisting and furthering clients' compliance with legal requirements. Efforts by the government to impose responsibility upon lawyers to assure the quality of their clients' compliance with the law or to compel lawyers to give advice resolving all doubts in favor of regulatory restrictions would evoke serious and far-reaching disruption in the role of the lawyer as counselor, which would be detrimental to the public, clients and the legal profession. In fulfillment of their responsibility to clients under the CPR, lawyers must be free to advise clients as to the full range of their legitimately available courses of action and the relative attendant risks involved. Furthermore, it is often desirable for the lawyer to point out those factors which may suggest a decision that is morally just as well as legally permissible. However, the decision as to the course to be taken should be made by the client. The client's actions should

not be improperly narrowed through the insistence of an attorney who may, perhaps unconsciously, eliminate available choices from consideration because of his concern over possible personal risks if the position is taken which, though supportable, is subject to uncertainty or contrary to a known, but perhaps erroneous, position of the SEC or a questionable lower court decision. Public policy, we strongly believe, is best served by lawyers acting in conformance with their obligations to their clients and others as prescribed under the CPR. Accordingly, liability should not be imposed upon lawyers whose conduct is in conformance with the CPR.

REPORT

I. INTRODUCTION

Lawyers are often called upon for legal advice when the answer is not clear. The statute or regulation in question may be ambiguous; judicial opinions may be in conflict or not directly in point; counsel may be of the opinion that an existing precedent is wrong and should be reversed on appeal; or the issue, in the absence of a precedent directly in point, may involve a high degree of subjective judgment, particularly when considering various central concepts deliberately imprecise in laws administered by the Securities and Exchange Commission ("SEC"). Illustrative are concepts such as "materiality," "control," "adequate disclosure," "average prudent investor," "public distribution," "care of a prudent man," "manipulative or deceptive device or contrivance," and "untrue statement of a material fact or to omit to state a material fact necessary in order to make the statements made, in light of the circumstances in which they were made, not misleading." Furthermore, there are often questions of fact presented, sometimes involving technical problems in diversified and complicated industries, regarding which clients or others are better qualified to determine than lawyers.

Various proceedings by the SEC, speeches by members and staff of the Commission, and certain statements in recent judicial opinions have caused many lawyers serious concern as to their responsibility to their clients and to the public when advising in the areas of SEC laws. Their advice is, of course, reviewed by the SEC with the benefit of "hindsight" when something has gone wrong. Must the lawyer in such matters resolve all uncertainties in favor of the law having application, e. g., if there is any question whether something may be "material" it should be treated as "material," and if the client fails to follow such advice must the lawyer report such failure to the SEC?

II. PUBLIC POLICY

It is a basic principle that the lawyer's role is essentially that of counselor to his client. The effectiveness of this role is highly dependent upon the long-accepted confidentiality of the attorney-client relationship. For this reason a role for the lawyer as investigator or informant would be a seriously inconsistent one, and the Bar should critically scrutinize any proposal, however limited, that the lawyer can be so regarded.

Whenever a proposal is made that a lawyer go beyond his fundamental role of advising his client and assume a function that could require him publicly to contradict his client or disclose possible deficiencies, on the basis of information gained in the course of his professional engagement, there is cause for concern on the part of the public as well as the Bar, since the attorney-client relationship is of fundamental importance to our legal system.

The lawyer's ability to serve his client and the public by assisting and furthering the client's compliance with legal requirements rests largely on the effectiveness of his relationship with his client. This relationship is undermined to the extent that client communications with lawyers are made with the risk that the lawyer will, if not satisfied with the client's response to his advice or if concerned over his own potential personal liabilities, report possible deficiencies to third parties. Accordingly, it has long been recognized by the Code of Professional Responsibility ("CPR") and its predecessor Canons of Ethics that only in the clearest cases of illegal or fraudulent activities by a client in the course of the lawyer's representation should the lawyer be called upon or permitted to take such action. (The text of relevant provisions of the CPR is attached).

We do not believe that the policy of disclosure as embodied in the SEC laws warrants an exception to the basic confidentiality of the attorney-client relationship. Such exceptions have to date been carefully reserved by the CPR for far more critical and limited situations. The statutes administered by the SEC give it no power to require disclosure by lawyers concerning their clients beyond what is provided in the CPR.

For the foregoing reasons we strongly urge that the American Bar Association adopt a general statement of policy concerning lawyers' responsibilities and liabilities regarding a client's failure to comply with a law administered by the SEC which will reflect the basic principles we, as lawyers, believe are essential to the preservation of the concept of the attorney-client relationship as part of our legal system.

The statement should recognize that the lawyer has a duty to advise his client candidly and responsibly as to the client's legal obligations, including the obligation to make appropriate disclosures as required by various laws and regulations administered by the SEC, and that a lawyer must take appropriate action, as required by the CPR (as adopted in his particular State), when faced with conduct of a client which clearly establishes his prospective commission of a crime, or the past or prospective perpetration of a fraud, in the course of the lawyer's representation. Similarly, the lawyer should consider appropriate action, as required or permitted by the CPR, in cases where the lawyer's opinion is expected to be relied on by third parties and the opinion is discovered to be not correct, whether because it is based on erroneous information or otherwise. The statement should also acknowledge that a lawyer need not confine his advice to purely legal considerations, but in appropriate cases should bring to the attention of the client considerations of fairness and avoidance of infliction of needless harm.

We firmly believe that such an approach will be in the long-term public interest and will provide for greater assurance of compliance with our laws, including those relating to disclosure, than would an approach requiring lawyers to disclose possible SEC violations by clients.

The Recommendation preceding this Report has been adopted by the Council of the Section of Corporation, Banking and Business Law.

CODE OF PROFESSIONAL RESPONSIBILITY

CANON 4. A LAWYER SHOULD PRESERVE THE CONFIDENCES AND SECRETS OF A CLIENT

*   *   *

DISCIPLINARY RULES

DR 4-101 Preservation of Confidence and Secrets of a Client.

*   *   *

(C) A lawyer may reveal:

* * *

(3) The intention of his client to commit a crime and the information necessary to prevent the crime.

* * *

CANON 7. A LAWYER SHOULD REPRESENT A CLIENT ZEALOUSLY WITHIN THE BOUNDS OF THE LAW

* * *

DISCIPLINARY RULES

* * *

DR 7-102 Representing a Client Within the Bounds of the Law.

* * *

(B) A lawyer who receives information clearly establishing that:
   (1) His client has, in the course of the representation, perpetrated a fraud upon a person or tribunal shall promptly
call upon his client to rectify the same, and if his client
refuses or is unable to do so, he shall reveal the fraud to
the affected person or tribunal except when the information is protected as a privileged communication.

* * *

This last provision presents a number of nice questions. For
example: Is the "clearly establishing" phrase satisfied in the SEC
context by the client's negligent failure to provide accurate or
required data? Does the lawyer have a duty to investigate when
he suspects a "fraud"? What is "fraud" in the SEC context? The
word "person" aside, is the SEC a "tribunal" when it is not sitting
in a quasi-judicial capacity? And doesn't the "except" clause,
which was added by amendment in 1974,[2] come close to eating up
the rule?[3]

[2] Am. B. Foundation, Annotated Code of Professional Responsibility (1979)
307.
  [3] For a discussion of these and other questions, see the commentary in id.

In any event, even apart from the limitation to "the course of the representation," the accent is pretty clearly on the "may" in DR4-101(C), on the past tense in the mandatory DR7-102(B)(1), and on the "except" clause. This generally permissive rather than mandatory mode reflects the historical development of these ethical precepts in a simpler era in which the lawyer's practice consisted far more of defending persons charged with common crimes and far less of counseling on complex economic regulations. Against the possibility of a client's (or would-be client's) seeking a lawyer's advice on how to find a poison that would leave no trace, all that is necessary (so the argument goes) is to *permit* the lawyer to telephone the police; for, freed of any restraint as a lawyer, his moral obligation as a citizen will impel him to do so. But, when a lawyer advises that certain shares received in a merger are not yet transferable and the client is defiant, the call is much closer. Besides, it is contended, anything that is conducive to clients' being less than completely frank with their lawyers will result in *more* harm in the long run — harm that counsel might have presented. At any rate, it is apparently considerations of that sort that are fueling the vigorous opposition to the proposed revision of the Code of Professional Responsibility, which many lawyers apparently perceive would limit their discretion in this area.[4]

Questions of attorney-client relationship aside, we must still ask just what the SEC lawyer's duty is when, say, he drafts a registration statement or report.

The issuer's counsel has been aptly called the "quarterback" in preparing the nonfinancial portions of a 1933 Act registration statement,[5] though the underwriter's counsel may play a substantial role if the issuer's counsel is inexperienced. This does not give the lawyer the statutory status of an "expert" on virtually the

---

at 321-26. Only some ten states have adopted the "except" clause. And see DR7-102(A)(7): "In his representation of a client, a lawyer shall not * * * Counsel or assist his client in conduct that the lawyer knows to be illegal or fraudulent."

[4] See ABA Commission on Evaluation of Professional Standards, Report to the House of Delegates (1982) App. A, Rules 1.6(b) (exceptions to confidentiality rule), 1.13 (the organization as the client), 3.3 (candor toward the tribunal). Final action on the report was put over at the August 1982 meeting of the American Bar Association. See 14 Sec. Reg. L. Rep. 1474-77 (1982).

[5] R. Jennings and H. Marsh, Securities Regulation Cases and Materials (5th ed. 1982) 106. For a set of guidelines on the lawyer's role in the preparation of registration statements, see Assn. of the Bar of the City of N. Y., Report by Special Committee on Lawyers' Role in Securities Transactions, 32 Record A. B. C. N. Y. 345 (1977), 32 Bus. Law. 1879 (1977).

whole registration statement.[6] Normally he is an "expert" only with respect to his required opinion that the stock being offered will be legally issued, fully paid and nonassessable, or any additional opinions he might give on such questions as title to property or the validity of a patent. Although counsel is not doing his job unless he asks searching questions of management — clients seldom come into a lawyer's office in any branch of the law with all the relevant facts neatly arranged on a silver platter — the truthfulness and completeness of a registration statement are in the last analysis management's responsibility.

Here again, however, the Commission has repeatedly cautioned that "the task of enforcing the securities laws rests in overwhelming measure on the bar's shoulders."[7] And, if a Commissioner's statement in an address to a Bar group that "a lawyer preparing a registration statement has an obligation to do more than simply act as the blind scrivener of the thoughts of his client" can be discounted as an able lawyer's rhetoric, it is not quite so easy to discount the further suggestion that "in securities matters (other than those where advocacy is clearly proper) the attorney will have to function in a manner more akin to that of the auditor than to that of the advocate."[8]

The suggestion has been heard that the SEC lawyer is counsel to "the situation." The phrase is not new. Louis Brandeis used it as a practicing lawyer in Boston. But an admirer has termed it "one of the most unfortunate phrases he ever casually uttered."[9] And surely some of his Beacon Hill adversaries must have asked, as some lawyers ask today, where they should address their bills to "the situation."[10]

---

[6] Escott v. BarChris Construction Corp., 283 F. Supp. 643, 683 (S. D. N. Y. 1968); see pp. 1034-35 supra.

[7] Emanuel Fields, 45 SEC 262, 266 n. 20 (1973), aff'd without opinion sub nom. Fields v. SEC, 495 F. 2d 1075 (D. C. Cir. 1974), quoted in William R. Carter, Sec. Ex. Act Rel. 17,597, 22 SEC Dock. 292, 297 n. 21 (1981), set out infra p. 1243, at p. 297 n. 21; see also SEC v. Spectrum, Ltd., 489 F. 2d 535, 541-42 (2d Cir. 1973), quoted infra p. 1260.

[8] Sommer, The Emerging Responsibilities of the Securities Lawyer, CCH Fed. Sec. L. Rep. ¶79,631 at 83,689, 83,690 (1974).

[9] Frank, The Legal Ethics of Louis D. Brandeis, 17 Stan. L. Rev. 683, 702 (1965); see also id. at 698-703; A. Mason, Brandeis: A Free Man's Life (1956) 236.

[10] R. Jennings and H. Marsh, Securities Regulation Cases and Materials (5th ed. 1982) 1209.

For a comprehensive review, see Small, An Attorney's Responsibilities under Federal and State Securities Laws: Private Counselor or Public Servant?, 61 Calif. L. Rev. 1189 (1973); for a philosophical analysis, see Rosenfeld, Between Rights and Consequences: A Philosophical Inquiry into the Foundations of

B. DISCIPLINARY PROCEEDINGS

WILLIAM R. CARTER

Securities and Exchange Commission, 1981
Sec. Ex. Act Rel. 17,597, 22 SEC Dock. 292

William R. Carter and Charles J. Johnson, Jr. [partners in a New York law firm referred to in the opinion as Brown, Wood], respondents, appeal from the initial decision of the Administrative Law Judge in this proceeding brought under Rule 2(e) of the Commission's Rules of Practice. In an opinion dated March 7, 1979, the Administrative Law Judge found that, in connection with their representation of National Telephone Company, Inc. during the period from May 1974 to May 1975, Carter and Johnson willfully violated and willfully aided and abetted violations of Sections 10(b) and 13(a) of the Securities Exchange Act of 1934 (the "Exchange Act") and Rules 10b-5, 12b-20 and 13a-11 thereunder and that they engaged in unethical and improper professional conduct. In light of these findings, the Administrative Law Judge concluded that Carter and Johnson should be suspended from appearing or practicing before the Commission for periods of one year and nine months, respectively.

* * *

I. JURISDICTION

Respondents challenge the Commission's authority to promulgate Rule 2(e). Because this is an issue of great significance to the bar, we issued a blanket order permitting the filing of *amicus curiae* briefs on general legal and policy issues.

* * *

* * * As set out more fully below in the discussions on Aiding and Abetting and Ethical and Professional Responsibilities, we are extremely sensitive to the role of the securities lawyer in the disclosure process and to the need to fashion a rule that is neither excessive in scope nor beyond our expertise. Nevertheless, we conclude that the enactment of Rule 2(e) and our application of that Rule in this case are clearly within our jurisdictional grant

---

Legal Ethics in the Changing World of Securities Regulation, 49 Geo. Wash. L. Rev. 462 (1981).

of authority and reflect an entirely appropriate discharge of our statutory mandates. * * *

A. AUTHORITY

The Commission's authority to adopt Rule 2(e) has been before a number of courts. No court, having considered the question, has found the Commission not to have the authority to adopt Rule 2(e). In the most recent case to address the issue,[6] the Second Circuit Court of Appeals concluded:

> we reject [the] assertion that the Commission acted without authority in promulgating Rule 2(e). Although there is no express statutory provision authorizing the Commission to discipline professionals appearing before it, Rule 2(e), promulgated pursuant to its statutory rulemaking authority, represents an attempt by the Commission to protect the integrity of its own processes. It provides the Commission with the means to ensure that those professionals, on whom the Commission relies heavily in the performance of its statutory duties, perform their tasks diligently and with a reasonable degree of competence. As such the Rule is "reasonably related" to the purposes of the securities laws. *Mourning* v. *Family Publications Service, Inc.,* [411 U. S. 356 (1973)]. Moreover, we hold that the Rule does not violate, nor is it inconsistent with, any other provision of the securities laws. We therefore sustain the validity of the Rule as a necessary adjunct to the Commission's power to protect the integrity of its administrative procedures and the public in general. *Goldsmith* v. *Board of Tax Appeals,* [270 U. S. 117 (1926)].

B. THE ADMINISTRATIVE PRACTICE ACT

Subsection (b) of the Administrative Practice Act, 5 U. S. C. 500(b), expressly states that

> An individual who is a member in good standing of the bar of the highest court of a State may represent a person before an agency on filing with the agency written declaration that he is currently qualified as provided by this subsection and is authorized to represent the particular person on whose behalf he acts.

The primary purpose of this 1965 legislation was to provide "for the right of persons to be represented by any attorney in good standing in matters before Federal agencies."[7] * * *

*   *   *

C. 11B [6][Touche Ross & Co. v. SEC, 609 F. 2d 570, 582 (2d Cir. 1979).]
    [7]H. R. Rep. No. 1141, 89th Cong., 1st Sess. (1965), reprinted in 2 U. S. Code Con. & Ad. News 4170, 4171 (1965).

C. PROSECUTORIAL CONSIDERATIONS

We are sensitive to the abuses that may occur when an administrative agency with prosecutorial responsibilities has the power to discipline attorneys representing regulated entities. We are constrained to point out, however, that each administrative agency is charged with responsibilities and vested with powers that are fraught with potential for abuse. As is the case with other administrative agencies, the Commission performs legislative, prosecutorial, judicial, and general administrative functions. Although the potential for abuse does exist, "it is neither so great nor so unique to this agency that the Commission should decline to exercise its authority in this area."[10]

We have considered the potential for abuse and we have considered the way Rule 2(e) has actually been used, as well as the substantial internal safeguards we have established to protect against its abuse. We are convinced that, at this time, our responsibilities do not permit us to

> ignore or refuse to exercise an effective professional disciplinary tool under the appropriate circumstances. The important role which professionals, particularly attorneys and accountants, play in assuring adherence to the federal securities laws has long been recognized. Clearly, the Commission would be unable to administer effectively those laws in an environment in which issuers, underwriters, and others involved in the capital raising process were not routinely served by professionals of the highest integrity and competence, well-versed in the requirements of the statutory scheme Congress has created. An incompetent or unethical practitioner has the ability to inflict substantial damage on the Commission's processes, and thus the investing public, and to the level of trust and confidence in our capital markets. [We believe] that Rule 2(e) should not be utilized as an enforcement tool against those who violate the federal securities laws and happen coincidentally also to be lawyers or accountants. But where such individuals engage in professional misconduct which impairs the integrity of the Commission's processes, the Commission has an obligation to respond through the application of Rule 2(e).[11]

D. THE COMMISSION'S EXPERTISE

As discussed in the section on Ethical and Professional Responsibilities, infra, in this decision the Commission interprets Rule

---

[10] In the Matter of Keating, Muething & Klekamp, Securities Exchange Act Release No. 15982 (July 2, 1979), 17 SEC Docket 1149, 1165 (concurring opinion of Chairman Williams).

[11] Id. at 1165-6.

2(e)(1)(ii) in cases limited to securities lawyers performing disclo-
sure-related professional services, an area within our responsibility
and our expertise. At the same time, we do not view our efforts
in this regard as an attempt to preempt the recodification efforts
of the American Bar Association or the ongoing standard-setting
of the various state bar disciplinary and ethics bodies. We view
private sector initiatives to clarify the difficult problems in these
areas as a useful — indeed necessary — response to the need for
predictable and generally applicable standards governing lawyers
in the discharge of their professional responsibilities. Our attention today is directed only to the narrow range of lawyers engaged
in a federal securities practice, to the specific factual context of an
ongoing disclosure program of a corporate client, and to the limited question of when it is appropriate for a lawyer to make further efforts within the corporation to forestall continuing violative
conduct.

II.   BACKGROUND OF RULE 2(e)

A.   THE HISTORY OF RULE 2(e)

[The Commission in 1938 amended Rule 2 of its original Rules
of Practice to disestablish its formal "SEC Bar," with specific admission requirements, but preserved the provision that authorized
the Commission to "deny admission to, suspend, or disbar, any
person who does not possess the requisite qualifications to represent others, or who is lacking in character, integrity, or proper
professional conduct."]

*　　　*　　　*

In September 1970, Rule 2(e) was again amended to provide for
an automatic suspension from appearance or practice before the
Commission by a person who (1) had been suspended or disbarred
from practice or who has had his license to practice suspended or
revoked by a state licensing authority; (2) had been convicted of a
felony or of a misdemeanor involving moral turpitude; or (3) had
been suspended or disbarred by a court of competent jurisdiction.
In addition, a third category — subparagraph (1)(iii) of the Rule
— was added to provide that the Commission may deny a professional the privilege of appearing or practicing before it for the
willful violation, or the willful aiding and abetting of a violation,

of the federal securities laws or the rules and regulations thereunder.

B. THE PURPOSE OF RULE 2(e)

The Commission promulgated Rule 2(e) pursuant to its general rulemaking powers in order to protect the integrity of its processes. These powers were not exercised with a view to the creation of new administrative proceedings to fill gaps in the Commission's current statutory panoply of remedies. Rule 2(e) is not intended to provide an administrative remedy as an alternative to our power to seek injunctive relief for violations of provisions of the securities laws which do not already provide for an administrative remedy. For example, it does not reach any of the myriad of non-professionals who may have been involved in violations of the securities laws for which an administrative remedy is not available. It is addressed to a different problem — professional misconduct — and its sanction is limited to that necessary to protect the investing public and the Commission from the future impact on its processes of professional misconduct.

Rule 2(e) represents a balancing of public benefits. It rests upon the recognition that the privilege of practicing before the Commission is a mechanism that generates great leverage — for good or evil — in the administration of the securities laws.[21] A significant failure to perform properly the professional's role has implications extending beyond the particular transaction involved, for wrongdoing by a lawyer or an accountant raises the spectre of a replication of that conduct with other clients.

---

[21] We have previously noted

the peculiarly strategic and especially central place of the private practicing lawyer in the investment process and in the enforcement of the body of federal law aimed at keeping that process fair . . . . [T]he task of enforcing the securities laws rests in over-whelming measure on the bar's shoulders . . . . Very little of a securities lawyer's work is adversary in character. He doesn't work in courtrooms where the pressure of diligent adversaries and alert judges checks him. He works in his office where he prepares prospectuses, proxy statements, opinions of counsel, and other documents that we, our staff, the financial community and the investing public must take on faith. This is a field where unscrupulous lawyers can inflict irreparable harm on those who rely on the disclosure documents that they produce. Hence we are under a duty to hold our bar to appropriately rigorous standards of professional honor.

In the Matter of Emanuel Fields, 45 S. E. C. 262, 266, n.20 (1973), *aff'd without opinion*, 495 F. 2d 1085 (C. A. D. C. 1974). * * *

Recognition of the public implications of the securities professional's role does not mean that the Commission has, by rule, imposed duties to the public on lawyers where such duties would not otherwise exist. Accountants, of course, issue audit reports that speak directly to the investing public and publicly represent that the code of conduct embodied in the statements of auditing standards promulgated by the AICPA has been followed. The duty of accountants to those who justifiably rely on those reports is well-recognized. But the traditional role of the lawyer as counselor is to advise his client, not the public, about the law. Rule 2(e) does not change the nature of that obligation. Nevertheless, if a lawyer violates ethical or professional standards, or becomes a conscious participant in violations of the securities laws, or performs his professional function without regard to the consequences, it will not do to say that because the lawyer's duty is to his client alone, this Commission must stand helplessly by while the lawyer carries his privilege of appearing and practicing before the Commission on to the next client.

C.   THE OPERATION OF RULE 2(e)

The operation of subparagraphs (i) and (ii) of Rule 2(e)(1) responds to the policy considerations stated in Part B above. * * *

The operation of subparagraph (iii) of the Rule reflects the same concerns. * * * Not every violation of law, however, may be sufficient to justify invocation of the sanctions available under Rule 2(e). The violation must be of a character that threatens the integrity of the Commission's processes in the way that the activities of unqualified or unethical professionals do.

Against that background, we turn to an analysis of respondents' conduct. In our judgment, that conduct presents difficult questions under the applicable legal and professional standards.

III.   RESPONDENTS' CONDUCT

[The Commission here discusses, for 15 double-column pages in the SEC Docket, the events that led the client, National Telephone Company, Inc., to file a petition under Chapter X of the then Bankruptcy Act. The picture is one of misleading filings, letters to stockholders, and press releases, with the respondents "in the uncomfortable position of attempting to provide disclosure advice to an aggressive client whose unreceptive management actively frustrated the giving of advice and ignored what advice managed to get through."]

IV. AIDING AND ABETTING

*   *   *

A. THE FINDINGS BELOW

The initial decision makes no precise distinction between its stated conclusions as to findings of willful primary violations by respondents and its findings of secondary, that is, aiding and abetting, liability. It is clear that respondents, as individuals, could not on the instant facts be found to have directly violated Section 13(a) or Rules 13a-11 and 12b-20 because they are not an "issuer," as that term is defined in Section 3(a)(8) of the Exchange Act, the only direct object of those provisions. Moreover, given the circumstances of this case, we do not believe that respondents' involvement in the affairs or decisionmaking processes of the company was sufficient to justify a finding against them as direct, primary violators of Section 10(b) or Rule 10b-5 as a result of the antifraud violations growing out of National's statements. We therefore will consider respondents' conduct only as it may constitute willful aiding and abetting of a federal securities law violation by National.

B. SECURITIES LAW VIOLATIONS BY NATIONAL

We have no doubt that [National violated Rule 10b-5 and various disclosure provisions]. * * *

C. AIDING AND ABETTING

Our primary concern, however, is with the respondents' relationship to these violations of the securities laws. Although "[t]he elements of an aiding and abetting claim have not yet crystallized into a set pattern,"[56] we have examined the decisions of the various circuits and conclude that certain legal principles are common to all the decisions.

In the context of the federal securities laws, these principles hold generally that one may be found to have aided and abetted a violation when the following three elements are present.

  1. there exists an independent securities law violation committed by some other party;

  2. the aider and abettor knowingly and substantially assisted the conduct that constitutes the violation; and

---

[56] Woodward v. Metro Bank of Dallas, 522 F. 2d 84, 94 (C. A. 5 1975).

3.   the aider and abettor was aware or knew that his role was part of an activity that was improper or illegal.

* * * The second element — substantial assistance — is generally satisfied in the context of a securities lawyer performing professional duties, for he is inevitably deeply involved in his client's disclosure activities and often participates in the drafting of the documents, as was the case with Carter. And he does so knowing that he is participating in the preparation of disclosure documents — that is his job.

In this connection, we do not distinguish between the professional advice of a lawyer given orally or in writing and similar advice which is embodied in drafting documents to be filed with the Commission. Liability in these circumstances should not turn on such artificial distinctions, particularly in light of the almost limitless range of forms which legal advice may take. Moreover, the opposite approach, which would permit a lawyer to avoid or reduce his liability simply by avoiding participation in the drafting process, may well have the undesirable effect of reducing the quality of the disclosure by the many to protect against the defalcations of the few.

For these reasons, the crucial inquiry in a Rule 2(e) proceeding against a lawyer inevitably tends to focus on the awareness or the intent element of the offense of aiding and abetting. It is that element which has been the source of the most disagreement among commentators and the courts. We do not seek to resolve that disagreement today. We do hold, however, that a finding of *willful aiding and abetting* within the meaning of Rule 2(e)(1)(iii) requires a showing that respondents were aware or knew that their role was part of an activity that was improper or illegal.

It is axiomatic that a lawyer will not be liable as an aider and abettor merely because his advice, followed by the client, is ultimately determined to be wrong. What is missing in that instance is a wrongful intent on the part of the lawyer. It is that element of intent which provides the basis for distinguishing between those professionals who may be appropriately considered as subjects of professional discipline and those who, acting in good faith, have merely made errors of judgment or have been careless.

Significant public benefits flow from the effective performance of the securities lawyer's role. The exercise of independent, careful and informed legal judgment on difficult issues is critical to the flow of material information to the securities markets. Moreover, we are aware of the difficulties and limitations attendant upon that role. In the course of rendering securities law advice, the lawyer is called upon to make difficult judgments, often under great pressure and in areas where the legal signposts are far apart and only faintly discernible.

If a securities lawyer is to bring his best independent judgment to bear on a disclosure problem, he must have the freedom to make innocent — or even, in certain cases, careless — mistakes without fear of legal liability or loss of the ability to practice before the Commission. Concern about his own liability may alter the balance of his judgment in one direction as surely as an unseemly obeisance to the wishes of his client can do so in the other. While one imbalance results in disclosure rather than concealment, neither is, in the end, truly in the public interest. Lawyers who are seen by their clients as being motivated by fears for their personal liability will not be consulted on difficult issues.

Although it is a close judgment, after careful review, we conclude that the available evidence is insufficient to establish that either respondent acted with sufficient knowledge and awareness or recklessness to satisfy the test for willful aiding and abetting liability. * * *

* * *

E.   SUBSEQUENT CONDUCT

* * * The Administrative Law Judge also found that respondents willfully aided and abetted these [company] violations [through the continued nondisclosure of its deteriorating cash position and so on] by failing to ensure that the required disclosures were made or to communicate to National's board of directors concerning management's refusal to make such disclosures. Our review of the record does not reveal a sufficient basis for sustaining respondents' liability as aiders and abettors of these violations.

* * *

The courts have differed with respect to the circumstances under which inaction or silence may constitute the requisite assistance to the primary wrongdoer. Some cases require a showing that the alleged aider and abettor deliberately intended to assist the primary violation by his silence or inaction. Other cases have held that inaction or silence may constitute "substantial assistance" when the alleged aider and abettor was under a duty to act or disclose, but failed to do so.

Finally, some courts synthesize the two approaches as follows:

> When it is impossible to find any duty of disclosure, an aider and abettor should be found liable only if scienter of the high "conscious intent" variety can be found. Where some special duty of disclosure exists, then liability should be possible with a lesser degree of scienter.

Accordingly, in order to sustain the law judge's finding, we must find that respondents either consciously intended to assist National's violation, or that they breached a duty to disclose or act and had some degree of scienter.

On the basis of the record before us, we think that it is a close question, but in the final analysis we are unable to infer that respondents intended to aid the violations by not acting. The level of intent required by this test is higher than that required by some courts to show the appropriate mental state for the third element of aiding and abetting. There, some courts require only that an aider and abettor be "aware" that his role was part of an illegal or improper activity. Here, the test requires a showing that he "intended" to foster the illegal activity. This is a find distinction, but we think it is an important one.

Our review of the record, which includes respondents' periodic exhortations * * * to improve the quality of National's disclosure, leads us to believe that respondents did not intend to assist the violations by their inaction or silence. Rather, they seemed to be at a loss for how to deal with a difficult client.

Association of a law firm with a client lends an air of legitimacy and authority to the actions of a client. There are occasions when, but for the law firm's association, a violation could not have occurred. Under those circumstances, if the firm were cognizant of how it was being used and acquiesced, or if it gained some benefit from the violation beyond that normally obtained in a legal relationship, inaction would probably give rise to an inference of intent. This, however, is not such a case, and we find that respondents did not intend to assist the violation by their inaction.

V. ETHICAL AND PROFESSIONAL RESPONSIBILITIES

A. THE FINDINGS OF THE ADMINISTRATIVE LAW JUDGE

*   *   *

Respondents argue that the Commission has never promulgated standards of professional conduct for lawyers and that the Commission's application in hindsight of new standards would be fundamentally unfair. Moreover, even if it is permissible for the Commission to apply — without specific adoption or notice — generally recognized professional standards, they argue that no such standards applicable to respondents' conduct existed in 1974-75, nor do they exist today.

We agree that, in general, elemental notions of fairness dictate that the Commission should not establish new rules of conduct and impose them retroactively upon professionals who acted at the time without reason to believe that their conduct was unethical or improper. At the same time, however, we perceive no unfairness whatsoever in holding those professionals who practice before us to generally recognized norms of professional conduct, whether or not such norms had previously been explicitly adopted or endorsed by the Commission. To do so upsets no justifiable expectations, since the professional is already subject to those norms.

The ethical and professional responsibilities of lawyers who become aware that their client is engaging in violations of the securities laws have not been so firmly and unambiguously established that we believe all practicing lawyers can be held to an awareness of generally recognized norms. We also recognize that the Commission has never articulated or endorsed any such standards. That being the case, we reverse the Administrative Law Judge's findings under subparagraph (ii) of Rule 2(e)(1) with respect to both respondents. Nevertheless, we believe that respondents' conduct raises serious questions about the obligations of securities lawyers, and the Commission is hereby giving notice of its interpretation of "unethical or improper professional conduct" as that term is used in Rule 2(e)(1)(ii). The Commission intends to issue a release soliciting comment from the public as to whether this interpretation should be expanded or modified.

B.   INTERPRETIVE BACKGROUND

Our concern focuses on the professional obligations of the lawyer who gives essentially correct disclosure advice to a client that does not follow that advice and as a result violates the federal securities laws. The subject of our inquiry is not a new one by any means and has received extensive scholarly treatment as well as consideration by a number of local bar ethics committees and disciplinary bodies. Similar issues are also presently under consideration by the ABA's Commission on Evaluation of Professional Standards in connection with the review and proposed revision of the ABA's Code of Professional Responsibility.

While precise standards have not yet emerged, it is fair to say that there exists considerable acceptance of the proposition that a lawyer must, in order to discharge his professional responsibilities, make all efforts within reason to persuade his client to avoid or terminate proposed illegal action. Such efforts could include, where appropriate, notification to the board of directors of a corporate client. In this connection, it is noteworthy that a number of commentators responding to the Commission's request, in Securities Exchange Act Release No. 16045,[70] for written comments on a rulemaking petition concerning the disclosure of relationships between registrants and their lawyers (the "Georgetown Petition"), volunteered their beliefs that such a professional obligation already exists. This informal expression of views is, of course, not conclusive, and there continues to be a lively debate surrounding the lawyer's proper reaction to his client's wrongdoings.

We are mindful that, when a lawyer represents a corporate client, the client — and the entity to which he owes his allegiance — is the corporation itself and not management or any other individual connected with the corporation. Moreover, the lawyer should try to "insure that decisions of his client are made only after the client has been informed of relevant considerations."[74] These unexceptionable principles take on a special coloration when a lawyer becomes aware that one or more specific members of a corporate client's management is deciding not to follow his disclosure advice, especially if he knows that those in control, such as the board of directors, may not have participated in or been aware of that decision. Moreover, it is well established that no lawyer, even in the most zealous pursuit of his client's interests, is privileged to assist his client in conduct the lawyer knows to be illegal. The application of these recognized principles to the special role of the securities lawyer giving disclosure advice, however, is not a simple task.

The securities lawyer who is an active participant in a company's ongoing disclosure program will ordinarily draft and revise disclosure documents, comment on them and file them with the Commission. He is often involved on an intimate, day-to-day basis in the judgments that determine what will be disclosed and what will be withheld from the public markets. When a lawyer serving in such a capacity concludes that his client's disclosures are not adequate to comply with the law, and so advises his client, he is

[70] (July 25, 1979), 17 SEC Docket 1376.
[74] ABA Code of Professional Responsibility, E. C. 7-8.

"aware," in a literal sense, of a continuing violation of the securities laws. On the other hand, the lawyer is only an adviser, and the final judgment — and, indeed, responsibility — as to what course of conduct is to be taken must lie with the client. Moreover, disclosure issues often present difficult choices between multiple shades of gray, and while a lawyer's judgment may be to draw the disclosure obligation more broadly than his client, both parties recognize the degree of uncertainty involved.

The problems of professional conduct that arise in this relationship are well-illustrated by the facts of this case. In rejecting Brown, Wood's advice to include the assumptions underlying its projections in its 1974 Annual Report, in declining to issue two draft stockholders letters offered by respondents and in ignoring the numerous more informal urgings by both respondents and Socha [an associate in their firm] to make disclosure, Hart and Lurie [chief executive officer and in-house counsel] indicated that they were inclined to resist any public pronouncements that were at odds with the rapid growth which had been projected and reported for the company.

If the record ended there, we would be hesitant to suggest that any unprofessional conduct might be involved. Hart and Lurie were, in effect, pressing the company's lawyers hard for the minimum disclosure required by law. That fact alone is not an appropriate basis for a finding that a lawyer must resign or take some extraordinary action. Such a finding would inevitably drive a wedge between reporting companies and their outside lawyers; the more sophisticated members of management would soon realize that there is nothing to gain in consulting outside lawyers.

However, much more was involved in this case. In sending out a patently misleading letter to stockholders on December 23 in contravention of Socha's plain and express advice to clear all such disclosure with Brown, Wood, in deceiving respondents about Johnson's approval of the company's quarterly report of its stockholders in early December and in dissembling in response to respondents' questions about the implementation of the LMP ["lease maintenance plan"], the company's management erected a wall between National and its outside lawyers — a wall apparently designed to keep out good legal advice in conflict with management's improper disclosure plans.

Any ambiguity in the situation plainly evaporated in late April and early May of 1975 when Hart first asked Johnson for a legal opinion flatly contrary to the express disclosure advice Johnson had given Hart only five days earlier, and when Lurie soon thereafter prohibited Kay [his assistant] from delivering a copy of the company's April 1975 Form 8-K to Brown, Wood.

These actions reveal a conscious desire on the part of National's management no longer to look to Brown, Wood for independent disclosure advice, but rather to embrace the firm within Hart's fraud and use it as a shield to avoid the pressures exerted by the banks toward disclosure. Such a role is a perversion of the normal lawyer-client relationship, and no lawyer may claim that, in these circumstances, he need do no more than stubbornly continue to suggest disclosure when he knows his suggestions are falling on deaf ears.

C. "UNETHICAL OR IMPROPER PROFESSIONAL CONDUCT"

The Commission is of the view that a lawyer engages in "unethical or improper professional conduct" under the following circumstances: When a lawyer with significant responsibilities in the effectuation of a company's compliance with the disclosure requirements of the federal securities laws becomes aware that his client is engaged in a substantial and continuing failure to satisfy those disclosure requirements, his continued participation violates professional standards unless he takes prompt steps to end the client's noncompliance. The Commission has determined that this interpretation will be applicable only to conduct occurring after the date of this opinion.

We do not imply that a lawyer is obliged, at the risk of being held to have violated Rule 2(e), to seek to correct every isolated disclosure action or inaction which he believes to be at variance with applicable disclosure standards, although there may be isolated disclosure failures that are so serious that their correction becomes a matter of primary professional concern. It is also clear, however, that a lawyer is not privileged to unthinkingly permit himself to be co-opted into an ongoing fraud and cast as a dupe or a shield for a wrongdoing client.

Initially, counselling accurate disclosure is sufficient, even if his advice is not accepted. But there comes a point at which a reasonable lawyer must conclude that his advice is not being followed, or even sought in good faith, and that his client is involved in a continuing course of violating the securities laws. At this critical juncture, the lawyer must take further, more affirmative steps in order to avoid the inference that he has been co-opted, willingly or unwillingly, into the scheme of nondisclosure.

The lawyer is in the best position to choose his next step. Resignation is one option, although we recognize that other considerations, including the protection of the client against forseeable prejudice, must be taken into account in the case of withdrawal. A direct approach to the board of directors or one or more individual directors or officers may be appropriate; or he may choose to try to enlist the aid of other members of the firm's management. What is required, in short, is some prompt action[77] that leads to the conclusion that the lawyer is engaged in efforts to correct the underlying problem, rather than having capitulated to the desires of a strong-willed, but misguided client.

Some have argued that resignation is the only permissible course when a client chooses not to comply with disclosure advice. We do not agree. Premature resignation serves neither the end of an effective lawyer-client relationship nor, in most cases, the effective administration of the securities laws. The lawyer's continued interaction with his client will ordinarily hold the greatest promise of corrective action. So long as a lawyer is acting in good faith and exerting reasonable efforts to prevent violations of the law by his client, his professional obligations have been met. In general, the best result is that which promotes the continued, strong-minded and independent participation by the lawyer.

We recognize, however, that the "best result" is not always obtainable, and that there may occur situations where the lawyer must conclude that the misconduct is so extreme or irretrievable, or the involvement of his client's management and board of directors in the misconduct is so thoroughgoing and pervasive that any action short of resignation would be futile. We would anticipate that cases where a lawyer has no choice but to resign would be rare and of an egregious nature.[78]

D. CONCLUSION

As noted above, because the Commission has never adopted or endorsed standards of professional conduct which would have

---

[77] In those cases where resignation is not the only alternative, should a lawyer choose not to resign, we do not believe the action taken *must be successful* to avoid the inference that the lawyer had improperly participated in his client's fraud. Rather, the acceptability of the action must be considered in the light of all relevant surrounding circumstances. Similarly, what is "prompt" in any one case depends on the situation then facing the lawyer.

[78] This case does not involve, nor do we here deal with, the additional question of when a lawyer, aware of his client's intention to commit fraud or an illegal act, has a professional duty to disclose that fact either publicly or to an affected third party. * * *

applied to respondents' activities during the period here in question, and since generally accepted norms of professional conduct which existed outside the scope of Rule 2(e) did not, during the relevant time period, unambiguously cover the situation in which respondents found themselves in 1974-75, no finding of unethical or unprofessional conduct would be appropriate. That being the case, we reverse the findings of the Administrative Law Judge under Rule 2(e)(1)(ii). In future proceedings of this nature, however, the Commission will apply the interpretation of subparagraph (ii) of Rule 2(e)(1) set forth in this opinion.

An appropriate order will issue.

By the Commission (Chairman WILLIAMS and Commissioners LOOMIS and FRIEDMAN); Commissioner EVANS concurring in part and dissenting in part; and Commissioner THOMAS not participating.

Query:

(1) Can the *Touche Ross* case,[1] which involved an accounting firm, be distinguished with respect to lawyers? Commissioner Karmel (as she then was) thought it might because of the Commission's express statutory authority to define accounting terms and require certification:[2]

> When Rule 2(e) is invoked to discipline attorneys for misconduct which does not directly obstruct the administrative process, in my opinion it is done so improperly as a matter of law and as a matter of policy. In the *Emanuel Fields* case[3] the Commission barred an attorney on the theory that the Commission can regulate the manner in which lawyers counsel clients and render opinions in securities transactions in order to protect investors. A primary rationale for so using Rule 2(e) has been that "the task of enforcing the securities laws rests in overwhelming measure on the bar's shoulders" and that given "its small staff, limited resources, and onerous tasks, the Commission is peculiarly dependent on the probity and diligence of the professionals who practice before it."[4] However, Congress did not authorize the Commission to conscript attorneys to enforce their clients' re-

[1] Touche, Ross & Co. v. SEC, 609 F. 2d 570, 582 (2d Cir. 1979). It was a stipulation of the final settlement of this action that the respondents would not seek judicial review of the court's injunction. Touche, Ross & Co., Acctg. Ser. Rel. 153A, 17 SEC Dock. 1107, 1115 (1979).

[2] Keating, Muething & Klekamp, Sec. Ex. Act Rel. 15,982, 17 SEC Dock. 1149, 1161-62 (1979) (dissenting opinion), supra n. 10.

[3] Emanuel Fields, 45 SEC 262, *aff'd without opinion* sub nom. Fields v. SEC, 495 F. 2d 1085 (D. C. Cir. 1974).

[4] Id., 45 SEC at 6 n. 20.

sponsibilities under the federal securities laws. Furthermore, institutional limitations alone cannot justify the creation of a new remedy not contemplated by the Congress.

I am firmly convinced that such conscription, or the promulgation and enforcement of regulatory standards of conduct for securities lawyers by the Commission, is very bad policy. It undermines the willingness and ability of the bar to exercise professional responsibility and sows the seeds for government abuse of power.

A person's right to counsel is protected by various common law principles, the Administrative Procedure Act and the Sixth Amendment to the U. S. Constitution. When a prosecutorial agency like the Commission disciplines attorneys acting in a representative capacity, it necessarily impinges upon and interferes with a client's right to counsel. Because of the importance of the right to counsel to persons in their dealings with the government, it seems to me that government agencies, especially those with a prosecutorial function, should exercise caution in taking administrative action against attorneys. Such regulation necessarily gives an advocate pause, whether he is acting as an advisor or an adversary.[5]

Again, when the Commission invited comment on whether its *Carter* interpretation should be expanded or modified, expressly stating that the invitation did not extend to the "previously considered * * * issue of its authority to adopt and administer Rule 2(e),"[6] an American Bar Association committee in its highly critical response expressed surprise "that the Commission thought that assertion could be dispositive of the issue presented by the Release."[7]

The fact is that for the first forty years or so there was only a handful of Rule 2(e) proceedings, involving egregious interference with the Commission's processes, whereas the volume later increased geometrically, with the Commission using the rule as a basis for regulating lawyers and accountants, even when there was no proceeding before the Commission, as long as the respondent's alleged conduct could be said somehow to have facilitated some violation of the federal securities laws.[8]

---

[5] See also Daley and Karmel, Attorneys' Responsibilities at the Bar of the SEC, 24 Emory L. J. 747 (1975). For the opposite point of view, see, in addition to the majority opinion in *Keating,* Sommer [then a Commissioner], Introduction [to Symposium: Enforcement of the Federal Securities Laws], 24 Emory L. J. 557, 564-66 (1975); Sondé, Professional Responsibility — A New Religion, or the Old Gospel?, 24 Emory L. J. 827 (1975).

[6] Sec. Act Rel. 6344, 23 SEC Dock. 826 (1981).

[7] SEC Standard of Conduct for Lawyers, 37 Bus. Law. 915, 917 (1982).

[8] Marsh, Rule 2(e) Proceedings, 35 Bus. Law. 987, 990-93 (1980). The other side of this coin is that the vast majority of the more than a hundred proceed-

(2) *Should* the SEC as an enforcement agency with prosecutorial functions have authority to discipline lawyers *as lawyers?* Does the possibility of Rule 2(e) proceedings militate against vigorous advocacy on the part of counsel for persons who are under investigation or the subject of administrative proceedings? If the lawyer in such a case may himself become a subject of the investigation, isn't his self-interest brought into conflict with his client's? And what about the possibility of inconsistent requirements between the Commission on the one hand and the states or other agencies on the other hand? The Commission's staff, at least, has been heard to disclaim any attempt to criticize lawyers' actions as advocates as distinct from their actions as advisers? Will such a distinction stand up?[9]

(3) What about the Commission's proceeding against lawyers by way of injunctive relief? Fair enough if they have acted with scienter, even with its connotation of recklessness rather than knowledge of falsity with intent to defraud. But all that the Second Circuit required in a 1973 case was a showing of negligence in the preparation of legal opinions that permitted the distribution of unregistered securities in violation of the 1933 Act:

> In assessing liability as an aider and abettor * * * , the district judge formulated a requisite standard of culpability — actual knowledge of the improper scheme plus an intent to further that scheme — which we find to be a sharp and unjustified departure from the negligence standard which we have repeatedly held to be sufficient in the context of enforcement proceedings seeking equitable or prophylactic relief. * * *
>
> * * * The legal profession plays a unique and pivotal role in the effective implementation of the securities laws.[10]

Surely lawyers ought not to be held to *less* strict standards than others. Quite the contrary, they should be exemplars. Yet there

---

ings in the history of the rule have been either consent cases or based on injunctions, convictions, or disbarments. Indeed, many of the consent cases have been by way of settling injunctive actions. Greene, Lawyer Disciplinary Proceedings before the Securities and Exchange Commission, 14 Sec. Reg. L. Rep. 168 (1982). But, of course, the pressure to consent in order to avoid the risk of a more harsh disposition is considerable.

[9] For an examination of these disparate roles that lawyers play, see Lorne, The Corporate and Securities Adviser, the Public Interest, and Professional Ethics, 76 Mich. L. Rev. 428 (1978).

[10] SEC v. Spectrum, Ltd., 489 F. 2d 535, 541-42 (2d Cir. 1973); see also SEC v. Management Dynamics, Inc., 515 F. 2d 801, 811 (2d Cir. 1975) (court referred to "the high degree of carelessness" in *Spectrum*); SEC v. Universal Major Industries Corp., 546 F. 2d 1044, 1047 (2d Cir. 1976), *cert. denied* sub nom. Homans v. SEC, 434 U. S. 834 (court referred to the lawyer's conduct in giving a private offering opinion as in fact "reckless"); but cf. SEC v. Haswell, 654 F. 2d 698 (10th Cir. 1981). For citations to a considerable number

is something disquieting about a court's telling a lawyer, under penalty of contempt: "Go thou and be nevermore negligent." If the lawyer, having had his fingers burned, is resolved to bend over backwards in advising future clients — as the Commission must surely hope — will he be able to do justice to his clients? Although the Commission need not allege more than negligence if it confines its complaint to §17(a)(2) and (3) of the 1933 Act,[11] presumably the Government would have to show more to get a conviction for criminal contempt. And we must rely here on the prosecutorial discretion of the Commission and the good sense of the courts.[12]

(4) Is there a solution that might achieve a consensus? Since the summer of 1980 the SEC and the American Bar Association's Standing Committee on Professional Discipline have been trying to create a model disciplinary mechanism for lawyers who practice before federal and state agencies, so far without success.[13] The subject has generated so much emotion that those who worked on the Federal Securities Code — exhibiting either cowardice or statesmanship depending on the point of view — ultimately decided, after trying and abandoning various formulas, that "doing nothing seems the least imperfect course."[14] And this is one of six "separable issues" that the Commission, in announcing its approval of the Code, reserved the right to bring to the attention of Congress at any time.[15]

In 1982 the Commission's General Counsel, in a considered address, suggested among other propositions that, as a general matter, the Commission should institute 2(e) proceedings only if

---

of injunctive proceedings against lawyers in 1966-72, see Mathews, SEC Civil Injunctive Actions, 5 Rev. Sec. Reg. 969, 970 n. 2 (1972).

[11] Aaron v. SEC, 446 U. S. 680 (1980), set out supra p. 887.

[12] See cases cited supra n. 10.

[13] See 14 Sec. Reg. L. Rep. 1400, 1477-78 (1982). The Commission favors a federal statute that would give the federal courts jurisdiction to discipline lawyers for improper professional practices before federal agencies. But, because "the states, for a variety of reasons * * * , have not adequately disciplined lawyers who practice before federal agencies," the Commission is not willing to accept a statute that would merely give the appropriate state bar association exclusive jurisdiction, on complaint by a federal agency, to investigate and prosecute the complaint before a United States District Court, but without any *requirement* that the state authorities take any action. And the judges of the District Court for the District of Columbia unanimously rejected the Standing Committee's further proposal that their court promulgate standards of conduct for practitioners' direct appearance before an agency. See letter from Paul Gonson, Solicitor, SEC, to Michael Franck, Chairman, Standing Committee on Professional Discipline, ABA, CCH Fed. Sec. L. Rep. ¶ 83,241 (1982).

[14] 2 Code 832; see generally 2 id. at 832-33, Comment (10).

[15] Sec. Act Rel. 6242, 20 SEC Dock. 1483, 1484-85, 1512 (1980), reprinted in 2 Code (2d Supp.) 7, 15-16.

the alleged misconduct was a violation of established ethical rules at the state level *and* had a direct impact on the Commission's internal processes (for example, participation in the preparation of filed disclosure documents); that ordinarily invocation of Rule 2(e) with respect to lawyers who do not actually appear before the Commission and are not involved in the preparation of filed documents "could entangle the Commission in the regulation of lawyers' routine office practice"; that he would not recommend proceedings against lawyers appearing as advocates, because the threat of their institution could have a seriously chilling effect on zealous representation; and that the Commission should likewise be sensitive to the problems of parallel proceedings against client and attorney.[16]

C. MISCELLANEOUS ASPECTS OF THE SEC LAWYER'S WORK

Lawyer *qua* director aside,[1] there are two aspects of his work that are peculiar to the securities field:

(1) The first has to do with his preparation of written opinions — to the effect, for example, that an exemption from §5 is available for a proposed transaction. Here the Bar has the benefit of guidelines prepared by a committee of The Association of the Bar of the City of New York:

REPORT BY THE SPECIAL COMMITTEE ON LAWYERS' ROLE IN SECURITIES TRANSACTIONS
The Association of the Bar of the City of New York
32 Bus. Law. 1879 (1977)[a]

*   *   *

GUIDELINE ONE

Before rendering an opinion, a lawyer should ascertain the purpose for which the opinion is sought; whether the opinion is to be

---

[16] Greene, Lawyer Disciplinary Proceedings before the Securities and Exchange Commission, 14 Sec. Reg. L. Rep. 168, 169 (1982).

C. 11C   [1] See Escott v. BarChris Construction Corp., 283 F. Supp. 643 (S. D. N. Y. 1968), supra p. 1040; Feit v. Leasco Data Processing Equipment Corp., 332 F. Supp. 544 (E. D. N. Y. 1971), supra p. 1046. On the lawyer's liability as aider and abettor, see SEC v. National Student Marketing Corp., 457 F. Supp. 682 (D. D. C. 1978), set out supra p. 1217; William R. Carter, Sec. Ex. Act Rel. 17,597, 22 SEC Dock. 292 (1981), set out supra p. 1243.

[a] ED.: Copyright 1977 by the American Bar Association and reprinted with

addressed to the client or another recipient; whether any persons other than the client or other addressee are intended to be entitled to rely on the opinion and, if so, their identity; and whether use by and reliance on the opinion should be expressly limited to a specific person or group of persons or to a particular purpose. * * *

GUIDELINE TWO

A lawyer should not give an opinion (including one based on hypothetical facts or one that is legally correct as to the limited matters to which it is addressed), if he knows or suspects that the opinion is being sought to further an illegal securities transaction.

GUIDELINE THREE

The lawyer should identify, consider and reach a conclusion concerning the legal questions posed by the requested opinion, performing such legal research as is reasonable to enable the lawyer to reach the opinion. In order to do so, he will in most instances have to identify and obtain factual information on which his legal analysis will depend. The lawyer generally obtains such factual information through inquiry of the client and, where appropriate, from others, and by reviewing materials provided to him for this purpose by the client or others. The lawyer should, therefore, satisfy himself that the client (and, if appropriate, others providing the lawyer with factual information or materials) is aware of the extent to which the lawyer is relying upon such information or materials in rendering the opinion and that there could be serious consequences if such information and materials are inaccurate or incomplete and, as a result, the legal opinion proves inapplicable or incorrect.

GUIDELINE FOUR

A lawyer should not render an opinion based on factual information or material which he knows or suspects to be inaccurate in any material respect. Subject to the foregoing and except as stated in (a) and (b) below, a lawyer has no obligation independently to verify factual matters underlying his legal opinion, but in such opinion or otherwise he should make clear to the client and any other intended recipients of the opinion that he has not done so and, where appropriate, he should identify the factual

---

the permission of the Association and its Section of Corporation, Banking, and Business Law. The commentary is omitted.

information he has accepted or assumed without verification. A statement in the opinion as to reliance on officers' certificates and other documents will normally serve as adequate notice of the absence of independent verification by the lawyer of the factual matters to which such documents relate.

(a) A lawyer has no obligation to verify statements made, or other information provided, to him by a client or other intended recipient of an opinion unless he is aware of inconsistent information, or of experience or circumstances which reasonably alert him that such statements and information may be erroneous or incomplete in a material respect. Where he is aware of such inconsistencies, experience or circumstances, the doubts which they create should be resolved to the lawyer's satisfaction through further inquiry or other appropriate investigation before an opinion is given which is based on such statements or other information.

(b) When the lawyer's opinion requires his interpretation or checking of legal documents, such as contracts, certificates of incorporation, or the terms of securities, he should examine the relevant documents (or copies thereof) and should not rely on the client or others to summarize or paraphrase documents for this purpose unless otherwise warranted by accepted legal practice (such as reliance on real estate title abstracts) and disclosed in the opinion.

*   *   *

GUIDELINE SEVEN

If in the lawyer's opinion the applicable law, or the application of that law to the particular facts, is sufficiently uncertain or unresolved so that there is a substantial possibility of differences of view among knowledgeable lawyers, the lawyer's own legal conclusion should be expressed in the context of that possibility. If the lawyer believes that the position reflected in his opinion is not in accordance with a position of responsible officials of the cognizant regulatory or administrative agency which is known to the lawyer, the lawyer should bring this to the attention of the client or other intended recipients of the opinion.

GUIDELINE EIGHT

If an opinion does not purport to address itself to an actual set of facts, it may be given on the basis of hypothetical facts if it states clearly the extent to which it is addressed only to hypothetical facts and that the opinion might be incorrect if the actual facts differ from the hypothetical facts. Opinions based on hypothetical facts, even though clearly identified as such, should not normally be given except when clearly limited, as to use and reliance, to the client or some other limited group with respect to whom the lawyer believes there will be no misunderstanding or misuse of the opinion.

*   *   *

These guidelines, together with other authority, inevitably leave room for the lawyer's exercise of discretion in particular cases.

The Commission cautioned in 1962 that, "if an attorney furnishes an opinion based solely upon hypothetical facts which he has made no effort to verify, and if he knows that his opinion will be relied upon as the basis for a substantial distribution of unregistered securities, a serious question arises as to the propriety of his professional conduct."[2] But presumably lawyers who give opinions on securities questions do not have to hire private detectives; for the same announcement referred to "the practice of responsible counsel not to furnish an opinion concerning the availability of an exemption from registration under the Securities Act for a contemplated distribution unless such counsel have themselves carefully examined all of the relevant circumstances and satisfied themselves, *to the extent possible,* that the contemplated transaction is, in fact, not a part of an unlawful distribution."[3]

The Eighth Circuit, in holding that it was not reckless for a lawyer to rely on a description of his corporate client's business by an officer who was a convicted felon, said: "To impose a standard of independent factual inquiry in these circumstances would make it unreasonably difficult for clients to obtain expeditious legal advice, or for lawyers to maintain a busy practice."[4] And Judge Friendly covered both ends as well as the middle when he stated *obiter* that a lawyer had no privilege to assist in circulating a statement with regard to securities that he knew to be false simply because his client had furnished it to him; that, at the other extreme, it would be unreasonable to hold a lawyer who was putting his client's description of a chemical process in understandable

---

[2] Sec. Act Rel. 4445 (1962).
[3] Ibid. Italics are supplied.
[4] Stokes v. Lokken, 644 F. 2d 779, 783 n. 3 (8th Cir. 1981).

English to be guilty of fraud simply because of his failure to detect discrepancies between that description and the technical reports available to him in a physical sense but beyond his ability to understand; and that the case at Bar was in between.[5]

(2) In the last decade or so the Commission's relatively small enforcement arm has managed to extend its reach in a series of consent injunction cases by having the court appoint special counsel to supervise an investigation[6] and sometimes institute all necessary lawsuits on behalf of the corporate defendant,[7] or to administer a reimbursement fund and approve the corporate defendant's continued operations with authority in counsel's discretion to seek the Commission's approval of the institution of bankruptcy proceedings,[8] or to determine whether the defendant violated suitability standards and if so to order restitution to particular buyers.[9] Sometimes it is the corporate defendant that selects special counsel satisfactory to the Commission.[10]

Although the vast majority of these judgments have been entered by consent,[11] there are several reported cases that bless the procedure.[12] But it is not clear what status special counsel has or whom he represents — the court, the Commission, or the defendant whom he sometimes investigates and sometimes champions in actions against third persons.[13] Since he is a hybrid between pri-

---

[5] SEC v. Frank, 388 F. 2d 486, 489 (2d Cir. 1968).

[6] SEC v. Clinton Oil Co., Litig. Rel. 5798.

[7] SEC v. Charter Diversified Services, Litig. Rel. 6507.

[8] SEC v. Holiday Magic, Inc., CCH Fed. Sec. L. Rep. ¶94,526 (N. D. Cal. 1974).

[9] SEC v. American Agronomics Corp., Litig. Rels. 5372, 5539, 5568 (N. D. Ohio 1972).

[10] SEC v. Canadian Javelin, Ltd., CCH Fed. Sec. L. Rep. ¶94,720 (S. D. N. Y. 1974).

[11] For a criticism of this practice whereby "the agency quickly builds up numerous uncontested precedents justifying a novel theory or procedure," see Karmel, address to Securities Law Committee of Young Lawyers Division of ABA, Sec. Reg. L. Rep. No. 489, p. H-1.

[12] United States v. Handler, CCH Fed. Sec. L. Rep. ¶96,519 at 94,023-24 (C. D. Cal. 1978) (although the unlimited nature of the special counsel procedure set forth in a prior consent injunction might have created due process problems, counsel's self-initiated safeguards cured any defect); Handler v. SEC, 610 F. 2d 656 (9th Cir. 1979) (there was no unlawful delegation of governmental power to a private person in the consent appointment of special counsel whose report led to the conviction in United States v. Handler, supra); International Controls Corp. v. Hogan & Hartson, summarized in CCH Fed. Sec. L. Rep. ¶97,183 (S. D. N. Y. 1979) (special counsel monitoring a consent judgment was permitted to employ his own law firm to litigate claims held by the monitored company); cf. also cases cited supra c. 10J n. 6; but cf. Brick v. Dominion Mortgage & Realty Trust, 442 F. Supp. 283, 307-08 (W. D. N. Y. 1977).

[13] See Gruenbaum and Oppenheimer, Special Investigative Counsel: Conflicts and Roles, 33 Rutgers L. Rev. 865 (1981).

vately retained counsel and government investigator, nice questions have arisen with respect to attorney-client privilege and counsel's work product.[14]

D.   LAWYER *VERSUS* ACCOUNTANT: CONTINGENT LIABILITIES

This last aspect of the securities lawyer's role pitted the legal and accounting professions against each other for some five years until a *modus vivendi* was reached in 1976.

Accountants have always disclosed contingent liabilities (which for some reason they now prefer to call "loss contingencies") in notes to the financial statements. But contingent liabilities traditionally were confined to those arising out of lawsuits already filed or clearly threatened.[1] Controversy arose in the early 1970s when the accounting fraternity, out of concern presumably for their own liability, began to demand that their clients instruct counsel (thus avoiding the question of attorney-client privilege that would arise if counsel were quizzed directly) to inform the auditors with respect to *potential* lawsuits. Since this would be inviting lawsuits to be filed, the Bar balked. This impasse raised the specter that the auditors might qualify their opinions not merely as to certainty but as to scope, thus indicating that an essential audit step had not been completed; and opinions qualified as to scope are not acceptable to the Commission.[2]

A compromise was approved by the ABA and the AICPA in

---

[14] See SEC v. Canadian Javelin, Ltd., 451 F. Supp. 594 (D. D. C. 1978), *remanded on other grounds,* CCH Fed. Sec. L. Rep. ¶96,742 (D. C. Cir. 1978) (no attorney-client relationship between defendant and compliance counsel); Osterneck v. E. T. Barwick Industries, Inc., 82 F. R. D. 81 (N. D. Ga. 1979) (same, and also no work product privilege, with respect to special counsel to Special Review Committee); but cf. Diversified Industries, Inc. v. Meredith, 572 F. 2d 596 (8th Cir. *en banc* 1978) (special counsel retained by corporation itself to investigate and report on charges of corporate bribery of purchasing agents of other companies); In re LTV Securities Litigation, 89 F. R. D. 595, 619 (N. D. Tex. 1981) ("it is likely that corporations will be less willing to engage in the sort of self-investigation [by an Audit Committee that retained special counsel pursuant to a consent injunction] if the results of such an investigation can be discovered in parallel civil litigation"). For a general review, see In re International Systems & Controls Corp. Securities Litigation, 91 F. R. D. 552 (S. D. Tex. 1981).

C. 11D [1] The Commission has always required the financial statements in a 1933 Act registration statement to disclose a contingent liability under §12(1) arising out of any violation of §5 disclosed in the registration statement.

[2] See Sommer, Two Problems for Lawyers (address to Dallas B. Assn., Nov. 4, 1975).

January, 1976. The statement issued by the two organizations is fairly lengthy.[3] Among other things, it states:[4]

(5) *Loss Contingencies.* When properly requested by the client, it is appropriate for the lawyer to furnish to the auditor information concerning the following matters if the lawyer has been engaged by the client to represent or advise the client professionally with respect thereto and he has devoted substantive attention to them in the form of legal representation or consultation:

(a) *overtly threatened or pending litigation,* whether or not specified by the client;

(b) *a contractually assumed obligation* which the client has specifically identified and upon which the client has specifically requested, in the inquiry letter or a supplement thereto, comment to the auditor;

(c) *an unasserted possible claim or assessment* which the client has specifically identified and upon which the client has specifically requested, in the inquiry letter or a supplement thereto, comment to the auditor.

* * *

(6) *Lawyer's Professional Responsibility.* * * * The lawyer also may be required under the Code of Professional Responsibility to resign his engagement if his advice concerning disclosures is disregarded by the client. The auditor may properly assume that whenever, in the course of performing legal services for the client with respect to a matter recognized to involve an unasserted possible claim or assessment which may call for financial statement disclosure, the lawyer has formed a professional conclusion that the client must disclose or consider disclosure concerning such possible claim or assessment, the lawyer, as a matter of professional responsibility to the client, will so advise the client and will consult with the client concerning the question of such disclosure and the applicable requirement* of FAS 5.[5]

---

[3] ABA, Statement of Policy Regarding Lawyers' Responses to Auditors' Requests for Information, 31 Bus. Law. 1709 (1976). Several weeks later the AICPA approved a coordinating Statement on Auditing Standards No. 12.

[4] Id. at 1712, 1714.

* Under FAS [Financial Accounting Standards Board] 5, when there has been no manifestation by a potential claimant of an awareness of a possible claim or assessment, disclosure of an unasserted possible claim is required only if the enterprise concludes that (i) it is probable that a claim will be asserted, (ii) there is a reasonable possibility, if the claim is in fact asserted, that the outcome will be unfavorable, and (iii) the liability resulting from such unfavorable outcome would be material to its financial condition.

[5] See also Introductory Analysis and Guides to Statement of Policy Regarding Lawyers' Responses to Auditors' Requests for Information — Prepared

Be all this as it may, neither of the two priesthoods can absolve from legal liability when it exists. Both continue to face a conundrum that is inherent in a system of compulsory disclosure: You are counsel for a company whose annual report is due in a month. You have just stumbled on facts indicating that for a considerable period ending some years ago the company used a process on which another company held the dominant patent. An action for patent infringement would probably succeed and come close to bankrupting the company. But apparently you are the only person who knows of this contingent liability. The statute of limitations expires in two months. It is a crime under §32(a) of the 1934 Act (1) willfully to fail to file a required report (or to file it late) in violation of §13(a) or (2) "willfully and knowingly" to make or cause any statement in a required report that is "false or misleading with respect to any material fact."[6] Under the circumstances how much weight will the word "material" bear?

This is not a case of the lady or the tiger. It is a case of two equally ferocious tigers. Which door do you open?

---

by the Committee on Audit Inquiry Responses, 31 Bus. Law. 1737 (1976); ABA Statement of Policy Regarding Lawyers' Responses to Auditors' Request for Information: Second Report of the Committee on Audit Inquiry Responses Regarding Initial Implementation, 32 Bus. Law. 177 (1976); Deer, Practical Problems and Procedures in Preparing Responses to Auditors' Inquiry Letters, in Practising Law Institute, Eighth Annual Institute on Securities Regulation (1977) c. 3.

[6] This, of course, is apart from the risk of potentially crushing civil liability under Rule 10b-5.

SEC STATUTES
IN THE UNITED STATES CODE

SECURITIES ACT OF 1933

| §1 | 15 U. S. C. | §77a |
| §2 | | §77b |

*　　*　　*

§26		§77z
Sch. A		§77aa
Sch. B		§77aa

SECURITIES EXCHANGE ACT OF 1934

| §1 | 15 U. S. C. | §78a |
| §2 | | §78b |

*　　*　　*

§11		§78k
§11A		§78k-1
§12		§78l

*　　*　　*

§15		§78o
§15A		§78o-3[1]
§15B		§78o-4
§16		§78p
§17		§78q

| §17A | | §78q-1 |
| §18 | | §78r |

*　　*　　*

| §26 | | §78z |
| §27 | | §78aa |

*　　*　　*

§30		§78dd
§30A		§78dd-1
§31		§78ee

*　　*　　*

| §34 | | §78hh |

PUBLIC UTILITY HOLDING COMPANY ACT OF 1935

| §1 | 15 U. S. C. | §79a |
| §2 | | §79b |

*　　*　　*

| §26 | | §79z |
| §27 | | §79z-1 |

*　　*　　*

[1] 15 U. S. C. §§78o-1 and 78o-2, which are not properly part of the 1934 Act, were mechanically incidental to the 1936 amendments.

§32		§79z-6
§33 (short title)		§79

Trust Indenture Act of 1939

§301	15 U. S. C.	§77aaa
§302		§77bbb

*   *   *

§26	§77zzz
§27	§77aaaa
§28	§77bbbb

Investment Company Act of 1940

§1	15 U. S. C.	§80a-1
§2		§80a-2

*   *   *

§28	§80a-28
§29	—²
§30	§80a-29
§31	§80a-30

*   *   *

§65	§80a-64

Investment Advisers Act of 1940

§201	15 U. S. C.	§80b-1
§202		§80b-2

*   *   *

§206A	§80b-6a

*   *   *

§221	§80b-21
§222	§80b-18a

Securities Investor Protection Act of 1970

§1	15 U. S. C.	§78aaa
§2		§78bbb

*   *   *

§6	§78fff
§7	§78fff-1
§8	§78fff-2
§9	§78fff-3
§10	§78fff-4
§11	§78ggg

*   *   *

§16	§78lll

---

²Since §29 amended §§44 and 67 of the then Bankruptcy Act, it does not appear in 15 U. S. C.

SEC, SIPC, AND FEDERAL RESERVE RULES IN THE CODE OF FEDERAL REGULATIONS

The SEC rules under the 1933 and 1935 Acts simply begin with 100 and 1, respectively, and run consecutively. Those under the 1934, 1939, and 1940 Acts are keyed into the sections under which they are adopted (except for a few preliminary rules designated 0-1, 0-2, etc.). Thus Rule 10b-5 under the 1934 Act is the fifth rule adopted under §10(b) of that statute. In the case of the 1939 Act, whose first section is 301, the first two digits of the section numbers are ignored in numbering the rules.

All the rules of the SEC are officially reported in 17 Code Fed. Regs., c. II. The Commission's rule numbers (as well as SIPC's under the Securities Investor Protection Act of 1970) correlate with the U. S. C. numbers as follows:

Set of Rules	Part Number of C. F. R.	Typical SEC Rule Number	Typical Section Number of 12 C. F. R.
Organization; Conduct and Ethics; Information and Requests	200	—	§200.1
Rules of Practice	201	6(e)	§201.6(e)
Informal and Other Procedures	202	—	§202.1
Investigations	203	—	§203.1
Reg. S-X	210	1-01	§210.1-01
Reg. S-K	229	Item 101	§229.101

Set of Rules	Part Number of C. F. R.	Typical SEC Rule Number	Typical Section Number of 12 C. F. R.
Sec. Act	230	140	§230.140
Sec. Ex. Act	240	10b-5	§240.10b-5
Holding Co. Act	250	50	§250.50
Trust Ind. Act	260	10b-1	§260.10b-1
Inv. Co. Act	270	8b-1	§270.8b-1
Inv. Adv. Act	275	203-1	§275.203-1
Sec. Inv. Prot. Act (SIPC rules)	300	100	§300.100

The margin rules adopted by the Board of Governors of the Federal Reserve System under §§7 and 8 of the Securities Exchange Act of 1934 appear in 12 Code Fed. Regs.:

Reg.	Part Number of 12 C. F. R.
G	207
T	220
U	221
X	224

TABLE OF CASES

This table is incomplete. It includes only those cases and other materials that are set out substantially in full, together with a number of other leading cases. Cases that are set out substantially in full, together with the pages at which they appear, are printed in italics.

TABLE OF SEC RELEASES

*Releases that are set out substantially in full, together with
the pages at which they appear, are printed in italics.*

11,396	471	15,345	198
11,406	768	15,348	579
11,424	677, 693	15,376	783
11,468	717	15,384	524
11,497	705	15,548	582
11,604	991	15,570	163
11,628	781	15,671	759
11,742	680	15,723	710
11,766	1002	15,769	784, 785
11,935	704	15,772	163
11,942	782	15,926	789, 791
12,278	974	15,982	1245, 1258
12,344	701	15,984	1194
12,352	710	16,045	1254
12,361	507	16,075	586
12,384	717	16,112	582, 587
12,396	754	16,214	774
12,532	710	16,356	520, 524
12,670	769	16,371	75
12,676	582	16,384	587
12,935	710	16,385	583, 584, 588
12,999	540	16,420	578
13,030	519	16,422	670
13,091	717	16,443	560
13,163	695	16,623	585
13,346	*484*	16,682	508
13,391	783	16,701	795
13,437	831	16,738	508
13,482	524	16,817	1002
13,508	804	16,877	163
13,542	783	16,888	785, 787
13,626	769	16,889	785
13,629	677, 678	17,120	572, 868, 869
13,662	782	17,169	78
13,719	559	17,208	705
13,787	589	17,222	579, 993, 1005
13,901	524	17,347	717
14,056	991	17,353	585
14,149	970	17,383	693
14,185	587	17,480	816
14,384	991	17,516	785, 786
14,416	769	17,518	524
14,970	524	17,549	790
14,981	495	17,562	695
15,191	710	17,577	257
15,230	570	17,580	767
15,250	767	17,583	770, 771

17,584	670	18,713	786
17,597	1187, 1188, 1242, *1243,*	18,738	787
	1262	18,853	469
17,601	786	18,878	512
17,704	775	18,927	183
17,709	957	19,005	955
17,719	587	19,125-34	257
17,744	786	19,135	539
18,114	612, 639, 649, 650, 655	*19,244*	1003, *1004*
18,278	445	19,263	258
18,417	*704*	19,264	258
18,451	163	19,274	258
18,482	771	19,284	271
18,528	1004	19,291	559
18,536	786	19,336	576
18,647	465, 496	19,346	197
18,666	1004	19,372	787
18,710	677	19,431	523

INDEX